Random House
Webster's
Large Print
Dictionary

RANDOM HOUSE
NEW YORK

Random House Webster's Large Print Dictionary

Copyright © 1998, 1997 by Random House, Inc.

This work was originally published in hardcover and paperback by Random House, Inc. in 1997 and in different form.

This work is based on the Random House American Dictionary, Second Edition, published in 1995.

Library of Congress Cataloging-in-Publication Data

Random House Webster's dictionary. --Large print ed., 1st ed.

    p.   cm.

    Based on the Random House American dictionary, 2nd ed., 1995.

    ISBN 0-679-45810-7 (hc). --ISBN 0-679-77710-5 (pbk.).

    1. English Language--Dictionaries. 2. Large print type books.

    I. Random House American Dictionary.

    [PE1628.R294 1997]

    423--dc21   96-47193
                                                      CIP

Random House Reference Web site: www.randomwords.com

Typeset and printed in the United States of America.

Updated Large Print Edition

0 9

ISBN 0-375-40114-8 (Hardcover)

ISBN 0-375-70106-0 (Paperback)

        New York Toronto London Sydney Auckland

Foreword

I am delighted Random House adds to its roster of publications a dictionary in large type for readers who need or prefer larger than regulation size print. In undertaking this project, the editors have exerted every effort to conform to criteria set by the National Association for Visually Handicapped (NAVH).

As the pioneer in large print, NAVH encourages and oversees publication of government and corporate forms and informational materials, in addition to offering consultation to publishers of large print books. When requirements are met, NAVH grants its prestigious "Seal of Approval."

The extremely readable *Random House Webster's Dictionary* conforms to NAVH's strict standards and will, I am certain, be warmly welcomed by all who use and enjoy large print.

—Lorraine H. Marchi
Founder/Executive Director,
NAVH

New Words in English

The Random House family of dictionaries has kept up with the remarkable growth of the English language by recording Newer Words Faster. New terms enter the language mostly as a result of recent inventions or knowledge in the fields of science and technology, but social and cultural trends have also contributed to the great expansion of English vocabulary. These new terms represent a variety of subject categories, both general and specialized.

New terms are popularized and given life in our newspapers, magazines, books, and electronic documents, not to mention television shows, movies, and plays. Some new terms last only for the moment, as a passing fad, and are forgotten soon after their introduction. Other new terms are controversial because of their slang status, or because they are perceived to be offensive. It is not possible to predict the future of a particular word. As for the future of English, the language is likely to continue its expansion in the course of the 21st century.

A study of the following selection of words on the next page, which have recently gained currency, will reveal a great deal about our changing world. You will find the definitions for these and many more new words in the A–Z dictionary.

abs	global warming
African-American	HMO
ageism	househusband
ATM	infomercial
bar code	Internet
basmati	in-your-face
biological clock	life-care
caregiver	liposuction
cellular phone	minoxidil
cyberspace	mountain bike
designated driver	paper trail
dis	politically correct
downsize	quality time
e-mail	significant other
ergonomics	spin control
ERT	superstore
fajitas	virtual reality
Generation X	voice mail
glass ceiling	wannabe

Abbreviations Used in This Book

adj.	adjective		*interj.*	interjection
adv.	adverb		*l.c.*	lower case
art.	article		*n.*	noun
aux.	auxiliary		*pl.*	plural
Brit.	British		*prep.*	preposition
cap.	capital		*pron.*	pronoun
conj.	conjunction		*pt.*	past tense
def.	definition		*sing.*	singular
esp.	especially		*usu.*	usually
fem.	feminine		*v.*	verb

A

a, *adj. or indef. art.* **1.** some. **2.** one. **3.** any.

a-, prefix indicating: **1.** not, as *atypical.* **2.** without, as *amorality.*

AA, 1. administrative assistant. **2.** Alcoholics Anonymous. **3.** anti-aircraft.

A.A., Associate in Arts.

aard′vark′, *n.* African ant-eating mammal.

AARP (*pronounced as initials or* ärp), American Association of Retired Persons.

A.B., Bachelor of Arts.

A.B.A., American Bar Association.

a•back′, *adv.* by surprise.

ab′a•cus, *n.* **1.** calculating device using movable beads. **2.** slab at top of column.

a•baft′, *prep. Naut.* **1.** behind. —*adv.* **2.** at the stern.

ab′a•lo′ne (ab′ə lō′nē), *n.* edible mollusk with mother-of-pearl shell.

a•ban′don, *v.* **1.** leave completely; forsake. **2.** give up. —*n.* **3.** freedom from constraint. —**a•ban′doned,** *adj.* —**a•ban′don•ment,** *n.*

a•base′, *v.,* **abased, abasing.** lower; degrade. —**a•base′ment,** *n.*

a•bash′, *v.* to embarrass.

a•bate′, *v.,* **abated, abating.** lessen or subside. —**a•bate′ment,** *n.*

ab•at•toir′ (-twär′), *n.* slaughterhouse.

ab′bé (-ā), *n.* abbot; priest.

ab′bess, *n.* convent head.

ab′bey (-ē), *n.* monastery or convent.

ab′bot, *n.* monastery head.

abbr., abbreviation.

ab•bre′vi•ate′, *v.,* **-ated, -ating.** shorten. —**ab•bre′vi•a′tion,** *n.*

ABC, *n., pl.* **ABC's, ABCs. 1.** alphabet. **2.** (*pl.*) basics.

ab′di•cate′, *v.,* **-cated, -cating.** give up (power or office). —**ab′di•ca′tion,** *n.*

ab′do•men (-də-), *n.* part of body between thorax and pelvis; belly. —**ab•dom′i•nal** (-dom′-), *adj.*

ab•dom′i•nals, *n.pl.* muscles of abdomen. Also, **abs.**

ab•duct′, *v.* kidnap.
—**ab•duc′tion,** *n.*
—**ab•duc′tor,** *n.*

a•beam′, *adv. Naut.* across a ship.

a•bed′, *adv.* in bed.

ab′er•ra′tion, *n.* **1.** deviation from normal or right course. **2.** mental lapse.

a•bet′, *v.,* **abetted, abetting.** encourage in wrongdoing.
—**a•bet′tor, a•bet′ter,** *n.*

a•bey′ance, *n.* temporary inactivity.

ab•hor′, *v.,* **-horred, -horring.** loathe; consider repugnant.
—**ab•hor′rence,** *n.*
—**ab•hor′rent,** *adj.*

a•bide′, *v.,* **abode** or **abided, abiding. 1.** remain; stay. **2.** dwell. **3.** wait for. **4.** agree; conform. **5.** *Informal.* tolerate.

a•bid′ing, *adj.* steadfast; lasting.

a•bil′i•ty, *n., pl.* **-ties. 1.** talent. **2.** competence.

ab′ject, *adj.* **1.** humiliating. **2.** despicable. —**ab′ject•ly,** *adv.*
—**ab•jec′tion,** *n.*

ab•jure′, *v.,* **-jured, -juring.** renounce or forswear.
—**ab′ju•ra′tion,** *n.*

ab′la•tive, *adj. Gram.* denoting origin, means, etc.

a•blaze′, *adv., adj.* burning.

a′ble, *adj.,* **abler, ablest. 1.** having sufficient power or qualification. **2.** competent.
—**a′bly,** *adv.*

-able, suffix indicating: **1.** able to be, as *readable.* **2.** tending to, as *changeable.* **3.** worthy of, as *loveable.*

a′ble-bod′ied, *adj.* healthy.

ab•lu′tion, *n.* ritual washing.

ab′ne•gate′, *v.,* **-gated, -gating.** deny to oneself.
—**ab′ne•ga′tion,** *n.*

ab•nor′mal, *adj.* not normal; not usual or typical.
—**ab′nor•mal′i•ty,** *n.*
—**ab•nor′mal•ly,** *adv.*

a•board′, *adv.* **1.** on a ship, train, etc. —*prep.* **2.** on.

a•bode′, *n.* **1.** home. **2.** stay.

a•bol′ish, *v.* make void.

ab′o•li′tion, *n.* **1.** act of abolishing. **2.** end of slavery in the U.S. —**ab′o•li′tion•ist,** *n.*

A′-bomb′, *n.* atomic bomb.

a•bom′i•na•ble, *adj.* hateful; loathsome.
—**a•bom′i•na•bly,** *adv.*

a·bom′i·nate′, *v.*, **-nated, -nating.** abhor or hate. —**a·bom′i·na′tion**, *n.*

ab′o·rig′i·nal, *adj.* **1.** original. —*n.* **2.** aborigine.

ab′o·rig′i·ne′ (-rij′ə nē′), *n.* original inhabitant of a land.

a·bort′, *v.* **1.** have or cause abortion. **2.** end prematurely. —**a·bor′tive**, *adj.*

a·bor′tion, *n.* expulsion of fetus before it is viable. —**a·bor′tion·ist**, *n.*

a·bound′, *v.* be or have plentifully; teem.

a·bout′, *prep.* **1.** concerning. **2.** near, in, on, or around. **3.** ready. —*adv.* **4.** approximately. **5.** *Informal.* almost. **6.** on all sides. **7.** oppositely. —*adj.* **8.** active.

a·bout-face, *n.* reversal of position.

a·bove′, *adv.* **1.** higher. **2.** previously. **3.** in or to heaven. —*prep.* **4.** higher or greater than. —*adj.* **5.** foregoing.

a·bove′board′, *adv., adj.* honest; fair.

ab′ra·ca·dab′ra, *n.* **1.** word used in magic. **2.** drivel.

a·brade′, *v.*, **abraded, abrading.** wear or scrape off. —**a·bra′sion**, *n.*

a·bra′sive, *adj.* **1.** abrading. **2.** annoying. —*n.* **3.** material or substance used to grind or smooth. —**a·bra′sive·ly**, *adv.*

a·breast′, *adv., adj.* next to.

a·bridge′, *v.*, **abridged, abridging.** shorten. —**a·bridg′ment**, *n.*

a·broad′, *adv., adj.* **1.** out of one's own country. **2.** in circulation.

ab′ro·gate′, *v.*, **-gated, -gating.** end, annul, or repeal. —**ab′ro·ga′tion**, *n.*

ab·rupt′, *adj.* **1.** sudden; unexpected. **2.** steep. —**ab·rupt′ly**, *adv.* —**ab·rupt′ness**, *n.*

abs, *n.pl.* abdominals.

ab′scess, *n.* infected, pus-filled place.

ab·scond′, *v.* depart suddenly and secretly.

ab′sent, *adj.* **1.** not present. **2.** lacking. —*v.* (ab sent′). **3.** keep away. —**ab′sence**, *n.*

ab′sen·tee′, *n.* absent person.

ab′sent-mind′ed, *adj.* forgetful or preoccupied. —**ab′sent-mind′ed•ly,** *adv.* —**ab′sent-mind′ed•ness,** *n.*

ab′sinthe, *n.* bitter liqueur.

ab′so•lute′, *adj.* **1.** complete; perfect. **2.** pure. **3.** unrestricted. **4.** despotic. —**ab′so•lute′ly,** *adv.*

absolute pitch, ability to identify exact musical pitch.

absolute zero, temperature at which molecular activity ceases.

ab•solve′ (-zolv′), *v.,* **-solved, -solving. 1.** release or free. **2.** remit sins of. **3.** forgive. —**ab′so•lu′tion,** *n.*

ab•sorb′, *v.* **1.** take in. **2.** occupy completely; fascinate. —**ab•sor′bent,** *adj., n.* —**ab•sorp′tion,** *n.* —**ab•sorp′tive,** *adj.*

ab•stain′, *v.* refrain (from). —**ab•sten′tion,** *n.*

ab•ste′mi•ous, *adj.* moderate in eating, drinking, etc.

ab′sti•nence, *n.* forebearance; self-restraint. —**ab′sti•nent,** *adj.*

ab′stract, *adj.* **1.** apart from specific matter. **2.** theoretical. **3.** hard to understand. **4.** (of art) not representing natural forms. —*n.* **5.** summary. **6.** essence. —*v.* (ab strakt′). **7.** remove or steal. **8.** summarize. —**ab•strac′tion,** *n.*

ab•stract′ed, *adj.* preoccupied.

ab•struse′, *adj.* hard to understand.

ab•surd′, *adj.* ridiculous. —**ab•surd′ly,** *adv.* —**ab•surd′i•ty,** *n.*

a•bun′dance, *n.* plentiful supply. —**a•bun′dant,** *adj.* —**a•bun′dant•ly,** *adv.*

a•buse′, *v.,* **abused, abusing,** *n.* —*v.* (-byōōz′) **1.** use or treat wrongly. —*n.* (-byōōs′) **2.** wrong use or treatment. **3.** insult. —**a•bu′sive,** *adj.* —**a•bu′sive•ness,** *n.*

a•but′, *v.,* **abutted, abutting.** be adjacent to.

a•but′ment, *n.* structural part sustaining pressure.

a•buzz′, *adj.* full of activity.

a•bys′mal (-biz′-), *adj.* deep; measureless.

a•byss′, *n.* **1.** chasm. **2.** hell. Also, **a•bysm′** (ə biz′əm).

Ab′ys•sin′i•an (ab′ə sin′ē ən), *adj.* **1.** from ancient Ethiopia. —*n.* **2.** type of cat.

AC, 1. air conditioning. **2.** Also, **ac., a.c., A.C.** alternating current.

a·ca'cia (-kā'shə), *n.* tropical tree or shrub.

ac'a·dem'ic, *adj.* Also, **ac'a·dem'i·cal. 1.** of a school, college, etc. **2.** theoretical. —*n.* **2.** college student or teacher.

a·cad'e·my, *n., pl.* **-mies. 1.** school. **2.** cultural society.

a·can'thus, *n.* Mediterranean plant.

a cap·pel'la (ä kə pel'ə), *adv., adj. Music.* without instrumental accompaniment.

ac·cede', *v.,* **-ceded, -ceding. 1.** consent. **2.** reach.

ac·cel'er·ate', *v.,* **-ated, -ating.** speed up; hasten. —**ac·cel'er·a'tion,** *n.*

ac·cel'er·a'tor, *n.* pedal that controls vehicle's speed.

ac'cent, *n.* **1.** emphasis. **2.** characteristic pronunciation. **3.** mark showing stress, etc. —*v.* (ak sent') **4.** emphasize.

ac·cen'tu·ate', *v.,* **-ated, -ating.** stress or emphasize. —**ac·cen'tu·a'tion,** *n.*

ac·cept', *v.* **1.** take or receive. **2.** agree to. **3.** believe.

—**ac·cept'a·ble,** *adj.*
—**ac·cept'ed,** *adj.*
—**ac·cept'a·bil'i·ty,** *n.*
—**ac·cept'a·bly,** *adv.*
—**ac·cept'ance,** *n.*

ac'cess, *n.* **1.** right or means of approach. **2.** attack.

ac·ces'si·ble, *adj.* easy to reach or influence.
—**ac·ces'si·bil'i·ty,** *n.*

ac·ces'sion, *n.* **1.** attainment of an office, etc. **2.** increase.

ac·ces'so·ry, *n., pl.* **-ries. 1.** something added for convenience, decoration, etc. **2.** one who abets a felony.

ac'ci·dence, *n.* part of grammar dealing with inflection.

ac'ci·dent, *n.* unexpected event, usually unfortunate.
—**ac'ci·den'tal,** *adj.*
—**ac'ci·den'tal·ly,** *adv.*

ac'ci·dent-prone', *adj.* inclined to have accidents.

ac·claim', *v.* **1.** salute with applause, cheers, etc. —*n.* **2.** applause, cheers, etc.
—**ac'cla·ma'tion,** *n.*

ac·cli'mate, *v.,* **-ated, -ating.** accustom to new conditions. Also, **ac·cli'ma·tize'.**

ac•cliv′i•ty, *n., pl.* **-ties.** upward slope.

ac′co•lade′, *n.* award, honor, or applause.

ac•com′mo•date′, *v.,* **-dated, -dating. 1.** do a favor for. **2.** supply. **3.** provide with room, food, etc. **4.** adjust.

ac•com′mo•dat′ing, *adj.* helpful; obliging.

ac•com′mo•da′tion, *n.* **1.** act of accommodating. **2.** (*pl.*) space for lodging or travel.

ac•com′pa•ni•ment, *n.* **1.** something added as decoration, etc. **2.** subsidiary music for performer.

ac•com′pa•ny, *v.,* **-nied, -nying. 1.** go or be with. **2.** provide musical accompaniment for. **—ac•com′pa•nist,** *n.*

ac•com′plice, *n.* partner in crime.

ac•com′plish, *v.* do or finish.

ac•com′plished, *adj.* **1.** done; finished. **2.** expert.

ac•com′plish•ment, *n.* **1.** completion. **2.** skill.

ac•cord′, *v.* **1.** agree; be in harmony. **2.** cause to agree. **3.** grant; allow. **—***n.* **4.** agreement; harmony. **—ac•cord′ance,** *n.* **—ac•cord′ant,** *adj.*

ac•cord′ing•ly, *adv.* therefore.

according to, 1. in proportion to. **2.** on authority of.

ac•cor′di•on, *n.* bellowslike musical instrument.

ac•cost′, *v.* confront.

ac•count′, *n.* **1.** story; report. **2.** explanation. **3.** reason. **4.** importance. **5.** consideration. **6.** record of transactions. **—***v.* **7.** explain. **8.** report. **9.** consider.

ac•count′a•ble, *adj.* **1.** responsible. **2.** explainable. **—ac•count′a•bly,** *adv.*

ac•count′ing, *n.* maintenance of transaction records. **—ac•count′ant,** *n.* **—ac•count′an•cy,** *n.*

ac•cou′ter′ments (-trə mənts, -tər-), *n.pl.* personal clothing or equipment. Also, **ac•cou′tre•ments.**

ac•cred′it, *v.* **1.** attribute. **2.** certify with credentials. **—ac•cred′i•ta′tion,** *n.*

ac•cre′tion (-krē′-), *n.* increase by addition.

ac•crue′, *v.*, **-crued, -cruing.** be added (to). —**ac•cru′al**, *n.*

ac•cul′tur•ate′, *v.*, **-at•ed, -at•ing.** adopt cultural traits of another group. —**ac•cul′tur•a•tion**, *n.*

ac•cu′mu•late′, *v.*, **-lated, -lating.** gather; collect. —**ac•cu′mu•la′tion**, *n.* —**ac•cu′mu•la′tive**, *adj.* —**ac•cu′mu•la′tor**, *n.*

ac′cu•rate, *adj.* exact; correct. —**ac′cu•rate•ly**, *adv.* —**ac′cu•ra•cy**, *n.*

ac•curs′ed, *adj.* **1.** cursed. **2.** hateful. Also, **ac•curst′.**

ac•cu′sa•tive, *adj. Gram.* denoting verb's direct object.

ac•cuse′, *v.*, **-cused, -cusing.** blame; charge. —**ac′cu•sa′tion**, *n.* —**ac•cus′er**, *n.* —**ac•cus′a•to′ry**, *adj.*

ac•cus′tom, *v.* make used to.

ac•cus′tomed, *adj.* **1.** usual; habitual. **2.** habituated.

ace, *n.* **1.** playing card with single spot. **2.** expert. **3.** *Tennis.* serve opponent cannot touch. —*v.* **4.** score ace against. **5.** do very well on.

a•cer′bic (ə sûr′bik), *adj.* **1.** sour. **2.** sharp or severe. —**a•cer′bi•ty**, *n.*

a•ce′ta•min′o•phen (ə sē′tə min′ə fən), *n.* substance used to reduce pain or fever.

ac′e•tate′, *n.* salt or ester of acetic acid.

a•ce′tic (-sē′-), *adj.* of or producing vinegar.

acetic acid, sharp-tasting acid found in vinegar.

ac′e•tone′ (as′i tōn′), *n.* flammable liquid; solvent.

a•cet′y•lene′, *n.* gas used in welding, etc.

ache, *v.*, **ached, aching**, *n.* —*v.* **1.** suffer dull pain. —*n.* **2.** dull pain.

a•chieve′, *v.*, **achieved, achieving.** accomplish; bring about. —**a•chieve′ment**, *n.*

A•chil′les heel (ə kil′ēz), vulnerable spot.

ach′ro•mat′ic (ak′-), *adj.* colorless.

ac′id, *n.* **1.** chemical compound containing hydrogen replaceable by a metal to form a salt. **2.** sour substance. —*adj.* **3.** of acids. **4.** sour. —**a•cid′i•ty**, *n.*

ac•i•do′sis, *n.* acidic poisoning.

acid rain, rain containing chemicals from industrial pollution.

a•cid′u•lous (-sij′-), *adj.* sour or sharp.

ack′-ack′, *n. Slang.* anti-aircraft fire.

ac•knowl′edge, *v.,* **-edged, -edging.** 1. recognize; admit. 2. show appreciation for. **—ac•knowl′edg•ment,** *n.*

ac′me, *n.* highest point.

ac′ne, *n.* skin eruption.

ac′o•lyte′, *n.* altar attendant.

ac′o•nite′, *n.* plant yielding medicine and poison.

a′corn, *n.* fruit of the oak.

acorn squash, acorn-shaped winter squash.

a•cous′tic, *adj.* of sound. **—a•cous′ti•cal•ly,** *adv.*

a•cous′tics, *n.* 1. science of sound. 2. sound qualities.

ac•quaint′, *v.* make familiar.

ac•quaint′ance, *n.* 1. someone personally known. 2. general knowledge.

ac′qui•esce′, *v.,* **-esced, -escing.** agree or comply.

—ac′qui•es′cence, *n.*
—ac′qui•es′cent, *adj.*

ac•quire′, *v.,* **-quired, -quiring.** obtain. **—ac•quire′ment,** *n.*

ac′qui•si′tion, *n.* 1. acquiring. 2. something acquired.

ac•quis′i•tive, *adj.* eager to acquire.
—ac•quis′i•tive•ness, *n.*

ac•quit′, *v.,* **-quitted, -quitting.** 1. free of blame or guilt. 2. behave or conduct.
—ac•quit′tal, *n.*

a′cre, *n.* unit of land area (1/640 sq. mi. or 43,560 sq. ft.). **—a′cre•age,** *n.*

ac′rid, *adj.* sharp; biting.

ac′ri•mo•ny, *n.* harshness of manner or speech.
—ac′ri•mo′ni•ous, *adj.*

ac′ro•bat′, *n.* performer on trapeze. **—ac′ro•bat′ic,** *adj.*

ac′ro•bat′ics, *n.* (*used with a pl. v.*) 1. acrobat's feats. 2. any feats requiring skill.

ac′ro•nym, *n.* word formed from successive initials or groups of letters, as NATO, UNICEF.

ac′ro•pho′bi•a, *n.* fear of heights.

a•cross', *prep.* **1.** from side to side of. **2.** on the other side of. —*adv.* **3.** from one side to another.

across-the-board, *adj.* applying to all members or categories.

a•cryl'ic, *n.* synthetic fiber.

act, *n.* **1.** something done. **2.** law or decree. **3.** part of a play or opera. —*v.* **4.** do something. **5.** behave. **6.** pretend. **7.** perform on stage.

act'ing, *adj.* substitute.

ac'tin•ism, *n.* action of radiant energy in causing chemical changes. —**ac•tin'ic,** *adj.*

ac•tin'i•um, *n.* radioactive metallic element.

ac'tion, *n.* **1.** process or state of being active. **2.** something done. **3.** behavior. **4.** combat. **5.** lawsuit.

ac'tion•a•ble, *adj.* providing grounds for a lawsuit.

ac'ti•vate', *v.,* **-vated, -vating.** make active; start. —**ac'ti•va'tion,** *n.*

ac'tive, *adj.* **1.** in action; busy, nimble, or lively. **2.** *Gram.* indicating that the subject performs the action of the verb. —**ac'tive•ly,** *adv.* —**ac•tiv'i•ty,** *n.*

ac'tiv•sim, *n.* vigorous action toward political or social goals. —**ac'tiv•ist,** *n.*

ac'tor, *n.* performer in play. —**ac'tress,** *n.fem.*

ac'tu•al (-chōō-), *adj.* real. —**ac'tu•al•ly,** *adv.* —**ac'tu•al'i•ty,** *n.*

ac'tu•ar'y, *n., pl.* **-aries.** calculator of insurance rates, etc. —**ac'tu•ar'i•al,** *adj.*

ac'tu•ate', *v.,* **-ated, -ating.** cause to act; effect.

a•cu'i•ty (ə kyōō'i tē), *n.* sharpness of perception.

a•cu'men (-kyōō'-), *n.* mental keenness.

ac'u•punc'ture, *n.* Chinese art of healing by inserting needles into the skin. —**ac'u•punc'tur•ist,** *n.*

a•cute', *adj.* **1.** sharp; pointed. **2.** severe. **3.** crucial. **4.** keen, clever. **5.** high-pitched. **6.** (of an angle) less than 90 degrees. —**a•cute'ly,** *adv.* —**a•cute'ness,** *n.*

a•cy'clo•vir', *n.* drug used to treat genital herpes.

ad, *n. Informal.* advertisement.

A.D., anno Domini: in the year of our Lord.

ad′age, *n.* proverb.

a•da′gio (ə dä′ jō), *adj., adv. Music.* slow.

ad′a•mant′, *n.* **1.** hard substance. —*adj.* **2.** Also, **ad′a•man′tine.** unyielding.

Ad′am's ap′ple, projection of cartilage in front of neck.

a•dapt′, *v.* adjust to. —**a•dapt′a•ble,** *adj.* —**a•dapt′a•bil′i•ty,** *n.* —**ad′ap•ta′tion,** *n.* —**a•dapt′er, a•dap′tor,** *n.*

add, *v.* **1.** unite or join. **2.** find the sum (of). **3.** increase.

ad′dend, *n.* number to be added to another.

ad•den′dum, *n., pl.* **-da.** something to be added.

ad′der, *n.* venomous snake.

ad′dict, *n.* **1.** person habituated to a drug, etc. —*v.* (ə dikt′). **2.** habituate (to). —**ad•dic′tion,** *n.* —**ad•dic′tive,** *adj.*

ad•di′tion, *n.* **1.** adding. **2.** anything added. **3. in addition to,** besides. —**ad•di′tion•al,** *adj.* —**ad•di′tion•al•ly,** *adv.*

ad′di•tive, *n.* added ingredient.

ad′dle, *v.,* **-dled, -dling. 1.** confuse. **2.** spoil.

ad•dress′, *n.* **1.** formal speech. **2.** place of residence. **3.** manner of speaking. **4.** skill. —*v.* **5.** speak or write (to). **6.** send. **7.** apply (oneself). —**ad′dress•ee′,** *n.*

ad•duce′, *v.,* **-duced, -ducing.** present; cite.

ad′e•noid′, *n.* mass of tissue in upper pharynx.

a•dept′, *adj.* **1.** skilled. —*n.* (ad′ ept). **2.** expert.

ad′e•quate, *adj.* sufficient; fit. —**ad′e•quate•ly,** *adv.* —**ad′e•qua•cy,** *n.*

ad•here′, *v.,* **-hered, -hering. 1.** stick or cling. **2.** be faithful or loyal. —**ad•her′ence,** *n.* —**ad•her′ent,** *n., adj.* —**ad•he′sion,** *n.*

ad•he′sive, *adj.* **1.** coated with a sticky substance. **2.** sticky. —*n.* adhesive substance.

ad hoc, for a purpose.

ad ho′mi•nem, attacking an opponent personally instead of answering an argument.

a•dieu′ (ə dyōō′, ə dōō′), *interj., n. French.* (good-by!)

ad in′fi•ni′tum, to infinity; without end.

ad′i•os′, *interj. Spanish.* (good-by!)

ad′i•pose′, *adj.* fatty.

adj., 1. adjective. 2. adjustment. 3. adjutant.

ad•ja′cent, *adj.* adjoining.

ad′jec•tive, *n.* word describing a noun.
—**ad′jec•ti′val,** *adj.*

ad•join′, *v.* be next to.

ad•journ′, *v.* suspend (meeting) till another time.
—**ad•journ′ment,** *n.*

ad•judge′, *v.,* -judged, -judging. 1. decree or decide. 2. award.

ad•ju′di•cate′, *v.,* -cated, -cating. decide on as a judge.
—**ad•ju′di•ca′tion,** *n.*

ad′junct, *n.* something added.

ad•jure′, *v.,* -jured, -juring. request or command, esp. under oath.

ad•just′, *v.* 1. fit; adapt. 2. regulate. 3. settle.
—**ad•just′a•ble,** *adj.*
—**ad•just′er, ad•jus′tor,** *n.*
—**ad•just′ment,** *n.*

ad′ju•tant, *n.* military assistant to commandant.

ad-lib′, *v.,* -libbed, -libbing. *Informal.* improvise.

Adm., admiral.

adm. or **admn.,** 1. administration. 2. administrative. 3. administrator.

ad′man′, *n.* advertising professional.

ad•min′is•ter, *v.* 1. manage; direct. 2. dispense or give.

ad•min′is•tra′tion, *n.* 1. management. 2. dispensing. 3. executive officials.
—**ad•min′is•tra′tive,** *adj.*

ad•min′is•tra′tor, *n.* manager.

ad′mi•ral, *n.* 1. high-ranking navy officer. 2. brightly colored type of butterfly.

ad′mi•ral•ty, *n., pl.* -ties. navy department.

ad•mire′, *v.,* -mired, -miring. to hold in high regard.
—**ad•mir′er,** *n.*
—**ad′mi•ra′tion,** *n.*
—**ad′mi•ra•ble,** *adj.*

ad•mis′si•ble, *adj.* allowable.

ad•mis′sion, *n.* 1. act of admitting. 2. entrance price. 3. confession.

ad•mit′, *v.*, -mitted, -mitting. 1. allow to enter. 2. permit. 3. confess or acknowledge. —**ad•mit′tance**, *n.*

ad•mit′ted•ly, *adv.* without evasion or doubt.

ad•mix′ture, *n.* thing added. —**ad•mix′**, *v.*

ad•mon′ish, *v.* 1. warn. 2. reprove. —**ad′mo•ni′tion**, *n.* —**ad•mon′i•to′ry**, *adj.*

ad nau′se•am (ad nô′zē əm), to a sickening degree.

a•do′, *n.* activity; fuss.

a•do′be (-bē), *n.* sun-dried brick.

ad′o•les′cence, *n.* period between childhood and adulthood. —**ad′o•les′cent**, *adj.*, *n.*

a•dopt′, *v.* take or accept as one's own. —**a•dop′tion**, *n.* —**a•dopt′ive**, *adj.*

a•dore′, *v.*, adored, adoring. regard highly; worship. —**a•dor′a•ble**, *adj.* —**ad′o•ra′tion**, *n.*

a•dorn′, *v.* decorate. —**a•dorn′ment**, *n.*

ad•re′nal (ə drēn′l), *adj.* of glands near the kidneys.

ad•ren′al•in, *n.* glandular secretion that speeds heart.

a•drift′, *adv.*, *adj.* floating about, esp. helplessly.

a•droit′, *adj.* expert; deft. —**a•droit′ly**, *adv.* —**a•droit′ness**, *n.*

ad•sorb′, *v.* hold on a surface in a condensed layer.

ad′u•late′ (aj′ə lāt′), *v.*, -lated, -lating. flatter excessively. —**ad′u•la′tion**, *n.* —**ad′u•la•to′ry**, *adj.*

a•dult′, *adj.* 1. full-grown; mature. —*n.* 2. full-grown person. —**a•dult′hood**, *n.*

a•dul′ter•ate′, *v.*, -ated, -ating. make impure. —**a•dul′ter•a′tion**, *n.* —**a•dul′ter•ant**, *n.*

a•dul′ter•y, *n.*, *pl.* -teries. marital infidelity. —**a•dul′ter•er**, *n.* —**a•dul′ter•ess**, *n.fem.* —**a•dul′ter•ous**, *adj.*

adv., 1. advance 2. adverb 3. adverbial. 4. advertisement.

ad va lo′rem (ad və l′ôr′əm), fixed at a percentage of the value.

ad•vance′, *v.*, -vanced, -vancing. 1. move forward. 2.

propose. 3. raise in rank, price, etc. 4. supply beforehand; lend. —*n.* 5. forward move. 6. promotion. 7. increase. 8. loan. 9. friendly gesture. —*adj.* 10. early. —**ad•vance′ment,** *n.*

ad•vanced′, *adj.* 1. progressive. 2. relatively learned, old, etc.

ad•van′tage, *n.* 1. more favorable condition. —**ad′van•ta′geous,** *adj.*

ad′vent, *n.* 1. arrival. 2. coming of Christ. 3. (*cap.*) month before Christmas.

ad′ven•ti′tious, *adj.* accidentally added.

ad•ven′ture, *n., v.,* **-tured, -turing.** —*n.* 1. risky undertaking. 2. exciting event. —*v.* 3. risk or dare. —**ad•ven′tur•er,** *n.* —**ad•ven′tur•ous,** *adj.*

ad′verb, *n. Gram.* word modifying a verb, verbal noun, or other adverb. —**ad•ver′bi•al,** *adj.*

ad′ver•sar′y, *n., pl.* **-saries.** opponent.

ad•verse′, *adj.* antagonistic. —**ad•verse′ly,** *adv.*

ad•ver′si•ty, *n., pl.* **-ties.** misfortune.

ad•vert′, *v.* refer.

ad′ver•tise′, *v.,* **-tised, -tising.** bring to public notice. —**ad′ver•tis′er,** *n.* —**ad′ver•tise′ment,** *n.* —**ad′ver•tis′ing,** *n.*

ad•vice′, *n.* 1. opinion offered. 2. news.

ad•vis′a•ble, *adj.* prudent. —**ad•vis′a•bil′i•ty,** *n.*

ad•vise′, *v.* **-vised, -vising.** 1. offer an opinion. 2. recommend. 3. consult (with). 4. give news. —**ad•vis′er, ad•vi′sor,** *n.*

ad•vis′ed•ly, *adv.* after consideration; deliberately.

ad•vi′so•ry, *adj.* 1. giving advice. —*n.* 2. report on conditions.

ad′vo•cate′, *v.,* **-cated, -cating,** *n.* —*v.* (-kāt′). 1. urge; recommend. —*n.* (-kit). 2. supporter of cause. 3. lawyer. —**ad′vo•ca•cy,** *n.*

adz, *n.* axlike tool.

ae′gis (ē′jis) *n.* sponsorship.

ae′on (ē′ən), *n.* eon.

aer′ate, *v.,* **-ated, -ating.** expose to air.

aer′i•al, *adj.* **1.** of or in air. **2.** lofty. —*n.* **3.** radio antenna.

aer′ie (âr′ē, ēr′ē), *n, pl.* **-ies.** high nest, as of an eagle.

aero- prefix indicating: **1.** air. **2.** aircraft. Also, **aer-.**

aer•o′bic (â rō′bik), *adj.* **1.** needing oxygen to live. **2.** of aerobics.

aer•o′bics, *n.pl.* exercises designed to strengthen the heart and lungs.

aer′o•dy•nam′ics, *n.* science of action of air against solids. —**aer′o•dy•nam′ic,** *adj.*

aer′o•naut′, *n.* pilot.

aer′o•nau′tics, *n.* science of flight in aircraft. —**aer′o•naut′i•cal,** *adj.*

aer′o•plane′, *n. Brit.* airplane.

aer′o•space′, *n.* **1.** earth's atmosphere and the space beyond. —*adj.* **2.** operating in aerospace.

aer′o•sol′, *n.* **1.** liquid distributed through a gas. **2.** spray of such liquid.

aer′o•space′, *n.* **1.** the earth's atmosphere and space beyond. —*adj.* of missiles, aircraft, and spacecraft.

aes•thet′ic (es-), *adj.* **1.** of beauty. **2.** appreciating beauty. —**aes′thete** (-thēt), *n.*

aes•thet′ics, *n.* study of beauty.

a•far′, *adv.* at a distance.

af′fa•ble, *adj.* friendly; cordial. —**af′fa•bil′i•ty,** *n.*

af•fair′, *n.* **1.** matter of business. **2.** event. **3.** amorous relationship.

af•fect′, *v.* **1.** act on. **2.** impress (feelings). **3.** pretend to possess or feel.

af′fec•ta′tion, *n.* pretense.

af•fect′ed, *adj.* **1.** vain; haughty. **2.** diseased; infected. —**af•fect′ed•ly,** *adv.*

af•fec′tion, *n.* **1.** love. **2.** disease.

af•fec′tion•ate, *adj.* fond of. —**af•fec′tion•ate•ly,** *adv.*

af•fi′ance (ə fī′-), *v.* **-anced, -ancing.** become engaged to.

af′fi•da′vit, *n.* written statement under oath.

af•fil′i•ate′, *v.,* **-ated, -ating,** *n.* —*v.* **1.** join; connect. —*n.* (-ē it). **2.** associate. —**af•fil′i•a′tion,** *n.*

af•fin′i•ty, *n., pl.* **-ties. 1.** attraction. **2.** similarity.

af•firm′, *v.* 1. state; assert. 2. ratify. —**af′fir•ma′tion,** *n.*

af•firm′a•tive, *adj.* saying yes; affirming.

affirmative action, policy to increase employment opportunities for women and minorities.

af•fix′, *v.* 1. attach. —*n.* (af′iks). 2. added part.

af•flict′, *v.* distress; trouble. —**af•flic′tion,** *n.*

af′flu•ent, *adj.* rich; abundant. —**af′flu•ence,** *n.*

af•ford′, *v.* 1. have resources enough. 2. provide.

af•fray′, *n.* fight.

af•front′, *n., v.* insult.

af′ghan, *n.* woolen blanket.

a•field′, *adv.* astray.

a•fire′, *adv., adj.* on fire.

a•flame′, *adv., adj.* in flames.

AFL-CIO, American Federation of Labor and Congress of Industrial Organizations.

a•float′, *adv., adj.* 1. floating. 2. in circulation.

a•foot′, *adv., adj.* 1. on foot. 2. in existence.

a•fore′said′, *adj.* said before. Also, **a•fore′men′tioned.**

a•foul′, *adv., adj.* colliding; entangled; in conflict.

a•fraid′, *adj.* full of fear.

a•fresh′, *adj.* again.

Af′ri•can, *n.* native of Africa. —**Af′ri•can,** *adj.*

African-American, *n., adj.* black American.

African violet, *n.* hairy-leaved African houseplant with purple, pink, or white flowers.

Af′ri•kaans′ (af′ri käns′, -känz′), *n.* language of South Africa, derived from Dutch.

Af′ri•kan′er, *n.* white South African.

Af′ro, *n.* full, bushy hairstyle.

Af′ro-A•mer′i•can, *n., adj.* African-American.

aft, *adv.* *Naut.* at the stern.

af′ter, *prep.* 1. behind. 2. about. 3. later than. 4. next to. 5. in imitation of. —*adv.* 6. behind. 7. later.

af′ter•birth′, *n.* placenta and other matter expelled from uterus after childbirth.

af′ter•care′, *n.* care of recovering patient.

af′ter•ef•fect′, *n.* reaction.

af′ter•glow′, *n.* 1. glow after sunset. 2. pleasant memory.

af′ter•life′, *n.* life after death.

af′ter•math′, *n.* results.

af′ter•noon′, *n.* period between noon and evening.

af′ter•taste′, *n.* taste remaining in the mouth.

af′ter•thought′, *n.* later thought.

af′ter•ward, *adv.* later.

a•gain′, *adv.* 1. once more. 2. besides.

a•gainst′, *prep.* 1. opposed to. 2. in or into contact with.

a•gape′, *adv., adj.* wide open.

a′gar (ä′gär, ag′ər), *n.* seaweed gel used as food thickener.

ag′ate, *n.* 1. kind of quartz. 2. child's marble.

a•ga′ve (ə gä′vē), *n.* thick-leaved desert plant.

agcy., agency.

age, *n., v.,* **aged, aging.** —*n.* 1. length of time in existence. 2. stage; period. 3. legal maturity. —*v.* 4. make or become older.

ag′ed, *adj.* 1. having lived long. 2. matured. —*n.pl.* 3. elderly persons.

age′ism, *n.* discrimination against elderly persons. —**age′ist**, *n.*

age′less, *adj.* 1. apparently not aging. 2. not outdated.

a′gen•cy, *n., pl.* **-cies.** 1. office. 2. action. 3. means.

a•gen′da, *n.* matters to be dealt with.

a′gent, *n.* 1. person acting for another. 2. cause; means. 3. official.

ag•glom′er•ate′, *v.,* **-ated, -ating,** *adj., n.* —*v.* 1. collect into a mass. —*adj.* (-ər it). 2. collected in a mass. —*n.* (-ər it). 3. such a mass. —**ag•glom′er•a′tion**, *n.*

ag′gran•dize′, *v.,* **-dized, -dizing.** increase in size, rank, etc. —**ag•gran′dize•ment**, *n.*

ag′gra•vate′, *v.,* **-vated, -vating.** 1. make worse. 2. anger. —**ag′gra•va′tion**, *n.*

ag′gre•gate, *adj., n., v.,* **-gated, -gating.** —*adj.* 1. combined. —*n.* 2. whole amount. —*v.* (-gāt′). 3. gather. —**ag′gre•ga′tion**, *n.*

ag•gres′sion, *n.* hostile act. —**ag•gres′sor**, *n.*

ag•gres′sive, *adj.* 1. boldly energetic. 2. hostile.

ag•grieve′, *v.,* **-grieved, -grieving.** wrong severely.

a•ghast′ (ə gast′), *adj.* struck with fear or horror.

ag′ile (aj′əl), *adj.* quick; nimble. —**a•gil′i•ty,** *n.*

ag′i•tate′, *v.,* -tated, -tating. 1. shake. 2. disturb; excite. 3. discuss. —**ag′i•ta′tion,** *n.* —**ag′i•ta′tor,** *n.*

a•glow′, *adj., adv.* glowing.

ag•nos′tic, *n.* one who believes God is beyond human knowledge. —**ag•nos′ti•cism,** *n.*

a•go′, *adj., adv.* in the past.

a•gog′, *adj.* eagerly excited.

ag′o•nize′, *v.,* -nized, -nizing. 1. torture. 2. suffer anxiety.

ag′o•ny, *n., pl.* -nies. intense pain or suffering.

ag′o•ra•pho′bi•a (ag′ər ə fō′bē ə), *n.* fear of open spaces.

a•grar′i•an, *adj.* of the land.

a•gree′, *v.,* agreed, agreeing. 1. consent or promise. 2. be in harmony. 3. be similar. 4. be pleasing. —**a•gree′ment,** *n.*

a•gree′a•ble, *adj.* 1. pleasant. 2. willing. —**a•gree′a•bly,** *adv.*

ag′ri•busi′ness, large-scale business of growing, processing, and distributing farm products.

ag′ri•cul′ture, *n.* farming. —**ag′ri•cul′tur•al,** *adj.*

a•gron′o•my, *n.* science of farm management and crop production.

a•ground′, *adv., adj. Naut.* onto the bottom.

a′gue (ā′gyo͞o), *n.* fever, usu. malarial.

ah (ä), *interj.* (exclamation of pain, surprise, or satisfaction)

a•head′, *adv.* 1. in front; forward. 2. winning.

a•hoy′, *interj. Naut.* (hey there!)

aid, *v., n.* help.

aide (ād), *n.* assistant.

aide-de-camp, *n., pl.* **aides-de-camp.** military assistant.

AIDS (ādz), *n.* acquired immunity deficiency syndrome, a disease making one increasingly susceptible to diseases.

ail, *v.* 1. trouble. 2. be sick.

ai′ler•on′, *n.* flap on airplane wing.

ail'ment, *n.* illness.

aim, *v.* **1.** point or direct. **2.** intend. —*n.* **3.** act of aiming. **4.** target. **5.** purpose. —**aim'less,** *adj.*

ain't, *v. Illiterate or Dial.* am, is, or are not.

air, *n.* **1.** mixture of gases forming atmosphere of earth. **2.** appearance; manner. **3.** tune. —*v.* **4.** expose to air. **5.** broadcast.

air bag, bag that inflates automatically to protect passengers in a car collision.

air'borne', *adj.* carried by air.

air'brush', *n.* **1.** atomizer for spraying paint. —*v.* **2.** paint with an airbrush.

air conditioning, control of interior air for temperature, humidity, etc. —**air-conditioned,** *adj.*

air'craft', *n.* vehicle or vehicles for flight.

air'field', *n.* ground area for airplanes to land on and take off from.

air' force', military branch for air operations.

air gun, gun operated by compress air.

air'head', *n. Slang.* scatterbrained person.

air'lift', *n.* **1.** major transport by air. —*v.* **2.** move by airlift.

air'line', *n.* air transport company.

air'lin'er, *n.* large passenger airplane operated by airline.

air'mail', *n.* **1.** system of sending mail by airplane. **2.** mail sent by airmail. Also, **air'mail'.** —**air'mail',** *v.*

air'man, *n., pl.* **-men.** aviator.

air'plane', *n.* powered heavier-than-air craft.

air'port', *n.* airfield for loading, repairs, etc.

air raid, attack by aircraft.

air rifle, air gun with rifled bore.

air'ship', *n.* lighter-than-air aircraft.

air'sick'ness, *n.* nausea from motion in air travel. —**air'sick',** *adj.*

air'space', *n.* space above a nation, city, etc., over which it has jurisdiction or control.

air'tight', *adj.* **1.** impermeable to air. **2.** perfect; free of error.

air'waves', *n.pl.* medium of broadcasting.

air′wor′thy, *adj.,* **-thier, -thiest.** safe or fit to fly.

air′y, *adj.,* **airier, airiest. 1.** of or like air. **2.** delicate. **3.** unrealistic. **4.** well ventilated. **5.** light; gay. **—air′i•ly,** *adv.* **—air′i•ness,** *n.*

aisle, *n.* passageway.

a•jar′, *adj., adv.* partly opened.

AK, Alaska.

a.k.a., also known as.

a•kim′bo, *adj., adv.* with hands at hips.

a•kin′, *adj.* **1.** related. **2.** alike.

AL, Alabama.

à la or **a la** (ä′ là, ä′ lə), *prep.* in the manner or style of.

Ala., Alabama.

al′a•bas′ter, *n.* white gypsum.

à la carte, separately priced.

a•lac′ri•ty, *n.* quickness.

à la mode, 1. in the fashion. **2.** with ice cream.

a•larm′, *n.* **1.** fear of danger. **2.** sudden warning. **3.** call to arms. **—***v.* **4.** fill with fear.

alarm clock, clock with device to awaken sleeper.

a•larm′ist, *n.* sensationalist.

a•las′, *interj.* (cry of sorrow.)

al′ba•core′, *n.* type of tuna.

al′ba•tross′, *n.* sea bird.

al•be′it (ôl-), *conj.* though.

al•bi′no (-bī′-), *n., pl.* **-nos.** one lacking in pigmentation.

al′bum, *n.* **1.** blank book for pictures, stamps, etc. **2.** container with recordings.

al•bu′men (-byo͞o′-), *n.* egg white.

al•bu′min (-byo͞o′-), *n.* water-soluble protein.

al′che•my (-kə mē), *n.* medieval chemistry. **—al′che•mist,** *n.*

al′co•hol′, *n.* colorless intoxicating liquid formed by fermentation.

al′co•hol′ic, *adj.* **1.** of alcohol. **—***n.* **2.** one addicted to alcohol.

al′co•hol•ism, *n.* addiction to alcohol.

al′cove, *n.* recessed space.

al′der, *n.* small tree, usually growing in moist places.

al′der•man, *n., pl.* **-men.** representative on city council.

ale, *n.* dark, bitter beer.

ale′wife′, *n., pl.* **-wives.** North American shadlike fish.

a·lert′, *adj.* 1. vigilant. —*n.* 2. air-raid alarm. —*v.* 3. warn. —**a·lert′ly,** *adv.* —**a·lert′ness,** *n.*

al·fal′fa, *n.* forage plant also grown as food.

al·fres′co (al fres′kō), *adv., adj.* in the open air. Also, **al fres′co.**

al′ga, *n., pl.* **-gae** (-jē). water plant; seaweed.

al′ge·bra, *n.* branch of mathematics using symbols rather than specific numbers. —**al′ge·bra′ic,** *adj.*

ALGOL (al′gol, -gôl), *n.* computer language using mathematical symbols.

Al·gon′qui·an (al gong′kē ən, -kwē əen), *n.* North American Indian people. Also, **Al·gon′ki·an.**

al′go·rithm (al′gə riŧh əm), *n.* set of rules or steps to solve mathematical problem, program computer, etc. —**al′go·rith′mic,** *adj.*

a′li·as, *adv.* 1. otherwise known as. —*n.* 2. assumed name.

al′i·bi′ (-bī′), *n.* defense of accused one as being elsewhere. 2. excuse.

al′ien (āl′yən), *n.* 1. foreigner. —*adj.* 2. foreign.

al′ien·ate′, *v.,* -ated, -ating. lose friendship of; repel. —**al′ien·a′tion,** *n.*

al′ien·ist, *n.* psychiatrist who gives legal testimony.

a·light′, *v.* 1. dismount after travel. 2. descend to perch or sit. —*adv., adj.* 3. lighted up.

a·lign′ (ə līn′), *v.* bring into line. —**a·lign′ment,** *n.*

a·like′, *adv.* 1. similarly. —*adj.* 2. similar.

al′i·men′ta·ry, *adj.* of or for food.

alimentary canal, tube-shaped bodily passage for digestion of food.

al′i·mo′ny, *n.* money for support of a wife after separation or divorce.

a·live′, *adj.* 1. living. 2. active. 3. lively. 4. teeming.

al′ka·li′ (-lī′), *n.* chemical that neutralizes acids to form salts. —**al′ka·line′,** *adj.*

al′ka·loid′, *n.* organic compound in plants.

all, *adj.* 1. the whole of. 2. every. —*n., pron.* 3. the whole; everything. —*adv.* 4. entirely.

Al'lah, *n.* Muslim name for God.

All'-Amer'ican, *adj.* 1. best in the U.S., as in a sport. 2. typically American. —*n.* 3. all-American player or team.

all'-around', *adj.* 1. versatile. 2. having many uses.

al·lay', *v.* quiet or lessen.

al·lege' (ə lej'), *v.,* **-leged, -leging.** declare; state, often without proof. —**al'le·ga'tion,** *n.* —**al·leg'ed·ly,** *adv.*

al·le'giance, *n.* loyalty.

al'le·go'ry, *n., pl.* **-ries.** symbolic story. —**al'le·gor'i·cal,** *adj.*

al·le'gro, *adv. Music.* fast.

al'le·lu'ia (al'ə l 'yə), *interj.* (hallelujah.)

al'ler·gen, *n.* substance that causes allergic reaction. —**al'ler·gen'ic,** *adj.*

al'ler·gist, *n.* doctor who treats allergies.

al'ler·gy, *n., pl.* **-gies.** bodily sensitiveness to certain substances. —**al·ler'gic,** *adj.*

al·le'vi·ate', *v.,* **-ated, -ating.** lessen; relieve. —**al·le'vi·a'tion,** *n.*

al'ley, *n.* narrow street.

alley cat, stray cat.

al·li'ance, *n.* 1. union; joining. 2. marriage. 3. treaty. 4. parties to treaty.

al·lied', *adj.* 1. joined by treaty. 2. related.

al'li·ga'tor, *n.* broad-snouted type of crocodile.

all'-im·por'tant, *adj.* supremely necessary.

all'-in·clu'sive, *adj.* comprehensive.

al·lit'er·a'tion, *n.* series of words starting with the same sound.

al'lo·cate', *v.,* **-cated, -cating.** allot. —**al'lo·ca'tion,** *n.*

al·lot', *v.,* **-lotted, -lotting.** 1. divide; distribute. 2. assign. —**al·lot'ment,** *n.*

all'-out', *adj.* unrestricted.

al·low', *v.* 1. permit. 2. give. 3. admit. —**al·low'a·ble,** *adj.* —**al·low'ance,** *n.*

al'loy, *n.* 1. mixture of metals. —*v.* (ə loi'). 2. mix (metals). 3. adulterate.

all right, 1. yes; I agree. 2. in a satisfactory way. 3. safe; sound. 4. acceptable.

All Saints' Day, church festival Nov. 1 in honor of saints.

all′spice′, *n.* fragrant spice.

all′-star′, *adj.* 1. consisting of star performers. —*n.* 2. member of all-star group.

all′-time′, *adj.* never equaled.

al•lude′, *v.,* -luded, -luding. refer (to) in words. —**al•lu′sion,** *n.*

al•lure′, *v.,* -lured, -luring. attract; tempt. —**al•lure′ment,** *n.*

al•lu′vi•um, *n.* earth deposited by rivers, etc. —**al•lu′vi•al,** *adj.*

al•ly′, *v.,* -lied, -lying, *n., pl.* -lies. —*v.* 1. unite in an alliance. —*n.* (al′ī). 2. person or nation bound to each other.

al′ma ma′ter, one's school.

al′ma•nac′, *n.* calendar showing special events, etc.

al•might′y, *adj.* 1. having all power. —*n.* 2. (*cap.*) God.

al′mond (ä′mənd), *n.* edible nut of the almond tree.

al′most, *adv.* nearly.

alms (ämz), *n.pl.* charity.

al′oe, *n.* plant with fleshy leaves.

a•loft′, *adv., adj.* high up.

a•lo′ha (ə lō′ə, ä lō′hä), *n., interj.* 1. (hello). 2. (farewell.)

a•lone′, *adj., adv.* 1. apart. 2. by oneself.

a•long′, *prep.* 1. through length of. —*adv.* 2. onward. 3. together; with one.

a•long′side′, *adv.* 1. to one's side. —*prep.* 2. beside.

a•loof′, *adv.* 1. at a distance. —*adj.* 2. reserved; indifferent. —**a•loof′ness,** *n.*

a•loud′, *adv.* loudly.

al•pac′a, *n.* South American sheep with soft, silky wool.

al′pha, *n.* first letter of Greek alphabet.

al′pha•bet′, *n.* letters of a language in order. —**al′pha•bet′i•cal,** *adj.* —**al′pha•bet•ize′,** *v.*

al′pha•nu•mer′ic, *adj.* using both letters and numbers. Also, **al′pha•nu•mer′i•cal.** —**al′pha•nu•mer′i•cal•ly,** *adv.*

al′pine (al′pīn, -pin), *adj.* 1. of or like a high mountain. 2. above the timberline.

al•read′y, *adv.* previously.

al′so, *adv.* in addition.

alt., 1. alteration. 2. alternate. 3. altitude. 4. alto.

al′tar, *n.* 1. platform for religious rites. 2. communion table.

al′ter, *v.* change. —**al′ter•a′tion,** *n.*

al′ter•ca′tion, *n.* dispute.

al′ter e′go, 1. intimate friend. 2. perfect substitute for oneself. 3. one's other side.

al′ter•nate′, *v.,* -nated, -nating, *adj., n.* —*v.* (-nāt′). 1. occur or do in turns. —*adj.* (-nit). 2. being by turns. —*n.* (-nit). 3. substitute. —**al′ter•na′tion,** *n.*

alternating current, electric current that regularly reverses its direction.

al′ter•na′tor, *n.* generator of alternating current.

al•ter′na•tive, *n.* 1. other choice. —*adj.* 2. offering a choice.

al•though′, *conj.* even though.

al•tim′e•ter, *n.* device for measuring altitude.

al′ti•tude′, *n.* height.

al′to, *n., pl.* -tos. lowest female voice.

al′to•geth′er, *adv.* entirely.

al′tru•ism′, *n.* devotion to others. —**al′tru•ist,** *n.* —**al′tru•is′tic,** *adj.*

al′um, *n.* astringent substance, used in medicine, etc.

a•lu′mi•num, *n.* light, silvery metal. Also, *Brit.,* **al′u•min′i•um.**

a•lum′nus, *n., pl.* -ni (-nī). graduate. —**a•lum′na,** *n.fem., pl.* -nae (-nē).

al′ways, *adv.* 1. all the time. 2. every time.

Alz′hei•mer's disease′ (älts′hī mərz, ôlts′-), disease marked by increasing memory loss and mental deterioration, usually in old age.

am, *v.* 1st pers. sing. pres. indic. of **be.**

Am., 1. America. 2. American.

a.m., the period before noon. Also, **A.M.**

A.M.A., American Medical Association.

a•mal′gam, *n.* mixture, esp. one with mercury.

a•mal′gam•ate′, *v.,* -ated, -ating. combine. —**a•mal′gam•a′tion,** *n.*

a•man′u•en′sis, *n., pl.* -ses. secretary.

am′a·ranth′, *n.* plant grown as food and for its flowers.

am′a·ret′to (am′ə ret′ō, ä′mə-), almond liqueur.

am′a·ryl′lis, *n.* plant with large, lilylike flowers.

a·mass′, *v.* collect.

am′a·teur′ (-chŏŏr′), *n.* nonprofessional artist, athlete, etc. —**am′a·teur′ish**, *adj.* —**am′a·teur·ism**, *n.*

am′a·to′ry, *adj.* of love.

a·maze′, *v.*, amazed, amazing. awe. —**a·maze′ment**, *n.*

Am′a·zon′, *n.* 1. female warrior of Greek legend. 2. tall, powerful woman.

am·bas′sa·dor, *n.* diplomat of highest rank.

am′ber, *n.* 1. yellowish fossil resin. —*adj.* 2. yellowish.

am′ber·gris′ (-grēs′), *n.* gray secretion of sperm whale, used in perfumes.

am′bi·dex′trous, *adj.* using both hands equally well.

am′bi·ence (-bē-), *n.* surroundings; atmosphere. Also, **am′bi·ance**. —**am′bi·ent**, *adj.*

am·big′u·ous, *adj.* unclear in meaning. —**am′bi·gu′i·ty**, *n.*

am·bi′tion, *n.* 1. desire for success, power, etc. 2. object so desired. —**am·bi′tious**, *adj.*

am·biv′a·lent, *adj.* with conflicting emotions. —**am·biv′a·lence**, *n.*

am′ble, *v.*, -bled, -bling, *n.* —*v.* 1. to go at an easy gait. —*n.* 2. easy gait.

am·bro′sia (-zhə), *n.* food of classical gods.

am′bu·lance, *n.* vehicle for sick or wounded.

am′bu·la·to′ry, *adj.* able to walk.

am′bus·cade′, *n.* ambush.

am′bush, *n.* 1. concealment for a surprise attack. 2. surprise attack. 3. place of such concealment. —*v.* 4. attack thus.

a·me′ba (ə mē′bə), *n.*, *pl.* **-bas** *or* **-bae** (-bē). microscopic one-celled animal. Also, **a·moe′ba**.

a·mel′io·rate′, *v.*, -rated, -rating. improve. —**a·mel′io·ra′tion**, *n.*

a′men′, *interj.* (so be it!)

a·me′na·ble, *adj.* willing.

a•mend′, *v.* **1.** change or correct. **2.** improve. —**a•mend′ment,** *n.*

a•mends′, *n.pl.* reparation.

a•men′i•ty, *n., pl.* **-ties.** pleasant feature, etc.

Am′er•a′sian (am′ə rā′zhən), *n.* person of mixed American and Asian descent.

A•mer′i•can, *n.* **1.** citizen of the U.S. **2.** native of N. or S. America. —*adj.* **3.** of the U.S. **4.** of N. or S. America.

American Indian, member of the aboriginal peoples of N. or S. America.

A•mer′i•can•ism, *n.* **1.** devotion to the U.S. **2.** custom, etc., of the U.S.

A•mer′i•can•ize′, *v.,* become American in character.

American plan, payment of fixed hotel rate for room, service, and meals.

American Sign Language, visual-gesture language used by deaf people in U.S. and parts of Canada.

am′e•thyst, *n.* violet quartz.

a′mi•a•ble, *adj.* friendly. —**a′mi•a•bil′i•ty,** *n.* —**a′mi•a•bly,** *adv.*

am′i•ca•ble, *adj.* not hostile. —**am′i•ca•bly,** *adv.*

a•mid′, *prep.* among. Also, **a•midst′.**

a•mid′ships′ or **-ship′,** *adv.* the middle part of a ship.

a•mi′go (-mē′-), *n., pl.* **-gos.** *Spanish.* friend.

a•mi′no ac′id, type of organic compound from which proteins are made.

a•miss′, *adv.* **1.** wrongly. —*adj.* **2.** wrong.

am′i•ty, *n.* friendship.

am′me•ter, *n.* instrument for measuring current in amperes.

am•mo (am′ō), *n. Slang.* ammunition.

am•mo′nia, *n.* colorless, pungent, water-soluble gas.

am′mu•ni′tion, *n.* bullets, shot, etc., for weapons.

am•ne′sia, *n.* loss of memory. —**am•ne′si•ac′** (-zhē ak′, -zē-), **am•ne′sic,** *adj., n.*

am′nes•ty, *n.* pardon for political crimes.

am′ni•o•cen•te′sis (am′nē ō sen tē′sis) *n., pl.* **-ses** (-sēz). surgical procedure of withdrawing fluid from pregnant woman for genetic diagnosis of fetus.

a•mok′, *adv.* amuck.

a•mong′, *prep.* **1.** in the group of. Also, **a•mongst′.**

a•mor′al (ā-), *adj.* indifferent to moral standards. —**a′mo•ral′i•ty,** *n.*

am′o•rous, *adj.* inclined to, or showing, love.

a•mor′phous, *adj.* formless.

am′or•tize′, *v.,* -tized, -tizing. pay off. —**am′or•ti•za′tion,** *n.*

a•mount′, *n.* **1.** sum total. **2.** quantity. —*v.* **3.** add up (to).

a•mour′, *n.* love affair.

am′per•age (am′pər ij, am pēr′-), *n.* strength of an electric current in amperes.

am′pere (-pēr), *n.* unit measuring electric current.

am′per•sand′, *n.* sign (&) meaning "and."

am•phet′a•mine (-mēn), *n.* drug stimulating nervous system.

am•phib′i•an, *n.* **1.** animal living both in water and on land. —*adj.* **2.** Also, **am•phib′i•ous.** operating on land or water.

am′phi•the′a•ter, *n.* theater with seats tiered around its center.

am′ple, *adj.,* -pler, -plest. **1.** sufficient. **2.** abundant. —**am′ply,** *adv.*

am′pli•fy′, *v.,* -fied, -fying. make larger or louder. —**am′pli•fi′er,** *n.* —**am′pli•fi•ca′tion,** *n.*

am′pli•tude′, *n.* **1.** extent. **2.** abundance.

am′pule (am′pyōōl, -pōōl), *n.* sealed glass or plastic vial containing solution for hypodermic injection. Also, **am′pul, am′poule.**

am′pu•tate′, *v.,* -tated, -tating. cut off (a limb). —**am′pu•ta′tion,** *n.* —**am′pu•tee′,** *n.*

a•muck′, *adv.* maniacally.

am′u•let, *n.* magical charm.

a•muse′, *v.,* amused, amusing. **1.** entertain. **2.** cause mirth in. —**a•muse′ment,** *n.*

amusement park, park with rides and recreations.

an, *adj. or indef. art. before initial vowel sounds.* See **a.**

a•nach′ro•nism, *n.* chronological discrepancy. —**a•nach′ro•nis′tic,** *adj.*

an′a•con′da, *n.* large South American snake.

an′a•gram′, *n.* word formed from letters of another.

a′nal, *adj.* of the anus.

an′al•ge′sic (an′əl jē′zik), *n.* drug for relieving pain.

analog computer, computer that solves problems by using voltages as analogies of numerical variables.

an′a•logue′ (an′l ôg′, -og′), *n.* something analogous to something else. Also, **an′a•log′.**

a•nal′o•gy (-jē), *n., pl.* **-gies.** similarity in some respects. —**a•nal′o•gous** (-gəs), *adj.*

a•nal′y•sis, *n., pl.* **-ses. 1.** separation into constituent parts. **2.** summary. **3.** psychoanalysis. —**an′a•lyst,** *n.* —**an′a•lyt′ic, an′a•lyt′i•cal,** *adj.* —**an′a•lyze′,** *v.*

an′ar•chy (-kē), *n.* lawless society. —**an′ar•chism,** *n.* —**an′ar•chist,** *n.*

a•nath′e•ma, *n.* **1.** solemn curse. **2.** object detested.

a•nat′o•my, *n., pl.* **-mies. 1.** structure of an animal or plant. **2.** science dealing with such structure. —**an′a•tom′i•cal,** *adj.*

an′ces•tor, *n.* person from whom one is descended. —**an′ces•try,** *n.* —**an•ces′tral,** *adj.*

an′chor, *n.* **1.** heavy device for keeping boats, etc., in place. **2.** main broadcaster who coordinates TV or radio newscast. —*v.* **3.** fasten by an anchor. **4.** serve as anchor for (newscast). —**an′chor•age,** *n.*

an′chor•man′, *n., pl.* **-men.** person who anchors a newscast. Also, *fem.,* **an′chor•wom′an;** *masc.* or *fem.,* **an′chor•per′son.**

an′cho•vy (-chō vē), *n., pl.* **-vies.** small herringlike fish.

an′cient, *adj.* **1.** of long ago. **2.** very old. —*n.* **3.** person who lived long ago.

an′cil•lar′y (an′sə ler′ē), *adj.* subordinate; auxiliary.

and, *conj.* **1.** with; also. **2.** *Informal.* (used in place of **to** in infinitive): *Try and stop me.*

an•dan′te (-tä), *adv. Music.* at moderate speed.

and′i′rons, *n.pl.* metal supports for logs in fireplace.

an'dro·gen, *n.* male sex hormone, as testosterone.

an·drog'y·nous (an droj'ə nəs), *adj.* having both masculine and feminine characteristics.

an'droid, *n.* automaton in human form.

an'ec·dote', *n.* short story.

a·ne'mi·a, *n.* inadequate supply of hemoglobin and red blood cells. —**a·ne'mic,** *adj.*

an'e·mom'e·ter, *n.* instrument for measuring wind speed.

a·nem'o·ne', *n.* buttercuplike plant with colorful flowers.

an'es·the'sia (-zhə), *n.* insensibility to pain, usually induced by a drug (**an'es·thet'ic**). —**an·es'the·tize',** *v.*

an'eu·rysm (an'yə riz'əm), *n.* permanent pouch formed in a weakened artery wall. Also, **an'eu·rism'.**

a·new', *adv.* again.

an'gel, *n.* **1.** spiritual being who is messenger of God. **2.** very kind and helpful person.

angel food cake, light, spongy cake made with egg whites.

an'ger, *n.* **1.** outrage. —*v.* **2.** cause anger in.

an·gi'na pec'to·ris (an jī'nə pek'tə ris), coronary attack.

an'gle, *n., v.,* **-gled, -gling.** —*n.* **1.** spread between converging lines. —*v.* **2.** fish with a hook on a line. **3.** try for something by artful means. **4.** bend in angles. —**an'gler,** *n.*

an'gle·worm', *n.* worm used in fishing.

An'gli·can, *adj.* **1.** of the Church of England. —*n.* **2.** member of this church.

An'gli·cize', *v.,* **-cized, -ciz·ing.** make or become English in form or character.

An'glo-Sax'on, *n.* **1.** person of English descent. **2.** inhabitant of England before 1066. —*adj.* **3.** of Anglo-Saxons.

An·go'ra, *n.* **1.** cat, goat, or rabbit with long, silky hair. **2.** (*l.c.*) yarn or fabric from Angora goat or rabbit.

an'gry, *adj.,* **-grier, -griest. 1.** full of anger. **2.** inflamed. —**an'gri·ly,** *adv.*

angst (ängkst), *n.* feeling of dread, anxiety, or anguish.

ang′strom (ang′strəm), *n.* *(often cap.)* unit of measure for wavelengths of light.

an′guish, *n.* intense grief.

an′gu•lar, *adj.* having angles. —**an•gu•lar′i•ty,** *n.*

an′i•line (-lin), *n.* oily liquid used in dyes, plastics, etc.

an′i•mad•vert′, *v.* criticize. —**an′i•mad•ver′sion,** *n.*

an′i•mal, *n.* **1.** non-vegetative living thing. —*adj.* **3.** of animals.

an′i•mate′, *v.,* -mated, -mating, *adj.* —*v.* (-māt′). **1.** make alive or lively. —*adj.* (-mit). **2.** alive. —**an′i•ma′tion,** *n.*

an′i•mism, *n.* belief that animals and natural objects have souls. —**an′i•mist,** *n.,* *adj.* —**an′i•mis′tic,** *adj.*

an′i•mos′i•ty, *n.,* *pl.* -ties. strong ill will or enmity.

an′i•mus, *n.* strong dislike.

an′ise (an′is), *n.* plant yielding aromatic seed (**an′i•seed′**).

an′kle, *n.* joint between foot and leg.

an′let, *n.* **1.** short, ankle-length sock. **2.** ornament for ankle.

an′nals, *n.pl.* record of events.

an•neal′, *v.* to toughen.

an•nex′, *v.* **1.** add; join. —*n.* (an′ eks). **2.** part, etc., attached. —**an′nex•a′tion,** *n.*

an•ni′hi•late′, *v.,* -lated, -lating. destroy completely. —**an•ni′hi•la′tion,** *n.*

an′ni•ver′sa•ry, *n.,* *pl.* -ries. annual recurrence of the date of a past event.

an′no•tate′, *v.,* -tated, -tating. supply with notes. —**an′no•ta′tion,** *n.*

an•nounce′, *v.,* -nounced, -nouncing. make known. —**an•nounce′ment,** *n.* —**an•nounc′er,** *n.*

an•noy′, *v.* irritate or trouble. —**an•noy′ance,** *n.*

an′nu•al, *adj.* **1.** yearly. **2.** living only one season. —*n.* **3.** annual plant. **4.** yearbook. —**an′nu•al•ly,** *adv.*

an•nu′i•tant, *n.* person who receives an annuity.

an•nu′i•ty, *n.,* *pl.* -ties. income in annual payments.

an•nul′, *v.,* -nulled, -nulling. make void. —**an•nul′ment,** *n.*

an′nu•lar, *adj.* ring shaped.

An·nun'ci·a'tion, *n.* announcement to Virgin Mary of incarnation of Christ (March 25).

an'ode (an'ōd), *n.* **1.** electrode with positive charge. **2.** negative terminal of a battery.

an'o·dyne' (-dīn'), *n.* medication that relieves pain.

a·noint', *v.* to oil; consecrate.

a·nom'a·ly, *n., pl.* **-lies.** something irregular. **—a·nom'a·lous,** *adj.*

a·non', *adv. Archaic.* soon.

anon., anonymous.

a·non'y·mous, *adj.* by someone unnamed. **—an'o·nym'i·ty,** *n.* **—a·non'y·mous·ly,** *adv.*

an'o·rak, *n.* hooded jacket.

an'o·rex'i·a (an'ə rek'sē ə), *n.* **1.** loss of appetite. **2.** Also, **anorexia ner·vos'a** (nûr vō'sə). eating disorder marked by excessive dieting.

an·oth'er, *adj.* **1.** additional. **2.** different. **—n. 3.** one more. **4.** different one.

an'swer, *n.* **1.** reply. **2.** solution. **—v. 3.** reply to. **4.** suit. **5.** be responsible. **6.** correspond.

an'swer·a·ble, *adj.* **1.** able to be answered. **2.** responsible.

ant, *n.* common small insect.

ant·ac'id, *n.* medicine to counteract acids.

an·tag'o·nism', *n.* hostility. **—an·tag'o·nist,** *n.* **—an·tag'o·nis'tic,** *adj.* **—an·tag'o·nize',** *v.*

ant·arc'tic, *adj. (often cap.)* of or at the South Pole.

an'te (an'tē), *n.* **1.** (in poker) stake put in pot before cards are dealt. **2.** price or cost of something. **—v. 3.** (in poker) put (one's ante) into the pot. **4.** pay (one's share).

ante-, prefix indicating: **1.** happening before, as *antediluvian.* **2.** in front of, as *anteroom.*

ant'eat'er, *n.* tropical American mammal having long snout and feeding on ants and termites.

an'te·bel'lum, *adj.* before a war.

an'te·ced'ent (-sēd'-), *adj.* **1.** prior. **—n. 2.** anything that precedes.

an'te·date', *v.,* **-dated, -dating. 1.** happen earlier than. **2.** predate.

an′te·di·lu′vi·an, *adj.* before the Flood.

an′te·lope′, *n.* deerlike animal.

an·ten′na, *n., pl.* **-nae** (-nē), *for 1.* **1.** feeler on the head of an insect, etc. **2.** wires for transmitting radio waves.

an·te′ri·or, *adj.* **1.** earlier. **2.** frontward.

an′te·room′, *n.* room before the main room.

an′them, *n.* patriotic hymn.

an′ther, *n.* pollen-bearing part of stamen.

an·thol′o·gy, *n., pl.* **-gies.** collection of writings.

an′thra·cite′, *n.* hard coal.

an′thrax, *n.* cattle disease.

an′thro·poid′, *adj.* manlike.

an′thro·pol′o·gy, *n.* science of humankind. **—an′thro·pol′o·gist,** *n.*

an′thro·po·mor′phic (an′thrə pə môr′fik), *adj.* ascribing human qualities to a nonhuman thing or being. **—an′thro·po·mor′phism,** *n.*

anti- prefix indicating: **1.** against or opposed to, as *antisocial.* **2.** acting against, as *antihistamine.*

an′ti·bi·ot′ic, *n.* substance used to destroy organisms.

an′ti·bod′y, *n., pl.* **-bodies.** substance in the blood that destroys bacteria.

an′tic, *n.* **1.** odd behavior. **—***adj.* **2.** playful.

an·tic′i·pate′, *v.,* **-pated, -pating. 1.** expect and prepare for. **2.** foresee. **—an·tic′i·pa′tion,** *n.*

an′ti·cli′max, *n.* undramatic outcome.

an′ti·co·ag′u·lant, *n.* substance that prevents coagulation of blood.

an′ti·de·pres′sant, *n.* drug for relieving depression.

an′ti·dote′, *n.* medicine counteracting poison, etc.

an′ti·freeze′, *n.* liquid used in engine's radiator to prevent freezing of cooling fluid.

an′ti·gen (an′ti jən, -jen′), *n.* substance that stimulates production of antibodies.

an′ti·his′ta·mine′ (-mēn′), *n.* substance used esp. against allergic reactions.

an′ti·mat′ter, *n.* matter with charges opposite to those of common particles.

an′ti•mo′ny, *n.* brittle white metallic element.

an′ti•ox′i•dant, *n.* organic substance counter-acting oxidation.

an′ti•pas′to, *n., pl.* **-pas′tos, -pas′ti.** Italian appetizer.

an•tip′a•thy, *n., pl.* **-thies.** dislike; aversion.

an′ti•per′spi•rant, *n.* astringent product for reducing perspiration.

an•tip′o•des (an tip′ə dēz′), *n.pl.* places opposite each other on the globe.

an′ti•quar′i•an, *adj.* **1.** of the study of antiquities. —*n.* **2.** antiquary.

an′ti•quar′y (-kwer′ē), *n., pl.* **-ries.** collector of antiquities.

an′ti•quat′ed, *adj.* old.

an•tique′ (-tēk′), *adj.* **1.** old-fashioned. —*n.* **2.** old valuable object.

an•tiq′ui•ty, *n., pl.* **-ties. 1.** ancient times. **2.** something ancient.

an′ti-Sem′ite (an′tē sem′īt, an′tī-), *n.* person hostile to Jews. —**an′ti-Se•mit′ic,** *adj.* —**an′ti-Sem′i•tism,** *n.*

an′ti•sep′tic, *adj.* **1.** destroying certain germs. —*n.* **2.** antiseptic substance.

an′ti•so′cial, *adj.* **1.** hostile to society. **2.** not sociable.

an•tith′e•sis, *n., pl.* **-ses.** direct opposite.

an′ti•tox′in, *n.* substance counteracting germ-produced poisons in the body.

an′ti•trust′, *adj.* opposing or intended to restrain business trusts or monopolies.

ant′ler, *n.* horn on deer, etc.

an′to•nym, *n.* word of opposite meaning.

a′nus, *n.* opening at lower end of alimentary canal.

an′vil, *n.* iron block on which hot metals are shaped.

anx•i′e•ty (ang zī′-), *n., pl.* **-ties. 1.** worried distress. **2.** eagerness. —**anx′ious** (angk′shəs), *adj.* —**anx′ious•ly,** *adv.*

an′y, *adj.* **1.** one; some. **2.** every. —*pron.* **3.** any person, etc. —**an′y•bod′y, an′y•one′,** *pron.* —**an′y•thing′,** *pron.*

an′y•how′, *adv.* in any way. Also, **an′y•way′.**

an′y•place′, *adv.* anywhere.

an′y·time′, *adv.* at any time.

an′y·where′, *adv.* at any place.

A′-OK′ (ā′ō kā′), *adj., adv.* OK; perfect. Also, **A′-O·kay′**.

A′ one′ (ā′ wun′), *adj.* excellent. Also, **A′ 1′, A′-1′**.

a·or′ta, *n., pl.* **-tas, -tae** (-tē). main blood vessel from heart.

a·pace (ə pās′), *adv.* quickly.

A·pach′e (ə pach′ē), *n., pl.* **A·pach·e, A·pach·es.** member of a group of American Indian peoples of the U.S. Southwest.

a·part′, *adv.* 1. into pieces. 2. separately.

a·part′heid (ə pärt′hīt), *n.* separation of and discrimination against blacks.

a·part′ment, *n.* set of rooms in a dwelling.

ap′a·thy, *n., pl.* **-thies.** lack of emotion or interest. —**ap′a·thet′ic**, *adj.*

ape, *n., v.,* **aped, aping.** —*n.* 1. large monkeylike animal. —*v.* 2. imitate stupidly.

a·pé·ri·tif (ə per′i tēf′), *n.* liquor served before meal.

ap′er·ture (-chər), *n.* opening.

a′pex, *n.* tip; summit.

a·pha′sia (ə fā′zhə), *n.* loss of ability to speak or to understand language. —**a·pha′sic** (-zik), *adv.*

a·phe′li·on (ə fē′lē ən, ap hē′-), *n.* point farthest from sun in orbit of planet or comet.

a′phid, *n.* plant-sucking insect.

aph′o·rism′, *n.* brief maxim.

aph′ro·dis′i·ac′, *adj.* 1. sexually exciting. —*n.* 2. aphrodisiac food, drug, etc.

a′pi·ar′y, *n., pl.* **-ries.** place where bees are kept.

a·piece′, *adv.* for each.

a·plen′ty, *adv., adv.* in generous amounts.

a·plomb (ə plom′, ə plum′), *n.* poise; self-possession.

A·poc′a·lypse, *n.* 1. revelation of the apostle John. 2. *(l.c.)* prophetic revelation. —**a·poc′a·lyp′tic**, *adj.*

A·poc′ry·pha, *n.* uncanonical parts of the Bible.

a·poc′ry·phal, *adj.* dubious.

ap′o·gee, *n.* remotest point of satellite orbit.

a′po·lit′i·cal, *adj.* not interested in politics.

a·pol′o·gist (-jist), *n.* advocate; defender.

a·pol′o·gize′, *v.,* **-gized, -gizing.** offer apology.

a·pol′o·gy, *n., pl.* **-gies. 1.** statement of regret for one's act. **2.** stated defense. —**a·pol′o·get′ic,** *adj.*

ap′o·plex′y, *n.* sudden loss of bodily function due to bursting of blood vessel. —**ap′o·plec′tic,** *adj.*

a·pos′tate, *n.* deserter of one's faith, cause, etc. —**a·pos′ta·sy,** *n.*

a′ pos·te′·ri·o′ri (ā′ po stēr′ē ôr′ī, -ôr′ē), *adj.* **1.** from particular instances to a general principle. **2.** based on observation or experiment.

a·pos′tle, *n.* **1.** disciple sent by Jesus to preach gospel. **2.** moral reformer. —**ap′os·tol′ic,** *adj.*

a·pos′tro·phe, *n.* **1.** sign (') indicating an omitted letter, the possessive, or certain plurals. **2.** words in passing to one person or group. —**a·pos′tro·phize′,** *v.*

a·poth′e·car′y, *n., pl.* **-ries.** druggist.

a·poth′e·o′sis (ə poth′ē ō′sis), *n., pl.* **-ses** (-sēz). **1.** elevation to the rank of a god. **2.** ideal example; epitome.

ap·pall′, *v.* fill with horror. Also, **ap·pal′.** —**ap·pall′ing,** *adj.*

ap′pa·ra′tus, *n.* **1.** instruments and machines for some task. **2.** organization.

ap·par′el, *n.* **1.** clothes. —*v.* **2.** dress.

ap·par′ent, *adj.* **1.** obvious. **2.** seeming. —**ap·par′ent·ly,** *adv.*

ap′pa·ri′tion, *n.* specter.

ap·peal′, *n.* **1.** call for aid. **2.** request for corroboration or review. **3.** attractiveness. —*v.* **4.** make an appeal.

ap·pear′, *v.* **1.** come into sight. **2.** seem.

ap·pear′ance, *n.* **1.** act of appearing. **2.** outward look.

ap·pease′, *v.,* **-peased, -peasing. 1.** placate. **2.** satisfy. —**ap·pease′ment,** *n.*

ap·pel′lant, *n.* one who appeals.

ap·pel′late, *adj.* dealing with appeals.

ap′pel·la′tion, *n.* name or title.

ap·pend′, *v.* add; join.

ap·pend′age, *n.* subordinate attached part.

ap′pen·dec′to·my, *n., pl.* **-mies.** removal of the appendix.

ap·pen′di·ci′tis (-sī′-), *n.* inflammation of appendix.

ap·pen′dix, *n., pl.* **-dixes, -dices. 1.** supplement. **2.** closed tube off intestines.

ap′per·tain′, *v.* belong.

ap′pe·tite′, *n.* a desire for.

ap′pe·tiz′er, *n.* portion of food or drink served before meal to stimulate appetite. —**ap′pe·tiz′·ing,** *adj.*

ap·plaud′, *v.* clapping praise. —**ap·plause′,** *n.*

ap′ple, *n.* common fruit.

ap′ple·jack′, *n.* brandy made from fermented cider.

ap′ple·sauce′, *n.* apples stewed to a pulp.

ap·pli′ance, *n.* special device.

ap′pli·ca·ble, *adj.* that can be applied.

ap′pli·cant, *n.* one who applies.

ap′pli·ca′tion, *n.* **1.** act of applying. **2.** use to which something is put. **3.** relevance. **4.** petition; request. **5.** form filled out by applicant. **6.** persistent attention.

ap′pli·ca′tor, *n.* device for applying a substance.

ap′pli·qué′ (ap′li kā′), *n., v.,* **-quéd, -quéing.** —*n.* **1.** cutout design of one material applied to another. —*v.* **2.** decorate with appliqué.

ap·ply′, *v.* **-plied, -plying. 1.** put on. **2.** put into practice. **3.** use or devote. **4.** be relevant. **5.** make request.

ap·point′, *v.* **1.** choose; name. **2.** furnish. —**ap·point·ee′,** *n.* —**ap·poin′tive,** *adj.*

ap·point′ment, *n.* **1.** act of choosing or naming. **2.** prearranged meeting. **3.** equipment.

ap·por′tion, *v.* divide. —**ap·por′tion·ment,** *n.*

ap′po·site, *adj.* suitable.

ap·praise′, *v.,* **-praised, -praising.** estimate the value of. —**ap·prais′al,** *n.* —**ap·prais′er,** *n.*

ap·pre′ci·a·ble (-shē-), *adj.* noticeable; significant.

ap•pre′ci•ate′ (-shē-), *v.,* -ated, -ating. 1. value at true worth. 2. increase in value. —**ap•pre′ci•a′tion,** *n.* —**ap•pre′cia•tive** (-shə-), *adj.*

ap•pre•hend′, *v.* 1. take into custody. 2. understand.

ap′pre•hen′sion, *n.* 1. anxiety. 2. comprehension. 3. arrest.

ap′pre•hen′sive, *adj.* worried; anxious.

ap•pren′tice, *n., v.,* -ticed, -ticing. —*n.* 1. assistant learning a trade. —*v.* 2. bind as such an assistant. —**ap•pren′tice•ship′,** *n.*

ap•prise′, *v.,* -prised, -prising. notify. Also, **ap•prize′.**

ap•proach′, *v.* 1. come near to. 2. make a proposal to. —*n.* 3. coming near. 4. access. 5. method.

ap′pro•ba′tion, *n.* approval.

ap•pro′pri•ate′, *adj., v.,* -ated, -ating. —*adj.* (-prē it). 1. suitable; proper. —*v.* (-prē āt′). 2. designate for use. 3. take possession of. —**ap•pro′pri•ate•ly,** *adv.* —**ap•pro′pri•ate•ness,** *n.* —**ap•pro′pri•a′tion,** *n.*

ap•prove′, *v.,* -proved, -proving. 1. think well of. 2. confirm. —**ap•prov′al,** *n.*

approx., approximate.

ap•prox′i•mate, *adj., v.,* -mated, -mating. —*adj.* (-mit). 1. near; similar. —*v.* (-māt′). 2. come near to. —**ap•prox′i•mate′ly,** *adv.* —**ap•prox′i•ma′tion,** *n.*

ap•pur′te•nance, *n.* accessory.

ap•pur′te•nant, *adj.* pertaining.

Apr., April.

a′pri•cot′, *n.* peachlike fruit.

A′pril, *n.* fourth month of year.

a′ pri•o′ri (ā′ prē ôr′ī, -ôr′ē), *adj.* 1. from a general law to a particular instance. 2. existing independent of experience.

a′pron, *n.* protective garment for the front of one's clothes.

ap′ro•pos′ (ap′rə pō′), *adv.* 1. opportunely. 2. with reference. —*adj.* 3. timely.

apse, *n. Arch.* vaulted recess.

apt, *adj.* 1. prone. 2. likely. 3. skilled; able. —**apt′ly,** *adv.* —**apt′ness,** *n.*

apt., apartment.

ap′ti•tude′, *n.* skill; talent.

aq'ua·cul'ture, *n.* cultivation of aquatic animals or plants.

Aq'ua·lung', *n. Trademark.* underwater breathing device using compressed air.

aq'ua·ma·rine', *n.* 1. greenish blue. 2. beryl of this color.

a·quar'i·um, *n., pl.* **-iums, -ia.** place for exhibiting aquatic animals and plants.

a·quat'ic, *adj.* of water.

aq'ue·duct', *n.* artificial channel for conducting water.

a'que·ous, *adj.* of water.

aq'ui·line', *adj.* (of a nose) curved upward.

AR, Arkansas.

Ar'ab, *n.* 1. member of a people living or originating in Arabia. —*adj.* 2. of Arabs. Also, **A·ra'bi·an.**

Ar'a·bic, *n.* 1. Semitic language spoken chiefly in S.W. Asia and N. Africa. —*adj.* 2. of Arabic, Arabia, or Arabs.

Arabic numeral, any of the numerals 0 through 9.

ar'a·ble, *adj.* plowable.

a·rach'nid (əe rak'nid), *n.* small eight-legged arthropod.

A·rap'a·ho or **-hoe,** *n., pl.* **-hos** or **-hoes,** or **hoe.** member of a North American Indian people.

ar'bit·er, *n.* judge.

ar'bi·trage' (-träzh'), *n.* simultaneous sale of security or commodity in different markets to profit from unequal prices. —**ar'bi·trag'er, ar'bi·tra·geur'** (-trä zhûr'), *n.*

ar·bit'ra·ment, *n.* judgment by an arbiter.

ar'bi·trar'y, *adj.* 1. subject to personal judgment. 2. capricious. 3. abusing powers. —**ar'bi·trar'i·ly,** *adv.*

ar'bi·trate', *v.,* **-trated, -trating.** adjudicate as, or submit to, an arbiter. —**ar'bi·tra'tion,** *n.* —**ar'bi·tra'tor,** *n.*

ar'bor, *n.* tree-shaded garden.

ar·bo're·al, *adj.* of trees.

ar'bo·re'tum (är'bə rē'təm), *n., pl.* **-tums, -ta** (-tə). parklike area with trees or shrubs for study or display.

ar'bor·vi'tae (är'bər vī'tē), *n.* evergreen tree.

ar·bu'tus (-byōō'-), *n.* 1. variety of evergreen shrub. 2. creeping flowering plant.

arc, *n.* 1. part of circle. 2. luminous current between two electric conductors.

ar·cade', *n.* 1. row of archways. 2. covered passage with stores.

ar·cane', *adj.* known only to those with special knowledge.

arch, *n.* 1. upwardly curved structure. —*v.* 2. cover with an arch. —*adj.* 3. chief. 4. roguish.

ar'chae·ol'o·gy (-kē-), *n.* study of past cultures from artifacts. Also, **ar'che·ol'·o·gy.** —**ar'chae·o·log'i·cal,** *adj.* —**ar'chae·ol'o·gist,** *n.*

ar·cha'ic, *adj.* 1. no longer used. 2. ancient.

arch'an'gel (ärk'-), *n.* chief angel.

arch'bish'op, *n.* bishop of highest rank.

arch'di'o·cese, *n.* diocese of archbishop. —**arch'di·oc'e·san,** *adj., n.*

arch'en'e·my, *n., pl.* -mies. chief enemy.

arch'duke', *n.* royal prince.

arch'er, *n.* shooter of a bow and arrow. —**arch'er·y,** *n.*

ar'che·type' (är'ki tīp'), *n.* original pattern or model.

ar'chi·pel'a·go' (är'kə-), *n., pl.* -gos, -goes. 1. body of water with many islands. 2. the islands.

ar'chi·tect', (är'kə-), *n.* designer of buildings. —**ar'chi·tec'ture,** *n.* —**ar'chi·tec'tur·al,** *adj.*

ar'chives (är'kīvz), *n.pl.* 1. documents. 2. place for documents.

arch'way', *n.* entrance covered by arch.

arc'tic, *adj. (often cap.)* of or at the North Pole.

ar'dent, *adj.* earnest; zealous. —**ar'dent·ly,** *adv.*

ar'dor, *n.* zeal.

ar'du·ous (-jōō-), *adj.* 1. difficult. 2. steep. 3. severe.

are, *v.* pres. indic. pl. of **be.**

ar'e·a, *n.* 1. extent of surface; region. 2. scope.

area code, three-digit number used in telephone dialing.

a·re'na, *n.* space for contests.

aren't, contraction of **are not.**

ar′go•sy, *n., pl.* **-sies.** *Poetic.* large merchant ship or fleet.

ar′got (är′gō, -gət), *n.* jargon.

ar′gue, *v.,* **-gued, -guing. 1.** present reasons for or against something. **2.** dispute. **3.** persuade. —**ar′gu•ment,** *n.* —**ar′gu•men•ta′tion,** *n.*

ar′gu•men′ta•tive, *adj.* tending to dispute.

ar′gyle (är′gīl), *n. (often cap.)* diamond-shaped knitting pattern, as of socks.

a′ri•a, *n.* operatic solo.

-arian, suffix indicating: **1.** one connected with, as *librarian.* **2.** one supporting or practicing, as *vegetarian.*

ar′id, *adj.* dry. —**a•rid′i•ty,** *n.*

a•right′, *adv.* rightly.

a•rise′, *v.,* **arose, arisen, arising. 1.** move or get up. **2.** occur.

ar′is•toc′ra•cy, *n., pl.* **-cies. 1.** state governed by nobility. **2.** nobility. —**a•ris′to•crat,** *n.* —**a•ris′to•crat′ic,** *adj.*

a•rith′me•tic, *n.* computation with figures. —**ar′ith•met′i•cal,** *adj.* —**ar′ith•met′i•cal•ly,** *adv.*

Ariz., Arizona.

ark, *n. Archaic.* large ship.

Ark., Arkansas.

arm, *n.* **1.** upper limb from hand to shoulder. **2.** weapon. **3.** combat branch. **4.** armlike part. —*v.* **5.** outfit; fortify.

ar•ma′da (-mä′-), *n.* fleet of warships.

ar•ma•dil′lo (är′mə dil′ō), *n.* burrowing mammal covered with plates of bone and horn.

ar′ma•ged′don (-ged′-), *n.* crucial or final conflict.

ar′ma•ment, *n.* **1.** military weapons. **2.** arming for war.

arm′chair′, *n.* chair with supports for the arms.

arm′ful, *n., pl.* **-fuls.** capacity of both arms.

ar′mi•stice, *n.* truce.

ar′mor, *n.* protective covering.

ar′mor•y, *n., pl.* **-ries. 1.** storage place for weapons. **2.** military drill hall.

arm′pit′, *n.* hollow part under arm at shoulder.

ar′my, *n., pl.* **-mies. 1.** force for land combat. **2.** large group.

a•ro′ma, *n.* odor. —**ar′o•mat′ic,** *adj.*

a·round′, *adv., prep.* **1.** on every side of. **2.** somewhere in or near. **3.** about.

a·rouse′, *v.,* aroused, arousing. **1.** awaken. **2.** stir to act. —**a·rous′al,** *n.*

ar·peg′gi·o′ (är pej′ē ō′, -pej′ō), *n.* sounding of notes in a chord in succession.

ar·raign′ (ə rān′), *v.* **1.** call to court. **2.** accuse. —**ar·raign′ment,** *n.*

ar·range′, *v.,* -ranged, -ranging. **1.** place in order. **2.** plan or prepare. —**ar·range′ment,** *n.*

ar′rant, *adj.* downright.

ar·ray′, *v.* **1.** arrange. **2.** clothe. —*n.* **3.** arrangement, as for battle. **4.** clothes.

ar·rears′, *n.pl.* overdue debt.

ar·rest′, *v.* **1.** seize (person) by law. **2.** stop. —*n.* **3.** seizure.

ar·rest′ing, *adj.* engaging.

ar·rive′, *v.,* -rived, -riving. reach a place. —**ar·riv′al,** *n.*

ar′ro·gant, *adj.* insolently proud. —**ar′ro·gance,** *n.* —**ar′ro·gant·ly,** *adv.*

ar′ro·gate′, *v.,* -gated, -gating. appropriate. —**ar′ro·ga′tion,** *n.*

ar′row, *n.* pointed stick shot by a bow.

ar′row·head′, *n.* pointed tip of arrow.

ar′row·root′, *n.* edible starch from tropical plant root.

ar·roy′o (ə roi′ō), *n., pl.* **-os.** steep, dry gulch.

ar′se·nal, *n.* military storehouse or factory.

ar′se·nic, *n.* **1.** metallic element. **2.** poisonous powder.

ar′son, *n.* malicious burning of.

art, *n.* **1.** production of something beautiful or extraordinary. **2.** skill; ability. **3.** cunning. —**art′ful,** *adj.*

art dec′o (dek′ō), *n. (often caps.)* 1920s decorative art.

ar·te′ri·o·scle·ro′sis, *n.* hardening of arteries.

ar′ter·y, *n., pl.* **-ries. 1.** blood vessel from the heart. **2.** main channel. —**ar·te′ri·al,** *adj.*

ar·te′sian (-zhən) **well,** deep well whose water rises under its own pressure.

ar·thri′tis, *n.* inflammation of a joint. —**ar·thrit′ic,** *adj.*

ar′thro•pod′, *n.* invertebrate with segmented body and jointed legs, as the lobster.

ar′ti•choke′, *n.* plant with an edible flower head.

ar′ti•cle, *n.* 1. literary composition. 2. thing; item. 3. the words *a, an,* or *the.*

ar•tic′u•late, *adj., v.,* **-lated, -lating.** —*adj.* (-lit). 1. clear. 2. able to speak. 3. jointed. —*v.* (-lāt′). 4. speak distinctly. 5. joint. —**ar•tic′u•la′tion,** *n.*

ar′ti•fact′, *n.* object made by human being or beings.

ar′ti•fice, *n.* trick.

ar•tif′i•cer, *n.* craftsperson.

ar′ti•fi′cial (-shəl), *adj.* 1. manufactured, esp. as an imitation. 2. affected. —**ar′ti•fi′cial•ly,** *adv.* —**ar′ti•fi′ci•al′i•ty,** *n.*

artificial respiration, forcing of air into and out of lungs of a nonbreathing person.

ar•til′ler•y, *n.* mounted guns.

ar′ti•san (är′tə zən), *n.* person skilled in a practical art.

art′ist, *n.* practitioner of fine art. —**ar•tis′tic,** *adj.* —**art′ist•ry,** *n.*

art′less, *adj.* natural.

art′y, *adj.,* **artier, artiest.** *Informal.* self-consciously artistic.

as, *adv.* 1. to such an extent. —*conj.* 2. in the manner that. 3. while. 4. because. —*pron.* 5. that.

ASAP, as soon as possible. Also, **A.S.A.P., a.s.a.p.**

as•bes′tos, *n.* fibrous material formerly used in fireproofing.

as•cend′, *v.* climb. —**as•cent′,** *n.*

as•cend′an•cy, *n.* domination; power. —**as•cend′ant,** *adj., n.*

As•cen′sion, *n.* bodily passing of Christ to heaven.

as′cer•tain′ (as′ər-), *v.* find out.

as•cet′ic (ə set′ik), *n.* 1. one who lives austerely. —*adj.* 2. austere or abstemious. —**as•cet′i•cism′,** *n.*

ASCII (as′kē), *n.* standardized code for computer storage and transmission.

as•cor′bic ac′id, vitamin C.

as′cot (as′kət, -kot), *n.* tie or scarf with broad ends.

as•cribe′, *v.,* **-cribed, -cribing.** attribute. —**as•crip′tion,** *n.*

a·sep′sis, *n.* absence of certain harmful bacteria. —**a·sep′tic,** *adj.*

a·sex′u·al (ā-), *adj.* sexless.

ash, *n.* **1.** (*pl.* **ashes**) residue of burned matter. **2.** a common tree. —**ash′y,** *adj.*

a·shamed′, *adj.* feeling shame.

ash′en, *adj.* pale gray.

a·shore′, *adv., adj.* on or to shore.

ash′tray′, *n.* container for tobacco ashes.

A′sian (ā′zhən), *n.* native of Asia. —**Asian,** *adj.*

A′si·at′ic, *adj., n. Offensive.* Asian.

a·side′, *adv.* **1.** on or to one side. **2.** separate.

as′i·nine′, *adj.* stupid.

ask, *v.* **1.** put a question to. **2.** request. **3.** invite. **4.** inquire.

a·skance′, *adv.* with doubt.

a·skew′, *adv., adj.* twisted.

a·sleep′, *adj., adv.* sleeping.

a·so′cial (ā sō′shəl), *adj.* **1.** not sociable. **2.** selfish.

asp, *n.* poisonous snake.

as·par′a·gus, *n.* plant with edible shoots.

as·par′tame (ə spär′tām, as′pər tām′), *n.* artificial low-calorie sweetener.

as′pect, *n.* **1.** appearance. **2.** phase. **3.** direction faced.

as′pen, *n.* variety of poplar.

as·per′i·ty, *n., pl.* **-ties.** roughness.

as·per′sion, *n.* derogatory criticism.

as′phalt, *n.* hard, black material used for pavements.

as·phyx′i·ate′, *v.,* **-ated, -ating.** affect by a lack of oxygen; choke or smother. —**as·phyx′i·a′tion,** *n.*

as′pic, *n.* jelly made from meat, fish, or vegetable stock.

as·pire′, *v.,* **-pired, -piring.** long, aim, or seek for. —**as·pir′ant,** *n.* —**as′pi·ra′tion,** *n.*

as′pi·rin, *n.* crystalline derivative of salicylic acid, used for relief of headaches.

ass, *n.* **1.** donkey. **2.** fool.

as·sail′, *v.* attack. —**as·sail′ant,** *n.*

as·sas′sin, *n.* murderer, esp. of an important person. —**as·sas′si·nate′,** *v.* —**as·sas′si·na′tion,** *n.*

as•sault′, *n., v.* attack.

as•say′, *v.* analyze or evaluate. —**as•say′**, *n.* —**as•say′er**, *n.*

as•sem′blage (ə sem′blij), *n.* 1. assembly. 2. act of assembling.

as•sem′ble, *v.,* -bled, -bling. come or bring together.

as•sem′bly, *n., pl.* -blies. 1. group gathered together. 2. legislative body. 3. putting together of parts.

as•sem′bly•man, *n., pl.* -men. member of legislative assembly. Also, *fem.,* **as•sem′bly•wom′an**; *masc.* or *fem.,* **as•sem′bly•per′son.**

as•sent′, *v.* 1. agree. —*n.* 2. agreement.

as•sert′, *v.* 1. state; declare. 2. claim. 3. present (oneself) boldly. —**as•ser′tion**, *n.* —**as•ser′tive**, *adj.* —**as•ser′tive•ly**, *adv.* —**as•ser′tive•ness**, *n.*

as•sess′, *v.* evaluate, as for taxes. —**as•sess′ment**, *n.* —**as•ses′sor**, *n.*

as′set, *n.* 1. item of property. 2. quality.

as•sid′u•ous (ə sij′-), *adj.* persistent; devoted. —**as•sid′u•ous•ly**, *adv.*

as•sign′ (ə sīn′), *v.* 1. give. 2. appoint. 3. transfer. —*n.* 4. one to whom something is transferred. —**as•sign′a•ble**, *adj.* —**as•sign•ee′**, *n.* —**as•sign′ment**, *n.*

as′sig•na′tion (-sig-), *n.* appointment; rendezvous.

as•sim′i•late′, *v.,* -lated, -lating. absorb or merge. —**as•sim′i•la′tion**, *n.*

as•sist′, *v., n.* help; aid. —**as•sist′ant**, *n., adj.* —**as•sist′ance**, *n.*

assn., association.

as•so′ci•ate′, *v.,* -ated, -ating, *n., adj.* —*v.* (-āt′). 1. connect or join. 2. keep company. —*n.* (-it). 3. partner; colleague. —*adj.* (-it). 4. allied. —**as•so′ci•a′tion**, *n.*

as′so•nance (as′ə nəns), *n.* similarity of sound in words. —**as′so•nant**, *adj.*

as•sort′, *v.* 1. classify. 2. vary. —**as•sort′ed**, *adj.* —**as•sort′ment**, *n.*

asst., assistant.

as•suage′ (ə swāj′), *v.,* -suaged, -suaging. lessen (pain, grief, etc.).

as•sume′, *v.*, **-sumed, -suming.**
1. take without proof. 2.
undertake. 3. pretend. 4. take
upon oneself.

as•sump′tion, *n.* 1. belief. 2.
undertaking. 3. (*cap.*) ascent
to heaven of Virgin Mary.

as•sure′, *v.*, **-sured, -suring.** 1.
affirm to. 2. convince; make
sure. 3. encourage. 4. insure.
—**as•sur′ance**, *n.*
—**as•sured′**, *adj., n.*

as′ter, *n.* plant with many
petals around a center disk.

as′ter•isk, *n.* star (*) symbol.

a•stern′, *adv., adj.* Naut.
toward or at the rear.

as′ter•oid′, *n.* planetlike body
beyond Mars.

asth′ma (az′mə), *n.* painful
respiratory disorder.
—**asth•mat′ic**, *adj., n.*

a•stig′ma•tism, *n.* eye defect
resulting in imperfect images.
—**a′stig•mat′ic**, *adj.*

a•stir′, *adj., adv.* active.

as•ton′ish, *v.* surprise greatly;
amaze. —**as•ton′ish•ing**, *adj.*
—**as•ton′ish•ing•ly**, *adv.*
—**as•ton′ish•ment**, *n.*

as•tound′, *v.* amaze greatly.

a•strad′dle, *adv., prep.*
astride.

as′tral, *adj.* of the stars.

a•stray′, *adj., adv.* straying.

a•stride′, *adv., adj., prep.*
straddling.

as•trol′o•gy, *n.* study of star's
influence on human affairs.
—**as′tro•log′i•cal**, *adj.*
—**as•trol′o•ger**, *n.*

as′tro•naut, *n.* traveler
outside earth's atmosphere.

as′tro•nau′tics, *n.* science of
space travel. —**as′tro•nau′tic,
as′tro•nau′ti•cal**, *adj.*

as′tro•nom′i•cal, *adj.* 1. of
astronomy. 2. extremely great.
—**as′tro•nom′i•cal•ly**, *adv.*

as•tron′o•my, *n.* science of all
the celestial bodies.
—**as′tron′o•mer**, *n.*

as′tro•phys′ics, *n.* branch of
astronomy about physical
properties of celestial bodies.
—**as′tro•phys′i•cist**, *n.*

as•tute′, *adj.* shrewd; clever.
—**as•tute′ly**, *adv.*
—**as•tute′ness**, *n.*

a•sun′der, *adv., adj.* apart.

a•sy′lum, *n.* home for persons
needing care.

a•sym'me•try (ā sim'i trē), *n.* lack of symmetry.
—**a'sym•met'ric,**
a'sym•met'ri•cal, *adj.*

at, *prep.* (word used in indicating place, time, etc.)

at'a•vism, *n.* reappearance of ancestral traits. —**at'a•vist,** *n.*
—**at'a•vis'tic,** *adj.*

ate, *v.* pt. of **eat.**

at'el•ier' (at'l yā'), *n.* studio, esp. of an artist.

a'the•ism, *n.* belief that there is no God. —**a'the•ist,** *n.*
—**a'the•is'tic,** *adj.*

ath'lete, *n.* expert in sports. —**ath•let'ic,** *adj.*

athlete's foot, ringworm of the feet.

a•thwart', *adv., prep.* from side to side of.

at'las, *n.* book of maps.

ATM, automated teller machine, which provides certain bank services.

at'mos•phere', *n.* 1. air surrounding earth. 2. pervading mood.
—**at'mos•pher'ic,** *adj.*

at'oll, *n.* ring-shaped coral island.

at'om, *n.* smallest unit making up chemical element.
—**a•tom'ic,** *adj.*
—**a•tom'i•cal•ly,** *adv.*

atomic bomb, bomb whose force is derived from nuclear fission of atoms, causing the conversion of mass to energy (**atomic energy**). Also, **atom bomb.**

at'om•iz'er, *n.* device for making a fine spray.

a•ton'al (ā tōn'l), *adj.* lacking tonality. —**a'to•nal'i•ty,** *n.*

a•tone', *v.,* atoned, atoning. make amends.
—**a•tone'ment,** *n.*

a•top', *adj., adv., prep.* on or at the top of.

a'tri•um (ā'trē əm), *n., pl.* **-a, -ums.** 1. enclosed court in building. 2. either of two upper chambers of the heart.

a•tro'cious, *adj.* 1. wicked. 2. very bad. —**a•troc'i•ty,** *n.*

at'ro•phy, *n., v.,* **-phied, -phying.** —*n.* 1. wasting away of the body. —*v.* 2. cause or undergo atrophy.

at'ro•pine' (a'trə pēn', -pin), *n.* poisonous alkaloid of belladonna.

at•tach′, *v.* **1.** fasten or join. **2.** take by legal authority.

at′ta•ché′ (at′ə shā′), *n.* embassy official.

at•tach′ment, *n.* **1.** an attaching. **2.** thing fastened on. **3.** affectionate tie.

at•tack′, *v.* **1.** act against with sudden force **2.** do vigorously. —*n.* **3.** an attacking; onset. —**at•tack′er**, *n.*

at•tain′, *v.* **1.** reach; arrive at. **2.** accomplish; fulfill. —**at•tain′a•ble**, *adj.* —**at•tain′ment**, *n.*

at′tar, *n.* perfume from flowers.

at•tempt′, *v., n.* try.

at•tend′, *v.* **1.** be present at. **2.** go with. **3.** take care of. **4.** give heed to. —**at•tend′ance**, *n.* —**at•tend′ant**, *n., adj.*

at•ten′tion, *n.* **1.** act of attending. **2.** careful notice. —**at•ten′tive**, *adj.* —**at•ten′tive•ly**, *adv.*

at•ten′u•ate′, *v., -ated, -ating.* **1.** make thin. **2.** lessen; abate. —**at•ten′u•a′tion**, *n.*

at•test′, *v.* declare as true. —**at′tes•ta′tion**, *n.*

at′tic, *n.* room under the roof.

at•tire′, *v., -tired, -tiring, n.* —*v.* **1.** dress. —*n.* **2.** clothes.

at′ti•tude′, *n.* **1.** expressed opinion. **2.** posture.

attn., attention.

at•tor′ney, *n.* lawyer.

attorney general, *pl.* **attorneys general, attorney generals.** chief law officer of a country or state.

at•tract′, *v.* **1.** draw toward. **2.** invite; allure. —**at•trac′tion**, *n.* —**at•tract′tive**, *adj.* —**at•trac′tive•ly**, *adv.* —**at•trac′tive•ness**, *n.*

at•tract′ant, *n.* substance that attracts.

at•trib′ute, *v., -uted, -uting, n.* —*v.* (ə trib′yoot). **1.** ascribe; credit; impute. —*n.* (at′rə byoot′). **2.** special quality, aspect. —**at′tri•bu′tion**, *n.*

at•tri′tion (ə trish′ən), *n.* wearing down.

at•tune′, *v., -tuned, -tuning.* harmonize.

atty., attorney.

ATV, *n.* all-terrain vehicle.

a•twit′ter, *adj.* nervous.

a•typ′i•cal (ā tip′i kəl), *adj.* not typical; irregular. —**a•typ′i•cal•ly**, *adv.*

au'burn, *adj.* reddish brown.

auc'tion, *n.* 1. sale of goods to highest bidders. —*v.* 2. sell by auction. —**auc'tion•eer',** *n., v.*

au•da'cious, *adj.* bold; daring. —**au•dac'i•ty** (-das'-), *n.*

au'di•ble, *adj.* that can be heard. —**au'di•bil'i•ty,** *n.* —**au'di•bly,** *adv.*

au'di•ence, *n.* 1. group of hearers or spectators. 2. formal hearing or interview.

au'di•o', *adj.* 1. of sound reception or reproduction. —*n.* 2. audible part of TV.

au'di•ol'o•gy (-ol'ə jē), *n.* study of hearing disorders. —**au'di•ol'o•gist,** *n.*

au'di•om'e•ter, *n.* instrument for testing hearing.

au'di•o•tape', *n.* magnetic tape for recording sound.

au'di•o•vis'u•al, *adj.* using films, TV, and recordings.

au'dit, *n.* official examination of accounts. —**au'dit,** *v.* —**au'di•tor,** *n.*

au•di'tion, *n.* 1. hearing. —*v.* 2. give a hearing to.

au'di•to'ri•um, *n.* large meeting room.

au'di•to'ry, *adj.* of hearing.

Aug., August.

au'ger, *n.* drill.

aught, *n.* 1. anything. 2. zero (0). —*adv.* 3. at all.

aug•ment', *v.* increase. —**aug'men•ta'tion,** *n.*

au'gur (ô'gər), *v.* predict; bode. —**au'gu•ry** (-gyə-), *n.*

Au'gust, *n.* eighth month of year.

au•gust', *adj.* majestic.

au jus (ō zhoos'), *adj.* (of meat) served in the natural juices.

auk, *n.* northern diving bird.

auld lang syne, fondly remembered times.

aunt, *n.* 1. sister of a parent. 2. wife of an uncle.

au pair (ō pâr'), person who does household tasks in exchange for room and board.

au'ra, *n.* 1. atmosphere, quality, etc. 2. radiance coming from the body.

au'ral, *adj.* of or by hearing.

au're•ole', *n.* halo.

Au•re•o•my•cin (ô'rē ō mī'sin), *n. Trademark.* antibiotic drug effective against some diseases.

au′ re•voir′ (ō′ rə vwär′), *French.* good-by.

au′ri•cle, *n.* 1. outer part of ear. 2. chamber in heart. —**au•ric′u•lar,** *adj.*

au•rif′er•ous, *adj.* with gold.

au•ror′a (ə rôr′ə), *n.* display of bands of light in the night sky.

aus′pice (ô′spis), *n.* (*usually pl.*) patronage.

aus•pi′cious, *adj.* favorable. —**aus•pi′cious•ly,** *adv.*

aus•tere′, *adj.* 1. harsh; stern. 2. severely simple. —**aus•ter′i•ty,** *n.*

Aus•tral′ian (-trāl′-), *n.* native or citizen of Australia. —**Australian,** *adj.*

Aus′tri•an, *n.* native of Austria. —**Austrian,** *adj.*

au•then′tic, *adj.* reliable; genuine. —**au•then′ti•cal•ly,** *adv.* —**au′then•tic′i•ty,** *n.* —**au•then′ti•cate′,** *v.*

au′thor, *n.* writer or creator. —**au′thor•ship′,** *n.*

au•thor′i•tar′i•an, *adj.* requiring total obedience.

au•thor′i•ta′tive, *adj.* to be accepted as true.

au•thor′i•ty, *n., pl.* -ties. 1. right to order. 2. one with such right. 3. respected source of information.

au′thor•ize′, *v.,* -ized, -izing. permit officially. —**auth′or•i•za′tion,** *n.*

au•tism (ô′tiz əm), *n.* disorder characterized by extreme self-absorption and detachment from reality. —**au•tis′tic,** *adj.*

au′to, *n.* automobile.

auto-, prefix meaning self or same, as *autograph.*

au′to•bi•og′ra•phy, *n., pl.* -phies. story of one's own life.

au•toc′ra•cy, *n., pl.* -cies. absolute political power. —**au′to•crat′,** *n.* —**au′to•crat′ic,** *adj.*

au′to•di′dact, *n.* self-taught person.

au′to•graph′, *n.* signature.

au′to•im•mune′, *adj.* of the body's immune response to its own components.

au′to•mat′, *n.* restaurant with coin-operated service.

au′to•mate, *v.,* -mated, -mating. make automatic.

au′to·mat′ic, *adj.* 1. self-acting. 2. inevitably following.
—**au′to·mat′i·cal·ly,** *adv.*

automatic pilot, automatic electronic control system for piloting aircraft.

au′to·ma′tion, *n.* automatically controlled.

au·tom′a·ton, *n.* mechanical device or figure; robot.

au′to·mo·bile′, *n.* motorized passenger vehicle.

autonomic nervous system, system of nerves controlling involuntary functions such as heartbeat.

au·ton′o·my, *n.* self-government.
—**au′to·nom′ic,** *adj.*
—**au·ton′o·mous,** *adj.*

au′top·sy, *n., pl.* -sies. examination of body for causes of death.

au′tumn, *n.* season before winter; fall. —**au·tum′nal,** *adj.*

aux·il′ia·ry (ôg zil′yə rē), *adj., n., pl.* -ries. —*adj.* 1. assisting. 2. subsidiary. —*n.* 3. aid. 4. noncombat naval vessel. 5. verb preceding other verbs to express tense, etc.

a·vail′, *v.* 1. be of use, value, etc. 2. take to (oneself) advantageously. —*n.* 3. benefit; advantage.

a·vail′a·ble, *adj.* present for use. —**a·vail′a·bil′i·ty,** *n.*

av′a·lanche′, *n.* mass of snow, ice, etc., falling down mountain.

a·vant′-garde′, *adj.* progressive, esp. in art.

av′a·rice, *n.* greed.
—**av′a·ri′cious,** *adj.*

ave., avenue.

a·venge′, *v.,* avenged, avenging. take vengeance for.
—**a·veng′er,** *n.*

av′e·nue′, *n.* 1. broad street. 2. approach.

a·ver′, *v.,* averred, averring. affirm; declare.

av′er·age (-ij), *n., adj., v.,* -aged, -aging. —*n.* 1. sum of a series of numbers divided by the number of terms in the series. —*adj.* 2. of or like an average. 3. typical. —*v.* 4. find average of.

a·verse′, *adj.* unwilling.
—**a·verse′ly,** *adv.*
—**a·verse′ness,** *n.*

a·ver′sion, *n.* dislike.

a•vert', *v.* **1.** turn away. **2.** prevent.

avg., average.

a'vi•ar'y (ā'-), *n., pl.* **-aries.** place in which birds are kept.

a'vi•a'tion, *n.* science of flying aircraft. —**a'vi•a'tor**, *n.* —**a'vi•a'trix**, *n.fem.*

av'id, *adj.* eager. —**a•vid'i•ty**, *n.* —**av'id•ly**, *adv.*

av'o•ca'do (-kä'-), *n., pl.* **-dos.** tropical pear-shaped fruit.

av'o•ca'tion, *n.* hobby.

a•void', *v.* shun; evade. —**a•void'a•ble**, *adj.* —**a•void'ance**, *n.*

av'oir•du•pois' (av'ər də poiz'), *n.* system of weights with 16-ounce pounds.

a•vow', *v.* declare; confess. —**a•vow'al**, *n.* —**a•vowed'**, *adj.*

a•vun'cu•lar (ə vung'kyə lər), *adj.* of or like an uncle.

a•wait', *v.* wait for.

a•wake', *v.,* **awoke** or **awaked, awaking,** *adj.* —*v.* **1.** Also, **a•wak'en.** rouse from sleep. —*adj.* **2.** not asleep.

a•wak'en, *v.* awake. —**a•wak'en•ing**, *n., adj.*

a•ward', *v.* **1.** bestow; grant. —*n.* **2.** thing bestowed.

a•ware', *adj.* conscious (of). —**a•ware'ness**, *n.*

a•wash', *adj.* overflowing with water.

a•way', *adv.* **1.** from this or that place. **2.** apart. **3.** aside. —*adj.* **4.** absent. **5.** distant.

awe, *n., v.,* **awed, awing.** —*n.* **1.** respectful fear. —*v.* **2.** fill with awe. —**awe'some**, *adj.*

awe'struck', *adj.* filled with awe. Also, **awe'strick'en.**

aw'ful, *adj.* **1.** fearful. **2.** bad.

aw'ful•ly, *adv.* **1.** very badly.

a•while', *adv.* for a short time.

awk'ward, *adj.* **1.** clumsy. **2.** embarrassing. **3.** difficult; risky. —**awk'ward•ly**, *adv.* —**awk'ward•ness**, *n.*

awl, *n.* small drill.

awn, *n.* bristlelike part plant.

awn'ing, *n.* canvas overhang.

AWOL (ā'wôl, -wol) *adj., adv.* absent without leave.

a•wry' (ə rī'), *adv., adj.* **1.** twisted. **2.** wrong.

ax, *n.* small chopping tool. Also, **axe.**

ax′i•om, *n.* accepted truth. —**ax′i•o•mat′ic,** *adj.*

ax′is, *n., pl.* **axes** (ak′sēz). line about which something turns. —**ax′i•al,** *adj.*

ax′le, *n.* bar on which a wheel turns.

ay (ā), *adv. Poetic.* always. Also, **aye.**

a′ya•tol′lah, *n.* chief Muslim leader.

aye (ī), *adv., n.* yes.

a•zal′ea, *n.* flowering shrub.

AZT, *n. Trademark.* drug used in AIDS treatment.

Az′tec, *n.* American Indian people whose Mexican empire was conquered by Spaniards in 1521. —**Az′tec•an,** *adj.*

az′ure (azh′-), *adj., n.* sky-blue.

B, b, *n.* second letter of English alphabet.

B.A., Bachelor of Arts.

bab′ble, *v.,* **-bled, -bling. 1.** talk indistinctly or foolishly. **2.** make a murmuring sound. —**bab′ble,** *n.*

babe, *n.* **1.** baby. **2.** naïf.

ba•boon′, *n.* large monkey of Africa and Arabia.

ba•bush′ka, *n.* woman's head scarf.

ba′by, *n., pl.* **-bies,** *v.,* **-bied, -bying.** —*n.* **1.** infant. **2.** childish person. —*v.* **3.** pamper. —**ba′by•hood′,** *n.* —**ba′by•ish,** *adj.*

baby boom, period of increase in the rate of births. —**baby boomer,** *n.*

ba′by-sit′, *v.,* **-sat, -sitting.** tend another's child for a few hours. —**ba′by-sit′ter,** *n.*

bac′ca•lau′re•ate (-lôr′ē it), *n.* bachelor's degree.

bac′cha•nal′ (bak′ə nal′), *n.* drunken revelry. —**bac′cha•na′li•an,** *adj., n.*

bach′e•lor (bach′-), *n.* **1.** unmarried man. **2.** person holding first degree at a college. —**bach′e•lor•hood′,** *n.* —**bach′e•lor•ship′,** *n.*

B

ba•cil′lus (-sil′əs), *n., pl.* **-cilli** (-sil′ī). type of bacteria.

back, *n.* **1.** hinder part of human and animal body. **2.** rear. **3.** spine. —*v.* **4.** sponsor. **5.** move backward. **6.** bet in favor of. **7.** furnish or form a back. —*adj.* **8.** being behind. **9.** in the past. **10.** overdue. —*adv.* **11.** at or toward the rear. **12.** toward original point or condition. **13.** in return. —**back′er,** *n.* —**back′ing,** *n.*

back′bite′, *v.,* **-bit, -bitten, -biting.** discuss (someone) maliciously.

back′board′, *n.* in basketball, vertical board behind basket.

back′bone′, *n.* **1.** spine. **2.** strength of character. —**back′boned′,** *adj.*

back′break′ing, *adj.* fatiguing.

back′drop′, *n.* **1.** curtain at the back of a stage. **2.** background of an event; setting.

back′field′, *n.* football players behind the line.

back′fire′, *v.,* **-fired, firing. 1.** (of an engine) ignite prematurely. 2. bring opposite results. —**back'fire'**, *n.*

back'gam'mon, *n.* board game for two persons.

back'ground', *n.* 1. parts in the rear. 2. distant portions in a picture. 3. origins.

back'hand', *n.* 1. sports stroke made with back of hand facing direction of movement. —*adj.* 2. backhanded. —*adv.* 3. in a backhanded way. —*v.* 4. hit with a backhand.

back'hand'ed, *adj.* 1. with upper part of hand forward. 2. ambiguous.

back'lash', *n.* retaliatory reaction.

back'log', *n.* reserve or accumulation, as of work.

back'pack', *n.* 1. knapsack. —*v.* 2. hike using backpack.

back'-ped'al *v.,* -aled, -aling. 1. slow a bicycle by pressing backward on pedals. 2. retreat from or reverse a previous stand or opinion.

back'side', *n.* 1. rear. 2. rump.

back'slap'ping, *n.* exaggerated friendliness. —**back'slap'per,** *n.*

back'slide', *v.,* -slid, -slidden or -slid, -sliding. relapse into bad habits. —**back'slid'er,** *n.*

back'stage', *adv.* 1. in theater wings or dressing rooms. —**adj.** 2. of secret activities.

back'stroke', *n.* swimming stroke performed while lying on back.

back talk, impertinent talk.

back'track', *v.* retreat slowly.

back'up', *n.* 1. person or thing that reinforces another. 2. accumulation caused by a stopping. 3. alternate kept in reserve.

back'ward, *adv.* Also, **back'wards.** 1. toward the back. 2. back foremost. 3. toward or in the past. —*adj.* 4. toward the back or past. 5. behind in progress. 6. bashful. —**back'ward•ly,** *adv.* —**back'ward•ness,** *n.*

back'wa'ter, *n.* place that is backward or stagnant.

back'woods', *n.pl.* wooded or unsettled districts. —**back'woods'man,** *n.*

ba'con, *n.* cured back and sides of a hog.

bac·ter′i·a (-tēr′ē ə), *n., pl. of* **bacterium.** simplest type of vegetable organism, involved in fermentation, production of disease, etc. —**bac·te′ri·al,** *adj.* —**bac·te′ri·al·ly,** *adv.*

bac·te′ri·ol′o·gy, *n.* science dealing with bacteria. —**bac·te′ri·o·log′i·cal,** *adj.* —**bac·te′ri·ol′o·gist,** *n.*

bad, *adj.,* **worse, worst,** *n., v.* —*adj.* **1.** not good. —*n.* **2.** bad thing, condition, or quality. —*v.* **3.** Also, **bade.** pt. of **bid.** —**bad′ly,** *adv.* —**bad′ness,** *n.*

bad blood, hostility.

badge, *n.* emblem or insignia.

badg′er, *n.* **1.** burrowing mammal. —*v.* **2.** harass.

bad′min·ton, *n.* game similar to lawn tennis.

bad′-mouth′, *v.* criticize. Also, **bad′mouth′.**

baf′fle, *v.,* **-fled, -fling,** *n.* —*v.* **1.** thwart; confuse. —*n.* **2.** obstacle; obstruction. —**baf′fle·ment,** *n.*

bag, *n., v.,* **bagged, bagging.** —*n.* **1.** sack or receptacle of flexible material. **2.** purse. —*v.* **3.** bulge. **4.** put into a bag. **5.** kill or catch. —**bag′gy,** *adj.* —**bag′gi·ness,** *n.*

bag′a·telle′, *n.* article of small value.

ba′gel, *n.* hard ringlike roll.

bag′gage, *n.* cases for travel.

bag′pipe′, *n.* (*often pl.*) musical instrument with windbag and two or more pipes. —**bag′pip′er,** *n.*

bah, *interj.* (exclamation of contempt or annoyance).

bail, *Law* (1, 2, 4). —*n.* **1.** security for the return of a prisoner to custody. **2.** person giving bail. **3.** handle of kettle or pail. —*v.* **4.** give or obtain liberty by bail. **5.** dip water out of boat. **6. bail out,** make a parachute jump. —**bail′a·ble,** *adj.* —**bail′ee′,** *n.* —**bail′ment,** *n.* —**bail′or,** *n.* —**bail′er,** *n.*

bail′iff, *n.* public officer similar to sheriff or deputy.

bail′i·wick, *n.* **1.** district under bailiff's jurisdiction. **2.** person's area of authority.

bait, *n.* **1.** item used as lure. —*v.* **2.** prepare with bait. **3.** set dogs upon for sport.

bake, *v.,* **baked, baking. 1.** cook by dry heat. **2.** harden by heat. —**bak′er,** *n.*

baker's dozen, a dozen plus one; 13.

bak′er•y, *n., pl.* **-eries.** place for baking; baker's shop.

baking powder, powder used as leavening agent in baking.

baking soda, sodium bicarbonate, powder used as an antacid and in baking.

bal′a•lai′ka (-lī′-), *n.* musical instrument similar to guitar.

bal′ance, *n., v.,* **-anced, -ancing.** —*n.* **1.** instrument for weighing. **2.** equilibrium. **3.** harmonious arrangement. **4.** act of balancing. **5.** remainder, as of money due. —*v.* **6.** weigh. **7.** set or hold in equilibrium. **8.** be equivalent to. **9.** reckon or adjust accounts. —**bal′anc•er,** *n.*

bal′co•ny, *n., pl.* **-nies. 1.** platform projecting from wall of building. **2.** theater gallery.

bald, *adj.* **1.** lacking hair on scalp. **2.** plain; undisguised. —**bald′ly,** *adv.* —**bald′ness,** *n.*

bal′der•dash′ (bôl′dər dash′), *n.* nonsense.

bale, *n., v.,* **baled, baling.** —*n.* **1.** large bundle or package. —*v.* **2.** make into bales. —**bal′er,** *n.*

bale′ful, *adj.* evil; menacing. —**bale′ful•ly,** *adv.* —**bale′ful•ness,** *n.*

balk (bôk), *v.* **1.** stop short. **2.** hinder; thwart. —*n.* **3.** hindrance. **4.** in baseball, illegal stop in pitcher's motion. —**balk′y,** *adj.*

ball, *n.* **1.** round or roundish body. **2.** game played with ball. **3.** social assembly for dancing. **4.** *Informal.* good time. —*v.* **5.** form into ball.

bal′lad, *n.* **1.** narrative folk song or poem. **2.** sentimental popular song.

bal′last, *n.* **1.** heavy material carried to ensure stability. —*v.* **2.** furnish with ballast.

ball bearing, 1. bearing in which a moving part turns on steel balls. **2.** ball so used.

bal′le•ri′na (-rē′-), *n.* leading woman ballet dancer.

bal•let′ (ba lā′), *n.* theatrical entertainment by dancers.

ballistic missile, guided missile completing its trajectory in free fall.

bal•lis′tics, *n.* study of the motion of projectiles. —**bal•lis′tic,** *adj.*

bal·loon', *n.* 1. bag filled with a light gas, designed to float in atmosphere. —*v.* 2. go up in balloon. —**bal·loon'ist**, *n.*

bal'lot, *n., v.,* **-loted, -loting.** —*n.* 1. paper used in voting. 2. vote. —*v.* 3. vote by ballot.

ball'park', *n.* baseball arena.

ball'point' pen, pen laying down ink with small ball.

ball'room', *n.* room for dances.

bal'ly·hoo', *n.* 1. *Informal.* inflated news. —*v.* 2. tout.

balm (bäm), *n.* 1. fragrant, oily substance obtained from tropical trees. 2. aromatic ointment or fragrance.

balm'y, *adj.,* **balmier, balmiest.** 1. mild; refreshing. 2. fragrant. —**balm'i·ly**, *adv.* —**balm'i·ness**, *n.*

ba·lo'ney, *n. Informal.* 1. bologna. 2. foolish talk.

bal'sa (bôl'-), *n.* tropical tree with light wood.

bal'sam, *n.* 1. fragrant substance exuded from certain trees. 2. any of these trees. —**bal·sam'ic**, *adj.*

bal'us·ter, *n.* pillarlike support for railing.

bal'us·trade', *n.* series of balusters supporting a railing.

bam·boo', *n., pl.* **-boos.** treelike tropical grass having a hollow woody stem.

bam·boo'zle, *v.,* **-zled, -zling.** *Informal.* confuse or trick.

ban, *v.,* **banned, banning,** *n.* —*v.* 1. prohibit. —*n.* 2. prohibition.

ba'nal, *adj.* trite. —**ba·nal'i·ty**, *n.*

ba·nan'a, *n.* 1. tropical plant. 2. fruit of this plant.

band, *n.* 1. strip of material for binding. 2. stripe. 3. company of persons. 4. group of musicians. —*v.* 5. mark with bands. 6. unite. —**band'mas'ter**, *n.* —**bands'man**, *n.*

band'age, *n., v.,* **-aged, -aging.** —*n.* 1. material for binding wound. —*v.* 2. bind with bandage. —**band'ag·er**, *n.*

Band'-Aid', *n.* 1. *Trademark.* small adhesive bandage with gauze center. 2. *(often l.c.)* makeshift aid or solution.

ban·dan'na, *n.* colored handkerchief with figures. Also, **ban·dan'a.**

ban′dit, *n., pl.* **-dits, -dit′ti.** robber. —**ban′dit•ry,** *n.*

band′stand′, *n.* platform on which band performs.

band′wag′on, *n.* 1. large wagon for carrying band in parade. 2. cause that appears popular and successful.

ban′dy, *v.,* **-died, -dying,** *adj.* —*v.* 1. strike to and fro. 2. exchange (words) back and forth. —*adj.* 3. bent outward. —**ban′dy-leg′ged,** *adj.*

bane, *n.* thing causing death or destruction.

bane′ful, *adj.* destructive. —**bane′ful•ly,** *adv.* —**bane′ful•ness,** *n.*

bang, *n.* 1. loud, sudden noise. 2. (*often pl.*) fringe of hair across forehead. —*v.* 3. make loud noise. 4. strike noisily.

ban′gle, *n.* bracelet.

bang′-up′, *adj. Informal.* excellent.

ban′ish, *v.* 1. exile. 2. drive or put away. —**ban′ish•ment,** *n.*

ban′is•ter, *n.* 1. baluster. 2. (*pl.*) balustrade.

ban′jo, *n., pl.* **-jos, -joes.** musical instrument similar to guitar, with circular body. —**ban′jo•ist,** *n.*

bank, *n.* 1. pile; heap. 2. slope bordering stream. 3. place or institution for receiving and lending money. 4. store of something, such as blood, for future use. —*v.* 5. border with or make into bank. 6. cover fire to make burn slowly. 7. act as bank. 8. deposit or keep money in bank. **9.** rely (on). —**bank′er,** *n.* —**bank′ing,** *n.*

bank′roll′, *n.* 1. money possessed. —*v.* 2. fund.

bank′rupt, *n.* 1. insolvent person. —*adj.* 2. insolvent. 3. lacking. —*v.* 4. make bankrupt. —**bank′rupt•cy,** *n.*

ban′ner, *n.* flag.

banns, *n.pl.* notice of intended marriage. Also, **bans.**

ban′quet, *n.* 1. feast. —*v.* 2. dine or entertain at banquet. —**ban′quet•er,** *n.*

ban′shee, *n.* female spirit of folklore whose wailing means a loved one is about to die.

ban′tam, *n.* 1. breed of small domestic fowl. —*adj.* 2. tiny.

ban′ter, *n.* 1. teasing; raillery. —*v.* 2. address with or use banter. —**ban′ter•er,** *n.*

ban′yan, *n.* East Indian fig tree.

ba′o•bab′ (bā′ō bab′, bä′ō-), *n.* tropical tree with thick trunk and gourdlike fruit.

bap′tism, *n.* immersion in or application of water, esp. as initiatory rite in Christian church. —**bap•tis′mal,** *adj.*

Bap′tist, *n.* Christian who undergoes baptism only after profession of faith.

bap•tize′, *v.,* -tized, -tizing. 1. administer baptism. 2. christen. —**bap•tiz′er,** *n.*

bar, *n., v.,* barred, barring, *prep.* —*n.* 1. long, evenly shaped piece of wood or metal. 2. band; stripe. 3. long ridge in shallow waters. 4. hindrance. 5. line marking division between two measures of music. 6. place where liquors are served. 7. legal profession or its members. 8. railing in courtroom between public and court officers. 9. place in courtroom where prisoners are stationed. —*v.* 10. provide or fasten with a bar. 11. block; hinder. —*prep.* 12. except for. —**barred,** *adj.*

barb, *n.* 1. point projecting backward. —*v.* 2. furnish with barb. —**barbed,** *adj.*

bar•bar′i•an, *n.* 1. savage person. —*adj.* 2. uncivilized. —**bar•bar′i•an•ism,** *n.* —**bar•bar′ic,** *adj.* —**bar•bar′i•cal•ly,** *adv.*

bar′ba•rism, *n.* barbarian state or act.

bar•bar′i•ty, *n., pl.* -ties. 1. cruelty. 2. crudity.

bar′ba•rous, *adj.* 1. barbarian. 2. harsh; harsh-sounding. —**bar′ba•rous•ly,** *adv.* —**bar′ba•rous•ness,** *n.*

bar′be•cue′, *n., v.,* -cued, -cuing. —*n.* 1. outdoor meal at which foods are roasted over an open fire. 2. animal roasted whole. —*v.* 3. broil or roast over an open fire. Also, **bar′be•que′.**

bar′ber, *n.* 1. one who gives haircuts, shaves, etc. —*v.* 2. shave or cut the hair.

bar•bi′tu•rate′ (bär bich′ə rāt′), *n.* sedative drug.

bar code, line series placed on item for identification by computer scanner.

bard, *n.* 1. ancient Celtic poet. 2. any poet. —**bard′ic,** *adj.*

bare, *adj.,* barer, barest, *v.,* bared, baring. —*adj.* 1.

uncovered; unclothed. 2. unfurnished. 3. unconcealed. 4. mere. —*v.* 5. make bare. —**bare′ness,** *n.* —**bare′foot′,** *adj., adv.*

bare′back′, *adv., adj.* saddleless.

bare′faced′, *adj.* 1. undisguised. 2. impudent.

bare′ly, *adv.* 1. no more than; only. 2. nakedly.

bar′gain, *n.* 1. agreement. 2. advantageous purchase. —*v.* 3. discuss or arrive at agreement. —**bar′gain•er,** *n.*

barge, *n., v.,* **barged, barging.** —*n.* 1. unpowered vessel for freight. —*v.* 2. carry by barge. 3. move clumsily. 4. *Informal.* intrude. —**barge′man,** *n.*

bar′i•tone′, *n.* 1. male voice between tenor and bass. 2. baritone instrument.

bar′i•um (bâr′ē əm, bar′-), *n.* metallic element.

bark, *n.* 1. cry of a dog. 2. external covering of woody plants. 3. Also, **barque.** three-masted vessel. —*v.* 4. sound a bark. 5. utter with barking sound. 6. strip off bark of. 7. rub off the skin of.

bark′er, *n.* person who stands at the entrance to a show, shouting out its attractions.

bar′ley, *n.* edible cereal plant.

bar mitz′vah (bär), Jewish religious ceremony recognizing manhood.

barn, *n.* farm building for storage and stabling. —**barn′yard′,** *n.*

bar′na•cle, *n.* type of shellfish that clings to passing objects. —**bar′na•cled,** *adj.*

barn′storm′, *v.* tour rural areas performing or giving speeches.

ba•rom′e•ter, *n.* instrument for measuring atmospheric pressure. —**bar′o•met′ric, bar′o•met′ri•cal,** *adj.*

bar′on, *n.* member of lowest nobility. Also, *n.fem.* **bar′on•ess.** —**bar′on•age,** *n.* —**ba•ro′ni•al,** *adj.*

bar′on•et, *n.* member of hereditary British commoner order, ranking below baron. —**bar′on•et•cy,** *n.*

Ba•roque′ (-rōk′), *n.* artistic style marked by exuberant decoration.

bar′rack, *n. (usually pl.)* **1.** building for lodging soldiers. —*v.* **2.** lodge in barracks.

bar′ra•cu′da (-koo′-), *n.* edible eellike fish.

bar•rage′, *n.* barrier of concentrated artillery fire.

bar′rel, *n., v.,* **-reled, -reling.** —*n.* **1.** wooden cylindrical vessel with bulging sides. **2.** quantity held in such vessel. —*v.* **3.** put in barrel or barrels.

bar′ren, *adj.* **1.** sterile; unfruitful. **2.** dull. —**bar′ren•ness,** *n.*

bar•rette′, *n.* clasp for hair.

bar′ri•cade′, *n., v.,* **-caded, -cading.** —*n.* **1.** defensive barrier. —*v.* **2.** block or defend with barricade.

bar′ri•er, *n.* obstacle.

bar′ring (bär-′), *prep.* excepting.

bar′ris•ter, *n.* in England, lawyer in higher courts.

bar′room′, *n.* room with a bar for serving liquor.

bar′row, *n.* **1.** flat frame for carrying load. **2.** artificial mound, as over a grade.

bar′tend′er, *n.* person mixing and serving drinks at a bar.

bar′ter, *v.* **1.** exchange. —*n.* **2.** act of bartering.

ba′sal, *adj.* basic.

ba•salt′ (-sôlt′), *n.* dark, hard rock. —**ba•sal′tic,** *adj.*

base, *n., v.,* **based, basing,** *adj.,* **baser, basest.** —*n.* **1.** foundation. **2.** fundamental principle. **3.** starting point. **4.** *Mil.* **a.** protected place from which operations proceed. **b.** supply installation. **5.** chemical compound which unites with an acid to form a salt. —*v.* **6.** make foundation for. —*adj.* **7.** despicable. **8.** inferior. **9.** counterfeit. —**base′ness,** *n.*

base′ball′, *n.* **1.** game of ball played by two teams of nine players on diamond-shaped field. **2.** ball used.

base′board′, *n.* board or molding at the base of a room's walls.

base′less, *adj.* unfounded.

base′line′, *n.* **1.** line between bases on baseball diamond. **2.** line at each end of tennis court. **3.** basic standard or level; guideline. Also, **base line.**

base′ment, *n.* story of building below the ground floor.

base on balls, *pl.* **bases on balls.** awarding of first base to a batter after four pitches not strikes.

bash, *v.* **1.** hit hard. **2.** attack with blows or words. —*n.* **3.** hard blow. **4.** big, lively party.

bash′ful, *adj.* shy; timid. —**bash′ful•ly,** *adv.* —**bash′ful•ness,** *n.*

ba′sic, *adj.* **1.** rudimentary. **2.** essential. —*n.* **3.** (*pl.*) rudiments. —**ba′si•cal•ly,** *adv.*

bas′il (baz′-), *n.* mintlike herb.

BASIC (ā′sik), *n.* computer programming language using English words, punctuation, and algebraic notation.

ba•sil′i•ca, *n.* **1.** ancient church. **2.** Roman Catholic church.

ba′sin, *n.* **1.** circular vessel for liquids. **2.** area drained by river. **3.** area of lower land, not drained to outside.

ba′sis, *n., pl.* -ses. **1.** base (defs. 1, 2). **2.** principal ingredient.

bask, *v.* expose to warmth.

bas′ket, *n.* receptacle woven of twigs, strips of wood, etc.

bas′ket•ball′, *n.* **1.** game of ball played by two teams of five players on rectangular court. **2.** ball used.

bas•ma′ti (bäs mä′tē), *n.* variety of long-grain rice that is notably fragrant.

bas′-re•lief′ (bä′ri lēf′), *n.* sculpture in which figures project slightly.

bass, *adj., n., pl.* (for 3) **basses, bass.** —*adj.* **1.** (bās). of the lowest musical part or range. —*n.* **2.** (bās). bass part, voice, instrument, etc. **3.** (bas). various edible, spiny fishes.

basset hound, short-legged hound with drooping ears.

bas′si•net′, *n.* basket with hood, used as cradle.

bas•soon′, *n.* baritone woodwind instrument.

bas′tard, *n.* **1.** illegitimate child. **2.** *Informal.* mean person. —*adj.* **3.** illegitimate in birth. **4.** not pure. —**bas′tard•i•za′tion,** *n.* —**bas′tard•ize′,** *v.*

baste, *v.,* **basted, basting. 1.** sew with temporary stitches. **2.** moisten while cooking.

bas′tion (bas′chən), *n.* **1.** projecting part of fortification. **2.** fortified place. **3.** something that protects.

bat, *n., v.,* **batted, batting.** —*n.* **1.** stick or club, esp. as used in ball games. **2.** nocturnal flying mammal. —*v.* **3.** strike with bat. **4.** take turn in batting. **5.** blink; flutter.

batch, *n.* material, esp. bread, prepared in one operation.

bat′ed, *adj.* (of breath) held back in suspense.

bath, *n., pl.* **baths. 1.** washing of entire body. **2.** water used. —**bath′room′, bath′tub′,** *n.*

bathe, *v.,* **bathed, bathing. 1.** take a bath. **2.** immerse in liquid; moisten. —**bath′er,** *n.*

bathing suit, garment worn for swimming; swimsuit.

ba′thos (bā′thos, -thōs), *n.* **1.** ludicrous change in tone from lofty to commonplace. **2.** false pathos; trite sentiment. —**ba•thet′ic,** *adj.*

bath′robe′, *n.* robe worn going to and from bath.

ba•tik′ (-tēk′), *n.* cloth partly waxed to resist dye.

bat mitz′vah (bät), Jewish religious ceremony for a girl, paralleling the bar mitzvah.

ba•ton′, *n.* rod, esp. one used by orchestral conductor.

bat•tal′ion, *n.* military unit of three or more companies.

bat′ten, *n.* **1.** strip of wood. —*v.* **2.** fasten or furnish with battens. **3.** fatten or grow fat.

bat′ter, *v.* **1.** beat persistently. **2.** damage by hard usage. —*n.* **3.** semiliquid cooking mixture. **4.** one who bats.

battering ram, heavy beam for beating down walls, gates, etc.

bat′ter•y, *n., pl.* **-teries. 1.** device for producing electricity. **2.** combination of artillery pieces. **3.** illegal attack by beating.

bat′tle, *n., v.,* **-tled, -tling.** —*n.* **1.** hostile encounter. —*v.* **2.** fight. —**bat′tle•field′,** *n.* —**bat′tle•ground′,** *n.* —**bat′tler,** *n.*

bat′tle•ment, *n.* indented parapet.

bat′tle•ship′, *n.* heavily armed warship.

bat′ty, *adj.,* **-tier, -tiest.** *Slang.* crazy or eccentric.

bau′ble, *n.* trinket.

baud (bôd), *n.* unit used to measure speed of a signal or data transfer, as in computers.

baux'ite (bôk'sīt), *n.* principal ore of aluminum.

bawd'y, *adj.,* **bawdier, bawdiest.** obscene. —**bawd'i•ness,** *n.*

bawl, *v.* 1. shout out. —*n.* 2. shout.

bay, *n.* 1. inlet of sea or lake. 2. vertical section of window. 3. compartment or recess in a building. 4. deep, prolonged bark. 5. stand made by hunted animal or person. 6. reddish brown. 7. laurel tree. —*v.* 8. bark. 9. bring to bay (def. 5). —*adj.* 10. of the color bay.

bay'ber'ry, *n., pl.* **-ries.** fragrant shrub with berries.

bay leaf, dried leaf of the laurel, used in cooking.

bay'o•net, *n., v.,* **-neted, -neting.** —*n.* 1. daggerlike instrument attached to rifle muzzle. —*v.* 2. kill or wound with bayonet.

bay'ou (bī'oo), *n., pl.* **bayous.** arm of river, etc.

ba•zaar', *n.* market place.

ba•zoo'ka, *n.* hand-held rocket launcher.

BB, *n., pl.* **BB's.** small metal shot fired from a BB gun.

bbl., barrel.

B.C., before Christ.

be, *v.* 1. exist. 2. occur.

beach, *n.* 1. sand or pebbles of seashore. —*v.* 2. run or pull a ship onto beach.

beach'comb'er, *n.* 1. person who gathers salable jetsam or refuse on a beach. 2. vagrant living on a beach.

beach'head', *n.* part of beach landed on and seized by military force.

bea'con, *n.* 1. signal, esp. a fire. —*v.* 2. serve as beacon.

bead, *n.* 1. small ball of glass, pearl, etc., designed to be strung. 2. (*pl.*) necklace. —*v.* 3. ornament with beads. —**bead'ing,** *n.* —**bead'y,** *adj.*

bea'gle, *n.* short-legged hunting dog.

beak, *n.* 1. bill of bird. 2. beaklike object.

beak'er, *n.* large glass.

beam, *n.* 1. horizontal support secured at both ends. 2. breadth of ship. 3. ray of light or other radiation. —*v.* 4. emit

beams. 5. smile radiantly.
—**beam'ing,** *adj.*

bean, *n.* 1. edible seed of certain plants. 2. plant producing such seed.

bear, *v.,* **bore** (for 1–5) or **beared** (for 6), **bearing,** *n.* —*v.* 1. support. 2. carry. 3. undergo; endure. 4. move; go. 5. give birth. 6. act as bear (def. 9). —*n.* 7. large shaggy mammal. 8. clumsy or rude person. 9. speculator who counts on falling prices. —**bear'er,** *n.* —**bear'a•ble,** *adj.* —**bear'ish,** *adj.* —**bear'ish•ly,** *adv.*

beard, *n.* 1. hair on face of man. 2. similar growth or part. —*v.* 3. defy. —**beard'ed,** *adj.* —**beard'less,** *adj.*

bear hug, tight embrace.

bear'ing, *n.* 1. manner. 2. reference; relation. 3. *Mach.* part in which another part moves. 4. position; direction. 5. **bearings,** orientation.

bear market, stock market with falling prices.

beast, *n.* 1. animal. 2. coarse or inhuman person.

beast'ly, *adj.,* **-lier, -liest.** 1. brutish. 2. nasty. —**beast'li•ness,** *n.*

beat, *v.,* **beat, beaten** or **beat, beating,** *n.* —*v.* 1. strike repeatedly. 2. dash against. 3. mark time in music. 4. defeat. 5. throb. —*n.* 6. blow. 7. sound of a blow. 8. habitual rounds. 9. musical time. —**beat'a•ble,** *adj.* —**beat'en,** *adj.* —**beat'er,** *n.*

be'a•tif'ic, *adj.* blissful. —**be'a•tif'i•cal•ly,** *adv.*

be•at'i•tude', *n.* 1. blessedness. 2. (*often cap.*) declaration of blessedness made by Christ (Matthew 5).

beat'nik, *n.* disillusioned, unconventional person, esp. of the 1950s.

beau (bō), *n., pl.* **beaus, beaux.** 1. lover. 2. fop.

beau'te•ous (byoo'-), *adj.* beautiful. —**beau'te•ous•ly,** *adv.* —**beau'te•ous•ness,** *n.*

beau•ti'cian, *n.* person who works in beauty parlor.

beau'ti•ful, *adj.* having beauty. —**beau'ti•ful•ly,** *adv.*

beau'ti•fy', *v.,* **-fied, -fying.** make beautiful. —**beau'ti•fi•ca'tion,** *n.*

beau′ty, *n., pl.* **-ties. 1.** quality that excites admiration. **2.** beautiful thing or person.

beauty parlor, salon for women's haircuts and styling. Also, **beauty shop.**

bea′ver, *n.* **1.** amphibious rodent. **2.** the fur.

be•cause′, *conj.* **1.** for the reason that. —*adv.* **2.** by reason (of).

beck, *n.* beckoning gesture.

beck′on, *v.* signal by gesture. —**beck′on•er,** *n.*

be•cloud′, *v.* **1.** obscure with clouds. **2.** confuse.

be•come′, *v.,* **became, become, becoming. 1.** come to be. **2.** suit. —**be•com′ing,** *adj.* —**be•com′ing•ly,** *adv.*

bed, *n., v.,* **bedded, bedding.** —*n.* **1.** piece of furniture on or in which a person sleeps. **2.** sleep. **3.** piece of ground for planting. **4.** foundation. —*v.* **5.** plant in bed. —**bed′time′,** *n.*

bed′bug′, *n.* bloodsucking insect.

bed′ding, *n.* blankets, sheets, etc., for a bed.

be•dev′il, *v.,* **-iled, -il•ing. 1.** torment maliciously. **2.** confuse; confound.

bed′fast′, *adj.* bedridden.

bed′fel′low, *n.* **1.** sharer of bed. **2.** ally.

bed′lam, *n.* **1.** scene of loud confusion. **2.** lunatic asylum.

Bed′ou•in (-oo in), *n.* **1.** desert Arab. **2.** nomad.

bed′pan′, *n.* shallow pan used as toilet for bedridden person.

be•drag′gled, *adj.* soiled.

bed′rid•den′, *adj.* confined to bed.

bed′rock′, *n.* **1.** continuous solid rock under soil. **2.** firm foundation or basis.

bed′room′, *n.* sleeping room.

bed′sore′, *n.* skin ulcer caused by long confinement in bed.

bed′spread′, *n.* cover for bed.

bed′stead′, *n.* frame for bed.

bee, *n.* **1.** four-winged, nectar-gathering insect. **2.** local gathering. —**bee′hive′,** *n.* —**bee′keep′er,** *n.*

beech, *n.* tree bearing small edible nuts (**beech′nuts′**). —**beech′en,** *adj.*

beef, *n., pl.* **beeves. 1.** bull, cow, or steer. **2.** edible flesh of such an animal. **3.** brawn. —**beef′y,** *adj.* —**beef′i•ness,** *n.* —**beef′steak′,** *n.*

bee′line′, *n.* direct course.

beep, *n.* **1.** short tone, usu. high in pitch, as from automobile horn or electronic device. —*v.* **2.** make or cause to make a beep.

beep′er, *n.* small electronic device that signals wearer of telephone message.

beer, *n.* beverage brewed and fermented from cereals.

beet, *n.* biennial edible plant.

bee′tle, *v.,* **-tled, -tling,** *n.* —*v.* **1.** project. —*n.* **2.** insect with hard, horny forewings.

be•fall′, *v.,* **-fell, -fallen, -falling.** happen; happen to.

be•fit′, *v.,* **-fitted, -fitting.** be fitting for. —**be•fit′ting,** *adj.*

be•fore′, *adv.* **1.** in front. **2.** earlier. —*prep.* **3.** in front of. **4.** previously to. **5.** in future of. **6.** in preference to. **7.** in precedence of. **8.** in presence of. —*conj.* **9.** previously to time when.

be•fore′hand′, *adv.* earlier.

be•friend′, *v.* act as friend toward.

be•fud′dle, *v.,* **-dled, -dling.** confuse thoroughly. —**be•fud′dle•ment,** *n.*

beg, *v.,* **begged, begging. 1.** ask for charity. **2.** ask humbly.

be•get′, *v.,* **begot, begotten** or **begot, begetting.** procreate. —**be•get′ter,** *n.*

beg′gar, *n.* **1.** one who begs alms. **2.** penniless person. —*v.* **3.** reduce to poverty. —**beg′gar•y,** *n.*

beg′gar•ly, *adj.* penurious.

be•gin′, *v.,* **began, begun, beginning. 1.** start. **2.** originate. —**be•gin′ner,** *n.* —**be•gin′ning,** *n.*

be•gone′, *interj.* (depart!)

be•gon′ia (bi gōn′yə), *n.* tropical flowering plant.

be•grudge′, *v.,* **-grudged, -grudging. 1.** be envious of. **2.** give or allow reluctantly.

be•guile′ (-gīl′), *v.,* **-guiled, -guiling. 1.** delude. **2.** charm; divert. —**be•guile′ment,** *n.* —**be•guil′er,** *n.*

be•half′, *n.* **1.** side; part. **2.** interest; favor.

be•have′, *v.,* **-haved, -having. 1.** conduct oneself. **2.** act properly.

be•hav′ior, *n.* manner of behaving.

be•head′, *v.* cut off head of.

be·he'moth (bi hē' məth), *n.* any huge or extremely powerful creature or thing.

be·hest', *n.* urgent request.

be·hind', *prep.* 1. at the back of. 2. later than. —*adv.* 3. at the back. 4. in arrears. —*n.* 5. *Informal.* buttocks.

be·hold', *v.,* **beheld, beholding,** *interj.* —*v.* 1. look at; see. —*interj.* 2. look! —**be·hold'er,** *n.*

be·hold'en, *adj.* obliged.

be·hoove', *v.,* **-hooved, -hooving.** be necessary for.

beige (bāzh), *n.* light brown.

be'ing, *n.* 1. existence. 2. something that exists.

be·la'bor, *v.* 1. discuss, etc., excessively. 2. beat.

be·lat'ed, *adj.* late. —**be·lat'ed·ly,** *adv.*

belch, *v.* 1. eject gas from stomach. 2. emit violently. —*n.* 3. act of belching.

be·lea'guer (bi lē'gər), *v.* beset with difficulties.

bel'fry, *n., pl.* **-fries.** bell tower.

be·lie', *v.,* **-lied, -lying.** 1. misrepresent. 2. show to be false. 3. lie. —**be·li'er,** *n.*

be·lief', *n.* 1. thing believed. 2. conviction. 3. faith.

be·lieve', *v.,* **-lieved, -lieving.** 1. trust. 2. accept as true. 3. regard as likely. —**be·liev'a·ble,** *adj.* —**be·liev'er,** *n.*

be·lit'tle, *v.,* **-littled, -littling.** disparage.

bell, *n.* 1. metal instrument producing ringing sound. —*v.* 2. put bell on. 3. flare outward. —**bell'-like',** *adj.*

bel'la·don'na, *n.* poisonous plant yielding medicinal drug.

belle, *n.* beautiful woman.

bell'hop', *n.* person who carries luggage and runs errands in a hotel. Also, **bell'boy'.**

bel'li·cose', *adj.* warlike.

bel·lig'er·ent (-lij'-), *adj.* 1. warlike. 2. engaged in war. —*n.* 3. nation at war. —**bel·lig'er·ence, bel·lig'er·en·cy,** *n.* —**bel·lig'er·ent·ly,** *adv.*

bel'low, *v.* 1. roar, as a bull. 2. utter in deep, loud voice. —*n.* 3. act or sound of bellowing.

bel'lows, *n.sing. and pl.* collapsing device producing strong current of air.

bell pepper, plant yielding a mild, bell-shaped pepper.

bell′weth′er, *n.* 1. male sheep leading a flock. 2. one that leads or marks a trend.

bel′ly, *n., pl.* **-lies,** *v.,* **-lied, -lying.** —*n.* 1. abdomen. 2. inside. 3. protuberant surface. —*v.* 4. swell out.

bel′ly•ache′, *n., v.,* **-ached, aching.** —*n.* 1. pain in the abdomen. —*v.* 2. *Informal.* complain.

be•long′, *v.* 1. be a member of. 2. **belong to,** be property of.

be•long′ings, *n.pl.* effects.

be•lov′ed, *adj.* 1. greatly loved. —*n.* 2. object of love.

be•low′, *adv.* 1. beneath. 2. in lower rank. —*prep.* 3. lower than.

belt, *n.* 1. band for encircling waist. 2. any flexible band. —*v.* 3. gird or furnish with belt. —**belt′ing,** *n.*

belt′way′, *n.* highway around perimeter of urban area.

be•moan′, *v.* lament.

be•mused′, *adj.* preoccupied.

bench, *n.* 1. long seat. 2. judge's seat. 3. body of judges. 4. work table.

bench′mark′, *n.* standard against which others can be measured or judged. Also, **bench′ mark′.**

bend, *v.,* **bent, bending,** *n.* —*v.* 1. curve. 2. become curved. 3. cause to submit. 4. turn or incline. —*n.* 5. a bending. 6. something bent.

be•neath′, *adj.* 1. in a lower place. —*prep.* 2. under. 3. lower than. 4. unworthy of.

ben′e•dic′tion, *n.* blessing.

ben′e•fac′tion, *n.* 1. doing of good. 2. benefit conferred. —**ben′e•fac′tor,** *n.* —**ben′e•fac′tress,** *n.fem.*

be•nef′i•cent, *adj.* doing good. —**benef′i•cence,** *n.* —**be•nef′i•cent•ly,** *adv.*

ben•e•fi′cial, *adj.* helpful. —**ben′e•fi′cial•ly,** *adv.*

ben•e•fi′ci•ar•y, *n., pl.* **-aries.** recipient of benefits.

ben′e•fit, *n., v.,* **-fited, -fiting.** —*n.* 1. act of kindness. 2. entertainment for worthy cause. —*v.* 3. do good to. 4. gain advantage.

be•nev′o•lent, *adj.* desiring to do good. —**be•nev′o•lence,** *n.*

be•night′ed, *adj.* ignorant.

be·nign' (bi nīn'), *adj.* **1.** kind. **2.** favorable. —**be·nign'ly,** *adv.*

be·nig'nant (-nig'-), *adj.* **1.** kind. **2.** beneficial. —**be·nig'nan·cy,** *n.* —**be·nig'nant·ly,** *adv.* —**be·nig'ni·ty,** *n.*

bent, *adj.* **1.** curved. **2.** determined. —*n.* **3.** curve. **4.** inclination.

be·numb' (bi num'), *v.* **1.** make numb. **2.** make inactive.

ben'zene (-zēn), *n.* inflammable liquid, used as solvent.

ben'zine (-zēn), *n.* liquid used in cleaning and dyeing.

be·queath', *v.* dispose of by will. —**be·queath'al,** *n.*

be·quest', *n.* legacy.

be·rate', *v.,* **-rated, -rating.** scold.

be·reave', *v.,* **-reaved** or **-reft, -reaving. 1.** deprive of. **2.** make desolate. —**be·reave'ment,** *n.*

be·ret' (-rā'), *n.* cloth cap.

ber'i·ber'i, *n.* disease caused by vitamin deficiency.

berm, *n.* **1.** shoulder of road. **2.** mound of snow or dirt.

ber'ry, *n., pl.* **-ries,** *v.,* **-ried, -rying.** —*n.* **1.** small juicy fruit. —*v.* **2.** gather berries.

ber·serk', *adj.* wild; frenzied.

berth, *n.* **1.** sleeping space for traveler. **2.** mooring space for vessel. —*v.* **3.** assign berth.

ber'yl, *n.* green mineral.

be·seech', *v.,* **-sought, -seeching.** implore; beg. —**be·seech'ing·ly,** *adv.*

be·set', *v.,* **-set, -setting. 1.** attack on all sides. **2.** surround.

be·side', *prep.* **1.** at the side of. **2.** compared with. **3.** in addition to. —*adv.* **4.** in addition.

be·sides', *adv.* **1.** moreover. **2.** otherwise. —*prep.* **3.** in addition to. **4.** other than.

be·siege', *v.,* **-sieged, -sieging.** lay siege to. —**be·sieg'er,** *n.*

be·smirch', *v.* defile.

be·sot'ted (bi sot'id), *adj.* **1.** drunk. **2.** infatuated.

be·speak', *v.,* **-spoke, -spoken** or **-spoke, -speaking. 1.** ask for in advance. **2.** imply.

best, *adj.* **1.** of highest quality. **2.** most suitable. —*adv.* **3.** most excellently. **4.** most fully. —*n.* **5.** best thing. —*v.* **6.** defeat.

bes'tial (-chəl), *adj.* **1.** beastlike. **2.** brutal. —**bes·ti·al'i·ty,** *n.* —**bes'tial·ly,** *adv.*

be·stir', *v.,* -stirred, -stirring. stir up.

best man, chief attendant of the bridegroom at a wedding.

be·stow', *v.* **1.** present. **2.** apply.

be·strew', *v.,* -strewed, -strewed or -strewn, -strewing. **1.** cover. **2.** scatter.

bet, *v.,* **bet** or **betted, betting,** *n.* —*v.* **1.** risk on a chance result. —*n.* **2.** thing or amount bet. —**bet'ter, bet'tor,** *n.*

be·take', *v.,* -took, -taken, -taking. **betake oneself, 1.** go. **2.** resort (to).

be'tel nut (bēt'l), seed of a palm, often chewed in tropics.

bête' noire' (bet' nwär'), most dreaded person or thing.

be·tide', *v.,* -tided, -tiding. happen.

be·times', *adv. Archaic.* **1.** early. **2.** soon.

be·to'ken, *v.* indicate.

be·tray', *v.* **1.** expose by treachery. **2.** be unfaithful to. **3.** reveal. **4.** deceive. **5.** seduce. —**be·tray'al,** *n.* —**be·tray'er,** *n.*

be·troth' (bi trōth'), *v.* promise to marry. —**be·troth'al,** *n.* —**be·trothed',** *adj., n.*

bet'ter, *adj.* **1.** of superior quality. **2.** healthier. —*adv.* **3.** in a more excellent way. **4.** more. —*n.* **5.** something better. **6.** one's superior. —*v.* **7.** improve on. —**bet'ter·ment,** *n.*

be·tween', *prep.* **1.** in the space separating. **2.** intermediate to. **3.** connecting. —*adv.* **4.** in the intervening space or time.

be·twixt', *prep., adv.* between.

bev'el, *n., v.,* -eled, -eling. —*n.* **1.** surface cutting off a corner. **2.** device for drawing angles. —*v.* **3.** cut or slant at a bevel.

bev'er·age, *n.* drink.

bev'y, *n., pl.* **bevies. 1.** flock of birds. **2.** group.

be·wail', *v.* lament.

be•ware', *v.*, -wared, -waring. be wary (of).

be•wil'der, *v.* confuse.
—**be•wil'dered**, *adj.*
—**be•wil'der•ing**, *adj.*
—**be•wil'der•ing•ly**, *adv.*
—**be•wil'der•ment**, *n.*

be•witch', *v.* enchant.
—**be•witch'ing**, *adj.*

be•yond', *prep.* **1.** on the farther side of. **2.** farther, more, or later on. —*adv.* **3.** farther on.

bi-, prefix meaning twice or two.

bi•an'nu•al, *adj.* occurring twice a year.
—**bi•an'nu•al•ly**, *adv.*

bi'as, *n.* **1.** slant. **2.** prejudice. —*v.* **3.** prejudice.

bi•ath'lon (bī ath'lon), *n.* athletic contest comprising two consecutive events.

bib, *n.* cloth to protect dress.

Bi'ble, *n.* Old and New Testaments. —**Bib'li•cal**, *adj.* —**Bib'li•cal•ly**, *adv.*

bib'li•og'ra•phy, *n.*, *pl.* -phies. list of sources.

bib'u•lous (bib'yə ləs), *adj.* fond of or addicted to drink.

bi•cam'er•al, *adj.* composed of two legislative bodies.

bi•car'bo•nate of soda, baking soda.

bi'cen•ten'ni•al, *n.* two-hundredth anniversary. Also, **bi'cen•ten'a•ry**.

bi'ceps (-seps), *n.* muscle of upper arm.

bick'er, *v.* squabble.

bi•cus'pid, *n.* tooth having two cusps or points.

bi'cy•cle (-si-), *n.*, *v.*, -cled, -cling. —*n.* **1.** two-wheeled vehicle. —*v.* **2.** ride a bicycle. —**bi'cy•cler, bi'cy•clist**, *n.*

bid, *v.*, **bade** or **bad** (for 1, 2) or **bid** (for 3), **bidden** or **bid**, **bidding**, *n.* —*v.* **1.** command. **2.** say. **3.** offer. —*n.* **4.** offer. —**bid'der**, *n.* —**bid'ding**, *n.*

bid'da•ble, *adj.* **1.** worth bidding. **2.** *Archaic.* obedient.

bide, *v.*, **bided, biding.** —**bide one's time,** await opportunity.

bi•det' (bē dā'), *n.* tub for bathing genital areas.

bi•en'ni•al, *adj.* occurring every two years.
—**bi•en'ni•al•ly**, *adv.*

bier, *n.* stand for a coffin.

bi·fo′cal, *adj.* **1.** having two focuses. **2.** (of eyeglass lens) having areas for near and far vision. —*n.* **3.** (*pl.*) eyeglasses with bifocal lenses.

big, *adj.,* **bigger, biggest. 1.** large. **2.** important. —**big′ness,** *n.*

big′a·my, *n., pl.* **-mies.** crime of marrying again while legally married. —**big′a·mist,** *n.* —**big′a·mous,** *adj.*

big bang theory, theory that universe began with explosion of dense mass of matter and is still expanding.

big′horn′, *n.* wild sheep of western U.S.

bight (bīt), *n.* **1.** loop of rope. **2.** deep bend in seashore.

big′ot, *n.* bigoted person. —**big′ot·ry,** *n.*

big′ot·ed, *adj.* intolerant. —**big′ot·ed·ly,** *adv.*

big shot, *Informal.* important person.

bike, *n.* **1.** bicycle, motorbike, or motorcycle. —*v.* **2.** ride a bike. —**bik′er,** *n.*

bi·ki′ni (-kē′-), *n.* woman's brief two-piece bathing suit.

bi·lat′er·al, *adj.* on or affecting two sides.

bile, *n.* **1.** digestive secretion of the liver. **2.** ill nature.

bilge, *n., v.,* **bilged, bilging.** —*n.* **1.** outer part of ship bottom. **2.** water in a bilge. **3.** wide part of cask. —*v.* **4.** cause to leak at the bilge.

bi·lin′gual, speaking or expressed in two languages. —**bi·lin′gual·ly,** *adv.*

bil′ious (-yəs), *adj.* **1.** pertaining to bile or excess bile. **2.** peevish.

bilk, *v.* cheat; defraud.

bill, *n.* **1.** account of money owed. **2.** piece of paper money. **3.** draft of proposed statute. **4.** written list. **5.** horny part of bird's jaw. **6.** poster. —*v.* **7.** charge.

bill′board′, *n.* large outdoor advertising display panel.

bil′let, *n., v.,* **-leted, -leting.** —*n.* **1.** lodging for a soldier. —*v.* **2.** provide with lodging.

bil′let-doux′ (bil′ā doo′), *n., pl.* **billets-doux** (-dooz′), love letter.

bill′fold′, *n.* wallet.

bil′liards, *n.* game played with hard balls (**billiard balls**) on a table. —**bil′liard,** *adj.* —**bil′liard·ist,** *n.*

bil′lion, *n.* thousand million. —**bil′lionth,** *adj., n.*

bil′lion•aire′, *n.* owner of billion dollars or more.

bill of fare, menu.

bill of sale, document transferring personal property from seller to buyer.

bil′low, *n.* 1. great wave. —*v.* 2. surge. —**bil′low•y,** *adj.* —**bil′low•i•ness,** *n.*

billy goat, male goat.

bim′bo′, *n.pl.* -bos, -boes. *Slang.* 1. inept person. 2. floozie.

bi•month′ly, *adv., adj.* every two months.

bin, *n., v.,* **binned, binning.** —*n.* 1. storage box. —*v.* 2. store in bin.

bi′na•ry (bī′-), *adj.* 1. involving two parts. 2. of a numerical system in which each place of a number is expressed as 0 or 1.

bind, *v.,* **bound, binding.** 1. tie or encircle with band. 2. unite. 3. oblige. 4. attach cover to book. —**bind′er,** *n.*

bind′ing, *n.* 1. something that binds. —*adj.* 2. obligatory.

binge, *n., v.,* **binged, binging.** —*n.* 1. bout of excess. —*v.* 2. go on binge.

bin′go, *n.* game using cards with numbered squares.

bin′na•cle, *n.* compass stand.

bin•oc′u•lars, *n.pl.* field glasses.

bio-, prefix meaning life or living organisms, as *biodegradable.*

bi′o•chem′is•try, *n.* chemistry of living matter. —**bi′o•chem′i•cal,** *adj.* —**bi•o′chem′i•cal•ly,** *adv.* —**bi′o•chem′ist,** *n.*

bi′o•de•grad′a•ble, *adj.* decaying and being absorbed into environment.

bi′o•en′gi•neer′ing, *n.* 1. application of engineering principles to problems in biology. 2. application of biological principles to engineering processes.

bi′o•eth′ics, *n.* study of ethical implications of biological procedures.

bi′o•feed′back, *n.* method for achieving self-control through observation of one's waves, blood pressure, etc.

bi·og′ra·phy, *n., pl.* **-phies.** written account of person's life. —**bi·og′ra·pher,** *n.* —**bi′o·graph′i·cal, bi′o·graph′ic,** *adj.* —**bi′o·graph′i·cal·ly,** *adv.*

bi′o·haz′ard, *n.* **1.** anything connected with biological research that poses a health hazard. **2.** risk posed by a biohazard.

biol., biology.

biological clock, **1.** natural mechanism regulating bodily cycles.

biological warfare, use of toxic organisms as weapons.

bi·ol′o·gy, *n.* science of living matter. —**bi′o·log′i·cal,** *adj.* —**bi′o·log′i·cal·ly,** *adv.* —**bi·ol′o·gist,** *n.*

bi·on′ics, *n.* use of electronic devices to increase human ability. —**bi·on′ic,** *adj.*

bi′op·sy, *n., pl.* **-sies.** examination of specimen of living tissue.

bi′o·rhythm, *n.* natural, periodic bodily cycle.

bi′o·sphere′ (bī′ə-), *n.* the part of the earth's surface and atmosphere that supports life.

bi′o·tech·nol′o·gy (bī′ō-), *n.* use of biological systems in pharmaceutical and environmental problem solving.

bi·par′ti·san, *adj.* representing two parties. —**bi·par′ti·san·ship′,** *n.*

bi·par′tite (-pär′tī), *adj.* **1.** having two parts. **2.** shared by two; joint.

bi′ped, *n.* **1.** two-footed animal. —*adj.* **2.** having two feet.

birch, *n.* tree with light bark. —**birch′en,** *adj.*

bird, *n.* vertebrate with feathers and wings.

bird′ie, *n.* score of one under par on a golf hole.

bird's′-eye′, *adj.* seen from above.

birth, *n.* **1.** being born. **2.** lineage. **3.** origin. —**birth′day′,** *n.* —**birth′place′,** *n.*

birth control, contraception.

birth′mark′, *n.* mark on skin had since birth.

birth′rate′, *n.* number of births in given time and place.

birth′right′, *n.* inheritance.

bis′cuit, *n.* small bread cakes.

bi•sect′, *v.* cut into two parts.
—**bi•sec′tion,** *n.*
—**bi•sec′tion•al,** *adj.*
—**bi•sec′tor,** *n.*

bi•sex′u•al, *adj.* 1. being both heterosexual and homosexual. —*n.* 2. bisexual person.
—**bi•sex′u•al′i•ty,** *n.*

bish′op, *n.* 1. overseer of a diocese. 2. piece in chess.

bish′op•ric, *n.* office of bishop.

bi′son, *n.,* *pl.* **bisons, bison.** oxlike mammal.

bisque (bisk), *n.* creamy soup.

bis′tro (bis′trō, bē′strō), *n.* French café.

bit, *n., v.,* **bitted, bitting.** —*n.* 1. mouthpiece of bridle. 2. small amount. 3. drill. 4. unit of computer information. —*v.* 5. restrain with a bit.

bitch, *n.* 1. female dog. 2. *Slang.* mean woman. —*v.* 3. *Slang.* complain.

bite, *v.,* **bit, bitten** or **bit, biting,** *n.* —*v.* 1. cut or grip with teeth. 2. sting. 3. corrode. —*n.* 4. act of biting. 5. wound made by biting. 6. sting. 7. piece bitten off. —**bit′er,** *n.*

bit′ing, *adj.* 1. harsh to the senses. 2. severely critical.
—**bit′ing•ly,** *adv.*

bit′ter, *adj.* 1. of harsh taste. 2. hard to receive or bear. 3. intensely hostile. —*n.* 4. something bitter.
—**bit′ter•ish,** *adj.*
—**bit′ter•ly,** *adv.*
—**bit′ter•ness,** *n.*

bit′tern, *n.* type of heron.

bit′ters, *n.pl.* liquor with bitter vegetable ingredients.

bit′ter•sweet′, *adj.* 1. tasting both bitter and sweet. 2. being both painful and pleasant.

bi•tu′men (-too′-), *n.* asphalt or asphaltlike substance.
—**bi•tu′mi•nous,** *adj.*

bituminous coal, soft coal.

bi′valve′, *n.* mollusk with two shells hinged together.
—**bi′valve′, bi•val′vular,** *adj.*

biv′ou•ac′ (-oo ak′), *n., v.,* **-acked, -acking.** —*n.* 1. temporary resting or assembly place for troops. —*v.* 2. dispose or meet in bivouac.

bi•week′ly, *adv., adj.* 1. every two weeks. 2. twice a week.

bi•zarre′ (-zär′), *adj.* strange.

blab, *v.,* **blabbed, blabbing.** 1. talk idly. 2. reveal secrets.

black, *adj.* **1.** without brightness or color. **2.** having dark skin color. **3.** without light. **4.** gloomy. **5.** wicked. —*n.* **6.** member of a dark-skinned people, esp. of Africa or African ancestry. **7.** black clothing. **8.** something black. —*v.* **9.** make or become black. —**black′ness,** *n.* —**black′ly,** *adv.* —**black′ish,** *adj.*

black′-and-blue′, *adj.* discolored, as by bruising.

black′ball′, *n.* **1.** adverse vote. —*v.* **2.** ostracize.

black′ber′ry, *n., pl.* **-ries. 1.** dark-purple fruit. **2.** plant bearing it.

black′bird′, *n.* black-feathered American bird.

black′board′, *n.* dark board for writing on with chalk.

black′en, *v.* **1.** black (def. 9). **2.** defame.

black-eyed Susan, yellow daisy with dark center.

black′guard (blag′ärd), *n.* **1.** despicable person. —*v.* **2.** revile.

black′head′, *n.* small fatty mass in a skin follicle.

black hole, area in outer space whose great density prevents radiation of light.

black′jack′, *n.* **1.** short flexible club. **2.** game of cards. —*v.* **3.** strike with a blackjack.

black′list′, *n.* list of persons in disfavor. —**black′list′,** *v.*

black magic, sorcery.

black′mail′, *n.* **1.** extortion by intimidation. —*v.* **2.** extort by blackmail. —**black′mail′•er,** *n.*

black market, illegal buying and selling of goods in violation of laws.

black′out′, *n.* **1.** loss of lights. **2.** loss of consciousness.

black′smith′, *n.* **1.** person who shoes horses. **2.** ironcrafter.

black sheep, person who causes embarrassment or shame to his or her family.

black′thorn′, *n.* thorny shrub with plumlike fruit.

black′top′, *n., v.,* **-topped, -topping.** —*n.* **1.** bituminous paving substance, as asphalt. —*v.* **2.** pave with blacktop.

black widow, poisonous spider.

blad′der, *n.* sac in body holding urine.

blade, *n.* **1.** cutting part of knife, sword, etc. **2.** leaf. **3.** thin, flat part. **4.** dashing young man. —**blad′ed,** *adj.* —**blade′like′,** *adj.*

blame, *v.,* **blamed, blaming,** *n.* —*v.* **1.** hold responsible for fault. **2.** find fault with. —*n.* **3.** censure. **4.** responsibility for censure. —**blam′a•ble, blame′ful, blame′wor′thy,** *adj.* —**blame′less,** *adj.*

blanch, *v.* whiten.

bland, *adj.* **1.** not harsh. **2.** not flavorful. —**bland′ly,** *adv.* —**bland′ness,** *n.*

blan′dish, *v.* coax. —**blan′dish•ment,** *n.*

blank, *adj.* **1.** not written on. **2.** without interest. **3.** white. **4.** unrhymed. —*n.* **5.** place lacking something. **6.** space to be filled. **7.** paper with such space. —*v.* **8.** make blank. —**blank′ly,** *adv.* —**blank′ness,** *n.*

blan′ket, *n.* **1.** warm bed covering. —*v.* **2.** cover.

blare, *v.,* **blared, blaring,** *n.* —*v.* **1.** sound loudly. —*n.* **2.** loud, raucous noise.

blar′ney, *n.* **1.** wheedling talk. —*v.* **2.** wheedle.

bla•sé′ (blä zā′), *adj.* bored; unimpressed.

blas•pheme′ (-fēm′), *v.* speak impiously or evilly. —**blas•phem′er,** *n.* —**blas′phe•mous,** *adj.* —**blas′phe•my,** *n.*

blast, *n.* **1.** gust of wind. **2.** loud trumpet tone. **3.** stream of air. **4.** explosion. **5.** charge of explosive. —*v.* **6.** blow. **7.** blight; destroy. **8.** explode. —**blast′er,** *n.*

blast furnace, forced-air furnace for smelting iron ore.

blast′off′, *n.* rocket launching.

bla′tant, *adj.* brazenly obvious. —**bla′tan•cy,** *n.* —**bla′tant•ly,** *adv.*

blaze, *n., v.,* **blazed, blazing.** —*n.* **1.** bright flame. **2.** bright glow. **3.** brightness. **4.** mark cut on tree. **5.** white spot on animal's face. —*v.* **6.** burn or shine brightly. **7.** mark (def. 4).

blaz′er, *n.* sports jacket.

bla′zon (blā′zən), *v.* proclaim.

bldg., building.

bleach, *v.* **1.** whiten. —*n.* **2.** bleaching agent.

bleach'ers, *n.pl.* tiers of spectators' seats.

bleak, *adj.* 1. bare. 2. cold. 3. dreary; depressing. —**bleak'ly,** *adv.* —**bleak'ness,** *n.*

blear, *v.* 1. dim, esp. with tears. —*n.* 2. bleared state. —**blear'y,** *adj.*

bleat, *v.* 1. cry, as sheep, goat, etc. —*n.* 2. such a cry. —**bleat'er,** *n.*

bleed, *v.,* **bled, bleeding.** lose or cause to lose blood.

bleep, *v.* delete from a recording.

blem'ish, *v.* 1. mar. —*n.* 2. defect. —**blem'ish•er,** *n.*

blend, *v.* 1. mix. —*n.* 2. mixture.

blend'er, *n.* electric appliance that purées or mixes food.

bless, *v.,* **blessed** or **blest, blessing.** 1. consecrate. 2. request divine favor on. 3. extol as holy. —**bless'ed,** *adj.* —**bless'ing,** *n.*

blight, *n.* 1. plant disease. 2. ruin. —*v.* 3. wither. 4. ruin.

blimp, *n.* small dirigible.

blind, *adj.* 1. sightless. 2. uncomprehending. 3. hidden.

4. without an outlet. 5. without advance knowledge. —*v.* 6. make blind. —*n.* 7. something that blinds. 8. ruse or disguise. —**blind'ly,** *adv.* —**blind'ness,** *n.*

blind date, arranged meeting between two strangers.

blind'fold', *v.* 1. cover eyes. —*n.* 2. covering over eyes. —*adj.* 3. with covered eyes.

blind'side', *v.,* **-sided, -siding.** hit someone unawares.

blink, *v.* 1. wink. 2. ignore. —*n.* 3. act of blinking. 4. gleam.

blip, *n.* 1. point of light on radar screen, indicating an object. 2. brief interruption or upward turn in a continuity.

bliss, *n.* 1. gladness. 2. supreme happiness. —**bliss'ful,** *adj.* —**bliss'ful•ly,** *adv.* —**bliss'ful•ness,** *n.*

blis'ter, *n.* 1. vesicle on the skin. —*v.* 2. raise blisters on. —**blis'ter•y,** *adj.*

blithe, *adj.* joyous; cheerful. —**blithe'ly,** *adv.*

blithe'some, *adj.* cheerful.

blitz, *n.* Also, **blitz'krieg'** (-krēg'). 1. swift, violent war, waged by surprise. —*v.* 2. attack by blitz.

bliz'zard, *n.* severe snowstorm.

bloat, *v.* swell.

blob, *n.* 1. small lump or drop. 2. shapeless mass.

bloc, *n.* political or economic confederation.

block, *n.* 1. solid mass. 2. platform. 3. obstacle. 4. single quantity. 5. unit of city street pattern. —*v.* 6. obstruct. 7. outline roughly. —**block'er,** *n.*

block•ade', *n., v.,* **-aded, -ading.** —*n.* 1. shutting-up of place by armed force. 2. obstruction. —*v.* 3. subject to blockade.

block'bust'er, *n.* successful commercial release.

block'head', *n.* stupid person.

block'house', *n.* fortified structure.

blond, *adj.* 1. light-colored. 2. having light-colored hair, skin, etc. —*n.* 3. blond person. —**blonde,** *adj., n.fem.*

blood, *n.* 1. red fluid in arteries and veins. 2. bloodshed. 3. extraction. —**blood'y,** *adj.* —**blood'i•ness,** *n.* —**blood'less,** *adj.*

blood count, number of red and white blood cells in specific volume of blood.

blood'cur'dling, *adj.* causing terror or horror.

blood'hound', *n.* large dog with acute sense of smell.

blood'mo•bile', *n.* truck for receiving blood donations.

blood pressure, pressure of blood against inner walls of blood vessels.

blood'shed', *n.* slaughter.

blood'shot', *adj.* with eye veins conspicuous.

blood'stream', *n.* blood flowing through the body's circulatory system.

blood'suck'er, *n.* 1. leech. 2. extortionist.

blood'thirst'y, *adj.* savage.

blood vessel, artery, vein, or capillary.

bloom, *n.* 1. flower. 2. health. 3. healthy glow. —*v.* 4. blossom. 5. flourish. —**bloom'ing,** *adj.*

bloom'ers, *n.pl.* undergarments.

bloop'er, *n.* blunder.

blos'som, *n.* 1. flower. —*v.* 2. produce blossoms. 3. develop.

blot, *n., v.,* **blotted, blotting.** —*n.* **1.** spot; stain. —*v.* **2.** stain; spot. **3.** dry with absorbent material. **4.** destroy.

blotch, *n.* **1.** large spot or stain. —*v.* **2.** blot (def. 2). —**blotch'y,** *adj.*

blot'ter, *n.* **1.** piece of paper for blotting. **2.** book in which events are recorded.

blouse, *n.* women's upper garment.

blow, *v.,* **blew, blown, blowing,** *n.* —*v.* **1.** (of air) move. **2.** drive by current of air. **3.** sound a wind instrument. **4.** go bad. **5.** explode. **6.** blossom. —*n.* **7.** blast of air. **8.** sudden stroke. **9.** sudden shock. **10.** blossoming. —**blow'er,** *n.* —**blow'y,** *adj.*

blow'-by-blow', *adj.* detailed.

blow'out', *n.* rupture of tire.

blow'pipe', *n.* pipe used to direct stream of gas.

blow'torch', *n.* device producing hot flame.

blow'up', *n.* **1.** explosion. **2.** photographic enlargement.

blub'ber, *n.* **1.** fat of whales. —*v.* **2.** weep.

bludg'eon (bluj'ən), *n.* **1.** heavy club. —*v.* **2.** strike with a bludgeon.

blue, *n., adj.,* **bluer, bluest,** *v.,* **blued, bluing** or **blueing.** —*n.* **1.** color of sky. —*adj.* **2.** (skin) discolored. **3.** melancholy. —*v.* **4.** make blue. —**blue'ness,** *n.* —**blu'ish,** *adj.*

blue'ber'ry, *n., pl.* **-ries.** edible berry, usually bluish.

blue'bird', *n.* small, blue North American bird.

blue blood, aristocrat. —**blue'blood'ed,** *adj.*

blue chip', high-priced stock yielding regular dividends.

blue'-col'lar, *adj.* of manual laborers.

blue'jay', *n.* crested North American jay.

blue jeans, trousers of blue denim.

blue law, law against certain practices on Sunday.

blue'print', *n.* white-on-blue photocopy of line drawing. —**blue'print',** *v.*

blue ribbon, highest award.

blues, *n.pl.* **1.** melancholy. **2.** melancholy jazz song.

bluff, *v.* **1.** mislead by show of boldness. —*n.* **2.** act of bluffing. **3.** one who bluffs. **4.** steep cliff or hill. —*adj.* **5.** vigorously frank. **6.** steep. —**bluff′ly,** *adv.* —**bluff′ness,** *n.* —**bluff′er,** *n.*

blu′ing, *n.* bleaching agent. Also, **blue′ing.**

blun′der, *n.* **1.** mistake. —*v.* **2.** err. **3.** move blindly. —**blun′der•er,** *n.*

blunt, *adj.* **1.** having a dull edge or point. **2.** abrupt in manner. —*v.* **3.** make blunt. —**blunt′ly,** *adv.* —**blunt′ness,** *n.*

blur, *v.,* **blurred, blurring,** *n.* —*v.* **1.** obscure. **2.** make or become indistinct. —*n.* **3.** smudge. —**blur′ry,** *adj.*

blurb, *n.* brief advertisement.

blurt, *v.* utter suddenly.

blush, *v.* **1.** redden. **2.** feel shame. —*n.* **3.** reddening. **4.** reddish tinge. —**blush′ful,** *adj.* —**blush′ing•ly,** *adv.*

blus′ter, *v.* **1.** be tumultuous. **2.** be noisy or swaggering. —*n.* **3.** tumult. **4.** noisy talk. —**blus′ter•er,** *n.*

blvd., boulevard.

bo′a, *n.* **1.** large snake. **2.** long scarf of silk or feathers.

boar, *n.* male of swine.

board, *n.* **1.** thin flat piece of timber. **2.** table, esp. for food. **3.** daily meals. **4.** official controlling body. —*v.* **5.** cover or close with boards. **6.** furnish with food. **7.** take meals. **8.** enter (a ship, train, etc.). —**board′er,** *n.*

board′ing•house′, *n.* house where one can get room and board for payment.

board′walk′, *n.* wooden walk along beach.

boast, *v.* **1.** speak with pride; be proud of. **2.** speak with excessive pride. —*n.* **3.** thing boasted. —**boast′er,** *n.* —**boast′ful,** *adj.*

boat, *n.* **1.** vessel. —*v.* **2.** go or move in boat. —**boat′house′,** *n.* —**boat′man,** *n.* —**boat′ing,** *n.*

boat′swain (bō′sən), *n.* petty officer on ship.

bob, *n., v.,* **bobbed, bobbing.** —*n.* **1.** short jerky motion. **2.** short haircut. —*v.* **3.** move jerkily. **4.** cut short. —**bob′ber,** *n.*

bob′by pin, flat metal hairpin.

bob′bin, *n.* reel; spool.

bob′cat′, *n., pl.* **-cats, -cat.** North American lynx.

bob′o•link′, *n.* songbird.

bob′sled′, *n., v.,* **-sledded, -sledding.** —*n.* **1.** long sled with two pairs of runners and a steering mechanism. —*v.* **2.** ride on a bobsled.

bob′tail′, *n.* **1.** short tail. —*v.* **2.** cut short.

bob′white′, *n.* quail.

bode, *v.,* **boded, boding.** portend.

bo•de′ga (bō dā′gə), *n.* grocery store.

bod′ice, *n.* fitted waist.

bod′y, *n., pl.* **bodies,** *v.,* **bodied, bodying.** —*n.* **1.** animal's physical structure. **2.** corpse. **3.** main mass. **4.** collective group. —*v.* **5.** invest with body. —**bod′i•ly,** *adj., adv.*

bod′y•guard′, *n.* guard for personal safety.

body language, communication through gestures or attitudes.

bog, *n., v.,* **bogged, bogging.** —*n.* **1.** swampy ground. —*v.* **2.** sink or catch in a bog. —**bog′gy,** *adj.*

bog′gle, *v.,* **-gled, -gling. 1.** refuse to act. **2.** overwhelm with surprise.

bo′gus, *adj.* counterfeit; fake.

bo′gy, *n., pl.* **-gies.** hobgoblin. Also, **bo′gey, bo′gie.**

bo•he′mi•an (bō hē′mē ən), *n.* **1.** person who leads an unconventional life. —*adj.* **2.** of or characteristic of a bohemian.

boil, *v.* **1.** heat to bubbling point. **2.** be agitated. **3.** cook by boiling. —*n.* **4.** act or state of boiling. **5.** inflamed sore. —**boil′er,** *n.*

bois′ter•ous, *adj.* rough; noisy. —**bois′ter•ous•ly,** *adv.* —**bois′ter•ous•ness,** *n.*

bok′ choy′ (bok′ choy′), Asian plant whose leaves are used as a vegetable. Also, **bok′-choy′.**

bold, *adj.* **1.** fearless. **2.** conspicuous. —**bold′ly,** *adv.* —**bold′ness,** *n.*

bo•le′ro (bə lâr′ō, bō-), *n., pl.* **-ros. 1.** lively Spanish dance. **2.** waist-length, open vest.

boll (bōl), *n.* seed vessel.

boll weevil, beetle that attacks bolls of cotton.

bo•lo'gna (bə lō'nē), *n.* beef and pork sausage.

Bol'she•vik, *n., pl.* -viks, -viki. Russian communist. Also, **Bol'she•vist.** —**Bol'she•vism'**, *n.* —**Bol'she•vik, Bol'she•vis'tic,** *adj.*

bol'ster, *n.* 1. long pillow. —*v.* 2. support. —**bol'ster•er,** *n.*

bolt, *n.* 1. bar fastening a door. 2. similar part in a lock. 3. threaded metal pin. 4. sudden flight. 5. roll of cloth. 6. thunderbolt. —*v.* 7. fasten. 8. swallow hurriedly. 9. move or leave suddenly. 10. sift. —**bolt'er,** *n.*

bomb, *n.* 1. projectile with explosive charge. 2. *Slang.* total failure. —*v.* 3. attack with bombs. 4. *Slang.* fail totally. —**bomb'proof'**, *adj.*

bom•bard', *v.* attack with artillery or bombs. —**bom'bar•dier'**, *n.* —**bom•bard'ment,** *n.*

bom'bast, *n.* high-sounding words. —**bom•bas'tic, bom•bas'ti•cal,** *adj.*

bomb'er, *n.* 1. airplane that drops bombs. 2. one who plants bombs.

bomb'shell', *n.* object having a sensational effect.

bo'na fide' (bō'nə fīd'), real.

bo•nan'za, *n.* 1. rich mass of ore. 2. good luck.

bon'bon', *n.* piece of candy.

bond, *n.* 1. something that binds or unites. 2. bondsman. 3. written contractual obligation. 4. certificate held by creditor. —*v.* 5. put on or under bond. 6. mortgage.

bond'age, *n.* slavery.

bond'man, *n., pl.* -men. man in bondage; male slave. Also, **bond'wom'an,** *n.fem.*

bonds'man, *n., pl.* -men. person who gives surety for another by bond.

bone, *n., v.,* **boned, boning.** —*n.* 1. piece of the skeleton. 2. hard substance composing it. —*v.* 3. remove bones of. —**bon'y,** *adj.*

bon'fire', *n.* outdoor fire.

bon'go, *n., pl.* -gos, -goes. small hand drum.

bon'kers, *adj. Slang.* crazy.

bon'net, *n.* woman's or child's head covering.

bon'sai (-sī) *n., pl.* **bonsai.** dwarf tree or shrub.

bo′nus, *n.* extra payment.

boo, *interj.* (exclamation used to frighten or express contempt.)

boo′-boo′, *n. Slang.* **1.** stupid mistake. **2.** minor injury.

boo′by, *n., pl.* **-bies.** *Informal.* fool. Also, **boob.**

booby prize, prize given to worst player in contest.

booby trap, trap set for any person who happens on it.

book, *n.* **1.** printed or blank sheets bound together. **2.** (*pl.*) accounts. **3.** division of literary work. —*v.* **4.** enter in book. **5.** engage beforehand. —**book′bind′er,** *n.* —**book′case′,** *n.* —**book′keep′er,** *n.* —**book′let,** *n.* —**book′sell′er,** *n.* —**book′store′, book′shop′,** *n.*

book′end′, *n.* prop for books.

book′ie, *n.* bookmaker.

book′ing, *n.* engagement of professional entertainer.

book′ish, *adj.* fond of reading. —**book′ish•ness,** *n.*

book′mak′er, *n.* professional bettor.

book′mark′, *n.* page holder.

book′worm′, *n.* bookish person.

boom, *v.* **1.** make a loud sound. **2.** flourish. —*n.* **3.** loud hollow sound. **4.** rapid development. **5.** spar extending sail. **6.** beam on derrick.

boom′er•ang′, *n.* **1.** Australian throwing stick that returns in flight. —*v.* **2.** turn back on plotter.

boon, *n.* benefit.

boon′docks′, *n.pl.* **1.** backwoods. **2.** remote area.

boon′dog′gle, *n. Informal.* useless work paid for with public money.

boor, *n.* clownish, rude person. —**boor′ish,** *adj.*

boost, *v.* **1.** lift by pushing. **2.** praise; advocate. **3.** increase. —*n.* **4.** upward push. **5.** assistance. —**boost′er,** *n.*

boot, *n.* **1.** covering for foot and leg. **2.** kick. —*v.* **3.** kick. **4.** dismiss or discharge.

booth, *n.* **1.** light structure for exhibiting goods, etc. **2.** small compartment.

boot′leg′, *n., v.,* **-legged, -legging,** *adj.* —*n.* **1.** illicit liquor. —*v.* **2.** deal in illicit

goods. —*adj.* 3. illicit.
—**boot'leg'ger,** *n.*

boot'less, *adj.* futile; useless.

boo'ty, *n., pl.* **-ties.** plunder.

booze (bo͞oz) *n., v.,* **boozed,
boozing.** *Informal.* —*n.* 1.
liquor. —*v.* 2. drink liquor
excessively. —**booz'er,** *n.*

bop, *v.,* **bopped, bopping,** *n.*
Slang. —*v.* 1. hit. —*n.* 2. a
blow.

bo'rax (bôr'aks), *n.* white
crystalline substance used as
cleanser, in glassmaking, etc.

bor•del'o, *n., pl.* **-os.** brothel.

bor'der, *n.* 1. edge; margin. 2.
frontier. —*v.* 3. make a
border. 4. adjoin.
—**bor'der•land',** *n.*
—**bor'der•line',** *n.*

bore, *v.,* **bored, boring,** *n.* —*v.*
1. drill into. 2. be dull. —*n.* 3.
bored hole. 4. inside diameter.
5. dull person. —**bore'dom,** *n.*
—**bor'er,** *n.*

bo'ric acid, antiseptic acid.

born, *adj.* brought from the
womb.

born'-a•gain', *adj.* having
experienced Christian
spiritual revival.

bor'ough, *n.* 1. small
incorporated municipality. 2.
division of city.

bor'row, *v.* 1. obtain on loan.
2. adopt.

borscht (bôrsht), *n.* beet soup.

bos'om, *n.* 1. breast. —*adj.* 2.
intimate. —**bos'om•y,** *adj.*

boss, *n.* 1. employer. 2.
powerful politician. —*v.* 3.
control; manage. 4. be
domineering. —**boss'y,** *adj.*

bot'a•ny, *n.* science of plant
life. —**bo•tan'i•cal,** *adj.*
—**bot'a•nist,** *n.*

botch, *v.* 1. bungle. 2. do
clumsily. —*n.* 3. botched
work. —**botch'y,** *adj.*
—**botch'er,** *n.* —**botch'er•y,**
n.

both, *adj., pron.* 1. the two.
—*conj., adv.* 2. alike.

both'er, *v.* 1. annoy. 2. worry.
—*n.* 3. annoying thing.
—**both'er•some,** *adj.*

bot'tle, *n., v.,* **-tled, -tling.** —*n.*
1. sealed container for liquids.
—*v.* 2. put into bottle.
—**bot'tler,** *n.*

bot'tle•neck', *n.* 1. narrow
passage. 2. place of impeded
progress.

bot′tom, *n.* 1. deepest part. 2. underside. 3. lowest rank. —*v.* 4. reach bottom.

bot′tom·less, *adj.* 1. without bottom. 2. without limit.

bottom line, basic point.

bot′u·lism′ (boch′ə-), *n.* disease caused by spoilage.

bou′doir (bōō′dwär, -dwôr), *n.* woman's bedroom.

bouf·fant′ (bōō fänt′), *adj.* puffed out, as a hairdo.

bough (bou), *n.* branch of tree.

bouil′la·baisse′ (bōō′yə bäs′, bōōl′-), *n.* fish stew.

bouil′lon (bōōl′yon, -yən, bōō′-), *n.* clear broth.

boul′der, *n.* large rock.

boul′e·vard′, *n.* broad avenue.

bounce, *v.,* **bounced, bouncing,** *n.* —*v.* 1. spring back. —*n.* 2. act of bouncing. —**boun′ci·ness,** *n.* —**bounc′y,** *adj.*

bounc′ing, *adj.* healthy.

bound, *adj.* 1. in bonds. 2. made into book. 3. obligated. 4. going toward. —*v.* 5. jump. 6. limit. 7. adjoin. 8. name boundaries of. —*n.* 9. jump. 10. (*usually pl.*) boundary.

bound′a·ry, *n., pl.* **-ries.** borderline; limit.

bound′less, *adj.* unlimited.

boun′te·ous, *adj.* 1. generous. 2. plentiful. Also, **boun′ti·ful.** —**boun′te·ous·ly,** *adv.* —**boun′te·ous·ness,** *n.*

boun′ty, *n., pl.* **-ties.** 1. generosity. 2. gift.

bou·quet′ (bō kā′, bōō-), *n.* 1. bunch of flowers. 2. aroma.

bour′bon (bûr′bən), *n.* corn whiskey.

bour·geois′ (bŏŏr zhwä′), *n., pl.* **-geois.** 1. one of the middle class. —*adj.* 2. of the middle class.

bour′geoi·sie′ (-zē′), *n.* middle class.

bout, *n.* 1. contest. 2. attack.

bou·tique′ (bōō tēk′), *n.* small shop with fashionable items.

bo′vine, *adj.* oxlike.

bow (bou, *for 1, 2, 3, 5, 9;* bō, *for 4, 6, 7, 8*), *v.* 1. bend down. 2. bend in worship, respect, etc. 3. subdue. 4. curve. —*n.* 5. inclination of head or body. 6. strip of bent wood for shooting arrow. 7. looped knot. 8. rod for playing violin. 9. front of ship. —**bow′man,** *n.*

bowd′ler•ize′ (bōd′lə rīz′, boud-′), *v.*, **-ized, -izing.** to prudishly expunge.

bow′el, *n.* 1. intestine. Also, **bow′els.**

bow′er, *n.* leafy shelter.

bowl, *n.* 1. deep round dish. 2. rounded hollow part. 3. ball rolled at pins in various games. —*v.* 4. roll a ball underhand. 5. play bowling games. —**bowl′ing,** *n.*

bow′leg′ged (bō leg′id), *adj.* having legs curved outward.

box, *n.* 1. receptacle of wood, metal, etc. 2. compartment. 3. blow, as of the hand or fist. 4. Also, **box′wood′.** evergreen tree or shrub. —*v.* 5. put into box. 6. fight with fists. —**box′er,** *n.* —**box′ing,** *n.* —**box′like,** *adj.*

box′car′, *n.* completely enclosed railroad freight car.

box office, office at which tickets are sold.

boy, *n.* male child. —**boy′hood,** *n.* —**boy′ish,** *adj.*

boy′cott, *v.* 1. abstain from dealing with or using. —*n.* 2. instance of boycotting.

boy′friend′, *n.* 1. male sweetheart.

boy scout, member of organization for boys **(Boy Scouts)** promoting self-reliance and service.

boy′sen•ber′ry, *n., pl.* **-ries.** blackberrylike fruit.

bra, *n.* brassiere.

brace, *n., v.,* **braced, bracing.** —*n.* 1. stiffening device. 2. pair. 3. character, { or }. —*v.* 4. fasten with brace. 5. make steady. 6. stimulate. —**brac′er,** *n.*

brace′let, *n.* wrist jewelery.

brack′et, *n.* 1. armlike support for ledge. 2. mark, [or], for enclosing parenthetical words. —*v.* 3. furnish with or place within brackets.

brack′ish, *adj.* salty.

brad, *n.* small wire nail.

brag, *v.,* **bragged, bragging,** *n.* boast. —**brag′ger,** *n.*

brag′gart, *n.* boastful person.

braid, *v.* 1. weave together. —*n.* 2. something braided.

braille, *n.* alphabet for blind.

brain, *n.* 1. soft mass of nerves in cranium. 2. intelligence. —*v.* 3. dash out the brains. —**brain′y,** *adj.* —**brain′less,** *adj.*

brain death, complete ending of brain function, used as legal definition of death. —**brain'-dead,** *adj.*

brain drain, loss of trained professional personnel to another company, nation, etc.

brain'storm', *n.* sudden idea.

brain'wash', *v.* indoctrinate under stress. —**brain'wash'ing,** *n.*

braise (brāz), *v.,* **braised, braising.** cook slowly in moisture.

brake, *n., v.,* **braked, braking.** —*n.* **1.** device for arresting motion. **2.** thicket. **3.** large fern. —*v.* **4.** slow or stop with a brake. —**brake'man,** *n.*

bram'ble, *n.* **1.** rose plant. **2.** prickly shrub. —**bram'bly,** *adj.*

bran, *n.* husk of grain.

branch, *n.* **1.** division of plant's stem or trunk. **2.** limb; offshoot. **3.** local office, store, etc. **4.** division of body, system, family, etc. —*v.* **5.** put forth or divide into branches.

brand, *n.* **1.** trademark. **2.** kind; make. **3.** burned mark. **4.** burning piece of wood. —*v.* **5.** mark with a brand.

brand'ish, *v.* shake; wave.

brand'-new', *adj.* just new.

bran'dy, *n., pl.* **-dies.** spirit from fermented grapes.

brash, *adj.* **1.** impudent; tactless. **2.** rash; impetuous.

brass, *n.* **1.** alloy of copper and zinc. **2.** musical instrument such as trumpet or horn. **3.** *Informal.* high-ranking officials. **4.** impudence. —**brass'y,** *adj.*

bras·siere' (-zēr'), *n.* breast support garment.

brass tacks, *n.pl.* basics.

brat, *n.* spoiled or rude child.

brat'wurst' (brat'wûrst', -vŏŏrst', brät'-), *n.* pork sausage.

bra·va'do, *n., pl.* **-does, -dos.** boasting; swaggering.

brave, *adj.,* **braver, bravest,** *n., v.,* **braved, braving.** —*adj.* **1.** courageous. —*n.* **2.** North American Indian warrior. —*v.* **3.** meet courageously. **4.** defy. —**brave'ly,** *adv.* —**brave'ness, brav'er·y,** *n.*

bra'vo, *interj.* well done!

brawl, *n.* **1.** quarrel. —*v.* **2.** quarrel noisily. —**brawl'er,** *n.*

brawn, *n.* 1. muscles. 2. muscular strength. —**brawn'y,** *adj.*

bray, *n.* 1. cry of or like a donkey. —*v.* 2. sound a bray. —**bray'er,** *n.*

braze, *v.,* **brazed, brazing.** work in brass. —**bra'zier** (-zhər), *n.*

bra'zen, *adj.* 1. of or like brass. 2. shameless; impudent. —*v.* 3. face boldly. —**bra'zen•ly,** *adv.* —**bra'zen•ness,** *n.*

bra'zier (-zhər), *n.* receptacle for burning charcoal.

Bra•zil' nut, three-sided edible seed.

breach, *n.* 1. a breaking. 2. gap. 3. infraction; violation. 4. break in friendship. —*v.* 5. make breach.

bread, *n.* 1. baked dough. 2. livelihood. 3. *Slang.* money. —*v.* 4. cover with breadcrumbs.

bread'crumb', *n.* (*usually pl.*) a crumb of bread.

breadth, *n.* width.

bread'win'ner, *n.* main money earner in family.

break, *v.,* **broke, broken, breaking,** *n.* —*v.* 1. separate into parts. 2. dissolve. 3. fracture. 4. lacerate. 5. interrupt. 6. disclose. 7. fail; disable. 8. (*pp.* **broke**) ruin financially. 9. weaken. 10. tame. —*n.* 11. forcible disruption. 12. gap. 13. attempt to escape. 14. marked change. 15. brief rest. 16. *Informal.* opportunity. —**break'a•ble,** *adj.* —**break'age,** *n.*

break'down', *n.* 1. failure to operate. 2. nervous crisis. 3. analysis of figures.

break'er, *n.* wave breaking on land.

break'fast, *n.* 1. first meal of day. —*v.* 2. eat breakfast.

break'-in', *n.* illegal forcible entry into home, office, etc.

break'neck', *adj.* reckless.

break'through', *n.* discovery.

break'up', *n.* 1. dispersal or disintegration. 2. ending of a personal relationship.

break'wa'ter, *n.* barrier against the force of waves.

breast, *n.* 1. chest. 2. milk gland. 3. seat of thoughts and feelings. —*v.* 4. oppose boldly.

breast'bone', *n.* sternum.

breast'stroke', *n.* swimming stroke in which the arms

move forward, outward, and rearward while the legs kick.

breath, *n.* 1. air inhaled and exhaled. 2. light breeze. —**breath′less,** *adj.*

breathe, *v.,* **breathed, breathing.** 1. inhale and exhale. 2. blow lightly. 3. live. 4. whisper. —**breath′a•bil′i•ty,** *n.* —**breath′a•ble,** *adj.*

breath′er (brē′th ər), *n. Informal.* short rest.

breath′tak′ing (breth′-), *adj.* awesome or exciting.

breech′es, *n.pl.* trousers.

breed, *v.,* **bred, breeding,** *n.* —*v.* 1. produce. 2. raise. —*n.* 3. related animals. 4. lineage. 5. sort. —**breed′er,** *n.*

breed′ing, *n.* 1. ancestry. 2. training. 3. manners.

breeze, *n.* light current of air. —**breez′y,** *adj.*

breeze′way′, *n.* open-sided roofed passageway joining two buildings.

breth′ren, *n.* a pl. of **brother.**

bre•vet′, *n.* 1. promotion without increase of pay. —*v.* 2. appoint by brevet.

bre′vi•ar′y, *n., pl.* **-aries.** book of daily prayers and readings.

brev′i•ty, *n.* shortness.

brew, *v.* 1. prepare beverage such as beer or ale. 2. concoct. —*n.* 3. quantity brewed. 4. act or instance of brewing. —**brew′er,** *n.* —**brew′er•y,** *n.*

bri′ar (brī′ər), *n.* brier.

bribe, *n., v.,* **bribed, bribing.** —*n.* 1. gift made for corrupt performance of duty. —*v.* 2. give or influence by bribe. —**brib′er,** *n.* —**brib′er•y,** *n.*

bric′-a-brac′, *n.* trinkets.

brick, *n.* 1. building block of baked clay. —*v.* 2. fill or build with brick. —**brick′lay′er,** *n.* —**brick′lay′ing,** *n.*

brick′bat′, *n.* 1. fragment of brick. 2. caustic criticism.

bride, *n.* woman newly married or about to be married. —**brid′al,** *adj.*

bride′groom′, *n.* man newly married or about to be married.

brides′maid′, *n.* bride's wedding attendant.

bridge, *n., v.,* **bridged, bridging.** —*n.* 1. structure spanning river, road, etc. **2.** card game for four players. **3.** artificial replacement for tooth or teeth. —*v.* **4.** span.

bridge'head', *n.* military position held on hostile river shore.

bridge'work', *n.* dental bridges.

bri'dle, *n., v.,* **-dled, -dling.** —*n.* **1.** harness at horse's head. **2.** restraining thing. —*v.* **3.** put bridle on. **4.** restrain.

bridle path, wide path for riding horses.

brief, *adj.* **1.** short. **2.** concise. —*n.* **3.** concise statement. **4.** outline of arguments and facts. —*v.* **5.** instruct in advance. —**brief'ly,** *adv.* —**brief'ness,** *n.*

brief'case', *n.* flat carrier for business papers, etc.

bri'er, *n.* **1.** prickly plant. **2.** plant with woody root.

brig, *n.* **1.** two-masted square-rigged ship. **2.** ship's jail.

bri•gade', *n., v.* **-gaded, -gading.** —*n.* **1.** large military unit or body of troops. —*v.* **2.** form into brigade.

brig'a•dier', *n.* military officer between colonel and major general. Also, **brigadier general.**

brig'and, *n.* bandit.

bright, *adj.* **1.** shining. **2.** filled with light. **3.** brilliant. **4.** clever. —**bright'en,** *v.* —**bright'ly,** *adv.* —**bright'ness,** *n.*

bril'liant, *adj.* **1.** sparkling. **2.** illustrious. **3.** highly intelligent. —*n.* **4.** brilliant diamond. —**bril'liant•ly,** *adv.* —**bril'liance, bril'lian•cy, bril'liant•ness,** *n.*

brim, *n., v.,* **brimmed, brimming.** —*n.* **1.** upper edge; rim. —*v.* **2.** fill or be full to brim. —**brim'ful,** *adj.*

brim'stone', *n.* sulfur.

brin'dle, *n.* brindled coloring or animal.

brin'dled, *adj.* having dark streaks or spots.

brine, *n., v.,* **brined, brining.** —*n.* **1.** salt water. **2.** sea. —*v.* **3.** treat with brine. —**brin'y,** *adj.*

bring, *v.,* **brought, bringing. 1.** fetch. **2.** cause to come. **3.** lead.

brink, *n.* edge.

bri•quette′ (bri ket′), *n.* small block of compressed coal dust or charcoal used as fuel. Also, **bri•quet′.**

brisk, *adj.* 1. lively. 2. stimulating. —**brisk′ly,** *adv.* —**brisk′ness,** *n.*

bris′ket, *n.* animal's breast.

bris′tle, *n., v.,* **-tled, -tling.** —*n.* 1. short, stiff, coarse hair. —*v.* 2. rise stiffly. 3. show indignation. —**bris′tly,** *adv.*

britch′es (brich′iz), *n. (used with a pl. v.)* breeches.

Brit′ish, *adj.* of Great Britain or its inhabitants. —**Brit′ish•er,** *n.*

British thermal unit, amount of heat needed to raise temperature of 1 lb. (0.4 kg) water ° F. *Abbr.:* Btu, BTU

Brit′on, *n.* native of Great Britain.

brit′tle, *adj.* breaking readily. —**brit′tle•ness,** *n.*

broach (brōch), *n.* 1. tool for enlarging hole. —*v.* 2. use broach. 3. pierce. 4. mention for first time.

broad, *adj.* 1. wide. 2. main. 3. liberal. —**broad′ly,** *adv.*

broad′cast′, *v.,* **-cast** or **-casted, -casting,** *n., adj.* —*v.* 1. send by radio or television. 2. scatter widely. —*n.* 3. something broadcasted. 4. radio or television program. —*adj.* 5. sent by broadcasting. —**broad′cast′er,** *n.*

broad′cloth′, *n.* fine cotton material.

broad′en, *v.* widen.

broad jump, long jump.

broad′loom′, *n.* carpet woven on wide loom.

broad′-mind′ed, *adj.* tolerant.

broad′side′, *n., adv., v.,* **-sided, -siding.** —*n.* 1. simultaneous firing of all guns on one side of warship. 2. verbal attack. —*adv.* 3. directly on the side. —*v.* 4. hit broadside.

broad′-spec′trum, *adj.* (of antibiotics) effective against wide range of organisms.

bro•cade′, *n., v.,* **-caded, -cading.** —*n.* 1. figured fabric. —*v.* 2. weave with figure.

broc′co•li, *n.* green plant with edible flower heads.

bro•chure′ (-shoŏr′), *n.* pamphlet; booklet.

brogue, *n.* Irish accent.

broil, *v.* cook by direct heat. —**broil′er,** *n.*

broke, *adj.* **1.** without money. **2.** bankrupt.

bro′ken, *v.* **1.** pp. of **break.** —*adj.* **2.** in fragments. **3.** fractured. **4.** incomplete. **5.** weakened. **6.** imperfectly spoken.

bro′ken·heart′ed, *adj.* sorrowing deeply.

bro′ker, *n.* commercial agent. —**bro′ker·age,** *n.*

bro′mide, *n.* **1.** soothing compound. **2.** trite saying.

bro′mine (brō′mēn, -min), *n.* reddish, toxic liquid element.

bron′chi·al (brong′kē əl), *adj.* of the bronchi, two branches of the trachea.

bron·chi′tis, *n.* inflammation in windpipe and chest. —**bron·chit′ic,** *adj.*

bron′co, *n., pl.* **-cos.** pony or small horse of western U.S. Also, **bron′cho.**

bronze, *n., v.,* **bronzed, bronzing.** —*n.* **1.** alloy of copper and tin. **2.** brownish color. —*v.* **3.** make bronzelike.

brooch (brōch), *n.* clasp or ornament.

brood, *n.* **1.** group of animals born at one time. —*v.* **2.** hatch. **3.** think moodily.

brook, *n.* **1.** small stream. —*v.* **2.** tolerate.

broom, *n.* **1.** sweeping implement. **2.** shrubby plant.

broom′stick, *n.* handle of a broom.

bros., brothers.

broth, *n.* thin soup.

broth′el (broth′əl), *n.* bordelo.

broth′er, *n., pl.* **brothers, brethren. 1.** male child of same parents. **2.** member of same group. —**broth′er·hood′,** *n.* —**broth′er·ly,** *adj.*

broth′er-in-law′, *n., pl.* **brothers-in-law. 1.** husband's or wife's brother. **2.** sister's husband.

brou′ha·ha′ (broo′hä hä′), *n., pl.* **-has.** uproar.

brow, *n.* **1.** eyebrow. **2.** forehead. **3.** edge of a height.

brow′beat′, *v.,* **-beat, -beaten, -beating.** bully.

brown, *n.* **1.** dark reddish or yellowish color. —*adj.* **2.** of this color. —*v.* **3.** make or become brown.

brown′-bag′, *v.,* **-bagged, -bagging.** bring (one's lunch)

to work or school.
—**brown'-bag'ger,** *n.*

brown'ie, *n.* 1. elf who secretly helps with chores. 2. small, chewy chocolate cake. 3. (cap.) girl scout aged 6 to 8.

brown'out', *n.* reduction of power to prevent a blackout.

brown study, deep thought.

browse, *v.,* **browsed, browsing.** 1. graze; feed. 2. examine books, etc., at leisure. —**brows'er,** *n.*

bru'in (broo'in), *n.* bear.

bruise, *v.,* **bruised, bruising,** *n.* —*v.* 1. injure without breaking. —*n.* 2. bruised injury.

bruis'er, *n. Informal.* strong, tough man.

bruit (broot), *v.* rumor.

brunch, *n.* 1. meal that serves as both breakfast and lunch. —*v.* 2. eat brunch.

bru•net', *adj.* dark brown, esp. of skin or hair.

bru•nette', *n.* brunet woman.

brunt, *n.* main force.

brush, *n.* 1. instrument with bristles. 2. bushy tail. 3. brief encounter. 4. dense bushes, shrubs, etc. —*v.* 5. use brush. 6. touch lightly.

brush'-off', *n.* abrupt rebuff.

brusque, *adj.* abrupt; blunt. Also, **brusk.** —**brusque'ly,** *adv.* —**brusque'ness,** *n.*

Brus'sels sprouts, plant with small, edible heads.

bru'tal•ize', *v.,* **-ized, -izing.** 1. make brutal. 2. treat brutally.

brute, *n.* 1. beast. 2. beastlike person. —*adj.* 3. not human. 4. irrational. 5. like animals. 6. savage. —**bru'tal,** *adj.* —**bru•tal'i•ty,** *n.* —**bru'tal•ly,** *adv.* —**brut'ish,** *adj.*

B.S., Bachelor of Science.

Btu, British thermal unit. Also, **BTU**

bu., bushel.

bub'ble, *n.,* *v.,* **-bled, -bling.** —*n.* 1. globule of gas, esp. in liquid. 2. something infirm or unsubstantial. —*v.* 3. make or give off bubbles. —**bub'bly,** *adj.*

buc'ca•neer', *n.* pirate.

buck, *v.* 1. leap to unseat a rider. 2. resist. —*n.* 3. male of the deer, rabbit, goat, etc.

buck'et, *n.* pail.

buck′le, *n., v.,* **-led, -ling.** —*n.*
1. clasp for two loose ends.
—*v.* 2. fasten with buckle. 3.
bend. 4. set to work.

buck′ler, *n.* shield.

buck′ram, *n.* stiff cotton.

buck′shot′, *n.* large lead shot.

buck′skin′, *n.* skin of buck.

buck′tooth′, *n., pl.* **-teeth.**
projecting tooth.

buck′wheat′, *n.* plant with
edible triangular seeds.

bu•col′ic (byōō kol′ik), *adj.*
rustic; rural.
—**bu•col′i•cal•ly,** *adv.*

bud, *n., v.,* **budded, budding.**
—*n.* 1. protuberance on plant.
2. small rounded part. —*v.* 3.
produce buds. 4. begin to
grow.

Bud′dhism (bŏŏd′iz əm), *n.*
Eastern religion. —**Bud′dhist,**
n.

bud′dy, *n., pl.* **-dies.** *Informal.*
friend; comrade.

budge, *v.,* **budged, budging.**
move slightly with effort.

budg′et, *n.* estimate of income
and expense. 2. itemized
allotment of funds. —*v.* 3.
plan allotment of. 4. allot.
—**budg′et•ar′y,** *adv.*

buff, *n.* 1. thick light-yellow
leather. 2. yellowish brown.
—*adj.* 3. made or colored like
buff. —*v.* 4. polish brightly.

buf′fa•lo′, *n., pl.* **-loes, -los,
-lo.** large bovine mammal.

buff′er, *n.* 1. cushioning
device. 2. polishing device.

buf′fet, *n.* 1. blow. 2. (bə fā′).
cabinet for china, etc. 3. (bə
fā′). food counter. —*v.* 4.
strike. 5. struggle.

buf•foon′, *n.* clown.
—**buf•foon′er•y,** *n.*
—**buf•foon′ish,** *adj.*

bug, *n., v.,* **bugged, bugging.**
—*n.* 1. insect, esp. a beetle. 2.
microorganism. 3. defect or
imperfection. 4. enthusiast. 5.
hidden electronic
eavesdropping device. —*v.* 6.
install secret listening device
in. 7. *Informal.* pester.

bug′bear′, *n.* any source, real
or imaginary, of fright or fear.
Also, **bug′a•boo′.**

bug′gy, *n., pl.* **-gies.** carriage.

bu′gle, *n., v.,* **-gled, -gling.** —*n.*
1. cornetlike wind instrument.
—*v.* 2. sound a bugle.
—**bu′gler,** *n.*

build, *v.,* **built, building,** *n.* —*v.* 1. construct. 2. form. 3. develop. —*n.* 4. manner or form of construction. —**build′er,** *n.*

build′ing, *n.* shelter.

build′up′, *n. Informal.* 1. steady increase. 2. publicity.

built′-in′, *adj.* 1. built as part of a structure. 2. filled in with buildings.

built′-up′, *adj.* 1. made bigger or higher by addition. 2. filled in with buildings.

bulb, *n.* 1. subterranean bud. 2. rounded enlarged part. 3. electric lamp. —**bulb′ar, bulb′ous,** *adj.*

bulge, *n., v.,* **bulged, bulging.** —*n.* 1. rounded projection. —*v.* 2. swell out. —**bulg′y,** *adj.*

bul′gur (bo͞ol′gər), *n.* wheat.

bu•lim′i•a (byo͞o lim′ē ə, -lē′mē ə, bo͞o-), *n.* disorder marked by eating binges followed by purging.

bulk, *n.* 1. magnitude. 2. main mass. —*v.* 3. be of or increase in magnitude.

bulk′head′, *n.* wall-like partition in a ship.

bulk′y, *adj.,* **bulkier, bulkiest.** of great bulk. —**bulk′i•ness,** *n.*

bull, *n.* 1. male bovine. 2. bull-like person. 3. speculator who depends on rise in prices. 4. papal document. 5. *Slang.* lying talk. —*adj.* 6. male. 7. marked by rise in prices. —**bull′ish,** *adj.*

bull′dog′, *n.* heavily built dog.

bull′doz′er, *n.* powerful earth-moving tractor.

bul′let, *n.* projectile of gun.

bul′le•tin, *n.* news item.

bull′fight′, *n.* combat between man and a bull. —**bull′fight′er,** *n.*

bull′finch′, *n.* songbird.

bull′frog′, *n.* large frog.

bull′head′ed, *adj.* stubborn.

bull′horn′, *n.* megaphone.

bul′lion (bo͞ol′yən), *n.* uncoined gold or silver.

bull market, stock market with rising prices.

bull′ock, *n.* castrated bull.

bull′pen′, *n.* place where relief pitchers warm up.

bull′s′-eye′, *n.* center of target.

bull terrier, dog bred from bulldog and terrier.

bul'ly, *n., pl.* **-lies,** *v.,* **-lied, -lying.** —*n.* **1.** overbearing person. —*v.* **2.** intimidate.

bul'rush', *n.* rushlike plant.

bul'wark, *n.* **1.** rampart. **2.** protection.

bum, *n. Informal.* **1.** tramp or hobo. **2.** loafer; idler. —*v.* **3.** *Informal.* beg. —*adj.* **4.** of poor quality. **5.** false or misleading. **6.** lame.

bum'ble, *v.,* **-bled, -bling. 1.** blunder. **2.** bungle; botch.

bum'ble•bee', *n.* large bee.

bum'mer, *n. Slang.* frustrating or bad experience.

bump, *v.* **1.** strike; collide. —*n.* **2.** act or shock of bumping. **3.** swelling. —**bump'y,** *adj.*

bump'er, *n.* **1.** device for protection in collisions. **2.** glass filled to brim. —*adj.* **3.** abundant.

bump'kin, *n.* awkward, simple person from rural area.

bun, *n.* kind of bread roll.

bunch, *n.* **1.** cluster. **2.** group. —*v.* **3.** group; gather.

bun'dle, *n., v.,* **-dled, -dling.** —*n.* **1.** group bound together. **2.** package. —*v.* **3.** wrap in bundle. **4.** dress warmly.

bun'ga•low', *n.* cottage.

bun'gle, *v.,* **-gled, -gling,** *n.* —*v.* **1.** fail to do properly. —*n.* **2.** something bungled. —**bun'gler,** *n.*

bun'ion (-yən), *n.* swelling on foot.

bunk, *n.* **1.** built-in bed. **2.** bunkum.

bunk'er, *n.* **1.** bin. **2.** underground refuge.

bun'kum (bung'kəm), *n.* nonsense. Also, **bunk.**

bun'ny, *n., pl.* **-nies.** *Informal.* rabbit.

bunt, *v.* push or tap forward.

bun'ting, *n.* **1.** fabric for flags, etc. **2.** flags. **3.** finchlike bird.

buoy (boi), *n.* **1.** float used as support or navigational marker. —*v.* **2.** support by buoy. **3.** mark with buoy.

buoy'ant, *adj.* **1.** tending to float. **2.** cheerful. —**buoy'an•cy,** *n.* —**buoy'ant•ly,** *adv.*

bur, *n.* prickly seed case.

bur., bureau.

bur′den, *n.* **1.** load. —*v.* **2.** load heavily. —**bur′den•some,** *adj.*

bur′dock, *n.* prickly plant.

bu′reau (byŏŏr′ō), *n., pl.* **-eaus, -eaux. 1.** chest of drawers. **2.** government department.

bu•reauc′ra•cy (byŏŏ rok′rə sē), *n., pl.* **-cies. 1.** government by bureaus. **2.** bureau officials.

bu′reau•crat′, *n.* official of a bureaucracy. —**bu′reau•crat′ic,** *adj.*

burg, *n. Informal.* small, quiet city or town.

bur′geon (bûr′jən), *v.* **1.** grow quickly. **2.** begin to grow.

burg′er, *n.* hamburger.

bur′glar, *n.* thief who breaks and enters. —**bur′glar•ize′,** *v.* —**bur′gla•ry,** *n.*

Bur′gun•dy, *n., pl.* **-dies.** dry red wine. Also, **bur′gun•dy.**

bur′i•al, *n.* act of burying.

bur′lap, *n.* coarse fabric.

bur•lesque′, *n., v.,* **-lesqued, -lesquing.** —*n.* **1.** artistic travesty. **2.** sexually suggestive entertainment. —*v.* **3.** make a burlesque of.

bur′ly, *adj.,* **-lier, -liest. 1.** of great size. **2.** brusque.

burn, *v.,* **burned** or **burnt, burning,** *n.* —*v.* **1.** be on fire. **2.** consume with fire; be afire. **3.** heat; feel heat. **4.** glow. **5.** feel passion. —*n.* **6.** burned place. —**burn′er,** *n.*

bur′nish, *v.* **1.** polish. —*n.* **2.** gloss.

burn′out′, *n.* **1.** point at which rocket engine stops because it runs out of fuel. **2.** fatigue and frustration from too much work and stress.

burp, *n.* light belch. —**burp,** *v.*

burr, *n.* **1.** drilling tool. **2.** rough protuberance. **3.** bur.

bur′ro, *n., pl.* **-ros.** donkey.

bur′row, *n.* **1.** animal's hole in ground. —*v.* **2.** make or lodge in burrow. —**bur′row•er,** *n.*

bur′sar (bûr′sər, -sär), *n.* treasurer, esp. of a college.

bur•si′tis (bər sī′tis), *n.* condition in which a bursa becomes inflamed.

burst, *v.,* **burst, bursting,** *n.* —*v.* **1.** break open or issue forth violently. **2.** rupture. —*n.* **3.** act or result of bursting. **4.** sudden display.

bur′y, *v.,* **buried, burying. 1.** put into ground and cover. **2.** conceal. **—bur′i•er,** *n.*

bus, *n., pl.* **buses, busses,** *v.,* **bused** or **bussed, busing** or **bussing. —***n.* **1.** large passenger motor vehicle. **—***v.* **2.** move by bus.

bus′boy′, *n.* helper of waiter.

bush, *n.* **1.** shrubby plant. **2.** land covered by bushes. **—bush′y,** *adj.* **—bush′i•ness,** *n.*

bushed, *adj. Informal.* exhausted; tired.

bush′el, *n.* unit of 4 pecks.

bush league, secondary baseball league. **—bush leaguer**

busi′ness (biz′nis), *n.* **1.** occupation; profession. **2.** trade. **3.** trading enterprise. **4.** affair; matter. **—busi′ness•man′, busi′ness•wom•an,** *n.*

busi′ness•like′, *adj.* practical and efficient.

bus′ing, *n.* moving of pupils by bus to achieve racially balanced classes. Also, **bus′sing.**

bust, *n.* **1.** sculpture of head and shoulders. **2.** bosom. **—***v. Informal.* **3.** burst. **4.** become bankrupt. **5.** arrest. **6.** hit.

bus′tle, *v.,* **-tled, -tling. 1.** move or act energetically. **—***n.* **2.** energetic activity.

bus′y, *adj.,* **busier, busiest,** *v.,* **busied, busying. —***adj.* **1.** actively employed. **2.** full of activity. **—***v.* **3.** make or keep busy. **—bus′i•ly,** *adv.* **—bus′y•ness,** *n.*

bus′y•bod′y, *n., pl.* **-bodies.** meddler.

but, *conj.* **1.** on the contrary. **2.** except. **3.** except that. **—***prep.* **4.** except. **—***adv.* **5.** only.

bu′tane (byoo′tān), *n.* colorless gas used as fuel.

butch (booch), *adj. Slang.* **1.** (of a woman) having traits usu. associated with men. **2.** (of a man) having exaggerated masculine traits.

butch′er, *n.* **1.** dealer in meat. **2.** slaughterer. **—***v.* **3.** kill for food. **4.** bungle. **—butch′er•y,** *n.*

but′ler, *n.* chief male servant.

butt, *n.* **1.** thick end. **2.** object of ridicule. **3.** large cask. **4.**

cigarette end. 5. *Slang.* buttocks. —*v.* 6. push with head. 7. be adjacent; join. 8. strike with head.

but′ter, *n.* 1. Also, **but′ter•fat′.** solid fatty part of milk. —*v.* 2. put butter on. —**but′ter•y,** *adj.*

but′ter•cup′, *n.* plant with yellow cup-shaped flowers.

but′ter•fin′gers, *n., pl.* **-gers.** clumsy person.

but′ter•fly′, *n., pl.* **-flies.** insect with colorful wings.

but′ter•milk′, *n.* milk with its butter extracted.

but′ter•nut′, *n.* nut of walnutlike tree.

but′ter•scotch′, *n.* kind of taffy.

but′tock, *n.* protuberance of rump.

but′ton, *n.* 1. disk or knob for fastening. 2. buttonlike object. —*v.* 3. fasten with button.

but′ton•down′, *adj.* 1. (of a collar) having buttonholes for attachment to shirt. 2. conventional.

but′ton•hole′, *n., v.,* **-holed, -holing.** —*n.* 1. slit through which a button is passed. —*v.* 2. detain in conversation.

but′tress, *n.* 1. structure steadying wall. —*v.* 2. support.

bux′om, *adj.* (of a woman) attractively plump. —**bux′om•ness,** *n.*

buy, *v.,* **bought, buying.** 1. acquire by payment. 2. bribe. —**buy′er,** *n.*

buy′back′, *n.* repurchase by a company of its own stock.

buy′out′, *n.* purchase of a majority of shares in a company.

buzz, *n.* 1. low humming sound. —*v.* 2. make or speak with buzz. —**buz′zer,** *n.*

buz′zard, *n.* carnivorous bird.

buzz′word′, *n. Informal.* fashionable cliché used to give specious weight to argument.

by, *prep.* 1. near to. 2. through. 3. not later than. 4. past. 5. using as means or method. —*adv.* 6. near. 7. past.

bye (bī), *n.* (in a tournament) automatic advancement to the next round.

by′-elec′tion, *n.* special election to fill vacancy.

by′gone′, *adj.* 1. past. —*n.* 2. something past.

by′law′, *n.* standing rule.

by′line′, *n.* line, as in a newspaper, giving the writer or reporter's name.

BYOB, bring your own booze/beer/bottle.

by′pass′, *n.* **1.** detour. **2.** surgical procedure in which diseased or blocked organ is circumvented. —*v.* **3.** avoid through bypass.

by′play′, *n.* action or speech aside from the main action.

by′-prod′uct, *n.* secondary product.

by′road′, *n.* side road; byway.

by′stand′er, *n.* chance looker-on.

byte (bīt), *n.* unit of computer information, larger than bit.

by′way′, *n.* little-used road.

by′-word′, *n.* **1.** catchword. **2.** proverb.

Byz′an•tine′ (biz′ən tēn′), *adj.* *(sometimes l.c.)* **1.** complex; intricate. **2.** marked by intrigue.

C, c, *n.* third letter of English alphabet.

C, Celsius, Centigrade.

c., 1. centimeter. 2. century. 3. copyright.

CA, California.

ca., circa.

cab, *n.* 1. taxicab. 2. one-horse carriage. 3. part of locomotive where operator sits.

ca·bal′, *n.* group of plotters.

ca·ban′a, *n.* small structure for changing clothes at beach or pool.

cab′a·ret′ (-rā′), *n.* restaurant providing entertainment.

cab′bage, *n.* plant with edible head of leaves.

cab′in, *n.* 1. small house. 2. room in a ship or plane.

cab′i·net, *n.* 1. advisory council. 2. piece of furniture with drawers, etc. —**cab′i·net·mak′er,** *n.*

ca′ble, *n., v.,* **-bled, -bling.** —*n.* 1. strong rope. 2. cablegram. —*v.* 3. send cablegram (to).

ca′ble·gram′, *n.* telegram sent by underwater wires.

cable TV, distribution of television programs over coaxial cables.

C

ca·boose′ (kə bōōs′), *n.* car at the end of a train.

cab′ri·o·let′ (kab′rē ə lā′), *n.* 1. type of one-horse carriage. 2. convertible car.

ca·ca′o (kə kā′ō), *n., pl.* **-caos.** tropical tree whose seeds yield cocoa, etc.

cache (kash), *n., v.,* **cached, caching.** —*n.* 1. hiding place for treasure, etc. —*v.* 2. hide.

ca·chet′ (ka shā′), *n.* 1. official seal or sign. 2. superior status; prestige.

cack′le, *v.,* **-led, -ling,** *n.* —*v.* 1. utter shrill, broken cry. —*n.* 2. act or sound of cackling.

ca·coph′o·ny (kə kof′ə nē), *n., pl.* **-nies.** harsh sound.

cac′tus, *n., pl.* **-tuses, -ti.** leafless, spiny plant.

cad, *n.* ungentlemanly person.

ca·dav′er, *n.* corpse. —**ca·dav′er·ous,** *adj.*

CAD/CAM (kad′kam′), *n.* computer-aided design and computer-aided manufacturing.

cad′die, *n., v.,* **-died, -dying.**
—*n.* **1.** person who carries
one's golf clubs. —*v.* **2.** work
as caddie. Also, **cad′dy.**

ca′dence, *n.* rhythmic beat.

ca•det′, *n.* military student.

cadge, *v.,* **cadged, cadging.**
obtain by begging.

cad′mi•um, *n.* metallic
element used in plating.

ca′dre (kad′rē, kä′drā), *n.*
highly trained group around
which an organization is built.

Cae•sar′e•an (si zâr′ē ən), *n.*
Cesarean.

ca•fé′ (ka fā′), *n.* restaurant.

caf′e•te′ri•a, *n.* self-service
restaurant.

caf′feine (kaf′ēn), *n.* chemical
in coffee, etc., used as
stimulant. Also, **caf′fein.**

caf′tan, *n.* long wide-sleeved
garment.

cage, *n., v.,* **caged, caging.** —*n.*
1. barred box or room. —*v.* **2.**
put in cage.

cag′ey, *adj.* **-ier, -iest.**
cautious. Also, **cag′y.**
—**cag′i•ly,** *adv.* —**cag′i•ness,**
n.

cais′son (kā′sən), *n.* **1.**
ammunition wagon. **2.** airtight
underwater chamber.

ca•jole′, *v.,* **-joled, -joling.**
wheedle. —**ca•jol′er•y,** *n.*

Ca′jun (kā′jən), *n.* Louisianan
of Nova Scotia-French origin.

cake, *n., v.,* **caked, caking.** —*n.*
1. sweet baked dough. **2.**
compact mass. —*v.* **3.** form
into compact mass.

Cal., California. Also, **Calif.**

cal., **1.** caliber. **2.** calorie.

cal′a•bash′, *n.* kind of gourd.

ca′la•ma′ri, *n.* cooked squid.

cal′a•mine′ (kal′ə mīn′), *n.*
powder used in skin lotions.

ca•lam′i•ty, *n., pl.* **-ties.**
disaster. —**ca•lam′i•tous,**
adj.

cal′ci•fy′, *v.* **-fied, -fying.**
harden by the deposit of
calcium salts.
—**cal′ci•fi•ca′tion,** *n.*

cal′ci•mine′ (kal′sə mīn′), *n.,*
v., **-mined, -mining.** —*n.* **1.**
type of paint for ceilings, etc.
—*v.* **2.** cover with calcimine.

cal′ci•um, *n.* white metallic
chemical element.

cal′cu•late′, v., -lated, -lating. compute or estimate by mathematics. —**cal′cu•la′tor**, n. —**cal′cu•la′tion**, n.

cal′cu•la′ting, adj. shrewd.

cal′cu•lus, n. branch of mathematics.

cal′dron (kôl-), n. cauldron.

cal′en•dar, n. 1. list of days, weeks, and months of year. 2. list of events.

cal′en•der, n. 1. press for paper, cloth, etc. —v. 2. press in such a machine.

calf, n., pl. **calves**. 1. young of cow, etc. 2. fleshy part of leg below knee.

cal′i•ber, n. 1. diameter of bullet or gun bore. 2. quality. Also **cal′i•bre**.

cal′i•brate′, v., -brated, -brating. mark for measuring purposes. —**cal′i•bra′tion**, n.

cal′i•co′, n., pl. -coes, -cos. printed cotton cloth.

cal′i•per, n. (usu. pl.) compass for measuring.

ca′liph, n. Muslim leader.

cal′is•then′ics, n.pl. physical exercises.

calk (kôk), v. caulk.

call, v. 1. cry out loudly. 2. announce. 3. summon. 4. telephone. 5. name. 6. visit briefly. —n. 7. cry or shout. 8. summons. 9. brief visit. 10. need; demand. —**call′er**, n.

call girl, female prostitute who is called for services.

cal•lig′ra•phy, n. fancy penmanship; art of beautiful writing. —**cal•lig′ra•pher**, n.

call′ing, n. 1. trade. 2. summons.

cal′lous (kal′əs), adj. 1. unsympathetic. —v. 2. harden.

cal′low, adj. immature.

cal′lus, n. hardened skin.

calm, adj. 1. undisturbed. 2. not windy. —n. 3. calm state. —v. 4. make calm. —**calm′ly**, adv. —**calm′ness**, n.

cal′o•mel′, n. white powder used as cathartic.

ca•lor′ic, adj. of heat.

cal′o•rie, n. measured unit of heat or energy value.

ca•lum′ni•ate′, v., -ated, -ating. slander. —**ca•lum′ni•a′tor**, n. —**cal′um•ny**, n.

ca•lyp′so (kə lip′sō), *n.* **1.** musical style of the West Indies. **2.** song in this style.

ca′lyx (kā′liks), *n.* small leaflets around flower petals.

cam, *n.* device for changing circular movement to straight.

ca′ma•ra′de•rie (kä′mə rä′də rē, kam′ə-), *n.* comradeship; fellowship.

cam′ber, *v.* **1.** curve upward slightly. —*n.* **2.** slight upward curve; convexity.

cam′bric, *n.* close-weave.

cam′cord′er, *n.* hand-held television camera with an incorporated VCR.

cam′el, *n.* Large humped quadruped.

ca•mel′lia (kə mēl′yə, -mē′lē ə), *n.* shrub with glossy leaves and roselike flowers.

cam′e•o′, *n., pl.* **-eos.** carved stone with colored layers.

cam′er•a, *n.* device for making photographs.

cam′i•sole′, *n.* woman's sleeveless undershirt.

cam′o•mile′, *n.* chamomile.

cam′ou•flage′ (kam′ə fläzh′), *n., v.,* **-flaged, -flaging.** —*n.* **1.** deceptive covering. —*v.* **2.** hide by camouflage.

camp, *n.* **1.** place of temporary lodging. **2.** faction. **3.** something that amuses by being overdone or tasteless. —*adj.* **4.** Also, **camp′y.** amusing as camp. —*v.* **5.** form camp. —**camp′er,** *n.*

cam•paign′, *n.* **1.** military operation. **2.** competition for office. —*v.* **3.** engage in campaign. —**cam•paign′er,** *n.*

cam′phor, *n.* substance used as repellent, medicine, etc.

cam′pus, *n.* school area.

cam′shaft′, *n.* engine shaft fitted with cams.

can, *v.,* **canned** (**could** for def. 1), **canning** (for def. 2), *n.* —*v.* **1.** be able. **2.** put in airtight container. —*n.* **3.** cylindrical metal container. —**can′ner,** *n.*

Ca•na′di•an, *n.* citizen of Canada. —**Canadian,** *adj.*

ca•nal′, *n.* **1.** artificial waterway. **2.** tubular passage. —**can′al•ize′,** *v.*

can′a•pé (kan′ə pē), *n.* morsel of food served as appetizer.

ca•nard′, *n.* rumor.

ca•nar′y, *n., pl.* **-ries.** yellow cage bird.

ca·nas′ta, *n. Cards.* rummy whose object is to establish sets of seven or more cards.

can′cel, *v.,* **-celed, -celing. 1.** cross out. **2.** make void. —**can′cel·la′tion,** *n.*

can′cer, *n.* malignant growth. —**can′cer·ous,** *adj.*

can′de·la′brum (-lä′-), *n., pl.* **-bra.** branched candlestick. Also, **can′de·la′bra,** *pl.* **-bras.**

can′did, *adj.* frank or honest. —**can′did·ly,** *adv.* —**can′did·ness,** *n.*

can′di·da (kan′ di də), *n.* disease-causing fungus.

can′di·date′, *n.* one seeking to be elected or chosen. —**can′di·da·cy,** *n.*

can′di·di′a·sis (-dī′ə sis), *n.* infection caused by candida.

can′dle, *n.* waxy cylinder with wick for burning. —**can′dle·stick′,** *n.*

can′dor, *n.* frankness.

can′dy, *n., pl.* **-dies,** *v.,* **-died, -dying.** —*n.* **1.** confection. —*v.* **2.** cover with sugar.

cane, *n., v.,* **caned, caning.** —*n.* **1.** stick used in walking. **2.** long, woody stem. —*v.* **3.** beat with a cane.

ca′nine (kā′nīn), *adj.* **1.** of dogs. —*n.* **2.** animal of dog family.

canine tooth, one of the four somewhat pointed teeth next to the incisors.

can′is·ter, *n.* small box.

can′ker, *n.* ulcerous sore. —**can′ker·ous,** *adj.*

can′na·bis (kan′ə bis), *n.* **1.** hemp plant; marijuana. **2.** part of plant used as a drug.

canned, *adj.* **1.** put into cans or sealed jars. **2.** *Informal.* recorded.

can′ner·y, *n., pl.* **-ies.** factory where foods are canned.

can′ni·bal, *n.* person who eats human flesh. —**can′ni·bal·ism,** *n.*

can′ni·bal·ize′, *v.,* **ized, -izing.** strip of reusable parts.

can·nol′i (kə nō′lē), *n.* pastry filled with sweet cheese.

can′non, *n.* large mounted gun. —**can′non·eer′,** *n.*

can′non·ade′, *n.* long burst of cannon fire.

can′not, *v.* to be unable to.

can′ny, *adj.,* **-nier, -niest. 1.** careful. **2.** shrewd. —**can′ni·ness,** *n.*

ca•noe′, *n.* paddle-propelled boat. —**canoe′**, *v.*

can′on, *n.* 1. rule or law. 2. recognized books of Bible. 3. church official. —**ca•non′i•cal**, *adj.*

can′on•ize′, *v.*, -ized, -izing. declare as saint. —**can′on•i•za′tion**, *n.*

can′o•py, *n.*, *pl.* -pies. overhead covering.

cant, *n.* 1. insincerely virtuous talk. 2. special jargon.

can′t, *v.* *Informal.* cannot.

can′ta•loupe′ (-lōp′), *n.* small melon.

can•tan′ker•ous, *adj.* ill-natured.

can•ta′ta (-tä′-), *n.* dramatic choral composition.

can•teen′, *n.* 1. container for water, etc. 2. military supply store. 3. entertainment place for soldiers, etc.

can′ter, *n.* 1. easy gallop. —*v.* 2. go at easy gallop.

can′ti•cle, *n.* hymn.

can′ti•le′ver, *n.* structure secured at one end only.

can′to, *n.*, *pl.* -tos. section of a long poem.

can′ton (kan′tn, kan ton′), *n.* small territorial district.

can′tor, *n.* precentor; hazan.

can′vas, *n.* 1. cloth used for sails, tents, etc. 2. sails.

can′vas•back′, *n.*, *pl.* -backs, -back. wild duck with a whitish or grayish back.

can′vass, *v.* 1. investigate. 2. solicit votes, etc. —**can′vass•er**, *n.*

can′yon, *n.* narrow valley. Also, **cañon**.

cap, *n.*, *v.*, **capped, capping.** —*n.* 1. brimless hat. 2. cover. —*v.* 3. cover. 4. surpass.

cap., 1. capacity. 2. capital(ize). 3. capital letter.

ca′pa•ble, *adj.* able; qualified. —**ca′pa•bly**, *adv.* —**ca′pa•bil′i•ty**, *n.*

ca•pa′cious, *adj.* roomy.

ca•pac′i•tor, *n.* device for collecting and holding an electrical charge.

ca•pac′i•ty, *n.*, *pl.* -ties. 1. volume. 2. capability. 3. role.

cape, *n.* 1. sleeveless coat. 2. projecting point of land.

ca′per, *v.* 1. leap playfully. —*n.* 2. playful leap. 3. bud of shrub, used as seasoning.

cap′il·lar′y, *adj., n., pl.* **-laries.** —*adj.* 1. of or in a thin tube. —*n.* 2. tiny blood vessel.

cap′i·tal, *n.* 1. city in which government is located. 2. large letter. 3. money and property available for business use. 4. decorative head of structural support. —*adj.* 5. important or chief. 6. excellent. 7. (of letters) large. 8. punishable by death.

capital gain, profit from the sale of an asset.

capital goods, *n.pl.* machines for production of goods.

cap′i·tal·ism′, *n.* system of private investment in and ownership of business. —**cap′i·tal·ist,** *n.* —**cap′i·tal·is′tic,** *adj.*

cap′i·tal·ize′, *v.,* **-ized, -izing.** 1. put in large letters. 2. use as capital. 3. take advantage. —**cap′i·tal·i·za′tion,** *n.*

cap′i·tal·ly, *adv.* well.

cap′i·tol, *n.* building used by legislature.

ca·pit′u·late′, *v.,* **-lated, -lating.** surrender. —**ca·pit′u·la′tion,** *n.*

cap′let, *n.* oval-shaped medicinal tablet, coated for easy swallowing.

ca′pon, *n.* castrated rooster.

cap′puc·ci′no (kap′ə chē′nō, kä′-pə-), *n.* espresso coffee mixed with steamed milk.

ca·price′ (kə prēs′), *n.* whim. —**ca·pri′cious,** *adj.*

cap′size, *v.,* **-sized, -sizing.** overturn; upset.

cap′stan, *n.* device turned to pull cables.

cap′stone, *n.* stone that finishes off a structure.

cap′sule, *n.* small sealed container. —**cap′su·lar,** *adj.*

capt., captain.

cap′tain, *n.* 1. officer below major or rear admiral. 2. ship master. —**cap′tain·cy,** *n.*

cap′tion, *n.* heading.

cap′tious, *adj.* noting trivial faults. —**cap′tious·ly,** *adv.* —**cap′tious·ness,** *n.*

cap′ti·vate′, *v.,* **-vated, -vating.** charm. —**cap′ti·va′tion,** *n.* —**cap′ti·va′tor,** *n.*

cap′tive, *n.* prisoner. —**cap·tiv′i·ty,** *n.*

cap′ture, *v.,* **-tured, -turing,** *n.*
—*v.* **1.** take prisoner. —*n.* **2.**
act or instance of capturing.
—**cap′tor,** *n.*

car, *n.* automobile.

ca•rafe′ (kə raf′), *n.*
broad-mouthed bottle.

car′a•mel, *n.* confection made
of burnt sugar.

car′at, *n.* **1.** unit of weight for
gems. **2.** karat.

car′a•van′, *n.* group traveling
together, esp. over deserts.

car′a•way, *n.* herb bearing
aromatic seeds.

car′bide, *n.* carbon
compound.

car′bine (kär′bīn), *n.* rifle.

car′bo•hy′drate, *n.* organic
compound group including
starches and sugars.

car•bol′ic acid, brown
germicidal liquid.

car′bon, *n.* chemical element.
—**car•bon•if′er•ous,** *adj.*

car′bon•ate′, *v.,* **-ated, -ating.**
charge with carbon dioxide.
—**car′bon•a′tion,** *n.*

carbon dioxide, compound of
carbon and oxygen.

carbon monoxide, compound
of carbon and oxygen.

carbon paper, paper coated
with a carbon prepartion,
used to make copies of typed
or written material.

Car′bo•run′dum, *n.*
Trademark. abrasive material.

car′bun•cle, *n.* painful
inflammation under skin.

car′bu•re′tor, *n.* mechanism
that mixes gasoline and air in
motor.

car′cass, *n.* dead body. Also,
car′case.

car•cin′o•gen (kär sin′ə jən),
n. cancer-producing
substance.
—**car′cin•o•gen′ic,** *adj.*

car′ci•no′ma (kär sə nō′mə),
n. malignant tumor.

card, *n.* **1.** piece of stiff paper,
with one's name **(calling card)**,
marks for game purposes
(playing card), etc. **2.** comb for
wool, flax, etc. —*v.* **3.** dress
(wool, etc.) with card.

card′board, *n.* **1.** thin, stiff
pasteboard. —*adj.* **2.** flimsy. **3.**
seeming fake.

card′-car′ry•ing, *adj.* **1.**
officially enrolled, esp. in the
Communist Party. **2.** strongly
dedicated.

car′di•ac′, *adj.* of the heart.

cardiac arrest, heart failure.

car′di•gan, *n.* front-buttoning sweater.

car′di•nal, *adj.* 1. main; chief. 2. (of numbers) used to express quantities or positions in series, e.g., 3, 15, 45. 3. deep red. —*n.* 4. red bird. 5. high official of Roman Catholic Church.

cardio-, prefix meaning heart, as *cardiology.*

car′di•o•graph′, *n.* instrument for recording movements of heart. —**car′di•o•gram′,** *n.*

car′di•ol′o•gy, *n.* study of the heart and its functions. —**car′di•ol′o•gist,** *n.*

car′di•o•pul′mo•nar′y, *adj.* of the heart and lungs.

car′di•o•vas′cu•lar, *adj.* of the heart and blood vessels.

card′sharp′, *n.* person who cheats at card games. Also, **card shark.**

care, *n., v.,* **cared, caring.** —*n.* 1. worry. 2. caution. —*v.* 3. be concerned or watchful. —**care′free′,** *adj.* —**care′ful,** *adj.* —**care′less,** *adj.*

ca•reen′, *v.* tip; sway.

ca•reer′, *n.* 1. profession. 2. life work. 3. speed. —*v.* 4. speed.

care′giv′er, *n.* person who cares for a child or an invalid.

ca•ress′, *v., n.* touch in expressing affection.

car′et, *n.* insertion mark (∧).

care′tak′er, *n.* 1. maintenance person. 2. caregiver.

care′worn′, *adj.* haggard from worry.

car′fare′, *n.* cost of ride.

car′go, *n., pl.* **-goes, -gos.** goods carried by vessel.

car′i•bou′ (-bōō′), *n.* North American reindeer.

car′i•ca•ture, *n.* mocking portrait. —**car′i•ca•ture,** *v.*

car′ies (kâr′ēz), *n., pl.* **-ies.** tooth decay.

car′il•lon′, *n.* musical bells.

car′jack′ing, *n.* theft of car by force. —**car′jack′er,** *n.*

car′mine (-min), *n., adj.* crimson or purplish red.

car′nage, *n.* massacre.

car′nal, *adj.* of the body.

car•na′tion, *n.* common fragrant flower.

car′ni•val, *n.* **1.** amusement fair. **2.** festival before Lent.

car′ni•vore′ (-vōr′), *n.* flesh-eating mammal. —**car•niv′o•rous,** *adj.*

car′ob (kar′əb), *n.* **1.** tree bearing long pods. **2.** pulp from the pods, used as chocolate substitute.

car′ol, *n., v.,* **-oled, -oling.** —*n.* **1.** Christmas song. —*v.* **2.** sing joyously. —**car′ol•er,** *n.*

car′om (kar′əm), *v.* **1.** hit and rebound. —*n.* **2.** rebound.

ca•rot′id, *n.* either of two large arteries in the neck.

ca•rouse′ (kə rouz′), *n., v.,* **-roused, -rousing.** —*n.* **1.** noisy or drunken feast. —*v.* **2.** engage in a carouse. —**ca•rous′al,** *n.*

carp, *v.* **1.** find fault. —*n.* **2.** large fresh-water fish.

car′pal, *adj.* **1.** of the carpus. —*n.* **2.** wrist bone.

carpal tunnel syndrome, chronic wrist pain associated esp. with repetitive movements, as at a keyboard.

car′pel, *n.* seed-bearing leaf.

car′pen•ter, *n.* builder in wood. —**car′pen•try,** *n.*

car′pet, *n.* **1.** fabric covering for floors. —*v.* **2.** cover with carpet. —**car′pet•ing,** *n.*

car′pool′, *n.* **1.** group of automobile owners who share driving duties. —*v.* **2.** participate in a carpool.

car′port′, *n.* roof that provides shelter for a car.

car′pus, *n., pl.* **-pi** (pī). **1.** wrist. **2.** wrist bones as a group.

car′rel, *n.* small study space. Also, **car′rell.**

car′riage, *n.* **1.** wheeled vehicle. **2.** posture. **3.** conveyance.

car′ri•on, *n.* dead flesh.

car′rot, *n.* plant with orange edible root.

car′rou•sel′, *n.* merry-go-round.

car′ry, *v.,* **-ried, -rying. 1.** convey; transport. **2.** support; bear. **3.** behave. **4.** win. **5.** extend. **6.** have in stock. **7. carry out,** accomplish. —**car′ri•er,** *n.*

car′ry-out′, *adj.* bought at a restaurant to be eaten elsewhere. —**car′ry-out′,** *n.*

car′sick′, *adj.* nauseated and dizzy from car travel.

cart, *n.* small wagon.
—**cart′age,** *n.*

carte blanche (kärt′ blänch′), complete freedom to choose.

car•tel′, *n.* syndicate controlling production.

car′ti•lage, *n.* flexible connective body tissue.
—**car′ti•lag′i•nous,** *adj.*

car•tog′ra•phy, *n.* map production.
—**car•tog′ra•pher,** *n.*

car′ton, *n.* cardboard box.

car•toon′, *n.* 1. comic drawing. 2. design for large art work. —**car•toon′ist,** *n.*

car′tridge, *n.* 1. case containing bullet and explosive. 2. container with frequently replaced machine parts.

cart′wheel′, *n.* 1. sideways handspring. —*v.* 2. roll forward end over end.

carve, *v.,* **carved, carving.** cut into form. —**carv′er,** *n.*

ca•sa′ba (kə sä′bə, *n., pl.* **-bas.** melon with yellow rind.

cas•cade′, *n.* waterfall.

case, *n., v.,* **cased, casing.** —*n.* 1. example. 2. situation. 3. event. 4. statement of arguments. 5. medical patient. 6. lawsuit. 7. category in inflection of nouns, adjectives, and pronouns. 8. **in case,** if. 9. container. —*v.* 10. put in case.

ca′sein (kā′sēn), *n.* milk derivative used in cheese.

case′ment, *n.* hinged window.

cash, *n.* 1. money. —*v.* 2. give or get cash for.

cash′ew, *n.* small curved nut.

cash•ier′, *n.* 1. person in charge of money. —*v.* 2. dismiss in disgrace.

cash′mere (-mēr), *n.* soft wool fabric.

cas′ing, *n.* 1. covering. 2. framework. 3. skin of a sausage.

ca•si′no, *n., pl.* **-nos.** amusement or gambling hall.

cask, *n.* barrel for liquids.

cas′ket, *n.* coffin.

cas•sa′va, *n.* tropical plant with starchy roots.

cas′se•role′, *n.* covered baking dish.

cas•sette′, *n.* compact case that holds recording tape.

cas′sock, *n.* long ecclesiastical vestment.

cast, *v.,* **cast, casting,** *n.* —*v.* **1.** throw. **2.** deposit. **3.** pour and mold. **4.** compute. —*n.* **5.** act of casting. **6.** thing cast. **7.** actors in play. **8.** mold. **9.** rigid surgical dressing. **10.** tinge. **11.** twist. —**cast'ing,** *n.*

cas'ta•net', *n.* pieces of bone shell, etc., held in the palm and struck together as musical accompaniment.

cast'a•way', *n.* shipwrecked person.

caste (kast), *n.* social level.

cast'er, *n.* swivel-mounted wheel. Also, **cast'or.**

cas'ti•gate', *v.,* **-gated, -gating.** scold severely. —**cas'ti•ga'tion,** *n.* —**cas'ti•ga'tor,** *n.*

cast'ing, *n.* metal cast in a mold.

cast iron, hard, brittle alloy of carbon, iron, and silicon.

cas'tle, *n., v.,* **-tled, -tling.** —*n.* **1.** royal or noble residence, usually fortified. **2.** chess piece; rook. —*v.* **3.** *Chess.* transpose rook and king.

cas'tor oil, cathartic oil.

cas'trate, *v.,* **-trated, -trating.** remove testicles of. —**cas•tra'tion,** *n.*

cas'u•al, *adj.* **1.** accidental; not planned. **2.** not caring.

cas'u•al•ty, *n., pl.* **-ties. 1.** accident injurious to person. **2.** soldier missing in action, killed, wounded, or captured.

cas'u•ist•ry (kazh'oo-), *n., pl.* **-ries.** adroit, specious argument. —**cas'u•ist,** *n.*

cat, *n.* common domestic animal. —**cat'like',** *adj.*

cat'a•clysm', *n.* upheaval. —**cat'a•clys'mic,** *adj.*

cat'a•comb', *n.* underground cemetery.

cat'a•logue', *n., v.,* **-logued, -loguing.** —*n.* **1.** organized list. —*v.* **2.** enter in catalogue. Also, **cat'a•log'.**

ca•tal'pa, *n.* tree with bell-shaped white flowers.

cat'a•lyst, *n.* **1.** substance that causes or speeds a chemical reaction without itself being affected. **2.** anything that precipitates an event.

cat'a•ma•ran', *n.* two-hulled boat.

cat'a•mount', *n.* wild cat, as the cougar.

cat'a•pult', *n.* **1.** device for launching. —*v.* **2.** hurl.

cat'a·ract', *n.* **1.** waterfall. **2.** opacity of eye lens.

ca·tarrh' (-tär'), *n.* inflammation of respiratory mucous membranes.

ca·tas'tro·phe (-fē), *n.* great disaster. —**cat'a·stroph'ic,** *adj.*

cat'bird', *n.* songbird with catlike call.

cat'call', *n.* jeer.

catch, *v.,* **caught, catching,** *n.* —*v.* **1.** capture. **2.** trap. **3.** hit. **4.** seize and hold. **5.** be in time for. **6.** get or contract. **7.** be entangled. —*n.* **8.** act of catching. **9.** thing that catches. **10.** thing caught. **11.** snag. —**catch'er,** *n.*

catch'ing, *adj.* contagious.

Catch'-22', *n.* frustrating situation involving contradictions.

catch'up, *n.* a tomato sauce.

catch'word', *n.* slogan.

catch'y, *adj.,* **catchier, catchiest.** memorable.

cat'e·chism' (-kiz'əm), *n.* set of questions and answers on religious principles. —**cat'e·chize'**, *v.*

cat'e·gor'i·cal, *adj.* unconditional. —**cat'e·gor'i·cal·ly,** *adv.*

cat'e·go'ry, *n., pl.* **-ries.** division; class. —**cat'e·go·rize'**, *v.*

ca'ter, *v.* **1.** provide food. **2.** be accommodating. —**ca'ter·er,** *n.*

cat'er-cor'nered (kat'i-, kat'ē-, kat'ər-), *adj.* **1.** diagonal. —*adv.* **2.** diagonally.

cat'er·pil'lar, *n.* **1.** wormlike larva of butterfly. **2.** type of tractor.

cat'er·waul' (kat'ər wôl'), *v.* **1.** utter long wails. —*n.* **2.** such a wail.

cat'fish', *n.* fresh-water fish.

cat'gut', *n.* string made from animal intestine.

ca·thar'sis, *n.* **1.** purging of emotions, as through art. **2.** evacuation of bowels.

ca·thar'tic, *adj.* **1.** effecting a catharsis. **2.** evacuating the bowels. —*n.* **3.** medicine doing this.

ca·the'dral, *n.* main church of diocese.

cath'e·ter, *n.* tube inserted into a body passage, as to provide or drain fluids.

cath′ode, *n.* **1.** electrode with negative charge. **2.** positive terminal of a battery.

cathode ray, beam of electrons coming from a cathode.

cathode-ray tube, vacuum tube generating cathode rays directed at screen, used to display images on receiver or monitor. *Abbr.*: CRT.

Cath′o•lic, *adj.* **1.** of or belonging to Roman Catholic Church. **2.** (*l.c.*) universal. —*n.* **3.** member of Roman Catholic Church. —**Ca•thol′i•cism′,** *n.*

cat′kin, *n.* spike of bunched small flowers.

cat′nap′, *n.* **1.** short, light sleep. —*v.* **2.** sleep briefly.

cat′nip, *n.* plant with scented leaves.

CAT scan, 1. examination using x-rays at various angles to show cross section of body. **2.** image produced by CAT scan. —**CAT scanner**

cat′s′-paw′, *n.* dupe used by another.

cat′sup, *n.* catchup.

cat′tail′, *n.* marsh plant.

cat′tle, *n.* livestock, esp. cows. —**cat′tle•man,** *n.*

cat′ty, *adj.,* **-tier, -tiest.** maliciously gossiping.

cat′walk′, *n.* access walk.

Cau•ca′sian, *adj.* **1.** of the so-called "white race." —*n.* **2.** Caucasian person. Also, **Cau′ca•soid.**

cau′cus, *n.* political meeting.

cau′dal, *adj.* of the tail.

caul′dron (kôl′drən), *n.* large kettle.

cau′li•flow′er, *n.* plant with an edible head.

caulk (kôk), *v.* **1.** fill or close seams of to keep water or air out. —*n.* **2.** Also, **caulk′ing.** material used to caulk.

cause, *n., v.,* **caused, causing.** —*n.* **1.** person or thing producing an effect. **2.** reason. **3.** aim; purpose. —*v.* **4.** bring about; produce. —**caus′al,** *adj.* —**cau•sa′tion,** *n.*

cause′ cé•lè•bre′ (kôz′ sə leb′), *n., pl.* **causes cé•lè•bres** (kôz′ sə leb′). controversy attracting great attention.

cause′way′, *n.* raised road.

caus′tic (kôs′-) *adj.,* 1. corroding. 2. sharply critical. —**caus′ti•cal•ly,** *adv.*

cau′ter•ize′, *v.,* -ized, -izing. burn. —**cau′ter•y, cau′ter•i•za′tion,** *n.*

cau′tion, *n.* 1. carefulness. 2. warning. —*v.* 3. warn. —**cau′tious,** *adj.*

cav′al•cade′, *n.* procession.

cav′a•lier′, *n.* 1. knight or horseman. 2. courtly gentleman. —*adj.* 3. haughty; indifferent. 4. offhand.

cav′al•ry, *n., pl.* -ries. troops on horseback or in armored vehicles. —**cav′al•ry•man,** *n.*

cave, *n., v.,* caved, caving. —*n.* 1. hollow space in the earth. —*v.* 2. fall or sink.

ca′ve•at′ (kav′ē ät′, kä′vē-, kā′-), *n.* warning.

cave man, 1. Stone Age cave dweller. 2. rough, brutal man.

cav′ern, *n.* large cave. —**cav′ern•ous,** *adj.*

cav′i•ar′, *n.* roe of sturgeon, etc., eaten as a delicacy.

cav′il, *v.,* -iled, -iling, *n.* —*v.* 1. find trivial faults. —*n.* 2. trivial objection.

cav′i•ty, *n., pl.* -ties. a hollow.

ca•vort′, *v.* prance about.

caw (kô), *n.* 1. harsh call of a crow. —*v.* 2. make a caw.

cay•enne′ (kī en′), *n.* sharp condiment.

cay•use′ (kī yōos′), *n.* pony.

CB, citizens band: private two-way radio.

cc, 1. carbon copy. 2. cubic centimeter.

CCU, coronary-care unit.

CD, 1. certificate of deposit. 2. Civil Defense. 3. compact disc.

CD-ROM (sē′de′rom′), *n.* compact disc for storing digitized read-only data.

cease, *v.,* ceased, ceasing, *n.* stop; end. —**cease′less,** *adj.*

cease′-fire′, *n.* truce.

ce′dar, *n.* coniferous tree.

cede, *v.,* ceded, ceding. yield.

ceil′ing, *n.* 1. upper surface of room. 2. maximum altitude.

cel′e•brate′, *v.,* -brated, -brating. 1. commemorate. 2. act rejoicingly. 3. perform ritually. 4. extol. —**cel′e•bra′tion,** *n.* —**cel′e•bra′tor,** *n.*

ce•leb′ri•ty, *n., pl.* -ties. 1. famous person. 2. fame.

ce•ler′i•ty (sə ler′-), *n.* speed.

cel′er•y, *n.* plant with edible leaf stalks.

ce•les′tial, *adj.* of heaven or the sky.

cel′i•ba•cy (sel′ə bə sē), *n.* sexual abstinence. —**cel′i•bate,** *n., adj.*

cell, *n.* 1. a small room or compartment. 2. microscopic biological structure. 3. electric battery. 4. organizational unit. —**cel′lu•lar,** *adj.*

cel′lar, *n.* basement.

cel′lo (chel′ō), *n., pl.* **-los.** large violinlike instrument. —**cel′list,** *n.*

cel′lo•phane′, *n.* transparent wrapping material.

cellular phone, mobile telephone using radio transmission. Also, **cell phone.**

cel′lu•lite′ (sel′yə līt′, -lēt), *n.* lumpy fat deposits, esp. in the thighs and buttocks.

cel′lu•loid′, *n.* hard, flammable substance.

cel′lu•lose′, *n.* carbohydrate of plant origin.

Cel′si•us, *n.* temperature scale in which water freezes at 0° and boils at 100°.

ce•ment′, *n.* 1. clay-lime mixture that hardens into stonelike mass. 2. binding material. —*v.* 3. treat with cement. 4. unite.

cem′e•ter′y, *n., pl.* **-teries.** burial ground.

cen′o•taph′ (sen′ə taf′), *n.* monument for one buried elsewhere.

Ce′no•zo′ic, *adj.* noting the present geologic era.

cen′ser, *n.* incense burner.

cen′sor, *n.* 1. person eliminating undesirable words, pictures, etc. 2. official responsible for reforms. —*v.* 3. deal with as a censor. —**cen′sor•ship′,** *n.*

cen•so′ri•ous, *adj.* severely critical.

cen′sure (-shər), *n., v.,* **-sured, -suring.** —*n.* 1. disapproval. —*v.* 2. rebuke.

cen′sus, *n.* count of persons.

cent, *n.* 1/100 of a dollar; penny.

cent., century.

cen′taur (-tôr), *n.* mythological creature, half horse and half man.

cen′te·nar′i·an, *n.* person 100 years old.

cen′te·nar′y, *n., pl.* **-naries.** 100th anniversary.

cen·ten′ni·al, *n.* 1. 100th anniversary. —*adj.* 2. of 100 years.

cen′ter, *n.* 1. middle. —*v.* 2. place at center. 3. concentrate. Also, **cen′tre.**

cen′ter·fold′, *n.* page that folds out from magazine center.

cen′ter·piece′, *n.* decoration for center of table.

cen′ti·grade′, *adj.* Celsius.

cen′ti·gram′, *n.* $\frac{1}{100}$ of gram.

cen′ti·li′ter (-lē′tər), *n.* $\frac{1}{100}$ of liter.

cen′ti·me′ter, *n.* $\frac{1}{100}$ of meter.

cen′ti·pede′, *n.* insect with many legs.

cen′tral, *adj.* 1. of or at center. 2. main. —**cen′tral·ly,** *adv.*

cen′tral·ize′, *v.,* **-ized, -izing.** 1. gather at a center. 2. concentrate control of. —**cen′tral·i·za′tion,** *n.*

central nervous system, brain and spinal cord.

cen·trif′u·gal (sen trif′yə gəl), *adj.* moving away from center.

cen′tri·fuge′ (-fyōōj′), *n.* high-speed rotating apparatus for separating substances of different densities.

cen·trip′e·tal, *adj.* moving toward center.

cen′trist (sen′trist), *n.* 1. person with political views that are not extreme. —*adj.* 2. of views that are not extreme.

cen′tu·ry, *n., pl.* **-ries.** period of one hundred years.

CEO, chief executive officer.

ce·ram′ic, *adj.* of clay and similar materials. —**ce·ram′ics,** *n.*

ce′re·al, *n.* 1. plant yielding edible grain. 2. food from such grain.

cer′e·bel′lum (ser′ə-), *n.* rear part of brain.

cer′e·bral (ser′ə brəl, sə rē′-), *adj.* 1. of brain. 2. intellectual.

cerebral palsy, paralysis due to brain injury.

cer′e•brum, *n., pl.* **-brums, -bra.** front, upper part of brain.

cer′e•mo′ny, *n., pl.* **-nies.** formal act or ritual.
—**cer′e•mo′ni•al,** *adj., n.*
—**cer′e•mo′ni•ous,** *adj.*

ce•rise′ (sə rēs′, -rēz′), *adj., n.* medium to deep red.

cer′tain, *adj.* 1. without doubt; sure. 2. agreed upon. 3. definite but unspecified.
—**cer′tain•ly,** *adv.*
—**cer′tain•ty,** *n.*

cer•tif′i•cate, *n.* document of proof.

certificate of deposit, bank receipt showing interest paid for certain period on money deposited.

cer′ti•fy′, *v.,* **-fied, -fying.** 1. guarantee as certain. 2. vouch for in writing.
—**cer′ti•fi•ca′tion,** *n.*

cer′ti•tude′, *n.* sureness.

ce•ru′le•an (sə rōōlē ən), *adj.* deep blue.

cer′vix (sûr′viks), *n., pl.* **cer•vix•es, cer•vi•ces** (sûr′və sēz′, sər vī′sēz). necklike part, esp. lower end of uterus. —**cer′vi•cal,** *adj.*

Ce•sar′e•an (si zâr′ē ən), *n.* delivery of baby by cutting through abdomen and uterus. Also, **Cesarean section, C-section, Cae•sar′e•an.**

ces•sa′tion, *n.* stop.

ces′sion, *n.* ceding.

cess′pool′, *n.* receptacle for waste, etc., from house.

cf., compare.

cg., centigram.

ch., 1. chapter. 2. church.

Cha•blis′ (shä blē′), *n.* dry white wine. Also, **cha•blis′.**

chafe, *v.,* **chafed, chafing.** make sore by rubbing.

chaff, *n.* 1. grain husks. 2. worthless matter. —*v.* 3. tease.

chaf′fer, *v.* bargain.

chafing dish, device for warming food at table.

cha•grin′ (shə grin′), *n.* 1. shame or disappointment. —*v.* 2. cause chagrin to.

chain, *n.* 1. connected series. 2. any series. 3. mountain range. —*v.* 4. fasten with chain.

chain reaction, process which automatically continues.

chain saw, power saw with teeth set on endless chain.

chair, *n.* **1.** seat with a back and legs. **2.** place of official. **3.** chairperson. —*v.* **4.** preside over.

chair'man, *n., pl.* **-men.** presiding officer. Also, *fem.,* **chair'wom'an;** *masc.* or *fem.,* **chair'per'son.**

chaise (shāz), *n.* light, open carriage.

chaise longue (shāz' lông'), type of couch.

cha·let' (sha lā'), *n.* mountain house.

chal'ice, *n.* cup for ritual wine.

chalk (chôk), *n.* **1.** soft limestone used to write on chalkboards. —*v.* **2.** mark with chalk. —**chalk'board',** *n.*

chal'lenge, *n., v.,* **-lenged, -lenging.** —*n.* **1.** call to fight, contest, etc. **2.** demand for identification. **3.** objection to juror. —*v.* **4.** make challenge to. —**chal'leng·er,** *n.*

chal'lenged, *adj.* (used as a euphemism) disabled.

cham'ber, *n.* **1.** room. **2.** assembly hall. **3.** legislative body. **4.** space for ammunition.

cham'ber·maid', *n.* maid who cleans bedrooms.

chamber music, music for performance by a small ensemble in a room or parlor.

cha·me'le·on (kə mē'lē ən), *n.* lizard able to change color.

cham'ois (sham'ē), *n.* **1.** European antelope. **2.** soft leather from its skin.

cham'o·mile' (kam'ə mīl', -mēl'), *n.* plant whose flowers are used in medicine and as a tea. Also, **cam'o·mile'.**

champ, *n.* **1.** *Informal.* champion. —*v.* **2.** bite.

Cham·pagne' (sham pān'), *n.* effervescent white wine. Also, **cham·pagne'.**

cham'pi·on, *n.* **1.** best competitor. **2.** supporter. —*v.* **3.** advocate. —*adj.* **4.** best. —**cham'pi·on·ship',** *n.*

chance, *n., v.,* **chanced, chancing,** *adj.* —*n.* **1.** fate; luck. **2.** possibility. **3.** opportunity. **4.** risk. —*v.* **5.** occur by chance. **6.** risk. —*adj.* **7.** accidental.

chan'cel, *n.* space around church altar.

chan'cel·ler·y, *n., pl.* **-leries.** offices of chancellor.

chan'cel•lor, *n.* **1.** high government official. **2.** university head.

chan'cer•y, *n., pl.* **-ceries. 1.** high law court. **2.** helpless position.

chan'cre (shang'kər), *n.,* lesion, as of syphilis.

chanc'y, *adj.,* **chancier, chanciest,** risky; uncertain.

chan'de•lier', *n.* hanging lighting fixture.

chan'dler, *n.* **1.** dealer in candles. **2.** grocer.

change, *v.,* **changed, changing,** *n.* —*v.* **1.** alter in condition, etc. **2.** substitute for. **3.** put on other clothes. —*n.* **4.** alteration. **5.** substitution. **6.** novelty. **7.** coins of low value. —**chang'er,** *n.* —**change'a•ble,** *adj.* —**change'a•bil'i•ty,** *n.*

change of life, menopause.

change'o'ver, *n.* change from one system to another.

chan'nel, *n., v.,* **-neled, -neling.** —*n.* **1.** bed of stream. **2.** wide strait. **3.** access; route. **4.** specific frequency band. —*v.* **5.** direct in channel.

chant, *n.* **1.** song; psalm. —*v.* **2.** sing, esp. slowly. —**chant'er,** *n.*

chant'ey (shan'-), *n., pl.* **-eys, -ies.** sailors' song. Also, **chant'y.**

chan'ti•cleer', *n.* rooster.

Cha'nu•kah (hä'nə kə), *n.* Hanukkah.

cha'os, *n.* utter disorder. —**cha•ot'ic,** *adj.*

chap, *v.,* **chapped, chapping,** *n.* —*v.* **1.** roughen and redden. —*n.* **2.** *Informal.* fellow.

chap., chapter.

chap'el, *n.* small church.

chap'er•on' (shap'ə rōn'), *n., v.,* **-oned, -oning.** —*n.* **1.** escort of young unmarried woman for propriety. —*v.* **2.** older person at young people's social affair. **3.** be a chaperon to or for. Also, **chap'er•one'.**

chap'lain, *n.* clergyman.

chap'let, *n.* garland.

chaps, *n.pl.* leather leg protectors worn by cowboys.

chap'ter, *n.* **1.** division. **2.** branch of society.

char, *v.,* **charred, charring.** burn.

char′broil′, *v.* broil over charcoal fire.

char′ac•ter, *n.* 1. personal nature. 2. reputation. 3. person in fiction. 4. written or printed symbol.

char′ac•ter•is′tic, *adj.* 1. typical. —*n.* 2. special trait.

char′ac•ter•ize′, *v.*, **-ized, -izing.** 1. distinguish. 2. describe. —**char′ac•ter•i•za′tion**, *n.*

cha•rade′ (shə rād′), *n.* riddle in pantomime.

char′coal′, *n.* carbonized wood.

chard, *n.* plant with edible green leafy stalks.

Char′don•day′ (shär′-), *n.* dry white wines.

charge, *v.*, **charged, charging,** *n.* —*v.* 1. load or fill. 2. put electricity through or into. 3. command or instruct. 4. accuse. 5. ask payment of. 6. attack. —*n.* 7. load or contents. 8. unit of explosive. 9. care; custody. 10. command or instruction. 11. accusation. 12. expense. 13. price. 14. attack. —**charge′a•ble**, *adj.*

charg′er, *n.* battle horse.

char′i•ot, *n.* two-wheeled carriage. —**char′i•ot•eer′**, *n.*

cha•ris′ma (kə-), *n.* power to charm and inspire people. —**char′is•mat′ic**, *adj.*

char′i•ty, *n., pl.* **-ties.** 1. aid to needy. 2. benevolent institution. —**char′i•ta•ble**, *adj.*

char′la•tan (shär′-), *n.* fraud.

char′ley horse′, cramp or sore muscle, esp. in the leg.

charm, *n.* 1. power to attract and please. 2. magical object, verse, etc. —*v.* 3. attract; enchant. —**charm′er**, *n.* —**charm′ing**, *adj.*

char′nel house, place for dead bodies.

chart, *n.* 1. sheet exhibiting data. 2. map. —*v.* 3. make a chart of.

char′ter, *n.* 1. document of authorization. —*v.* 2. establish by charter. 3. hire; lease.

charter member, original member of an organization.

char•treuse′ (shär trōōz′), *adj., n.* yellowish green.

char′wom′an, *n.* woman who cleans offices, houses, etc.

char'y, *adj.,* **charier, chariest.** careful.

chase, *v.,* **chased, chasing,** *n.* —*v.* **1.** go after. **2.** drive away. **3.** engrave metal. —*n.* **4.** instance of chasing. —**chas'er,** *n.*

chasm (kaz'əm), *n.* deep cleft in earth.

chas'sis (shas'ē), *n.* frame, wheels, and motor of vehicle.

chaste, *adj.,* **chaster, chastest. 1.** virtuous. **2.** simple. —**chas'ti•ty,** *n.*

chas'ten (chā'sən), *v.* punish to improve.

chas•tise', *v.,* **-tised, -tising.** punish; beat.

chat, *v.,* **chatted, chatting,** *n.* —*v.* **1.** talk informally. —*n.* **2.** informal talk.

cha•teau' (sha tō'), *n., pl.* **-teaux.** stately residence.

chat'tel, *n.* article of property other than real estate.

chat'ter, *v.* **1.** talk rapidly or foolishly. **2.** rattle rapidly. —*n.* **3.** foolish talk.

chat'ter•box', *n.* talkative person.

chat'ty, *adj.,* **-tier, -tiest.** loquacious.

chauf'feur (shō'fər), *n.* hired driver.

chau'vin•ism' (shō'-), *n.* **1.** blind patriotism. **2.** fanatic devotion to one's race, gender, etc. —**chau'vin•ist,** *n., adj.* —**chau'vin•is'tic,** *adj.*

cheap, *adj.* of low price or value. —**cheap'ly,** *adv.* —**cheap'en,** *v.*

cheat, *v.* **1.** defraud; deceive. —*n.* **2.** fraud. **3.** one who defrauds. —**cheat'er,** *n.*

check, *v.* **1.** stop or restrain. **2.** investigate; verify. **3.** note with a mark. **4.** leave or receive for temporary custody. —*n.* **5.** stop; restraint. **6.** written order for bank to pay money. **7.** bill. **8.** identification tag. **9.** square pattern. **10.** *Chess.* direct attack on king.

check'er, *n.* **1.** piece used in checkers. —*v.* **2.** diversify.

check'er•board', *n.* board with 64 squares on which the game of **checkers** is played.

check'ered, *adj.* **1.** marked with squares. **2.** varied. **3.** dubious.

check'list', *n.* list of items for comparison, verification, etc.

check′mate′, *n., v.,* **-mated, -mating.** *Chess.* —*n.* **1.** inescapable check. —*v.* **2.** subject to inescapable check.

check′out′, *n.* **1.** act of leaving and paying for hotel room. **2.** counter where customers pay for purchases.

check′point′, *n.* place, as at a border, where travelers are stopped for inspection.

check′up′, *n.* physical examination.

ched′dar, *n.* sharp cheese.

cheek, *n.* **1.** soft side of face. **2.** *Informal.* impudence. —**cheek′•i•ly**, *adv.* —**cheek′i•ness**, *n.* —**cheek′y**, *adj.*

cheer, *n.* **1.** shout of support. **2.** gladness. —*v.* **3.** shout encouragement to. **4.** gladden. —**cheer′ful**, *adj.* —**cheer′less**, *adj.* —**cheer′y**, *adj.*

cheese, *n.* milk product.

cheese′burg′er, *n.* hamburger with melted cheese.

cheese′cloth′, *n.* open cotton fabric.

chee′tah, *n.* wild cat resembling leopard.

chef (shef), *n.* chief cook.

chem′i•cal, *adj.* **1.** of chemistry. —*n.* **2.** substance in chemistry. —**chem′i•cal•ly**, *adv.*

chemical warfare, warfare with the use of chemicals.

che•mise′ (shə mēz′), *n.* woman's undershirt.

chem′is•try, *n.* science of composition of substances. —**chem′ist**, *n.*

che′mo•ther′a•py, *n.* treatment of disease, esp. cancer, with chemicals.

chem′ur•gy, *n.* chemistry of industrial use of organic substances, as soybeans.

cheque (chek), *n. Brit.* bank check.

cher′ish, *v.* treat as dear.

Cher′o•kee′, *n., pl.* **-kee, -kees.** member of an American Indian people.

cher′ry, *n., pl.* **-ries.** small red fruit of certain trees.

cher′ub, *n.* **1.** (*pl.* **-ubim**) celestial being. **2.** (*pl.* **-ubs**) angelic child.

chess, *n.* board game for two, each using 16 pieces.

chest, *n.* **1.** part of body between neck and abdomen. **2.** large box.

chest'nut', *n.* **1.** edible nut of certain trees. **2.** reddish brown. **3.** *Informal.* stale joke.

chev'i•ot (shev'ē ət), *n.* sturdy worsted fabric.

chev'ron (shev'-), *n.* insignia indicating military rank.

chew, *v.* crush repeatedly with teeth. —**chew'er,** *n.*

chewing gum, flavored preparation for chewing.

chew'y, *adj.,* **chewier, chewiest.** not easily chewed.

Chey•enne' (shī en', -an'), *n.,* *pl.* **-enne, e-ennes.** member of an American Indian people.

Chi•an'ti (kē än'tē), *n.* dry red wine. Also, **chi•an'ti.**

chic (shēk), *adj.* stylish.

chi•can'er•y (shi kā'nə rē, chi-), *n.,* *pl.* **-ies. 1.** deception; trickery. **2.** trick.

Chi•ca'no (chi kä'nō), *n., pl.* **-nos.** Mexican-American. Also, *n.fem.,* **Chi•ca'na.**

chick, *n.* **1.** young chicken. **2.** *Slang.* young woman.

chick'a•dee', *n.* small gray North American bird.

Chick'a•saw' (chik'ə sô'), *n.,* *pl.* **-saw, -saws.** member of an American Indian people.

chick'en, *n.* common fowl.

chicken pox, viral disease.

chick'pea', *n.* **1.** legume with pealike seeds. **2.** its seed.

chic'le, *n.* natural substance used in making chewing gum.

chic'o•ry, *n., pl.* **-ries.** plant with edible leaves and root.

chide, *v.,* **chided, chiding.** scold. —**chid'er,** *n.*

chief, *n.* **1.** head; leader. —*adj.* **2.** principal. —**chief'ly,** *adv.*

chief'tain, *n.* leader.

chif•fon' (shi fon'), *n.* sheer silk or rayon fabric.

chif'fo•nier' (shif'ə nēr'), *n.* tall chest of drawers.

chig'ger, *n.* larva of mites.

chil'blains', *n.pl.* inflammation caused by overexposure to cold, etc.

child, *n., pl.* **children. 1.** baby. **2.** son or daughter. —**child'bear'ing,** *n., adj.* —**child'birth,** *n.* —**child'hood,** *n.* —**child'ish,** *adj.* —**child'less,** *adj.* —**child'like',** *adj.*

child'bed', *n.* condition of giving birth.

chil'i (chil'ē), *n., pl.* **-ies.** 1. pungent pod of a red pepper. 2. dish made with these peppers. Also, **chil'e.**

chill, *n.* 1. coldness. —*adj.* 2. cold. 3. shivering. 4. not cordial. —*v.* 5. make or become cool. —**chil'ly,** *adv.*

chill factor, chill to skin from low temperature and wind.

chime, *n., v.,* **chimed, chiming.** —*n.* 1. set of musical tubes. —*v.* 2. sound harmoniously.

chi•me'ra (ki mēr'ə e, kī-), *n.* 1. (*cap.*) mythical monster with lion's head, goat's body, and serpent's tail. 2. dream.

chi•mer'i•cal, *adj.* 1. unreal; imaginary. 2. wildly fanciful.

chim'ney, *n.* passage for smoke.

chim'pan•zee', *n.* large, intelligent African ape.

chin, *n.* part of face below mouth.

chi'na, *n.* ceramic ware.

chin•chil'la, *n.* small rodent valued for its fur.

Chi•nese', *n., pl.* **-nese.** native or language of China.

chink, *n.* 1. crack. 2. short ringing sound. —*v.* 3. make such a sound.

Chi•nook', *n., pl.* **-nook** or **nooks.** member of an American Indian people.

chintz, *n.* printed fabric.

chintz'y, *adj.,* **chintzier, chintziest.** cheap-looking.

chip, *n., v.,* **chipped, chipping.** —*n.* 1. small flat piece. 2. broken place. 3. small plate carrying electric circuit. —*v.* 4. break off bits. 5. dent. 6. **chip in,** contribute.

chip'munk, *n.* small striped rodent resembling squirrel.

chip'per, *adj. Informal.* lively.

chi•rop'o•dy (kī-), *n.* treatment of foot ailments. —**chi•rop'o•dist,** *n.*

chi•ro•prac'tor (kī'-), *n.* one who practices therapy based upon adjusting body structures, esp. the spine. —**chi'ro•prac'tic,** *n.*

chirp, *n.* 1. short, sharp sound of birds, etc. —*v.* 2. make such sound. Also, **chir'rup.**

chis'el, *n.* 1. tool with broad cutting tip. —*v.* 2. cut with such tool. 3. *Informal.* cheat. —**chis'el•er,** *n.*

chit′chat′, *n.* light talk.

chiv′al•ry (shiv′-), *n., pl.* **-ries.**
1. qualities such as courtesy
and courage. 2. knightly way
of life. —**chiv′al•ric,**
chiv′al•rous, *adj.*

chive, *n. (usually pl.)* onionlike
plant with slender leaves.

chlo′rine, *n.* green gaseous
element. —**chlo′ric,** *adj.*
—**chlor′in•ate′,** *v.*

chlo′ro•form′, *n.* 1. liquid
used as anesthetic. —*v.* 2.
administer chloroform to.

chlo′ro•phyll, *n.* green
coloring matter of plants.

chock, *n.* wedge; block.

choc′o•late, *n.* 1. product
made from cacao seeds. 2.
dark brown.

Choc′taw (chok′tö), *n., pl.*
taw, -taws. member of an
American Indian people.

choice, *n.* 1. act of choosing.
2. thing chosen. —*adj.* 3.
excellent. —**choice′ness,** *n.*

choir, *n.* group of singers.

choke, *v.,* **choked, choking,** *n.*
—*v.* 1. stop breath of. 2.
obstruct. 3. be unable to
breathe. —*n.* 4. act of
choking.

chol′er•a (kol′ər ə), *n.* acute,
often deadly disease.

chol′er•ic (kol′ər ik, kə
ler′ik), *adj.* easily irritated.

cho•les′te•rol′ (kə les′tə
rôl′), *n.* biochemical in many
bodily fluids and tissues.

chomp, *v.* chew noisily; champ.

choose, *v.,* **chose, chosen,**
choosing. take as one thinks
best. —**choos′er,** *n.*

choos′y, *adj.,* **choosier,**
choosiest. particular.

chop, *v.,* **chopped, chopping,** *n.*
—*v.* 1. cut with blows. 2. cut
in pieces. —*n.* 3. act of
chopping. 4. slice of meat
with rib. 5. jaw.

chop′per, *n.* 1. thing that
chops. 2. *Informal.* helicopter.

chop′py, *adj.,* **-pier, -piest.**
forming short waves.

chop′sticks′, *n.pl.* sticks used
in eating.

chop su′ey, Chinese-style
vegetable dish.

cho′ral, *adj.* of or for chorus.

cho•rale′ (kə ral′, -räl′), *n.* 1.
type of hymn. 2. group singing
church music.

chord (kôrd), *n.* 1. harmony. 2.
straight line across circle.

chore, *n.* routine job.

cho're·og'ra·phy, *n.* art of composing dances. —**cho're·o·graph',** *v.* —**cho're·og'ra·pher,** *n.*

chor'is·ter, *n.* choir singer.

chor'tle, *v.,* **-tled, -tling,** *n.* chuckle.

cho'rus (kô'-), *n.* 1. group of singers. 2. recurring melody.

chow, *n. Slang.* food.

chow'der, *n.* vegetable soup usu. containing clams or fish.

chow mein, Chinese-style dish served on fried noodles.

Christ, *n.* Jesus Christ; (in Christian belief) the Messiah.

chris'ten, *v.* baptize; name.

Chris'ten·dom (-ən-), *n.* all Christians.

Chris'tian, *adj.* 1. of Jesus Christ, his teachings, etc. —*n.* 2. believer in Christianity. —**Chris'tian·ize',** *v.*

Chris'ti·an'i·ty, *n.* religion based on teachings of Christ.

Christ'mas, *n.* festival in honor of birth of Christ.

chro·mat'ic, *adj.* 1. of color. 2. *Music.* using semitones.

chro'mi·um, *n.* metallic element. Also, **chrome.**

chro'mo·some' (-sōm'), *n.* structure carrying the genes. —**chro'mo·so'mal,** *adj.*

chron'ic, *adj.* constant; habitual. Also, **chron'i·cal.** —**chron'i·cal·ly,** *adv.*

chron'i·cle, *n., v.,* **-cled, -cling.** —*n.* 1. record of events in order. —*v.* 2. record in chronicle. —**chron'i·cler,** *n.*

chrono-, prefix meaning time, as *chronometer.*

chro·nol'o·gy, *n., pl.* **-gies.** historical order of events. —**chron'o·log'i·cal,** *adj.*

chro·nom'e·ter, *n.* very exact clock.

chrys'a·lis (kris'ə-), *n.* pupa.

chry·san'the·mum, *n.* large, colorful flower of aster family.

chub, *n.* fresh-water fish.

chub'by, *adj.,* **-bier, -biest.** plump.

chuck, *v.* 1. pat lightly. —*n.* 2. light pat. 3. cut of beef.

chuck'le, *v.,* **-led, -ling,** *n.* —*v.* 1. laugh softly. —*n.* 2. soft laugh.

chum, *n.* close friend. —**chum'my,** *adj.*

chump, *n. Informal.* fool.

chunk, *n.* big lump.

chunk′y, *adj.,* **chunkier, chunkiest. 1.** thick or stout; stocky. **2.** full of chunks.

church, *n.* **1.** place of Christian worship. **2.** sect.

churl, *n.* **1.** peasant. **2.** boor. —**churl′ish,** *adj.*

churn, *n.* **1.** agitator for making butter. —*v.* **2.** agitate.

chute (sho͞ot), *n.* sloping slide.

chut′ney, *n.* East Indian relish.

chutz′pa (кно͝ot′spə, ho͝ot′-), *n. Slang.* nerve; impudence; gall. Also, **chutz′pah.**

CIA, Central Intelligence Agency.

ci•ca′da (si kā′də), *n.* large insect with shrill call.

-cide, suffix indicating: **1.** killer, as *pesticide.* **2.** act of killing, as *homicide.*

ci′der, *n.* apple juice.

ci•gar′, *n.* roll of tobacco for smoking.

cig′a•rette′, *n.* roll of smoking tobacco in paper.

cinch, *n.* **1.** firm hold. **2.** *Informal.* sure or easy thing.

cin′der, *n.* burned piece; ash.

cin′e•ma (sin′-), *n.* **1.** motion pictures. **2.** movie theater.

cin′e•ma•tog′ra•phy, *n.* art or technique of motion-picture photography. —**cin′e•ma•tog′ra•pher,** *n.*

cin′na•mon, *n.* brown spice from bark of trees.

ci′pher (sī′-), *n.* **1.** the symbol (0) for zero. **2.** secret writing, using code. —*v.* **3.** calculate.

cir′ca (sûr′kə), *prep.* approximately.

cir′cle, *n., v.,* **-cled, -cling.** —*n.* **1.** closed curve of uniform distance from its center. **2.** range; scope. **3.** group of friends or associates. —*v.* **4.** enclose or go in circle.

cir′cuit, *n.* **1.** set of rounds, esp. in connection with duties. **2.** electrical path or arrangement. —**cir′cuit•ry,** *n.*

circuit breaker, device that interrupts electrical circuit to prevent excessive current.

cir•cu′i•tous (sər kyo͞o′ə-), *adj.* roundabout. —**cir•cu′i•tous•ly,** *adv.*

cir′cu•lar, *adj.* **1.** of or in circle. —*n.* **2.** advertisement distributed widely. —**cir′cu•lar•ize′,** *v.*

cir′cu•late′, *v.,* **-lated, -lating.** move or pass around.

—cir′cu•la′tion, *n.*
—cir′cu•la•to′ry, *adj.*

circum-, prefix indicating around or about, as *circumnavigate.*

cir′cum•cise′, *v.,* **-cised, -cising.** remove foreskin of. —cir′cum•ci′sion, *n.*

cir•cum′fer•ence (sər kum′fər əns), *n.* **1.** outer boundary of a circle. **2.** length of such a boundary. —cir•cum′fer•en′tial, *adj.*

cir′cum•flex′, *n.* diacritical mark (ˆ).

cir′cum•lo•cu′tion, *n.* roundabout expression.

cir′cum•nav′i•gate′, *v.,* **-gated, -gating.** sail around.

cir′cum•scribe′, *v.,* **-scribed, -scribing. 1.** encircle. **2.** confine.

cir′cum•spect′, *adj.* cautious. —cir′cum•spec′tion, *n.*

cir′cum•stance′, *n.* **1.** condition accompanying or affecting event. **2.** detail. **3.** condition. **4.** ceremony.

cir′cum•stan′tial, *adj.* **1.** of or from circumstances. **2.** detailed. **3.** with definite implications.

cir′cum•vent′, *v.* outwit or evade. —cir′cum•ven′tion, *n.*

cir′cus, *n.* show with animals, acrobats, etc.

cir•rho′sis (si rō′sis), *n.* chronic liver disease.

cir′rus (sir′-), *n.* fleecy cloud.

cis′tern (sis′-), *n.* reservoir.

cit′a•del, *n.* fortress.

cite, *v.,* **cited, citing. 1.** mention in proof, etc. **2.** summon. **3.** commend. —ci•ta′tion, *n.*

cit′i•zen, *n.* **1.** subject of a country. **2.** inhabitant. **3.** civilian. —cit′i•zen•ry, *n.* —cit′i•zen•ship′, *n.*

citizens band, CB.

citric acid, white powder in citrus fruits.

cit′ron (sit′rən), *n.* lemonlike Asian fruit.

cit′ro•nel′la (si′trə nel′la), *n.* pungent oil.

cit′rus, *adj.* of the genus including the orange, lemon, etc.

cit′y, *n., pl.* **cities.** large town.

civ′ic, *adj.* **1.** of cities. **2.** of citizens.

civ′ics, *n.* study of civil affairs and duties of citizens.

civ′il, *adj.* 1. of citizens. 2. civilized. 3. polite. —**civ′il•ly,** *adv.* —**ci•vil′i•ty,** *n.*

ci•vil′ian, *n.* 1. nonmilitary or nonpolice person. —*adj.* 2. of such persons.

civ′i•li•za′tion, *n.* 1. act of civilizing. 2. civilized territory.

civ′i•lize, *v.,* **-lized, -lizing.** convert from primitive state.

civil liberty, fundamental right guaranteed by law.

civil rights, rights of all people to freedom and equality.

civil servant, employee of civil service.

civil service, branches of governmental administration outside the armed services.

civil war, war between parts of same state.

cl., centiliter.

claim, *v.* 1. demand as one's right, property, etc. 2. assert. —*n.* 3. demand. 4. assertion. 5. something claimed. —**claim′ant,** *n.*

clair•voy′ant (klâr voi′ənt), *adj.* seeing beyond physical vision. —**clair•voy′ant,** *n.* —**clair•voy′ance,** *n.*

clam, *n.* common mollusk.

clam′ber, *v.* climb.

clam′my, *adj.,* **-mier, -miest.** cold and moist. —**clam′mi•ness,** *n.*

clam′or, *n.* 1. loud outcry or noise. —*v.* 2. raise clamor. —**clam′or•ous,** *adj.*

clamp, *n.* 1. clasping device. —*v.* 2. fasten with clamp.

clan, *n.* 1. related families. 2. clique. —**clan′nish,** *adj.*

clan•des′tine (-des′tin), *adj.* done in secret.

clang, *v.* 1. ring harshly. —*n.* 2. Also, **clang′or.** harsh ring.

clank, *v.* 1. ring dully. —*n.* 2. dull ringing.

clap, *v.,* **clapped, clapping,** *n.* —*v.* 1. strike together, as hands in applause. 2. apply suddenly. —*n.* 3. act or sound of clapping. —**clap′per,** *n.*

clap′board (klab′ərd), *n.* overlapping boards.

clap′trap′, *n.* empty speech.

claque (klak), *n.* hired applauders.

clar′et, *n.* dry red wine.

clar′i•fy′, *v.,* **-fied, -fying.** make or become clear. —**clar′i•fi•ca′tion,** *n.*

clar′i•net′, *n.* musical wind instrument.

clar′i•on, *adj.* clear and loud.

clar′i•ty, *n.* clearness.

clash, *v.* **1.** conflict. **2.** collide. —*n.* **3.** collision. **4.** conflict.

clasp, *n.* **1.** fastening device. **2.** hug. —*v.* **3.** fasten with clasp. **4.** hug.

class, *n.* **1.** group of similar persons or things. **2.** social rank. **3.** group of students ranked together. **4.** division. **5.** *Slang.* excellence. —*v.* **6.** place in classes. —**class′mate′**, *n.* —**class′room′**, *n.*

class action, lawsuit on behalf of persons with complaint in common.

clas′sic, *adj.* Also, **clas′si•cal. 1.** of finest or fundamental type. **2.** in Greek or Roman manner. —*n.* **3.** author, book, etc., of acknowledged superiority. —**clas′si•cal•ly**, *adv.* —**clas′si•cism′**, *n.*

clas′si•fied, *adj.* limited to authorized persons.

clas′si•fy′, *v.*, **-fied, -fying.** arrange in classes. —**clas′si•fi•ca′tion**, *n.*

class•y, *adj.*, **classier, classiest.** *Slang.* stylish; elegant. —**class′i•ness**, *n.*

clat′ter, *v., n.* rattle.

clause, *n.* part of sentence with its own subject and predicate.

claus′tro•pho′bi•a, *n.* dread of closed places. —**claus′tro•pho′bic**, *adj., n.*

clav′i•chord′ (klav′i kôrd′), *n.* early keyboard instrument.

clav′i•cle (klav′i kəl), *n.* collarbone.

claw, *n.* **1.** sharp, curved nail on animal's foot. —*v.* **2.** tear or scratch roughly.

clay, *n.* soft earth. —**clay′ey**, *adj.*

clean, *adj.* **1.** free from dirt. **2.** trim. **3.** complete. —*adv.* **4.** in clean manner. —*v.* **5.** make clean. —**clean′er**, *n.*

clean′-cut′, *adj.* **1.** neat. **2.** clear-cut.

clean•ly (klen′lē), *adj.* keeping or kept clean. —**clean′li•ness**, *n.*

cleanse, *v.*, **cleansed, cleansing.** make clean. —**cleans′er**, *n.*

clear, *adj.* **1.** free from darkness or obscurity. **2.** easily perceived. **3.** evident. **4.** unobstructed. **5.** free of obligations or encumbrances. **6.** blameless. —*adv.* **7.** in a clear manner. —*v.* **8.** make or become clear. **9.** pay in full. **10.** pass beyond. —**clear'ly,** *adv.* —**clear'ness,** *n.*

clear'ance, *n.* **1.** space between objects. **2.** authorization.

clear'-cut', *adj.* apparent; obvious.

clear'ing, *n.* treeless space.

cleat, *n.* metal piece to which ropes, etc., are fastened.

cleave, *v.,* **cleft** or **cleaved, cleaving.** split. —**cleav'er,** *n.* —**cleav'age,** *n.*

cleave, *v.,* **cleaved, cleaving. 1.** cling. **2.** remain faithful.

clef, *n.* musical symbol indicating pitch.

cleft, *n.* split.

cleft palate, fissure in the roof of the mouth.

clem'a•tis, *n.* flowering vine.

clem'ent, *adj.* **1.** lenient. **2.** mild. —**clem'en•cy,** *n.*

clench, *v.* close tightly.

cler'gy, *n., pl.* **-gies.** religious officials. —**cler'gy•man,** *n.* —**cler'gy•wom•an,** *n.fem.*

cler'ic, *n.* clergy member.

cler'i•cal, *adj.* **1.** of clerks. **2.** of clergy.

clerk, *n.* **1.** employee who keeps records, etc. **2.** retail sales person.

clev'er, *adj.* nimble of mind. —**clev'er•ly,** *adv.* —**clev'er•ness,** *n.*

clew, *n.* **1.** ball of yarn, etc. **2.** *Brit.* clue.

CLI or **cli,** cost-of-living index.

cli•ché' (klē shā'), *n.* trite expression.

click, *n.* **1.** slight, sharp noise. —*v.* **2.** make a click. **3.** *Slang.* succeed.

cli'ent, *n.* customer.

cli'en•tele' (-tel'), *n.* patrons.

cliff, *n.* steep bank.

cliff'-hang'er, *n.* **1.** melodramatic serial in which each part ends in suspense. **2.** suspenseful situation.

cli•mac'ter•ic (klī mak'tər ik, klīmak ter'ik), *n.* period of decreasing reproductive capacity.

cli′mate, *n.* weather conditions. —**cli•mat′ic,** *adj.*

cli′max, *n.* apex; culmination. —**cli•mac′tic,** *adj.*

climb, *v.* 1. ascend; rise. 2. **climb down, a.** descend. **b.** *Informal.* retreat; compromise. —*n.* 3. ascent. —**climb′er,** *n.*

clinch, *v.* 1. fasten (a nail) by bending the point. 2. hold tightly. —*n.* 3. act of clinching. —**clinch′er,** *n.*

cling, *v.,* **clung, clinging.** hold firmly to.

clin′ic, *n.* hospital for nonresident or charity patients. —**clin′i•cal,** *adj.*

clink, *v.* 1. make light, ringing sound. —*n.* 2. such a sound.

clink′er, *n.* fused mass of incombustible residue.

clip, *v.,* **clipped, clipping,** *n.* —*v.* 1. cut with short snips. 2. hit sharply. —*n.* 3. act of clipping. 4. clasp. 5. cartridge holder. —**clip′ping,** *n.*

clip′per, *n.* 1. cutting device. 2. fast sailing vessel.

clique (klēk), *n.* elitist group.

clit′o•ris (klit′ər is), *n., pl.* **clitorises** or **clitorides** (kli tôr′i dēz′). erectile organ of vulva.

cloak, *n.* 1. loose outer garment. —*v.* 2. cover with cloak. 3. hide.

cloak′-and-dag′ger, *adj.* of espionage or intrigue.

clob′ber, *v. Informal.* maul.

clock, *n.* device for telling time.

clock′wise′, *adv., adj.* in direction of clock hands.

clock′work′, *n.* 1. mechanism of a clock. 2. perfectly regular function, like that of a clock.

clod, *n.* piece of earth.

clog, *v.,* **clogged, clogging,** *n.* —*v.* 1. hamper; obstruct. —*n.* 2. obstruction, etc. 3. heavy wooden shoe.

clois′ter, *n.* 1. covered walk. 2. monastery or nunnery.

clone, *n., v.,* **cloned, cloning.** —*n.* 1. organism created by asexual reproduction. 2. *Informal.* duplicate. —*v.* 3. grow as clone.

close, *v.,* **closed, closing,** *adj.,* **closer, closest,** *adv., n.* —*v.* (klōz) 1. shut, obstruct, or end. 2. come to terms. —*adj.* (klōs) 3. shut. 4. confined. 5. lacking fresh air. 6. secretive. 7. stingy. 8. compact. 9. near.

10. intimate. —*adv.* (klōs) 11. in a close manner. —*n.* (klōz) 12. end. —**close'ly,** *adv.* —**close'ness,** *n.* —**clo'sure,** *n.*

close call, narrow escape.

closed'-cap'tioned, *adj.* broadcast with captions visible only with decoding device.

closed shop, place where workers must belong to union.

close'out', *n.* sale at greatly reduced prices.

clos'et, *n.* 1. small room or cabinet for clothes, etc. —*adj.* 2. *Slang.* clandestine.

close'up' (klōs'-), *n.* 1. photograph taken at close range. 2. intimate view.

clot, *n., v.,* **clotted, clotting.** —*n.* 1. mass, esp. of dried blood. —*v.* 2. form clot.

cloth, *n.* fabric of threads.

clothe, *v.,* **clothed** or **clad, clothing.** dress.

clothes, *n.pl.* garments; apparel. Also, **cloth'ing.**

cloud, *n.* 1. mass of water particles, etc., high in the air. —*v.* 2. grow dark or gloomy. 3. lose or deprive of transparency. —**cloud'y,** *adj.* —**cloud'i•ness,** *n.*

clout, *n.* 1. blow from hand. 2. *Informal.* influence. —*v.* 3. strike with hand.

clove, *n.* 1. tropical spice. 2. section of plant bulb.

clo'ver, *n.* three-leaved plant.

clown (kloun), *n.* 1. comic performer. 2. prankster. 3. fool. —*v.* 4. act like a clown. —**clown'ish,** *adj.*

cloy, *v.* weary by excess sweetness.

club, *n., v.,* **clubbed, clubbing.** —*n.* 1. bat. 2. organized group. 3. playing-card figure (♣). —*v.* 4. beat with club.

club'foot', *n.* deformed foot.

club soda, soda water.

cluck, *n.* 1. call of hen. —*v.* 2. utter such call.

clue, *n.* hint.

clump, *n.* cluster.

clum'sy, *adj.,* **-sier, -siest.** awkward. —**clum'si•ly,** *adv.* —**clum'si•ness,** *n.*

clus'ter, *n.* 1. group; bunch. —*v.* 2. gather into cluster.

clutch, *v.* 1. seize; snatch. 2. hold tightly. —*n.* 3. grasp. 4. (*pl.*) capture or mastery. 5. device for engaging or disengaging machinery.

clut′ter, *v., n.* heap or litter.

cm., centimeter.

CO, 1. Colorado. 2. Commanding Officer.

co-, prefix indicating: 1. together, as *cooperate.* 2. joint or jointly, as *coauthor.*

Co., 1. Company. 2. County.

c/o, care of.

coach, *n.* 1. enclosed carriage. 2. adviser, esp. in sports. —*v.* 3. advise.

co•ag′u•late′, *v.,* -lated, -lating. thicken, clot, or congeal. —**co•ag′u•la′tion,** *n.*

coal, *n.* 1. mineral burned as fuel. —*v.* 2. get coal.

co′a•lesce′ (-les′), *v.,* -lesced, -lescing. unite or ally. —**co′a•les′cence,** *n.*

co′a•li′tion, *n.* alliance.

coarse, *adj.,* coarser, coarsest. 1. rough. 2. vulgar. —**coarse′ly,** *adv.* —**coars′en,** *v.* —**coarse′ness,** *n.*

coast, *n.* 1. seashore. —*v.* 2. drift easily. 3. sail along coast. —**coast′al,** *adj.*

coast′er, *n.* 1. something that coasts. 2. object protecting surfaces from moisture.

coast guard, military service that enforces maritime laws.

coat, *n.* 1. outer garment. 2. covering, as fur or bark. —*v.* 3. cover or enclose.

coat′ing, *n.* outer layer.

coat of arms, emblems, motto, etc., of one's family.

co•au′thor (kō ô′thər, kō′ô-), *n.* one of two or more joint authors. —**co•au′thor,** *v.*

coax, *v.* cajole. —**coax′er,** *n.*

co•ax′i•al (-ak′sē əl), *adj.* having a common axis.

cob, *n.* corncob.

co′balt, *n.* 1. silvery metallic element. 2. deep blue.

cob′ble, *v.,* -bled, -bling, *n.* —*v.* 1. mend (shoes). —*n.* 2. Also, **cob′ble•stone′.** round stone for paving, etc. —**cob′bler,** *n.*

co′bra, *n.* venomous snake.

cob′web′, *n.* spider web.

co•caine′, *n.* narcotic drug.

cock, *n.* 1. male bird, esp. rooster. 2. valve. 3. hammer in lock of a gun. 4. pile of hay. —*v.* 5. set cock of (a gun). 6. set aslant.

cock•ade′, *n.* hat ornament.

cock'a•too', *n.* colorful crested parrot.

cock'er, *n.* small spaniel.

cock'eyed', *adj.* **1.** having an eye that cannot look straight. **2.** tilted to one side. **3.** absurd. **4.** drunk.

cock'le, *n.* **1.** mollusk with radially ribbed valves. **2.** inmost part.

cock'ney, *n.* **1.** resident of London, esp. East End. **2.** accent of such persons.

cock'pit', *n.* **1.** space for pilot. **2.** pit where cocks fight.

cock'roach', *n.* common bug.

cock'tail', *n.* **1.** drink containing mixture of liquors. **2.** mixed appetizer.

cock'y, *adj.,* **cockier, cockiest.** saucy and arrogant; too sure of oneself. —**cock'i•ness,** *n.*

co'coa, *n.* **1.** powdered seeds of cacao. —*adj.* **2.** brown.

co'co•nut', *n.* large seed of the **co'co palm.**

co•coon', *n.* larval covering.

cod, *n.* edible Atlantic fish. Also, **cod'fish'.**

C.O.D., cash, or collect, on delivery.

co'da (kō'də), *n.* final passage of a musical movement.

cod'dle, *v.,* **-dled, -dling. 1.** pamper. **2.** cook in almost boiling water.

code, *n., v.,* **coded, coding.** —*n.* **1.** collection of laws or rules. **2.** system of signals or secret words. —*v.* **3.** put in code.

co'deine (-dēn), *n.* opiate.

codg'er (koj'ər), *n.* eccentric man, esp. an old one.

cod'i•cil (kod'ə səl), *n.* supplement, esp. to a will.

cod'i•fy', *v.,* **-fied, -fying.** organize into legal or formal code. —**cod'i•fi•ca'tion,** *n.*

co'ed', *n.* female student, esp. in coeducational school.

co'ed•u•ca'tion, *n.* education in classes of both sexes. —**co'ed•u•ca'tion•al,** *adj.*

co'ef•fi'cient, *n.* number by which another is multiplied.

co•erce', *v.,* **-erced, -ercing.** force; compel. —**co•er'cion,** *n.* —**co•er'cive,** *adj.*

co•e'val, *adj.* of same period.

co'ex•ist', *v.* **1.** exist simultaneously. **2.** exist together peacefully.

—**co′ex•ist′ence,** *n.*
—**co′ex•ist′ent,** *adj.*

cof′fee, *n.* powdered brown seeds of certain tropical trees, used in making a beverage.

cof′fer, *n.* chest.

cof′fin, *n.* box for a corpse.

cog, *n.* tooth on wheel (**cog′wheel′**), connecting with another such wheel.

co′gent (kō′jənt), *adj.* convincing. —**co′gen•cy,** *n.* —**co′gent•ly,** *adv.*

cog′i•tate′ (koj′-), *v.,* **-tated, -tating.** ponder. —**cog′i•ta′tion,** *n.* —**cog′i•ta′tor,** *n.*

co′gnac (kōn′yak), *n.* brandy.

cog′nate, *adj.* 1. related. —*n.* 2. a cognate word.

cog•ni′tion, *n.* knowing.

cog′ni•zance, *n.* notice, esp. official. —**cog′ni•zant,** *adj.*

cog•no′men, *n.* surname.

co′gno•scen′ti (kon′yə shen′tē, kog′nə-), *n.pl., sing.* **-te** (-tā, -tē). those having superior knowledge.

co•hab′it, *v.* live together. —**co•hab′i•ta′tion,** *n.*

co•here′, *v.,* **-hered, -hering.** stick together. —**co•he′sion,** *n.* —**co•he′sive,** *adj.*

co•her′ent, *adj.* making sense. —**co•her′ence,** *n.*

co′hort, *n.* 1. associate; companion. 2. group.

coif•fure′ (kwä fyŏŏr′), *n.* arrangement of hair.

coil, *v.* 1. wind spirally. —*n.* 2. ring. 3. series of spirals.

coin, *n.* 1. piece of metal issued as money. —*v.* 2. make metal into money. 3. invent. —**coin′age,** *n.* —**coin′er,** *n.*

co•in•cide′, *v.,* **-cided, -ciding.** 1. occur at same time, place, etc. 2. match. —**co•in′ci•dence,** *n.* —**co•in′ci•den′tal,** *adj.* —**co•in′ci•den′tal•ly,** *adv.*

co′i•tus (kō′i təs), *n.* sexual intercourse. —**co′i•tal,** *adj.*

coke, *n., v.,* **coked, coking.** —*n.* 1. solid carbon produced from coal. 2. *Slang.* cocaine. —*v.* 3. convert into coke.

Col., 1. Colonel. 2. Colorado.

co′la, *n.* soft drink containing extract from kola nuts.

COLA (kōlə), *n.* adjustment in payments to offset changes in cost of living.

col'an•der (kul'-), *n.* large strainer.

cold, *adj.* **1.** without warmth. **2.** not cordial. —*n.* **3.** absence of heat. **4.** common illness. —**cold'ly,** *adv.* —**cold'ness,** *n.*

cold'-blood'ed, *adj.* **1.** frigid. **2.** with blood at same temperature as environment. —**cold'-blood'ed•ly,** *adv.* —**cold'-blood'ed•ness,** *n.*

cold cream, preparation for cleansing or soothing the skin.

cold cuts, *n.pl.* various sliced cold meats and cheeses.

cold feet, *Informal.* lack of courage.

cold shoulder, deliberate show of indifference.

cold turkey, *Informal.* —*n.* **1.** abrupt withdrawal. —*adv.* **2.** impromptu.

cold war, rivalry between nations just short of armed conflict.

cole'slaw', *n.* sliced raw cabbage.

col'ic, *n.* pain in bowels. —**col'ick•y,** *adj.*

col'i•se'um, *n.* large stadium.

co•li'tis (kə lī'tis, ko-), *n.* inflammation of the colon.

col•lab'o•rate', *v.,* **-rated, -rating.** work together. —**col•lab'o•ra'tion,** *n.* —**col•lab'o•ra'tor,** *n.*

col•lage' (kə läzh'), *n.* work of art made with various materials pasted on a surface.

col•lapse', *v.,* **-lapsed, -lapsing,** *n.* —*v.* **1.** fall in or together. **2.** fail abruptly. —*n.* **3.** a falling-in. **4.** sudden failure. —**col•laps'i•ble,** *adj.*

col'lar, *n.* **1.** part of garment around neck. —*v.* **2.** seize by collar.

col'lar•bone', *n.* slender bone connecting sternum and scapula; clavicle.

col'lard (kol'ərd), *n.* type of kale.

col•lat'er•al, *n.* **1.** security pledged on loan. —*adj.* **2.** additional. **3.** on side.

col'league, *n.* associate.

col•lect', *v.* **1.** gather together. **2.** take payment of. —*adj., adv.* **3.** payable on delivery. —**col•lec'tion,** *n.* —**col•lec'tor,** *n.*

col•lect'i•ble, *n.* **1.** object collected. —*adj.* **2.** able to be collected.

col•lec′tive, *adj.* **1.** joint; by a group. —*n.* **2.** socialist productive group.

collective bargaining, negotiation between union and employer.

col•lec′tiv•ism′, *n.* principle of communal control. —**col•lec′tiv•ist,** *n.*

col′lege, *n.* school of higher learning. —**col•le′giate,** *adj.*

col•lide′, *v.,* **-lided, -liding.** come together violently.

col′lie, *n.* long-haired dog.

col′lier (-yər), *n.* **1.** ship for carrying coal. **2.** coal miner.

col•li′sion, *n.* **1.** crash. **2.** conflict.

col•lo′qui•al, *adj.* appropriate to casual rather than formal speech or writing. —**col•lo′qui•al•ism′,** *n.* —**col•lo′qui•al•ly,** *adv.*

col•lo′qui•um (-kwē əm), *n., pl.* **-quiums, -quia.** focused conference.

col′lo•quy (-kwē), *n., pl.* **-quies.** conversation.

col•lu′sion, *n.* illicit agreement.

Colo., Colorado.

co•logne′ (kə lōn′), *n.* perfumed toilet water.

co′lon, *n.* **1.** punctuation (:). **2.** part of large intestine. —**co•lon′ic,** *adj.*

colo′nel (kûr′nəl), *n.* military officer below general. —**colo′nel•cy,** *n.*

co•lo′ni•al•ism, *n.* policy of extending national authority over foreign territories. —**co•lo′ni•al•ist,** *n., adj.*

col′on•nade′ (-nād′), *n.* series of columns.

col′o•ny, *n., pl.* **-nies. 1.** group of people settling in another land. **2.** territory subject to outside ruling power. **3.** community. —**co•lo′ni•al,** *adj., n.* —**col′o•nist,** *n.* —**col′o•nize′,** *v.*

col′or, *n.* **1.** quality of light perceived by human eye. **2.** pigment; dye. **3.** complexion. **4.** vivid description. **5.** (*pl.*) flag. **6.** race. —*v.* **7.** apply color to. **8.** distort in telling. Also, *Brit.,* **col′our.** —**col′or•a′tion,** *n.* —**col′or•ing,** *n.*

col′o•ra•tu′ra (-tyŏŏr′ə), *n.* soprano specializing in music containing ornamental trills.

col′or-blind′, *adj.* **1.** unable to distinguish certain colors. **2.** without racial bias.

col′ored, *adj. Often Offensive.* other than Caucasian.

col′or·ful, *adj.* **1.** full of color. **2.** vivid; interesting. —**col′or·ful·ly,** *adv.*

col′or·less, *adj.* **1.** without color. **2.** uninteresting. —**col′or·less·ly,** *adv.*

co·los′sal, *adj.* huge; vast. —**co·los′sal·ly,** *adv.*

co·los′sus, *n.* anything colossal.

colt, *n.* young male horse.

col′um·bine′, *n.* branching plant with bright flowers.

col′umn, *n.* **1.** upright shaft or support. **2.** long area of print. **3.** regular journalistic piece. **4.** long group. —**co·lum′nar,** *adj.* —**col′umn·ist,** *n.*

com-, prefix indicating: **1.** with or together, as *commingle.* **2.** completely, as *commit.*

co′ma, *n.* unconscious state. —**com′a·tose′,** *adj.*

Co·man′che (kə man′chē, kō-), *n., pl.* **-che, -ches.** member of an American Indian people.

comb, *n.* **1.** toothed object, for straightening hair or fiber. **2.** growth on a cock's head. **3.** crest. **4.** honeycomb. —*v.* **5.** dress with comb. **6.** search.

com·bat′, *v.,* **-bated, -bating,** *n.* —*v.* **1.** fight. —*n.* (kom′bat). **2.** battle. —**com·bat′ant,** *n.* —**com·bat′ive,** *adj.*

com′bi·na′tion, *n.* **1.** act of combining. **2.** mixture. **3.** alliance. **4.** sets of figures dialed to operate a lock.

com·bine′, *v.,* **-bined, -bining,** *n.* —*v.* **1.** unite; join. —*n.* (kom′bīn). **2.** combination. **3.** machine that cuts and threshes grain.

com′bo, *n.* **1.** *Informal.* small jazz band. **2.** combination.

com·bus′ti·ble, *adj.* **1.** inflammable. —*n.* **2.** inflammable substance.

com·bus′tion, *n.* burning.

come, *v.,* **came, come, coming. 1.** approach or arrive. **2.** happen. **3.** emerge.

come′back′, *n.* **1.** return to former status. **2.** retort.

co·me′di·an, *n.* comic. —**co·me′di·enne′,** *n.fem.*

com′e·dy, *n., pl.* **-dies. 1.** humorous drama. **2.** drama with happy ending.

come′ly (kum′lē), *adj.,* **-lier, -liest.** attractive. —**come′li·ness,** *n.*

com′er, *n. Informal.* one likely to have great success.

com′et, *n.* celestial body orbiting around and lighted by sun, often with misty tail.

com′fort, *v.* **1.** console or cheer. —*n.* **2.** consolation. **3.** ease. —**com′fort·a·ble,** *adj.* —**com′fort·a·bly,** *adv.*

com′fort·er, *n.* **1.** one who comforts. **2.** warm quilt.

com′ic, *adj.* **1.** of comedy. **2.** Also, **com′i·cal.** funny. —*n.* **3.** comedian. **4.** *(pl.)* comic strips.—**com′i·cal·ly,** *adv.*

comic strip, sequence of drawings relating comic incident or story.

com′ma, *n.* mark of punctuation (,).

com·mand′, *v.* **1.** order. **2.** be in control of. **3.** overlook. —*n.* **4.** order. **5.** control. **6.** troops, etc., under commander.

com′man·dant′ (-dant′, -dänt′), *n.* **1.** local commanding officer. **2.** director of Marine Corps.

com′man·deer′, *v.* seize for official use.

com·mand′er, *n.* **1.** chief officer. **2.** *Navy.* officer below captain.

com·mand′ment, *n.* **1.** command. **2.** precept of God.

com·man′do, *n., pl.* **-dos, -does.** soldier making brief raids against enemy.

com·mem′o·rate′, *v.,* **-rated, -rating.** honor memory of. —**com·mem′o·ra′tion,** *n.* —**com·mem′o·ra′tive,** *adj.*

com·mence′, *v.,* **-menced, -mencing.** start.

com·mence′ment, *n.* **1.** beginning. **2.** graduation day or ceremonies.

com·mend′, *v.* **1.** praise. **2.** entrust. —**com·mend′a·ble,** *adj.* —**com′men·da′tion,** *n.* —**com·mend′a·to′ry,** *adj.*

com·men′su·rate (-shə rit, -sə-), *adj.* corresponding. —**com·men′su·rate·ly,** *adv.*

com′ment, *n.* **1.** remark. —*v.* **2.** make remarks.

com′men·tar′y, *n., pl.* **-taries. 1.** comment. **2.** explanatory essay.

com'men·ta'tor, *n.* one who discusses news events, etc.

com'merce, *n.* sale or barter.

com·mer'cial, *adj.* **1.** of or in commerce. —*n.* **2.** *Radio or TV* advertisement. —**com·mer'cial·ly,** *adv.*

com·mer'cial·ize', *v.,* -ized, -izing. treat as a business. —**com·mer'cial·i·za'tion,** *n.*

com·min'gle, *v.,* -gled, -gling. blend.

com·mis'er·ate', *v.,* -ated, -ating. feel sympathy. —**com·mis'er·a'tion,** *n.*

com'mis·sar', *n.* Soviet government official.

com'mis·sar'y, *n., pl.* -saries. store selling materials.

com·mis'sion, *n.* **1.** act of committing. **2.** document giving authority. **3.** group of persons with special task. **4.** usable condition. **5.** fee for agent's services. —*v.* **6.** give commission to. **7.** authorize. **8.** put into service.

com·mis'sion·er, *n.* government official.

com·mit', *v.,* -mitted, -mitting. **1.** give in trust or custody. **2.** refer to committee. **3.** do. **4.** obligate. —**com·mit'ment,** *n.*

com·mit'tee, *n.* group assigned to special duties. —**com·mit'tee·man,** *n., pl.* -men. —**com·mit'tee·wom'an,** *n., pl.* -wom·en.

com·mode', *n.* small cabinet.

com·mo'di·ous, *adj.* roomy.

com·mod'i·ty, *n., pl.* -ties. article of commerce.

com'mo·dore', *n.* officer below rear admiral.

com'mon, *adj.* **1.** shared by all; joint. **2.** ordinary; usual. **3.** vulgar. —*n.* **4.** area of public land. —**com'mon·ly,** *adv.*

com'mon·er, *n.* one of common people.

common law, system of law based on custom and court decisions.

com'mon·place', *adj.* **1.** ordinary; trite. —*n.* **2.** commonplace remark.

com'mons, *n.* **1.** (*cap.*) elective house of certain legislatures. **2.** large dining room.

common sense, sound practical judgments. —**com'mon·sense',** *adj.*

com'mon·weal', *n.* public welfare.

com′mon•wealth′, *n.* 1. democratic state. 2. people of a state.

com•mo′tion, *n.* disturbance.

com•mu′nal, *adj.* of or belonging to a community.

com•mune′ (kə myōōn′), *v.,* -muned, -muning, *n.* —*v.* 1. talk together. —*n.* (kom′yōōn), 2. small community with shared property. 3. district.

com•mu′ni•cate′, *v.,* -cated, -cating. 1. make known. 2. transmit. 3. exchange news, etc. —**com•mu′ni•ca•ble,** *adj.* —**com•mu′ni•ca′tion,** *n.* —**com•mu′ni•ca′tive,** *adj.* —**com•mu′ni•cant,** *n.*

com•mun′ion, *n.* 1. act of sharing. 2. group with same religion. 3. sacrament commemorating Jesus' last supper; Eucharist.

com•mu′ni•qué′ (-kā′), *n.* official bulletin.

com′mu•nism, *n.* 1. social system based on collective ownership of all productive property. 2. (*cap.*) political doctrine advocating this. —**com′mu•nist,** *n., adj.* —**com′mu•nis′tic,** *adj.*

com•mu′ni•ty, *n., pl.* -ties. 1. people with common culture. 2. public.

com•mute′, *v.,* -muted, -muting. 1. exchange. 2. reduce (punishment). 3. travel between home and work. —**com′mu•ta′tion,** *n.* —**com•mut′er,** *n.*

com•pact′, *adj.* 1. packed together. 2. pithy. —*v.* 3. pack together. —*n.* (kom′pakt). 4. small cosmetic case. 5. agreement. —**com•pact′ly,** *adv.* —**com•pact′ness,** *n.*

compact disc, optical disc on which data is digitally recorded. Also, **CD.**

com•pac′tor (kəm pak′tər, kom′pak-), *n.* appliance that compresses trash into small bundles.

com•pan′ion, *n.* 1. associate. 2. mate. —**com•pan′ion•a•ble,** *adj.* —**com•pan′ion•ate,** *adj.* —**com•pan′ion•ship′,** *n.*

com′pa•ny, *n., pl.* -nies. 1. persons associated for business or social purposes, etc. 2. companionship. 3. guests. 4. military unit.

com•par′a•tive, *adj.* **1.** of or based on comparison. —*n.* **2.** *Gram.* intermediate degree of comparison.
—**com•par′a•tive•ly,** *adv.*

com•pare′, *v.,* **-pared, -paring.**
1. consider for similarities. **2.** *Gram.* inflect to show degree.
—**com′pa•ra•ble,** *adj.*
—**com•par′i•son,** *n.*

com•part′ment, *n.* separate room, space, etc.
—**com•part•men′tal,** *adj.*
—**com•part•men′tal•ize′,** *v.*

com′pass, *n.* **1.** instrument for finding direction. **2.** extent. **3.** tool for making circles.

com•pas′sion, *n.* sympathy.
—**com•pas′sion•ate,** *adj.*
—**com•pas′sion•ate•ly,** *adv.*

com•pat′i•ble, *adj.* congenial.
—**com•pat′i•bil′i•ty,** *n.*

com•pa′tri•ot, *n.* person from one's own country.

com•pel′, *v.,* **-pelled, -pelling.**
force.

com•pel′ling, *adj.* **1.** forceful.
2. demanding attention.

com•pen′di•ous, *adj.*
concise.

com•pen′di•um, *n., pl.,*
-diums, -dia. 1. summary. **2.**
full list.

com′pen•sate′, *v.,* **-sated,**
-sating. 1. make up for. **2.** pay.
—**com′pen•sa′tion,** *n.*
—**com•pen′sa•to′ry,** *adj.*

com•pete′, *v.,* **-peted, -peting.**
contend; rival.

com′pe•tent, *adj.* **1.** able enough. **2.** legally qualified. **3.**
sufficient. —**com′pe•tence,**
com′pe•ten•cy, *n.*
—**com′pe•tent•ly,** *adv.*

com′pe•ti′tion, *n.* **1.** contest.
2. rivalry. —**com•pet′i•tive,**
adj. —**com•pet′i•tor,** *n.*

com•pile′, *v.,* **-piled, -piling.**
put together; assemble.
—**com•pil′er,** *n.*
—**com′pi•la′tion,** *n.*

com•pla′cen•cy, *n., pl.* **-cies.**
satisfaction, esp. with self.
Also, **com•pla′cence.**
—**compla′cent,** *adj.*
—**com•pla′cent•ly,** *adv.*

com•plain′, *v.* **1.** express pain, dissatisfaction, etc. **2.** accuse.
—**com•plain′er,**
com•plain′ant, *n.*
—**com•plaint′,** *n.*

com•plai′sant, *adj.* obliging.

com′ple•ment, *n.* (-mənt). **1.**
that which completes. **2.** full amount. —*v.* (-ment′). **3.**

complete.
—**com′ple•men′ta•ry,** *adj.*

com•plete′, *adj., v.,* **-pleted, -pleting.** —*adj.* **1.** entire; perfect. —*v.* **2.** make complete. —**com•plete′ly,** *adv.* —**com•plete′ness,** *n.* —**com•ple′tion,** *n.*

com•plex′, *adj.* **1.** having many parts; intricate. —*n.* (kom′pleks). **2.** complex whole. **3.** obsession. —**com•plex′i•ty,** *n.*

com•plex′ion, *n.* color of skin.

com′pli•cate′, *v.,* **-cated, -cating.** make complex or difficult. —**com′pli•cat′ed,** *adj.* —**com′pli•ca′tion,** *n.*

com•plic′i•ty (-plis′ə-), *n., pl.* **-ties.** partnership in crime.

com′pli•ment, *n.* (-mənt). **1.** expression of praise. —*v.* (-ment′). **2.** express praise.

com′pli•men′ta•ry, *adj.* **1.** praising. **2.** free.

com•ply′, *v.,* **-plied, -plying.** act in accordance. —**com•pli′ance,** *n.* —**com•pli′ant, com•pli′a•ble,** *adj.*

com•po′nent, *adj.* **1.** composing. —*n.* **2.** part of whole.

com•port′, *v.* **1.** conduct (oneself). **2.** suit. —**com•port′ment,** *n.*

com•pose′, *v.,* **-posed, -posing. 1.** make by uniting parts. **2.** constitute. **3.** put in order; calm. **4.** create and write. **5.** set printing type. —**com′po•si′tion,** *n.*

com•posed′, *adj.* calm.

com•pos′er, *n.* writer, esp. of music.

com•pos′ite, *adj.* made of many parts.

com′post, *n.* decaying mixture of leaves, etc.

com•po′sure, *n.* calm.

com′pote (kom′pōt), *n.* stewed fruit.

com′pound, *adj.* **1.** having two or more parts, functions, etc. —*n.* **2.** something made by combining parts. **3.** enclosure with buildings. —*v.* (kəm pound′). **4.** combine. **5.** condone (crime) for a price.

com′pre•hend′, *v.* **1.** understand. **2.** include. —**com′pre•hen′si•ble,** *adj.* —**com′pre•hen′sion,** *n.*

com′pre•hen′sive, *adj.* inclusive.

—**com′pre•hen′sive•ly,** *adv.*
—**com′pre•hen′sive•ness,** *n.*

com•press′, *v.* **1.** press together. —*n.* (kom′pres). **2.** pad applied to affected part of body. —**com•pres′sion,** *n.* —**com•pres′sor,** *n.*

com•prise′, *v.,* -prised, -prising. consist of. Also, **com•prize′.** —**com•pris′al,** *n.*

com′pro•mise′, *n., v.,* -mised, -mising. —*n.* **1.** agreement to mutual concessions. **2.** something intermediate. —*v.* **3.** settle by compromise. **4.** endanger.

comp•trol′ler (kən-), *n.* controller.

com•pul′sion, *n.* compelling force. —**com•pul′so•ry,** *adj.*

com•pul′sive, *adj.* due to or acting on inner compulsion.

com•punc′tion, *n.* remorse.

com•pute′, *v.,* -puted, -puting. calculate; figure. —**com′pu•ta′tion,** *n.*

com•put′er, *n.* electronic apparatus for storing and manipulating data.

com•pu′ter•ize′, *v.,* -ized, -izing. **1.** do by computer. **2.** automate by computer, as a business. —**com•put′er•i•za′tion,** *n.*

computer virus, virus (def. 3).

com′rade, *n.* companion. —**com′rade•ship′,** *n.*

con, *adv., n., v.,* **conned, conning.** —*adv.* **1.** opposed to a plan, etc. —*n.* **2.** argument against. —*v.* **3.** study. **4.** *Informal.* deceive; swindle.

con•cave′, *adj.* curved inward. —**con•cave′ly,** *adv.* —**con•cav′i•ty,** *n.*

con•ceal′, *v.* hide. —**con•ceal′ment,** *n.*

con•cede′, *v.,* -ceded, -ceding. **1.** admit. **2.** yield.

con•ceit′, *n.* **1.** excess self-esteem. **2.** fanciful idea. —**con•ceit′ed,** *adj.*

con•ceive′, *v.,* -ceived, -ceiving. **1.** form (plan or idea). **2.** understand. **3.** become pregnant. —**con•ceiv′a•ble,** *adj.* —**con•ceiv′a•bly,** *adv.*

con′cen•trate′, *v.,* -trated, -trating, *n.* —*v.* **1.** bring to one point. **2.** intensify. **3.** give full attention. —*n.* **4.** product of concentration. —**con′cen•tra′tion,** *n.*

concentration camp, guarded compound where political prisoners are confined.

con·cen'tric, *adj.* having common center.

con'cept, *n.* general notion.

con·cep'tion, *n.* 1. act of conceiving. 2. idea.

con·cep'tu·a·lize' (-choo ə līz'), *v.,* **-lized, -lizing.** 1. form a concept of. 2. think in concepts. —**con·cep'tu·al·i·za'tion,** *n.*

con·cern', *v.* 1. relate to. 2. involve. 3. worry. —*n.* 4. matter that concerns. 5. business firm.

con·cerned', *adj.* 1. affected. 2. troubled; anxious.

con·cern'ing, *prep.* about.

con'cert, *n.* 1. musical performance. 2. accord.

con·cert'ed, *adj.* 1. planned together. 2. performed together or in cooperation. —**con·cert'ed·ly,** *adv.*

con'cer·ti'na (-tē'-), *n.* small accordion.

con·cer'to (kən cher'tō), *n., pl.* **-tos** or **-ti** (-tē). musical piece for principal instruments and orchestra.

con·ces'sion, *n.* 1. act of conceding. 2. what is conceded. 3. privilege conceded by authority.

conch (kongk), *n.* spiral shell.

con·cil'i·ate', *v.,* **-ated, -ating.** win over; reconcile. —**con·cil'i·a'tion,** *n.* —**con·cil'i·a'tor,** *n.* —**con·cil'i·a·to'ry,** *adj.*

con·cise', *adj.* brief; succinct. —**con·cise'ly,** *adv.* —**con·cise'ness,** *n.*

con'clave, *n.* private meeting.

con·clude', *v.,* **-cluded, -cluding.** 1. finish; settle. 2. infer. —**con·clu'sion,** *n.* —**con·clu'sive,** *adj.* —**con·clu'sive·ly,** *adv.*

con·coct', *v.* make by combining. —**con·coc'tion,** *n.*

con·com'i·tant, *adj.* 1. accompanying. —*n.* 2. anything concomitant. —**con·com'i·tant·ly,** *adv.*

con'cord, *n.* agreement.

con·cord'ance, *n.* 1. concord. 2. index of key words.

con·cor'dat, *n.* agreement, esp. between Pope and a government.

con'course, *n.* 1. assemblage. 2. place for crowds in motion.

con′crete, *adj., n., v.,* **-creted, -creting.** —*adj.* 1. real; objective. 2. made of concrete. —*n.* 3. material of cement and hard matter. —*v.* 4. (kon krēt′). become solid. —**con•crete′ly,** *adv.* —**con•crete′ness,** *n.* —**con•cre′tion,** *n.*

con′cu•bine′, *n.* woman living with but not married to man.

con•cu′pis•cent (-pi sənt), *adj.* lustful. —**con•cu′pis•cence,** *n.*

con•cur′, *v.,* **-curred, -curring.** 1. agree. 2. coincide. 3. cooperate. —**con•cur′rence,** *n.* —**con•cur′rent,** *adj.* —**con•cur′rent•ly,** *adv.*

con•cus′sion, *n.* shock or jarring from blow.

con•demn′, *v.* 1. denounce. 2. penalize. 3. judge unfit. 4. acquire for public purpose. —**con′dem•na′tion,** *n.*

con•dense′, *v.,* **-densed, -densing.** 1. reduce to denser form. 2. make or become compact. —**con′den•sa′tion,** *n.* —**con•dens′er,** *n.*

condensed milk, thick, sweetened milk.

con′de•scend′, *v.* 1. pretend equality with an inferior. 2. deign. —**con′de•scen′sion,** *n.*

con′di•ment, *n.* seasoning.

con•di′tion, *n.* 1. state of being or health. 2. fit state. 3. requirement. —*v.* 4. put in condition. —**con•di′tion•al,** *adj.* —**con•di′tion•al•ly,** *adv.* —**con•di′tion•er,** *n.*

con•dole′, *v.,* **-doled, -doling.** sympathize in sorrow. —**con•do′lence,** *n.*

con′dom (kon′dəm, kun′-), *n.* contraceptive device worn over penis; prophylactic.

con′do•min′i•um, *n.* apartment house in which units are individually owned. Also, *Informal,* **con′do.**

con•done′, *v.,* **-doned, -doning.** excuse.

con′dor, *n.* vulture.

con•duce′, *v.,* **-duced, -ducing.** contribute; lead. —**con•du′cive,** *adj.*

con′duct, *n.* 1. behavior. 2. management. —*v.* (kən dukt′). 3. behave. 4. manage. 5. lead or carry. 6. transmit. —**con•duc′tion,** *n.* —**con•duc′tive,** *adj.* —**con′duc•tiv′i•ty,** *n.*

con·duct'ance, *n.* ability of conductor to transmit electricity.

con·duc'tor, *n.* 1. guide. 2. director of an orchestra. 3. official on trains. 4. substance that conveys.

con'duit (-dwit), *n.* pipe for water, etc.

cone, *n.* 1. form tapering from round base to single point. 2. fruit of fir, pine, etc.

cone'flow'er, *n.* plants with cone-shaped center disks.

con'fab, *n.* conversation.

con·fec'tion, *n.* candy or other sweet preparation. —**con·fec'tion·er,** *n.* —**con·fec'tion·er'y,** *n.*

con·fed'er·a·cy, *n., pl.* **-cies.** 1. league. 2. (*cap.*) Confederate States of America.

con·fed'er·ate, *adj., n., v.,* **-ated, -ating.** —*adj.* (-ər it). 1. in league. 2. (*cap.*) of **Confederate States of America,** separated from U.S. during Civil War. —*n.* (-ər it). 3. ally. 4. accomplice. 5. (*cap.*) citizen of Confederate States of America. —*v.* (-ə rāt'). 6. be allied. —**con·fed'er·a'tion,** *n.*

con·fer', *v.,* **-ferred, -ferring.** 1. bestow. 2. consult. —**con'fer·ee',** *n.* —**con·fer'ment,** *n.* —**con·fer'rer,** *n.*

con'fer·ence, *n.* 1. meeting. 2. discussion.

con·fess', *v.* 1. admit. 2. declare one's sins, as to priest. —**con·fes'sion,** *n.*

con·fess'ed·ly, *adv.* by confession; admittedly.

con·fes'sion·al, *adj.* 1. characteristic of confession. —*n.* 2. place in church set apart for confession.

con·fes'sor, *n.* 1. one who confesses. 2. one who hears confessions.

con·fet'ti, *n.* bits of colored paper.

con'fi·dant', *n.* one to whom secrets are told. —**con'fi·dante',** *n.fem.*

con·fide', *v.,* **-fided, -fiding.** 1. trust with secret. 2. entrust.

con'fi·dence, *n.* 1. full trust. 2. assurance. —**con'fi·dent,** *adj.* —**con'fi·dent·ly,** *adv.*

confidence game, swindle in which the swindler first gains the victim's confidence.

con′fi•den′tial, *adj.* **1.** entrusted as secret. **2.** private. —**con′fi•den′tial•ly,** *adv.*

con•fig′u•ra′tion, *n.* external form.

con•fine′, *v.,* **-fined, -fining,** *n.* —*v.* **1.** keep within bounds. **2.** shut or lock up. —*n.* (*pl.*) (kon′fīnz). **3.** boundary.

con•fined′, *adj.* **1.** restricted. **2.** stuffy.

con•fine′ment, *n.* **1.** imprisonment. **2.** childbirth. **3.** period of being confined.

con•firm′, *v.* **1.** make sure. **2.** make valid. **3.** strengthen. **4.** admit into church. —**con′fir•ma′tion,** *n.*

con•firmed′, *adj.* verified.

con′fis•cate′ (kon′fis kāt′), *v.,* **-cated, -cating.** seize by public authority. —**con′fis•ca′tion,** *n.*

con′fla•gra′tion, *n.* fierce fire.

con•flict′, *v.* **1.** oppose; clash. —*n.* (kon′flikt). **2.** battle. **3.** antagonism.

con′flu•ence, *n.* act or place of flowing together. —**con′flu•ent,** *adj.*

con•form′, *v.* **1.** accord; adapt. **2.** make similar.

—**con•form′a•ble,** *adj.*
—**con•form′ist,** *n.*
—**con•form′ity,** *n.*

con′for•ma′tion, *n.* form.

con•found′, *v.* **1.** confuse. **2.** perplex.

con•found′ed, *adj.* **1.** bewildered. **2.** damned.

con•front′, *v.* **1.** meet or set facing. **2.** challenge openly. —**con′fron•ta′tion,** *n.* —**con′fron•ta′tion•al,** *adj.*

con•fuse′, *v.,* **-fused, -fusing. 1.** throw into disorder. **2.** associate wrongly. **3.** disconcert. —**con•fu′sion,** *n.*

con•fute′, *v.,* **-futed, -futing.** prove to be wrong. —**con′fu•ta′tion,** *n.*

Cong., 1. Congregational. **2.** Congress. **3.** Congressional.

con•geal′, *v.* make solid or thick. —**con•geal′ment,** *n.*

con•gen′ial, *adj.* agreeable; suited. —**con•ge′ni•al′i•ty,** *n.*

con•gen′i•tal, *adj.* innate. —**con•gen′i•tal•ly,** *adv.*

con•gest′, *v.* fill to excess. —**con•ges′tion,** *n.*

con•glom′er•ate, *n., adj., v.,* **-ated, -ating.** —*n.* (-ər it). **1.**

mixture. **2.** rock formed of pebbles, etc. **3.** company owning variety of other companies. —*adj.* (-ər it). **4.** gathered into a ball. **5.** mixed. —*v.* (-ə rāt′). **6.** gather into round mass. —**con·glom′er·a′tion,** *n.*

con·grat′u·late′, *v.,* -lated, -lating. express sympathetic joy. —**con·grat′u·la′tion,** *n.* —**con·grat′u·la·to′ry,** *adj.*

con′gre·gate′, *v.,* -gated, -gating. assemble. —**con′gre·ga′tion,** *n.*

con′gre·ga′tion·al, *adj.* **1.** of congregations. **2.** (*cap.*) denoting church denomination wherein each church acts independently. —**con′gre·ga′tion·al·ism,** *n.* —**con′gre·ga′tion·al·ist,** *n.*

con′gress, *n.* **1.** national legislative body, esp. (*cap.*) of the U.S. **2.** formal meeting. —**con·gres′sion·al,** *adj.* —**con′gress·man,** *n.* —**con′gress·per′son,** *n.* —**con′gress·wom′an,** *n.fem.*

con′gru·ent, *adj.* coinciding. —**con′gru·ence,** *n.*

con·gru′i·ty, *n., pl.* -ties. agreement. —**con′gru·ous,** *adj.*

con′ic, *adj.* of or like cone. Also, **con′i·cal.**

co′ni·fer, *n.* tree bearing cones. —**co·nif′er·ous,** *adj.*

con·jec′ture, *n., v.,* -tured, -turing. guess. —**con·jec′tur·al,** *adj.*

con·join′, *v.* join together.

con′ju·gal, *adj.* of marriage. —**con′ju·gal·ly,** *adv.*

con′ju·gate′, *v.,* -gated, -gating, *adj.* —*v.* (-gāt′). **1.** *Gram.* give forms of in order (verb). —*adj.* (-git). **2.** coupled. —**con′ju·ga′tion,** *n.*

con·junc′tion, *n.* **1.** union. **2.** *Gram.* word that joins. —**con·junc′tive,** *adj.*

con·junc′ti·vi′tis (kən jungk′tə vī′tis), *n.* inflammation of mucous membrane of the eye.

con′jure, *v.,* -jured, -juring. invoke or produce by magic. —**con′jur·er,** *n.*

conk (kongk, kôngk), *v. Slang.* **1.** strike on the head. **2. conk out. a.** break down. **b.** sleep. —*n.* **3.** blow on the head.

Conn., Connecticut.

con·nect′, *v.* join; link.
—**con·nec′tion;** *Brit.*
con·nex′ion, *n.*
—**con·nec′tive**, *adj., n.*

con·nive′, *v., -nived, -niving.*
conspire. —**con·niv′ance**, *n.*
—**con·niv′er**, *n.*

con′nois·seur′ (kon′ə sûr′),
n. skilled judge.

con·note′, *v., -noted, -noting.*
signify in addition; imply.
—**con′no·ta′tion**, *n.*

con·nu·bi·al, *adj.* nuptial.
—**con·nu′bi·al·ly**, *adv.*

con′quer, *v.* 1. acquire by
force. 2. defeat.
—**con′quer·or**, *n.*
—**con′quest**, *n.*

con·quis′ta·dor′ (kong
kwis′tə dôr′, -kēs-′, *n., pl.*
-**quis′ta·dors, -quis′ta·do′res**
(-kēs′tə dôr′ēz, -āz).
16th-century Spanish
conqueror of the Americas.

con′san·guin′e·ous, *adj.*
related by birth.
—**con′san·guin′i·ty**, *n.*

con′science, *n.* recognition of
right or wrong in oneself.
—**con′sci·en′tious**, *adj.*

conscientious objector,
person who refuses to serve in
military for moral reasons.

con′scion·a·ble (-shən-), *adj.*
approved by conscience.

con′scious, *adj.* 1. in
possession of one's senses. 2.
aware. 3. deliberate.
—**con′scious·ly**, *adv.*
—**con′scious·ness**, *n.*

con′script, *adj.* 1. drafted.
—*n.* 2. one drafted. —*v.* (kən
skript′). 3. draft for military
service. —**con·scrip′tion**, *n.*

con′se·crate′, *v., -crated,
-crating.* 1. make sacred. 2.
devote. —**con′se·cra′tion**, *n.*

con·sec′u·tive, *adj.* 1.
successive. 2. logical.
—**con·sec′u·tive·ly**, *adv.*

con·sen′sus, *n.* agreement.

con·sent′, *v.* 1. agree; comply.
—*n.* 2. assent.

con′se·quence′, *n.* 1. effect.
2. importance.

con′se·quent′, *adj.* following;
resulting. —**con′se·quen′tial**,
adj. —**con′se·quent·ly**, *adv.*

con′ser·va′tion, *n.*
preservation of resources.
—**con′ser·va′tion·ism**, *n.*
—**con′ser·va′tion·ist**, *n.*

con·serv′a·tive, *adj.* 1.
favoring status quo. 2.
cautious. —*n.* 3. conservative

person. —**con·serv′a·tive·ly,**
adv. —**con·serv′a·tism,** *n.*

con·serv′a·to′ry, *n., pl.* **-ries.**
1. school of music or drama.
2. hothouse.

con·serve′, *v.,* **-served,**
-serving, *n.* —*v.* 1. keep intact.
—*n.* (kon′sûrv). 2. preserves.

con·sid′er, *v.* 1. think over. 2.
deem. 3. respect.
—**con·sid′er·ate,** *adj.*
—**con·sid′er·ate·ly,** *adv.*

con·sid′er·a·ble, *adj.*
important or sizable.
—**con·sid′er·a·bly,** *adv.*

con·sid′er·a′tion, *n.* 1.
thought. 2. regard. 3. fee.

con·sid′er·ing, *prep.* in view
of.

con·sign′, *v.* 1. deliver. 2.
entrust. 3. ship.
—**con·sign′ment,** *n.*

con·sist′, *v.* be composed.

con·sist′en·cy, *n., pl.* **-cies.**
1. firmness. 2. density. 3.
adherence to principles,
behavior, etc. —**con·sist′ent,**
adj. —**con·sist′ent·ly,** *adv.*

con·sis′to·ry, *n., pl.* **-ries.**
church council.

con·sole′, *v.,* **-soled, -soling,**
n. —*v.* 1. cheer in sorrow. —*n.*
(kon′sōl). 2. control panel.

—**con′so·la′tion,** *n.*
—**con·sol′a·ble,** *adj.*
—**con·sol′er,** *n.*

con·sol′i·date′, *v.,* **-dated,**
-dating. 1. make firm. 2. unite.
—**con·sol′i·da′tion,** *n.*

con′som·mé′ (kon′sə mā′), *n.*
clear soup.

con′so·nant, *n.* 1. letter for
sound made by obstruction of
breath. —*adj.* 2. in agreement.
—**con′so·nance,** *n.*

con′sort, *n.* 1. spouse. —*v.*
(kən sôrt′). 2. associate.

con·sor′ti·um (kən sôr′shē
əm, -tē-, -shəm,), *n., pl.* **-tia.** 1.
combination for business
purposes. 2. association.

con·spic′u·ous, *adj.* 1. easily
seen. 2. notable.
—**con·spic′u·ous·ly,** *adv.*
—**con·spic′u·ous·ness,** *n.*

con·spire′, *v.,* **-spired,**
-spiring. plot together.
—**con·spir′a·cy,** *n.*
—**con·spir′a·tor,** *n.*

con′sta·ble, *n.* police officer.

con·stab′u·lar′y, *n., pl.*
-laries. police.

con′stant, *adj.* 1. uniform. 2.
uninterrupted. 3. faithful. —*n.*
4. something unchanging.

—**con′stan•cy,** *n.*

—**con′stant•ly,** *adv.*

con′stel•la′tion, *n.* group of stars.

con′ster•na′tion, *n.* dismay.

con′sti•pate′, *v.,* **-pated, -pating.** cause difficult evacuation of bowels. —**con′sti•pa′tion,** *n.*

con•stit′u•ent, *adj.* **1.** being part; composing. —*n.* **2.** ingredient. **3.** represented voter. —**con•stit′u•en•cy,** *n.*

con′sti•tute′, *v.,* **-tuted, -tuting. 1.** compose. **2.** make.

con′sti•tu′tion, *n.* **1.** make-up. **2.** physical condition. **3.** system of governmental principles. —**con′sti•tu′tion•al,** *adj.*

con•strain′, *v.* **1.** force or oblige. **2.** confine. —**con•strained′,** *adj.* —**con•straint′,** *n.*

con•strict′, *v.* draw together; shrink. —**con•stric′tion,** *n.* —**con•stric′tor,** *n.*

con•struct′, *v.* build or devise. —**con•struc′tion,** *n.*

con•struc′tion•ist, *n.* person who interprets laws in specified manner.

con•struc′tive, *adj.* **1.** of construction. **2.** helpful. —**con•struc′tive•ly,** *adv.*

con•strue′, *v.,* **-strued, -struing.** interpret.

con′sul, *n.* local diplomatic official. —**con′su•lar,** *adj.* —**con′su•late,** *n.*

con•sult′, *v.* **1.** ask advice of. **2.** refer to. **3.** confer. —**con•sult′ant,** *n.* —**con′sul•ta′tion,** *n.*

con•sume′, *v.,* **-sumed, -suming. 1.** use up. **2.** devour. **3.** engross.

con•sum′er, *n.* **1.** one that consumes. **2.** purchaser of goods for personal use.

con•sum′er•ism, *n.* policies protecting consumers.

con′sum•mate′, *v.,* **-mated, -mating,** *adj.* (kən sum′it *for adj.*). complete or perfect. —**con′sum•ma′tion,** *n.*

con•sump′tion, *n.* **1.** act of consuming. **2.** amount consumed. **3.** wasting disease, esp. tuberculosis of lungs. —**con•sump′tive,** *adj., n.*

cont., continued.

con′tact, *n.* **1.** a touching. **2.** association. **3.** business acquaintance. —*v.* 4. put or bring into contact. 5. communicate with.

contact lens, corrective lens put directly on eye.

con•ta′gion, *n.* spread of disease by contact. —**con•ta′gious,** *adj.*

con•tain′, *v.* 1. have within itself. 2. have space for. —**con•tain′er,** *n.*

con•tam′i•nate′, *v.,* -nated, -nating. make impure. —**con•tam′i•na′tion,** *n.*

contd., continued.

con•temn′, *v.* scorn.

con′tem•plate′, *v.,* -plated, -plating. 1. consider. 2. observe. 3. intend. —**con′tem•pla′tion,** *n.* —**con•tem′pla•tive** (kən tem′ plə tiv′), *adj.*

con•tem′po•rar′y, *adj., n., pl.* -raries. —*adj.* 1. Also, **con•tem′po•ra′ne•ous.** of same age or period. —*n.* 2. contemporary person.

con•tempt′, *n.* 1. scorn. 2. disgrace. 3. disrespect of court. —**con•tempt′i•ble,** *adj.* —**con•temp′tu•ous,** *adj.*

con•tend′, *v.* 1. be in struggle. 2. assert. —**con•tend′er,** *n.*

con•tent′, *adj.* 1. Also, **con•tent′ed.** satisfied. 2. willing. —*v.* 3. make content. —*n.* 4. Also, **con•tent′ment.** ease of mind. 5. (kon′tent) (*often pl.*). what is contained. 6. (kon′tent) capacity. —**con•tent′ed•ly,** *adv.*

con•ten′tion, *n.* 1. controversy. 2. assertion. —**con•ten′tious,** *adj.*

con′test, *n.* 1. struggle; competition. —*v.* (kən test′). 2. fight for. 3. dispute. —**con•test′ant,** *n.*

con′text, *n.* surrounding words or circumstances. —**con•tex′tu•al,** *adj.*

con•tig′u•ous, *adj.* 1. touching. 2. near.

con′ti•nent, *n.* 1. major land mass. —*adj.* 2. temperate. —**con′ti•nen′tal,** *adj.* —**con′ti•nence,** *n.*

con•tin′gen•cy, *n., pl.* -cies. chance; event.

con•tin′gent, *adj.* 1. conditional; possible. —*n.* 2. group. 3. contingency.

con•tin′ue, *v.,* -tinued, -tinuing. 1. go or carry on. 2. stay. 3. extend. 4. carry over.

—**con·tin'u·al,** *adj.*
—**con·tin'u·al·ly,** *adv.*
—**con·tin'u·ance,**
con·tin'u·a'tion, *n.*

con'ti·nu'i·ty, *n., pl.* **-ties. 1.** continuous whole. **2.** script.

con·tin'u·ous, *adj.* unbroken.
—**con·tin'u·ous·ly,** *adv.*

con·tin'u·um (-yoo əm), *n., pl.* **-ua.** continuous series.

con·tort', *v.* twist; distort.
—**con·tor'tion,** *n.*

con·tor'tion·ist, *n.* person able to contort their body.

con'tour (-toor), *n.* outline.

contra-, prefix meaning against, *contradict.*

con'tra·band', *n.* goods prohibited from shipment.
—**con'tra·band',** *adj.*

con'tra·cep'tion, *n.* prevention of pregnancy.
—**con'tra·cep'tive,** *adj., n.*

con'tract, *n.* **1.** agreement.
—*v.* (kən trakt'). **2.** shorten. **3.** acquire. **4.** agree.
—**con·trac'tion,** *n.*
—**con·trac'tu·al,** *adj.*

con'trac·tor, *n.* one who supplies work by contract.

con'tra·dict', *v.* deny as true.
—**con'tra·dic'tion,** *n.*
—**con'tra·dic'to·ry,** *adj.*

con·tral'to, *n., pl.* **-tos.** lowest female voice.

con·trap'tion, *n.* gadget.

con'tra·pun'tal, *adj.* of or relating to counterpoint.

con'tra·ry, *adj., n., pl.* **-ries.**
—*adj.* **1.** opposite. **2.** (kən trâr'ē). perverse. —*n.* **3.** something contrary.
—**con'tra·ri·ness,** *n.*
—**con'tra·ri·ly,**
—**con'tra·ri·wise',** *adv.*

con·trast', *v.* **1.** show unlikeness. **2.** compare. —*n.* (kon'trast). **3.** show of unlikeness. **4.** unlike item.

con'tra·vene', *v.,* **-vened, -vening. 1.** oppose. **2.** violate.
—**con'tra·ven'tion,** *n.*

con·trib'ute, *v.,* **-uted, -uting.** give in part; donate.
—**con'tri·bu'tion,** *n.*
—**con·trib'u·tor,** *n.*
—**con·trib'u·to'ry,** *adj.*

con·trite', *adj.* penitent.
—**con·tri'tion,** *n.*

con·trive', *v.,* **-trived, -triving. 1.** plan; devise. **2.** plot.
—**con·triv'ance,** *n.*

con•trol′, *v.,* **-trolled, -trolling,** *n.* —*v.* **1.** have direction over. **2.** restrain. —*n.* **3.** power of controlling. **4.** restraint. **5.** regulating device. —**con•trol′la•ble,** *adj.*

con•trol′ler, *n.* **1.** officer who superintends finances. **2.** regulator.

con′tro•ver′sy, *n., pl.* **-sies.** dispute or debate. —**con′tro•ver′sial,** *adj.* —**con′tro•ver′sial•ly,** *adv.*

con′tro•vert′, *v.* **1.** dispute. —**con′tro•vert′i•ble,** *adj.*

con′tu•ma′cious (-tŏŏ-), *adj.* stubbornly disobedient. —**con′tu•ma•cy,** *n.*

con′tu•me•ly, *n., pl.* **-lies.** contemptuous treatment.

con•tu′sion, *n.* bruise.

co•nun′drum, *n.* riddle involving pun.

con′ur•ba′tion, *n.* continuous mass of urban settlements.

con′va•lesce′, *v.,* **-lesced, -lescing.** recover from illness. —**con′va•les′cence,** *n.* —**con′va•les′cent,** *adj., n.*

con•vec′tion, *n.* transference of heat by movement of heated matter.

con•vene′, *v.,* **-vened, -vening.** assemble.

con•ven′ient, *adj.* handy or favorable. —**con•ven′ience,** *n.* —**con•ven′ient•ly,** *adv.*

con′vent, *n.* community of nuns.

con•ven′tion, *n.* **1.** meeting. **2.** accepted usage. —**con•ven′tion•al,** *adj.*

con•verge′, *v.,* **-verged, -verging.** meet in a point. —**con•ver′gence,** *n.* —**con•ver′gent,** *adj.*

con•ver′sant, *adj.* acquainted.

con′ver•sa′tion, *n.* informal discussion. —**con′ver•sa′tion•al,** *adj.* —**con′ver•sa′tion•al•ist,** *n.*

con•verse′, *v.,* **-versed, -versing,** *adj., n.* —*v.* **1.** talk informally. —*adj., n.* (*adj.* kən vûrs′; *n.* kon′vûrs). **2.** opposite. —**con•verse′ly,** *adv.*

con•vert′, *v.* **1.** change. **2.** persuade to different beliefs. **3.** exchange. —*n.* (kon′vûrt). **4.** converted person. —**con•ver′sion,** *n.* —**con•vert′er,** *n.*

con•vert′i•ble, *adj.* **1.** able to be converted. —*n.* **2.** automobile with folding top.

con•vex′, *adj.* curved outward. —**con•vex′i•ty**, *n.*

con•vey′, *v.* 1. transport. 2. transmit. —**con•vey′or**, —**con•vey′er**, *n.*

con•vey′ance, *n.* 1. act of conveying. 2. vehicle. 3. transfer of property.

con•vict′, *v.* 1. find guilty. —*n.* (kon′vikt). 2. convicted person.

con•vic′tion, *n.* 1. a convicting. 2. firm belief.

con•vince′, *v.*, -vinced, -vincing. cause to believe. —**con•vinc′ing**, *adj.* —**con•vinc′ing•ly**, *adv.*

con•viv′i•al, *adj.* sociable. —**con•viv′i•al′i•ty**, *n.*

con•voke′, *v.*, -voked, -voking. call together. —**con′vo•ca′tion**, *n.*

con′vo•lu′tion, *n.* coil. —**con′vo•lut′ed**, *adj.*

convoy, *v.* 1. escort for protection. —*n.* 2. ship, etc., that convoys. 3. group of ships with convoy.

con•vulse′, *v.*, -vulsed, -vulsing. shake violently. —**con•vul′sion**, *n.* —**con•vul′sive**, *adj.* —**con•vul′sive•ly**, *adv.*

co′ny, *n., pl.* -nies. rabbit fur.

coo, *v.*, **cooed, cooing.** murmur softly. —**coo**, *n.*

cook, *v.* 1. prepare by heating. —*n.* 2. person who cooks. —**cook′book′**, *n.* —**cook′er•y**, *n.*

cook′ie, *n.* small sweet cake. Also, **cook′y.**

cook′out′, *n.* outdoor gathering at which food is cooked and eaten.

cool, *adj.* 1. moderately cold. 2. calm. 3. not enthusiastic. 4. *Slang.* great; excellent. —*v.* 5. make or become cool. —**cool′ant**, *n.* —**cool′er**, *n.* —**cool′ly**, *adv.* —**cool′ness**, *n.*

coo′lie, *n.* Asian laborer.

coop, *n.* 1. cage for fowls. —*v.* 2. keep in coop.

coop′er, *n.* barrel maker.

co•op′er•ate′, *v.*, -ated, -ating. work or act together. Also, **co-op′er•ate′.** —**co•op′er•a′tion**, *n.*

co•op′er•a•tive (-ə tiv), *adj.* 1. involving cooperation. 2. willing to act with others. —*n.* 3. Also, **co-op.** jointly owned apartment house or business.

co-opt' (kō opt'), *v.* **1.** choose as fellow member. **2.** win over into larger group.

co·or'di·nate', *v.,* **-nated, -nating,** *adj., n.* —*v.* (-nāt'). **1.** put in same or due order. **2.** adjust. —*adj., n.* (-nit). **3.** equal. Also, **co-or'di·nate.** —**co·or'di·na'tion,** *n.* —**co·or'di·na'tor,** *n.*

coot, *n.* aquatic bird.

cop, *n. Slang.* police officer.

co'pay', *n.* percentage of a fee, paid by an insured to insurance carrier. Also, **co'pay'ment.**

cope, *v.,* **coped, coping,** *n.* —*v.* **1.** struggle successfully. —*n.* **2.** cloak worn by priests.

cop'i·er, *n.* duplicator.

co'pi'lot, *n.* aircraft pilot second in command.

cop'ing, *n.* top course of wall.

co'pi·ous, *adj.* abundant. —**co'pi·ous·ly,** *adv.*

cop'per, *n.* metallic element.

cop'per·head', *n.* venomous snake.

cop'ra, *n.* dried coconut meat.

copse (kops), *n.* thicket. Also, **cop'pice.**

cop'u·late', *v.,* **-lated, -lating.** have sexual intercourse. —**cop'u·la'tion,** *n.*

cop'y, *n., pl.* **copies,** *v.,* **copied, copying.** —*n.* **1.** reproduction. **2.** material to be reproduced. —*v.* **3.** make copy of. —**cop'y·ist,** *n.*

cop'y·cat', *n.* imitator.

cop'y·right', *n.* **1.** exclusive rights over. —*v.* **2.** secure copyright on. —*adj.* **3.** covered by copyright.

co·quette' (-ket'), *n.* female flirt. —**co·quet'tish,** *adj.*

cor'al, *n.* **1.** substance formed of skeletons of a marine animal. **2.** reddish yellow.

cord, *n.* **1.** small rope. **2.** *Elect.* small insulated cable. **3.** unit of measurement of wood.

cord'less, *adj.* having self-contained power supply.

cor'dial, *adj.* **1.** friendly. —*n.* **2.** liqueur. —**cor·dial'i·ty,** *n.* —**cor'dial·ly,** *adv.*

cor'don, *n.* **1.** honorary ribbon. **2.** line of sentinels.

cor'do·van, *n.* soft leather.

cor'du·roy', *n.* ribbed fabric.

core, *n., v.,* **cored, coring.** —*n.* 1. central part. —*v.* 2. remove core of.

co′ri•an′der, *n.* herb with pungent leaves and seeds.

cork, *n.* 1. bark of an oak tree. 2. stopper of cork. —*v.* 3. stop with a cork.

cork′screw′, *n.* spiral, pointed instrument for pulling corks.

cor′mo•rant, *n.* water bird.

corn, *n.* 1. maize. 2. any edible grain. 3. single seed. 4. horny callus, esp. on toe. —*v.* 5. preserve, esp. in brine.

corn bread, *n.* bread made with cornmeal.

corn′cob′, *n.* core of an ear of corn which holds grains.

cor′ne•a, *n.* transparent part of coat of the eye. —**cor′ne•al,** *adj.*

cor′ner, *n.* 1. place where two lines meet. 2. exclusive control. —*v.* 3. put in corner. 4. gain exclusive control of.

cor′ner•stone′, *n.* 1. stone representing start of construction. 2. starting point.

cor•net′, *n.* wind instrument resembling trumpet.

cor′nice, *n.* horizontal projection at top of a wall.

corn′meal′, *n.* meal made from corn.

corn′starch′, *n.* starchy flour made from corn.

cor′nu•co′pi•a, *n.* horn-shaped container of food, etc.; horn of plenty.

corn′y, *adj.,* **cornier, corniest.** trite or old-fashioned.

co•rol′la, *n.* petals of a flower.

cor′ol•lar′y, *n., pl.* **-laries.** proposition proved in proving another.

co•ro′na, *n., pl.* **-nas, -nae.** circle of light.

cor′o•nar′y, *adj., n., pl.* **-naries.** —*adj.* 1. of arteries supplying heart tissues. —*n.* 2. heart attack.

cor′o•na′tion, *n.* crowning.

cor′o•ner, *n.* official who investigates deaths.

cor′o•net, *n.* small crown.

corp., corporation.

cor′po•ral, *adj.* 1. physical. 2. *Mil.* officer below sergeant.

cor′po•ra′tion, *n.* legally formed association. —**cor′po•rate,** *adj.*

cor•po′re•al, *adj.* tangible.

corps (kōr), *n., pl.* **corps.** 1. military unit. 2. any group.

corpse, *n.* dead body.

cor'pu•lent, *adj.* fat. —**cor'pu•lence**, *n.*

cor'pus (kôr'pəs), *n., pl.* **-pora.** 1. comprehensive collection of writings. 2. body, esp. when dead.

cor'pus•cle (-pə səl), *n.* minute body in blood.

cor•ral', *n., v.*, **-ralled, -ralling.** —*n.* 1. pen for stock. —*v.* 2. keep in corral. 3. capture.

cor•rect', *v.* 1. mark or remove errors. 2. rebuke or punish. 3. counteract. —*adj.* 4. right. —**cor•rec'tion**, *n.* —**cor•rec'tion•al**, *adj.* —**cor•rec'tive**, *adj., n.* —**cor•rect'ly**, *adv.*

cor're•late', *v.*, **-lated, -lating.** bring into mutual relation. —**cor're•la'tion**, *n.* —**cor•rel'a•tive**, *adj., n.*

cor'res•pond', *v.* 1. be similar. 2. communicate by letters. —**cor're•spond'ence**, *n.*

cor're•spond'ent, *n.* 1. writer of letters. 2. reporter in field. —*adj.* 3. corresponding.

cor'ri•dor, *n.* passageway.

cor•rob'o•rate', *v.*, **-rated, -rating.** confirm. —**cor•rob'o•ra'tion**, *n.* —**cor•rob'o•ra'tive**, *adj.*

cor•rode', *v.*, **-roded, -roding.** 1. eat away gradually. 2. be eaten away. —**cor•ro'sion**, *n.* —**cor•ro'sive**, *adj., n.*

cor'ru•gate', *v.*, **-gated, -gating.** bend into folds. —**cor'ru•ga'tion**, *n.*

cor•rupt', *adj.* 1. dishonest. 2. tainted. —*v.* 3. make corrupt. —**cor•rupt'i•ble**, *adj.* —**cor•rup'tion, cor•rupt'ness**, *n.*

cor•sage' (kôr säzh'), *n.* small bouquet to be worn.

cor'sair, *n.* pirate.

cor'set, *n.* undergarment for confining figure.

cor•tege' (kôr tezh'), *n.* procession.

cor'tex, *n.* 1. bark. 2. outer covering of brain or other organ. —**cor'ti•cal**, *adj.*

cor'ti•sone' (-sōn', -zōn'), *n.* hormone used esp. in treating inflammatory diseases.

cor•vette', *n.* small fast vessel.

cos•met'ic, *n.* 1. product used for beautification. —*adj.* 2. of

cosmetics. 3. superficial.
—**cos′me•tol′o•gist,** *n.*
—**cos′me•tol′o•gy,** *n.*

cos′mic, *adj.* 1. of the cosmos. 2. vast.

cos•mol′o•gy, *n.* study of the universe. —**cos′mo•log′i•cal,** *adj.*

cos′mo•pol′i•tan, *adj.* worldly.

cos′mos, *n.* ordered universe.

cost, *n.* 1. price paid. 2. loss or penalty. —*v.* 3. require as payment. —**cost′ly,** *adj.*

cost′-ef•fec′tive, *adj.* producing optimum results.

cost of living, average amount paid for basic necessities.

cos′tume, *n., v.,* **-tumed, -tuming.** —*n.* 1. historical or theatrical dress. —*v.* 2. supply with costume.

co′sy, *adj.,* **-sier, -siest.** cozy.

cot, *n.* light bed.

cote, *n.* shelter for animals.

co′te•rie, *n.* group of social acquaintances.

co•til′lion (-til′yən), *n.* 1. elaborate dance. 2. ball.

cot′tage, *n.* small house.

cottage cheese, soft, mild cheese made from skim milk.

cot′ter, *n.* pin fitting into machinery opening.

cot′ton, *n.* downy plant substance made into fabric.

cot′ton•mouth′, *n.* venomous snake. Also, **water moccasin.**

cot′ton•seed′, *n.* oily seed of cotton plant. yielding an oil (**cottonseed oil**).

cot′ton•wood′, *n.* species of poplar.

couch, *n.* 1. bed. —*v.* 2. express.

couch potato, person who watches much television.

cou′gar (ko͞o′-), *n.* large American feline.

cough, *v.* 1. expel air from lungs suddenly and loudly. —*n.* 2. act of coughing.

cough drop, lozenge for relieving sore throat, etc.

could, *v.* pt. of **can.**

coun′cil, *n.* advisory body. —**coun′cil•man,** *n.* —**coun′cil•wo′man,** *n.fem.* —**coun′ci•lor, coun′cil•lor,** *n.*

coun′sel, *n., v.,* **-seled, -seling.** —*n.* 1. advice. 2. consultation. 3. lawyer. —*v.* 4. advise. —**coun′se•lor, coun′sel•lor,** *n.*

count, *v.* **1.** find total number. **2.** name numbers to. **3.** esteem. **4.** rely. **5.** be noticed. —*n.* **6.** a counting. **7.** total number. **8.** item in indictment. **9.** European nobleman.

count′down′, *n.* backward counting in time units to scheduled event.

coun′te·nance, *n., v.,* **-nanced, -nancing.** —*n.* **1.** appearance; face. **2.** encouragement. —*v.* **3.** tolerate.

count′er, *n.* **1.** table or display case. **2.** one that counts. **3.** anything opposite. —*v.* **4.** oppose. **5.** return (blow). —*adv., adj.* **6.** contrary.

counter-, prefix indicating: **1.** against, as *counterintelligence.* **2.** in response to, as *counterattack.* **3.** opposite, as *counterclockwise.* **4.** complementary, as *counterbalance.*

coun′ter·act′, *v.* act against. —**coun′ter·ac′tion,** *n.*

coun′ter·at·tack′, *n., v.* attack in response.

coun′ter·bal′ance, *n., v.,* **-anced, -ancing.** —*n.* **1.** anything that balances another. —*v.* (koun′tər bal′əns). **2.** offset.

coun′ter·clock′wise′, *adv., adj.* opposite to direction of turning clock hands.

coun′ter·cul′ture, *n.* culture opposed to prevailing culture.

coun′ter·feit, *adj.* **1.** fraudulently imitative. —*n.* **2.** fraudulent imitation. —*v.* **3.** make counterfeits. **4.** feign. —**coun′ter·feit′er,** *n.*

coun′ter·in·tel′li·gence, *n.* thwarting of espionage of a foreign power.

coun′ter·mand′, *v.* revoke (command).

coun′ter·part′, *n.* match or complement.

coun′ter·point′, *n.* combining of melodies.

coun′ter·pro·duc′tive, *adj.* giving contrary results.

coun′ter·sign′, *n.* **1.** secret signal. —*v.* **2.** sign to confirm another signature.

count′ess, *n.* woman spouse or equal of count or earl.

count′less, *adj.* innumerable.

coun′try, *n., pl.* **-tries. 1.** region. **2.** nation. **3.** rural districts. —**coun′try•man,** *n.* —**coun′try•wom′an,** *n.fem.* —**coun′try•side′,** *n.*

coun′ty, *n., pl.* **-ties.** political unit within state.

coup (ko͞o), *n., pl.* **coups.** daring and successful stroke.

coup d'é•tat′ (-dā tä′), *pl.* **coups d'état** (-dā täz′, -tä′). overthrow of a government.

coupe (ko͞op), *n.* small, two-door car. Also, **cou•pé′** (ko͞o pā′).

cou′ple, *n., v.,* **-pled, -pling.** —*n.* **1.** pair. —*v.* **2.** unite. —**cou′pler,** *n.* —**cou′pling,** *n.*

cou′plet, *n.* pair of rhyming lines.

cou′pon (ko͞o′pon, kyo͞o′-), *n.* certificate entitling holder to a gift or discount.

cour′age, *n.* bravery. —**cou•ra′geous,** *adj.* —**cou•ra′geous•ly,** *adv.*

cour′i•er, *n.* messenger.

course, *n., v.,* **coursed, coursing.** —*n.* **1.** continuous passage. **2.** route. **3.** manner. **4.** series of studies. **5.** one part of meal. —*v.* **6.** run.

cours′er, *n.* swift horse.

court, *n.* **1.** enclosed space. **2.** level area for games. **3.** palace. **4.** assembly held by sovereign. **5.** attention. **6.** place where justice is dealt. **7.** judge or judges. —*v.* **8.** woo. —**court′house,** *n.* —**court′room′,** *n.* —**court′ship,** *n.* —**court′yard′,** *n.*

cour′te•san (kôr′tə zən, kûr′-), *n.* prostitute with noble or wealthy clientele.

cour′te•sy, *n., pl.* **-sies. 1.** good manners. **2.** indulgence. —**cour′te•ous,** *adj.* —**cour′te•ous•ly,** *adv.*

cour′ti•er, *n.* person in attendance at court.

court′ly, *adj.* elegant.

court′-mar′tial, *n., pl.* **courts-martial,** *v.,* **-tialed, -tialing.** —*n.* **1.** military court. —*v.* **2.** try by court-martial.

cous′in, *n.* child of uncle or aunt.

cou•tu•ri•er (ko͞o to͞oy′ē ər, -ē ā′), *n.* designer of custom-made clothes for women.

cove, *n.* recess in shoreline.

cov′en (kuv′ən, kō′vən), *n.* assembly of witches.

cov′e•nant, *n.* oath or pact.

cov′er, *v.* 1. put something over. 2. include. 3. have in range. 4. meet or offset. —*n.* 5. thing that covers. 6. concealment. —**cov′er•ing,** *n.*

cov′er•age, *n.* 1. protection by insurance. 2. awareness and reporting of news.

cov′er•let, *n.* quilt.

cov′ert (kō′vərt), *adj.* secret or covered. —**cov′ert•ly,** *adv.*

cov′er-up′, *n.* concealing of illegal activity, a blunder, etc.

cov′et, *v.* desire greatly or wrongfully. —**cov′et•ous,** *adj.*

cov′ey, *n.* small flock.

cow, *n.* 1. female of bovine or other large animal. —*v.* 2. intimidate.

cow′ard, *n.* person who lacks courage. —**cow′ard•ice,** *n.* —**cow′ard•ly,** *adj., adv.*

cow′boy′, *n.* cattle herder. Also, **cow′hand′; cow′girl′,** *n. fem.*

cow′er, *v.* crouch in fear.

cowl, *n.* 1. hooded garment. 2. hoodlike part.

cow′lick′, *n.* tuft of hair growing in a different direction.

cow′slip′, *n.* plant with yellow flowers.

cox′comb′, *n.* dandy.

cox′swain (kok′sən), *n.* person who steers boat or racing shell. Also, **cox.**

coy, *adj.* affectedly shy. —**coy′ly,** *adv.* —**coy′ness,** *n.*

coy•o′te (kī ō′tē), *n.* animal related to wolf.

coz′en, *v.* cheat or deceive.

co′zy, *adj.,* **-zier, -ziest.** comfortable; snug. —**co′zi•ly,** *adv.* —**co′zi•ness,** *n.*

CPA, certified public accountant.

CPI, consumer price index.

CPR, cardiopulmonary resuscitation.

CPU, central processing unit, the key component of a computer system.

crab, *n.* crustacean with broad flat body.

crab apple, small tart apple.

crab′by, *adj.,* **-bier, biest.** grouchy. —**crab′bi•ness,** *n.*

crack, *v.* 1. make sharp sound. 2. break without separating. —*n.* 3. sharp sound. 4. break without separation. 5. smokable form of cocaine.

crack′down′, *n.* stern enforcement of regulations.

crack′er, *n.* **1.** crisp biscuit. **2.** firecracker. **3.** *Disparaging and Offensive.* yokel.

crack′le, *v.,* **-led, -ling,** *n.* —*v.* **1.** crack repeatedly. —*n.* **2.** crackling sound.

crack′pot′, *n.* person with irrational theories.

crack′up′, *n.* breakdown.

cra′dle, *n., v.,* **-dled, -dling.** —*n.* **1.** bed on rockers for baby. —*v.* **2.** place in a cradle. **3.** hold protectively.

craft, *n.* **1.** skill; skilled trade. **2.** cunning. **3.** vessels or aircraft. —**crafts′man**, *n.* —**crafts′wom•an**, *n.fem.* —**crafts′man•ship′**, *n.*

craft′y, *adj.,* **craftier, craftiest.** sly. —**craft′i•ly**, *adv.*

crag, *n.* steep rough rock. —**crag′gy**, *adj.*

cram, *v.,* **crammed, cramming.** **1.** fill tightly. **2.** study hard.

cramp, *n.* **1.** involuntary muscular contraction. —*v.* **2.** affect with a cramp. **3.** hamper.

cramped, *adj.* **1.** confined or limited. **2.** small and crowded.

cran′ber′ry, *n., pl.* **-ries.** red acid edible berry.

crane, *n.* **1.** tall wading bird. **2.** lifting device or machine.

cra′ni•um, *n., pl.* **-niums, -nia.** skull. —**cra′ni•al**, *adj.*

crank, *n.* **1.** right-angled arm for communicating motion. **2.** *Informal.* grouchy person. —*v.* **3.** turn with a crank.

crank′y, *adj.,* **crankier, crankiest.** ill-tempered. —**crank′i•ness**, *n.*

cran′ny, *n., pl.* **-nies.** cleft.

crap, *n. Slang.* **1.** worthless material. **2.** false or meaningless statements.

crape (krāp), *n.* crepe (defs. 1, 2).

crap′pie, *n.* small fish.

craps, *n.* dice game.

crash, *v.* **1.** strike noisily. **2.** land or fall with damage. —*n.* **3.** noise or act of crashing. **4.** collapse. **5.** act or instance of crashing. **6.** rough fabric.

crass, *adj.* crude. —**crass′ly**, *adv.* —**crass′ness**, *n.*

crate, *n., v.,* **crated, crating.** —*n.* **1.** box or frame for packing. —*v.* **2.** put in crate.

cra′ter, *n.* cup-shaped hole.

cra•vat′, *n.* necktie.

crave, *v.*, **craved, craving.** yearn or beg for.

cra′ven, *adj.* 1. cowardly. —*n.* 2. coward.

crav′ing, *n.* intense yearning.

craw, *n.* crop of bird.

crawl, *v.* 1. move slowly, as on stomach. —*n.* 2. act of crawling. 3. swimming stroke. —**crawl′er**, *n.*

cray′fish′, *n.* crustacean resembling a lobster. Also, **craw′fish′.**

cray′on, *n.* stick of colored wax or chalk for drawing.

craze, *v.*, **crazed, crazing,** *n.* —*v.* 1. make insane. 2. mark with fine cracks, as glaze. —*n.* 3. mania.

cra′zy, *adj.*, **-zier, -ziest.** insane. —**cra′zi•ly**, *adv.* —**cra′zi•ness**, *n.*

creak, *v.* 1. squeak sharply. —*n.* 2. creaking sound. —**creak′y**, *adj.*

cream, *n.* 1. fatty part of milk. 2. best part of anything. —*v.* 3. make with cream. 4. work to a creamy state. 5. *Informal.* defeat utterly. —**cream′er**, *n.* —**cream′y**, *adj.*

cream′er•y, *n., pl.* **-eries.** producer of dairy goods.

crease, *n., v.*, **creased, creasing.** —*n.* 1. fold mark. —*v.* 2. make creases in.

cre•ate′, *v.*, **-ated, -ating.** cause to exist. —**cre•a′tion**, *n.* —**cre•a′tive**, *adj.* —**cre•a′tor**, *n.*

crea′ture, *n.* 1. animate being. 2. anything created.

cre′dence, *n.* belief.

cre•den′tial, *n.* (*usually pl.*) verifying document.

cre•den′za, *n.* sideboard, esp. one without legs.

cred′i•ble, *adj.* believable. —**cred′i•bil′i•ty**, *n.* —**cred′i•bly**, *adv.*

cred′it, *n.* 1. belief. 2. trustworthiness. 3. honor. 4. time allowed for payment. —*v.* 5. believe. 6. ascribe to.

cred′it•a•ble, *adj.* worthy. —**cred′it•a•bly**, *adv.*

credit card, card entitling holder to charge purchases.

cred′i•tor, *n.* person owed.

credit union, cooperative group that makes loans to its members at low interest rates.

cred'u·lous, *adj.* overwilling to believe. —**cre·du'li·ty,** *n.*

creed, *n.* formula of belief. Also, **cre'do** (krē'dō).

creek (krēk, krik), *n.* brook.

creel, *n.* wickerwork basket for carrying fish.

creep, *v.,* **crept** or **creeped, creeping,** *n.* —*v.* **1.** move stealthily; crawl. —*n.* **2.** *Slang.* disagreeable person.

creep'y, *adj.,* **creepier, creepiest.** causing uneasiness.

cre'mate, *v.,* -mated, -mating. burn (corpse) to ashes. —**cre·ma'tion,** *n.* —**cre'ma·to'ry,** *adj., n.*

Cre'ole, *n.* **1.** one of French and Spanish blood born in Louisiana. **2.** (*l.c.*) pidgin that has become native language of a group.

cre'o·sote', *n.* oily liquid from tar.

crepe (krāp), *n.* **1.** light crinkled fabric. **2.** Also, **crepe paper.** thin, wrinkled paper used for decorating. **3.** thin, light pancake.

cre·scen'do (krə shen'dō), *n., pl.* -dos. *Music.* gradual increase in loudness.

cres'cent (kres'ənt), *n.* **1.** moon in its first or last quarter. **2.** object having this shape.

cress, *n.* plant with pungent leaves.

crest, *n.* **1.** tuft or plume. **2.** figure above coat of arms.

crest'fal'len, *adj.* abruptly discouraged or depressed.

cre'tin (krēt'n), *n.* **1.** person affected with cretinism, congenital thyroid deficiency. **2.** obtuse or boorish person.

cre·tonne' (kri ton'), *n.* heavily printed cotton.

cre·vasse', *n.* fissure, esp. in glacier.

crev'ice, *n.* fissure.

crew, *n.* **1.** group of persons working together, as on ship. —*v.* **2.** form crew of.

crew cut, haircut in which the hair is cut close to the head.

crew'el, *n.* worsted yarn for embroidery and edging.

crib, *n., v.,* **cribbed, cribbing.** —*n.* **1.** child's bed. **2.** rack or bin. —*v.* **3.** put in a crib. **4.** plagiarize.

crib'bage, *n.* card game using score-board with pegs.

crick, *n.* muscular spasm.

crick'et, *n.* **1.** leaping, noisy insect. **2.** British open-air ball game with bats.

cri'er, *n.* one who announces.

crime, *n.* **1.** unlawful act. **2.** sin. —**crim'i•nal,** *adj., n.* —**crim'i•nal•ly,** *adv.* —**crim'i•nol'o•gist,** *n.* —**crim'i•nol'o•gy,** *n.*

crimp, *v.* **1.** make wavy. —*n.* **2.** crimped form.

crim'son, *n., adj.* deep red.

cringe, *v.,* **cringed, cringing.** shrink in fear or servility.

crin'kle, *v.,* **-kled, -kling,** *n.* wrinkle. —**crin'kly,** *adj.*

crin'o•line (krin'l in), *n.* **1.** stiff, coarse fabric used as lining. **2.** petticoat.

crip'ple, *n., v.,* **-pled, -pling.** —*n.* **1.** *Sometimes Offensive.* lame person. —*v.* **2.** make lame.

cri'sis, *n., pl.* **-ses.** decisive stage or point.

crisp, *adj.* **1.** brittle. **2.** fresh. **3.** brisk. **4.** curly. —*v.* **5.** make or become crisp. —**crisp'ly,** *adv.* —**crisp'ness,** *n.*

criss'cross', *adj.* **1.** marked with crossed lines. —*n.* **2.** crisscross pattern. —*v.* **3.** mark with crossed lines.

cri•te'ri•on, *n., pl.* **-teria.** standard for judgment.

crit'ic, *n.* **1.** skilled judge. **2.** faultfinding person.

crit'i•cal, *adj.* **1.** severe in judgment. **2.** involving criticism. **3.** crucial. —**crit'i•cal•ly,** *adv.*

crit'i•cize', *v.,* **-cized, -cizing.** **1.** discuss as a critic. **2.** find fault with. —**crit'i•cism',** *n.*

cri•tique' (-tēk'), *n.* critical article.

crit'ter, *n. Dial.* creature.

croak, *v.* utter a hoarse cry.

cro•chet' (krō shā'), *v.* form thread into designs with hooked needle.

crock, *n.* earthen jar. —**crock'er•y,** *n.*

croc'o•dile', *n.* large aquatic legged reptile with long, powerful jaws and tail.

cro'cus, *n.* small bulbous plant blooming in early spring.

crois•sant' (kʀwä säɴ'; krə sänt'), *n.* crescent-shaped roll of flaky pastry.

crone, *n.* witchlike old woman.

cro'ny, *n., pl.* **-nies.** close friend.

crook, *n.* 1. tight curve. 2. bend. 3. *Informal.* dishonest person. —*v.* 4. bend. —**crook'ed,** *adj.*

croon, *v.* 1. sing softly. —*n.* 2. such singing. —**croon'er,** *n.*

crop, *n., v.,* **cropped, cropping.** —*n.* 1. produce from the soil. 2. short whip. 3. pouch in gullet of bird. —*v.* 4. remove ends. 5. cut short. 6. reap. 7. **crop up,** show. —**crop'per,** *n.*

cro•quet' (-kā'), *n.* game with wooden balls and mallets.

cro•quette', *n.* fried or baked piece of chopped food.

cro'sier (krō'zhər), *n.* staff of bishop.

cross, *n.* 1. structure whose basic form has an upright with transverse piece. 2. emblem of Christianity. 3. figure resembling cross. 4. trouble. 5. mixture of breeds. —*v.* 6. make sign of cross over. 7. put, lie, or pass across. 8. oppose or frustrate. 9. mark (out). 10. mix (breeds). —*adj.* 11. transverse. 12.

ill-humored. —**cross'ly,** *adv.* —**cross'ness,** *n.*

cross'bow', *n.* weapon consisting of a bow fixed on a stock like that of a rifle.

cross' breed', *v.,* **-bred, -breeding,** *n.* —*v.* 1. cross varieties of in breeding; hybridize. —*n.* hybrid.

cross'-coun'try, *adj.* 1. proceeding off-road rather than on a road or track. 2. from one end of a country to the other. —*n.* 3. sport of cross-country racing.

cross'-ex•am'ine, *v.,* **-ined, -ining.** examine closely, as opposing witness. Also, **cross'-ques'tion.** —**cross'-ex•am'in•a'tion,** *n.*

cross'-eye', *n.* visual disorder. —**cross'-eyed',** *adj.*

cross reference, reference to another part of book.

cross'road', *n.* 1. road that crosses another. 2. (*pl.*) **a.** intersection. **b.** decisive point.

cross section, 1. section made by cutting across something. 2. picture representing such a section. 3. representative sample of a whole.

cross′word puz′zle, puzzle in which words determined from numbered clues are fitted into pattern of horizontal and vertical squares.

crotch, *n.* forked part.

crotch′et (kroch′it), *n.* **1.** small hook. **2.** whim.

crotch′et•y, *adj.* grumpy. —**crotch′et•i•ness,** *n.*

crouch, *v.* **1.** stoop or bend low. —*n.* **2.** act of crouching.

croup (kroōp), *n.* inflammation of throat.

crou′pi•er (kroō′pē ər, -pē ā′), *n.* attendant who handles bets and money at gambling table.

crou′ton (kroō′ton), *n.* small cube of toasted bread.

crow, *v.* **1.** cry, as cock. **2.** boast. —*n.* **3.** cry of cock. **4.** black, harsh-voiced bird. **5.** (*cap.*) member of an American Indian people.

crow′bar′, *n.* iron bar for prying.

crowd, *n.* **1.** large group of people. —*v.* **2.** throng. **3.** press or push. —**crowd′ed,** *adj.*

crown, *n.* **1.** cover for royal head. **2.** power of a sovereign. **3.** top. —*v.* **4.** put crown on. **5.** reward.

crow′s′-foot′, *n., pl.* **-feet.** (*usually pl.*) tiny wrinkle at outer corner of the eye.

CRT, 1. cathode-ray tube. **2.** computer monitor that includes cathode-ray tube.

cru′cial, *adj.* **1.** decisive. **2.** severe. —**cru′cial•ly,** *adv.*

cru′ci•ble, *n.* vessel for melting metals, etc.

cru′ci•fix, *n.* cross with figure of Jesus crucified.

cru′ci•fy′, *v.,* **-fied, -fying.** put to death on cross. —**cru′ci•fix′ion,** *n.*

crude, *adj.,* **cruder, crudest,** *n.* —*adj.* **1.** unrefined. **2.** unfinished. —*n.* **3.** *Informal.* unrefined petroleum. —**crude′ly,** *adv.* —**crude′ness, cru′di•ty,** *n.*

cru′di•tés′ (kroō′ di tā′), *n.pl.* cut-up raw vegetables served with a dip.

cru′el, *adj.* **1.** disposed to inflict pain. **2.** causing pain. —**cru′el•ly,** *adv.* —**cru′el•ness, cru′el•ty,** *n.*

cru′et, *n.* stoppered bottle for vinegar, etc.

cruise, *v.,* **cruised, cruising,** *n.* —*v.* **1.** sail or fly at moderate

speed. 2. travel for pleasure.
—*n.* 3. cruising trip.

cruis′er, *n.* 1. kind of warship.
2. small pleasure boat.

crul′ler, *n.* doughnutlike cake.

crumb, *n.* small bit of bread.

crum′ble, *v.,* **-bled, -bling.**
break into fragments; decay.

crum′my, *adj.,* **-mier, -miest.**
Informal. 1. shabby. 2. cheap.
3. miserable.

crum′ple, *v.,* **-pled, -pling,** *n.*
wrinkle; rumple.

crunch, *v.* 1. chew or crush
noisily. —*n.* 2. *Informal.*
reduction of resources.

cru•sade′, *n., v.,* **-saded,
-sading.** —*n.* 1. Christian
expedition to Holy Land. 2.
campaign for good cause. —*v.*
3. engage in crusade.
—**cru•sad′er**, *n.*

crush, *v.* 1. bruise or break by
pressing. 2. subdue. —*n.* 3.
dense crowd. 4. infatuation.

crust, *n.* 1. hard outer part. 2.
Informal. impertinence. —*v.* 3.
cover with crust. —**crust′i•ly,**
adv. —**crust′i•ness,** *n.*
—**crust′y,** *adj.*

crus•ta′cean (-shən), *n.* sea
animal having hard shell. —
crus•ta′cean, *adj.*

crutch, *n.* 1. staff fitting under
the armpit for support in
walking. 2. *Informal.*
temporary aid or expedient.

crux, *n., pl.* **cruxes, cruces.**
vital point.

cry, *v.,* **cried, crying,** *n., pl.*
cries. —*v.* 1. make sounds of
grief, etc. 2. utter
characteristic sounds. 3.
shout. —*n.* 4. act of crying.

cry′o•gen′ics (krī′ə jen′iks),
n. study or use of extremely
low temperatures.
—**cry′o•gen′ic,** *adj.*

crypt, *n.* underground
chamber.

cryp′tic, *adj.* mysterious.
—**cryp′ti•cal•ly,** *adv.*

cryp•tog′ra•phy (krip tog′rə
fē), *n.* study or use of code
and cipher systems.
—**cryp•tog′ra•pher,** *n.*

crys′tal, *n.* 1. clear transparent
mineral. 2. body with
symmetrical plane faces. 3.
fine glass. 4. cover of watch
face. —**crys′tal•line,** *adj.*

crys′tal•lize′, *v.,* **-lized,
-lizing.** 1. form or cause to
form into crystals. 2. assume
or cause to assume definite
form. —**crys′tal•li•za′tion,** *n.*

C′-sec′tion, *n.* Cesarean.

CST, Central Standard Time.

CT, Connecticut.

Ct., 1. Connecticut. 2. Count.

ct., 1. carat. 2. cent. 3. court.

cu., cubic.

cub, *n.* young fox, bear, etc.

cub′by•hole′, *n.* small enclosed space.

cube, *n., v.,* **cubed, cubing.** —*n.* 1. solid bounded by six squares. 2. *Math.* third power of a quantity. —*v.* 3. make into cubes. 4. *Math.* raise to third power. —**cu′bic, cu′bi•cal,** *adj.*

cu′bi•cle, *n.* small room.

cub′ism, *n.* artistic style marked by reduction of natural forms to geometric shapes. —**cub′ist,** *adj., n.*

cub scout, (*sometimes caps.*) boy scout aged 8 to 10.

cuck′old, *n.* husband of unfaithful wife.

cuck′oo, *n.* small bird.

cu′cum•ber, *n.* green-skinned cylindrical fruit.

cud, *n.* food that cow returns to mouth for further chewing.

cud′dle, *v.,* **-dled, -dling.** hold tenderly. —**cud′dly,** *adj.*

cudg′el, *n., v.,* **-eled, -eling.** —*n.* 1. short thick stick. —*v.* 2. beat with cudgel.

cue, *n.* 1. (esp. on stage) something that signals speech or action. 2. rod for billiards.

cuff, *n.* 1. fold or band at end of sleeve or trouser leg. 2. slap. —*v.* 3. slap.

cui•sine′ (kwi zēn′), *n.* cookery.

cu′li•nar′y (kyōō′-), *adj.* of cooking.

cull, *v.* select best parts of.

cul′mi•nate′, *v.,* **-nated, -nating.** reach highest point. —**cul′mi•na′tion,** *n.*

cul′pa•ble, *adj.* deserving blame. —**cul′pa•bil′i•ty,** *n.*

cul′prit, *n.* person arraigned for or guilty of an offense.

cult, *n.* religious sect or system.

cul′ti•vate′, *v.,* **-vated, -vating.** 1. prepare and care for (land). 2. develop possibilities of. —**cul′ti•va′tion,** *n.* —**cul′ti•va′tor,** *n.*

cul′ti•vat′ed, *adj.* educated and well-mannered.

cul′ture, *n.* 1. raising of plants or animals. 2. development of mind. 3. state or form of civilization. —**cul′tur•al,** *adj.* —**cul′tur•al•ly,** *adv.*

culture shock, distress of person exposed to new culture.

cul′vert, *n.* channel under road, etc.

cum′ber•some, *adj.* clumsy.

cu′mu•la•tive, *adj.* increasing by accumulation.

cu′mu•lus (kyoo′myə ləs), *n.,* *pl.* **-li.** cloud in form of rounded heaps on flat base. —**cu′mu•lous,** *adj.*

cu•ne′i•form′ (kyoo nē′ə fôrm′), *adj.* 1. composed of wedge-shaped elements, as some ancient writing. —*n.* 2. cuneiform writing.

cun′ning, *n.* 1. skill. 2. guile. —*adj.* 3. clever. 4. sly.

cup, *n., v.,* **cupped, cupping.** —*n.* 1. small open drinking vessel. —*v.* shape like a cup.

cup′board (kub′ərd), *n.* closet for dishes, etc.

Cu′pid (kyoo′pid), *n.* Roman god of carnal love.

cu•pid′i•ty, *n.* greed.

cu′po•la (kyoo′-), *n.* rounded dome.

cu′prous, *adj.* containing copper.

cur, *n.* worthless dog.

cu′rate, *n.* clergyman assisting rector or vicar.

cu•ra′tor, *n.* person in charge of museum collection.

curb, *n.* 1. strap for restraining horse. 2. restraint. 3. edge of sidewalk. —*v.* 4. control.

curd, *n.* 1. substance formed when milk coagulates. —*v.* 2. change into curd.

cur′dle, *v.,* **-dled, -dling.** congeal.

cure, *n., v.,* **cured, curing.** —*n.* 1. treatment of disease. 2. restoration to health. —*v.* 3. restore to health. 4. prepare for use. —**cur′a•ble,** *adj.* —**cur′a•tive,** *adj., n.*

cure′-all′, *n.* panacea.

cur′few, *n.* time to leave streets.

cu′ri•o′, *n., pl.* **-rios.** odd valuable article.

cu′ri•os′i•ty, *n., pl.* **-ties.** 1. desire to know. 2. odd thing.

cu′ri•ous, *adj.* **1.** wanting to know. **2.** prying. **3.** strange. —**cu′ri•ous•ly,** *adv.*

curl, *v.* **1.** form in ringlets. **2.** coil. —*n.* **3.** ringlet. —**curl′er,** *n.* —**curl′y,** *adj.*

cur′lew, *n.* shore bird.

curl′i•cue′, *n.* fancy curl.

cur•mudg′eon (kər muj′ən), *n.* difficult person.

cur′rant, *n.* **1.** small seedless raisin. **2.** edible acid berry.

cur′ren•cy, *n., pl.* **-cies. 1.** money in use in a country. **2.** prevalence. **3.** circulation.

cur′rent, *adj.* **1.** present. **2.** generally known or believed. —*n.* **3.** stream; flow. **4.** water, air, etc., moving in one direction. **5.** movement of electricity. —**cur′rent•ly,** *adv.*

cur•ric′u•lum, *n., pl.* **-lums, -la.** course of study.

cur′ry, *n., pl.* **-ries,** *v.,* **-ried, -rying.** —*n.* **1.** East Indian hot sauce or powder **(curry powder).** —*v.* **2.** prepare with curry. **3.** rub and comb (horse, etc.). **4.** seek (favor) with servility. —**cur′ry•comb′,** *n.*

curse, *n., v.,* **cursed** or **curst, cursing.** —*n.* **1.** wish that evil befall another. **2.** evil so invoked. **3.** profane oath. **4.** cause of evil. —*v.* **5.** wish evil upon. **6.** swear. **7.** afflict. —**curs′ed,** *adj.*

cur′sive, *adj.* (of handwriting) in flowing strokes with letters joined together.

cur′sor (kûr′sər), *n.* symbol on computer screen indicating where data may be input.

cur′so•ry, *adj.* superficial. —**cur′so•ri•ly,** *adv.*

curt, *adj.* brief, esp. rudely so. —**curt′ly,** *adv.*

cur•tail′, *v.* cut short. —**cur•tail′ment,** *n.*

cur′tain, *n.* **1.** piece of fabric hung to adorn, conceal, etc. —*v.* **2.** cover with curtains.

curt′sy, *n., pl.* **-sies,** *v.,* **-sied, -sying.** —*n.* **1.** bow by women. —*v.* **2.** make curtsy.

cur′va•ture, *n.* **1.** a curving. **2.** degree of curving.

curve, *n., v.,* **curved, curving.** —*n.* **1.** bending line. —*v.* **2.** bend or move in a curve.

cush′ion, *n.* **1.** soft bag of feathers, air, etc. —*v.* **2.** lessen the effects of.

cush′y (koŏsh′ē), *adj. Informal.* **1.** easy and

profitable. **2.** soft and comfortable.

cusp, *n.* pointed end.

cus′pid, *n.* canine tooth.

cus′pi•dor′, *n.* spittoon.

cuss, *v. Informal.* curse.

cus′tard, *n.* cooked dish of eggs and milk.

cus′to•dy, *n., pl.* **-dies. 1.** keeping. **2.** imprisonment. —**cus•to′di•al,** *adj.* —**cus•to′di•an,** *n.*

cus′tom, *n.* **1.** usual practice. **2.** set of such practices. **3.** (*pl.*) **a.** duties on imports. **b.** agency collecting these. —*adj.* **4.** made for the individual. —**cus′tom•ar′y,** *adj.* —**cus′tom•ar′i•ly,** *adv.*

cus′tom•er, *n.* **1.** purchaser or prospective purchaser. **2.** *Informal.* person.

cus′tom•ize′, *v.,* **-ized, -iz•ing.** make to individual specifications. —**cus′tom•i•za′tion,** *n.*

cut, *v.,* **cut, cutting,** *n.* —*v.* **1.** sever, as with knife. **2.** wound feelings of. **3.** reap or trim. **4.** shorten by omitting part. **5.** dilute. **6.** move or cross. **7.** be absent from. —*n.* **8.** a cutting.

9. result of cutting. **10.** straight passage. **11.** engraved plate for printing.

cu•ta′ne•ous, *adj.* of the skin.

cut′back′, *n.* reduction.

cute, *adj.,* **cuter, cutest.** *Informal.* pretty or pleasing.

cu′ti•cle, *n.* epidermis, esp. around nails.

cut′lass, *n.* short curved sword.

cut′ler•y, *n.* knives collectively.

cut′let, *n.* slice of meat for frying or broiling.

cut′off′, *n.* **1.** point beyond which something is no longer possible. **2.** road that leaves another to make a shortcut.

cut′-rate′, *adj.* offered at reduced prices.

cut′ter, *n.* **1.** one that cuts. **2.** small fast vessel. **3.** sleigh.

cut′throat′, *n.* **1.** murderer. —*adj.* **2.** ruthless.

cut′tle•fish′, *n., pl.* **-fish, -fish•es.** mollusk with ten arms and hard internal shell (**cut′tle•bone′**).

cy′a•nide′ (sī′ə nīd′), *n.* salt of hydrocyanic acid.

cyber-, prefix meaning computer as *cyberspace*.

cy'ber•net'ics (sī'bər net'iks), *n.* study of organic control and communications systems and mechanical or electronic systems analogous to them, such as robots.

cy'ber•space', *n.* 1. realm of electronic communication. 2. virtual reality.

cy'cla•mate', *n.* artificial sweetening agent.

cy'cle, *n., v.,* **-cled, -cling.** —*n.* 1. recurring time or process. 2. complete set. 3. bicycle, etc. —*v.* 4. ride bicycle. —**cy'clic, cyc'li•cal,** *adj.* —**cy'clist,** *n.*

cy'clone, *n.* 1. rotary weather system. 2. tornado. —**cy•clon'ic,** *adj.*

cy'clo•pe'di•a, *n.* encyclopedia.

cy'clo•tron', *n.* device used in splitting atoms.

cyl'in•der, *n.* 1. round elongated solid with ends that are equal parallel circles. 2. part or opening in this form. —**cy•lin'dri•cal,** *adj.*

cym'bal, *n.* brass plate used in orchestras.

cyg'net, *n.* young swan.

cyn'ic, *n.* person who doubts or lacks goodness of motive. —**cyn'i•cal,** *adj.* —**cyn'i•cism,** *n.*

cy'no•sure' (sī'nə-), *n.* object that attracts by its brilliance.

cy'press, *n.* evergreen tree of pine family.

cyst (sist), *n.* sac containing morbid matter formed in live tissue. —**cys'tic,** *adj.*

cys'tic fi•bro'sis (sis'tik fī brō'sis), hereditary disease marked by breathing difficulties and growth of excess fibrous tissue.

czar (zär), *n.* former emperor of Russia. Also, **tsar.**

cza•ri'na (zä rē' nə), *n.* wife of a czar.

Czech (chek), *n.* native or language of Czech Republic.

D, d, *n.* fourth letter of English alphabet.

d., 1. date. 2. deceased. 3. degree. 4. diameter. 5. dose.

D.A., District Attorney.

dab, *v.,* **dabbed, dabbing.** 1. apply lightly. —*n.* 2. small moist lump. —**dab′ber,** *n.*

dab′ble, *v.,* **-bled, -bling.** 1. splatter. 2. play in water. 3. be interested superficially. —**dab′bler,** *n.*

dachs′hund′ (däks′hŏond′), *n.* long, short-legged dog.

Da′•cron, *n. Trademark.* strong synthetic fabric.

dad, *n. Informal.* father.

dad′dy, *n., pl.* **-dies.** *Informal.* father.

dad′dy-long′legs′, *n., pl.* **-legs.** spiderlike arachnid with long, slender legs. Also, **dad′dy long′legs′.**

daf′fo•dil, *n.* plant with yellow flowers.

daft, *adj.* 1. insane. 2. foolish. Also, **daf′fy.** —**daft′ly,** *adv.*

dag′ger, *n.* short knife.

dahl′ia (dal′yə). showy cultivated flowering plant.

D

dai′ly, *adj.* 1. of or occurring each day. —*n.* 2. daily newspaper.

dain′ty, *adj.,* **-tier, -tiest,** *n., pl.* **-ties.** —*adj.* 1. delicate. —*n.* 2. delicacy. —**dain′ti•ly,** *adv.* —**dain′ti•ness,** *n.*

dai′qui•ri (dak′ə rē, dīkə-), *n., pl.* **-ris.** cocktail of rum, lime juice, sugar, and fruit.

dair′y, *n., pl.* **dairies.** place for making or selling milk, butter, etc. —**dair′y•man,** *n.* —**dair′y•wom•an,** *n. fem.*

da′is (dā′is), *n.* raised platform.

dai′sy, *n., pl.* **-sies.** yellow-and-white flower.

Da•ko′ta, *n., pl.* **-ta, -tas.** Member of a North American Indian people.

dale, *n.* valley.

dal′ly, *v.,* **-lied, -lying.** 1. flirt. 2. delay. —**dal′li•ance,** *n.*

Dal•ma′tian, *n.* large white-and-black dog.

dam, *n., v.,* **dammed, damming.** —*n.* 1. barrier to obstruct water. 2. female quadruped parent. —*v.* **3.** obstruct with dam.

dam′age, *n., v.,* **-aged, -aging.** —*n.* **1.** injury. **2.** (*pl.*) payment for injury. —*v.* **3.** injure. —**dam′age•a•ble,** *adj.*

dam′ask, *n.* **1.** woven figured fabric. —*adj.* **2.** pink.

dame, *n.* **1.** woman of rank. **2.** *Slang (sometimes offensive).* any woman.

damn, *v.* **1.** declare bad. **2.** condemn to hell. —**dam′na•ble,** *adj.* —**dam•na′tion,** *n.*

damp, *adj.* **1.** moist. —*n.* **2.** moisture. **3.** noxious vapor. —*v.* Also, **damp′en. 4.** moisten. **5.** depress. **6.** deaden. —**damp′ness,** *n.*

damp′er, *n.* **1.** control for air or smoke currents. **2.** discouraging influence.

dam′sel, *n.* maiden.

dam′son, *n.* small plum.

dance, *v.,* **danced, dancing,** *n.* —*v.* **1.** move rhythmically. —*n.* **2.** act of dancing. **3.** gathering or music for dancing. —**danc′er,** *n.* —**dance′a•ble,** *adj.*

dan′de•li′on, *n.* plant with yellow flowers.

dan′der, *n.* **1.** loose skin scales from various animals. **2.** *Informal.* anger; temper.

dan′dle, *v.,* **-dled, -dling.** move (a child) lightly up and down.

dan′druff, *n.* scales on scalp.

dan′dy, *n., pl.* **-dies,** *adj.,* **-dier, -diest.** —*n.* **1.** fashionable dresser. —*adj.* **2.** fine.

Dane, *n.* native of Denmark.

dan′ger, *n.* exposure to harm. —**dan′ger•ous,** *adj.* —**dan′ger•ous•ly,** *adv.*

dan′gle, *v.,* **-gled, -gling.** hang loosely.

Dan′ish, *adj.* **1.** of Denmark, the Danes, or their language. —*n.* **2.** the language of the Danes. **3.** (*sometimes l.c.*) filled pastry.

dank, *adj.* unpleasantly damp. —**dank′ness,** *n.*

dap′per, *adj.* neat.

dap′ple, *n., adj., v.,* **-pled, -pling.** —*n.* **1.** mottled marking. —*adj.* **2.** mottled. Also, **dap′pled.** —*v.* **3.** mottle.

dare, *v.,* **dared** or **durst, dared, daring,** *n.* —*v.* **1.** be bold enough. **2.** challenge. —*n.* **3.** challenge. —**dar′ing,** *adj., n.*

dare′dev′il, *n.* **1.** recklessly daring person. —*adj.* **2.** recklessly daring.

dark, *adj.* **1.** lacking light. **2.** blackish. **3.** ignorant. —*n.* **4.** absence of light. —**dark′en,** *v.* —**dark′ness,** *n.*

Dark Ages, Middle Ages, esp. from A.D. 476 to about 1000.

dark horse, little-known competitor.

dark′room′, *n.* **1.** place for developing and printing films.

dar′ling, *n.* **1.** loved one. **2.** favorite. —*adv.* **3.** cherished. **4.** charming.

darn, *v.* mend with rows of stitches. —**darn′er,** *n.*

dart, *n.* **1.** slender pointed missile. —*v.* **2.** move swiftly.

dash, *v.* **1.** strike violently. **2.** frustrate. —*n.* **3.** violent blow. **4.** small quantity. **5.** punctuation mark (—) noting abrupt break. **6.** rush.

dash′board′, *n.* instrument board on motor vehicle.

dash′ing, *adj.* **1.** lively. **2.** stylish. —**dash′ing•ly,** *adv.*

das′tard, *n.* coward. —**das′tard•ly,** *adj.*

da′ta, *n.pl.* (*sing.* **datum**) facts or other information.

da′ta•base′, *n.* collection of computerized data.

data processing, high-speed handling of information by computer. —**data processor.**

date, *n., v.,* **dated, dating.** —*n.* **1.** particular time. **2.** fleshy, edible fruit of **date palm. 3.** appointment. **4.** social engagement arranged beforehand, esp. one of a romantic nature. **5.** person with whom one shares such an engagement. —*v.* **6.** exist from particular time. **7.** fix date for or with.

dat′ed, *adj.* **1.** having or showing a date. **2.** out-of-date.

daub, *v.* **1.** cover with mud, etc. **2.** paint clumsily. —*n.* **3.** daubed. —**daub′er,** *n.*

daugh′ter, *n.* female child. —**daugh′ter•ly,** *adj.*

daugh′ter-in-law′, *n., pl.* **daughters-in-law.** son's wife.

daunt, *v.* **1.** frighten. **2.** dismay. —**daunt′ing•ly,** *adv.*

daunt′less, *adj.* bold; fearless. —**daunt′less•ly,** *adv.*

dav′en•port′, *n.* large sofa.

dav′it, *n.* crane for boat, etc.

daw'dle, *v.,* **-dled, -dling.** waste time. **—daw'dler,** *n.*

dawn, *n.* **1.** break of day. **—v. 2.** begin to grow light. **3.** become apparent.

day, *n.* **1.** period between two nights. **2.** period (24 hours) of earth's rotation on its axis.

day'break', *n.* first appearance of light; dawn.

day care, supervised care for young children or the elderly, usu. in daytime and at a center outside the home. **—day'-care',** *adj.*

day'dream', *n.* **1.** reverie; fancy. **—v. 2.** indulge in reveries. **—day'dream'er,** *n.*

day'light', *n.* **1.** light of day. **2.** openness. **3.** *(pl.)* wits; sanity.

daylight-saving time, time one hour later than standard time.

day'time', *n.* time from sunrise to sunset.

day'-to-day', *adj.* **1.** occurring each day. **2.** routine; normal.

daze, *v.,* **dazed, dazing,** *n.* **—v. 1.** stun. **—n. 2.** dazed state.

daz'zle, *v.,* **-zled, -zling.** overwhelm with light.

dba, doing business as.

dbl, **1.** decibel. **2.** double.

DC, **1.** direct current. **2.** District of Columbia.

D.D., Doctor of Divinity.

D.D.S., **1.** Doctor of Dental Science. **2.** Doctor of Dental Surgery.

DDT, strong insecticide.

de-, prefix indicating: **1.** reverse, as *deactivate.* **2.** remove, as *decaffeinate.* **3.** reduce, as *degrade.*

dea'con, *n.* **1.** cleric inferior to priest. **2.** lay church officer. **—dea'con•ess,** *n.fem.* **—dea'con•ry,** *n.*

de•ac'ti•vate', *v.,* **-vated, -vating. 1.** making inactive. **2.** demobilize.

dead, *adj.* **1.** no longer alive or active. **2.** infertile. **3.** complete; absolute **—n. 4.** dead person or persons. **—adv. 5.** completely. **6.** directly. **—dead'en,** *v.*

dead end, **1.** street, corridor, etc., that has no exit. **2.** position with no hope of progress. **—dead'-end',** *adj.*

dead'beat', *n.* **1.** person who avoids paying. **2.** sponger.

dead heat, race that finishes in a tie.

dead'line', *n.* last allowable time.

dead'lock', *n.* standstill.

dead'ly, *adj.*, **-lier, -liest. 1.** fatal. **2.** dreary. **3.** extremely accurate. —*adv.* **4.** extremely.

dead'pan', *adj.* without expression; appearing serious.

dead'wood', *n.* useless or extraneous persons or things.

deaf, *adj.* unable to hear. —**deaf'en**, *v.* —**deaf'ness**, *n.*

deaf'-mute', *n. Often Offensive.* person unable to hear or speak.

deal, *v.*, **dealt, dealing**, *n.* —*v.* **1.** conduct oneself toward. **2.** do business. **3.** distribute. —*n.* **4.** transaction. **5.** quantity. —**deal'er**, *n.*

deal'ing, *n. (usually pl.)* interactions with others.

dean, *n.* **1.** head of academic faculty. **2.** head of cathedral organization.

dear, *adj.* **1.** loved. **2.** expensive. —*n.* **3.** dear one. —**dear'ly**, *adv.*

dearth, *n.* scarcity.

death, *n.* end of life. —**death'ly**, *adj., adv.* —**death'bed'**, *n.*

death'less, *adj.* enduring.

de·ba'cle (də bä'kəl), *n.* **1.** breakup; rout. **2.** utter failure.

de·bar', *v.*, **-barred, -barring.** exclude. —**de·bar'ment**, *n.*

de·bark', *v.* disembark. —**de'bar·ka'tion**, *n.*

de·base', *v.*, **-based, -basing.** reduce in quality. —**de·base'ment**, *n.*

de·bate', *n., v.*, **-bated, -bating.** —*n.* **1.** controversial discussion. —*v.* **2.** argue; discuss. —**de·bat'a·ble**, *adj.* —**de·bat'er**, *n.*

de·bauch' (-bôch'), *v.* **1.** corrupt; pervert. —*n.* **2.** period of corrupt indulgence. —**de·bauch'er·y**, *n.*

de·ben'ture (di ben'chər), *n.* short-term, negotiable, interest-producing note representing debt.

de·bil'i·tate', *v.*, **-tated, -tating.** weaken. —**de·bil'i·ta'tion**, *n.*

de·bil'i·ty, *n., pl.* **-ties.** weakness.

deb'it, *n.* **1.** recorded debt. **2.** account of debts. —*v.* **3.** charge as debt.

deb'o·nair', *adj.* **1.** suave; urbane. **2.** relaxed; calm.

de·brief′, *v.* gather information from someone about a completed mission.

de·bris′ (də brē′, dā′brē), *n.* rubbish; ruins.

debt, *n.* 1. something owed. 2. obligation to pay. —**debt′or**, *n.*

de·bug′, *v.*, **-bugged, -bugging.** 1. remove defects or errors from (computer program). 2. remove electronic bugs from (room or building).

de·bunk′, *v.* expose as false.

de·but′ (-byoo′), *n.* first public appearance. —**deb′u·tante′**, *n.fem.*

Dec., December.

dec′ade, *n.* 10-year period.

dec′a·dence, *n.* 1. decline in quality of power. 2. decline in morality; corruption. —**dec′a·dent**, *adj.*

de·caf′fein·at′ed (dē kaf′ə nā′təd), *adj.* having the caffeine removed.

dec′a·gon′, *n.* polygon with 10 angles and 10 sides.

dec′a·he′dron, *n., pl.* **-drons, -dra.** solid figure with 10 faces.

de′cal (dē′kal, di kal′), *n.* picture or design on specially prepared paper for transfer to wood, metal, etc.

Dec′a·logue′, *n.* Ten Commandments.

de·camp′, *v.* depart.

de·cant′, *v.* pour off.

de·cant′er, *n.* bottle.

de·cap′i·tate′, *v.*, **-tated, -tating.** behead. —**de·cap′i·ta′tion**, *n.*

de·cath′lon, *n.* contest of 10 events.

de·cay′, *v., n.* decline in quality, health, etc.

de·cease′, *n., v.*, **-ceased, -ceasing.** —*n.* 1. death. —*v.* 2. die. —**de·ceased′**, *adj., n.*

de·ce′dent (di sēd′nt), *n. Law.* deceased person.

de·ceit′, *n.* 1. fraud. 2. trick. —**de·ceit′ful**, *adj.*

de·ceive′, *v.*, **-ceived, -ceiving.** mislead.

de·cel′er·ate′ (dē sel′ə rāt′), *v.* slow down.

De·cem′ber, *n.* 12th month of year.

de′cen·cy, *n., pl.* **-cies.** 1. conformity to standards of morality. 2. respectability. 3. adequacy. 4. kindness. —**de′cent**, *adj.* —**de′cent•ly,** *adv.*

de•cen′tral•ize′, *v.,* **-ized, -izing.** end central control of. —**de•cen′tral•i•za′tion,** *n.*

de•cep′tion, *n.* 1. act of deceiving. 2. fraud. —**de•cep′tive,** *adj.*

dec′i•bel′, *n.* unit of intensity of sound.

de•cide′, *v.,* **-cided, -ciding.** settle; resolve.

de•cid′ed, *adj.* unambiguous. —**de•cid′ed•ly,** *adv.*

de•cid′u•ous (di sij′oo əs), *adj.* shedding leaves annually.

dec′i•mal, *adj.* 1. of tenths. 2. proceeding by tens. —*n.* 3. fraction in tenths, hundredths, etc., indicated by dot (**decimal point**) before numerator.

dec′i•mate′ (des′ə māt′), *v.* **-mated, -mating.** kill or destroy large part of.

de•ci′pher (-sī′-), *v.* decode. —**de•ci′pher•a•ble,** *adj.*

de•ci′sion, *n.* 1. something decided. 2. firmness of mind.

de•ci′sive, *adj.* 1. determining. 2. resolute.

—**de•ci′sive•ly,** *adv.* —**de•ci′sive•ness,** *n.*

deck, *n.* 1. level on ship. 2. pack of playing cards. —*v.* 3. array.

de•claim′, *v.* speak rhetorically. —**de•claim′er,** *n.*

dec′la•ma′tion, *n.* speech. —**de•clam′a•to′ry,** *adj.*

de•clare′, *v.,* **-clared, -claring.** 1. make known; proclaim. 2. affirm. —**dec′la•ra′tion,** *n.* —**de•clar′a•tive, de•clar′a•to′ry,** *adj.*

de•clen′sion, *n.* grammatical inflection or set of inflections.

dec′li•na′tion, *n.* 1. slope. 2. angular height of heavenly body.

de•cline′, *v.,* **-clined, -clining,** *n.* —*v.* 1. refuse. 2. slant down. 3. give grammatical inflections. 4. fail; diminish. —*n.* 5. downward slope. 6. deterioration.

de•cliv′i•ty, *n, pl.* **-ties.** downward slope.

de•code′, *v.,* **-coded, -coding.** decipher from code.

de′com•mis′sion, *v.* retire vessel from active service.

de′com•pose′, *v.*, -posed, -posing. **1.** separate into constituent parts. **2.** rot. —**de′com•po•si′tion**, *n.*

de′con•ges′tant, *adj.* **1.** relieving congestion of the upper respiratory tract. —*n.* **2.** decongestant agent.

de′con•tam′i•nate, *v.*, -nated, -nating. make safe by removing or neutralizing harmful contaminants. —**de′con•tam′i•na′tion**, *n.*

dé•cor′ (dā kôr′, di-), *n.* style of decoration. Also, **de•cor′**.

dec′o•rate′, *v.*, -rated, -rating. furnish with ornament. —**dec′o•ra′tion**, *n.* —**dec′o•ra′tive**, *adj.* —**dec′o•ra′tor**, *n.*

dec′o•rous, *adj.* dignified. —**dec′o•rous•ly**, *adv.*

de•co′rum, *n.* propriety.

de•coy′, *n.*, *v.* lure.

de•crease′, *v.*, -creased, -creasing, *n.* —*v.* **1.** lessen. —*n.* (dē′krēs). **2.** lessening.

de•cree′, *n.*, *v.*, -creed, -creeing. —*n.* **1.** published command. —*v.* **2.** proclaim.

de•crep′it, *adj.* feeble with age. —**de•crep′i•tude′**, *n.*

de′cre•scen′do (dē′kri shen′dō, dā′-), *adj.*, *adv. Music.* gradually decreasing in loudness.

de•crim′i•nal•ize′, *v.*, -ized, -izing. cease to treat as crime. —**de•crim′i•nal•i•za′tion**, *n.*

de•cry′, *v.*, -cried, -crying. disparage.

ded′i•cate′, *v.*, -cated, -cating. **1.** set apart. **2.** devote. **3.** inscribe in honor of. —**ded′i•ca′tion**, *n.*

de•duce′, *v.*, -duced, -ducing. derive logically; infer. —**de•duc′i•ble**, *adj.*

de•duct′, *v.* subtract. —**de•duct′i•ble**, *adj.*

de•duc′tion, *n.* act or result of deducting or deducing. —**de•duc′tive**, *adj.*

deed, *n.* **1.** act. **2.** written conveyance of property. —*v.* **3.** transfer by deed.

dee′jay′, *n.* disc jockey.

deem, *v.* think; estimate.

de-em′pha•size′, *v.*, -sized, -sizing. place less emphasis on. —**de-em′pha•sis**, *n.*

deep, *adj.* **1.** extending far down or in. **2.** difficult to understand. **3.** profound. **4.**

low in pitch. —*n.* **5.** deep part. —*adv.* **6.** at great depth. —**deep'en,** *v.* —**deep'ly,** *adv.*

deep'-freeze', *v.,* **-froze, -frozen, -freezing,** *n.* —*v.* **1.** freeze rapidly for preservation. —*n.* **2.** refrigerator that deep-freezes.

deep'-fry', *v.,* **-fried, -frying.** cook in boiling fat. —**deep'-fry'er,** *n.*

deep'-seat'ed, *adj.* firmly fixed. Also, **deep'-root'ed.**

deep space, space beyond the solar system.

deer, *n., pl.* **deer.** hoofed, ruminant animal, the male of which is usually horned.

de•face', *v.,* **-faced, -facing.** mar. —**de•face'ment,** *n.*

de fac'to (dē fak'tō, dā-), **1.** in reality. **2.** actually existing, esp. without legal authority.

de•fame', *v.,* **-famed, -faming.** attack reputation of. —**def'a•ma'tion,** *n.* —**de•fam'a•to'ry,** *adj.*

de•fault', *n.* **1.** failure; neglect. —*v.* **2.** fail to meet obligation.

de•feat', *v., n.* overthrow.

de•feat'ism, *n.* expectance of defeat. —**de•feat'ist,** *n.*

def'e•cate' (def'i kāt'), *v.,* **-cated, -cating.** void from bowels. —**def'e•ca'tion,** *n.*

de'fect, *n.* **1.** fault; imperfection. —*v.* (di fekt'). **2.** desert a cause, country, etc. —**de•fec'tive,** *adj.*

de•fec'tion, *n.* desertion.

de•fend', *v.* **1.** protect against attack. **2.** uphold. —**de•fend'er,** *n.*

de•fend'ant, *n.* party accused of a crime or sued in court.

de•fense', *n.* **1.** resistance to attack. **2.** defending argument. —**de•fense'less,** *adj.* —**de•fen'sive,** *adj., n.*

defense mechanism, unconscious process that protects person from painful ideas or impulses.

de•fer', *v.,* **-ferred, -ferring. 1.** postpone. **2.** yield in opinion. **3.** show respect. —**de•fer'ment,** *n.*

def'er•ence, *n.* act of showing respect. —**def'er•en'tial,** *adj.*

de•fi'ance, *n.* **1.** bold resistance. **2.** disregard. —**de•fi'ant,** *adj.* —**de•fi'ant•ly,** *adv.*

de•fi'cien•cy, *n., pl.* **-cies.** lack. —**de•fi'cient,** *adj.*

def′i·cit, *n.* deficiency of funds.

de·file′, *v.,* **-filed, -filing,** *n.* —*v.* 1. befoul. 2. desecrate. 3. march in file. —*n.* 4. narrow pass. —**de·file′ment,** *n.*

de·fine′, *v.,* **-fined, -fining.** 1. state meaning of. 2. outline. —**def′i·ni′tion,** *n.*

def′i·nite, *adj.* 1. exact. 2. with fixed limits. —**def′i·nite·ly,** *adv.*

de·fin′i·tive, *adj.* conclusive. —**de·fin′i·tive·ly,** *adv.*

de·flate′, *v.,* **-flated, -flating.** release gas from.

de·fla′tion, *n.* sharp fall in prices. —**de·fla′tion·ar′y,** *adj.*

de·flect′, *v.* turn from true course. —**de·flec′tion,** *n.*

de·fo′li·ate′, *v.,* **-ated, -ating.** 1. strip of leaves. 2. clear of vegetation, as to expose hidden enemy forces. —**de·fo′li·a′tion,** *n.* —**de·fo′li·ant,** *n.*

de·for′est, *v.* clear of forests. —**de·for′es·ta′tion,** *n.*

de·form′, *v.* mar form of. —**de·form′i·ty,** *n.*

de·fraud′, *v.* cheat. —**de·fraud′er,** *n.*

de·fray′, *v.* pay (expenses).

de·frost′, *v.* 1. remove frost or ice from. 2. thaw.

deft, *adj.* skillful. —**deft′ly,** *adv.* —**deft′ness,** *n.*

de·funct′, *adj.* dead.

de·fuse′, *v.* 1. remove detonating fuse from. 2. make less dangerous or tense.

de·fy′, *v.,* **-fied, -fying.** challenge; resist.

de·gen′er·ate′, *v.,* **-ated, -ating,** *adj., n.* —*v.* (-ə rāt′). 1. decline; deteriorate. —*adj.* (-ər it). 2. having declined. 3. corrupt. —*n.* (-ər it). 4. degenerate person. —**de·gen′er·a′tion,** *n.* —**de·gen′er·a·cy,** *n.*

de·grade′, *v.,* **-graded, -grading.** reduce in status. —**deg′ra·da′tion,** *n.*

de·gree′, *n.* 1. stage or extent. 2. 360th part of a complete revolution. 3. unit of temperature. 4. title conferred by college.

de·hu′man·ize′, *v.,* **-ized, -izing.** treat as lacking human qualities or requirements. —**de·hu′man·i·za′tion,** *n.*

de′hu·mid′i·fi′er, *n.* device for removing moisture from air. —**de′hu·mid′i·fy,** *v.*

de·hy′drate′, *v.,* -drated, -drating. deprive of moisture. —**de′hy·dra′tion,** *n.*

de′i·fy′, *v.,* -fied, -fying. make a god of. —**de′i·fi·ca′tion,** *n.*

deign (dān), *v.* condescend.

de·in′sti·tu′tion·al·ize′, *v.,* -ized, -izing. release from an institution to community care. —**de·in′sti·tu′tion·al·i·za′tion,** *n.*

de′ism (dē′iz əm), *n.* belief in the existence of a God based on reason and evidence in nature, rather than on divine revelation. —**de′ist,** *n.* —**de·is′tic,** *adj.*

de′i·ty, *n, pl.* -ties. god or goddess.

dé′jà vu′ (dā′zhä vo͞o′), feeling of having lived through same moment before.

de·ject′ed, *adj.* disheartened. —**de·jec′tion,** *n.*

de ju′re (di jo͝or′ĕ, dā jo͝or′ā), by right or according to law.

Del., Delaware.

de·lay′, *v.* 1. postpone. 2. hinder. —**de·lay′,** *n.* —**de·lay′er,** *n.*

de·lec′ta·ble, *adj.* delightful. —**de·lec′ta·bly,** *adv.* —**de′lec·ta′tion,** *n.*

del′e·gate, *n., v.,* -gated, -gating. —*n.* 1. deputy. 2. legislator. —*v.* (-gāt′). 3. send as deputy. 4. commit to another. —**del′e·ga′tion,** *n.*

de·lete′, *v.,* -leted, -leting. cancel; erase. —**de·le′tion,** *n.*

del′e·te′ri·ous, *adj.* harmful.

del′i (del′ē), *n.* delicatessen.

de·lib′er·ate, *adj., v.,* -ated, -ating. —*adj.* (-ər it). 1. intentional. 2. unhurried. —*v.* (-ə rāt′). 3. consider. 4. confer. —**de·lib′er·a′tion,** *n.* —**de·lib′er·ate·ly,** *adv.* —**de·lib′er·ate·ness,** *n.* —**de·lib′er·a′tive,** *adj.* —**de·lib′er·a′tor,** *n.*

del′i·ca·cy, *n., pl.* -cies. 1. fineness. 2. nicety. 3. choice food.

del′i·cate, *adj.* 1. fine. 2. dainty. 3. fragile. 4. tactful. —**del′i·cate·ly,** *adv.*

del·i·ca·tes′sen, *n.* store that sells cooked or prepared food.

de·li′cious, *adj.* pleasing, esp. to taste. —**de·li′cious·ly,** *adv.* —**de·li′cious·ness,** *n.*

de·light′, *n.* 1. joy. —*v.* 2. please highly. 3. take joy. —**de·light′ed**, *adj.* —**de·light′ful**, *adj.*

de·lim′it, *v.* mark limits of. —**de·lim′i·ta′tion**, *n.*

de·lin′e·ate′, *v.,* -ated, -ating. sketch; outline. —**de·lin′e·a′tion**, *n.*

de·lin′quent, *adj.* 1. neglectful; guilty. —*n.* 2. delinquent one. —**de·lin′quen·cy**, *n.*

de·lir′i·um, *n.* mental disorder marked by excitement, visions, etc. —**de·lir′i·ous**, *adj.*

de·liv′er, *v.* 1. give up. 2. carry and turn over. 3. utter. 4. direct. 5. save. 6. give birth. 7. assist at birth. —**de·liv′er·ance**, *n.* —**de·liv′er·y**, *n.*

dell, *n.* small, wooded valley.

del·phin′i·um, *n., pl.* -iums, -ia. blue garden flower.

del′ta, *n.* 1. 4th letter of Greek alphabet. 2. triangular area between branches of river mouth.

de·lude′, *v.,* -luded, -luding. mislead.

del′uge, *n., v.,* -uged, -uging. —*n.* 1. great flood. —*v.* 2. flood. 3. overwhelm.

de·lu′sion, *n.* false opinion or conception. —**de·lu′sive**, *adj.*

de·luxe′ (-luks′), *adj.* of finest quality.

delve, *v.,* delved, delving. dig. —**delv′er**, *n.*

Dem., 1. Demcorat. 2. Democratic.

dem′a·gogue′ (-gôg′), *n.* unscrupulous popular leader. —**dem′a·gogu′er·y**, *n.*

de·mand′, *v.* 1. claim. 2. require. 3. ask for in urgent or peremptory manner. —*n.* 4. claim. 5. requirement.

de·mar′cate, *v.,* -cated, -cating. 1. delimit. 2. set apart. —**de′mar·ca′tion**, *n.*

de·mean′, *v.* 1. conduct (oneself). 2. lower in dignity.

de·mean′or, *n.* conduct; behavior; deportment.

de·ment′ed, *adj.* crazed.

de·men′tia (-shə, -shē ə), *n.* severe mental impairment.

de·mer′it, *n.* 1. fault. 2. rating for misconduct.

demi-, prefix indicating half or lesser, as *demigod.*

dem′i•god′, *n.* one partly divine and partly human.

de•mil′i•ta•rize′, *v.*, **-rized, -rizing.** free from military influence. —**de•mil′i•ta•ri•za′tion,** *n.*

de•mise′ (di mīz′), *n., v.,* **-mised, -mising.** —*n.* 1. death. 2. transfer of estate. —*v.* 3. transfer.

dem′i•tasse′, *n.* small coffee cup.

dem′o (dem′ō), *n.* product offered for trial.

de•mo′bi•lize′, *v.*, **-lized, -lizing.** disband (army). —**de•mo′bi•li•za′tion,** *n.*

Democratic Party, a major political party in the U.S.

de•moc′ra•cy, *n., pl.* **-cies.** 1. government in which the people hold supreme power. 2. social equality. —**dem′o•crat′,** *n.* —**dem′o•crat′ic,** *adj.* —**de•moc′ra•tize′,** *v.*

dem′o•graph′ic, *adj.* of statistics on population. —**dem′o•graph′i•cal•ly,** *adv.* —**dem′o•graph′ics,** *n.pl.* —**de•mog′ra•phy,** *n.*

de•mol′ish, *v.* destroy. —**dem′o•li′tion,** *n.*

de′mon, *n.* evil spirit.

de•mon′ic, *adj.* 1. inspired. 2. like a demon. Also, **de′mo•ni′a•cal.**

dem′on•strate′, *v.*, **-strated, -strating.** 1. prove. 2. describe and explain. 3. manifest. 4. parade in support or opposition. —**de•mon′stra•ble,** *adj.* —**dem′on•stra′tion,** *n.* —**dem′on•stra′tor,** *n.*

de•mon′stra•tive, *adj.* 1. expressive. 2. explanatory. 3. conclusive.

de•mor′al•ize′, *v.*, **-ized, -izing.** destroy morale. —**de•mor′al•i•za′tion,** *n.*

de•mote′, *v.*, **-moted, -moting.** reduce rank. —**de•mo′tion,** *n.*

de•mur′, *v.*, **-murred, -murring,** *n.* —*v.* 1. object. —*n.* 2. objection. —**de•mur′ral,** *n.*

de•mure′, *adj.* modest. —**de•mure′ly,** *adv.*

den, *n.* 1. cave of wild beast. 2. squalid place. 3. room in a home for relaxation.

de•na′ture, *v.*, **-tured, -turing.** make (alcohol) unfit to drink.

de•ni′al, *n.* 1. contradiction. 2. refusal to agree or give.

den′i•grate′, *v.,* **-grated, -grating.** speak badly of. **—den′i•gra′tion,** *n.*

den′im, *n.* 1. heavy cotton fabric. 2. (*pl.*) trousers of this.

den′i•zen, *n.* inhabitant.

de•nom′i•nate′, *v.,* **-nated, -nating.** name specifically.

de•nom′i•na′tion, *n.* 1. name or designation. 2. sect. 3. value of piece of money. **—de•nom′i•na′tion•al,** *adj.*

de•nom′i•na′tor, *n.* lower term in fraction.

de•note′, *v.,* **-noted, -noting.** 1. indicate. 2. mean. **—de′no•ta′tion,** *n.*

de′noue•ment′ (dā′noo män′), *n.* 1. final resolution. 2. outcome of events. Also, **dé′noue•ment′.**

de•nounce′, *v.,* **-nounced, -nouncing.** 1. condemn. 2. inform against. **—de•nounce′ment,** *n.*

dense, *adj.,* **denser, densest.** 1. compact. 2. stupid. **—den′si•ty,** *n.* **—dense′ly,** *adv.* **—dense′ness,** *n.*

dent, *n.* 1. hollow. **—***v.* 2. make a dent.

den′tal, *adj.* of teeth.

den′ti•frice, *n.* teeth-cleaning substance.

den′tin, *n.* hard tissue that forms most of a tooth. Also, **den′tine** (-tēn).

den′tist, *n.* person who prevents and treats oral disease. **—den′tist•ry,** *n.*

den′ture, *n.* artificial tooth.

de•nude′, *v.,* **-nuded, -nuding.** strip. **—den′u•da′tion,** *n.*

de•nun′ci•a′tion, *n.* 1. condemnation. 2. accusation.

de•ny′, *v.,* **-nied, -nying.** 1. declare not to be true. 2. refuse to agree or give.

de•o′dor•ant, *n.* agent for destroying odors.

de•o′dor•ize′, *v.,* **-ized, -izing.** rid of odors. **—de•o′dor•iz′er,** *n.*

de•part′, *v.* 1. go away. 2. die. **—de•par′ture,** *n.*

de•part′ment, *n.* 1. part; section. 2. branch. **—de′part•men′tal,** *adj.*

de•pend′, *v.* 1. rely. 2. be contingent. **—de•pend′ence,** *n.* **—de•pend′en•cy,** *n.* **—de•pend′ent,** *adj., n.*

de·pend′a·ble, *adj.* reliable.
—**de·pend′a·bil′i·ty,** *n.*
—**de·pend′a·bly,** *adv.*

de·pict′, *v.* 1. portray. 2.
describe. —**de·pic′tion,** *n.*

de·pil′a·to′ry (di pil′ə tôr′ē),
adj., n., pl. **-ries.** —*adj.* 1.
capable of removing hair. —*n.*
2. depilatory agent.

de·plete′, *v.,* **-pleted, -pleting.**
to empty. —**de·ple′tion,** *n.*

de·plore′, *v.,* **-plored, -ploring.**
lament. —**de·plor′a·ble,** *adj.*

de·ploy′, *v.* place strategically.
—**de·ploy′ment,** *n.*

de′po·lit′i·cize′, *v.,* **-cized,**
-cizing. remove from politics.

de·pop′u·late′, *v.,* **-lated,**
-lating. deprive of inhabitants.
—**de·pop′u·la′tion,** *n.*

de·port′, *v.* 1. banish. 2.
conduct (oneself).
—**de′por·ta′tion,** *n.*

de·port′ment, *n.* conduct.

de·pose′, *v.,* **-posed, -posing.**
1. remove from office. 2.
testify. —**dep′o·si′tion,** *n.*

de·pos′it, *v.* 1. place. 2. place
for safekeeping. —*n.* 3.
sediment. 4. something
deposited. —**de·pos′i·tor,** *n.*

de·pos′i·to′ry, *n., pl.* **-ries.**
place for safekeeping.

de′pot (dē′pō), *n.* 1. station. 2.
storage base.

de·prave′, *v.,* **-praved,**
-praving. corrupt.
—**de·praved′,** *adj.*
—**de·prav′i·ty,** *n.*

dep′re·cate′, *v.,* **-cated,**
-cating. disapprove of.
—**dep′re·ca′tion,** *n.*
—**dep′re·ca·to′ry,** *adj.*

de·pre′ci·ate′ (-shi āt′), *v.,*
-ated, -ating. 1. reduce or
decline in value. 2. belittle.
—**de·pre′ci·a′tion,** *n.*

dep′re·da′tion, *n.* plunder.

de·press′, *v.* 1. deject. 2.
weaken. 3. press down.
—**de·press′ant,** *adj., n.*
—**de·pressed′,** *adj.*

de·pres′sion, *n.* 1. act of
depressing. 2. depressed state.
3. depressed place. 4. decline
in business. —**de·pres′sive,**
adj.

de·prive′, *v.,* **-prived, -priving.**
1. divest. 2. withhold from.
—**dep′ri·va′tion,** *n.*

dept., 1. department. 2.
deputy.

depth, *n.* 1. distance down. 2. profundity. 3. lowness of pitch. 4. deep part.

dep•u•ta′tion, *n.* delegation.

dep•u•ty, *n., pl.* **-ties.** agent; substitute. **—dep′u•tize′,** *v.*

de•rail′, *v.* cause to run off rails. **—de•rail′ment,** *n.*

de•range′, *v.,* **-ranged, -ranging.** 1. disarrange. 2. make insane. **—de•range′ment,** *n.*

der′by, *n., pl.* **-bies.** 1. stiff, rounded hat. 2. race.

de•reg′u•late′, *v.,* **-lated, -lating.** free of regulation. **—de•reg′u•la′tion,** *n.*

der′e•lict, *adj.* 1. abandoned. 2. neglectful. **—***n.* 3. abandoned. 4. vagrant.

der′e•lic′tion, *n.* neglect.

de•ride′, *v.,* **-rided, -riding.** mock. **—de•ri′sion,** *n.* **—de•ri′sive,** *adj.* **—de•ri′sive•ly,** *adv.*

de•rive′, *v.,* **-rived, -riving.** 1. get from source. 2. trace. 3. deduce. 4. originate. **—der′i•va′tion,** *n.* **—de•riv′a•tive,** *n., adj.*

der′ma•ti′tis (dûr′mə tī′tis), *n.* inflammation of the skin.

der′ma•tol′o•gy, *n.* medical study and treatment of the skin. **—der′ma•tol′o•gist,** *n.*

der′o•gate′, *v.,* **-gated, -gating.** detract. **—der′o•ga′tion,** *n.* **—de•rog′a•to′ry,** *adj.*

der′rick, *n.* crane with boom pivoted at one end.

der′ri•ère′ (der′ē âr′), *n.* buttocks.

de•scend′ (di send′), *v.* 1. move down. 2. be descendant. **—de•scent′,** *n.*

de•scend′ant, *n.* person descended from specific ancestor; offspring.

de•scribe′, *v.,* **-scribed, -scribing.** 1. set forth in words. 2. trace. **—de•scrib′a•ble,** *adj.* **—de•scrip′tion,** *n.* **—de•scrip′tive,** *adj.*

de•scry′ (de skrī′), *v.,* **-scried, -scrying.** happen to see.

des′e•crate′, *v.,* **-crated, -crating.** divest of sacredness. **—des′e•cra′tion,** *n.*

de•seg′re•gate′, *v.,* **-gated, -gating.** eliminate racial segregation in. **—de•seg′re•ga′tion,** *n.*

de•sen′si•tize′, *v.*, **-tized,** **-tizing.** make less sensitive. —**de•sen′si•ti•za′tion,** *n.*

des′ert, *n.* **1.** arid region. **2.** (di zûrt′). due reward or punishment. —*adj.* **3.** desolate; barren. —*v.* **4.** (di zûrt′). abandon. —**de•sert′er,** *n.* —**de•ser′tion,** *n.*

de•serve′, *v.,* **-served,** **-serving.** have due one.

des′ic•cate′, *v.,* **-cated,** **-cating.** dry up. —**des′ic•ca′tion,** *n.*

de•sid′er•a′tum (di sid′ə rā′təm, -rä′-, -zid′-), *n., pl.* **-ta.** something wanted.

de•sign′, *v.* **1.** plan. **2.** conceive form of. —*n.* **3.** sketch or plan. **4.** art of designing. **5.** scheme. **6.** purpose. —**de•sign′er,** *n.*

des′ig•nate′, *v.,* **-nated,** **-nating. 1.** indicate. **2.** name. —**des′ig•na′tion,** *n.*

designated driver, person who abstains from alcohol at a gathering in order to drive companions home safely.

de•sign′ing, *adj.* scheming.

de•sire′, *v.,* **-sired, -siring,** *n.* —*v.* **1.** wish for. **2.** request. —*n.* **3.** longing. **4.** request. **5.**

thing desired. **6.** lust. —**de•sir′a•ble,** *adj.* —**de•sir′ous,** *adj.* —**de•sir′a•bil′i•ty,** *n.*

de•sist′, *v.* stop.

desk, *n.* **1.** table for writing. **2.** specialized section of an organization or office.

desk′top′ publishing, design and production of publications using a microcomputer.

des′o•late, *adj., v.,* **-lated,** **-lating.** —*adj.* (-ə lit). **1.** barren. **2.** lonely. **3.** dismal. —*v.* (-ə lāt′). **4.** lay waste. **5.** make hopeless. —**des′o•la′tion,** *n.*

de•spair′, *n.* **1.** hopelessness. —*v.* **2.** lose hope.

des′per•a′do (-rā′-, -rä′-), *n., pl.* **-does, -dos.** wild outlaw.

des′per•ate, *adj.* **1.** reckless from despair. **2.** despairing. —**des′per•ate•ly,** *adv.* —**des′per•a′tion,** *n.*

des′pi•ca•ble, *adj.* contemptible. —**des′pi•ca•bly,** *adv.*

de•spise′, *v.,* **-spised, -spising.** scorn.

de•spite′, *prep.* **1.** in spite of. —*n.* **2.** insult.

de·spoil′, *v.* plunder.

de·spond′, *v.* lose courage or hope. —**de·spond′en·cy**, *n.* —**de·spond′ent**, *adj.*

des′pot, *n.* tyrant. —**des·pot′ic**, *adj.* —**des′pot·ism′**, *n.*

des·sert′, *n.* sweet course of meal.

des′ti·na′tion, *n.* goal of journey.

des′tine (-tin), *v.*, **-tined, -tining. 1.** set apart. **2.** predetermine by fate.

des′ti·ny, *n., pl.* **-nies. 1.** predetermined future. **2.** fate.

des′ti·tute′, *adj.* **1.** without means of support. **2.** deprived. —**des′ti·tu′tion**, *n.*

de·stroy′, *v.* **1.** ruin. **2.** end. **3.** kill.

de·stroy′er, *n.* **1.** one that destroys. **2.** naval vessel.

de·struct′, *v.* be destroyed automatically.

de·struc′tion, *n.* **1.** act or means of destroying. **2.** fact of being destroyed. —**de·struct′i·ble**, *adj.* —**de·struc′tive**, *adj.*

des′ue·tude′ (des′wi tood′, -tyood′), *n.* state of disuse.

des′ul·to′ry, *adj.* disjointed. —**des′ul·to′ri·ly**, *adv.*

de·tach′, *v.* take off or away. —**de·tach′a·ble**, *adj.*

de·tached′, *adj.* **1.** separate. **2.** uninterested.

de·tach′ment, *n.* **1.** act of detaching. **2.** unconcern. **3.** impartiality. **4.** special troops.

de·tail′, *n.* **1.** minute part. **2. in detail,** with all details specified. **3.** troops for special duty. —*v.* **4.** relate in detail. **5.** assign.

de·tain′, *v.* **1.** delay. **2.** keep in custody. —**de·ten′tion**, *n.*

de·tect′, *v.,* **1.** discover. **2.** perceive. —**de·tec′tion**, *n.* —**de·tec′tor**, *n.*

de·tec′tive, *n.* professional investigator of crimes, etc.

dé·tente (dā tänt′), *n.* lessening of hostility.

de·ter′, *v.,* **-terred, -terring.** discourage or restrain. —**de·ter′ment**, *n.*

de·ter′gent, *adj.* **1.** cleansing. —*n.* **2.** cleansing agent.

de·te′ri·o·rate′, *v.,* **-rated, -rating.** become worse. —**de·te′ri·o·ra′tion**, *n.*

de•ter′mi•nant′, *n.* determining agent or factor.

de•ter′mi•nate, *adj.* able to be specified.

de•ter′mi•na′tion, *n.* 1. act of determining. 2. firmness of purpose.

de•ter′mine, *v.,* -mined, -mining. 1. settle; decide. 2. ascertain. 3. limit. —**de•ter′mi•na•ble,** *adj.*

de•ter′mined, *adj.* resolved.

de•ter′rence, *n.* discouragement. —**de•ter′rent,** *adj., n.*

de•test′, *v.* hate or despise. —**de•test′a•ble,** *adj.* —**de•test′a•bly,** *adv.* —**de′tes•ta′tion,** *n.*

de•throne′, *v.,* -throned, -throning. remove from a throne.

det′o•nate′, *v.,* -nated, -nating. explode. —**det′o•na′tion,** *n.*

de′tour, *n.* 1. roundabout course. —*v.* 2. make detour.

de′tox (*n.* dē′toks; *v.* dētoks′), *n., v.,* -toxed, -toxing. *Informal.* —*n.* 1. detoxification. 2. hospital unit for patients undergoing detoxification. —*v.* 3. detoxify.

de•tox′i•fy, *v.,* -fied, -fying. rid of effects of alcohol or drug use. —**de•tox′i•fi•ca′tion,** *n.*

de•tract′, *v.* take away quality or reputation. —**de•trac′tion,** *n.* **de•trac′tor,** *n.*

det′ri•ment, *n.* damage. —**det′ri•men′tal,** *adj.*

de•tri′tus (di trī′təs), *n.* 1. rock particles worn away from a mass. 2. debris.

deuce (do̅o̅s, dyo̅o̅s), *n.* 1. card or die with two pips. 2. tie score as in tennis.

de•val′u•ate′, *v.,* -ated, -ating. reduce in value; depreciate. Also, **de•val′ue.** —**de•val′u•a′tion,** *n.*

dev′as•tate′, *v.,* -tated, -tating. lay waste. —**dev′as•ta′tion,** *n.*

de•vel′op, *v.* 1. mature; perfect. 2. elaborate. 3. bring into being. 4. make (images on film) visible. 5. acquire. —**de•vel′op•ment,** *n.* —**de•vel′op•men′tal,** *adj.* —**de•vel′op•er,** *n.*

de′vi•ate′, *v.,* -ated, -ating. 1. digress. 2. depart from normal. —**de′vi•a′tion,** *n.* —**de′vi•ant,** *adj., n.*

de·vice′, *n*. 1. contrivance. 2. plan. 3. slogan or emblem.

dev′il, *n*. 1. Satan. 2. evil spirit or person. —**dev′il·ish**, *adj*. —**dev′il·try**, *n*.

dev′il-may-care′, *adj*. reckless.

devil's advocate, person who takes opposing view for the sake of argument.

devil's food cake, rich chocolate cake.

de′vi·ous, *adj*. 1. circuitous. 2. with low cunning. —**de′vi·ous·ly**, *adv*.

de·vise′, *v.*, **-vised, -vising.** 1. plan; contrive. 2. bequeath. —**de·vis′er**, *n*.

de·vi′tal·ize′, *v.*, **-ized, -izing.** remove vitality of. —**de·vi′tal·i·za′tion**, *n*.

de·void′, *adj*. destitute.

de·volve′, *v.*, **-volved, -volving.** 1. delegate. 2. fall as a duty.

de·vote′, *v.*, **-voted, -voting.** 1. give of oneself. 2. dedicate.

de·vot′ed, *adj*. 1. zealous. 2. dedicated.

dev′o·tee′ (dev′ə tē′), *n*. devoted one.

de·vo′tion, *n*. 1. consecration. 2. attachment or dedication. 3. (*pl.*) worship. —**de·vo′tion·al**, *adj*.

de·vour′, *v*. consume ravenously.

de·vout′, *adj*. pious.

dew, *n*. atmospheric moisture condensed in droplets. —**dew′y**, *adj*.

dex·ter′i·ty, *n*. 1. physical skill. 2. cleverness. —**dex′ter·ous**, *adj*.

dex′trose, *n*. type of sugar.

di′a·be′tes, *n*. disease causing body's inability to use sugar. —**di′a·bet′ic**, *adj., n.*

di′a·bol′ic, *adj*. fiendish. Also, **di′abol′i·cal.**

di′a·crit′ic, *n*. mark added to a letter to give it a particular phonetic value. Also, **di′a·crit′i·cal mark.**

di′a·dem′, *n*. crown.

di′ag·nose′, *v.*, **-nosed, -nosing.** determine nature of (disease). —**di′ag·no′sis**, *n*. —**di′ag·nos′tic**, *adj*.

di·ag′o·nal, *adj*. 1. connecting two angles. 2. oblique. —**di·ag′o·nal·ly**, *adv*.

di′a•gram, *n., v.,* **-gramed, -graming.** chart or plan. —**di′a•gram•mat′ic,** *adj.*

di′al, *n., v.,* **-aled, -aling.** —*n.* **1.** numbered face, as on a watch. —*v.* **2.** select or contact with use of dial.

di′a•lect′, *n.* language of district or class. —**di′a•lec′tal,** *adj.*

di′a•lec′tic, *n.* art or practice of debate or conversation by which truth of theory or opinion is arrived at logically. Also, **di′a•lec′tics.** —**di′a•lec′ti•cal,** *adj.*

di′a•logue′, *n.* conversation between two or more people. Also, **di′a•log′.**

di•al′y•sis (dī al′ə sis), *n.* process of removing waste products from blood of someone with kidney disease.

di•am′e•ter, *n.* straight line through center of a circle.

di′a•met′ri•cal, *adj.* **1.** of diameters. **2.** completely in contrast.

dia′mond, *n.* **1.** hard, brilliant precious stone. **2.** rhombus or square. **3.** (*pl.*) suit of playing cards. **4.** baseball field.

dia′mond•back′, *n.* venomous rattlesnake.

di′a•per, *n.* **1.** infant's underpants. —*v.* **2.** put diaper on.

di•aph′a•nous (dī af′ə nəs), *adj.* very sheer and light.

di′a•phragm′ (-fram′), *n.* **1.** wall in body, as between thorax and abdomen. **2.** vibrating membrane. **3.** contraceptive device.

di′ar•rhe′a (dī′ə rē′ə), *n.* intestinal disorder. Also, **di′ar•rhoe′a.**

di′a•ry, *n., pl.* **-ries.** personal daily record. —**di′a•rist,** *n.*

di′a•ther′my, *n.* heating of body by electric currents.

di′a•ton′ic (dī′ə ton′ik), *adj. Music.* made up of the eight notes of the major or minor scale.

di′a•tribe′, *n.* denunciation.

dib′ble, *n.* pointed instrument for planting.

dice, *n.pl., sing.* **die,** *v.,* **diced, dicing.** —*n.* **1.** small cubes, used in games. —*v.* **2.** cut into small cubes.

dic′ey, *adj.,* **-ier, -iest.** not certain; risky.

di•chot'o•my, *n., pl.* **-mies.** division into two irreconcilable groups.

dick'er, *v.* bargain.

di•cot'y•le'don, *n.* plant having two embryonic seed leaves.

Dic'ta•phone', *n. Trademark.* brand name for machine that records and plays back dictated speech.

dic'tate, *v.,* **-tated, -tating,** *n.* —*v.* **1.** say something to be written down. **2.** command. —*n.* **3.** command. —**dic•ta'tion,** *n.*

dic'ta•tor, *n.* absolute ruler. —**dic'ta•to'ri•al,** *adj.* —**dic'ta•tor•ship',** *n.*

dic'tion, *n.* style of speaking.

dic'tion•ar'y, *n., pl.* **-aries.** book on meaning, spelling, pronunciation, of words.

dic'tum, *n., pl.* **-ta, -tums. 1.** authoritative declaration. **2.** saying; maxim.

di•dac'tic, *adj.* instructive. —**di•dac'ti•cism,** *n.*

did'n't, *v. Informal.* did not.

die, *v.,* **died, dying,** *n., pl.* (for 3) **dies.** —*v.* **1.** cease to be. **2.** fade. —*n.* **3.** shaping device. **4.** sing. of **dice.**

die'hard', *n.* defender of lost cause.

di•er'e•sis (dī er'ə sis), *n., pl.* **-ses.** sign (¨) over a vowel indicating separate pronunciation, as in Noël.

die'sel (dē'-), *n.* **1.** engine using air compression for ignition. **2.** machine powered by such an engine. **3.** fuel consumed by a diesel engine.

di'et, *n.* **1.** food. **2.** food specially chosen for health. **3.** formal assembly. —*v.* **4.** adhere to diet. —**di'e•tar'y,** *adj.* —**di'e•tet'ic,** *adj.* —**di'e•tet'ics,** *n.*

di'e•ti'tian (dī'i tish'ən), *n.* expert in nutrition and dietary requirements. Also, **di'e•ti'cian.**

dif'fer, *v.* **1.** be unlike. **2.** disagree.

dif'fer•ence, *n.* **1.** unlikeness. **2.** disagreement. **3.** amount separating two quantities. —**dif'fer•ent,** *adj.* —**dif'fer•ent•ly,** *adv.*

dif'fer•en'ti•ate', *v.,* **-ated, -ating. 1.** alter. **2.** distinguish between. —**dif'fer•en'ti•a'tion,** *n.*

dif′fi·cult′, *adj.* 1. hard to do or understand. 2. unmanageable.

dif′fi·cul′ty, *n., pl.* -ties. 1. condition of being difficult. 2. embarrassing or difficult situation. 3. trouble; struggle. 4. disagreement or dispute.

dif′fi·dent, *adj.* timid; shy. —**dif′fi·dence**, *n.*

dif·frac′tion, *n.* breaking up of rays of light to produce spectrum.

dif·fuse′, *v.,* -fused, -fusing, *adj.* —*v.* (-fyo͞oz′). 1. spread or scatter. —*adj.* (-fyo͞os′). 2. not to the point. 3. spread or scattered. —**dif·fu′sion**, *n.* —**dif·fu′sive**, *adj.*

dig, *v.,* **dug** or **digged, digging,** *n.* —*v.* 1. thrust down. 2. lift to extract. 3. form by extraction. 4. *Slang.* understand. —*n.* 5. sarcastic remark. —**dig′ger**, *n.*

di·gest′, *v.* 1. prepare (food) for assimilation. 2. assimilate mentally. —*n.* (dī′jest). 3. collection or summary, esp. of laws. —**di·ges′tion**, *n.* —**di·gest′ive**, *adj.* —**di·gest′i·ble**, *adj.* —**di·gest′i·bil′i·ty**, *n.*

dig′it, *n.* 1. finger or toe. 2. any Arabic numeral.

dig′it·al, *adj.* of, using, or expressing data in numerals. —**dig′it·al·ly**, *adv.*

dig′i·tal′is (dij′i tal′is, -tā′lis), *n.* medicine derived from the leaves of the foxglove, used to stimulate the heart.

dig′·i·tize′, *v.* convert (data) to digital form.

dig′ni·fied, *adj.* stately.

dig′ni·fy′, *v.,* -fied, -fying. 1. honor. 2. honor more than is deserved.

dig′ni·ta′ry, *n., pl.* -ries. high-ranking person.

dig′ni·ty, *n., pl.* -ties. 1. nobility. 2. worthiness. 3. high rank, office, or title.

di·gress′, *v.* wander from main purpose, theme, etc. —**di·gres′sion**, *n.* —**di·gres′ive**, *adj.*

dike, *n.* 1. bank for restraining waters. 2. ditch.

di·lap′i·dat′ed, *adj.* decayed.

di·lap′i·da′tion, *n.* decay.

di·late′, *v.,* -lated, -lating. expand. —**di·la′tion**, *n.*

dil′a·to′ry, *adj.* delaying; tardy. —**dil′a·to′ri·ness**, *n*

di·lem′ma, *n.* predicament.

dil′et·tante′ (-tänt′), *n.* superficial practitioner.

dil′i·gence, *n.* earnest effort. —**dil′i·gent,** *adj.*

dill, *n.* plant with aromatic seeds and leaves.

dil′ly-dal′ly, *v.,* -lied, -lying. waste time, esp. by indecision.

di·lute′, *v.,* -luted, -luting. thin, as with water; weaken. —**di·lu′tion,** *n.*

dim, *adj.,* **dimmer, dimmest,** *v.,* **dimmed, dimming.** —*adj.* 1. not bright. 2. indistinct. —*v.* 3. make or become dim. —**dim′ly,** *adv.* —**dim′ness,** *n.*

dime, *n.* coin worth 10 cents.

di·men′sion, *n.* 1. property of space; extension in a given direction. 2. magnitude. —**di·men′sion·al,** *adj.*

di·min′ish, *v.* lessen; reduce. —**dim′i·nu′tion,** *n.*

di·min′u·en′do (di min′yoo en′dō), *adj., adv. Music.* gradually reducing in loudness.

di·min′u·tive, *adj.* 1. small. 2. denoting smallness, etc. —*n.* 3. diminutive form.

dim′i·ty, *n., pl.* -ties. thin cotton fabric.

dim′ple, *n.* small hollow, esp. in cheek.

dim′wit′, *n. Slang.* stupid person. —**dim′wit′ted,** *adj.*

din, *n., v.,* **dinned, dinning.** —*n.* 1. confused noise. —*v.* 2. assail with din.

dine, *v.,* **dined, dining.** 1. eat dinner or another meal. 2. provide dinner.

din′er, *n.* 1. person who dines. 2. railroad dining car. 3. eatery shaped like such a car.

di·nette′, *n.* small area or alcove for dining.

din′ghy (ding′gē), *n., pl.* -ghies. small boat. Also, **din′gey, din′gy.**

din′gy (-jē), *adj.,* -gier, -giest. dark; dirty.

din′ner, *n.* main meal.

di′no·saur′, *n.* extinct reptile.

dint, *n.* 1. force. 2. dent.

di′o·cese′ (dī′ə sēs′), *n.* district under a bishop. —**di·oc′e·san,** *adj., n.*

di′o·ram′a, *n.* miniature three-dimensional scene against painted background.

di•ox′ide (dī ok′sīd, -sid), *n.* oxide with two atoms of oxygen.

di•ox′in, *n.* toxic by-product of pesticide.

dip, *v.,* **dipped, dipping,** *n.* —*v.* 1. plunge temporarily in liquid. 2. bail or scoop. 3. slope down. —*n.* 4. act of dipping. 5. downward slope. 6. substance into which something is dipped.

diph•the′ri•a (dif thēr′ē ə), *n.* infectious disease of air passages, esp. throat.

diph′thong (dif′-), *n.* sound containing two vowels.

di•plo′ma, *n.* document of academic qualifications.

di•plo′ma•cy, *n., pl.* **-cies.** 1. conduct of international relations. 2. skill in negotiation. —**dip′lo•mat′,** *n.*

dip′lo•mat′ic, *adj.* 1. of diplomacy. 2. tactful. —**dip′lo•mat′i•cal•ly,** *adv.*

dip′per, *n.* 1. one that dips. 2. ladle.

dip′so•ma′ni•a, *n.* morbid craving for alcohol. —**dip′so•ma′ni•ac,** *n.*

dir., director.

dire, *adj.,* **direr, direst.** dreadful.

di•rect′, *v.* 1. guide. 2. command. 3. manage. 4. address. —*adj.* 5. straight. 6. straightforward. —**di•rect′ly,** *adv.* —**di•rect′ness,** *n.* —**di•rec′tor,** *n.*

direct current, electric current flowing in one direction.

di•rec′tion, *n.* 1. act of directing. 2. line along which a thing lies or moves. —**di•rec′tion•al,** *adj.*

di•rec′tive, *n.* order or instruction from authority.

di•rec′to•ry, *n., pl.* **-ries.** guide to locations.

dire′ful, *adj.* dire.

dirge, *n.* funeral song.

dir′i•gi•ble, *n.* airship.

dirk, *n.* dagger.

dirt, *n.* 1. filth. 2. earth.

dirt′y, *adj.* **dirtier, dirtiest,** *v.,* **dirtied, dirtying.** —*adj.* 1. soiled. 2. indecent. —*v.* 3. soil. —**dirt′i•ness,** *n.*

dis, *v.,* **dissed, dissing.** *Slang.* 1. disrespect. 2. disparage.

dis-, prefix indicating: 1. reversal, as *disconnect.* 2.

negation or lack, as *distrust*. 3. removal, as *disbar*.

dis•a′ble, *v.*, **-bled, -bling.** damage capability of. —**dis′a•bil′i•ty**, *n.*

dis•a•buse′, *v.*, **-bused, -busing.** free from deception.

dis′ad•van′tage, *n.* 1. drawback; handicap. 2. injury. —**dis•ad′van•ta′geous**, *adj.*

dis′ad•van′taged, *adj.* lacking opportunity.

dis′af•fect′, *v.* alienate. —**dis′af•fec′tion**, *n.*

dis′a•gree′, *v.*, **-greed, -greeing.** differ in opinion. —**dis′a•gree′ment**, *n.*

dis′a•gree′a•ble, *adj.* unpleasant. —**dis′a•gree′a•bly**, *adv.*

dis′al•low′, *v.* refuse to allow.

dis′ap•pear′, *v.* 1. vanish. 2. cease to exist. —**dis′ap•pear′ance**, *n.*

dis′ap•point′, *v.* fail to fulfill hopes or wishes of. —**dis′ap•point′ment**, *n.*

dis′ap•pro•ba′tion, *n.* disapproval.

dis′ap•prove′, *v.*, **-proved, -proving.** condemn; censure. —**dis′ap•prov′al**, *n.*

dis•arm′, *v.* 1. deprive of arms. 2. reduce one's own armed power. —**dis•ar′ma•ment**, *n.*

dis′ar•range′, *v.*, **-ranged, -ranging.** disorder. —**dis′ar•range′ment**, *n.*

dis′ar•ray′, *n.* lack of order.

dis′as•so′ci•ate, *v.*, **-ated, -ating.** dissociate.

dis•as′ter, *n.* extreme misfortune. —**dis•as′trous**, *adj.*

dis′a•vow′, *v.* disown. —**dis′a•vow′al**, *n.* —**dis′a•vow′er**, *n.*

dis•band′, *v.* terminate as organization. —**dis•band′ment**, *n.*

dis•bar′, *v.*, **-barred, -barring.** expel from law practice. —**dis•bar′ment**, *n.*

dis′be•lieve′, *v.*, **-lieved, -lieving.** reject as untrue. —**dis′be•lief′**, *n.*

dis•burse′, *v.*, **-bursed, -bursing.** pay out. —**dis•burse′ment**, *n.*

disc, *n.* 1. disk. 2. phonograph record.

dis•card′, *v.* 1. reject. —*n.* (dis′kärd). 2. something discarded. 3. discarded state.

dis•cern' (di sûrn'), *v.* 1. see. 2. distinguish.
—**dis•cern'ible,** *adj.*
—**dis•cern'ing,** *adj.*
—**dis•cern'ment,** *n.*

dis•charge', *v.,* **-charged, -charging.** 1. rid of load. 2. send forth. 3. shoot. 4. end employment of. 5. fulfill. —*n.* (dis'chärj). 6. act of discharging. 7. something discharged.

dis•ci'ple (di sī'pəl), *n.* follower.

dis'ci•pline, *n., v.,* **-plined, -plining.** —*n.* 1. training in rules. 2. punishment. 3. subjection to rules. 4. branch of instruction or learning. —*v.* 5. train. 6. punish.
—**dis'ci•pli•nar'y,** *adj.*
—**dis'ci•pli•nar'i•an,** *n.*

disc jockey, person who plays and comments on recorded music on a radio program. Also, **disk jockey.**

dis•claim', *n.* disown.

dis•close', *v.,* **-closed, -closing.** reveal.
—**dis•clo'sure,** *n.*

dis'co, *n., pl.* **-cos.** 1. discotheque. 2. style of dance music.

dis•col'or, *v.* change in color.
—**dis•col'or•a'tion,** *n.*

dis'com•bob'u•late', *v.,* **-lated, -lating.** confuse.
—**dis'com•bob'u•la'tion,** *n.*

dis•com'fit, *v.* 1. defeat. 2. thwart. —**dis•com'fi•ture,** *n.*

dis•com'fort, *n.* lack of comfort.

dis'com•mode', *v.,* **-moded, -moding.** cause inconvenience.

dis'com•pose', *v.,* **-posed, -posing.** 1. upset the order of. 2. disturb the composure of.
—**dis'com•po'sure,** *n.*

dis'con•cert', *v.* perturb.

dis'con•nect', *v.* break connection of.

dis•con'so•late, *adj.* sad.
—**dis•con'so•late•ly,** *adv.*

dis'con•tent', *adj.* Also **dis'con•tent'ed.** 1. not contented. —*n.* 2. lack of contentment.

dis'con•tin'ue, *v.,* **-tinued, -tinuing.** end; stop.
—**dis'con•tin'u•ance,** *n.*
—**dis'con•tin'u•ous,** *adj.*

dis'cord, *n.* 1. lack of harmony. 2. disagreement; strife. —**dis•cord'ance,** *n.*
—**dis•cord'ant,** *adj.*

dis′co•theque′ (dis′kō tek′), *n.* nightclub where recorded dance music is played.

dis′count, *v.* 1. deduct. 2. advance money after deduction of interest. 3. disregard. 4. allow for bias. —*n.* 5. deduction.

dis•coun′te•nance, *v.,* **-nanced, -nancing. 1.** disconcert regularly. 2. show disapproval of.

dis•cour′age, *v.,* **-aged, -aging. 1.** deprive of resolution. 2. hinder. —**dis•cour′age•ment,** *n.*

dis′course, *n., v.,* **-coursed, -coursing.** —*n.* 1. talk. 2. formal discussion. —*v.* (dis kōrs′). 3. talk.

dis•cour′te•sy, *n., pl.* **-sies. 1.** lack of courtesy. 2. impolite act. —**dis•cour′te•ous,** *adj.*

dis•cov′er, *v.* learn or see for first time. —**dis•cov′er•y,** *n.* —**dis•cov′er•a•ble,** *adj.* —**dis•cov′er•er,** *n.*

dis•cred′it, *v.* 1. defame. 2. give no credit to. —*n.* 3. lack of belief. 4. disrepute.

dis•creet′, *adj.* wise; prudent. —**dis•creet′ly,** *adv.*

dis•crep′an•cy, *n., pl.* **-cies.** difference; inconsistency. —**dis•crep′ant,** *adj.*

dis•crete′, *adj.* separate.

dis•cre′tion, *n.* 1. freedom of choice. 2. prudence. —**dis•cre′tion•ar′y,** *adj.*

dis•crim′i•nate′, *v.,* **-nated, -nating,** *adj.* —*v.* (-ə nāt′). 1. distinguish accurately. 2. show bias. —*adj.* (-ə nit). 3. making distinctions. —**dis•crim′i•na′tion,** *n.* —**dis•crim′i•na•to′ry,** *adj.*

dis•cur′sive, *adj.* rambling.

dis′cus (dis′kəs), *n.* disk for throwing in athletic competition.

dis•cuss′, *v.* talk about. —**dis•cus′sion,** *n.*

dis•dain′, *v., n.* scorn. —**dis•dain′ful,** *adj.*

dis•ease′, *n., v.,* **-eased, -easing.** —*n.* 1. ailment. —*v.* 2. affect with disease. —**dis•eased′,** *adj.*

dis′em•bark′, *v.* land. —**dis•em′bar•ka′tion,** *n.*

dis′em•bod′y, *v.,* **-bodied, -bodying.** free from the body.

dis′en•chant′, *v.* free from enchantment or illusion. —**dis′en•chant′ment,** *n.*

dis′en·gage′, *v.,* **-gaged, -gaging.** separate; disconnect. —**dis′en·gage′ment,** *n.*

dis·fa′vor, *n.* 1. displeasure. 2. disregard. —*v.* 3. slight.

dis·fig′ure, *v.,* **-ured, -uring.** mar. —**dis·fig′ure·ment′,** *n.*

dis·fran′chise, *v.,* **-chised, -chising.** deprive of franchise.

dis·gorge′, *v.,* **-gorged, -gorging.** 1. vomit forth. 2. yield up.

dis·grace′, *n., v.,* **-graced, -gracing.** —*n.* 1. state or cause of dishonor. —*v.* 2. bring shame upon. —**dis·grace′ful,** *adj.* —**dis·grace′ful·ly,** *adv.*

dis·grun′tle, *v.,* **-tled, -tling.** make discontented.

dis·guise′, *v.,* **-guised, -guising,** *n.* —*v.* 1. conceal true identity of. —*n.* 2. something that disguises.

dis·gust′, *v.* 1. cause loathing in. —*n.* 2. loathing. —**dis·gust′ed,** *adj.* —**dis·gust′ing,** *adj.*

dish, *n.* 1. open shallow container. 2. article of food.

dis′ha·bille′ (dis′ə bēl′, -bē′), *n.* state of being partially or carelessly dressed.

dis·heart′en, *v.* discourage.

di·shev′el, *v.,* **-eled, -eling.** let hang in disorder.

dis·hon′est, *adj.* not honest. —**dis·hon′est·ly,** *adv.* —**dis·hon′es·ty,** *n.*

dis·hon′or, *n.* 1. lack of honor. 2. disgrace. —*v.* 3. disgrace. 4. fail to honor. —**dis·hon′or·a·ble,** *adj.*

dish′wash′er, *n.* person or machine that washes dishes.

dis′il·lu′sion, *v.* free from illusion. —**dis′il·lu′sion·ment,** *n.*

dis′in·cline′, *v.,* **-clined, -clining.** make or be averse. —**dis·in′cli·na′tion,** *n.*

dis′in·fect′, *v.* destroy disease germs in. —**dis′in·fect′ant,** *n., adj.*

dis·in′for·ma′tion, *n.* false information released by a government to mislead rivals.

dis′in·gen′u·ous, *adj.* lacking frankness.

dis′in·her′it, *v.* exclude from inheritance.

dis·in′te·grate′, *v.,* **-grated, -grating.** separate into parts. —**dis·in′te·gra′tion,** *n.*

dis′in·ter′, *v.,* **-terred, -terring.** take out of interment. —**dis′in·ter′ment,** *n.*

dis•in′ter•est, *n.* indifference.

dis•in′ter•est′ed, *adj.* 1. impartial. 2. not interested. —**dis•in′ter•est′ed•ly,** *adv.*

dis•joint′ed, *adj.* 1. separated at joints. 2. incoherent.

disk, *n.* 1. flat circular plate. 2. phonograph record. 3. plate for storing electronic data. 4. roundish, flat anatomical part, as in the spine.

disk•ette′, *n.* floppy disk.

disk jockey, *n.* disc jockey.

dis•like′, *v.,* -liked, -liking, *n.* —*v.* 1. regard with displeasure. —*n.* 2. distaste.

dis′lo•cate′, *v.,* -cated, -cating. 1. displace. 2. put out of order. —**dis′lo•ca′tion,** *n.*

dis•lodge′, *v.,* -lodged, -lodging. force from place. —**dis•lodg′ment,** *n.*

dis•loy′al, *adj.* not loyal; traitorous. —**dis•loy′al•ty,** *n.*

dis′mal, *adj.* 1. gloomy. 2. terrible. —**dis′mal•ly,** *adv.*

dis•man′tle, *v.,* -tled, -tling. 1. deprive of equipment. 2. take apart. —**dis•man′tle•ment,** *n.*

dis•may′, *v.* 1. dishearten. —*n.* 2. disheartenment.

dis•mem′ber, *v.* remove limbs. —**dis•mem′ber•ment,** *n.*

dis•miss′, *v.* 1. direct or allow to go. 2. discharge. 3. reject. —**dis•mis′sal,** *n.*

dis•mount′, *v.* 1. get or throw down from saddle. 2. remove from mounting.

dis′o•be′di•ent, *adj.* not obedient. —**dis′o•be′di•ence,** *n.* —**dis′o•bey′,** *v.*

dis•or′der, *n.* 1. lack of order. 2. illness or disease. —*v.* 3. create disorder in. —**dis•or′der•ly,** *adj.*

dis•or′gan•ize′, *v.,* -ized, -izing. throw into disorder. —**dis•or′gan•i•za′tion,** *n.*

dis•o′ri•ent′, *v.* 1. cause to lose one's way. 2. confuse. —**dis•o′ri•en•ta′tion,** *n.*

dis•own′, *v.* repudiate.

dis•par′age, *v.,* -aged, -aging. speak slightly of; belittle. —**dis•par′age•ment,** *n.*

dis′par•ate (dis′pər it, di spar′-), *adj.* distinct in kind; dissimilar. —**dis•par′i•ty,** *n.*

dis•pas′sion•ate, *adj.* impartial; calm. —**dis•pas′sion•ate•ly,** *adv.*

dis•patch′, *v.* 1. send off. 2. transact quickly. 3. kill. —*n.* 4. act of sending off. 5. killing. 6. speed. 7. message or report. —**dis•patch′er**, *n.*

dis•pel′, *v.,* -**pelled, -pelling.** drive off; scatter.

dis•pen′sa•ry, *n., pl.* -**ries.** place for dispensing medicines.

dis′pen•sa′tion, *n.* 1. act of dispensing. 2. divine order. 3. relaxation of law.

dis•pense′, *v.,* -**pensed, -pensing.** 1. distribute. 2. administer. 3. forgo. 4. do away. —**dis•pen′sa•ble**, *adj.* —**dis•pens′er**, *n.*

dis•perse′, *v.,* -**persed, -persing.** scatter. —**dis•per′sion, dis•per′sal,** *n.*

dis•pir′i•ted, *adj.* dejected.

dis•place′, *v.,* -**placed, -placing.** 1. put out of place. 2. replace. —**dis•place′ment**, *n.*

dis•play′, *v., n.* exhibit.

dis•please′, *v.,* -**pleased, -pleasing.** offend. —**dis•pleas′ure** (-plezh′-), *n.*

dis•pose′, *v.,* -**posed, -posing.** 1. arrange. 2. incline. 3. decide. 4. get rid.

—**dis•pos′a•ble**, *adj., n.*
—**dis•pos′al**, *n.*

dis′po•si′tion, *n.* 1. personality or mood. 2. tendency. 3. disposal.

dis′pos•sess′, *v.* deprive of possession. —**dis′pos•ses′sion**, *n.*

dis′pro•por′tion, *n.* lack of proportion. —**dis′pro•por′tion•ate**, *adj.* —**dis′pro•por′tion•ate•ly**, *adv.*

dis•prove′, *v.,* -**proved, -proving.** prove false.

dis•pute′, *v.,* -**puted, -puting,** *n.* —*v.* 1. argue or quarrel. —*n.* 2. argument; quarrel. —**dis•put′a•ble**, *adj.* —**dis•pu′tant**, *adj., n.* —**dis′pu•ta′tion**, *n.*

dis•qual′i•fy′, *v.,* -**fied, -fying.** make ineligible. —**dis•qual′i•fi•ca′tion**, *n.*

dis•qui′et, *v.* 1. disturb. —*n.* 2. lack of peace.

dis′qui•si′tion, *n.* formal discourse or treatise.

dis′re•gard′, *v.* 1. ignore. —*n.* 2. neglect.

dis′re•pair′, *n.* impaired condition.

dis′re•pute′, *n.* ill repute. —**dis•rep′u•ta•ble**, *adj.*

dis′re•spect′, *n.* lack of respect. —**dis′re•spect′ful**, *adj.* —**dis′re•spect′ful•ly**, *adv.*

dis•robe′, *v.,* -robed, -robing. undress.

dis•rupt′, *v.* break up. —**dis•rup′tion**, *n.* —**dis•rup′tive**, *adj.*

dis•sat′is•fy′, *v.,* -fied, -fying. make discontented. —**dis′sat•is•fac′tion**, *n.*

dis•sect′, *v.* cut apart for examination; analyze in detail. —**dis•sec′tion**, *n.*

dis•sem′ble, *v.,* -bled, -bling. feign. —**dis•sem′bler**, *n.*

dis•sem′i•nate′, *v.,* -nated, -nating. scatter. —**dis•sem′i•na′tion**, *n.*

dis•sen′sion, *n.* 1. disagreement. 2. discord.

dis•sent′, *v.* 1. disagree. —*n.* 2. difference of opinion. —**dis•sent′er**, *n.*

dis′ser•ta′tion, *n.* formal essay or treatise.

dis•serv′ice, *n.* injury.

dis′si•dent, *adj.* 1. refusing to conform. —*n.* 2. dissident person. —**dis′si•dence**, *n.*

dis•sim′i•lar, *adj.* not similar. —**dis•sim′i•lar′i•ty**, *n.*

dis•sim′u•late′, *v.,* -lated, -lating. disguise; dissemble. —**dis•sim′u•la′tion**, *n.*

dis′si•pate′, *v.,* -pated, -pating. 1. scatter. 2. squander. 3. live dissolutely. —**dis′si•pa′tion**, *n.*

dis•so′ci•ate′, *v.,* -ated, -ating. separate.

dis′so•lute′, *adj.* licentious. —**dis′so•lute′ly**, *adv.*

dis•solve′, *v.,* -solved, -solving. 1. make solution of. 2. terminate. 3. destroy. —**dis′so•lu′tion**, *n.*

dis′so•nance, *n.* harsh sound. —**dis′so•nant**, *adj.*

dis•suade′, *v.,* -suaded, -suading. persuade against.

dist., 1. distance. 2. district.

dis′taff, *n.* 1. staff held in spinning. —*adj.* 2. of women.

dis′tance, *n.* 1. space between. 2. remoteness. 3. aloofness.

dis′tant, *adj.* 1. remote. 2. reserved. —**dis′tant•ly**, *adv.*

dis•taste′, *n.* dislike; aversion. —**dis•taste′ful,** *adj.*

dis•tem′per, *n.* infectious disease of dogs and cats.

dis•tend′, *v.* expand abnormally. —**dis•ten′tion,** *n.*

dis•till′, *v.* 1. obtain by evaporation and condensation. 2. purify. 3. fall in drops. —**dis′til•la′tion,** —**dis•till′er,** *n.* —**dis•till′er•y,** *n.*

dis•tinct′, *adj.* 1. clear. 2. separate. —**dis•tinct′ly,** *adv.*

dis•tinc′tion, *n.* 1. act or instance of distinguishing. 2. discrimination. 3. difference. 4. eminence. —**dis•tinc′tive,** *adj.*

dis•tin′guish, *v.* 1. identify as different. 2. perceive. 3. make eminent. —**dis•tin′guish•a•ble,** *adj.*

dis•tin′guished, *adj.* dignified or elegant.

dis•tort′, *v.* 1. twist out of shape. 2. hide truth or true meaning of. —**dis•tor′tion,** *n.*

dis•tract′, *v.* 1. divert attention of. 2. trouble. —**dis•trac′tion,** *n.*

dis•traught′, *adj.* crazed with anxiety.

dis•tress′, *n.* 1. torment. 2. state of emergency. —*v.* 3. afflict with sorrow.

dis•trib′ute, *v.,* **-uted, -uting.** 1. divide in shares. 2. spread. 3. sort. —**dis′tri•bu′tion,** *n.* —**dis•trib′u•tor,** *n.*

dis′trict, *n.* 1. political division. 2. region.

district attorney, attorney for the government within a given district, whose job is primarily prosecuting.

dis•trust′, *v.* 1. suspect. —*n.* 2. doubt. —**dis•trust′ful,** *adj.*

dis•turb′, *v.* 1. interrupt peace of. 2. unsettle. —**dis•turb′ance,** *n.*

dis•use′, *n.* absence of use.

ditch, *n.* 1. trench; channel. —**v.** 2. *Slang.* get rid of.

dith′er (dith ′er), *n.* 1. flustered. —*v.* 2. fail to act resolutely; vacillate.

dit′to, *n., pl.* **-tos,** *adv.* —*n.* 1. the same. —*adv.* 2. likewise.

ditto mark, mark (″) indicating repetition.

dit′ty, *n., pl.* **-ties.** simple song.

di′u•ret′ic, *adj.* promoting urination. —**di′u•ret′ic,** *n.*

di•ur′nal, *adj.* daily.

div., 1. dividend. 2. division. 3. divorced.

di′va (de′və, -vä), *n.* prima donna (def. 1).

di′van, *n.* sofa.

dive, *v.,* **dived** or **dove, dived, diving,** *n.* —*v.* 1. plunge into water. 2. plunge deeply. —*n.* 3. act of diving. —**div′er,** *n.*

di•verge′, *v.,* **-verged, -verging.** 1. move or lie in different directions. 2. differ. —**di•ver′gence,** *n.* —**di•ver′gent,** *adj.*

di′vers (dī′vərz), *adj.* various.

di•verse′, *adj.* assorted. —**di•ver′si•fy′,** *v.* —**di•ver′si•ty,** *n.* —**di•ver′si•fi•ca′tion,** *n.*

di•vert′, *v.* 1. turn aside. 2. amuse. —**di•ver′sion,** *n.* —**di•ver′sion•ar′y,** *adj.*

di•vest′, *v.* dispossess.

di•vide′, *v.,* **-vided, -viding,** *n.* —*v.* 1. separate into parts. 2. apportion. —*n.* 3. zone separating drainage basins. —**di•vid′a•ble,** *adj.* —**di•vid′er,** *n.*

div′i•dend′, *n.* 1. number to be divided. 2. share in profits.

di•vine′, *adj., n., v.,* **-vined, -vining.** —*adj.* 1. of or from God or a god. 2. religious. 3. godlike. —*n.* 4. theologian or clergyman. —*v.* 5. prophesy. 6. perceive. —**div′i•na′tion,** *n.* —**di•vine′ly,** *adv.*

divining rod, forked stick for finding water deposits.

di•vin′i•ty, *n., pl.* **-ties.** 1. divine nature. 2. god.

di•vi′sion, *n.* 1. act or result of dividing. 2. thing that divides. 3. section. 4. military unit under major general. —**di•vis′i•ble,** *adj.* —**di•vi′sion•al,** *adj.* —**di•vi′sive,** *adj.*

di•vi′sor, *n.* number dividing dividend.

di•vorce′, *n., v.,* **-vorced, -vorcing.** —*n.* 1. dissolution of marriage. 2. separation. —*v.* 3. separate by divorce. —**di•vor′cee′** (-sē′), *n.fem.*

div′ot, *n.* turf gouged out by a golf club stroke.

di•vulge′, *v.,* **-vulged, -vulging.** disclose.

Dix′ie (dik′sē), *n.* southern states of the U.S., esp. those that joined Confederacy.

Dix′ie•land′, *n.* style of jazz marked by accented four-four rhythm and improvisation.

diz'zy, *adj.,* **-zier, -ziest. 1.** giddy. **2.** confused. **3.** *Informal.* foolish; silly. —**diz'zi•ly,** *adv.* —**diz'zi•ness,** *n.*

D.J., disc jockey. Also, **DJ, deejay.**

DNA, deoxyribonucleic acid, substance that carries genes along its strands.

do, *v.,* **did, done, doing,** *n.* —*v.* **1.** perform; execute. **2.** behave. **3.** fare. **4.** finish. **5.** effect. **6.** render. **7.** suffice. —*n.* **8.** *Informal.* social gathering. **9.** (dō). first note of musical scale.

DOA, dead on arrival.

do'cent (dō'sənt), *n.* lecturer or guide, esp. in museum.

doc'ile (dos'əl), *adj.* **1.** willing. **2.** tractable. —**do•cil'i•ty,** *n.*

dock, *n.* **1.** wharf. **2.** place for ship. **3.** fleshy part of tail. **4.** prisoner's place in courtroom. —*v.* **5.** put into dock. **6.** cut off end of. **7.** deduct from (pay).

dock'et, *n.* **1.** list of court cases. **2.** label.

doc'tor, *n.* **1.** medical practitioner. **2.** holder of highest academic degree. —*v.* **3.** treat medicinally.

doc'tor•ate (-it), *n.* doctor's degree.

doctor's degree, degree of the highest rank awarded by universities.

doc'tri•naire', *adj.* orthodox.

doc'trine, *n.* **1.** principle. **2.** teachings. —**doc'tri•nal,** *adj.*

doc'u•ment, *n.* paper with information or evidence.

doc'u•dra'ma, *n.* fictionalized TV drama depicting actual events.

doc'u•men'ta•ry, *adj., n., pl.* **-ries.** —*adj.* **1.** of or derived from documents. —*n.* **2.** film on factual subject.

dod'der, *v.* shake; tremble; totter. —**dod'der•ing,** *adj.*

dodge, *v.,* **dodged, dodging,** *n.* —*v.* **1.** elude. —*n.* **2.** act of dodging. **3.** con. —**dodg'er,** *n.*

do'do, *n., pl.* **-dos, -does.** extinct bird.

doe, *n.* female deer, etc. —**doe'skin',** *n.*

does (duz), *v.* third pers. sing. pres. indic. of **do.**

does'n't (duz'-), *v. Informal.* does not.

doff, *v.* remove.

dog, *n., v.,* **dogged, dogging.**
—*n.* **1.** domesticated carnivore. —*v.* **2.** follow.

dog′-ear′, *n.* folded-down corner of book page.
—**dog′-eared′,** *adj.*

dog′ged, *adj.* persistent.

dog′ger•el, *n.* bad verse.

dog′house′, *n.* **1.** shelter for dog. **2.** place of disfavor.

dog′ma, *n.* doctrine.

dog•mat′ic, *adj.* **1.** of dogma. **2.** opinionated.
—**dog•mat′i•cal•ly,** *adv.*

dog′ma•tism′, *n.* aggressive assertion of opinions.

dog′wood′, *n.* flowering tree.

doi′ly, *n., pl.* **-lies.** small napkin.

Dol′by (dōl′bē, dôl′-), *n. Trademark.* system for reducing high-frequency noise in a tape recording.

dol′drums (dōl′-), *n. pl.* **1.** flat calms at sea. **2.** listless mood.

dole, *n., v.,* **doled, doling.** —*n.* **1.** portion of charitable gift. —*v.* **2.** give out sparingly.

dole′ful, *adj.* sorrowful; gloomy. —**dole′ful•ly,** *adv.*

doll, *n.* **1.** toy representing baby or other human being. **2.** attractive or nice person.

dol′lar, *n.* monetary unit equal to 100 cents.

dol′lop, *n.* lump or blob of soft substance, as whipped cream.

dol′ly, *n., pl.* **-lies. 1.** cart for moving heavy loads. **2.** movable platform.

dol′or•ous, *adj.* grievous.

dol′phin, *n.* whalelike animal.

dolt, *n.* fool. —**dolt′ish,** *adj.*

-dom, suffix indicating: **1.** domain, as *kingdom.* **2.** rank or station, as *dukedom.* **3.** general condition, as *freedom.*

do•main′, *n.* **1.** ownership of land. **2.** realm.

dome, *n.* spherical roof.

do•mes′tic, *adj.* **1.** of or devoted to the home. **2.** not foreign. —*n.* **3.** household servant. —**do′mes•tic′i•ty,** *n.*

do•mes′ti•cate′, *v.,* **-cated, -cating.** tame.
—**do•mes′ti•ca′tion,** *n.*

domestic partner, unmarried person who cohabits with another.

dom′i•cile′ (-sīl′, -səl), *n.* home.

dom′i•nate′, *v.*, **-nated, -nating. 1.** rule. **2.** tower above. **—dom′i•na′tion, dom′i•nance,** *n.* **—dom′i•nant,** *adj.*

dom′i•neer′, *v.* rule oppressively. **—dom′i•neer′ing,** *adj.*

do•min′ion, *n.* **1.** power of governing. **2.** territory governed.

dom′i•no′, *n., pl.* **-noes.** oblong dotted piece used in game of **dominoes.**

don, *v.,* **donned, donning.** put on.

do′nate, *v.,* **-nated, -nating.** give. **—do•na′tion,** *n.*

don′key, *n.* **1.** ass. **2.** fool.

don′ny•brook′, *n. (often cap.)* brawl; melee.

do′nor, *n.* giver.

doo′dle, *v.,* **-dled, -dling.** to scribble. **—doo′dler,** *n.*

doom, *n.* **1.** fate. **2.** ruin. **3.** judgment. **—***v.* **4.** condemn.

dooms′day′, *n.* day the world ends; Judgment Day.

door, *n.* **1.** movable barrier. **2.** Also, **door′way′.** entrance. **—door′bell′,** *n.* **—door′step′,** *n.*

door′yard′, *n.* yard near front door of house.

dope, *n.* **1.** liquid substance used to prepare a surface. **2.** *Informal.* narcotic. **3.** *Slang.* information; news. **4.** *Informal.* stupid person.

dop′ey, *adj.,* **-ier, -iest.** *Informal.* **1.** stupid; silly. **2.** sluggish or confused, as from drug use. Also, **dop′y.**

dor′mant, *adj.* **1.** asleep. **2.** inactive. **—dor′man•cy,** *n.*

dor′mer, *n.* vertical window projecting from sloping roof.

dor′mi•to′ry, *n., pl.* **-ries.** group sleeping place. Also, **dorm.**

dor′mouse′, *n., pl.* **-mice.** small rodent.

dor′sal, *adj.* of or on the back.

do′ry, *n., pl.* **-ries.** flat-bottomed rowboat.

DOS (dôs, dos), *n.* disk operating system for microcomputers.

dose, *n., v.,* **dosed, dosing. —***n.* **1.** amount to be taken. **—***v.* **2.** give doses to. **—dos′age,** *n.*

dos′si•er′ (dos′ē ā′), *n.* file.

dot, *n., v.,* **dotted, dotting.** —*n.* **1.** small spot. —*v.* **2.** mark with or make dots.

do′tard (dō′tərd), *n.* senile person.

dote, *v.,* **doted, doting. 1.** be overfond. **2.** be senile. —**dot′age,** *n.*

dou′ble, *adj., n., v.,* **-bled, -bling.** —*adj.* **1.** twice as great, etc. **2.** of two parts. **3.** deceitful. —*n.* **4.** double quantity. **5.** duplicate. —*v.* **6.** make double. **7.** bend. **8.** turn back. —**doub′ly,** *adv.*

double bass (bās), lowest-pitched instrument of violin family.

doub′le-cross′, *v. Informal.* cheat or betray. —**doub′le-cross′er,** *n.*

doub′le-dig′it, *adj.* involving two-digit numbers.

dou′ble en•ten′dre (än tän′drə, -tänd′), *n., pl.* **-ten′dres** (-tän′drəz, -tändz′). saying with two meanings.

dou′ble•head′er, *n.* two games played on the same day in rapid succession.

double play, baseball play in which two players are put out.

double standard, standard that differs for different persons or groups.

double take, delayed response, as to something not immediately recognized.

doub′le-talk′, *n.* evasive talk.

doubt (dout), *v.* **1.** be uncertain about. —*n.* **2.** uncertainty. —**doubt′less,** *adv., adj.*

doubt′ful, *adj.* **1.** having doubts. **2.** causing doubts or suspicion. —**doubt′ful•ly,** *adv.*

douche (dōōsh), *n., v.,* **douched, douching.** —*n.* **1.** jet of liquid applied to a body part or cavity. —*v.* **2.** apply a douche.

dough, *n.* mixture of flour, liquid, etc., for baking.

dough′nut, *n.* ringlike cake of fried, sweet dough. —**dough′nut•like′,** *adj.*

dour (dŏŏr, dour), *adj.* sullen.

douse, *v.,* **doused, dousing. 1.** plunge; dip. **2.** extinguish.

dove, *n.* pigeon.

dove′cote′, *n.* structure for tame pigeons. Also, **dove′cot′.**

dove′tail′, *n.* **1.** tenon-and-mortise joint. —*v.*

2. join by dovetail. 3. fit together harmoniously.

dow·a·ger (dou′ə jər), *n.* 1. titled or wealthy widow. 2. dignified elderly woman.

dow′dy, *adj.,* **-dier, -diest.** not stylish or attractive.

dow′el, *n.* wooden pin fitting into hole.

dow′er, *n.* widow's share of husband's property.

down, *adv.* 1. to, at, or in lower place or state. 2. on or to ground. 3. on paper. —*prep.* 4. in descending direction. —*n.* 5. descent. 6. soft feathers. —*v.* 7. subdue. —**down′wards,** *adv.* —**down′ward,** *adv., adj.* —**down′y,** *adj.*

down′cast′, *adj.* dejected.

down′er, *n. Informal.* 1. depressing experience or person. 2. sedative drug.

down′fall′, *n.* 1. ruin. 2. fall. —**down′fall′en,** *adj.*

down′grade′, *v.,* **-graded, -grading,** *n.* —*v.* 1. reduce in classification. —*n.* 2. downward slope.

down′heart′ed, *adj.* dejected. —**down′heart′ed·ly,** *adv.*

down′hill′, *adv., adj.* in downward direction.

down′play′, *v.* minimize.

down′pour′, *n.* heavy rain.

down′right′, *adj.* 1. thorough. —*adv.* 2. completely.

down′scale′, *adj.* of or for people at lower end of economic scale.

down′size′, *v.,* **-sized, -sizing.** 1. make smaller version of. 2. reduce in size or number.

down′stage′ (*adv.* -stāj′; *adj.* -stāj′), *adv., adj.* at or toward front of stage.

down′stairs′, *adv., adj.* to or on lower floor.

down′stream′, *adv., adj.* with current of stream.

Down syndrome, genetic disorder characterized by mental retardation, a wide, flattened skull, and slanting eyes. Also, **Down's syndrome.**

down′-to-earth′, *adj.* objective; practical.

down′town′, *n.* 1. central part of town. —*adj.* 2. of this part. —*adv.* 3. to or in this part.

down′trod′den, *adj.* oppressed.

down′turn′, *n.* decline.

dow′ry, *n., pl.* **-ries.** bride's estate.

dowse, *v.,* **dowsed, dowsing.** use divining rod. —**dows'er,** *n.*

dox·ol'o·gy, *n., pl.* **-gies.** hymn praising God.

doz., dozen.

doze, *v.,* **dozed, dozing,** *n.* —*v.* **1.** sleep lightly. —*n.* **2.** light sleep.

doz'en, *n., pl.* **dozen, dozens.** group of 12.

Dr., **1.** Doctor. **2.** Drive.

drab, *n., adj.,* **drabber, drabbest.** —*n.* **1.** dull color. —*adj.* **2.** colored drab. **3.** uninteresting. —**drab'ness,** *n.*

draft, *n.* **1.** drawing; sketch. **2.** rough version. **3.** current of air. **4.** haul. **5.** swallow of liquid. **6.** depth in water. **7.** selection for military service. **8.** written request for payment. —*v.* **9.** plan. **10.** write. **11.** enlist by draft. —**draft'y,** *adj.* —**draft·ee',** *n.*

drafts'man, *n.* person who draws plans, etc.

drag, *v.,* **dragged, dragging,** *n.* —*v.* **1.** haul. **2.** dredge. **3.** trail on ground. **4.** pass slowly. —*n.* **5.** thing used in dragging. **6.** hindrance.

drag'net', *n.* **1.** net for dragging. **2.** system for catching criminal.

drag'on, *n.* fabled reptile.

drag'on·fly', *n., pl.* **-flies.** large four-winged insect.

dra·goon', *n.* **1.** heavily armed mounted soldier, formerly common in European armies. —*v.* **2.** force; coerce.

drag race, race with cars accelerating from a standstill.

drain, *v.* **1.** flow off gradually. **2.** empty. **3.** exhaust. —*n.* **4.** channel for draining. —**drain'er,** *n.* —**drain'age,** *n.*

drake, *n.* male duck.

dram, *n.* **1.** apothecaries' weight, equal to ⅛ ounce. **2.** small drink of liquor.

dra'ma, *n.* **1.** story acted on stage. **2.** vivid series of events.

dra·mat'ic, *adj.* **1.** of plays or theater. **2.** highly vivid. —**dra·mat'i·cal·ly,** *adv.*

dra·mat'ics, *n.* **1.** theatrical art. **2.** exaggerated emotion.

dram'a·tist, *n.* playwright.

dram'a·tize', *v.,* **-tized, -tizing.** put in dramatic form. —**dram'a·ti·za'tion,** *n.*

drape, *v.,* **draped, draping,** *n.* —*v.* **1.** cover with fabric. **2.** arrange in folds. —*n.* **3.** hanging. —**dra'per•y,** *n.*

dras'tic, *adj.* extreme. —**dras'ti•cal•ly,** *adv.*

draught (draft), *n. Brit.* draft.

draw, *v.,* **drew, drawn, drawing,** *n.* —*v.* **1.** pull; lead. **2.** take out. **3.** attract. **4.** sketch. **5.** take in. **6.** deduce. **7.** stretch. **8.** make or have as draft. —*n.* **9.** act of drawing. **10.** part that is drawn. **11.** equal score. **12.** *Informal.* attraction to public.

draw'back', *n.* disadvantage.

draw'bridge', *n.* bridge that can be drawn up.

draw'er, *n.* **1.** sliding compartment. **2.** (*pl.*) trouserlike undergarment. **3.** person who draws.

draw'ing, *n.* drawn picture.

drawl, *v.* **1.** speak slowly. —*n.* **2.** drawled utterance.

drawn, *adj.* tense; haggard.

dray, *n.* low, strong cart. —**dray'man,** *n.*

dread, *v.* **1.** fear. —*n.* **2.** fear. **3.** awe. —*adj.* **4.** feared. **5.** revered.

dread'ful, *adj.* **1.** very bad. **2.** inspiring dread.

dread'ful•ly, *adv. Informal.* very.

dread'locks', *n.* hairstyle with many long, ropelike locks.

dream, *n.* **1.** ideas imagined during sleep. **2.** reverie. —*v.* **3.** have dream (about). **4.** fancy. —**dream'er,** *n.* —**dream'y,** *adj.*

dream team, group of experts associated in some joint action.

drear'y, *adj.,* **drearier, dreariest.** gloomy or boring. —**drear'i•ly,** *adv.* —**drear'i•ness,** *n.*

dredge, *n., v.,* **dredged, dredging.** —*n.* **1.** machine for moving earth at the bottom of river, etc. —*v.* **2.** move with dredge. **3.** sprinkle with flour.

dregs, *n.pl.* sediment.

drench, *v.* soak.

dress, *n.* **1.** woman's garment. **2.** clothing. —*v.* **3.** clothe. **4.** ornament. **5.** prepare. **6.** treat (wounds). —**dress'mak'er,** *n.* —**dress'mak'ing,** *n.*

dres•sage' (drə säzh', dre-), *n.* art of training a horse in obedience and precision.

dress circle, semicircular division of seats in a theater.

dress'er, *n.* 1. bureau; chest of drawers. 2. person who dresses another. 3. person who dresses in a certain way.

dress'ing, *n.* 1. sauce or stuffing. 2. application for wound.

dress rehearsal, final rehearsal.

dress'y, *adj.,* **-ier, -iest.** fancy.

drib'ble, *v.,* **-bled, -bling,** *n.* —*v.* 1. fall in drops. 2. bounce repeatedly. —*n.* 3. trickle.

dri'er, *n.* dryer.

drift, *n.* 1. deviation from set course. 2. tendency. 3. something driven, esp. into heap. —*v.* 4. carry by currents.

drift'er, *n.* person who moves frequently.

drill, *n.* 1. boring tool. 2. methodical training. 3. furrow for seeds. 4. sowing machine. 5. strong twilled cotton. —*v.* 6. pierce with drill. 7. train methodically. —**drill'er,** *n.*

drink, *v.,* **drank, drunk, drinking,** *n.* —*v.* 1. swallow liquid. 2. swallow alcoholic liquids. —*n.* 3. liquid for quenching thirst. 4. alcoholic beverage. —**drink'er,** *n.*

drip, *v.,* **dripped, dripping.** 1. fall or let fall in drops. —*n.* 2. act of dripping.

drive, *v.,* **drove, driven, driving,** *n.* —*v.* 1. send by force. 2. control; guide. 3. convey or travel in vehicle. 4. impel. —*n.* 5. military offensive. 6. strong effort. 7. trip in vehicle. 8. road for driving. —**driv'er,** *n.*

drive'-by', *n., pl.* **-bys.** 1. action of driving by something specified. 2. shooting that occurs from vehicle driving by. —**drive'-by',** *adj.*

drive'-in', *adj.* 1. designed for persons in automobiles. —*n.* 2. a drive-in business.

driv'el, *v.,* **-eled, -eling,** *n.* —*v.* 1. droll. 2. talk foolishly. —*n.* 3. foolish talk.

drive'way', *n.* road on private property.

driz'zle, *v.,* **-zled, -zling,** *n.* rain in fine drops.

droll (drōl), *adj.* amusingly odd. —**droll'er•y,** *n.*

drom'e•dar'y, *n., pl.* **-daries.** one-humped camel.

drone, *v.,* **droned, droning,** *n.* —*v.* **1.** make humming sound. **2.** speak dully. —*n.* **3.** monotonous tone. **4.** male of honeybee.

drool, *v.* **1.** salivate. —*n.* **2.** saliva dripping from the mouth.

droop, *v.* **1.** sink or hang down. **2.** lose spirit. —*n.* **3.** act of drooping. —**droop′y,** *adj.*

drop, *n., v.,* **dropped, dropping.** —*n.* **1.** small mass of liquid. **2.** small quantity. **3.** fall. **4.** steep slope. —*v.* **5.** fall or let fall. **6.** cease. **7.** visit. —**drop′per,** *n.*

drop kick, kick made by dropping ball to the ground and kicking it as it starts to bounce up. —**drop′kick′,** *v.* —**drop′-kick′er,** *n.*

drop′out′, *n.* student who quits before graduation.

drop′sy, *n.* edema.

dross, *n.* refuse.

drought (drout), *n.* dry weather. Also, **drouth.**

drove, *n.* **1.** group of driven cattle. **2.** crowd.

drown, *v.* suffocate by immersion in liquid.

drowse, *v.,* **drowsed, drowsing.** be sleepy. —**drow′sy,** *adj.* —**drow′si•ness,** *n.*

drub, *v.,* **drubbed, drubbing. 1.** beat. **2.** defeat.

drudge, *n., v.,* **drudged, drudging.** —*n.* **1.** person doing tedious work. —*v.* **2.** do such work. —**drudg′er•y,** *n.*

drug, *n., v.,* **drugged, drugging.** —*n.* **1.** therapeutic chemical. **2.** narcotic. —*v.* **3.** affect with drug. —**drug′store′,** *n.*

drug′gist, *n.* **1.** prepares drugs; pharmacist. **2.** person who owns or operates drugstore.

dru′id (droo′id), *n.* (*often cap.*) member of a pre-Christian religious order in Europe. —**dru′id•ism,** *n.*

drum, *n., v.,* **drummed, drumming.** —*n.* **1.** percussion musical instrument. **2.** eardrum. —*v.* **3.** beat on or as on drum. —**drum′mer,** *n.*

drum major, leader of marching band.

drum majorette, majorette.

drum′stick′, *n.* **1.** stick for beating a drum. **2.** leg of a cooked fowl.

drunk, *adj.* intoxicated. Also, **drunk′en.**

drunk′ard, *n.* habitually drunk person.

dry, *adj.,* **drier, driest,** *v.,* **dried, drying.** —*adj.* 1. not wet. 2. rainless. 3. not yielding liquid. 4. thirsty. 5. boring. 6. not expressing emotion. 7. not sweet. —*v.* 8. make or become dry. —**dry′ly,** *adv.* —**dry′ness,** *n.*

dry′ad, *n.* *(often cap.)* nymph of the woods.

dry′-clean′, *v.* clean with solvents. —**dry′-clean′er,** *n.*

dry′er, *n.* machine for drying.

dry ice, solid carbon dioxide, used esp. as a refrigerant.

dry run, rehearsal or trial.

DST, daylight-saving time.

du′al, *adj.* 1. of two. 2. double, two-fold. —**du′al•ism,** *n.* —**du•al′i•ty,** *n.*

dub, *v.,* **dubbed, dubbing.** 1. name formally. 2. furnish with new sound track.

du′bi•ous, *adj.* doubtful. —**du′bi•ous•ly,** *adv.*

du′cal, *adj.* of dukes.

duch′ess, *n.* 1. duke's wife. 2. woman equal in rank to duke.

duch′y (duch′ē), *n., pl.* **duchies.** 1. territory of duke. 2. small state.

duck, *v.* 1. plunge under water. 2. stoop quickly. 3. avoid. —*n.* 4. act of ducking. 5. swimming bird. 6. heavy cotton fabric. —**duck′ling,** *n.*

duck′bill′, *n.* small, egg-laying mammal.

duct, *n.* tube or canal in body. —**duct′less,** *adj.*

duc′tile, *adj.* 1. flexible. 2. compliant. —**duc•til′i•ty,** *n.*

duct tape, strongly adhesive tape, used in plumbing, household repairs, etc.

dud, *n. Informal.* failure.

dude (dōōd, dyōōd), *n.* 1. fop; dandy. 2. *Slang.* fellow; guy. 3. urban vacationer on ranch.

dudg′eon, *n.* indignation.

due, *adj.* 1. payable. 2. proper. 3. attributable. 4. expected. —*n.* 5. something due. 6. *(sometimes pl.).* regularly payable fee for membership. —*adv.* 7. in a straight line.

du′el, *n., v.* **-eled, -eling.** —*n.* 1. prearranged combat between two persons. —*v.* 2. fight in duel. —**du′el•er, du′el•ist,** *n.*

du·et′, *n.* music for two performers.

duf′fel bag′, cylindrical bag for carrying belongings.

duff′er, *n.* **1.** *Informal.* plodding, incompetent person. **2.** person inept at a specific sport, as golf.

dug′out′, *n.* **1.** boat made by hollowing a log. **2.** roofed structure where baseball players sit when not on the field. **3.** rough shelter dug in the ground, as by soldiers.

duke, *n.* **1.** ruler of duchy. **2.** nobleman below prince. —**duke′dom**, *n.*

dul′cet (dul′sit), *adj.* melodious.

dul′ci·mer (dul′sə mər), *n.* musical instrument with metal strings.

dull, *adj.* **1.** stupid. **2.** not brisk. **3.** tedious. **4.** not sharp. **5.** dim. —*v.* **6.** make or become dull. —**dul′ly**, *adv.* —**dull′ness, dul′ness**, *n.*

du′ly, *adv.* **1.** properly. **2.** punctually.

dumb, *adj.* **1.** temporarily unable to speak. **2.** *Often Offensive.* lacking the power of speech. **3.** *Informal.* stupid.

dumb′bell′, *n.* **1.** weighted bar for exercising. **2.** *Informal.* stupid person.

dumb·found′, *v.* strike dumb with awe. Also, **dum·found′**.

dumb′wait′er, *n.* small elevator for moving food, etc.

dum′my, *n., pl.* **-mies**, *adj.* —*n.* **1.** model or copy. **2.** *Informal.* **a.** *Offensive.* mute. **b.** stupid person. —*adj.* **3.** counterfeit.

dump, *v.* **1.** drop heavily. **2.** empty. —*n.* **3.** place for dumping. **4.** *Informal.* dilapidated, dirty place.

dump′ling, *n.* **1.** mass of steamed dough. **2.** dough wrapper with filling.

dump′y, *adj.,* **dumpier, dumpiest.** squat. —**dump′i·ness**, *n.*

dun, *v.,* **dunned, dunning**, *n.* —*v.* **1.** demand payment of. —*n.* **2.** demand for payment. **3.** dull brown.

dunce, *n.* stupid person.

dune, *n.* sand hill formed by wind.

dung, *n.* manure; excrement.

dun′ga·ree′, *n.* fabric for work clothes (**dungarees**).

dun′geon, *n.* underground cell.

dunk, *v.* **1.** dip in beverage before eating. **2.** submerge briefly in liquid. **3.** thrust downward.

duo (dōō′ō, dyōō′ō), *n.* **1.** duet. **2.** couple or pair.

du′o•de′num (dōō′ə dē′nəm), *n.* uppermost part of small intestine.

dupe, *n., v.,* **duped, duping.** —*n.* **1.** deceived person. —*v.* **2.** deceive.

du′plex (dōō′pleks, dyōō-), *n.* **1.** apartment with two floors. **2.** house for two families.

du′pli•cate, *adj., n., v.,* **-cated, -cating.** —*adj.* (-kit). **1.** exactly like. **2.** double. —*n.* (-kit). **3.** copy. —*v.* (-kāt′). **4.** copy. **5.** double. —**du′pli•ca′tion,** *n.* —**du′pli•ca′tor,** *n.*

du•plic′i•ty (-plis′-), *n., pl.* **-ties.** deceitfulness.

du′ra•ble, *adj.* enduring. —**du′ra•bil′i•ty,** *n.* —**du′ra•bly,** *adv.*

du•ra′tion, *n.* continuance.

du•ress′, *n.* compulsion.

dur′ing, *prep.* in the course of.

du′rum (dōō′əm), *n.* kind of wheat flour used in pasta.

dusk, *n.* twilight. —**dusk′y,** *adj.*

dust, *n.* **1.** fine particles of earth, etc. **2.** dead body. —*v.* **3.** free from dust. **4.** sprinkle. —**dust′y,** *adj.*

Dutch (duch), *n.* people or language of the Netherlands.

Dutch uncle, mentor who criticizes very frankly.

du′ti•ful, *adj.* doing one's duties. Also, **du′te•ous.** —**du′ti•ful•ly,** *adv.*

du′ty, *n., pl.* **-ties. 1.** obligation. **2.** function. **3.** tax.

dwarf, *n.* **1.** abnormally small person, etc. —*v.* **2.** make or make to seem small.

dwell, *v.,* **dwelt** or **dwelled, dwelling. 1.** reside. **2.** linger, esp. in words. —**dwell′ing,** *n.*

dwin′dle, *v.,* **-dled, -dling.** shrink; lessen.

dye, *n., v.,* **dyed, dyeing.** —*n.* **1.** coloring material. —*v.* **2.** color with dye. —**dye′ing,** *n.* —**dy′er,** *n.*

dyed′-in-the-wool′, *adj.* uncompromising.

dyke, *n.* dike.

dy•nam′ic, *adj.* 1. of force. 2. energetic. Also, **dy•nam′i•cal.** —**dy•nam′i•cal•ly,** *adv.* —**dyn′a•mism,** *n.*

dy′na•mite′, *n., v.,* **-mited, -miting.** —*n.* 1. explosive. —*v.* 2. blow up with dynamite.

dy′na•mo′, *n., pl.* **-mos.** 1. machine for generating electricity. 2. forceful person.

dy′nas•ty (dī′-), *n., pl.* **-ties.** rulers of same family. —**dy•nas′tic,** *adj.*

dys′en•ter′y (dis′-), *n.* infectious disease of bowels.

dys-, prefix meaning ill or bad, as *dysfunction.*

dys•func′tion, *n.* ineffective functioning. —**dys•func′tion•al,** *adj.*

dys•lex′i•a (dis lek′sē ə), *n.* impairment of ability to read. —**dys•lex′ic,** *adj., n.*

dys•pep′sia, *n.* indigestion. —**dys•pep′tic,** *adj. z.,* dozen.

dz., dozen.

E, e, *n.* fifth letter of English alphabet.

E, 1. east, eastern. 2. English.

ea., each.

each, *adj., pron.* 1. every one. —*adv.* 2. apiece.

ea′ger, *adj.* ardent. —**ea′ger•ly,** *adv.* —**ea′ger•ness,** *n.*

ea′gle, *n.* large bird of prey.

ea′gle-eyed′, *adj.* having unusually sharp eyesight.

ear, *n.* 1. organ of hearing. 2. grain-containing part of cereal plant.

ear′drum′, *n.* sensitive membrane in ear.

earl, *n.* nobleman ranking below marquis. —**earl′dom,** *n.*

ear′ly, *adv.,* **-lier, -liest,** *adj.* 1. in first part of. 2. before usual time.

ear′mark′, *n.* 1. identifying mark. —*v.* 2. designate.

ear′muffs′, *n.pl.* warm coverings for the ears.

earn, *v.* gain by labor or merit.

ear′nest, *adj.* 1. serious. —*n.* 2. portion given to bind bargain. —**ear′nest•ly,** *adv.*

earn′ings, *n.pl.* profits.

E

ear′phone′, *n.* sound receiver held to the ear.

ear′ring′, *n.* ornament worn on ear lobe.

ear′shot′, *n.* hearing range.

ear′split′ting, *adj.* extremely loud or shrill.

earth, *n.* 1. planet we inhabit. 2. dry land. 3. soil.

earth′en, *adj.* made of clay or earth. —**earth′en•ware′,** *n.*

earth′ly, *adj.,* **-lier, -liest.** of or in this world.

earth′quake′, *n.* vibration of earth's surface.

earth′shak′ing, *adj.* seriously affecting something basic.

earth′work′, *n.* 1. fortification formed of moved earth. 2. work of art involving large land area.

earth′worm′, *n.* burrowing worm.

earth′y, *adj.,* **earthier, earthiest.** 1. practical; realistic. 2. coarse; unrefined. —**earth′i•ness,** *n.*

ease, *n., v.,* **eased, easing.** —*n.* 1. freedom from work, pain, etc. 2. facility. —*v.* 3. relieve.

ea′sel, *n.* support stand.

ease′ment, *n.* right of one property owner to use land of another for some purpose.

east, *n.* 1. direction from which sun rises. 2. (*sometimes cap.*) region in this direction. —*adj., adv.* 3. toward, in, or from east. —**east′er•ly,** *adj., adv.* —**east′ern,** *adj.* —**east′ward,** *adv., adj.* —**East′ern•er,** *n.*

East′er, *n.* anniversary of resurrection of Christ.

eas′y, *adj.,* **easier, easiest.** 1. not difficult. 2. at ease. 3. affording comfort. —**eas′i•ly,** *adv.* —**eas′i•ness,** *n.*

eas′y-go′ing, *adj.* 1. casual; relaxed. 2. lenient.

eat, *v.,* **ate, eating, eaten.** 1. take into the mouth and swallow. 2. dissolve.

eat′er•y, *n., pl.* **-eries.** *Informal.* restaurant.

eating disorder, disorder characterized by severe disturbances in eating habits.

eaves, *n.pl.* overhang of roof.

eaves′drop′, *v.,* **-dropped, -dropping.** listen secretly. —**eaves′drop′per,** *n.*

ebb, *n.* 1. fall of tide. 2. decline. —*v.* 3. flow back. 4. decline.

eb′on•y, *n.* 1. hard black wood. —*adj.* 2. very dark.

e•bul′lient, *adj.* full of enthusiasm. —**e•bul′lience,** *n.*

ec•cen′tric (ik sen′-), *adj.* 1. odd. 2. off center. —*n.* 3. odd person. —**ec′cen•tric′i•ty** (-tris′-), *n.*

ec•cle′si•as′tic, *n.* 1. member of the clergy. —*adj.* 2. Also, **ec•cle′si•as′ti•cal.** of church or clergy.

ech′e•lon (esh′-), *n.* level of command.

ech′o, *n., pl.* **echoes,** *v.,* **echoed, echoing.** —*n.* 1. repetition of sound, esp. by reflection. —*v.* 2. emit or repeat as echo.

é•clair′, (ā-), *n.* cream- or custard-filled pastry.

é•clat′ (ā klä′), *n.* 1. brilliance, as of success. 2. showy display. 3. acclaim.

ec•lec′tic, *adj.* chosen from various sources.

e·clipse′, *n., v.,* **eclipsed, eclipsing.** —*n.* **1.** obscuring of light of sun or moon by passage of body in front of it. **2.** oblivion. —*v.* **3.** obscure.

e·clip′tic, *n.* path of sun.

eco-, prefix meaning ecology or environment, as *ecocide.*

e′co·cide′, *n.* destruction of natural environment.

e·col′o·gy, *n.* science of relationship between organisms and environment. —**e·col′o·gist,** *n.* —**ec′·o·log′i·cal,** *adj.*

e′co·nom′i·cal, *adj.* thrifty. —**e′co·nom′i·cal·ly,** *adv.*

e′co·nom′ics, *n.* production, distribution, and use of wealth. —**e′co·nom′ic,** *adj.* —**e·con′o·mist,** *n.*

e·con′o·mize′, *v.,* **-mized, -mizing.** save; be thrifty.

e·con′o·my, *n., pl.* **-mies. 1.** thrifty management. **2.** system of producing and distributing weath.

ec′o·sys′tem (ek′-), *n.* distinct ecological system.

ec′ru (ek′rōō), *n., adj.* beige. Also, **éc·ru** (ā′krōō).

ec′sta·sy, *n., pl.* **-sies. 1.** overpowering emotion. **2.** rapture. —**ec·stat′ic,** *adj.*

-ectomy, suffix meaning surgical removal of, as *tonsillectomy.*

ec′u·men′i·cal, *adj.* **1.** universal. **2.** of or pertaining to universal Christian unity. —**e·cu′men·ism,** *n.*

ec′ze·ma, *n.* disease of skin.

E′dam (ē′dəm, ē′dam), *n.* mild yellow cheese.

ed′dy, *n., pl.* **-dies,** *v.,* **-died, -dying.** —*n.* **1.** current at variance with main current. —*v.* **2.** whirl in eddies.

e′del·weiss′ (ād′l vīs′, -wīs′), *n.* flowering Alpine plant.

e·de′ma (i dē′mə), *n.* abnormal accumulation of fluid in body.

E′den, *n.* garden where Adam and Eve first lived; paradise.

edge, *n., v.,* **edged, edging.** —*n.* **1.** border; brink. **2.** cutting side. —*v.* **3.** border. **4.** move sidewise. —**edge′wise′,** *adv.* —**edg′ing,** *n.*

edg′y, *adj.,* **edgier, edgiest.** nervous or tense.

ed′i·ble, *adj.* fit to be eaten. —**ed′i·bil′i·ty,** *n.*

e′dict, *n.* official decree.

ed′i•fice (-fis), *n.* building.

ed′i•fy′, *v.,* -fied, -fying. instruct. —**ed′i•fi•ca′tion,** *n.*

ed′it, *v.* prepare for or direct publication of. —**ed′i•tor,** *n.*

e•di′tion, *n.* one of various printings of a book.

ed′i•to′ri•al, *n.* 1. article in periodical presenting its point of view. —*adj.* 2. of or written by editor. —**ed′i•to′ri•al•ize′,** *v.*

EDP, electronic data processing.

ed′u•cate′, *v.,* -cated, -cating. develop by instruction. —**ed′u•ca′tion,** *n.* —**ed′u•ca′tion•al,** *adj.* —**ed′u•ca′tor,** *n.*

-ee, suffix denoting person who is the object, beneficiary, or performer of an act, as *addressee; grantee; escapee.*

EEG, electroencephalogram.

eel, *n.* snakelike fish.

e′er, *adv. Poetic.* ever.

ee′rie, *adj.,* -rier, -riest. weird; unsettling. —**ee′ri•ly,** *adv.* —**ee′ri•ness,** *n.*

ef•face′, *v.,* -faced, -facing. wipe out. —**ef•face′ment,** *n.*

ef•fect′, *n.* 1. result. 2. power to produce results. 3. operation. 4. (*pl.*) personal property. —*v.* 5. bring about.

ef•fec′tive, *adj.* 1. producing intended results. 2. in force.

ef•fec′tive•ly, *adv.* 1. in an effective way. 2. for all practical purposes.

ef•fec′tu•al, *adj.* 1. capable; adequate. 2. valid or binding.

ef•fem′i•nate, *adj.* (of a man) having feminine traits.

ef′fer•vesce′, *v.,* -vesced, -vescing. give off bubbles of gas. —**ef′fer•ves′cence,** *n.* —**ef′fer•ves′cent,** *adj.*

ef•fete′ (i fēt′), *adj.* worn out.

ef′fi•ca′cious, *adj.* effective. —**ef′fi•ca•cy,** *n.*

ef•fi′cient, *adj.* acting effectively. —**ef•fi′cien•cy,** *n.* —**ef•fi′cient•ly,** *adv.*

ef′fi•gy, *n., pl.* -gies. visual representation of person.

ef′flu•ent (ef′lōō ənt), *n.* 1. something that flows out. —*adj.* 2. flowing out.

ef′fort, *n.* 1. force. 2. attempt.

ef•fron′ter•y, *n., pl.* -teries. impudence.

ef•fu′sion, *n.* free expression of feelings. —**ef•fu′sive,** *adj.*

e.g., for example.

e•gal′i•tar′i•an, *adj.* having all persons equal in status. —**e•gal′i•tar′i•an•ism,** *n.*

egg, *n.* **1.** reproductive body produced by animals. —*v.* **2.** encourage.

egg′head′, *n. Slang.* impractical intellectual.

egg′nog′, *n.* drink containing eggs, milk, etc.

egg′plant′, *n.* purple, egg-shaped vegetable.

e′go, *n.* self.

e′go•cen′tric (-sen′trik), *adj.* self-centered.

e′go•ism′, *n.* thinking only in terms of oneself. —**e′go•ist,** *n.* —**e′go•is′tic, e′go•is′ti•cal,** *adj.*

e′go•tism′, *n.* vanity. —**e′go•tist,** *n.* —**e′go•tis′tic, e′go•tis′ti•cal,** *adj.*

e•gre′gious (i grē′jəs), *adj.* flagrant; glaring. —**e•gre′gious•ly,** *adv.*

e′gress, *n.* exit.

e′gret, *n.* kind of heron.

E•gyp′tian (i jip′shən), *n.* native or citizen of Egypt. —**E•gyp•tian,** *adj.*

eh (ā, e), *interj.* (exclamation of surprise or doubt).

ei′der duck (ī′dər), sea duck yielding **eiderdown.**

eight, *n., adj.* seven plus one. —**eighth,** *adj., n.*

eight′een′, *n., adj.* ten plus eight. —**eight•eenth′,** *adj., n.*

eight′y, *n., adj.* ten times eight. —**eight′i•eth,** *adj., n.*

ei′ther (ē′ th ər, ī′ th ər), *adj., pron.* **1.** one or the other of two. —*conj.* **2.** (introducing an alternative.) —*adv.* **3.** (after negative clauses joined by **and, or, nor.**)

e•jac′u•late′, *v.,* **-lated, -lating. 1.** exclaim. **2.** eject. —**e•jac′u•la′tion,** *n.*

e•ject′, *v.* force out. —**e•jec′tion,** *n.* —**e•jec′tor,** *n.*

eke, *v.,* **eked, eking. eke out, 1.** supplement. **2.** make (livelihood) with difficulty.

EKG, 1. electrocardiogram. **2.** electrocardiograph.

e•lab′o•rate, *adj., v.,* **-rated, -rating.** —*adj.* (-ə rit). **1.** done with care and detail. —*v.* (-ə rāt′). **2.** supply details; work out. —**e•lab′o•ra′tion,** *n.*

é•lan′ (ā län′, ā läN′), *n.* lively zeal; dashing spirit.

e•lapse′, *v.,* **elapsed, elapsing.** (of time) pass; slip by.

e•las′tic, *adj.* **1.** springy. —*n.* **2.** material containing rubber. —**e•las′tic′i•ty** (-tis′-), *n.*

e•late′, *v.,* **elated, elating.** put in high spirits. —**e•la′tion,** *n.*

el′bow, *n.* **1.** joint between forearm and upper arm. —*v.* **2.** jostle.

elbow grease, hard work.

el′bow•room′, *n.* space to move or work freely.

eld′er, *adj.* **1.** older. —*n.* **2.** older person. **3.** small tree bearing clusters of **el′der•ber′ries.**

el′der•ly, *adj.* rather old.

eld′est, *adj.* oldest; first-born.

e•lect′, *v.* **1.** select by vote. —*adj.* **2.** selected. —*n.* **3.** (*pl.*) persons chosen. —**e•lec′tion,** *n.* —**e•lec′tive,** *adj.*

e•lec′tion•eer′, *v.* work for candidate in an election.

e•lec′tor•al college, body of special voters (**electors**) chosen to elect president and vice-president of U.S.

e•lec′tor•ate, *n.* voters.

e•lec′tri′cian, *n.* one who repairs electrical systems.

e•lec′tric′i•ty (-tris′-), *n.* **1.** agency producing light, heat, attraction, etc. **2.** electric current. —**e•lec′tric, e•lec′tri•cal,** *adj.* —**e•lec′tri•cal•ly,** *adv.* —**e•lec′tri•fy′,** *v.*

e•lec′tro•car′di•o•gram′, *n.* graphic record of heart action.

e•lec′tro•car′di•o•graph′, *n.* instrument for making electrocardiograms.

e•lec′tro•cute′, *v.,* **-cuted, -cuting.** kill by electricity. —**e•lec′tro•cu′tion,** *n.*

e•lec′trode, *n.* conductor through which current enters or leaves electric device.

e•lec′tro•en•ceph′a•lo•gram (i lek′trō en sef′ə lə gram′), *n.* graphic record of brain action.

e•lec′tro•en•ceph′a•lo•graph′, *n.* instrument for

making electroencephalo-grams.

e•lec•trol′o•gist, *n.* person trained in electrolysis for removing unwanted hair, moles, etc.

e•lec′trol′y•sis, *n.* 1. decomposition by electric current. 2. destruction by electric current.

e•lec′tro•lyte′, *n.* substance that conducts electricity when melted or dissolved. —**e•lec′tro•lyt′ic**, *adj.*

e•lec′tro•mag′net, *n.* device with iron or steel core made magnetic by electric current in surrounding coil. —**e•lec′tro•mag•net′ic**, *adj.* —**e•lec′tro•mag′net•ism**, *n.*

e•lec′tro•mo′tive, *adj.* of or producing electric current.

e•lec′tron, *n.* minute particle supposed to be or contain a unit of negative electricity.

electronic mail, system for sending messages between computers. Also, **e-mail**.

e•lec′tron′ics, *n.* science dealing with development of devices involving flow of electrons. —**e•lec′tron′ic**,

adj. —**e•lec′tron′i•cal•ly**, *adv.*

el′ee•mos′y•nar′y (el′ə-), *adj.* charitable.

el′e•gant, *adj.* luxurious or refined. —**el′e•gance**, *n.* —**el′e•gant•ly**, *adv.*

el′e•gy, *n., pl.* -**gies**. poem of mourning. —**el′e•gi′ac** (el′i jī′ək, i lē′jē ak′), *adj.*

el′e•ment, *n.* 1. part of whole. 2. rudiment. 3. suitable environment. 4. (*pl.*) atmospheric forces. 5. substance that cannot be broken down chemically. 6. (*pl.*) bread and wine of the Eucharist. —**el′e•men′tal**, *adj.*

el′e•men′ta•ry, *adj.* of or dealing with elements or rudiments.

elementary school, school giving elementary instruction in six or eight grades.

el′e•phant, *n.* large mammal with long trunk and tusks.

el′e•phan′tine (-fan′tēn, -tīn), *adj.* 1. huge. 2. clumsy.

el′e•vate′, *v.*, -**vated**, -**vating**. 1. raise higher. 2. exalt.

el′e•va′tion, *n.* 1. elevated place. 2. height. 3. measured drawing of vertical face.

el′e•va′tor, *n.* 1. platform for lifting. 2. grain storage place.

e•lev′en, *n., adj.* ten plus one. —**e•lev′enth,** *adj., n.*

elf, *n., pl.* **elves.** mischievous sprite. —**elf′in,** *adj.*

e•lic′it (-lis′-), *v.* evoke.

e•lide′ (i līd′), *v.,* **-lided, -liding.** 1. omit in pronunciation. 2. pass over. —**e•li′sion** (i lizh′ən), *n.*

el′i•gi•ble, *adj.* qualified. —**el′i•gi•bil′i•ty,** *n.*

e•lim′i•nate′, *v.,* **-nated, -nating.** get rid of. —**e•lim′i•na′tion,** *n.*

e•lite′ (i lēt′), *adj.* 1. regarded as finest. —*n.* (*sing.* or *pl.*) elite group of persons.

e•lit′ism, *n.* favoritism of elite. —**e•lit′ist,** *n., adj.*

e•lix′ir, *n.* 1. preparation supposed to prolong life. 2. kind of medicine.

elk, *n.* large deer.

el•lipse′, *n.* closed plane curve forming regular oblong figure. —**el•lip′ti•cal,** *adj.*

el•lip′sis, *n., pl.* **-ses.** omission of word or words.

elm, *n.* large shade tree.

el′o•cu′tion, *n.* art of speaking in public. —**el′o•cu′tion•ar′y,** *adj.* —**el′o•cu′tion•ist,** *n.*

e•lon′gate, *v.,* **-gated, -gating.** lengthen. —**e•lon′ga′tion,** *n.*

e•lope′, *v.,* **eloped, eloping.** run off with lover to be married. —**e•lope′ment,** *n.*

el′o•quent, *adj.* fluent and forcible. —**el′o•quence,** *n.* —**el′o•quent•ly,** *adv.*

else, *adv.* 1. instead. 2. in addition. 3. otherwise.

else′where′, *adv.* somewhere else.

e•lu′ci•date′ (-loo′sə-), *v.,* **-dated, -dating.** explain. —**e•lu′ci•da′tion,** *n.* —**e•lu′ci•da′tor,** *n.*

e•lude′, *v.,* **eluded, eluding.** 1. avoid cleverly. 2. baffle. —**e•lu′sive,** *adj.* —**e•lu′sive•ly,** *adv.*

e•ma′ci•ate′ (-mā′shē-), *v.,* **-ated, -ating.** make lean. —**e•ma′ci•a′tion,** *n.*

e′-mail′, *n.* electronic mail. Also, **E-mail.**

em'a·nate', *v.*, **-nated,
-nating.** come forth.
—**em'a·na'tion**, *n.*

e·man'ci·pate', *v.*, **-pated,
-pating.** liberate.
—**e·man'ci·pa'tion**, *n.*
—**e·man'ci·pa'tor**, *n.*

e·mas'cu·late', *v.*, **-lated,
-lating.** castrate.
—**e·mas'cu·la'tion**, *n.*

em·balm', *v.* treat (dead body)
to prevent decay. —**em·balm'
er**, *n.*

em·bank'ment, *n.* long
earthen mound.

em·bar'go, *n., pl.* **-goes.**
government restriction of
movement of ships or goods.

em·bark', *v.* 1. put or go on
board ship. 2. start.
—**em'bar·ka'tion**, *n.*

em·bar'rass, *v.* 1. make
ashamed. 2. complicate.
—**em·bar'rass·ment**, *n.*

em'bas'·sy, *n., pl.* **-sies.** 1.
ambassador and staff. 2.
headquarters of ambassador.

em·bat'tled, *adj.* engaged in
conflict.

em·bed', *v.*, **-bedded,
-bedding.** fix in surrounding
mass.

em·bel'lish, *v.* decorate.
—**em·bel'lish·ment**, *n.*

em'ber, *n.* live coal.

em·bez'zle, *v.*, **-zled, -zling.**
steal (money entrusted).
—**em·bez'zle·ment**, *n.*
—**em·bez'zler**, *n.*

em·bit'ter, *v.* make bitter.

em·bla'zon, *v.* decorate, as
with emblems.

em'blem, *n.* symbol.
—**em'blem·at'ic**, *adj.*

em·bod'y, *v.*, **-bodied,
-bodying.** 1. put in concrete
form. 2. comprise.
—**em·bod'i·ment**, *n.*

em'bo·lism, *n.* closing off of
blood vessel, as by gas
bubble.

em·boss', *v.* ornament with
raised design.

em·brace', *v.*, **-braced,
-bracing**, *n.* —*v.* 1. clasp in
arms. 2. accept willingly. 3.
include. —*n.* 4. act of
embracing.

em·broi'der, *v.* decorate with
stitches. —**em·broi'der·y**, *n.*

em·broil', *v.* involve in strife.
—**em·broil'ment**, *n.*

em′bry•o′, *n., pl.* **-bryos.** organism in first stages of growth. —**em′bry•on′ic**, *adj.*

em′cee′ (em′sē′) *n., v.,* **-ceed, -ceeing.** —*n.* 1. master of ceremonies. —*v.* 2. serve as emcee.

e•mend′, *v.* correct. —**e′men•da′tion**, *n.*

em′er•ald, *n.* 1. green gem.—*adj.* 2. of a deep green.

e•merge′, *v.,* **emerged, emerging.** come forth or into notice. —**e•mer′gence**, *n.*

e•mer′gen•cy, *n., pl.* **-cies.** urgent occasion for action.

e•mer′i•tus, *adj.* retaining title after retirement.

em′er•y, *n.* mineral used for grinding, etc.

e•met′ic, *n.* medicine that induces vomiting.

em′i•grate′, *v.,* **-grated, -grating.** leave one's country to settle in another. —**em′i•grant**, *n.* —**em′i•gra′tion**, *n.*

é′mi•gré′ (em′i grā′, em′i grā′), *n.* emigrant who flees esp. for political reasons.

em′i•nence, *n.* high repute. —**em′i•nent**, *adj.* —**em′i•nent•ly**, *adv.*

eminent domain, power of the state to take private property for public use.

em′is•sar′y, *n., pl.* **-saries.** agent on mission.

e•mit′, *v.,* **emitted, emitting.** 1. send forth. —**e•mis′sion**, —**e•mit′ter**, *n.*

e•mol′lient (i mol′yənt), *adj.* 1. softening; soothing. —*n.* 2. emollient substance.

e•mol′u•ment (-yə-), *n.* wage.

e•mote, *v.,* **emoted, emoting.** show emotion in or as if in acting. —**e•mot′er**, *n.*

e•mo′tion, *n.* state of feeling. —**e•mo′tion•al**, *adj.*

em′pa•thy, *n.* sensitive awareness of another's feelings. —**em′pa•thet′ic**, *adj.* —**em′pa•thize′**, *v.*

em′per•or, *n.* ruler of empire. —**em′press**, *n.fem.*

em′pha•sis, *n., pl.* **-ses.** greater importance; stress. —**em•phat′ic**, *adj.* —**em•phat′i•cal•ly**, *adv.* —**em′pha•size′**, *v.*

em′phy•se′ma (em′fə sē′mə, -zē′-,), *n.* lung disease.

em′pire, *n.* nations under one ruler.

em·pir′i·cal (em pir′i kəl), *adj.* drawing on experience.

em·ploy′, *v.* 1. use or hire. —*n.* 2. employment. —**em·ploy′ee**, *n.* —**em·ploy′er**, *n.* —**em·ploy′ment**, *n.*

em·po′ri·um, *n.* large store.

em·pow′er, *v.* 1. authorize to act for one. 2. enable. —**em·pow′er·ment**, *n.*

emp′ty, *adj.*, **-tier, -tiest**, *v.*, **-tied, -tying**. —*adj.* 1. containing nothing. —*v.* 2. deprive of contents. 3. become empty. —**emp′ti·ness**, *n.*

empty nest syndrome, depressed state felt by some parents after their children have grown up and left home.

EMT, emergency medical technician.

e′mu (ē′myo͞o), *n.* large flightless Australian bird.

em′u·late′, *v.*, **-lated, -lating**. try to equal or excel. —**em′u·la′tion**, *n.*

e·mul′si·fy′, *v.*, **-fied, -fying**. make into emulsion.

e·mul′sion, *n.* 1. milklike mixture of liquids. 2. light-sensitive layer on film.

en-, prefix meaning: 1. put into or on, as *enthrone*. 2. cover or surround with, as *encircle*. 3. cause to be, as *enlarge*.

en·a′ble, *v.*, **-bled, -bling**. give power, means, etc., to.

en·act′, *v.* 1. make into law. 2. act part of. —**en·act′ment**, *n.*

e·nam′el, *n.*, *v.*, **-eled, -eling**. —*n.* 1. glassy coating fused to metal, etc. 2. paint giving a glossy surface. 3. surface of teeth. —*v.* 4. apply enamel to. —**en·am′el·ware′**, *n.*

en·am′or, *v.* fill with love.

en·camp′, *v.*, settle in camp. —**en·camp′ment**, *n.*

en·cap′su·late′, *v.*, **-lated, -lating**. place as if in a capsule; summarize.

en·case′, *v.*, **-cased, -casing**. enclose in or as if in a case.

en·ceph′a·li′tis (en sef′ə lī′tis), *n.* inflammation of the brain.

en·chant′, *v.* bewitch; beguile; charm. —**en·chant′ment**, *n.*

en′chi·la′da, *n.* food consisting of a tortilla rolled around a filling, usu. with a chili-flavored sauce.

en·cir′cle, *v.*, **-cled, -cling**. surround.

encl., 1. enclosed. 2. enclosure.

en′clave, *n.* country, etc., surrounded by alien territory.

en•close′, *v.,* -closed, -closing. 1. close in on all sides. 2. put in envelope. —**en•clo′sure,** *n.*

en•code′, *v.,* -coded, -coding. convert into code.

en•co′mi•um (-kō′-), *n., pl.* -miums, -mia. praise; eulogy.

en•com′pass, *v.* 1. encircle. 2. contain.

en′core, *interj.* 1. again! bravo! —*n.* 2. additional song, etc.

en•coun′ter, *v.* 1. meet. —*n.* 2. casual meeting. 3. combat.

en•cour′age, *v.,* -aged, -aging. inspire or help. —**en•cour′age•ment,** *n.*

en•croach′, *v.* trespass. —**en•croach′ment,** *n.*

en•cum′ber, *v.* impede; burden. —**en•cum′brance,** *n.*

en•cyc′li•cal (-sik′-), *n.* letter from Pope to bishops.

en•cy′clo•pe′di•a, *n.* reference book giving information on many topics. Also, **en•cy′clo•pae′di•a.** —**en•cy′clo•pe′dic,** *adj.*

end, *n.* 1. extreme or concluding part. 2. close. 3. purpose. 4. result. —*v.* 5. bring or come to an end. 6. result. —**end′less,** *adj.*

en•dan′ger, *v.* expose to danger.

en•dear′, *v.* make beloved. —**en•dear′ment,** *n.*

en•deav′or, *v., n.* attempt.

en•dem′ic, *adj.* of a particular people or place.

end′ing, *n.* close.

en′dive, *n.* plant for salad.

en′do•crine (en′də krin, -krīn′), *adj.* 1. secreting internally into the blood or lymph. 2. of glands involved in such secretion.

en•dorse′, *v.,* -dorsed, -dorsing. 1. support. 2. sign. —**en•dorse′ment,** *n.*

en•dow′, *v.* 1. grant fund to. 2. equip. —**en•dow′ment,** *n.*

en•dure′, *v.,* -dured, -during. 1. tolerate. 2. last. —**en•dur′a•ble,** *adj.* —**en•dur′ance,** *n.*

en′e•ma, *n.* liquid injection into rectum.

en′em•y, *n., pl.* -mies. adversary; opponent.

en′er·gize′, *v.*, -gized, -gizing. give energy. —**en′er·giz′er**, *n.*

en′er·gy, *n., pl.* -gies. capacity for activity; vigor. —**en·er·get′ic**, *adj.*

en′er·vate′, *v.*, -vated, -vating. weaken.

en·fee′ble, *v.*, -bled, -bling. weaken.

en·fold′, *v.* wrap around.

en·force′, *v.* -forced, -forcing. compel obedience to. —**en·force′a·ble**, *adj.* —**en·force′ment**, *n.* —**en·forc′er**, *n.*

en·fran′chise, *v.*, -chised, -chising. admit to citizenship.

en·gage′, *v.*, -gaged, -gaging. 1. occupy. 2. hire. 3. please. 4. betroth. 5. interlock with. 6. enter into conflict with. —**en·gaged′**, *adj.* —**en·gage′ment**, *n.*

en·gag′ing, *adj.* charming. —**en·gag′ing·ly**, *adv.*

en·gen′der (-jen′-), *v.* cause.

en′gine, *n.* 1. machine for converting energy into mechanical work. 2. locomotive.

en′gi·neer′, *n.* 1. expert in engineering. 2. engine operator. —*v.* 3. contrive.

en′gi·neer′ing, *n.* art of practical application of physics, chemistry, etc.

Eng′lish, *n.* language of the people of England, Australia, the U.S., etc. —**Eng′lish**, *adj.* —**Eng′lish·man**, *n.* —**Eng′lish·wom′an**, *n.fem.*

en·gorge′, *v.*, -gorged, -gorging. congest, esp. with blood. —**en·gorge′ment**, *n.*

en·grave′, *v.*, -graved, -graving. cut into hard surface for printing. —**en·grav′er**, *n.* —**en·grav′ing**, *n.*

en·gross′, *v.* occupy wholly.

en·gulf′, *v.* swallow up.

en·hance′, *v.*, -hanced, -hancing. increase.

e·nig′ma, *n.* something puzzling. —**en′ig·mat′ic**, **en′ig·mat′i·cal**, *adj.*

en·join′, *v.* prohibit. —**en·join′der**, *n.*

en·joy′, *v.* find pleasure in or for. —**en·joy′a·ble**, *adj.* —**en·joy′ment**, *n.*

en·large′, *v.*, -larged, -larging. make or grow larger. —**en·large′ment**, *n.*

en·light′en, *v.* impart knowledge to. —**en·light′en·ment**, *n.*

en·list', *v.* enroll for service.
—**en·list'ment**, *n.*

en·liv'en, *v.* make active.

en masse' (än mas', äN), in a
mass; all together.

en·mesh', *v.* entangle.

en'mi·ty, *n., pl.* **-ties.** hatred.

en'nui' (än'wē'), *n.* boredom.

e·nor'mi·ty, *n., pl.* **-ties. 1.**
extreme wickedness. **2.**
grievous crime; atrocity.

e·nor'mous, *adj.* gigantic.
—**e·nor'mous·ly**, *adv.*

e·nough', *adj.* **1.** adequate.
—*n.* **2.** adequate amount.
—*adv.* **3.** sufficiently.

en·plane', *v.,* **-planed,**
-planing. board an airplane.

en·quire', *v.,* **-quired, -quiring.**
inquire. —**en·quir'y**, *n.*

en·rage', *v.,* **-raged, -raging.**
make furious.

en·rap'ture, *v.,* **-tured, -turing.**
delight.

en·rich', *v.* make rich or
better. —**en·rich'ment**, *n.*

en·roll', *v.* take into group.
—**en·roll'ment**, *n.*

en route (än root'), on the
way.

en·sconce' (en skons'), *v.,*
-sconced, -sconcing. settle
securely or snugly.

en·sem'ble (än säm'bəl), *n.*
assembled whole.

en·shrine', *v.,* **-shrined,**
-shrining. cherish.

en·shroud', *v.* conceal.

en'sign (-sīn; *Mil.* -sən), *n.* **1.**
flag. **2.** lowest commissioned
naval officer.

en·slave', *v.,* **-slaved, -slaving.**
make slave of.
—**en·slave'ment**, *n.*

en·snare', *v.,* **-snared,**
-snaring. entrap.

en·sue', *v.,* **-sued, -suing.**
follow.

en·sure', *v.,* **-sured, -suring.**
make certain; secure.

en·tail', *v.* involve.

en·tan'gle, *v.,* **-gled, -gling.**
involve; entrap.
—**en·tan'gle·ment**, *n.*

en·tente' (än tänt'), *n.* **1.**
agreement. **2.** alliance of
parties to an entente.

en'ter, *v.* **1.** come or go in. **2.**
begin. **3.** record.

en'ter·i'tis, *n.* inflammation
of the intestines.

en'ter·prise', *n.* 1. project. 2. initiative.

en'ter·pris'ing, *adj.* showing initiative.

en'ter·tain', *v.* 1. amuse. 2. treat as guest. 3. hold in mind. —**en'ter·tain'er**, *n.* —**en'ter·tain'ing**, *adj.* —**en'ter·tain'ment**, *n.*

en·thrall', *v.* 1. captivate. 2. enslave.

en·throne, *v.*, -throned, -throning. place on a throne. —**en·throne'ment**, *n.*

en·thuse', *v.*, -thused, -thus·ing. show enthusiasm.

en·thu'si·asm', *n.* lively interest. —**en·thu'si·ast**, *n.* —**en·thu'si·as'tic**, *adj.*

en·tice', *v.*, -ticed, -ticing. lure. —**en·tice'ment**, *n.*

en·tire', *adj.* whole. —**en·tire'ly**, *adv.* —**en·tire'ty**, *n.*

en·ti'tle, *v.*, -tled, -tling. permit to claim something. —**en·ti'tle·ment**, *n.*

en'ti·ty, *n.*, *pl.* -ties. real or whole thing.

en·tomb', *v.* bury.

en'to·mol'o·gy, *n.* study of insects. —**en'to·mol'o·gist**, *n.*

en'tou·rage' (än'tŏŏ räzh'), *n.* group of attendants.

en'trails, *n.pl.* internal parts of body, esp. intestines.

en'trance, *n.*, *v.*, -tranced, -trancing. —*n.* (en'trəns). 1. act of entering. 2. place for entering. 3. admission. —*v.* (en trans'). 4. charm.

en'trant, *n.* person who enters competition or contest.

en·trap', *v.*, -trapped, -trapping. 1. catch in a trap. 2. entice into guilty situation. —**en·trap'ment**, *n.*

en·treat', *v.* implore. —**en·treat'ing·ly**, *adv.*

en·treat'y, *n.*, *pl.* -ies. earnest request.

en'tree (än'trā), *n.* 1. main dish of meal. 2. access.

en·trench', *v.* fix in position. —**en·trench'ment**, *n.*

en'tre·pre·neur' (än'trə prə nûr'), *n.* independent business manager. —**en'tre·pre·neur'i·al**, *adj.*

en'tro·py (en'trə pē), *n.* 1. measure of the amount of

energy unavailable for useful work in a thermodynamic process. **2.** tendency toward disorder.

en•trust′, *v.* give in trust.

en′try, *n., pl.* **-tries. 1.** entrance. **2.** recorded statement, etc. **3.** contestant.

en•twine′, *v.,* **-twined, -twining.** twine together.

e•nu′mer•ate′, *v.,* **-ated, -ating.** list; count. —**e•nu′mer•a′tion**, *n.*

e•nun′ci•ate′ (-sē-), *v.,* **-ated, -ating.** say distinctly. —**e•nun′ci•a′tion**, *n.*

en•vel′op, *v.* wrap; surround. —**en•vel′op•ment**, *n.*

en′ve•lope′, *n.* **1.** covering for letter. **2.** covering; wrapper.

en•vi′ron•ment, *n.* surrounding conditions. —**en•vi′ron•men′tal**, *adj.*

en•vi′ron•men′tal•ist, *n.* person working to protect environment.

en•vi′rons, *n.pl.* outskirts.

en•vis′age, *v.,* **-aged, -aging.** form mental picture of. Also, **en•vi′sion.**

en′voy, *n.* **1.** diplomatic agent. **2.** messenger.

en′vy, *n., pl.* **-vies**, *v.,* **-vied, -vying.** —*n.* **1.** discontent at another's good fortune. **2.** thing coveted. —*v.* **3.** regard with envy. —**en′vi•a•ble**, *adj.* —**en′vi•ous**, *adj.* —**en′vi•ous•ly**, *adv.*

en′zyme (-zīm), *n.* bodily substance capable of producing chemical change in other substances. —**en′zy•mat′ic**, *adj.*

e′on, *n.* long period of time.

EPA, Environmental Protection Agency.

ep′au•let′ (ep′ə-), *n.* shoulder piece worn on uniform. Also, **ep′au•lette′.**

e•phem′er•al, *adj.* brief.

ep′ic, *adj.* **1.** describing heroic deeds. —*n.* **2.** epic poem.

ep′i•cen′ter, *n.* point directly above center of earthquake.

ep′i•cure′, *n.* connoisseur of food and drink. —**ep′i•cu•re′an**, *adj., n.*

ep′i•dem′ic, *adj.* **1.** affecting many persons at once. —*n.* **2.** epidemic disease.

ep′i•der′mis, *n.* outer layer of skin. —**ep′i•der′mal, ep′i•der′mic**, *adj.*

ep'i·glot'tis, *n.* thin structure that covers larynx during swallowing.

ep'i·gram', *n.* witty statement. —**ep'i·gram·mat'ic,** *adj.*

ep'i·lep'sy, *n.* nervous disease often marked by convulsions. —**ep'i·lep'tic,** *adj., n.*

ep'i·logue', *n.* afterward.

e·piph'a·ny, *n.* 1. act of showing oneself; appearance. 2. sudden perception or realization. 3. (*cap.*) festival, Jan. 6, commemorating the Wise Men's visit to Christ.

e·pis'co·pa·cy, *n., pl.* **-cies.** church government by bishops.

e·pis'co·pal, *adj.* 1. governed by bishops. 2. (*cap.*) designating Anglican Church. —**E·pis'co·pa'lian,** *n., adj.*

ep'i·sode', *n.* incident. —**ep'i·sod'ic,** *adj.*

e·pis'tle, *n.* letter.

ep'i·taph', *n.* inscription on tomb.

ep'i·thet', *n.* descriptive term for person or things.

e·pit'o·me, *n.* 1. summary. 2. typical specimen. —**e·pit'o·mize',** *v.*

e plu'ri·bus u'num, *Latin.* out of many, one (motto of the U.S.).

ep'och (ep'ək), *n.* distinctive period of time. —**ep'och·al,** *adj.*

ep·ox'y, *n., pl.* **-ies.** tough synthetic resin used in glues.

Ep'som salts, salt used esp. as a cathartic. Also, **Ep'som salt.**

eq'ua·ble, *adj.* even; temperate. —**eq'ua·bly,** *adv.*

e'qual, *adj., n., v.,* **equaled, equaling.** —*adj.* 1. alike in quantity, rank, size, etc. 2. uniform. 3. adequate. —*n.* 4. one that is equal to. —*v.* 5. be equal to. —**e·qual'i·ty,** *n.* —**e'qual·ize',** *v.* —**e'qual·ly,** *adv.*

equal (or **equals**) **sign,** symbol (=) indicating equality between terms.

e'qua·nim'i·ty, *n.* calmness.

e·quate', *v.,* **equated, equating.** consider as equal.

e·qua'tion, *n.* expression of equality of two quantities.

e·qua'tor, *n.* imaginary circle around earth midway between poles. —**e'qua·to'ri·al,** *adj.*

e•ques'tri•an, *adj.* **1.** of horse riders or horsemanship. —*n.* **2.** Also, *fem.,* **e•ques'tri•enne'.** horse rider.

e'qui•dis'tant, *adj.* equally distant.

e'qui•lat'er•al, *adj.* having all sides equal.

e'qui•lib'ri•um, *n., pl.* **-riums, -ria.** balance.

e'quine, *adj.* of horses.

e'qui•nox', *n.* time when night and day are of equal length. —**e'qui•noc'tial,** *adj., n.*

e•quip', *v.,* **equipped, equipping.** furnish; provide. —**e•quip'ment,** *n.*

eq'ui•ta•ble, *adj.* just; fair. —**eq'ui•ta•bly,** *adv.*

eq'ui•ty, *n., pl.* **-ties. 1.** fairness. **2.** share.

e•quiv'a•lent, *adj., n.* equal.

e•quiv'o•cal, *adj.* **1.** ambiguous. **2.** questionable.

e•quiv'o•cate', *v.,* **-cated, -cating.** express oneself ambiguously or indecisively. —**e•quiv'o•ca'tion,** *n.* —**e•quiv'o•ca'tor,** *n.*

e'ra, *n.* period of time.

ERA, 1. Also, **era.** earned run average. **2.** Equal Rights Amendment.

e•rad'i•cate', *v.,* **-cated, -cating.** remove completely. —**e•rad'i•ca'tion,** *n.*

e•rase', *v.,* **erased, erasing.** rub out. —**e•ras'a•ble,** *adj.* —**e•ras'er,** *n.* —**e•ra'sure,** *n.*

ere, *prep., conj. Archaic.* before.

e•rect', *adj.* **1.** upright. —*v.* **2.** build.

e•rec'tion, *n.* **1.** something erected. **2.** erect state of an organ. —**e•rec'tile** (i rek'tl, -tīl), *adj.*

erg, *n.* unit of work or energy.

er'go (ûr'gō, er'gō), *conj., adv.* therefore.

er'go•nom'ics, *n.* applied science that coordinates workplace design and equipment with workers' needs. —**er'go•nom'ic,** *adj.*

er'mine, *n.* kind of weasel.

e•rode', *v.,* **eroded, eroding.** wear away. —**e•ro'sion,** *n.*

e•rog'e•nous (i roj'ə nəs), *adj.* sensitive to sexual stimulation.

e•rot′ic, *adj.* **1.** of sexual love. **2.** arousing sexual desire. —**e•rot′i•cal•ly,** *adv.* —**e•rot′i•cism,** *n.*

e•rot′i•ca, *n.pl.* erotic literature and art.

err (ûr), *v.* **1.** be mistaken. **2.** sin.

er′rand, *n.* special trip.

er′rant, *adj.* roving.

er•rat′ic, *adj.* irregular.

er•ra′tum, *n., pl.* **-ta.** (*usually pl.*) error in printing.

er•ro′ne•ous, *adj.* incorrect. —**er•ro′ne•ous•ly,** *adv.*

er′ror, *n.* **1.** mistake. **2.** sin.

er•satz′ (er zäts′), *n., adj.,* substitute.

erst′while, *adj.* former.

ERT, estrogen replacement therapy.

er′u•dite′, *adj.* learned. —**er′u•di′tion,** *n.*

e•rupt′, *v.* burst forth. —**e•rup′tion,** *n.*

er′y•sip′e•las, *n.* infectious skin disease.

e•ryth′ro•cyte′ (i rith′rə sīt′), *n.* red blood cell.

es′ca•late′, *v.,* **-lated, -lating.** increase in intensity or size. —**es′ca•la′tion,** *n.*

es′ca•la′tor, *n.* moving stairway.

es•cal′lop, *v.* **1.** finish with scallops (def. 2) **2.** bake in breadcrumb-topped sauce. —*n.* **3.** scallop.

es′ca•pade′, *n.* wild prank.

es•cape′, *v.,* **-caped, -caping,** *n.* —*v.* **1.** get away. **2.** elude. —*n.* **3.** act or means of escaping. —**es•cap′ee,** *n.*

es•cape′ment, *n.* part of clock that controls speed.

es•cap′ism, *n.* attempt to forget reality through fantasy. —**es•cap′ist,** *n., adj.*

es′ca•role′, *n.* broad-leaved endive.

es•carp′ment, *n,* long ridge.

es•chew′, *v.* avoid.

es′cort, *n.* (es′kôrt). **1.** accompanying person or persons for guidance, courtesy, etc. —*v.* (es kôrt′). **2.** accompany as escort.

es′crow, *n.* legal contract kept by third person until its provisions are fulfilled.

es•cutch′eon, *n.* coat of arms.

Es′ki•mo, *n.* Arctic North American people or language.

ESL, English as a second language.

e•soph'a•gus, *n., pl.* **-gi.** tube connecting mouth and stomach.

es'o•ter'ic, *adj.* intended for select few.

ESP, extrasensory perception.

esp., especially.

es'pa•drille' (es'pə dril'), *n.* flat shoe with cloth upper and rope sole.

es•pe'cial, *adj.* special. **—es•pe'cial•ly,** *adv.*

Es'pe•ran'to, *n.* artificial language based on major European languages.

es'pi•o•nage' (-näzh', -nij), *n.* work or use of spies.

es'pla•nade' (es'plə näd', -nād'), *n.* open level space, as for public walks.

es•pouse', *v.,* **-poused, -pousing.** 1. advocate. 2. marry. **—es•pous'al,** *n.*

es•pres'so, *n.* strong coffee made with steam.

es•prit' de corps' (ē sprē' də kôr'), sense of group unity and common purpose.

es•py', *v.,* **-pied, -pying.** catch sight of.

Es•quire', *n. Brit.* title of respect after man's name., in the U.S. chiefly applied to lawyers. *Abbr.:* Esq.

es'say, *n.* 1. short treatise. 2. attempt. —*v.* (ə sā'). 3. try.

es'say•ist, *n.* writer of essays.

es'sence, *n.* 1. intrinsic nature. 2. concentrated form of substance or thought.

es•sen'tial, *adj.* 1. necessary. —*n.* 2. necessary thing.

es•sen'tial•ly, *adv.* basically.

EST, Eastern Standard Time.

est., 1. established. 2. estimate. 3. estimated.

es•tab'lish, *v.* 1. set up permanently. 2. prove.

es•tab'lish•ment, *n.* 1. act of establishing. 2. institution or business. 3. (*often cap.*) group controlling government and social institutions.

es•tate', *n.* 1. landed property. 2. one's possessions.

es•teem', *v.* 1. regard. —*n.* 2. opinion.

es'ter, *n.* chemical compound produced by reaction between an acid and an alcohol.

es'thete, *n.* aesthete. **—es•thet'ic,** *adj.*

es′ti·ma·ble, *adj.* worthy of high esteem.

es′ti·mate′, *v.,* **-mated, -mating,** *n.* —*v.* (-māt′). 1. calculate roughly. —*n.* (es′tə mit). 2. rough calculation. 3. opinion. —**es′ti·ma′tion,** *n.*

es·trange′, *v.,* **-tranged, -tranging.** alienate. —**es·trange′ment,** *n.*

es′tro·gen (es′trə jən), *n.* female sex hormone.

es′tu·ar′y, *n., pl.* **-aries.** part of river affected by sea tides.

ETA, estimated time of arrival.

et al. (et al′, äl′, ôl′), and others.

et cet′er·a (set′-), and so on. *Abbr.:* etc.

etch, *v.* cut design into (metal, etc.) with acid. —**etch′ing,** *n.*

e·ter′nal, *adj.* 1. without beginning or end. —*n.* 2. (*cap.*) God. —**e·ter′ni·ty,** *n.* —**e·ter′nal·ly,** *adv.*

eth′ane, *n.* flammable gas used chiefly as a fuel.

e′ther, *n.* 1. colorless liquid used as an anesthetic. 2. upper part of space.

e·the′re·al, *adj.* 1. delicate. 2. heavenly.

eth′ics, *n.pl.* principles of conduct. —**eth′i·cal,** *adj.* —**eth′i·cal·ly,** *adv.*

eth′nic, *adj.* 1. sharing a common culture. —*n.* 2. member of minority group. —**eth′ni·cal·ly,** *adv.*

eth·nic′i·ty, *n.* ethnic traits.

eth·nol′o·gy, *n.* branch of anthropology dealing with cultural comparisons. —**eth·nol′o·gist,** *n.*

e·thol′o·gy, *n.* scientific study of animal behavior. —**e·thol′o·gist,** *n.*

e′thos (ē′thos, eth′os), *n.* distinguishing characteristics of person or group.

eth′yl, *n.* fluid containing lead.

e′ti·ol′o·gy (ē′tē ol′ə jē), *n., pl.* **-gies.** 1. study of causes, esp. of diseases. 2. cause or origin, esp. of a disease.

et′i·quette′, *n.* conventions of social behavior.

et seq., and the following.

é·tude (ā′tōōd, ā′tyōōd), *n.* musical composition played to improve technique but also for its artistic merit.

et′y·mol′o·gy, *n., pl.* **-gies.** history of word or words. —**et′y·mol′o·gist,** *n.*

eu-, prefix meaning good, as *eugenics.*

eu′ca•lyp′tus, *n., pl.* **-ti.** Australian tree.

Eu′cha•rist (ū′kə-), *n.* Holy Communion.

eu•gen′ics, *n.* science of improving human race. —**eu•gen′ic,** *adj.*

eu′lo•gy, *n., pl.* **-gies.** formal praise. —**eu′lo•gize′,** *v.*

eu′nuch (-nək), *n.* castrated man.

eu′phe•mism, *n.* substitution of mild expression for blunt one. —**eu′phe•mis′tic,** *adj.*

eu′pho•ny, *n., pl.* **-nies.** pleasant sound. —**eu•pho′ni•ous,** *adj.*

eu•pho′ri•a (yoo fôr′ē ə), *n.* strong feeling of happiness or well-being. —**eu•phor′ic,** *adj.*

Eur•a′sian, *adj.* of or originating in both Europe and Asia.

eu•re′ka (yoo rē′kə, yə-), *interj.* (exclamation of triumph at a discovery.)

Eu′ro•pe′an, *n.* native of Europe. —**Eu′ro•pe′an,** *adj.*

European plan, system of paying a fixed hotel rate that covers lodging only.

Eu•sta′chian tube (yoo stā′ shən), (*often l.c.*) canal between middle ear and pharynx.

eu′tha•na′sia, *n.* mercy killing.

e•vac′u•ate′, *v.,* **-ated, -ating.** 1. vacate. 2. remove. 3. help to flee. —**e•vac′u•a′tion,** *n.*

e•vade′, *v.,* **evaded, evading.** avoid or escape from by cleverness. —**e•va′sion,** *n.* —**e•va′sive,** *adj.*

e•val′u•ate′, *v.,* **-ated, -ating.** appraise. —**e•val′u•a′tion,** *n.*

ev′a•nes′cent, *adj.* fading away.

e′van•gel′i•cal, *adj.* 1. of or in keeping with Gospel. 2. of those Protestant churches that stress personal conversion through faith.

e•van′ge•list, *n.* 1. preacher. 2. One of the writers of Gospel. —**e•van′ge•lism′,** *n.* —**e•van′ge•lize′,** *v.*

e•vap′o•rate′, *v.,* **-rated, -rating.** change into vapor. —**e•vap′o•ra′tion,** *n.*

eve, *n.* evening before.

e′ven, *adj.* **1.** smooth. **2.** uniform. **3.** equal. **4.** divisible by 2. **5.** calm. —*adv.* **6.** hardly. **7.** indeed. —*v.* **8.** make even. —**e′ven•ly,** *adv.* —**e′ven•ness,** *n.*

e′ven•hand′ed, *adj.* impartial; fair.

eve′ning, *n.* early part of night; end of day.

evening star, bright planet visible around sunset.

e•vent′, *n.* anything that happens. —**e•vent′ful,** *adj.*

e•ven′tu•al, *adj.* final. —**e•ven′tu•al•ly,** *adv.*

e•ven′tu•al′i•ty, *n., pl.* **-ties.** possible event.

ev′er, *adv.* at all times.

ev′er•glade′, *n.* tract of low, swampy ground.

ev′er•green′, *adj.* **1.** having its leaves always green. —*n.* **2.** evergreen plant.

ev′er•last′ing, *adj.* lasting forever or indefinitely.

eve′ry, *adj.* **1.** each. **2.** all possible. —**eve′ry•bod′y, eve′ry•one′,** *pron.* —**eve′ry•thing′,** *pron.* —**eve′ry•where′,** *adv.* —**eve′ry•day′,** *adj.*

e•vict′, *v.* expel from property. —**e•vic′tion,** *n.*

e′vi•dence, *n., v.,* **-denced, -dencing.** —*n.* **1.** grounds for belief. —*v.* **2.** prove.

ev′i•dent, *adj.* clearly so. —**ev′i•dent•ly,** *adv.*

e′vil, *adj.* **1.** wicked. **2.** unfortunate. —**e′vil•do′er,** *n.* —**e′vil•ly,** *adv.*

evil eye, look thought capable of doing harm.

e•vince′, *v.,* **evinced, evincing. 1.** prove. **2.** show.

e•vis′cer•ate′ (i vis′ə rāt′), *v.,* **-ated, -ating. 1.** remove entrails of. **2.** deprive of vital or essential parts.

e•voke′, *v.,* **evoked, evoking.** call forth. —**ev′o•ca′tion,** *n.* —**e•voc′a•tive,** *adj.*

e•volve′, *v.,* **evolved, evolving.** develop gradually. —**ev′o•lu′tion,** *n.* —**ev′o•lu′tion•ar′y,** *adj.*

ewe (yōō), *n.* female sheep.

ew′er, *n.* wide-mouthed pitcher.

ex-, prefix meaning: **1.** out of or from, as *export.* **2.** utterly or thoroughly, as *exacerbate* **3.** former, as *ex-governor.*

ex., 1. example. 2. except. 3. except ion. 4. exchange.

ex•ac′er•bate′ (ig zas′ər bāt′, ek sas′-), *v.,* **-bated, -bating.** make more severe, violent. —**ex•ac′er•ba′tion,** *n.*

ex•act′, *adj.* 1. precise; accurate. —*v.* 2. demand; compel. —**ex•act′ly,** *adv.*

ex•act′ing, *adj.* severe.

ex•ag′ger•ate′, *v.,* **-ated, ating.** magnify beyond truth. —**ex•ag′ger•a′tion,** *n.*

ex•alt′, *v.* 1. elevate. 2. extol. —**ex′al•ta′tion,** *n.*

ex•am′, *n. Informal.* examination.

ex•am′ine, *v.,* **-ined, -ining.** 1. investigate. 2. test. 3. query. —**ex•am′i•na′tion,** *n.* —**ex•am′in•er,** *n.*

ex•am′ple, *n.* 1. typical one. 2. model. 3. illustration.

ex•as′per•ate′, *v.,* **-ated, -ating.** make angry. —**ex•as′per•a•tion,** *n.*

ex′ca•vate′, *v.,* **-vated, -vating.** 1. dig out. 2. unearth. —**ex•ca•va′tion,** *n.* —**ex′ca•va′tor,** *n.*

ex•ceed′, *v.* surpass.

ex•ceed′ing•ly, *adv.* very.

ex•cel′, *v.,* **-celled, -celling.** be superior (to).

ex′cel•len•cy, *n., pl.* **-cies.** 1. (*cap.*) title of honor. 2. excellence.

ex′cel•lent, *adj.* remarkably good. —**ex′cel•lence,** *n.*

ex•cel′si•or, *n.* wood shavings.

ex•cept′, *prep.* 1. Also, **ex•cept′ing.** excluding. —*v.* 2. exclude. 3. object. —**ex•cep′tion,** *n.*

ex•cep′tion•a•ble, *adj.* causing objections.

ex•cep′tion•al, *adj.* unusual. —**ex•cep′tion•al•ly,** *adv.*

ex′cerpt, *n.* (ek′sûrpt). 1. passage from longer writing. —*v.* (ik sûrpt′, ek′sûrpt). 2. take (passage) from.

ex•cess′, *n.* (ik ses′). 1. amount over that required. —*adj.* (ek′ses). 2. more than necessary, usual, or desirable.

ex•ces′sive, *adj.* profuse. —**ex•ces′sive•ly,** *adv.*

ex•change′, *v.,* **-changed, -changing,** *n.* —*v.* 1. change for something else. —*n.* 2. act of exchanging. 3. thing exchanged. 4. trading place. —**ex•change′a•ble,** *adj.*

ex•cheq′uer, *n. Brit.* treasury.

ex′cise, *n., v.,* **-cised, -cising.** —*n.* (ek′sīz). **1.** tax on certain goods. —*v.* (ik sīz′). **2.** cut out. —**ex•ci′sion,** *n.*

ex•cite′, *v.,* **-cited, -citing. 1.** stir up. (emotions, etc.). **2.** cause. —**ex•cit′a•ble,** *adj.* —**ex•cite′ment,** *n.*

ex•claim′, *v.* cry out. —**ex′cla•ma′tion,** *n.*

ex•clude′, *v.,* **-cluded, -cluding.** shut out. —**ex•clu′sion,** *n.*

ex•clu′sive, *adj.* **1.** belonging or pertaining to one. **2.** excluding others. **3.** stylish; chic. —**ex•clu′sive•ly,** *adv.*

ex′com•mu′ni•cate′, *v.,* **-cated, -cating.** cut off from membership. —**ex′com•mu′ni•ca′tion,** *n.*

ex•co′ri•ate′, *v.,* **-ated, -ating.** denounce. —**ex•co′ri•a′tion,** *n.*

ex′cre•ment, *n.* bodily waste.

ex•cres′cence, *n.* abnormal growth. —**ex•cres′cent,** *adj.*

ex•crete′, *v.,* **-creted, -creting.** eliminate from body. —**ex•cre′tion,** *n.* —**ex′cre•to′ry,** *adj.*

ex•cru′ci•at′•ing (ik skrōō′shē ā′ting), *adj.* **1.** causing suffering. **2.** intense. —**ex•cru′ci•at′ing•ly,** *adv.*

ex′cul•pate′, *v.,* **-pated, -pating.** free of blame. —**ex′cul•pa′tion,** *n.*

ex•cur′sion, *n.* short trip.

ex•cuse′, *v.,* **-cused, -cusing,** *n.* —*v.* (ik skyōōz′). **1.** pardon. **2.** apologize for. **3.** justify. **4.** seek or grant release. —*n.* (ik skyōōs′). **5.** reason for being excused. —**ex•cus′a•ble,** *adj.*

ex′e•crate′, *v.,* **-crated, -crating. 1.** abominate. **2.** curse. —**ex′e•cra•ble,** *adj.*

ex′e•cute′, *v.,* **-cuted, -cuting. 1.** do. **2.** kill legally. —**ex′e•cu′tion,** *n.* —**ex′e•cu′tion•er,** *n.*

ex•ec′u•tive, *adj.* **1.** responsible for directing affairs. —*n.* **2.** administrator.

ex•ec′u•tor, *n.* person named to carry out provisions of a will. —**ex•ec′u•trix′,** *n.fem.*

ex′e•ge′sis (ek′si jē′ sis), *n.,* *pl.* **-ses** (sēz). critical interpretation.

ex•em′plar, *n.* **1.** model or pattern. **2.** typical example.

ex•em′pla•ry, *adj.* 1. worthy of imitation. 2. warning.

ex•em′pli•fy′, *v.*, -fied, -fying. show or serve as example. —**ex•em′pli•fi•ca′tion**, *n.*

ex•empt′, *v.*, *adj.* free from obligation. —**ex•emp′tion**, *n.*

ex′er•cise′, *n.*, *v.*, -cised, -cising. —*n.* 1. action to increase skill or strength. 2. performance. 3. (*pl.*) ceremony. —*v.* 4. put through exercises. 5. use. —**ex′er•cis′er**, *n.*

ex•ert′, *v.* put into action. —**ex•er′tion**, *n.*

ex•hale′, *v.*, -haled, -haling. breathe out; emit breath. —**ex′ha•la′tion**, *n.*

ex•haust′, *v.* 1. use up. 2. fatigue greatly. —*n.* 3. used gases from engine. —**ex•haus′ti•ble**, *adj.* —**ex•haus′tion**, *n.*

ex•haus′tive, *adj.* thorough.

ex•hib′it, *v.*, *n.* show; display. —**ex′hi•bi′tion**, *n.* —**ex•hib′i•tor**, *n.*

ex′hi•bi′tion•ism′, *n.* desire or tendency to display onself. —**ex′hi•bi′tion•ist**, *n.*

ex•hil′a•rate′, *v.*, -rated, -rating. cheer; stimulate. —**ex•hil′a•ra′tion**, *n.*

ex•hort′, *v.* advise earnestly. —**ex′hor•ta′tion**, *n.*

ex•hume′ (ig zyōōm′), *v.*, -humed, -huming. dig up body.

ex′i•gen•cy, *n.*, *pl.* -cies. urgent requirement. —**ex′i•gent**, *adj.*

ex′ile, *n.*, *v.*, -iled, -iling. —*n.* 1. enforced absence from one's country. 2. one so absent. —*v.* 3. send into exile.

ex•ist′, *v.* be; live. —**ex•ist′ence**, *n.* —**ex•ist′ent**, *adj.*

ex′is•ten′tial, *adj.* of human life; based on experience.

ex′is•ten′tial•ism, *n.* philosophy that stresses personal liberty and responsibility. —**ex′is•ten′tial•ist**, *n.*, *adj.*

ex′it, *n.* 1. way out. 2. departure. —*v.* 3. leave.

exo-, prefix meaning outside or outer, as *exosphere*.

ex′o•crine (ek′s ə krin, -krīn′), *adj.* 1. secreting through a duct. 2. of glands involved in such secretion.

ex′o•dus, *n.* departure.

ex of·fi′ci·o′ (-fish′ē-), because of one's office.

ex·on′er·ate, *v.*, -ated, -ating. free of blame. —**ex·on′er·a′tion**, *n.*

ex·or′bi·tant (ig zôr′bi tənt), *adj.* excessive, esp. in cost. —**ex·or′bi·tance**, *n.*

ex′or·cise′, *v.*, -cised, -cising. expel (evil spirit). —**ex′or·cism′**, *n.* —**ex′or·cist**, *n.*

ex′o·sphere′, *n.* highest region of the atmosphere.

ex·ot′ic, *adj.* 1. foreign; alien. 2. strikingly unusual.

ex·pand′, *v.* increase; spread out. —**ex·pan′sion**, *n.* —**ex·pan′sive**, *adj.*

ex·panse′, *n.* wide extent.

ex·pa′ti·ate′ (-pā′shē-), *v.*, -ated, -ating. talk at length.

ex·pa′tri·ate′, *v.*, -ated, -ating, *n.*, *adj.* —*v.* (-āt′). 1. exile. 2. remove (oneself) from homeland. —*n.* (-ət). 3. expatriated person. —*adj.* (-ət). 4. exiled; banished.

ex·pect′, *v.* look forward to. —**ex·pect′an·cy**, *n.* —**ex·pect′ant**, *adj.* —**ex′pec·ta′tion**, *n.*

ex·pec′to·rate′, *v.*, -rated, -rating. spit. —**ex·pec′to·rant**, *n.*

ex·pe′di·ent, *adj.* 1. desirable in given circumstances. 2. conducive to advantage. —*n.* 3. expedient means. —**ex·pe′di·en·cy**, *n.*

ex′pe·dite′, *v.*, -dited, -diting. speed up. —**ex′pe·dit′er**, *n.*

ex′pe·di′tion, *n.* 1. journey to explore. 2. promptness. —**ex′pe·di′tion·ar′y**, *adj.*

ex′pe·di′tious, *adj.* prompt. —**ex′pe·di′tious·ly**, *adv.*

ex·pel′, *v.*, -pelled, -pelling. force out.

ex·pend′, *v.* 1. use up. 2. spend. —**ex·pend′i·ture**, *n.*

ex·pend′a·ble, *adj.* 1. available for spending. 2. that can be sacrificed if necessary.

ex·pense′, *n.* 1. cost. 2. cause of spending.

ex·pen′sive, *adj.* costing much. —**ex·pen′sive·ly**, *adv.*

ex·pe′ri·ence, *n.*, *v.*, -enced, -encing. —*n.* 1. something lived through. 2. knowledge from such things. —*v.* 3. have experience of.

ex·pe′ri·enced, *adj.* wise or skillful through experience.

ex•per′i•ment, *n.* (-ə mənt). **1.** test to discover or check something. —*v.* (-ment′). **2.** perform experiment.
—**ex•per′i•men′tal,** *adj.*
—**ex•per′i•men•ta′tion,** *n.*
—**ex•per′i•ment′er,** *n.*

ex′pert, *n.* (eks′pûrt). **1.** skilled person. —*adj.* **2.** skilled. —**ex•pert′ly,** *adv.*
—**ex•pert′ness,** *n.*

ex′per•tise′ (-tēz′), *n.* skill.

ex′pi•ate′, *v.,* -ated, -ating. atone for. —**ex′pi•a′tion,** *n.*

ex•pire′, *v.,* -pired, -piring. **1.** end. **2.** die. **3.** breathe out.
—**ex′pi•ra′tion,** *n.*

ex•plain′, *v.* **1.** make plain. **2.** account for. —**ex′pla•na′tion,** *n.* —**ex•plan′a•to′ry,** *adj.*

ex′ple•tive, *n.* exclamatory oath, usu. profane.

ex′pli•cate, *v.,* -cated, -cating. explain in detail.

ex•plic′it (-plis′-), *adj.* **1.** clearly stated. **2.** outspoken. **3.** having sexual acts or nudity clearly depicted.
—**ex•plic′it•ly,** *adv.*

ex•plode′, *v.,* -ploded, -ploding. **1.** burst violently. **2.** disprove; discredit.

—**ex•plo′sion,** *n.*
—**ex•plo′sive,** *n., adj.*

ex′ploit, *n.* (eks′ploit). **1.** notable act. —*v.* (ik sploit′). **2.** use, esp. selfishly.
—**ex′ploi•ta′tion,** *n.*
—**ex•ploit′a•tive,** *adj.*
—**ex•ploit′er,** *n.*

ex•plore′, *v.,* -plored, -ploring. examine from end to end.
—**ex′plo•ra′tion,** *n.*
—**ex•plor′er,** *n.*
—**ex•plor′a•to′ry,** *adj.*

ex•po′nent, *n.* **1.** person who explains. **2.** symbol. **3.** *Math.* Symbol placed to the upper right of another to indicate the power to which the latter is to be raised.

ex•port′, *v.* (ik spōrt′). **1.** send to other countries. —*n.* (eks′pōrt). **2.** what is sent.
—**ex′por•ta′tion,** *n.*

ex•pose′, *v.,* -posed, -posing. **1.** lay open to harm, etc. **2.** reveal. **3.** allow light to reach (film). —**ex•po′sure,** *n.*

ex′po•sé′ (-zā′), *n.* exposure of wrongdoing.

ex′po•si′tion, *n.* **1.** public show. **2.** explanation.

ex•pos′i•to′ry (-poz′i-), *adj.* serving to expound or explain.

ex post facto, *adj.* made or done after the fact.

ex•pos′tu•late′ (-pos′chə-), *v.,* -lated, -lating. protest. —**ex•pos′tu•la′tion,** *n.*

ex•pound′, *v.* state in detail.

ex•press′, *v.* 1. convey in words, art, etc. 2. press out. —*adj.* 3. definite. —*n.* 4. fast or direct train, etc. 5. delivery system. —**ex•pres′sion,** *n.* —**ex•pres′sive,** *adj.* —**ex•press′ly,** *adv.*

ex•press′way′, *n.* road for high-speed traffic.

ex•pro′pri•ate′, *v.,* -ated, -ating. take for public use. —**ex•pro′pri•a′tion,** *n.* —**ex•pro′pri•a′tor,** *n.*

ex•pul′sion, *n.* eviction.

ex•punge′, *v.,* -punged, -punging. obliterate.

ex′pur•gate′, *v.,* -gated, -gating. remove objectionable parts. —**ex′pur•ga′tion,** *n.*

ex′qui•site, *adj.* delicately beautiful. —**ex•quis′ite•ly,** *adv.*

ex′tant (ek′stənt), *adj.* still existing.

ex•tem′po•ra′ne•ous, *adj.* impromptu. —**ex•tem′po•re** (ik stem′pə rē), *adv.*

ex•tend′, *v.* 1. stretch out. 2. offer. 3. reach. 4. increase. —**ex•ten′sion,** *n.*

extended family, family comprising a married couple, their children, and relatives.

ex•ten′sive, *adj.* far-reaching; broad. —**ex•ten′sive•ly,** *adv.*

ex•tent′, *n.* degree; breadth.

ex•ten′u•ate′, *v.,* -ated, -ating. lessen (fault).

ex•te′ri•or, *adj.* 1. outer. —*n.* 2. outside.

ex•ter′mi•nate′, *v.,* -nated, -nating. destroy. —**ex•ter′mi•na′tion,** *n.* —**ex•ter′mi•na•tor,** *n.*

ex•ter′nal, *adj.* outer.

ex•tinct′, *adj.* no longer existing. —**ex•tinc′tion,** *n.*

ex•tin′guish, *v.* put out; end. —**ex•tin′guish•a•ble,** *adj.* —**ex•tin′guish•er,** *n.*

ex′tir•pate′, *v.,* -pated, -pating. destroy totally.

ex•tol′, *v.,* -tolled, -tolling. praise.

ex•tort′, *v.* get by force, threat, etc. —**ex•tor′tion,** *n.* —**ex•tor′tion•ate,** *adj.*

ex′tra, *adj.* additional.

extra-, prefix meaning outside or beyond, as *extrasensory.*

ex•tract', *v.* (ik strakt'). 1. draw out. —*n.* (eks'trakt). 2. something extracted. —**ex•trac'tion,** *n.*

ex'tra•cur•ric'u•lar, *adj.* outside the regular curriculum, as of a school.

ex'tra•dite', *v.,* -dited, -diting. deliver (fugitive) to another state. —**ex'tra•di'tion,** *n.*

ex'tra•le'gal, *adj.* beyond the authority of law.

ex'tra•mu'ral, *adj.* involving members of different groups.

ex•tra'ne•ous, *adj.* irrelevant. —**ex•tra'ne•ous•ly,** *adv.*

ex•traor'di•nar'y, *adj.* unusual. —**ex•traor'di•nar'i•ly,** *adv.*

ex•trap'o•late, *v.,* -lated, -lating. infer from known data. —**ex•trap'o•la'tion,** *n.*

ex'tra•sen'so•ry, *adj.* beyond one's physical senses.

ex'tra•ter•res'tri•al, *adj.* outside the earth's limits. —*n.* extraterrestrial being.

ex•trav'a•gant, *adj.* 1. spending imprudently. 2. immoderate.

—**ex•trav'a•gance,** *n.*
—**ex•trav'a•gant•ly,** *adv.*

ex•trav'a•gan'za, *n.* lavish production.

ex•treme', *adj.* 1. farthest from ordinary. 2. very great. 3. outermost. —*n.* 4. utmost degree. —**ex•treme'ly,** *adv.*

ex•trem'ism, *n.* tendency to go to extremes, esp. in politics. —**ex•trem'ist,** *n., adj.*

ex•trem'i•ty, *n., pl.* -ties. 1. extreme part. 2. limb of body. 3. distress.

ex'tri•cate', *v.,* -cated, -cating. disentangle.

ex•trin'sic, *adj.* 1. not inherent or essential. 2. being or coming from without.

ex'tro•vert', *n.* outgoing person. —**ex'tro•ver'sion,** *n.* —**ex'tro•vert'ed,** *adj.*

ex•trude', *v.,* -truded, -truding. 1. force or press out. 2. shape by forcing through a die. —**ex•tru'sion,** *n.* —**ex•tru'sive,** *adj.*

ex•u'ber•ant, *adj.* 1. joyful; vigorous. 2. lavish. —**ex•u'ber•ance,** *n.* —**ex•u'ber•ant•ly,** *adv.*

ex•ude', *v.,* -uded, -uding. ooze out. —**ex'u•da'tion,** *n.*

ex•ult′, *v.* rejoice.
—**ex•ult′ant,** *adj.*
—**ex′ul•ta′tion,** *n.*

eye, *n., v.,* **eyed, eying** or
eyeing. —*n.* **1.** organ of sight.
2. power of seeing. **3.** close
watch. —*v.* **4.** watch closely.
—**eye′ball′,** *n., v.*
—**eye′sight′,** *n.*

eye′brow′, *n.* ridge and fringe
of hair over eye.

eye′ful, *n.* **1.** thorough view. **2.**
Informal. attractive person.

eye′glass′es, *n.pl.* pair of
corrective lenses in a
frame.

eye′lash′, *n.* short hair at edge
of eyelid.

eye′let, *n.* small hole.

eye′lid′, *n.* movable skin
covering the eye.

eye′o′pen•er, *n.* sudden
awareness.

eye′sore′, *n.* something
unpleasant to look at.

eye′tooth′, *n.* canine tooth in
upper jaw.

eye′wash′, *n.* **1.** soothing
solution for eyes. **2.** nonsense.

eye′wit′ness, *n.* person who
sees event.

ey′rie (âr′ē, ēr′ē), *n., pl.* **-ies.**
aerie.

F, f, *n.* sixth letter of English alphabet.

F, 1. Fahrenheit. 2. female.

f., 1. feet. 2. female. 3. folio. 4. foot. 5. franc.

FAA, Federal Aviation Administration.

fa′ble, *n.* 1. short tale with moral. 2. untrue story.

fab′ric, *n.* cloth.

fab′ri•cate′, *v.,* -cated, -cating. 1. construct. 2. devise (lie). —**fab′ri•ca′tion,** *n.*

fab′u•lous, *adj.* 1. marvelous. 2. suggesting fables.

fa•çade′ (fə säd′), *n.* 1. building front. 2. superficial appearance.

face, *n., v.,* **faced, facing.** —*n.* 1. front part of head. 2. surface. 3. appearance. 4. dignity. —*v.* 5. look toward. 6. confront. —**fa′cial,** *adj.*

face′less, *adj.* lacking distinction or identity.

face′-lift′, *n.* 1. surgery to eliminate facial sagging or wrinkling. 2. renovation to improve appearance, as of a building. Also, **face′-lift′ing.**

face′-sav′ing, *adj.* saving one's prestige or dignity.

F

fac′et (fas′it), *n.* 1. surface of cut gem. 2. aspect.

fa•ce′tious, *adj.* joking, esp. annoyingly so.
—**fa•ce′tiously,** *adv.*
—**fa•ce′tious•ness,** *n.*

face value (fās′ val′yoo *for 1;* fās′ val′yoo *for 2*). 1. value printed on the face of a stock, bond, etc. 2. apparent value.

fac′ile (fas′il), *adj.* glibly easy.

fa•cil′i•tate′, *v.,* -tated, -tating. make easier.
—**fa•cil′i•ta′tion,** *n.*
—**fa•cil′i•ta′tor,** *n.*

fa•cil′i•ty, *n., pl.* -ties. 1. resource. 2. dexterity.

fac′ing, *n.* outer material.

fac•sim′i•le (fak sim′ə lē), *n., pl.* -les, *v.,* -led, -leing. —*n.* 1. exact copy. 2. fax. —*v.* 3. make facsimile of.

fact, *n.* truth. —**fac′tu•al,** *adj.*

fac′tion, *n.* competing internal group. —**fac′tion•al,** *adj.* —**fac′tion•al•ism,** *n.*

fac′tious, *adj.* causing strife.

fac′tor, *n.* 1. element. 2. one of two numbers multiplied.

fac′to•ry, *n., pl.* **-ries.** place where goods are made.

fac′ul•ty, *n., pl.* **-ties. 1.** special ability. **2.** power. **3.** body of teachers.

fad, *n.* temporary fashion; craze. —**fad′dish,** *adj.*

fade, *v.,* **faded, fading. 1.** lose freshness, color, or vitality. **2.** disappear gradually.

fag, *v.,* **fagged, fagging,** *n.* —*v.* **1.** exhaust. —*n.* **2.** Also, **fag′got.** *Offensive.* homosexual.

fag′ot, *n.* bundle of firewood.

Fahr′en•heit′ (far′ən hīt′), *adj.* measuring temperature so that water freezes at 32° and boils at 212°.

fail, *v.* **1.** be unsuccessful. **2.** become weaker. **3.** cease functioning. —**fail′ure,** *n.*

fail′ing, *n.* **1.** weak point of character. —*prep.* **2.** in the absence of.

faille (fīl, fāl), *n.* ribbed fabric.

fail′-safe′, *adj.* ensured against failure or against consequences of its failure.

faint, *adj.* **1.** lacking strength. —*v.* **2.** lose consciousness. —**faint′ly,** *adv.* —**faint′ness,**

faint′heart′ed, *adj.* cowardly.

fair, *adj.* **1.** behaving justly. **2.** average. **3.** sunny. **4.** light-hued. **5.** attractive. —*n.* **6.** exhibition. —**fair′ly,** *adv.* —**fair′ness,** *n.*

fair shake, just treatment.

fair′y, *n., pl.* **fairies. 1.** tiny supernatural being. **2.** *Offensive.* homosexual. —**fair′y•land′,** *n.*

fairy tale, 1. story, usu. for children, about magical creatures. **2.** misleading account.

faith, *n.* **1.** confidence. **2.** religious belief. **3.** loyalty. —**faith′less,** *adj.*

faith′ful, *adj.* **1.** loyal. **2.** having religious belief. **3.** copying accurately. —**faith′ful•ly,** *adv.* —**faith′ful•ness,** *n.*

fa•ji′tas (fä hē′təz, fə-), *n. (used with a sing. or pl. v.)* thin strips of marinated and grilled meat, served with tortillas.

fa•la′fel (fə lä′fəl), *n.* fried ball of ground chickpeas.

fake, *v.,* **faked, faking,** *n., adj. Informal.* —*v.* **1.** counterfeit. —*n.* **2.** thing faked. —*adj.* **3.** deceptive. —**fak′er,** *n.*

fa•kir′ (fə kēr′), *n.* Muslim or Hindu monk.

fal′con (fôl′kən), *n.* bird of prey. —**fal′con•ry,** *n.*

fall, *v.,* **fell, fallen, falling,** *n.* —*v.* 1. drop. 2. happen. —*n.* 3. descent. 4. autumn.

fal′la•cy, *n., pl.* **-cies.** 1. false belief. 2. unsound argument. —**fal•la′cious,** *adj.*

fall guy, *Slang.* 1. easy victim. 2. scapegoat.

fal′li•ble, *adj.* liable to error. —**fal′li•bil′i•ty,** *n.*

fall′ing-out′, *n., pl.* **fallings-out, falling-outs.** quarrel or estrangement.

fal•lo′pian tube, either of pair of ducts in female abdomen that transport ova from ovary to uterus. Also, **Fallopian tube.**

fall′out′, *n.* 1. radioactive particles carried by air. 2. incidental outcome or product.

fal′low, *adj.* plowed and not seeded.

fallow deer, Eurasian deer with yellowish coat that is white-spotted in summer.

false, *adj.,* **falser, falsest.** 1. not true. 2. faithless. 3. deceptive. —**false′hood,** *n.* —**false′ly,** *adv.* —**false′ness,** *n.* —**fal′si•fy,** *v.*

fal•set′to, *n., pl.* **-tos.** unnaturally high voice.

fal′ter, *v.* hesitate; waver. —**fal′ter•ing•ly,** *adv.*

fame, *n.* wide reputation. —**famed,** *adj.*

fa•mil′iar, *adj.* 1. commonly known. 2. intimate. —**fa•mil′i•ar′i•ty,** *n.* —**fa•mil′iar•ize′,** *v.* —**fa•mil′iar•ly,** *adv.*

fam′i•ly, *n., pl.* **-lies.** 1. parents and their children. 2. relatives. —**fa•mil′i•al,** *adj.*

family tree, genealogical chart of a family.

fam′ine, *n.* scarcity of food.

fam′ish, *v.* starve.

fa′mous, *adj.* renowned.

fa′mous•ly, *adv.* very well.

fan, *n., v.,* **fanned, fanning.** —*n.* 1. device for causing current of air. 2. *Informal.* devotee. —*v.* 3. blow upon with fan. 4. stir up.

fa•nat′ic, *n.* excessive devote. —**fa•nat′i•cal,** *adj.* —**fa•nat′i•cism′,** *n.*

fan′ci•er, *n.* person interested in something, as dogs.

fan′cy, *n., pl.* **-cies,** *adj.,* **-cier, -ciest,** *v.,* **-cied, -cying.** —*n.* **1.** imagination. **2.** thing imagined. **3.** whim. **4.** taste. —*adj.* **5.** ornamental. —*v.* **6.** imagine. **7.** crave. —**fan′ci•ful,** *adj.* —**fan′ci•ly,** *adv.* —**fan′ci•ness,** *n.*

fan′cy-free′, *adj.* free from emotional ties, esp. from love.

fan′cy•work′, *n.* ornamental needlework.

fan′fare′, *n.* **1.** chorus of trumpets. **2.** showy flourish.

fang, *n.* long, sharp tooth. —**fanged,** *adj.*

fan′ny, *n., pl.* **-nies.** *Informal.* buttocks.

fan•ta′sia (fan tā′zhə), *n.* fanciful musical work.

fan′ta•size′, *v.,* **-sized, -sizing.** have fantasies.

fan•tas′tic, *adj.* **1.** wonderful and strange. **2.** fanciful. Also, **fan•tas′ti•cal.** —**fan•tas′ti•cal•ly,** *adv.*

fan′ta•sy, *n., pl.* **-sies. 1.** imagination. **2.** daydream.

far, *adv., adj.,* **farther, farthest.** at or to great distance.

far′a•way′, *adj.* **1.** distant; remote. **2.** preoccupied.

farce, *n.* light comedy. —**far′ci•cal,** *adj.*

fare, *n., v.,* **fared, faring.** —*n.* **1.** price of passage. **2.** food. —*v.* **3.** eat. **4.** get along. **5.** go.

Far East, countries of east and southeast Asia.

fare′well′, *interj., n., adj.* good-by.

far′-fetched′, *adj.* not reasonable or probable.

far′-flung′, *adj.* **1.** extending over a great distance or wide area. **2.** widely distributed.

fa•ri′na (fə rē′nə), *n.* flour or meal cooked as a cereal. —**far′i•na′ceous,** *adj.*

farm, *n.* **1.** land for agriculture. —*v.* **2.** cultivate land. —**farm′a•ble,** *adj.* —**farm′er,** *n.* —**farm′house′,** *n.* —**farm′ing,** *n.* —**farm′yard′,** *n.*

far′o, *n.* gambling game in which players bet on cards.

far′-off′, *adj.* distant.

far′-out′, *adj. Slang.* extremely unconventional.

far•ra′go (fə rë′gō, -rā-), *n., pl.* **-goes.** confused mixture.

far'-reach'ing, *adj.* of widespread influence.

far'row, *n.* 1. litter of pigs. —*v.* 2. (of swine) bear.

far'-sight'ed, *adj.* 1. seeing distant objects best. 2. planning for future. —**far'sigh'ed•ness,** *n.*

far'ther, *compar. of* **far.** *adv.* 1. at or to a greater distance. —*adj.* 2. more distant. 3. additional.

far'thest, *superl. of* **far.** *adv.* 1. at or to the greatest distance. —*adj.* 2. most distant.

fas'ci•nate', *v.,* **-nated, -nating.** attract irresistibly. —**fas'ci•na'tion,** *n.*

fas'cism (fash'iz əm), *n.* dictatorship. —**fas'cist,** *n., adj.* —**fa•scis'tic,** *adj.*

fash'ion, *n.* 1. prevailing style. 2. manner. —*v.* 3. make.

fash'ion•a•ble, *adj.* stylish. —**fash'ion•a•bly,** *adv.*

fast, *adj.* 1. quick; swift. 2. secure. —*adv.* 3. tightly. 4. swiftly. —*v.* 5. abstain from food. —*n.* 6. such abstinence.

fast'back', *n.* rear of automobile, curved downward.

fas'ten, *v.* 1. fix securely. 2. seize. —**fas'ten•er, fas'ten•ing,** *n.*

fast'-food', *adj.* specializing in food that can be prepared and served quickly.

fas•tid'i•ous, *adj.* highly critical and demanding. —**fas•tid'i•ous•ly,** *adv.* —**fas•tid'i•ous•ness,** *n.*

fast'ness, *n.* fortified place.

fat, *n., adj.,* **fatter, fattest.** —*n.* 1. greasy substance. —*adj.* 2. fleshy. —**fat'ty,** *adj.*

fa'tal, *adj.* causing death or ruin. —**fa'tal•ly,** *adv.*

fa'tal•ism, *n.* belief in destiny. —**fa'tal•ist,** *n.* —**fa'tal•is'tic,** *adj.*

fa•tal'i•ty, *n., pl.* **-ties.** 1. death by a disaster. 2. fate.

fate, *n., v.,* **fated, fating.** —*n.* 1. destiny. 2. death or ruin. —*v.* 3. destine.

fat'ed, *adj.* subject to fate; destined.

fate'ful, *adj.* involving decisive events.

fa'ther, *n.* 1. male parent. 2. (*cap.*) God. 3. priest. —**fa'ther•hood',** *n.* —**fa'ther•less,** *adj.* —**fa'ther•ly,** *adv.*

fa′ther-in-law′, *n., pl.*
fathers-in-law. spouse's
father.

fa′ther•land′, *n.* 1. one's
native country. 2. land of
one's ancestors.

fath′om, *n.* 1. nautical measure
equal to six feet. —*v.* 2.
understand.

fa•tigue′, *n., v.,* **-tigued,**
-tiguing. —*n.* 1. weariness. 2.
(*pl.*) military work clothes.
—*v.* 3. weary.

fat′ten, *v.* grow fat or wealthy.

fatty acid, organic acid found
in animal and vegetable fats.

fat′u•ous (fach′-), *adj.* 1.
foolish or stupid. 2. unreal.
—**fa•tu′i•ty,** *n.*

fau′cet, *n.* valve for liquids.

fault, *n.* defect. —**fault′i•ly,**
adv. —**fault′i•ness,** *n.*
—**faul′ty,** *adj.*

faun, *n.* Roman deity, part
man and part goat.

fau′na (fô′nə), *n., pl.* **-nas, -nae**
(-nē). animals or animal life of
particular region or period.

faux pas′ (fō pä′), social error.

fa′vor, *n.* 1. kind act. 2. high
regard. —*v.* 3. prefer. 4.

oblige. 5. resemble. Also,
fa′vour. —**fa′vor•a•ble,** *adj.*
—**fa′vor•ite,** *adj., n.*

fa′vor•it•ism, *n.* preference
shown toward certain
persons.

fawn, *n.* 1. young deer. —*v.* 2.
seek favor by servility.

fax, *n.* 1. method of
transmitting written or
graphic material by telephone
or radio. 2. item transmitted
in this way. —*v.* 3. send by
fax. 4. communicate by fax.

faze, *v.,* **fazed, fazing.** *Informal.*
daunt.

FBI, Federal Bureau of
Investigation.

FCC, Federal Communications
Commission.

FDA, Food and Drug
Administration.

FDIC, Federal Deposit
Insurance Corporation.

fear, *n.* 1. feeling of coming
harm. 2. awe. —*v.* 3. be afraid
of. 4. hold in awe. —**fear′ful,**
adj. —**fear′less,** *adj.*

fea′si•ble, *adj.* able to be
done. —**fea′si•bil′i•ty,** *n.*

feast, *n.* 1. sumptuous meal. 2.
religious celebration. —*v.* 3.
provide with or have feast.

feat, *n.* remarkable deed.

feath′er, *n.* one of the growths forming bird's plumage. —**feath′er•y,** *adj.*

fea′ture, *n., v.,* **-tured, -turing.** —*n.* **1.** part of face. **2.** special part, article, etc. —*v.* **3.** give prominence to.

Feb., February.

Feb′ru•ar′y, *n., pl.* **-aries.** second month of year.

fe′ces (fē′sēz), *n.pl.* excrement. —**fe′cal** (fē′ kəl), *adj.*

feck′less, *adj.* **1.** incompetent. **2.** irresponsible and lazy.

fe′cund (fē′kund), *adj.* productive. —**fe•cun′di•ty,** *n.*

fed., **1.** federal. **2.** federated. **3.** federation.

fed′er•al, *adj.* **1.** of states in permanent union. **2.** (*sometimes cap.*) of U.S. government. —**fed′er•al•ly,** *adv.*

fed′er•ate′, *v.,* **-ated, -ating.** unite. —**fed′er•a′tion,** *n.*

fed′ex′ (fed′eks′), *v.,* **-exed, -exing,** *n. Informal.* —*v.* **1.** send by Federal Express. —*n.* **2.** letter or parcel sent by Federal Express.

FedEx, *n. Trademark.* Federal Express.

fe•do′ra, *n.* soft felt hat.

fee, *n.* **1.** payment for services, etc. **2.** ownership.

fee′ble, *adj.,* **-bler, -blest.** weak. —**fee′bly,** *adv.*

feed, *v.,* **fed, feeding,** *n.* —*v.* **1.** give food to. **2.** eat. —*n.* **3.** food. —**feed′er,** *n.*

feed′back′, *n.* **1.** return of part of output of a process to its input. **2.** informative response.

feel, *v.,* **felt, feeling,** *n.* —*v.* **1.** perceive or examine by touch. **2.** be conscious of. **3.** have emotions. —*n.* **4.** touch. —**feel′ing,** *adj., n.*

feel′er, *n.* **1.** proposal designed to elicit reaction. **2.** organ of touch.

feign (fān), *v.* pretend.

feint (fānt), *n.* **1.** deceptive move. —*v.* **2.** make feint.

feist′y (fī′stē), *adj.,* **feistier, feistiest. 1.** full of energy; spirited. **2.** pugnacious. —**feist′i•ly,** *adv.* —**feist′i•ness,** *n.*

feld′spar′, *n.* hard crystalline mineral.

fe·lic′i·tate′, *v.,* **-tated,**
-tating. congratulate.
—**fe·lic′i·ta′tion,** *n.*

fe·lic′i·tous, *adj.* suitable.

fe·lic′i·ty, *n., pl.* **-ties.**
happiness.

fe′line (fē′līn), *adj.* **1.** of or
like cats. —*n.* **2.** animal of the
cat family.

fell, *v.* cut or strike down.

fel′low, *n.* **1.** man. **2.**
companion. **3.** equal. **4.**
member of group.
—**fel′low·ship′,** *n.*

fel′on, *n.* criminal.

fel′o·ny, *n., pl.* **-nies.** serious
crime. —**fe·lo′ni·ous,** *adj.*

felt, *n.* **1.** matted fabric. —*adj.*
2. of felt.

fem., **1.** female. **2.** feminine.

fe′male, *adj.* **1.** belonging to
sex that brings forth young.
—*n.* **2.** female person or
animal.

fem′i·nine, *adj.* of women.
—**fem′i·nin′i·ty,** *n.*

fem′in·ism, *n.* support of
feminine causes. —**fem′in·ist,**
adj., n.

fe′mur (fē′-), *n.* thigh bone.
—**fem′o·ral,** *adj.*

fen, *n.* swampy ground; marsh.

fence, *n., v.,* **fenced, fencing.**
—*n.* **1.** wall-like enclosure. **2.**
person who receives and
disposes of stolen goods. —*v.*
3. fight with sword for sport.
4. sell to a fence. —**fenc′er,** *n.*
—**fenc′ing,** *n.*

fend, *v.* ward off.

fend′er, *n.* metal part over
automobile wheel.

fen′nel, *n.* plant with seeds
used for flavoring.

fe′ral (fēr′əl, fer′-), *adj.* **1.** in a
wild state. **2.** having returned
to a wild state.

fer′ment, *n.* **1.** substance
causing fermentation. **2.**
agitation. —*v.* (fər ment′). **3.**
undergo fermentation.

fer′men·ta′tion, *n.* chemical
change involving
effervescence or
decomposition.

fern, *n.* plant with feathery
leaves.

fe·ro′cious, *adj.* savagely
fierce. —**fe·ro′cious·ly,** *adv.*
—**fe·roc′i·ty,** *n.*

fer′ret, *n.* **1.** kind of weasel.
—*v.* **2.** search intensively.

Fer′ris wheel, amusement ride
consisting of large upright
wheel with suspended seats.

fer′rous, *adj.* of or containing iron. Also, **fer′ric.**

fer′ry, *n., pl.* **-ries,** *v.,* **-ried, -rying.** —*n.* **1.** Also, **fer′ry•boat′.** boat making short crossings. **2.** place where ferries operate. —*v.* **3.** carry or pass in ferry.

fer′tile, *adj.* **1.** producing abundantly. **2.** able to bear young. —**fer•til′i•ty,** *n.* —**fer′ti•li•za′tion,** *n.* —**fer′ti•lize′,** *v.* —**fer′ti•liz′er,** *n.*

fer′vent, *adj.* ardent; passionate. —**fer′ven•cy, fer′vor,** *n.* —**fer′vent•ly,** *adv.*

fer′vid, *adj.* vehement. —**fer′vid•ly,** *adv.*

fes′tal, *adj.* of feasts.

fes′ter, *v.* **1.** generate pus. **2.** rankle.

fes′ti•val, *n.* celebration. Also, **fes•tiv′i•ty.** —**fes′tive,** *adj.* —**fes′tive•ly,** *adv.*

fes•toon′, *n.* **1.** garland hung between two points. —*v.* **2.** adorn with festoons.

fet′a (fet′ə), *n.* Greek cheese usu. from goat's milk.

fetch, *v.* go and bring.

fetch′ing, *adj.* captivating. —**fetch′ing•ly,** *adv.*

fete (fāt, fet), *n., v.,* **feted, feting.** —*n.* **1.** festival. **2.** party. —*v.* **3.** honor with a fete.

fet′id, *adj.* stinking; rank.

fe′tish, *n.* object worshiped. —**fet′ish•ism,** *n.* —**fet′ish•ist,** *n.* —**fet′ish•ist′ic,** *adj.*

fet′lock, *n.* **1.** part of horse's leg behind hoof. **2.** tuft of hair on this part.

fet′ter, *n.* **1.** shackle for feet. **2.** (*pl.*) anything that restrains. —*v.* **3.** put fetters on. **4.** restrain from action.

fet′tle, *n.* condition.

fe′tus, *n.* unborn offspring. —**fe′tal,** *adj.*

feud, *n.* **1.** lasting hostility. —*v.* **2.** engage in feud.

feu′dal•ism, *n.* system by which land is held in return for service. —**feu′dal,** *adj.*

fe′ver, *n.* **1.** bodily condition marked by high temperature. **2.** intense nervous excitement. —**fe′ver•ish,** *adj.* —**fe′ver•ish•ly,** *adv.*

few, *adj., n.* not many.

fey (fā), *adj.* **1.** strange; whimsical. **2.** enchanted.

fez, *n., pl.* **fezzes.** felt cap.

ff, 1. folios. **2.** (and the) following (pages, verses, etc.).

FG, field goal(s).

fi'an·cé' (fē'än sā'), *n.* betrothed man. —**fi'an·cée',** *n.fem.*

fi·as'co (fē as'kō), *n., pl.* **-cos, -coes.** failure.

fi'at (fī'ət), *n.* decree.

fib, *n., v.,* **fibbed, fibbing.** —*n.* **1.** mild lie. —*v.* **2.** tell a fib. —**fib'ber,** *n.*

fi'ber, *n.* **1.** threadlike piece. **2.** threadlike structures that form plant or animal tissue. **3.** roughage. Also, **fi'bre.** —**fi'brous,** *adj.* —**fi'broid,** *adj.*

fi'ber·glass', *n.* material composed of fine glass fibers.

fiber optics, technology of sending light and images through glass or plastic fibers. —**fi'ber-op'tic,** *adj.*

fi'bril·la'tion (fī'brə lā'shən, fib'rə-), *n.* abnormally fast and irregular heartbeat. —**fi'bril·late,** *v.*

fi·bro'sis, *n.* excess fibrous connective tissue in an organ.

fib'u·la, *n., pl.* **-lae, -las.** outer thinner bone from knee to ankle.

FICA, Federal Insurance Contributions Act.

fiche (fēsh), *n.* microfiche.

fick'le, *adj.* inconstant.

fic'tion, *n.* **1.** narrative of imaginary events. **2.** something made up. —**fic'tion·al,** *adj.* —**fic·ti'tious,** *adj.*

fid'dle, *n., v.,* **-dled, -dling.** —*n.* **1.** violin. —*v.* **2.** play folk or popular tunes on violin. **3.** trifle. —**fid'dler,** *n.*

fid'dle·sticks', *interj.* (exclamation of impatience, disbelief, etc.).

fi·del'i·ty, *n., pl.* **-ties.** faithfulness.

fidg'et, *v.* **1.** move restlessly. —*n.* **2.** (*pl.*) restlessness. —**fidg'et·y,** *adj.*

fi·du'cial (-shəl), *adj.* based on trust, as paper money not backed by precious metal.

fi·du'ci·ar'y (-shē-), *adj., n., pl.* **-aries.** —*adj.* **1.** being a trustee. **2.** held in trust. —*n.* **3.** trustee.

field, *n.* **1.** open ground. **2.** area of interest.

field day, 1. day for outdoor sports or contests. 2. chance for unrestricted enjoyment.

fiend, *n.* 1. devil. 2. cruel person. 3. *Informal.* addict. —**fiend′ish,** *adj.* —**fiend′ish•ly,** *adv.*

fierce, *adj.,* **fiercer, fiercest.** wild; violent. —**fierce′ly,** *adv.*

fier′y, *adj.,* **fierier, fieriest.** 1. of or like fire. 2. ardent.

fi•es′ta, *n.* festival.

fife, *n.* high-pitched flute.

fif′teen′, *n., adj.* ten plus five. —**fif•teenth′,** *adj., n.*

fifth, *adj.* 1. next after fourth. —*n.* 2. fifth part.

fifth column, traitorous group within a country.

fifth wheel, one that is unnecessary or unwanted.

fif′ty, *n., adj.* ten times five. —**fif′ti•eth,** *adj., n.*

fig, *n.* fruit of semitropical tree.

fig., 1. figurative. 2. figuratively. 3. figure.

fight, *n., v.,* **fought, fighting.** battle. —**fight′er,** *n.*

fig′ment, *n.* imagined story.

fig′ur•a•tive, *adj.* not literal. —**fig′ur•a•tive•ly,** *adv.*

fig′ure, *n., v.,* **-ured, -uring.** —*n.* 1. written symbol, esp. numerical. 2. amount. 3. shape. —*v.* 4. compute. 5. be prominent.

fig′ure•head′, *n.* powerless leader.

figure of speech, use of words in nonliteral sense.

fig′ur•ine′, *n.* miniature statue.

fil′a•ment, *n.* fine fiber.

fil′bert, *n.* kind of nut.

filch, *v.* steal.

file, *n., v.,* **filed, filing.** —*n.* 1. storage place for documents. 2. line of persons, etc. 3. metal rubbing tool. —*v.* 4. arrange in file. 5. march in file. 6. rub with file. —**fil′er,** *n.*

fi•let′ mi•gnon′ (fi lā min yon′), *n.* round of beef tenderloin cut thick.

fil′i•al, *adj.* befitting sons and daughters.

fil′i•bus′ter, *n.* 1. obstruction of legislation by prolonged speaking. —*v.* 2. use filibuster to impede legislation. —**fil′i•bus ter•er,** *n.*

fil′i•gree′, *n.* ornamental work of fine wires.

Fil′i•pi′no (fil′ə pē′no), *n.* native of the Philippines.

fill, *v.* 1. make full. 2. pervade. 3. supply. —*n.* 4. full supply. —**fill′ing,** *n.*

fil•let′ (fi lā′), *n.* narrow strip, esp. of meat or fish. Also, **fi′let.**

fil′lip, *n.* thing that excites.

fil′ly, *n., pl.* **-lies.** young female horse.

film, *n.* 1. thin coating. 2. roll or sheet with photographically sensitive coating. 3. motion picture. —*v.* 4. make motion picture of.

film′strip′, *n.* length of film containing still pictures for projecting on screen.

film′y, *adj.,* **filmier, filmiest.** 1. partly transparent. 2. blurred. —**film′i•ness,** *n.*

fil′ter, *n.* 1. device for straining substances. —*v.* 2. remove by or pass through filter. —**fil•tra′tion,** *n.*

filth, *n.* 1. dirt. 2. obscenity; offensive indecency. —**filth′y,** *adj.* —**filth′i•ness,** *n.*

fin, *n.* winglike organ on fishes. —**finned,** *adj.*

fi•na′gle (fi nā gəl), *v.,* **-gled, -gling.** practice or obtain by trickery. —**fi•na′gler,** *n.*

fi′nal, *adj.* last. —**fi′nal•ist,** *n.* —**fi•nal′i•ty,** *n.* —**fi′nal•ize′,** *v.* —**fi′nal•ly,** *adv.*

fi•na′le (fi nä′lē), *n.* last part.

fi•nance′, *n., v.,* **-nanced, -nancing.** —*n.* 1. money matters. 2. (*pl.*) funds. —*v.* 3. supply with money. —**fi•nan′cial,** *adj.* —**fi•nan′cial•ly,** *adv.*

fin′an•cier′ (-sēr′), *n.* professional money handler.

finch, *n.* small bird.

find, *v.,* **found, finding,** *n.* —*v.* 1. come upon. 2. learn. —*n.* 3. discovery.

fine, *adj.,* **finer, finest,** *n., v.,* **fined, fining.** —*adj.* 1. excellent. 2. delicate; thin. —*n.* 3. money exacted as penalty. —*v.* 4. subject to fine.

fine art, (*usually pl.*) painting, sculpture, etc., created primarily for beauty.

fin′er•y, *n.* showy dress.

fi•nesse′, *n.* artful delicacy.

fin′ger, *n.* one of five terminal parts of hand. —**fin′ger•nail′,** *n.* —**fin′ger•tip,** *n.*

fin′ger•print′, *n.* 1. impression of markings of surface of finger, used for identification. —*v.* 2. take or record fingerprints of.

fin′ick•y, *adj.*, **-ickier, -ickiest.** fussy. Also, **fin′ic•al.**

fi′nis (fin′is, fī′nis), *n.* end.

fin′ish, *v.* 1. end. 2. perfect. 3. give desired surface to. —*n.* 4. completion. 5. surface coating or treatment.

fi′nite (fīnīt), *adj.* having limits. —**fi′nite•ly**, *adv.*

Finn, *n.* native of Finland.

fin′nan had′die, smoked haddock.

Finn′ish, *n.* 1. language of Finland. —*adj.* 2. of Finland, the Finns, or Finnish.

fiord (fyôrd, fē ôrd′), *n.* narrow arm of sea. Also, **fjord.**

fir, *n.* evergreen tree.

fire, *n., v.,* **fired, firing.** —*n.* 1. burning. 2. ardor. 3. discharge of firearms. —*v.* 4. set on fire. 5. discharge. 6. *Informal.* dismiss.

fire′arm′, *n.* gun.

fire′bomb′, *n.* 1. incendiary bomb. —*v.* 2. attack with firebombs.

fire′fight′er, *n.* person who fights destructive fires. —**fire′fight′ing**, *n., adj.*

fire′fly′, *n., pl.* **-flies.** nocturnal beetle with light-producing organ.

fire′man (fīr′mən), *n., pl.* **-men.** 1. firefighter. 2. person maintaining fires.

fire′place′, *n.* place for fire.

fire′plug′, *n.* hydrant with water for fighting fires.

fire′proof′, *adj.* safe against fire.

fire′side′, *n.* hearth.

fire′trap′, *n.* dilapidated building.

fire′works′, *n.pl.* devices ignited for display of light.

firm, *adj.* 1. hard or stiff. 2. fixed. 3. resolute. —*v.* 4. make or become firm. —*n.* 5. business organization. —**firm′ly**, *adv.* —**firm′ness**, *n.*

fir′ma•ment, *n.* sky.

first, *adj., adv.* 1. before all others. —*n.* 2. first thing, etc.

first aid, immediate treatment.

first class, 1. highest grade. 2. most expensive class in travel. 3. class of mail sealed against inspection. —**first'-class'**, *adj.*

first'hand', *adj., adv.* from the first source. Also, **first'-hand'**.

first'-rate', *adj.* 1. of the highest quality, rank, etc. —*adv.* 2. very well.

fis'cal (-kəl), *adj.* financial.

fish, *n., pl.* **fish, fishes**, *v.* —*n.* 1. aquatic vertebrate. —*v.* 2. try to catch fish. —**fish'er•man**, *n.* —**fish'er•y**, *n.*

fish'y, *adj.,* **fishier, fishiest.** 1. like a fish, esp. in taste or smell. 2. questionable; dubious. —**fish'i•ness**, *n.*

fis'sion (fish'ən), *n.* division. —**fis'sion•a•ble**, *adj.*

fis'sure (fish'ər), *n.* crack.

fist, *n.* closed hand.

fist'ful, *n., pl.* **fuls.** handful.

fist'i•cuffs', *n.pl.* fistfight.

fit, *adj.,* **fitter, fittest**, *v.,* **fitted, fitting**, *n.* —*adj.* 1. well suited. 2. in good condition. —*v.* 3. be or make suitable. 4. equip. —*n.* 5. manner of fitting. 6. sudden attack of illness or emotion. —**fit'ness**, *n.*

fit'ful, *adj.* irregular.

fit'ting, *adj.* 1. appropriate. —*n.* 2. attached part. 3. trial of new clothes, etc., for fit.

five, *n., adj.* four plus one.

fix, *v.* 1. make fast or steady. 2. repair. 3. prepare. —**fix'a•ble**, *adv.* —**fixed**, *adj.* —**fix'ed•ly**, *adv.* —**fix'er**, *n.*

fix•a'tion, *n.* obsession.

fix'ings, *n.pl. Informal.* things accompanying main item.

fix'ture, *n.* thing fixed in place.

fizz, *v., n.* hiss.

fiz'zle, *v.,* **-zled, -zling**, *n.* —*v.* 1. hiss weakly. 2. *Informal.* fail. —*n.* 3. act of fizzling.

fjord (fyôrd, fē ôrd'), *n.* fiord.

FL, Florida.

fla., 1. (he or she) flourished. 2. fluid.

Fla., Florida.

flab, *n.* loose, excessive flesh.

flab'ber•gast', *v. Informal.* astound.

flab'by, *adj.,* **-bier, -biest.** not firm. —**flab'bi•ness**, *n.*

flac'cid (flak'sid, flas'id), *adj.* flabby.

flag, *n., v.,* **flagged, flagging.** —*n.* 1. cloth with symbolic colors or design. 2. plant with long narrow leaves. 3. Also, **flag′stone′**. paving stone. —*v.* 4. signal with flags (def. 1). 5. fall off in vigor, energy, etc.

flag′el•late′ (flaj′-), *v.*, **-lated, -lating.** whip; flog. —**flag′el•la′tion,** *n.*

flag′on, *n.* large bottle.

fla′grant, *adj.* glaring. —**fla′gran•cy,** *n.* —**fla′grant•ly,** *adv.*

flag′ship′, *n.* ship of senior naval officer.

flail, *n.* **1.** hand instrument for threshing. —*v.* **2.** strike or strike at as with flail.

flair, *n.* aptitude; talent.

flak, *n.* **1.** antiaircraft fire. **2.** critical or hostile reaction.

flake, *n., v.,* **flaked, flaking.** —*n.* **1.** small thin piece. —*v.* **2.** separate into flakes.

flak′y, *adj.,* **flakier, flakiest. 1.** of or like flakes. **2.** lying or coming off in flakes. **3.** *Slang.* eccentric; odd. Also, **flak′ey.** —**flak′i•ness,** *n.*

flam•blé (fläm bā′), *adj.* served in flaming liquor.

flam•boy′ant, *adj.* showy; colorful. —**flam•boy′ance,** *n.* —**flam•boy′ant•ly,** *adv.*

flame, *n., v.,* **flamed, flaming.** blaze.

fla•men′co (flä meng′kō, flə-), *n.* Spanish gypsy dance and music style.

fla•min′go, *n., pl.* **-gos, -goes.** tall, red, aquatic bird.

flam′ma•able, *adj.* easily set on fire. —**flam′ma•bil′i•ty,** *n.*

flange, *n.* projecting rim.

flank, *n.* **1.** side. —*v.* **2.** be at side of. **3.** pass around side of.

flan′nel, *n.* soft wool fabric.

flap, *v.,* **flapped, flapping,** *n.* —*v.* **1.** swing loosely and noisily. **2.** move up and down. —*n.* **3.** flapping movement. **4.** something hanging loosely. **5.** *Informal.* agitated state.

flare, *v.,* **flared, flaring,** *n.* —*v.* **1.** burn with unsteady or sudden flame. **2.** spread outward. —*n.* **3.** signal fire.

flare′up′, *n.* sudden outburst.

flash, *n.* **1.** brief light. **2.** instant. **3.** news dispatch. —*v.* **4.** gleam suddenly.

flash′back′, *n.* **1.** earlier event inserted out of order in a story or dramatic work. **2.** sudden recollection of a past event.

flash′bulb′, *n.* bulb giving burst of light for photography.

flash′cube′, *n.* device containing four flashbulbs.

flash′ing, *n.* protective metal for roof joints and angles.

flash′light′, *n.* portable light.

flash′y, *adj.*, **flashier, flashiest.** showy. —**flash′i•ness**, *n.*

flask, *n.* kind of bottle.

flat, *adj.*, **flatter, flattest**, *n.* —*adj.* 1. level. 2. horizontal. 3. not thick. 4. staunch. 5. dull. 6. below musical pitch. —*n.* 7. something flat. 8. apartment. —**flat′ly**, *adv.* —**flat′ness**, *n.* —**flat′ten**, *v.*

flat′bed′, *n.* truck with trailer platform open on all sides.

flat′car′, *n.* railroad car without sides or top.

flat′fish′, *n.* fish with broad, flat body, as flounder.

flat′foot′, *n.*, *pl.* **-feet** for 2, **-foots** for 3. 1. flattened condition of arch of foot. 2. feet with flattened arches. 3. *Slang.* police officer.

flat′-out′, *adj. Informal.* 1. using full speed, resources, etc. 2. downright.

flat′ter, *v.* praise insincerely. —**flat′ter•y**, *n.*

flat′u•lent (flach′ə lənt), *adj.* 1. having an accumulation of gas in the intestines. 2. inflated and empty; pompous.

flat′ware′, *n.* table utensils and dishes.

flaunt, *v.* display boldly.

fla′vor, *n.* 1. taste. —*v.* 2. give flavor to. —**fla′vor•ing**, *n.*

flaw, *n.* defect. —**flawed**, *adj.* —**flaw′less**, *adj.* —**flaw′less•ly**, *adv.*

flax, *n.* linen plant. —**flax′en**, *adj.*

flay, *v.* strip skin from.

flea, *n.* bloodsucking insect.

flea market, market, often outdoors, where used articles, antiques, etc., are sold.

fleck, *n.* 1. speck. —*v.* 2. spot.

fledg′ling, *n.* young bird.

flee, *v.*, **fled, fleeing.** run from.

fleece, *n.*, *v.*, **fleeced, fleecing.** —*n.* 1. wool of sheep. —*v.* 2. swindle. —**fleec′y**, *adj.*

fleet, *n.* 1. organized group of ships, aircraft, or road vehicles. —*adj.* 2. swift.

fleet′ing, *adj.* temporary.

flesh, *n.* 1. muscle and fat of animal body. 2. body. 3. soft part of fruit or vegetable. —**flesh′y,** *adj.*

flesh′ly, *adj.* carnal.

flesh′pot′, *n.* place of unrestrained pleasure.

flex, *v.* bend. —**flex′i•ble,** *adj.* —**flex′i•bil′i•ty,** *n.*

flick, *n.* 1. light stroke. —*v.* 2. strike lightly.

flick′er, *v.* 1. glow unsteadily. —*n.* 2. unsteady light.

fli′er, *n.* aviator.

flight, *n.* 1. act or power of flying. 2. trip through air. 3. steps between two floors. 4. hasty departure.

flight′less, *adj.* incapable of flying.

flight′y, *adj.,* **flightier, flightiest.** capricious. —**flight′i•ness,** *n.*

flim′sy, *adj.,* **-sier, -siest.** weak or thin. —**flim′si•ness,** *n.*

flinch, *v.* shrink.

fling, *v.,* **flung, flinging,** *n.* —*v.* 1. throw violently. —*n.* 2. act of flinging.

flint, *n.* hard stone that strikes sparks. —**flint′y,** *adj.*

flip, *v.,* **flipped, flipping,** *n.,* *adj.,* **flipper, flippest.** —*v.* 1. move, as by snapping finger. 2. turn over with sudden stroke. —*n.* 3. such movement. —*adj.* 4. flippant.

flip′-flop′, *n.* 1. sudden reversal, as of opinion. 2. backward somersault.

flip′pant, *adj.* pert; disrespectful. —**flip′pant•ly,** *adv.* —**flip′pan•cy,** *n.*

flip′per, *n.* broad flat limb.

flirt, *v.* 1. act amorously without serious intentions. —*n.* 2. person who flirts. —**flir•ta′tion,** *n.* —**flir•ta′tious,** *adj.* —**flir•ta′tious•ly,** *adv.*

flit, *v.,* **flitted, flitting.** scurry.

float, *v.* 1. rest or move on or in liquid, air, etc. —*n.* 2. something that floats. 3. decorated parade wagon. —**flo•ta′tion,** *n.*

flock, *n.* 1. group of animals. —*v.* 2. gather in flock.

floe, *n.* field of floating ice.

flog, *v.,* **flogged, flogging.** beat.

flood, *n.* 1. overflowing of water. —*v.* 2. overflow or cover with water, etc.

flood′light′, *n.* artificial light for large area.

floor, *n.* 1. bottom surface of room, etc. 2. level in building. 3. right to speak. —*v.* 4. furnish with floor. 5. knock down.

floor′ing, *n.* floor covering.

flop, *v.,* **flopped, flopping,** *n. Informal.* —*v.* 1. fall flatly. 2. fail. 3. flap. —*n.* 4. act of flopping.

flop′py, *adj.* **-pier, -piest.** limp. —**flop′pi•ness,** *n.*

floppy disk, thin plastic disk for storing computer data.

flo′ra (flôr′ə), *n., pl.* **-ras, -rae** (-ē). plants or plant life of a particular region or period.

flo′ral, *adj.* of flowers.

flor′id, *adj.* ruddy. —**flo•rid′i•ty,** *n.*

flo′rist, *n.* dealer in flowers.

floss, *n.* 1. silky fiber from certain plants. 2. fiber for cleaning between teeth. —**floss′y,** *adj.*

flo•til′la, *n.* small fleet.

flot′sam, *n.* floating wreckage.

flounce, *v.,* **flounced, flouncing,** *n.* —*v.* 1. go with an angry fling. —*n.* 2. flouncing movement. 3. trim; ruffle.

floun′der, *v.* 1. struggle clumsily. —*n.* 2. clumsy effort. 3. flat edible fish.

flour, *n.* finely ground meal.

flour′ish (flûr′-), *v.* 1. thrive. 2. brandish. —*n.* 3. act of brandishing. 4. decoration.

flout, *v.* mock; scorn.

flow, *v.* 1. move in stream. —*n.* 2. act or rate of flowing.

flow chart, chart showing steps in procedure or system.

flow′er, *n., v.* blossom; bloom. —**flow′er•y,** *adj.*

flu, *n.* influenza.

flub, *v.,* **flubbed, blubbing.** botch; bungle.

fluc′tu•ate′, *v.,* **-ated, -ating.** vary irregularly. —**fluc′tu•a′tion,** *n.*

flue, *n.* duct for smoke, etc.

flu′ent, *adj.* command of a language. —**flu′en•cy,** *n.* —**flu′ent•ly,** *adv.*

fluff, *n.* downy particles. —**fluff′y,** *adj.*

flu′id, *n.* 1. substance that flows. —*adj.* 2. liquid or gaseous. —**flu•id′i•ty,** *n.*

fluke, *n.* 1. lucky chance. 2. flounder (def. 3).

flume, *n.* channel; trough.

flunk, *v. Informal.* fail, esp. in a course or examination.

flun′ky, *n., pl.* **-kies.** servant.

fluo•res′cence, *n.* emission of light upon exposure to radiation, etc. **—fluo•res′cent,** *adj.*

fluorescent lamp, tubular lamp using phosphors to produce radiation of light.

fluor′i•da′tion (floor′ə dā′shən), *n.* addition of fluorides to drinking water to reduce tooth decay. **—fluor′i•date′,** *v.*

fluor•ide′, *n.* compound containing fluorine.

fluor′ine, *n.* yellowish toxic gaseous element.

fluor′o•scope′ (floor′ə-), *n.* device for examining the body with x-rays.

flur′ry, *n., pl.* **-ries.** 1. light snowfall. 2. agitated state.

flush, *n.* 1. rosy glow. —*v.* 2. redden. 3. wash out. —*adj.* 4. even with surface. 5. well supplied.

flus′ter, *v.* confuse.

flute, *n., v.,* **fluted, fluting.** —*n.* 1. musical wind instrument. 2. groove. —*v.* 3. form flutes in. **—flut′ing,** *n.*

flut′ist, *n.* flute player. Also, **flau′tist** (flû′tist, flou′-).

flut′ter, *v.* 1. wave in air. —*n.* 2. agitation. **—flut′tery,** *adj.*

flux, *n.* 1. a flowing. 2. continuous change. 3. substance that promotes fusion of metals.

fly, *v.,* **flew, flown, flying,** *n., pl.* **flies.** —*v.* 1. move or direct through air. 2. move swiftly. —*n.* 3. winged insect. **—fly′er,** *n.*

fly′-blown′, *adj.* tainted.

fly′-by-night′, *adj.* 1. unreliable. 2. not lasting.

flying saucer, disk-shaped missile or plane, thought to come from outer space.

fly′leaf′, *n., pl.* **-leaves.** blank page in a book.

fly′wheel′, *n.* wheel for equalizing speed.

foal, *n.* young horse.

foam, *n.* 1. mass of tiny bubbles. —*v.* 2. form foam. **—foam′y,** *adj.*

foam rubber, spongy rubber used in cushions.

fob, *n.* watch chain.

fo′cus, *n., pl.* **-cuses, -ci** (-sī), *v.,* **-cused, -cusing.** —*n.* **1.** point at which refracted rays meet. **2.** state of sharpness for image from optical device. **3.** central point. —*v.* **4.** bring into focus. —**fo′cal,** *adj.*

fod′der, *n.* livestock food.

foe, *n.* enemy.

fog, *n., v.,* **fogged, fog•ging.** —*n.* **1.** thick mist. **2.** mental confusion. —*v.* **3.** become enveloped with fog. —**fog′gy,** *adj.* —**fog′gi•ness,** *n.*

fo′gy, *n., pl.* **-gies.** old-fashioned person.

foi′ble, *n.* weak point.

foil, *v.* **1.** frustrate. —*n.* **2.** thin metallic sheet. **3.** thing that sets off another by contrast. **4.** thin sword for fencing.

foist, *v.* impose unjustifiably.

fold, *v.* **1.** bend over upon itself. **2.** wrap. **3.** collapse. —*n.* **4.** folded part. **5.** enclosure for sheep.

-fold, suffix meaning: **1.** having so many parts, as *a fourfold plan.* **2.** times as many, as *to increase tenfold.*

fold′er, *n.* **1.** folded printed sheet. **2.** outer cover.

fo′li•age, *n.* leaves.

folic acid (fō′lik, fol′ik), vitamin used in treating anemia.

fo′li•o′, *n., pl.* **-ios. 1.** sheet of paper folded once. **2.** book printed on such sheets.

folk, *n., pl.* **folk** or **folks. 1.** people. —*adj.* **3.** of or from the common people.

folk′lore′, *n.* customs and beliefs of people.

folk′lor′ist, *n.* expert on folklore. —**folk′lor•is′tic,** *adj.*

folk song, 1. song originating among the common people. **2.** song of similar character written by a known composer. —**folk singer**

folk′sy, *adj.,* **-sier, -siest.** *Informal.* suggesting genial simplicity. —**folk′si•ness,** *n.*

fol′li•cle, *n.* **1.** seed vessel. **2.** small cavity, sac, or gland.

fol′low, *v.* **1.** come or go after. **2.** conform to. **3.** work at. **4.** move along. **5.** watch or understand. **6.** result.

fol′low•er, *n.* **1.** person who follows. **2.** disciple.

fol′low·ing, *n.* group of admirers or disciples.

fol′low-through′, *n.* **1.** last part of a motion, as after a ball has been struck. **2.** act of continuing a plan, program, etc., to completion.

fol′ly, *n., pl.* **-lies.** foolishness.

fo·ment′, *v.* foster. —**fo′men·ta′tion,** *n.* **fo·ment′er,** *n.*

fond, *adj.* **1.** having affection. **2.** foolish. —**fond′ly,** *adv.* —**fond′ness,** *n.*

fon′dant, *n.* sugar paste.

fon′dle, *v.,* **-dled, -dling.** caress.

fon·due′, *n.* dip of melted cheese.

font (font), *n.* **1.** receptacle for baptismal water. **2.** printing type style.

food, *n.* what is taken in for nourishment.

food processor, appliance for chopping food.

fool, *n.* **1.** person acting stupidly. —*v.* **2.** trick. **3.** act frivolously. —**fool′ish,** *adj.*

fool′har′dy, *adj.,* **-dier, -diest.** rash.

fool′proof′, *adj.* proof against accident.

foot, *n., pl.* **feet,** *v.* —*n.* **1.** part of leg on which body stands. **2.** unit of length equal to 12 inches. **3.** lowest part; base. —*v.* **4.** walk. —**foot′print′,** *n.*

foot′ball′, *n.* game played with pointed leather ball.

foot′hill′, *n.* hill at foot of mountains.

foot′hold′, *n.* **1.** secure place for foot to rest. **2.** firm basis for progress.

foot′ing, *n.* **1.** secure position. **2.** basis for relationship.

foot′less, *adj.* **1.** having no basis. **2.** inefficient.

foot′lights′, *n.pl.* **1.** lights at the front of a stage floor. **2.** acting.

foot′lock′er, *n.* small trunk kept at the foot of a bed.

foot′loose′, *adj.* free to go.

foot′man, *n.* male servant.

foot′note′, *n.* note at foot of page.

foot′-pound′, *n.* work done by force of one pound moving through distance of one foot.

foot′step′, *n.* sound of walking.

foot'stool', *n.* low stool for resting the feet.

fop, *n.* haughty, overdressed man. —**fop'pish**, *adj.*

for, *prep.* **1.** with the purpose of. **2.** in the interest of. **3.** in place of. **4.** in favor of. **5.** during. —*conj.* **6.** seeing that. **7.** because.

for'age, *n., v.,* **-aged, -aging.** —*n.* **1.** food for stock. —*v.* **2.** search for supplies.

for'ay, *n.* **1.** raid. **2.** venture.

for•bear', *v.,* **-bore, -borne, -bearing. 1.** refrain from. **2.** be patient. —**for•bear'ance**, *n.*

for•bid', *v.,* **-bade** or **-bad, -bidden** or **-bid, -bidding.** give order against.

for•bid'ding, *adj.* intimidating or discouraging.

force, *n., v.,* **forced, forcing.** —*n.* **1.** strength. **2.** coercion. **3.** armed group. **4.** influence. —*v.* **5.** compel. **6.** make yield. —**force'ful**, *adj.*

for'ceps, *n.* medical tool for seizing and holding.

for'ci•ble, *adj.* by means of force. —**for'ci•bly**, *adv.*

ford, *n.* **1.** place for crossing water by wading. —*v.* **2.** cross at ford. —**ford'a•ble**, *adj.*

fore, *adj., adv.* **1.** at the front. **2.** earlier. —*n.* **3.** front.

fore-, prefix meaning: **1.** before, as forewarn. **2.** front, as *forehead.* **3.** preceding, as *forefather.* **4.** chief, as *foreman.*

fore'arm', *n.* arm between elbow and wrist.

fore'bear', *n.* ancestor.

fore•bode', *v.,* **-boded, -boding.** portend.

fore'cast', *v.,* **-cast, -casting,** *n.* —*v.* **1.** predict. —*n.* **2.** prediction.

fore'cas•tle (fōk'səl, fōr'kas'əl), *n.* forward part of vessel's upper deck.

fore•close', *v.,* **-closed, -closing.** deprive of the right to redeem (mortgage, etc.). —**fore•clo'sure**, *n.*

fore'fa'ther, *n.* ancestor. —**fore'moth'er**, *n.fem.*

fore'fin'ger, *n.* finger next to thumb.

fore'front', *n.* foremost place.

fore•go'ing, *adj.* previous.

fore'gone' conclusion, inevitable result.

fore'ground', *n.* nearest area.

fore′hand′, *n.* in sports, stroke made with palm of hand facing direction of movement. —**fore′hand′**, *adj.*

fore′head, *n.* part of face above eyes.

for′eign, *adj.* 1. of or from another country. 2. from outside. —**for′eign•er**, *n.*

fore′man or **-wom′an** or **per′son** *n., pl.* **-men** or **-women** or **-persons.** person in charge of work crew or jury.

fore′most′, *adj., adv.* first.

fore′noon′, *n.* daylight time before noon.

fo•ren′sic, *adj.* of or for public discussion or courtroom procedure.

fore′play′, *n.* sexual stimulation leading to intercourse.

fore′run′ner, *n.* predecessor.

fore•see′, *v.,* **-saw, -seen, -seeing.** see beforehand. —**fore′sight′**, *n.*

fore•shad′ow, *v.* hint.

fore′skin′, *n.* skin on end of penis.

for′est, *n.* land covered with trees. —**for′est•er**, *n.* —**for′est•ry**, *n.*

fore•stall′, *v.* thwart by earlier action.

for′est•a′tion, *n.* planting of forests.

forest ranger, officer who supervises care and preservation of forests.

fore•tell′, *v.,* **-told, -telling.** predict.

fore′thought′, *n.* 1. prudence. 2. previous calculation.

for•ev′er, *adv.* always.

fore•warn′, *v.* warn in good time.

fore′word′, *n.* introduction.

for′feit, *n.* 1. penalty. —*v.* 2. lose as forfeit. —*adj.* 3. forfeited. —**for′fei•ture**, *n.*

for•gath′er, *v.* assemble.

forge, *n., v.,* **forged, forging.** —*n.* 1. place for heating metal before shaping. —*v.* 2. form by heating and hammering. 3. imitate fraudulently. 4. move ahead persistently. —**forg′er**, *n.* —**for′ger•y**, *n.*

for•get′, *v.,* **-got, -gotten, -getting.** fail to remember. —**for•get′ful**, *adj.* —**for•get′ta•ble**, *adj.*

for•get′-me-not′, *n.* small plant with blue flowers.

for•give′, *v.*, **-gave, -given, -giving.** grant pardon. —**for•giv′a•ble**, *adj.* —**for•give′ness**, *n.* —**for•giv′ing**, *adj.*

for•go′, *v.*, **-went, -gone, -going.** do without.

fork, *n.* **1.** pronged instrument. **2.** point of division. —*v.* **3.** branch.

fork′lift′, *n.* vehicle with two power-operated prongs.

for•lorn′, *adj.* abandoned. —**for•lorn′ly**, *adv.*

form, *n.* **1.** shape. **2.** mold. **3.** custom; standard practice. **4.** document to be filled in. —*v.* **5.** shape. —**form′less**, *adj.*, —**form′less•ness**, *n.*

for′mal, *adj.* **1.** according to custom or standard practice. **2.** ceremonious. **3.** precisely stated. —**for′mal•ly**, *adv.* —**for′mal•ize′**, *v.*

form•al′de•hyde′, *n.* solution used as disinfectant, etc.

for•mal′i•ty, *n.*, *pl.* **-ties. 1.** custom. **2.** act done as matter of standard practice.

for′mat, *n.*, *v.*, **-matted, -matting.** —*n.* **1.** general arrangement. —*v.* **2.** prepare for writing and reading.

for•ma′tion, *n.* **1.** act of forming. **2.** material that forms. **3.** pattern of moving bodies together.

form′a•tive, *adj.* **1.** giving or acquiring form. **2.** relating to formation and development.

for′mer, *adj.* **1.** earlier. **2.** first-mentioned. —**for′mer•ly**, *adv.*

form′fit′ting, *adj.* snug.

for′mi•da•ble, *adj.* awesome. —**for′mi•da•bly**, *adv.*

form letter, standardized letter that can be sent to many people.

for′mu•la, *n.*, *pl.* **-las, -lae. 1.** scientific description in figures and symbols. **2.** set form of words.

for′mu•late′, *v.*, **-lated, -lating.** state systematically. —**for′mu•la′tion**, *n.*

for′ni•cate′, *v.*, **-cated, -cating.** have illicit sexual relations. —**for′ni•ca′tion**, *n.* —**for′ni•ca′tor**, *n.*

for•sake′, *v.*, **-sook, -saken, -saking.** desert; abandon.

for•swear′, *v.*, **-swore, -sworn, -swearing. 1.** renounce. **2.** perjure.

for•syth′i•a, *n.* shrub bearing yellow flowers.

fort, *n.* fortified place.

forte (fôrt), *n.* 1. one's strong point. —*adv.* (fôr′tā). 2. *Music.* loudly.

forth, *adv.* 1. onward. 2. into view. 3. abroad.

forth′com′ing, *adj.* about to appear.

forth′right′, *adj.* direct in manner or speech.

forth′with′, *adv.* at once.

for′ti•fi•ca′tion, *n.* defensive military construction.

for′ti•fy′, *v.,* -fied, -fying. strengthen.

for•tis′si•mo′, *adj., adv. Music.* very loud.

for′ti•tude′, *n.* endurance.

fort′night′, *n.* two weeks.

for′tress, *n.* fortified place.

for•tu′i•tous (-tyōō′-), *adj.* 1. accidental. 2. lucky.
   —**for•tu′i•tous•ly,** *adv.*
   —**for•tu′i•ty,** *n.*

for′tu•nate, *adj.* lucky.
   —**for′tu•nate•ly,** *adv.*

for′tune, *n.* 1. wealth. 2. luck.

for′tune-tell′er, *n.* person who claims to read the future.
   —**for′tune-tell′ing,** *n.*

for′ty, *n., adj.* ten times four.
   —**for′ti•eth,** *adj., n.*

fo′rum, *n.* assembly for public discussion.

for′ward, *adv.* 1. onward.
   —*adj.* 2. advanced. 3. bold.
   —*v.* 4. send on.
   —**for′ward•er,** *n.*
   —**for′ward•ly,** *adv.*
   —**for′ward•ness,** *n.*

fos′sil, *n.* petrified remains of animal or plant.
   —**fos′sil•i•za′tion,** *n.*
   —**fos′sil•ize′,** *v.*

fos′ter, *v.* 1. promote growth. —*adj.* 2. reared in a family but not related.

foul, *adj.* 1. filthy; dirty. 2. abominable. 3. unfair. —*n.* 4. violation of rules in game. —*v.* 5. make or become foul. 6. entangle. —**foul′ly,** *adv.*

foul′-up′, *n.* mix-up.

found, *v.* establish.

foun•da′tion, *n.* 1. base for building, etc. 2. organization endowed for public benefit. 3. act of founding.

foun′der, *v.* 1. fill with water and sink. 2. go lame. —*n.* 3. person who founds.

found′ling, *n.* abandoned child.

found'ry, *n., pl.* **-ries.** place where molten metal is cast.

foun'tain, *n.* 1. spring of water. 2. source. Also, **fount.**

foun'tain·head', *n.* source.

four, *n., adj.* three plus one. —**fourth,** *n., adj.*

four'-flush', *v.* bluff. —**four'flush'er,** *n.*

four'-score', *adj.* eighty.

four'some, *n.* 1. set or group of four. 2. golf match between two pairs of players.

four'square', *adj.* firm; forthright. —*adv.* 3. firmly.

four'teen', *n., adj.* ten plus four. —**four'teenth',** *adj., n.*

fowl, *n.* 1. bird, esp. hen or rooster.

fox, *n.* carnivorous animal of dog family. 2. crafty person. —*v.* 3. trick.

fox'glove', *n.* tall plant with bell-shaped flowers.

fox'hole', *n.* small pit used for cover in battle.

fox trot, dance for couples.

fox'y, *adj.,* **foxier, foxiest.** 1. cunning. 2. *Slang.* attractive.

foy'er, *n.* lobby.

FPO, 1. field post office. 2. fleet post office.

Fr., 1. Father. 2. French. 3. Friar. 4. Friday.

fra'cas (frā'-), *n.* tumult.

frac'tion, *n.* part of whole. —**frac'tion·al,** *adj.*

frac'tious, *adj.* unruly.

frac'ture, *n., v.,* **-tured, -turing.** break or crack.

frag'ile, *adj.* easily damaged. —**fra·gil'i·ty,** *n.*

frag'ment, *n.* 1. broken part. 2. bit. —*v.* 3. break into fragments. —**frag'men·tar'·y,** *adj.* —**frag'men·ta'tion,** *n.*

fra'grance, *n.* pleasant smell. —**fra'grant,** *adj.*

frail, *adj.* weak; fragile. —**frail'ty,** *n.*

frame, *n., v.,* **framed, framing.** —*n.* 1. enclosing border. 2. skeleton. —*v.* 3. devise. 4. put in frame. —**frame'work',** *n.*

frame'-up', *n.* fraudulent incrimination.

franc (frangk), *n.* French coin.

fran'chise (-chīz), *n.* 1. right to vote. 2. right to do business.

frank, *adj.* 1. candid. —*v.* 2. stamp mail. —**frank'ly,** *adv.* —**frank'ness,** *n.*

frank'furt·er, *n.* sausage.

frank'in•cense' (-sens'), *n.* aromatic resin.

fran'tic, *adj.* wildly excited. —**fran'ti•cal•ly,** *adv.*

fra•ter'nal, *adj.* brotherly. —**fra•ter'nal•ly,** *adv.*

fra•ter'ni•ty, *n., pl.* **-ties.** male society.

frat'er•nize', *v.,* **-nized, -nizing.** associate fraternally. —**frat'er•ni•za'tion,** *n.*

frat'ri•cide' (fra'tri sīd', frā'-), *n.* **1.** act of killing one's brother. **2.** person who kills his or her brother. —**frat'ri•cid'al,** *adj.*

fraud, *n.* trickery. —**fraud'u•lent,** *adj.* —**fraud'u•lent•ly,** *adv.*

fraught, *adj.* full; charged.

fray, *n.* **1.** brawl. —*v.* **2.** ravel.

fraz'zle, *v.,* **-zled, -zling,** *n.* *Informal.* —*v.* **1.** fray. **2.** fatigue. —*n.* **3.** state of fatigue.

freak, *n.* abnormal phenomenon. —**freak'ish, freak'y,** *adj.*

freck'le, *n.* small brownish spot on skin. —**freck'led,** *adj.*

free, *adj.,* **freer, freest,** *adv., v.,* **freed, freeing.** —*adj.* **1.** having liberty. **2.** independent. **3.** open. **4.** without charge. —*adv.* **5.** without charge. —*v.* **6.** make free. —**free'dom,** *n.* —**free'ly,** *adv.*

free'boot'er, *n.* pirate.

free'-for-all', *n. Informal.* brawl; melee.

free'lance', *adj., n., v.,* **-lanced, -lancing.** *adj.* **1.** hiring out one's work job by job. —*n.* **2.** Also, **free'lanc'er.** freelance worker. —*v.* **3.** work as freelance.

free'load', *v. Informal.* take advantage of the generosity of others. —**free'load'er,** *n.*

Free'ma'son, *n.* member of secret fraternal association. —**Free'ma'son•ry,** *n.*

free radical, molecule capable of multiplying rapidly and harming the immune system.

free'think'er, *n.* person with original religious opinions. —**free'think'ing,** *adj., n.*

free'way', *n.* major highway.

freeze, *v.,* **froze, frozen, freezing,** *n.* —*v.* **1.** harden into ice. **2.** fix (prices, etc.) at a specific level. **3.** make unnegotiable. —*n.* **4.** act of freezing. —**freez'er,** *n.*

freight, *n.* 1. conveyance of goods. 2. goods conveyed. 3. price paid.

freight'er, *n.* ship carrying mainly freight.

French, *n.* language or people of France. —**French,** *adj.* —**French'man,** *n.* —**French'wom'an,** *n.fem.*

French dressing, 1. salad dressing of oil and vinegar. 2. creamy orange salad dressing.

French fries, strips of potato that have been deep-fried.

French horn, coiled brass wind instrument.

fre•net'ic, *adj.* frantic.

fren'zy, *n., pl.* **-zies.** wild excitement. —**fren'zied,** *adj.*

fre'quen•cy, *n., pl.* **-cies.** 1. state of being frequent. 2. rate of recurrence. 3. *Physics.* number of cycles in a unit of time.

fre'quent, *adj.* 1. occurring often. —*v.* (fri kwent'). 2. visit often.

fres'co, *n., pl.* **-coes, -cos.** painting on damp plaster.

fresh, *adj.* 1. new. 2. not salt. 3. *Informal.* impudent. —**fresh'en,** *v.* —**fresh'ly,** *adv.* —**fresh'ness,** *n.*

fresh'wa'ter, *adj.* of or living in water that is not salty.

fresh'et, *n.* sudden flooding of a stream.

fresh'man, *n., pl.* **-men.** first-year student.

fret, *n., v.,* **fretted, fretting.** —*n.* 1. vexation. 2. interlaced design. 3. metal or wood ridge across strings of an instrument, as a guitar. —*v.* 4. ornament with fret. 5. worry. —**fret'ful,** *adj.* —**fret'work',** *n.*

Freud'i•an (froi'dē ən), *adj.* 1. of or relating to psychoanalytic theories of Sigmund Freud. —*n.* 2. person, esp. a psychoanalyst, who follows Freud's theories.

Fri., Friday.

fri'a•ble, *adj.* crumbly.

fri'ar, *n.* member of Roman Catholic monastic order. —**fri'ar•y,** *n.*

fric'as•see', *n.* stewed meat.

fric'tion, *n.* 1. act or effect of rubbing together. 2. conflict. —**fric'tion•al,** *adj.*

Fri'day, *n.* sixth day of week.

friend, *n.* 1. person attached to another by personal regard. 2. (*cap.*) Quaker; member of

Society of Friends, a Christian sect. —**friend'ly,** *adj.* —**friend'ship,** *n.*

frieze (frēz), *n.* decorative, often carved band.

frig'ate (frig'it), *n.* **1.** fast sailing warship. **2.** destroyerlike warship.

fright, *n.* **1.** sudden fear. **2.** shocking thing. —**fright'en,** *v.* —**fright'en•ing•ly,** *adv.*

fright'ful, *adj.* **1.** causing fright. **2.** *Informal.* ugly.

fright'ful•ly, *adv. Informal.* very.

frig'id, *adj.* **1.** very cold. **2.** coldly disapproving. **3.** lacking sexual appetite. —**fri•gid'i•ty, frig'id•ness,** *n.*

frill, *n.* **1.** ruffle. **2.** trim. —*v.* **3.** ruffle. —**frill'y,** *adj.*

fringe, *n.* border of lengths of thread, etc.

frip'per•y, *n., pl.* **-peries.** cheap finery.

frisk, *v.* frolic. —**frisk'i•ness,** *n.* —**frisk'y,** *adj.*

frit'ter, *v.* **1.** squander little by little. —*n.* **2.** fried batter cake.

friv'o•lous, *adj.* not serious or appropriate. —**fri•vol'i•ty,** *n.*

frizz, *n., v.,* curl. Also, **friz'zle.** —**friz'zy,** *adj.*

fro, *adv.* from; back.

frock, *n.* **1.** dress. **2.** robe.

frog, *n.* **1.** small, tailless amphibian. **2.** hoarseness.

frol'ic, *n., v.,* **-icked, -icking.** —*n.* **1.** fun; gaiety. —*v.* **2.** play merrily. —**frol'ic•some,** *adj.*

from, *prep.* **1.** out of. **2.** because of. **3.** starting at.

frond, *n.* divided leaf.

front, *n.* **1.** foremost part. **2.** area of battle. **3.** appearance; pretense. **4.** false operation concealing illegal activity. —*adj.* **5.** of or at the front. —*v.* **6.** face. —**fron'tal,** *adj.*

front'age, *n.* front extent of property.

front burner, condition of top priority.

fron•tier', *n.* **1.** border of a country. **2.** edges of civilization. —**fron•tiers'man,** *n.*

fron'tis•piece', *n.* picture preceding title page.

front'-run'ner, *n.* person who leads in a competition.

frost, *n.* **1.** state of freezing. **2.** cover of ice particles. —*v.* **3.** cover with frost or frosting. —**frost′y,** *adj.*

frost′bite′, *n.* gangrenous condition caused by extreme cold. —**frost′-bit′ten,** *adj.*

frost′ing, *n.* **1.** sweet preparation for covering cakes. **2.** lusterless finish.

froth, *n., v.* foam. —**froth′y,** *adj.*

fro′ward, *adj.* perverse.

frown, *v.* **1.** show concentration or displeasure on face. —*n.* **2.** frowning look.

frowz′y, *adj.* **frowzier, frowziest.** slovenly.

fruc′ti•fy′, *v.,* **-fied, -fying. 1.** bear fruit. **2.** make productive. —**fruc′ti•fi•ca′tion,** *n.*

fruc′tose (-tōs), *n.* sweet sugar in honey and many fruits.

fru′gal, *adj.* thrifty. —**fru•gal′i•ty,** *n.* —**fru′gal•ly,** *adv.*

fruit, *n.* **1.** edible product of a plant. **2.** result.

fruit′ful, *adj.* productive.

fruit′less, *adj.* unsuccessful.

fru•i′tion, *n.* attainment.

frump, *n.* dowdy, unattractive woman. —**frump′y,** *adj.*

frus′trate′, *v.,* **-trated, -trating.** thwart. —**frus•tra′tion,** *n.*

frus′tum, *n.* segment of conical solid with parallel top and base.

fry, *v.,* **fried, frying,** *n., pl.* **fries,** (for 4) **fry.** —*v.* **1.** cook in fat over direct heat. —*n.* **2.** something fried. **3.** feast of fried things. **4.** young fish.

ft., 1. feet. **2.** foot. **3.** fort.

FTC, Federal Trade Commission.

fuch′sia (fyoo′shə), *n.* **1.** plant with drooping flowers. **2.** bright purplish red color.

fudge, *n.* kind of candy.

fuel, *n., v.,* **fueled, fueling.** —*n.* **1.** substance that maintains fire. —*v.* **2.** supply with or take in fuel.

fu′gi•tive, *n.* **1.** fleeing person. —*adj.* **2.** fleeing. **3.** fleeting.

fugue (fyoog), *n.* musical composition in which themes are performed by different voices in turn. —**fu′gal,** *adj.*

-ful, suffix meaning: **1.** full of or characterized by, as *beautiful.* **2.** tending to or able to, as *harmful*. 3. as much as will fill, as *spoonful*.

ful'crum, *n., pl.* **-crums, -cra.** support on which lever turns.

ful•fill', *v.* 1. carry out. 2. satisfy. —**ful•fill'ment, ful•fil'ment**, *n.*

full, *adj.* 1. filled. 2. complete. 3. abundant. —*adv.* 4. completely. 5. very. —**ful'ly,** *adv.* —**full'ness**, *n.*

full'back', *n.* (in football) running back positioned behind the quarterback.

full'-bod'ied, *adj.* of full strength, flavor, or richness.

full'-fledged', *adj.* mature.

full'-scale', *adj.* 1. of exact size as an original. 2. all-out.

ful'mi•nate', *v.,* **-nated, -nating,** *n.* —*v.* 1. explode loudly. 2. issue denunciations. —*n.* 3. explosive chemical salt. —**ful'mi•na'tion**, *n.*

ful'some, *adj.* excessive.

fum'ble, *v.,* **-bled, -bling,** *n.* —*v.* 1. grope clumsily. 2. drop. —*n.* 3. act of fumbling.

fume, *n., v.,* **fumed, fuming.** —*n.* 1. vapor. —*v.* 2. emit fumes. 3. show anger.

fu'mi•gate', *v.,* **-gated, -gating.** disinfect with fumes. —**fu'mi•ga'tion**, *n.*

fun, *n.* play; joking.

func'tion, *n.* 1. proper activity. 2. formal social gathering. —*v.* 3. act; operate. —**func'tion•al**, *adj.*

func'tion•ar'y, *n., pl.* **-aries.** official.

fund, *n.* 1. stock of money. —*v.* 2. pay for.

fun'da•men'tal, *adj.* 1. basic. —*n.* 2. basic principle. —**fun'da•men'tal•ly**, *adv.*

fun'da•men'tal•ist, *n.* believer in literal interpretation of a religious text, as the Bible. —**fun'da•men'tal•ism**, *n.*

fu'ner•al, *n.* burial rite. —**fu'ner•al**, *adj.*

fu•ne're•al, *adj.* 1. mournful. 2. of funerals.

fun'gus, *n., pl.* **-gi** (-jī). plant of group including mushrooms and molds. —**fun'gous**, *adj.*

funk, *n. Informal.* depression.

funk'y, *adj.,* **funkier, funkiest.** 1. earthy, as blues-based jazz. 2. *Slang.* offbeat.

fun′nel, *n., v.,* **-neled, -neling.** —*n.* **1.** cone-shaped tube. **2.** smokestack of vessel. —*v.* **3.** channel or focus.

fun′ny, *adj.,* **-nier, -niest. 1.** amusing. **2.** *Informal.* strange.

funny bone, part of elbow that tingles when the nerve is hit.

fur, *n., v.,* **furred, furring.** —*n.* **1.** thick hairy skin of animal. **2.** garment made of fur. —*v.* **3.** trim with fur. —**fur′ry,** *adj.*

fur′be•low′, *n.* showy trim.

fur′bish, *v.* polish; renew.

fu′ri•ous, *adj.* **1.** full of fury. **2.** violent. —**fu′ri•ous•ly,** *adv.*

furl, *v.* roll tightly.

fur′long, *n.* ⅛ of mile; 220 yards.

fur′lough, *n.* **1.** leave of absence. **2.** temporary layoff. —*v.* **3.** give a furlough to.

fur′nace, *n.* structure in which to generate heat.

fur′nish, *v.* **1.** provide. **2.** fit out with furniture.

fur′nish•ing, *n.* **1.** article of furniture, etc. **2.** clothing accessory.

fur′ni•ture, *n.* tables, chairs, beds, etc.

fu′ror, *n.* general excitement.

fur′ri•er, *n.* dealer in furs.

fur′row, *n.* **1.** trench made by plow. **2.** wrinkle. —*v.* **3.** make furrows in.

fur′ther, *adv.* **1.** to a greater extent. **2.** moreover. —*adj.* **3.** more. —*v.* **4.** promote. —**fur′ther•ance,** *n.*

fur′ther•more′, *adv.* in addition.

fur′ther•most′, *adj.* most distant.

fur′thest, *adj.* **1.** most distant or remote. —*adv.* **2.** to greatest distance.

fur′tive, *adj.* stealthy. —**fur′tive•ly,** *adv.* —**fur′tive•ness,** *n.*

fu′ry, *n., pl.* **-ries. 1.** violent passion. **2.** violence.

furze, *n.* low evergreen shrub.

fuse, *n., v.,* **fused, fusing.** —*n.* **1.** safety device that breaks an electrical connection under excessive current. **2.** Also, **fuze.** device for igniting explosive. —*v.* **3.** blend, esp. by melting together. —**fu′si•ble,** *adj.* —**fu′sion,** *n.*

fu′se•lage′ (fyoo′sə läzh′), *n.* framework of an airplane.

fu′sil•lade′ (fyoo′sə läd′), *n.* simultaneous gunfire.

fuss, *n.* **1.** needless concern or activity. —*v.* **2.** make or put into fuss. —**fuss'y,** *adj.*

fus'tian, *n.* **1.** stout fabric. **2.** turgid writing or speech.

fus'ty, *adj.,* **-tier, -tiest. 1.** musty. **2.** out-of-date.

fu'tile, *adj.* useless; unsuccessful. —**fu•til'i•ty,** *n.*

fu'ton (foo'ton), *n.* thin, quiltlike mattress.

fu'ture, *n.* **1.** time to come. —*adj.* **2.** that is to come. —**fu'tur•is'tic,** *adj.* —**fu•tu'ri•ty,** *n.*

fuzz, *n.* fluff.

fuzz'y, *adj.,* **fuzzier, fuzziest. 1.** covered with fuzz. **2.** blurred. —**fuzz'i•ly,** *adv.* —**fuzz'i•ness,** *n.*

FYI, for your information.

G

G, g, *n.* **1.** seventh letter of English alphabet. **2.** suitable for all ages.

g, 1. good. **2.** gram. **3.** gravity.

GA, 1. Gamblers Anonymous. **2.** general of the army. **3.** Georgia.

Ga., Georgia.

gab, *n., v.,* **gabbed, gabbing.** *Informal.* chatter. —**gab'by,** *adj.*

gab'ar•dine' (-dēn'), *n.* twill fabric.

gab'ble, *n., v.,* **-bled, -bling.** —*n.* **1.** rapid, unintelligible talk. —*v.* **2.** talk gabble.

ga'ble, *n.* triangular wall from eaves to roof ridge.

gad, *v.,* **gadded, gadding.** wander restlessly.

gad'a•bout', *n.* person who flits about socially.

gad'fly', *n., pl.* **-flies.** annoyingly critical person.

gadg'et, *n. Informal.* any ingenious device. —**gad'get•ry,** *n.*

gaff, *n.* **1.** hook for landing fish. **2.** spar on the upper edge of fore-and-aft sail.

gaffe (gaf), *n.* social blunder.

gaf'fer, *n.* **1.** chief electrician on a film or TV show. **2.** *Informal.* old man.

gag, *v.,* **gagged, gagging,** *n.* —*v.* **1.** stop up mouth to keep (person) silent. **2.** suppress statements of. **3.** retch. —*n.* **4.** something that gags. **5.** *Informal.* joke.

gage, *n., v.,* **gaged, gaging.** —*n.* **1.** token of challenge. **2.** pledge. **3.** gauge. —*v.* **4.** gauge.

gag'gle, *n.* flock of geese.

gai'e•ty, *n., pl.* **-ties.** merriment.

gai'ly, *adv.* merrily.

gain, *v.* **1.** obtain. **2.** earn. **3.** improve. **4.** move faster. —*n.* **5.** profit. —**gain'ful,** *adj.* —**gain'ful•ly,** *adv.*

gain'say', *v.,* **-said, -saying.** contradict.

gait, *n.* manner of walking.

gai'ter, *n.* **1.** covering for lower leg, worn over the shoe. **2.** kind of shoe.

gal, *n. Informal.* girl.

gal., gallon.

ga′la, *adj.* **1.** festive. —*n.* **2.** festive occasion.

gal′ax•y, *n., pl.* **-axies. 1.** (*often cap.*) Milky Way. **2.** brilliant assemblage. —**ga•lac′tic,** *adj.*

gale, *n.* **1.** strong wind. **2.** noisy outburst, as of laughter.

gall (gôl), *v.* **1.** chafe. **2.** irritate. —*n.* **3.** sore due to rubbing. **4.** bile. **5.** *Informal.* impudence. **6.** abnormal growth on plants.

gal′lant, *adj.* chivalrous. —**gal′lant•ly,** *adv.* —**gal′lant•ry,** *n.*

gall bladder, sac in which bile is stored.

gal′le•on, *n.* sailing vessel.

gal′ler•y, *n.* **1.** corridor. **2.** balcony. **3.** place for exhibits.

gal′ley, *n.* **1.** vessel propelled by many oars. **2.** kitchen of ship.

gal′li•vant′, *v.* gad frivolously.

gal′lon, *n.* unit of capacity equal to 4 quarts.

gal′lop, *v.* **1.** run at full speed. —*n.* **2.** fast gait.

gal′lows, *n.* wooden frame for execution by hanging.

gall′stone′, *n.* stone formed in bile passages.

ga•lore′, *adv.* in abundance.

ga•losh′es, *n.pl.* overshoes.

gal•van′ic, *adj.* **1.** producing or caused by electric current. **2.** stimulating; exciting.

gal′va•nize′, *v.,* **-nized, -nizing. 1.** stimulate by or as by galvanic current. **2.** coat with zinc.

gam′bit, *n.* **1.** sacrificial move in chess. **2.** clever tactic.

gam′ble, *v.,* **-bled, -bling,** *n.* —*v.* **1.** play for stakes at game of chance. **2.** wager; risk. —*n.* **3.** *Informal.* uncertain venture. —**gam′bler,** *n.*

gam′bol, *v.,* **-boled, -boling,** *n.* frolic.

game, *n.* **1.** pastime or contest. **2.** wild animals, hunted for sport. —*adj.* **3.** brave and willing. **4.** lame.

game plan, carefully planned strategy or course of action.

gam′ete (gam′ēt), *n.* mature sexual reproductive cell that unites with another to form a new organism.

gam′in, *n.* street urchin. —**gam′ine** (-ēn), *n.fem.*

gam′ut, *n.* full range.

gam'y, *adj.*, **gamier, gamiest. 1.** having the strong flavor of game, esp. slightly tainted game. **2.** showing pluck; game. **3.** risqué. —**gam'i•ness**, *n.*

gan'der, *n.* male goose.

gang, *n.* **1.** group; band. **2.** work crew. **3.** band of criminals.

gan'gling, *adj.* awkwardly tall and thin.

gan'gli•on (-ən), *n., pl.* **-glia, -glions.** nerve center.

gang'plank', *n.* temporary bridge to docked vessel.

gan'grene (gang'grēn), *n.* dying of tissue. —**gan'gre•nous**, *adj.*

gang'ster, *n.* gang member.

gang'way', *n.* **1.** entrance to ship. **2.** narrow passage. —*interj.* (gang'wā'). **3.** (make way!)

gan'try, *n.pl.* **-tries. 1.** spanning framework for traveling crane. **2.** wheeled framework with scaffolds for erecting rocket.

gaol (jāl), *n., v. Brit.* jail.

gap, *n.* **1.** opening; vacant space. **2.** ravine.

gape, *v.*, **gaped, gaping. 1.** open mouth as in wonder. **2.** open wide.

gar, *n.* long, slim fish.

ga•rage', *n.* place where motor vehicles are kept or repaired.

garb, *n.* **1.** clothes. —*v.* **2.** clothe.

gar'bage, *n.* refuse; trash.

gar•ban'zo, *n., pl.* **-zos.** chickpea.

gar'ble, *v.*, **-bled, -bling.** misquote or mix up.

gar'den, *n.* **1.** area for growing plants. —*v.* **2.** make or tend garden. —**gar'den•er**, *n.*

gar•de'nia, *n.* flowering evergreen shrub.

gar'den-vari'ety, *adj.* common; ordinary.

gar•gan'tu•an (gär gan'choo ən), *adj.* gigantic; colossal.

gar'gle, *v.*, **-gled, -gling,** *n.* —*v.* **1.** rinse throat. —*n.* **2.** liquid for gargling.

gar'goyle, *n.* grotesquely carved figure.

gar'ish, *adj.* glaring; showy. —**gar'ish•ly**, *adv.* —**gar'ish•ness**, *n.*

gar′land, *n.* **1.** wreath of flowers, etc. —*v.* **2.** deck with garland.

gar′lic, *n.* plant with edible bulb. —**gar′lick•y,** *adj.*

gar′ment, *n.* article of dress.

gar′ner, *v.* gather; acquire.

gar′net, *n.* deep-red gem.

gar′nish, *v.* **1.** adorn. **2.** decorate (food). —*n.* **3.** decoration for food.

gar′nish•ee′, *v.,* **-nisheed, -nisheeing.** attach (money or property of defendant).

gar′ret, *n.* attic.

gar′ri•son, *n.* **1.** body of defending troops. —*v.* **2.** provide with garrison.

gar•rote′ (-gə rot′), *n., v.,* **-roted, -roting.** —*n.* **1.** strangulation. —*v.* **2.** strangle.

gar′ru•lous, *adj.* talkative. —**gar•ru′li•ty,** *n.*

gar′ter, *n.* fastening to hold up stocking.

garter snake, common, harmless striped snake.

gas, *n., pl.* **gases,** *v.,* **gassed, gassing.** —*n.* **1.** fluid substance, often burned for light or heat. **2.** gasoline. —*v.*

3. overcome with gas. —**gas′e•ous,** *adj.*

gash, *n.* **1.** long deep cut. —*v.* **2.** make gash in.

gas′ket, *n.* ring or strip used as packing.

gas′o•hol′, *n.* fuel mixture of gasoline and alcohol.

gas′o•line′, *n.* inflammable liquid from petroleum.

gasp, *n.* **1.** short breath. —*v.* **2.** breathe in gasps.

gas′tric, *adj.* of stomachs.

gas•tri′tis, *n.* inflammation of the stomach.

gas′tro•nom′i•cal, *adj.* of good eating. Also, **gas′tro•nom′ic.** —**gas•tron′o•my,** *n.*

gate, *n.* movable hinged barrier.

gate′way′, *n.* entrance.

gath′er, *v.* **1.** come together. **2.** infer. **3.** harvest. —*n.* **4.** pucker.—**gath′er•ing,** *n.*

gauche (gōsh), *adj.* socially clumsy.

gaud′y, *adj.,* **gaudier, gaudiest.** vulgarly showy. —**gaud′i•ly,** *adv.* —**gaud′i•ness,** *n.*

gauge (gāj), *v.,* **gauged, gauging,** *n.* —*v.* 1. estimate. 2. measure. —*n.* 3. standard of measure. 4. distance between railroad rails.

gaunt, *adj.* haggard; bleak.

gaunt′let, *n.* 1. large-cuffed glove. 2. Also, **gant′let.** *n.* double row of persons beating offender passing between them.

gauze (gôz), *n.* transparent fabric. —**gauz′y,** *adj.*

gav′el, *n.* chairperson's mallet.

gawk, *v.* stare stupidly.

gawk′y, *adj.,* **gawkier, gawkiest.** clumsy. —**gawk′i•ness.** *n.*

gay, *adj.,* **gayer, gayest,** *n.* —*adj.* 1. joyous. 2. bright. 3. *Slang.* homosexual. —*n.* 4. *Slang.* homosexual. —**gay′ly,** *adv.*

gaze, *v.,* **gazed, gazing,** *n.* —*v.* 1. look steadily. —*n.* 2. stare.

ga•ze′bo (gə zā′bō, -zē′-), *n.,* *pl.* **-bos, -boes.** structure on a site with a pleasant view.

ga•zelle′, *n.* small antelope.

ga•zette′, *n.* newspaper.

gaz′et•teer′ (-tēr′), *n.* geographical dictionary.

gaz•pa′cho (gäz pä′chō), *n.* Spanish chilled vegetable soup.

gear, *n.* 1. toothed wheel that engages with another. 2. equipment. —*v.* 3. connect by gears. 4. adjust.

gear′shift′, *n.* gear-changing lever in transmission system.

geck′o, *n.,* *pl.* **-os** or **-oes.** small tropical lizard.

GED, general equivalency diploma.

gee (jē), *interj.* (exclamation of surprise or disappointment.)

gee′zer, *n.* odd or eccentric man, esp. an older one.

Gei′ger counter (gī′gər), instrument for measuring radioactivity.

gei′sha (gā′shə), *n.* Japanese woman trained to provide entertainment for men.

gel (jel), *n.,* *v.,* **gelled, gel•ling.** —*n.* 1. jellylike or gluelike substance. —*v.* 2. become gel.

gel′a•tin, *n.* substance from animals, used in glue, etc. —**ge•lat′i•nous,** *adj.*

geld′ing, *n.* castrated male horse. —**geld,** *v.*

gel′id (jel′id), *adj.* icy.

gem, *n.* precious stone.

Gen., General.

gen., genl., general.

gen'darme (zhän'därm), *n.* French police officer.

gen'der, *n.* **1.** *Gram.* set of classes including all nouns, distinguished as masculine, feminine, neuter. **2.** sex.

gene, *n.* biological unit that carries inherited traits.

ge'ne•al'o•gy, *n., pl.* **-gies.** study or account of ancestry. —**ge'ne•a•log'i•cal,** *adj.* —**ge'ne•al'o•gist,** *n.*

gen'er•al, *adj.* **1.** of or including all. **2.** usual. **3.** undetailed. —*n.* **4.** highest-ranking army officer. —**gen'er•al•ly,** *adv.*

gen'er•al'i•ty, *n., pl.* **-ties.** general statement.

gen'er•al•ize', *v.,* **-ized, -izing.** make generalities. —**gen'er•al•i•za'tion,** *n.*

general practitioner, doctor whose practice is not limited to any specific branch.

gen'er•ate', *v.,* **-ated, -ating.** produce. —**gen'er•a'tive,** *adj.*

gen'er•a'tion, *n.* **1.** all individuals born in one period. **2.** such period (about 30 years). **3.** production. —**gen'er•a'tion•al,** *adj.*

Generation X, the generation born in the U.S. after 1965.

gen'er•a'tor, *n.* device for producing electricity, gas, etc.

ge•ner'ic, *adj.* **1.** of entire categories. **2.** unbranded. —**ge•ner'i•cal•ly,** *adv.*

gen'er•ous, *adj.* **1.** giving freely. **2.** abundant. —**gen'er•os'i•ty,** *n.*

gen'e•sis (jen'-), *n.* origin.

ge•net'ics, *n.* science of heredity. —**ge•net'ic,** *adj.* —**ge•net'i•cal•ly,** *adv.* —**ge•net'i•cist,** *n.*

gen'ial (jēn'-), *adj.* openly friendly. —**ge'ni•al'i•ty,** *n.* —**gen'ial•ly,** *adv.*

ge'nie (jē'nē), *n.* spirit, often appearing in human form.

gen'i•ta'li•a (-tā'lē ə, -tāl'yə), *n.pl.* genitals.

gen'i•tals, *n.pl.* sexual organs. —**gen'i•tal,** *adj.*

gen'i•tive (jen'i tiv), *n.* **1.** grammatical case usu. indicating possession, origin, or other close association. —*adj.* **2.** of this case.

gen'ius (jēn'-), *n.* 1. exceptional natural ability. 2. person having such ability.

gen'o•cide' (jen'ə-), *n.* planned extermination of national or racial group.

gen're (zhän'rə), *n.* class or category of artistic work.

gen•teel', *adj.* well-bred; refined. —**gen•til'i•ty**, *n.*

gen'tian (jen'shən), *n.* plant with blue flowers.

gen'tile (-tīl), *adj.* (*sometimes cap.*) not Jewish or Mormon. —**gentile**, *n.*

gen'tle, *adj.*, **-tler, -tlest.** 1. mild; kindly. 2. respectable. 3. careful. —**gen'tle•ness**, *n.* —**gen'tly**, *adv.*

gen'tle•man, *n., pl.* **-men.** 1. man of good breeding and manners. 2. (used as polite term) any man.

gen'tri•fi•ca'tion, *n.* replacement of existing population by others with more wealth or status. —**gen'tri•fy**, *v.*

gen'try, *n.* wellborn people.

gen'u•flect' (jen'yoo-), *v.* kneel partway in reverence. —**gen'u•flec'tion**, *n.*

gen'u•ine (-in), *adj.* real. —**gen'u•ine•ly**, *adv.* —**gen'u•ine•ness**, *n.*

ge'nus (jē'-), *n., pl.* **genera, genuses.** biological group including species.

Gen X (jen' eks'), Generation X. Also, **GenX.**

geo-, prefix meaning the earth or ground, as *geography.*

ge'ode (jē'ōd), *n.* hollow stone often lined with crystals.

ge'o•des'ic dome, dome with framework of straight members that form grid.

ge•og'ra•phy, *n.* study of earth's surface, climate, etc. —**ge•og'ra•pher**, *n.* —**ge'o•graph'i•cal, ge'o•graph'ic**, *adj.*

ge•ol'o•gy, *n.* science of earth's structure. —**ge'o•log'i•cal**, *adj.* —**ge•ol'o•gist**, *n.*

ge'o•mag•net'ic, *adj.* of the earth's magnetism. —**ge'o•mag'net•ism**, *n.*

ge•om'e•try, *n.* branch of mathematics dealing with shapes. —**ge'o•met'ric, ge'o•met'ri•cal**, *adj.*

ge′o•phys′ics, *n.* science of the physics of the earth and its atmosphere. —**ge′o•phys′i•cal,** *adj.*

ge′o•pol′i•tics, *n.* study of politics in relation to geography. —**ge′o•po•lit′i•cal,** *adj.*

ge′o•sta′tion•ar′y, *adj.* of an orbiting satellite remaining in same spot over the earth. Also, **ge′o•syn′chro•nous.**

ge′o•ther′mal, *adj.* of the earth's internal heat.

ge•ra′ni•um, *n.* small plant with showy flowers.

ger′bil (jûr′bəl), *n.* rodent, popular as a pet.

ger′i•at′rics (jer′-), *n.* branch of medicine dealing with aged persons. —**ger′i•at′ric,** *adj.*

germ, *n.* **1.** microscopic disease-producing organism. **2.** seed or origin.

Ger′man, *n.* native or language of Germany. —**German,** *adj.*

ger•mane′, *adj.* pertinent.

German measles, rubella.

German shepherd, large dog with thick black-and-tan coat.

ger′mi•cide′, *n.* agent that kills germs. —**ger′mi•cid′al,** *adj.*

ger′mi•nate′, *v.,* **-nated, -nating.** begin to grow. —**ger′mi•na′tion,** *n.*

ger′on•tol′o•gy (jer′ən tol′ə jē, jēr′-), *n.* study of aging. —**ge•ron′to•log′i•cal,** *adj.* —**ger′on•tol′o•gist,** *n.*

ger′ry•man′der (jer′-), *v.* divide into voting districts so as to give one group or area an unequal advantage.

ger′und (jer′-), *n.* noun form of a verb.

ges•ta′tion (jes-), *n.* period of being carried in womb.

ges•tic′u•late′, *v.,* **-lated, -lating.** make gestures. —**ges•tic′u•la′tion,** *n.*

ges′ture, *n., v.,* **-tured, -turing.** —*n.* **1.** expressive movement of body, head, etc. **2.** act demonstrating attitude or emotion. —*v.* **3.** make expressive movements.

get, *v.,* **got, got** or **gotten, getting. 1.** obtain. **2.** cause to be or do. **3.** be obliged to. **4.** arrive. **5.** become.

get′a•way, *n.* 1. escape. 2. start of race. 3. place for relaxing, etc.

get′-up, *n. Informal.* costume.

gew′gaw (gyo͞o′-), *n.* gaudy ornament.

gey′ser (gī′zər), *n.* hot spring that emits jets of water.

ghast′ly, *adj.,* **-lier, -liest.** 1. frightful. 2. deathly pale.

gher′kin (gûr′-), *n.* 1. small cucumber. 2. small pickle.

ghet′to, *n., pl.* **-tos, -toes.** 1. (formerly) Jewish part of city. 2. city area in which mostly poor minorities live. —**ghet′to•ize,** *v.*

ghost, *n.* disembodied soul of dead person. —**ghost′ly,** *adj.*

ghost′writ′er, *n.* person who writes for another who is presumed to be the author. —**ghost′write′,** *v.*

ghoul (go͞ol), *n.* 1. spirit that preys on dead. 2. person morbidly interested in misfortunes. —**ghoul′ish,** *adj.*

G.I., *Informal.* enlisted soldier.

gi′ant, *n.* 1. being of superhuman size. 2. person of great accomplishments. —**gi′ant•ess,** *n.fem.*

gib′ber (jib′-), *v.* speak nonsense. —**gib′ber•ish,** *n.*

gib′bet (jib′-), *n.* gallows with projecting arm.

gib′bon (gib′-), *n.* small ape.

gibe (jīb), *v.,* **gibed, gibing,** *n.* jeer.

gib′lets (jib′-), *n.pl.* heart, liver, and gizzard of a fowl.

gid′dy, *adj.,* **-dier, -diest.** 1. frivolous. 2. dizzy. —**gid′di•ly,** *adv.* —**gid′di•ness,** *n.*

gift, *n.* 1. present. 2. act of giving. 3. power of giving. 4. talent.

gift′ed, *adj.* 1. talented. 2. highly intelligent.

gig (gig), *n.* 1. carriage drawn by one horse. 2. light boat. 3. *Slang.* engagement, as of musician. 4. *Slang.* job.

gi•gan′tic, *adj.* befitting a giant. —**gi•gan′ti•cal•ly,** *adv.*

gig′gle, *v.,* **-gled, -gling,** *n.* —*v.* 1. laugh lightly. —*n.* 2. silly laugh.

GIGO (gī′gō), *n.* axiom that faulty data input to a computer will result in faulty output.

gig′o•lo′ (jig′-), *n., pl.* **-los. 1.** male professional escort. **2.** man supported by his lover.

Gi′la monster (hē′lə), large, venomous lizard.

gild, *v.,* **gilded** or **gilt, gilding.** coat with gold.

gill (gil), *n.* **1.** breathing organ on fish. **2.** (jil). unit of liquid measure, ¼ pint.

gilt, *n.* gold used for gilding.

gilt′-edged′, *adj.* of the highest quality. Also, **gilt′-edge′.**

gim′crack′ (jim′-), *n.* trifle.

gim′let (gim′-), *n.* small tool for boring holes.

gim′mick, *n.* device or trick.

gimp′y, *adj.,* **gimpier, gimpiest.** *Slang.* limping or lame.

gin, *n., v.,* **ginned, ginning. —n. 1.** flavored alcoholic drink. **2.** machine for separating cotton from its seeds. **3.** trap. —*v.* **4.** put (cotton) through gin.

gin′ger, *n.* **1.** plant with spicy root used in cookery. **2.** spirit.

ginger ale, carbonated soft drink flavored with ginger.

gin′ger•bread′, *n.* **1.** cake flavored with ginger and molasses. **2.** elaborate architectural ornamentation.

gin′ger•ly, *adj.* **1.** wary. —*adv.* **2.** warily.

gin′ger•snap′, *n.* crisp cookie flavored with ginger.

ging′ham, *n.* checked fabric.

gin′gi•vi′tis, *n.* inflammation of the gums.

gink′go (ging′kō, jing-′), *n., pl.* **-goes.** tree with fan-shaped leaves. Also, **ging′ko,** *pl.* **-koes.**

gin′seng (jin′-), *n.* plant with a medicinal root.

gi•raffe′, *n.* tall, long-necked animal of Africa.

gird, *v.,* **girt** or **girded, girding. 1.** encircle with or as with belt. **2.** prepare.

gird′er, *n.* horizontal beam.

gir′dle, *n., v.,* **-dled, -dling. —n. 1.** encircling band. **2.** light corset. —*v.* **3.** encircle.

girl, *n.* female child. —**girl′hood′,** *n.* —**girl′ish,** *adj.*

girl′friend′, *n.* **1.** frequent or favorite female companion; sweetheart. **2.** female friend.

girl scout, *(sometimes caps.)* member of organization for girls (**Girl Scouts**).

girth, *n.* **1.** distance around. —*v.* **2.** gird.

gis'mo (giz′mō), *n.* gadget. Also, **giz'mo.**

gist (jist), *n.* essential meaning.

give, *v.,* **gave, given, giving,** *n.* —*v.* **1.** bestow. **2.** emit. **3.** present. **4.** yield. —*n.* **5.** elasticity.

give'a•way', *n. Informal.* **1.** revealing act, remark, etc. **2.** TV show in which contestants compete for prizes.

giv'en, *adj.* **1.** stated; fixed. **2.** inclined; disposed. —*n.* **3.** established fact or condition.

giz'zard, *n.* stomach of birds.

gla'cier, *n.* mass of ice moving slowly down slope.

gla'cial, *adj.* **1.** of glaciers or ice sheets. **2.** bitterly cold.

glad, *adj.,* **gladder, gladdest. 1.** pleased; happy. **2.** causing joy. —**glad'den,** *v.* —**glad'ness,** *n.*

glade, *n.* open space in forest.

glad'i•a'tor, *n.* Roman swordsman fighting for public entertainment.

glad'i•o'lus (glad′ē ō′ləs), *n.,* *pl.* **lus, li** (lī), **luses.** plant bearing tall spikes of flowers. Also, **glad'i•o'la.**

glad'ly, *adv.* **1.** with pleasure. **2.** willingly.

glam'or•ize, *v.,* **-ized, -izing.** make glamorous. —**glam'or•i•za'tion,** *n.*

glam'our, *n.* alluring charm. —**glam'or•ous,** *adj.* —**glam'or•ous•ly,** *adv.*

glance, *v.,* **glanced, glancing,** *n.* —*v.* **1.** look briefly. **2.** strike obliquely. —*n.* **3.** brief look.

gland, *n.* body organ that secretes some substance. —**glan'du•lar,** *adj.*

glan'ders, *n.* disease of horses.

glare, *n.,* *v.,* **glared, glaring.** —*n.* **1.** strong light. **2.** fierce look. **3.** bright, smooth surface. —*v.* **4.** shine with strong light. **5.** stare fiercely.

glar'ing, *adj.* very obvious. —**glar'ing•ly,** *adv.*

glass, *n.* **1.** hard, brittle, substance. **2.** (*pl.*) eyeglasses. **3.** drinking vessel of glass. **4.** anything made of glass. —*adj.* **5.** of glass. —*v.* **6.** cover with glass. —**glass'ware',** *n.*

glass ceiling, not generally acknowledged upper limit to professional advancement, esp. for women or minorities.

glass′y, *adj.,* **glassier, glassiest. 1.** like glass, as in transparency. **2.** without expression; dull.

glau•co′ma (glô kō′mə, glou-), *n.* condition of elevated fluid pressure within the eyeball.

glaze, *v.,* **glazed, glazing,** *n.* —*v.* **1.** furnish with glass. **2.** put glossy surface on. **3.** make (eyes) expressionless. —*n.* **4.** glossy coating.

gla′zier (-zhər), *n.* person who installs glass.

gleam, *n.* **1.** flash of light. —*v.* **2.** emit gleams.

glean, *v.* gather laboriously, as grain left by reapers. —**glean′ing,** *n.*

glee, *n.* joy; mirth. —**glee′ful,** *adj.* —**glee′ful•ly,** *adj.*

glee club, singing club.

glen, *n.* narrow valley.

glib, *adj.* suspiciously fluent. —**glib′ly,** *adv.* —**glib′ness,** *n.*

glide, *v.,* **glided, gliding,** *n.* —*v.* **1.** move smoothly. —*n.* **2.** gliding movement.

glid′er, *n.* motorless aircraft.

glim′mer, *n.* **1.** faint unsteady light. —*v.* **2.** shine faintly. —**glim′mer•ing,** *n.*

glimpse, *n., v.,* **glimpsed, glimpsing.** —*n.* **1.** brief view. —*v.* **2.** catch glimpse of.

glint, *n., v.* gleam.

glis′ten, *v., n.* sparkle.

glitch, *n. Informal.* malfunction; hitch.

glit′ter, *v.* **1.** reflect light with a brilliant sparkle. **2.** make a brilliant show. —*n.* **3.** sparkling light or luster. **4.** showy brilliance. **5.** small glittering ornaments. —**glit′ter•y,** *adj.*

glitz′y, *adj.,* **glitzier, glitziest.** *Informal.* tastelessly showy. —**glitz,** *n.*

gloam′ing, *n.* dusk.

gloat, *v.* gaze or speak with unconcealed triumph.

glob, *n.* rounded lump or mass.

global warming, increase in the average temperature of the earth's atmosphere.

globe, *n.* **1.** earth; world. **2.** sphere depicting the earth. **3.** any sphere. —**glob′al,** *adj.* —**glob′al•ly,** *adv.*

globe′trot′ter, *n.* one who travels regularly all over the world.

glob′ule, (glob′yōol), *n.* small sphere. —**glob′u•lar,** *adj.*

gloom, *n.* 1. low spirits. 2. darkness.

gloom′y, *adj.,* **gloomier, gloomiest.** 1. low-spirited. 2. depressing. 3. dark; dismal.

glor′i•fied, *adj.* made to seem better than is really so.

glo′ri•fy′, *v.,* **-fied, -fying.** 1. extol. 2. make glorious. —**glor′i•fi•ca′tion,** *n.*

glo′ry, *n., pl.* **-ries,** *v.,* **-ried, -rying.** —*n.* 1. great praise or honor. 2. magnificence. 3. heaven. —*v.* 4. exult. —**glor′i•ous,** *adj.* —**glor′i•ous•ly,** *adv.*

gloss, *n.* 1. external show. 2. shine. 3. explanation of text. —*v.* 4. put gloss on. 5. annotate. 6. explain away. —**glos′sy,** *adj.*

glos′sa•ry, *n., pl.* **-ries.** list of key words with definitions.

glot′tis, *n.* opening at upper part of larynx. —**glot′tal,** *adj.*

glove, *n., v.,* **gloved, gloving.** —*n.* 1. mitt with sheath for each finger. —*v.* 2. cover with glove. —**gloved,** *adj.*

glow, *n.* 1. light emitted by substance. 2. brightness or warmth. —*v.* 3. shine.

glow′er (glou′-), *v.* 1. frown sullenly. —*n.* 2. frown.

glow′worm′, *n.* kind of firefly.

glu′cose′, *n.* sugar found in fruits and animal tissues.

glue, *n., v.,* **glued, gluing.** —*n.* 1. adhesive substance. —*v.* 2. fasten with glue. —**glue′like′,** *adj.* —**glue′y,** *adj.*

glum, *adj.,* **glummer, glummest.** gloomily sullen.

glut, *v.,* **glutted, glutting,** *n.* —*v.* 1. feed or fill to excess. —*n.* 2. full supply. 3. surfeit.

glu′ten (glōo′-), *n.* substance left in flour after starch is removed.

glu′tin•ous, *adj.* gluelike.

glut′ton, *n.* greedy person. —**glut′ton•ous,** *adj.* —**glut′ton•y,** *n.*

glyc′er•in, *n.* thick liquid used as a sweetener, lotion, etc. Also, **glyc′er•ine.**

glyc′er•ol, *n.* glycerin.

gly′co•gen, *n.* carbohydrate in animal tissues, changed into glucose when needed.

gnarl (närl), *n.* knot on a tree.

gnarled (närld), *adj.* contorted.

gnash (nash), *v.* grind (the teeth) together, as in rage.

gnat (nat), *n.* small fly.

gnaw (nô), *v.* **1.** wear away by biting. **2.** distress. —**gnaw′ing,** *adj.*

gnome (nōm), *n.* dwarf in superstition.

GNP, gross national product.

gnu (noo), *n., pl.* **gnus, gnu.** African antelope.

go, *v.,* **went, gone, going. 1.** move; depart. **2.** act. **3.** become. **4.** harmonize.

goad, *n.* **1.** pointed stick. **2.** stimulus. —*v.* **3.** drive with goad. **4.** tease; taunt.

goal, *n.* **1.** aim. **2.** terminal or target in race or game. **3.** single score in various games.

goal′keep′er, *n.* in sports, player whose chief duty is to prevent opposition from scoring a goal. Also, **goal′tend′er;** *Informal,* **goal′ie.**

goat, *n.* horned mammal related to sheep.

goat•ee′, *n.* pointed beard.

goat′herd′, *n.* person who tends goats.

gob, *n.* **1.** mass. **2.** *Slang.* sailor.

gob′ble, *v.,* **-bled, -bling,** *n.* —*v.* **1.** eat greedily. **2.** make cry of male turkey. —*n.* **3.** this cry.

gob′ble•de•gook′, *n.* meaningless speech.

gob′bler, *n.* male turkey.

go′-be•tween′, *n.* intermediary.

gob′let, *n.* stemmed glass.

gob′lin, *n.* elf.

God, *n.* **1.** Supreme Being. **2.** (*l.c.*) deity. —**god′dess,** *n.fem.* —**god′like′,** *adj.*

god′ly, *adj.,* **-lier, -liest. 1.** of God or gods. **2.** conforming to religion. —**god′li•ness,** *n.*

god′par′ent, *n.* sponsor of child at baptism. —**god′child′,** *n.* —**god′daugh′ter,** *n.* —**god′fath′er,** *n.* —**god′moth′er,** *n.* —**god′son′,** *n.*

god′send′, *n.* anything unexpected but welcome.

goes (gōz), third pers. sing. pres. indic. of **go.**

go'fer (gō'fər), *n. Slang.* employee who mainly runs errands.

gog'gle, *n., v.,* -**gled, -gling.** —*n.* **1.** (*pl.*) protective eyeglasses. —*v.* **2.** stare wtih wide-open eyes.

goi'ter, *n.* enlargement of thyroid gland.

gold, *n.* **1.** precious yellow metal. **2.** bright yellow. —**gold, gold'en,** *adj.*

gold'brick', *Slang.* —*n.* **1.** Also, **gold'brick'er.** person who loafs on the job. —*v.* **2.** shirk work.

gold'en•rod', *n.* plant bearing clusters of yellow flowers.

gold'finch', *n.* yellow-feathered finch.

gold'fish', *n.* small, gold-colored fish.

golf, *n.* game played on outdoor course with special clubs and small ball. —**golf'er,** *n.*

go'nad, *n.* ovary or testis. —**go•nad'al,** *adj.*

gon'do•la (gon'də lə, gon dō'lə), *n.* **1.** narrow canal boat used in Venice. **2.** low-sided freight car. —**gon'do•lier'** (-lēr'), *n.*

gon'er, *n. Informal.* person or thing that is past recovery.

gong, *n.* brass or bronze disk sounded with soft hammer.

gon'or•rhe'a (gon'ə rē'ə), *n.* contagious venereal disease.

goo, *n., pl.* **goos. 1.** thick or sticky substance. **2.** sentimentality. —**goo'ey,** *adj.*

goo'ber, *n.* peanuts.

good, *adj.* **1.** morally excellent. **2.** of high or adequate quality. **3.** kind. **4.** skillful. —*n.* **5.** benefit. **6.** excellence. **7.** (*pl.*) possessions. **8.** (*pl.*) cloth. —**good'ness,** *n.*

good'ly, *adj.,* -**lier, -liest.** numerous; abundant.

good'-by', *interj., n., pl.* -**bys.** farewell. Also, **good'-bye'.**

good Sa•mar'i•tan, person who helps those in need.

good'will', *n.* friendly intentions.

Good Friday, Friday before Easter.

good'y, *n., pl.* -**ies.** food pleasing to eat, as candy.

goof, *Informal.* —*n.* **1.** fool. **2.** blunder. —*v.* **3.** blunder. —**goof′y,** *adj.*

goon, *n. Slang.* **1.** hoodlum hired to threaten or commit violence. **2.** stupid person.

goose, *n., pl.* **geese.** web-footed water bird.

goose′ber′ry, *n., pl.* **-ries.** tart, edible acid fruit.

goose flesh, bristling of hair on the skin, as from cold or fear. Also, **goose pimples, goose bumps.**

G.O.P., Grand Old Party (Republican Party epithet).

go′pher, *n.* burrowing rodent.

gore, *n., v.,* **gored, goring.** —*n.* **1.** clotted blood. **2.** triangular insert of cloth. —*v.* **3.** pierce with horn. **4.** finish with gores (def. 2). —**gor′y,** *adj.*

gorge, *n., v.,* **gorged, gorging.** —*n.* **1.** narrow rocky cleft. —*v.* **2.** stuff with food.

gor′geous, *adj.* splendid. —**gor′geous•ly,** *adv.*

go•ril′la, *n.* large African ape.

gos′ling, *n.* young goose.

gos′pel, *n.* **1.** teachings of Christ and apostles. **2.** absolute truth.

gos′sa•mer, *n.* **1.** filmy cobweb. —*adj.* **2.** like gossamer.

gos′sip, *n., v.,* **-siped, -siping.** —*n.* **1.** idle talk, esp. about others. **2.** person given to gossip. —*v.* **3.** talk idly about others. —**gos′sip•y,** *adj.*

Goth′ic, *adj.* **1.** of a style of European architecture from the 12th to 16th centuries. **2.** (*often l.c.*) of a style of literature marked by gloomy settings and sinister events.

Gou′da (gou′də, gōō′-), *n.* mild, yellowish Dutch cheese.

gouge, *n., v.,* **gouged, gouging.** —*n.* **1.** chisel with hollow blade. —*v.* **2.** dig out with gouge. **3.** extract by coercion. —**goug′er,** *n.*

gou′lash, *n.* seasoned stew.

gourd (gōrd), *n.* dried shell of kind of cucumber.

gour•mand′ (gŏŏr mänd′), *n.* enthusiastic or greedy eater.

gour′met (gŏŏr′mā), *n.* lover of fine food.

gout, *n.* painful disease of joints. —**gout′y,** *adj.*

gov., **1.** government. **2.** governor.

gov′ern, *v.* 1. rule. 2. influence. 3. regulate.

gov′ern•ess, *n.* woman who teaches children in their home.

gov′ern•ment, *n.* 1. system of rule. 2. political governing body. —**gov′ern•men′tal,** *adj.*

gov′er•nor, *n.* 1. person who governs. 2. device that controls speed.

govt., government.

gown, *n.* 1. woman's dress. 2. loose robe.

G.P., General Practitioner.

grab, *v.,* **grabbed, grabbing,** *n.* —*v.* 1. seize eagerly. —*n.* 2. act of grabbing.

grace, *n.,* *v.,* **graced, gracing.** —*n.* 1. beauty of form, movement, etc. 2. goodwill. 3. God's love. 4. prayer said at table. —*v.* 5. lend grace to; favor. —**grace′ful,** *adj.* —**grace′ful•ly,** *adv.* —**grace′less,** *adj.* —**grace′less•ly,** *adv.*

gra′cious, *adj.* kind. —**gra′cious•ly,** *adv.* —**gra′cious•ness,** *n.*

grack′le, *n.* blackbird with iridescent black plumage.

gra•da′tion, *n.* change in series of stages.

grade, *n.,* *v.,* **graded, grading.** —*n.* 1. degree in a scale. 2. scholastic division. 3. Also, **gra′di•ent.** slope. —*v.* 4. arrange in grades. 5. level.

grade crossing, intersection of a railroad track and another track, a road, etc.

grade school, elementary school.

grad′u•al, *adj.* changing by degrees. —**grad′u•al•ly,** *adv.*

grad′u•ate, *n.,* *adj.,* *v.,* **-ated, -ating.** —*n.* (-it). 1. recipient of diploma. —*adj.* (-it). 2. graduated. 3. of or academic study beyond the baccalaureate level. —*v.* (-āt′). 4. receive or confer degree. 5. mark in measuring degrees. —**grad′u•a′tion,** *n.*

graf•fi′ti (-fē′tē), *n.pl.,* *sing.* **-to.** markings written on public surfaces.

graft, *n.* 1. twig, etc., inserted in another plant to unite with it. 2. profit through dishonest use of one's position. —*v.* 3. make graft. 4. make dishonest profits. —**graft′er,** *n.*

gra′ham, *adj.* made of unsifted whole-wheat flour.

Grail (grāl), *n.* in medieval legend, the cup or chalice used at the last supper of Christ with the apostles.

grain, *n.* 1. seed of cereal plant. 2. particle. 3. pattern of wood fibers. —**grain′y,** *adj.*

gram, *n.* metric unit of weight.

-gram, suffix meaning something written or drawn, as *diagram.*

gram′mar, *n.* 1. features of a language as a whole. 2. knowledge or usage of the preferred forms in speaking or writing. —**gram•mar′i•an,** *n.* —**gram•mat′i•cal,** *adj.*

gran′a•ry (gran′-), *n., pl.* **-ries.** storehouse for grain.

grand, *adj.* 1. large; major. 2. impressive. —*n.* 3. grand piano. 4. *Informal.* a thousand dollars. —**grand′ly,** *adv.* —**grand′ness,** *n.*

grand′child′, *n.* child of one's son or daughter. —**grand′son′,** *n.* —**grand′daugh′ter,** *n.fem.*

gran•dee′ (-dē′), *n.* nobleman.

gran′deur, *n.* splendor.

gran•dil′o•quence, *n.* lofty, often pompous speech. —**gran•dil′o•quent,** *adj.*

gran′di•ose′, *adj.* pompous.

grand jury, jury designated to determine if a law has been violated and whether the evidence warrants prosecution.

grand′par′ent, *n.* parent of parent. —**grand′fa′ther,** *n.* —**grand′moth′er,** *n.fem.*

grand piano, large piano with a horizontal case on three legs.

grand slam, home run with three runners on base.

grand′stand′, *n.* 1. sloped open-air place for spectators. —*v.* 2. conduct oneself or perform to impress onlookers.

grange, *n.* farmers' organization.

gran′ite, *n.* granular rock.

gra•no′la, *n.* cereal of dried fruit, grains, nuts, etc.

grant, *v.* 1. bestow. 2. admit. —*n.* 3. thing granted.

gran•tee′, *n.* grant receiver.

grants′man•ship′, *n.* skill in securing grants.

gran'u·late', *v.*, **-lated, -lating.** form into granules. —**gran'u·la'tion**, *n.*

gran'ule, *n.* small grain. —**gran'u·lar**, *adj.*

grape, *n.* smooth-skinned fruit that grows in clusters.

grape'fruit', *n.* large yellow citrus fruit.

grape'vine', *n.* **1.** vine on which grapes grow. **2.** route by which gossip spreads.

graph, *n.* diagram showing relations by lines, etc.

-graph, suffix meaning: **1.** something written or drawn, as *autograph.* **2.** instrument that writes or records, as *seismograph.*

graph'ic, *adj.* **1.** vivid. **2.** of writing, painting, etc. —**graph'i·cal·ly**, *adv.*

graph'ite (-īt), *n.* soft, dark mineral.

graph·ol'o·gy (gra fol'ə jē), *n.* study of handwriting. —**graph·ol'o·gist**, *n.*

-graphy, suffix meaning: **1.** process or form of writing, printing, recording, or describing, as *biography.* **2.** art or science concerned with these, as *geography.*

grap'nel, *n.* hooked device for grasping.

grap'ple, *n., v.,* **-pled, -pling.** —*n.* **1.** hook for grasping. —*v.* **2.** try to grasp. **3.** try to cope.

grasp, *v.* **1.** seize and hold. **2.** understand. —*n.* **3.** act of gripping. **4.** mastery.

grasp'ing, *adj.* greedy.

grass, *n.* **1.** ground-covering herbage. **2.** cereal plant. —**grass'y**, *adj.*

grass'hop'per, *n.* leaping insect.

grass'land', *n.* open grass-covered land; prairie.

grass roots, ordinary citizens, as contrasted with leadership or elite. —**grass'-roots'**, *adj.*

grass widow, woman who is separated or divorced.

grate, *v.,* **grated, grating,** *n.* —*v.* **1.** irritate. **2.** make harsh sound. **3.** rub into small bits. —*n.* **4.** Also, **grat'ing.** metal framework. —**grat'er**, *n.*

grate'ful, *adj.* **1.** thankful. **2.** welcome as news. —**grate'ful·ly**, *adv.*

grat'i·fy', *v.,* **-fied, -fying.** please. —**grat'i·fi·ca'tion**, *n.*

gra′tis (grat′is), *adv., adj.* free of charge.

grat′i•tude′, *n.* thankfulness.

gra•tu′i•tous (-tōō′-), *adj.* **1.** free of charge. **2.** without reasonable cause.

gra•tu′i•ty, *n., pl.* **-ties.** tip.

grave, *n., adj.* **graver, gravest.** —*n.* **1.** place of or excavation for burial. —*adj.* **2.** solemn. **3.** important. —**grave′yard′**, *n.*

graveyard shift, work shift starting late at night.

grav′el, *n.* small stones.

grav′el•ly, *adj.* **1.** like gravel. **2.** harsh-sounding; raspy.

grav′i•ta′tion, *n.* force of attraction between bodies. —**grav′i•tate′**, *v.*

grav′i•ty, *n., pl.* **-ties. 1.** force attracting bodies to the earth's center. **2.** seriousness.

gra′vy, *n., pl.* **-vies.** juices from cooking meat.

gray, *n.* **1.** color between black and white. —*adj.* **2.** of this color. **3.** ambiguous. **4.** depressing. —**gray′ish**, *adj.* —**gray′ness**, *n.*

gray′beard′, *n.* old man.

gray matter, **1.** nerve tissue of brain and spinal cord. **2.** *Informal.* brains; intelligence.

graze, *v.*, **grazed, grazing. 1.** feed on grass. **2.** brush past.

grease, *n., v.*, **greased, greasing.** —*n.* **1.** animal fat. **2.** fatty matter. —*v.* **3.** put grease on or in. —**greas′y**, *adj.*

great, *adj.* **1.** very large. **2.** important. —**great′ly**, *adv.* —**great′ness**, *n.*

Great Dane, large dog.

grebe (grēb), *n.* diving bird.

greed, *n.* excessive desire. —**greed′i•ly**, *adv.* —**greed′y**, *adj.*

Greek, *n.* native or language of Greece. —**Greek**, *adj.*

green, *adj.* **1.** of color of vegetation. **2.** unripe. **3.** inexperienced. —*n.* **4.** green color. **5.** grassy land. —**green′ish**, *adj.* —**green′ness**, *n.*

green′back′, *n.* U.S. legal-tender note.

green′belt′, *n.* area of woods, parks, or open land surrounding a community.

green′er•y, *n., pl.* **-eries.** plants; foliage.

green'-eyed', *adj.* envious.

green'gro'cer, *n.* retailer of fresh fruit and vegetables.

green'horn', *n.* **1.** novice. **2.** naive or gullible person.

green'house', *n.* building where plants are grown.

greenhouse effect, heating of atmosphere resulting from absorption by certain gases of solar radiation.

green'room', *n.* lounge in theater for use by performers.

green thumb, exceptional skill for growing plants.

greet, *n.* **1.** address in meeting. **2.** react to; receive. —**greet'ing**, *n.*

gre•gar'i•ous (gri gâr'-), *adj.* fond of company.

grem'lin, *n.* mischievous elf.

gre•nade', *n.* hurled explosive.

gren'a•dier', *n. Brit.* member of special infantry regiment.

grey, *n., adj.* gray.

grey'hound', *n.* slender dog.

grid, *n.* **1.** covering of crossed bars. **2.** system of crossed lines.

grid'dle, *n.* shallow frying pan.

grid'i'ron, *n.* **1.** grill. **2.** football field.

grid'lock', *n.* **1.** complete stoppage of movement in all directions due to traffic. **2.** stoppage of a process.

grief, *n.* keen sorrow.

griev'ance, *n.* **1.** wrong. **2.** complaint against wrong.

griev'ous, *adj.* causing grief, pain, etc. —**grie'vous•ly**, *adv.*

grieve, *v.,* grieved, grieving. feel sorrow; inflict sorrow on.

grif'fin, *n.* monster of fable with head and wings of eagle and body of lion. Also, **gryph'on.**

grill, *n.* **1.** barred utensil for broiling. —*v.* **2.** broil on grill. **3.** question persistently.

grille (gril), *n.* metal barrier.

grim, *adj.,* grimmer, grimmest. **1.** stern. **2.** harshly threatening. —**grim'ly**, *adv.* —**grim'ness**, *n.*

gri•mace' (*n.* grim'əs, *v.* gri mās'), *n., v.,* -maced, -macing. smirk.

grime, *n.* dirt. —**grim'y**, *adj.*

grin, *v.,* grinned, grinning, *n.* —*v.* **1.** smile openly and broadly. —*n.* **2.** broad smile.

grind, *v.,* **ground, grinding,** *n.* —*v.* **1.** wear, crush, or sharpen by friction. **2.** turn crank. —*n.* **3.** *Informal.* dreary routine. —**grind′stone,** *n.*

grip, *n., v.,* **gripped, gripping.** —*n.* **1.** grasp. **2.** handclasp. **3.** small suitcase. **4.** handle. —*v.* **5.** grasp. —**grip′per,** *n.*

gripe, *v.,* **griped, griping,** *n.* —*v.* **1.** grasp. **2.** produce pain in bowels. **3.** *Informal.* complain. —*n.* **4.** *Informal.* complaint. —**grip′er,** *n.*

grippe (grip), *n.* influenza.

gris′ly, *adj.,* **-lier, -liest.** gruesome.

grist, *n.* grain to be ground. —**grist′mill′,** *n.*

gris′tle, *n.* cartilage. —**gris′tly,** *adj.*

grit, *n., v.,* **gritted, gritting.** —*n.* **1.** fine particles. **2.** courage. —*v.* **3.** cause to grind together. —**grit′ty,** *adj.*

grits, *n.pl.* ground grain.

griz′zly, *adj.,* **-zlier, -zliest.** gray, as hair or fur. Also, **griz′zled.**

grizzly bear, large bear with coarse, gray-tipped fur.

groan, *n.* **1.** moan of pain, derision, etc. —*v.* **2.** utter groans. —**groan′er,** *n.*

gro′cer, *n.* dealer in foods, etc.

gro′cer•y, *n., pl.* **-ceries. 1.** store selling food. **2.** (*usually pl.*) food bought at such a store.

grog, *n.* **1.** mixture of rum and water. **2.** any alcoholic drink.

grog′gy, *adj.,* **-gier, -giest.** dizzy. —**grog′gi•ness,** *n.*

groin, *n.* hollow where thigh joins abdomen.

grom′met, *n.* eyelet.

groom, *n.* **1.** person in charge of stables. **2.** bridegroom. —*v.* **3.** make neat.

grooms′man, *n., pl.* **-men.** attendant of bridegroom.

groove, *n., v.,* **grooved, grooving.** —*n.* **1.** furrow. —*v.* **2.** form groove in.

grope, *v.,* **groped, groping.** feel blindly.

gros′beak′, *n.* finch with a thick, conical bill.

gross, *adj.* **1.** before deductions. **2.** flagrant. —*n.* **3.** amount before deductions. **4.** twelve dozen. —**gross′ly,** *adv.* —**gross′ness,** *n.*

gross national product, total monetary value of all goods and services produced in a country during one year.

gro·tesque′, *adj.* **1.** fantastically ugly or absurd. **2.** fantastic.

grot′to, *n., pl.* **-tos, -toes.** cave.

grouch, *Informal.* —*v.* **1.** sulk. —*n.* **2.** sulky person. **3.** sullen mood. —**grouch′y,** *adj.*

ground, *n.* **1.** earth's solid surface. **2.** tract of land. **3.** motive. **4.** (*pl.*) dregs. **5.** rational basis. —*adj.* **6.** of or on ground. —*v.* **7.** instruct in elements. **8.** run aground.

ground ball, batted baseball that rolls or bounces along the ground. Also, **ground′er.**

ground′hog′, *n.* woodchuck.

ground′less, *adj.* without rational basis.

ground rules, basic rule of conduct in a situation.

ground′swell′, *n.* surge of feelings, esp. among the general public.

ground′work′, *n.* basic work.

group, *n.* **1.** number of persons or things placed or considered together. —*v.* **2.** place in or form group.

group′er, *n., pl.* **-ers, -er.** large sea bass of warm waters.

group′ie, *n., pl.* **-ies. 1.** young female fan of rock group. **2.** ardent fan of any celebrity.

grouse, *n.* game bird.

grout (grout), *n.* thin, coarse mortar, used between tiles.

grove, *n.* small wood.

grov′el, *v.,* **-eled, -eling.** humble oneself, esp. by crouching.

grow, *v.,* **grew, grown, growing.** increase in size; develop. —**grow′er,** *n.*

growl, *n.* **1.** guttural, angry sound. —*v.* **2.** utter growls.

grown′up′, *n.* adult. —**grown′-up′,** *adj.*

growth, *n.* **1.** act of growing. **2.** something that has grown.

grub, *n., v.,* **grubbed, grubbing.** —*n.* **1.** larva. **2.** drudge. **3.** *Informal.* food. —*v.* **4.** dig.

grub′by, *adj.,* **-bier, -biest. 1.** dirty. **2.** sordid. —**grub′bi·ness,** *n.*

grudge, *n. v.,* **grudged, grudging.** —*n.* **1.** lasting malice. —*v.* **2.** begrudge. —**grudg′ing·ly,** *adv.*

gru′el, *n.* thin cereal.

gru•el•ing, *adj.* exhausting.

grue'some, *adj.* revoltingly sinister. —**grue'some•ly,** *adv.* —**grue'some•ness,** *n.*

gruff, *adj.* surly. —**gruff'ly,** *adv.* —**gruff'ness,** *n.*

grum'ble, *v.,* **-bled, -bling.** murmur in discontent. —**grum'bler,** *n.*

grump'y, *adj.,* **grumpier, grumpiest.** surly. —**grump'i•ness,** *n.*

grun'gy (grun'jē), *adj.,* **-gier, -giest.** *Slang.* grimy.

grunt, *n.* 1. guttural sound. 2. *Slang.* foot soldier. 3. *Slang.* low-ranking worker. —*v.* 4. utter grunts.

gryph'on, *n.* griffin.

gua'no (gwä'nō), *n.* manure; excrement of sea birds.

guar., guarantee(d).

guar'an•tee', *n., v.,* **-teed, -teeing.** —*n.* 1. pledge given as security. —*v.* 2. pledge. 2. assure. Also, **guar'an•ty'.** —**guar'an•tor',** *n.*

guard, *v.* 1. watch over. —*n.* 2. person who guards. 3. body of guards. 4. close watch.

guard'ed, *adj.* 1. cautious; prudent. 2. protected. —**guard'ed•ly,** *adv.*

guard'i•an, *n.* 1. person who guards. 2. person entrusted with care of another. —**guard'i•an•ship',** *n.*

gua'va (gwä'və), *n.* large yellow fruit of tropical tree.

gu'ber•na•to'ri•al, *adj.* of governors.

guer•ril'la (gə ril'ə), *n.* independent soldier.

guess, *v.* 1. form opinion on incomplete evidence. 2. be right in such opinion. —*n.* 3. act of guessing. —**guess'er,** *n.*

guess'work', *n.* 1. act of guessing. 2. conclusions from guesses.

guest, *n.* 1. visitor. 2. customer at hotel, restaurant, etc.

guf•faw', *n.* 1. loud laughter. —*v.* 2. laugh loudly.

guid'ance, *n.* 1. act or instance of guiding. 2. advice over period of time.

guide, *v.,* **guided, guiding,** *n.* —*v.* 1. show the way. —*n.* 2. one that guides. —**guid'er,** *n.*

guide'book', *n.* book of directions and information.

guided missile, radio-controlled missile.

guide′line′, *n.* indication of course of action.

gui′don (gī′dən), *n.* small flag.

guild, *n.* organization for common interest.

guile, *n.* cunning. —**guile′less,** *adj.*

guil′lo•tine′ (gil′ə tēn′), *n.* machine for beheading.

guilt, *n.* fact or feeling of having committed a wrong. —**guilt′i•ly,** *adv.* —**guilt′y,** *adj.*

guin′ea (gin′ē), *n., pl.* **-eas.** former British coin.

guinea fowl, domesticated fowl. Also, **guinea hen.**

guinea pig, 1. South American rodent. **2.** subject of experiment.

guise (gīz), *n.* appearance.

gui•tar′, *n.* stringed musical instrument. —**gui•tar′ist,** *n.*

gulch, *n.* ravine.

gulf, *n.* **1.** arm of sea. **2.** abyss.

gull, *n.* **1.** web-footed sea bird. **2.** dupe. —*v.* **3.** cheat; trick.

gul′let, *n.* throat.

gul′li•ble, *adj.* easily deceived. —**gul′li•bil′i•ty,** *n.*

gul′ly, *n., pl.* **-lies.** deep channel cut by running water.

gulp, *v.* **1.** consume hastily. —*n.* **2.** act of gulping.

gum, *n., v.,* **gummed, gumming.** —*n.* **1.** sticky plant excretion. **2.** chewing gum. **3.** tissue around teeth. —*v.* **4.** smear with gum. —**gum′my,** *adj.*

gum′bo, *n., pl.* **-bos.** soup made with okra.

gum′drop′, *n.* chewy candy.

gump′tion, *n.* **1.** initiative. **2.** courage; spunk.

gum′shoe′, *n., pl.* **-shoes. 1.** *Slang.* detective. **2.** rubber overshoe.

gun, *n., v.,* **gunned, gunning.** —*n.* **1.** tubular weapon which shoots missiles with explosives. —*v.* **2.** hunt with gun. **3.** cause (an engine) to speed up quickly. —**gun′ner,** *n.* —**gun′ner•y,** *n.*

gun′cot′ton, *n.* explosive made of cotton and acids.

gung′-ho′, *adj. Informal.* enthusiastic and loyal.

gunk (gungk), *n. Slang.* sticky or greasy matter.

gun′man, *n., pl.* **-men.** armed criminal.

gun'ny, *n., pl.* **-nies.** coarse material used for sacks.

gun'pow'der, *n.* explosive mixture.

gun'shot', *n.* shot fired from gun.

gun'smith', *n.* person who makes or repairs firearms.

gun'wale (gun'əl), *n.* upper edge of vessel's side.

gup'py, *n., pl.* **-pies.** tiny tropical fish.

gur'gle, *v.,* **-gled, -gling,** *n.* —*v.* 1. flow noisily. —*n.* 2. sound of gurgling.

gur'ney, *n.* wheeled table or stretcher for transporting patients.

gu'ru, *n.* 1. Hindu spiritual teacher. 2. teacher; leader.

gush, *v.* 1. flow suddenly. 2. talk effusively. —*n.* 3. sudden flow. —**gush'y,** *adj.*

gush'er, *n.* jet of petroleum from underground.

gus'set, *n.* angular insertion.

gus'sy, *v.,* **-sied, -sying.** dress up or decorate showily.

gust, *n.* 1. blast of wind. 2. outburst. —**gust'y,** *adj.*

gus'ta·to'ry, *adj.* of taste.

gus'to, *n., pl.* **-toes.** zest.

gut, *n., v.,* **gutted, gutting.** —*n.* 1. intestine. 2. (*pl.*) *Informal.* courage. —*v.* 3. destroy interior of.

gut'less, *adj.* lacking courage.

guts'y, *adj.,* **gutsier, gutsiest.** daring. —**guts'i·ness,** *n.*

gut'ter, *n.* channel for leading off rainwater.

gut'tur·al, *adj.* 1. of or in throat. —*n.* 2. guttural sound. —**gut'tur·al·ly,** *adv.*

guy, *n.* 1. rope, etc., used to guide or steady object. 2. *Informal.* fellow.

guz'zle, *v.,* **-zled, -zling.** drink greedily. —**guz'zler,** *n.*

gym·na'si·um (jim-), *n., pl.* **-siums, -sia.** place for physical exercise. *Informal,* **gym.**

gym'nast, *n.* performer of gymnastics.

gym·nas'tics, *n.pl.* physical exercises. —**gym·nas'tic,** *adj.*

gy'ne·col'o·gy (gī'nə-), *n.* branch of medicine dealing with care of women. —**gy'ne·co·log'ic, gy'ne·co·log'i·cal,** *adj.* —**gy'ne·col'o·gist,** *n.,*

gyp (jip), *v.*, **gypped, gypping.**
Informal. cheat.

gyp′sum, *n.* soft mineral.

Gyp′sy, *n., pl.* **-sies.** member of wandering people.

gy′rate, *v.,* **-rated, -rating.**
whirl. —**gy•ra′tion,** *n.*

gy′ro•scope′ (jī′rə-), *n.*
rotating wheel mounted to maintain absolute direction in space. —**gy′ro•scop′ic,** *adj.*

H, h, *n.* eighth letter of English alphabet.

h. or **H., 1.** height. **2.** high. **3.** (in baseball) hit. **4.** hour. **5.** hundred. **6.** husband.

ha, *interj.* (exclamation of surprise, suspicion, etc.).

ha′be•as cor′pus (hā′bē əs kôr′pəs), writ requiring that arrested person be brought before court to determine whether he or she is legally detained.

hab′er•dash′er•y, *n., pl.* **-eries.** shop selling men's items. —**hab′er•dash′er,** *n.*

hab′it, *n.* **1.** customary practice or act. **2.** garb. —**ha•bit′u•al** (hə bich′oo əl), *adj.* —**ha•bit′u•al•ly,** *adv.* —**ha•bit′u•a′tion,** *n.*

hab′it•a•ble, *adj.* livable. —**hab′it•a•bly,** *adv.*

hab′i•tant, *n.* resident.

hab′i•tat′, *n.* natural dwelling.

hab′i•ta′tion, *n.* abode.

ha•bit′u•ate′, *v.,* **-ated, -ating.** accustom; make used to. —**ha•bit′u•a′tion,** *n.*

ha•bit′u•é′ (hə bich′oo ā′), *n.* habitual visitor.

hack, *v.* **1.** cut or chop roughly. **2.** cough sharply. —*n.* **3.** cut or notch. **4.** artistic drudge. **5.** vehicle for hire. —*adj.* **6.** routine.

hack′er, *n. Slang.* **1.** skilled computer enthusiast. **2.** computer user who tries to gain unauthorized access to systems.

hack′les, *n.pl.* **1.** hair that can bristle on the back of an animal's neck. **2.** anger.

hack′ney, *n., pl.* **-neys.** horse or carriage for hire.

hack′neyed, *adj.* trite.

hack′saw′, *n.* saw for cutting metal.

had′dock, *n.* food fish of northern Atlantic.

Ha′des (hā′dēz), *n.* hell.

haft, *n.* handle.

hag, *n.* repulsive old woman.

hag′gard, *adj.* fatigued.

hag′gle, *v.,* **-gled, -gling.** argue over price.

hai′ku (hī′koo), *n., pl.* **-ku.** Japanese poem consisting of 3 lines of 5, 7, and 5 syllables, respectively.

hail, *n.* **1.** ice pellets (**hail'stones'**) **2.** shout. **3.** salutation. —*v.* **4.** pour down hail. **5.** greet. **6.** call out to.

hair, *n.* **1.** filament on human head, animal body, etc. **2.** hairs collectively. —**hair'y,** *adj.* —**hair'i•ness,** *n.* —**hair'dres'ser,** *n.* —**hair'less,** *adj.* —**hair'pin',** *n.*

hair'breadth', *n.* narrow margin. Also, **hairs'breadth'.**

hair'cut', *n.* **1.** act of cutting hair. **2.** hair style.

hair'do', *n., pl.* **-dos.** hair arrangement.

hair'piece', *n.* toupee or wig.

hair'-rais'ing, *adj.* terrifying.

hair'spray', *n.* liquid spray for holding the hair in place.

hair'style', *n.* way of wearing hair. —**hair'styl'ist,** *n.*

hair'-trig'ger, *adj.* easily activated or set off.

hake, *n.* codlike fish.

hal'cy•on (hal'sē ən), *adj.* peaceful; happy; carefree.

hale, *v.,* **haled, haling,** *adj.* —*v.* **1.** summon. —*adj.* **2.** healthy.

half, *n., pl.* **halves,** *adj., adv.* —*n.* **1.** one of two equal parts. —*adj.* **2.** being half. **3.** incomplete. —*adv.* **4.** partly.

half'back', *n.* (in football) one of two backs who line up on each side of the fullback.

half'-baked', *adj.* **1.** ill-prepared. **2.** foolish.

half'-breed', *n. Offensive.* offspring of parents of two races.

half brother, brother related through one parent only.

half'-cocked', *adj.* ill-considered or ill-prepared.

half'-heart'ed, *adj.* unenthusiastic. —**half'-heart'ed•ly,** *adv.* —**half-heart'ed•ness,** *n.*

half'-life', *n., pl.* **-lives.** time required for one half the atoms of a radioactive substance to decay.

half sister, sister related through one parent only.

half'-truth', *n.* statement that is only partly true.

half'way', *adv.* **1.** to the midpoint. **2.** partially or almost. —*adj.* **3.** midway. **4.** partial or inadequate.

halfway house, residence for persons released from hospital, prison, etc., to ease their return to society.

half′-wit′, *n.* stupid or foolish person. —**half′-wit′ted,** *adj.*

hal′i•but, *n.* large edible fish.

hal′i•to′sis, *n.* bad breath.

hall, *n.* **1.** corridor. **2.** large public room.

hal′le•lu′jah (-loo′yə), *interj.* Praise ye the Lord! Also, **hal′le•lu′iah.**

hall′mark′, *n.* **1.** mark of genuineness or quality. **2.** distinguishing characteristic.

hal′low, *v.* consecrate. —**hal′lowed,** *adj.*

Hal′low•een′, *n.* the evening of October 31, observed by dressing in costumes. Also, **Hal′low•e′en′.**

hal•lu′ci•na′tion, *n.* illusory perception. —**hal•luc′ci•nate′,** *v.* —**hal•lu′ci•na•to′ry,** *adj.*

hal•lu′ci•no•gen, *n.* substance that produces halluciations. —**hal•lu′ci•no•gen′ic,** *adj.*

hall′way′, *n.* corridor.

ha′lo, *n., pl.* **-los, -loes.** radiance surrounding a head.

halt, *v.* **1.** falter; limp. **2.** stop. —*adj.* **3.** lame. —*n.* **4.** stop. —**halt′ing,** *adj.* —**halt′ing•ly,** *adv.*

hal′ter, *n.* **1.** strap for horse. **2.** noose. **3.** woman's top tied behind the neck and back.

halve, *v.,* **halved, halving.** divide in half.

hal′yard (-yərd), *n.* line for hoisting sail or flag.

ham, *n., v.* **hammed, hamming.** —*n.* **1.** meat from rear thigh of hog. **2.** amateur radio operator. **3.** performer who overacts. —*v.* **4.** overact. —**ham′my,** *adj.*

ham′burg′er, *n.* sandwich of ground beef in bun.

ham′let, *n.* small village.

ham′mer, *n.* **1.** tool for pounding. —*v.* **2.** pound with hammer. —**ham′mer•er,** *n.*

ham′mock, *n.* hanging bed of canvas, etc.

ham′per, *v.* **1.** impede. —*n.* **2.** large basket.

ham′ster, *n.* small burrowing rodent kept as a pet.

ham′string′, *n.*, *v.*, **-strung,
-stringing.** —*n.* **1.** tendon
behind the knee. —*v.* **2.**
disable by cutting hamstring.
3. make ineffective.

hand, *n.* **1.** terminal part of
arm. **2.** worker. **3.** side as
viewed from certain point. **4.**
style of handwriting. **5.** pledge
of marriage. **6.** cards held by
player. —*v.* **7.** pass by hand.

hand′bag′, *n.* woman's purse.

hand′ball′, *n.* ball game
played against a wall.

hand′bill′, *n.* small printed
notice distributed by hand.

hand′book′, *n.* guide or
manual.

hand′clasp′, *n.* handshake.

hand′cuff′, *n.* **1.** shackle for
wrist. —*v.* **2.** put handcuff on.

hand′ful, *n.* **1.** amount hand
can hold. **2.** difficult problem.

hand′gun′, *n.* pistol.

hand′i•cap′, *n.*, *v.*, **-capped,
-capping.** —*n.* **1.**
disadvantage. —*v.* **2.** subject
to disadvantage.

hand′i•craft′, *n.* **1.** manual
skill. **2.** work or products
requiring such skill. Also,
hand′craft′.

hand′i•work′, *n.* **1.** work done
by hand. **2.** personal work or
accomplishment.

hand′ker•chief (hang′kər-), *n.*
small cloth for wiping face.

han′dle, *n.*, *v.*, **-dled, -dling.**
—*n.* **1.** part to be grasped. —*v.*
2. feel or grasp. **3.** manage. **4.**
Informal. endure. **5.** deal in.
—**han′dler**, *n.*

hand′made′, *adj.* made
individually by worker.

hand′out′, *n.* **1.** something
given to a beggar. **2.** flyer.

hand′shake′, *n.* clasping of
hands in greeting or
agreement.

hands′-off′, *adj.* characterized
by nonintervention.

hand′some, *adj.* **1.** of fine
appearance. **2.** generous.
—**hand′some•ly**, *adv.*

hands′-on′, *adj.* characterized
by personal participation.

hand′spring′, *n.* complete
flipping of body, landing first
on hands, then on feet.

hand′-to-mouth′, *adj.*
precarious, bare existence.

hand′writ′ing, *n.* writing done
by hand. —**hand′writ′ten**, *adj.*

hand′y, *adj.,* **handier, handiest.** 1. convenient. 2. dexterous. 3. useful. —**hand′i•ly,** *adv.*

han′dy•man′, *n., pl.* **-men.** worker at miscellaneous physical chores.

hang, *v.,* **hung** or **hanged, hanging,** *n.* —*v.* 1. suspend. 2. suspend by neck until dead. —*n.* 3. manner of hanging. —**hang′ing,** *n.* —**hang′man,** *n.* —**hang′er,** *n.*

hang′ar, *n.* shed for aircraft.

hang′dog′, *adj.* shamefaced.

hang glider, kitelike glider for soaring through the air from hilltops, etc. (**hang gliding**).

hang′nail′, *n.* small piece of skin around fingernail.

hang′o′ver, *n.* ill feeling from too much alcohol.

hang′up′, *n. Informal.* obsessive problem.

hank, *n.* skein of yarn.

han′ker, *v.* yearn. —**han′ker•ing,** *n.*

hank′y-pank′y, *n. Informal.* 1. mischief. 2. illicit relations.

han′som, *n.* two-wheeled cab.

Ha′nuk•kah (hä′-), *n.* annual Jewish festival.

hap′haz′ard, *adj.* 1. accidental. —*adv.* 2. by chance. —**hap•haz′ard•ly,** *adv.*

hap′less, *adj.* unlucky.

hap′pen, *v.* occur. —**hap′pen•ing,** *n.*

hap′pen•stance′, *n.* chance happening or event.

hap′py, *adj.,* **-pier, -piest.** 1. pleased; glad. 2. pleasurable. 3. bringing good luck. —**hap′pi•ly,** *adv.* —**hap′pi•ness,** *n.*

ha′ra•ki′ri (här′ə kēr′ē), *n.* Japanese ritual suicide by cutting the abdomen.

ha•rangue′, *n., v.,* **-rangued, -ranguing.** —*n.* 1. diatribe. —*v.* 2. address in harangue.

ha•rass′ (hə ras′, har′əs), *v.* annoy; disturb. —**ha•rass′er,** *n.* —**har•ass′ment,** *n.*

har′bin•ger (-bin jər), *n., v.* herald.

har′bor, *n.* 1. sheltered water for ships. 2. shelter. —*v.* 3. give shelter.

hard, *adj.* 1. firm. 2. difficult. 3. severe. 4. indisputable. —**hard′en,** *v.* —**hard′ness,** *n.*

hard′-bit′ten, *adj.* tough.

hard′-boiled′, *adj.* **1.** boiled long enough for yolk and white to solidify. **2.** tough.

hard cider, fermented cider.

hard′-core′, *adj.* **1.** dedicated. **2.** graphic; explicit.

hard′hat′, *n.* **1.** worker's helmet. **2.** working-class conservative.

hard′head′ed, *adj.* **1.** practical. **2.** obstinate; willful.

hard′heart′ed, *adj.* unfeeling.

hard′-line′, *adj.* staunch. Also, **hard′line′.** —**hard′-lin′er,** *n.*

hard′ly, *adv.* barely.

hard′-nosed′, *adj. Informal.* **1.** practical and shrewd. **2.** tough. —**hard′nose′,** *n.*

hard′ship, *n.* severe condition.

hard′tack′, *n.* hard biscuit.

hard′ware′, *n.* **1.** metalware. **2.** the machinery of a computer.

hard′wood′, *n.* hard, compact wood of various trees.

har′dy, *adj.,* **-dier, -diest. 1.** fitted to endure hardship. **2.** daring. —**har′di•ness,** *n.*

hare, *n.* rabbit-like mammal.

hare′brained′, *adj.* foolish.

hare′lip′, *n.* split upper lip.

har′em (hâr′əm), *n.* **1.** women's section of Muslim palace. **2.** the women there.

hark, *v.* listen. Also, **hark′en.**

har′le•quin (här′lə kwin, -kin), *n.* masked clown in theater and pantomime.

har′lot, *n.* prostitute. —**har′lot•ry,** *n.*

harm, *n.* **1.** injury. **2.** evil. —*v.* **3.** injure. —**harm′ful,** *adj.*

harm′less, *adj.* **1.** causing no harm. **2.** immune from legal action. —**harm′less•ly,** *adv.* —**harm′less•ness,** *n.*

har•mon′i•ca, *n.* musical reed instrument.

har′mo•ny, *n., pl.* **-nies. 1.** agreement. **2.** combination of agreeable musical sounds. —**har•mon′ic,** *adj.* —**har•mon′i•cal•ly,** *adv.* —**har′mo•nize′,** *v.* —**har•mon′i•ous,** *adj.*

har′ness, *n.* **1.** horse's working gear. —*v.* **2.** put harness on.

harp, *n.* **1.** plucked musical string instrument. —*v.* **2.** dwell persistently in one's words. —**harp′ist, harp′er,** *n.*

har•poon′, *n.* **1.** spear used against whales. —*v.* **2.** strike with harpoon.

harp′si•chord′, *n.* keyboard instrument with plucked strings. —**harp′si•chord′ist**, *n.*

har′ri•dan (här′i dn), *n.* scolding, vicious woman.

har′ri•er, *n.* hunting dog.

har′row, *n.* 1. implement for leveling or breaking up plowed land. —*v.* 2. draw a harrow over. 3. distress. —**har′row•ing**, *adj.*

har′ry, *v.*, **-ried, -rying.** harass.

harsh, *adj.* 1. rough. 2. unpleasant. 3. highly severe. —**harsh′ly**, *adv.* —**harsh′ness**, *n.*

hart, *n.* male deer.

har′vest, *n.* 1. gathering of crops. 2. season for this. 3. crop. —*v.* 4. reap. —**har′vest•er**, *n.*

has (haz), *v.* third pers. sing. pres. indic. of **have.**

has′-been′, *n.* one that is no longer effective or successful.

hash, *n.* 1. chopped meat and potatoes. 2. *Slang.* hashish. —*v.* 3. chop.

hash′ish, *n.* narcotic of Indian hemp.

hasn't, contraction of **has not.**

hasp, *n.* clasp for door, lid, etc.

has′sle, *n., v.*, **-sled, -sling.** *Informal.* —*n.* 1. disorderly dispute. 2. troublesome situation. —*v.* 3. bother.

has′sock, *n.* cushion; footstool.

has′ten, *v.* hurry. —**haste, hast′i•ness**, *n.* —**hast′y**, *adj.* —**hast′i•ly**, *adv.*

hat, *n.* covering for head. —**hat′ter**, *n.*

hatch, *v.* 1. bring forth young from egg. 2. be hatched. —*n.* 3. cover for opening. —**hatch′er•y**, *n.*

hatch′et, *n.* small ax.

hatchet job, maliciously destructive critiques.

hatch′way′, *n.* opening in ship's deck.

hate, *v.*, **hated, hating**, *n.* —*v.* 1. feel enmity. —*n.* 2. Also, **hat′red.** strong dislike.

hate′ful, *adj.* 1. full of hate. 2. arousing hate. —**hate′ful•ly**, *adv.* —**hate′ful•ness**, *n.*

haugh′ty, *adj.*, **-tier, -tiest.** disdainfully proud. —**haugh′ti•ly**, *adv.* —**haugh′ti•ness**, *n.*

haul, *v.* 1. pull; drag. —*n.* 2. pull. 3. distance of carrying. 4. thing hauled. 5. thing gained.

haunch, *n.* hip.

haunt, *v.* 1. visit, esp. as ghost. —*n.* 2. place of frequent visits. —**haunt′ed,** *adj.*

haunt′ing, *adj.* persist in the mind.

haute cou·ture′ (ōt′ kōō tōōr′), high fashion.

haute cui·sine′ (ōt′ kwi zēn′), gourmet cooking.

have, *v.,* **had, having. 1.** possess; contain. **2.** get. **3.** be forced or obligated. **4.** be affected by. **5.** give birth to.

ha′ven, *n.* 1. harbor. 2. shelter.

have′-not′, *n.* (*usually pl.*) group without wealth.

haven′t, contraction of **have not.**

hav′er·sack′, *n.* bag for rations, etc.

hav′oc, *n.* devastation.

Haw., Hawaii.

hawk, *n.* 1. bird of prey. —*v.* 2. hunt with hawks. 3. peddle.

hawk′er, *n.* peddler.

haw′ser, *n.* cable for mooring or towing ship.

haw′thorn′, *n.* small tree with thorns and small, bright fruit.

hay, *n.* grass cut and dried for fodder. —**hay′field′,** *n.* —**hay′stack′,** *n.*

hay fever, disorder of eyes and respiratory tract, caused by pollen.

hay′wire′, *adj. Informal.* amiss.

haz′ard, *n., v.* risk. —**haz′ard·ous,** *adj.*

haze, *v.,* **hazed, hazing,** *n.* —*v.* 1. play abusive tricks on. —*n.* 2. blur. —**ha′zy,** *adj.*

ha′zel, *n.* 1. tree bearing edible nut (**ha′zel·nut′**). 2. light reddish brown.

H′-bomb′, *n.* hydrogen bomb.

hdqrs., headquarters.

he, *pron.* 1. male mentioned. —*n.* 2. male.

head, *n.* 1. part of body joined to trunk by neck. 2. leader. 3. top or foremost part. —*adj.* 4. at the head. 5. leading or main. —*v.* 6. lead. 7. move in certain direction.

head′ache′, *n.* 1. pain in upper part of head. 2. worrying problem.

head′dress, *n.* covering or decoration for the head.

head′first′, *adv.* headlong.

head'ing, *n.* caption.

head'light', *n.* light with reflector at front of vehicle.

head'line', *n.* title of newspaper article.

head'long', *adj., adv.* **1.** with the head foremost. **2.** in impulsive manner.

head'-on', *adj., adv.* with the head or front foremost.

head'phone', *n.* (*usually pl.*) device worn over the ears for listening to an audiotape, etc.

head'quar'ters, *n.* center of command or operations.

head'strong', *adj.* willful.

head'stone', *n.* stone marker at head of grave.

head'way', *n.* progress.

head'y, *adj.,* **headier, headiest. 1.** impetuous. **2.** intoxicating.

heal, *v.* **1.** restore to health. **2.** get well.

health, *n.* **1.** soundness. **2.** physical condition. —**health'ful,** —**health'y,** *adj.*

heap, *n., v.* pile.

hear, *v.,* **heard, hearing. 1.** perceive by ear. **2.** listen. **3.** receive report. —**hear'er,** *n.* —**hear'ing,** *n.*

heark'en, *v.* listen.

hear'say', *n.* indirect report.

hearse, *n.* funeral vehicle.

heart, *n.* **1.** muscular organ keeping blood in circulation. **2.** seat of life or emotion. **3.** compassion. **4.** vital part. —**heart'less,** *adj.* —**heart'less•ly,** *adv.* —**heart'less•ness,** *n.*

heart'ache', *n.* grief.

heart attack, sudden insufficiency of oxygen supply to heart that results in heart muscle damage.

heart'break', *n.* great sorrow or anguish. —**heart'break'ing,** *adj.* —**heart'bro'ken,** *adj.*

heart'burn', *n.* burning sensation in stomach and esophagus, sometimes caused by rising stomach acid.

heart'en, *v.* encourage.

heart'felt', *adj.* deeply felt.

heart'-rend'ing, *adj.* causing sympathetic grief.

hearth, *n.* place for fires.

heart'sick', *adj.* sorrowful.

heart'-to-heart', *adj.* intimate.

heart'y, *adj.,* **heartier, heartiest. 1.** cordial. **2.**

genuine. 3. vigorous. 4. substantial. —**heart'i•ly,** *adv.* —**heart'i•ness,** *n.*

heat, *n.* 1. warmth. 2. form of energy raising temperature. 3. intensity of emotion. 4. sexual arousal, esp. female. —*v.* 5. make or become hot. 6. excite. —**heat'er,** *n.*

heat'ed, *adj.* 1. supplied with heat. 2. emotionally charged. —**heat'ed•ly,** *adv.*

heath, *n.* 1. Also, **heath'er.** low evergreen shrub. 2. open land overgrown with shrubs.

hea'then, *n., adj.* pagan. —**hea'then•ish,** *adj.*

heat'stroke', *n.* condition caused by too much heat.

heave, *v.,* **heaved, heaving,** *n.* —*v.* 1. raise with effort. 2. lift and throw. 3. *Slang.* vomit. 4. rise and fall. —*n.* 5. act or instance of heaving.

heav'en, *n.* 1. abode of God, angels, and spirits of righteous dead. 2. (*often pl.*) sky. 3. bliss. —**heav'en•ly,** *adj.*

heav'y, *adj.,* **heavier, heaviest.** 1. of great weight. 2. substantial. 3. clumsy; indelicate. —**heav'i•ly,** *adv.* —**heav'i•ness,** *n.*

heav'y-du'ty, *adj.* made for hard use.

heav'y-hand'ed, *adj.* tactless.

heav'y-heart'ed, *adj.* sorrowful; worried. —**heav'y-heart'ed•ness,** *n.*

heav'y-set', *adj.* large body.

He'brew, *n.* 1. member of people of ancient Palestine. 2. their language, now the national language of Israel. —**He'brew,** *adj.*

heck'le, *v.,* **-led, -ling.** harass with comments. —**heck'ler,** *n.*

hec'tare (hek'târ), *n.* 10,000 square meters (2.47 acres).

hec'tic, *adj.* marked by excitement, passion, etc. —**hec'ti•cal•ly,** *adv.*

hec'tor, *v., n.* bully.

hedge, *n., v.,* **hedged, hedging.** —*n.* 1. Also, **hedge'row'.** fence of greenery. —*v.* 2. surround with hedge. 3. offset (risk, bet, etc.).

hedge'hog', *n.* spiny mammal.

he'don•ist, *n.* person living for pleasure. —**he'do•nis'tic,** *adj.* —**he'don•ism,** *n.*

heed, *v.* 1. notice. 2. pay serious attention to. —**heed,**

n. —**heed′ful,** *adj.*
—**heed′less,** *adj.*
—**heed′less•ly,** *adv.*

heel, *n.* **1.** back of foot below ankle. **2.** part of shoe, etc., covering this. —*v.* **3.** furnish with heels. **4.** lean to one side.

heft, *n.* **1.** heaviness. **2.** import. —*v.* **3.** weigh by lifting.

hef′ty, *adj.,* **-tier, -tiest. 1.** heavy. **2.** sturdy. **3.** substantial. —**heft′i•ness,** *n.*

he•gem′o•ny (hi jem′ə nē), *n., pl.* **-nies.** domination.

heif′er (hef′ər), *n.* young cow without issue.

height, *n.* **1.** state of being high. **2.** altitude. **3.** apex. —**height′en,** *v.*

Heim′lich maneuver (hīm′lik), procedure to aid choking person by applying pressure to upper abdomen.

hei′nous (hā′nəs), *adj.* hateful.

heir (âr), *n.* inheritor. —**heir′ess,** *n.fem.*

heir′loom′, *n.* possession long kept in family.

heist (hīst), *Slang.* —*n.* **1.** robbery. —*v.* **2.** rob.

hel′i•cop′ter, *n.* heavier-than-air craft lifted by horizontal propeller.

he′li•o•trope′ (hē′lē ə trōp′), *n.* **1.** shrub with fragrant flowers. **2.** light purple color.

he′li•um, *n.* gaseous element.

he′lix (hē′liks), *n., pl.* **hel′i•ces** (hel′ə sēz′), **helixes.** spiral.

hell, *n.* abode of condemned spirits. —**hell′ish,** *adj.* —**hell′ish•ly,** *adv.*

Hel•len′ic, *adj.* Greek.

hel•lo′, *interj.* (exclamation of greeting.)

helm, *n.* **1.** control of rudder. **2.** steering apparatus. —**helms′man,** *n.*

hel′met, *n.* protective head covering.

help, *v.* **1.** aid. **2.** save. **3.** relieve. **4.** avoid. —*n.* **5.** aid; relief. **6.** helping person or thing. —**help′er,** *n.* —**help′ful,** *adj.* —**help′ful•ly,** *adv.* —**help′ful•ness,** *n.*

help′ing, *n.* portion served.

help′less, *adj.* unable to act for oneself. —**help′less•ly,** *adv.* —**help′less•ness,** *n.*

help′mate′, *n.* companion and helper. Also, **help′meet′**.

hel′ter-skel′ter, *adv.* in a disorderly way.

hem, *v.*, **hemmed, hemming**, *n.* —*v.* 1. confine. 2. fold and sew down edge of cloth. 3. make throat-clearing sound. —*n.* 4. hemmed border.

hem′i•sphere′, *n.* 1. half the earth or sky. 2. half sphere. —**hem′i•spher′i•cal**, *adj.*

hem′lock, *n.* 1. coniferous tree. 2. poisonous plant.

he′mo•glo′bin (hh′mə glō′bin, hem′ə-), *n.* oxygen-carrying compound in red blood cells.

he′mo•phil′i•a (hē′mə fil′ē ə), *n.* genetic disorder marked by excessive bleeding. —**he′mo•phil′i•ac′**, *n.*

hem′or•rhage (hem′ə rij), *n.* discharge of blood.

hem′or•rhoid′ (hem′ə roid′), *n.* (*usually pl.*) painful dilation of blood vessels in anus. —**hem′or•rhoi′dal**, *adj.*

hemp, *n.* 1. herb fiber used for rope. 2. intoxicating drug made from hemp plant.

hen, *n.* 1. female fowl. 2. female bird. —**hen′ner•y**, *n.*

hence, *adv.* 1. therefore. 2. from now on. 3. from this place, etc.

hence′forth′, *adv.* from now on.

hench′man, *n., pl.* **-men**. 1. associate in wrongdoing. 2. trusted attendant.

hen′na, *n.* red dye.

hen′pecked′, *adj.* nagged or controlled by one's wife.

hep′a•rin, *n.* anticoagulant found esp. in liver.

hep′a•ti′tis (hep′ə tī′tis), *n.* inflammation of the liver.

her, *pron.* 1. objective case of **she**. —*adj.* 2. of female.

her′ald, *n.* 1. messenger. 2. proclaimer. —*v.* 3. proclaim. 4. give promise of.

her′ald•ry, *n.* art of devising and describing coats of arms. —**he•ral′dic**, *adj.*

herb (ûrb, hûrb), *n.* flowering plant with nonwoody stem. —**her•ba′ceous**, *adj.* —**herb′al**, *adj.* —**herb′al•ist**, *n.*

herb′age, *n.* 1. nonwoody plants. 2. leaves and stems of herbs.

herb′i·cide (hûr′bə sīd′, ûr′-), *n.* substance for killing plants. —**her′bi·cid′al,** *adj.*

her·biv′o·rous (hûr biv′ər əs, ûr-), *adj.* feeding on plants. —**her′bi·vore′,** *n.*

her′cu·le′an (hûr′kyə lē′ən, hûr kyoo′lē-), *adj.* **1.** requiring extraordinary strength or effort. **2.** having extraordinary strength, courage, or size.

herd, *n.* **1.** animals feeding or moving together. —*v.* **2.** go in herd. **3.** tend herd. —**herd′er, herds′man,** *n.*

here, *adv.* **1.** in or to this place. **2.** present.

here′a·bout′ *adv.* in this vicinity. Also, **here′a·bouts′.**

here·af′ter, *adv.* **1.** in the future. —*n.* **2.** future life.

here·by′, *adv.* by this.

he·red′i·tar′y, *adj.* **1.** passing from parents to offspring. **2.** of heredity. **3.** by inheritance. —**he·red′i·tar′i·ly,** *adv.*

he·red′i·ty, *n.* passage of traits from parents to offspring.

here·in′, *adv.* in this place.

her′e·sy, *n., pl.* **-sies.** unorthodox opinion or doctrine. —**her′e·tic,** *n.* —**he·ret′i·cal,** *adj.*

here′to·fore′, *adv.* before.

here′with′, *adv.* along with this.

her′it·a·ble, *adj.* capable of being inherited.

her′it·age, *n.* **1.** inheritance. **2.** traditions and history.

her·maph′ro·dite′ (hûr maf′rə dīt′), *n.* animal or plant with reproductive organs of both sexes. —**her·maph′ro·dit′ic,** *adj.*

her·met′ic, *adj.* airtight. Also, **hermet′i·cal.** —**her·met′i·cal·ly,** *adv.*

her′mit, *n.* recluse.

her′mit·age, *n.* hermit's abode.

her′ni·a (hûr′nē ə), *n.* rupture in abdominal wall, etc.

he′ro, *n., pl.* **-roes. 1.** man of valor, nobility, etc. **2.** main male character in story. —**her′oine,** *n.fem.* —**he·ro′ic,** *adj.* —**her′o·ism′,** *n.*

her′o·in, *n.* narcotic.

her′on, *n.* long-legged bird.

hero sandwich, sandwich of cold cuts in long roll.

her′pes (hûr′pēz), *n.* viral disease characterized by blisters on skin.

her′ring, *n.* north Atlantic food fish.

her′ring·bone′, *n.* **1.** pattern of slanting lines in vertical rows. **2.** fabric of this.

hers, *pron.* **1.** form of possessive **her. 2.** her belongings or family.

her·self′, *pron.* emphatic or reflexive form of **her.**

hertz, *n., pl.* **hertz.** radio frequency of one cycle per second.

hes′i·tate′, *v.,* **-tated, -tating. 1.** be reluctant. **2.** pause. **3.** stammer. —**hes′i·tant,** *adj.* —**hes′i·ta′tion, hes′i·tan·cy,** *n.*

het′er·o·dox′, *adj.* unorthodox. —**het′er·o·dox′y,** *n.*

het′er·o·ge′ne·ous, *adj.* **1.** unlike. **2.** varied.

het′er·o·sex′u·al, *adj.* sexually attracted to opposite sex. —**het′er·o·sex′u·al,** *n.*

heu·ris′tic (hyŏŏ ris′tik; *often.* yŏŏ-), *adj.* **1.** serving to indicate. **2.** denoting learning esp. by experiment.

hew, *v.,* **hewed, hewed** or **hewn, hewing. 1.** chop or cut. **2.** cut down. —**hew′er,** *n.*

hex, *v.* **1.** cast spell on. **2.** bring bad luck to. —*n.* **3.** spell; jinx.

hex′a·gon′, *n.* six-sided polygon. —**hex·ag′o·nal,** *adj.*

hey′day′, *n.* prime time.

hgt., height.

hgwy., highway.

HI, Hawaii.

hi·a′tus (hī ā′təs), *n., pl.* **-tuses, -tus.** interruption in a series.

hi·ba′chi (hi bä′chē), *n.* small charcoal brazier.

hi′ber·nate′, *v.,* **-nated, -nating.** spend winter in dormant state. —**hi′ber·na′tion,** *n.* —**hi′ber·na′tor,** *n.*

hi·bis′cus (hī bis′kəs, hi-), *n.* plant with large flowers.

hic′cup, *n.* **1.** sudden involuntary drawing in of breath. —*v.* **2.** have hiccups. Also, **hic′cough** (hik′up).

hick, *n.* provincial person.

hick′o·ry, *n., pl.* **-ries.** tree bearing nut (**hickory nut**).

hide, *v.,* **hid, hidden** or **hid, hiding,** *n.* —*v.* **1.** conceal. —*n.* **2.** animal's skin.

hide′a•way, *n.* private retreat.

hide′bound′, *adj.* narrow and rigid in opinion.

hid′e•ous, *adj.* **1.** very ugly. **2.** revolting.

hide′-out′, *n.* safe place to hide, esp. from the law.

hie, *v.,* **hied, hieing** or **hying.** *Archaic.* go hastily.

hi′er•ar′chy, *n., pl.* **-chies.** graded system of officials. —**hi′er•ar′chi•cal, hi′er•ar′chic,** *adj.* —**hi′er•ar′chi•cal•ly,** *adv.*

hi′er•o•glyph′ic, *adj.* **1.** of picture writing, as among ancient Egyptians. —*n.* **2.** hieroglyphic symbol. **3.** *(usually pl.)* symbol, sign, etc., difficult to decipher.

hi′-fi′ *adj.* of high fidelity. —**hi′-fi′,** *n.*

high, *adj.* **1.** tall. **2.** lofty. **3.** expensive. **4.** shrill. **5.** *Informal.* exuberant with drink or drugs. **6.** greater than normal. **7.** elevated in pitch. —*adv.* **8.** at or to high place.

high′ball′, *n.* drink of whiskey with a mixer.

high′brow′, *n.* **1.** sophisticate. —*adj.* typical of a highbrow.

high fidelity, reproduction of sound without distortion. —**high′ fi•del′i•ty,** *adj.*

high′-flown′, *adj.* **1.** pretentious. **2.** bombastic.

high frequency, radio frequency between 3 and 30 megahertz. —**high′-fre′quen•cy,** *adj.*

high′-hand′ed, *adj.* overbearing.

high′lands (-ləndz), *n.* elevated part of country.

high′light′, *v.* **1.** emphasize. —*n.* **2.** important event, scene, etc. **3.** area of strong reflected light.

high′ly, *adv.* **1.** in high place, etc. **2.** very; extremely

high′-mind′ed, *adj.* noble in feelings or principles.

high′ness, *n.* **1.** high state. **2.** *(cap.)* title of royalty.

high′-pres′sure, *adj., v.,* **-sured, -suring.** —*adj.* **1.** stressful. **2.** aggressive. —*v.* **3.** persuade aggressively.

high′rise′, *n.* high building. —**high′rise′,** *adj.*

high′road′, *n.* highway.

high′ school′, *n.* school for grades 9 through 12.

high seas, open ocean.

high′-spir′it•ed, *adj.* lively.

high′-strung′, *adj.* nervous.

high′-tech′, *n.* **1.** technology using highly sophisticated and advanced equipment and techniques. —*adj.* **2.** using or suggesting high-tech.

high′-ten′sion, *adj.* of relatively high voltage.

high′way′, *n.* main road.

high′way′man, *n., pl.* **-men.** highway robber.

hi′jack′, *v.* seize (plane, truck, etc.) by force. —**hi′jack′er,** *n.*

hike, *v.,* **hiked, hiking,** *n.* —*v.* **1.** walk long distance. —*n.* **2.** long walk. —**hik′er,** *n.*

hi•lar′i•ous, *adj.* **1.** very funny. **2.** very cheerful. —**hi•lar′i•ous•ly,** *adv.* —**hi•lar′i•ty,** *n.*

hill, *n.* high piece of land. —**hill′y,** *adj.*

hill′bil′ly, *n., pl.* **-lies.** *Sometimes Offensive.* **1.** Southern mountaineer. **2.** yokel; rustic.

hill′ock, *n.* little hill.

hilt, *n.* sword handle.

him, *pron.* objective case of **he.**

him•self′, *pron.* reflexive or emphatic form of **him.**

hind, *adj.* **1.** rear. —*n.* **2.** female deer.

hin′der, *v.* **1.** retard. **2.** stop. —**hin′drance,** *n.*

hind′most′, *adj.* last.

hind′sight′, *n.* keen awareness of how one should have avoided past mistakes.

Hin′du, *n.* adherent of Hinduism. —**Hindu,** *adj.*

Hin′du•ism, *n.* a major religion of India.

hinge, *n., v.,* **hinged, hinging.** —*n.* **1.** joint on which door, lid, etc., turns. —*v.* **2.** depend. **3.** furnish with hinges.

hint, *n.* **1.** indirect suggestion. —*v.* **2.** give hint.

hin′ter•land′, *n.* area remote from cities.

hip, *n.* **1.** projecting part of each side of body below waist. —*adj. Slang.* **2.** familiar with the latest styles or ideas.

hip′-hop′, *n. Slang.* popular subculture as characterized by rap music.

hip′pie, *n.* person of 1960s who rejected conventional cultural and moral values.

hip′po, *n., pl.* **-pos.** hippopotamus.

hip′po•drome′, *n.* arena.

hip′po•pot′a•mus, *n., pl.* **-muses, -mi.** large African water mammal.

hire, *v.,* **hired, hiring,** *n.* —*v.* **1.** purchase services or use of. —*n.* **2.** payment for services.

hire′ling, *n.* person whose loyalty can be bought.

hir′sute (hûr′soot), *adj.* hairy. —**hir′sute•ness,** *n.*

his, *pron.* **1.** possessive form of **he. 2.** his belongings.

His•pan′ic, *n.* person of Spanish or Latin-American descent. —**Hispanic,** *adj.*

hiss, *v.* **1.** make prolonged *s* sound. **2.** express disapproval in this way. —*n.* **3.** hissing sound.

his′ta•mine′ (-mēn′, -min), *n.* organic compound released during allergic reactions.

his•tor′ic, *adj.* **1.** Also, **his•tor′i•cal.** of history. **2.** important in the past. —**his•tor′i•cal•ly,** *adv.*

his′to•ry, *n., pl.* **-ries. 1.** knowledge, study, or record of past events. **2.** pattern of events determining future. —**his•to′ri•an,** *n.*

his′tri•on′ics, *n.pl.* exaggerated behavior. —**his′tri•on′ic,** *adj.* —**his′tri•on′i•cal•ly,** *adv.*

hit, *v.,* **hit, hitting,** *n.* —*v.* **1.** strike. **2.** collide with. **3.** meet. **4.** guess. —*n.* **5.** collision. **6.** blow. **7.** success. **8.** *Slang.* murder. —**hit′ter,** *n.*

hitch, *v.* **1.** fasten. **2.** harness to cart, etc. **3.** raise or move jerkily. —*n.* **4.** fastening or knot. **5.** obstruction. **6.** jerk.

hitch′hike′, *v.,* **-hiked, -hiking.** beg a ride. —**hitch′hik′er,** *n.*

hith′er, *adv.* to this place. —**hith′er•ward,** *adv.*

hith′er•to′, *adv.* until now.

HIV, human immunodeficiency virus, a cause of AIDS.

hive, *n.* shelter for bees.

hives, *n.pl.* eruptive skin condition.

HMO, *pl.* **HMOs, HMO's.** health maintenance organization, health care plan that provides comprehensive services to subscribers.

H.M.S., Her (or His) Majesty's Ship.

hoa′gie, *n.* mixed sandwich in long roll. Also, **hoa′gy.**

hoard, *n.* **1.** accumulation for future use. —*v.* **2.** accumulate as hoard. —**hoard′er,** *n.*

hoar′frost′, *n.* frost (def. 2).

hoarse, *adj.* gruff in tone.

hoary, *adj.* **1.** white with age or frost. **2.** old. Also, **hoar.**

hoax, *n.* **1.** mischievous deception. —*v.* **2.** deceive.

hob′ble, *v.,* **-bled, -bling. 1.** limp. **2.** fasten legs to prevent free movement.

hob′by, *n., pl.* **-bies.** favorite avocation or pastime. —**hob′by•ist,** *n.*

hob′by•horse′, *n.* **1.** rocking toy for riding. **2.** favorite subject for discussion.

hob′gob′lin, *n.* something causing superstitious fear.

hob′nob′, *v.,* **-nobbed, -nobbing.** associate socially.

ho′bo, *n., pl.* **-bos, -boes.** tramp; vagrant.

hock, *n.* **1.** joint in hind leg of horse, etc. —*v.* **2.** pawn.

hock′ey, *n.* game played with bent clubs (**hockey sticks**) and ball or disk.

hock′shop′, *n.* pawnshop.

ho′cus-po′cus, *n.* **1.** sleight of hand. **2.** trickery.

hod, *n.* **1.** trough for carrying mortar, bricks, etc. **2.** coal scuttle.

hodge′podge′, *n.* mixture.

hoe, *n., v.,* **hoed, hoeing.** —*n.* **1.** tool for breaking ground, etc. —*v.* **2.** use hoe on.

hog, *n., v.,* **hogged, hogging.** —*n.* **1.** domesticated swine. **2.** greedy or filthy person. —*v.* **3.** take greedily. —**hog′gish,** *adj.*

hogs′head′, *n.* large cask.

hog′tie′, *v.,* **-tied, -tying. 1.** tie with all four feet or arms together. **2.** hamper; thwart.

hog′wash′, *n.* nonsense; bunk.

hog′-wild′, *adj.* enthusiastic.

hoi′ pol•loi′, common people.

hoist, *v.* **1.** lift, esp. by machine. —*n.* **2.** hoisting apparatus. **3.** act of lifting.

hok′ey (hō′kē), *adj.,* **hokier, hokiest. 1.** mawkish. **2.** obviously contrived. —**hok′i•ness,** *n.*

hold, *v.,* **held, holding,** *n.* —*v.* **1.** have in hand. **2.** possess. **3.** sustain. **4.** adhere. **5.** celebrate. **6.** restrain or detain. **7.** believe. **8.** consider. —*n.* **9.** grasp. **10.** influence. **11.** cargo space below ship's deck. —**hold'er,** *n.*

hold'ing, *n.* **1.** leased land, esp. for farming. **2.** *(pl.)* legally owned property.

hold'out', *n.* one who refuses to take part, give in, etc.

hold'o'ver, *n.* one remaining from a former period.

hold'up', *n.* **1.** delay. **2.** robbery at gunpoint.

hole, *n., v.,* **holed, holing.** —*n.* **1.** opening. **2.** cavity. **3.** burrow. **4.** in golf, one of the cups into which the ball is driven. —*v.* **5.** drive into hole.

hol'i•day', *n.* **1.** period without work. —*adj.* **2.** festive.

ho'li•ness, *n.* holy character.

ho•lis'tic, *adj.* of or using therapies that consider the body and the mind as an integrated whole.

hol'lan•daise', *n.* rich egg-based sauce.

hol'low, *adj.* **1.** empty within. **2.** sunken. **3.** dull. **4.** unreal. —*n.* **5.** cavity. —*v.* **6.** make hollow.

hol'ly, *n., pl.* **-lies.** shrub with bright red berries.

hol'ly•hock', *n.* tall flowering plant.

hol'o•caust' (hol'ə kôst'), *n.* **1.** great destruction, esp. by fire. **2.** (*cap.*) Nazi killing of Jews during World War II.

ho'lo•gram', *n.* three-dimensional image made by a laser.

ho•log'ra•phy, *n.* process of making holograms.

hol'ster, *n.* case for pistol.

ho'ly, *adj.,* **-lier, -liest. 1.** sacred. **2.** dedicated to God.

Holy Ghost, third member of Trinity. Also, **Holy Spirit.**

hom'age, *n.* reverence.

home, *n.* **1.** residence. **2.** native place or country. —*adv.* **3.** to or at home. —**home'land',** *n.* —**home'ward,** *adv., adj.* —**home'less,** *adj.* —**home'made',** *adj.*

home'ly, *adj.,* **-lier, -liest. 1.** plain; not beautiful. **2.** simple. —**home'li•ness,** *n.*

home′mak′er, *n.* person who manages a home.

ho′me·op′a·thy, *n.* method of treating disease with small doses of drugs that in a healthy person would cause symptoms like those of the disease. —**ho′me·o·path′ic,** *adj.*

ho′me·o·sta′sis, *n.* tendency of a system to maintain internal stability. —**ho′me·o·stat′ic,** *adj.*

home′sick′, *adj.* longing for home. —**home′sick′ness,** *n.*

home′spun′, *adj.* 1. spun at home. 2. unpretentious. —*n.* 3. cloth made at home.

home′stead, *n.* dwelling with its land and buildings.

home′stretch′, *n.* last part of racetrack, endeavor, etc.

hom′ey, *adj.,* **homier, homiest.** cozy.

hom′i·cide′, *n.* killing of one person by another. —**hom′i·cid′al,** *adj.*

hom′i·ly, *n., pl.* **-lies.** sermon. —**hom′i·let′ic,** *adj.*

hom′i·ny, *n.* 1. hulled corn. 2. coarse flour from corn.

homo-, prefix meaning same or identical, as *homogeneous.*

ho′mo·ge′ne·ous, *adj.* 1. unvaried in content. 2. alike. —**ho′mo·ge·ne′i·ty,** *n.*

ho·mog′e·nize′, *v.,* **-nized, -nizing.** form by mixing and emulsifying. —**ho·mog′e·ni·za′tion,** *n.*

ho′mo·graph′, *n.* word spelled the same as another but having a different meaning.

hom′o·nym, *n.* word like another in sound, but not in meaning.

ho′mo·pho′bi·a, *n.* unreasoning fear or hatred of homosexuals.

Ho′mo sa′pi·ens (hō′mo sā′pē ənz), human being.

ho′mo·sex′u·al, *adj.* 1. sexually attracted to same sex. —*n.* 2. homosexual person. —**ho′mo·sex′u·al′i·ty,** *n.*

Hon., 1. Honorable. 2. Honorary.

hon′cho, *n., pl.* **-chos.** *Slang.* 1. leader; boss. 2. important or influential person.

hone, *n., v.,* **honed, honing.** —*n.* 1. fine whetstone. —*v.* 2. sharpen to fine edge.

hon′est, *adj.* 1. trustworthy. 2. sincere. 3. virtuous.

—**hon′est•ly,** *adv.*
—**hon′es•ty,** *n.*

hon′ey, *n.* fluid produced by bees (**hon′ey•bees′**).

hon′ey•comb′, *n.* wax structure built by bees to store honey.

hon′ey•dew′ melon, sweet muskmelon.

hon′eyed (-ēd), *adj.* sweet or flattering, as speech.

hon′ey•moon′, *n.* holiday trip of newly married couple. —**hon′ey•moon′er,** *n.*

hon′ey•suck′le, *n.* shrub bearing tubular flowers.

honk, *n.* 1. sound of automobile horn. 2. nasal sound of goose, etc. —*v.* 3. make such sound.

hon′or, *n.* 1. public or official esteem. 2. something as token of this. 3. good reputation. 4. high ethical character. 5. chastity. —*v.* 6. revere. 7. confer honor. 8. show regard for. 9. accept as valid.

hon′or•a•ble, *adj.* 1. worthy of honor. 2. of high principles. —**hon′or•a•bly,** *adv.*

hon′o•rar′i•um (ôn′ə râr′ē əm), *n., pl.* **-iums, -ia.** fee paid for professional services customarily not recompensed.

hon′or•ar′y, *adj.* conferred as honor.

hood, *n.* 1. covering for head and neck. 2. automobile engine cover. 3. hoodlum. —**hood′ed,** *adj.*

hood′lum, *n.* petty criminal.

hood′wink′, *v.* deceive.

hoof, *n., pl.* **hoofs, hooves.** horny covering of animal foot. —**hoofed,** *adj.*

hook, *n.* 1. curved piece of metal for catching, etc. 2. fishhook. 3. sharp curve. —*v.* 4. seize, etc., with hook.

hook′er, *n. Slang.* prostitute.

hook′up′, *n.* connection of apparatus into system.

hoo′li•gan, *n.* hoodlum.

hoop, *n.* circular band.

hoop′la, *n. Informal.* 1. commotion. 2. excitement.

hoo•ray′, *interj., n.* (hurrah.)

hoot, *v.* 1. shout in derision. 2. (of owl) utter cry. —*n.* 3. owl's cry. 4. shout of derision.

hop, *v.,* **hopped, hopping,** *n.* —*v.* 1. leap, esp. on one foot. —*n.* 2. such a leap. 3. plant bearing cones used in brewing. **4.** (*pl.*) the cones of this plant.

hope, *n., v.,* **hoped, hoping.** —*n.* **1.** feeling that something desired is possible. **2.** object of this. **3.** confidence. —*v.* **4.** look forward to with hope. —**hope′ful,** *adj.* —**hope′ful•ly,** *adv.* —**hope′less,** *adj.* —**hope′less•ly,** *adv.*

Ho′pi (hō′pē), *n., pl.* **-pi, -pis.** member of an American Indian people of the southwest.

hop′per, *n.* funnel-shaped trough for grain, etc.

horde, *n.* **1.** multitude. **2.** nomadic group.

hore′hound′, *n.* herb containing bitter juice.

ho•ri′zon, *n.* apparent line between earth and sky.

hor′i•zon′tal, *adj.* **1.** at right angles to vertical. **2.** level. —*n.* **3.** horizontal line, etc.

hor′mone, *n.* endocrine gland secretion that activates specific organ, mechanism, etc. —**hor•mo′nal,** *adj.*

horn, *n.* **1.** hard growth on heads of cattle, goats, etc. **2.** hornlike part. **3.** musical wind instrument. —**horned,** *adj.* —**horn′y,** *adj.*

hor′net, *n.* large wasp.

horn′pipe′, *n.* **1.** lively dance. **2.** music for it.

hor′o•scope′, *n.* chart of heavens used in astrology.

hor•ren′dous, *adj.* horrible. —**hor•ren′dous•ly,** *adv.*

hor′ri•ble, *adj.* dreadful. —**hor′ri•bly,** *adv.*

hor′rid, *adj.* abominable. —**hor′rid•ly,** *adv.*

hor′ror, *n.* intense fear or repugnance. —**hor′ri•fy′,** *v.*

hors-d'oeuvre′ (ôr dûrv′), *n., pl.* **-d'oeuvres′** (-dûrv′). tidbit served before meal.

horse, *n.* **1.** large domesticated quadruped. **2.** cavalry. **3.** frame with legs for bearing work, etc. —**horse′back′,** *n., adv.* —**horse′man,** *n.* —**horse′wo′man,** *n.fem.* —**horse′hair′,** *n.*

horse′play′, *n.* rough play.

horse′pow′er, *n.* unit of power, equal to 550 foot-pounds per second.

horse′rad′ish, *n.* cultivated plant with pungent root.

horse sense, common sense.

horse'shoe', *n.* **1.** ∪-shaped iron plate nailed to horse's hoof. **2.** arrangement in this form. **3.** (*pl.*) game in which horseshoes are tossed.

hors'y, *adj.,* **horsier, horsiest. 1.** of or like a horse. **2.** dealing with or interested in horses.

hor'ta•to'ry, *adj.* urging strongly.

hor'ti•cul'ture, *n.* cultivation of gardens. —**hor'ti•cul'tur•al,** *adj.* —**hor'ti•cul'tur•ist,** *n.*

ho•san'na, *interj.* (praise the Lord!)

hose, *n.* **1.** stockings. **2.** flexible tube for water, etc.

ho'sier•y (-zhə rē), *n.* stockings.

hos'pice (hos'pis), *n.* **1.** shelter for pilgrims, strangers, etc. **2.** facility for supportive care of dying persons.

hos'pi•ta•ble, *adj.* showing hospitality. —**hos'pi•ta•bly,** *adv.*

hos'pi•tal, *n.* institution for treatment of sick and injured. —**hos'pi•tal•i•za'tion,** *n.* —**hos'pi•tal•ize',** *v.*

hos'pi•tal'i•ty, *n., pl.* **-ties.** warm reception of guests, etc.

host, *n.* **1.** entertainer of guests. **2.** great number. **3.** (*cap.*) bread consecrated in Eucharist. —**host'ess,** *n.fem.*

hos'tage, *n.* person given or held as security.

hos'tel, *n.* inexpensive inn.

hos'tile (-təl), *adj.* **1.** opposed; unfriendly. **2.** of enemies. —**hos•til'i•ty,** *n.*

hot, *adj.,* **hotter, hottest. 1.** of high temperature. **2.** feeling great heat. **3.** sharp-tasting. **4.** ardent. **5.** fresh or new. **6.** *Informal.* currently popular. **7.** *Informal.* performing very well. **8.** *Slang.* recently stolen. —**hot'ly,** *adv.* —**hot'ness,** *n.*

hot'bed', *n.* **1.** covered and heated bed of earth for growing plants. **2.** place where something thrives.

hot'-blood'ed, *adj.* excitable.

hot cake, pancake.

hot dog, 1. frankfurter. **2.** *Slang.* person who acts flamboyantly; show-off.

ho•tel', *n.* house offering food, lodging, etc.

hot flash, sudden, brief feeling of heat experienced by some menopausal women.

hot'head', *n.* impetuous person. —**hot'head'ed,** *adj.*

hot'house', *n.* greenhouse.

hot line, system for instantaneous communications of major importance.

hot plate, portable electrical appliance for cooking.

hot potato, *Informal.* unpleasant or risky situation.

hot rod, *Slang.* car with speeded-up engine. —**hot rodder.**

hot'shot', *n. Slang.* skillful and often vain person.

hot tub, tank of hot water big enough for several persons.

hot water, *Informal.* trouble.

hound, *n.* 1. hunting dog. —*v.* 2. hunt or track.

hour, *n.* period of 60 minutes. —**hour'ly,** *adj., adv.*

hour'glass', *n.* timepiece operating by visible fall of sand.

house, *n., v.,* **housed, housing.** —*n.* (hous). 1. building, esp. for residence, rest, etc. 2. family. 3. legislative or deliberative body. 4. commercial firm. —*v.* (houz). 5. provide with a house.

house'break'er, *n.* person who breaks into another's house to steal. —**house'break'ing,** *n.*

house'bro'ken, *adj.* trained to excrete outdoors or to behave appropriately indoors.

house'fly', *n., pl.* **-flies.** common insect.

house'hold', *n.* 1. people of house. —*adj.* 2. domestic.

house'hold'er, *n.* 1. person who owns house. 2. head of household.

house'hus'band, *n.* married man who stays at home to manage the household.

house'keep'er, *n.* person who manages a house. —**house'keeping,** *n.*

house'plant', *n.* ornamental plant grown indoors.

house'warm'ing, *n.* party to celebrate a new home.

house'wife', *n., pl.* **-wives.** woman in charge of the home. —**house'wife'ly,** *adj.*

house'work', *n.* housekeeping.

hous′ing, *n.* **1.** dwellings collectively. **2.** container.

hov′el, *n.* small mean dwelling.

hov′er, *v.* **1.** stay suspended in air. **2.** linger about.

Hov′er·craft′, *n. Trademark.* vehicle that can skim over water on cushion of air.

how, *adv.* **1.** in what way. **2.** to, at, or in what extent, price, or condition. **3.** why.

how·ev′er, *conj.* **1.** nevertheless. —*adj.* **2.** to whatever extent.

how′itz·er, *n.* cannon for firing shells at an elevated angle.

howl, *v.* **1.** utter loud long cry. **2.** wail. —*n.* **3.** cry of wolf, etc. **4.** wail.

how′so·ev′er, *adv.* however.

hoy′den (hoid′n), *n.* tomboy. —**hoy′den·ish,** *adj.*

HP or **hp,** horsepower.

HQ or **hq,** headquarters.

hr., hour.

H.R., House of Representatives.

H.S., High School.

ht., height.

hub, *n.* central part of wheel.

hub′bub, *n.* confused noise.

hu′bris (hyōō′bris, hōō′-), *n.* excessive pride.

huck′le·ber′ry, *n., pl.* **-ries.** berry of heath shrub.

huck′ster, *n.* **1.** peddler. **2.** aggressive seller or promoter.

HUD, Department of Housing and Urban Development.

hud′dle, *v.,* **-dled, -dling,** *n.* —*v.* **1.** crowd together. —*n.* **2.** confused heap or crowd.

hue, *n.* **1.** color. **2.** outcry.

huff, *n.* angry fit. —**huf′fy,** *adj.*

hug, *v.,* **hugged, hugging,** *n.* —*v.* **1.** clasp in arms. **2.** stay close to. —*n.* **3.** tight clasp.

huge, *adj.,* **huger, hugest.** very large in size. —**huge′ly,** *adv.* —**huge′ness,** *n.*

hu′la (hōō′lə), *n.* Hawaiian dance with intricate arm movements.

hulk, *n.* hull from old ship.

hulk′ing, *adj.* bulky; clumsy. Also, **hulk′y.**

hull, *n.* **1.** outer covering of seed or fruit. **2.** body of ship. —*v.* **3.** remove hull of.

hul′la·ba·loo′, *n., pl.* **-loos.** *Informal.* uproar.

hum, *v.,* **hummed, humming,** *n.*
—*v.* **1.** make low droning sound. **2.** sing with closed lips. **3.** be busy. —*n.* **4.** murmur. —**hum′mer,** *n.*

hu′man, *adj.* **1.** of or like people or their species. —*n.* **2.** Also, **human being.** a person. —**hu′man•ness,** *n.*

hu•mane′, *adj.* tender; compassionate. —**hu•mane′ly,** *adv.*

hu′man•ism, *n.* system of thought focusing on human interests, values, and dignity. —**hu′man•ist,** *n., adj.* —**hu′man•is′tic,** *adj.*

hu•man′i•tar′i•an, *adj.* **1.** philanthropic. —*n.* **2.** philanthropist.

hu•man′i•ty, *n., pl.* **-ties. 1.** humankind. **2.** human state or quality. **3.** kindness. **4.** (*pl.*) literature, philosophy, etc., as distinguished from the sciences.

hu′man•ize′, *v.,* **-ized, -izing.** become human or humane. —**hu′man•i•za′tion,** *n.*

hu′man•kind′, *n.* people collectively.

hu′man•ly, *adv.* by human means.

hum′ble, *adj.,* **-bler, -blest,** *v.,* **-bled, -bling.** —*adj.* **1.** low in rank, etc. **2.** meek. —*v.* **3.** abase. —**hum′ble•ness,** *n.* —**hum′bly,** *adv.*

hum′bug, *n.* **1.** hoax. **2.** falseness.

hum′drum′, *adj.* dull.

hu′mid, *adj.* (of air) moist. —**hu•mid′i•fi′er,** *n.* —**hu•mid′i•fy′,** *v.* —**hu•mid′i•ty,** *n.*

hu′mi•dor′, *n.* humid box or chamber.

hu•mil′i•ate′, *v.,* **-ated, -ating.** lower pride of. —**hu•mil′i•a′tion,** *n.*

hu•mil′i•ty, *n.* humbleness.

hum′ming•bird′, *n.* very small American bird.

hum′mock, *n.* hillock or knoll.

hu•mon′gous (hyoo mung′gəs, -mong′-; *often* yoo-), *adj. Slang.* huge.

hu′mor, *n.* **1.** funniness. **2.** mental disposition. **3.** whim. —*v.* **4.** indulge mood or whim of. —**hu′mor•ist,** *n.* —**hu′mor•ous,** *adj.* —**hu′mor•ous•ly,** *adv.*

hump, *n.* **1.** protuberance. —*v.* **2.** raise in hump.

hump′back′, *n.* **1.** back with hump. **2.** person with such a back. Also, **hunch′back′.**

hu′mus (hyōo′məs), *n.* dark organic material in soils, produced by decomposing vegetable or animal matter.

hunch, *v.* **1.** push out or up in a hump. —*n.* **2.** hump. **3.** guess.

hun′dred, *n., adj.* ten times ten. —**hun′dredth,** *adj., n.*

Hun•gar′i•an, *n.* native or language of Hungary. —**Hun•gar′ian,** *adj.*

hun′ger, *n.* **1.** need of food. —*v.* **2.** be hungry.

hun′gry, *adj.,* **-grier, -griest. 1.** craving food. **2.** desirous. —**hun′gri•ly,** *adv.* —**hung′ri•ness,** *n.*

hunk, *n.* **1.** large piece. **2.** *Slang.* handsome man.

hun′ker, *v.* squat down.

hunt, *v.* **1.** chase to catch. **2.** search for. —*n.* **3.** act of hunting. **4.** search. —**hunt′er,** *n.* —**hunt′ress,** *n.fem.*

hur′dle, *n., v.,* **-dled, -dling.** —*n.* **1.** barrier in race track. —*v.* **2.** leap over.

hurl, *v.* drive or throw forcefully. —**hurl′er,** *n.*

hurl′y-burl′y, *n.* disorder.

hur•rah′, *interj., n.* (exclamation of joy, triumph, etc.) Also, **hur•ray′.**

hur′ri•cane′, *n.* violent storm.

hur′ry, *v.,* **-ried, -rying,** *n., pl.* **-ries.** —*v.* **1.** act with haste. —*n.* **2.** need for haste. **3.** haste. —**hur′ried•ly,** *adv.*

hurt, *v.,* **hurt, hurting,** *n.* —*v.* **1.** injure or pain. **2.** harm. **3.** offend. —*n.* **4.** injury or damage. —**hurt′ful,** *adj.*

hur′tle, *v.,* **-tled, -tling.** strike or rush violently.

hus′band, *n.* **1.** man of married pair. —*v.* **2.** manage prudently.

hus′band•ry, *n.* farming and raising of livestock.

hush, *interj.* **1.** (command to be silent.) —*n.* **2.** silence.

husk, *n.* **1.** dry covering of fruits and seeds. —*v.* **2.** remove husk.

husk′y, *adj.,* **huskier, huskiest,** *n., pl.* **-ies.** —*adj.* **1.** big and strong. **2.** hoarse. —*n.* **3.** *(sometimes cap.)* sturdy sled dog of arctic regions.

hus′sy, *n., pl.* **-sies. 1.** ill-behaved girl. **2.** lewd woman.

hus'tle, *v.*, **-tled, -tling**, *n.* —*v.* 1. work energetically. 2. force or shove violently. —*n.* 3. energetic activity. 4. discourteous shoving.

hus'tler, *n. Slang.* 1. person eager for success. 2. swindler. 3. prostitute.

hut, *n.* small humble dwelling.

hutch, *n.* 1. pen for small animals. 2. chestlike cabinet with open shelves above.

hwy., highway.

hy'a•cinth, *n.* bulbous flowering plant.

hy'brid, *n.* offspring of organisms of different breeds.

hy'brid•ize, *v.*, **-ized, -izing**, produce hybrids. —**hy'brid•i•za'tion**, *n.*

hy•dran'gea (-jə), *n.* flowering shrub.

hy'drant, *n.* water pipe with outlet.

hy•drau'lic, *adj.* 1. of or operated by liquid. 2. of hydraulics.

hy•drau'lics, *n.* science of moving liquids.

hydro-, prefix meaning: 1. water. 2. hydrogen.

hy'dro•car'bon, *n.* compound containing only hydrogen and carbon.

hy'dro•e•lec'tric, *adj.* of electricity generated by hydraulic energy. —**hy'dro•e•lec'tric'i•ty**, *n.*

hy'dro•foil', *n.* powered vessel that can skim on water.

hy'dro•gen, *n.* inflammable gas, lightest of elements.

hy'dro•gen•ate' (hī'drə jə nāt', hī droj'ə-), *v.*, **-ated, -ating.** treat with hydrogen. —**hy•drog'e•nat'ed**, *adj.*

hydrogen peroxide, liquid used as antiseptic and bleach.

hydrogen bomb, powerful bomb utilizing thermonuclear fusion.

hy'dro•pho'bi•a, *n.* 1. rabies. 2. fear of water.

hy'dro•plane', *n.* 1. airplane that lands on water. 2. light, high-speed motorboat.

hy'dro•pon'ics, *n.* cultivation of plants in liquids rather than in soil. —**hy'dro•pon'ic**, *adj.*

hy'dro•ther'a•py, *n.* use of water externally in the treatment of disease or injury.

hy•e'na, *n.* African mammal.

hy′giene, *n.* science of preserving health. —**hy′gi•en′ic,** *adj.*

hy•grom′e•ter, *n.* instrument for measuring humidity.

hy′men, *n.* fold of mucous membrane partly enclosing the vagina in a virgin.

hymn, *n.* song of praise.

hym′nal, *n.* book of hymns. Also, **hymn′book′.**

hype (hīp), *v.,* **hyped, hyping,** *n. Informal.* —*v.* **1.** stimulate or agitate. **2.** create interest in by flamboyant or questionable methods. —*n.* **3.** intensive or exaggerated promotion.

hyper-, *prefix.* excessive.

hy′per•ac′tive, *adj.* abnormally active. —**hy′per•ac•tiv′i•ty,** *n.*

hy•per′bo•le′ (-bə lē′), *n.* exaggeration for rhetorical effect. —**hy′per•bol′ic,** *adj.*

hy′per•crit′i•cal, *adj.* excessively critical.

hy′per•gly•ce′mi•a (-sē′mē ə), *n.* abnormally high level of glucose in the bloods. —**hy′per•gly•ce′mic,** *adj.*

hy′per•ten′sion, *n.* high blood pressure. —**hy′per•ten′sive,** *adj., n.*

hy′per•ven′ti•la′tion, *n.* rapid breathing. —**hy′per•ven′ti•late′,** *v.*

hy′phen, *n.* short line (-) connecting parts or syllables of a word. —**hy′phen•ate′,** *v.* —**hy′phen•a′tion,** *n.*

hyp•no′sis, *n., pl.* **-ses.** artificially produced sleeplike state. —**hyp•not′ic,** *adj.* —**hyp′no•tism′,** *n.* —**hyp′no•tist,** *n.* —**hyp′no•tize′,** *v.*

hy′po, *n., pl.* **-pos.** hypodermic needle or injection.

hypo-, *prefix* meaning: **1.** under or beneath, as *hypodermic.* **2.** lacking or insufficient, as *hypothermia.*

hy′po•al′ler•gen′ic, *adj.* designed to minimize the chance of an allergic reaction.

hy′po•chon′dri•a (-kon′-), *n.* morbid fancies of ill health. —**hy′po•chon′dri•ac′,** *n., adj.*

hy•poc′ri•sy, *n., pl.* **-sies.** pretense of virtue, piety, etc.

hyp′o•crite, *n.* person given to hypocrisy. —**hyp′o•crit′i•cal,** *adj.*

hy′po•der′mic, *adj.* **1.** introduced under the skin, as needle. 2. syringe and needle for hypodermic injections.

hy′po•gly•ce′mi•a, *n.* abnormally low level of glucose in the blood. —**hy′po•gly•ce′mic,** *adj.*

hy•pot′e•nuse, *n.* side of right triangle opposite right angle.

hy′po•ther′mi•a, *n.* body temperature below normal.

hy•poth′e•sis, *n., pl.* **-ses.** 1. proposed explanation. 2. guess. —**hy′po•thet′i•cal,** *adj.*

hys′ter•ec′to•my, *n., pl.* **-mies.** removal of uterus.

hys•te′ri•a (-ster′-, -stēr′-), *n.* 1. uncontrollable emotion. 2. psychological disorder. —**hys•ter′i•cal** (-ster′-), *adj.* —**hys•ter′i•cal•ly,** *adv.*

hys•ter′ics (-ster′-), *n.pl.* fit of hysteria.

Hz, hertz.

I, i, *n.* 1. ninth letter of English alphabet. —*pron.* 2. subject form of first pers. sing. pronoun.

IA or **Ia.,** Iowa.

-iatrics, suffix meaning medical care, as *geriatrics.*

-iatry, suffix meaning medical practice, as *psychiatry.*

i′bex (ī′beks), *n., pl.* **i′bex•es, ib′i•ces′** (ib′ə sēz′, ī′bə-), **i′bex.** wild goat with backward-curving horns.

ibid. (ib′id), ibidem.

i′bi•dem′ (ib′i dəm, i bī′dəm), *adv.* in the same book, chapter, etc., previously cited.

i′bis, *n.* wading bird.

i′bu•pro′fen (ī′byoo prō′fən), *n.* anti-inflammatory drug that reduces pain and swelling.

ICC, Interstate Commerce Commission.

ice, *n., v.,* **iced, icing.** —*n.* 1. water frozen solid. 2. frozen dessert. —*v.* 3. cover with ice or icing. 4. cool with ice. —**iced,** *adj.* —**i′ci•ly,** *adv.* —**i′ci•ness,** *n.* —**i′cy,** *adj.*

ice′berg′, *n.* mass of ice floating at sea.

ice′box′, *n.* food chest cooled by ice.

ice cream, frozen dessert made with cream or milk, sweeteners, and flavorings.

ice skate, shoe with metal blade for skating on ice. —**ice-skate,** *v.* —**ice skater.**

ich′thy•ol′o•gy (ik′thi-), *n.* study of fishes. —**ich′thy•ol′o•gist,** *n.*

i′ci•cle, *n.* hanging tapering mass of ice.

ic′ing, *n.* preparation for covering cakes.

i′con, *n.* sacred image.

i•con′o•clast′, *n.* attacker of cherished beliefs. —**i•con′o•clas′tic,** *adj.*

-ics, suffix meaning: 1. art, science, or field, as *physics.* 2. activities or practices of a certain kind, as *acrobatics.*

ICU, intensive care unit.

id, *n.* part of the psyche that is the source of unconscious and instinctive impulses.

ID (ī′dē′), *pl.* **IDs, ID's.** document, card, or other means of identification.

ID Idaho. Also, **Id.**

Ida., Idaho.

i•de•a, *n.* conception in mind.

i•de′al, *n.* 1. conception or standard of perfection. —*adj.* 2. being an ideal. 3. not real. —**i•de′al•ly,** *adv.* —**i•de′al•ize′,** *v.*

i•de′al•ism′, *n.* belief in or behavior according to ideals. —**i•de′al•ist,** *n.* —**i•de′al•is′tic,** *adj.*

i•den′ti•cal, *adj.* same. —**i•den′ti•cal•ly,** *adv.*

i•den′ti•fy′, *v.,* **-fied, -fying.** 1. recognize as particular person or thing. 2. regard as or prove to be identical. —**i•den′ti•fi•ca′tion,** *n.*

i•den′ti•ty, *n., pl.* **-ties.** 1. fact of being same. 2. self.

i′de•ol′o•gy, *n., pl.* **-gies.** beliefs of group, esp. political. —**i′de•o•log′i•cal,** *adj.*

id′i•om, *n.* 1. expression peculiar to a language. 2. dialect. —**id′i•o•mat′ic,** *adj.*

id′i•o•path′ic, *adj.* of unknown cause, as a disease.

id′i•o•syn′cra•sy, *n., pl.* **-sies.** unusual individual trait. —**id′i•o•syn•crat′ic,** *adj.*

id′i•ot, *n.* utterly foolish person. —**id′i•ot′ic,** *adj.* —**id′i•ot′i•cal•ly,** *adv.* —**id′i•o•cy,** *n.*

i′dle, *adj., v.,* **idled, idling.** —*adj.* 1. doing nothing. 2. valueless. 3. groundless. —*v.* 4. do nothing. —**i′dler,** *n.* —**i′dly,** *adv.*

i′dol, *n.* object worshiped or adored. —**i′dol•ize′,** *v.*

i•dol′a•try, *n., pl.* **-tries.** worship of idols. —**i•dol′a•ter,** *n.* —**i•dol′a•trous,** *adj.*

i′dyll, *n.* composition describing pastoral scene. Also, **i′dyl. —i•dyl′lic,** *adj.*

i.e., that is.

if, *conj.* 1. in case that. 2. whether. 3. though.

if′fy, *adj.,* **-fier, -fiest.** *Informal.* indefinite.

ig′loo, *n., pl.* **-loos.** snow hut.

ig′ne•ous, *adj.* 1. produced by great heat. 2. of fire.

ig•nite′, *v.,* **-nited, -niting.** set on fire. —**ig•ni′tion,** *n.*

ig•no′ble, *adj.* 1. dishonorable. 2. humble. —**ig•no′bly,** *adv.*

ig′no•min′i•ous, *adj.* **1.** humiliating. **2.** contemptible. —**ig′no•min′y,** *n.*

ig′no•ra′mus (-rā′-), *n.* ignorant person.

ig′no•rant, *adj.* **1.** lacking knowledge. **2.** unaware. —**ig′no•rance,** *n.*

ig•nore′, *v.,* **-nored, -noring.** disregard.

i•gua′na (i gwä′nə), *n.* large tropical lizard.

IL, Illinois.

ilk, *n.* family or kind.

ill, *adj.* **1.** not well; sick. **2.** evil. **3.** unfavorable. —*n.* **4.** evil; harm. **5.** ailment. —*adv.* **6.** badly. **7.** with difficulty.

Ill. Illinois.

ill′-ad•vised′, *adj.* showing bad judgment.

ill′-bred′, *adj.* rude.

ill′-fat′ed, *adj.* doomed.

il•le′gal, *adj.* unlawful. —**il•le′gal•ly,** *adv.*

il•leg′i•ble, *adj.* hard to read. —**il•leg′i•bil′i•ty,** *n.* —**il•leg′i•bly,** *adv.*

il′le•git′i•mate, *adj.* **1.** unlawful. **2.** born to unmarried parents. —**il′le•git′i•ma•cy,** *n.*

il•lib′er•al, *adj.* **1.** not generous. **2.** narrow in attitudes or beliefs.

il•lic′it, *adj.* not allowed.

il•lim′it•a•ble, *adj.* boundless.

il•lit′er•ate, *adj.* **1.** unable to read and write. —*n.* **2.** illiterate person. —**il•lit′er•a•cy,** *n.*

ill′-man′nered, *adj.* having bad manners.

ill′ness, *n.* bad health.

il•log′i•cal, *adj.* not logical. —**il•log′i•cal•ly,** *adv.*

ill′-starred′, *adj.* unlucky.

ill′-treat′, *v.* abuse. —**ill′-treat′ment,** *n.*

il•lu′mi•nate′, *v.,* **-nated, -nating.** supply with light. Also, **il•lu′mine.** —**il•lu′mi•na′tion,** *n.*

illus., **1.** illustrated. **2.** illustration.

ill′-use′ (*v.* il′yōōz′; *n.* -yōōs′), *v.,* **-used, -using,** *n.* —*v.* **1.** treat badly or unjustly. —*n.* **2.** Also, **ill′-us′age.** bad or unjust treatment.

il•lu′sion, *n.* false appearance. —**il•lu′sive, il•lu′so•ry,** *adj.*

il′lus·trate′, *v.*, **-trated, -trating.** 1. explain with examples, etc. 2. furnish with pictures. —**il′lus·tra′tion**, *n.* —**il·lus′tra·tive**, *adj.* —**il′lus·tra′tor**, *n.*

il·lus′tri·ous, *adj.* 1. famous. 2. glorious.

ill will, hostile feeling.

im-, *prefix.* variant of **in-**.

im′age, *n.* 1. likeness. 2. idea. 3. conception of one's character. —*v.* 4. mirror.

im′age·ry, *n.*, *pl.* **-ries.** 1. mental images collectively. 2. use of figures of speech.

im·ag′ine, *v.*, **-ined, -ining.** 1. form mental images. 2. think; guess. —**im·ag′i·na′tion**, *n.* —**im·ag′i·na′tive**, *adj.* —**im·ag′i·nar′y**, *adj.* —**im·ag′i·na·ble**, *adj.*

i·mam′ (i mäm′), *n.* Muslim religious leader.

im·bal′ance, *n.* lack of balance.

im′be·cile (-sil), *n.* 1. *Obsolete.* a retarded person having a mental age of up to eight years. 2. a foolish or stupid person. —**im′be·cil′ic**, *adj.* —**im′be·cil′i·ty**, *n.*

im·bibe′, *v.*, **-bibed, -bibing.** drink. —**im·bib′er**, *n.*

im·bro′glio (-brōl′yō), *n.*, *pl.* **-glios.** complicated affair.

im·bue′, *v.*, **-bued, -buing.** 1. inspire. 2. saturate.

im′i·tate′, *v.*, **-tated, -tating.** 1. copy. 2. counterfeit. —**im′i·ta′tive**, *adj.* —**im′i·ta′tor**, *n.* —**im′i·ta′tion**, *n.*

im·mac′u·late, *adj.* 1. spotlessly clean. 2. pure.

im′ma·nent, *adj.* being within. —**im′ma·nence**, *n.*

im′ma·te′ri·al, *adj.* 1. unimportant. 2. spiritual.

im′ma·ture′, *adj.* not mature. —**im′ma·tu′ri·ty**, *n.*

im·meas′ur·a·ble, *adj.* limitless. —**im·meas′ur·a·bly**, *adv.*

im·me′di·ate, *adj.* 1. without delay. 2. nearest. 3. present. —**im·me′di·a·cy**, *n.* —**im·me′di·ate·ly**, *adv.*

im′me·mo′ri·al, *adj.* beyond memory or record.

im·mense′, *adj.* 1. vast. 2. boundless. —**im·men′si·ty**, *n.* —**im·mense′ly**, *adv.*

im•merse′, *v.,* **-mersed, -mersing. 1.** plunge into liquid. **2.** absorb, as in study. **—im•mer′sion,** *n.*

im′mi•grant, *n.* person who immigrates.

im′mi•grate′, *v.,* **-grated, -grating.** come to new country. **—im′mi•gra′tion,** *n.*

im′mi•nent, *adj.* about to happen. **—im′mi•nence,** *n.*

im•mo′bile, *adj.* not moving. **—im′mo•bil′i•ty,** *n.* **—im•mo′bi•lize′,** *v.*

im•mod′er•ate, *adj.* excessive. **—im•mod′er•ate•ly,** *adv.*

im•mod′est, *adj.* not modest. **—im•mod′es•ty,** *n.*

im′mo•late′, *v.,* **-lated, -lating. 1.** sacrifice. **2.** destroy by fire. **—im′mo•la′tion,** *n.*

im•mor′al, *adj.* not moral. **—im′mo•ral′i•ty,** *n.* **—im•mor′al•ly,** *adv.*

im•mor′tal, *adj.* **1.** living forever. **—***n.* **2.** immortal being. **—im′mor•tal′i•ty,** *n.* **—im•mor′tal•ize′,** *v.*

im•mov′a•ble, *adj.* **1.** fixed. **2.** unchanging.

im•mune′, *adj.* **1.** protected from disease. **2.** exempt.

—im•mu′ni•ty, *n.*
—im′mu•ni•za′tion, *n.*
—im′mu•nize′, *v.*

immune system, network that protects the body from infection.

im′mu•nol′o•gy, *n.* branch of science dealing with the immune system. **—im′mu•nol′o•gist,** *n.*

im•mure′, *v.,* **-mured, -muring.** confine within walls.

im•mu′ta•ble, *adj.* unchangeable. **—im•mu′ta•bil′i•ty,** *n.* **—im•mu′ta•bly,** *adv.*

imp, *n.* **1.** little demon. **2.** mischievous child. **—imp′ish,** *adj.* **—imp′ish•ly,** *adv.*

im′pact, *n.* **1.** collision. **2.** influence; effect. **—***v.* **3.** collide with. **4.** have effect.

im•pact′ed, *adj.* (of a tooth) wedged too tightly in its socket to erupt properly.

im•pair′, *v.* damage; weaken. **—im•pair′ment,** *n.*

im•pale′, *v.,* **-paled, -paling.** fix upon sharp stake, etc.

im•pal′pa•ble, *adj.* that cannot be felt or understood.

im•pan′el, *v.,* **-eled, -eling.** list for jury duty.

im·part′, *v*. 1. tell. 2. give.

im·par′tial, *adj*. unbiased.
—**im′par·ti·al′i·ty**, *n*.
—**im·par′tial·ly**, *adv*.

im·pas′sa·ble, *adj*. not able to be passed through or along.

im′passe (-pas), *n*. deadlock.

im·pas′sioned, *adj*. full of passion.

im·pas′sive, *adj*. 1. emotionless. 2. calm.
—**im·pas′sive·ly**, *adv*.

im·pa′tience, *n*. lack of patience. —**im·pa′tient**, *adj*.
—**im·pa′tient·ly**, *adv*.

im·peach′, *v*. charge with misconduct in office.
—**im·peach′ment**, *n*.

im·pec′ca·ble, *adj*. faultless.
—**im·pec′ca·bly**, *adv*.

im′pe·cu′ni·ous, *adj*. without money.

im·ped′ance (im pēd′ns), *n*. total opposition to alternating current by an electric circuit.

im·pede′, *v*., -peded, -peding. hinder. —**im·ped′i·ment**, *n*.

im·ped′i·men′ta, *n.pl.* baggage carried with one.

im·pel′, *v*., -pelled, -pelling. urge forward.

im·pend′, *v*. be imminent.

im·pen′e·tra·ble, *adj*. that cannot be penetrated.
—**im·pen′e·tra·bil′i·ty**, *n*.
—**im·pen′e·tra·bly**, *adv*.

im·per′a·tive, *adj*. 1. necessary. 2. *Gram*. denoting command.

im′per·cep′ti·ble, *adj*. 1. very slight. 2. not perceptible.
—**im′per·cep′ti·bly**, *adv*.

im·per′fect, *adj*. 1. having defect. 2. not complete. 3. *Gram*. denoting action in progress. —**im′per·fec′tion**, *n*. —**im·per′fect·ly**, *adv*.

im·pe′ri·al (-pēr′-), *adj*. of an empire or emperor.

im·pe′ri·al·ism′, *n*. policy of extending rule over other peoples. —**im·pe′ri·al·ist**, *n., adj*. —**im·pe′ri·al·is′tic**, *adj*.

im·per′il, *v*., -iled, -iling. endanger.

im·pe′ri·ous, *adj*. domineering.
—**im·pe′ri·ous·ly**, *adv*.

im·per′ish·a·ble, *adj*. not subject to decay.
—**im·per′ish·a·bly**, *adv*.

im·per′me·a·ble, *adj*. not permitting penetration.
—**im·per′me·a·bil′i·ty**, *n*.

im•per′son•al, *adj.* without personal reference or bias. —**im•per′son•al•ly,** *adv.*

im•per′son•ate′, *v.,* **-ated, -ating.** act the part of. —**im•per′son•a′tion,** *n.* —**im•per′son•a′tor,** *n.*

im•per′ti•nence, *n.* **1.** rude presumption. **2.** irrelevance. —**im•per′ti•nent,** *adj.* —**im•per′ti•nent•ly,** *adv.*

im′per•turb′a•ble, *adj.* calm. —**im′per•turb′a•bly,** *adv.*

im•per′vi•ous, *adj.* **1.** not allowing penetration.**2.** incapable of being affected. —**im•per′vi•ous•ly,** *adv.*

im′pe•ti′go (im′pi tī′gō), *n.* contagious skin infection characterized by pustules.

im•pet′u•ous, *adj.* rash or hasty. —**im•pet′u•os′i•ty,** *n.* —**im•pet′u•ous•ly,** *adv.*

im′pe•tus, *n.* **1.** stimulus. **2.** force of motion.

im•pi′e•ty, *n., pl.* **-ties. 1.** lack of piety. **2.** act showing this.

im•pinge′, *v.,* **-pinged, -pinging. 1.** collide. **2.** encroach.

im′pi•ous (im′pē əs, im pī′-), *adj.* **1.** irreligious. **2.** disrespectful.

im•pla′ca•ble, *adj.* not to be placated.

im•plant′, *v.* **1.** instill. —*n.* (im′plant). **2.** material used to repair part of the body.

im•plaus′i•ble, *adj.* not plausible. —**im•plau′si•bil′i•ty,** *n.*

im′ple•ment, *n.* **1.** instrument or tool. —*v.* **2.** put into effect. —**im′ple•men•ta′tions,** *n.*

im′pli•cate′, *v.,* **-cated, -cating.** involve as guilty.

im′pli•ca′tion, *n.* **1.** act of implying. **2.** thing implied. **3.** act of implicating.

im•plic′it (-plis′it), *adj.* **1.** unquestioning; complete. **2.** implied. —**im•plic′it•ly,** *adv.*

im•plode′, *v.,* **-ploded, -ploding.** burst inward. —**im•plo′sion,** *n.*

im•plore′, *v.,* **-plored, -ploring.** urge or beg.

im•ply′, *v.,* **-plied, -plying. 1.** indicate. **2.** suggest.

im′po•lite′, *adj.* rude.

im•pol′i•tic, *adj.* not wise.

im•pon′der•a•ble, *adj.* that cannot be evaluated.

im·port', *v.* 1. bring in from another country. 2. matter; signify. —*n.* (im'pōrt). 3. anything imported. 4. significance. —**im'por·ta'tion**, *n.* —**im·port'er**, *n.*

im·por'tant, *adj.* 1. of some consequence. 2. prominent. —**im·por'tance**, *n.* —**im·por'tant·ly**, *adv.*

im'por·tune' (-tyoon'), *v.,* -tuned, -tuning. persistently beg. —**im·por'tu·nate**, *adj.*

im·pose', *v.,* -posed, -posing. 1. set as obligation. 2. intrude (oneself). 3. deceive. —**im'po·si'tion**, *n.*

im·pos'ing, *adj.* impressive.

im·pos'si·ble, *adj.* that cannot be done or exist. —**im·pos'si·bil'i·ty**, *n.* —**im·pos'si·bly**, *adv.*

im'post, *n.* tax or duty.

im·pos'tor, *n.* person who deceives under false name. Also, **im·pos'ter**. —**im·pos'ture**, *n.*

im'po·tence, *n.* 1. lack of power. 2. lack of sexual powers. —**im'po·tent**, *adj.*

im·pound', *v.* seize by law.

im·pov'er·ish, *v.* make poor.

im·prac'ti·ca·ble, *adj.* not able to be put into use.

im·prac'ti·cal, *adj.* not usable or useful.

im'pre·ca'tion, *n.* curse. —**im'pre·cate**, *v.*

im'pre·cise', *adj.* not precise.

im·preg'na·ble, *adj.* resistant to or proof against attack.

im·preg'nate, *v.,* -nated, -nating. 1. make pregnant. 2. saturate; infuse. —**im'preg·na'tion**, *n.*

im'pre·sa'ri·o, *n.* person who organizes or manages entertainment events.

im·press', *v.* 1. affect with respect, etc. 2. fix in mind. 3. stamp. 4. force into public service. —*n.* (im'pres). 5. act of impressing. —**im·pres'sive**, *adj.* —**im·pres'sive·ly**, *adv.*

im·pres'sion, *n.* 1. effect on mind or feelings. 2. notion. 3. printed or stamped mark.

im·pres'sion·a·ble, *adj.* easily influenced. —**im·pres'sion·a·bly**, *adv.*

im·pres'sion·ism, *n.* (*often cap.*) style of painting characterized by short brush strokes to represent the effect

of light on objects.
—**im•pres′sion•ist,** *n., adj.*
—**im•pres′sion•is′tic,** *adj.*

im′pri•ma′tur (im′pri mä′tər, -mā′-), *n.* **1.** permission to print or publish. **2.** sanction.

im′print, *n.* **1.** mark made by pressure. **2.** impression.

im•pris′on, *v.* put in prison.
—**im•pris′on•ment,** *n.*

im•prob′a•ble, *adj.* unlikely.
—**im•prob′a•bil′i•ty,** *n.*
—**im•prob′a•bly,** *adv.*

im•promp′tu, *adj., adv.* without preparation.

im•prop′er, *adj.* not right, suitable, or proper.
—**im′pro•pri′e•ty,** *n.*
—**im•prop′er•ly,** *adv.*

im•prove′, *v.,* **-proved, -proving.** make or become better. —**im•prove′ment,** *n.*

im•prov′i•dent, *adj.* not providing for the future.
—**im•prov′i•dence,** *n.*
—**im•prov′i•dent•ly,** *adv.*

im′pro•vise′, *v.,* **-vised, -vising.** prepare for or perform at short notice.
—**im′pro•vi•sa′tion,** *n.*

im•pru′dent, *adj.* not prudent.

im′pu•dent, *adj.* shamelessly bold. —**im′pu•dence,** *n.*
—**im′pu•dent•ly,** *adv.*

im•pugn′ (-py o͞o n′), *v.* cast doubt on.

im′pulse, *n.* **1.** inciting influence. **2.** sudden inclination. —**im•pul′sive,** *adj.* —**im•pul′sive•ly,** *adv.*

im•pu′ni•ty, *n.* exemption from punishment.

im•pure′, *adj.* **1.** not pure. **2.** immoral. —**im•pu′ri•ty,** *n.*

im•pute′, *v.,* **-puted, -puting.** attribute.

in, *prep.* **1.** within. **2.** into. **3.** while; during. **4.** into some place. —*adv.* **5.** inside; within.

IN, Indiana.

in-, common prefix meaning "not" or "lacking." See list on following pages.

in., inch.

in ab•sen′tia (in ab sen′shə, -shē ə), *adv. Latin.* in absence.

in•ac′ti•vate′, *v.,* **-vated, -vating.** make inactive.
—**in•ac′ti•va′tion,** *n.*

in′ad•vert′ent, *adj.* **1.** heedless. **2.** unintentional.
—**in′ad•vert′ence,** *n.*
—**in′ad•vert′ent•ly,** *adv.*

in•al'ien•a•ble, *adj.* not to be taken away or transferred.

in•am'o•ra'ta (in am′ə rä′tə, in′am-), *n.* female lover.

in•ane', *adj.* silly; ridiculous. —**in•an'i•ty,** *n.*

in'ar•tic'u•late, *adj.* not clear in expression.

in'as•much' as, 1. seeing that. 2. to the extent that.

in•au'gu•rate', *v.,* -rated, -rating. 1. induct into office. 2. begin. —**in•au'gu•ral,** *adj., n.* —**in•au'gu•ra'tion,** *n.*

in'board', *adj., adv.* 1. inside a hull or aircraft. 2. nearer the center, as of an airplane.

in'born', *adj.* innate.

in'bound', *adj.* inward bound.

in'breed', *v.* produce by breeding of related individuals. —**in'breed'ing,** *n.* —**in'bred',** *adj.*

inc., 1. incomplete. 2. incorporated. 3. increase.

In'ca, *n., pl.* -cas. member of South American Indian people dominant in Peru before the Spanish conquest. —**In'can,** *adj.*

in'can•des'cence (-des′əns), *n.* glow of intense heat. —**in'can•des'cent,** *adj.*

in'can•ta'tion, *n.* 1. magic ritual. 2. spell.

in'ca•pac'i•tate', *v.,* -tated, -tating. make unfit. —**in'ca•pac'i•ty,** *n.*

---

in'a•bil'i•ty
in'ac•ces'si•ble
in•ac'cu•ra•cy
in•ac'cu•rate
in•ac'tive
in•ad'e•qua•cy
in•ad'e•quate
in'ad•mis'si•ble
in'ad•vis'a•ble
in•an'i•mate
in'ap•pro'pri•ate

in•apt'i•tude'
in'ar•tis'tic
in'at•ten'tion
in'at•ten'tive
in•au'di•ble
in'aus•pi'cious
in•cal'cu•la•ble
in•ca'pa•ble
in'ca•pac'i•ty
in•cau'tious
in'ci•vil'i•ty

in•car′cer•ate′, *v.,* -ated, -ating. imprison. —**in•car′cer•a′tion**, *n.*

in•car′nate (-nit), *adj.* embodied in flesh. —**in′car•na′tion**, *n.*

in•cen′di•ar′y (-sen′-), *adj., n., pl.* -aries. —*adj.* 1. of or for setting fires. 2. arousing strife. —*n.* 3. person who maliciously sets fires.

in•cense′, *v.,* -censed, -censing, *n.* —*v.* (in sens′). 1. enrage. —*n.* (in′sens). 2. substance burned to give a sweet odor.

in•cen′tive, *n.* motivation.

in•cep′tion, *n.* beginning.

in•ces′sant, *adj.* unceasing. —**in•ces′sant•ly**, *adv.*

in′cest, *n.* sexual relations between close relatives. —**in•ces′tu•ous**, *adj.*

inch, *n.* unit of length, $\frac{1}{12}$ foot.

in•cho′ate (-kō′it), *adj.* just begun; incomplete.

inch′worm′, *n.* moth larva that moves in looping motion.

in′ci•dence, *n.* range of occurrence or effect.

in′ci•dent, *n.* 1. happening. 2. side event. —*adj.* 3. likely. 4. naturally belonging. —**in′ci•den′tal**, *adj., n.* —**in′ci•den′tal•ly**, *adv.*

in•cin′er•ate′, *v.,* -ated, -ating. burn to ashes. —**in•cin′er•a′tor**, *n.*

in•cip′i•ent (-sip′-), *adj.* beginning. —**in•cip′i•ence**, *n.*

in•clem′ent
in′co•her′ence
in′co•her′ent
in′com•men′su•rate
in′com•pat′i•bil′i•ty
in′com•pat′i•ble
in•com′pe•tence
in•com′pe•tent
in′com•plete′
in′com•pre•hen′si•ble
in′con•ceiv′a•ble

in′con•clu′sive
in•con′gru•ous
in′con•se•quen′tial
in′con•sist′en•cy
in′con•sist′ent
in′con•sol′a•ble
in′con•spic′u•ous
in•con′stan•cy
in•con′stant
in′con•test′a•ble
in′con•tro•vert′i•ble

in•cise' (-sīz'), *v.*, **-cised, -cising.** cut into; engrave. —**in•ci'sion,** *n.*

in•ci'sive, *adj.* **1.** sharp. **2.** uncomfortably sharp.

in•ci'sor, *n.* cutting tooth.

in•cite', *v.,* **-cited, -citing.** urge to action. —**in•cite'ment,** *n.*

incl., including.

in•cline', *v.,* **-clined, -clining,** *n.* —*v.* **1.** tend. **2.** slant. **3.** dispose. —*n.* (in'klīn). **4.** slanted surface. —**in'cli•na'tion,** *n.*

in•close', *v.,* **-closed, -closing.** enclose.

in•clude', *v.,* **-cluded, -cluding. 1.** contain. **2.** have among others. —**in•clu'sion,** *n.* —**in•clu'sive,** *adj.*

in•cog'ni•to' (in kog'nə tō'), *adj., adv.* hiding identity.

in'com•bus'ti•ble, *adj.* incapable of being burned.

in'come, *n.* money received.

in'com'ing, *adj.* coming in.

in'com•mu'ni•ca'do (in'kə myōō'ni kä'dō), *adv., adj.* without means of communicating.

in•com'pa•ra•ble, *adj.* unequaled. —**in•com'pa•ra•bly,** *adv.*

in'con•sid'er•ate, *adj.* thoughtless.

in'con•ven'ience
in'con•ven'ient
in'cor•rect'
in'cor•rupt'i•ble
in•cur'a•ble
in•de'cen•cy
in•de'cent
in•de•ci'sive
in•dec'o•rous
in'de•fen'si•ble
in•de•fin'a•ble

in•def'i•nite
in•del'i•ca•cy
in•del'i•cate
in'de•scrib'a•ble
in'de•ter'mi•nate
in'di•gest'i•ble
in'di•rect'
in'dis•creet'
in'dis•cre'tion
in'dis•pen'sa•ble
in'dis•put'a•ble

in•con'ti•nent, *adj.* 1. unable to control bodily discharges. 2. lacking sexual self-restraint. —**in•con'ti•nence,** *n.*

in•cor'po•rate', *v.,* -rated, -rating. 1. form a corporation. 2. include as part. —**in•cor'po•ra'tion,** *n.*

in'cor•po're•al, *adj.* not corporeal or material.

in•cor'ri•gi•ble, *adj.* not to be reformed.

in•crease', *v.,* -creased, -creasing, *n.* —*v.* 1. make or become more or greater. —*n.* (in'krēs). 2. instance of increasing. 3. growth. —**in•creas'ing•ly,** *adv.*

in•cred'i•ble, *adj.* amazing. —**in•cred'i•bly,** *adv.*

in•cred'u•lous, *adj.* not believing. —**in•cred'u•lous•ly,** *adv.*

in'cre•ment, *n.* increase. —**in'cre•men'tal,** *adj.*

in•crim'i•nate', *v.,* -nated, -nating. charge with a crime. —**in•crim'i•na'tion,** *n.*

in•crust', *v.* cover with crust. —**in'crus•ta'tion,** *n.*

in'cu•bate', *v.,* -bated, -bating. keep warm for hatching. —**in'cu•ba'tion,** *n.*

in'cu•ba'tor, *n.* 1. heated case for incubating. 2. apparatus in which premature infants are cared for.

in•cul'cate, *v.,* -cated, -cating. teach; instill.

in'dis•tinct'
in'dis•tin'guish•a•ble
in'di•vis'i•ble
in•ed'i•ble
in'ef•fec'tive
in'ef•fi'cien•cy
in'ef•fi'cient
in•el'i•gi•ble
in'e•qual'i•ty
in•eq'ui•ta•ble
in'es•cap'a•ble

in•es'ti•ma•ble
in'ex•act'
in'ex•cus'a•ble
in'ex•haust'i•ble
in'ex•pen'sive
in'ex•pe'ri•enced
in'ex•pres'si•ble
in•fea'si•ble
in'fe•lic'i•tous
in•fer'tile
in'fi•del'i•ty

in·cum′bent, *adj.* 1. obligatory. —*n.* 2. office holder. —**in·cum′ben·cy,** *n.*

in·cur′, *v.,* -curred, -curring. bring upon oneself.

in·cur′sion, *n.* raid.

Ind., Indiana

in·debt′ed, *adj.* obligated by debt. —**in·debt′ed·ness,** *n.*

in′de·ci′pher·a·ble, *adj.* illegible.

in′de·ci′sion, *n.* inability to decide.

in·deed′, *adv.* 1. in fact. —*interj.* 2. (used to express surprise, contempt, etc.)

in′de·fat′i·ga·ble, *adj.* tireless.

in·del′i·ble, *adj.* unerasable.

in·dem′ni·fy′, *v.,* -fied, -fying. compensate for loss. —**in·dem′ni·ty,** *n.*

in·dent′, *v.* 1. notch. 2. set in from margin. —**in′den·ta′tion,** *n.*

in·den′ture (in den′chər) *n.,* *v.,* -tured, -turing. —*n.* 1. contract binding one to service. —*v.* 2. bind by indenture.

in′de·pend′ent, *adj.* 1. free. 2. not dependent on others. —**in′de·pend′ence,** *n.*

in′-depth′, *adj.* intensive.

in′de·struct′i·ble, *adj.* that cannot be destroyed.

in′dex, *n.,* *pl.* -dexes, -dices, *v.* —*n.* 1. list of topics with page

in·flex′i·ble
in·for′mal
in′for·mal′i·ty
in·fre′quen·cy
in·fre′quent
in·glo′ri·ous
in·grat′i·tude′
in′har·mon′ic
in′har·mo′ni·ous
in·hos′pi·ta·ble
in′hu·mane′

in′ju·di′cious
in·jus′tice
in′of·fen′sive
in·op′er·a·tive
in·op′por·tune′
in′or·gan′ic
in′se·cure′
in·sen′si·tive
in·sep′a·ra·ble
in′sig·nif′i·cance
in′sig·nif′i·cant

references. 2. indicator. —*v.* 3. provide with index.

In′dian, *n.* 1. native of India. 2. Also, **Amer′ican In′dian.** member of the aboriginal peoples of N. and S. America. —**Indian,** *adj.*

Indian summer, period of mild weather in late fall.

in′di•cate′, *v.,* -**cated, -cating.** 1. be a sign of. 2. point to. —**in′di•ca′tion,** *n.* —**in•dic′a•tive,** *adj.* —**in′di•ca′tor,** *n.*

in•dict′ (-dīt′), *v.* charge with crime. —**in•dict′ment,** *n.*

in•dif′fer•ent, *adj.* 1. without concern. 2. moderate. —**in•dif′fer•ence,** *n.*

in•dig′e•nous (-dij′ə nəs), *adj.* native.

in′di•gent, *adj.* needy; destitute. —**in′di•gence,** *n.*

in′di•ges′tion, *n.* difficulty in digesting food.

in′dig•na′tion, *n.* righteous anger. —**in•dig′nant,** *adj.*

in•dig′ni•ty, *n., pl.* -**ties.** 1. loss of dignity. 2. cause of this.

in′di•go′, *n., pl.* -**gos, -goes.** blue dye.

in′dis•crim′i•nate, *adj.* done at random; haphazard

in′dis•pose′, *v.,* -**posed, -posing.** 1. make ill. 2. make unwilling.

in′sin•cere′
in′sin•cer′i•ty
in•sol′u•ble
in′sta•bil′i•ty
in′sub•or′di•nate
in′sub•or′di•na′tion
in′suf′fer•a•ble
in′suf•fi′cient
in′sup•press′i•ble
in′sur•mount′a•ble
in′sus•cep′ti•ble

in•tan′gi•ble
in•tem′per•ance
in•tem′per•ate
in•tol′er•a•ble
in•tol′er•ance
in•tol′er•ant
in•var′i•a•ble
in•vis′i•ble
in•vis′i•bly
in•vol′un•tar′y
in•vul′ner•a•ble

in′dis·posed′, *adj.* 1. mildly ill. 2. unwilling. —**in′dis·po·si′tion**, *n.*

in′dis·sol′u·ble, *adj.* that cannot be dissolved, undone, or destroyed.

in·dite′, *v.,* -dited, -diting. write.

in′di·vid′u·al, *adj.* 1. single. 2. of or for one only. —*n.* 3. single thing. —**in′di·vid′u·al′i·ty**, *n.* —**in′di·vid′u·al·ly**, *adv.*

in′di·vid′u·al·ist, *n.* person dependent only on self. —**in′di·vid′u·al·ism′**, *n.*

in·doc′tri·nate′, *v.,* -nated, -nating. train to accept doctrine. —**in·doc′tri·na′tion**, *n.*

in′do·lent, *adj.* lazy. —**in′do·lence**, *n.*

in·dom′i·ta·ble, *adj.* that cannot be dominated.

in′door′, *adj.* inside a building. —**in·doors′**, *adv.*

in·du′bi·ta·ble, *adj.* undoubted. —**in·du′bi·ta·bly**, *adv.*

in·duce′, *v.,* -duced, -ducing. 1. persuade; influence. 2. cause. —**in·duce′ment**, *n.*

in·duct′, *v.* bring into office. —**in′duc·tee′**, *n.*

in·duc′tion, *n.* 1. reasoning from particular facts. 2. act of inducting. —**in·duc′tive**, *adj.*

in·dulge′, *v.,* -dulged, -dulging. 1. accommodate whims of. 2. accommodate one's own whims. —**in·dul′gence**, *n.* —**in·dul′gent**, *adj.*

in·dus′tri·al·ist, *n.* owner of industrial plant.

in·dus′tri·al·ize′, *v.,* -ized, -izing. convert to modern industrial methods.

in·dus′tri·ous, *adj.* hard-working. —**in·dus′tri·ous·ly**, *adv.*

in′dus·try, *n., pl.* -tries. 1. trade or manufacture, esp. with machinery. 2. diligent work. —**in·dus′tri·al**, *adj.*

in·e′bri·ate′, *v.,* -ated, -ating, *n.* —*v.* (in ē′bri āt′). 1. make drunk. —*n.* (-it). 2. drunken person. —**in·e′bri·a′tion**, *n.*

in·ef′fa·ble, *adj.* that cannot be described.

in′ef·fec′tu·al, *adj.* futile.

in·ept′, *adj.* careless; unskilled. —**in·ept′i·tude′**, *n.*

—**in•ept′ly,** *adv.*
—**in•ept′ness,** *n.*

in•eq′ui•ty, *n., pl.* **-ties.**
injustice.

in•ert′, *adj.* **1.** without
inherent power to move,
resist, or act. **2.** slow-moving.
—**in•er′tia,** *n.*

in•ev′i•ta•ble, *adj.* not to be
avoided.
—**in•ev′i•ta•bil′i•ty,** *n.*
—**in•ev′i•ta•bly,** *adv.*

in•ex′o•ra•ble, *adj.* stubborn.
—**in•ex′o•ra•bly,** *adv.*

in•ex′pert, *adj.* unskilled.

in•ex′pli•ca•ble, *adj.* not to
be explained.
—**in•ex′pli•ca•bly,** *adv.*

in•ex′tri•ca•ble, *adj.* that
cannot be disentangled.
—**in•ex′tri•ca•bly,** *adv.*

in•fal′li•ble, *adj.* never failing
or making mistakes.
—**in•fal′li•bly,** *adv.*

in′fa•my, *n., pl.* **-mies.** evil
repute. —**in′fa•mous,** *adj.*

in′fant, *n.* small baby.
—**in′fan•cy,** *n.* —**in′fan•tile′,**
adj.

in′fan•try, *n., pl.* **-tries.**
soldiers who fight on foot.
—**in′fan•try•man,** *n.*

in′farct′ (in′ färkt′, in färkt′),
n. area of dead or dying
tissue, as in the heart. Also,
in•farc′tion.
—**in•fat′u•a′tion,** *n.*

in•fat′u•ate′, *v.,* **-ated, -ating.**
inspire with foolish passion.
—**in•fat′u•a′tion,** *n.*

in•fect′, *v.* affect with disease
germs. —**in•fec′tion,** *n.*

in•fec′tious, *adj.* spreading
readily.

in•fer′, *v.,* **-ferred, -ferring.**
conclude or deduce.
—**in′fer•ence,** *n.*

in•fe′ri•or, *adj.* **1.** less good,
important, etc. —*n.* **2.** person
inferior to others.
—**in•fe′ri•or′i•ty,** *n.*

in•fer′nal, *adj.* **1.** of hell. **2.**
Informal. outrageous.

in•fer′no, *n., pl.* **-nos.** hell.

in•fest′, *v.* overrun; trouble.
—**in′fes•ta′tion,** *n.*

in′fi•del, *n.* unbeliever.

in′field′, *n.* **1.** area of baseball
field inside base lines. **2.**
players in infield.
—**in′field′er,** *n.*

in′fight′ing, *n.* conflict within
group.

in•fil′trate, *v.,* **-trated, -trating.** pass in, as by filtering. —**in′fil•tra′tion,** *n.*

in′fi•nite, *adj.* 1. vast; endless. —*n.* 2. that which is infinite. —**in•fin′i•ty,** *n.*

in′fin•i•tes′i•mal, *adj.* immeasurably small. —**in′fin•i•tes′i•mal•ly,** *adv.*

in•fin′i•tive, *n.* simple form of verb.

in•firm′, *adj.* feeble; weak. —**in•fir′mi•ty,** *n.*

in•fir′ma•ry, *n., pl.* **-ries.** hospital.

in•flame′, *v.,* **-flamed, -flaming.** 1. set afire. 2. redden. 3. excite. 4. cause bodily reaction marked by redness, pain, etc. —**in•flam′ma•ble,** *adj.* —**in•flam′ma•to′ry,** *adj.* —**in′flam•ma′tion,** *n.*

in•flate′, *v.,* **-flated, -flating.** 1. swell or expand with air or gas. 2. increase unduly. —**in•flat′a•ble,** *adj.*

in•fla′tion, *n.* 1. rise in prices when currency expands faster than available goods or services. 2. act of inflating. —**in•fla′tion•ar′y,** *adj.*

in•flect′, *v.* 1. bend. 2. modulate. 3. display forms of a word. —**in•flec′tion,** *n.* —**in•flec′tion•al,** *adj.*

in•flict′, *v.* impose harmfully. —**in•flic′tion,** *n.*

in′flu•ence, *n., v.,* **-enced, -encing.** —*n.* 1. power to affect another. 2. something that does this. —*v.* 3. move, affect, or sway. —**in′flu•en′tial,** *adj.*

in′flu•en′za, *n.* contagious disease caused by virus.

in′flux′, *n.* a flowing in.

in′fo•mer′cial, *n.* program-length television commercial designed to appear to be standard programming rather than an advertisement.

in•form′, *v.* supply with information. —**in•form′ant,** *n.* —**in•form′er,** *n.* —**in•form′a•tive,** *adj.*

in′for•ma′tion, *n.* factual knowledge. —**in′for•ma′tion•al,** *adj.*

information superhighway, large-scale communications network linking computers, television sets, etc.

in′fo·tain′ment, *n.* broadcasting or publishing that strives to treat factual matter in an entertaining way, as by dramatizing or fictionalizing real events.

in·frac′tion, *n.* violation.

in′fra·red′, *n.* part of invisible spectrum.

in′fra·struc′ture, *n.* **1.** basic framework of system or organization. **2.** basic facilities, as transportation and communications systems.

in·fringe′, *v.,* **-fringed, -fringing.** violate; encroach. **—in·fringe′ment,** *n.*

in·fu′ri·ate′, *v.,* **-ated, -ating.** enrage.

in·fuse′, *v.,* **-fused, -fusing. 1.** instill; fortify. **2.** steep. **—in·fu′sion,** *n.*

in·gen′ious (-jēn′-), *adj.* inventive; clever. **—in·gen′ious·ly,** *adv.* **—in·ge·nu′i·ty,** *n.*

in′ge·nue′ (an′zhə noo′), *n.* **1.** role of an innocent young woman in a play. **2.** actress who plays this role.

in·gen′u·ous (-jen′-), *adj.* artlessly sincere. **—in·gen′u·ous·ly,** *adv.*

in·gest′ (-jest′), *v.* take into the body, as food or liquid. **—in·ges′tion,** *n.*

in′got (ing′gət), *n.* cast metal.

in·grained′, *adj.* fixed firmly.

in′grate, *n.* ungrateful person.

in·gra′ti·ate′ (-grā′shē āt′), *v.,* **-ated, -ating.** get (oneself) into someone's good graces.

in·gre′di·ent, *n.* element or part of mixture.

in′gress, *n.* entrance.

in·hab′it, *v.* live in. **—in·hab′it·ant,** *n.*

in·hal′ant, *n.* substance inhaled, as a medicine.

in′ha·la′tor, *n.* **1.** apparatus to help one inhale medicine, etc. **2.** respirator.

in·hale′, *v.,* **-haled, -haling.** breathe in. **—in′ha·la′tion,** *n.*

in·hal′er, *n.* inhalator.

in·here′, *v.,* **-hered, -hering.** be inseparable part or element. **—in·her′ent,** *adj.*

in·her′it, *v.* become heir to. **—in·her′it·ance,** *n.*

in·hib′it, *v.* restrain or hinder. **—in′hi·bi′tion,** *n.*

in·hib′i·tor, *n.* substance that stops a chemical reaction.

in'house' (*adj.* in'hous'; *adv.* -hous'), *adj.*, *adv.* within or using an organization's own staff or resources.

in•hu'man, *adj.* 1. brutal; heartless. 2. not human. —**in'hu•man'i•ty,** *n.*

in•im'i•cal, *adj.* 1. adverse. 2. hostile.

in•im'i•ta•ble, *adj.* not to be imitated.

in•iq'ui•ty, *n.*, *pl.* -ties. 1. wicked injustice. 2. sin. —**in•iq'ui•tous,** *adj.*

in•i'tial, *adj.*, *n.*, *v.*, -tialed, -tialing. —*adj.* 1. of or at beginning. —*n.* 2. first letter of word. —*v.* 3. sign with initials of one's name. —**in•i'tial•ly,** *adv.*

in•i'ti•ate', *v.*, -ated, -ating. 1. begin. 2. admit with ceremony. —**in•i'ti•a'tion,** *n.*

in•i'ti•a•tive, *n.* 1. beginning action. 2. readiness to proceed.

in•ject', *v.* force, as into tissue. —**in•jec'tion,** *n.* —**in•jec'tor,** *n.*

in•junc'tion, *n.* admonition.

in'jure, *v.*, -jured, -juring. 1. hurt. 2. do wrong to.

—**in•ju'ri•ous,** *adj.*
—**in•ju'ri•ous•ly,** *adv.*
—**in'ju•ry,** *n.*

ink, *n.* 1. writing fluid. —*v.* 2. mark with ink. —**ink'y,** *adj.*

ink'ling, *n.* hint.

in'land, *adj.* 1. of or in the interior of a region. 2. not foreign. —*adv.* 3. of or toward inland area. —*n.* 4. inland area.

in'-law', *n.* relative by marriage.

in•lay', *v.*, -laid, -laying, *n.* —*v.* 1. ornament with design set in surface. —*n.* (in'lā'). 2. inlaid work.

in'let, *n.* narrow bay.

in-line skate, roller skate with four wheels in a straight line.

in'mate', *n.* person confined in prison, hospital, etc.

in me•mo'ri•am (in mə môr'ē əm), in memory (of).

in'most', *adj.* farthest within. Also, **in'ner•most'.**

inn, *n.* 1. hotel. 2. tavern.

in•nards, *n.pl.* 1. internal parts of the body. 2. internal parts, structure, etc., of something.

in•nate', *adj.* born into one.

in′ner, *adj.* **1.** being farther within. **2.** spiritual.

inner city, central part of city.

in′ner-direct′ed, *adj.* guided by one's own values.

in′ning, *n. Baseball.* one round of play for both teams.

in′no•cence, *n.* **1.** freedom from guilt. **2.** lack of worldly knowledge. —**in′no•cent,** *adj., n.*

in•noc′u•ous, *adj.* harmless.

in′no•vate′, *v.,* **-vated, -vating.** bring in something new. —**in′no•va′tion,** *n.* —**in′no•va′tor,** *n.* —**in′no•va′tive,** *adj.*

in′nu•en′do, *n., pl.* **-dos, -does.** hint of wrong.

in•nu′mer•a•ble, *adj.* **1.** very numerous. **2.** uncountable.

in•oc′u•late′, *v.,* **-lated, -lating.** immunize. —**in•oc′u•la′tion,** *n.*

in•or′di•nate, *adj.* excessive. —**in•or′di•nate•ly,** *adv.*

in′pa′tient, *n.* patient who stays in hospital while receiving care or treatment.

in′put′, *n., v.,* **-putted** or **-put, putting.** —*n.* **1.** power, etc., supplied to machine. **2.**

information given computer. —*v.* **3.** enter (data) into computer. —**in′put′ter,** *n.*

in′quest, *n.* legal inquiry.

in•quire′, *v.,* **-quired, -quiring. 1.** ask. **2.** make investigation. —**in•quir′y,** *n.*

in′qui•si′tion, *n.* probe. —**in•quis′i•tor,** *n.*

in•quis′i•tive, *adj.* having great curiosity.

in re (in rē′, rā′), in the matter of.

in′road′, *n.* encroachment.

ins., 1. inches. **2.** insurance.

in•sane′, *adj.* mentally deranged. —**in•san′i•ty,** *n.*

in•sa′ti•a•ble, *adj.* impossible to satisfy.

in•scribe′, *v.,* **-scribed, -scribing. 1.** write or engrave. **2.** dedicate. —**in•scrip′tion,** *n.*

in•scru′ta•ble, *adj.* that cannot be understood. —**in•scru′ta•bil′i•ty,** *n.*

in′sect, *n.* small six-legged animal with body in three parts.

in•sec′ti•cide′, *n.* chemical for killing insects.

in·sem′i·nate′, *v.*, **-nated,
-nating. 1.** sow seed in. **2.**
impregnate.
—**in·sem′i·na′tion,** *n.*

in·sen′sate, *adj.* without
feeling.

in·sen′si·ble, *adj.* **1.**
incapable of feeling or
perceiving. **2.** not aware;
unconscious. **3.** not
perceptible by the senses.

in·sert′, *v.* **1.** put or set in.
—*n.* (in′sûrt). **2.** something
inserted. —**in·ser′tion,** *n.*

in′shore′, *adj.* **1.** on or close to
the shore. —*adv.* **2.** toward
the shore.

in′side′, *prep., adv.* **1.** within.
—*n.* (in′sīd′). **2.** inner part.
—*adj.* (in′sīd′). **3.** inner.

in′sid′er, *n.* **1.** member of
certain organization, society,
etc. **2.** person who has
influence, esp. because privy
to confidential information.

in·sid′i·ous, *adj.* artfully
treacherous.
—**in·sid′i·ous·ly,** *adv.*

in′sight′, *n.* discernment.

in·sig′ni·a, *n.pl.* badges of
rank, honor, etc.

in·sin′u·ate′, *v.,* **-ated, -ating.
1.** hint slyly. **2.** put into mind.
3. make one's way artfully.
—**in·sin′u·a′tion,** *n.*

in·sip′id, *adj.* without
distinctive qualities; vapid.
—**in·sip′id·ly,** *adv.*

in·sist′, *v.* be firm or
persistent. —**in·sist′ence,** *n.*
—**in·sist′ent,** *adj.*

in′so·far′, *adv.* to such extent.

in′sole′, *n.* **1.** inner sole of
shoe. **2.** removable inner sole.

in′so·lent, *adj.* boldly rude.
—**in′so·lence,** *n.*

in·sol′vent, *adj.* without funds
to pay one's debts.
—**in·sol′ven·cy,** *n.*

in·som′ni·a, *n.* sleeplessness.

in′so·much′, *adv.* **1.** to such a
degree. **2.** inasmuch.

in·sou′ci·ant (in soo′sē ənt),
adj. free from concern or
anxiety. —**in·sou′ci·ance,** *n.*

in·spect′, *v.* view critically or
officially. —**in·spec′tion,** *n.*

in·spec′tor, *n.* **1.** person with
duty to inspect. **2.** minor
police official.

in·spire′, *v.,* **-spired, -spiring.
1.** arouse (emotion, etc.). **2.**

prompt to extraordinary actions. 3. inhale.
—**in'spi•ra'tion,** *n.*
—**in'spi•ra'tion•al,** *adj.*

Inst., 1. Institute. 2. Institution.

in•stall', *v.* 1. put in position for use. 2. establish.
—**in'stal•la'tion,** *n.*

in•stall'ment, *n.* division, as of payment or story. Also, **in•stal'ment.**

installment plan, system for paying in installments.

in'stance, *n., v.,* **-stanced, -stancing.** —*n.* 1. case; example. —*v.* 2. cite.

in'stant, *n.* 1. moment. 2. point of time now present. —*adj.* 3. immediate.
—**in'stant•ly,** *adv.*

in'stan•ta'ne•ous, *adj.* occurring, etc., in an instant.
—**in'stan•ta'ne•ous•ly,** *adv.*

in•stead', *adv.* in place of.

in'step', *n.* upper arch of foot.

in'sti•gate', *v.,* **-gated, -gating.** incite to action.
—**in'sti•ga'tion,** *n.*
—**in'sti•ga'tor,** *n.*

in•still', *v.* present slowly.
—**in•still'ment,** *n.*

in'stinct, *n.* natural impulse or talent. —**in•stinc'tive,** *adj.*

in'sti•tute', *v.,* **-tuted, -tuting,** *n.* —*v.* 1. establish. 2. put into effect. —*n.* 3. society or organization. 4. established law, custom, etc.

in'sti•tu'tion, *n.* 1. organization with purpose. 2. established tradition, etc. 3. act of instituting.
—**in'sti•tu'tion•al,** *adj.*
—**in'sti•tu'tion•al•ize',** *v.*

in•struct', *v.* 1. order. 2. teach. —**in•struc'tion,** *n.*
—**in•struc'tive,** *adj.*
—**in•struc'tor,** *n.*

in'stru•ment, *n.* 1. tool. 2. device for producing music. 3. means; agent. 4. legal document. —**in'stru•men'tal,** *adj.* —**in'stru•men•tal'i•ty,** *n.*

in'su•lar, *adj.* 1. of islands. 2. narrow in viewpoint.
—**in'su•lar'i•ty,** *n.*

in'su•late', *v.,* **-lated, -lating.** cover with nonconducting material. —**in'su•la'tion,** *n.*
—**in'su•la'tor,** *n.*

in'su•lin, *n.* hormone used to treat diabetes.

in•sult′, *v*. 1. treat with open contempt. —*n*. (in′sult). 2. such treatment.

in•su′per•a•ble, *adj*. that cannot be overcome.

in•sure′, *v*., **-sured, -suring.** 1. make certain. 2. guarantee payment in case of harm to or loss of. —**in•sur′ance**, *n*. —**in•sured′**, *n., adj.* —**in•sur′er**, *n*.

in•sur′gent, *n*. 1. rebel. —*adj*. 2. rebellious.

in′sur•rec′tion, *n*. revolt. —**in′sur•rec′tion•ist**, *n*.

int., 1. interest. 2. interior 3. interjection. 4. international. 5. intransitive.

in•tact′, *adj*. undamaged.

in′take′, *n*. 1. point at which something is taken in. 2. what is taken in.

in•tagl′io (in tal′yō, -täl′-), *n., pl.* **-taglios, -tagli** (-tal′yē, -täl′-). design carved into a surface.

in′te•ger (-jər), *n*. 1. whole number. 2. entity.

in′te•gral, *adj*. 1. necessary to completeness. 2. entire.

in′te•grate′, *v.,* **-grated, -grating.** 1. bring into whole.

2. complete. 3. abolish segregation by race. —**in′te•gra′tion**, *n*.

in•teg′ri•ty, *n*. 1. soundness of character; honesty. 2. perfect condition.

in•teg′u•ment, *n*. skin or rind.

in′tel•lect′, *n*. 1. reasoning. 2. mental capacity.

in′tel•lec′tu•al, *adj*. 1. of intellect. 2. devising concepts in dealing with problems. —*n*. 3. person who pursues intellectual interests. —**in′tel•lec′tu•al•ly**, *adv*.

in•tel′li•gence, *n*. 1. ability to learn. 2. news. 3. gathering of secret information. —**in•tel′li•gent**, *adj*.

in•tel′li•gi•ble, *adj*. understandable. —**in•tel′li•gi•bil′i•ty**, *n*. —**in•tel′li•gi•bly**, *adv*.

in•tend′, *v*. plan; design.

in•tend′ed, *n. Informal.* person one plans to marry.

in•tense′, *adj*. 1. extremely powerful. 2. emotional. —**in•ten′si•fi•ca′tion**, *n*. —**in•ten′si•fy′**, *v*. —**in•ten′si•ty**, *n*.

in•ten′sive, *adj*. thorough.

in·tent′, *n.* 1. purpose. —*adj.* 2. firmly concentrated. 3. firmly purposeful. —**in·tent′ly,** *adv.*

in·ten′tion, *n.* 1. purpose. 2. meaning. —**in·ten′tion·al,** *adj.*

in·ter′ (-tûr′), *v.,* **-terred, -terring.** bury.

inter-, prefix meaning: 1. between or among, as *interdepartmental.* 2. reciprocally, as *interdependent.*

in′ter·act′, *v.* act upon one another. —**in′ter·ac′tion,** *n.* —**in′ter·ac′tive,** *adj.*

in′ter·breed′, *v.,* **-bred, -breeding.** crossbreed.

in′ter·cede′, *v.,* **-ceded, -ceding.** act or plead in behalf. —**in′ter·ces′sion,** *n.*

in′ter·cept′, *v.* stop or check passage. —**in′ter·cep′tion,** *n.* —**in′ter·cep′tor,** *n.*

in′ter·change′, *v.,* **-changed, -changing,** *n.* —*v.* (in′tər chānj′). 1. exchange. 2. alternate. —*n.* (in′tər chānj′). 3. act or place of interchanging.

in′ter·con′ti·nen′tal, *adj.* 1. between or among continents. 2. capable of traveling between continents.

in′ter·course′, *n.* 1. dealings. 2. sexual relations.

in′ter·de·nom′i·na′tion·al, *adj.* involving different religious denominations.

in′ter·de′part·men′tal, *adj.* involving or existing between two or more departments.

in′ter·de·pend′ent, *adj.* mutually dependent. —**in′ter·de·pend′ence,** *n.*

in′ter·dict′, *n.* 1. decree that prohibits. —*v.* (in′tər dikt′). 2. prohibit. —**in′ter·dic′tion,** *n.*

in′ter·est, *n.* 1. feeling of curiosity. 2. business or ownership. 3. benefit. 4. payment for use of money. —*v.* 5. excite interest of.

interest group, group acting together because of a common interest, etc.

in′ter·est·ing, *adj.* engaging the attention or curiosity.

in′ter·face′, *n.* 1. surface forming common boundary between two spaces. 2. common boundary between people, concepts, etc. 3. computer hardware or software that communicates information between entities. —*v.* 4. interact smoothly.

in′ter•fere′, *v.*, **-fered, -fering.** 1. hamper. 2. intervene. 3. meddle. —**in′ter•fer′ence**, *n.*

in′ter•im, *n.* 1. meantime. —*adj.* 2. temporary.

in•te′ri•or, *adj.* 1. inside. 2. inland. —*n.* 3. interior part.

in′ter•ject′, *v.* add abruptly.

in′ter•jec′tion, *n.* 1. act of interjecting. 2. something interjected. 3. interjected word that forms a complete utterance, as *indeed!*

in′ter•lace′, *v.*, **-laced, -lacing.** unite by or as if by weaving together; intertwine.

in′ter•lard′, *v.* mix in.

in′ter•lock′, *v.*, join together.

in′ter•loc′u•tor, *n.* participant in conversation.

in′ter•loc′u•to′ry, *adj.* 1. of or in conversation. 2. *Law.* not final.

in′ter•lop′er, *n.* intruder.

in′ter•lude′, *n.* 1. intervening episode, time, etc. 2. performance in intermission.

in′ter•mar′ry, *v.*, **-ried, -rying.** 1. (of groups) become connected by marriage. 2. marry outside one's group. —**in′ter•mar′riage**, *n.*

in′ter•me′di•ar′y, *adj., n., pl.* **-aries.** —*adj.* 1. intermediate. —*n.* 2. mediator.

in′ter•me′di•ate, *adj.* being or acting between two others.

in•ter′ment, *n.* burial.

in′ter•mez′zo (in′tər met′sō, -med′zō), *n., pl.,* **-mezzos, -mezzi.** short musical composition, as between divisions of a longer work.

in•ter′mi•na•ble, *adj.* seeming to be without end. —**in•ter′mi•na•bly**, *adv.*

in′ter•mis′sion, *n.* interval between acts in drama, etc.

in′ter•mit′tent, *adj.* alternately ceasing and starting again. —**in′ter•mit′tent•ly**, *adv.*

in•tern′, *v.* 1. hold within certain limits. —*n.* (in′tûrn). 2. Also, **in′terne.** resident assistant physician on hospital staff. —**in•tern′ment**, *n.*

in•ter′nal, *adj.* 1. interior; inner. 2. domestic. —**in•ter′nal•ly**, *adv.*

internal medicine, branch of medicine dealing with diagnosis and nonsurgical treatment of diseases.

in·ter·na'tion·al, *adj.* 1. among nations. 2. of many nations.
—**in'ter·na'tion·al·ly,** *adv.*

in'ter·na'tion·al·ism', *n.* principle of international cooperation.
—**in'ter·na'tion·al·ist,** *n.*

in'ter·na'tion·al·ize', *v.,* -ized, -izing. 1. make international. 2. bring under international control.

in'ter·ne'cine (-nē'sīn), *adj.* 1. of conflict within a group. 2. mutually destructive.

Internet, *n.* large computer network linking smaller networks worldwide.

in'tern·ist, *n.* doctor specializing in internal medicine.

in'ter·per'son·al, *adj.* between persons.

in'ter·plan'e·tar'y, *adj.* between planets.

in'ter·play', *n.* reciprocal action.

in·ter'po·late', *v.,* -lated, -lating. insert to alter or clarify meaning.
—**in·ter'po·la'tion,** *n.*

in'ter·pose', *v.,* -posed, -posing. 1. place between things. 2. intervene.

in·ter'pret, *v.* 1. explain. 2. construe. 3. translate.
—**in·ter'pre·ta'tion,** *n.*
—**in·ter'pret·er,** *n.*

in'ter·ra'cial, *adj.* of, for, or between persons of different races.

in'ter·re·lat'ed, *adj.* closely associated.

in·ter'ro·gate', *v.,* -gated, -gating. question.
—**in·ter'ro·ga'tion,** *n.*
—**in'ter·rog'a·tive,** *adj.*
—**in·ter'ro·ga'tor,** *n.*

in'ter·rupt', *v.* break in; stop.
—**in'ter·rup'tion,** *n.*

in'ter·scho·las'tic, *adj.* occurring between schools.

in'ter·sect', *v.* divide by crossing; cross.

in'ter·sec'tion, *n.* 1. place where roads meet. 2. act of intersecting.

in'ter·sperse' (-spûrs'), *v.,* -spersed, -spersing. 1. scatter at random. **2.** vary with something scattered.

in′ter•state′, *adj.* involving number of states.

in′ter•stel′lar, *adj.* situated or occurring between the stars.

in•ter′stice (-tûr′stis), *n.* chink or opening.

in′ter•twine′, *v.,* **-twined, -twining.** unite by twining together.

in′ter•ur′ban, *adj.* between cities.

in′ter•val, *n.* **1.** intervening time or space. **2.** difference in musical pitch between tones.

in′ter•vene′, *v.,* **-vened, -vening. 1.** come or be between. **2.** mediate. —**in′ter•ven′tion,** *n.* —**in′ter•ven′tion•ist,** *n.*

in′ter•view′, *n.* **1.** conversation to obtain information. **2.** meeting. —*v.* **3.** have interview with. —**in′ter•view′er,** *n.*

in•tes′tate, *adj.* **1.** without having made a will. **2.** not disposed of by will.

in•tes′tine, *n.* lower part of alimentary canal. —**in•tes′ti•nal,** *adj.*

in′ti•mate, *adj., n., v.,* **-mated, -mating.** —*adj.* **1.** close; friendly. **2.** private. **3.** thorough. —*n.* **4.** intimate friend. —*v.* (-māt′). **5.** imply. —**in′ti•ma•cy,** *n.* —**in′ti•ma′tion,** *n.* —**in′ti•mate•ly,** *adv.*

in•tim′i•date′, *v.,* **-dated, -dating.** make timid; frighten. —**in•tim′i•da′tion,** *n.*

in′to, *prep.* to inside of.

in•tone′, *v.,* **-toned, -toning. 1.** use particular spoken tone. **2.** chant. —**in′to•na′tion,** *n.*

in to′to (in tō′tō), completely.

in•tox′i•cate′, *v.,* **-cated, -cating.** affect with liquor. —**in•tox′i•ca′tion,** *n.*

in•trac′ta•ble, *adj.* stubborn.

in′tra•mu′ral, *adj.* within one school.

in•tran′si•gent (-sə jənt), *adj.* uncompromising. —**in•tran′si•gence,** *n.*

in•tran′si•tive, *adj.* (of verb) not having a direct object.

in′tra•ve′nous, *adj.* within vein.

in•trep′id, *adj.* fearless. —**in′tre•pid′i•ty,** *n.*

in′tri•cate, *adj.* complicated.
—**in′tri•ca•cy,** *n.*
—**in′tri•cate•ly,** *adv.*

in•trigue′ (in trēg′), *v.,*
 -trigued, -triguing, *n.* —*v.* 1.
 interest by puzzling. 2. plot.
 —*n.* 3. crafty design or plot.

in•trin′sic, *adj.* inherent.
—**in•trin′si•cal•ly,** *adv.*

in′tro•duce′, *v.,* **-duced,**
 -ducing. 1. bring to notice,
 use, etc. 2. be preliminary to.
 3. make (person) known to
 another. —**in′tro•duc′tion,** *n.*
 —**in′tro•duc′to•ry,** *adj.*

in′tro•spec′tion, *n.*
 examination of one's own
 thoughts and motives.
 —**in′tro•spec′tive,** *adj.*

in′tro•vert′, *n.* person
 concerned chiefly with inner
 thoughts or feelings.
 —**in′tro•ver′sion,** *n.*
 —**in′tro•vert′ed,** *adj.*

in•trude′, *v.,* **-truded, -truding.**
 come or bring in without
 welcome. —**in•trud′er,** *n.*
 —**in•tru′sion,** *n.*
 —**in•tru′sive,** *adj.*
 —**in•tru′sive•ly,** *adv.*

in′tu•i′tion, *n.* instinctive
 perception. —**in•tu′i•tive,**
 adj. —**in•tu′i•tive•ly,** *adv.*

in′un•date′, *v.,* **-dated,**
 -dating. flood.
 —**in′un•da′tion,** *n.*

in•ure′ (in yŏŏr′), *v.,* **-ured,**
 -uring. accustom; harden.

in•vade′, *v.,* **-vaded, -vading.**
 enter hostilely. —**in•vad′er,** *n.*
 —**in•va′sion,** *n.*

in′va•lid, *n.* 1. sick person.
 —*adj.* 2. sick. 3. for invalids.
 4. (in val′id). not valid.
 —**in•val′i•date′,** *v.*

in•val′u•a•ble, *adj.* beyond
 valuing; priceless.

in•vec′tive, *n.* 1. censure. 2.
 harsh taunts or accusations.

in•veigh′ (-vā′), *v.* attack
 violently in words.

in•vei′gle (-vē′gəl -vā′-), *v.*
 -gled, -gling. lure into action.
 —**in•vei′gler,** *n.*

in•vent′, *v.* devise (something
 new). —**in•ven′tion,** *n.*
 —**in•ven′tive,** *adj.*
 —**in•ven′tor,** *n.*

in′ven•to′ry, *n., pl.* **-tories.** list
 or stock of goods.

in•verse′, *adj.* 1. reversed. 2.
 opposite. 3. inverted.
 —**in•verse′ly,** *adv.*

in•vert′, *v.* 1. turn upside
 down. 2. reverse. 3. make
 contrary. —**in•ver′sion,** *n.*

in·ver′te·brate (-brit), *adj.* **1.** without backbone. —*n.* **2.** invertebrate animal.

in·vest′, *v.* **1.** spend money, esp. so as to get larger amount in return. **2.** give or devote (time, etc.). **3.** furnish with power or authority. —**in·vest′ment,** *n.* —**in·ves′tor,** *n.*

in·ves′ti·gate′, *v.,* **-gated, -gating.** examine in detail. —**in·ves′ti·ga′tion,** *n.* —**in·ves′ti·ga′tive,** *adj.* —**in·ves′ti·ga′tor,** *n.*

in·vet′er·ate, *adj.* confirmed in habit.

in·vid′i·ous, *adj.* **1.** likely to arouse envy. **2.** unjust.

in·vig′or·ate′, *v.,* **-ated, -ating.** give vigor to.

in·vin′ci·ble, *adj.* unconquerable. —**in·vin′ci·bil′i·ty,** *n.*

in·vi′o·la·ble, *adj.* that must not or cannot be violated. —**in·vi′o·la·bil′i·ty,** *n.*

in·vi′o·late, *adj.* **1.** not hurt or desecrated. **2.** undisturbed.

in·vite′, *v.,* **-vited, -viting. 1.** ask politely. **2.** act so as to make likely. **3.** attract. —**in′vi·ta′tion,** *n.*

in·vit′ing, *adj.* attractive.

in vi′tro (in vē′trō), developed or maintained in a controlled nonliving environment, as a laboratory vessel.

in′vo·ca′tion, *n.* prayer for aid, guidance, etc.

in′voice, *n., v.,* **-voiced, -voicing.** —*n.* **1.** list with prices of goods sent to buyer. —*v.* **2.** list on invoice.

in·voke′, *v.,* **-voked, -voking. 1.** beg for. **2.** call on in prayer. **3.** cite as authoritative.

in·vol′un·tar′y, *adj.* **1.** not done intentionally. **2.** not under conscious control.

in·volve′, *v.,* **-volved, -volving. 1.** include as necessary. **2.** complicate. **3.** implicate. **4.** engross. —**in·volve′ment,** *n.*

in·vul′ner·a·ble, *adj.* **1.** that cannot be damaged. **2.** proof against attack.

in′ward, *adv.* **1.** Also, **in′wards.** toward the interior. —*adj.* **2.** toward the interior. **3.** inner. —*n.* **4.** inward part. —**in′ward·ly,** *adv.*

in′-your-face′, *adj. Informal.* involving confrontation.

Io., Iowa.

I/O, input/output.

i′o•dine′, *n.* nonmetallic element used in medicine.

i′on, *n.* charged particle.

i′o•nize′ (ī′ə nīz′), *v.,* **-nized, -nizing.** 1. separate or change into ions. 2. produce ions in. 3. become ionized. —**i′on•i•za′tion,** *n.*

i•on′o•sphere (ī on′ə sfēr′), *n.* outermost region of earth's atmosphere, consisting of ionized layers.

i•o′ta (ī ō′tə), *n.* very small quantity.

IOU, written acknowledgment of debt.

IQ, intelligence quotient.

ip′e•cac′, *n.* drug from root of South American shrub.

ip′so fac′to (ip′sō fak′tō), by the fact itself.

IRA, individual retirement account.

I•ra′ni•an, *n.* native of Iran. —**I•ra′ni•an,** *adj.*

I•ra′qi (i rak′ē, i rä′ kē), *n., pl.* **-qis.** native of Iraq. —**Iraqi,** *adj.*

i•ras′ci•ble (i ras′ə bəl), *adj.* easily angered.

ire, *n.* anger. —**i′rate,** *adj.*

ir′i•des′cence (-des′əns), *n.* play of rainbowlike colors. —**ir′i•des′cent,** *adj.*

i′ris, *n.* 1. colored part of the eye. 2. perennial plant with showy flowers.

I′rish, *n.* language or people of Ireland. —**I′rish,** *adj.*

irk, *v.* annoy. —**irk′some,** *adj.*

i′ron, *n.* 1. metallic element. 2. implement for pressing cloth. 3. (*pl.*) shackles. —*adj.* 4. of or like iron. —*v.* 5. press with iron (def. 2).

i′ron-clad′, *adj.* 1. iron-plated, as a ship. 2. very rigid.

iron curtain, (formerly) barrier between Communist and non-Communist areas.

i′ro•ny, *n., pl.* **-nies.** 1. figure of speech in which meaning is opposite to what is said. 2. unexpected outcome. —**i•ron′i•cal, i•ron′ic,** *adj.* —**i•ron′i•cal•ly,** *adv.*

Ir′o•quois′ (ir′ə kwoi′, -kwoiz′), *n., pl.* **-quois.** member of a group of North American Indian peoples.

ir•ra′di•ate′, *v.,* **-ated, -ating.** 1. illuminate. 2. expose to radiation. 3. shine. —**ir•ra′di•a′tion,** *n.*

ir·ra′tion·al, *adj.* without reason or judgment.

ir·rec′on·cil′a·ble, *adj.* 1. that cannot be brought into agreement. 2. bitterly opposed.

ir′re·deem′a·ble, *adj.* that cannot be redeemed.

ir′re·duc′i·ble, *adj.* that cannot be reduced.

ir·ref′u·ta·ble, *adj.* not refutable.

ir·reg′u·lar, *adj.* 1. not symmetrical. 2. not fixed. 3. not conforming to rule. —**ir·reg′u·lar′i·ty,** *n.*

ir·rel′e·vant, *adj.* not relevant. —**ir·rel′e·vance,** *n.*

ir′re·li′gious, *adj.* 1. not religious. 2. hostile to religion.

ir·rep′a·ra·ble, *adj.* that cannot be rectified. —**ir·rep′a·ra·bly,** *adv.*

ir′re·press′i·ble, *adj.* that cannot be repressed. —**ir′re·press′i·bly,** *adv.*

ir′re·proach′a·ble, *adj.* blameless.

ir′re·sist′i·ble, *adj.* not to be withstood. —**ir′re·sist′i·bly,** *adv.*

ir′res′o·lute′, *adj.* undecided.

ir′re·spec′tive, *adj.* without regard to.

ir′re·spon′si·ble, *adj.* not concerned with responsibilities. —**ir′re·spon′si·bly,** *adv.*

ir′re·triev′a·ble, *adj.* that cannot be recovered.

ir·rev′er·ent, *adj.* lacking respect. —**ir·rev′er·ent·ly,** *adv.*

ir·rev′o·ca·ble, *adj.* not to be revoked or annulled. —**ir·rev′o·ca·bly,** *adv.*

ir′ri·gate′, *v.,* -gated, -gating. supply with water. —**ir′ri·ga′tion,** *n.*

ir′ri·ta·ble, *adj.* easily angered. —**ir′ri·ta·bil′i·ty,** *n.* —**ir′ri·ta·bly,** *adv.*

ir′ri·tate′, *v.,* -tated, -tating. 1. annoy. 2. make sensitive. 3. excite to action. —**ir′ri·tant,** *n.* —**ir′ri·ta′tion,** *n.*

ir·rup′tion, *n.* 1. bursting in. 2. invasion.

IRS, Internal Revenue Service.

-ish, suffix meaning: 1. of or belonging to, as *British.* 2. like or having characteristics of, as *babyish.* 3. inclined to, as *bookish.* 4. near or about, as *fiftyish.* **5.** somewhat, as *reddish.*

is, *v.* third pers. sing. pres. indic. of **be.**

i′sin•glass′, *n.* **1.** transparent substance from some fish. **2.** mica.

Is•lam′, *n.* religious faith founded by Muhammad (A.D. 570–632). —**Is•lam′ic,** *adj.*

is′land, *n.* body of land surrounded by water. —**is′land•er,** *n.*

isle, *n.* small island.

is′let (ī′lit), *n.* tiny island.

ism, *n.* doctrine.

i′so•bar (ī′sə bär′), *n.* line on map connecting points at which barometric pressure is the same.

i′so•late′, *v.,* **-lated, -lating.** set apart. —**i′so•la′tion,** *n.*

i′so•la′tion•ist, *n.* person opposed to participation in world affairs. —**i′so•la′tion•ism,** *n.*

i′so•met′rics, *n.pl.* exercises in which one body part is tensed against another. —**i′so•met′ric,** *adj.*

i•sos′ce•les′ (ī sos′ə lēz′), *adj.* (of triangle) having two sides equal.

i′so•tope′, *n.* one of two or more forms of an element that vary in atomic weight.

Is•rae′li *(-ā′ lē),* *n., pl.* **-lis, -li.** native of Israel. —**Is•rae′li,** *adj.*

is′sue, *v.,* **-sued, -suing,** *n.* —*v.* **1.** send out. **2.** publish. **3.** distribute. **4.** emit. **5.** emerge. —*n.* **6.** act of issuing. **7.** thing issued. **8.** point in question. **9.** offspring. **10.** result. —**is′su•ance,** *n.*

-ist, suffix meaning: **1.** one who makes or produces, as *novelist.* **2.** one who operates, as *machinist.* **3.** advocate, as *socialist.*

isth′mus (is′məs), *n.* strip of land surrounded by water and connecting two larger bodies.

it, *pron.* third pers. sing. neuter pronoun.

ital., italic.

I•tal′ian, *n.* native or language of Italy. —**Italian,** *adj.*

i•tal′ic, *n.* typeface that slopes to right. Also, **i•tal′ics.** —**i•tal′i•cize′,** *v.* —**i•tal′ic,** *adj.*

itch, *v.* **1.** feel irritation of skin. —*n.* **2.** itching sensation. **3.** restless desire. —**itch′y,** *adj.*

i′tem, *n.* separate article.

i′tem•ize′, *v.,* **-ized, -izing.** state by items; list. —**i′tem•i•za′tion,** *n.*

it′er•ate, *v.,* **-ated, -ating.** say or do repeatedly. —**it′er•a′tion,** *n.* —**it′er•a′tive,** *adj.*

i•tin′er•ant, *adj.* **1.** traveling. —*n.* **2.** person who goes from place to place.

i•tin′er•ar′y, *n., pl.* **-aries. 1.** route. **2.** plan of travel.

-itis, suffix meaning inflammation of a body part, as *tonsillitis.*

its, *adj.* possessive form of **it.**

it's, contraction of **it is.**

itself, *pron.* reflexive form of it.

IV (ā′nē′), *n., pl.,* **IVs, IV's.** apparatus for intravenous delivery of medicines, etc.

i′vo•ry, *n., pl.* **-ries. 1.** hard white substance in tusks. **2.** yellowish white.

ivory tower, remoteness or aloofness from wordly affairs.

i′vy, *n., pl.* **ivies.** climbing evergreen vine. —**i′vied,** *adj.*

-ize, suffix meaning: **1.** engage in, as *economize.* **2.** treat in a certain way, as *idolize.* **3.** become or form into, as *unionize.* **4.** make or cause to be, as *civilize.*

J, j, *n.* tenth letter of English alphabet.

jab, *v.,* **jabbed, jabbing,** *n.* poke; thrust.

jab′ber, *v.* **1.** talk rapidly or indistinctly. —*n.* **2.** such talk.

jack, *n.* **1.** lifting device. **2.** person. **3.** knave in playing cards. **4.** male. **5.** flag; ensign. —*v.* **6.** raise with jack.

jack′al, *n.* wild dog of Asia and Africa.

jack′ass′, *n.* **1.** male donkey. **2.** fool.

jack′et, *n.* **1.** short coat. **2.** any covering.

Jack Frost, frost personified.

jack′ham′mer, compressed-air portable drill for rock, etc.

jack′-in-the-box′, *n., pl.* **-boxes.** toy consisting of box from which figure springs up when the lid is opened.

jack′-in-the-pul′pit, *n., pl.* **-pulpits.** plant with upright spike enclosed by leaflike part.

jack′knife′, *n., pl.* **-knives,** *v.,* **-knifed, -knifing.** —*n.* **1.** large folding pocketknife. **2.** dive in which diver bends over, then straightens out. —*v.* **3.** (of a trailer truck) have or cause to have the cab and trailer swivel into a V.

jack′pot′, *n.* cumulative prize in contest, lottery, etc.

jack rabbit, large rabbit of western America.

Ja·cuz′zi (jə kōō′zē), *n., pl.* **-zis.** *Trademark.* brand name for type of whirlpool bath.

jade, *n., v.,* **jaded, jading.** —*n.* **1.** green stone. **2.** old horse. —*v.* **3.** weary. —**jad′ed,** *adj.*

jag, *n.* **1.** ragged edge. **2.** *Slang.* drunken spree. —**jag′ged,** *adj.*

jag′uar (-wär), *n.* large South American wildcat.

jai′ a·lai′ (hī′ lī′, hī′ ə lī′), *n.* game played on three-walled court with basketlike rackets.

jail, *n.* **1.** prison. —*v.* **2.** put in prison. —**jail′er,** *n.*

ja′la·pe′ño (hä′lə pān′yāo), *n., pl.* **-ños.** hot pepper.

ja·lop′y, *n., pl.* **-pies.** old, decrepit automobile.

jam, *v.,* **jammed, jamming,** *n.* —*v.* **1.** push or squeeze. **2.** become unworkable. —*n.* **3.**

objects jammed together. **4.** *Informal.* difficult situation. **5.** preserve of entire fruit.

jamb, *n.* side post of door or window.

jam′bo•ree′, *n.* festivity.

Jan., January.

jan′gle, *v.,* **-gled, -gling,** *n.* —*v.* **1.** sound harshly. —*n.* **2.** harsh sound.

jan′i•tor, *n.* caretaker of building. —**jan′i•tress,** *n.fem.* —**jan′i•to′ri•al,** *adj.*

Jan′u•ar′y, *n.* first month of year.

Jap′a•nese′, *n., pl.* **-nese.** native or language of Japan. —**Japanese,** *adj.*

jar, *n., v.,* **jarred, jarring.** —*n.* **1.** broad-mouthed bottle. **2.** unpleasant sound. **3.** sudden shock or shake. —*v.* **4.** shock or shake. **5.** conflict.

jar′gon, *n.* language of a particular trade, etc.

jas′mine, *n.* fragrant shrub.

jas′per, *n.* precious quartz.

jaun′dice (jôn′-), *n.* illness causing yellowed skin, etc.

jaun′diced, *adj.,* **1.** skeptical. **2.** envious.

jaunt, *n.* short trip.

jaun′ty, *adj.* **-tier, -tiest.** sprightly. —**jaun′ti•ly,** *adv.* —**jaun′ti•ness,** *n.*

jave′lin, *n.* spear.

jaw, *n.* either of two bones forming mouth.

jaw′bone′, *n., v.,* **-boned, -boning.** —*n.* **1.** bone of the jaw. —*v.* **2.** influence by persuasion.

jaw′break′er. *n.* **1.** word that is hard to pronounce. **2.** very hard candy.

jay, *n.* noisy colorful bird.

jay′walk′, *v.* cross street improperly. —**jay′walk′er,** *n.*

jazz, *n.* **1.** popular music of black American origin. **2.** *Slang.* insincere talk.

jazz′y, *adj.,* **jazzier, jazziest. 1.** of or like jazz music. **2.** flashy.

J.D., 1. Doctor of Jurisprudence; Doctor of Law. **2.** Doctor of Laws **3.** Justice Department.

jeal′ous, *adj.* **1.** resentful of another's success, etc.; envious. **2.** vigilant, esp. against rivalry. —**jeal′ous•ly,** *adv.* —**jeal′ous•y,** *n.*

jeans, *n.pl.* cotton trousers.

Jeep, *n. Trademark.* small rugged type of automobile.

jeer, *v.* **1.** deride. —*n.* **2.** deriding shout.

Je•ho′vah, *n.* God.

je•june′ (ji jōōn′), *adj.* **1.** lacking interest or significance; insipid. **2.** lacking maturity; childish.

jell (jel), *v.* **1.** become like jelly in consistency. **2.** become clear or definite.

jel′ly, *n., pl.* **-lies,** *v.,* **-lied, -lying.** —*n.* **1.** soft, semisolid food, as fruit juice boiled down with sugar. —*v.* **2.** make into, or provide with, jelly.

jel′ly•bean′, *n.* small, bean-shaped, chewy candy.

jel′ly•fish′, *n., pl.* **-fish, -fishes.** marine animal with soft, jellylike body.

jelly roll, thin cake spread with jelly and rolled up.

jen′ny, *n., pl.* **-nies. 1.** spinning machine. **2.** female donkey.

jeop′ard•ize′ (jep′-), *v.,* **-ized, -izing.** risk; endanger. —**jeop′ard•y,** *n.*

jer′e•mi′ad (jer′ə mī′əd, -ad), *n.* prolonged lament.

jerk, *n.* **1.** quick pull, etc. **2.** *Slang.* stupid person. —*v.* **3.** give jerk to. —**jerk′y,** *adj.*

jer′kin, *n.* close-fitting, usu. sleeveless jacket.

jerk′wa′ter, *adj.* insignificant and remote.

jer′ry-built′, *adj.* flimsily made.

jer′sey, *n.* type of shirt.

jest, *n., v.* joke. —**jest′er,** *n.*

Je′sus, *n.* founder of Christian religion. Also called **Jesus Christ.**

jet, *n., v.,* **jetted, jetting,** *adj.* —*n.* **1.** stream under pressure. **2.** Also, **jet plane.** plane operated by jet propulsion. —*v.* **3.** spout. —*adj.* **4.** deep black.

jet lag, fatigue after jet flight to different time zone.

jet′lin′er, *n.* jet plane carrying passengers.

jet propulsion, propulsion of plane, etc., by reactive thrust of jet. —**jet′ pro•pelled′,** *adj.*

jet′sam, *n.* goods thrown overboard to lighten ship.

jet′ti•son, *v.* cast (jetsam) out.

jet′ty, *n., pl.* **-ties.** wharf; pier.

Jew, *n.* **1.** follower of Judaism. **2.** descendant of Biblical Hebrews. —**Jew'ish,** *adj.*

jew'el, *n.* precious stone; gem. —**jew'el•er,** *n.* —**jew'el•ry,** *n.*

jib, *n.* triangular sail on forward mast.

jibe, *v.,* **jibed, jibing. 1.** gibe. **2.** *Informal.* be consistent.

jif'fy, *n., pl.* **-fies.** short time.

jig, *n., v.,* **jigged, jigging.** —*n.* **1.** lively folk dance. —*v.* **2.** dance a jig.

jig'ger, *n.* glass measure of 1½ oz. (45 ml) for liquors.

jig'gle, *v.,* **-gled, -gling,** *n.* —*v.* **1.** move back and forth, etc. —*n.* **2.** act of jiggling.

jig'saw', *n.* saw with narrow blade for cutting curves.

jigsaw puzzle, set of irregularly cut flat pieces that form a picture when fitted together.

jilt, *v.* reject (a previously encouraged suitor).

Jim Crow, *(sometimes l.c.)* discrimination against blacks. —**Jim'-Crow',** *adj.*

jim'my, *n., pl.* **-mies,** *v.,* **-mied, -mying.** —*n.* **1.** short crowbar.

—*v.* **2.** force open with or as if with a jimmy.

jim'son•weed', *n.* coarse weed with poisonous leaves.

jin'gle, *v.,* **-gled, -gling,** *n.* —*v.* **1.** make repeated clinking sound. —*n.* **2.** clink; tinkle. **3.** very simple verse.

jin'go•ism', *n.* chauvinism marked by aggressive foreign policy. —**jin'go•ist,** *n.* —**jin'go•is'tic,** *adj.*

jin•rik'i•sha (jin rik'shô), *n.* rickshaw. Also, **jin•rik'sha.**

jinx, *n.* **1.** cause of bad luck. —*v.* **2.** cause bad luck.

jit'ter•bug', *n.* jazz dance.

jit'ters, *n.pl. Informal.* nervousness. —**jit'ter•y,** *adj.*

jive (jīv), *n., v.,* **jived, jiving.** —*n.* **1.** swing music or early jazz. **2.** deceptive or meaningless talk. —*v.* **3.** *Slang.* fool or kid.

job, *n., v.,* **jobbed, jobbing.** —*n.* **1.** piece of work. **2.** employment. —*v.* **3.** sell wholesale. —**job'less,** *adj.*

job action, work slowdown by employees to win demands.

job'ber, *n.* **1.** wholesaler. **2.** dealer in odd lots of goods.

job lot, large assortment of goods sold as a single unit.

jock, *n. Informal.* **1.** athlete. **2.** enthusiast.

jock′ey, *n.* **1.** rider of race horses. —*v.* **2.** maneuver.

jo·cose′, *adj.* jesting. Also, **joc′und.** —**jo·cos′i·ty,** *n.*

joc′u·lar, *adj.* joking. —**joc′u·lar′i·ty,** *n.*

jodh′purs (jod′pərz), *n.pl.* riding breeches.

jog, *v.,* **jogged, jogging,** *n.* —*v.* **1.** nudge; shake. **2.** run at slow, steady pace. —*n.* **3.** nudge. **4.** steady pace. **5.** projection. —**jog′ger,** *n.*

joie de vi′vre (zhwʌd° vē′vʀ°), *n. French.* delight in being alive.

join, *v.* **1.** put together. **2.** become member of.

join′er, *n.* **1.** assembler of woodwork. **2.** *Informal.* person who likes to join clubs, etc. —**join′er·y,** *n.*

joint, *n.* **1.** place or part in which things join. **2.** movable section. **3.** cheap, sordid place. **4.** *Slang.* marijuana cigarette. —*adj.* **5.** shared or sharing. —*v.* **6.** join or divide at joint. —**joint′ly,** *adv.*

joist, *n.* floor beam.

joke, *n., v.,* **joked, joking.** —*n.* **1.** amusing remark, story, etc. —*v.* **2.** make or tell joke. **3.** speak only to amuse. —**jok′er,** *n.* —**jok′ing·ly,** *adv.*

jol′ly, *adj.,* **-lier, -liest,** *v.,* **-lied, -lying,** *adv.* —*adj.* **1.** gay; merry. —*v.* **2.** try to keep (someone) in good humor. —*adv.* **3.** *Brit. Informal.* very. —**jol′li·ness, jol′li·ty,** *n.*

jolt, *v., n.* jar; shake.

jon′quil, *n.* fragrant narcissus.

josh, *v. Informal.* tease.

jos′tle, *v.,* **-tled, -tling,** *n.* —*v.* **1.** push rudely. —*n.* **2.** rude push.

jot, *n., v.,* **jotted, jotting.** —*n.* **1.** bit. —*v.* **2.** write.

jounce, *v.,* **jounced, jouncing,** *n.* —*v.* **1.** move joltingly. —*n.* **2.** jouncing movement. —**jounc′y,** *adj.*

jour′nal, *n.* **1.** daily record. **2.** periodical. **3.** part of shaft in contact with bearing.

jour′nal·ese′ (-ēz′, -ēs′), *n.* writing style typical of newspapers and magazines.

jour′nal·ism′, *n.* newspaper writing. —**jour′nal·ist,** *n.* —**jour′nal·is′tic,** *adj.*

jour′ney, *n.* **1.** act or course of traveling. —*v.* **2.** travel.

jour′ney·man, *n., pl.* **-men.** hired skilled worker.

joust (joust), *n.* fight between mounted knights.

jo′vi·al, *adj.* vigorously cheerful. —**jo′vi·al′i·ty,** *n.*

jowl, *n.* jaw or cheek.

joy, *n.* gladness; delight. —**joy′ful, joy′ous,** *adj.*

joy′ride′, *n.* ride for pleasure, esp. recklessly.

joy′stick′, *n.* **1.** *Informal.* control stick of airplane. **2.** lever for controlling cursor.

JP, Justice of the Peace.

Jr. or **jr.,** junior.

ju′bi·lant, *adj.* rejoicing. —**ju′bi·la′tion,** *n.*

ju′bi·lee′, *n.* celebration, esp. of anniversary.

Ju′da·ism′, *n.* religion of the Jewish people.

judge, *n., v.,* **judged, judging.** —*n.* **1.** person who decides cases in court of law. **2.** person making authoritative decisions. **3.** discriminating person; connoisseur. —*v.* **4.** decide on. —**judg′er,** *n.*

judg′ment, *n.* **1.** decision, as in court of law. **2.** good sense.

judg·men′tal, *adj.* making judgments, esp. on morality.

ju·di′cial, *adj.* **1.** of justice or judges. **2.** thoughtful; wise. —**ju·di′cial·ly,** *adv.*

ju·di′ci·ar′y, *n., pl.* **-aries,** *adj.* —*n.* **1.** legal branch of government. —*adj.* **2.** of judges, etc.

ju·di′cious, *adj.* wise; prudent. —**ju·di′cious·ly,** *adv.* —**ju·di′cious·ness,** *n.*

ju′do, *n.* martial art.

jug, *n.* **1.** container for liquids. **2.** *Slang.* prison.

jug′ger·naut′ (jug′ər nôt′, -not′), *n.* any large, overpowering force.

jug′gle, *v.,* **-gled, -gling.** perform tricks tossing things. —**jug′gler,** *n.*

jug′u·lar, *adj.* **1.** of the neck. —*n.* **2.** large vein in neck.

juice, *n.* liquid part of plant, fruit, etc. —**juic′i·ly,** *adv.* —**juic′i·ness,** *n.* —**juic′y,** *adj.*

juic′er, *n.* **1.** appliance for squeezing fruit and vegetable juice. **2.** *Slang.* heavy drinker.

ju•jit′su, *n.* Japanese method of wrestling and self-defense.

ju′jube (jōō′joob, jōō′joo bē′), *n.* chewy fruity lozenge.

juke box, coin-operated music player.

Jul., July.

ju′li•enne′ (jōō′lē en′), *adj., v.* cut into thin strips.

Ju•ly′, *n.* seventh month of year.

jum′ble, *n., v.,* **-bled, -bling.** —*n.* **1.** confused mixture. —*v.* **2.** make jumble of.

jum′bo, *adj.* very large.

jump, *v.* **1.** spring up; leap. **2.** raise. —*n.* **3.** spring; leap. **4.** rise. **5.** *Informal.* advantage.

jump′er, *n.* **1.** one that jumps. **2.** sleeveless dress worn over blouse. **3.** electric cable for starting dead car battery.

jump′-start′, *n.* **1.** starting of car engine with jumpers (def. 3). —*v.* **2.** give a jump-start to. **3.** enliven or revive.

jump′suit′, *n.* **1.** one-piece suit worn by parachutist. **2.** garment fashioned after it.

jump′y, *adj.* **jumpier, jumpiest.** nervous. —**jump′i•ly,** *adv.* —**jump′i•ness,** *n.*

Jun., June.

jun′co (jung′kō), *n., pl.* **-cos.** small North American finch.

junc′tion, *n.* **1.** union. **2.** place of joining.

junc′ture, *n.* **1.** point of time. **2.** crisis. **3.** joint.

June, *n.* sixth month of year.

jun′gle, *n.* wildly overgrown tropical land.

jun′ior, *adj.* **1.** younger. **2.** lower. —*n.* **3.** third-year high school or college student.

junior college, two-year college.

junior high school, school for grades 7 through 9.

ju′ni•per, *n.* coniferous evergreen shrub or tree.

junk, *n.* **1.** useless material; rubbish. **2.** type of Chinese ship. **3.** narcotics, esp. heroin. —*v.* **4.** discard. —**junk′y,** *adj.*

junk′er, *n. Informal.* old vehicle ready to be scrapped.

jun′ket, *n.* **1.** custard. **2.** pleasure excursion. **3.** trip by government official at public expense. —*v.* **4.** entertain. —**jun′ke•teer′, jun′ket•er,** *n.*

junk food, high-calorie food of little nutritional value.

junk′ie, *n. Informal.* 1. drug addict. 2. person who craves something.

junk mail, commercial material mailed in bulk.

jun′ta (hŏŏn′tə), *n.* military group that seizes power.

Ju′pi•ter, *n.* largest of sun's planets.

ju′ris•dic′tion, *n.* range of control. —**ju′ris•dic′tion•al,** *adj.*

ju′ris•pru′dence, *n.* science of law.

ju′rist, *n.* expert in law.

ju′ror, *n.* member of jury. Also, **ju′ryman,** *fem.* **jur′y•wom′an.**

ju′ry, *n., pl.* **-ries.** group of persons selected to make decisions, esp. in law court.

just, *adj.* 1. fair; right. 2. legal. 3. true. —*adv.* 4. exactly. 5. barely. 6. only. —**just′ly,** *adv.*

jus′tice, *n.* 1. fairness; rightness. 2. administration of law. 3. high judge.

justice of the peace, local public officer who performs marriages, tries minor cases, etc.

jus′ti•fy′, *v.,* **-fied, -fying.** 1. show to be true, right, etc. 2. defend. —**jus′ti•fi•ca′tion,** *n.* —**jus′ti•fi′a•ble,** *adj.* —**jus′ti•fi′a•bly,** *adv.*

jut, *v.,* **jutted, jutting,** *n.* —*v.* 1. project. —*n.* 2. projection.

jute, *n.* plant whose fibers are used for fabrics, etc.

ju′ve•nile, *adj.* 1. young. —*n.* 2. young person. 3. youthful theatrical role. 4. book for children.

juvenile delinquency, illegal or antisocial behavior by a minor. —**juvenile delinquent.**

jux′ta•pose′, *v.* **-posed, -posing.** place close for comparison. —**jux′ta•po•si′tion,** *n.*

K, k, *n.* eleventh letter of English alphabet.

K, 1. karat. 2. Kelvin. 3. kilobyte. 4. kilometer. 5. thousand.

k., 1. karat. 2. kilogram.

ka·bu′ki (kə bōō′ kē, kä′bōō kē′), *n.* drama of Japan.

kai′ser (kī′-), *n.* German emperor.

kale, *n.* type of cabbage.

ka·lei′do·scope′ (-lī′-), *n.* optical device in which colored bits change patterns continually. —**ka·lei′do·scop′ic,** *adj.*

kan′ga·roo′, *n., pl.* **-roos, -roo.** marsupial with long hind legs used for leaping.

kangaroo court, self-appointed tribunal disregarding law.

Kans., Kansas.

ka′o·lin, *n.* fine white clay used to make porcelain.

ka′pok, *n.* silky down from seeds of certain trees.

ka·put′ (-pŏŏt′), *adj. Informal.* 1. extinct. 2. out of order.

ka′ra·o′ke (kar′ē ō′kē), *n.* act of singing along to music in which original vocals have been eliminated.

kar′at, *n.* 1/24 part: unit for measuring purity of gold.

ka·ra′te (kə rä′tē), *n.* Japanese technique of unarmed combat.

kar′ma, *n.* fate as the result of one's actions in successive incarnations. —**kar′mic,** *adj.*

Kas., Kansas.

ka′ty·did, *n.* large green grasshopper.

kay′ak (kī′ak), *n.* Eskimo canoe, esp. of skin.

ka·zoo′, *n.* tubular musical toy that vibrates and buzzes when one hums into it.

KB, kilobyte.

kc, kilocycle.

Ke·bab′ (kə bob′), *n.* cubes of marinated meat broiled on a skewer. Also, **ke·bob′.**

keel, *n.* 1. central framing member of ship's bottom. —*v.* 2. fall sideways.

keen, *adj.* 1. sharp. 2. excellent. 3. intense. 4. eager. —*v.* 5. lament. —**keen′ly,** *adv.* —**keen′ness,** *n.*

keep, *v.,* **kept, keeping,** *n.* —*v.* 1. continue. 2. detain. 3. support. 4. maintain. 5. withhold. 6. observe. 7. last. —*n.* 8. board and lodging. —**keep′er,** *n.*

keep′ing, *n.* 1. conformity. 2. care.

keep′sake′, *n.* souvenir.

keg, *n.* small barrel.

kelp, *n.* large brown seaweed.

Kel′vin, *adj.* of or noting an absolute scale of temperature in which 0° equals −273.16° Celsius.

ken, *n.* knowledge.

Ken., Kentucky.

ken′nel, *n.* 1. doghouse. 2. establishment where dogs are boarded and cared for.

ker′chief, *n.* scarf for head.

ker′nel, *n.* center part of nut.

ker′o•sene′, *n.* type of oil.

kes′trel, *n.* small falcon that hovers as it hunts.

ketch′up, *n.* catchup.

ket′tle, *n.* pot for boiling.

ket′tle•drum′, *n.* large drum with round copper bottom.

key, *n.* 1. part for operating lock. 2. explanation. 3. operating lever. 4. musicial tonality. 5. reef. —*adj.* 6. chief. —*v.* 7. intensify; excite.

key′board′, *n.* 1. row of keys on piano, computer, etc. —*v.* 2. insert (data) into computer. —**key′board′er,** *n.*

key′note′, *n.* 1. basic note of a musical piece; tonic. 2. theme of meeting, etc.

key′stone′, *n.* stone forming summit of arch.

kg, kilogram.

khak′i (kak′ē), *adj., n.* yellowish brown.

khan (kän), *n.* Asian ruler.

kHz, kilohertz.

KIA, killed in action.

kib•butz′ (-bŏŏts′), *n., pl.* **-but′zim.** Israeli collective community.

kib′itz•er, *n. Informal.* person offering unwanted advice. —**kib′itz,** *v.*

kick, *v.* 1. strike with foot. 2. recoil. 3. *Informal.* complain. —*n.* 4. act of kicking. 5. *Informal.* thrill. —**kick′er,** *n.*

kick′back′, *n.* portion of an income given to someone who made the income possible.

kick′off′, *n.* **1.** kick that begins play in football or soccer. **2.** beginning of anything.

kick′stand′, *n.* pivoting bar for holding cycle upright when not in use.

kid, *n., v.,* **kidded, kidding.** —*n.* **1.** young goat. **2.** leather from its skin. **3.** *Informal.* child. —*v.* **4.** *Informal.* fool; tease. —**kid′der**, *n.*

kid′nap, *v.,* **-napped** or **-naped, -napping** or **-naping.** abduct. —**kid′nap•per, kid′nap•er**, *n.*

kid′ney, *n.* **1.** gland that secretes urine. **2.** kind.

kidney bean, plant cultivated for its edible seeds.

kidney stone, abnormal stony mass formed in kidney.

kiel•ba′sa (kil bä′sə, kēl-), *n., pl.* **-sas, -sy** (-sē). smoked Polish sausage.

kill, *v.* **1.** end life of; murder. **2.** destroy; cancel. —*n.* **3.** animal slain. —**kill′er**, *n.*

killer whale, large, predatory, black-and-white dolphin.

kill′ing, *n.* **1.** act of one that kills. **2.** quick, large profit. —*adj.* **3.** fatal. **4.** exhausting.

kill′-joy′, *n.* person who spoils pleasure of others.

kiln (kil, kiln), *n.* large furnace for making bricks, etc.

ki′lo (kē′lō, kil′ō), *n., pl.* **-los. 1.** kilogram. **2.** kilometer.

kilo-, prefix meaning thousand, as *kilowatt.*

kil′o•byte, *n.* **1.** 1024 bytes. **2.** (loosely) 1000 bytes.

kil′o•cy′cle, *n.* kilohertz.

kil′o•gram′, *n.* 1000 grams. Also, **kilo.**

kil′o•hertz′, *n., pl.* **-hertz.** radio frequency of 1000 cycles per second. Also, *formerly,* **kil′o•cy′cle.**

kil′o•li′ter (-lē′-), *n.* 1000 liters.

ki•lom′e•ter, *n.* 1000 meters.

kil′o•watt′, *n.* 1000 watts.

kilt, *n.* man's skirt, worn in Scotland.

ki•mo′no (-nə), *n., pl.* **-nos.** loose dressing gown.

kin, *n.* relatives. Also, **kins′folk′.** —**kins′man**, *n.* —**kins′wom′an**, *n.fem.*

kind, *adj.* **1.** compassionate; friendly. —*n.* **2.** type; group. —**kind′ness**, *n.*

kin′der•gar′ten, *n.* school for very young children.

kind'heart'ed, *adj.* having or showing kindness.
—**kind'heart'ed•ly,** *adv.*
—**kind'heart'ed•ness,** *n.*

kin'dle, *v.,* **-dled, -dling. 1.** set afire. **2.** rouse.

kin'dling, *n.* material for starting fire.

kind'ly, *adj.,* **-lier, -liest,** *adv.* —*adj.* **1.** kind; gentle. —*adv.* **2.** in kind manner. **3.** cordially; favorably.
—**kind'li•ness,** *n.*

kin'dred, *adj.* **1.** related; similar. —*n.* **2.** relatives.

kin'e•scope', *n.* **1.** television tube. **2.** filmed recording of television show.

ki•net'ic, *adj.* of motion.

king, *n.* sovereign male ruler.
—**king'ly,** *adj.*

king'dom, *n.* government ruled by king or queen.

king'fish'er, *n.* colorful, fish-eating bird.

king'-size', *adj.* extra large.

kink, *n., v.* twist; curl. —**kink'y,** *adj.*

kin'ship, *n.* **1.** family relationship. **2.** affinity.

ki•osk (kē'osk), *n.* small open structure where newspapers, refreshments, etc., are sold.

kip'per, *n.* salted, dried fish.

kis'met (kiz'met), *n.* fate.

kiss, *v.* **1.** touch with lips in affection, etc. —*n.* **2.** act of kissing. **3.** type of candy.
—**kiss'a•ble,** *adj.*

kit, *n.* set of supplies.

kitch'en, *n.* room for cooking.
—**kitch'en•ware',** *n.*

kitch'en•ette', *n.* small, compact kitchen.

kite, *n.* **1.** light, paper-covered frame flown in wind on long string. **2.** type of falcon.

kith and kin, friends and relations.

kitsch (kich), *n.* something tawdry designed to appeal to undiscriminating persons.

kit'ten, *n.* young cat.

kit'ten•ish, *adj.* playfully coy.

kit'ty-cor'nered, *adj.* cater-cornered. Also, **kit'ty-cor'ner.**

ki'wi (kē' wē), *n.* **1.** flightless bird of New Zealand. **2.** egg-sized brown berry with edible green pulp.

KKK, Ku Klux Klan.

Klee′nex, *Trademark.* soft paper tissue.

klep′to•ma′ni•a, *n.* irresistible desire to steal. —**klep′to•ma′ni•ac′,** *n.*

klutz (kluts), *n. Slang.* clumsy person. —**klutz′y,** *adj.* —**klutz′i•ness,** *n.*

km, kilometer.

knack, *n.* special skill.

knack′wurst (näk′ wûrst, -wŏorst), *n.* spicy sausage.

knap′sack′, *n.* backpack.

knave, *n.* rogue. —**knav′er•y,** *n.* —**knav′ish,** *adj.*

knead (nēd), *v.* mix (dough).

knee, *n.* middle joint of leg.

knee′cap′, *n.* flat bone at front of knee.

knee′-jerk′, *adj. Informal.* reacting in habitual way.

kneel, *v.,* **knelt** or **kneeled, kneeling.** be on one's knees.

knell, *n.* deep sound of bell.

knick′ers, *n.pl.* breeches.

knick′knack′, *n.* trinket.

knife, *n., pl.* **knives.** cutting blade in handle.

knight, *n.* **1.** chivalrous medieval soldier of noble birth. **2.** holder of honorary rank. **3.** piece in chess. —*v.* **4.** name man a knight. —**knight′hood,** *n.* —**knight′ly,** *adj., adv.*

knit, *v.,* **knitted** or **knit, knitting.** form netlike fabric. —**knit′ting,** *n.*

knob, *n.* rounded handle. —**knob′by,** *adj.*

knock, *v.* **1.** strike hard; pound. **2.** *Informal.* criticize. —*n.* **3.** hard blow, etc. **4.** *Informal.* criticism. —**knock′er,** *n.*

knock′-knee′, *n.* inward curvature of the legs at the knees. —**knock′-kneed′,** *adj.*

knock′out′, *n.* **1.** boxing blow that knocks opponent to the canvas. **2.** *Informal.* one that is extremely attractive.

knock′wurst, *n.* knackwurst.

knoll (nōl), *n.* small hill.

knot, *n., v.,* **knotted, knotting.** —*n.* **1.** intertwining of cords to bind. **2.** cluster. **3.** lump. **4.** hard mass where branch joins tree trunk. **5.** one nautical mile per hour. —*v.* **6.** tie or tangle. —**knot′ty,** *adj.*

knout, *n.* whip.

know, *v.,* **knew, known, knowing,** *n.* —*v.* **1.**

understand, remember, or experience. —*n.* **2.** *Informal.* state of knowledge, esp. of secrets. —**know′a•ble,** *adj.*

know′-how′, *n. Informal.* skill.

know′ing, *adj.* **1.** having knowledge. **2.** shrewd. **3.** deliberate. —**know′ing•ly,** *adv.*

knowl′edge, *n.* facts known.

know′ledge•a•ble, *adj.* well-informed.

knuck′le, *n.* **1.** joint of a finger. —*v.* **2. knuckle down,** apply oneself earnestly. **3. knuckle under,** submit; yield.

knuck′le•head′, *n. Informal.* stupid, inept person.

KO, knockout.

ko•al′a (kō ö′lə), *n.* gray, tree-dwelling marsupial.

kohl′ra′bi (kōl′rä′bē), *n., pl.* **-bies.** variety of cabbage.

koi (koi), *n., pl.* **kois, koi.** colorful carp.

ko′la (kō′lə), *n.* tropical African tree grown for its nuts.

kook (kook), *n. Slang.* eccentric. —**kook′y,** *adj.*

Ko•ran′, *n.* sacred scripture of Islam.

Ko•re′an (kə rē′ən), *n.* native or language of Korea. —**Ko•re′an,** *adj.*

ko′sher, *adj.* (among Jews) permissible to eat.

kow′tow′, *v.* act obsequiously.

kryp′ton, *n.* inert gas, an element found in very small amounts in the atmosphere.

KS, Kansas.

ku′dos (-dōs, -dōz), *n.* praise.

kud′zu (kood′zoo), *n.* fast-growing vine planted for fodder and to retain soil.

kum′quat, *n.* small citrus fruit.

kung′ fu′, Chinese technique of unarmed combat.

KW or **kw,** kilowatt.

KY, Kentucky. Also, **ky.**

L, l, *n.* twelfth letter of English alphabet.

L., 1. lake. 2. large. 3. Latin. 4. left. 5. length. 6. *Brit.* pound. 7. long.

l., 1. left. 2. length. 3. *pl.* **ll.** line. 4. liter.

LA, Louisiana. Also, **La.**

lab, *n.* laboratory.

la′bel, *n., v.,* **-beled, -beling.** —*n.* 1. information tag. —*v.* 2. put label on.

la′bi•um, *n., pl.* **-bia.** folds of skin bordering the vulva. —**la′bi•al,** *adj.*

la′bor, *n.* 1. bodily toil; work. 2. childbirth. 3. workers as a group. —*v.* 4. work. Also, *Brit.,* **la′bour.** —**la′bor•er,** *n.*

la′bored, *adj.* done with difficulty.

lab′o•ra•to′ry, *n., pl.* **-ries.** place for scientific work.

la•bo′ri•ous, *adj.* involving much labor.

labor union, organization of workers for mutual aid.

la•bur′num, *n.* poisonous tree with drooping yellow flowers.

lab′y•rinth (lab′ə-), *n.* 1. maze. 2. internal ear. —**lab′y•rin′thine** (-rin′ thin, -thīn), *adj.*

lac, *n.* resinous secretion of Asian insect.

lace, *n., v.,* **laced, lacing.** —*n.* 1. fancy network of threads. 2. cord. —*v.* 3. fasten with lace. —**lac′y,** *adj.*

lac′er•ate′ (las′ə-), *v.,* **-ated, -ating.** tear; wound. —**lac′er•a′tion,** *n.*

lach′ry•mal (lak′rə məl), *adj.* of or producing tears.

lach′ry•mose′, *adj.* tearful.

lack, *n.* 1. deficiency. —*v.* 2. be wanting.

lack′a•dai′si•cal, *adj.* listless.

lack′ey, *n.* servile follower.

lack′lus′ter, *adj.* dull.

la•con′ic (lə kon′ik), *adj.* using few words. —**la•con′i•cal•ly,** *adv.*

lac′quer, *n.* 1. kind of varnish. —*v.* 2. coat with lacquer.

la•crosse′ (lə krôs′), *n.* game played with long rackets.

lac′tate, *v.,* **-tated, -tating.** secrete milk. —**lac•ta′tion,** *n.*

lac′tic, *adj.* of or from milk.

lac′tose (-tōs), *n.* sweet crystalline substance in milk.

la·cu′na (lə kyōō′nə), *n., pl.* **-nae** (-nē), **-nas.** 1. cavity. 2. gap.

lad, *n.* boy.

lad′der, *n.* structure of two sidepieces with steps between.

lad′en, *adj.* loaded heavily.

lad′ing, *n.* cargo; freight.

la′dle, *n., v.,* **-dled, -dling.** —*n.* 1. large deep-bowled spoon. —*v.* 2. dip with ladle.

la′dy, *n., pl.* **-dies.** 1. refined woman. 2. mistress of household. 3. title of noblewoman.

la′dy·bug′, *n.* small spotted beetle. Also, **la′dy·bird′.**

la′dy·fin′ger, *n.* small cake.

la′dy's-slip′per, *n.* orchid with slipper-shaped flower lips. Also, **la′dy-slip′per.**

lag, *v.,* **lagged, lagging,** *n.* —*v.* 1. move slowly or belatedly. —*n.* 2. instance of lagging.

la′ger (lä′gər), *n.* kind of beer.

lag′gard, *adj.* 1. lagging. —*n.* 2. person who lags.

la·gniappe′ (lan yap′, lan′yap), *n.* 1. small gift given with a purchase. 2. gratuity. Also, **la·gnappe′.**

la·goon′, *n.* shallow pond connected with a body of water.

laid′-back′, *adj. Informal.* relaxed; easygoing.

lair, *n.* den of beast.

lais′sez-faire′ (les′ā fer′), *adj.* without interfering.

la′i·ty, *n.* laypersons.

lake, *n.* large body of water enclosed by land.

La·ko′ta, *n., pl.* **-tas** or **-ta.** Member of a Plains Indian people.

lam, *n., v.,* **lammed, lamming.** *Slang.* —*n.* 1. hasty escape. —*v.* 2. escape; flee. —3. **on the lam,** fleeing from the police.

la′ma, *n.* Tibetan or Mongolian Buddhist priest.

La·maze′ method (lə mäz′), method by which expectant mother is prepared for birth.

lamb, *n.* young sheep.

lam·baste′ (lam bāst′, -bast′), *v.,* **-basted, -basting.** *Informal.* 1. beat severely. 2. reprimand.

lam′bent, *adj.* glowing lightly. —**lam′ben•cy,** *n.*

lame, *adj.,* lamer, lamest, *v.,* lamed, laming. —*adj.* **1.** crippled. **2.** inadequate. —*v.* **3.** make lame.

la•mé′ (la mā′, lä-), *n.* fabric with metallic threads.

lame duck, elected official completing term after election of successor.

la•ment′, *v.* **1.** mourn; regret. —*n.* **2.** Also, **lam′en•ta′tion.** expression of lament. —**lam′en•ta•ble,** *adj.*

lam′i•na, *n., pl.* **-nae** (-nē), **-nas.** thin layer.

lam′i•nate′, *v.,* -nated, -nating, *adj.* —*v.* **1.** split into thin layers. **2.** cover or form with layers. —*adj.* **3.** Also, **lam′i•nat′ed.** made of layers. —**lam′i•na′tion,** *n.*

lamp, *n.* light source. —**lamp′shade′,** *n.* —**lamp′post′,** *n.*

lamp′black′, *n.* pigment from soot.

lam•poon′, *n.* **1.** vicious satire. —*v.* **2.** satirize.

lam′prey, *n.* eellike fish.

lance, *n., v.,* lanced, lancing. —*n.* **1.** long spear. —*v.* **2.** open with lancet.

lan′cet, *n.* sharp surgical tool.

land, *n.* **1.** part of the earth's surface above water. **2.** region. —*v.* **3.** bring or come to land. **4.** fall to earth or floor.

lan′dau (-dô), *n.* carriage with folding top.

land′ed, *adj.* **1.** owning land. **2.** consisting of land.

land′fall′, *n.* **1.** approach to land. **2.** land reached.

land′fill′, *n.* **1.** area of land built up from refuse material. **2.** material deposited on landfill.

land′ing, *n.* **1.** act of one that lands. **2.** place for landing persons and goods. **3.** platform between stairs.

land′locked′, *adj.* **1.** shut in completely or almost completely by land. **2.** having no access to sea. **3.** living in waters shut off from sea.

land′lord′, *n.* person who owns and leases property. —**land′la′dy,** *n.fem.*

land′lub′ber, *n.* person unused to sea.

land′mark′, *n.* **1.** prominent object serving as a guide. **2.** anything prominent.

land′mass′, *n.* large area of land, as a continent.

land′scape′, *n., v.,* **-scaped, -scaping.** —*n.* **1.** broad view of rural area. —*v.* **2.** arrange trees, shrubs, etc., for effects. —**land′scap′er**, *n.*

land′slide′, *n.* fall of earth.

lane, *n.* narrow road.

lan′guage, *n.* **1.** speech. **2.** any means of communication.

lan′guid, *adj.* without vigor.

lan′guish, *v.* **1.** become weak. **2.** pine. —**lan′guish•ing,** *adj.* —**lan′guor,** *n.* —**lan′guor•ous,** *adj.*

lank, *adj.* lean. Also, **lank′y.**

lan′o•lin, *n.* fat from wool.

lan′tern, *n.* case for enclosing light.

lantern jaw, long, thin jaw. —**lan′tern-jawed′,** *adj.*

lan′yard (lan′yərd), *n.* short rope.

lap, *v.,* **lapped, lapping,** *n.* —*v.* **1.** lay or lie partly over. **2.** wash against. **3.** take up with tongue. —*n.* **4.** overlapping part. **5.** one circuit of racecourse. **6.** part of body of sitting person from waist to knees.

la•pel′, *n.* folded-back part on front of a garment.

lap′i•dar′y, *n., pl.* **-daries,** *adj.* —*n.* **1.** worker in gems. —*adj.* **2.** meticulous in detail.

lap′in, *n.* rabbit.

lap′is laz′u•li (lap′is laz′ŏŏ lē, -lī′, laz′yŏŏ-), **1.** deep blue gem. **2.** sky-blue color; azure.

lapse, *n., v.,* **lapsed, lapsing.** —*n.* **1.** slight error; negligence. **2.** slow passing. —*v.* **3.** pass slowly. **4.** make error. **5.** slip downward. **6.** become void.

lap′top′, *n.* portable computer that fits on lap.

lar′ce•ny, *n., pl.* **-nies.** theft. —**lar′ce•nist,** *n.* —**lar′ce•nous,** *adj.*

larch, *n.* tree of pine family.

lard, *n.* **1.** rendered fat of hogs. —*v.* **2.** apply lard to.

lard′er, *n.* pantry.

large, *adj.,* **larger, largest. 1.** great in size or number. **2. at large, a.** at liberty. **b.** in general. —**large′ness,** *n.*

large′ly, *adv.* 1. in large way. 2. generally.

large′-scale′, *adj.* extensive.

lar•gess′, *n.* generous gifts. Also, **lar•gesse′.**

lar′go, *adj., adv. Music.* slowly.

lar′i•at, *n.* long, noosed rope.

lark, *n.* 1. songbird. 2. frolic.

lark′spur, *n.* plant with flowers on tall stalks.

lar′va, *n., pl.* **-vae** (-vē). young of insect between egg and pupal stages. —**lar′val,** *adj.*

lar•yn•gi′tis (-jī′-), *n.* inflammation of larynx.

lar′ynx, *n., pl.* **-ynges, -ynxes.** cavity at upper end of windpipe. —**la•ryn′ge•al,** *adj.*

la•sa′gna (lə zän′yə, lä-), *n.* baked dish of wide strips of pasta layered with cheese, tomato sauce, and usu. meat. Also, **la•sa′gne.**

las•civ′i•ous (lə siv′-), *adj.* lewd; wanton. —**las•civ′i•ous•ness,** *n.*

la′ser, *n.* device for amplifying radiation of frequencies of visible light.

lash, *n.* 1. flexible part of whip. 2. blow with whip. 3. eyelash. —*v.* 4. strike with or as with lash. 5. bind.

lass, *n.* girl.

las′si•tude′, *n.* 1. listlessness. 2. indifference.

las′so, *n., pl.* **-sos, soes,** *v.,* **-soed, -soing.** —*n.* 1. lariat. —*v.* 2. catch with lasso.

last, *adj.* 1. latest. 2. final. —*adv.* 3. most recently. 4. finally. —*n.* 5. that which is last. 6. foot-shaped form on which shoes are made. —*v.* 7. endure. —**last′ly,** *adv.*

last′ing, *adj.* going on or enduring a long time. —**last′ing•ly,** *adv.*

lat., latitude.

latch, *n.* 1. device for fastening. —*v.* 2. fasten with latch.

late, *adj., adv.,* **later, latest.** 1. after proper time. 2. being or lasting well along in time. 3. recent. 4. deceased.

late′ly, *adv.* recently.

la′tent, *adj.* hidden; dormant. —**la′ten•cy,** *n.*

lat′er•al, *adj.* on or from the side. —**lat′er•al•ly,** *adv.*

la′tex, *n.* milky plant juice yielding rubber.

lath (lath), *n.* **1.** wood strip. **2.** material for holding plaster. —*v.* **3.** cover with laths.

lathe (lāth), *n.* machine for turning wood, etc., against a shaping tool.

lath'er, *n.* **1.** froth made with soap and water. **2.** froth from sweating. —*v.* **3.** form or cover with lather.

Lat'in, *n.* **1.** language of ancient Rome. **2.** member of any people speaking Latin-based language. —**Latin**, *adj.*

Latin America, countries in South and Central America where Spanish or Portuguese is spoken. —**Lat'in-A•mer'i•can**, *adj., n.*

La•ti'no (lə tē'nō, la-), *n.* Hispanic.

lat'i•tude', *n.* **1.** distance from equator. **2.** freedom.

la•trine' (-trēn'), *n.* toilet.

lat'ter, *n.* **1.** being second of two. **2.** later.

lat'tice, *n.* structure of crossed strips. —**lat'tice•work'**, *n.*

laud, *v.* praise. —**laud'a•ble**, *adj.* —**laud'a•to'ry**, *adj.*

lau'da•num (lô'də nəm), *n.* tincture of opium.

laugh, *v.* **1.** express mirth audibly. —*n.* **2.** act or sound of laughing. —**laugh'ing•ly**, *adv.* —**laugh'ter**, *n.*

laugh'a•ble, *adj.* ridiculous.

laugh'ing•stock', *n.* object of ridicule.

launch, *v.* **1.** set afloat. **2.** start. **3.** throw. —*n.* **4.** large open motorboat. —**launch'er**, *n.*

launch pad, platform for launching rockets. Also, **launch'ing pad**.

laun'der, *v.* wash and iron. —**laun'der•er**, *n.* —**laun'dress**, *n.fem.*

Laun'dro•mat', *n. Trademark.* self-service laundry with coin-operated machines.

laun'dry, *n., pl.* **-dries. 1.** clothes to be washed. **2.** place where clothes are laundered.

lau're•ate (lôr'ē it, lor'-), *n.* person who has been honored in a particular field.

lau'rel, *n.* **1.** small glossy evergreen tree. **2.** (*pl.*) honors.

la'va, *n.* molten rock from volcano.

lav'a•to'ry, *n., pl.* **-ries. 1.** bathroom. **2.** washbowl.

lave, *v.,* **laved, laving.** bathe.

lav′en•der, *n.* **1.** pale purple. **2.** fragrant shrub yielding **oil of lavender.**

lav′ish, *adj.* **1.** extravagant. —*v.* **2.** expend or give abundantly. —**lav′ish•ly,** *adv.*

law, *n.* **1.** rules established by government under which people live. **2.** rule. **3.** legal action. —**law′-a•bid′ing,** *adj.* —**law′break′er,** *n.* —**law′break′ing,** *n., adj.* —**law′less,** *adj.* —**law′mak′er,** *n.*

law′ful, *adj.* permitted by law. —**law′ful•ly,** *adv.*

lawn, *n.* **1.** grass-covered land kept mowed. **2.** thin cotton or linen fabric.

law′suit′, *n.* prosecution of claim in court.

law′yer, *n.* person trained in law.

lax, *adj.* **1.** careless. **2.** slack. —**lax′i•ty,** *n.*

lax′a•tive, *adj.* **1.** purgative. —*n.* **2.** laxative agent.

lay, *v.,* **laid, laying,** *n., adj.* —*v.* **1.** put down. **2.** produce eggs. **3.** ascribe. **4.** devise. **5.** pt. of **lie.** —*n.* **6.** position. **7.** song. —*adj.* **8.** not clerical or professional. —**lay′man, lay′per•son,** *n.* —**lay′wom•an,** *n.fem.*

lay′a•way plan, method of purchasing in which store reserves item until customer has completed a series of payments.

lay′er, *n.* one thickness.

lay•ette′, *n.* outfit for newborn child.

lay′off′, *n.* temporary dismissal of employees.

lay′out′, *n.* arrangement.

lay′o•ver, *n.* stopover.

laze, *v.,* **lazed, lazing.** pass (time) lazily.

la′zy, *adj.,* **-zier, -ziest. 1.** unwilling to work. **2.** slow-moving. —**la′zi•ly,** *adv.* —**la′zi•ness,** *n.*

lb., *pl.* **lbs., lb.** pound.

l.c., lowercase.

lea, *n.* meadow.

leach, *v.* **1.** soak through or in. **2.** dissolve from a material by soaking it.

lead (lēd *for 1–4;* led *for 5–7*), *v.,* **led, leading,** *n.* —*v.* **1.** guide by going before or with. **2.** influence. **3.** afford passage.

—*n.* **4.** foremost place. **5.** malleable metal. **6.** plummet. **7.** graphite used in pencils. —**lead′en**, *adj.* —**lead′er**, *n.* —**lead′er•ship′**, *n.*

leading question, question worded to suggest the desired answer.

lead poisoning, toxic condition produced by contact with lead or lead compounds.

lead time (lēd), time between beginning of a process and appearance of results.

leaf, *n., pl.* **leaves,** *v.* —*n.* **1.** flat green part on stem of plant. **2.** thin sheet. —*v.* **3.** thumb through. —**leaf′y**, *adj.*

leaf′let, *n.* **1.** pamphlet. **2.** small leaf.

league, *n., v.,* **leagued, leaguing.** —*n.* **1.** alliance; pact. **2.** unit of distance, about three miles. —*v.* **3.** unite in league.

leak, *n.* **1.** unintended hole. —*v.* **2.** pass or let pass through leak. **3.** allow to be known unofficially. —**leak′age**, *n.* —**leak′y**, *adj.*

lean, *v.,* **leaned** or **leant, leaning,** *n., adj.* —*v.* **1.** bend.

2. depend. —*n.* **3.** inclination. **4.** lean flesh. —*adj.* **5.** not fat. —**lean′ness**, *n.*

lean′ing, *n.* inclination.

lean′-to′, *n., pl.* **-tos.** structure with single-sloped roof abutting a wall.

leap, *v.,* **leaped** or **leapt, leaping,** *n.* —*v.* **1.** spring through air. —*n.* **2.** jump.

leap′frog′, *n., v.,* **-frogged, -frogging.** —*n.* **1.** game in which players leap over each other's backs. —*v.* **2.** jump over as in leapfrog.

leap year, year of 366 days.

learn, *v.* acquire knowledge or skill. —**learn′er**, *n.* —**learn′ing**, *n.*

learn′ed, *adj.* knowing much.

learning disability, difficulty in reading, writing, etc., associated with impairment of central nervous system. —**learn′ing-dis•a′bled**, *adj.*

lease, *n., v.,* **leased, leasing.** —*n.* **1.** contract conveying property for certain time. —*v.* **2.** get by means of lease.

leash, *n.* line for holding dog.

least, *adj.* **1.** smallest. —*n.* **2.** least amount, etc. —*adv.* **3.** to least extent, etc.

leath′er, *n.* prepared skin of animals. —**leath′er•y,** *adj.*

leath′er•neck′, *n. Informal.* U. S. marine.

leave, *v.,* **left, leaving,** *n.* —*v.* **1.** depart from. **2.** let remain or be. **3.** have remaining. **4.** bequeath. —*n.* **5.** permission. **6.** farewell. **7.** furlough.

leav′en (lev′-), *n.* **1.** Also, **leav′en•ing.** fermenting agency to raise dough. —*v.* **2.** produce fermentation.

lech′er•ous (lech′ər əs), *adj.* lustful. —**lech′er•y,** *n.* —**lech′er,** *n.*

lec′i•thin (les′ ə thin), *n.* fatty substances in nerve tissue and egg yolk.

lec′tern, *n.* stand for speaker's papers.

lec′ture, *n., v.,* **-tured, -turing.** —*n.* **1.** instructive speech. —*v.* **2.** give lecture; moralize. —**lec′tur•er,** *n.*

ledge, *n.* narrow shelf.

ledg′er, *n.* account book.

lee, *n.* **1.** shelter. **2.** side away from the wind. **3.** (*pl.*) dregs. —**lee,** *adj.* —**lee′ward,** *adj., adv., n.*

leech, *n.* bloodsucking worm.

leek, *n.* plant resembling onion.

leer, *n.* **1.** sly or insinuating glance. —*v.* **2.** look with leer.

leer′y, *adj.,* **leerier, leeriest.** wary; suspicious. —**leer′i•ness,** *n.*

lee′way′, *n.* **1.** *Naut.* drift due to wind. **2.** extra space.

left, *adj.* **1.** on side toward west when facing north. **2.** still present; remaining. —*n.* **3.** left side. **4.** political side favoring liberal or radical reform. —**left′-hand′,** *adj.* —**left′-hand′ed,** *adj.* —**left′ist,** *n., adj.*

leg, *n.* **1.** one of limbs supporting a body. **2.** any leglike part.

leg′a•cy, *n., pl.* **-cies.** anything bequeathed.

le′gal, *adj.* of or according to law. —**le•gal′i•ty,** *n.* —**le′gal•ize′,** *v.*

le′gal•ese′ (-gə lēz′, -lēs′), *n.* excessive legal jargon.

leg′a•tee′, *n.* person bequeathed legacy.

le•ga′tion, *n.* **1.** diplomatic minister and staff. **2.** official residence of minister.

le·ga'to (lə gä'to), *adj., adv. Music.* smooth and connected; without breaks.

leg'end, *n.* 1. story handed down by tradition. 2. key. —**leg'end·ar'y,** *adj.*

leg'er·de·main' (lej'ər də mān'), *n.* sleight of hand.

leg'ging, *n.* covering for leg.

leg'i·ble, *adj.* easily read. —**leg'i·bil'i·ty,** *n.* —**leg'i·bly,** *adv.*

le'gion, *n.* 1. military unit. 2. multitude. —*adj.* 3. great in number. —**le'gion·naire',** *n.*

leg'is·late', *v.,* -lated, -lating. 1. make laws. 2. effect by law. —**leg'is·la'tion,** *n.* —**leg'is·la'tive,** *adj.* —**leg'is·la'tor,** *n.*

leg'is·la'ture, *n.* law-making body.

le·git'i·mate, *adj.* 1. lawful. 2. after right or established principles. 3. born to a married couple. —**le·git'i·ma·cy,** *n.*

le·git'i·mize', *v.,* -mized, -mizing. show to be legitimate.

leg'ume (leg'yoom), *n.* plant of group including peas and beans. —**le·gu'mi·nous,** *adj.*

lei (lā), *n.* flower wreath for neck.

lei'sure (lē'zhər), *n.* 1. freedom from work. —*adj.* 2. unoccupied; at rest.

lei'sure·ly, *adj.* unhurried.

leit'mo·tif' (līt'mō tēf'), *n.* 1. recurring musical phrase in an opera. 2. dominant theme or underlying pattern.

lem'ming, *n.* rodent noted for mass migrations.

lem'on, *n.* 1. yellowish fruit of citrus tree. 2. *Informal.* person or thing that is defective or unsatisfactory.

lem'on·ade', *n.* beverage of lemon juice and water.

le'mur (lē'mər), *n.* small monkeylike animal.

lend, *v.,* **lent, lending.** 1. give temporary use of. 2. give; provide. —**lend'er,** *n.*

length, *n.* size or extent from end to end. —**length'en,** *v.* —**length'wise',** *adv., adj.* —**length'y,** *adj.*

le'ni·ent, *adj.* merciful; not severe. —**le'ni·ence, le'ni·en·cy,** *n.*

lens, *n., pl.* **lenses.** glass for manipulating light rays.

Lent, *n.* season of fasting before Easter. —**Lent'en,** *adj.*

len'til, *n.* pealike plant.

le'o•nine' (lē'ə nīn'), *adj.* of or like the lion.

leop'ard, *n.* large spotted cat.

le'o•tard' (lē'ə tärd'), *n.* tight, flexible, one-piece garment.

lep'er (lep'ər), *n.* person afflicted with leprosy.

lep're•chaun', *n.* Irish sprite.

lep'ro•sy, *n.* disease marked by skin ulcerations.

les'bi•an (lez'-), *n.* **1.** female homosexual. —*adj.* **2.** pertaining to female homosexuals.

lese majesty or **lèse maj'es•té** (lēz' maj'əs tē), *n.* **1.** offense against the dignity of a ruler. **2.** attack on a revered custom.

le'sion (lē'zhən), *n.* **1.** injury. **2.** morbid change in bodily part.

less, *adv.* **1.** to smaller extent. —*adj.* Also, **les'ser. 2.** smaller. **3.** lower in importance. —*n.* **4.** Also, **lesser.** smaller amount, etc. —*prep.* **5.** minus. —**less'en,** *v.*

-less, suffix indicating: **1.** without, as *childless.* **2.** not able to, as *sleepless.* **3.** not able to be, as *useless.*

les•see', *n.* recipient of lease.

les'ser, *adj.* **1.** compar. of **little. 2.** minor.

les'son, *n.* **1.** something to be studied. **2.** reproof. **3.** useful experience.

les'sor, *n.* granter of lease.

lest, *conj.* for fear that.

let, *v.,* **let, letting,** *n.* —*v.* **1.** permit. **2.** rent out. **3.** contract for work. —*n.* **4.** hindrance.

-let, suffix indicating: **1.** small, as *booklet.* **2.** article worn on, as *anklet.*

let'down', *n.* **1.** disappointment. **2.** decrease in volume, force, energy, etc.

le'thal, *adj.* deadly.

leth'ar•gy, *n., pl.* **-gies.** drowsy dullness. —**le•thar'gic,** *adj.* —**le•thar'gi•cal•ly,** *adv.*

let'ter, *n.* **1.** written communication. **2.** written component of word. **3.** actual wording. **4.** (*pl.*) literature. —*v.* **5.** write with letters.

let'tered, *adj.* literate; learned.

let'ter·head', *n.* 1. printed information on stationery. 2. paper with a letterhead.

let'ter-per'fect, *adj.* perfect.

let'tuce, *n.* plant with large leaves used in salad.

let'up', *n.* pause; relief.

leu·ke'mi·a, *n.* cancerous disease of blood cells.

leu'ko·cyte, *n.* white blood cell.

lev'ee, *n.* 1. embankment to prevent floods. 2. (Also, le vē'). reception.

lev'el, *adj., n., v.,* -eled, -eling. —*adj.* 1. even. 2. horizontal. 3. well-balanced. —*n.* 4. height; elevation. 5. level position. 6. device for determining horizontal plane. —*v.* 7. make or become level. 8. aim. —**lev'el·er**, *n.*

lev'el·head'ed, *adj.* sensible. —**lev'el·head'ed·ness**, *n.*

lev'er, *n.* bar moving on fixed support to exert force.

lev'er·age, *n.* power of lever.

le·vi'a·than (-vī'-), *n.* 1. Biblical sea monster. 2. something of great power.

Le'vi's (lē'vīz), *n. (used with a pl. v.) Trademark.* brand of jeans, esp. blue jeans.

lev'i·tate', *v.,* -tated, -tating. rise or cause to rise into the air, esp. in apparent defiance of gravity. —**lev'i·ta'tion**, *n.*

lev'i·ty, *n.* lack of seriousness.

lev'y, *v.,* levied, levying, *n., pl.* levies. —*v.* 1. raise or collect by authority. 2. make (war). —*n.* 3. act of levying. 4. something levied.

lewd, *adj.* obscene. —**lewd'ly**, *adv.* —**lewd'ness**, *n.*

lex'i·cog'ra·phy, *n.* writing of dictionaries. —**lex'i·cog'ra·pher**, *n.*

lex'i·con, *n.* dictionary.

lg., 1. large. 2. long.

li'a·bil'i·ty, *n., pl.* -ties. 1. debt. 2. disadvantage. 3. state of being liable.

li'a·ble, *adj.* 1. likely. 2. subject to penalty.

li'ai·son' (lē'ə zon'), *n.* 1. contact to ensure cooperation. 2. intimacy.

li'ar, *n.* person who tells lies.

li·ba'tion (lī bā'shən), *n.* 1. pouring out of wine or oil to honor a deity. **2.** the liquid poured. **3.** alcoholic drink.

li′bel, *n., v.,* **-beled, -beling.** —*n.* **1.** defamation in writing or print. —*v.* **2.** publish libel against. —**li′bel•ous,** *adj.*

lib′er•al, *adj.* **1.** favoring extensive individual liberty. **2.** tolerant. **3.** generous. —*n.* **4.** liberal person.
—**lib′er•al•ism,** *n.*
—**lib′er•al′i•ty,** *n.*
—**lib′er•al•ize′,** *v.*

liberal arts, college courses comprising the arts, humanities, and natural and social sciences.

lib′er•ate′, *v.,* **-ated, -ating.** set free. —**lib′er•a′tion,** *n.* —**lib′er•a′tor,** *n.*

lib′er•tar′i•an, *n.* person who advocates liberty.

lib′er•tine′ (-tēn′), *n.* dissolute person.

lib′er•ty, *n., pl.* **-ties. 1.** freedom; independence. **2.** right to use place. **3.** impertinent freedom.

li•bi′do (-bē-), *n., pl.* **-dos. 1.** sexual desire. **2.** instinctual energies and drives derived from the id. —**li•bid′i•nal,** *adj.* —**li•bid′i•nous,** *adj.*

li′brar′y, *n., pl.* **-ries. 1.** place for collection of books, etc. **2.** collection of books, etc.
—**li•brar′i•an,** *n.*

li•bret′to (li-), *n., pl.* **-tos, -ti.** words of musical drama.
—**li•bret′tist,** *n.*

li′cense, *n., v.,* **-censed, -censing.** —*n.* **1.** formal permission. **2.** undue freedom. —*v.* **3.** grant license to. Also, **li′cence.**

li′cen•see′, *n.* person to whom a license is granted.

li•cen′tious, *adj.* lewd.
—**li•cen′tious•ly,** *adv.*

li′chen (lī′kən), *n.* crustlike plant on rocks, trees, etc.

lic′it (lis′it), *adj.* lawful.

lick, *v.* **1.** pass tongue over. **2.** *Informal.* beat or defeat. —*n.* **3.** act of licking. **4.** place where animals lick salt.

lick′e•ty-split′, *adv. Informal.* at great speed.

lick′ing, *n. Informal.* **1.** beating or thrashing. **2.** setback.

lic′o•rice, *n.* plant root used in candy, etc.

lid, *n.* **1.** movable cover. **2.** eyelid. —**lid′ded,** *adj.*

lie, *n., v.,* **lied, lying.** —*n.* **1.** deliberately false statement. —*v.* **2.** tell lie.

lie, *v.,* **lay, lain, lying,** *n.* —*v.* **1.** assume or have reclining position. **2.** be or remain. —*n.* **3.** manner of lying.

lie detector, polygraph.

lief, *adv.* gladly.

liege (lēj), *n.* **1.** lord. **2.** vassal.

lien (lēn), *n.* right in another's property as payment on claim.

lieu (lo͞o), *n.* stead.

lieu•ten′ant, *n.* **1.** commissioned officer in army or navy. **2.** aide. —**lieu•ten′an•cy,** *n.*

life, *n., pl.* **lives. 1.** distinguishing quality of animals and plants. **2.** period of being alive. **3.** living things. **4.** mode of existence. **5.** animation. —**life′long′,** *adj.* —**life′time′,** *n.* —**life′less,** *adj.*

life′blood′ *n.* **1.** blood. **2.** vital element.

life′boat′, *n.* boat carried on ship to save passengers in the event of sinking.

life′-care′, *adj.* providing the basic needs of elderly residents. Also, **life′care′.**

life′guard′, *n.* person employed to protect swimmers, as at a beach.

life preserver, buoyant device to keep a person afloat.

lif′er, *n.* person serving a term of imprisonment for life.

life′sav′er, *n.* person or thing that saves from death or a difficult situation. —**life′sav′ing,** *adj., n.*

life′-size′, *adj.* of the actual size of a person, etc.

life′style′, person's general pattern of living. Also, **life′-style′.**

life′-sup•port′, *adj.* of equipment or techniques that sustain or substitute for essential body functions.

life′work′, *n.* complete or principal work of a lifetime.

lift, *v.* **1.** move or hold upward. **2.** raise or rise. —*n.* **3.** act of lifting. **4.** help. **5.** ride. **6.** exaltation. **7.** *Brit.* elevator.

lift′-off′, *n.* departure from ground by rocket, etc.

lig′a•ment, *n.* band of tissue.

lig′a•ture, *n.* **1.** two or more letters combined, as *fl*. **2.** surgical thread or wire for tying blood vessels.

light, *n., adj., v.,* **lighted** or **lit, lighting.** —*n.* **1.** that which gives illumination. **2.** daylight. **3.** aspect. **4.** enlightenment. —*adj.* **5.** not dark. **6.** not heavy. **7.** not serious. —*v.* **8.** ignite. **9.** illuminate. **10.** alight; land. **11.** happen (upon). —**light′ly,** *adv.* —**light′ness,** *n.*

light′en, *v.* **1.** become or make less dark. **2.** lessen in weight. **3.** mitigate. **4.** cheer.

light′er, *n.* **1.** something that lights. **2.** barge.

light′-fin′gered, *adj.* given to pilfering.

light′-head′ed, *adj.* as if about to faint.

light′-heart′ed, *adj.* cheerful; without worry. —**light′-heart′ed•ly,** *adv.* —**light′-heart′ed•ness,** *n.*

light′house′, *n.* tower displaying light to guide mariners.

light′ning, *n.* flash of light in sky caused by electrical discharge.

lightning bug, firefly.

lightning rod, rod to divert lightning into ground.

light′-year′, *n.* distance that light travels in one year.

lig′nite (lig′nīt), *n.* kind of coal.

lig′ne•ous, *adj.* of the nature of or resembling wood.

like, *v.,* **liked, liking,** *adj., prep., conj., n.* —*v.* **1.** find agreeable. **2.** wish. —*adj.* **3.** resembling; similar to. —*prep.* **4.** in like manner with. —*conj.* **5.** *Informal.* as; as if. —*n.* **6.** like person or thing; match. **7.** preference. —**lik′a•ble, like′a•ble,** *adj.*

-like, suffix indicating: like or characteristic of, as *childlike.*

like′ly, *adj.,* **-lier, -liest,** *adv.* —*adj.* **1.** probable. **2.** suitable; promising. —*adv.* **3.** probably. —**like′li•hood′,** *n.*

lik′en, *v.* compare.

like′ness, *n.* **1.** image; picture. **2.** fact of being like.

like′wise′, *adv.* **1.** also. **2.** in like manner.

li′lac (lī′lək), *n.* fragrant flowering shrub.

Lil′li•pu′tian *adj.* **1.** very small. **2.** trivial.

lilt, *n.* rhythmic cadence. —**lilt′ing,** *adj.*

lil′y, *n., pl.* **lilies.** plant with erect stems and showy flowers.

lil′y-liv′ered, *adj.* cowardly.

lily of the valley, *n., pl.* **lilies of the valley.** plant with spike of bell-shaped flowers.

li′ma bean, flat, edible bean.

limb, *n.* **1.** jointed part of an animal body. **2.** branch.

lim′ber, *adj.* **1.** flexible; supple. —*v.* **2.** become limber.

lim′bo, *n., pl.* **-bos. 1.** region on border of hell or heaven. **2.** state of oblivion. **3.** midway state or place. **4.** dance involving bending backward to pass under horizontal bar.

Lim′burg′er, *n.* strong cheese.

lime, *n., v.,* **limed, liming.** —*n.* **1.** oxide of calcium, used in mortar, etc. **2.** small, greenish, acid fruit of tropical tree. —*v.* **3.** treat with lime.

lime′light′, *n.* **1.** fame. **2.** strong light formerly used on stage.

lim′er•ick (lim′-), *n.* humorous five-line verse.

lime′stone′, *n.* rock consisting chiefly of powdered calcium.

lim′it, *n.* **1.** farthest extent; boundary. —*v.* **2.** fix or keep within limits. —**lim′i•ta′tion,** *n.* —**lim′it•less,** *adj.*

lim′it•ed, *adj.* **1.** restricted **2.** (of trains, etc.) making few stops. —*n.* **3.** limited train.

limn (lim), *v.* **1.** represent in pictures. **2.** describe.

lim′o (lim′ō), *n., pl.* **-os.** *Informal.* limousine.

lim′ou•sine′ (lim′ə zēn′), *n.* luxurious automobile for several passengers.

limp, *v.* **1.** walk unevenly. —*n.* **2.** lame movement. —*adj.* **3.** not stiff or firm. —**limp′ly,** *adv.* —**limp′ness,** *n.*

lim′pet, *n.* small cone-shelled marine animal.

lim′pid, *adj.* clear. —**lim•pid′i•ty, lim′pid•ness,** *n.* —**lim′pid•ly,** *adv.*

linch′pin′, *n.* **1.** pin inserted through end of axle to keep wheel on. **2.** something that holds parts together.

lin′den, *n.* tree with heart-shaped leaves.

line, *n., v.,* **lined, lining.** —*n.* **1.** long thin mark. **2.** row; series. **3.** course of action, etc. **4.**

boundary. **5.** string, cord, etc. **6.** occupation. —*v.* **7.** form line. **8.** mark with line. **9.** cover inner side of.

lin′e•age (lin′ē ij), *n.* ancestry.

lin′e•al, *adj.* **1.** of direct descent. **2.** Also, **lin′e•ar.** in or of a line.

lin′e•a•ment, *n.* feature, as of face.

line drive, batted baseball that travels low, fast, and straight.

line′man, *n., pl.* **-men.** worker who repairs telegraph wires.

lin′en, *n.* **1.** fabric made from flax. **2.** articles of linen.

lin′er, *n.* **1.** ship or airplane on regular route. **2.** lining.

line′-up′, *n.* order.

-ling, suffix meaning: **1.** person connected with, as *hireling.* **2.** little, as *duckling.*

lin′ger, *v.* **1.** stay on. **2.** persist. **3.** delay. —**lin′ger•ing•ly,** *adv.*

lin′ge•rie′ (län′zhə rā′), *n.* women's undergarments.

lin′go, *n., pl.* **-goes.** *Informal.* language.

lin′gual, *adj.* **1.** of the tongue. **2.** of languages.

lin•gui′ni (-gwē′nē), *n. pl.* pasta in slender flat form.

lin′guist, *n.* person skilled in languages.

lin•guis′tics, *n.* science of language. —**lin•guis′tic,** *adj.*

lin′i•ment, *n.* liquid applied to bruises, etc.

lin′ing, *n.* inner covering.

link, *n.* **1.** section of chain. **2.** bond. —*v.* **3.** unite. —**link′age,** *n.*

links, *n.pl.* golf course.

link′up′, *n.* **1.** contact set up between military units. **2.** linking element or system.

lin′net, *n.* small songbird.

li•no′le•um, *n.* floor covering made of cork, oil, etc.

Lin′o•type′, *n. Trademark.* keyboard machine for casting solid type.

lin′seed′, *n.* seed of flax.

lin′sey-wool′sey, *n.* fabric of linen and wool.

lint, *n.* bits of thread. —**lint′y,** *adj.*

lin′tel, *n.* beam above door or window.

li′on, *n.* **1.** large tawny animal of Africa and Asia. **2.** person of note. —**li′on•ess,** *n.fem.*

li′on•heart′ed, *adj.* exceptionally courageous.

li′on·ize′, *v.,* -ized, -izing. treat as a celebrity.

lip, *n.* **1.** fleshy margin of the mouth. **2.** projecting edge. **3.** *Slang.* impudent talk.

lip′o·suc′tion (lip′ə·suk′shən, lī′pə-), *n.* surgical withdrawal of excess fat from under skin.

lip′read′ing, method of understanding spoken words by interpreting speaker's lip movements. **lip′read′er,** *n.*

lip service, insincere profession of support.

lip′stick′, *n.* coloring for lips.

liq′ue·fy′, *v.,* -fied, -fying. become liquid. —**liq′ue·fac′tion,** *n.*

li·queur′ (li kûr′), *n.* strong sweet alcoholic drink.

liq′uid, *n.* **1.** fluid of molecules remaining together. —*adj.* **2.** of or being a liquid. **3.** in or convertible to cash.

liq′ui·date′, *v.,* -dated, -dating. **1.** settle, as debts. **2.** convert into cash. **3.** eliminate. —**liq′ui·da′tion, liq′ui·da′tor,** *n.*

liq′uor, *n.* **1.** alcoholic beverage. **2.** liquid.

lisle (līl), *n.* strong cotton thread.

lisp, *n.* **1.** pronunciation of *s* and *z* like *th.* —*v.* **2.** speak with lisp. —**lisp′er,** *n.*

lis′some (lis′əm), *adj.* **1.** gracefully supple. **2.** nimble. Also, **lis′som.**

list, *n.* **1.** series of words. **2.** inclination to side. —*v.* **3.** make list. **4.** incline.

lis′ten, *v.* attend with ear. —**lis′ten·er,** *n.*

list′less, *adj.* spiritless. —**list′less·ly,** *adv.* —**list′less·ness,** *n.*

list price, retail price.

lit., **1.** literally. **2.** literature.

lit′a·ny, *n., pl.* -nies. **1.** form of prayer. **2.** tedious account.

li′ter (lē′-), *n.* metric unit of capacity, = 1.0567 U.S. quarts. Also, *Brit.,* **li′tre.**

lit′er·al, *adj.* **1.** in accordance with strict meaning of words. **2.** exactly as written or stated. —**lit′er·al·ly,** *adv.*

lit′er·al-mind′ed, *adj.* unimaginative.

lit′er·ar′y, *adj.* of literature.

lit′er·ate, *adj.* **1.** able to read. **2.** educated. —*n.* **3.** literate person. —**lit′er·a·cy,** *n.*

lit′e•ra′ti (lit′ə rä′tē, -rā-′), *n.pl.* persons of scholarly or literary attainments.

lit′er•a•ture, *n.* writings of notable expression and thought.

lithe (līth), *adj.* limber. Also, **lithe′some.**

lith′i•um (lith′ē əm), *n.* soft silver-white metallic element.

lith′o•graph′, *n.* print made from prepared stone or plate. —**li•thog′ra•pher,** *n.* —**li•thog′ra•phy,** *n.*

lith′o•sphere′, *n.* crust and upper mantle of the earth.

lit′i•gant, *n.* person engaged in lawsuit.

lit′i•gate′, *v.,* **-gated, -gating.** carry on lawsuit. —**lit′i•ga′tion,** *n.*

lit′mus, *n.* blue coloring matter turning red in acid solution.

litmus paper, paper treated with litmus for use as a chemical indicator.

litmus test, use of single factor as basis for judgment.

Litt. D., Doctor of Letters; Doctor of Literature.

lit′ter, *n.* **1.** disordered array. **2.** young from one birth. **3.** stretcher. **4.** bedding for animals. **5.** scattered rubbish, etc. —*v.* **6.** strew in disorder.

lit′ter•bug′, *n.* person who litters places with trash.

lit′tle, *adj.,* **-tler, -tlest. 1.** small. **2.** mean. —*adv.* **3.** not much. —*n.* **4.** small amount.

lit′tor•al, *adj.* of the shore.

lit′ur•gy (lit′ər jē), *n., pl.* **-gies.** form of worship. —**li•tur′gi•cal,** *adj.*

liv′able, *adj.* habitable or endurable. —**liv′a•bil′i•ty,** *n.*

live (liv *for* 1–5; līv *for* 6–8), *v.,* **lived, living,** *adj.* —*v.* **1.** be alive. **2.** endure in reputation. **3.** rely for food, etc. **4.** dwell. **5.** pass (life). —*adj.* **6.** alive. **7.** energetic. **8.** effective.

live′li•hood′, *n.* means of supporting oneself.

live′long′, *adj.* entire; whole.

live′ly, *adj.,* **-lier, -liest,** *adv.* —*adj.* **1.** active; spirited. —*adv.* **2.** vigorously. —**live′li•ness,** *n.*

liv′er, *n.* abdominal organ.

liv′er•wurst′, *n.* liver sausage.

liv′er•y, *n., pl.* **-eries. 1.** uniform of male servants. **2.** keeping of horses for hire.

live′stock′, *n.* farm animals.

live wire, *Informal.* energetic, keenly alert person.

liv′id, *adj.* **1.** dull blue. **2.** mad.

liv′ing, *adj.* **1.** live. **2.** sufficient for living. —*n.* **3.** condition of life. **4.** livelihood.

living room, room in home used for leisure activities.

living will, document stipulating that no extraordinary measures be taken to prolong signer's life during terminal illness.

liz′ard, *n.* four-legged reptile.

lla′ma (lä′mə), *n.* South American animal.

LL.B., Bachelor of Laws.

L.L.D., Doctor of Laws.

lo, *interj.* (behold!)

load, *n.* **1.** cargo. **2.** charge of firearm. —*v.* **3.** put load on. **4.** oppress. **5.** charge (firearm). —**load′er,** *n.*

loaf, *n., pl.* **loaves,** *v.* —*n.* **1.** shaped mass of bread, etc. —*v.* **2.** idle. —**loaf′er,** *n.*

loam, *n.* loose fertile soil. —**loam′y,** *adj.*

loan, *n.* **1.** act of lending. **2.** something lent. —*v.* **3.** lend.

loan shark, *Informal.* usurer. —**loan′shark′ing,** *n.*

loan′word′, *n.* word borrowed from another language.

loath, *adj.* reluctant.

loathe, *v.,* **loathed, loathing.** feel disgust at; despise. —**loath′some,** *adj.*

lob, *v.,* **lobbed, lobbing,** *n.* —*v.* **1.** hurl in a high curve. —*n.* **2.** tennis ball so struck.

lob′by, *n., pl.* **-bies,** *v.,* **-bied, -bying.** —*n.* **1.** vestibule or entrance hall. **2.** group that tries to influence legislators. —*v.* **3.** try to influence legislators. —**lob′by•ist,** *n.*

lobe, *n.* roundish projection. —**lo′bar, lo′bate,** *adj.*

lo•bot′o•my (lə bot′ə mē, lō-), *n., pl.* **-mies.** surgical incision of brain lobe to treat mental disorder. —**lo•bot′o•mize′,** *v.*

lob′ster, *n.* edible shellfish.

lo′cal, *adj.* **1.** of or in particular area. —*n.* **2.** local branch of trade union. **3.** train that makes all stops. —**lo′cal•ly,** *adv.*

lo•cale′ (-kal′), *n.* setting.

lo·cal'i·ty, *n., pl.* **-ties.** area.

lo'cal·ize', *v.,* **-ized, -izing.** confine to particular place. —**lo'cal·i·za'tion,** *n.*

lo'cate, *v.,* **-cated, -cating.** find or establish place of.

lo·ca'tion, *n.* **1.** act or instance of locating. **2.** place where something is.

loc. cit. (lok'sit'), in the place cited.

lock, *n.* **1.** fastener preventing access. **2.** place in canal for moving vessels from one water level to another. **3.** part of firearm. **4.** tress of hair. —*v.* **5.** secure with lock. **6.** shut in or out. **7.** join firmly.

lock'er, *n.* closet with lock.

lock'et, *n.* small case worn on necklace.

lock'jaw', *n.* disease in which jaws become tightly locked.

lock'out', *n.* business closure to force acceptance of employer's terms of work.

lock'smith', *n.* person who makes or repairs locks.

lock'step', *n.* **1.** way of marching in close file. **2.** rigidly inflexible pattern.

lock'up', *n.* jail.

lo'co, *adj. Slang.* crazy.

lo'co·mo'tion, *n.* act of moving about.

lo'co·mo'tive, *n.* engine that pulls railroad cars.

lo'co·weed', *n.* plant causing a disease in livestock.

lo'cust, *n.* **1.** kind of grasshopper. **2.** flowering American tree.

lo·cu'tion (lō kyoo'shən), *n.* phrase; expression.

lode, *n.* veinlike mineral deposit.

lode'star', *n.* guiding star.

lode'stone', *n.* magnetic stone. Also, **load'stone'.**

lodge, *n., v.,* **lodged, lodging.** —*n.* **1.** hut or house. **2.** members or meeting place of fraternal organization. —*v.* **3.** live or house temporarily. **4.** fix or put; become fixed. —**lodg'er,** *n.*

lodg'ing, *n.* **1.** temporary housing. **2.** (*pl.*) rooms.

lodg'ment, *n.* **1.** lodging. **2.** something lodged. Also, **lodge'ment.**

loft, *n.* attic or gallery.

loft'y, *adj.,* **loftier, loftiest. 1.** tall. **2.** elevated. —**loft'i•ly,** *adv.* —**loft'i•ness,** *n.*

log, *n., v.,* **logged, logging.** —*n.* **1.** trunk of felled tree. **2.** Also, **log'book'.** record of events. —*v.* **3.** fell and cut up trees. **4.** record in log. **5. log in** or **on,** gain access to computer system. —**log'ger,** *n.*

lo'gan•ber'ry, *n., pl.* **-ries.** dark red acid fruit.

log'a•rithm, *n. Math.* symbol of number of times a number must be multiplied by itself to equal a given number.

loge (lōzh), *n.* box in theater.

log'ger•head', *n.* **1.** stupid person. **2. at loggerheads,** disputing.

log'ic, *n.* science of reasoning. —**log'i•cal,** *adj.* —**log'i•cal•ly,** *adv.* —**lo•gi'cian,** *n.*

lo•gis'tics, *n.* science of military supply. —**lo•gis'tic, lo•gis'ti•cal,** *adj.*

log'jam', *n.* **1.** pileup of logs, as in a river. **2.** blockage.

lo'go, *n.* representation or symbol of company name, trademark, etc. Also, **lo'go•type'.**

log'roll'ing, *n.* exchange of support or favors.

lo'gy (lō'gē), *adj.,* **-gier, -giest.** heavy; dull.

-logy, suffix meaning science or study of, as *theology.*

loin, *n.* part of body between ribs and hipbone.

loin'cloth', *n.* cloth worn around the loins or hips.

loi'ter, *v.* linger. —**loi'ter•er,** *n.*

loll, *v.* **1.** recline indolently. **2.** hang loosely.

lol'li•pop', *n.* candy on stick.

lone, *adj.* alone.

lone'ly, *adj.,* **-lier, -liest. 1.** alone. **2.** wishing for company. **3.** isolated. —**lone'li•ness,** *n.*

lon'er, *n.* person who spends much time alone.

lone'some, *adj.* **1.** depressed by solitude. **2.** lone.

long, *adj.* **1.** of great or specified length. —*adv.* **2.** for long space of time. —*v.* **3.** yearn. —**long'ing,** *n.*

lon•gev'i•ty (lon jev'-), *n.* long life.

long'hand', *n.* ordinary handwriting.

lon′gi•tude′, *n.* distance east and west on earth's surface.

lon′gi•tu′di•nal, *adj.* **1.** of longitude. **2.** lengthwise.

long jump, jump for distance.

long′-lived′ (-līvd′, -livd′), *adj.* having a long life.

long′-range′, *adj.* spanning a long distance or time.

long′shore′man, *n.* person who loads and unloads ships. **—long′shore′wom•an,** *n.fem.*

long shot, 1. racehorse, team, etc., with little chance for winning. **2.** undertaking with little chance for success.

long′-term′, *adj.* involving a long time.

long′-wind′ed, *adj.* speaking or spoken at excessive length.

look, *v.,* **1.** direct the eyes. **2.** seem. **3.** face. **4.** seek. **—n. 5.** act of looking. **6.** appearance.

looking glass, mirror.

look′out′, *n.* **1.** watch. **2.** person for keeping watch. **3.** place for keeping watch.

loom, *n.* **1.** device for weaving fabric. **—v. 2.** weave on loom. **3.** appear as large and indistinct.

loon, *n.* diving bird.

loon′y, *adj.,* **loonier, looniest.** *Informal.* **1.** lunatic; insane. **2.** extremely foolish.

loop, *n.* **1.** circular form from length of material or line. **—v. 2.** form a loop.

loop′hole′, *n.* **1.** small opening. **2.** means of evasion.

loose, *adj.,* **looser, loosest,** *v.,* **loosed, loosing. —***adj.* **1.** free; unconfined. **2.** not firm. **3.** not exact. **4.** dissolute. **—v. 5.** free. **6.** shoot (missiles). **—loos′en,** *v.* **—loose′ly,** *adv.* **—loose′ness,** *n.*

loot, *n.* **1.** spoils. **—v. 2.** plunder. **—loot′er,** *n.*

lop, *v.,* **lopped, lopping.** cut off.

lope, *v.,* **loped, loping,** *n.* **—v. 1.** move with long, easy stride. **—n. 2.** long, easy stride.

lop′sid′ed, *adj.* uneven.

lo•qua′cious, *adj.* talkative. **—lo•quac′i•ty** (-kwas′ə tē), *n.*

lord, *n.* **1.** master. **2.** British nobleman. **3.** (*cap.*) God. **4.** (*cap.*) Jesus Christ. **—v. 5.** domineer. **—lord′ly,** *adj.* **—lord′ship,** *n.*

lore, *n.* learning.

lor•gnette′ (lôr nyet′), *n.* eyeglasses on long handle.

lor'ry, *n., pl.* **-ries.** *Brit.* truck.

lose, *v.,* **lost, losing. 1.** fail to keep. **2.** misplace. **3.** be deprived of. **4.** fail to win. —**los'er,** *n.*

loss, *n.* **1.** disadvantage from losing. **2.** thing lost. **3.** waste.

lot, *n.* **1.** object drawn to decide question by chance. **2.** allotted share. **3.** piece of land. **4.** large amount.

Lo•thar'i•o, *n., pl.* **-os.** *(often l.c.)* man who obsessively seduces women.

lo'tion, *n.* liquid for skin.

lot'ter•y, *n., pl.* **-teries.** sale of tickets on prizes to be awarded by lots.

lot'to, *n.* **1.** game of chance similar to bingo. **2.** lottery in which players choose numbers that are matched against those of the official drawing.

lo'tus, *n.* water lily.

loud, *adj.* **1.** strongly audible. **2.** blatant. —**loud'ly,** *adv.* —**loud'ness,** *n.*

loud'-mouth', *n.* a braggart; gossip. —**loud'-mouthed',** *adj.*

loud'speak'er, *n.* device for increasing volume of sound.

lounge, *v.,* **lounged, lounging,** *n.* —*v.* **1.** pass time idly. **2.** loll. —*n.* **3.** kind of sofa. **4.** parlor.

louse, *n., pl.* **lice.** bloodsucking insect.

lous'y, *adj.,* **lousier, lousiest. 1.** *Informal.* bad; poor. **2.** troubled with lice. —**lous'i•ness,** *n.*

lout, *n.* boor. —**lout'ish,** *adj.*

lou'ver (lo͞o'vər), *n.* arrangement of slits for ventilation. —**lou'vered,** *adj.*

lov'a•ble, *adj.* attracting love. Also, **love'a•ble.** —**lov'a•bly,** *adv.*

love, *n., v.,* **loved, loving.** —*n.* **1.** strong affection. **2.** sweetheart. —*v.* **3.** have love for. —**lov'er,** *n.* —**love'less,** *adj.* —**lov'ing,** *adj.* —**lov'ing•ly,** *adv.*

love'lorn', *adj.* deprived of love or a lover.

love'ly, *adj.,* **-lier, -liest.** charming. —**love'li•ness,** *n.*

love'sick', *adj.* sick from intensity of love.

loving cup, large two-handled drinking cup.

low, *adj.* **1.** not high or tall. **2.** prostrate. **3.** weak. **4.** humble or inferior. **5.** not loud. —*adv.* **6.** in low position. **7.** in quiet tone. —*n.* **8.** thing that is low. **9.** moo. —*v.* **10.** moo.

low′brow′, *n.* **1.** uncultured person. —*adj.* **2.** typical of a lowbrow.

low′-cal′, *adj.* with fewer calories than usual.

low′down′, *n.* **1.** real and unadorned facts. —*adj.* (low′down′). **2.** contemptible.

low′er (lō′ər *for 1, 2;* lou′ər *for 3–5*), *v.* **1.** reduce or diminish. **2.** make or become lower. **3.** be threatening. **4.** frown. —*n.* **5.** lowering appearance.

low′er•case′, *adj.* **1.** (of a letter) of a form often different from and smaller than its corresponding capital letter. —*n.* **2.** lowercase letter.

low frequency, radio frequency between 30 and 300 kilohertz. —**low′-fre′quen•cy,** *adj.*

low′-key′, *adj.* understated.

low′life′, *n., pl.* **-lifes.** disreputable person.

low′ly, *adj.,* **-lier, -liest.** humble; meek.

low′-mind′ed, *adj.* vulgar.

low profile, deliberately inconspicuous manner.

lox, *n.* salmon cured in brine.

loy′al, *adj.* faithful; steadfast. —**loy′al•ly,** *adv.* —**loy′al•ty,** —**loy′al•ness,** *n.*

loz′enge (loz′inj), *n.* **1.** flavored candy, often medicated. **2.** diamond shape.

LPN, licensed practical nurse.

LSD, lysergic acid diethylamide, a powerful psychedelic drug.

Lt., lieutenant.

Ltd. limited.

lu′au (lōō′ou), *n., pl.* **-aus.** feast of Hawaiian food.

lub′ber, *n.* clumsy person.

lu′bri•cant, *n.* lubricating substance.

lu′bri•cate′, *v.,* **-cated, -cating.** oil or grease, esp. to diminish friction. —**lu′bri•ca′tion,** *n.* —**lu′bri•ca′tor,** *n.* —**lu′bri•cant,** *adj., n.*

lu•bri′cious (-brish′əs), *adj.* **1.** lewd. **2.** slippery. Also, **lu′bri•cous** (-kəs).

lu′cid (lōō′sid), *adj.* **1.** bright. **2.** clear in thought or

expression. 3. rational.
—**lu•cid′i•ty, lu′cid•ness,** *n.*
—**lu′cid•ly,** *adv.*

Lu′cite, *n. Trademark.* transparent plastic.

luck, *n.* 1. chance. 2. good fortune. —**luck′less,** *adj.*

luck′y, *adj.,* **luckier, luckiest.** having or due to good luck. —**luck′i•ly,** *adv.*

lu′cra•tive, *adj.* profitable.

lu′cre (loo′kər), *n.* wealth.

lu′di•crous, *adj.* ridiculous. —**lu′di•crous•ly,** *adv.*

luff, *v.* 1. sail into wind. —*n.* 2. act of luffing.

lug, *v.,* **lugged, lugging,** *n.* —*v.* 1. pull or carry with effort. 2. haul. —*n.* 3. projecting handle. 4. *Slang.* awkward, clumsy fellow.

luge (loozh), *n., v.,* **luged, luging.** —*n.* 1. small racing sled for one or two persons. —*v.* 2. race on a luge.

lug′gage, *n.* baggage.

lug nut, large nut, esp. for attaching a wheel to a vehicle.

lu•gu′bri•ous (loo goo′-), *adj.* excessively gloomy. —**lu•gu′bri•ous•ly,** *adv.*

luke′warm′, *adj.* slightly warm.

lull, *v.* 1. soothe, esp. to sleep. —*n.* 2. brief stillness.

lull′a•by, *n., pl.* **-bies.** song to lull baby.

lum•ba′go, *n.* pain in back.

lum′bar, *adj.* of or close to the loins.

lum′ber, *n.* 1. timber made into boards, etc. —*v.* 2. cut and prepare timber. 3. encumber. 4. move heavily. —**lum′ber•man,** *n.*

lum′ber•jack′, *n.* person who fells trees.

lum′ber•yard′, *n.* yard where lumber is stored for sale.

lu′mi•nar′y, *n., pl.* **-naries.** 1. celestial body. 2. person who inspires many.

lu′min•es′cent, *adj.* luminous at relatively low temperatures. —**lu′min•es′cence,** *n.*

lu′mi•nous, *adj.* giving or reflecting light. —**lu′mi•nos′i•ty,** *n.*

lum′mox (lum′əks), *n. Informal.* oafish person.

lump, *n.* 1. irregular mass. 2. swelling. 3. aggregation.

—*adj.* **4.** including many. —*v.* **5.** put together. **6.** endure. —**lump'y,** *adj.*

lu'na•cy, *n., pl.* **-cies.** insanity.

lu'nar, *adj.* **1.** of or according to moon. **2.** Also, **lu'nate.** crescent-shaped.

lu'na•tic, *n.* **1.** insane person. —*adj.* **2.** for the insane. **3.** crazy.

lunch, *n.* **1.** Also, **lunch'eon.** mid-day meal. —*v.* **2.** eat lunch.

lunch'eon•ette', *n.* restaurant for quick, simple lunches.

lung, *n.* respiratory organ.

lunge, *n., v.,* **lunged, lunging.** —*n.* **1.** sudden forward movement. —*v.* **2.** make lunge.

lu'pine (loo'pin), *n.* **1.** plant with tall, dense clusters of flowers. —*adj.* **2.** of or resembling the wolf.

lu'pus (loo'pəs), *n.* any of several diseases characterized by skin eruptions.

lurch, *n.* **1.** sudden lean to one side. **2.** helpless plight. —*v.* **3.** make lurch.

lure, *n., v.,* **lured, luring.** —*n.* **1.** bait. —*v.* **2.** decoy; entice.

lu'rid, *adj.* **1.** glaringly lighted. **2.** intended to be exciting; sensational. —**lu'rid•ly,** *adv.*

lurk, *v.* **1.** loiter furtively. **2.** exist unperceived.

lus'cious, *adj.* delicious. —**lus'cious•ly,** *adv.* —**lus'cious•ness,** *n.*

lush, *adj.* **1.** tender and juicy. **2.** abundant.

lust, *n.* **1.** strong desire. —*v.* **2.** have desire. —**lust'ful,** *adj.*

lus'ter, *n.* gloss; radiance. Also, **lus'tre.** —**lus'ter•less,** *adj.* —**lus'trous,** *adj.*

lust'y, *adj.,* **lustier, lustiest.** vigorous. —**lust'i•ly,** *adv.*

lute, *n.* stringed musical instrument.

Lu'ther•an, *adj.* of Protestant sect named for Martin Luther. —**Lu'ther•an•ism,** *n.*

lux•u'ri•ant (lug zhoor'ē ənt), *adj.* profuse; abundant. —**lux•u'ri•ance,** *n.*

lux•u'ri•ate' (-ē āt'), *v.,* **-ated, -ating.** revel; delight.

lux'u•ry (luk'shə rē), *n., pl.* **-ries.** something enjoyable but not necessary. —**lux•u'ri•ous,** *adj.* —**lux•u'ri•ous•ly,** *adv.* —**lux•u'ri•ous•ness,** *n.*

ly•ce′um, *n.* hall for lectures.

lye, *n.* alkali solution.

ly′ing-in′, *adj.* 1. of or for childbirth. —*n.* 2. childbirth.

Lyme disease (līm), tick-transmitted disease characterized esp. by joint pains and fatigue.

lymph, *n.* yellowish matter from body tissues. —**lym•phat′ic,** *adj.*

lym′pho•cyte′ (-fə sīt′), *n.* white blood cell producing antibodies.

lynch, *v.* put to death without legal authority.

lynx, *n., pl.* **lynxes, lynx.** kind of wild cat.

lyre, *n.* harplike instrument.

lyr′ic, *adj.* Also, **lyr′i•cal.** 1. (of poetry) musical. 2. of or writing such poetry. 3. ardently expressive. —*n.* 4. lyric poem. 5. (*pl.*) words for song. —**lyr′i•cal•ly,** *adv.* —**lyr′i•cism,** *n.* —**lyr′i•cist,** *n.*

M, m, *n.* thirteenth letter of English alphabet.

ma, *n. Informal.* mother.

MA, Massachusetts.

M.A., Master of Arts.

ma'am, *n. Informal.* madam.

ma·ca'bre, *adj.* gruesome.

mac·ad'am, *n.* road-making material containing broken stones. —**mac·ad'am·ize',** *v.*

mac'a·ro'ni, *n.* **1.** tube-shaped food made of wheat. **2.** 18th-century fop.

mac'a·roon', *n.* small cookie, usually containing almonds.

ma·caw', *n.* tropical parrot.

mace, *n.* **1.** spiked war club. **2.** staff of office. **3.** spice from part of nutmeg seed. **4.** (*cap.*) *Trademark.* chemical for subduing rioters, etc.

mac'er·ate (mas'-), *v.,* **-ated, -ating.** soften by steeping in liquid. —**mac'er·a'tion,** *n.*

ma·che'te (mə shet'ē), *n.* heavy knife.

Mach'i·a·vel'li·an (mak'-), *adj.* wily.

mach'i·na'tion (mak'-), *n.* cunning plan.

ma·chine', *n.* **1.** mechanical device. **2.** group controlling political organization.

machine gun, firearm capable of firing continuous stream of bullets.

ma·chin'er·y, *n., pl.* **-eries.** machines or mechanisms.

ma·chin'ist, *n.* operator of machines.

ma·chis'mo (-chēz'-), *n.* exaggerated masculinity as basis for code of behavior.

Mach' num'ber (mäk), ratio of speed of object to speed of sound.

ma'cho (mä'-), *adj.* exaggeratedly virile.

mack'er·el, *n.* common fish.

mack'i·naw', *n.* woolen coat.

mack'in·tosh', *n.* raincoat.

mac'ra·mé', *n.* decorative work of knotted cords.

macro-, prefix meaning large, as *macrocosm.*

mac'ro·bi·ot'ic, *adj.* of or giving long life.

mac'ro·cosm, *n.* universe.

ma′cron (mā′kron), *n.* horizontal line over vowel to show it is long.

mad, *adj.,* **madder, maddest. 1.** insane. **2.** *Informal.* angry. **3.** violent. —**mad′man′,** *n.* —**mad′den,** *v.* —**mad′ly,** *adv.* —**mad′ness,** *n.*

mad′am, *n.* **1.** female term of address. **2.** woman in charge of brothel.

mad′ame, *n., pl.* **mesdames** (mā dam′). French term of address for a married woman.

mad′cap′, *adj.* impulsive; rash.

mad′e•moi•selle′ (mad′mwə zel′), *n., pl.* **mademoiselles, mesdemoiselles.** French term of address for unmarried woman.

Ma•don′na, *n.* Virgin Mary.

mad′ras, *n.* light cotton fabric.

mad′ri•gal, *n.* song for several voices unaccompanied.

mael′strom (māl′-), *n.* **1.** whirlpool. **2.** confusion.

mae′nad (mē′-), *n.* female votary of Dionysus.

maes′tro (mīs′-), *n., pl.* **-tros.** master, esp. of music.

Ma′fi•a, *n.* criminal society.

mag′a•zine′, *n.* **1.** periodical publication. **2.** storehouse for ammunition, etc. **3.** cartridge receptacle in weapon.

ma•gen′ta (-jen′-), *n.* fuschia.

mag′got, *n.* larva of fly.

Ma′gi (mā′jī), *n.pl. Bible.* the three wise men.

mag′ic, *n.* **1.** seemingly supernatural production of effects. —*adj.* Also, **mag′i•cal. 2.** of magic. **3.** enchanting. —**ma•gi′cian,** *n.*

mag′is•te′ri•al, *adj.* masterlike.

mag′is•trate′, *n.* public official.

mag′ma, *n.* molten material beneath the earth's surface, from which igneous rocks and lava are formed.

mag•nan′i•mous, *adj.* generous; high-minded. —**mag′na•nim′i•ty,** *n.*

mag′nate (-nāt), *n.* tycoon.

mag•ne′sia, *n.* magnesium oxide, used as laxative.

mag•ne′si•um (-zē-), *n.* light, silvery, metallic element.

mag′net, *n.* metal body that attracts iron or steel. —**mag•net′ic,** *adj.*

magnetic field, space near magnet, electric current, moving charged particle in which magnetic force acts.

mag′net•ism′, *n.* 1. characteristic property of magnets. 2. science of magnets. 3. great personal charm. —**mag′net•ize′,** *v.*

mag′net•ite′, *n.* common black mineral.

mag•ne′to, *n., pl.* **-tos.** small electric generator.

mag•nif′i•cence, *n.* 1. splendor; grandeur. 2. nobility. 3. excellence. —**mag•nif′i•cent,** *adj.*

mag′ni•fy′, *v.,* **-fied, -fying.** 1. increase apparent size. 2. enlarge. —**mag′ni•fi•ca′tion,** *n.* —**mag′ni•fi′er,** *n.*

mag•nil′o•quent, *adj.* pompous in expression. —**mag•nil′o•quence,** *n.*

mag′ni•tude′, *n.* 1. size or extent. 2. brightness.

mag•no′li•a, *n.* tree with large fragrant flowers.

mag′num o′pus, chief work of writer, composer, or artist.

mag′pie′, *n.* bird that steals.

ma′ha•ra′jah, *n.* (formerly) ruling prince in India. —**ma′ha•ra′nee,** *n.fem.*

ma•hat′ma (mə hät′mə, -hat′-), *n.* person, esp. in India, held in highest esteem for wisdom and saintliness.

mah′-jongg′, *n.* Chinese game.

ma•hog′a•ny, *n., pl.* **-nies.** tropical American tree.

Ma•hom′et, *n.* Muhammad.

maid, *n.* 1. unmarried woman. 2. female servant.

maid′en, *n.* 1. young unmarried woman. —*adj.* 2. of maidens. 3. unmarried. 4. initial. —**maid′en•ly,** *adj.* —**maid′en•li•ness,** *n.*

maid′en•hair′, *n.* fern with finely divided fronds.

mail, *n.* 1. material delivered by postal system. 2. postal system. 3. armor, usually flexible. —*adj.* 4. of mail. —*v.* 5. send by mail. —**mail′box′,** *n.* —**mail′man′,** *n.*

mail•lot′ (mä yō′), *n.* one-piece bathing suit.

maim, *v.* cripple; impair.

main, *adj.* 1. chief; principal. —*n.* 2. chief pipe. 3. strength. 4. ocean. —**main′ly,** *adv.*

main′frame′, *n.* large computer, often the hub of a system serving many users.

main′land′, *n.* continental land rather than island.

main′spring′, *n.* chief spring of mechanism.

main′stay′, *n.* chief support.

main′stream′, *n.* customary trend of behavior.

main·tain′, *v.* 1. support. 2. assert. 3. keep in order. —**main′te·nance**, *n.*

mai′tre d'hô·tel′ (me′tr dō tel′), headwaiter. Also, **mai′tre d′′** (mā′tər dē′).

maize (māz), *n.* corn.

maj′es·ty, *n., pl.* **-ties.** 1. regal grandeur. 2. sovereign. —**ma·jes′tic**, *adj.* —**ma·jes′ti·cal·ly**, *adv.*

ma·jol′i·ca, *n.* pottery type.

ma′jor, *n.* 1. army officer above captain. 2. person of legal age. —*adj.* 3. larger.

ma′jor-do′mo, *n.* steward.

ma′jor·ette′, *n.* female leader of marchers.

major general, army officer above brigadier general.

ma·jor′i·ty, *n., pl.* **-ties.** 1. greater number. 2. legal age.

make, *v.*, **made, making**, *n.* —*v.* 1. bring into existence; form. 2. cause; force. 3. earn. 4. accomplish. —*n.* 5. style. 6. manufacture. —**mak′er**, *n.*

make′-be·lieve′, *n.* 1. pretending that fanciful thing is true. —*adj.* 2. fictitious.

make′shift′, *n., adj.* make-do.

make′up′, *n.* 1. cosmetics. 2. organization; composition.

mal-, prefix meaning bad or ill, as *maladjustment.*

mal′a·chite′ (-kīt′), *n.* green mineral, an ore of copper.

mal′ad·just′ment, *n.* 1. faulty adjustment. 2. inability to adapt to social conditions. —**mal′ad·just′ed**, *adj.*

mal′ad·min′is·ter, *v.* mismanage.

mal′a·droit′, *adj.* awkward.

mal′a·dy, *n., pl.* **-dies.** illness.

ma·laise′ (-lāz′), *n.* 1. weakness; discomfort. 2. uneasiness.

mal′a·mute′, *n.* Alaskan breed of large dogs.

mal′a·prop·ism, *n.* ludicrous misuse of similar words.

ma·lar′i·a, *n.* mosquito-borne disease. —**ma·lar′i·al**, *adj.*

ma·lar′key, *n. Informal.* nonsense.

mal′a·thi′on (-thī′on), *n.* organic insecticide of low toxicity for mammals.

mal′con·tent′, *n.* dissatisfied person.

mal de mer′, seasickness.

male, *adj.* 1. of sex that begets young. —*n.* 2. male person.

mal′e·dic′tion, *n.* curse.

mal′e·fac′tor, *n.* wrong doer.

ma·lev′o·lent, *adj.* wishing evil. —**ma·lev′o·lence,** *n.*

mal·fea′sance (-fē′-), *n.* misconduct in office.

mal·formed′, *adj.* badly formed. —**mal′for·ma′tion,** *n.*

mal′ice, *n.* evil intent. —**ma·li′cious,** *adj.*

ma·lign′ (-līn′), *v.* 1. speak ill of. —*adj.* 2. evil.

ma·lig′nan·cy, *n., pl.* **-cies.** 1. malignant state. 2. cancerous growth.

ma·lig′nant, *adj.* 1. causing harm or suffering. 2. deadly.

ma·lin′ger, *v.* feign sickness. —**ma·lin′ger·er,** *n.*

mall, *n.* 1. shaded walk. 2. covered shopping center.

mal′lard, *n.* wild duck.

mal′le·a·ble, *adj.* 1. that may be hammered or rolled into shape. 2. readily influenced. —**mal′le·a·bil′i·ty,** **mal′le·a·ble·ness,** *n.*

mal′let, *n.* wooden hammer.

mal′nu·tri′tion, *n.* improper nutrition.

mal′oc·clu′sion, *n.* irregular contact between upper and lower teeth.

mal·o′dor·ous, *adj.* smelling bad.

mal·prac′tice, *n.* improper professional behavior.

malt, *n.* germinated grain used in liquor-making.

malt′ose, *n.* sugar formed by action of enzyme on starch.

mal·treat′, *v.* abuse.

ma′ma, *n. Informal.* mother.

mam′bo (mäm′bō), *n.* Latin-American dance style.

mam′mal, *n.* vertebrate animal whose young are suckled.

mam′ma·ry, *adj.* of breasts.

mam′mo·gram′, *n.* x-ray photograph of a breast, for detection of tumors.

mam′mon, *n.* 1. material wealth. 2. greed for riches.

mam′moth, *n.* **1.** extinct kind of elephant. —*adj.* **2.** huge.

mam′my, *n., pl.* **-mies.** *Informal.* mother.

man, *n., pl.* **men,** *v.,* **manned, manning.** —*n.* **1.** male person. **2.** person. **3.** human race. —*v.* **4.** supply with crew. **5.** serve.

man′a•cle, *n., v.,* **-cled, -cling.** handcuff.

man′age, *v.,* **-aged, -aging. 1.** take care of. **2.** direct. —**man′age•a•ble,** *adj.* —**man′a•ger,** *n.* —**man′a•ge′ri•al,** *adj.*

man′age•ment, *n.* **1.** direction. **2.** persons in charge.

ma•ña′na (mä nyä′nä), *n. Spanish.* tomorrow.

man′a•tee′ (man′ə tē′), *n.* plant-eating aquatic mammal. Also, **sea cow.**

man•da′mus, *n., pl.* **-mus•es.** *Law.* writ commanding that a thing be done.

man′da•rin, *n.* **1.** public official in Chinese Empire. **2.** (*cap.*) spoken form of Chinese language.

man′date, *n.* **1.** authority over territory granted to nation by other nations. **2.** territory under such authority. **3.** command, as to take office. —**man′date,** *v.*

man′da•to′ry, *adj.* required.

man′di•ble, *n.* bone comprising the lower jaw.

man′do•lin′, *n.* plucked stringed musical instrument.

man′drake, *n.* narcotic herb.

man′drel, *n.* rod or axle in machinery.

man′drill, *n.* kind of baboon.

mane, *n.* long hair at neck of some animals.

ma•nège′ (ma nezh′), *n.* art of training and riding horses.

ma•neu′ver (-noo′-), *n.* **1.** planned movement, esp. in war. —*v.* **2.** change position by maneuver. **3.** put in certain situation by intrigue. —**ma•neu′ver•a•ble,** *adj.*

man Friday, *pl.* **men Friday.** reliable male assistant.

man′ful, *adj.* resolute. —**man′ful•ly,** *adv.*

man′ga•nese′, *n.* hard metallic element.

mange (mānj), *n.* skin disease of animals. —**man′gy,** *adj.*

man′ger, *n.* trough for feeding.

man′gle, *v.*, **-gled, -gling,** *n.* —*v.* **1.** disfigure. **2.** put through mangle. —*n.* **3.** device with rollers for removing water in washing clothes.

man′go, *n., pl.* **-goes.** fruit of tropical tree.

man′grove, *n.* tropical tree.

man′han′dle, *v.*, **-dled, -dling.** handle roughly.

man·hat′tan, *n.* cocktail of whiskey and vermouth.

man′hole′, *n.* access hole to sewer, drain, etc.

man′hood, *n.* **1.** manly qualities. **2.** state of being a man.

man′-hour′, *n.* amount of work done by one person in an hour.

man′hunt′, *n.* search for fugitive.

ma′ni·a, *n.* **1.** excitement. **2.** violent insanity.

ma′ni·ac′, *n.* lunatic. —**ma·ni′a·cal** (-nī′-), *adj.*

man′ic, *adj.* irrationally lively.

man′ic-depress′ive, *adj.* suffering from mental disorder in which mania alternates with depression.

man′i·cure′, *n.* skilled care of fingernails and hands. —**man′i·cure′,** *v.* —**man′i·cur′ist,** *n.*

man′i·fest′, *adj.* **1.** evident. —*v.* **2.** show plainly. —*n.* **3.** list of cargo and passengers. —**man′i·fes·ta′tion,** *n.*

man′i·fes′to, *n., pl.* **-toes.** declaration of philosophy.

man′i·fold′, *adj.* **1.** of many kinds or parts. —*v.* **2.** copy.

man′i·kin, *n.* model of body.

Ma·nil′a paper, strong, light brown or buff paper.

man in the street, ordinary person.

ma·nip′u·late′, *v.*, **-lated, -lating.** handle with skill or cunning. —**ma·nip′u·la′tion,** *n.* —**ma·nip′u·la′tor,** *n.*

man′kind′, *n.* **1.** human race. **2.** men.

man′ly, *adj.*, **-lier, -liest.** virile.

man′na, *n.* divine food.

man′ne·quin (-kin), *n.* model for displaying clothes.

man′ner, *n.* **1.** way of doing, acting, etc. **2.** (*pl.*) way of acting in society. **3.** sort.

man′ner·ism, *n.* peculiarity of manner.

man′ner•ly, *adj.* polite.

man′nish, *adj.* like a man.

man′-of-war′, *n., pl.* **men-of-war.** warship.

man′or, *n.* large estate. —**ma•no′ri•al,** *adj.*

man′pow′er, *n.* labor force.

man•qué′ (mäng kā′), *adj.* unfulfilled.

man′sard, *n.* roof with two slopes of different pitch on all sides.

manse, *n.* house and land of parson.

man′serv′ant, *n.* male servant.

man′sion, *n.* stately house.

man′slaugh′ter, *n.* killing of person without malice.

man′sue•tude′ (man′swi tōōd′), *n.* mildness.

man′ta, *n.* huge ray with pectoral fins.

man′tel, *n.* ornamental structure around fireplace.

man•til′la, *n.* lace head scarf of Spanish women.

man′tis, *n.* carnivorous insect.

man•tis′sa, *n.* decimal part of common logarithm.

man′tle, *n., v.,* **-tled, -tling.** —*n.* 1. loose cloak. —*v.* 2. envelop. 3. blush.

man′tra, *n.* Hindu or Buddhist verbal formula for recitation.

man′u•al, *adj.* 1. of or done with hands. —*n.* 2. small informational book. 3. hand powered typewriter. —**man′u•al•ly,** *adv.*

man′u•fac′ture, *n., v.,* **-tured, -turing.** —*n.* 1. making of things, esp. in great quantity. 2. thing made. —*v.* 3. make. —**man′u•fac′tur•er,** *n.*

man′u•mit′ (man′yə mit′), *v.,* **-mitted, -mitting.** release from slavery. —**man′u•mis′sion,** *n.*

ma•nure′, *n., v.,* **-ured, -uring.** —*n.* 1. fertilizer, esp. dung. —*v.* 2. apply manure to.

man′u•script′, *n.* document.

man′y, *adj.* 1. comprising a large number; numerous. —*n.* 2. large number.

Mao′ism (mou′iz əm), *n.* policies of Chinese Communist leader Mao Zedong. —**Mao′ist,** *n., adj.*

map, *n., v.,* **mapped, mapping.** —*n.* 1. flat representation of earth, etc. —*v.* 2. show by map. 3. plan.

ma′ple, *n.* northern tree.

mar, *v.,* **marred, marring.** damage.

Mar., March.

mar′a•bou′, *n., pl.* **-bous.** bare-headed stork.

ma•ra′ca, *n.* gourd-shaped rattle filled with seeds or pebbles, used as rhythm instrument.

mar′a•schi′no (-skē′-), *n.* cordial made from fermented juice of wild cherry.

maraschino cherry, cherry preserved in maraschino.

mar′a•thon′, *n.* long contest, esp. a foot race of 26 miles, 385 yards.

ma•raud′, *v.* plunder. —**ma•raud′er,** *n.*

mar′ble, *n.* **1.** crystalline limestone used in sculpture and building. **2.** small glass ball used in children's game. —*adj.* **3.** of marble.

mar′bling, *n.* intermixture of fat with lean in meat.

march, *v.* **1.** walk with measured tread. **2.** advance. —*n.* **3.** act of marching. **4.** distance covered in march. **5.** music for marching.

March, *n.* third month of year.

mar′chion•ess, *n.* **1.** wife or widow of marquess. **2.** woman of rank equal to marquess.

Mar′di Gras (mär′dē grä′, grä′), the day before Lent, often celebrated as a carnival.

mare, *n.* female horse.

mare′s′-nest′, *n.* discovery that proves to be delusion.

mar′ga•rine (-jə-), *n.* oleomargarine.

mar′gin, *n.* **1.** edge. **2.** amount more than necessary. **3.** difference between cost and price. —**mar′gin•al,** *adj.*

mar′gi•na′li•a (-jə nā′-), *n.pl.* marginal notes.

mar′gue•rite′ (-gə rēt′), *n.* daisylike chrysanthemum.

mar′i•gold′, *n.* common, yellow-flowered plant.

ma′ri•jua′na (mä′rə wä′nə), *n.* narcotic plant.

ma•rim′ba, *n.* xylophone.

ma•ri′na (-rē′-), *n.* docking area for small boats.

mar′i•nade′, *n.* pungent liquid mixture for steeping food.

mar′i•nate′, *v.* -nated, -nating. season by steeping. —**mar′i•na′tion**, *n.*

ma•rine′, *adj.* **1.** of the sea. —*n.* **2.** member of U.S. Marine Corps. **3.** fleet of ships.

Marine Corps, military branch of U.S. Navy.

mar′i•ner, *n.* sailor.

mar′i•o•nette′, *n.* puppet on strings.

mar′i•tal, *adj.* of marriage. —**mar′i•tal•ly**, *adv.*

mar′i•time′, *adj.* of sea or shipping.

mar′jo•ram, *n.* seasoning herb.

mark, *n.* **1.** any visible sign. **2.** object aimed at. **3.** rating; grade. **4.** lasting effect. **5.** German monetary unit. —*v.* **6.** be feature of. **7.** put mark on, as grade or price. **8.** pay attention to. —**mark′er**, *n.*

mark′down′, *n.* cut price.

marked, *adj.* **1.** conspicuous. **2.** ostentatious. **3.** singled out for revenge. —**mark′ed•ly**, *adv.*

mar′ket, *n.* **1.** place for selling and buying. —*v.* **2.** sell or buy. —**mar′ket•a•ble**, *adj.*

mar′ket•place′, *n.* **1.** open area where market is held. **2.** the world of business, trade, and economics.

marks′man, *n., pl.* -men. good shooter. —**marks′man•ship′**, *n.* —**marks′wom′an**, *n.fem.*

mark′up′, *n.* price increase by retailer.

marl, *n.* earth used as fertilizer.

mar′lin, *n.* large game fish.

mar′line•spike′, *n.* iron tool used to separate strands of rope.

mar′ma•lade′, *n.* preserve.

mar′mo•set′, *n.* small, tropical American monkey.

mar′mot (-mət), *n.* bushy-tailed rodent.

ma•roon′, *n., adj.* **1.** brown-red. —*v.* **2.** abandon ashore.

mar•quee′ (-kē′), *n.* projecting shelter over outer door.

mar′que•try (mär′ki trē), *n.* inlaid work forming pattern.

mar′quis (-kwis), *n.* rank of nobility below duke. Also, *Brit.* **mar′quess.** —**mar•quise′** (-kēz′), *n.fem.*

mar′qui•sette′ (-ki zet′), *n.* delicate open fabric.

mar′riage, *n.* 1. legal union of man and woman. 2. wedding. —**mar′riage•a•ble,** *adj.*

mar′row, *n.* inner tissue of bone.

mar′ry, *v.*, **-ried, -rying.** take, give, or unite in marriage.

Mars, *n.* one of the planets.

marsh, *n.* low, wet land. —**marsh′y,** *adj.*

mar′shal, *n.*, *v.*, **-shaled, -shaling.** —*n.* 1. federal officer. —*v.* 2. rally; organize.

marsh gas, decomposition product of organic matter.

marsh′mal′low, *n.* soft confection.

marsh marigold, yellow-flowered plant of buttercup family.

mar•su′pi•al, *n.* animal carrying its young in pouch, as the kangaroo. —**mar•su′pi•al,** *adj.*

mart, *n.* market.

mar′ten, *n.* small, American, fur-bearing animal.

mar′tial, *adj.* warlike; military. —**mar′tial•ly,** *adv.*

martial art, East Asian self-defense or combat.

martial law, law imposed by military forces.

mar′tin, *n.* bird of swallow family.

mar′ti•net′, *n.* disciplinarian.

mar•ti′ni (-tē′nē), *n.* cocktail of gin and vermouth.

mar′tyr, *n.* 1. person who willingly dies or suffers for a belief. —*v.* 2. make martyr of. —**mar′tyr•dom,** *n.*

mar′vel, *n.*, *v.*, **-veled, -veling.** —*n.* 1. wonderful thing. —*v.* 2. wonder (at). —**mar′vel•ous,** *adj.*

Marx′ism, *n.* doctrine of classless society; communism. —**Marx′ist,** *n.*, *adj.*

mar′zi•pan′, *n.* confection of almond paste and sugar.

mas•car′a, *n.* cosmetic for eyelashes.

mas′cot, *n.* source of luck.

mas′cu•line, *adj.* of or like men. —**mas′cu•lin′i•ty,** *n.*

ma′ser (mā′zər), *n.* device for producing electromagnetic waves.

mash, *n.* 1. soft pulpy mass. —*v.* 2. crush.

mash′ie, *n.* golf club.

mask, *n.* **1.** disguise for face. —*v.* **2.** disguise.

mas′och•ism (mas′ə kiz′əm), *n.* willful suffering. —**mas′och•ist,** *n.* —**mas′och•is′tic,** *adj.*

ma′son, *n.* builder with stone, brick, etc. —**ma′son•ry,** *n.*

mas′quer•ade′, *n., v.,* **-aded, -ading.** —*n.* **1.** disguise. **2.** party at which guests wear disguise. —*v.* **3.** wear disguise. —**mas′quer•ad′er,** *n.*

mass, *n.* **1.** body of coherent matter. **2.** quantity or size. **3.** weight. **4.** (*cap.*) celebration of the Eucharist. **5. the masses,** common people as a whole. —*v.* **6.** form into a mass. —*adj.* **7.** of or affecting the masses. **8.** done on a large scale.

Mass., Massachusetts.

mas′sa•cre, *n., v.,* **-cred, -cring.** —*n.* **1.** killing of many. —*v.* **2.** slaughter.

mas•sage′, *v.,* **-saged, -saging,** *n.* —*v.* **1.** treat body by rubbing or kneading. —*n.* **2.** such treatment. —**mas•seur′** (mə sûr′), *n.* —**mas•seuse′** (mə sōōs′), *n.fem.*

mas′sive, *adj.* large; heavy. —**mas′sive•ly,** *adv.*

mass media, means of communication that reaches large numbers of people.

mass noun, noun referring to indefinitely divisible substance or abstract noun.

mass number, number of nucleons in atomic nucleus.

mass′-produce′, *v.,* **-duced, -ducing.** produce in large quantities. —**mass production.**

mast, *n.* upright pole.

mas•tec′to•my, *n., pl.* **-mies.** surgical removal of a breast.

mas′ter, *n.* **1.** person in control. **2.** employer or owner. **3.** skilled person. —*adj.* **4.** chief. —*v.* **5.** conquer.

mas′ter•ful, *adj.* asserting power or authority. —**mas′ter•ful•ly,** *adv.*

mas′ter•ly, *adj.* highly skilled.

mas′ter•mind′, *n.* **1.** supreme planner. —*v.* **2.** plan as such.

master of ceremonies, person who conducts events.

mas′ter•piece′, *n.* work of highest skill.

master's degree, academic degree awarded to student who has completed at least one year of graduate study.

master sergeant, noncommissioned officer of highest rank.

mas'ter•stroke', *n.* extremely skillful action.

mas'ter•y, *n., pl.* **-teries.** control; skill.

mast'head', *n.* box in newspaper, etc., giving names of owners and staff.

mas'ti•cate', *v.,* **-cated, -cating.** chew. **—mas'ti•ca'tion,** *n.*

mas'tiff, *n.* powerful dog.

mas'to•don', *n.* large extinct elephantlike mammal.

mas'toid, *n.* protuberance of bone behind ear.

mas'tur•bate', *v.,* **-bated, -bating.** practice sexual self-gratification. **—mas'tur•ba'tion,** *n.*

mat, *n., v.,* **matted, matting,** *adj.* **—n. 1.** covering for floor or other surface. **2.** border for picture. **3.** padding. **4.** thick mass. **5.** matte. **—v. 6.** cover with mat. **7.** form into mat. **—adj. 8.** matte.

mat'a•dor', *n.* bullfighter.

match, *n.* **1.** stick chemically tipped to strike fire. **2.** thing equaling another. **3.** game. **4.** marriage. **—v. 5.** equal. **6.** fit together. **7.** arrange marriage for.

match'less, *adj.* unequaled. **—match'less•ly,** *adv.*

match'mak'er, *n.* arranger of marriages.

mate, *n., v.,* **mated, mating.** **—n. 1.** one of pair. **2.** officer of merchant ship. **3.** assistant. **4.** female member of couple. **—v. 5.** join; pair.

ma'té (mä'tā), *n., pl.* **-tés.** tealike beverage.

ma•te'ri•al, *n.* **1.** substance of which thing is made. **2.** fabric. **—adj. 3.** physical. **4.** germane. **—ma•te'ri•al•ly,** *adv.*

ma•te'ri•al•ism', *n.* **1.** devotion to material objects or wealth. **2.** belief that all reality is material. **—ma•te'ri•al•ist,** *n.* **—ma•te'ri•al•is'tic,** *adj.*

ma•te'ri•al•ize', *v.,* **-ized, -izing.** assume material form.

ma•te'ri•el', *n.* supplies.

ma•ter'ni•ty, *n.* motherhood. **—ma•ter'nal,** *adj.*

math′e•mat′ics, *n.* science of numbers.
—**math′e•mat′i•cal,** *adj.*
—**math′e•ma•ti′cian,** *n.*

mat′i•née′ (-nā′), *n.* afternoon performance.

mat′ins, *n.* morning prayer.

ma′tri•arch′, *n.* female ruler.
—**ma′tri•ar′chy,** *n.*

mat′ri•cide′, *n.* killing one's mother. —**mat′ri•cid′al,** *adj.*

ma•tric′u•late′, *v.,* -lated, -lating. enroll.
—**ma•tric′u•la′tion,** *n.*

mat′ri•mo′ny, *n., pl.* -nies. marriage. —**mat′ri•mo′ni•al,** *adj.*

ma′trix (mā′triks, ma′-), *n., pl.* -trices (-tri sēz′), -trixes. 1. point where something originates. 2. mold; model.

ma′tron, *n.* 1. married woman. 2. female institutional officer.
—**ma′tron•ly,** *adj.*

matte (mat), *adj.* 1. having a dull surface. —*n.* 2. dull surface or finish. Also, **mat.**

mat′ter, *n.* 1. material. 2. affair. 3. pus. 4. importance.
—*v.* 5. be of importance.

mat′ter-of-fact′, *adj.* objective; realistic.

mat′ting, *n.* mat of rushes.

mat′tock, *n.* digging implement with one broad and one pointed end.

mat′tress, *n.* thick filled case for sleeping on.

ma•ture′ (-tyo͞or′), *adj.,* -turer, -turest, *v.,* -tured, -turing.
—*adj.* 1. grown or developed. 2. adult in manner or thought. 3. payable. —*v.* 4. become or make mature. —**ma•tu′ri•ty,** *n.* —**ma•ture′ly,** *adv.*
—**mat′u•ra′tion,** *n.*

mat′zo (mät′sə), *n., pl.* -zos. unleavened bread.

maud′lin, *adj.* sentimental.

maul, *v.* handle roughly.

maun′der, *v.* 1. talk meanderingly. 2. wander.

mau′so•le′um, *n., pl.* -leums, -lea. tomb in form of building.

mauve (mōv), *n.* pale purple.

ma′ven (mā′-), *n.* expert.

mav′er•ick, *n.* 1. unbranded calf. 2. nonconformist.

maw, *n.* mouth.

mawk′ish, *adj.* sickly sentimental. —**mawk′ish•ly,** *adv.* —**mawk′ish•ness,** *n.*

max′i, *n., pl.* -is. ankle-length coat or skirt.

max•il′la, *n., pl.* **maxillae.** upper jaw. —**max′il•lar′y**, *adj.*

max′im, *n.* general truth.

max′i•mum, *n.* **1.** greatest degree or quantity. —*adj.* **2.** greatest possible.

may, *v., pt.* **might.** (auxiliary verb of possibility or permission.)

May, *n.* fifth month of year.

may′be, *adv.* perhaps.

May′day′, *n.* international radio distress call.

may′flow′er, *n.* plant that blossoms in May.

may′fly′, *n., pl.* **-flies.** insect with large forewings.

may′hem, *n.* random violence.

may′on•naise′, *n.* salad dressing made chiefly of egg yolks, oil, and vinegar. Also, *Informal,* **may′o.**

may′or, *n.* chief officer of city. —**may′or•al•ty**, *n.*

maze, *n.* confusing arrangement of paths.

ma•zur′ka, *n.* Polish dance.

MD, Maryland. Also, **Md.**

M.D., Doctor of Medicine.

me, *pers. pronoun.* objective case of **I.**

ME, Maine.

mead, *n.* liquor of honey.

mead′ow, *n.* level grassland.

mead′ow•lark′, *n.* common American songbird.

mea′ger, *adj.* poor; scanty. Also, **mea′gre.**

meal, *n.* **1.** food eaten. **2.** coarse grain. —**meal′y**, *adj.*

meal′y-mouthed′, *adj.* avoiding candid speech.

mean, *v.,* **meant, meaning,** *adj., n.* —*v.* **1.** intend (to do or signify). **2.** signify. —*adj.* **3.** poor; shabby. **4.** hostile; malicious. **5.** middle. —*n.* **6.** (*pl.*) method of achieving purpose. **7.** (*pl.*) money or property. **8.** intermediate quantity. —**mean′ness**, *n.*

me•an′der, *v.* wander.

mean′ing, *n.* **1.** significance. —*adj.* **2.** significant. —**mean′ing•ful**, *adj.* —**mean′ing•less**, *adj.* —**mean′ing•ly**, *adv.*

mean′time′, *n.* **1.** time between. —*adv.* Also, **mean′while′**. **2.** in time between.

mea′sles, *n.* infectious disease marked by small red spots.

mea'sly, *adj.,* **-slier, -sliest.** *Informal.* miserably small.

meas'ure, *v.,* **-ured, -uring.** *n.* —*v.* **1.** ascertain size or extent. —*n.* **2.** process of measuring. **3.** dimensions. **4.** instrument or system of measuring. **5.** action. —**meas'ur•a•ble,** *adj.* —**meas'ure•ment,** *n.*

meas'ured, *adj.* in distinct sequence.

meat, *n.* **1.** flesh of animals used as food. **2.** edible part of fruit. **3.** essential part.

meat'y, *adj.,* **meatier, meatiest. 1.** with much meat. **2.** rewarding attention.

Mec'ca (mek'ə), *n.* **1.** city in Saudi Arabia, spiritual center of Islam. **2.** (*often l.c.*) place that attracts many.

me•chan'ic, *n.* skilled worker with machinery.

me•chan'i•cal, *adj.* of or operated by machinery. —**me•chan'i•cal•ly,** *adv.*

me•chan'ics, *n.* science of motion and of action of forces on bodies.

mech'an•ism', *n.* **1.** structure of machine. **2.** piece of machinery. —**mech'a•nist,** *n.*

mech'a•nis'tic, *adj.* of or like machinery.

mech'a•nize', *v.,* **-nized, -nizing.** adapt to machinery. —**mech'a•ni•za'tion,** *n.*

med'al, *n.* badgelike metal object given for merit.

med'al•ist, *n.* medal winner.

me•dal'lion, *n.* large medal.

med'dle, *v.,* **-dled, -dling.** interfere; tamper. —**med'dler,** *n.* —**med'dle•some,** *adj.*

me'di•a, *n. pl.* the means of mass communication, as radio or television.

me'di•al, *adj.* average.

me'di•an, *adj., n.* middle.

me'di•ate', *v.,* **-ated, -ating.** settle (dispute) between parties. —**me'di•a'tion,** *n.* —**me'di•a'tor,** *n.*

med'ic, *n. Informal.* doctor.

Med'i•caid', *n.* state- and federal-supported medical care for low-income persons.

med'i•cal, *adj.* **1.** of medicine. **2.** curative. —**med'i•cal•ly,** *adv.*

me•dic'a•ment, *n.* healing substance.

Med′i•care′, *n.* government-supported medical insurance for those 65 years old or more.

med′i•cate′, *v.,* **-cated, -cating.** treat with medicine. —**med′i•ca′tion,** *n.*

me•dic′i•nal (-dis′-), *adj.* curative; remedial. —**me•dic′i•nal•ly,** *adv.*

med′i•cine, *n.* **1.** substance used in treating disease. **2.** art of preserving or restoring physical health.

medicine man, among American Indians, person believed to have magical powers.

me′di•e′val, *adj.* of the Middle Ages. Also, **me′di•ae′val.**

me′di•e′val•ism, *n.* **1.** a characteristic of the Middle Ages. **2.** devotion to medieval ideals, etc.

me′di•e′val•ist, *n.* **1.** expert in medieval history, etc. **2.** one devoted to medieval ideals, etc.

me′di•o′cre, *adj.* ordinary. —**me′di•oc′ri•ty,** *n.*

med′i•tate′, *v.,* **-tated, -tating.** think intensely; consider. —**med′i•ta′tion,** *n.* —**med′i•ta′tive,** *adj.*

me′di•um, *n., pl.* **-diums** *for 1–5,* **-dia** *for 1–3, 5, adj.* —*n.* **1.** something intermediate. **2.** means of doing. **3.** environment. **4.** person believed able to speak with dead. **5.** means of mass communication. —*adj.* **6.** intermediate.

med′ley, *n.* mixture.

me•dul′la, *n.* soft, marrowlike center of organ.

meek, *adj.* submissive.

meer′schaum (mir′shəm), *n.* claylike mineral, used for tobacco pipes.

meet, *v.,* **met, meeting,** *n., adj.* —*v.* **1.** come into contact with. **2.** make acquaintance of. **3.** satisfy. —*n.* **4.** equal. **5.** meeting. —*adj.* **6.** proper.

meet′ing, *n.* **1.** a coming together. **2.** persons gathered.

meg′a-, *prefix.* **1.** one million. **2.** large.

meg′a•hertz′, *n., pl.* **-hertz.** *Elect.* one million cycles per second.

meg′a·lo·ma′ni·a, *n.* delusion of greatness.

meg′a·lop′o·lis, *n.* large urban area. Also, **me·gap′o·lis.**

meg′a·phone′, *n.* device for magnifying sound.

meg′a·ton′, *n.* one million tons, esp. of TNT, as equivalent in explosive force.

mei·o′sis (mī ō′sis), *n.* part of process of gamete formation.

mel′a·mine, *n.* solid used in manufacturing resins.

mel′an·cho′li·a, *n.* state of great depression.

mel′an·chol′y, *n., pl.* **-cholies.** 1. low spirits; depression. —*adj.* 2. sad.

mé·lange′ (mā länj′), *n.* mixture.

mel′a·nin, *n.* pigment accounting for dark color of skin, hair, etc.

mel′a·nism, *n.* high concentration of melanin in skin.

mel′a·no′ma, *n.* darkly pigmented skin tumor.

meld, *v.* display combination of cards for a score.

me′lee (mā′lā), *n.* confused, general fight.

mel′io·rate′ (mēl′yə rāt′), *v.,* **-rated, -rating.** improve. —**mel′io·ra′tion,** *n.* —**mel′io·ra′tive,** *adj.*

mel·lif′lu·ous, *adj.* soft and sweet in speech.

mel′low, *adj.* 1. soft and rich. 2. genial. —*v.* 3. make or become mellow.

me·lo′de·on, *n.* reed organ.

me·lo′di·ous, *adj.* tuneful.

mel′o·dra′ma, *n.* play emphasizing theatrical effects and strong emotions. —**mel′o·dra·mat′ic,** *adj.*

mel′o·dy, *n., pl.* **-dies.** arrangement of musical sounds. —**me·lod′ic,** *adj.*

mel′on, *n.* edible fruit of certain annual vines.

melt, *v.,* **melted, melted** or **molten, melting.** 1. become liquid. 2. soften.

melt′down′, *n.* melting of nuclear reactor core.

melting pot, place where blending of peoples, races, or cultures takes place.

mel′ton, *n.* woolen fabric.

mem'ber, *n.* **1.** part of structure or body. **2.** one belonging to organization. —**mem'ber•ship'**, *n.*

mem'brane, *n.* thin film of tissue in animals and plants.

me•men'to, *n., pl.* **-tos, -toes.** reminder.

mem'oir (-wär), *n.* **1.** (*pl.*) personal recollection. **2.** biography.

mem•o•ra•bil'i•a, *n.pl.* souvenirs.

mem'o•ra•ble, *adj.* worth remembering. —**mem'o•ra•bly,** *adv.*

mem'o•ran'dum, *n., pl.* **-dums, -da.** written statement or reminder. Also, **mem'o.**

me•mo'ri•al, *n.* **1.** something honoring memory of a person or event. —*adj.* **2.** serving as memorial.

mem'o•rize', *v.,* **-rized, -rizing.** commit to memory.

mem'o•ry, *n., pl.* **-ries. 1.** faculty of remembering. **2.** something that is remembered. **3.** length of time of recollection. **4.** reputation after death. **5.** capacity of computer to store data.

men'ace, *v.,* **-aced, -acing,** *n.* —*v.* **1.** threaten evil to. —*n.* **2.** something that threatens.

mé•nage' (mā näzh'), *n.* household.

me•nag'er•ie, *n.* collection of animals.

mend, *v.* repair. —**mend'er,** *n.*

men•da'cious, *adj.* untruthful. —**men•dac'i•ty,** *n.*

men'di•cant, *n.* beggar.

men•ha'den (-hād'n), *n., pl.* **-den.** herringlike Atlantic fish.

me'ni•al, *adj.* **1.** humble; servile. —*n.* **2.** servant.

me•nin'ges (mi nin'jēz), *n.pl., sing.* **me'ninx.** membranes covering brain and spinal cord.

men'in•gi'tis (-jī'-), *n.* inflammation of meninges.

men'o•pause', *n.* cessation of menses.

me•nor'ah (mə nôr'ə), *n.* symbolic candelabrum used by Jews during Hanukkah.

men'ses (-sēz), *n.pl.* monthly discharge of blood from uterus. —**men'stru•al,** *adj.* —**men'stru•ate',** *v.* —**men•stru•a'tion,** *n.*

men'sur•a•ble (-shər-), *adj.* measurable.
—**men'su•ra'tion**, *n.*

mens'wear', *n.* men's clothing.

men'tal, *adj.* of or in mind.
—**men'tal•ly**, *adv.*

men•tal'i•ty, *n., pl.* **-ties. 1.** mental ability. **2.** characteristic mental attitude.

men'thol, *n.* colorless alcohol from peppermint oil.
—**men'thol•at'ed**, *adj.*

men'tion, *v.* **1.** speak or write of. —*n.* **2.** reference.
—**men'tion•a•ble**, *adj.*

men'tor, *n.* adviser; teacher.

men'u, *n.* list of dishes that can be served.

me•ow', *n.* **1.** sound cat makes. —*v.* **2.** make such sound.

mer'can•tile' (-tēl, -tīl), *adj.* of or engaged in trade.

mer'ce•nar'y (-sə-), *adj., n., pl.* **-naries.** —*adj.* **1.** acting only for profit. —*n.* **2.** hired soldier.

mer'cer•ize', *v.,* **-ized, -izing.** treat (cottons) for strength.

mer'chan•dise', *n., v.,* **-dised, -dising.** —*n.* **1.** goods; wares. —*v.* **2.** buy and sell.

mer'chant, *n.* person who deals in goods for profit.

mer'chant•man, *n., pl.* **-men.** trading ship.

merchant marine, commercial vessels of nation.

mer•cu'ri•al, *adj.* **1.** of mercury. **2.** sprightly. **3.** changeable in emotion.

mer'cu•ry, *n.* **1.** heavy metallic element. **2.** (*cap.*) one of the planets.

mer'cy, *n., pl.* **-cies. 1.** pity; compassion. **2.** act of compassion. —**mer'ci•ful**, *adj.* —**mer'ci•less**, *adj.*

mere, *adj.* only; simple.
—**mere'ly**, *adv.*

mer'e•tri'cious, *adj.* falsely attractive.

mer•gan'ser, *n.* diving duck.

merge, *v.,* **merged, merging.** combine. —**merg'er**, *n.*

me•rid'i•an, *n.* circle on earth's surface passing through the poles.

me•ringue' (-rang'), *n.* egg whites and sugar beaten together.

me·ri′no, *n., pl.* **-nos.** kind of sheep.

mer′it, *n.* **1.** excellence or good quality. —*v.* **2.** deserve. —**mer′i·to′ri·ous,** *adj.*

mer′maid′, *n.* imaginary sea creature, half woman and half fish. —**mer′man′,** *n.masc.*

mer′ry, *adj.,* **-rier, -riest.** gay; joyous. —**mer′ri·ly,** *adv.* —**mer′ri·ment,** *n.*

mer′ry-go-round′, *n.* revolving amusement ride.

mer′ry·mak′ing, *n.* festivities; hilarity. —**mer′ry-ma′ker,** *n.*

me′sa (mā′-), *n.* high, steep-walled plateau.

mé′sal·li′ance (mā′zə lī′əns), *n.* marriage with social inferior.

mesh, *n.* **1.** open space of net. **2.** net itself. **3.** engagement of gears. —*v.* **4.** catch in mesh. **5.** engage. **6.** match or interlock.

mes′mer·ize′, *v.,* **-ized, -izing.** hypnotize; spellbind. —**mes′mer·ism′,** *n.*

mes′o·sphere′, *n.* region between stratosphere and thermosphere.

Mes′o·zo′ic, *adj.* pertaining to geologic era occurring between 230 and 65 million years ago.

mes·quite′ (-kēt′), *n.* tree of southwest U.S.

mess, *n.* **1.** dirty condition. **2.** group taking meals together regularly. **3.** meals so taken. —*v.* **4.** make dirty. **5.** eat in company. —**mess′y,** *adj.*

mes′sage, *n.* communication.

mes′sen·ger, *n.* bearer of message.

Mes·si′ah, *n.* **1.** expected deliverer. **2.** (in Christian theology) Jesus Christ.

mes·ti′zo (mes tē′zō), *n., pl.* **-zos, -zoes.** person part-Spanish, part-Indian. Also, **mes·ti′za,** *fem.*

meta-, prefix meaning: **1.** after or beyond, as *metaphysics*. **2.** behind, as *metacarpus*. **3.** change, as *metamorphosis*.

me·tab′o·lism′, *n.* biological processes of converting food into matter and matter into energy. —**met′a·bol′ic,** *adj.*

met′a·car′pus, *n., pl.* **-pi.** bones of forelimb between wrist and fingers. —**met′a·car′pal,** *adj., n.*

met′al, *n.* **1.** substance such as gold or copper. **2.** mettle. —**me·tal′lic,** *adj.* —**met′al·ware′,** *n.*

met′al·lur′gy, *n.* science of working with metals. —**met′al·lur′gist,** *n.*

met′a·mor′phose, *v.,* **-phosed, -phosing.** transform.

met′a·mor′pho·sis, *n., pl.* **-ses.** change.

met′a·phor, *n.* figure of speech using analogy. —**met′a·phor′i·cal,** *adj.*

met′a·phys′ics, *n.* branch of philosophy concerned with ultimate nature of reality. —**met′a·phys′ical,** *adj.* —**met′a·phy·si′cian,** *n.*

me·tas′ta·size′, *v.,* **-sized, -sizing.** spread from one to another part of the body. —**me·tas′ta·sis′,** *n.* —**met′a·stat′ic,** *adj.*

met′a·tar′sus, *n., pl.* **-si.** bones between tarsus and toes. —**met′a·tar′sal,** *adj., n.*

mete, *v.,* **meted, meting.** allot.

me′te·or, *n.* celestial body passing through earth's atmosphere. —**me′te·or′ic,** *adj.*

me′te·or·ite′, *n.* meteor reaching earth.

me′te·or·ol′o·gy, *n.* science of atmospheric phenomena. —**me′te·or·olog′i·cal,** *adj.* —**me′te·orol′o·gist,** *n.*

me′ter, *n.* **1.** unit in metric system, equal to 39.37 inches. **2.** rhythmic arrangement of words. **3.** device for measuring flow. —*v.* **4.** measure. Also, *Brit.,* **me′tre.** —**met′ric, met′ri·cal,** *adj.*

meth′a·done′, *n.* synthetic narcotic used in treating heroin addiction.

meth′ane, *n.* colorless, odorless, flammable gas.

meth′a·nol′, *n.* liquid used as solvent or fuel. Also, **meth′yl alcohol.**

meth′od, *n.* system of doing. —**me·thod′i·cal, me·thod′ic,** *adj.* —**me·thod′i·cal·ly,** *adv.*

meth′od·ol′o·gy, *n., pl.* **-gies.** system of methods.

meth′yl, *n.* univalent group derived from methane.

methyl alcohol, colorless, poisonous liquid used as solvent, fuel, and antifreeze.

me·tic′u·lous, *adj.* detailed.

mé′tier (mā′tyā), *n.* field of activity in which one has special ability. Also, **me′tier.**

metric, *adj.* of decimal system of weights and measures. —**met′ri•cize′,** *v.* —**met′ri•ca′tion,** *n.*

met′ro•nome′, *n.* device for marking tempo.

me•trop′o•lis, *n.* great city.

met′ro•pol′i•tan, *adj.* 1. of or in city. 2. of urban areas.

met′tle, *n.* 1. spirit. 2. disposition.

met′tle•some, *adj.* spirited; courageous.

mew (myōo), *n.* 1. cry of a cat. —*v.* 2. emit a mew.

mews, *n.* street with dwellings converted from stables.

Mex′i•can, *n.* native of Mexico. —**Mexican,** *adj.*

mez′za•nine′, *n.* low story between two main floors.

mez′zo-so•pran′o (met′sō-, med′zo-), *n.* voice, musical part, or singer intermediate in range between soprano and contralto.

M.F.A., Master of Fine Arts.

MI, Michigan.

mi•as′ma (mī-), *n., pl.* **-mata,** **-mas.** vapors from decaying organic matter.

mi′ca, *n.* shiny mineral occurring in thin layers.

Mich., Michigan.

mi′cro-, prefix meaning: 1. extremely small. 2. one millionth.

mi′crobe, *n.* microorganism.

mi′cro•chip′, *n.* chip (def. 3).

mi′cro•com•put′er, *n.* compact computer with less capability than minicomputer.

mi′cro•cosm, *n.* world in miniature.

mi′cro•fiche′ (-fēsh′), *n.* small sheet of microfilm.

mi′cro•film′, *n.* 1. very small photograph of book page, etc. —*v.* 2. make microfilm of.

mi•crom′e•ter, *n.* device for measuring minute distances.

mi′cron, *n.* millionth part of a meter.

mi′cro•or′gan•ism′, *n.* microscopic organism.

mi′cro•phone′, *n.* instrument for changing sound waves into changes in electric current.

mi′cro•proc′es•sor, *n.* computer circuit that performs all functions of CPU.

mi′cro•scope′, *n.* instrument for inspecting minute objects.

mi′cro•scop′ic, *adj.* 1. of microscopes. 2. very small.

mi′cro•sur′ger•y, *n.* surgery performed under magnification.

mi′cro•wave′, *n.* 1. short radio wave used in radar, cooking, etc. 2. oven that uses microwaves to generate heat in the food. —*v.* 3. cook in microwave oven.

mid, *adj.* 1. middle. —*prep.* 2. amid.

mid′day′, *n.* noon.

mid′dle, *adj.* 1. equally distant from given limits. 2. medium. —*n.* 3. middle part.

Middle Ages, period of European history, about A.D. 476 to 1500.

middle class, class of people intermediate between the poor and the wealthy, usu. educated working people.

Middle East, area including Israel and Arab countries of NE Africa and SW Asia.

Middle English, English language of period c1150–1475.

mid′dle•man′, *n.* merchant who buys direct from producer.

middle-of-the-road, *adj.* moderate.

middle school, school for grades 5 or 6 through 8.

mid′dling, *adj.* 1. medium. —*n.* 2. (*pl.*) coarse parts of grain.

mid′dy, *n., pl.* **-dies.** blouse with square back collar.

midge, *n.* minute fly.

midg′et, *n.* very small person.

mid′land, *n.* interior of country.

mid′night′, *n.* 12 o'clock at night.

midnight sun, sun visible at midnight in summer in arctic and antarctic regions.

mid′point′, *n.* point at or near the middle.

mid′riff, *n.* part of body between the chest and abdomen.

mid′ship′man, *n., pl.* **-men.** rank of student at U.S. Naval or Coast Guard academy.

midst, *n.* middle.

mid′sum′mer, *n.* **1.** middle of the summer. **2.** summer solstice, around June 21.

mid′term, *n.* **1.** halfway point of school term. **2.** examination given at midterm.

mid′way′, *adj., adv.* **1.** in or to middle. —*n.* **2.** area of games and shows at carnival.

mid′wife′, *n., pl.* **-wives.** woman who assists at childbirth.

mid′win′ter, *n.* **1.** middle of winter. **2.** winter solstice, around December 22.

mien (mēn), *n.* air; bearing.

miff, *n.* **1.** petty quarrel. —*v.* **2.** offend.

might, *v.* **1.** pt. of **may.** —*n.* **2.** strength; power.

might′y, *adj.,* **mightier, mightiest,** *adv.* —*adj.* **1.** powerful; huge. —*adv.* **2.** *Informal.* very. —**might′i•ness,** *n.*

mi′gnon•ette′ (min′yə net′), *n.* plant with small flowers.

mi′graine, *n.* painful headache.

mi′grate′, *v.,* **-grated, -grating.** go from one region to another. —**mi•gra′tion,** *n.* —**mi′gra•to′ry,** *adj.* —**mi′grant,** *adj., n.*

mi•ka′do, *n., pl.* **-dos.** a title of emperor of Japan.

mike, *n. Informal.* microphone.

mil, *n.* one thousandth of inch.

mi•la′dy, *n., pl.* **-dies.** English noblewoman (often used as term of address).

milch, *adj.* giving milk.

mild, *adj.* gentle; temperate. —**mild′ly,** *adv.* —**mild′ness,** *n.*

mil′dew′, *n.* **1.** discoloration caused by fungus. —*v.* **2.** affect with mildew.

mile, *n.* unit of distance, equal on land to 5280 ft.

mile′age, *n.* **1.** miles traveled. **2.** travel allowance.

mile′stone′, *n.* **1.** marker showing road distance. **2.** important event.

mi•lieu′ (mēl yo͝o′), *n., pl.* **-lieus, -lieux.** environment.

mil′i•tant, *adj.* aggressive.

mil′i•ta•rism, *n.* **1.** military spirit. **2.** domination by military. —**mil′i•ta•rist,** *n.* —**mil′i•ta•ris′tic,** *adj.*

mil′i•tar•ize′, *v.,* **-ized, -izing.** equip with military weapons.

mil′i•tar′y, *adj., n., pl.* **-taries.** —*adj.* **1.** of armed forces, esp. on land. —*n.* **2.** armed forces or soldiers collectively.

military police, soldiers who perform police duties within army.

mil′i•tate′, *v.,* **-tated, -tating.** act (for or against).

mi•li′tia (-lish′ə), *n.* organization for emergency military service. —**mi•li′tia•man**, *n.*

milk, *n.* **1.** liquid secreted by female mammals to feed their young. —*v.* **2.** draw milk from. —**milk′y**, *adj.* —**milk′maid′**, *n.* —**milk′man′**, *n.*

milk glass, opaque white glass.

milk′weed′, *n.* plant with milky juice.

Milk′y Way′, *Astron.* galaxy containing sun and earth.

mill, *n.* **1.** place where manufacturing is done. **2.** device for grinding. **3.** one tenth of a cent. —*v.* **4.** grind or treat with mill. **5.** groove edges of (coin). **6.** move about in confusion. —**mill′er**, *n.*

mil•len′ni•um, *n., pl.* **-niums, -nia. 1.** future period. **2.** future reign of Christ on earth.

mil′let, *n.* cereal grass.

milli-, prefix meaning thousand or thousandth.

mil′li•gram′, *n.* one thousandth of gram.

mil′liard, *n. Brit.* one billion.

mil′li•li′ter, *n.* one thousandth of liter.

mil′li•me′ter, *n.* one thousandth of meter.

mil′li•ner, *n.* person who makes or sells women's hats.

mil′li•ner′y, *n.* **1.** women's hats. **2.** business of milliner.

mil′lion, *n., adj.* 1000 times 1000. —**mil′lionth**, *adj., n.*

mil′lion•aire′, *n.* person having million dollars.

mill′race′, *n.* channel for water driving mill wheel.

mill′stone′, *n.* **1.** stone for grinding grain. **2.** heavy mental or emotional burden.

mill′stream′, *n.* stream in millrace.

mill′wright′, *n.* person who designs mill machinery.

milque′toast′ (milk′-), *n.* (*often cap.*) timid person.

milt, *n.* male secretion of fish.

mime, *n.* pantomimist; clown.

mim′e•o•graph′, *n.* **1.** stencil device for duplicating. —*v.* **2.** copy with mimeograph.

mim′ic, *v.,* **-icked, -icking,** *n.* —*v.* **1.** imitate speech or actions of. —*n.* **2.** person who mimics. —**mim′ic•ry,** *n.*

mi•mo′sa, *n.* semitropical tree.

min′a•ret′, *n.* tower for calling Muslims to prayer.

min′a•to′ry, *adj.* threatening.

mince, *v.,* **minced, mincing. 1.** chop fine. **2.** speak, move, or behave with affected elegance. —**minc′ing•ly,** *adv.*

mince′meat′, *n.* cooked mixture of finely chopped meat, raisins, spices, etc.

mind, *n.* **1.** thinking part of human or animal. **2.** intellect. **3.** inclination. —*v.* **4.** heed; obey.

mind′-blow′ing, *adj.* **1.** astounding. **2.** producing hallucinogenic effect.

mind′ed, *adj.* **1.** having a certain kind of mind. **2.** inclined.

mind′ful, *adj.* careful.

mind′less, *adj.* **1.** heedless. **2.** without intelligence.

mine, *pron., n., v.,* **mined, mining.** —*pron.* **1.** possessive form of **I.** —*n.* **2.** excavation in earth for resources. **3.** stationary explosive device used in war. **4.** abundant source. **5.** dig or work in mine. —*v.* **6.** lay explosive mines. —**min′er,** *n.*

min′er•al, *n.* **1.** inorganic substance. **2.** substance obtained by mining. —*adj.* **3.** of minerals.

min′er•al′o•gy, *n.* science of minerals. —**min′er•al•og′i•cal,** *adj.* —**min′er•al′o•gist,** *n.*

mineral water, water with dissolved mineral salts or gases.

min′e•stro′ne (min′i strō′nē), *n.* thick vegetable soup.

mine′sweep′er, *n.* ship used to remove explosive mines.

min′gle, *v.,* **-gled, -gling.** associate; mix.

min′i, *n.* small version.

mini-, prefix meaning: **1.** smaller than others of its kind. **2.** very short.

min′i•a•ture, *n.* **1.** greatly reduced form. **2.** tiny painting. —*adj.* **3.** on small scale.

min′i•a•tur•ize′, *v.,* **-ized, -izing.** make in very small size. —**min′i•a•tur•i•za′tion,** *n.*

min′i•com•put′er, *n.* computer with capabilities between those of microcomputer and mainframe.

min′im, *n.* smallest unit of liquid measure.

min′i•mal•ism, *n.* style that is spare and simple.

min′i•mize′, *v.,* **-mized, -mizing.** make minimum.

min′i•mum, *n.* **1.** least possible quantity, degree, etc. —*adj.* **2.** Also, **min′i•mal.** lowest.

min′ion, *n.* servile follower.

min′is•ter, *n.* **1.** person authorized to conduct worship. **2.** government representative abroad. **3.** head of governmental department. —*v.* **4.** give care. —**min′is•te′ri•al,** *adj.* —**min′is•tra′tion,** *n.*

min′is•try, *n., pl.* **-tries. 1.** religious calling. **2.** clergy. **3.** office of government. **4.** body of executive officials. **5.** act of ministering.

mink, *n.* fur-bearing animal.

Minn., Minnesota.

min′ne•sing′er, *n.* lyric poet of medieval Germany.

min′now, *n.* tiny fish.

mi′nor, *adj.* **1.** lesser in size or importance. **2.** under legal age. —*n.* **3.** person under legal age.

mi•nor′i•ty, *n., pl.* **-ties. 1.** smaller number or part. **2.** relatively small population group. **3.** state or time of being under legal age.

min•ox′i•dil′, *n.* drug used in treating hypertension and baldness.

min′strel, *n.* **1.** musician or singer, esp. in Middle Ages. **2.** comedian in blackface.

mint, *n.* **1.** aromatic herb. **2.** place where money is coined. —*v.* **3.** make coins.

min′u•end′, *n.* number from which another is to be subtracted.

min′u•et′, *n.* stately dance.

mi′nus, *prep.* **1.** less. —*adj.* **2.** less than.

mi′nus•cule′ (min′əs-), *adj.* tiny.

min′ute, *n.* **1.** sixty seconds. **2.** (*pl.*) record of proceedings. —*adj.* (mī nyo͞ot′). **3.** extremely small. **4.** attentive to detail. —**mi•nute′ly**, *adv.*

mi•nu′ti•ae′ (-shē ē′), *n.pl.* trifling matters.

minx, *n.* saucy girl.

mir′a•cle, *n.* supernatural act. —**mi•rac′u•lous**, *adj.*

mi•rage′, *n.* atmospheric illusion in which images of far-distant objects are seen.

mire, *n., v.*, **mired, miring.** —*n.* **1.** swamp. **2.** deep mud. —*v.* **3.** stick fast in mire. **4.** soil with mire. —**mir′y**, *adj.*

mir′ror, *n.* **1.** reflecting surface. —*v.* **2.** reflect.

mirth, *n.* gaiety. —**mirth′ful**, *adj.* —**mirth′less**, *adj.*

mis-, prefix meaning: **1.** wrong, as *misconduct.* **2.** lack of, as *mistrust.*

mis′ad•ven′ture, *n.* mishap.

mis′al•li′ance, *n.* incompatible association.

mis′an•thrope′, *n.* people hater. —**mis′an•throp′ic**, *adj.*

mis′ap•ply′, *v.*, **-plied, -plying.** use wrongly. —**mis′ap•pli•ca′tion**, *n.*

mis′ap•pre•hend′, *v.* misunderstand. —**mis′ap•pre•hen′sion**, *n.*

mis′ap•pro′pri•ate′, *v.*, **-ated, -ating.** use wrongly as one's own. —**mis′ap•pro′pri•a′tion**, *n.*

mis′be•got′ten, *adj.* ill-conceived.

mis′be•have′, *v.*, **-haved, -having.** behave badly. —**mis′be•hav′ior**, *n.*

misc., miscellaneous.

mis•cal′cu•late′, *v.*, **-lated, -lating.** judge badly. —**mis′cal•cu•la′tion**, *n.*

mis•call′, *v.* call by a wrong name.

mis•car′riage, *n.* **1.** premature birth resulting in death of fetus. **2.** failure.

mis•car′ry, *v.*, **-ried, -rying. 1.** go wrong. **2.** have miscarriage.

mis•cast′, *v.* wrongly cast.

mis′ce•ge•na′tion (mis′i jə-), *n.* sexual union between persons of different races.

mis′cel•la′ne•ous, *adj.* various. —**mis′cel•la•ny**, *n.*

mis•chance′, *n.* bad luck.

mis′chief, *n.* **1.** trouble. **2.** tendency to tease. —**mis′chie•vous,** *adj.*

mis′ci•ble, *adj.* capable of being mixed.

mis′con•ceive′, *v.,* **-ceived, -ceiving.** misunderstand. —**mis′con•cep′tion,** *n.*

mis•con′duct, *n.* improper or illegal conduct.

mis′con•strue′, *v.,* **-strued, -struing.** misinterpret.

mis′cre•ant, *n.* villain.

mis•deed′, *n.* immoral deed.

mis′de•mean′or, *n.* minor offense.

mis•do′ing, *n.* (*often pl.*) wrongful act.

mise-en-scène′ (mē zän sen′), *n., pl.* **-scènes** (-sens′). **1.** placement of actors, scenery, and properties on stage. **2.** surroundings.

mi′ser, *n.* hoarder of wealth. —**mi′ser•ly,** *adj.*

mis′er•a•ble, *adj.* **1.** wretched. **2.** deplorable. **3.** contemptible; despicable. —**mis′er•a•bly,** *adv.*

mis′er•y, *n., pl.* **-eries.** wretched condition.

mis•fea′sance, *n.* wrongful exercise of lawful authority.

mis•fire′, *v.,* **-fired, -firing.** fail to fire.

mis•fit′, *n.* **1.** poor fit. **2.** (mis′fit′). maladjusted person.

mis•for′tune, *n.* bad luck.

mis•giv′ing, *n.* apprehension.

mis•guide′, *v.,* **-guided, -guiding.** guide wrongly.

mis•han′dle, *v.,* **-dled, -dling. 1.** handle roughly. **2.** manage badly.

mis′hap, *n.* unlucky accident.

mish′mash′ (mish′mäsh′), *n.* jumble; hodgepodge.

mis′in•form′, *v.* give false information to. —**mis′in•for•ma′tion,** *n.*

mis′in•ter′pret, *v.* interpret wrongly. —**mis′in•ter′pre•ta′tion,** *n.*

mis•judge′, *v.,* **-judged, -judging.** judge wrongly. —**mis•judg′ment,** *n.*

mis•lay′, *v.,* **-laid, -laying. 1.** put in place later forgotten. **2.** misplace.

mis•lead′, *v.,* **-led, -leading. 1.** lead in wrong direction. **2.** lead into error, as in conduct.

mis•man′age, *v.,* **-aged, -aging.** manage badly. **—mis•man′age•ment,** *n.*

mis•match′ (mis mach′; *for 2 also* mis′mach′), *v.* **1.** match unsuitably. **—n. 2.** unsuitable match.

mis•no′mer, *n.* misapplied name.

mi•sog′a•my, *n.* hatred of marriage. **—mi•sog′a•mist,** *n.*

mi•sog′y•ny (-soj′ə-), *n.* hatred of women. **—mi•sog′y•nist,** *n.*

mis•place′, *v.,* **-placed, -placing. 1.** forget location of. **2.** place unwisely.

mis′print′, *n.* error in printing.

mis•pri′sion (-prizh′ən), *n.* neglect of official duty.

mis′pro•nounce′, *v.,* **-nounced, -nouncing.** pronounce wrongly. **—mis′pro•nun′ci•a′tion,** *n.*

mis•quote′, *v.,* **-quoted, -quoting.** quote incorrectly. **—mis′quo•ta′tion,** *n.*

mis•read′ (-rēd′), *v.,* **-read** (red′), **-reading. 1.** read wrongly. **2.** misinterpret.

mis′rep•re•sent′, *v.* give wrong idea of. **—mis′rep•re•sen•ta′tion,** *n.*

mis•rule′, *n.* bad or unwise rule. **—mis•rule′,** *v.*

miss, *v.* **1.** fail to hit or catch. **2.** feel absence of. **—n. 3.** (*cap.*) title of respect for unmarried woman. **4.** girl. **5.** failure to hit or catch.

Miss., Mississippi.

mis′sal, *n.* book of prayers, etc., for celebrating Mass.

mis•shap′en, *adj.* deformed.

mis′sile, *n.* object thrown or shot, as lance or bullet.

mis′sion, *n.* **1.** group sent abroad for specific work. **2.** duty. **3.** air operation against enemy. **4.** missionary post.

mis′sion•ar′y, *n., pl.* **-aries,** *adj.* **—n. 1.** person sent to propagate religious faith. **—adj. 2.** of religious missions.

mis′sive, *n.* written message.

mis•spell′, *v.* spell wrongly.

mis•spend′, *v.,* **-spent, -spending.** squander.

mis•state′, *v.,* **-stated, -stating.** state wrongly. **—mis′state′ment,** *n.*

mis•step′, *n.* error.

mist, *n.* light, thin fog. **—mist′y,** *adj.*

mis·take′, *n., v.,* **-took, -taken, -taking.** —*n.* **1.** error in judgment or action. —*v.* **2.** take wrongly. **3.** misunderstand. **4.** be in error.

Mis′ter, *n.* title of respect for man. *Abbr.:* **Mr.**

mis′tle·toe′, *n.* parasitic plant.

mis·treat′, *v.* treat badly. —**mis·treat′ment,** *n.*

mis′tress, *n.* **1.** female head of household. **2.** female owner. **3.** woman illicitly acting as wife.

mis·tri′al, *n.* trial ended without verdict because of legal error or inability of jury to agree on verdict.

mis·trust′, *n.* lack of trust. —**mis·trust′,** *v.*

mis′un·der·stand′, *v.,* **-stood, -standing.** misinterpret. —**mis′un·der·stand′ing,** *n.*

mis·use′, *n., v.,* **-used, -using.** —*n.* (-yoos′). **1.** improper use. —*v.* (-yooz′). **2.** use badly or wrongly. **3.** abuse.

mite, *n.* **1.** tiny parasitic insect. **2.** small thing or bit.

mi′ter, *v.* **1.** join two pieces on diagonal. —*n.* **2.** such joint. **3.** tall cap worn by bishops. Also, *Brit.,* **mi′tre.**

mit′i·gate′, *v.,* **-gated, -gating.** make less severe.

mi·to′sis (mī tō′-), *n.* cell division. —**mi·tot′ic,** *adj.*

mitt, *n.* thick glove.

mit′ten, *n.* fingerless glove.

mix, *v.,* **mixed** or **mixt, mixing,** *n.* —*v.* **1.** put together; combine. **2.** associate. **3.** confuse. —*n.* **4.** mixture. **5.** mess. —**mix′ture,** *n.*

mixed number, number consisting of whole number and fraction or decimal.

mix′-up′, *n.* state of confusion.

miz′zen·mast′, *n.* third mast from forward on ship.

ml, milliliter.

mm, millimeter.

MN, Minnesota.

mne·mon′ic (nē-), *adj.* aiding memory.

MO, 1. Also, **Mo.** Missouri. **2.** modus operandi.

moan, *n.* **1.** low groan. —*v.* **2.** utter moans.

moat, *n.* deep, water-filled ditch around fortification.

mob, *n., v.,* **mobbed, mobbing.** —*n.* **1.** crowd, esp. disorderly one. —*v.* **2.** attack as a mob.

mo′bile, *adj.* **1.** capable of moving or being moved. —*n.* (-bēl). **2.** abstract sculpture with parts that move, as with breezes. —**mo•bil′i•ty,** *n.*

mo′bi•lize′, *v.,* **-lized, -lizing.** make ready for war. —**mo′bi•li•za′tion,** *n.*

mob′ster, *n.* member of mob.

moc′ca•sin, *n.* **1.** soft shoe. **2.** poisonous snake.

mo′cha (-kə), *n.* **1.** kind of coffee. **2.** flavoring made from coffee and chocolate.

mock, *v.* **1.** mimic or ridicule. —*n.* **2.** derision. —*adj.* **3.** imitation.

mock′er•y, *n., pl.* **-ies. 1.** derision. **2.** travesty.

mock′ing•bird′, *n.* songbird with imitative voice.

mock′-up′, *n.* scale model.

mod, *adj. Informal.* stylish.

mode, *n.* prevailing style.

mod′el, *n., adj., v.,* **-eled, -eling.** —*n.* **1.** standard for imitation. **2.** person who poses, as for artist. —*adj.* **3.** serving as model. —*v.* **4.** pattern after model. **5.** wear as model. **6.** form.

mo′dem (mō′dəm, -dem), *n.* device enabling transmission of data from or to a computer via telephone or other communication lines.

mod′er•ate, *adj., n., v.,* **-ated, -ating.** —*adj.* (-it). **1.** not extreme. —*n.* (-it). **2.** person having moderate views. —*v.* (-ə rāt′). **3.** become less intense. **4.** preside over. —**mod′er•a′tion,** *n.* —**mod′er•ate•ly,** *adv.*

mod′er•a′tor, *n.* director of group discussion.

mod′ern, *adj.* of recent time. —**mo•der′ni•ty,** *n.* —**mod′ern•ize′,** *v.*

Modern English, English language since c1475.

mod′ern•ism, *n.* **1.** modern character or tendencies. **2.** modern usage. **3.** divergence from the past in the arts.

mod′ern•is′tic, *adj.* following modern trends.

mod′est, *adj.* **1.** humble in estimating oneself. **2.** simple; moderate. **3.** decent, moral. —**mod′est•ly,** *adv.* —**mod′es•ty,** *n.*

mod′i•cum, *n.* small amount.

mod′i•fy, *v.,* **-fied, -fying.** alter or moderate. —**mod′i•fi•ca′tion,** *n.* —**mod′i•fi′er,** *n.*

mod′ish (mō′-), *adj.* fashionable.

mo•diste′ (-dēst′), *n.fem.* maker of women's attire.

mod′u•late′, *v.,* **-lated, -lating. 1.** soften. **2.** *Radio.* alter (electric current) in accordance with sound waves. **3.** alter the pitch or key of. —**mod′u•la′tion,** *n.*

mod′ule, *n.* **1.** unit of measure. **2.** building unit. **3.** self-contained element of spacecraft. —**mod′u•lar,** *adj.*

mo′dus op′e•ran′di (mō′dəs op′ə ran′dē), *n., pl.* **mo′di op′e•ran′di** (mō′dē), method of operating.

mo′gul (mō′gəl), *n.* **1.** powerful person. **2.** bump on ski slope.

mo′hair′, *n.* fabric from fleece of the Angora goat.

Mo•ham′med•an•ism, *n.* Islam. —**Mo•ham′med•an,** *n., adj.*

moi′e•ty, *n., pl.* **-ties.** half.

moil, *n., v.* labor.

moi•ré′ (mwä rā′), *n., pl.* **-rés.** fabric with watery appearance.

moist, *adj.* damp. —**mois′ten,** *v.* —**mois′ten•er,** *n.*

mois′ture, *n.* dampness.

mo′lar, *n.* broad back tooth.

mo•las′ses, *n.* syrup produced in refining sugar.

mold, *n.* **1.** form for shaping molten material. **2.** thing so formed. **3.** fungus growth on matter. **4.** loose rich earth. —*v.* **5.** shape or form. **6.** become covered with mold (def. 3). —**mold′y,** *adj.*

mold′board′, *n.* curved metal plate on plow.

mold′er, *v.* **1.** decay. —*n.* **2.** person who molds.

mold′ing, *n.* decorative strip with special cross section.

mole, *n.* **1.** small spot on skin. **2.** small mammal. **3.** spy who works against agency he or she is employed by.

mol′e•cule′, *n.* smallest physical unit of a chemical element. —**mo•lec′u•lar,** *adj.*

mole′hill′, *n.* **1.** small mound of earth raised by moles. **2.** something insignificant.

mole′skin′, *n.* 1. fur of mole. 2. heavy cotton fabric with suedelike finish.

mo•lest′, *v.* 1. annoy by interfering with. 2. make indecent sexual advances to. —**mo′les•ta′tion**, *n.*

moll, *n. Slang.* female companion of gangster.

mol′li•fy′, *v.,* -**fied**, -**fying**. appease in temper.

mol′lusk, *n.* hard-shelled invertebrate animal. Also, **mol′lusc.**

mol′ly•cod′dle, *v.,* -**dled**, -**dling**. pamper.

molt, *v.* shed skin or feathers.

mol′ten, *adj.* melted.

mo•lyb′de•num (mə lib′də nəm), *n.* silver-white metallic element used in alloys.

mom, *n. Informal.* mother.

mo′ment, *n.* 1. short space of time. 2. importance.

mo′men•tar′y, *adj.* brief in time. —**mo′men•tar′i•ly**, *adv.*

mo•men′tous, *adj.* important.

mo•men′tum, *n., pl.* -**ta**, -**tums**. force of moving body.

mom′my, *n., pl.* -**mies**. *Informal.* mother.

Mon., Monday.

mon′ad, *n.* one-celled organism.

mon′arch, *n.* sovereign.

mon′ar•chy, *n., pl.* -**chies**. 1. government by monarch. 2. country governed by monarch. —**mon′ar•chism**, *n.*

mon′as•ter′y, *n., pl.* -**teries**. residence of monks. —**mo•nas′tic**, *adj.* —**mo•nas′ti•cism**, *n.*

Mon′day, *n.* second day of week.

mon′e•tar′y, *adj.* of money.

mon′ey, *n., pl.* **moneys**, **monies**. 1. pieces of metal or certificates issued as medium of exchange. 2. wealth.

mon′eyed (-ēd), *adj.* wealthy.

mon′ger, *n.* 1. person involved with something contemptible. 2. *Brit.* dealer.

mon′gol•ism, *n. Offensive.* (earlier term for) Down syndrome.

Mon′gol•oid′, *adj.* designating division of human race including most peoples of eastern Asia.

mon′goose, *n., pl.* -**gooses**. carnivorous animal of Asia.

mon′grel, *n.* **1.** animal or plant resulting from crossing of different breeds. —*adj.* **2.** of mixed breeds.

mon′i•ker, *n. Slang.* name. Also, **mon′ick•er.**

mon′ism, *n.* theory that reality consists of a single element. —**mon′ist,** *n.* —**mo•nis′tic,** *adj.*

mo•ni′tion, *n.* warning.

mon′i•tor, *n.* **1.** pupil who assists teacher. —*v.* **2.** check continuously.

mon′i•to′ry, *adj.* warning.

monk, *n.* man who is a member of a religious order.

mon′key, *n.* **1.** mammal strongly resembling a human being. —*v.* **2.** trifle idly.

monkey business, mischievous behavior.

monkey wrench, 1. wrench with adjustable jaws. **2.** something that interferes with process or operation.

mono-, prefix meaning one.

mon′o•chrome, *adj.* of one color. Also, **mon′o•chro•mat′ic.**

mon′o•cle, *n.* eyeglass for one eye.

mon′o•clo′nal, *adj.* pertaining to cell products derived from single biological clone.

mon′o•cot′y•le′don, *n.* plant having embryo containing single seed leaf.

mo•noc′u•lar, *adj.* **1.** having one eye. **2.** for use of only one eye.

mon′o•dy, *n., pl.* **-dies.** poem lamenting someone's death.

mo•nog′a•my, *n.* marriage of one woman with one man. —**mo•nog′a•mous,** *adj.* —**mo•nog′a•mist,** *n.*

mon′o•gram′, *n.* design made of one's initials. —**mon′o•grammed,** *adj.*

mon′o•graph′, *n.* treatise on one subject.

mon′o•lith, *n.* structure of single block of stone. —**mon′o•lith′ic,** *adj.*

mon′o•logue′, *n.* talk by single speaker. Also, **mon′o•log′.** —**mon′o•log′ist, mon′o•logu′ist,** *n.*

mon′o•ma′ni•a, *n.* obsessive zeal for or interest in single thing. —**mon′o•ma′ni•ac,** *n.*

mon′o•nu′cle•o′sis (-nŏŏ′klē ō′sis, -nyŏŏ′-), *n.* infectious disease characterized by fever, swelling of lymph nodes, etc.

mon′o·plane′, *n.* airplane with one wing on each side.

mo·nop′o·ly, *n., pl.* **-lies. 1.** exclusive control. **2.** thing so controlled. **3.** company having such control. —**mo·nop′o·lis′tic**, *adj.* —**mo·nop′o·lize′**, *v.*

mon′o·rail′, *n.* **1.** single rail serving as track for wheeled vehicles. **2.** car or train moving on such a rail.

mon′o·so′di·um glu′ta·mate′, white crystalline powder used to intensify flavor of foods.

mon′o·syl′la·ble, *n.* word of one syllable. —**mon′o·syl·lab′ic**, *adj.*

mon′o·the·ism, *n.* doctrine or belief that there is only one God. —**mon′o·the′ist**, *n., adj.* —**mon′o·the·is′tic**, *adj.*

mon′o·tone′, *n.* single tone of unvarying pitch.

mo·not′o·ny, *n.* wearisome uniformity. —**mo·not′o·nous**, *adj.*

mon·sieur′ (mə syoo′), *n., pl.* **mes·sieurs′** (mā-). French term of address for man.

mon·si′gnor (mon sē′nyər), *n., pl.* **-gnors, -gno′ri** (mon sē nyō′rē). title of certain dignitaries of Roman Catholic Church.

mon·soon′, *n.* seasonal wind of Indian Ocean.

mon′ster, *n.* **1.** animal or plant of abnormal form. **2.** wicked creature. **3.** anything huge.

mon′strance, *n.* receptacle used in churches for display of consecrated Host.

mon·stros′i·ty, *n., pl.* **-ties.** grotesquely abnormal thing.

mon′strous, *adj.* **1.** huge. **2.** frightful.

Mont., Montana.

mon·tage′ (-täzh′), *n.* blending of elements from several pictures into one.

month, *n.* any of twelve parts of calendar year.

month′ly, *adj., n., pl.* **-lies,** *adv.* —*adj.* **1.** occurring once a month. **2.** lasting for a month. —*n.* **3.** published once a month. —*adv.* **4.** once a month. **5.** by the month.

mon′u·ment, *n.* memorial structure.

mon′u•men′tal, *adj.* **1.** imposing. **2.** serving as monument.

moo, *n.* **1.** sound cow makes. —*v.* **2.** utter such sound.

mooch, *Slang.* —*v.* **1.** try to get without paying. —*n.* **2.** Also, **mooch′er.** person who mooches.

mood, *n.* frame of mind.

mood′y, *adj.,* **moodier, moodiest.** of uncertain mood. —**mood′i•ly,** *adv.*

moon, *n.* **1.** body which revolves around earth monthly. **2.** month. —*v.* **3.** gaze dreamily.

moon′light′, *n.* **1.** light from moon. —*v.* **2.** work at second job after principal one.

moon′shine′, *n.* illegally made liquor. —**moon′shin′er,** *n.*

moon′stone′, *n.* pearly gem.

moon′struck′, *adj.* **1.** deranged. **2.** dreamily bemused.

moor, *v.* **1.** secure (ship), as at a dock. —*n.* **2.** *Brit.* open peaty wasteland.

moor′ing, *n.* **1.** *(pl.)* cables, etc., by which ship is moored. **2.** place where ship is moored.

moose, *n., pl.* **moose.** large animal of deer family.

moot, *adj.* debatable.

mop, *n., v.,* **mopped, mopping.** —*n.* **1.** piece of cloth, etc., fastened to stick, for washing or dusting. —*v.* **2.** clean with mop. **3.** *Mil.* **mop up,** destroy final resisting elements.

mope, *v.,* **moped, moping.** be in low spirits.

mo′ped′, *n.* motorized bicycle.

mop′pet, *n.* child.

mo•raine′ (-rān′), *n.* mass of stone, etc., left by glacier.

mor′al, *adj.* **1.** of or concerned with right conduct. **2.** virtuous. —*n.* **3.** *(pl.)* principles of conduct. **4.** moral lesson. —**mor′al•ist,** *n.* —**mor′al•is′tic,** *adj.*

mo•rale′, *n.* spirits; mood.

mo•ral′i•ty, *n.* **1.** conformity to rules of right conduct. **2.** moral quality.

mor′al•ize′, *v.,* **-ized, -izing.** think on moral questions.

mor′al•ly, *adv.* **1.** according to morals. **2.** in one's belief.

mo•rass′, *n.* swamp.

mor'a·to'ri·um, *n., pl.* **-ria,** **-riums. 1.** legal permission to delay payment of debts. **2.** any temporary cessation.

mo'ray, *n.* tropical eel.

mor'bid, *adj.* **1.** unwholesome. **2.** of disease. —**mor·bid'i·ty,** *n.* —**mor'bid·ly,** *adv.*

mor'dant, *adj.* **1.** sarcastic; biting. **2.** burning; corrosive.

more, *adj.* **1.** in greater degree. **2.** additional. —*n.* **3.** additional quantity. —*adv.* **4.** in addition.

mo·rel', *n.* edible mushroom.

more·o'ver, *adv.* besides.

mo'res (mōr'āz), *n.pl.* social and moral customs of group.

mor'ga·nat'ic, *adj.* designating marriage between royal person and commoner.

morgue, *n.* place where corpses are taken for identification.

mor'i·bund', *adj.* dying.

Mor'mon·ism, *n.* religion founded in U.S. in 1830. —**Mor'mon,** *n., adj.*

morn, *n.* morning.

morn'ing, *n.* **1.** first part of day. —*adj.* **2.** done, or occurring, in the morning.

morn'ing-glo'ry, *n., pl.* **-ries.** vine with white flowers.

morning sickness, nausea occurring early in the day during the first months of pregnancy.

morning star, bright planet seen in east before sunrise.

mo·roc'co, *n.* fine leather.

mo'ron, *n.* stupid person. —**mo·ron'ic,** *adj.*

mo·rose', *adj.* gloomily ill-humored. —**mo·rose'ly,** *adv.* —**mo·rose'ness,** *n.*

mor'pheme, *n.* minimal grammatical unit. —**mor·phe'mic,** *adj.*

mor'phine (-fēn), *n.* narcotic found in opium.

mor·phol'o·gy (môr fol'ə jē), *n.* **1.** branch of biology dealing with form and structure of organisms. **2.** form and structure of an organism.

mor'row, *n.* *Poetic.* tomorrow.

Morse, *n.* telegraphic code of long and short signals.

mor'sel, *n.* small amount.

mor'tal, *adj.* **1.** liable to death. **2.** causing death. **3.** to death. —*n.* **4.** human being. —**mor'tal·ly,** *adv.*

mor·tal′i·ty, *n., pl.* **-ties. 1.** mortal nature. **2.** death rate.

mor′tar, *n.* **1.** bowl in which drugs, etc., are pulverized. **2.** short cannon. **3.** material used to bind masonry.

mor′tar·board′, *n.* **1.** board used to hold mortar. **2.** academic cap with square, flat top and tassel.

mort′gage (môr′-), *n., v.,* **-gaged, -gaging. —***n.* **1.** conditional transfer of property as security for debt. —*v.* **2.** put mortgage on. —**mort′ga·gee′,** *n.* —**mort′ga·gor,** *n.*

mor·ti′cian, *n.* undertaker.

mor′ti·fy′, *v.,* **-fied, -fying. 1.** humiliate or shame. **2.** subject (body) to austerity. —**mor′ti·fi·ca′tion,** *n.*

mor′tise, *n., v.,* **-tised, -tising.** —*n.* **1.** slot in wood for tenon. —*v.* **2.** fasten by mortise.

mor′tu·ar′y (-choo-), *n., pl.* **-aries.** place where bodies are prepared for burial.

mo·sa′ic, *n.* design made of small colored pieces.

mo′sey, *v. Informal.* stroll.

mosh, *v. Slang.* engage in frenzied, violent dancing.

Mos′lem, *n., adj.* Muslim.

mosque (mosk), *n.* Muslim place of prayer.

mos·qui′to, *n., pl.* **-toes, -tos.** common biting insect.

moss, *n.* small, leafy-stemmed plant growing on rocks, etc. —*v.* **2.** cover with moss. —**moss′y,** *adj.*

moss′back′, *n. Informal.* old-fashioned person.

most, *adj.* **1.** in greatest amount. **2.** majority of. —*n.* **3.** greatest quantity. —*adv.* **4.** to greatest extent.

most′ly, *adv.* **1.** in most cases. **2.** in greater part.

mote, *n.* small particle.

mo·tel′, *n.* roadside hotel for automobile travelers.

mo·tet′, *n.* unaccompanied choral composition.

moth, *n.* insect, some of whose larvae eat cloth.

moth′ball′, *n.* ball of camphor, etc., for repelling moths.

moth′er, *n.* **1.** female parent. **2.** head of group of nuns. **3.** stringy substance forming on fermenting liquids. —*adj.* **4.** of, like, or being mother. **5.**

native. —*v.* 6. act as or like mother to. —**moth'er•hood'**, *n.* —**moth'er•ly**, *adj.*

moth'er-in-law', *n., pl.* **mothers-in-law.** mother of one's spouse.

moth'er•land', *n.* 1. one's native land. 2. land of one's ancestors.

moth'er-of-pearl', *n.* inner layer of certain shells.

mo•tif' (-tēf'), *n.* recurring subject or theme.

mo'tile (mōt'l, mō'til), *adj.* *Biology.* capable of moving spontaneously, as cells and spores. —**mo•til'i•ty**, *n.*

mo'tion, *n.* 1. process of changing position. 2. action or power of movement. 3. formal proposal made in meeting. —*v.* 4. indicate by gesture. —**mo'tion•less**, *adj.*

motion picture, series of photographs projected so rapidly that objects seem to be moving.

mo'ti•vate', *v.,* **-vated, -vating.** give motive to. —**mo'ti•va'tion**, *n.*

mo'tive, *n.* 1. purpose; goal. —*adj.* 2. of or causing motion.

mot'ley, *adj.* widely varied.

mo'to•cross', *n.* motorcycle race over rough terrain.

mo'tor, *n.* 1. small engine. —*adj.* 2. of or causing motion. 3. of or operated by motor. —*v.* 4. travel by automobile.

mo'tor•bike', *n.* motorcycle.

mo'tor•boat', *n.* boat run by motor.

mo'tor•cade', *n.* procession of automobiles.

mo'tor•car', *n.* automobile.

mo'tor•cy'cle, *n.* heavy motor-driven bicycle.

mo'tor•ist, *n.* automobile driver.

mo'tor•ize', *v.,* **-ized, -izing.** furnish with motors or motor-driven vehicles.

mo'tor•man', *n., pl.* **-men.** person who drives electrically operated vehicle.

mot'tle, *v.,* **-tled, -tling.** mark with spots or blotches.

mot'to, *n., pl.* **-toes, -tos.** phrase expressing one's guiding principle.

moue (mo͞o), *n., pl.* **moues** (mo͞o). pouting grimace.

mould, *n.* mold.

mould'er, *v.* molder.

moult, *v., n.* molt.

mound, *n.* heap of earth; hill.

mount, *v.* 1. go up; get on; rise. 2. prepare for use or display. 3. fix in setting. —*n.* 4. act or manner of mounting. 5. horse for riding. 6. Also, **mounting.** support, setting, etc. 7. hill.

moun′tain, *n.* lofty natural elevation on earth's surface. —**moun′tain•ous,** *adj.*

mountain ash, small tree of rose family.

mountain bike, bicycle designed for off-road use.

moun′tain•eer′, *n.* 1. mountain climber. 2. dweller in mountains. —**moun′tain•eer′ing,** *n.*

mountain laurel, shrub bearing rose or white flowers.

mountain lion, cougar.

moun′te•bank′, *n.* charlatan.

mourn, *v.* grieve; feel sorrow. —**mourn′er,** *n.* —**mourn′ful,** *adj.* —**mourn′ing,** *n.*

mouse, *n., pl.* **mice,** *v.,* **moused, mousing.** —*n.* 1. small rodent. 2. device used to select items on computer screen. —*v.* (mouz). 3. hunt for mice.

mousse (mo͞os), *n.* 1. frothy dessert. 2. foamy preparation used to style hair.

mous•tache′, *n.* mustache.

mous′y, *adj.,* **mousier, mousiest.** drably quiet in manner or appearance. —**mous′i•ness,** *n.*

mouth, *n., pl.* **mouths,** *v.* —*n.* 1. opening through which animal takes in food. 2. any opening. —*v.* 3. utter pompously or dishonestly. —**mouth′ful′,** *n.*

mouth organ, harmonica.

mouth′piece′, *n.* 1. piece at or forming mouth. 2. person, newspaper, etc., speaking for others.

mouth′wash′, *n.* solution for cleaning the mouth.

mouth′-wa′tering, *adj.* appetizing.

mou′ton (mo͞o′-), *n.* sheepskin processed to resemble seal or beaver.

move, *v.,* **moved, moving,** *n.* —*v.* 1. change position. 2. change one's abode. 3. advance. 4. make formal proposal in meeting. 5. affect emotionally. —*n.* 6. act of moving. 7. purposeful action. —**mov′a•ble,** *adj., n.* —**mov′er,** *n.*

move′ment, *n.* **1.** act or process of moving. **2.** trend in thought. **3.** works of mechanism. **4.** principal division of piece of music.

moving picture, motion picture. Also, **mov′ie.**

mow, *v.,* **mowed, mowed** or **mown, mowing,** *n.* —*v.* (mō). **1.** cut (grass, etc.). **2.** kill indiscriminately. —*n.* (mou). **3.** place in barn where hay, etc., are stored. —**mow′er,** *n.*

moz′za•rel′la (mot′sə rel′lə, mōt′-), *n.* mild white cheese.

MP, 1. a member of Parliament. **2.** Military Police.

mph, miles per hour.

Mr. (mis′tər), *pl.* **Messrs.** (mes′ərz). mister.

MRI, magnetic resonance imaging: process of producing images of the body using strong magnetic field and low-energy radio waves.

Mrs. (mis′iz, miz′iz), *pl.* **Mmes.** (mā däm′, -dam′). title of address for married woman.

MS, 1. Also, **ms, ms.** manuscript. **2.** Mississippi. **3.** multiple sclerosis.

Ms. (miz), title of address for woman not to be distinguished as married or unmarried.

M.S., Master of Science.

MSG, monosodium glutamate.

MT, Montana.

much, *adj.* **1.** in great quantity or degree. —*n.* **2.** great quantity. **3.** notable thing. —*adv.* **4.** greatly. **5.** generally.

mu′ci•lage, *n.* adhesive. —**mu′ci•lag′i•nous,** *adj.*

muck, *n.* **1.** filth. **2.** moist barn refuse. —**muck′y,** *adj.*

muck′rake′, *v.,* **-raked, -raking.** expose scandal. —**muck′rak′er,** *n.*

mu′cous (-kəs), *adj.* **1.** secreting mucus. **2.** of mucus.

mucous membrane, membrane lining internal surface of organ.

mu′cus, *n.* sticky secretion of mucous membrane.

mud, *n.* **1.** wet soft earth. **2.** scandalous or malicious statements or information. —**mud′dy,** *adj., v.*

mud′dle, *v.,* **-dled, -dling,** *n.* —*v.* **1.** mix up; confuse. —*n.* **2.** confusion.

mud′dle•head′ed, *adj.* confused in one's thinking.

mud′sling′ing, *n.* efforts to discredit opponent by malicious remarks.

mu•ez′zin (myo͞o ez′in, mo͞o-), *n.* crier who summons Muslims to prayer.

muff, *n.* **1.** tubular covering for hands. —*v.* **2.** bungle. **3.** drop after catching.

muf′fin, *n.* small round bread.

muf′fle, *v.,* **-fled, -fling,** *n.* —*v.* **1.** wrap in scarf, cloak, etc. **2.** deaden (sound). —*n.* **3.** something that muffles.

muf′fler, *n.* **1.** heavy neck scarf. **2.** device for deadening sound, as on engine.

muf′ti, *n.* civilian dress.

mug, *n., v.,* **mugged, mugging.** —*n.* **1.** drinking cup. **2.** *Slang.* face. —*v.* **3.** assault, usually with intent to rob. **4.** *Slang.* grimace. —**mug′ger,** *n.*

mug′gy, *adj.,* **-gier, -giest.** hot and humid.

mug shot, photograph of the face of a criminal suspect.

mug′wump′, *n.* person who takes independent position.

Mu•ham′mad, *n.* founder of Islam, A.D. 570–632.

muk′luk, *n.* soft boot worn by Eskimos.

mu•lat′to, *n., pl.* **-toes. 1.** person with one white and one black parent. **2.** person with mixed black and white ancestry.

mul′ber′ry, *n., pl.* **-ries.** tree, the leaves of some of whose species are used as food by silkworms.

mulch, *n.* **1.** loose covering of leaves, straw, etc., on plants. —*v.* **2.** surround with mulch.

mulct (mulkt), *v.* **1.** deprive of by trickery. **2.** fine.

mule, *n.* **1.** offspring of donkey and mare. **2.** woman's slipper.

mule deer, deer with large ears and gray coat.

mu′le•teer′, *n.* mule-driver.

mul′ish, *adj.* obstinate.

mull, *v.* **1.** study or ruminate (over). **2.** heat and spice.

mul′lah, *n.* Muslim religious teacher.

mul′lein (-in), *n.* tall weed.

mul′let, *n.* common food fish.

mul′li•gan, *n.* stew of meat and vegetables.

mul′li•ga•taw′ny, *n.* curry-flavored soup.

mul′lion, *n.* vertical member separating lights of window.

multi-, prefix meaning many.

mul′ti•cul′tur•al•ism, *n.* recognition of different cultural identities within unified society.

mul′ti•far′i•ous, *adj.* many and varied.

mul′ti•me′di•a, *n.* (*used with sing. v.*) combined use of several media or mass media.

mul′ti•na′tion•al, *n.* 1. corporation with operations in many countries. —*adj.* 2. pertaining to several nations or multinationals.

mul′ti•ple, *adj.* 1. consisting of or involving many. —*n.* 2. number evenly divisible by stated other number.

multiple sclerosis, disease marked by destruction of areas of brain and spinal cord.

mul′ti•pli•cand′, *n.* number to be multiplied by another.

mul′ti•plic′i•ty, *n., pl.* -ties. great number or variety.

mul′ti•ply′, *v.,* -plied, -plying. 1. increase the number of.

2. add (number) to itself a stated number of times. —**mul′ti•pli′er,** *n.* —**mul′ti•pli•ca′tion,** *n.*

mul′ti•tude′, *n.* great number.

mul′ti•tu′di•nous, *adj.* 1. numerous. 2. having many parts.

mum, *adj.* silent.

mum′ble, *v.,* -bled, -bling, *n.* —*v.* 1. speak quietly and unintelligibly. —*n.* 2. mumbling sound.

mum′ble•ty•peg′, *n.* game in which pocketknife is flipped so it sticks in ground. Also, **mum′ble-the-peg′.**

mum′bo jum′bo, 1. strange ritual. 2. senseless language.

mum′mer, *n.* 1. person in festive disguise. 2. actor.

mum′mer•y, *n., pl.* -meries. mere show.

mum′my, *n., pl.* -mies. dead body treated to prevent decay.

mumps, *n.pl.* disease marked by swelling of salivary glands.

munch, *v.* chew.

mun•dane′, *adj.* banal.

mu•nic′i•pal, *adj.* of a city.

mu•nic′i•pal′i•ty, *n., pl.* -ties. self-governing city.

mu·nif′i·cent, *adj.* extremely generous. —**mu·nif′i·cence,** *n.* —**mu·nif′i·cent·ly,** *adv.*

mu·ni′tions, *n.* weapons and ammunition used in war.

mu′ral, *n.* 1. picture painted on wall. —*adj.* 2. of walls.

mur′der, *n.* 1. unlawful willful killing. —*v.* 2. commit murder. —**mur′der·er,** *n.* —**mur′der·ess,** *n.fem.* —**mur′der·ous,** *adj.*

murk, *n.* darkness.

murk′y, *adj.,* **murkier, murkiest.** dark and gloomy. —**murk′i·ness,** *n.*

mur′mur, *n.* 1. low, continuous sound. 2. complaint. —*v.* 3. speak softly or indistinctly. 4. complain.

mur′rain (mûr′in), *n.* disease of cattle.

mus′ca·dine, *n.* American grape.

mus′cat, *n.* sweet grape.

mus′ca·tel′, *n.* wine made from muscat grapes.

mus′cle, *n., v.,* **-cled, -cling.** —*n.* 1. bundle of fibers in animal body that contract to produce motion. 2. brawn. —*v.* 3. *Informal.* force one's way. —**mus′cu·lar,** *adj.*

mus′cle·bound′, *adj.* having enlarged muscles.

muscular dys′tro·phy (dis′trə fē), disease characterized by wasting of muscles.

muse, *v.,* **mused, musing.** 1. reflect quietly. 2. say or think meditatively.

Muse, *n.* one of nine goddesses of the arts.

mu·se′um, *n.* place for permanent public exhibits.

mush, *n.* 1. meal boiled in water until thick, used as food. 2. anything soft. 3. *Informal.* maudlin sentiment. —*v.* 4. travel on foot. —**mush′y,** *adj.*

mush′room, *n.* 1. fleshy fungus. —*adj.* 2. growing rapidly. —*v.* 3. grow quickly.

mu′sic, *n.* 1. art of arranging sounds for effect. 2. score of musical composition. —**mu·si′cian,** *n.*

mus′i·cal, *adj.* 1. of music. 2. pleasant-sounding. 3. sensitive to or skilled in music. —*n.* 4. Also, **mus′ical com′edy.** a play with music. —**mus′i·cal·ly,** *adv.*

mu′si·cale′ (-kal′), *n.* social occasion featuring music.

mu′si•col′o•gy, *n.* scholarly or scientific study of music. —**mu′si•col′o•gist,** *n.*

music video, videotape featuring dramatized rendition of popular song.

musk, *n.* fragrant animal secretion. —**musk′y,** *adj.*

mus′keg, *n.* bog.

mus′kel•lunge′ (-lunj′), *n., pl.* **-lung•es, -lunge.** large fish of pike family.

mus′ket, *n.* early rifle.

mus′ket•eer′, *n.* soldier armed with musket.

musk′mel′on, *n.* sweet melon.

musk′ox′, *n., pl.* **-oxen.** large mammal of arctic regions.

musk′rat′, *n.* large aquatic American rodent.

Mus′lim (muz′-), *n.* **1.** follower of Islam. —*adj.* **2.** of or pertaining to Islam.

mus′lin, *n.* cotton fabric.

muss, *Informal.* —*n.* **1.** disorder; mess. —*v.* **2.** rumple. —**muss′y,** *adj.*

mus′sel, *n.* bivalve mollusk, sometimes edible.

must, *aux. v.* **1.** be obliged to. **2.** may be assumed to. —*adj.*

3. necessary. —*n.* **4.** anything necessary. **5.** new wine not yet fermented.

mus′tache, *n.* hair growing on upper lip. Also, **mus•ta′chio** (-shō).

mus′tang, *n.* small wild horse of western U.S.

mus′tard, *n.* pungent yellow powder made from seeds of mustard plant.

mustard gas, oily liquid with irritating, poisonous properties, used in warfare.

mus′ter, *v.* **1.** assemble, as troops; gather. —*n.* **2.** assembly.

mus′ty, *adj.,* **-tier, -tiest. 1.** stale-smelling. **2.** out-dated. —**mus′ti•ness,** *n.*

mu′ta•ble, *adj.* subject to change. —**mu′ta•bil′i•ty,** *n.*

mu′tant (myōōt′nt), *n.* **1.** organism resulting from mutation. —*adj.* **2.** resulting from mutation.

mu′tate (myōō′tāt), *v.,* **-tated, -tating.** change.

mu•ta′tion, *n.* **1.** change in genetic characteristic. **2.** species characterized by such change. **3.** change.

mute, *adj.,* **muter, mutest,** *n.,* *v.,* **muted, muting.** —*adj.* **1.** silent. **2.** incapable of speech. —*n.* **3.** person unable to utter words. **4.** device for muffling musical instrument. —*v.* **5.** deaden sound of.

mu′ti•late′, *v.,* **-lated, -lating.** injure by damaging part. —**mu′ti•la′tion,** *n.*

mu′ti•ny, *n., pl.* **-nies,** *v.,* **-nied,** **-nying.** revolt against lawful authority. —**mu′ti•neer′,** *n.* —**mu′ti•nous,** *adj.*

mutt, *n. Slang.* mongrel dog.

mut′ter, *v.* **1.** speak low and indistinctly; grumble. —*n.* **2.** act or sound of muttering.

mut′ton, *n.* flesh of sheep.

mut′ton•chops′, *n.pl.* side whiskers that are narrow at temples and broad at jawline.

mu′tu•al (-cho͞o-), *adj.* **1.** done, etc., by two or more in relation to each other; reciprocal. **2.** common. —**mu′tu•al•ly,** *adv.*

mutual fund, investment company that invests money of its shareholders.

muu′muu′, *n., pl.* **-muus.** loose-fitting dress.

muz′zle, *n., v.,* **-zled, -zling.** —*n.* **1.** mouth of firearm. **2.** mouth part of animal's head. **3.** cage for this. —*v.* **4.** put muzzle on. **5.** silence; gag.

my, *pron.* possessive form of **I** used before noun.

my′as•the′ni•a (mī′əs thē′nē ə), *n.* muscle weakness. —**my′as•then′ic** (-then′-), *adj.*

my•col′o•gy, *n.* study of fungi. —**my•col′o•gist,** *n.*

my′e•li′tis, *n.* **1.** inflammation of spinal cord. **2.** inflammation of bone marrow.

my′na, *n.* Asiatic bird sometimes taught to talk.

my•o′pi•a, *n.* near-sightedness. —**my•op′ic,** *adj.*

myr′i•ad, *n., adj.* **1.** very great number. **2.** ten thousand.

myr′i•a•pod′, *n.* many-legged worm.

myrrh (mûr), *n.* aromatic substance from certain plants.

myr′tle, *n.* **1.** evergreen shrub. **2.** periwinkle (def. 2).

my•self′, *pron., pl.* **ourselves.** **1.** intensive form of **I** or **me.** **2.** reflexive form of **me.**

mys'ter•y, *n., pl.* **-teries. 1.** anything secret, unknown, or unexplained. **2.** obscurity. **3.** secret rite.
—**mys•te'ri•ous,** *adj.*
—**mys•te'ri•ous•ly,** *adv.*

mys'tic, *adj.* Also, **mys'ti•cal. 1.** occult. **2.** spiritual. —*n.* **3.** believer in mysticism.

mys'ti•cism, *n.* doctrine of direct spiritual intuition.

mys'ti•fy', *v.,* **-fied, -fying.** bewilder purposely.
—**mys'ti•fi•ca'tion,** *n.*

mys•tique' (mi stēk'), *n.* aura of mystery or power.

myth, *n.* **1.** legendary story, person, etc. **2.** false popular belief. —**myth'i•cal, myth'ic,** *adj.* —**myth'i•cal•ly,** *adv.*

my•thol'o•gy, *n., pl.* **-gies.** body of myths.
—**myth'o•log'i•cal,** *adj.*

N, n, *n.* fourteenth letter of English alphabet.

N, north, northern.

nab, *v.,* **nabbed, nabbing.** *Informal.* seize; arrest.

na·celle′ (-sel′), *n.* enclosed shelter for aircraft engine.

na′cre (nā′kər), *n.* mother-of-pearl. —**na′cre·ous,** *adj.*

na′dir (nā′dər), *n.* **1.** lowest point. **2.** point of celestial sphere opposite zenith.

nag, *v.,* **nagged, nagging,** *n.* —*v.* **1.** scold constantly. —*n.* **2.** person who nags. **3.** old horse.

nai′ad (nā′ad), *n.* water nymph.

nail, *n.* **1.** piece of metal for holding pieces of wood together. **2.** horny plate at end of finger or toe. —*v.* **3.** fasten with nails. **4.** *Informal.* seize.

na·ive′ (nä ēv′), *adj.* simple. Also, **na·ïve′.**

na·ive·té′ (-tā′), *n.* artless simplicity. Also, **na·ïve·té′.**

na′ked, *adj.* **1.** without clothing or covering. **2.** (of eye) unassisted in seeing. **3.** plain. —**na′ked·ness,** *n.*

N

name, *n., v.,* **named, naming.** —*n.* **1.** word or words by which a person, place, or thing is designated. **2.** reputation. **3.** behalf or authority. —*v.* **4.** give name to. **5.** specify. **6.** appoint. —**nam′a·ble, name′a·ble,** *adj.* —**nam′er,** *n.*

name′less, *adj.* **1.** having no name. **2.** not referred to by name. **3.** incapable of being described.

name′ly, *adv.* that is to say.

name′sake′, *n.* one having same name as another.

nan′ny, *n., pl.* **-nies.** child's nursemaid.

nanny goat, female goat.

nan′o·sec′ond, *n.* one billionth of a second.

nap, *n., v.,* **napped, napping.** —*n.* **1.** short sleep. **2.** short, fuzzy fibers on the surface of cloth. —*v.* **3.** raise fuzz on. **4.** have short sleep.

na′palm (nā′päm), *n.* **1.** highly incendiary jellylike substance used in bombs, etc. —*v.* **2.** bomb or attack with napalm.

nape, *n.* back of neck.

naph'tha (nap'-), *n.* petroleum derivative.

naph'tha•lene' (naf'-), *n.* substance used in mothballs.

nap'kin, *n.* piece of cloth or paper used at table to wipe lips or fingers.

na•po'le•on, *n.* rich, flaky pastry with cream filling.

nar'cis•sism, *n.* excessive admiration of oneself. —**nar'cis•sis'tic,** *adj.*

nar•cis'sus, *n.* spring-blooming plant.

nar•co'sis (-kō'-), *n.* stupor.

nar•cot'ic, *adj.* **1.** sleep-inducing. —*n.* **2.** substance that dulls pain, induces sleep, etc. **3.** addictive drug, esp. an illegal one.

nar'rate, *v.,* -rated, -rating. tell. —**nar•ra'tion,** *n.* —**nar'ra•tor,** *n.*

nar'ra•tive, *n.* **1.** story of events. —*adj.* **2.** that narrates. **3.** of narration.

nar'row, *adj.* **1.** not broad or wide. **2.** literal or strict in interpreting rules, etc. **3.** minute. —*v.* **4.** make or become narrow. —*n.* **5.** narrow place, thing, etc. —**nar'row-mind'ed,** *adj.*

nar'whal (-wəl), *n.* Arctic whale.

NASA (nas'ə), *n.* National Aeronautics and Space Administration.

na'sal, *adj.* **1.** of noses. **2.** spoken through nose. —*n.* **3.** nasal sound. —**na'sal•ly,** *adv.*

nas'cent (nas'ənt, nā'sənt), *adj.* beginning to exist or develop. —**nas'cence,** *n.*

na•stur'tium, *n.* garden plant with multi-colored flowers.

nas'ty, *adj.,* -tier, -tiest. **1.** disgustingly unclean. **2.** objectionable. —**nas'ti•ly,** *adv.* —**nas'ti•ness,** *n.*

na'tal, *adj.* of one's birth.

na'tion, *n.* **1.** people living in one territory under same government. **2.** people related by tradition or ancestry. —**na'tion•al,** *adj., n.* —**na'tion•al•ly,** *adv.*

na'tion•al•ism', *n.* devotion to one's nation. —**na'tion•al•ist,** *n., adj.* —**na'tion•al•is'tic,** *adj.*

na'tion•al'i•ty, *n., pl.* -ties. **1.** condition of being member of a nation. **2.** nation.

na′tion·al·ize′, *v.,* **-ized, -izing.** bring under national control or ownership. **—na′tion·al·i·za′tion,** *n.*

na′tion·wide′, *adj., adv.* across entire nation.

na′tive, *adj.* **1.** belonging to by birth, nationality, or nature. **2.** of natives. **3.** being the place of origin of a person or thing. **—***n.* **4.** person, animal, or plant native to region.

Native American, member of indigenous peoples of N. and S. America.

na·tiv′i·ty, *n., pl.* **-ties.** birth.

NATO (nā′tō), *n.* North Atlantic Treaty Organization.

nat′ty, *adj.,* **-tier, -tiest.** smart.

nat′u·ral, *adj.* **1.** of, existing in, or formed by nature. **2.** to be expected in circumstances. **3.** without affectation. **4.** *Music.* neither sharp nor flat. **—nat′u·ral·ly,** *adv.* **—nat′u·ral·ness,** *n.*

natural childbirth, childbirth without use of drugs.

natural gas, mixture of gaseous hydrocarbons that accumulates in porous sedimentary rocks.

natural history, study of natural objects.

nat′u·ral·ism, *n.* artistic or literary style that represents objects or events as they occur in nature or real life. **—nat′u·ral·is′tic,** *adj.*

nat′u·ral·ist, *n.* **1.** student of nature. **2.** adherent of naturalism.

nat′u·ral·ize′, *v.,* **-ized, -izing.** **1.** confer citizenship upon. **2.** introduce to region. **—nat′u·ral·i·za′tion,** *n.*

natural resource, source of wealth occurring in nature.

natural selection, process by which life forms having traits that enable them to adapt to the environment will survive in greater numbers.

na′ture, *n.* **1.** material world. **2.** universe. **3.** one's character.

naught, *n.* zero.

naugh′ty, *adj.,* **-tier, -tiest.** **1.** disobedient; bad. **2.** improper. **—naugh′ti·ly,** *adv.* **—naugh′ti·ness,** *n.*

nau′sea (nô′shə), *n.* **1.** feeling of impending vomiting. **2.** disgust. **—nau′se·ate′,** *v.* **—nau′seous,** *adj.*

nau′ti•cal, *adj.* of ships, sailors, or navigation.

nautical mile, unit of distance equal to 1.852 kilometers.

nau′ti•lus, *n.* mollusk having pearly shell.

Nav′a•jo′ (-hō′), *n., pl.* **-jo, -jos, -joes.** member of an American Indian people of the Southwest.

na′val, *adj.* of ships or navy.

nave, *n.* main lengthwise part of church.

na′vel, *n.* pit in center surface of belly.

nav′i•gate′, *v.,* **-gated, -gating. 1.** traverse (water or air). **2.** direct on a course. —**nav′i•ga′tion,** *n.* —**nav′i•ga′tor,** *n.* —**nav′i•ga•ble,** *adj.*

na′vy, *n., pl.* **-vies.** a nation's warships and crews.

navy bean, small white bean.

navy blue, dark blue.

nay, *adv., n.* no.

nay′say′er, *n.* person who is habitually negative.

Na′zi (nä′tsē), *n.* member of the National Socialist party in Germany, headed by Adolf Hitler. —**Na′zism,** *n.*

NB, nota bene.

NC, North Carolina. Also, **N.C.**

ND, North Dakota. Also, **N.D.**

N.Dak., North Dakota.

NE, 1. Nebraska. **2.** northeast.

Ne•an′der•thal′ man′, subspecies of humans that lived in Stone Age.

neap tide, tide having lowest high point.

near, *adv.* **1.** close by. —*adj.* **2.** close. **3.** intimate. —*v.* **4.** approach. —**near′ness,** *n.*

near′by′, *adj., adv.* close by.

near′ly, *adv.* almost.

near′-sight′ed, *adj.* myopic. —**near′-sight′ed•ness,** *n.*

neat, *adj.* **1.** orderly. **2.** skillful. **3.** undiluted. —**neat′ly,** *adv.* —**neat′ness,** *n.*

neb, *n.* bill or beak.

Nebr., Nebraska.

neb′u•la, *n., pl.* **-lae** (-lē′), **-las.** luminous mass of gas or stars. —**neb′u•lar,** *adj.*

neb′u•lous, *adj.* **1.** hazy; vague. **2.** cloudlike.

nec′es•sar′y, *adj., n., pl.* **-saries.** —*adj.* **1.** that cannot be dispensed with. **2.** unavoidable. —*n.* **3.**

something necessary. —**nec′es•sar′i•ly,** *adv.*

ne•ces′si•tate′, *v.,* **-tated, -tating.** make necessary.

ne•ces′si•ty, *n., pl.* **-ties. 1.** something necessary. **2.** fact of being necessary. **3.** poverty.

neck, *n.* **1.** part connecting head and trunk. —*v.* **2.** *Slang.* play amorously.

neck′er•chief, *n.* cloth worn around neck.

neck′lace, *n.* ornament of gems, etc., worn around neck.

neck′tie′, *n.* cloth strip worn under collar and tied in front.

ne•crol′o•gy, *n., pl.* **-gies.** list of persons who have died.

nec′ro•man′cy, *n.* magic. —**nec′ro•manc′er,** *n.*

ne•cro′sis, *n.* death of tissue.

nec′tar, *n.* **1.** sweet secretion of flower. **2.** drink of gods.

nec′tar•ine′, *n.* downless peach.

nee (nā), *adj.* (of woman) born; having as maiden name. Also, **née.**

need, *n.* **1.** requirement. **2.** condition marked by necessity. —*v.* **3.** depend on.

4. be obliged. —**need′ful,** *adj.* —**need′less,** *adj.*

nee′dle, *n., v.,* **-dled, -dling.** —*n.* **1.** slender pointed implement for sewing. **2.** anything similar, as gauge. **3.** hypodermic syringe. —*v.* **4.** prod; tease.

nee′dle•point′, *n.* embroidery on canvas.

nee′dle•work′, *n.* art or product of working with a needle, esp. in embroidery.

needs, *adv.* necessarily.

need′y, *adj.,* **needier, neediest.** very poor. —**need′i•ness,** *n.*

ne′er′-do-well′, *n.* person who habitually fails.

ne•far′i•ous, *adj.* wicked.

ne•gate′, *v.,* **-gated, -gating.** deny; nullify. —**ne•ga′tion,** *n.*

neg′a•tive, *adj.* **1.** expressing denial or refusal. **2.** undistinguished. **3.** *Math.* minus. **4.** *Photog.* having light and shade reversed. —*n.* **5.** negative statement, etc. **6.** *Photog.* negative image. —**neg′a•tive•ly,** *adv.*

ne•glect′, *v.* **1.** disregard; fail to do. —*n.* **2.** disregard. —**ne•glect′ful,** *adj.*

neg′li•gee′ (-zhā′), *n.* woman's house robe.

neg′li•gent, *adj.* neglectful. —**neg′li•gence,** *n.*

neg′li•gi•ble, *adj.* unimportant.

ne•go′ti•a•ble (-shē-), *adj.* transferable, as securities. —**ne•go′ti•a•bil′i•ty,** *n.*

ne•go′ti•ate′ (-shē āt′), *v.,* **-ated, -ating. 1.** deal with; bargain. **2.** dispose of. —**ne•go′ti•a′tion,** *n.* —**ne•go′ti•a′tor,** *n.*

Ne′gro, *n., pl.* **-groes.** member of racial group having brown to black skin. —**Ne′gro,** *adj.* —**Ne′groid,** *adj.*

neigh, *n.* **1.** cry of horse. —*v.* **2.** make cry of horse.

neigh′bor, *n.* **1.** person or thing near another. —*v.* **2.** be near. —**neigh′bor•ly,** *adj.*

neigh′bor•hood, *n.* **1.** surrounding area. **2.** district having separate identity.

nei′ther (nē′ th ər, nī′ th ər), *conj., adj.* not either.

nem′a•tode, *n.* unsegmented worm.

nem′e•sis, *n., pl.* **-ses.** cause of one's downfall.

neo-, prefix meaning new, recent, or revived.

Ne′o•lith′ic, *adj.* of the later Stone Age.

ne•ol′o•gism (-jiz′əm), *n.* new word or phrase.

ne′on, *n.* gas used in electrical signs.

ne′o•nate′, *n.* newborn child. —**ne′o•na′tal,** *adj.*

ne′o•phyte′, *n.* beginner.

ne′o•plasm, *n.* tumor.

ne•pen′the, *n.* anything inducing pleasurable sensation of forgetfulness.

neph′ew, *n.* son of one's brother or sister.

ne•phri′tis (nə frī′tis), *n.* inflammation of the kidneys. —**ne•phrit′ic** (-frit′ik), *adj.*

ne′plus′ul′tra (nē′ plus′ ul′trə), highest point.

nep′o•tism, *n.* favoritism toward one's relatives.

Nep′tune, *n.* planet eighth from the sun.

nerd, *n. Slang.* **1.** dull, ineffectual, or unattractive person. **2.** person devoted to nonsocial pursuit.

nerve, *n., v.,* **nerved, nerving.**
—*n.* **1.** bundle of fiber that conveys impulses between brain and other parts of body. **2.** courage. **3.** *Informal.* presumption. **4.** (*pl.*) anxiety. —*v.* **5.** give courage to.

nerve gas, poison gas that interferes with nerve functions, respiration, etc.

nerv'ous, *adj.* **1.** of nerves. **2.** having or caused by disordered nerves. **3.** anxious; uneasy. —**nerv'ous•ly,** *adv.* —**nerv'ous•ness,** *n.*

nerv'y, *adj.,* **nervier, nerviest.** *Informal.* presumptuous.

nest, *n.* **1.** place used by animal for rearing its young. **2.** group of things fitting tightly together. —*v.* **3.** settle in nest. **4.** fit one within another.

nest egg, money saved for emergencies, retirement, etc.

nes'tle, *v.,* **-tled, -tling.** lie close and snug.

net, *adj., n., v.,* **netted, netting.** —*adj.* **1.** exclusive of loss, expense, etc. —*n.* **2.** net profit. **3.** Also, **net'ting.** lacelike fabric of uniform mesh. **4.** bag of such fabric. —*v.* **5.** gain as clear profit. **6.** cover with net. **7.** ensnare.

neth'er, *adj.* lower. —**neth'er•most',** *adj.*

net'tle, *n., v.,* **-tled, -tling.** —*n.* **1.** plant with stinging hairs. —*v.* **2.** irritate; sting.

net'tle•some, *adj.* **1.** causing irritation. **2.** easily provoked.

net'work', *n.* **1.** netlike combination. **2.** group of associated radio or television stations, etc. **3.** any system of interconnected elements. —*v.* **4.** share information informally with others who have common interests.

neu'ral (ny$\overline{oo}$r'əl), *adj.* of nerves or nervous system.

neu•ral'gia, *n.* sharp pain along nerve.

neur'as•the'ni•a, *n.* pattern of symptoms often linked with depression.

neu•ri'tis, *n.* inflammation of nerve. —**neu•rit'ic,** *adj.*

neu•rol'o•gy, *n.* study of nerves. —**neu•rol'o•gist,** *n.* —**neu'ro•log'i•cal,** *adj.*

neu'ron (n$\overline{oo}$r'on, ny$\overline{oo}$r'-), *n.* cell that is basic to nervous system.

neu•ro'sis, *n., pl.* **-ses.** psychoneurosis. —**neu•rot'ic,** *adj., n.*

neu'ro•sur'ger•y, *n.* surgery of the brain or other nerve tissue.

neu'ro•trans'mit•ter, *n.* chemical substance that transmits nerve impulses across synapse.

neu'ter, *adj.* **1.** neither male nor female. —*v.* **2.** spay or castrate. —**neu'ter,** *n.*

neu'tral, *adj.* **1.** taking no side in controversy. **2.** not emphatic or positive. —*n.* **3.** neutral person or state. —**neu•tral'i•ty,** *n.* —**neu'tral•ize',** *v.* —**neu'tral•ly,** *adv.* —**neu'tral•i•za'tion,** *n.*

neu'tron, *n.* particle in nucleus of atom.

Nev., Nevada.

nev'er, *adv.* not ever.

nev'er•the•less', *adv.* in spite of what has been said.

new, *adj.* **1.** of recent origin or existence. **2.** unfamiliar. —*adv.* **3.** recently; freshly. —**new'ness,** *n.*

new'el, *n.* post at the head or foot of stair.

New England, group of states in northeast U.S.

new'fan'gled, *adj.* of a new kind or fashion.

new'ly, *adv.* **1.** recently. **2.** anew.

new'ly•wed', *n.* newly married person.

news, *n.* report of recent event.

news'cast', *n.* radio or television broadcast of news. —**news'cast'er,** *n.*

news'let'ter, *n.* periodical for specialized group.

news'man', *n.* journalist. Also, **news'wom'an,** *n.fem.*

news'pa'per, *n.* news journal. —**news'pa'per•man',** *n.* —**news'pa'per•wom'an,** *n.fem.*

news'print', *n.* paper on which newspapers are printed.

news'reel', *n.* motion picture of news events.

news'stand', *n.* sales booth for periodicals, etc.

news'wor'thy, *adj.* interesting enough to warrant coverage. —**news'wor'thi•ness,** *n.*

newt, *n.* salamander.

New Testament, portion of Christian Bible recording life and teachings of Christ and His disciples.

new'ton, *n.* unit of force.

new wave, movement that breaks with traditional values.

new year, 1. (*cap.*) first day of year. **2.** year approaching.

next, *adj.* **1.** nearest after. —*adv.* **2.** in nearest place after. **3.** at first subsequent time.

next'-door', *adj.* in the next house, apartment, etc.

nex'us, *n., pl.* **nexus.** link.

NH, New Hampshire. Also, **N.H.**

ni'a•cin, *n.* nicotinic acid.

nib, *n.* **1.** beak of bird. **2.** pen point.

nib'ble, *v.,* **-bled, -bling,** *n.* —*v.* **1.** bite off in small bits. —*n.* **2.** small morsel.

nib'lick, *n.* golf club.

nice, *adj.,* **nicer, nicest. 1.** agreeable. **2.** precise. **3.** fastidious. —**nice'ly,** *adv.*

ni'ce•ty, *n., pl.* **-ties. 1.** subtle point. **2.** refinement.

niche (nich), *n.* **1.** recess in wall. **2.** proper role.

nick, *n.* **1.** notch or hollow place in surface. **2.** precise or opportune moment. —*v.* **3.** make nick in.

nick'el, *n.* **1.** hard silver-white metal. **2.** five-cent coin.

nick'el•o'de•on, *n.* **1.** early motion-picture house. **2.** coin-operated automatic piano.

nick'name', *n., v.,* **-named, -naming.** —*n.* **1.** name used informally. —*v.* **2.** give nickname to.

nic'o•tine' (-tēn'), *n.* alkaloid found in tobacco.

nic'o•tin'ic acid, vitamin from nicotine.

niece, *n.* daughter of one's brother or sister.

nif'ty, *adj.,* **-tier, -tiest.** *Informal.* smart; fine.

nig'gard•ly, *adj.* **1.** stingy. **2.** meanly small.

nig'gling, *adj.* trivial.

nigh, *adv., adj.* near.

night, *n.* period between sunset and sunrise.

night'cap', *n.* **1.** alcoholic drink taken before bed. **2.** cap worn while sleeping.

night'club', *n.* establishment open at night, offering food, drink, and entertainment.

night crawler, earthworm.

night'fall', *n.* coming of night.

night'gown', *n.* gown for sleeping. Also, **night'dress'**.

night'hawk', *n.* nocturnal American bird.

night'in·gale', *n.* small bird noted for song.

night'ly, *adj., adv.* every night.

night'mare', *n.* **1.** bad dream. **2.** harrowing event.

night owl, *n.* person who often stays up late at night.

night'shade', *n.* plant sometimes used in medicine.

night'shirt', *n.* loose shirtlike garment worn in bed.

night stick, billy club.

ni'hil·ism (nī'ə liz'əm), *n.* disbelief in principles. —**ni'hil·ist**, *n.* —**ni'hil·is'tic**, *adj.*

nil, *n.* nothing.

nim'ble, *adj.,* -bler, -blest. agile; quick. —**nim'bly**, *adv.* —**nim'ble·ness**, *n.*

nim'bus, *n., pl.* -bi (-bī), -buses. **1.** halo. **2.** rain cloud.

nim'rod, *n.* hunter.

nin'com·poop', *n.* fool.

nine, *n., adj.* eight plus one. —**ninth**, *n., adj.*

nine'pins', *n.pl.* bowling game played with nine wooden pins.

nine'teen', *n., adj.* ten plus nine. —**nine'teenth'**, *n., adj.*

nine'ty, *n., adj.* ten times nine. —**nine'ti·eth**, *adj., n.*

nin'ny, *n., pl.* -nies. fool.

ni·o'bi·um, *n.* steel-gray metallic element.

nip, *v.,* nipped, nipping, *n.* —*v.* **1.** pinch or bite. **2.** check growth of. **3.** affect sharply. **4.** sip. —*n.* **5.** pinch. **6.** biting quality. **7.** sip.

nip'ple, *n.* **1.** milk-discharging protuberance on breast. **2.** nipple-shaped object.

nip'py, *adj.,* -pier, -piest. **1.** chilly. **2.** sharp.

nir·va'na (nir vä'nə), *n.* **1.** (in Buddhism) freedom from all passion. **2.** state of bliss.

nit, *n.* egg of louse.

ni'ter, *n.* white salt used in gunpowder, etc. Also, **ni'tre**.

nit'-pick', *v. Informal.* argue or find fault pettily.

ni′trate, *n.* **1.** salt of nitric acid. **2.** fertilizer containing nitrates.

nitric acid, caustic liquid used in manufacture of explosives, fertilizers, etc.

ni′tro•gen, *n.* gas used in explosives, fertilizers, etc.

ni′tro•glyc′er•in, *n.* colorless, highly explosive oil.

ni′trous, *adj.* **1.** of niter. **2.** Also, **ni′tric.** containing nitrogen.

nitrous oxide, colorless gas.

nit′ty-grit′ty, *n. Slang.* essentials of situation.

nit′wit′, *n.* simpleton.

nix, *adv. Informal.* no.

NJ, New Jersey. Also, **N.J.**

NM, New Mexico.

N. Mex., New Mexico.

no, *adv., n., pl.* **noes,** *adj.* —*adv.* **1.** word used to express dissent or refusal. —*n.* **2.** negative vote. —*adj.* **3.** not any.

no., **1.** north **2.** number.

no•bel′i•um, *n.* synthetic radioactive element.

no•bil′i•ty, *n., pl.* **-ties.** **1.** noble class. **2.** noble quality.

no′ble, *adj.,* **-bler, -blest,** *n.* —*adj.* **1.** of high rank by birth. **2.** admirable or magnificent. —*n.* **3.** person of noble rank. —**no′ble•man,** *n.* —**no′ble•wom′an,** *n.fem.* —**no′bly,** *adv.*

no•blesse′ o•blige′ (nō bles′ ō blēzh′), moral obligation of the rich to display generous conduct.

no′bod′y, *n., pl.* **-bodies.** **1.** no one. **2.** no one of importance.

noc•tur′nal, *adj.* **1.** of night. **2.** occurring or active by night.

noc′turne, *n.* dreamy or pensive musical composition.

nod, *v.,* **nodded, nodding,** *n.* —*v.* **1.** incline head briefly. **2.** become sleepy. **3.** sway gently. **4.** be absent-minded. —*n.* **5.** brief inclination of head, as in assent.

node, *n.* **1.** protuberance. **2.** difficulty. **3.** joint in plant stem.

nod′ule, *n.* small knob or lump. —**nod′u•lar,** *adj.*

No•el′, *n.* Christmas.

no′-fault′, *adj.* (of auto accident insurance, divorces, etc.) effective without establishing fault.

nog′gin, *n.* **1.** small mug. **2.** *Informal.* head.

noise, *n., v.,* **noised, nois•ing.** —*n.* **1.** sound, esp. loud or harsh. —*v.* **2.** spread rumors. —**noise′less,** *adj.* —**nois′y,** *adj.* —**nois′i•ly,** *adv.* —**nois′i•ness,** *n.*

noi′some, *adj.* offensive.

no′mad, *n.* wanderer. —**no•mad′ic,** *adj.*

no man's land, area between warring armies.

nom de plume (nom′ də plōōm′), name assumed by writer.

no′men•cla′ture (-klā′chər), *n.* set or system of names.

nom′i•nal, *adj.* **1.** in name only; so-called. **2.** trifling. —**nom′i•nal•ly,** *adv.*

nom′i•nate′, *v.,* **-nated, -nating. 1.** propose as candidate. **2.** appoint. —**nom′i•na′tion,** *n.* —**nom′i•na′tor,** *n.*

nom′i•na•tive, *adj.* **1.** denoting noun or pronoun used as the subject of a sentence. —*n.* **2.** nominative case.

nom′i•nee′, *n.* one nominated.

non-, prefix meaning not.

non′age (non′ij), *n.* period of legal minority.

non′a•ge•nar′i•an, *n.* person 90 to 99 years old.

nonce, *n.* present occasion.

non′cha•lant′ (non′shə länt′), *adj.* coolly unconcerned. —**non′cha•lance′,** *n.* —**non′cha•lant′ly,** *adv.*

non′com•bat′ant, *n.* **1.** member of military force who is not a fighter. **2.** civilian in wartime.

non′com•mis′sioned, *adj. Mil.* not commissioned.

non′com•mit′tal, *adj.* not committing oneself. —**non′com•mit′tal•ly,** *adv.*

non′ com′pos men′tis, *Law.* not of sound mind.

non′con•duc′tor, *n.* substance that does not readily conduct heat.

non′con•form′ist, *n.* person who refuses to conform.

non′de•script′, *adj.* of no particular kind.

none, *pron. sing. and pl.* **1.** not any. —*adv.* **2.** in no way.

non·en′ti·ty, *n., pl.* **-ties. 1.** unimportant person or thing. **2.** nonexistent thing.

none′such′, *n.* person or thing without equal.

none′the·less′, *adv.* nevertheless.

no′-no′, *n. Informal.* forbidden thing.

non′pa·reil′ (non′pə rel′), *adj.* **1.** having no equal. —*n.* **2.** person or thing without equal.

non·par′ti·san, *adj.* **1.** not taking sides. **2.** belonging to no party.

non·plus′, *v.* confuse.

non·prof′it, *adj.* not profit motivated.

non′rep·re·sen·ta′tion·al, *adj.* not resembling any object.

non′re·stric′tive, *adj.* noting word or clause describing modified element but not essential to its meaning.

non′sec·tar′i·an, *adj.* of no one sect. —**nonsectarian,** *n.*

non′sense, *n.* **1.** senseless or absurd words or action. **2.** anything useless. —**non·sen′si·cal,** *adj.*

non se′qui·tur, statement unrelated to preceding one.

non′stand′ard, *adj.* not conforming to usage considered acceptable by educated native speakers.

non′stop′, *adj., adv.* without intermediate stops. Also, **non-stop.**

non′sup·port′, *n.* failure to provide financial support.

non·un′ion, *adj.* **1.** not belonging to labor union. **2.** not produced by union workers.

non·vi′o·lence, *n.* policy of not using violence. —**non·vi′o·lent,** *adj.*

noo′dle, *n.* thin strip of dough, cooked in soup, etc.

nook, *n.* **1.** corner of room. **2.** secluded spot.

noon, *n.* 12 o'clock in daytime. —**noon′time′, noon′tide′,** *n.*

no one, not anyone.

noose, *n., v.,* **noosed, noosing.** —*n.* **1.** loop with running knot that pulls tight. —*v.* **2.** catch by noose.

nor, *conj.* or not: used with **neither.**

Nor'dic, *n.* person marked by tall stature, blond hair, and blue eyes. —**Nor'dic,** *adj.*

norm, *n.* standard.

nor'mal, *adj.* 1. of standard type; usual. 2. at right angles. —*n.* 3. standard; average. 4. perpendicular line. —**nor'mal•cy, nor•mal'i•ty,** *n.* —**nor'mal•ize',** *v.* —**nor'mal•i•za'tion,** *n.* —**nor'mal•ly,** *adv.*

normal school, school for training teachers.

nor'ma•tive, *adj.* establishing a norm.

Norse, *n.* inhabitants or speech of medieval Scandinavia.

north, *n.* 1. cardinal point of compass, on one's right facing the setting sun. 2. territory in or to north. —*adj.* 3. toward, in, or from north. —*adv.* 4. toward north. —**north'er•ly,** *adj., adv.* —**north'ern,** *adj.* —**north'ern•er,** *n.* —**north'ward,** *adj., adv.*

north'east', *n.* direction midway between north and east. —**north'east',** *adj., adv.* —**north'east'ern,** *adj.*

North Star, Polaris.

north'west', *n.* direction midway between north and west. —**north'west',** *adj., adv.* —**north'west'ern,** *adj.*

nose, *n., v.,* **nosed, nosing.** —*n.* 1. part of head containing nostrils. 2. sense of smell. 3. projecting part. —*v.* 4. smell. 5. pry or head cautiously.

nose'cone', *n.* forward section of rocket.

nose'dive', *n.* 1. downward plunge. —*v.* 2. go into a nosedive.

nose'gay', *n.* small bouquet.

nosh, *Informal.* —*v.* 1. snack (on). —*n.* 2. snack.

no'-show', *n.* person who does not show up for reservation.

nos•tal'gia, *n.* yearning for the past. —**nos•tal'gic,** *adj.*

nos'tril, *n.* external opening of nose for breathing.

nos'trum, *n.* charlatan's medicine; panacea.

nos'y, *adj.,* **nosier, nosiest.** *Informal.* unduly inquisitive. Also, **nos'ey.**

not, *adv.* word expressing negation, denial, or refusal.

no'ta be'ne, *Latin.* note well.

no'ta•ble, *adj.* **1.** worthy of note; important. —*n.* **2.** prominent person. —**no'ta•bly,** *adv.*

no'ta•rize', *v.,* **-rized, -rizing.** authenticate by notary.

no'ta•ry, *n., pl.* **-ries.** official authorized to verify documents. Also, **notary public.**

no•ta'tion, *n.* **1.** note. **2.** special symbol. —**no•ta'tion•al,** *adj.*

notch, *n.* **1.** angular cut. —*v.* **2.** make notch in.

note, *n., v.,* **noted, noting.** —*n.* **1.** brief record, comment, etc. **2.** short letter. **3.** importance. **4.** notice. **5.** paper promising payment. **6.** musical sound or written symbols. —*v.* **7.** write down. **8.** notice.

note'book', *n.* **1.** book with blank pages for writing notes. **2.** laptop computer.

not'ed, *adj.* famous.

note'wor'thy, *adj.* notable.

noth'ing, *n.* **1.** not anything. **2.** trivial action, thing, etc. —*adv.* **3.** not at all.

noth'ing•ness, *n.* **1.** lack of being. **2.** unconsciousness. **3.** absence of worth.

no'tice, *n., v.,* **-ticed, -ticing.** —*n.* **1.** information; warning. **2.** note, etc., that informs or warns. **3.** attention; heed. —*v.* **4.** pay attention to; perceive. **5.** mention. —**no'tice•a•ble,** *adj.* —**no'tice•a•bly,** *adv.*

no'ti•fy', *v.,* **-fied, -fying.** give notice to. —**no'ti•fi•ca'tion,** *n.* —**no'ti•fi'er,** *n.*

no'tion, *n.* **1.** idea; conception. **2.** opinion. **3.** whim. **4.** (*pl.*) small items, as pins or trim.

no•to'ri•ous, *adj.* widely known, esp. unfavorably. —**no'to•ri'e•ty,** *n.*

not'with•stand'ing, *prep.* **1.** in spite of. —*adv.* **2.** nevertheless. —*conj.* **3.** although.

nou'gat (nōō'gət), *n.* pastelike candy with nuts.

nought, *n.* naught.

noun, *n.* word denoting person, place, or thing.

nour'ish, *v.* sustain with food. —**nour'ish•ment,** *n.*

nou'veau riche' (nōō'vō rēsh'), *pl.* **nou'veaux riches.** newly rich person.

nou•velle' cui•sine' (nōō vel'), cooking that emphasizes fresh ingredients and light sauces.

Nov., November.

no′va, *n., pl.* **-vas, -vae** (-vē). star that suddenly becomes much brighter, then gradually fades.

nov′el, *n.* 1. fictitious narrative. —*adj.* 2. unfamiliar. —**nov′el•ist,** *n.*

nov′el•ty, *n., pl.* **-ties.** 1. unfamiliarity. 2. unfamiliar or amusing thing.

No•vem′ber, *n.* eleventh month of year.

no•ve′na (nō vē′-), *n., pl.* **-nae** (-nē), **-nas.** Roman Catholic devotion occurring on nine consecutive days.

nov′ice, *n.* 1. beginner. 2. person just received into a religious order.

no•vi′ti•ate (-vish′ē it), *n.* probationary period in religious order.

No′vo•caine′, *n. Trademark.* local anesthetic.

now, *adv.* 1. at present time. 2. immediately. —*conj.* 3. since. —*n.* 4. the present.

now′a•days′, *adv.* in these times.

no′where′, *adv.* not anywhere.

nox′ious, *adj.* harmful.

noz′zle, *n.* projecting spout.

nth (enth), *adj.* utmost.

nu′ance (nyo͞o′äns), *n.* shade of expression, etc.

nub, *n.* gist.

nu′bile (nyo͞o′bil, -bīl), *adj.* (of a young woman) 1. marriageable. 2. sexually developed and attractive.

nu′cle•ar, *adj.* of or forming a nucleus.

nuclear energy, energy released by reactions within atomic nuclei.

nuclear family, social unit composed of father, mother, and children.

nuclear physics, branch of physics dealing with atoms.

nuclear winter, devastation, darkness, and cold that could result from nuclear war.

nu′cle•on, *n.* proton or neutron.

nu′cle•us, *n., pl.* **-clei, -cleuses.** 1. central part about which other parts are grouped. 2. central body of living cell. 3. core of atom.

nude, *adj.* **1.** naked. —*n.* **2.** naked human figure.

nudge, *v.,* **nudged, nudging,** *n.* —*v.* **1.** push slightly. —*n.* **2.** slight push.

nud'ism, *n.* practice of going naked for health. —**nud'ist,** *n.*

nu'ga•to'ry, *adj.* **1.** trifling. **2.** futile.

nug'get, *n.* lump.

nui'sance, *n.* annoyance.

nuke, *n., v.,* **nuked, nuking.** *Slang.* —*n.* **1.** nuclear weapon or power plant. —*v.* **2.** attack with nuclear weapons.

null, *adj.* of no effect.

null'i•fy', *v.,* **-fied, -fying. 1.** make null. **2.** make legally void. —**nul'li•fi•ca'tion,** *n.*

numb, *adj.* **1.** deprived of feeling or movement. —*v.* **2.** make numb. —**numb'ness,** *n.*

num'ber, *n.* **1.** sum of group of units. **2.** numeral. **3.** one of series or group. **4.** large quantity. —*v.* **5.** mark with number. **6.** count. **7.** amount to in numbers.

num'ber•less, *adj.* too numerous to count.

nu'mer•al, *n.* **1.** word or sign expressing number. —*adj.* **2.** of numbers.

nu'mer•ate', *v.,* **-ated, -ating.** number; count. —**nu'mer•a'tion,** *n.*

nu'mer•a'tor, *n.* part of fraction written above the line, showing number to be divided.

nu•mer'i•cal, *adj.* of, denoting number. —**nu•mer'i•cal•ly,** *adv.*

nu'mer•ol'o•gy, *n.* study of numbers to determine supernatural meaning.

nu'mer•ous, *adj.* very many.

nu'mi•nous, *adj.* supernatural.

nu'mis•mat'ics, *n.* science of coins and medals.

num'skull', *n. Informal.* dunce. Also, **numb'skull'.**

nun, *n.* woman living with religious group under vows.

nun'ci•o' (nun'shē ō'), *n., pl.* **-cios.** diplomatic representative of a Pope.

nun'ner•y, *n., pl.* **-neries.** convent.

nup'tial, *adj.* **1.** of marriage. —*n.* **2.** (*pl.*) marriage ceremony.

nurse, *n., v.,* **nursed, nursing.** —*n.* **1.** person who cares for sick or children. —*v.* **2.** tend in sickness. **3.** look after carefully. **4.** suckle.

nurs'er•y, *n., pl.* **-eries. 1.** room set apart for young children. **2.** place where young plants are grown.

nursery school, school level below kindergarten age.

nurs'ling, *n.* nursing infant.

nur'ture, *v.,* **-tured, -turing,** *n.* —*v.* **1.** feed and care for during growth. —*n.* **2.** upbringing. **3.** nourishment.

nut, *n.* **1.** dry fruit consisting of edible kernel in shell. **2.** the kernel. **3.** perforated, threaded metal block used to screw on end of bolt. —**nut'crack'er,** *n.* —**nut'shell',** *n.*

nut'hatch', *n.* bird that seeks food along tree trunks.

nut'meg, *n.* aromatic seed.

nu'tri•a (nyoo′trē ə), *n.* fur.

nu'tri•ent, *adj.* **1.** nourishing. —*n.* **2.** nutrient substance.

nu'tri•ment, *n.* nourishment.

nu•tri'tion, *n.* **1.** process of nourishing or being nourished. **2.** study of dietary requirements. **3.** process by which organism converts food into living tissue. —**nu•tri'tious, nu'tritive,** *adj.* —**nu•tri'tion•al,** *adj.* —**nu•tri'tion•ist,** *n.*

nuts, *adj. Informal.* crazy.

nut'ty, *adj.,* **-tier, -tiest. 1.** tasting of or like nuts. **2.** *Informal.* insane; senseless. —**nut'ti•ness,** *n.*

nuz'zle, *v.,* **-zled, -zling. 1.** rub noses with. **2.** cuddle.

NV, Nevada.

NW, northwest. Also, **N.W.**

NY, New York. Also, **N.Y.**

ny'lon, *n.* **1.** tough, elastic synthetic substance used for yarn, bristles, etc. **2.** (*pl.*) stockings of nylon.

nymph, *n.* **1.** beautiful goddess living in woodlands and waters. **2.** beautiful young woman.

nym'pho•ma'ni•a, *n.* uncontrollable sexual desire in women. —**nym'pho•ma'ni•ac',** *n.*

O, o, *n.* **1.** fifteenth letter of English alphabet. —*interj.* **2.** (expression of surprise, gladness, pain, etc.) **3.** word used before name in archaic form of address.

o', *prep.* shortened form of **of.**

oaf, *n.* clumsy, rude person. —**oaf'ish,** *adj.*

oak, *n.* tree having hard wood. —**oak'en,** *adj.*

oa'kum, *n.* loose fiber used in calking seams.

oar, *n.* **1.** flat-bladed shaft for rowing boat. —*v.* **2.** row. —**oars'man,** *n.*

oar'lock', *n.* support on gunwale for oar.

o•a'sis, *n., pl.* **-ses.** fertile place in desert.

oat, *n.* cereal grass.

oath, *n.* **1.** vow. **2.** curse.

oat'meal', *n.* **1.** meal made from oats. **2.** cooked breakfast food made from this.

ob'bli•ga'to (ob'li gä'tō), *n., pl.* **-tos, -ti** (-tē). musical line performed by single instrument accompanying a solo part.

ob'du•rate, *adj.* stubborn. —**ob'du•ra•cy,** *n.*

o•bei'sance (-bā'-), *n.* **1.** bow or curtsy. **2.** homage.

ob'e•lisk, *n.* tapering, four-sided monumental shaft.

o•bese' (ō bēs'), *adj.* very fat. —**o•bes'i•ty,** *n.*

o•bey', *v.* **1.** do as ordered by. **2.** respond to, as controls. —**o•be'di•ence,** *n.* —**o•be'di•ent,** *adj.* —**o•be'di•ent•ly,** *adv.*

ob•fus'cate (-fus'kāt), *v.,* **-cated, -cating.** confuse; make unclear. —**ob'fus•ca'tion,** *n.*

ob'i•ter dic'tum (ob'i tər dik'təm), *pl.* **obiter dicta** (-tə). incidental remark.

o•bit'u•ar'y, *n., pl.* **-aries.** notice of death.

obj., 1. object. **2.** objective.

ob'ject, *n.* **1.** something solid. **2.** thing or person to which attention is directed. **3.** end; motive. **4.** noun or pronoun that represents goal of action. —*v.* (əb jekt'). **5.** make protest. —**ob•jec'tion,** *n.* —**ob•jec'tor,** *n.*

ob•jec'tion•a•ble, *adj.* causing disapproval.

ob•jec′tive, *n.* 1. something aimed at. 2. objective case. —*adj.* 3. real or factual. 4. unbiased. 5. being object of perception or thought. 6. denoting word used as object of sentence. —**ob•jec′tive•ly**, *adv.* —**ob′jec•tiv′i•ty**, *n.*

object lesson, practical illustration of principle.

ob•jet d'art (ob′zhā där′), *pl.* **objets d'art.** object of artistic worth.

ob′jur•gate′, *v.*, -gated, -gating. scold. —**ob′jur•ga′tion**, *n.* —**ob•jur′ga•to′ry**, *adj.*

ob′late, *adj.* (of spheroid) flattened at poles.

ob•la′tion, *n.* offering.

ob′li•gate′, *v.*, -gated, -gating. bind morally or legally. —**ob′li•ga′tion**, *n.* —**ob•lig′a•to′ry**, *adj.*

o•blige′, *v.*, obliged, obliging. 1. require; bind. 2. place under debt of gratitude.

o•blig′ing, *adj.* willing to help.

ob•lique′ (ə blēk′), *adj.* 1. slanting. 2. indirect. —**ob•lique′ly**, *adv.* —**ob•liq′ui•ty**, *n.*

ob•lit′er•ate′, *v.*, -ated, -ating. remove all traces of. —**ob•lit′er•a′tion**, *n.*

ob•liv′i•on, *n.* 1. state of being forgotten. 2. forgetfulness. —**ob•liv′i•ous**, *adj.* —**ob•liv′i•ous•ness**, *n.*

ob′long, *adj.* 1. longer than broad. —*n.* 2. oblong rectangle.

ob′lo•quy, *n.*, *pl.* -quies. public disgrace.

ob•nox′ious, *adj.* offensive. —**ob•nox′ious•ly**, *adv.*

o′boe, *n.* wind instrument. —**o′bo•ist**, *n.*

obs., obsolete.

ob•scene′, *adj.* offensive to decency. —**ob•scene′ly**, *adv.* —**ob•scen′i•ty**, *n.*

ob•scu′rant•ism, *n.* willful obscuring of something presented to public. —**ob•scu′rant•ist**, *n.*, *adj.*

ob•scure′, *adj.*, *v.*, -scured, -scuring. —*adj.* 1. not clear. 2. not prominent. 3. dark. —*v.* 4. make obscure. —**ob′scu•ra′tion**, *n.* —**ob•scu′ri•ty**, *n.* —**ob•scure′ly**, *adv.*

ob•se′qui•ous, *adj.* servile.

ob′se·quy, *n., pl.* **-quies.** funeral rite.

ob·serv′ance, *n.* 1. act of observing. 2. due celebration. —**ob·serv′ant,** *adj.*

ob·serv′a·to′ry, *n., pl.* **-ries.** building for observing stars.

ob·serve′, *v.,* **-served, -serving.** 1. see; notice; watch. 2. remark. 3. pay respect to. —**ob·serv′a·ble,** *adj.* —**ob′ser·va′tion,** *n.* —**ob·serv′er,** *n.*

ob·sess′, *v.* be constantly in thoughts of. —**ob·ses′sion,** *n.* —**ob·ses′sive,** *adj.* —**ob·ses′sive·ly,** *adv.*

ob·sid′i·an (əb sid′ē ən), *n.* dark volcanic glass.

ob′so·les′cent (-les′ənt), *adj.* becoming obsolete. —**ob′so·les′cence,** *n.*

ob′so·lete′, *adj.* out of use.

ob′sta·cle, *n.* impediment.

ob·stet′rics, *n.* branch of medicine concerned with childbirth. —**ob′ste·tri′cian,** *n.* —**ob·stet′ric, ob·stet′ri·cal,** *adj.*

ob′sti·nate, *adj.* 1. firm; stubborn. 2. not yielding to treatment. —**ob′sti·na·cy,** *n.* —**ob′sti·nate·ly,** *adv.*

ob·strep′er·ous, *adj.* unruly.

ob·struct′, *v.* block; hinder. —**ob·struc′tion,** *n.* —**ob·struc′tive,** *adj.*

ob·struc′tion·ism, *n.* desire to be obstructive. —**ob·struc′tion·ist,** *n., adj.*

ob·tain′, *v.* 1. acquire. 2. prevail. —**ob·tain′a·ble,** *adj.*

ob·trude′, *v.,* **-truded, -truding.** thrust forward; intrude. —**ob·tru′sion,** *n.* —**ob·tru′sive,** *adj.*

ob·tuse′, *adj.* 1. blunt. 2. not perceptive. 3. (of angle) between 90° and 180°.

ob′verse, *n.* 1. front. 2. side of coin having principal design. 3. counterpart. —*adj.* (ob vûrs′). 4. facing. 5. corresponding.

ob′vi·ate′, *v.,* **-ated, -ating.** take preventive measures against. —**ob′vi·a′tion,** *n.*

ob′vi·ous, *adj.* 1. readily perceptible. 2. not subtle. —**ob′vi·ous·ly,** *adv.* —**ob′vi·ous·ness,** *n.*

oc′a·ri′na (ok′ə rē′nə), *n.* egg-shaped wind instrument.

oc·ca′sion, *n.* 1. particular time. 2. important time.

3. opportunity. 4. reason. —*v.* 5. give cause for.
—**oc•ca'sion•al,** *adj.*
—**oc•ca'sion•al•ly,** *adv.*

Oc'ci•dent (ok'sə-), *n.* West, esp. Europe and Americas.
—**Oc'ci•den'tal,** *adj., n.*

oc•clude', *v.,* **-cluded, -cluding.** close; shut.
—**oc•clu'sion,** *n.*

oc•cult', *adj.* 1. outside ordinary knowledge. —*n.* 2. occult matters.

oc'cu•pa'tion, *n.* 1. trade; calling. 2. possession. 3. military seizure.
—**oc'cu•pa'tion•al,** *adj.*

occupational therapy, therapy utilizing activities for rehabilitation.

oc'cu•py, *v.,* **-pied, -pying.** 1. inhabit or be in. 2. require as space. 3. take possession of. 4. hold attention of.
—**oc'cu•pan•cy,** *n.*
—**oc'cu•pant,** *n.*

oc•cur', *v.,* **-curred, -curring.** 1. take place. 2. appear. 3. come to mind. —**oc•cur'rence,** *n.*

o'cean, *n.* 1. large body of salt water covering much of earth. 2. any of its five main parts.
—**o'ce•an'ic,** *adj.*

o'ce•a•nog'ra•phy, *n.* study of oceans.
—**o'ce•a•no•graph'ic,** *adj.*
—**o'ce•a•nog'ra•pher,** *n.*

o'ce•lot' (ō'sə-), *n.* small American wildcat.

o'cher (ō'kər), *n.* yellow-to-red color. Also, **o'chre.**

o'clock', *adv.* by the clock.

Oct., October.

oc'ta•gon', *n.* plane figure with eight sides and eight angles.

oc'tane, *n.* hydrocarbon found in petroleum.

octane number, designation of quality of gasoline.

oc'tave, *n. Music.* 1. eighth tone from given tone. 2. interval between such tones.

oc•ta'vo (-tā'-), *n., pl.* **-vos.** book whose pages are printed 16 to a sheet.

oc•tet', *n.* group of eight, esp. musicians. Also, **oc•tette'.**

Oc•to'ber, *n.* tenth month of year.

oc'to•ge•nar'i•an, *n.* person 80 to 89 years old.

oc'to•pus, *n., pl.* **-puses, -pi.** eight-armed sea mollusk.

oc'u•lar, *adj.* of eyes.

oc′u·list, *n.* eye doctor.

OD (ō′dē′), *n., pl.* **ODs** or **OD's,** *v.,* **OD'd** or **ODed, OD'ing.** *Slang.* —*n.* 1. overdose of a drug. —*v.* 2. take a drug overdose.

odd, *adj.* 1. eccentric; bizarre. 2. additional; not part of set. 3. not evenly divisible by two.

odd′ball′, *n. Informal.* peculiar person or thing.

odd′i·ty, *n., pl.* **-ties.** 1. queerness. 2. odd thing.

odds, *n.* 1. chances; probability for or against. 2. state of disagreement. 3. odd things.

odds and ends, 1. miscellany. 2. remnants.

odds′-on′, *adj.* most likely.

ode, *n.* poem of praise.

o′di·ous, *adj.* hateful.

o′di·um, *n.* 1. discredit; reproach. 2. hatred.

o·dom′e·ter (ō-), *n.* instrument that measures distance traveled.

o′dor, *n.* quality that affects sense of smell; scent. —**o′dor·ous,** *adj.*

o′dor·if′er·ous, *adj.* having odor, esp. unpleasant.

od′ys·sey (od′ə sē), *n.* long, adventurous journey.

oed′i·pal (ed′ə pəl), *adj.* (*often cap.*) resulting from the Oedipus complex.

Oedipus complex, libidinous feelings of son toward mother.

oe·nol′o·gy (ē-), *n.* science of winemaking.

oe′no·phile′ (ē′nə fīl′), *n.* connoisseur of wine.

o′er, *prep., adv. Poetic.* over.

oeu′vre (*Fr.* œ′vrˊ), *n., pl.* **oeu·vres** (*Fr.* œ′vrˊ). all the works of a writer, painter, etc.

of, *prep.* particle indicating: 1. being from. 2. belonging to.

off, *adv.* 1. up or away. 2. deviating. 3. out of operation or effect. —*prep.* 4. up or away from. —*adj.* 5. no longer in operation or effect. 6. in error. 7. on one's way.

of′fal, *n.* refuse; carrion.

off′beat′, *adj. Informal.* unconventional.

off′-col′or, *adj.* 1. not having the usual color. 2. of questionable taste; risqué.

of·fend′, *v.* displease greatly.

of·fend′er, *n.* 1. person who offends. 2. crimninal.

of·fense′, *n.* 1. wrong; sin. 2. displeasure. 3. attack. 4. (ô′fens, of′ens). attacking side. Also, **of·fence′**. —**of·fen′sive**, *adj., n.*

of′fer, *v.* 1. present. 2. propose; suggest. —*n.* 3. proposal; bid. —**of′fer·ing**, *n.*

of′fer·to′ry, *n., pl.* **-ries.** 1. *Rom. Cath. Ch.* offering to God of bread and wine during Mass. 2. collection at religious service.

off′hand′, *adj.* 1. Also, **off′hand′ed.** done without previous thought; informal. 2. curt. —**off′hand′ed·ly**, *adv.*

of′fice, *n.* 1. place of business. 2. position of authority. 3. duty; task. 4. religious service.

of′fice·hold′er, *n.* official.

of′fi·cer, *n.* person of authority.

of·fi′cial, *n.* 1. person who holds office. —*adj.* 2. authorized. 3. pertaining to office. —**of·fi′cial·ly**, *adv.*

of·fi′ci·ant (ə fish′ē ənt), *n.* cleric at religious service.

of·fi′ci·ate, *v.,* **-ated, -ating.** perform official duties. —**of·fi′ci·a′tor**, *n.*

of·fi′cious, *adj.* too forward in offering unwanted help.

off′ing, *n.* 1. distant area. 2. foreseeable future.

off′-key′, *adj.* 1. not in tune. 2. somewhat incongruous.

off′-lim′its, *adj.* forbidden to be patronized, used, etc.

off′-put′ting, *adj.* provoking uneasiness, annoyance, etc.

off′set′, *v.,* **-set, -setting.** compensate for.

off′shoot′, *n.* branch.

off′shore′, *adj., adv.* in water and away from shore.

off′spring′, *n.* children.

off′stage′, *adv., adj.* out of sight of audience.

off′-the-cuff′, *adj.* off hand.

off′-the-rec′ord, *adj.* not to be quoted.

off′-the-wall′, *adj. Informal.* bizarre.

off′track′, *adj.* occurring away from racetrack.

off year, 1. year without major election. 2. year marked by reduced production.

oft, *adv. Poetic.* often.

of′ten, *adv.* 1. frequently. 2. in many cases.

o'gle, *v.,* **ogled, ogling,** *n.* —*v.* 1. leer. —*n.* 2. ogling glance.

o'gre (ō'gər), *n.* 1. hideous giant who eats human flesh. 2. barbarous person. —**o'gre•ish,** *adj.* —**o'gress,** *n.fem.*

oh, *interj.* (exclamation of surprise, etc.)

OH, Ohio.

ohm (ōm), *n.* unit of electrical resistance.

-oid, suffix meaning resembling or like.

oil, *n.* 1. combustible liquid used for lubricating, and heating. —*v.* 2. supply with oil. —*adj.* 3. of oil. —**oil'er,** *n.* —**oil'y,** *adj.*

oil'cloth', *n.* fabric made waterproof with oil.

oil'skin', *n.* 1. fabric made waterproof with oil. 2. (*often pl.*) garment made of this.

oint'ment, *n.* salve.

OK, Oklahoma.

OK, *adj., adv., v.,* **OK'd, OK'ing,** *n., pl.* **OK's.** —*adj., adv.* (ō'kā'). 1. all right; correct. —*v.* (ō'kā'). 2. approve. —*n.* (ō'kā'). 3. agreement or approval. Also, **O.K., o'kay'.**

Okla., Oklahoma.

o'kra, *n.* plant with edible pods.

old, *adj.* 1. far advanced in years or time. 2. of age. 3. Also, **old'en.** former. 4. wise.—*n.* 5. former time.

Old English, English language before c1150.

old'-fash'ioned, *adj.* having ideas of an earlier time.

Old Guard, (*sometimes l.c.*) conservative members.

old hand, person with long experience.

old hat, old-fashioned; dated.

old school, supporters of established custom.

old'ster, *n. Informal.* elder.

Old Testament, complete Bible of the Jews, being first division of Christian Bible.

old'-tim'er, *n. Informal.* elderly person.

Old World, Europe, Asia, and Africa. —**old'-world',** *adj.*

o'le•ag'i•nous (ō'lē aj'ə nəs), *adj.* 1. oily. 2. fawning.

o'le•an'der, *n.* poisonous evergreen flowering shrub.

o′le•o•mar′ga•rine *n.* edible fat made of vegetable oils and skim milk. Also, **o′le•o′**, **o′le•o•mar′ga•rin**.

ol•fac′to•ry, *adj.* pertaining to sense of smell.

ol′i•garch′ (-gärk′), *n.* ruler in an oligarchy.

ol′i•gar′chy, *n., pl.* **-chies**. government by small group. —**ol′i•gar′chic**, *adj.*

ol′ive, *n.* **1.** tree valued for its fruit. **2.** fruit of this tree. **3.** yellowish green.

om′buds•man′, *n., pl.* **-men**. official who investigates private individuals' complaints against government. Also, *fem.* **om′buds•wom′an**.

o•me′ga (ō mē′gə), *n.* last letter of Greek alphabet.

om′e•let, *n.* eggs beaten and cooked with filling. Also, **om′e•lette**.

o′men, *n.* harbinger.

om′i•nous, *adj.* threatening evil. —**om′i•nous•ly**, *adv.*

o•mit′, *v.*, **omitted, omitting**. **1.** leave out. **2.** fail to do, etc. —**o•mis′sion**, *n.*

omni-, prefix meaning all.

om′ni•bus′, *n., pl.* **-buses**. **1.** bus. **2.** anthology.

om•nip′o•tent, *adj.* almighty. —**om•nip′o•tence**, *n.*

om′ni•pres′ent, *adj.* present everywhere at once.

om•nis′cient (om nish′ənt), *adj.* knowing all things. —**om•nis′cience**, *n.*

om•niv′o•rous, *adj.* eating all kinds of foods.

on, *prep.* particle expressing: **1.** position in contact with supporting surface. **2.** support; reliance. **3.** situation or direction. **4.** basis. —*adv.* **5.** onto a thing, place, or person. **6.** forward. **7.** into operation. —*adj.* **8.** near.

once, *adv.* **1.** formerly. **2.** single time. **3.** at any time. —*conj.* **4.** if ever; whenever.

once′-o′ver, *n. Informal.* quick survey.

on′co•gene′, *n.* gene causing beginning of cancerous growth.

on•col′o•gy, *n.* branch of medical science dealing with tumors and cancer. —**on•col′o•gist**, *n.*

on′com′ing, *adj.* approaching.

one, *adj.* 1. single. 2. some. 3. common to all. —*n.* 4. first and lowest whole number. 5. single person or thing. —*pron.* 6. person or thing.

one'ness, *n.* unity.

on'er·ous (on'-), *adj.* burdensome.

one·self', *pron.* person's self. Also, **one's self.**

one'-sid'ed, *adj.* 1. with all advantage on one side. 2. biased.

one'-time', *adj.* former.

one'-track', *adj. Informal.* obsessed with one subject.

one'-way', *adj.* moving in one direction only.

on'go'ing, *adj.* continuing.

on'ion, *n.* common plant having edible bulb.

on'-line', *adj.* operating under the direct control of a main computer.

on'look'er, *n.* spectator.

on'ly, *adv.* 1. solely. 2. merely. —*adj.* 3. sole. —*conj.* 4. but.

on'o·mat'o·poe'ia (on'ə mat'ə pē'ə), *n.* formation of word by imitation of a sound.

on'rush', *n.* rapid advance.

on'set', *n.* 1. beginning. 2. attack.

on'slaught', *n.* attack.

on'to, *prep.* upon; on.

on·tog'e·ny (on toj'ə nē), *n.* development of an organism.

on·tol'o·gy, *n.* branch of metaphysics studying existence or being.

o'nus (ō'nəs), *n.* burden.

on'ward, *adv.* 1. toward or at point ahead. —*adj.* 2. moving forward.

on'yx, *n.* varicolored quartz.

oo'dles, *n.pl. Informal.* large quantity.

ooze, *v.,* **oozed, oozing**, *n.* —*v.* 1. exude. —*n.* 2. something that oozes. 3. soft mud.

o·pac'i·ty (ō pas'-), *n., pl.* **-ties.** state of being opaque.

o'pal, *n.* stone.

o'pa·les'cent, *adj.* with opallike play of color. —**o'pa·les'cence**, *n.*

o·paque' (ō pāk'), *adj.* 1. not transmitting light. 2. not shining. 3. not clear.

op. cit., in the work cited.

OPEC (ō'pek), *n.* Organization of Petroleum Exporting Countries.

Op'-Ed', *n.* newspaper section for signed articles and letters.

o'pen, *adj.* 1. not shut. 2. not enclosed. 3. available; accessible. 4. candid. —*v.* 5. make or become open. 6. begin. 7. come apart. —*n.* 8. any open space.

o'pen-and-shut', *adj.* easily solved or decided; obvious.

o'pen-end'ed, *adj.* 1. unrestricted. 2. having no fixed answer.

o'pen-hand'ed, *adj.* generous.

o'pen•ing, *n.* 1. unobstructed place. 2. gap. 3. beginning. 4. opportunity.

o'pen-mind'ed, *adj.* without prejudice. —**o'pen-mind'ed•ness**, *n.*

open shop, business in which union membership is not a condition of employment.

op'er•a, *n.* sung drama. —**op'er•at'ic**, *adj.*

op'er•a•ble, *adj.* 1. able to be operated. 2. curable by surgery.

opera glasses, small, low-power binoculars.

op'er•ate', *v.*, **-ated, -ating.** 1. work or run. 2. exert force or influence. 3. use surgery. —**op'er•a'tion**, *n.* —**op'er•a'tor**, *n.*

operating system, software that directs computer's operations.

op'er•a'tion•al, *adj.* 1. concerning operations. 2. in working order. 3. in operation.

op'er•a'tive, *n.* 1. worker. 2. detective. 3. spy. —*adj.* 4. effective.

op'er•et'ta, *n.* light opera.

oph•thal'mi•a (of thal'mē ə), *n.* inflammation of eye.

oph'thal•mol'o•gy, *n.* branch of medicine dealing with eye. —**oph'thal•mol'o•gist**, *n.*

o'pi•ate (ō'pē it), *n.* medicine containing opium.

o•pine' (ō pīn'), *v.*, **-pined, -pining.** express an opinion.

o•pin'ion, *n.* belief or judgment.

o•pin'ion•at'ed, *adj.* stubborn in opinions.

o'pi•um, *n.* narcotic juice of poppy.

o•pos'sum, *n.* pouched mammal of southern U.S.

op•po′nent, *n.* **1.** person on opposite side, as in contest. **2.** person opposed to something.

op′por•tune′, *adj.* timely.

op′por•tun′ism, *n.* unprincipled use of opportunities. —**op′por•tun′ist,** *n.* —**op′por•tun•is′tic,** *adj.*

op′por•tu′ni•ty, *n., pl.* **-ties.** temporary possible advantage.

op•pose′, *v.,* **-posed, -posing. 1.** resist or compete with. **2.** hinder. **3.** set as an obstacle. **4.** cause to disfavor something. —**op′po•si′tion,** *n.*

op′po•site, *adj.* **1.** in corresponding position on other side. **2.** completely different. —*n.* **3.** one that is opposite.

op•press′, *v.* **1.** weigh down. **2.** treat harshly. —**op•pres′sion,** *n.* —**op•pres′sive,** *adj.* —**op•pres′sor,** *n.*

op•pro′bri•um, *n.* disgrace. —**op•pro′bri•ous,** *adj.*

opt, *v.* make a choice.

op′tic, *adj.* of eyes.

op′ti•cal, *adj.* **1.** acting by means of sight. **2.** made to assist sight. **3.** visual. **4.** of optics. —**op′ti•cal•ly,** *adv.*

optical disc, disk on which digital data is stored and read by laser.

optical scanner, device for scanning and digitizing printed material.

op•ti′cian, *n.* eyeglass maker.

op′tics, *n.* branch of science dealing with light and vision.

op′ti•mal, *adj.* optimum.

op′ti•mism′, *n.* **1.** disposition to hope for best. **2.** belief that good will prevail over evil. —**op′ti•mist,** *n.* —**op′ti•mis′tic,** *adj.*

op′ti•mum, *adj., n.* best.

op′tion, *n.* **1.** power of choosing. **2.** choice made. —**op′tion•al,** *adj.*

op•tom′e•try, *n.* art of testing eyes for eyeglasses. —**op•tom′e•trist,** *n.*

op′u•lent, *adj.* wealthy. —**op′u•lence,** *n.*

o′pus, (ō′pəs), *n., pl.* **opera.** work usually numbered.

or, *conj.* (particle used to connect alternatives.)

OR, 1. Oregon. **2.** operating room.

or′a•cle, *n.* **1.** answer by the gods to question. **2.** medium giving the answer. —**o•rac′u•lar,** *adj.*

o′ral, *adj.* **1.** spoken. **2.** of mouths. —**o′ral•ly,** *adv.*

or′ange, *n.* **1.** round, reddish-yellow citrus fruit. **2.** reddish yellow.

or′ange•ade′, *n.* drink with base of orange juice.

o•rang′u•tan′, *n.* large, long-armed ape. Also, **o•rang′ou•tang′, o•rang′.**

o•rate′, *v.,* -rated, -rating. deliver an oration.

o•ra′tion, *n.* formal speech.

or′a•tor, *n.* public speaker.

or′a•to′ri•o, *n., pl.* -rios. religious work for voices and orchestra in dramatic form.

or′a•to′ry, *n., pl.* -ries. **1.** eloquent speaking. **2.** small room for prayer. —**or′a•tor′i•cal,** *adj.*

orb, *n.* **1.** sphere. **2.** any of heavenly bodies.

or′bit, *n.* **1.** path of planet, etc., around another body. **2.** cavity in skull for eyeball. —*v.* **3.** travel in or send into orbit. —**or′bit•al,** *adj.*

or′chard, *n.* plot of fruit trees.

or′ches•tra, *n.* **1.** *Music.* large company of instrumental performers. **2.** space in theater for musicians. **3.** main floor of theater. —**or•ches′tral,** *adj.*

or′ches•trate′, *v.,* -trated, -trating. **1.** arrange music for orchestra. **2.** arrange elements of. —**or′ches•tra′tion,** *n.*

or′chid (ôr′kid), *n.* **1.** tropical plant with oddly shaped blooms. **2.** light purple.

or•dain′, *v.* **1.** invest as a member of the clergy. **2.** appoint or direct.

or•deal′, *n.* severe test.

or′der, *n.* **1.** authoritative command. **2.** harmonious arrangement. **3.** group bound by common religious rules. **4.** list of items desired. —*v.* **5.** give an order. **6.** arrange.

or′der•ly, *adj., adv., n., pl.* -lies. —*adj.* **1.** methodical. **2.** well-behaved. —*adv.* **3.** according to rule. —*n.* **4.** hospital attendant. —**or′der•li•ness,** *n.*

or′di•nal, *adj.* **1.** showing position in series. —*n.* **2.** ordinal number.

or′di•nance, *n.* law.

or′di•nar′y, *adj., n., pl.* **-naries.** —*adj.* **1.** usual. —*n.* **2.** ordinary condition. —**or′di•nar′i•ly,** *adv.*

or′di•na′tion, *n.* act of ordaining. Also, **or•dain′ment.**

ord′nance, *n.* military weapons of all kinds.

Or′do•vi′cian (-də vish′ən), *adj.* pertaining to geologic period of Paleozoic era.

or′dure, *n.* dung.

ore, *n.* metal-bearing rock.

Ore., Oregon.

o•reg′a•no, *n.* plant with leaves used as seasoning.

or′gan, *n.* **1.** large musical keyboard instrument sounded by air forced through pipes, etc. **2.** part of animal or plant with specific function. **3.** means of communication. —**or′gan•ist,** *n.*

or′gan•dy, *n., pl.* **-dies.** thin stiff cotton fabric.

or′gan•elle′, *n.* specialized cell structure.

or•gan′ic, *adj.* **1.** of carbon compounds. **2.** of living organisms. **3.** of produce grown without pesticides. —**or•gan′i•cal•ly,** *adv.*

or′gan•ism, *n.* anything living.

or′gan•ize′, *v.,* **-ized, -izing.** form into coordinated whole. —**or′gan•i•za′tion,** *n.* —**or′gan•iz′er,** *n.* —**or′gan•i•za′tion•al,** *adj.*

or•gan′za, *n.* sheer fabric of rayon, nylon, or silk.

or′gasm, *n.* sexual climax.

or′gy, *n., pl.* **-gies.** wild revelry. —**or′gi•as′tic,** *adj.*

o′ri•el, *n.* bay window.

o′ri•ent, *n.* (ōr′ē ənt). **1.** (*cap.*) countries of Asia. —*v.* (ōr′ē ent′). **2.** set facing certain way. **3.** inform about one's situation. —**O′ri•en′tal,** *adj.* —**o′ri•en•ta′tion,** *n.*

o′ri•en•teer′ing, *n.* sport of navigating unknown terrain.

or′i•fice (ôr′ə fis), *n.* opening.

o′ri•ga′mi (ôr′i gä′mē), *n.* Japanese art of folding paper into decorative forms.

or′i•gin, *n.* **1.** source. **2.** beginning. **3.** lineage.

o•rig′i•nal, *adj.* **1.** first. **2.** novel. **3.** being new work. **4.** capable of creating something original. —*n.* **5.** primary form. **6.** thing copied. **7.** beginning. —**o•rig′i•nal′i•ty,** *n.*

o·rig′i·nal·ly, *adv.* **1.** at first. **2.** in original manner.

o·rig′i·nate′, *v.,* **-nated, -nating. 1.** come to be. **2.** give origin to. **—o·rig′i·na′tor,** *n.* **—o·rig′i·na′tion,** *n.*

o′ri·ole′, *n.* bright-colored bird of Europe and America.

or′i·son (ôr′i zən), *n.* prayer.

Or′lon, *n. Trademark.* synthetic fabric resembling nylon.

or′mo·lu′, *n., pl.* **-lus.** copper-zinc alloy.

or′na·ment, *n.* **1.** decoration. **—v. 2.** adorn. **—or′na·men′tal,** *adj.* **—or′na·men·ta′tion,** *n.*

or·nate′, *adj.* lavish. **—or·nate′ly,** *adv.*

or′ner·y, *adj. Informal.* ill-tempered.

or′ni·thol′o·gy, *n.* study of birds. **—or′ni·thol′o·gist,** *n.* **—or′ni·tho·log′i·cal,** *adj.*

o′ro·tund′, *adj.* **1.** rich and clear in voice. **2.** pompous.

or′phan, *n.* **1.** child whose parents are both dead. **—adj. 2.** of or for orphans. **—v. 3.** bereave of parents.

or′phan·age, *n.* home for orphans.

or′ris, *n.* kind of iris.

or′tho·don′tics, *n.* branch of dentistry dealing with irregular teeth. Also, **or′tho·don′tia.** **—or′tho·don′tic,** *adj.* **—or′tho·don′tist,** *n.*

or′tho·dox′, *adj.* **1.** correct in doctrine. **2.** conventional. **3.** (*cap.*) of Christian churches common in eastern Europe. **—or′tho·dox′y,** *n.*

or·thog′ra·phy, *n., pl.* **-phies.** spelling. **—or′tho·graph′ic, or′tho·graph′i·cal,** *adj.*

or′tho·pe′dics, *n.* branch of medicine dealing with the skeletal system. **—or′tho·pe′dist,** *n.* **—or′tho·pe′dic,** *adj.*

-ory, suffix meaning: **1.** of, characterized by, or serving to, as *excretory.* **2.** place or instrument for, as *crematory.*

os′cil·late′ (os′ə-), *v.,* **-lated, -lating.** swing to and fro. **—os′cil·la′tion,** *n.* **—os′cil·la′tor,** *n.*

os·cil′lo·scope′, *n.* device that uses cathode-ray tube to display changes in electric quantity.

os′cu·late′ (os′kyə-), *v.,* -lated, -lating. kiss.
—**os′cu·la′tion,** *n.*
—**os′cu·la·to′ry,** *adj.*

o′sier (ō′zhər), *n.* tough twig.

-osis, suffix meaning: **1.** action or condition, as *osmosis.* **2.** abnormal state, as *tuberculosis.*

os′mi·um, *n.* metallic element used in alloys.

os·mo′sis, *n.* diffusion of liquid through membrane.

os′prey, *n.* large hawk.

os′se·ous, *adj.* of, like, or containing bone.

os′si·fy′, *v.,* -fied, -fying. make or become bone.
—**os′si·fi·ca′tion,** *n.*

os·ten′si·ble, *adj.* merely apparent or pretended.
—**os·ten′si·bly,** *adv.*

os′ten·ta′tion, *n.* pretention.
—**os′ten·ta′tious,** *adj.*

os′te·o·ar·thri′tis, *n.* arthritis marked by decay of cartilage in joints.

os′te·op′a·thy, *n.* treatment of disease by manipulating affected part.
—**os′te·o·path′,** *n.*
—**os′te·o·path′ic,** *adj.*

os′te·o·po·ro′sis (os′tē ō pə rō′sis), *n.* disorder in which bones become increasingly brittle and prone to fracture.

os′tra·cize′ (os′trə sīz′), *v.,* -cized, -cizing. exclude; banish. —**os′tra·cism,** *n.*

os′trich, *n.* large, swift-footed, flightless bird.

oth′er, *adj.* **1.** additional. **2.** different. **3.** or remaining. **4.** former. —*pron.* **5.** other person or thing.

oth′er·wise′, *adv.* **1.** in other ways. —*adj.* **2.** of other sort.

oth′er·world′ly, *adj.* concerned with spiritual or imaginary world.

o′ti·ose′ (ō′shē ōs′), *adj.* **1.** idle. **2.** futile.

ot′ter, *n.* aquatic mammal.

ot′to·man, *n.* low seat.

ought, *aux. v.* **1.** be bound by reasoning. —*n.* **2.** cipher (0).

ounce, *n.* unit of weight equal to 1/16 lb. avoirdupois or 1/12 lb. troy.

our, *pron.* possessive form of **we,** used before noun.

ours, *pron.* possessive form of **we,** used predicatively.

our•selves', *pron.* 1. reflexive substitute for **us.** 2. intensive with or substitute for **we** or **us.**

-ous, suffix meaning full of or characterized by.

oust, *v.* eject; force out.

oust'er, *n.* ejection.

out, *adv.* 1. away from some place. 2. so as to emerge or project. 3. until conclusion. 4. to depletion. 5. so as to be extinguished, etc. —*adj.* 6. away from some place. 7. extinguished, etc. —*prep.* 8. out from. 9. away along. —*n.* 10. means of evasion.

out-, prefix meaning: 1. outward, as *outburst.* 2. outside, as *outbuilding.* 3. surpass, as *outlast.*

out'age (ou'tij), *n.* failure in supply of power.

out'-and-out', *adj.* thorough.

out'back', *n.* remote area.

out'board', *adj., adv.* on exterior of ship or boat.

out'bound', *adj.* headed out.

out'break', *n.* 1. sudden occurrence. 2. riot.

out'build'ing, *n.* detached building from main building.

out'burst', *n.* bursting forth.

out'cast', *n.* exiled person.

out'class', *v.* outdo in style.

out'come', *n.* consequence.

out'crop', *n.* emerging stratum at earth's surface.

out'cry', *n., pl.* **-cries.** expression of protest.

out•dat'ed, *adj.* obsolete.

out•dis'tance, *v.,* **-tanced, -tancing.** leave behind.

out•do', *v.,* **-did, -done, -doing.** surpass.

out'door', *adj.* done in open air. —**out'doors',** *adv., n.*

out'er, *adj.* 1. farther out. 2. on outside.

out'er•most', *adj.* farthest out.

outer space, 1. space beyond the earth's atmosphere. 2. space beyond solar system.

out'er•wear', *n.* garments worn over other clothing.

out'field', *n.* part of baseball field beyond diamond. —**out'field'er,** *n.*

out'fit', *n., v.,* **-fitted, -fitting.** —*n.* 1. set of articles for any purpose. 2. organized group of persons. —*v.* 3. equip. —**out'fit'ter,** *n.*

out′flank′, *v.* go beyond flank.

out′fox′, *v.* outsmart.

out′go′, *n., pl.* **-goes.** expenditure.

out′go′ing, *adj.* **1.** departing. **2.** retiring from a position or office. **3.** friendly; sociable.

out′grow′, *v.,* **-grew, -grown, -growing.** grow too large for.

out′growth′, *n.* **1.** natural result. **2.** offshoot.

out′house′, *n.* separate building serving as toilet.

out′ing, *n.* pleasure trip.

out•land′ish, *adj.* strange.

out′last′, *v.* endure after.

out′law′, *n.* **1.** criminal. **2.** person excluded from protection of law. —*v.* **3.** prohibit by law. **4.** deny protection of law to. —**out′law′ry,** *n.*

out′lay′, *n.* expenditure.

out′let, *n.* **1.** passage out. **2.** market for goods.

out′line′, *n., v.,* **-lined, -lining.** —*n.* **1.** line by which object is bounded. **2.** drawing showing only outer contour. **3.** general description. —*v.* **4.** draw or represent in outline.

out′live′, *v.,* **-lived, -living.** live longer than.

out′look′, *n.* **1.** view. **2.** mental view. **3.** prospect.

out′ly′ing, *adj.* remote.

out′mod′ed, *adj.* obsolete.

out•num′ber, *v.* be more numerous than.

out′-of-bod′y, *adj.* characterized by sensation that mind has left body.

out′-of-date′, *adj.* obsolete.

out′-of-doors′, *adj.* **1.** outdoor. —*n.* **2.** outdoors.

out′-of-the-way′, *adj.* **1.** isolated. **2.** unusual.

out′pa′tient, *n.* patient visiting hospital to receive treatment.

out′place′ment, *n.* assistance in finding new job, provided by company for employee being let go.

out′post′, *n.* **1.** sentinel station away from main army. **2.** place away from main area.

out′put′, *n.* **1.** production. **2.** quantity produced.

out′rage, *n., v.,* **-raged, -raging.** —*n.* **1.** gross violation. —*v.* **2.** subject to outrage. —**out•ra′geous,** *adj.*

ou•tré′ (oo trā′), *adj.* bizarre.

out′reach′, *v.* 1. exceed. 2. reach out. —*n.* 3. act of reaching out. —*adj.* 4. concerned with extending services.

out′rig′ger, *n.* framework supporting float extended from side of boat.

out′right′, *adj.* 1. utter; thorough. —*adv.* (out′rīt′). 2. without concealment.

out′run′, *v.,* **-ran, -run, -running.** 1. run faster or farther than. 2. exceed.

out′sell′, *v.,* **-sold, -selling.** exceed in number of sales.

out′set′, *n.* beginning.

out′shine′, *v.,* **-shone** or **-shined, -shining.** 1. shine more brightly than. 2. surpass.

out′side′, *n.* 1. outer side, aspect, etc. 2. space beyond enclosure. —*adj.* 3. on the outside. —*adv.* 4. on or to the outside. —*prep.* (out′sīd′). 5. at the outside of.

out•sid′er, *n.* person not belonging.

out′skirts′, *n.pl.* fringes.

out•smart′, *v.* outwit.

out′spo′ken, *adj.* candid.

out′spread′, *adj.* extended.

out′stand′ing, *adj.* 1. prominent. 2. not yet paid.

out′strip′, *v.,* **-stripped, -stripping.** 1. excel. 2. exceed.

out′take′, *n.* segment edited from published version.

out′ward, *adj.* 1. external. —*adv.* 2. Also, **out′wards.** toward the outside. —**out′ward•ly**, *adv.*

out′weigh′, *v.* exceed in importance.

out′wit′, *v.,* **-witted, -witting.** defeat by superior cleverness.

out•worn′, *adj.* 1. no longer vital or appropriate. 2. useless because of wear.

o′va, *n.* pl. of OVUM.

o′val, *adj.* egg-shaped; elliptical. Also, **o′vate.**

o′va•ry, *n., pl.* **-ries.** female reproductive gland. —**o•var′i•an**, *adj.*

o′vate, *adj.* egg-shaped.

o•va′tion, *n.* applause.

ov′en, *n.* chamber for baking.

o′ver, *prep.* 1. above in place. 2. on. 3. across; through. 4. in excess of. 5. concerning. 6. during. —*adv.* 7. so as to affect whole surface. **8.** above. **9.** again. —*adj.* **10.** finished. **11.** remaining. **12.** upper. **13.** surplus.

o′ver•a•chieve′, *v.,* **-chieved, -chieving.** perform better than expected, esp. in school. —**o′ver•a•chiev′er,** *n.*

o′ver•act′, *v.* perform in an exaggerated manner.

o′ver•age (ō′vər ij), *n.* **1.** surplus. —*adj.* (ō′vər āj′). **2.** beyond desirable age.

o′ver•all′, *adj.* **1.** including everything. —*n.* **2.** (*pl.*) loose, stout trousers.

o′ver•awe′, *v.,* **-awed, -awing.** dominate; intimidate.

o′ver•bear′ing, *adj.* domineering.

o′ver•bite′, *n.* occlusion in which upper incisor teeth overlap lower ones.

o′ver•blown′, *adj.* **1.** excessive. **2.** pretentious.

o′ver•board′, *adv.* over side of ship into water.

o′ver•cast′, *adj.* **1.** cloudy. **2.** gloomy.

o′ver•charge′, *v.,* **-charged, -charging. 1.** charge too high a price. **2.** overload. —*n.* (ō′vər chärj′). **3.** charge exceeding fair price. **4.** excessive load.

o′ver•coat′, *n.* coat worn over ordinary clothing.

o′ver•come′, *v.,* **-came, -come, -coming.** overpower.

o′ver•do′, *v.,* **-did, -done, -doing. 1.** do to excess. **2.** exaggerate.

o′ver•dose′, *n., v.,* **-dosed, -dosing.** —*n.* **1.** excessive dose. —*v.* **2.** take such a dose.

o′ver•draw′, *v.,* **-drew, -drawn, -drawing.** draw upon in excess of. —**o′ver•draft′,** *n.*

o′ver•drive′, *n.* arrangement of gears providing propeller speed greater than engine crankshaft speed.

o′ver•due′, *adj.* past due.

o′ver•flow′, *v.,* **-flowed, -flown, -flowing,** *n.* —*v.* **1.** flow or run over; flood. —*n.* (ō′vər flō′). **2.** instance of flooding. **3.** something that runs over.

o′ver•grow′, *v.,* **-grew, -grown, -growing.** cover with growth.

o′ver•hand′, *adv.* with hand above shoulder.

o′ver•hang′, *v.,* **-hung, -hanging,** *n.* —*v.* **1.** project over. **2.** threaten. —*n.* (ō′vər hang′). **3.** projection.

o′ver·haul′, *v.* 1. investigate thoroughly. 2. overtake. —*n.* 3. complete examination.

o′ver·head′, *adv.* 1. aloft. —*n.* (ō′vər hed′). 2. general business expense.

o′ver·hear′, *v.,* -heard, -hearing. hearing unintentionally.

o′ver·joyed′, *adj.* very happy.

o′ver·kill′, *n.* 1. *Mil.* ability to kill more than is needed for victory. 2. any excessive amount.

o′ver·land′, *adv., adj.* across open country.

o′ver·lap′, *v.,* -lapped, -lapping, *n.* —*v.* 1. extend over and beyond. —*n.* (ō′vər lap′). 2. overlapping part.

o′ver·lay′, *v.,* -laid, -laying, *n.* —*v.* 1. spread over. —*n.* 2. something used in overlaying.

o′ver·lie′, *v.* -lay, -lain, -lying. lie over or on.

o′ver·look′, *v.* 1. fail to notice. 2. afford view over.

o′ver·ly, *adv. Informal.* excessively.

o′ver·night′, *adv.* 1. during the night. 2. on previous night. —*adj.* 3. done, made, etc., during the night. 4. staying for one night.

o′ver·pass′, *n.* bridge crossing other traffic.

o′ver·play′, *v.* exaggerate.

o′ver·pow′er, *v.* 1. overwhelm in feeling. 2. subdue.

o′ver·qual′i·fied′, *adj.* having more education or experience than required.

o′ver·rate′, *v.,* -rated, -rating. esteem too highly.

o′ver·reach′, *v.* 1. extend beyond. 2. defeat (oneself), as by excessive eagerness.

o′ver·re·act′, *v.* react too emotionally. —**o′ver·re·ac′tion**, *n.*

o′ver·ride′, *v.,* -rode, -ridden, -riding. supersede.

o′ver·rule′, *v.,* -ruled, -ruling. rule against.

o′ver·run′, *v.,* -ran, -run, -running. 1. swarm over. 2. overgrow.

o′ver·seas′, *adv.* over or across the sea.

o′ver·see′, *v.,* -saw, -seen, -seeing. supervise. —**o′ver·se′er**, *n.*

o′ver·shad′ow, *v.* be more important than.

o′ver‧shoe′, *n.* protective shoe worn over another shoe.

o′ver‧shoot′, *v.*, **-shot, -shooting.** 1. shoot over so as to miss. 2. go beyond.

o′ver‧sight′, *n.* 1. error of neglect. 2. supervision.

o′ver‧sleep′, *v.*, **-slept, -sleeping.** sleep beyond desired time.

o′ver‧state′, *v.*, **-stated, -stating.** exaggerate in describing. **—o′ver‧state′ment,** *n.*

o′ver‧stay′, *v.*, **-stayed, -staying.** stay too long.

o′ver‧step′, *v.*, **-stepped, -stepping.** exceed.

o′ver‧stuffed′, *adj.* (of furniture) having the frame padded and covered.

o‧vert′, *adj.* 1. not concealed. 2. giving perceptible cause.

o′ver‧take′, *v.*, **-took, -taken, -taking.** catch up with.

o′ver-the-count′er, *adj.* 1. not listed on an organized securities exchange. 2. sold legally without a prescription.

o′ver‧throw′, *v.*, **-threw, -thrown, -throwing,** *n.* **—v.** 1. defeat; put end to. **—n.** (ō′vər thrō′). 2. act of overthrowing.

o′ver‧time′, *n.* time worked in addition to regular hours. **—o′ver‧time′**, *adv., adj.*

o′ver‧tone′, *n.* 1. additional meaning. 2. musical tone added to basic tone.

o′ver‧ture, *n.* 1. offer. 2. musical prelude to opera, etc.

o′ver‧turn′, *v.* 1. tip off base. 2. defeat.

o′ver‧view′, *n.* overall perception or description.

o′ver‧ween′ing, *adj.* 1. conceited. 2. excessive.

o′ver‧weight′, *n.* 1. excess of weight. **—adj.** (ō′vər wāt′). 2. weighing more than is normal.

o′ver‧whelm′, *v.* 1. overpower. 2. stun.

o′ver‧work′, *v.*, **-worked** or **-wrought, -working,** *n.* **—v.** 1. work too hard. **—n.** (ō′vər wûrk′). 2. work beyond one's strength.

o′ver‧wrought′, *adj.* highly excited.

o′vi‧duct′, *n.* tube through which ova are transported.

o‧vip′a‧rous, *adj.* producing eggs that hatch outside body.

o′void, *adj.* egg-shaped.

ov′u•late, *v.,* **-lated, -lating.** produce and discharge eggs (ova) from ovary. —**ov′u•la′tion**, *n.*

ov′ule, *n.* 1. structure that develops into seed. 2. small egg.

o′vum, *n., pl.* **ova.** female reproductive cell.

owe, *v.,* **owed, owing.** be obligated to pay or give to another.

owl, *n.* nocturnal bird of prey. —**owl′ish**, *adj.*

owl′et, *n.* small owl.

own, *adj.* 1. of or belonging to. —*v.* 2. possess. 3. acknowledge. —**own′er**, *n.* —**own′er•ship′**, *n.*

ox, *n., pl.* **oxen.** adult castrated male bovine.

ox′blood′, *n.* deep red color.

ox′ bow′, *n.* ∪-shaped part of yoke placed under and around neck of ox.

ox′ford, *n.* low laced shoe.

ox′i•dant, *n.* chemical agent that oxidizes.

ox′ide, *n.* compound of oxygen and another element.

ox′i•dize′, *v.,* **-dized, -dizing.** 1. add oxygen to. 2. rust. —**ox′i•di•za′tion, ox′i•da′tion**, *n.*

ox′y•a•cet′y•lene′ (ok′sē ə set′ə lēn′), *adj.* denoting a mixture of oxygen and acetylene used with steel.

ox′y•gen, *n.* gas necessary to life and fire.

ox′y•gen•ate′, *v.,* **-ated, -ating.** enrich with oxygen. —**ox′y•gen•a′tion**, *n.*

ox′y•mo′ron, *n., pl.* **-mora.** figure of speech that uses seeming contradictions.

oys′ter, *n.* edible mollusk.

oz., ounce.

o′zone, *n.* form of oxygen in upper atmosphere.

ozone hole, part of ozone layer depleted by pollution.

ozone layer, layer of upper atmosphere where most ozone is concentrated.

P, p, *n.* sixteenth letter of English alphabet.

pab'lum, *n.* simplistic ideas.

PA, 1. Pennsylvania. **2.** public-address system. Also, **Pa.**

PAC (pak), *n., pl.* **PACs, PAC's.** political action committee.

pace, *n., v.,* **paced, pacing.** —*n.* **1.** rate of movement or progress. **2.** linear measure. **3.** step or gait. —*v.* **4.** set pace for. **5.** step regularly. —**pac'er,** *n.*

pace'mak'er, *n.* **1.** one that sets pace. **2.** electrical device for controlling heartbeat.

pace'set'ter, *n.* leader.

pach'y•derm' (pak'ə-), *n.* thick-skinned mammal.

pach'y•san'dra (pak'ə-), *n., pl.* **-dras.** low plant used as ground cover.

pa•cif'ic, *adj.* peaceful.

pac'i•fism', *n.* principle of abstention from violence. —**pac'i•fist,** *n.* —**pa'ci•fis'tic,** *adj.*

pac'i•fy', *v.,* **-fied, -fying. 1.** calm. **2.** appease. —**pac'i•fi'er,** *n.* —**pac'i•fi•ca'tion,** *n.*

P

pack, *n.* **1.** bundle. **2.** group or complete set. —*v.* **3.** make into compact mass. **4.** fill with objects. **5.** cram. —**pack'er,** *n.*

pack'age, *n., v.,* **-aged, -aging.** —*n.* **1.** parcel. **2.** container. —*v.* **3.** put into package.

pack'et, *n.* **1.** small package. **2.** boat with fixed route.

pack rat, 1. rat that carries off shiny articles to its nest. **2.** *Informal.* person who saves useless items.

pact, *n.* agreement.

pad, *n., v.,* **padded, padding.** —*n.* **1.** soft, cushionlike mass. **2.** bound writing paper. **3.** dull sound of walking. —*v.* **4.** furnish with padding. **5.** expand with useless matter. **6.** walk with dull sound.

pad'ding, *n.* material with which to pad.

pad'dle, *n., v.,* **-dled, -dling.** —*n.* **1.** short oar for two hands. —*v.* **2.** propel with paddle. **3.** play in water.

paddle wheel, wheel for propelling ship.

pad'dock, *n.* field for horses.

pad'dy, *n., pl.* **-dies.** rice field.

paddy wagon, van for transporting prisoners.

pad'lock', *n.* **1.** portable lock. —*v.* **2.** lock with padlock. **3.** forbid access to.

pa'dre (pä'drā), *n., pl.* **-dres.** clergyman.

pae'an (pē'ən), *n.* song of praise.

pa'gan, *n.* **1.** worshiper of idols. —*adj.* **2.** idolatrous; heathen. —**pa'gan•ism,** *n.*

page, *n., v.,* **paged, paging.** —*n.* **1.** written surface. **2.** boy servant. —*v.* **3.** number pages of. **4.** seek by calling by name.

pag'eant, *n.* spectacle. —**pag'eant•ry,** *n.*

pag'i•nate, *v.,* **-nated, -nating.** number pages. —**pag'i•na'tion,** *n.*

pa•go'da, *n.* Far Eastern temple tower, esp. Buddhist.

pail, *n.* bucket.

pain, *n.* **1.** suffering. **2.** (*pl.*) effort. **3.** penalty. —*v.* **4.** hurt. —**pain'ful,** *adj.* —**pain'ful•ly,** *adv.* —**pain'less,** *adj.* —**pain'less•ly,** *adv.*

pain'kil'ler, *n.* pain reliever.

pains'tak'ing, *adj.* careful.

paint, *n.* **1.** liquid coloring matter used as coating. —*v.* **2.** represent in paint. **3.** apply paint to. —**paint'er,** *n.* —**paint'ing,** *n.*

pair, *n., pl.* **pairs, pair,** *v.* —*n.* **1.** combination of two. —*v.* **2.** arrange in pairs.

pais'ley, *n.* fabric woven in colorful, detailed pattern.

pa•jam'as, *n.pl.* nightclothes.

pal, *n. Informal.* comrade.

pal'ace, *n.* official residence of sovereign.

pal'a•din, *n.* heroic champion.

pal'an•quin' (-kēn'), *n.* enclosed chair or bed carried on men's shoulders.

pal'at•a•ble, *adj.* agreeable.

pal'ate, *n.* **1.** roof of mouth. **2.** sense of taste. —**pal'a•tal,** *adj.*

pa•la'tial, *adj.* like a palace. —**pa•la'tial•ly,** *adv.*

pal'a•tine, *n.* vassal exercising royal privileges in province. —**pa•lat'i•nate',** *n.*

pa•lav'er, *n.* **1.** conference. **2.** flattery. **3.** idle talk.

pale, *adj.,* **paler, palest,** *v.,* **paled, paling,** *n.* —*adj.* **1.** without intensity of color. **2.** dim. —*v.* **3.** become pale. —*n.* **4.** stake; picket. **5.** bounds. **6.** enclosed area.

Pa′le•o•lith′ic, *adj.* denoting early Stone Age.

pa′le•on•tol′o•gy, *n.* science of early life forms.

Pa′le•o•zo′ic, *adj.* pertaining to geologic era 570 to 230 million years ago.

pal′ette (pal′it), *n.* board on which painter mixes colors.

pal′frey (pôl′-), *n., pl.* **-freys.** riding horse.

pal′i•mo′ny, *n.* alimony awarded to member of unmarried couple.

pal′imp•sest′, *n.* manuscript with text erased to make room for other text.

pal′in•drome′, *n.* word or verse reading the same backward as forward.

pal′ing, *n.* pale fence.

pal′i•sade′, *n.* **1.** fence of pales. **2.** line of tall cliffs.

pall (pôl), *n.* **1.** cloth spread on coffin. **2.** something gloomy. —*v.* **3.** become tiring.

pall′bear′er, *n.* person who attends the coffin at funeral.

pal′let, *n.* **1.** straw mattress. **2.** implement for shaping. **3.** projecting lip on pawl.

pal′li•ate′, *v.,* **-ated, -ating.** mitigate; excuse. —**pal′li•a′tive,** *n., adj.*

pal′lid, *adj.* pale.

pal′lor, *n.* paleness.

palm, *n.* **1.** inner surface of hand. **2.** tall tropical tree. —*v.* **3.** hide in palm of hand.

pal•met′to, *n., pl.* **-tos, -toes.** species of palm.

palm′is•try, *n.* art of telling fortunes lines on palms of hands. —**palm′ist,** *n.*

palm′y, *adj.,* **palmier, palmiest.** thriving.

pal′o•mi′no (-mē′-), *n., pl.* **-nos.** light-tan horse.

pal′pa•ble, *adj.* obvious; tangible. —**pal′pa•bly,** *adv.*

pal′pate, *v.,* **-pated, -pating.** examine by touch. —**pal•pa′tion,** *n.*

pal′pi•tate′, *v.,* **-tated, -tating.** pulsate with unnatural rapidity. —**pal′pi•ta′tion,** *n.*

pal'sy (pôl'zē), *n., pl.* **-sies,** *v.,* **-sied, -sying.** —*n.* **1.** paralysis. **2.** condition with tremors. —*v.* **3.** afflict with palsy.

pal'try, *adj.,* **-trier, -triest.** trifling. —**pal'tri•ness,** *n.*

pam'pas, *n.* vast South American plains.

pam'per, *v.* indulge; coddle.

pam'phlet, *n.* **1.** thin booklet. **2.** argumentative treatise.

pam'phlet•eer', *n.* writer of pamphlets.

pan, *n., v.,* **panned, panning.** —*n.* **1.** dish for cooking. —*v.* **2.** wash (gravel, etc.) in seeking gold. **3.** *Informal.* criticize harshly. **4.** film panoramically.

Pan, *n.* Greek god of shepherds.

pan-, prefix meaning all.

pan'a•ce'a (-sē'ə), *n.* cure-all.

pa•nache' (pə nash', -näsh'), *n.* grand manner; flair.

pan'cake', *n.* flat fried cake.

pan'chro•mat'ic, *adj.* sensitive to all visible colors.

pan'cre•as, *n.* gland near stomach secreting a digestive fluid. —**pan'cre•at'ic,** *adj.*

pan'da, *n.* bearlike animal.

pan•dem'ic, *adj.* epidemic over large area.

pan'de•mo'ni•um, *n.* uproar.

pan'der, *n.* **1.** person who caters to base passions of others. —*v.* **2.** act as pander. —**pan'der•er,** *n.*

pane, *n.* glass of window.

pan'e•gyr'ic (-jir'ik), *n.* eulogy.

pan'el, *n., v.,* **-eled, -eling.** —*n.* **1.** bordered section of wall, door, etc. **2.** list of persons called for jury duty. **3.** public discussion group. —*v.* **4.** arrange in or ornament with panels. —**pan'el•ing,** *n.* —**pan'el•ist,** *n.*

pang, *n.* sudden feeling.

pan'han'dle, *v.,* **-dled, -dling.** *Informal.* beg from passersby. —**pan'han'dler,** *n.*

pan'ic, *n.* demoralizing terror. —**pan'ick•y,** *adj.* —**pan'ic-strick'en,** *adj.*

pan'i•cle, *n.* flower cluster.

pan'nier (pan'yər), *n.* large basket for carrying goods.

pan'o•ply, *n., pl.* **-plies. 1.** wide array. **2.** suit of armor.

pan′o•ram′a, *n.* 1. view over wide area. 2. passing scene. —**pan′o•ram′ic**, *adj.*

pan′sy, *n., pl.* **-sies.** 1. species of violet. 2. *Brit.* (*Offensive*). homosexual.

pant, *v.* 1. breathe hard and quickly. 2. long eagerly.

pan′ta•loons′, *n.pl. Archaic.* trousers.

pan′the•ism′, *n.* religious belief that identifies God with the universe. —**pan′the•ist**, *n.* —**pan′the•is′tic**, *adj.*

pan′the•on, *n.* 1. building with tombs of illustrious dead. 2. heroes as a group.

pan′ther, *n.* cougar or leopard.

pan′ties, *n.pl.* women's underpants. Also, **pan′ty.**

pan′to•graph′, *n.* instrument for copying traced figures.

pan′to•mime′, *n., v.,* **-mimed, -miming.** —*n.* 1. expression by mute gestures. 2. play in this form. —*v.* 3. express in pantomime. —**pan′to•mim′ist**, *n.*

pan′try, *n., pl.* **-tries.** room for kitchen supplies.

pants, *n.pl. Informal.* trousers.

pant′y•hose′, *n.* one-piece stockings.

pant′y•waist, *n.* sissy.

pan′zer, *adj.* 1. armored. —*n.* 2. armored vehicle.

pap, *n.* soft food.

pa′pa, *n. Informal.* father.

pa′pa•cy, *n., pl.* **-cies.** office or dignity of the pope.

pa′pal, *adj.* of the pope.

pa•pa′ya, *n.* tropical fruit.

pa′per, *n.* 1. thin fibrous sheet for writing, etc. 2. document. 3. treatise. 4. newspaper. —*v.* 5. decorate with wallpaper. —*adj.* 6. of paper. —**pa′per•y**, *adj.* —**pa′per•weight′** *n.*

pa′per•back′, *n.* book cheaply bound in paper.

paper tiger, person or nation that has appearance of power but is actually weak.

paper trail, written record.

pa′per•weight′, *n.* small, heavy object placed on papers to keep them from scattering.

pa′pier-mâ•ché′ (pā′pər mə shā′), *n.* molded paper pulp.

pa•pil′la, *n., pl.* **-lae** (pil′ē). small protuberance on skin. —**pap′il•lar′y**, *adj.*

pa′pist (pā′pist), *n., adj.*
Disparaging. Roman Catholic.
—**pa′pism,** *n.*

pa•poose′, *n.* North American
Indian baby. Also,
pap•poose′.

pap•ri′ka (pa prē′-), *n.* spice
from pepper plant.

Pap test, test for cancer of the
cervix.

pa•py′rus (-pī′-), *n., pl.* **-ri.** tall
aquatic plant made into paper
by ancient Egyptians.

par, *n.* **1.** equality in value or
standing. **2.** average amount,
etc. **3.** in golf, standard
number of strokes.

para-, prefix meaning: **1.**
beside, as *paradigm*. **2.**
beyond, as *parapsychology*. **3.**
auxiliary, as *paralegal*.

par′a•ble, *n.* moral allegory.

pa•rab′o•la, *n.* a ∪-shaped
curve, surface, object, etc.
—**par•a•bol′ic,** *adj.*

par′a•chute′, *n., v.,* **-chuted,**
-chuting. —*n.* **1.** apparatus
used to fall safely through air.
—*v.* **2.** fall by parachute.
—**par′a•chut′ist,** *n.*

pa•rade′, *n., v.,* **-raded,**
-rading. —*n.* **1.** public
procession. —*v.* **2.** march in
display. **3.** display
ostentatiously. —**pa•rad′er,** *n.*

par′a•digm′ (-dīm′, -dim), *n.*
example or pattern.
—**par′a•dig•mat′ic,** *adj.*

par′a•dise′, *n.* **1.** heaven. **2.**
garden of Eden. **3.** ideal.
—**par′a•di•sa′i•cal,** *adj.*

par′a•dox′, *n.* statement that
seems self-contradictory.
—**par′a•dox′i•cal,** *adj.*

par′af•fin, *n.* waxy substance
from petroleum.

par′a•gon′, *n.* ideal model.

par′a•graph′, *n.* **1.** unit of
written or printed matter,
begun on new line. —*v.* **2.**
divide into paragraphs.

par′a•keet′, *n.* small parrot.

par′a•le′gal, *n.* attorney's
assistant.

par′al•lax′, *n.* apparent
displacement of object due to
changed position of viewer.

par′al•lel′, *adj., n., v.,* **-leled,**
-leling. —*adj.* **1.** having same
direction. **2.** having same
characteristics. —*n.* **3.** parallel
line or plane. **4.** anything
parallel. —*v.* **5.** be parallel to.
—**par′al•lel•ism,** *n.*

par′al·lel′o·gram, *n.* a four-sided figure whose opposite sides are parallel.

pa·ral′y·sis, *n., pl.* **-ses.** loss of voluntary muscular control. —**par′a·lyt′ic,** *n., adj.* —**par′a·lyze′,** *v.*

par′a·me′ci·um (-mē′shē-, -sē-), *n., pl.* **-cia.** protozoan.

par′a·med′ic, *n.* person with paramedical duties.

par′a·med′i·cal, *adj.* of supplementary medicine.

pa·ram′e·ter, *n.* determinant.

par′a·mil′i·ta·ry, *adj.* of organizations operating in place of or in addition to a regular military force.

par′a·mount′, *adj.* greatest.

par′a·mour′, *n.* lover of married person.

par′a·noi′a, *n.* mental disorder marked by severe distrust of others. —**par′a·noi′ac,** *adj., n.*

par′a·pet, *n.* wall at edge of roof or terrace.

par′a·pher·nal′ia, *n.pl.* 1. equipment. 2. belongings.

par′a·phrase′, *v.,* **-phrased, -phrasing,** *n.* —*v.* 1. rephrase. —*n.* 2. such restatement.

par′a·ple′gi·a (-plē′-), *n.* paralysis of lower part of body. —**par′a·pleg′ic** (-plēj′-), *n., adj.*

par′a·pro·fes′sion·al, *adj.* engaged in profession in partial or secondary capacity. —**paraprofessional,** *n.*

par′a·psy·chol′o·gy, *n.* branch of psychology that studies psychic phenomena.

par′a·site′, *n.* animal or plant that lives on another organism. —**par′a·sit′ic,** *adj.*

par′a·sol′, *n.* sun umbrella.

par′a·sym′pa·thet′ic, *adj.* nervous system that functions in opposition to sympathetic system.

par′a·thy′roid gland, gland that regulates blood levels of calcium and phosphate.

par′a·troops′, *n.* force of soldiers who reach battle by parachuting from planes.

par′boil′, *v.* precook.

par′cel, *n., v.,* **-celed, -celing.** —*n.* 1. package. 2. part. —*v.* 3. divide.

parch, *v.* dry by heat.

par·chee′si, *n.* game resembling backgammon.

parch′ment, *n.* skin of sheep, etc., prepared for writing on.

par′don, *n.* 1. indulgence. 2. forgiveness. —*v.* 3. forgive. —**par′don•a•ble,** *adj.*

pare, *v.,* **pared, paring.** cut off outer part of.

par′e•gor′ic, *n.* soothing medicine.

par′ent, *n.* father or mother. —**pa•ren′tal,** *adj.* —**par′ent•hood′,** *n.*

par′ent•age, *n.* descent.

pa•ren′the•sis, *n., pl.* **-ses.** 1. upright curves ( ) used to mark off interpolation. 2. material so interpolated. —**par′en•thet′ic, par′en•thet′i•cal,** *adj.* —**par′en•thet′i•cal•ly,** *adv.*

pa•re′sis, *n.* incomplete paralysis.

par excellence (pär ek′sə läns′), superior.

par•fait′ (pär fā′), *n.* frothy frozen dessert.

pa•ri′ah (-rī′-), *n.* outcast.

par′i-mu′tu•el, *n.* form of betting on races.

par′ish, *n.* ecclesiastical district. —**pa•rish′ion•er,** *n.*

par′i•ty, *n.* 1. equality. 2. similarity. 3. guaranteed level of farm prices.

park, *n.* 1. land set apart for public. —*v.* 2. place vehicle.

par′ka, *n.* hooded garment.

Par′kin•son's disease, neurological disease.

park′way′, *n.* thoroughfare landscaped with greenery.

par′lance, *n.* way of speaking.

par′lay, *v.* reinvest original amount and its earnings.

par′ley, *n.* 1. conference between combatants. —*v.* 2. hold parley.

par′lia•ment, *n.* legislative body.

par′lia•men•tar′ian, *n.* expert in parliamentary rules.

par′lia•men′ta•ry, *adj.* 1. of a parliament. 2. in accordance with rules of debate.

par′lor, *n.* room for reception.

Par′me•san, *n.* hard, dry Italian cheese.

par′mi•gia′na (pär′mə zhä′nə), *adj.* cooked with Parmesan cheese.

pa•ro′chi•al, *adj.* 1. of a parish. 2. narrow; provincial. —**pa•ro′chi•al•ism,** *n.*

parochial school, school run by religious organization.

par′o•dy, *n., pl.* **-dies,** *v.,* **-died, -dying.** —*n.* 1. humorous imitation. —*v.* 2. satirize.

pa•role′, *n., v.,* **-roled, -roling.** —*n.* 1. conditional release from prison. —*v.* 2. put on parole. —**pa•rol′a•ble,** *adj.* —**pa•rol•ee′** (-rō lē′), *n.*

par′ox•ysm, *n.* outburst. —**par′ox•ys′mal,** *adj.*

par•quet′ (-kā′), *n.* inlaid floor.

par′que•try, *n.* wooden mosaic work.

par′ri•cide′ (-sīd′), *n.* crime of killing one's close relative.

par′rot, *n.* 1. bird capable of being taught to talk. —*v.* 2. repeat senselessly.

par′ry, *v.,* **-ried, -rying,** *n., pl.* **-ries.** —*v.* 1. ward off; evade. —*n.* 2. act of parrying.

parse, *v.,* **parsed, parsing.** analyze grammatically.

par′si•mo′ny, *n.* frugality. —**par′si•mo′ni•ous,** *adj.*

pars′ley, *n.* seasoning herb.

pars′nip, *n.* plant with white edible root.

par′son, *n.* member of clergy.

par′son•age, *n.* house provided for parson.

part, *n.* 1. portion of a whole. 2. share. 3. (*pl.*) personal qualities. —*v.* 4. separate.

par•take′, *v.,* **-took, -taken, -taking.** have share.

par•terre′ (pär târ′), *n.* rear theater seats under balcony.

par′the•no•gen′e•sis, *n.* development of egg without fertilization.

par′tial, *adj.* 1. incomplete. 2. biased. 3. especially fond. —**par•tial′i•ty,** *n.* —**par′tial•ly,** *adv.*

par•tic′i•pate′, *v.,* **-pated, -pating.** take part; share (in). —**par•tic′i•pant,** *n.* —**par•tic′i•pa′tion,** *n.* —**par•tic′i•pa•to′ry,** *adj.*

par′ti•ci•ple, *n.* adjective derived from verb. —**par′ti•cip′i•al,** *adj.*

par′ti•cle, *n.* 1. tiny piece. 2. functional word.

par′ti•col′ored, *adj.* having areas of different colors.

par•tic′u•lar, *adj.* 1. pertaining to a specific. 2. noteworthy. 3. attentive to details. —*n.* 4. detail. —**par•tic′u•lar•ly,** *adv.*

par·tic′u·lar·ize′, *v.*, -ized, -izing. give details. —**par·tic′u·lar·i·za′tion**, *n.*

par·tic′u·late (-lit), *adj.* composed of particles.

part′ing, *n.* separation.

par′ti·san, *n.* 1. adherent. 2. guerrilla.

par·ti′tion, *n.* 1. division into portions. 2. interior wall. —*v.* 3. divide into parts.

part′ly, *adv.* not wholly.

part′ner, *n.* 1. sharer; associate. 2. joint owner. —**part′ner·ship′**, *n.*

part′-song′, *n.* song with parts for several voices.

par′tridge, *n.* game bird.

part′-time′, *adj.* 1. working less than full time. —*adv.* 2. on a part-time basis.

par′tu·ri′tion, *n.* childbirth.

par′ty, *n., pl.* -ties. 1. group with common purpose. 2. social gathering. 3. person concerned.

party line, 1. guiding policy of political party. 2. telephone line connecting telephones of several subscribers.

par′ve·nu′ (pär′və noo′), *n., pl.* -nus. person with new wealth but not social acceptance.

pas′chal (pas′kəl), *adj.* of Passover or Easter.

pa·sha′, *n.* (formerly) Turkish official.

pass, *v.,* **passed, passed** or **past, passing,** *n.* —*v.* 1. go past, by, or through. 2. omit. 3. approve. 4. convey. 5. proceed. 6. go by; elapse. 7. die. 8. be accepted. 9. go unchallenged. —*n.* 10. narrow route through barrier. 11. license. 12. free ticket. 13. state of affairs. —**pass′er**, *n.*

pas′sa·ble, *adj.* adequate. —**pas′sa·bly**, *adv.*

pas′sage, *n.* 1. section of writing. 2. freedom to pass. 3. transportation. 4. corridor. 5. lapse. 6. act of passing. —**pas′sage·way′**, *n.*

pass′book′, *n.* record of depositor's bank balance.

pas·sé′ (pa sā′), *adj.* out-of-date.

pas′sel, *n.* large group.

pas′sen·ger, *n.* riders.

pass′er·by′, *n., pl.* **passersby.** person who passes by.

pas′sim, *adv.* here and there.

pass′ing, *adj.* brief; transitory.

pas′sion, *n.* 1. very strong emotion. 2. sexual love. 3. (*cap.*) sufferings of Christ. —**pas′sion•ate,** *adj.* —**pas′sion•ate•ly,** *adv.* —**pas′sion•less,** *adj.*

pas′sive, *adj.* 1. not in action. 2. acted upon. 3. submitting without resistance. 4. designating voice of verbs indicating subject acted upon. —**pas′sive•ly,** *adv.* —**pas′sive•ness, pas•siv′i•ty,** *n.*

passive resistance, nonviolent opposition.

passive smoking, inhaling of other's smoke.

pass′key′, *n.* master key.

Pass′o′ver, *n.* Jewish festival.

pass′port, *n.* document giving permission to travel abroad.

pass′word′, *n.* secret word used to gain access.

past, *adj.* 1. previous. 2. of an earlier time. 3. designating a tense formation showing time gone by. —*n.* 4. time or events gone by. 5. past tense. —*adv.* 6. so as to pass by. —*prep.* 7. after. 8. beyond.

pas′ta (päs′-), *n.* Italian formed, unleavened dough.

paste, *n., v.,* **pasted, pasting.** —*n.* 1. sticky mixture. 2. glass used for gems. —*v.* 3. fasten with paste. —**past′y,** *adj.*

paste′board′, *n.* firm board made of layers of paper.

pas•tel′, *n.* soft color.

pas′tern, *n.* horse's foot between fetlock and hoof.

pas′teur•ize′, *v.,* **-ized, -izing.** heat to destroy bacteria. —**pas′teur•i•za′tion,** *n.*

pas•tiche′ (-tēsh′), *n.* work made up of borrowed details.

pas•tille′ (-tēl′), *n.* lozenge.

pas′time′, *n.* diversion.

past master, expert.

pas′tor, *n.* minister.

pas′to•ral, *adj.* 1. bucolic. 2. of shepherds. 3. of pastors.

pas′to•rale′ (-räl′), *n.* dreamy musical composition.

pas•tra′mi (-trä′-), *n.* seasoned smoked beef.

pas′try, *n., pl.* **-tries.** food made of rich paste, as pies.

pas′tur•age, *n.* pasture.

pas′ture, *n., v.,* **-tured, -turing.** —*n.* 1. ground for grazing. —*v.* 2. graze on pasture.

pat, *v.,* **patted, patting,** *n., adj., adv.* —*v.* **1.** strike gently with flat object. —*n.* **2.** light stroke. **3.** small mass. —*adj.* **4.** apt. —*adv.* **5.** perfectly. **6.** unwaveringly.

patch, *n.* **1.** piece of material used to mend or protect. **2.** any small piece. —*v.* **3.** mend. —**patch′work′,** *n.*

patch test, allergy test where allergen is applied to skin.

patch′y, *adj.,* **patchier, patchiest.** irregular in surface or quality. —**patch′i•ness,** *n.*

pate, *n.* crown of head.

pâ•té′ (pä tā′, pa-), *n.* paste of puréed or chopped meat.

pa•tel′la, *n., pl.* **-tellae** (tel′ē). kneecap.

pat′ent, *n.* **1.** exclusive right to invention. —*adj.* **2.** protected by patent. **3.** evident. —*v.* **4.** secure patent on.

patent leather, hard, glossy, smooth leather.

patent medicine, drug protected by trademark.

pa•ter′nal, *adj.* **1.** fatherly. **2.** related through father. —**pa•ter′nal•ly,** *adv.*

pa•ter′nal•ism, *n.* benevolent rule. —**pa•ter′nal•is′tic,** *adj.*

pa•ter′ni•ty, *n.* fatherhood.

pa′ter•nos′ter, *n.* Lord's Prayer.

path, *n.* **1.** Also, **path′way′.** narrow way. **2.** route. **3.** course of action.

pa•thet′ic, *adj.* arousing pity. —**pa•thet′i•cal•ly,** *adv.*

path′find′er, *n.* person who finds a path.

path′o•gen (path′ə jən, -jen′), *n.* disease-producing agent. —**path′o•gen′ic,** *adj.*

path′o•log′i•cal, *adj.* sick. —**path′o•log′i•cal•ly,** *adv.*

pa•thol′o•gy, *n.* study of disease. —**pa•thol′o•gist,** *n.*

pa′thos (pā′-), *n.* quality or power of arousing pity.

-pathy, suffix meaning: **1.** feeling, as *antipathy.* **2.** method of treatment, as *osteopathy.*

pa′tient, *n.* **1.** person under care of a doctor. —*adj.* **2.** enduring calmly. —**pa′tience,** *n.* —**pa′tient•ly,** *adv.*

pat′i•na (pə tē′nə), *n.* film on old bronze, etc.

pa′ti•o′, *n., pl.* **-tios.** inner open court.

pat′ois (pat′wä, pä′twä), *n.* regional form of a language.

pa′tri•arch′, *n.* **1.** venerable old man. **2.** male head of family. —**pa′tri•ar′chal**, *adj.*

pa′tri•ar′chy, *n., pl.* **-chies.** family group ruled by a father.

pa•tri′cian, *n.* **1.** aristocrat. —*adj.* **2.** aristocratic.

pat′ri•cide′, *n.* killing one's father. —**pat′ri•cid′al**, *adj.*

pat′ri•mo′ny, *n., pl.* **-nies.** inherited estate.

pa′tri•ot, *n.* person who supports country. —**pa′tri•ot′ic**, *adj.* —**pa′tri•ot′ism**, *n.* —**pa′tri•ot′i•cal•ly**, *adv.*

pa•trol′, *v.,* **-trolled, -trolling,** *n.* —*v.* **1.** pass through in guarding. —*n.* **2.** person or group assigned to patrol.

pa•trol′man, *n., pl.* **-men.** police officer who patrols.

pa′tron, *n.* **1.** supporter. **2.** regular customer.

pa′tron•age, *n.* **1.** support by patron. **2.** political control of appointments to office.

pa′tron•ize′, *v.,* **-ized, -izing.** **1.** buy from, esp. regularly. **2.** treat condescendingly.

patron saint, saint regarded as special guardian.

pat′ro•nym′ic, *n.* name derived from ancestor.

pat′sy, *n., pl.* **-sies.** *Slang.* person easily manipulated.

pat′ter, *v.* **1.** walk quickly. **2.** speak glibly. —*n.* **3.** pattering sound. **4.** rapid, glib speech.

pat′tern, *n.* **1.** surface design. **2.** characteristic mode. **3.** model for copying. —*v.* **4.** make after pattern.

pat′ty, *n., pl.* **-ties. 1.** thin piece of food. **2.** wafer.

pau′ci•ty (pô′sə tē), *n.* scarceness.

paunch, *n.* belly, esp. when large. —**paunch′y**, *adj.*

pau′per, *n.* poor person.

pause, *n., v.,* **paused, pausing.** —*n.* **1.** temporary stop. —*v.* **2.** make pause.

pave, *v.,* **paved, paving. 1.** cover with solid road surface. **2.** prepare. —**pave′ment**, *n.*

pa•vil′ion, *n.* **1.** light open shelter. **2.** tent.

paw, *n.* **1.** foot of animal. —*v.* **2.** scrape with paw.

pawl, *n.* pivoted bar engaging with teeth of ratchet wheel.

pawn, *v.* 1. deposit as security for loan. —*n.* 2. state of being pawned. 3. piece used in chess. —**pawn'shop',** *n.*

pawn'bro'ker, *n.* person who lends money on collateral.

paw'paw', *n.* small tree bearing purple flowers.

pay, *v.,* **paid, paying,** *n.* —*v.* 1. give money required to. 2. give as compensation. 3. yield profit. 4. let out (rope). —*n.* 5. wages. 6. paid employ. —**pay'a•ble,** *adj.* —**pay•ee',** *n.* —**pay'er,** *n.* —**pay'ment,** *n.*

pay dirt, 1. profitable soil to mine. 2. *Informal.* any source of wealth.

pay'load', *n.* 1. revenue-producing freight, etc. 2. contents to be carried.

pay'mas'ter, *n.* person in charge of paying out wages.

pay'off', *n.* 1. *Informal.* climax. 2. awaited payment.

pay•o'la, *n.* bribery.

pay'roll, *n.* 1. list of employees to be paid. 2. total of these amounts.

PC, 1. *pl.* **PCs** or **PC's.** personal computer. 2. politically correct.

PCB, *pl.* **PCBs, PCB's.** highly toxic compound.

PCP, phencyclidine: drug used as tranquilizer.

PE, physical education.

pea, *n.* edible seed of legume.

peace, *n.* freedom from war, trouble, or disturbance. —**peace'mak'er,** *n.* —**peace'time',** *n.*

peace'ful, *adj.* 1. at peace. 2. desiring peace. Also, **peace'a•ble.** —**peace'ful•ly,** *adv.* —**peace'ful•ness,** *n.*

peach, *n.* sweet juicy fruit.

pea'cock', *n.* male peafowl, having iridescent tail feathers.

pea'fowl', *n.* bird of pheasant family.

pea'hen', *n.* female peafowl.

pea jacket, short heavy coat.

peak, *n.* 1. pointed top. 2. highest point.

peaked, *adj.* 1. having peak. 2. (pē'kid). sickly, haggard.

peal, *n.* 1. prolonged sound. 2. bells. —*v.* 3. sound in a peal.

pea'nut', *n.* edible seed.

pear, *n.* elongated edible fruit.

pearl, *n.* gem formed within an oyster. —**pearl'y,** *adj.*

peas′ant, *n.* farm worker.

peat, *n.* organic soil dried for fuel. —**peat′y,** *adj.*

peat moss, moss from which peat may form, used as mulch.

peb′ble, *n.* small, rounded stone. —**peb′bly,** *adj.*

pe•can′ (pi kän′, -kan′), *n.* smooth-shelled nut.

pec′ca•dil′lo, *n., pl.* **-loes, -los.** trifling sin.

pec′ca•ry, *n., pl.* **-ries.** wild American pig.

peck, *v.* 1. strike with beak. —*n.* 2. pecking stroke. 3. dry measure of eight quarts.

pecking order, hierarchy.

pec′tin, *n.* substance in ripe fruit that forms jelly.

pec′to•ral, *adj.* 1. of the chest. —*n.* 2. pectoral muscle.

pec′u•late′, *v.,* **-lated, -lating.** embezzle. —**pec′u•la′tion,** *n.*

pe•cul′iar, *adj.* 1. strange; odd. 2. uncommon. 3. exclusive. —**pe•cu′liar′i•ty,** *n.* —**pe•cul′iar•ly,** *adv.*

pe•cu′ni•ar′y, *adj.* of money.

ped′a•gogue′, *n.* teacher. —**ped′a•go′gy,** *n.* —**ped′a•gog′ic,**

ped′a•gog′i•cal, *adj.* —**ped′a•gog′i•cal•ly,** *adv.*

ped′al, *n., v.,* **-aled, -aling,** *adj.* —*n.* 1. lever worked by foot. —*v.* 2. work pedals of. —*adj.* 3. (pē′dəl). of feet.

ped′ant, *n.* person excessively concerned with details. —**pe•dan′tic,** *adj.* —**ped′ant•ry,** *n.*

ped′dle, *v.,* **-dled, -dling.** carry about for sale. —**ped′dler,** *n.*

ped′er•as•ty, *n.* sexual relations between a man and a boy. —**ped′er•ast′,** *n.*

ped′es•tal, *n.* base for object.

pe•des′tri•an, *n.* 1. walker. —*adj.* 2. walking. 3. prosaic.

pe′di•at′rics, *n.* study of care and diseases of children. —**pe′di•a•tri′cian,** *n.* —**pe′di•at′ric,** *adj.*

ped′i•cab′, *n.* three-wheeled cab operated by pedals.

ped′i•cure′ (ped′i kyŏŏr′), *n.* grooming of the feet.

ped′i•gree′, *n.* 1. certificate of ancestry. 2. ancestry. —**ped′i•greed′,** *adj.*

ped′i•ment, *n.* gablelike architectural feature.

pe·dom′e·ter, *n.* device that measures distance walked.

pe·dun′cle, *n.* stalk that supports flower cluster.

peek, *v., n.* peep (defs. 1–3; 5).

peel, *v.* **1.** remove or lose skin, bark, etc. —*n.* **2.** skin of fruit.

peen, *n.* sharp end of hammer.

peep, *v.* **1.** look through small opening. **2.** look furtively. **3.** show slightly. **4.** utter shrill little cry. —*n.* **5.** quick look. **6.** weak sound. —**peep′er,** *n.*

peer, *n.* **1.** equal. **2.** noble. —*v.* **3.** look closely.

peer′age, *n.* **1.** rank of peer. **2.** list of peers.

peer′less, *adj.* without equal. —**peer′less·ness,** *n.*

peeve, *n., v.,* **peeved, peeving.** —*n.* **1.** annoyance. —*v.* **2.** annoy; vex.

pee′vish, *adj.* discontented.

pee·wee, *n. Informal.* person or thing that is very small.

peg, *n., v.,* **pegged, pegging.** —*n.* **1.** pin of wood, metal, etc. —*v.* **2.** fasten with pegs.

peg leg, wooden leg.

peign·oir′ (pān wär′), *n.* woman's loose dressing gown.

pe·jo′ra·tive (pi jôr′ə tiv, -jor′-), *adj.* disparaging.

Pe′king·ese′ (pē′kə nēz′), *n., pl.* **-ese.** long-haired Chinese dog with flat muzzle.

pe′koe, *n.* black tea.

pe·lag′ic (-laj′-), *adj.* of seas.

pel′i·can, *n.* large-billed bird.

pel·la′gra (pə lā′-), *n.* chronic disease from inadequate diet.

pel′let, *n.* little ball.

pell′-mell′, *adv.* in haste.

pel·lu′cid (pə l o͞o′sid), *adj.* **1.** translucent. **2.** clear.

pelt, *v.* **1.** throw. **2.** assail. —*n.* **3.** a blow. **4.** skin of beast.

pel′vis, *n.* **1.** cavity in lower body trunk. **2.** bones forming this cavity. —**pel′vic,** *adj.*

pem′mi·can (-kən), *n.* dried food.

pen, *n., v.,* **penned** or (for 4) **pent, penning.** —*n.* **1.** device for writing with ink. **2.** small enclosure. —*v.* **3.** write with pen. **4.** confine in pen.

pe′nal (pē′nəl), *adj.* of punishment. —**pe′nal·ize′,** *v.*

pen′al·ty, *n., pl.* **-ties. 1.** punishment. **2.** disadvantage.

pen′ance, *n.* punishment.

pence, *n. Brit. pl.* of **penny.**

pen′chant, *n.* liking.

pen′cil, *n.* enclosed stick of graphite, etc., for marking.

pend, *v.* remain undecided.

pend′ant, *n.* 1. hanging ornament. 2. counterpart.

pend′ent, *adj.* hanging.

pend′ing, *prep.* 1. until. —*adj.* 2. undecided.

pen′du•lous, *adj.* hanging.

pen′du•lum, *n.* hung weight.

pen′e•trate′, *v.,* **-trated, -trating.** 1. pierce; permeate. 2. enter. 3. understand; have insight. —**pen′e•tra•ble,** *adj.* —**pen′e•tra′tion,** *n.*

pen′guin, *n.* aquatic bird.

pen′i•cil′lin (pen′ə sil′in), *n.* antibacterial substance.

pen•in′su•la, *n.* piece of land nearly surrounded by water. —**pen•in′su•lar,** *adj.*

pe′nis, *n.* male sex organ. —**pe′nile** (pēn′l), *adj.*

pen′i•tent, *adj.* 1. sorry for sin or fault. —*n.* 2. penitent person. —**pen′i•tence,** *n.*

pen′i•ten′tia•ry, *n., pl.* **-ries.** prison.

pen′knife′, *n.* pocket knife.

pen′light′, *n.* flashlight shaped like fountain pen.

pen′man, *n., pl.* **-men.** one who writes. —**pen′man•ship′,** *n.*

Penn., Pennsylvania.

pen name, pseudonym.

pen′nant, *n.* flag, usually tapered. Also, **pen′non.**

pen′ny, *n., pl.* **-nies,** *Brit.* **pence.** small coin, equal to one cent in the U.S. and Canada, and to $\frac{1}{100}$ pound in United Kingdom. —**pen′ni•less,** *adj.*

penny pincher, stingy person. —**pen′ny-pinch′ing,** *adj.*

pen′ny•weight′, *n.* (in troy weight) 24 grains, or $\frac{1}{20}$ of an ounce.

pe•nol′o•gy, *n.* science of punishment of crime and management of prisoners. —**pe•nol′o•gist,** *n.*

pen pal, person with whom one exchanges letters.

pen′sion, *n.* 1. fixed periodic payment for past service, etc. 2. (pän sē ōn′). (in France) boarding house or school. —*v.* 3. give pension to.

pen′sion•er, *n.* person receiving pension.

pen′sive, *adj.* gravely thoughtful. —**pen′sive•ly,** *adv.* —**pen′sive•ness,** *n.*

pent, *adj.* confined.

penta-, prefix meaning five.

pen′ta·gon′, *n.* plane figure having five sides and five angles.

pen′ta·gram′, *n.* five-pointed, star-shaped symbol.

pen·tam′e·ter, *n.* verse or line of five feet.

Pen′ta·teuch′ (-tōōk′, -tyōōk′), *n. Bible.* first five books of the Old Testament.

pen·tath′lon, *n.* athletic contest of five events.

Pen′te·cost′, *n.* Christian festival; Whitsunday.

Pen′te·cos′tal, *adj.* of Christian groups that emphasize the Holy Spirit.

pent′house′, *n.* rooftop apartment or dwelling.

pe·nu′che (pə nōō′chē), *n.* brown-sugar fudge.

pent′-up′, *adj.* confined.

pe′nult, *n.* next to last syllable.

pe·nul′ti·mate (pi nul′tə mit), *adj.* being next to last.

pe·num′bra, *n., pl.* **-brae, -bras.** partial shadow outside complete shadow of celestial body in eclipse. —**pe·num′bral,** *adj.*

pe·nu′ri·ous (pə nyŏŏr′-), *adj.* **1.** meanly stingy. **2.** in great poverty.

pen′u·ry, *n.* poverty.

pe′on, *n.* **1.** unskilled worker. **2.** endentured worker.

pe′on·age, *n.* work of peon.

pe′o·ny, *n., pl.* **-nies.** perennial plant with large flowers.

peo′ple, *n., v.* **-pled, -pling.** —*n.* **1.** body of persons constituting nation. **2.** persons in general. **3.** person's relatives. —*v.* **4.** populate.

pep, *n., v.,* **pepped, pepping.** *Informal.* —*n.* **1.** vigor. —*v.* **2.** give vigor to. —**pep′py,** *adj.*

pep′per, *n.* **1.** condiment from dried berries. **2.** edible fruit of certain plants. —*v.* **3.** season with pepper. **4.** pelt with shot. —**pep′per·y,** *adj.*

pep′per·corn′, *n.* dried berry of pepper plant.

pepper mill, device for grinding peppercorns.

pep′per·mint′, *n.* oil of herb.

pep′per·o′ni, *n., pl.* **-nis.** highly seasoned sausage.

pep′sin, *n.* juice secreted in stomach that digests proteins.

pep′tic, *adj.* digestive.

per, *prep.* for; by means of.

per′ad·ven′ture, *adv. Archaic.* maybe.

per·am′bu·late′, *v.,* -lated, -lating. walk about. —**per·am′bu·la′tion,** *n.*

per·am′bu·la′tor, *n.* baby carriage.

per an′num, yearly.

per·cale′, *n.* smooth, closely woven cotton fabric.

per cap′i·ta, for each person.

per·ceive′, *v.,* -ceived, -ceiving. 1. gain knowledge of by seeing, hearing, etc. 2. understand. —**per·ceiv′a·ble, per·cep′ti·ble,** *adj.*

per·cent′, *n.* number of parts in each hundred.

per·cent′age, *n.* 1. rate per hundred. 2. *Informal.* profit.

per·cen′tile, *n.* value of statistical variable that divides distribution of variable into 100 equal parts.

per′cept, *n.* result of perceiving.

per·cep′tion, *n.* 1. act or faculty of perceiving. 2. intuition; insight. 3. result or product of perceiving.

per·cep′tive, *adj.* 1. keen. 2. showing perception.

per·cep′tu·al, *adj.* involving perception.

perch, *n.* 1. place for roosting. 2. linear measure of 5½ yards. 3. square rod (30¼ sq. yards). 4. common food fish. —*v.* 5. set or rest on perch.

per·chance′, *adv. Poetic.* maybe; by chance.

per′co·late′, *v.,* -lated, -lating. filter through. —**per′co·la′tion,** *n.*

per′co·la′tor, *n.* coffee pot.

per·cus′sion, *n.* 1. violent impact. —*adj.* 2. sounded by striking. —**per·cus′sion·ist,** *n.* —**per·cus′sive,** *adj.*

per di′em (pər dē′əm), *adv.* 1. by the day. —*n.* 2. daily pay or allowance for expenses. 3. person paid by the day. —*adj.* 4. paid by the day.

per·di′tion, *n.* ruin; hell.

per·dur′a·ble, *adj.* very durable.

per′e‧gri‧nate′, *v.*, **-nated, -nating.** travel on foot. —**per′e‧gri‧na′tion**, *n.*

per′e‧grine falcon (-grin), bird of prey.

per‧emp′to‧ry, *adj.* permitting no denial or refusal. —**per‧emp′to‧ri‧ly,** *adv.* —**per‧emp′to‧ri‧ness,** *n.*

per‧en′ni‧al, *adj.* **1.** lasting indefinitely. **2.** living more than two years. —*n.* **3.** perennial plant. —**per‧en′ni‧al‧ly,** *adv.*

per′fect, *adj.* **1.** faultless. **2.** *Gram.* of action already completed. —*n.* **3.** *Gram.* perfect tense. —*v.* (pər fekt′). **4.** make faultless. —**per‧fec′tion,** *n.* —**per′fect‧ly,** *adv.*

per‧fec′tion‧ism, *n.* insistence on perfection. —**per‧fec′tion‧ist,** *n.*

per′fi‧dy, *n., pl.* **-dies.** treachery; faithlessness. —**per‧fid′i‧ous,** *adj.*

per′fo‧rate′, *v.*, **-rated, -rating.** make holes through. —**per′fo‧ra′tion,** *n.*

per‧force′, *adv.* of necessity.

per‧form′, *v.* **1.** carry out; do. **2.** act, as on stage. —**per‧for′mance,** *n.* —**per‧form′er,** *n.*

performing arts, arts requiring public performance.

per′fume, *n., v.*, **-fumed, -fuming.** —*n.* **1.** sweet-smelling liquid. **2.** sweet smell. —*v.* (pər fyo͞om′). **3.** impart fragrance to. —**per‧fum′er‧y,** *n.*

per‧func′to‧ry, *adj.* done without care or attention. —**per‧func′to‧ri‧ly,** *adv.* —**per‧func′to‧ri‧ness,** *n.*

per‧haps′, *adv.* maybe.

peri-, prefix meaning around, surrounding, or near.

per′i‧car′di‧um, *n.* sac enclosing the heart.

per′i‧gee′ (-jē′), *n.* point nearest earth in orbit of a heavenly body.

per′i‧he′li‧on, *n.* point nearest sun in orbit.

per′il, *n.* **1.** danger. —*v.* **2.** endanger. —**per′il‧ous,** *adj.*

per‧im′e‧ter, *n.* **1.** outer boundary. **2.** length of boundary. —**pe‧rim′e‧tral, per′i‧met′ric,** *adj.*

per′i•ne′um, *n., pl.* **-nea.** area between genitals and anus.

pe′ri•od, *n.* **1.** portion of time. **2.** mark (.) ending sentence.

pe′ri•od′ic, *adj.* recurring regularly or intermittently. —**pe′ri•od′i•cal•ly,** *adv.*

pe′ri•od′i•cal, *n.* **1.** publication issued at regular intervals. —*adj.* **2.** periodic.

periodic table, table showing chemical elements.

per′i•o•don′tal (per′ē ə don′tl), *adj.* of tissue surrounding teeth.

per′i•pa•tet′ic, *adj.* walking or traveling about; itinerant.

pe•riph′er•al, *adj.* **1.** on periphery. **2.** partly relevant.

pe•riph′er•y, *n., pl.* **-eries. 1.** external boundary. **2.** external surface.

pe•riph′ra•sis (pə rif′rə sis), *n., pl.* **-ses** (-sēz′). roundabout. —**per′i•phras′tic,** *adj.*

per′i•scope′, *n.* optical tube in which mirrors reflect to give a view from below or behind an obstacle.

per′ish, *v.* **1.** die. **2.** decay. —**per′ish•a•ble,** *adj., n.*

per′i•stal′sis, *n., pl.* **-ses** (-sēz). muscle contractions and relaxations that move food along alimentary canal.

per′i•to′ne•um (-tō′-), *n.* lining of abdominal cavity. —**per′i•to•ne′al,** *adj.*

per′i•to•ni′tis (-nī′-), *n.* swelling of peritoneum.

per′i•win′kle, *n.* **1.** edible snail. **2.** trailing plant.

per′jure, *v.,* **-jured, -juring.** lie under oath. —**per′jur•er,** *n.*

per′ju•ry, *n., pl.* **-ries.** false statement made under oath.

perk, *v.* **1.** move or raise jauntily. **2.** become lively. —*n.* **3.** perquisite. —**perk′y,** *adj.*

per′ma•frost′, *n.* permanently frozen subsoil.

per′ma•nent, *adj.* **1.** lasting indefinitely. —*n.* **2.** curl permanently set in hair. —**per′ma•nence, per′ma•nen•cy,** *n.* —**per′ma•nent•ly,** *adv.*

per′me•ate′, *v.,* **-ated, -ating.** penetrate; pervade. —**per′me•a′tion,** *n.* —**per′me•a•ble,** *adj.*

per•mis′sion, *n.* authorization.

—**per•mis′si•ble,** *adj.*
—**per•mis′si•bly,** *adv.*

per•mis′sive, *adj.* 1. giving permission. 2. tolerant.

per•mit′, *v.,* -mitted, -mitting, *n.* —*v.* (pər mit′). 1. allow; agree to. —*n.* (pûr′mit). 2. written permission.

per′mu•ta′tion, *n.* alteration.

per•ni′cious, *adj.* 1. highly hurtful. 2. deadly.

per′o•ra′tion, *n.* concluding part of speech.

per•ox′ide, *n.* 1. oxide containing large amount of oxygen. 2. antiseptic liquid.

per′pen•dic′u•lar, *adj.* 1. upright; vertical. 2. meeting given line at right angles. —*n.* 3. perpendicular position.

per′pe•trate′, *v.,* -trated, -trating. commit (crime, etc.).
—**per′pe•tra′tion,** *n.*
—**per′pe•tra′tor,** *n.*

per•pet′u•al, *adj.* 1. lasting forever. 2. unceasing.
—**per•pet′u•ate′,** *v.*

per′pe•tu′i•ty, *n.* forever.

per•plex′, *v.* confuse mentally.
—**per•plex′i•ty,** *n.*

per′qui•site, *n.* incidental profit in addition to fixed pay.

per se (pûr sā′, sē′, pər), by, of, for, or in itself.

per′se•cute′, *v.,* -cuted, -cuting. oppress persistently.
—**per′se•cu′tion,** *n.*
—**per′se•cu′tor,** *n.*

per′se•vere′, *v.,* -vered, -vering. continue steadfastly.
—**per′se•ver′ance,** *n.*

per′si•flage′ (pûr′sə fläzh′, pär′-), *n.* light, bantering talk.

per•sim′mon, *n.* soft fruit.

per•sist′, *v.* 1. continue firmly in spite of opposition. 2. endure. —**per•sist′ence,** *n.*
—**per•sist′ent,** *adj.*
—**per•sist′ent•ly,** *adv.*

per•snick′et•y, *adj. Informal.* fussy.

per′son, *n.* 1. human being. 2. individual. 3. body.

per′son•a•ble, *adj.* attractive in appearance and manner.

per′son•age, *n.* dignitary.

per′son•al, *adj.* 1. of, by, or relating to a certain person. 2. *Gram.* denoting class of pronouns that refer to speaker, person addressed, or thing spoken of. 3. *Law.* of property that is movable.
—**per′son•al•ly,** *adv.*

personal computer, microcomputer designed for individual use.

personal effects, belongings.

per'son·al'i·ty, *n., pl.* **-ties.** 1. distinctive personal character. 2. famous person.

per'son·al·ize', *v.,* **-ized, -izing.** 1. make personal. 2. treat as if human.

per'son·al·ty, *n., pl.* **-ties.** personal property.

per·so'na non gra'ta (pər sō'nə non grä'tə), unwelcome.

per·son'i·fy', *v.,* **-fied, -fying.** 1. attribute character to. 2. embody. 3. impersonate. —**per·son'i·fi·ca'tion,** *n.*

per'son·nel', *n.* employees.

per·spec'tive, *n.* 1. depiction as to show space relationships. 2. mental view.

per'spi·ca'cious, *adj.* astute. —**per'spi·cac'i·ty,** *n.*

per·spic'u·ous, *adj.* lucid. —**per'spi·cu'i·ty,** *n.*

per·spire', *v.,* **-spired, -spiring.** sweat. —**per'spi·ra'tion,** *n.*

per·suade', *v.,* **-suaded, -suading.** 1. prevail on to act as suggested. 2. convince. —**per·sua'sive,** *adj.* —**per·sua'sive·ly,** *adv.*

per·sua'sion, *n.* 1. power of persuading. 2. conviction. 3. religious system.

pert, *adj.* bold; saucy. —**pert'ly,** *adv.* —**pert'ness,** *n.*

per·tain', *v.* have reference.

per'ti·na'cious, *adj.* holding tenaciously to purpose.

per'ti·nent, *adj.* relevant. —**per'ti·nence,** *n.* —**per'ti·nent·ly,** *adv.*

per·turb', *v.* disturb greatly. —**per'tur·ba'tion,** *n.*

pe·ruke', *n.* man's wig.

pe·ruse' (-rōōz'), *v.,* **-rused, -rusing.** read. —**pe·ru'sal,** *n.*

per·vade', *v.,* **-vaded, -vading.** be present throughout. —**per·va'sive,** *adj.*

per·verse', *adj.* 1. stubbornly contrary. 2. abnormal. —**per·ver'si·ty,** *n.* —**per·verse'ly,** *adv.*

per·vert', *v.* 1. turn from right or moral course or use. —*n.* (pûr'vûrt). 2. perverted person. —**per·ver'sion,** *n.*

pe·se'ta (pə sā'tə), *n., pl.* **-tas.** monetary unit of Spain.

pes′ky, *adj.,* **-kier, -kiest.** annoying; troublesome.

pe′so (pā′sō), *n.* monetary unit and coin in Latin America.

pes′si•mism, *n.* 1. disposition to expect worst. 2. belief that all things tend to evil. —**pes′si•mist,** *n.* —**pes′si•mis′tic,** *adj.* —**pes′si•mis′ti•cal•ly,** *adv.*

pest, *n.* troublesome thing.

pes′ter, *v.* annoy; harass.

pes′ti•cide′, *n.* poison used to kill harmful insects or weeds.

pes•tif′er•ous, *adj.* 1. bearing disease. 2. dangerous 3. troublesome.

pes′ti•lence, *n.* epidemic disease. —**pes′ti•lent,** *adj.*

pes′tle, *n.* instrument for pounding or crushing.

pes′to, *n.* sauce of basil.

pet, *n., adj., v.,* **petted, petting.** —*n.* 1. domestic animal. 2. favorite. 3. tantrum. —*adj.* 4. treated as pet. —*v.* 5. caress.

pet′al, *n.* leaf of blossom.

pe•tard′, *n.* explosive device.

pe′ter, *v. Informal.* diminish.

pet′i•ole′, *n.* stalk that attaches leaf to stem.

pet′it (pet′ē), *adj. Law.* petty.

pe•tite′ (-tēt′), *adj.* tiny.

pe•ti′tion, *n.* 1. request, esp. formal one. —*v.* 2. present petition. —**pe•ti′tion•er,** *n.*

pet′rel, *n.* small oceanic bird.

pet′ri•fy′, *v.,* **-fied, -fying.** 1. turn into stone. 2. paralyze with fear.

pet′ro•chem′i•cal, *n.* chemical from petroleum.

pet′ro•dol′lars, *n.pl.* petroleum-export revenues.

pet′rol, *n. Brit.* gasoline.

pet′ro•la′tum, *n.* gelatinous mass from petroleum.

pe•tro′le•um, *n.* oily liquid occurring naturally.

pe•trol′o•gy, *n.* study of rocks.

pet′ti•coat′, *n.* underskirt.

pet′ti•fog′, *v.,* **-fogged, -fogging.** quibble over trifles.

pet′tish, *adj.* petulant.

pet′ty, *adj.,* **-tier, -tiest.** 1. trivial 2. small-minded. —**pet′ti•ness,** *n.*

petty cash, fund for paying minor expenses.

petty jury, jury in civil trial.

petty officer, noncommissioned officer in navy or coast guard.

pet′u·lant (pech′-), *adj.* showing impatient irritation. —**pet′u·lance,** *n.*

pe·tu′ni·a, *n.* plant with funnel-shaped flowers.

pew, *n.* seats in church.

pe′wee, *n.* certain small birds.

pew′ter, *n.* alloy rich in tin.

pf., (of stock) preferred.

PG, motion picture rating: parental guidance recommended.

PG-13, motion-picture rating: material may be unsuitable for children under 13.

pg., page.

pH, symbol describing acidity or alkalinity of solution.

pha′e·ton (fā′ə tən), *n.* open carriage or automobile.

phag′o·cyte′, *n.* cell that ingests foreign particles.

pha·lan′ger (-jər), *n.* tree-dwelling marsupial.

pha′lanx, *n., pl.* **-lanxes, -langes** (fə lan′jēz). 1. compact body. 2. any bones of fingers or toes.

phal′lus, *n., pl.* **phalli.** 1. penis. 2. image of penis as symbol of fertility. —**phal′lic,** *adj.*

phan′tasm, *n.* apparition.

phan·tas′ma·go′ri·a, *n.* shifting series of illusions.

phan′tom, *n.* 1. ghostlike image. —*adj.* 2. unreal.

Phar′aoh (fâr′ō), *n.* title of ancient Egyptian kings.

Phar′i·see′, *n.* 1. member of ancient Jewish sect. 2. (*l.c.*) self-righteous person.

phar′ma·ceu′ti·cal (-sσ̄σ̄′-), *adj.* pertaining to pharmacy. Also, **phar′ma·ceu′tic.**

phar′ma·col′o·gy, *n.* study of drugs. —**phar′ma·col′o·gist,** *n.*

phar′ma·co·poe′ia (-pē′ə), *n.* book on medicines.

phar′ma·cy, *n., pl.* **-cies.** 1. art or practice of preparing medicines. 2. place for dispensing medicines. —**phar′ma·cist,** *n.*

phar′ynx, *n., pl.* **pharynges** (fə rin′jēz), **pharynxes.** tube connecting mouth and nasal passages with esophagus. —**pha·ryn′ge·al,** *adj.* —**phar′yn·gi′tis,** *n.*

phase, *n.* 1. stage of change. 2. aspect of changing thing.

phase′out′, *n.* gradual dismissal or termination.

Ph.D., Doctor of Philosophy.

pheas′ant, *n.* long-tailed bird.

phe′no•bar′bi•tal′, *n.* white powder used as sedative.

phe′nol, *n.* carbolic acid. —**phe•no′lic,** *adj.*

phe•nom′e•non′, *n., pl.* **-ena.** 1. something observable. 2. extraordinary thing or person. —**phe•nom′e•nal,** *adj.* —**phe•nom′e•nal•ly,** *adv.*

pher′o•mone′, *n.* chemical substance released by animal that influences behavior of other members of species.

phi′al, *n.* vial.

phil-, prefix meaning loving.

phi•lan′der, *v.* womanize. —**phi•lan′der•er,** *n.*

phi•lan′thro•py, *n., pl.* **-pies.** 1. love of humanity. 2. benevolent work. —**phil′an•throp′ic, phil′an•throp′i•cal,** *adj.* —**phi•lan′thro•pist,** *n.*

phi•lat′e•ly, *n.* collection and study of postage stamps, etc. —**phil′a•tel′ic,** *adj.* —**phi•lat′e•list,** *n.*

-phile, suffix meaning one that has strong enthusiasm for.

phil′har•mon′ic, *adj.* 1. music-loving. —*n.* 2. large orchestra.

phil′is•tine′ (fil′ə stēn′), *n.* person indifferent to culture.

phil′o•den′dron, *n., pl.* **-drons, -dra.** tropical climbing plant.

phi•lol′o•gy, *n.* linguistics. —**phi•lol′o•gist,** *n.*

phi•los′o•pher, *n.* 1. person versed in philosophy. 2. person guided by reason. 3. person who remains calm.

phi•los′o•phy, *n., pl.* **-phies.** 1. study of truths underlying being and knowledge. 2. system of philosophical belief. 3. principles of particular field of knowledge or action. 4. calmness. —**phil′o•soph′ic, phil′o•soph′i•cal,** *adj.* —**phi•los′o•phize′,** *v.*

phil′ter, *n.* magic potion.

phle•bi′tis (flə bī′tis), *n.* inflammation of a vein.

phle•bot′o•my, *n., pl.* **-mies.** *Med.* practice of opening a vein to let blood. —**phle•bot′o•mize′,** *v.*

phlegm (flem), *n.* 1. thick mucus in the respiratory passages. 2. apathy.

phleg•mat′ic, *adj.* unenthusiastic. —**phleg•mat′i•cal•ly,** *adv.*

phlo′em, *n.* tissue in plant which food passes.

phlox, *n.* flowering plant.

-phobe, suffix meaning one who hates or fears.

pho′bi•a, *n.* morbid fear.

-phobia, suffix meaning fear.

phoe′be (fē′bē), *n.* small American bird.

Phoe′bus (fē′-), *n.* Apollo as the sun god.

phoe′nix (fē′niks), *n.* mythical bird that burns, then rises from its ashes.

phone, *n., v.,* **phoned, phoning.** *Informal.* telephone.

pho′neme, *n.* minimal unit of speech that distinguishes one word from another.

pho•net′ics, *n.* science of speech sounds. —**pho•net′ic,** *adj.* —**pho•net′i•cal•ly,** *adv.*

phon′ics, *n.* method of teaching based on phonetics.

phono-, prefix meaning sound.

pho′no•graph′, *n.* sound-producing machine using records. —**pho′no•graph′ic,** *adj.*

pho•nol′o•gy, *n., pl.* **-gies.** study of sound changes in language. —**pho′no•log′i•cal,** *adj.* —**pho•nol′o•gist,** *n.*

pho′ny, *adj.,* **-nier, -niest,** *n., pl.* **-nies.** *Informal.* —*adj.* **1.** false. —*n.* **2.** something phony. —**pho′ni•ness,** *n.*

phos′gene (-jēn), *n.* poisonous gas.

phos′phate, *n.* **1.** salt of phosphoric acid. **2.** fertilizer containing phosphorus.

phos′phor (fos′fər), *n.* substance showing luminescence.

phos′pho•resce′, *v.,* **-resced, -rescing.** be luminous. —**phos′pho•res′cence,** *n.* —**phos′pho•res′cent,** *adj.*

phos′pho•rus, *n.* solid nonmetallic element. —**phos•phor′ic, phos′pho•rous,** *adj.*

pho′to, *n., pl.* **-tos.** *Informal.* photograph.

photo-, prefix meaning light.

pho′to•cop′y, *n., pl.* **-copies.** photographic copy. —**pho′to•cop′y,** *v.*

pho′to•e•lec′tric, *adj.* of or using electrical effects produced by light.

pho′to•en•grav′ing, *n.* process of obtaining a relief-printing surface by photographic reproduction. —**pho′to•en•grav′er,** *n.*

photo finish, finish of race so close as to require photograph to determine winner.

pho′to•gen′ic (-jen′-), *adj.* looking attractive in photos.

pho′to•graph′, *n.* **1.** picture produced by photography. —*v.* **2.** take photograph. —**pho•tog′ra•pher,** *n.*

pho•tog′ra•phy, *n.* process of obtaining images on sensitized surface by action of light. —**pho′to•graph′ic,** *adj.*

pho′ton, *n.* quantum of electromagnetic radiation.

pho′to•sen′si•tive, *adj.* sensitive to light.

Pho′to•stat′, *n.* **1.** *Trademark.* camera for photographing documents, etc. **2.** (*l.c.*) the photograph. —*v.* **3.** (*l.c.*) make photostatic copy. —**pho′to•stat′ic,** *adj.*

pho′to•syn′the•sis, *n.* conversion by plants of carbon dioxide and water into carbohydrates, aided by light and chlorophyll.

phrase, *n., v.,* **phrased, phrasing.** —*n.* **1.** sequence of words used as unit. **2.** minor division of musical composition. —*v.* **3.** express in particular way.

phra′se•ol′o•gy, *n.* **1.** manner of verbal expression. **2.** expressions.

phre•net′ic, *adj.* frenetic.

phre•nol′o•gy, *n.* theory that mental powers are shown by shape of skull. —**phre•nol′o•gist,** *n.*

phy•lac′ter•y, *n., pl.* **-teries.** leather cube containing Biblical verses.

phy•log′e•ny (-loj′-), *n.* development of particular group of organisms.

phy′lum, *n., pl.* **-la.** primary taxonomic classification.

phys′ic, *n.* cathartic medicine.

phys′i•cal, *adj.* **1.** of the body. **2.** of matter. **3.** of physics. —*n.* **4.** full examination of body. —**phys′i•cal•ly,** *adv.*

physical anthropology, study of evolutionary changes in human body structure.

physical science, science that deals with matter or energy.

physical therapy, treatment of physical disability or pain by techniques such as exercise.

phy·si′cian, *n.* medical doctor.

phys′ics, *n.* science of matter, motion, energy, and force. —**phys′i·cist,** *n.*

phys′i·og′no·my, *n., pl.* **-mies.** face.

phys′i·og′ra·phy, *n.* study of earth's surface.

phys′i·ol′o·gy, *n.* science dealing with functions of living organisms. —**phys′i·o·log′i·cal,** *adj.* —**phys′i·ol′o·gist,** *n.* —**phys′i·o·log′i·cal·ly,** *adv.*

phys′i·o·ther′a·py, *n.* treatment of disease by massage, exercise, etc.

phy·sique′ (-zēk′), *n.* physical structure.

pi (pī), *n.* the Greek letter π, used as symbol for ratio of circumference to diameter.

pi′a·nis′si·mo, *adv. Music.* very softly.

pi·an′o, *n., pl.* **-anos,** *adv.* —*n.* 1. Also, **pi·an′o·for′te.** musical keyboard instrument in which hammers strike upon metal strings. —*adv.* (pē ä′nō). 2. *Music.* softly. —**pi·an′ist,** *n.*

pi·az′za, *n.* 1. open public square. 2. veranda.

pi′ca (pī′-), *n.* 1. size of printing type. 2. unit of measure in printing.

pic′a·resque′, *adj.* of fiction that describes adventures of roguish hero.

pic′a·yune′, *adj.* petty.

pic′ca·lil′li, *n.* spiced relish.

pic′co·lo′, *n., pl.* **-los.** small shrill flute.

pick, *v.* 1. choose. 2. pluck. 3. dig or break into, esp. with pointed instrument. 4. nibble listlessly. —*n.* 5. choice. 6. right to choose. 7. Also, **pick′ax′, pick′axe′.** sharp-pointed tool. —**pick′er,** *n.*

pick′er·el, *n.* small pike.

pick′et, *n.* 1. pointed stake. 2. demonstration in front of workplace. 3. troops posted to warn of enemy attack. —*v.* 4. enclose with pickets. 5. put pickets in front of.

picket line, line of strikers or other pickets.

pick′le, *n., v.,* **-led, -ling. —***n.*
1. vegetable pserved in
vinegar. 2. predicament. —*v.*
3. preserve in vinegar.

pick′pock′et, *n.* person who
steals from others' pockets.

pick′up′, *n.* 1. ability to
accelerate rapidly. 2. small
open-body truck.

pick′y, *adj.,* **pickier, pickiest.**
extremely fussy or finicky.

pic′nic, *n., v.,* **-nicked,
-nicking. —***n.* 1. outing and
meal in the open. —*v.* 2. have
picnic. —**pic′nick•er,** *n.*

pi′cot (pē′kō), *n.* decorative
loop along edge of trim.

pic′ture, *n., v.,* **-tured, -turing.**
—*n.* 1. painting or
photograph. 2. motion
picture. —*v.* 3. represent in
picture. 4. imagine.
—**pic•to′ri•al,** *adj.*

pic′tur•esque′, *adj.* visually
charming or quaint.

pid′dle, *v.,* **-dled, -dling.** waste.

pid′dling, *adj.* trivial.

pidg′in (pij′in), *n.* language
developed to allow speakers
of two different languages to
communicate.

pidgin English, English jargon
used in other countries.

pie, *n.* baked dish of fruit,
meat, etc., in pastry crust.

pie′bald′, *adj.* having patches
of different colors.

piece, *n., v.,* **pieced, piecing.**
—*n.* 1. single portion. 2. one
part of a whole. 3. artistic
work. 4. rifle or cannon. —*v.*
5. make by joining pieces.

pièce de ré•sis•tance′ (pyes
də ʀā zē stäɴs′), *n., pl.* **pièces
de résistance** (pyes-), 1.
principal dish of meal. 2.
principal item of series.

piece goods, goods sold at
retail by linear measure.

piece′meal′, *adv.* 1. gradually.
2. into fragments.

piece′work′, *n.* work done
and paid for by the piece.

pie chart, graph in which
sectors of circle represent
quantities.

pied, *adj.* many-colored.

pied′-à-terre′ (pyā′də târ′),
n., pl. **pieds′-à-terre′** (pyā′-).
apartment for part-time use.

pie′-eyed′, *adj. Slang.* drunk.

pie′plant′, *n.* rhubarb.

pier, *n.* 1. structure at which
vessels are moored. 2.
masonry support.

pierce, *v.,* **pierced, piercing. 1.** make hole or way through. **2.** make (hole) in.

pi'e•ty, *n.* piousness.

pif'fle, *n. Informal.* nonsense. —**pif'fling,** *adj.*

pig, *n.* **1.** swine. **2.** bar of metal. —**pig'gish,** *adj.*

pi'geon, *n.* short-legged bird with compact body.

pi'geon•hole', *n., v.,* **-holed, -holing.** —*n.* **1.** small place. —*v.* **2.** classify. **3.** ignore.

pi'geon-toed', *adj.* having toes or feet turned inward.

pig'gy•back', *adv.* **1.** on the back. —*adj.* **2.** astride the back. **3.** attached to something else. **4.** of the carrying of truck trailers on trains.

pig'head'ed, *adj.* stubborn.

pig iron, iron from furnace.

pig'ment, *n.* coloring matter. —**pig'men•tar'y,** *adj.*

pig'men•ta'tion, *n.* color.

pig'my, *n., pl.* **-mies.** pygmy.

pig'pen', *n.* **1.** stall for pigs. **2.** filthy place. Also, **pig'sty'.**

pig'tail', *n.* hanging braid at back of head.

pike, *n.* **1.** large fresh-water fish. **2.** metal-headed shaft. **3.** highway.

pik'er, *n. Slang.* cheapskate.

pi'laf (pē'läf, pi läf'), *n.* Middle Eastern rice dish.

pi•las'ter, *n.* shallow imitation of column.

pil'chard (-chərd), *n.* marine fish.

pile, *n., v.,* **piled, piling.** —*n.* **1.** heap. **2.** device for producing energy by nuclear reaction. **3.** Also, **pil'ing.** upright driven into ground as foundation member. **4.** hair; down; wool; fur. **5.** nap (def. 2). **6.** *pl.* hemorrhoids. —*v.* **7.** lay in pile. **8.** accumulate.

pil'fer, *v.* steal, esp. from storage. —**pil'fer•age,** *n.*

pil'grim, *n.* **1.** traveler, esp. to sacred place. **2.** (*cap.*) early Puritan settler. —**pil'grim•age,** *n.*

pill, *n.* small mass of medicine to be swallowed.

pil'lage, *v.,* **-laged, -laging,** *n.* plunder.

pil'lar, *n.* upright shaft of masonry.

pill'box', *n.* **1.** small fort. **2.** box for pills.

pil′lo•ry, *n., pl.* **-ries,** *v.,* **-ried, -rying.** —*n.* **1.** wooden framework used to confine and expose offenders. —*v.* **2.** put in pillory. **3.** expose to public contempt.

pil′low, *n.* bag of feathers, etc., used as support for head. —**pil′low•case′,** *n.*

pi′lot, *n.* **1.** operator of aircraft. **2.** expert navigator. —*v.* **3.** steer. —*adj.* **4.** experimental.

pi′lot•house′, *n.* enclosed structure on deck of ship.

pilot light, small flame used to relight main burners.

pi•men′to, *n., pl.* **-tos.** dried fruit of tropical tree; allspice.

pi•mien′to (-myen′-), *n., pl.* **-tos.** variety of garden pepper.

pimp, *n., v.* —*n.* **1.** manager of prostitutes. —*v.* **2.** act as pimp.

pim′per•nel′, *n.* variety of primrose.

pim′ple, *n.* small swelling of skin. —**pim′ply,** *adj.*

pin, *n., v.,* **pinned, pinning.** —*n.* **1.** slender pointed piece of metal, wood, etc., for fastening. —*v.* **2.** fasten with pin. **3.** hold fast; bind.

PIN, *n.* identification number.

pin′a•fore′, *n.* **1.** child's apron. **2.** sleeveless dress.

pin′ball′, *n.* game in which spring-driven ball rolls against pins on sloping board.

pince′-nez′ (pans′ nā′), *n., pl.* **pince-nez.** eyeglasses supported by pinching the nose.

pin′cers, *n.* gripping tool with two pivoted limbs.

pinch, *v.* **1.** squeeze. **2.** cramp. **3.** economize. —*n.* **4.** act of pinching. **5.** tiny amount. **6.** distress. —**pinch′er,** *n.*

pinch′-hit′, *v.,* **-hit, -hitting.** substitute.

pine, *v.,* **pined, pining,** *n.* —*v.* **1.** long for. **2.** fail in health from grief. —*n.* **3.** evergreen tree with needle-shaped leaves. —**pin′y,** *adj.*

pin′e•al gland (pin′ē əl), organ involved in biorhythms and gonadal development.

pine′ap′ple, *n.* tropical fruit.

pin′feath′er, *n.* undeveloped feather.

ping, *v.* **1.** produce sharp sound like bullet striking metal. —*n.* **2.** pinging sound.

Ping'-Pong', *n. Trademark.* table tennis.

pin'head', *n.* 1. head of pin. 2. stupid person.

pin'ion (-yən), *n.* 1. feather or wing. 2. small cogwheel. —*v.* 3. bind (the arms).

pink, *n.* 1. pale red. 2. fragrant garden flower. 3. highest degree. —**pink**, *adj.*

pink'eye', *n.* inflammation of membrane covering eye.

pinking shears, shears with notched blades.

pin money, small sum set aside.

pin'na•cle, *n.* lofty peak.

pin'nate, *adj.* having leaflets on each side of common stalk.

pi'noch'le (pē'nuk əl, -nok-), *n.* game using 48 cards.

pin'point', *v.* identify.

pin'stripe', *n.* very thin stripe in fabric. —**pin'striped'**, *adj.*

pint, *n.* liquid and dry measure equal to one-half quart.

pin'tle, *n.* pin or bolt.

pin'to, *adj., n., pl.* **-tos.** —*adj.* 1. piebald. —*n.* 2. piebald horse.

pinto bean, bean with pinkish mottled seeds.

pin'up', *n.* large photograph of sexually attractive person.

pin'wheel', *n.* windmill-like toy that spins on stick.

pin'yin', *n.* system for transliterating Chinese into Latin alphabet.

pi'o•neer', *n.* 1. early arrival in new territory. 2. first one in any effort. —*v.* 3. act as pioneer.

pi'ous, *adj.* 1. reverential; devout. 2. sacred. —**pi'ous•ly**, *adv.* —**pi'ous•ness**, *n.*

pip, *n.* 1. small fruit seed. 2. spot on playing card, domino, etc. 3. disease of fowls.

pipe, *n., v.,* **piped, piping.** —*n.* 1. tube for conveying fluid. 2. tube for smoking tobacco. 3. tube used as musical instrument. —*v.* 4. play on pipe. 5. convey by pipe. —**pip'er**, *n.* —**pipe'line'**, *n.*

pipe dream, unrealistic hope.

pipe'line', *n.* 1. linked pipes for transporting fluids. 2. route for supplies. 3. channel.

pip'ing, *n.* 1. pipes. 2. sound of pipes. 3. kind of trimming.

pip'pin, *n.* kind of apple.

pip'squeak', *n. Informal.* small or unimportant person.

pi′quant (pē′kənt), *adj.* zesty.
—**pi′quan•cy**, *n.*

pique (pēk), *v.*, **piqued, piquing,**
n. —*v.* **1.** arouse resentment
in. **2.** excite (curiosity, etc.).
—*n.* **3.** irritated feeling.

pi•qué′ (pi kā′), *n.* corded
cotton fabric.

pi′ra•cy, *n., pl.* **-cies. 1.**
robbery at sea. **2.** illegal use of
material. —**pi′rate**, *n., v.*

pi•ra′nha (pi rän′yə, -ran′-,
-rä′nə), *n., pl.* **-nhas, -nha.**
small, fiercely predatory fish.

pir′ou•ette′ (pir′ o͞o et′), *v.,*
-etted, -etting, *n.* —*v.* **1.** whirl
about on the toes. —*n.* **2.** such
whirling.

pis′ca•to′ri•al (pis′kə-), *adj.*
of fishing.

pis′mire, *n.* ant.

pis•ta′chi•o′ (pis tä′shē ō′),
n., pl. **-chios.** edible nut.

pis′til, *n.* seed-bearing organ
of flower. —**pis′til•late**, *adj.*

pis′tol, *n.* short hand-held gun.

pis′tol-whip′, *v.,* **-whipped,**
-whipping. beat with pistol.

pis′ton, *n.* part moving back
and forth in cylinder.

pit, *n., v.,* **pitted, pitting.** —*n.* **1.**
hole in surface. **2.** hollow in
body. **3.** part of main floor of
theater. **4.** stone of fruit. —*v.*
5. mark with pits. **6.** set in
opposition. **7.** remove pit.

pi′ta (pē′tä, -tə), *n.* round, flat
bread with pocket.

pitch, *v.* **1.** throw. **2.** set at
certain point. **3.** fall forward.
4. drop and rise, as ship. —*n.*
5. relative point or degree. **6.**
musical tone. **7.** slope. **8.**
sticky dark substance from
coal tar. **9.** sap.

pitch′-black′, *adj.* jet black.

pitch′blende′, *n.* principal ore
of uranium and radium.

pitch′-dark′, *adj.* very dark.

pitched, *adj.* fought with all
available troops.

pitch′er, *n.* **1.** container with
spout for liquids. **2.** person
who pitches.

pitcher plant, insectivorous
plant.

pitch′fork′, *n.* sharp-tined fork
for handling hay.

pitch′man, *n., pl.* **-men.** person
who makes sales pitch.

pitch pipe, small pipe
producing pitches.

pit′e•ous, *adj.* pathetic.
—**pit′e•ous•ly**, *adv.*

pit′fall′, *n.* trap; hazard.

pith, *n.* 1. spongy tissue. 2. essence. 3. strength. —**pith′y**, *adj.* —**pith′i•ness**, *n.*

pit′i•a•ble, *adj.* 1. deserving pity. 2. contemptible. —**pit′i•a•bly**, *adv.*

pit′i•ful, *adj.* 1. deserving pity. 2. exciting contempt. 3. full of pity. —**pit′i•ful•ly**, *adv.* —**pit′i•ful•ness**, *n.*

pit′tance, *n.* meager income.

pi•tu•′i•tar′y (pi tyoo′ə ter′ē), *adj.* denoting gland at base of brain.

pit′y, *n., pl.* **pities,** *v.,* **pitied, pitying.** —*n.* 1. sympathetic sorrow. 2. cause for regret. —*v.* 3. feel pity for. —**pit′i•less**, *adj.* —**pit′i•less•ly**, *adv.*

piv′ot, *n.* 1. shaft on which something turns. —*v.* 2. turn on pivot. —**piv′ot•al**, *adj.*

pix′el, *n.* smallest element of image in video display system.

pix′y, *n., pl.* **pixies.** fairy. Also, **pix′ie.**

pi•zazz′, *n. Informal.* 1. vigor. 2. flair. Also, **piz•zazz′.**

piz′za (pēt′sə), *n.* dish of cheese, tomato sauce, etc., on baked crust.

piz′zer•i′a (pēt′sə rē′ə), *n.* restaurant serving pizza.

piz′zi•ca′to (pit′si kä′tō), *adj. Music.* played by plucking strings with fingers.

pkg., package.

pkwy., parkway.

pl., 1. place. 2. plural.

plac′a•ble, *adj.* forgiving.

plac′ard, *n.* public notice.

pla′cate, *v.,* **-cated, -cating.** appease. —**pla•ca′tion**, *n.*

place, *n., v.,* **placed, placing.** —*n.* 1. particular portion of space. 2. function. 3. social standing. 4. stead. —*v.* 5. put in place. 6. identify from memory. —**place′ment**, *n.*

pla•ce′bo (plə sē′bō), *n., pl.* **-bos, -boes.** pill, etc., containing no medication, given to reassure patient or as control in testing drug.

pla•cen′ta (-sen′-), *n.* organ in uterus which attaches to and nourishes fetus.

plac′er, *n.* surface gravel containing gold particles.

plac′id, *adj.* serene. —**pla•cid′i•ty**, *n.* —**plac′id•ly**, *adv.*

plack′et, *n.* slit at neck, waist, or wrist of garment.

pla′gia•rize′ (plā′jə rīz′), *v.,* **-rized, -rizing.** copy and claim as one's own work of another. —**pla′gia•rism,** *n.* —**pla′gia•rist,** *n.*

plague, *n., v.,* **plagued, plaguing.** —*n.* **1.** often fatal epidemic disease. **2.** affliction or vexation. —*v.* **3.** trouble.

plaid (plad), *n.* **1.** fabric woven in many-colored cross bars. —*adj.* **2.** having such pattern.

plain, *adj.* **1.** distinct. **2.** evident. **3.** candid. **4.** ordinary. **5.** bare. **6.** flat. —*adv.* **7.** clearly. **8.** candidly. —*n.* **9.** level area. —**plain′ly,** *adv.* —**plain′ness,** *n.*

plain′clothes′man, *n., pl.* **-men.** police officer who wears civilian clothes on duty.

plain′song′, *n.* unisonal music of early Christian Church.

plaint, *n.* complaint.

plain′tiff, *n.* one who brings suit in court.

plain′tive, *adj.* melancholy. —**plain′tive•ly,** *adv.* —**plain′tive•ness,** *n.*

plait, *n., v.* **1.** braid. **2.** pleat.

plan, *n., v.,* **planned, planning.** —*n.* **1.** scheme of action or arrangement. **2.** drawing of projected structure. —*v.* **3.** make plan. —**plan′ner,** *n.*

plane, *n., adj., v.,* **planed, planing.** —*n.* **1.** flat surface. **2.** level. **3.** airplane. **4.** tool for smoothing. —*adj.* **5.** flat. —*v.* **6.** glide. **7.** smooth with plane.

plan′et, *n.* solid heavenly body revolving about sun. —**plan′e•tar′y,** *adj.*

plan′e•tar′i•um, *n., pl.* **-iums, -ia.** **1.** optical device that projects a representation of heavens on a dome. **2.** museum with such device.

plane tree, large shade tree.

plan′gent (-jənt), *adj.* resounding loudly.

plank, *n.* **1.** long flat piece of timber. **2.** point in political platform. —**plank′ing,** *n.*

plank′ton, *n.* microscopic organisms floating in water.

plant, *n.* **1.** member of vegetable group. **2.** factory. —*v.* **3.** set in ground for growth. **4.** furnish with plants. —**plant′er,** *n.* —**plant′like′,** *adj.*

plan'tain (-tin), *n.* **1.** tropical bananalike plant. **2.** common flat-leaved weed.

plan'tar (plan'tər), *adj.* of the soles of the feet.

plan•ta'tion, *n.* large farm.

plaque (plak), *n.* **1.** monumental tablet. **2.** film formed on tooth surfaces.

plash, *n.* **1.** gentle splash. —*v.* **2.** splash gently.

plas'ma, *n.* clear liquid part of blood or lymph.

plas'ter, *n.* **1.** pasty mixture for covering walls. **2.** medicinal preparation spread on cloth and applied to body. —*v.* **3.** treat with plaster.

plas'ter•board', *n.* material for covering walls.

plaster of Par'is, form of gypsum in powdery form.

plas'tic, *adj.* **1.** of or produced by molding. **2.** moldable. **3.** three-dimensional. —*n.* **4.** organic material that is hardened after shaping. —**plas•tic'i•ty,** *n.*

plastic surgery, branch of surgery dealing with repair or reshaping of parts of body.

plate, *n., v.,* **plated, plating.** —*n.* **1.** shallow round dish for food. **2.** gold or silver ware. **3.** sheet of metal used in printing. **4.** shaped holder for false teeth. —*v.* **5.** coat with metal. —**plat'er,** *n.*

pla•teau', *n., pl.* **-teaus, -teaux.** raised plain.

plate glass, smooth glass.

plat'en (plat'-), *n.* plate in printing press that presses paper against inked surface.

plat'form, *n.* **1.** raised flooring. **2.** set of announced political principles.

plat'i•num, *n.* precious, malleable metallic element.

plat'i•tude', *n.* trite remark. —**plat'i•tud'i•nous,** *adj.*

pla•ton'ic, *adj.* without sexual involvement.

pla•toon', *n.* small military or police unit.

plat'ter, *n.* large serving dish.

plat'y•fish', *n., pl.* **-fish, -fishes.** freshwater fish.

plat'y•pus (-ə pəs), *n., pl.* **-puses, -pi.** duckbill.

plau'dit (plô'dit), *n. (usu. pl.)* applause.

plau'si•ble, *adj.* apparently true or trustworthy.

—**plau′si•bil′i•ty**, *n.*

—**plau′si•bly**, *adv.*

play, *n.* **1.** dramatic work. **2.** recreation. **3.** fun. **4.** change. **5.** movement. —*v.* **6.** act in a play. **7.** engage in game. **8.** perform on musical instrument. **9.** amuse oneself. **10.** move about lightly. —**play′er**, *n.* —**play′ful**, *adj.* —**play′ful•ly**, *adv.* —**play′ful•ness**, *n.* —**play′go′er**, *n.* —**play′mate′**, *n.*

play′back′, *n.* **1.** reproduction of a recording. **2.** apparatus used in producing playbacks.

play′bill′, *n.* program play.

play′boy′, *n.* man who pursues life of pleasure.

play′ground′, *n.* area used for outdoor recreation.

play′house′, *n.* **1.** theater. **2.** small house for children to play in.

play′-off′, *n.* extra game played to break a tie.

play on words, pun.

play′pen′, *n.* small enclosure in which baby can play.

play′thing′, *n.* toy.

play′wright′, *n.* writer of plays.

pla′za, *n.* public square, esp. in Spanish-speaking countries.

plea, *n.* **1.** defense. **2.** entreaty.

plea bargain, agreement in which criminal defendant pleads guilty to lesser charge.

plead, *v.*, **pleaded** or **pled**, **pleading. 1.** make earnest entreaty. **2.** allege formally in court. **3.** argue (case at law). **4.** allege in justification. —**plead′er**, *n.*

pleas′ant, *adj.* agreeable; pleasing. —**pleas′ant•ly**, *adv.*

pleas′ant•ry, *n., pl.* **-ries.** good-humored remark.

please, *v.*, **pleased, pleasing.** be or act to pleasure of; seem good. —**pleas′ing•ly**, *adv.*

pleas′ur•a•ble, *adj.* enjoyable.

pleas′ure, *n.* **1.** enjoyment. **2.** person's will or desire.

pleat, *n.* **1.** double fold of cloth. —*v.* **2.** fold in pleats.

ple•be′ian (plə bē′ən), *adj.* of common people.

pleb′i•scite′ (-sīt′), *n.* direct vote by citizens on question.

plec′trum, *n., pl.* **-tra, -trums.** object for picking strings of musical instrument.

pledge, *n., v.,* **pledged, pledging. —***n.* **1.** solemn promise. **2.** property delivered as security on a loan. **3.** toast. —*v.* **4.** bind by pledge. **5.** promise. **6.** deliver as pledge.

Pleis′to•cene′ (plī′stə sēn′), *adj.* pertaining to geologic epoch forming earlier half of Quaternary Period.

ple′na•ry, *adj.* full; complete.

plen′i•po•ten′ti•ar′y (-shē er′ē), *n., pl.* **-aries,** *adj.* —*n.* **1.** diplomat with full authority. —*adj.* **2.** having full authority.

plen′i•tude′, *n.* abundance.

plen′ty, *n.* **1.** abundant supply. —*adv. Informal.* **2.** very. —**plen′te•ous, plen′ti•ful,** *adj.*

pleth′o•ra, *n.* excess.

pleu′ra, *n., pl.* **pleurae** (-ē). membrane that covers lung and lines chest wall.

pleu′ri•sy, *n.* inflammation of pleura.

Plex′i•glas′, *n. Trademark.* light, durable plastic.

plex′us, *n., pl.* **-uses, -us.** network.

pli′a•ble, *adj.* easily bent or influenced. —**pli′a•bil′i•ty,** *n.* —**pli′a•bly,** *adv.*

pli′ant, *adj.* pliable. —**pli′an•cy,** *n.*

pli′ers, *n.pl.* small pincers.

plight, *n.* **1.** distressing condition. —*v.* **2.** promise.

PLO, Palestine Liberation Organization.

plod, *v.,* **plodded, plodding. 1.** walk heavily. **2.** work laboriously. —**plod′der,** *n.*

plop, *v.,* **plopped, plopping,** *n.* —*v.* **1.** drop with sound like that of object hitting water. **2.** drop with direct impact. —*n.* **3.** plopping sound or fall.

plot, *n., v.,* **plotted, plotting.** —*n.* **1.** secret scheme. **2.** main story of fictional work. **3.** small area of ground. —*v.* **4.** plan secretly. **5.** mark (chart course) on. **6.** divide into plots. —**plot′ter,** *n.*

plov′er (pluv′ər), *n.* shore bird.

plow, *n.* **1.** implement for cutting and turning soil. **2.** similar implement for removing snow. —*v.* **3.** cut or turn with plow. **4.** force way, as through water. Also, **plough. —plow′man,** *n.*

plow′share′, *n.* blade of plow.

ploy, *n.* stratagem; ruse.

pluck, *v.* **1.** pull out from fixed position. **2.** sound (strings of musical instrument). —*n.* **3.** pull or tug. **4.** courage.

pluck'y, *adj.,* **pluckier, pluckiest.** courageous. —**pluck'i•ness,** *n.*

plug, *n., v.,* **plugged, plugging.** —*n.* **1.** object for stopping hole. **2.** device on electrical cord that establishes contact in socket. **3.** *Slang.* favorable mention. —*v.* **4.** insert plug. **5.** *Slang.* mention favorably. **6.** work steadily. —**plug'ger,** *n.*

plum, *n.* **1.** oval juicy fruit. **2.** deep purple. **3.** *Informal.* favor widely desired.

plumb, *n.* **1.** plummet. —*adj.* **2.** perpendicular. —*adv.* **3.** vertically. **4.** exactly. **5.** *Informal.* completely. —*v.* **6.** make vertical. **7.** measure depth of.

plumb'ing, *n.* system of water pipes, etc. —**plumb'er,** *n.*

plume, *n., v.,* **plumed, pluming.** —*n.* **1.** feather. **2.** ornamental tuft. —*v.* **3.** preen. **4.** furnish with plumes. —**plum'age,** *n.*

plum'met, *n.* **1.** weight on line for sounding or establishing verticals. —*v.* **2.** plunge.

plump, *adj.* **1.** somewhat fat. —*v.* **2.** become plump. **3.** drop heavily. —*n.* **4.** heavy fall. —*adv.* **5.** directly. **6.** heavily. —**plump'ness,** *n.*

plun'der, *v.* **1.** rob. —*n.* **2.** act of plundering. **3.** loot.

plunge, *v.,* **plunged, plunging,** *n.* —*v.* **1.** dip. **2.** rush. **3.** pitch forward. —*n.* **4.** dive.

plung'er, *n.* **1.** pistonlike part. **2.** device to unclog drains.

plunk, *v.* **1.** drop heavily. **2.** give forth twanging sound. —*n.* **3.** sound of plunking.

plu'ral, *adj.* **1.** more than one. —*n.* **2.** plural form. —**plur'al•ize',** *v.*

plu'ral•ism, *n.* condition in which minority groups participate in society, yet maintain their distinctions. —**plu'ral•is'tic,** *adj.*

plu•ral'i•ty, *n., pl.* **-ties. 1.** in election with three or more candidates, the excess of votes given leading candidate over next candidate. **2.** majority.

plus, *prep.* **1.** increased by. —*adj.* **2.** involving addition. **3.** positive. —*n.* **4.** something additional.

plush, *n.* long-piled fabric.

Plu'to, *n.* planet ninth in order from the sun.

plu•to•crat', *n.* **1.** wealthy person. **2.** member of wealthy governing class.
—**plu•toc'ra•cy,** *n.*
—**plu'to•crat'ic,** *adj.*

plu•to'ni•um, *n.* radioactive element.

plu'vi•al (ploo'vē-), *adj.* of rain.

ply, *v.,* **plied, plying,** *n., pl.* **plies.** —*v.* **1.** work with by hand. **2.** carry on, as trade. **3.** offer repeatedly. **4.** travel regularly. —*n.* **5.** thickness.

ply'wood', *n.* sheets of wood.

p.m., after noon. Also, **P.M.**

PMS, premenstrual syndrome.

pneu•mat'ic (nyoo-), *adj.* **1.** of gases. **2.** operated by air.
—**pneu•mat'i•cal•ly,** *adv.*

pneu•mo'nia, *n.* inflammation of lungs.

P.O., post office.

poach, *v.* **1.** hunt illegally. **2.** cook in hot water.
—**poach'er,** *n.*

pock'et, *n.* **1.** small bag sewed into garment. **2.** pouch; cavity. —*adj.* **3.** small. —*v.* **4.** put into one's pocket. **5.** take as profit. **6.** suppress.

pock'et•book', *n.* purse.

pock'et•knife', *n.* small folding knife.

pock'mark', *n.* acne scar.

pod, *n., v.,* **podded, podding.** —*n.* **1.** seed covering. —*v.* **2.** produce pod.

po•di'a•try, *n.* treatment of foot disorders.
—**po•di'a•trist,** *n.*

po'di•um, *n., pl.* **-diums, -dia.** small raised platform.

po'em, *n.* composition in verse. —**po'et,** *n.*

po'e•sy (-ə sē), *n., pl.* **-sies.** poetry.

po'et•as'ter, *n.* inferior poet.

poetic justice, fitting rewards and punishments.

poetic license, liberty taken by writer in deviating from fact to produce desired effect.

po'et•ry, *n.* rhythmical composition of words.
—**po•et'ic, po•et'i•cal,** *adj.*

po•grom' (pə grum'), *n.* organized massacre.

poign′ant (poin′yənt), *adj.* keenly distressing. —**poign′an•cy,** *n.*

poin′ci•an′a, *n., pl.* **-as.** tropical tree.

poin•set′ti•a (poin set′ē ə), *n.* plant with scarlet flowers.

point, *n.* 1. sharp end. 2. projecting part. 3. dot. 4. definite position or time. 5. compass direction. 6. basic reason, assertion, etc. 7. detail. 8. unit of printing measure. —*v.* 9. indicate. 10. direct. —**point′less,** *adj.*

point′-blank′, *adj.* 1. direct; plain. —*adv.* 2. directly.

point′ed, *adj.* 1. having a point. 2. sharp. 3. aimed at a particular. 4. emphasized.

point′er, *n.* 1. one that points. 2. long stick for pointing. 3. breed of hunting dog.

poin′til•lism (pwan′-), *n.* technique in painting of using dots of pure color that are optically mixed into resulting hue by viewer.

poise, *n., v.,* **poised, poising.** —*n.* 1. balance. 2. composure. —*v.* 3. balance. 4. be in position for action.

poi′son, *n.* 1. substance that kills or harms seriously. —*v.* 2. harm with poison. —**poi′son•er,** *n.* —**poi′son•ous,** *adj.*

poison ivy, 1. vine or shrub having shiny leaves with three leaflets. 2. rash caused by touching poison ivy.

poke, *v.,* **poked, poking,** *n.* thrust.

pok′er, *n.* 1. rod for poking fires. 2. card game.

pok′er-faced′, *adj.* showing no emotion or intention.

pok′y, *adj.,* **pokier, pokiest.** *Informal.* slow; dull. Also, **poke′y.** —**pok′i•ness,** *n.*

po′lar, *adj.* 1. arctic or antarctic. 2. in opposition or contrast. 3. of magnetic poles. —**po•lar′i•ty,** *n.*

polar bear, large arctic bear.

Po•lar′is, *n.* bright star close to North Pole.

po′lar•i•za′tion, *n.* 1. division of group into opposing factions. 2. state in which rays of light exhibit different properties in different directions. —**po′lar•ize′,** *v.*

pole, *n., v.,* **poled, poling.** —*n.*
1. long slender rod. 2. unit of length equal to 16½ ft.; rod.
3. square rod, 30¼ sq. yards.
4. each end of axis.
5. each end showing strongest opposite force. 6. (*cap.*) native or citizen of Poland. —*v.* 7. propel with a pole.

pole′cat′, *n.* small bad-smelling mammal.

po•lem′ics (-lem′iks), *n.* art or practice of argument.
—**po•lem′ic,** *n., adj.*
—**po•lem′i•cist,** *n.*

pole vault, athletic event in which vault over horizontal bar is performed with aid of long pole.

po•lice′, *n., v.,* **-liced, -licing.**
—*n.* 1. organized civil force for enforcing law. —*v.*
2. keep in order.
—**po•lice′man,** *n.*
—**po•lice′wom′an,** *n.fem.*

pol′i•cy, *n., pl.* **-cies.** 1. definite course of action. 2. insurance contract.

pol′i•o•my′e•li′tis (pōl′ē ō mī′ə lī′tis), *n.* infantile paralysis. Also, **po′li•o′.**

pol′ish (pol′-), *v.* 1. make glossy. —*n.* 2. polishing substance. 3. gloss. 4. refinement.

Pol′ish (pōl′-), *n.* of Poland. —**Pol′ish,** *adj.*

po•lite′, *adj.* showing good manners; refined.
—**po•lite′ly,** *adv.*
—**po•lite′ness,** *n.*

pol′i•tesse′, *n.* politeness.

pol′i•tic, *adj.* 1. prudent; expedient. 2. political.

politically correct, marked by progressive attitude on issues of race, sex, etc. —**political correctness.**

political science, social science dealing with political institutions and government.

po•lit′i•cize′, *v.,* **-cized, -cizing.** give a political bias to.

pol′i•tick′ing, *n.* political self-aggrandizement.

pol′i•tics, *n.* 1. science or conduct of government. 2. political affairs, methods, or principles. —**po•lit′i•cal,** *adj.*
—**pol′i•ti′cian,** *n.*
—**po•lit′i•cal•ly,** *adv.*

pol′ka, *n.* lively dance.

polka dot, pattern of dots.

poll, *n.* **1.** voting or votes at election. **2.** list of individuals, as for voting. **3.** (*pl.*) place of voting. **4.** analysis of public opinion. —*v.* **5.** receive votes. **6.** vote. **7.** ask opinions of.

pol′len, *n.* powdery fertilizing element of flowers.
—**pol′li•nate′,** *v.*
—**pol′li•na′tion,** *n.*

pol′li•wog′, *n.* tadpole.

poll′ster, *n.* person who takes public-opinion polls.

pol•lute′, *v.,* **-luted, -luting.** contaminate. —**pol•lu′tion,** *n.* —**pol•lut′ant,** *n.* —**pol•lut′er,** *n.*

po′lo, *n., pl.* **-los.** game played on horseback.

pol′o•naise′ (-nāz′), *n.* slow dance.

pol′ter•geist′ (pōl′tər gīst′), *n.* boisterous ghost.

pol•troon′, *n.* coward.

poly-, prefix meaning many.

pol′y•an′dry, *n.* practice of having more than one husband at a time.

pol′y•es′ter, *n.* artificial material for synthetics.

pol′y•eth′yl•ene′, *n.* plastic polymer used for packaging.

po•lyg′a•my, *n.* practice of having many spouses, esp. wives, at one time.
—**po•lyg′a•mist,** *n.*
—**po•lyg′a•mous,** *adj.*

pol′y•glot′, *adj.* knowing several languages.

pol′y•gon′, *n.* figure having three or more straight sides.
—**po•lyg′o•nal,** *adj.*

pol′y•graph′, *n.* instrument recording variations in certain body activities, sometimes used to detect lying in response to questions.

pol′y•he′dron, *n., pl.* **-drons, -dra.** solid figure having four or more sides.

pol′y•math′, *n.* person of great learning in several fields.

pol′y•mer, *n.* compound formed by the combination of various molecules with water or alcohol eliminated.
—**pol′y•mer•i•za′tion,** *n.*

pol′y•no′mi•al, *n.* algebraic expression consisting of two or more terms.

pol′yp, *n.* **1.** projecting growth from mucous surface. **2.** simple aquatic animal form.

po·lyph'o·ny, *n.* music with two or more melodic lines in equitable juxtaposition. —**pol'y·phon'ic,** *adj.*

pol'y·sty'rene, *n.* polymer used in molded objects and as insulator.

pol'y·syl·lab'ic, *adj.* consisting of many syllables.

pol'y·tech'nic, *adj.* offering instruction in variety of technical subjects.

pol'y·the'ism, *n.* belief in more than one god. —**pol'y·the'ist,** *n., adj.* —**pol'y·the·ist'ic,** *adj.*

pol'y·un·sat'u·rat'ed, *adj.* of a class of fats associated with low cholesterol content.

po·made', *n.* hair ointment.

pome'gran'ate (pom'gran'it), *n.* red, many-seeded fruit.

pom'mel (pum'əl), *n., v.,* -meled, -meling. —*n.* 1. knob. —*v.* 2. strike; beat.

pomp, *n.* stately display.

pom'pa·dour' (-dōr'), *n.* arrangement of hair brushed up high from forehead.

pom'pa·no', *n., pl.* -nos, -no. fish inhabiting waters off the S. Atlantic and Gulf states.

pom'pom, *n.* ornamental tuft.

pomp'ous, *adj.* self-important. —**pom·pos'i·ty, pomp'ous·ness,** *n.* —**pomp'ous·ly,** *adv.*

pon'cho, *n., pl.* -chos. blanketlike cloak.

pond, *n.* small lake.

pon'der, *v.* meditate.

pon'der·ous, *adj.* heavy.

pone, *n.* corn bread.

pon·gee' (-jē'), *n.* silk fabric.

pon'iard (pon'yərd), *n.* dagger.

pon'tiff, *n.* 1. pope. 2. bishop. —**pon·tif'i·cal,** *adj.*

pon·tif'i·cate', *v.,* -cated, -cating. speak with affected air of authority.

pon·toon', *n.* floating support.

po'ny, *n., pl.* -nies. small horse.

po'ny·tail', *n.* hair pulled back and fastened so as to hang freely.

poo'dle, *n.* dog with curly hair.

pool, *n.* 1. body of still water. 2. group of persons or things available for use. 3. game resembling billiards. —*v.* 4. put into common fund.

poop, *n.* upper deck on afterpart of a ship.

poor, *adj.* **1.** having little wealth. **2.** wanting. **3.** inferior. **4.** unfortunate. —*n.* **5.** poor persons. —**poor′ly,** *adv.* —**poor′ness,** *n.*

poor′-mouth′, *v. Informal.* complain about poverty.

pop, *v.,* **popped, popping,** *n.,* *adv.* —*v.* **1.** make or burst with a short, quick sound. **2.** shoot. —*n.* **3.** short, quick sound. **4.** soft drink. —*adv.* **5.** suddenly.

pop′corn′, *n.* corn kernels that burst in dry heat.

pope, *n.* (*often cap.*) head of Roman Catholic Church.

pop′in·jay′, *n.* vain person.

pop′lar, *n.* fast-growing tree.

pop′lin, *n.* corded fabric.

pop′o′ver, *n.* very light muffin.

pop′py, *n., pl.* **-pies.** showy-flowered herbs, one species of which yields opium.

pop′py·cock′, *n.* nonsense.

pop′u·lace, *n.* population.

pop′u·lar, *adj.* **1.** generally liked and approved. **2.** of the people. **3.** prevalent. —**pop′u·lar′i·ty,** *n.* —**pop′u·lar·ize′,** *v.* —**pop′u·lar·ly,** *adv.*

pop′u·late′, *v.,* **-lated, -lating.** inhabit.

pop′u·la′tion, *n.* **1.** number of persons inhabiting area. **2.** body of inhabitants.

pop′u·lism, *n.* political philosophy promoting the interests of the common people. —**pop′u·list,** *n., adj.*

pop′u·lous, *adj.* with many inhabitants.

por′ce·lain, *n.* glassy ceramic ware; china.

porch, *n.* veranda.

por′cine (pôr′sīn), *adj.* of or like swine.

por′cu·pine′, *n.* rodent with stout quills.

pore, *v.,* **pored, poring,** *n.* —*v.* **1.** ponder or read intently. —*n.* **2.** minute opening in skin.

por′gy, *n., pl.* **-gies.** fleshy salt-water food fish.

pork, *n.* flesh of hogs as food.

pork barrel, government funds available for popular local improvements.

por·nog′ra·phy, *n.* obscene literature or art. —**por′no·graph′ic,** *adj.* —**por·nog′ra·pher,** *n.*

po′rous, *adj.* permeable.
—**po′rous•ness,** *n.*

por′phy•ry, *n., pl.* **-ries.** hard purplish red rock.

por′poise, *n.* aquatic mammal.

por′ridge, *n.* boiled cereal.

por′rin•ger, *n.* shallow bowl.

port, *n.* **1.** place where ships load and unload. **2.** harbor. **3.** left side of vessel. **4.** sweet red wine. —**port,** *adj.*

port′a•ble, *adj.* readily carried. —**port′a•bil′i•ty,** *n.*

por′tage, *n.* **1.** overland route between navigable streams. **2.** act of carrying.

por′tal, *n.* door or gate.

port•cul′lis, *n.* heavy iron grating at gateway of castle.

por•tend′, *v.* foretell.

por′tent, *n.* **1.** omen. **2.** ominous significance.
—**por•ten′tous,** *adj.*

por′ter, *n.* **1.** railroad attendant. **2.** baggage carrier. **3.** superintendent.

por′ter•house′, *n.* choice cut of beefsteak.

port•fo′li•o′, *n., pl.* **-lios. 1.** portable case for papers, etc. **2.** cabinet post.

port′hole′, *n.* opening in ship's side.

por′ti•co′, *n., pl.* **-coes, -cos.** roof supported by columns.

por•tiere′ (pôr tyâr′, -tēr′), *n.* curtain hung in doorway. Also, **por•tière′.**

por′tion, *n.* **1.** part of a whole. **2.** share. —*v.* **3.** divide into shares.

port′ly, *adj.,* **-lier, -liest. 1.** fat. **2.** stately. —**port′li•ness,** *n.*

port•man′teau (-tō), *n., pl.* **-teaus, -teaux.** leather trunk.

por′trait, *n.* picture, sculpture, etc., showing specific person.
—**por′trai•ture,** *n.*

por′trait•ist, *n.* person who makes portraits.

por•tray′, *v.* depict.
—**por•tray′al,** *n.*

Por′tu•guese′, *n., pl.* **-guese.** native or language of Portugal. —**Portuguese,** *adj.*

Portugese man′-of-war′, poisonous marine animal.

por′tu•lac′a (pōr′chə lak′ə), *n.* low-growing garden plant.

pose, *v.,* **posed, posing,** *n.* —*v.* **1.** feign position or character. **2.** take position. **3.** ask (question). —*n.* **4.** position consciously assumed.

po′ser, *n.* **1.** person who poses. **2.** difficult question.

po•seur′ (pō zûr′), *n.* affected person.

posh, *adj.* elegant; luxurious.

pos′it (poz′it), *v.* lay down or assume as a fact or principle.

po•si′tion, *n.* **1.** place or attitude. **2.** belief or argument on question. **3.** social or organizational standing. **4.** job. —*v.* **5.** place.

pos′i•tive, *adj.* **1.** explicit; not denying or questioning. **2.** emphatic. **3.** confident. **4.** showing lights and shades of original. **5.** *Gram.* denoting first degree of comparison. **6.** denoting more than zero. **7.** deficient in electrons. **8.** revealing presence of thing tested for. —*n.* **9.** something positive. **10.** photographic image. —**pos′i•tive•ly,** *adv.* —**pos′i•tive•ness,** *n.*

pos′i•tron′, *n.* particle with same mass as electron but with positive charge.

pos′se (pos′ē), *n.* body of persons assisting sheriff.

pos•sess′, *v.* **1.** have under ownership or domination. **2.** have as quality. **3.** obsess. —**pos•ses′sor,** *n.* —**pos•ses′sion,** *n.*

pos•sessed′, *adj.* controlled by strong feeling or power.

pos•ses′sive, *adj.* **1.** denoting possession. **2.** obsessed with dominating another.

pos′si•ble, *adj.* that may be, happen, etc. —**pos′si•bil′i•ty,** *n.* —**pos′si•bly,** *adv.*

pos′sum, *n.* opossum.

post, *n.* **1.** upright support. **2.** position of duty or trust. **3.** station for soldiers or traders. **4.** *Chiefly Brit.* mail. —*v.* **5.** put up. **6.** station at post. **7.** *Chiefly Brit.* mail. **8.** enter in ledger. **9.** hasten. **10.** inform. —*adv.* **11.** with speed.

post-, prefix meaning after.

post′age, *n.* charge.

post′al, *adj.* concerning mail.

post•bel′lum, *adj.* after war.

post′card′, *n.* small notecard.

post•date′, *v.,* -dated, -dating. **1.** mark with date later than actual date. **2.** follow in time.

post′er, *n.* large public notice.

pos·te′ri·or, *adj.* 1. situated behind. 2. later. —*n.* 3. buttocks.

pos·ter′i·ty, *n.* descendants.

post exchange, retail store on military base.

post·grad′u·ate, *adj.* 1. of postgraduates. —*n.* 2. student taking advanced work after graduation.

post′haste′, *adv.* speedily.

post′hu·mous (pos′chə məs), *adj.* 1. arising after one's death. 2. born after father's death. —**post′hu·mous·ly,** *adv.*

pos·til′ion, *n.* person who rides leading left horse of those pulling carriage.

post′man, *n.* mail carrier.

post′mark′, *n.* official mark on mail showing place and time of mailing. —**post′mark′,** *v.*

post′mas′ter, *n.* official in charge of post office.

post′mis′tress, *n.* woman in charge of post office.

post me·rid′i·em′, afternoon.

post·mod′ern, *adj.* pertaining to late 20th century artistic movement that developed in reaction to modernism.

post·mor′tem, *adj.* 1. following death. —*n.* 2. examination of dead body.

post·nat′al, *adj.* after childbirth.

post office, government office responsible for postal service.

post′paid′, *adv., adj.* with postage paid in advance.

post·par′tum, *adj.* following childbirth.

post·pone′, *v.,* -poned, -poning. delay till later. —**post·pone′ment,** *n.*

post·pran′di·al, *adj.* after a meal.

post′script′, *n.* note added to letter after signature.

pos′tu·late′, *v.,* -lated, -lating, *n.* —*v.* (pos′chə lāt′). 1. require. 2. assume. —*n.* (-lit). 3. something postulated.

pos′ture, *n., v.,* -tured, -turing. —*n.* 1. position of the body. —*v.* 2. place in particular position. 3. behave affectedly.

post′war′, *adj.* after a war.

po′sy, *n., pl.* -sies. flower.

pot, *n., v.,* **potted, potting.** —*n.* 1. round deep container for cooking, etc. 2. total stakes at cards. 3. *Slang.* marijuana. —*v.* 4. put into pot.

po′ta•ble, *adj.* drinkable.

pot′ash′, *n.* potassium carbonate.

po•tas′si•um, *n.* light metallic element.

po•ta′tion, *n.* drink.

po•ta′to, *n., pl.* **-toes.** edible tuber of garden plant.

pot′bel′ly, *n., pl.* **-lies.** belly that sticks out. —**pot′bel′lied,** *adj.*

pot′boil′er, *n.* mediocre work of literature or art produced merely for financial gain.

po′tent, *adj.* 1. powerful. 2. (of a male) capable of sexual intercourse. —**po′tence, po′ten•cy,** *n.* —**po′tent•ly,** *adv.*

po′ten•tate′, *n.* powerful person, as a sovereign.

po•ten′tial, *adj.* 1. possible. 2. latent. —*n.* 3. possibility. —**po•ten′ti•al′i•ty,** *n.* —**po•ten′tial•ly,** *adv.*

poth′er, *n., v.* fuss.

pot′hole′, *n.* hole formed in pavement.

po′tion, *n.* drink.

pot′luck′, *n.* 1. meal to which participants bring food to be shared. 2. whatever happens to be available.

pot′pour•ri′ (pō′pə rē′), *n.* 1. mixture of dried flowers and spices. 2. miscellany.

pot′sherd′, *n.* pottery fragment.

pot′shot′, *n.* 1. casual shot. 2. random criticism.

pot′tage, *n.* thick soup.

pot′ted, *adj.* 1. grown in a pot. 2. *Slang.* drunk.

pot′ter, *n.* 1. person who makes earthen pots. —*v.* 2. putter (def. 1).

potter's field, burial ground for the poor.

pot′ter•y, *n., pl.* **-teries.** ware made of clay and baked.

pouch, *n.* 1. bag or sack.

poul′tice (pōl′tis), *n.* moist mass applied as medicine.

poul′try, *n.* domestic fowls.

pounce, *v.,* **pounced, pouncing,** *n.* —*v.* 1. swoop down or spring suddenly. 2. seize eagerly. —*n.* 3. sudden swoop.

pound, *n., pl.* **pounds, pound,** *v.* —*n.* **1.** unit of weight: in U.S., **pound avoirdupois** (16 ounces) and **pound troy** (12 ounces). **2.** British monetary unit. **3.** enclosure for stray animals. —*v.* **4.** strike repeatedly and heavily. **5.** crush by pounding.

pound cake, rich, sweet cake.

pour, *v.* **1.** cause to flow; flow. —*n.* **2.** abundant flow.

pout, *v.* **1.** look sullen. —*n.* **2.** sullen look or mood.

pov′er·ty, *n.* **1.** poorness. **2.** lack.

POW, *pl.* **POWs, POW's.** prisoner of war.

pow′der, *n.* **1.** fine loose particles. —*v.* **2.** reduce to powder. **3.** apply powder to. —**pow′der·y,** *adj.*

powder keg, 1. container for gunpowder. **2.** explosive situation.

pow′er, *n.* **1.** ability to act; strength. **2.** faculty. **3.** authority; control. **4.** person, nation, etc., having great influence. **5.** mechanical energy. **6.** product of repeated multiplications of number by itself. **7.** magnifying capacity of an optical instrument.

—**pow′er·ful,** *adj.*
—**pow′er·ful·ly,** *adv.*
—**pow′er·less,** *adj.*
—**pow′er·less·ly,** *adv.*

pow′er·house′, *n.* **1.** building where electricity is generated. **2.** person or group with great potential for success.

power of attorney, legal authorization for another person to act in one's place.

pow′wow′, *n. Informal.* conference.

pox, *n.* disease marked by skin eruptions.

pp., 1. pages. **2.** past participle.

ppd., 1. postpaid. **2.** prepaid.

P.P.S., additional postscript. Also, **p.p.s.**

PR, public relations.

prac′ti·ca·ble, *adj.* able to be put into practice; feasible.

prac′ti·cal, *adj.* **1.** of or from practice. **2.** useful. **3.** level-headed. **4.** concerned with everyday affairs. **5.** virtual. —**prac′ti·cal′i·ty,** *n.* —**prac′ti·cal·ly,** *adv.*

prac′tice, *n., v.,* **-ticed, -ticing.** —*n.* **1.** custom. **2.** action carried out. **3.** repeated performance in learning. **4.**

professional activity. —*v.* Also, *Brit.,* **prac'tise. 5.** do as profession. **6.** to repeat to acquire skill. —**prac'ticed,** *adj.*

prac'ti•cum, *n.* course of study devoted to practical experience in a field.

prac•ti'tion•er, *n.* person engaged in a profession.

prag•mat'ic, *adj.* concerned with practical values and results. —**prag'ma•tism,** *n.* —**prag'ma•tist,** *n.* —**prag•mat'i•cal•ly,** *adv.*

prai'rie, *n.* flat grassland.

prairie dog, burrowing squirrel.

prairie schooner, covered wagon.

praise, *n., v.,* **praised, praising.** —*n.* **1.** words of approval. **2.** grateful homage. —*v.* **3.** give praise to. **4.** worship. —**praise'wor'thy,** *adj.* —**prais'er,** *n.*

pra'line, *n.* confection of caramelized nuts and sugar.

pram, *n. Brit. Informal.* baby carriage.

prance, *v.,* **pranced, prancing,** *n.* —*v.* **1.** step about gaily or

proudly. —*n.* **2.** act of prancing. —**pranc'er,** *n.*

prank, *n.* playful trick. —**prank'ster,** *n.*

prate, *v.,* **prated, prating.** talk foolishly.

prat'fall', *n.* fall on the buttocks.

prat'tle, *v.,* **-tled, -tling,** *n.* —*v.* **1.** chatter childishly. —*n.* **2.** chatter. —**prat'tler,** *n.*

prawn, *n.* large shrimplike shellfish.

pray, *v.* make prayer.

prayer, *n.* **1.** petition to God. **2.** petition. —**prayer'ful,** *adj.*

pre-, prefix meaning before.

preach, *v.* **1.** advocate. **2.** deliver (sermon). —**preach'er,** *n.* —**preach'y,** *adj.*

pre'am'ble, *n.* introduction.

Pre•cam'bri•an, *adj.* pertaining to earliest era of earth history.

pre•can'cer•ous, *adj.* showing changes that may be preliminary to malignancy.

pre•car'i•ous, *adj.* uncertain. —**pre•car'i•ous•ly,** *adv.*

pre•cau'tion, *n.* safeguard. —**pre•cau'tion•ar'y,** *adj.*

pre·cede′, *v.*, -ceded, -ceding. go before. —**prec′e·dence**, *n.*

prec′e·dent, *n.* past case used as example or guide.

pre′cept, *n.* rule of conduct.

pre·cep′tor, *n.* teacher.

pre′cinct, *n.* defined area.

pre′ci·os′i·ty (presh′ē os′-), *n., pl.* -ties. fastidious refinement.

pre′cious, *adj.* 1. valuable. 2. beloved. 3. affectedly refined. —**pre′cious·ly**, *adv.*

prec′i·pice (pres′ə pəs), *n.* sharp cliff.

pre·cip′i·tate′, *v.*, -tated, -tating, *adj., n.* —*v.* 1. hasten occurrence of. 2. separate (solid from solution). 3. condense (as vapor into rain). 4. fling down. —*adj.* (-tit). 5. rash or impetuous; hasty. —*n.* (-tit). 6. substance precipitated. 7. condensed moisture. —**pre·cip′i·tate·ly**, *adv.* —**pre·cip′i·ta′tion**, *n.*

pre·cip′i·tous, *adj.* 1. like a precipice. 2. precipitate.

pré·cis′ (prā sē′), *n.* summary.

pre·cise′, *adj.* 1. definite; exact. 2. distinct. 3. strict. —**pre·ci′sion, pre·cise′ness**, *n.* —**pre·cise′ly**, *adv.*

pre·clude′, *v.*, -cluded, -cluding. prevent. —**pre·clu′sion**, *n.* —**pre·clu′sive**, *adj.*

pre·co′cious, *adj.* advanced. —**pre·coc′i·ty**, *n.*

pre′cog·ni′tion, *n.* knowledge of future event through extrasensory means.

pre′-Co·lum′bi·an, *adj.* of the period before the arrival of Columbus in the Americas.

pre·con·ceive′, *v.*, -ceived, -ceiving. prejudge. —**pre′con·cep′tion**, *n.*

pre′con·di′tion, *n.* something necessary for desired result.

pre·cur′sor, *n.* 1. predecessor. 2. harbinger.

pre·da′cious, *adj.* predatory. Also, **pre·da′ceous.**

pred′a·tor, *n.* preying animal.

pred′a·tor′y (pred′ə tōr′ē), *adj.* 1. plundering. 2. feeding on other animals.

pred′e·ces′sor, *n.* one who precedes another.

pre·des′ti·na′tion, *n.* 1. determination beforehand. 2. destiny. —**pre·des′tine**, *v.*

pre′de·ter′mine, *v.,* **-mined, mining. 1.** decide in advance. **2.** predestine.
—**pre′de·ter′mi·na′tion,** *n.*

pre·dic′a·ment, *n.* trying or dangerous situation.

pred′i·cate, *v.,* **-cated, -cating,** *adj., n.* —*v.* (-kāt′). **1.** declare. **2.** find basis for. —*adj.* (-kit). **3.** *Gram.* belonging to predicate. —*n.* (-kit). **4.** *Gram.* part of sentence that expresses what is said of subject.
—**pred′i·ca′tion,** *n.*

pre·dict′, *v.* tell beforehand.
—**pre·dic′tion,** *n.*
—**pre·dict′a·ble,** *adj.*
—**pre·dic′tor,** *n.*

pre′di·lec′tion (pred′-), *n.* preference.

pre′dis·pose′, *v.,* **-posed, -posing. 1.** make susceptible. **2.** incline.
—**pre·dis′po·si′tion,** *n.*

pre·dom′i·nate′, *v.,* **-nated, -nating. 1.** be more powerful or common. **2.** control.
—**pre·dom′i·nance,** *n.*
—**pre·dom′i·nant,** *adj.*
—**pre·dom′i·nant·ly,** *adv.*

pre·em′i·nent, *adj.* superior.
—**pre·em′i·nence,** *n.*
—**pre·em′i·nent·ly,** *adv.*

pre·empt′, *v.* **1.** acquire or reserve before others. **2.** occupy to establish prior right to buy. Also, **pre-empt′.**
—**pre·emp′tion,** *n.*
—**pre·emp′tive,** *adj.*

preen, *v.* **1.** trim or clean (feathers or fur). **2.** dress (oneself) carefully.

pre·fab′ri·cate′, *v.,* **-cated, -cating.** build in parts for quick assembly.
—**pre′fab·ri·ca′tion,** *n.*
—**pre′fab,** *n. Informal.*

pref′ace, *n., v.,* **-aced, -acing.** —*n.* **1.** preliminary statement. —*v.* **2.** provide with preface.
—**pref′a·to′ry,** *adj.*

pre′fect, *n.* magistrate.
—**pre′fec·ture,** *n.*

pre·fer′, *v.,* **-ferred, -ferring. 1.** like better. **2.** put forward.

pref′er·a·ble, *adj.* more desirable. —**pref′er·a·bly,** *adv.*

pref′er·ence, *n.* **1.** liking of one above others. **2.** person or thing preferred. **3.** granting

of advantage to one.
—**pref′er•en′tial**, *adj.*

pre•fer′ment, *n.* promotion.

pre•fig′ure, *v.,* **-ured, -uring.** foreshadow.

pre′fix, *n.* **1.** syllable or syllables put before word to qualify its meaning. —*v.* (prē fiks′). **2.** put before.

preg′nant, *adj.* **1.** being with child. **2.** fraught. **3.** seminal. —**preg′nan•cy**, *n.*

pre•hen′sile (-sil), *adj.* adapted for grasping.

pre′his•tor′ic, *adj.* of time before recorded history.

pre•judge′, *v.,* **-judged, -judging.** judge prematurely.

prej′u•dice, *n., v.,* **-diced, -dicing.** —*n.* **1.** opinion formed without specific evidence. **2.** disadvantage. —*v.* **3.** affect with prejudice. —**prej′u•di′cial**, *adj.* —**prej′u•di′cial•ly**, *adv.*

prel′ate, *n.* church official.

pre•lim′i•nar′y, *adj., n., pl.* **-naries.** —*adj.* **1.** introductory. —*n.* **2.** preliminary stage.

pre•lit′er•ate, *adj.* lacking a written language.

prel′ude, *n.* **1.** *Music.* **a.** preliminary piece. **b.** brief composition. **2.** preliminary to major event.

pre•mar′i•tal, *adj.* before marriage.

pre′ma•ture′, *adj.* **1.** occurring too soon. **2.** overhasty. —**pre′ma•ture′ly**, *adv.* —**pre′ma•ture′ness, pre′ma•tu′ri•ty**, *n.*

pre•med′i•tate′, *v.,* **-tated, -tating.** plan in advance. —**pre′med•i•ta′tion**, *n.*

pre•mier′ (pri mēr′), *n.* **1.** prime minister. —*adj.* **2.** chief.

pre•miere′ (pri mēr′), *n.* first public performance.

prem′ise, *n.* **1.** *(pl.)* building with its grounds. **2.** thesis.

pre′mi•um, *n.* **1.** contest prize. **2.** bonus. **3.** insurance payment.

pre′mo•ni′tion, *n.* foreboding. —**pre•mon′i•to′ry**, *adj.*

pre•na′tal, *adj.* before birth.

pre•oc′cu•py′, *v.,* **-pied, -pying.** engross completely. —**pre•oc′cu•pa′tion**, *n.*

pre′or•dain′, *v.* decree in advance.

prep, *v.*, **prepped, prepping. 1.** get ready; prepare. **2.** attend preparatory school.

preparatory school, private school preparing students for college. Also, **prep school.**

pre·pare′, *v.*, **-pared, -paring. 1.** make or get ready. **2.** manufacture. —**prep′a·ra′tion,** *n.* —**pre·par′a·to′ry,** *adj.* —**pre·par′ed·ness,** *n.*

pre·pay′, *v.*, **-paid, -paying.** pay beforehand.

pre·pon′der·ant, *adj.* superior in force or numbers. —**pre·pon′der·ance,** *n.*

prep′o·si′tion, *n.* word placed before noun or adjective to indicate relationship of space, time, means, etc. —**prep′o·si′tion·al,** *adj.*

pre′pos·sess′ing, *adj.* impressing favorably.

pre·pos′ter·ous, *adj.* absurd.

prep′py, *n.*, *pl.* **-pies,** *adj.*, **-pier, -piest.** —*n.* **1.** student or graduate of a preparatory school. **2.** person who acts like a preppy. —*adj.* **3.** of or characteristic of a preppy.

pre′puce (prē′ py$\overline{oo}$s), *n.* skin covering head of penis.

pre′quel, *n.* sequel that prefigures the original.

pre·req′ui·site, *adj.* **1.** required in advance. —*n.* **2.** something prerequisite.

pre·rog′a·tive, *n.* special right or privilege.

pres., 1. present. **2.** president.

pres′age (pres′ij), *v.*, **-aged, -aging. 1.** portend. **2.** predict.

pres′by·o′pi·a (-bē ō′pē ə), *n.* farsightedness.

pres′by·ter, *n.* **1.** priest. **2.** elder.

pres′by·te′ri·an, *adj.* **1.** (of religious group) governed by presbytery. **2.** (*cap.*) designating Protestant church so governed. —*n.* **3.** (*cap.*) member of Presbyterian Church.

pres′by·ter′y, *n.*, *pl.* **-teries.** body of church elders and ministers.

pre′school′, *adj.* **1.** of or for children between infancy and kindergarten age. —*n.* **2.** school preschool children.

pre′sci·ence (prē′shē əns), *n.* foresight. —**pre′sci·ent,** *adj.*

pre·scribe′, *v.*, **-scribed, -scribing. 1.** order for use, as

medicine. **2.** order.
—**pre•scrip'tion,** *n.*
—**pre•scrip'tive,** *adj.*

pres'ence, *n.* **1.** fact of being present. **2.** vicinity. **3.** impressive personal quality.

presence of mind, ability to think clearly.

pres'ent, *adj.* **1.** being or occurring now. **2.** being at particular place. **3.** *Gram.* denoting action or state now in progress. —*n.* **4.** present time. **5.** *Gram.* present tense. **6.** thing bestowed as gift. —*v.* (pri zent'). **7.** give. **8.** exhibit. —**pres'en•ta'tion,** *n.*

pre•sent'a•ble, *adj.* suitable. —**pre•sent'a•bly,** *adv.*

pre•sen'ti•ment, *n.* feeling of something impending.

pres'ent•ly, *adv.* **1.** at present. **2.** soon.

pre•sent'ment, *n.* presentation.

pre•serve', *v.,* -served, -serving, *n.* —*v.* **1.** keep alive. **2.** keep safe. **3.** maintain. **4.** prepare (food) for long keeping. —*n.* **5.** (*pl.*) preserved fruit. **6.** place where game is protected. —**pres'er•va'tion,**

n. —**pres'er•va'tion•ist,** *n.*
—**pre•serv'a•tive,** *n., adj.*
—**pre•serv'er,** *n.*

pre•side', *v.,* -sided, -siding. act as chairman.

pres'i•dent, *n.* **1.** highest executive of republic. **2.** chief officer. —**pres'i•den•cy,** *n.*

pre•sid'i•um, *n., pl.* -iums, -ia. executive committee.

press, *v.* **1.** act upon with force. **2.** oppress. **3.** insist upon. **4.** urge to hurry or comply. —*n.* **5.** newspapers, etc., collectively. **6.** device for pressing or printing. **7.** crowd. **8.** urgency. —**press'er,** *n.*

press agent, person employed to obtain favorable publicity.

press conference, interview with reporters.

press'ing, *adj.* urgent.

press release, statement distributed to the press.

pres'sure, *n.* **1.** exertion of force upon thing. **2.** harassment. **3.** urgency.

pressure cooker, pot for cooking quickly by steam under pressure.

pressure group, group that tries to influence legislation in a particular way.

pres′sur•ize′, *v.*, **-ized, -izing.** produce normal air pressure at high altitudes. —**pres′sur•i•za′tion**, *n.*

pres′ti•dig′i•ta′tion (-dij′ə-), *n.* sleight of hand. —**pres′ti•dig′i•ta′tor**, *n.*

pres•tige′ (-tēzh′), *n.* distinguished reputation. —**pres′tig′ious** (-stij′əs), *adj.*

pres′to, *adv. Music.* quickly.

pre•sume′ (-zoom′), *v.*, **-sumed, -suming. 1.** take for granted. **2.** act with unjustified boldness. —**pre•sum′a•ble**, *adj.* —**pre•sum′a•bly**, *adv.* —**pre•sump′tion** (-zump′-), *n.* —**pre•sump′tive**, *adj.* —**pre•sump′tu•ous**, *adj.*

pre′sup•pose′, *v.*, **-posed, -posing.** assume. —**pre•sup′po•si′tion**, *n.*

pre•teen′, *n.* **1.** child between 10 and 13 years old. —*adj.* **2.** of or for preteens.

pre•tend′, *v.* **1.** make false appearance or claim. **2.** make believe. **3.** claim, as sovereignty. —**pre•tend′er**, *n.* —**pre•tense′**, *n.*

pre•ten′sion, *n.* **1.** ostentation. **2.** act of pretending. —**pre•ten′tious**, *adj.* —**pre•ten′tious•ly**, *adv.* —**pre•ten′tious•ness**, *n.*

pret′er•it, *Gram.* —*adj.* **1.** denoting action in past. —*n.* **2.** preterit tense.

pre′ter•nat′u•ral, *adj.* supernatural.

pre′text, *n.* ostensible reason.

pret′ty, *adj.*, **-tier, -tiest**, *adv.* —*adj.* **1.** pleasingly attractive. —*adv.* **2.** moderately. **3.** very. —**pret′ti•fy′**, *v.* —**pret′ti•ly**, *adv.* —**pret′ti•ness**, *n.*

pret′zel, *n.* crisp knotted biscuit.

pre•vail′, *v.* **1.** be widespread. **2.** reign. **3.** gain victory.

pre•vail′ing, *adj.* **1.** most common. **2.** having superior influence.

prev′a•lent, *adj.* widespread; general. —**prev′a•lence**, *n.*

pre•var′i•cate′, *v.*, **-cated, -cating.** speak evasively; lie. —**pre•var′i•ca′tion**, *n.* —**pre•var′i•ca′tor**, *n.*

pre•vent′, *n.* hinder; stop. —**pre•vent′a•ble**, **pre•vent′i•ble**, *adj.* —**pre•ven′tion**, *n.* —**pre•ven′tive**, **pre•vent′a•tive**, *adj.*, *n.*

pre′view′, *n., v.* view or show in advance.

pre′vi•ous, *adj.* occurring earlier. —**pre′vi•ous•ly**, *adv.*

prey, *n.* **1.** animal hunted as food. **2.** victim. —*v.* **3.** seize prey. **4.** victimize another. **5.** be obsessive.

pri•ap′ic, *adj.* phallic.

price, *n., v.,* **priced, pricing.** —*n.* **1.** amount for which thing is sold. **2.** value. —*v.* **3.** set price on. **4.** *Informal.* ask the price of.

price′less, *adj.* too valuable to set price on.

pric′ey, *adj.,* **pricier, priciest.** *Informal.* high-priced. —**pric′i•ness**, *n.*

prick, *n.* **1.** puncture by pointed object. —*v.* **2.** pierce. **3.** point.

prick′le, *n.* sharp point. —**prick′ly**, *adj.*

prickly heat, rash caused by inflammation of sweat glands.

pride, *n., v.,* **prided, priding.** —*n.* **1.** high opinion of worth of oneself or that associated with oneself. **2.** self-respect. **3.** that which one is proud of. **4.** group of lions. —*v.* **5.** feel pride. —**pride′ful**, *adj.*

priest, *n.* member of clergy. —**priest′ess**, *n.fem.* —**priest′hood**, *n.*

prig, *n.* self-righteous person. —**prig′gish**, *adj.*

prim, *adj.* stiffly proper. —**prim′ly**, *adv.* —**prim′ness**, *n.*

pri′ma•cy, *n., pl.* **-cies.** supremacy.

pri′ma don′na (prē′mə don′ə), **1.** principal female opera singer. **2.** fussy.

pri′ma fa′ci•e (prī′mə fā′shē ē′, fā′shē), *Law.* sufficient to establish a fact unless rebutted.

pri′mal, *adj.* **1.** first; original. **2.** most important.

pri•ma′ri•ly, *adv.* **1.** chiefly. **2.** originally.

pri′ma′ry, *adj., n., pl.* **-ries.** —*adj.* **1.** first in importance or in order. **2.** earliest. —*n.* **3.** preliminary election for choosing party candidates.

pri′mate (-māt), *n.* **1.** high church official. **2.** mammal of order including humans, apes, and monkeys.

prime, *adj., n., v.,* **primed, priming.** —*adj.* **1.** first in importance or quality. **2.**

original. —*n.* **3.** best stage or part. —*v.* **4.** prepare for special purpose or function.

prime meridian, meridian running through Greenwich, England, from which longitude east and west is reckoned.

prime minister, chief minister in some governments.

prim′er, *n.* elementary book.

prime rate, minimum interest rate charged by banks.

prime time, hours with largest audience.

pri•me′val, *adj.* of earliest time.

prim′i•tive, *adj.* **1.** earliest. **2.** simple; unrefined. —**prim′i•tive•ly,** *adv.* —**prim′i•tive•ness,** *n.*

pri′mo•gen′i•ture, *n.* **1.** state of being firstborn. **2.** inheritance by eldest son.

pri•mor′di•al (prī môr′dē əl), *adj.* existing at or from the very beginning.

primp, *v.* dress fussily.

prim′rose′, *n.* early-flowering garden perennial.

prince, *n.* high-ranking male member of royalty. —**prin′cess,** *n.fem.*

prince′ly, *adj.* lavish.

prin′ci•pal, *adj.* **1.** chief. —*n.* **2.** leader. **3.** head of school. **4.** person authorizing another to act for him. **5.** capital sum. —**prin′ci•pal•ly,** *adv.*

prin′ci•pal′i•ty, *n., pl.* **-ties.** state ruled by prince.

prin′ci•ple, *n.* **1.** rule of conduct or action. **2.** fundamental truth or doctrine. **3.** fundamental factor.

print, *v.* **1.** reproduce from inked types, plates, etc. **2.** write in letters like those of print. **3.** produce from negative. —*n.* **4.** printed state. **5.** (of book) stock available for sale. **6.** print lettering. **7.** anything printed. —**print′er,** *n.* —**print′a•ble,** *adj.*

print′out′, *n.* printed output.

pri′or, *adj.* **1.** earlier. —*adv.* **2.** previously. —*n.* **3.** officer in religious house. —**pri′or•ess,** *n.fem.* —**pri′o•ry,** *n.*

pri•or′i•tize′, *v.,* **-tized, -tizing.** arrange in order of priority.

pri·or′i·ty, *n., pl.* **-ties. 1.** state of being earlier. **2.** precedence.

prism (priz′əm), *n.* transparent body for dividing light into its spectrum. **—pris·mat′ic,** *adj.*

pris′on, *n.* building for confinement of criminals. **—pris′on·er,** *n.*

pris′sy, *adj.,* **-sier, -siest.** affectedly proper. **—pris′si·ness,** *n.*

pris′tine (-tēn), *adj.* pure.

pri′vate, *adj.* **1.** belonging to particular party. **2.** free of outside intrusion. **—n. 3.** soldier of lowest rank. **—pri′va·cy,** *n.* **—pri′vate·ly,** *adv.*

pri′va·teer′, *n.* privately owned vessel commissioned to fight. **—pri′va·teer′ing,** *n.*

private eye, *Informal.* private detective.

pri·va′tion, *n.* lack; need.

priv′et, *n.* evergreen shrub.

priv′i·lege, *n., v.,* **-leged, -leging. —n. 1.** special advantage. **—v. 2.** grant privilege to.

priv′y, *adj., n., pl.* **privies. —adj. 1.** participating in shared secret. **2.** private. **—n. 3.** outdoor toilet.

privy council, board of personal advisors.

prize, *n., v.,* **prized, prizing. —n. 1.** reward. **2.** thing worth striving for. **—v. 3.** esteem highly.

pro, *n., pl.* **pros,** *adv.* **—n. 1.** argument in favor of something. **2.** *Informal.* professional. **—adv. 3.** in favor of a plan, etc.

pro-, prefix meaning: **1.** favoring or supporting, as *prowar.* **2.** before or in front of, as *prognosis.*

prob′a·ble, *adj.* **1.** likely to occur, etc. **2.** affording ground for belief. **—prob′a·bil′i·ty,** *n.* **—prob′a·bly,** *adv.*

pro′bate, *n., adj., v.,* **-bated, -bating. —n. 1.** authentication of will. **—adj. 2.** of probate. **—v. 3.** establish will's validity.

pro·ba′tion, *n.* **1.** act of testing. **2.** period of such testing. **3.** conditional release, as from prison. **4.** period in which to redeem past mistakes. **—pro·ba′tion·er,** *n.* **—pro·ba′tion·ar′y,** *adj.*

probe, *v.*, **probed, probing**, *n.* —*v.* **1.** examine thoroughly. —*n.* **2.** device for exploring wounds. —**prob'er**, *n.*

pro'bi•ty, *n.* honesty.

prob'lem, *n.* matter involving uncertainty or difficulty. —**prob'lem•at'ic, prob'lem•at'i•cal**, *adj.*

pro•bos'cis (-bos'is), *n.*, *pl.* -**cises.** flexible snout.

pro•ced'ure (-sē'jər), *n.* course of action. —**pro•ced'ur•al**, *adj.*

pro•ceed', *v.* **1.** go forward. **2.** carry on action. **3.** issue forth. —*n.* (prō'sēd). **4.** (*pl.*). sum derived from sale, etc.

pro•ceed'ing, *n.* **1.** action or conduct. **2.** (*pl.*) **a.** records of society. **b.** legal action.

proc'ess, *n.* **1.** series of actions toward given end. **2.** continuous action. **3.** legal summons. **4.** projecting growth. —*v.* **5.** treat by particular process.

pro•ces'sion, *n.* ceremonial movement; parade.

pro•ces'sion•al, *n.* **1.** hymn sung during procession. **2.** hymnal.

pro-choice', *adj.* supporting the right to legalized abortion.

pro•claim', *v.* announce. —**proc'la•ma'tion**, *n.*

pro•cliv'i•ty, *n.*, *pl.* -**ties.** natural tendency.

pro•cras'ti•nate', *v.*, -**nated, -nating.** delay from temperamental causes. —**pro•cras'ti•na'tion**, *n.* —**pro•cras'ti•na'tor**, *n.*

pro'cre•ate', *v.* -**ated, -ating.** produce or have offspring. —**pro'cre•a'tion**, *n.*

proc•tol'o•gy, *n.* branch of medicine dealing with rectum. —**proc•tol'o•gist**, *n.*

proc'tor, *n.* **1.** person who watches over students at examinations. —*v.* **2.** supervise or monitor.

pro•cure', *v.* -**cured, -curing.** **1.** get; obtain. **2.** cause. **3.** hire prostitutes. —**pro•cur'a•ble**, *adj.* —**pro•cure'ment**, *n.*

pro•cur'er, *n.* **1.** one that procures. **2.** Also, **pro•cur'ess**, *fem.* Madam.

prod, *v.*, **prodded, prodding**, *n.* —*v.* **1.** poke. **2.** goad. —*n.* **3.** poke. **4.** goading tool.

prod′i•gal, *adj.* **1.** wastefully extravagant. **2.** lavish. —*n.* **3.** spendthrift.

prod′i•gal′i•ty, *n., pl.* **-ties.** extravagance; lavishness.

pro•di′gious (-dij′əs), *adj.* huge; wonderful. —**pro•di′gious•ly,** *adv.*

prod′i•gy, *n., pl.* **-gies. 1.** very gifted person. **2.** wonderful thing.

pro•duce′, *v.,* **-duced, -ducing,** *n.* —*v.* **1.** bring into existence; create. **2.** bear, as young, fruit. **3.** exhibit. —*n.* (prō′dōōs). **4.** product. **5.** agricultural products. —**pro•duc′er,** *n.* —**pro•duc′tion,** *n.* —**pro•duc′tive,** *adj.* —**pro′duc•tiv′i•ty,** *n.*

prod′uct, *n.* **1.** result. **2.** result obtained by multiplying.

pro•fane′, *adj., v.,* **-faned, -faning.** —*adj.* **1.** irreverent toward sacred things. **2.** secular. —*v.* **3.** defile. **4.** treat (sacred thing) with contempt. —**prof′a•na′tion,** *n.*

pro•fan′i•ty, *n., pl.* **-ties. 1.** profane quality. **2.** vulgar language.

pro•fess′, *v.* **1.** declare. **2.** affirm faith in. **3.** claim. —**pro•fessed′,** *adj.*

pro•fes′sion, *n.* **1.** learned vocation. **2.** assertion.

pro•fes′sion•al, *adj.* **1.** following occupation for gain. **2.** of or engaged in profession. —*n.* **3.** professional person. —**pro•fes′sion•al•ism,** *n.* —**pro•fes′sion•al•ly,** *adv.*

pro•fes′sor, *n.* college teacher of highest rank. —**pro′fes•so′ri•al,** *adj.*

prof′fer, *v., n.* offer.

pro•fi′cient, *adj.* expert. —**pro•fi′cien•cy,** *n.* —**pro•fi′cient•ly,** *adv.*

pro′file, *n.* **1.** side view. **2.** informal biographical sketch.

prof′it, *n.* **1.** revenue. **2.** benefit. —*v.* **3.** gain advantage. **4.** make profit. —**prof′it•a•ble,** *adj.* —**prof′it•a•bly,** *adv.* —**prof′it•less,** *adj.*

prof′it•eer′, *n.* **1.** person who makes unfair profit. —*v.* **2.** act as profiteer.

prof′li•gate (-git), *adj.* **1.** immoral. **2.** extravagant. —**prof′li•gate,** *n.* —**prof′li•ga•cy,** *n.*

pro for′ma, done as a matter of form.

pro•found′, *adj.* 1. thinking deeply. 2. intense. 3. deep.
—**pro•found′ly,** *adv.*
—**pro•fun′di•ty,** *n.*

pro•fuse′, *adj.* abundant.
—**pro•fuse′ly,** *adv.*
—**pro•fu′sion,** *n.*

pro•gen′i•tor, *n.* ancestor.

prog′e•ny, *n.pl.* offspring.

pro•ges′ter•one, *n.* female hormone that prepares uterus for fertilized ovum.

prog′na•thous, *adj.* having protrusive jaws.

prog•no′sis, *n., pl.* **-noses** (-nō′sēz). medical forecast.

prog•nos′ti•cate′, *v.,* **-cated, -cating.** predict.
—**prog•nos′ti•ca′tion,** *n.*

pro′gram, *n., v.,* **-grammed, -gramming.** —*n.* 1. plan of things to do. 2. schedule of entertainments. 3. show. 4. plan for computerized problem solving. —*v.* 5. make program for.
—**pro′gram•ma•ble,** *adj.*
—**pro′gram•mat′ic,** *adj.*
—**pro′gram•mer,** *n.*

prog′ress, *n.* 1. advancement. 2. improvement. 3. growth.

—*v.* 4. make progress.
—**pro•gres′sion,** *n.*
—**pro•gres′sive,** *adj., n.*
—**pro•gres′sive•ly,** *adv.*

pro•hib′it, *v.* forbid; prevent.

pro′hi•bi′tion, *n.* 1. act of prohibiting. 2. (*cap.*) period, 1920–33, when manufacture and sale of alcoholic drinks was forbidden in U.S.
—**pro′hi•bi′tion•ist,** *n.*

pro•hib′i•tive, *adj.* 1. serving to prohibit. 2. too expensive.

proj′ect, *n.* 1. something planned. —*v.* (prə jekt′). 2. plan; contemplate. 3. impel forward. 4. display upon surface. 5. protrude.
—**pro•jec′tion,** *n.*
—**pro•jec′tor,** *n.*

pro•jec′tile, *n.* object fired with explosive force.

pro•jec′tion•ist, *n.* operator of motion-picture projector.

pro′le•tar′i•at, *n.* working or impoverished class.
—**pro′le•tar′i•an,** *adj., n.*

pro-life′, *adj.* opposed to legalized abortion.

pro•lif′er•ate′, *v.,* **-ated, -ating.** spread rapidly.
—**pro•lif′er•a′tion,** *n.*

pro•lif′ic, *adj.* productive.

pro•lix′, *adj.* tediously long and wordy. —**pro•lix′i•ty,** *n.*

pro′logue, *n.* introductory part of novel, play, etc.

pro•long′, *v.* lengthen. —**pro′lon•ga′tion,** *n.*

prom, *n.* formal dance at high school or college.

prom′e•nade′ (-nād′, -näd′), *n., v.,* **-naded, -nading.** —*n.* 1. leisurely walk. 2. space for such walk. —*v.* 3. stroll.

prom′i•nent, *adj.* 1. conspicuous. 2. projecting. 3. well-known. —**prom′i•nence,** *n.* —**prom′i•nent•ly,** *adv.*

pro•mis′cu•ous, *adj.* 1. having numerous sexual partners. 2. indiscriminate. —**prom′is•cu′i•ty,** *n.* —**pro•mis′cu•ous•ly,** *adv.*

prom′ise, *n., v.,* **-ised, -ising.** —*n.* 1. assurance that one will act as specified. 2. indication of future excellence. —*v.* 3. assure by promise. 4. afford ground for expectation. —**prom′is•ing,** *adj.*

prom′is•so′ry, *adj.* containing promise, esp. of payment.

prom′on•to′ry, *n., pl.* **-ries.** high peak projecting into sea or overlooking low land.

pro•mote′, *v.,* **-moted, -moting.** 1. further progress of. 2. advance. 3. organize. —**pro•mot′er,** *n.* —**pro•mo′tion,** *n.*

prompt, *adj.* 1. ready to act. 2. done at once. —*v.* 3. incite to action. 4. suggest (action, etc.). —**prompt′er,** *n.* —**prompt′ly,** *adv.* —**prompt′ness, promp′ti•tude′,** *n.*

prom′ul•gate, *v.,* **-gated, -gating.** proclaim formally. —**prom′ul•ga′tion,** *n.* —**prom′ul•ga′tor,** *n.*

prone, *adj.* 1. likely; inclined. 2. lying flat.

prong, *n.* point.

pro′noun′, *n.* word used as substitute for noun. —**pro•nom′i•nal,** *adj.*

pro•nounce′, *v.,* **-nounced, -nouncing.** 1. articulate. 2. declare to be. 3. announce. —**pro•nounce′ment,** *n.*

pro•nounced′, *adj.* 1. strongly marked. 2. decided.

pron′to, *adv.* promptly.

pro•nun′ci•a′tion, *n.* articulation.

proof, *n.* 1. confirmation. 2. standard strength, as of liquors. 3. trial printing. —*adj.* 4. resisting perfectly.

-proof, suffix meaning resistant.

proof'read', *v.,* -read, -reading. read to mark errors. —**proof'read'er,** *n.*

prop, *n., v.,* **propped, propping.** —*n.* 1. support. 2. propeller. —*v.* 3. support with prop.

prop'a•gan'da, *n.* doctrines disseminated by organization. —**prop'a•gan'dist,** *n.* —**prop'a•gan'dize,** *v.*

prop'a•gate', *v.,* -gated, -gating. 1. reproduce. 2. transmit (doctrine, etc.). —**prop'a•ga'tion,** *n.*

pro'pane, *n.* flammable gas.

pro•pel', *v.,* -pelled, -pelling. drive forward. —**pro•pel'lant, pro•pel'lent,** *n.*

pro•pel'ler, *n.* screwlike propelling device.

pro•pen'si•ty, *n., pl.* -ties. inclination.

prop'er, *adj.* 1. suitable; fitting. 2. correct. 3. designating particular person, place, or thing. —**prop'er•ly,** *adv.*

prop'er•ty, *n., pl.* -ties. 1. that which one owns. 2. attribute.

proph'e•sy (-sī), *v.,* -sied, -sying. foretell; predict. —**proph'e•cy** (-sē), *n.*

proph'et, *n.* 1. person who speaks for God. 2. inspired leader. 3. person who predicts. —**pro•phet'ic,** *adj.* —**pro•phet'i•cal•ly,** *adv.*

pro'phy•lax'is (prō'fə lak'sis), *n.* prevention of disease. —**pro'phy•lac'tic,** *adj., n.*

pro•pin'qui•ty, *n.* nearness.

pro•pi'ti•ate' (prə pish'ē āt'), *v.,* -ated, -ating. appease.

pro•pi'tious, *adj.* favorable. —**pro•pi'tious•ly,** *adv.*

pro•po'nent, *n.* advocate.

pro•por'tion, *n.* 1. proper relation of dimensions. 2. symmetry. 3. (*pl.*) dimensions. —*v.* 4. adjust in proper relation. —**pro•por'tion•al,** *adj.*

pro•por'tion•ate, *adj.* being in due proportion. —**pro•por'tion•ate•ly,** *adv.*

pro•pos'al, *n.* 1. proposition. 2. offer of marriage.

pro•pose', *v.,* -posed, -posing. 1. suggest. 2. intend. 3. offer marriage.

prop′o•si′tion, *n.* 1. proposed plan. 2. statement that affirms or denies. 3. proposal of sex. —*v.* 4. make proposition to.

pro•pound′, *v.* offer for consideration.

pro•pri′e•tor, *n.* manager. —**pro•pri′e•tar′y,** *adj.*

pro•pri′e•ty, *n., pl.* **-ties.** 1. appropriateness. 2. (*pl.*) morality; correctness.

pro•pul′sion, *n.* propelling force. —**pro•pul′sive,** *adj.*

pro•rate′, *v.,* **-rated, -rating.** divide proportionately.

pro•sa′ic, *adj.* commonplace. —**pro•sa′i•cal•ly,** *adv.*

pro•sce′ni•um, *n., pl.* **-niums, -nia.** arch separating stage from auditorium. Also, **proscenium arch.**

pro•scribe′, *v.* **-scribed, -scribing.** prohibit. —**pro•scrip′tion,** *n.*

prose, *n.* ordinary language.

pros′e•cute′, *v.,* **-cuted, -cuting.** 1. begin legal proceedings against. 2. go on with (task, etc.). —**pros′e•cu′tion,** *n.* —**pros′e•cu′tor,** *n.*

pros′e•lyte′ (pros′ə līt′), *n., v.,* **-lyted, -lyting.** convert. —**pros′e•lyt•ize′,** *v.*

pros′o•dy (pros′ə dē), *n., pl.* **-dies.** study of poetic meters and versification.

pros′pect, *n.* 1. likelihood of success. 2. outlook; view. 3. potential customer. —*v.* 4. search. —**pro•spec′tive,** *adj.* —**pros′pec•tor,** *n.*

pro•spec′tus, *n.* description of new investment.

pros′per, *v.* be successful. —**pros•per′i•ty,** *n.* —**pros′per•ous,** *adj.* —**pros′per•ous•ly,** *adv.*

pros′tate, *n.* gland in males at base of bladder.

pros•the′sis (pros thē′sis), *n., pl.* **-ses** (-sēz). device that substitutes for body part. —**pros•thet′ic,** *adj.*

pros′ti•tute′, *n., v.,* **-tuted, -tuting.** —*n.* 1. person who engages in sexual intercourse for money. —*v.* 2. put to base use. —**pros′ti•tu′tion,** *n.*

pros′trate, *v.,* **-trated, -trating,** *adj.* —*v.* 1. lay (oneself) face downward, esp. in humility. 2. exhaust. —*adj.* 3. lying flat. 4.

helpless. 5. weak or exhausted. —**pros•tra′tion,** *n.*

pros′y, *adj.,* **prosier, prosiest.** dull.

pro•tag′o•nist, *n.* main character.

pro′te•an, *adj.* assuming different forms.

pro•tect′, *v.* shield; defend.
—**pro•tec′tion,** *n.*
—**pro•tec′tive,** *adj.*
—**pro•tec′tive•ly,** *adv.*
—**pro•tec′tor,** *n.*

pro•tec′tion•ism, *n.* practice of protecting domestic industries from foreign competition by imposing import duties.

pro•tec′tor•ate, *n.* **1.** relation by which strong state partly controls weaker state. **2.** such weaker state.

pro′té•gé′ (prō′tə zhā′), *n.* one under patronage of another. —**pro′té•gée′,** *n.fem.*

pro′tein, *n.* nitrogenous compound.

pro tempore, temporarily.

pro′test, *n.* **1.** objection. —*v.* **2.** express objection. **3.** declare. —**prot′es•ta′tion,** *n.* —**pro•test′er,** *n.*

Prot′es•tant, *n.* Christian who belongs to a church that began by breaking away from the Roman Catholic Church in the 16th century. —**Prot′es•tant•ism′,** *n.*

proto-, prefix meaning earliest or foremost.

pro′to•col′, *n.* propriety.

pro′ton, *n.* part of atom bearing positive charge.

pro′to•plasm′, *n.* basis of living matter.

pro′to•type′, *n.* model. —**pro′to•typ′i•cal,** *adj.*

pro′to•zo′an (-zō′ən), *n., pl.* **-zoans, -zoa.** any of various one-celled organisms that obtain nourishment by ingesting food. —**pro′to•zo′ic,** *adj.*

pro•tract′, *v.* lengthen. —**pro•trac′tion,** *n.*

pro•trac′tor, *n.* instrument for measuring angles.

pro•trude′, *v.,* **-truded, -truding.** project; extend. —**pro•tru′sion,** *n.* —**pro•tru′sive,** *adj.*

pro•tu′ber•ant, *adj.* bulging out. —**pro•tu′ber•ance,** *n.*

proud, *adj.* 1. having pride. 2. arrogant. 3. magnificent. —**proud′ly,** *adv.*

prove, *v.*, **proved, proving.** 1. establish as fact. 2. test. 3. be or become ultimately. —**prov′a•ble,** *adj.*

prov′e•nance, *n.* place or source of origin.

prov′en•der, *n.* fodder.

prov′erb, *n.* wise, long-current saying. —**pro•ver′bi•al,** *adj.*

pro•vide′, *v.*, **-vided, -viding.** 1. supply. 2. yield. 3. prepare beforehand. —**pro•vid′er,** *n.*

pro•vid′ed, *conj.* if.

prov′i•dence, *n.* 1. God's care. 2. economy.

prov′i•dent, *adj.* prudent.

prov′i•den′tial, *adj.* coming as godsend.

prov′ince, *n.* 1. administrative unit of country. 2. sphere.

pro•vin′cial, *adj.* 1. of province. 2. unsophisticated.

pro•vi′sion, *n.* 1. something stated as necessary or binding. 2. act of providing. 3. what is provided. 4. arrangement beforehand. 5. (*pl.*) food supply. —*v.* 6. supply with provisions.

pro•vi′sion•al, *adj.* temporary.

pro•vi′so, *n.*, *pl.* **-sos, -soes.** stipulation or condition.

pro•vo′ca•teur′ (prə vok′ə tûr′, -tŏŏr′), *n.* person who provokes trouble.

pro•voke′, *v.*, **-voked, -voking.** 1. exasperate. 2. arouse. —**prov′o•ca′tion,** *n.* —**pro•voc′a•tive,** *adj.* —**pro•voc′a•tive•ly,** *adv.*

pro′vost (prō′ vōst), *n.* 1. superintendent. 2. high-ranking university administrator.

pro′vost marshal (prō′vō), *Mil.* head of police.

prow, *n.* fore part of ship.

prow′ess, *n.* 1. exceptional ability. 2. bravery.

prowl, *v.* roam or search stealthily. —**prowl′er,** *n.*

prox•im′i•ty, *n.* nearness.

prox′y, *n.*, *pl.* **proxies.** agent.

prude, *n.* excessively proper person. —**prud′er•y,** *n.* —**prud′ish,** *adj.*

pru′dence, *n.* caution. —**pru′dent, pru•den′tial,** *adj.* —**pru′dent•ly,** *adv.*

prune, *v.,* **pruned, pruning,** *n.*
—*v.* **1.** cut off (branches, etc.).
—*n.* **2.** kind of plum.

pru′ri•ent (pro͞or′ē ənt), *adj.*
having lewd thoughts.
—**pru′ri•ence,** *n.*

pry, *v.,* **pried, prying,** *n.* —*v.* **1.**
look or inquire too curiously.
2. move with lever. —*n.* **3.** act
of prying. **4.** prying person. **5.**
lever.

P.S., 1. Also, **p.s.** postscript. **2.**
Public School.

psalm, *n.* sacred song.

pseu′do (so͞o′dō), *adj.* false.

pseu′do•nym, *n.* pen name.
—**pseu•don′y•mous,** *adj.*

psit′ta•co′sis, *n.* disease
affecting birds and
transmissible to humans.

pso•ri′a•sis (sə rī′ə sis), *n.*
chronic skin disease
characterized by scaly
patches.

psych, *v. Informal.* **1.**
intimidate. **2.** prepare
psychologically.

psy′che (sī′kē), *n.* human
mind.

psy′che•del′ic (sī′kə del′ik),
adj. noting a mental state of
distorted sense perceptions
and hallucinations.

psy•chi′a•try, *n.* science of
mental diseases.
—**psy′chi•at′ric,** *adj.*
—**psy•chi′a•trist,** *n.*

psy′chic, *adj.* **1.** of the psyche.
2. pertaining to an apparently
nonphysical force or agency.
—*n.* **3.** person sensitive to
psychic influences.

psy′cho•ac′tive, *adj.*
affecting mental state.

psy′cho•a•nal′y•sis, *n.* **1.**
study of conscious and
unconscious psychological
processes. **2.** treatment
according to such study.
—**psy′cho•an′a•lyst,** *n.*
—**psy′cho•an′a•lyze′,** *v.*

psy′cho•gen′ic, *adj.*
originating in mental process.

psy•chol′o•gy, *n.* science of
mental states and behavior.
—**psy′cho•log′i•cal,** *adj.*
—**psy′cho•log′i•cal•ly,** *adv.*
—**psy•chol′o•gist,** *n.*

psy′cho•neu•ro′sis, *n., pl.*
-ses. emotional disorder.
—**psy′cho•neu•rot′ic,** *adj., n.*

psy•chop′a•thy (-kop′-), *n.,*
pl. **-thies.** mental disease.
—**psy′cho•path′,** *n.*
—**psy′cho•path′ic,** *adj.*

psy·cho'sis, *n., pl.* **-ses.** severe mental disease. —**psy·chot'ic,** *adj., n.*

psy'cho·so·mat'ic, *adj.* (of physical disorder) caused by one's emotional state.

psy'cho·ther'a·py, *n., pl.* **-pies.** treatment of mental disorders. —**psy'cho·ther'a·pist,** *n.*

psy'cho·tro'pic, *adj.* affecting mental activity.

pt., **1.** part. **2.** pint. **3.** point.

ptar'mi·gan (tär'-), *n.* species of mountain grouse.

pter'o·dac'tyl (ter'ə dak'til), *n.* extinct flying reptile.

pto'maine (tō'-), *n.* substance produced during decay of plant and animal matter.

pub, *n. Brit. Informal.* tavern.

pu'ber·ty (pyoo'-), *n.* sexual maturity. —**pu'ber·tal,** *adj.*

pu·bes'cent, *adj.* arriving at puberty. —**pu·bes'cence,** *n.*

pu'bic, *adj.* of or near the genitals.

pub'lic, *adj.* **1.** of or for people generally. **2.** open to view or knowledge of all. —*n.* **3.** people. —**pub'lic·ly,** *adv.*

pub'li·ca'tion, *n.* **1.** publishing of book, etc. **2.** item published.

public defender, lawyer who represents indigent clients at public expense.

public domain, legal status of material not protected by copyright or patent.

pub·lic'i·ty, *n.* **1.** public attention. **2.** material promoting this.

pub'li·cize', *v.,* **-cized, -cizing.** bring to public notice. —**pub'li·cist,** *n.*

public relations, actions of organization in promoting goodwill with the public.

pub'lish, *v.* **1.** issue (book, paper, etc.) for general distribution. **2.** announce publicly. —**pub'lish·er,** *n.*

puck, *n.* black rubber disk hit into goal in hockey.

puck'er, *v., n.* wrinkle.

puck'ish, *adj.* mischievous.

pud'ding (pood'-), *n.* soft, creamy dish, usually dessert.

pud'dle (pud'-), *n., v.,* **-dled, -dling.** —*n.* **1.** small pool of water, esp. dirty water. —*v.* **2.** fill with puddles.

pudg′y, *adj.,* **pudgier, pudgiest.** chubby. —**pudg′i•ness,** *n.*

pueb′lo (pweb′lō), *n., pl.* **-los.** village of certain Southwestern Indians.

pu′er•ile (pyoo′ər il), *adj.* childish. —**pu′er•il′i•ty,** *n.*

puff, *n.* **1.** short blast of wind. **2.** inflated part. **3.** anything soft and light. —*v.* **4.** blow with puffs. **5.** breathe hard and fast. **6.** inflate. —**puff′i•ness,** *n.* —**puff′y,** *adj.*

puf′fin, *n.* sea bird.

pug, *n.* kind of dog.

pu′gil•ism, *n.* boxing. —**pu′gil•ist,** *n.* —**pu′gi•lis′tic,** *adj.*

pug•na′cious, *adj.* fond of fighting. —**pug•nac′i•ty,** *n.*

pug nose, short, broad, somewhat turned-up nose.

puke, *v.,* **puked, puking,** *n.* *Slang.* vomit.

pul′chri•tude′, *n.* beauty.

pule, *v.,* **puled, puling.** whine.

pull, *v.* **1.** draw; haul. **2.** tear. **3.** move with force. —*n.* **4.** act of pulling. **5.** force. **6.** handle. **7.** *Informal.* influence.

pul′let, *n.* young hen.

pul′ley, *n.* wheel for guiding rope.

Pull′man, *n.* sleeping car on railroad.

pull′out′, *n.* **1.** withdrawal. **2.** section that can be pulled out.

pull′o′ver, *adj.* **1.** put on by being drawn over the head. —*n.* **2.** pullover garment.

pul′mo•nar′y, *adj.* of lungs.

pulp, *n.* **1.** soft fleshy part, as of fruit or tooth. **2.** any soft mass. —*v.* **3.** make or become pulp. —**pulp′y,** *adj.*

pul′pit, *n.* platform in church from which service is conducted.

pul′sar (-sär), *n.* source of pulsating energy among stars.

pul′sate, *v.,* **-sated, -sating.** throb. —**pul•sa′tion,** *n.*

pulse, *n., v.,* **pulsed, pulsing.** —*n.* **1.** heartbeat. —*v.* **2.** pulsate.

pul′ver•ize′, *v.,* **-ized, -izing.** reduce to powder. —**pul′ver•i•za′tion,** *n.*

pu′ma, *n.* cougar.

pum′ice, *n.* porous volcanic glass used as abrasive.

pum′mel, *v.,* **-meled, -meling.** strike; beat.

pump, *n.* 1. apparatus for raising or driving fluids. 2. women's shoe. —*v.* 3. raise or drive with pump. 4. *Informal.* try to get information from.

pum′per•nick′el, *n.* hard, sour rye bread.

pump′kin, *n.* orange squash.

pun, *n., v.,* **punned, punning.** —*n.* 1. wordplay using homophones. —*v.* 2. make pun. —**pun′ster,** *n.*

punch, *n.* 1. thrusting blow. 2. tool for piercing material. 3. sweetened beverage. —*v.* 4. hit with thrusting blow. 5. drive (cattle). 6. cut or indent with punch. —**punch′er,** *n.*

punch′-drunk′, *adj.* 1. showing symptoms of cerebral injury. 2. dazed.

pun′cheon, *n.* large cask.

punch line, climactic phrase in a joke.

punch′y, *adj.,* **punchier, punchiest.** 1. dazed, as if having been punched. 2. forceful.

punc•til′i•ous, *adj.* exact or careful in conduct.

punc′tu•al, *adj.* on time. —**punc′tu•al′i•ty,** *n.* —**punc′tu•al•ly,** *adv.*

punc′tu•ate′, *v.,* **-ated, -ating.** 1. mark with punctuation. 2. accent periodically.

punc′tu•a′tion, *n.* use of commas, semicolons, etc.

punc′ture, *n., v.,* **-tured, -turing.** —*n.* 1. perforation. —*v.* 2. perforate.

pun′dit, *n.* learned person.

pun′gent, *adj.* 1. sharp in taste. 2. biting. —**pun′gen•cy,** *n.* —**pun′gent•ly,** *adv.*

pun′ish, *v.* subject to pain, confinement, loss, etc., for offense. —**pun′ish•a•ble,** *adj.* —**pun′ish•ment,** *n.*

pu′ni•tive, *adj.* punishing.

punk, *n.* 1. substance that will smolder, used esp. to light fires. 2. *Slang.* something or someone unimportant. 3. *Slang.* hoodlum. 4. Also, **punk rock.** rock music marked by loudness and aggressive lyrics. 5. style suggesting defiance of social norms. —*adj.* 6. *Informal.* poor in quality. 7. of punk rock or punk style.

punt, *n.* 1. kick in football. 2. shallow flat-bottomed boat. —*v.* 3. kick (dropped ball) before it touches ground. 4. propel (boat) with pole.

pu′ny, *adj.,* **-nier, -niest.** small and weak.

pup, *n.* young dog.

pu′pa (pyoo′pə), *n., pl.* **-pae, -pas.** insect in stage between larva and winged adult. —**pu′pal,** *adj.*

pu′pil, *n.* **1.** student. **2.** opening in iris of eye.

pup′pet, *n.* **1.** doll or figure manipulated by hand or strings. **2.** person, government, etc., whose actions are controlled by another. —**pup′pet•ry,** *n.*

pup′pet•eer′, *n.* person who manipulates puppets.

pup′py, *n., pl.* **-pies.** young dog.

pup tent, small tent.

pur′blind (pûr′-), *adj.* **1.** partially blind. **2.** lacking understanding.

pur′chase, *v.,* **-chased, -chasing,** *n.* —*v.* **1.** buy. —*n.* **2.** acquisition by payment. **3.** what is purchased. **4.** leverage. —**pur′chas•er,** *n.*

pure, *adj.,* **purer, purest. 1.** free of pollutants. **2.** abstract. **3.** absolute. **4.** chaste. —**pure′ly,** *adv.* —**pure′ness,** *n.*

pure′bred, *adj.* **1.** having ancestors over many generations from a recognized breed. —*n.* **2.** purebred animal.

pu•rée′ (pyoo rā′), *n., v.,* **-réed, -réeing.** —*n.* **1.** cooked food that has been blended. —*v.* **2.** make purée of.

pur′ga•to′ry, *n., pl.* **-ries. 1.** *Rom. Cath. Theol.* condition or place of purification, after death, from venial sins. **2.** any condition or place of temporary punishment.

purge, *v.,* **purged, purging,** *n.* —*v.* **1.** cleanse; purify. **2.** rid. **3.** clear by causing evacuation. —*n.* **4.** act or means of purging. —**pur•ga′tion,** *n.* —**pur′ga•tive,** *adj., n.*

pu′ri•fy′, *v.,* **-fied, -fying.** make or become pure. —**pu′ri•fi•ca′tion,** *n.*

Pu′rim (poor′im), *n.* Jewish commemorative festival.

pur′ism, *n.* insistence on purity. —**pur′ist,** *n.*

Pu′ri•tan, *n.* **1.** member of strict Protestant group originating in 16th-century

England. 2. (*l.c.*) person of strict moral views.
—**pu′ri•tan′i•cal,** *adj.*

pu′ri•ty, *n.* condition of being pure.

purl, *v.* invert stitch.

pur′lieu, *n., pl.* **-lieus.** 1. (*pl.*) neighborhood. 2. suburb.

pur•loin′, *v.* steal.

pur′ple, *n.* 1. color blended of red and blue. —*adj.* 2. of or like purple.

pur•port′, *v.* 1. claim. 2. imply. —*n.* (pûr′pōrt). 3. meaning.

pur′pose, *n., v.,* **-posed, -posing.** —*n.* 1. object; aim; intention. —*v.* 2. intend. —**pur′pose•ful,** *adj.* —**pur′pose•less,** *adj.*

purr, *v.* 1. utter low continuous sound. —*n.* 2. this sound.

purse, *n., v.,* **pursed, pursing.** —*n.* 1. small case for carrying money. 2. money offered as prize. —*v.* 3. pucker.

purs′er, *n.* financial officer.

pur•su′ant, *adv.* according.

pur•sue′, *v.,* **-sued, -suing.** 1. follow to catch. 2. carry on (studies, etc.). —**pur•su′ance,** *n.* —**pur•su′er,** *n.*

pur•suit′, *n.* 1. act of pursuing. 2. quest. 3. occupation.

pu′ru•lent (pyŏŏr′ə lənt), *adj.* full of pus. —**pu′ru•lence,** *n.*

pur•vey′, *n.* provide; supply. —**pur•vey′ance,** *n.* —**pur•vey′or,** *n.*

pur′view (pûr′vyŏŏ), *n.* 1. range of operation, authority, or concern. 2. range of vision, insight, or understanding.

pus, *n.* liquid found in sores.

push, *v.* 1. exert force. 2. urge. —*n.* 3. act of pushing. 4. strong effort. —**push′er,** *n.*

push′o′ver, *n. Informal.* one easily victimized or overcome.

push′y, *adj.,* **pushier, pushiest.** obnoxiously self-assertive. —**push′i•ness,** *n.*

pu′sil•lan′i•mous, *adj.* cowardly.

puss′y, *n., pl.* **pussies.** cat. Also, **puss.**

puss′y•foot′, *v.* 1. go stealthily. 2. act timidly.

pussy willow, small willow.

pus′tule (-chŏŏl), *n.* pimple.

put, *v.,* **put, putting,** *n.* —*v.* 1. place. 2. set, as to task. 3. express. 4. apply. 5. impose. 6. throw. —*n.* 7. throw.

pu′ta•tive, *adj.* reputed.

put′-down′, *n. Informal.* snubbing remark.

pu′tre•fy′, *v.,* **-fied, -fying.** rot. —**pu′tre•fac′tion,** *n.*

pu•tres′cent, *adj.* becoming putrid. —**pu•tres′cence,** *n.*

pu′trid, *adj.* rotten.

putsch (pŏŏch), *n.* sudden political revolt or uprising.

putt, *v.* **1.** strike (golf ball) gently. —*n.* **2.** such strike.

put′ter, *v.* **1.** dawdle. —*n.* **2.** club for putting.

put′ty, *n., v.,* **-tied, -tying.** —*n.* **1.** cement of whiting and oil. —*v.* **2.** secure with putty.

puz′zle, *n., v.,* **-zled, -zling.** —*n.* **1.** device or question offering difficulties. —*v.* **2.** perplex. —**puz′zle•ment,** *n.*

Pvt., Private.

PX, post exchange.

pyg′my, *n., pl.* **-mies.** dwarf.

py′lon, *n.* tall thin structure.

py•lo′rus, *n., pl.* **-lori.** opening between stomach and intestine. —**py•lor′ic,** *adj.*

py′or•rhe′a, *n.* gum disease.

pyr′a•mid, *n.* **1.** solid with triangular sides meeting in point. —*v.* **2.** increase gradually. —**py•ram′i•dal,** *adj.*

pyre, *n.* heap of wood, esp. for burning corpse.

py′rite, *n.* common yellow mineral of low value.

py′ro•ma′ni•a, *n.* mania for setting fires. —**py′ro•ma′ni•ac′,** *n.*

py′ro•tech′nics, *n.* fireworks. —**py′ro•tech′nic,** *adj.*

py′thon, *n.* large snake that kills by constriction.

pyx, *n.* container in which Eucharist is kept.

Q, q, *n.* seventeenth letter of English alphabet.

Q.E.D., which was to be shown or demonstrated.

qt., *pl.* **qt., qts.** quart.

qty., quantity.

quack, *n.* pretender to medical skill. —**quack′er•y,** *n.*

quad, *n.* **1.** quadrangle. **2.** quadruplet.

quad′ran′gle, *n.* **1.** plane figure with four angles and four sides. **2.** Also, *Informal,* **quad.** enclosed four-sided area. —**quad•ran′gu•lar,** *adj.*

quad′rant, *n.* **1.** arc of 90°. **2.** instrument for measuring altitudes.

quad′ra•phon′ic, *adj.* of sound reproduced through four recording tracks.

quad•ren′ni•al, *adj.* occurring every four years.

quad′ri•cen•ten′ni•al, *n.* 400th anniversary. —*adj.* of 400 years.

quad′ri•lat′er•al, *adj.* **1.** four-sided. —*n.* **2.** four-sided plane figure.

qua•drille′ (kwə dril′), *n.* square dance for four couples.

Q

quad′ri•ple′gi•a (kwod′rə plē′jē ə, -jə), *n.* paralysis of the body below the neck. —**quad′ri•ple′gic,** *n., adj.*

quad′ru•ped′, *n.* four-footed animal.

quad•ru′ple, *adj., n., v.,* **-pled, -pling.** —*adj.* **1.** of four parts. **2.** four times as great. —*n.* **3.** number, etc., four times as great as another. —*v.* **4.** increase fourfold.

quad•ru′plet, *n.* one of four children born at one birth.

quad•ru′pli•cate, *n.* group of four copies.

quaff (kwaf), *v.* drink heartily.

quag′mire′, *n.* boggy ground.

qua′hog (kwô′hog, kō′-), *n.* edible American clam.

quail, *n., pl.* **quails, quail,** *v.* —*n.* **1.** game bird resembling domestic fowls. —*v.* **2.** lose courage; show fear.

quaint, *adj.* pleasingly odd. —**quaint′ly,** *adv.* —**quaint′ness,** *n.*

quake, *v.,* **quaked, quaking,** *n.* —*v.* **1.** tremble. —*n.* **2.** earthquake.

Quak′er, *n.* member of Society of Friends.

qual′i•fy′, *v.,* **-fied, -fying. 1.** make proper or fit. **2.** modify. **3.** mitigate. **4.** show oneself fit. —**qual′i•fi•ca′tion,** *n.*

qual′i•ty, *n., pl.* **-ties. 1.** characteristic. **2.** relative merit. **3.** excellence. —**qual′i•ta′tive,** *adj.*

quality time, time devoted exclusively to activity.

qualm (kwäm), *n.* **1.** misgiving; scruple. **2.** feeling of illness.

quan′da•ry, *n., pl.* **-ries.** dilemma.

quan′ti•fy′, *v.,* **-fied, -fying.** indicate quantity of.

quan′ti•ty, *n., pl.* **-ties. 1.** amount; measure. **2.** *Math.* something having magnitude. —**quan′ti•ta′tive,** *adj.*

quan′tum, *n., pl.* **-ta,** *adj.* —*n.* **1.** quantity or amount. **2.** *Physics.* very small, indivisible quantity of energy. —*adj.* **3.** sudden and significant.

quar′an•tine′, *n., v.,* **-tined, -tining.** —*n.* **1.** strict isolation to prevent spread of disease. —*v.* **2.** put in quarantine.

quark (kwôrk, kwärk), *n.* subatomic particle having fractional electric charge.

quar′rel, *n., v.,* **-reled, -reling.** —*n.* **1.** angry dispute. —*v.* **2.** disagree angrily. —**quar′rel•some,** *adj.*

quar′ry, *n., pl.* **-ries,** *v.,* **-ried, -rying.** —*n.* **1.** pit from which stone is taken. **2.** object of pursuit. —*v.* **3.** get from quarry.

quart, *n.* measure of capacity: in liquid measure, ¼ gallon; in dry measure, ⅛ peck.

quar′ter, *n.* **1.** one of four equal parts. **2.** coin worth 25 cents. **3.** (*pl.*) place of residence. **4.** mercy. —*v.* **5.** divide into quarters. **6.** lodge. —*adj.* **7.** being a quarter.

quar′ter•back′, *n.* position in football.

quar′ter•deck′, *n.* rear part of ship's weather deck.

quarter horse, horse capable of great sprints of speed.

quar′ter•ly, *adj., n., pl.* **-lies,** *adv.* —*adj.* **1.** occurring, etc., each quarter year. —*n.* **2.** quarterly publication. —*adv.* **3.** once each quarter year.

quar′ter·mas′ter, *n.* 1. military officer in charge of supplies, etc. 2. naval officer in charge of signals, etc.

quar·tet′, *n.* group of four. Also, **quar·tette′.**

quar′to, *n., pl.* **-tos.** book page of sheets folded twice.

quartz, *n.* crystalline mineral.

qua′sar (kwā′zär), *n.* astronomical source of powerful radio energy.

quash, *v.* subdue; suppress.

qua′si (kwā′zī), *adj.* resembling.

quasi-, prefix meaning somewhat.

Quat′er·nar′y, *adj.* pertaining to present geologic period forming latter part of Cenozoic Era.

quat′rain, *n.* four-line stanza.

qua′ver, *v.* 1. quiver. 2. speak tremulously. —*n.* 3. quavering tone.

quay (kē), *n.* landing beside water.

quea′sy (kwē′zē), *adj.,* **-sier, -siest.** 1. nauseated. 2. uneasy.

queen, *n.* 1. wife of king. 2. female sovereign. 3. fertile female of bees, ants, etc. —*v.* 4. reign as queen.

queer, *adj.* 1. odd. —*n.* 2. *Offensive.* homosexual. —*v.* 3. *Slang.* impair. —**queer′ly,** *adv.* —**queer′ness,** *n.*

quell, *v.* suppress.

quench, *v.* slake or extinguish.

quer′u·lous, *adj.* peevish.

que′ry (kwēr′ē), *n., pl.* **-ries,** *v.,* **-ried, -rying.** question.

quest, *n., v.* search.

ques′tion, *n.* 1. sentence put in a form to elicit information. 2. problem for discussion or dispute. —*v.* 3. ask a question. 4. doubt. —**ques′tion·a·ble,** *adj.* —**ques′tion·er,** *n.*

ques′tion·naire′, *n.* list of questions.

queue (kyōo), *n., v.,* **queued, queuing.** —*n.* 1. line of persons. 2. braid of hair. —*v.* 3. form in a line.

quib′ble, *v.,* **-bled, -bling,** *n.* —*v.* 1. speak ambiguously in evasion. 2. make petty objections. —*n.* 3. act of quibbling. —**quib′bler,** *n.*

quiche (kēsh), *n.* pielike dish of cheese, onion, etc.

quick, *adj.* **1.** prompt; done promptly. **2.** swift. **3.** alert. —*n.* **4.** living persons. **5.** sensitive flesh. —*adv.* **6.** quickly. —**quick′ly,** *adv.* —**quick′ness,** *n.*

quick bread, bread made without yeast.

quick′en, *v.* **1.** hasten. **2.** rouse. **3.** become alive.

quick′ie, *n.* something done or enjoyed in only a short time.

quick′lime′, *n.* untreated lime.

quick′sand′, *n.* soft sand yielding easily to weight.

quick′sil′ver, *n.* mercury.

quid, *n.* **1.** portion for chewing. **2.** *Brit. Informal.* one pound sterling.

quid pro quo, *pl.* **quid pro quos, quids pro quo.** something given or taken for something else.

qui·es′cent (kwī es′ənt), *adj.* inactive. —**qui·es′cence,** *n.*

qui′et, *adj.* **1.** being at rest. **2.** peaceful. **3.** silent. **4.** restrained. —*v.* **5.** make or become quiet. **6.** tranquillity. —**qui′et·ly,** *adv.* —**qui′et·ness, qui′e·tude′,** *n.*

qui·e′tus (kwī ē′təs), *n.* **1.** final settlement. **2.** death.

quill, *n.* large feather.

quilt, *n.* padded and lined bed covering. —**quilt′ed,** *adj.* —**quilt′er,** *n.* —**quilt′ing,** *n.*

quince, *n.* yellowish acid fruit.

qui′nine, *n.* bitter substance used esp. in treating malaria.

quint, *n.* quintuplet.

quin·tes′sence, *n.* essential substance. —**quin′tes·sen′tial,** *adj.*

quin·tet′, *n.* group of five. Also, **quin·tette′.**

quin·tu′plet, *n.* one of five children born at one birth.

quip, *n., v.,* **quipped, quipping.** —*n.* **1.** witty or sarcastic remark. —*v.* **2.** make quip.

quire, *n.* set of 24 uniform sheets of paper.

quirk, *n.* peculiarity. —**quirk′y,** *adj.,* —**quirk′i·ness,** *n.*

quirt, *n.* short riding whip.

quis′ling, *n.* traitor.

quit, *v.,* **quitted, quitting. 1.** stop. **2.** leave. **3.** relinquish. —**quit′ter,** *n.*

quit′claim′, *n.* **1.** transfer of one's interest. —*v.* **2.** give up claim to.

quite, *adv.* **1.** completely. **2.** really.

quits, *adj.* with no further payment or revenge due.

quit′tance, *n.* 1. requital. 2. discharge from debt.

quiv′er, *v.* 1. tremble. —*n.* 2. trembling. 3. case for arrows.

quix•ot′ic, *adj.* extravagantly idealistic; impractical.

quiz, *v.,* **quizzed, quizzing,** *n., pl.* **quizzes.** —*v.* 1. question. —*n.* 2. informal questioning.

quiz′zi•cal, *adj.* 1. comical. 2. puzzled. —**quiz′zi•cal•ly,** *adv.*

quoin, *n.* 1. external solid angle. 2. cornerstone. 3. wedge for securing type.

quoit, *n.* flat ring thrown to encircle peg in game of **quoits.**

quon′dam, *adj.* former.

Quon′set hut, *n. Trademark.* semicylindrical metal shelter with end walls.

quo′rum, *n.* number of members needed to transact business legally.

quo′ta, *n.* share due.

quote, *v.,* **quoted, quoting,** *n.* —*v.* 1. repeat verbatim. 2. cite. 3. state (price of). —*n.* 4. *Informal.* quotation. —**quo•ta′tion,** *n.* —**quot′a•ble,** *adj.*

quoth, *v. Archaic.* said.

quo•tid′i•an (kwō tid′ē ən), *adj.* 1. daily. 2. ordinary.

quo′tient, *n. Math.* number of times one quantity is contained in another.

R, r, *n.* **1.** eighteenth letter of English alphabet. **2.** motion-picture rating: those less than 17 years old must be accompanied by adult.

rab′bi, *n.* Jewish religious leader. —**rab•bin′ic, rab•bin′i•cal,** *adj.*

rab′bin•ate, *n.* **1.** office of a rabbi. **2.** rabbis collectively.

rab′bit, *n.* long-eared mammal.

rab′ble, *n.* mob.

rab′ble-rous′er, *n.* demagogue.

rab′id, *adj.* **1.** irrationally intense. **2.** having rabies. —**rab′id•ly,** *adv.*

ra′bies (rā′bēz), *n.* fatal disease transmitted by bite of infected animal.

rac•coon′, *n.* small nocturnal carnivorous mammal.

race, *n., v.,* **raced, racing.** —*n.* **1.** contest of speed. **2.** onward course. **3.** group of persons of common origin. **4.** any kind. —*v.* **5.** engage in race. **6.** move swiftly. —**rac′er,** *n.* —**ra′cial,** *adj.*

ra•ceme′ (rā sēm′), *n.* cluster of flowers along stem.

R

rac′ism, *n.* prejudice against another race.

rack, *n.* **1.** structure for storage. **2.** toothed bar engaging with teeth of pinion. **3.** torture device. **4.** destruction. —*v.* **5.** torture. **6.** strain.

rack′et, *n.* **1.** noise. **2.** illegal or dishonest business. **3.** Also, **rac′quet.** framed network used as bat in tennis, etc.

rack′e•teer′, *n.* criminal engaged in racket.

rac′on•teur′ (rak′on tûr′), *n.* skilled storyteller.

ra•coon′, *n.* raccoon.

rac′quet•ball, *n.* game similar to handball, played with rackets on four-walled court.

rac′y, *adj.,* **racier, raciest. 1.** lively. **2.** risqué. —**rac′i•ly,** *adv.* —**rac′i•ness,** *n.*

ra′dar, *n.* device capable of locating objects by radio wave.

ra′di•al, *adj.* of rays or radii.

ra′di•ant, *adj.* **1.** emitting rays of light. **2.** bright; exultant. **3.**

emitted in rays, as heat.
—**ra′di•ance,** *n.*
—**ra′di•ant•ly,** *adv.*

ra′di•ate′, *v.,* **-ated, -ating. 1.** spread like rays from center. **2.** emit or issue in rays.
—**ra′di•a′tion,** *n.*

ra′di•a′tor, *n.* heating device.

rad′i•cal, *adj.* **1.** fundamental. **2.** favoring drastic reforms. —*n.* **3.** person with radical ideas. **4.** atom or group of atoms behaving as unit in chemical reaction.
—**rad′i•cal•ism,** *n.*
—**rad′i•cal•ly,** *adv.*

ra′di•o′, *n., pl.* **-dios. 1.** way of transmitting sound by electromagnetic waves. **2.** apparatus for sending or receiving such waves.

ra′di•o•ac′tive, *adj.* emitting radiation from the nucleus.
—**ra′di•o•ac•tiv′i•ty,** *n.*

ra′di•o•car′bon, *n.* radioactive isotope of carbon.

ra′di•ol′o•gy, *n.* use of radiation for medical diagnosis and treatment.
—**ra′di•ol′o•gist,** *n.*

rad′ish, *n.* root of garden plant.

ra′di•um, *n.* radioactive metallic element.

ra′di•us, *n., pl.* **-dii, -diuses. 1.** straight line from center of a circle to circumference. **2.** one of the bones of the forearm.

ra′don (rā′don), *n.* element produced by decay of radium.

RAF, Royal Air Force.

raf′fi•a, *n.* fiber made from leafstalks of palm tree.

raff′ish, *adj.* **1.** jaunty; rakish. **2.** gaudily vulgar or cheap.

raf′fle, *n., v.,* **-fled, -fling.** —*n.* **1.** lottery. —*v.* **2.** dispose of by raffle.

raft, *n.* floating platform.

raft′er, *n.* framing part of roof.

rag, *n.* worthless bit of cloth, esp. one torn. —**rag′ged,** *adj.*

ra′ga, *n., pl.* **-gas.** traditional melody of Hindu music.

rag′a•muf′fin, *n.* ragged child.

rage, *n., v.,* **raged, raging.** —*n.* **1.** violent anger. **2.** fad. —*v.* **3.** be violently angry. **4.** prevail violently.

rag′lan, *n.* loose garment with sleeves continuing to collar.

raglan sleeve, set-in sleeve with slanting seam from neckline to armhole.

ra•gout′ (ra g$\overline{oo}$′), *n.* stew.

rag′time′, *n.* style of jazz.

rag′weed′, *n.* plant whose pollen causes hay fever.

raid, *n.* **1.** sudden attack. —*v.* **2.** attack. —**raid′er,** *n.*

rail, *n.* **1.** horizontal bar. **2.** one of pair of railroad tracks. **3.** railroad as means of transport. **4.** wading bird. —*v.* **5.** complain bitterly.

rail′ing, *n.* barrier of rails.

rail′ler•y, *n.* banter.

rail′road′, *n.* **1.** road with fixed rails on which trains run. —*v.* **2.** transport by means of a railroad. **3.** coerce into action.

rail′way′, *n. Chiefly Brit.* railroad.

rai′ment, *n.* clothing.

rain, *n.* **1.** water falling from sky in drops. **2.** rainfall. —*v.* **3.** fall as rain. —**rain′y,** *adj.*

rain′bow′, *n.* arc of colors sometimes seen in sky opposite sun during rain. —**rain′bow•like,** *adj.*

rain check, 1. postponement of invitation. **2.** ticket for future admission to event postponed by rain.

rain′coat′, *n.* waterproof coat.

rain′fall′, *n.* amount of rain.

rain forest, tropical forest in area of high annual rainfall.

rain′mak′er, *n.* one who induces rain.

raise, *v.,* **raised, raising,** *n.* —*v.* **1.** lift up. **2.** set upright. **3.** cause to appear. **4.** grow. **5.** collect. **6.** rear. **7.** cause (dough) to expand. **8.** end (siege). —*n.* **9.** increase.

rai′sin, *n.* dried sweet grape.

rai′son d′ê′tre (rā′zōn de′trə), *n., pl.* **rai′sons d′ê′tre.** reason for existence.

ra′jah (-jə), *n.* (formerly) Indian king or prince.

rake, *n., v.,* **raked, raking.** —*n.* **1.** long-handled tool with teeth for gathering. **2.** dissolute person. **3.** slope. —*v.* **4.** gather or smooth with rake. **5.** fire guns the length of (target).

rak′ish, *adj.* **1.** jaunty. **2.** dissolute.

rake′-off′, *n.* amount received.

ral′ly, *v.,* **-lied, -lying,** *n., pl.* **-lies.** —*v.* **1.** bring into order again. **2.** come together. **3.** revive. **4.** come to aid. —*n.* **5.** renewed order. **6.** renewal of strength. **7.** mass meeting.

ram, *n., v.,* **rammed, ramming.** —*n.* **1.** male sheep. **2.** device for battering, forcing, etc. —*v.* **3.** strike forcibly.

RAM, random-access memory: computer memory available for running programs and storing data.

ram′ble, *v.,* **-bled, -bling,** *n.* —*v.* **1.** stroll idly. **2.** talk vaguely. —*n.* **3.** leisurely stroll. —**ram′bler,** *n.*

ram•bunc′tious, *adj.* difficult to control or handle.

ram′i•fy′, *v.,* **-fied, -fying.** divide into branches. —**ram′i•fi•ca′tion,** *n.*

ramp, *n.* sloping surface between two levels.

ram′page, *n., v.,* **-paged, -paging.** —*n.* (ram′pāj). **1.** violent behavior. —*v.* (ram pāj′). **2.** move furiously about.

ramp′ant, *adj.* **1.** unrestrained. **2.** standing on hind legs.

ram′part, *n.* mound of earth raised as bulwark.

ram′rod′, *n.* rod for cleaning or loading gun.

ram′shack′le, *adj.* rickety.

ranch, *n.* large farm, esp. for raising stock. —**ranch′er,** *n.*

ran′cid (-sid), *adj.* stale. —**ran•cid′i•ty,** *n.*

ran′cor (rang′kər), *n.* grudge. —**ran′cor•ous,** *adj.*

rand, *n., pl.* **rand.** monetary unit of South Africa.

ran′dom, *adj.* without aim. —**ran′dom•ly,** *adv.*

rand′y, *adj.,* **randier, randiest.** sexually aroused; lustful.

range, *n., v.,* **ranged, ranging.** —*n.* **1.** limits; extent. **2.** place for target shooting. **3.** distance between gun and target. **4.** row. **5.** mountain chain. **6.** grazing area. **7.** cooking stove. —*v.* **8.** arrange. **9.** pass over (area). **10.** vary.

rang′er, *n.* **1.** warden of forest tract. **2.** civil officer who patrols large area.

rang′y (rān′jē), *adj.,* **rangier, rangiest.** slender and long.

rank, *n.* **1.** class, group, or standing. **2.** high position. **3.** row. **4.** (*pl.*) enlisted personnel. —*v.* **5.** arrange. **6.**

put or be in particular rank. **7.** be senior in rank. —*adj.* **8.** growing excessively. **9.** offensively strong in smell. **10.** utter. **11.** grossly vulgar. —**rank′ly,** *adv.* —**rank′ness,** *n.*

rank and file, 1. members apart from leaders. **2.** enlisted soldiers.

rank′ing, *adj.* **1.** senior. **2.** renowned.

ran′kle, *v.,* **-kled, -kling.** irk.

ran′sack, *v.* plunder.

ran′som, *n.* **1.** sum demanded for prisoner. —*v.* **2.** pay ransom for.

rant, *v.* **1.** speak wildly. —*n.* **2.** violent speech. —**rant′er,** *n.*

rap, *v.,* **rapped, rapping,** *n.* —*v.* **1.** strike quickly and sharply. —*n.* **2.** sharp blow. **3.** music marked by intoning of rhymed verses over repetitive beat. —**rap′per,** *n.*

ra•pa′cious, *adj.* plundering.

rape, *n., v.,* **raped, raping.** —*n.* **1.** forcing of sexual intercourse on someone. **2.** abduction or seizure. —*v.* **3.** commit rape on. **4.** abduct or seize. —**rap′ist,** *n.*

rap′id, *adj.* **1.** swift. —*n.* **2.** (*pl.*) fast part of river. —**ra•pid′i•ty, rap′id•ness,** *n.* —**rap′id•ly,** *adv.*

ra′pi•er (rā′pē ər), *n.* slender sword.

rap′ine (rap′in), *n.* plunder.

rap•port′ (ra pôr′), *n.* sympathetic relationship.

rap′proche•ment′ (-rōsh mäN′), *n.* establishment of harmonious relations.

rap•scal′lion, *n.* rascal.

rap sheet, *Slang.* record of person's arrests.

rapt, *adj.* engrossed. —**rapt′ly,** *adv.* —**rapt′ness,** *n.*

rap′ture, *n.* ecstatic joy. —**rap′tur•ous,** *adj.*

ra′ra a′vis (râr′ə ā′vis), *n., pl.* **ra′rae a′ves** (-ē -vēz). rare person or thing.

rare, *adj.,* **rarer, rarest. 1.** unusual. **2.** thin, as air. **3.** (of meat) not thoroughly cooked. —**rar′i•ty,** *n.* —**rare′ly,** *adv.* —**rare′ness,** *n.*

rare′bit (râr′bit), *n.* dish of melted cheese.

rar′e•fy′, *v.,* **-fied, -fying.** make or become thin, as air.

rar′ing, *adj.* very eager.

ras′cal, *n.* dishonest person. —**ras•cal′i•ty,** *n.*

rash, *adj.* 1. thoughtlessly hasty. —*n.* 2. skin eruption. —**rash′ly,** *adv.* —**rash′ness,** *n.*

rash′er, *n.* thin slice of ham.

rasp, *v.* 1. scrape, as with file. 2. irritate. 3. speak gratingly. —*n.* 4. coarse file. 5. rasping sound. —**rasp′y,** *adj.*

rasp′ber′ry (raz′-), *n., pl.* **-ries.** small juicy red or black fruit.

rat, *n.* rodent.

ratch′et, *n.* wheel or bar having teeth that catch pawl to control motion.

rate, *n., v.,* **rated, rating.** —*n.* 1. charge in proportion to something that varies. 2. degree of speed, etc. —*v.* 3. estimate rate. 4. judge.

rath′er, *adv.* 1. somewhat. 2. in preference. 3. on the contrary.

raths′kel•ler (rät′skel-), *n.* pub below street level.

rat′i•fy′, *v.,* **-fied, -fying.** confirm formally. —**rat′i•fi•ca′tion,** *n.*

ra′tio (-shō, -shē ō′), *n., pl.* **-tios.** relative number or extent; proportion.

ra′ti•oc′i•na′tion (rash′ē os′-), *n.* reasoning.

ra′tion, *n.* 1. fixed allowance. —*v.* 2. apportion. 3. put on ration.

ra′tion•al, *adj.* 1. sensible. 2. sane. —**ra′tion•al•ly,** *adv.* —**ra′tion•al′i•ty,** *n.*

ra′tion•ale′ (rash′ə nal′), *n.* reasonable basis for action.

ra′tion•al•ism, *n.* advocacy of precise reasoning as source of truth. —**ra′tion•al•ist,** *n.* —**ra′tion•al•is′tic,** *adj.*

ra′tion•al•ize′, *v.,* **-ized, -izing.** 1. find reason for one's behavior. 2. make rational. —**ra′tion•al•i•za′tion,** *n.*

rat race, routine.

rat•tan′, *n.* hollow stem of climbing palm.

rat′tle, *v.,* **-tled, -tling,** *n.* —*v.* 1. make series of short sharp sounds. 2. chatter. 3. *Informal.* disconcert. —*n.* 4. sound of rattling. 5. toy that rattles.

rat′tle•snake′, *n.* venomous American snake.

rat′ty, *adj.,* **-tier, -tiest.** 1. of rats. 2. shabby.

rau′cous (rô′kəs), *adj.* 1. hoarse; harsh. 2. rowdy. —**rau′cous•ly,** *adv.*

raun'chy, *adj.* **-chier, -chiest.** 1. smutty. 2. lecherous. 3. dirty, slovenly.

rav'age, *n., v.,* **-aged, -aging.** ruin. —**rav'ag•er,** *n.*

rave, *v.,* **raved, raving.** talk wildly.

rav'el, *v.* 1. disengage threads. 2. tangle. 3. make clear. —*n.* 4. tangle. 5. loose thread.

ra'ven, *n.* large black bird.

rav'en•ing, *adj.* greedy for prey.

rav'en•ous, *adj.* very hungry; greedy. —**rav'en•ous•ly,** *adv.*

ra•vine', *n.* narrow valley.

ra'vi•o'li, *n.* small pockets of pasta filled with cheese.

rav'ish, *v.* 1. fill with joy. 2. rape. —**rav'ish•er,** *n.* —**rav'ish•ment,** *n.*

rav'ish•ing, *adj.* gorgeous.

raw, *adj.* 1. in the natural state. 2. uncooked. 3. open. 4. untrained. —*n.* 5. raw condition. —**raw'ness,** *n.*

raw'boned', *adj.* bony.

raw'hide', *n.* untanned hide.

ray, *n.* 1. narrow beam of light. 2. trace. 3. line outward from center. 4. flat-bodied fish.

ray'on, *n.* synthetic fabric.

raze, *v.,* **razed, razing.** demolish.

ra'zor, *n.* sharp-edged instrument for shaving.

razz, *v.* make fun of; mock.

R.C., Roman Catholic.

rd., road.

re, *n.* 1. (rā). *Music.* second tone of scale. —*prep.* 2. (rē). with reference to.

re-, prefix indicating: 1. repetition, as *reprint, rearm.* 2. withdrawal.

reach, *v.* 1. come to. 2. be able to touch. 3. extend. —*n.* 4. act of reaching. 5. extent.

re•act', *v.* 1. act upon each other. 2. respond.

re•ac'tant, *n.* substance that changes in chemical reaction.

re•ac'tion, *n.* 1. extreme conservatism. 2. responsive action. 3. chemical change. —**re•ac'tion•ar'y,** *n., adj.*

re•ac'tor, *n.* 1. one that reacts. 2. apparatus for producing useful nuclear energy.

read, *v.,* **read, reading.** 1. observe and understand (printed matter, etc.). 2. register. 3. utter aloud (something written or printed). 4. obtain and store, as in computer memory. —**read′a•ble,** *adj.* —**read′er,** *n.* —**read′er•ship′,** *n.*

read′ing, *n.* 1. amount read at one time. 2. interpretation of written or musical work.

read′-on′ly, *adj.* noting computer files or memory that can be read but not changed.

read′y, *adj.,* **readier, readiest,** *v.,* **readied, readying,** *n.* —*adj.* 1. fully prepared. 2. willing. 3. apt. —*v.* 4. make ready. —*n.* 5. state of being ready. —**read′i•ly,** *adv.* —**read′i•ness,** *n.*

read′y-made′, *adj.* ready for use when bought.

re•a′gent, *n.* chemical used in analysis and synthesis.

re′al, *adj.* 1. actual. 2. genuine. 3. denoting immovable property. —**re•al′i•ty, re′al•ness,** *n.* —**re′al•ly,** *adv.*

real estate, land with buildings. Also, **re′al•ty.**

re′al•ism, *n.* 1. tendency to see things as they really are. 2. representation of things as they really are. —**re′al•ist,** *n.*

—**re′al•is′tic,** *adj.* —**re′al•is′ti•cal•ly,** *adv.*

re′al•ize′, *v.,* **-ized, -izing.** 1. understand clearly. 2. make real. 3. get as profit. —**re′al•i•za′tion,** *n.*

realm (relm), *n.* 1. kingdom. 2. special field.

ream, *n.* 1. twenty quires of paper. —*v.* 2. enlarge (hole) with a **ream′er.**

reap, *v.* harvest. —**reap′er,** *n.*

rear, *n.* 1. back part. —*adj.* 2. of or at rear. —*v.* 3. care for to maturity. 4. raise; erect. 5. rise on hind legs.

rear admiral, naval officer above captain.

re•arm′, *v.* arm again. —**re•arm′a•ment,** *n.*

rear′most′, *adj.* farthest back.

rear′ward, *adv.* 1. Also, **rear′wards.** toward the rear. —*adj.* 2. located in the rear.

rea′son, *n.* 1. cause for belief, act, etc. 2. sound judgment. 3. sanity. —*v.* 4. think or argue logically. 5. infer. —**rea′son•ing,** *n.* —**rea′son•er,** *n.*

rea′son•a•ble, *adj.* showing sound judgment. —**rea′son•a•bly,** *adv.*

re′as•sure′, *v.*, -sured, -suring. restore confidence of. —**re′as•sur′ance**, *n.*

re′bate, *v.*, -bated, -bating, *n.* —*v.* 1. return (part of amount paid). —*n.* 2. amount rebated.

re•bel′, *v.*, -belled, -belling, *n.* —*v.* (ri bel′). 1. rise in arms against one's government. 2. resist any authority. —*n.* (reb′əl). 3. one who rebels. —**re•bel′lion**, *n.* —**re•bel′lious**, *adj.* —**re•bel′lious•ly**, *adv.* —**re•bel′lious•ness**, *n.*

re•bound′, *v.* 1. bound back after impact. —*n.* (rē′bound′). 2. act of rebounding.

re•buff′, *n.* 1. blunt check or refusal. —*v.* 2. check; repel.

re•buke′, *v.*, -buked, -buking, *n.* reprimand.

re′bus, *n.* puzzle in which pictures and symbols combine to represent a word.

re•but′, *v.*, -butted, -butting. refute. —**re•but′tal**, *n.*

re•cal′ci•trant (ri kal′sə trənt), *adj.* resisting control. —**re•cal′ci•trance**, *n.*

re•call′, *v.* 1. remember. 2. call back. 3. withdraw. —*n.* 4. act of recalling.

re•cant′, *v.* retract.

re′cap′, *n.*, *v.*, -capped, -capping. —*n.* 1. recapitulation. 2. tire reconditioned by adding strip of rubber. —*v.* 3. recapitulate. 4. recondition a tire.

re′ca•pit′u•late (-pich′ə-), *v.*, -lated, -lating. review; sum up. —**re′ca•pit′u•la′tion**, *n.*

re•cap′ture, *v.*, -tured, -turing, *n.* —*v.* 1. capture again. 2. experience again. —*n.* 3. recovery by capture.

recd. or **rec'd.**, received.

re•cede′, *v.*, -ceded, -ceding. move or appear to move back.

re•ceipt′, *n.* 1. written acknowledgment of receiving. 2. (*pl.*) amount received. 3. act of receiving.

re•ceiv′a•ble, *adj.* still to be paid.

re•ceive′, *v.*, -ceived, -ceiving. 1. take (something offered or delivered). 2. experience. 3. welcome (guests). 4. accept.

re•ceiv′er, *n.* 1. one that receives. 2. device that receives electricl signals and converts them. 3. person put in charge of property in litigation. —**re•ceiv′er•ship′,** *n.*

re′cent, *adj.* happening, etc., lately. —**re′cen•cy,** *n.* —**re′cent•ly,** *adv.*

re•cep′ta•cle, *n.* container.

re•cep′tion, *n.* **1.** act of receiving. **2.** manner of being received. **3.** social function.

re•cep′tion•ist, *n.* person who receives callers in an office.

re•cep′tive, *adj.* quick to consider ideas.

re•cep′tor, *n.* nerve ending that is sensitive to stimuli.

re•cess′, *n.* **1.** temporary cessation of work. **2.** alcove. **3.** (*pl.*) inner part. —*v.* **4.** take or make recess.

re•ces′sion, *n.* **1.** withdrawal. **2.** economic decline.

re•ces′sion•al, *n.* music at end of church service.

re•ces′sive, *adj.* **1.** receding. **2.** noting one of pair of hereditary traits that is masked by the other when both are present.

re•cher′ché (rə shâr′shā, rə shâr shā′), *adj.* **1.** very rare or choice. **2.** affectedly refined.

re•cid′i•vism (ri sid′ə viz′əm), *n.* repeated or habitual relapse, as into crime. —**re•cid′i•vist,** *n., adj.*

rec′i•pe′, *n.* formula.

re•cip′i•ent, *n.* **1.** receiver. —*adj.* **2.** receiving.

re•cip′ro•cal, *adj.* **1.** mutual. —*n.* **2.** thing in reciprocal position. —**re•cip′ro•cal•ly,** *adv.*

re•cip′ro•cate′, *v.,* **-cated, -cating. 1.** give, feel, etc., in return. **2.** move alternately backward and forward. —**re•cip′ro•ca′tion,** *n.*

rec′i•proc′i•ty, *n.* interchange.

re•cit′al, *n.* musical entertainment.

rec′i•ta•tive′ (res′i tə tēv′), *n.* style of vocal music intermediate between speaking and singing.

re•cite′, *v.,* **-cited, -citing. 1.** repeat from memory. **2.** narrate. —**rec′i•ta′tion,** *n.*

reck′less, *adj.* careless. —**reck′less•ly,** *adv.* —**reck′less•ness,** *n.*

reck′on, *v.* **1.** calculate. **2.** regard as; esteem. **3.** *Informal.*

suppose. 4. deal (with).
—**reck′on•er,** *n.*

reck′on•ing, *n.* 1. settling of accounts. 2. navigational calculation.

re•claim′, *v.* make usable, as land. —**rec′la•ma′tion,** *n.*

re•cline′, *v.,* -clined, -clining. lean back.

re•clin′er, *n.* chair with adjustable back and footrest.

rec′luse, *n.* hermit.

re•cog′ni•zance, *n.* bond pledging one to do an act.

rec′og•nize′, *v.,* -nized, -nizing. 1. identify or perceive from previous knowledge. 2. acknowledge formally. 3. greet. —**rec′og•ni′tion,** *n.* —**rec′og•niz′a•ble,** *adj.*

re•coil′, *v.* 1. shrink back. 2. spring back. —*n.* 3. act of recoiling.

re′col•lect′, *v.* remember. —**rec′ol•lec′tion,** *n.*

rec′om•mend′, *v.* 1. commend as worthy. 2. advise. —**rec′om•men•da′tion,** *n.*

rec′om•pense′, *v.,* -pensed, -pensing, *n.* —*v.* 1. repayment or reward. —*n.* 2. such compensation.

rec′on•cile′, *v.,* -ciled, -ciling. 1. bring into agreement. 2. restore to friendliness. —**rec′on•cil′i•a′tion,** *n.* —**rec′on•cil′a•ble,** *adj.*

rec′on•dite (rek′ən dīt′), *adj.* 1. very profound, difficult, or abstruse. 2. esoteric.

re′con•noi′ter, *v.* search area for information. —**re•con′nais•sance**

re•cord′, *v.* 1. set down in writing. 2. register for mechanical reproduction. —*n.* (rek′ərd). 3. what is recorded. 4. object from which sound is reproduced. 5. best yet attained. —*adj.* (rek′ərd). 6. being a record. —**re•cord′ing,** *n.*

re•cord′er, *n.* 1. person who records. 2. recording device. 3. flute with mouthpiece like a whistle and eight finger holes.

re•count′, *v.* 1. narrate. 2. count again. —*n.* (rē′kount′). 3. a second count.

re•coup′ (ri kōōp′), *v.* recover.

re′course, *n.* resort for help.

re•cov′er, *v.* 1. get back. 2. reclaim. 3. regain health. —**re•cov′er•a•ble,** *adj.* —**recov′er•y,** *n.*

rec′re·ant, *adj.* 1. cowardly. 2. disloyal. —*n.* 3. cowardly or disloyal person.

re′-cre·ate′, *v.,* -ated, -ating. create anew.

rec′re·ate′, *v.,* -ated, -ating. refresh physically or mentally.

rec′re·a′tion, *n.* enjoyment. —**rec′re·a′tion·al,** *adj.*

re·crim′i·nate′, *v.,* -nated, -nating. accuse in return. —**re·crim′i·na′tion,** *n.*

re′cru·des′cence, *n.* breaking out again. —**re′cru·des′cent,** *adj.*

re·cruit′, *n.* 1. new member of group. —*v.* 2. enlist. —**re·cruit′er,** *n.* —**re·cruit′ment,** *n.*

rec′tan′gle, *n.* parallelogram with four right angles. —**rec·tan′gu·lar,** *adj.*

rec′ti·fy′, *v.,* -fied, -fying. correct. —**rec′ti·fi·a·ble,** *adj.* —**rec′ti·fi′er,** *n.*

rec′ti·lin′e·ar, *adj.* 1. forming straight line. 2. formed by straight lines.

rec′ti·tude′, *n.* rightness.

rec′to, *n., pl.* -tos. right-hand page of book.

rec′tor, *n.* 1. member of clergy in charge of parish, etc. 2. head of university, etc.

rec′to·ry, *n., pl.* -ries. parsonage.

rec′tum, *n.* lowest part of intestine. —**rec′tal,** *adj.*

re·cum′bent, *adj.* lying down. —**re·cum′ben·cy,** *n.*

re·cu′per·ate′ (-kōō′-), *v.,* -ated, -ating. regain health. —**re·cu′per·a′tion,** *n.*

re·cur′, *v.,* -curred, -curring. 1. occur again. 2. return in thought, etc. —**re·cur′rence,** *n.* —**re·cur′rent,** *adj.* —**re·cur′rent·ly,** *adv.*

re·cy′cle, *v.* -cled, -cling. treat to extract reusable material.

red, *n., adj.,* **redder, reddest.** —*n.* 1. color of blood. 2. leftist radical in politics. —*adj.* 3. of or like red. 4. radically to left in politics. —**red′den,** *v.* —**red′dish,** *adj.* —**red′ness,** *n.*

re·dact′, *v.* edit.

red blood cell, blood cell that carries oxygen to cells.

red′cap′, *n.* baggage porter.

re·deem′, *v.* 1. pay off. 2. recover. 3. fulfill. 4. deliver

from sin by sacrifice.
—**re•deem′er,** *n.*
—**re•deem′a•ble,** *adj.*
—**re•demp′tion,** *n.*

red′-hand′ed, *adj., adv.* in the act of wrongdoing.

red′head′, *n.* person with red hair. —**red′head′ed,** *adj.*

red herring, something intended to distract attention from the real problem.

red′-let′ter, *adj.* memorable.

red′lin′ing, *n.* refusal by banks to grant mortgages in areas.

red′o•lent, *adj.* 1. odorous. 2. suggestive. —**red′o•lence,** *n.*

re•doubt′, *n.* isolated fort.

re•doubt′a•ble, *adj.* 1. evoking fear; formidable. 2. commanding respect.

re•dound′, *v.* occur as result.

re•dress′, *v.* 1. set right (a wrong). —*n.* (rē′dres). 2. act of redressing.

red tape, excessive attention to prescribed procedure.

re•duce′, *v.,* -duced, -ducing. 1. make less. 2. put into simpler form. 3. remove weight. —**re•duc′i•ble,** *adj.* —**re•duc′tion,** *n.* —**re•duc′er,** *n.*

re•dun′dant, *adj.* 1. excess. 2. wordy. —**re•dun′dance, re•dun′dan•cy,** *n.* —**re•dun′dant•ly,** *adv.*

red′wood′, *n.* huge evergreen tree of California.

reed, *n.* 1. tall marsh grass. 2. musical pipe made of hollow stalk. 3. small piece of cane or metal at mouth of wind instrument. —**reed′y,** *adj.*

reef, *n.* 1. narrow ridge near the surface of water. 2. *Naut.* part of sail rolled or folded to reduce area. —*v.* 3. shorten (sail) by rolling or folding.

reef′er, *n.* 1. short heavy coat. 2. *Slang.* marijuana cigarette.

reek, *v.* 1. smell strongly. —*n.* 2. such smell.

reel, *n.* 1. turning object for wound cord, film, etc. 2. lively dance. —*v.* 3. wind on reel. 4. tell easily and at length. 5. sway or stagger. 6. whirl.

re•en′try, *n., pl.* -tries. 1. second entry. 2. return into earth's atmosphere.

reeve, *v.,* **reeved** or **rove, reeved** or **roven, reeving.** pass (rope) through hole.

ref, *n., v.* referee.

re•fec'to•ry, *n., pl.* **-ries.**
dining hall.

re•fer', *v.,* **-ferred, -ferring. 1.**
direct attention. **2.** direct or
go for information. **3.** apply.
—**re•fer'ral,** *n.*

ref'er•ee', *n.* **1.** judge. —*v.* **2.**
act as referee.

ref'er•ence, *n.* **1.** act or fact
of referring. **2.** something
referred to. **3.** person giving
recommendation. **4.**
testimonial.

ref'er•en'dum, *n., pl.* **-dums,**
-da. submission to popular
vote of law passed by
legislature.

ref'er•ent, *n.* something
referred to.

re•fill', *v.* **1.** fill again. —*n.*
(rē'fil'). **2.** second filling.

re•fine', *v.,* **-fined, -fining. 1.**
free from impurities or error.
2. teach manners and taste.
—**re•fin'er,** *n.*
—**re•fine'ment,** *n.*

re•fin'er•y, *n., pl.* **-eries.**
establishment for refining.

re•flect', *v.* **1.** cast back. **2.**
show; mirror. **3.** bring (credit
or discredit) on one. **4.** think.
—**re•flec'tion,** *n.*

—**re•flec'tive,** *adj.*
—**re•flec'tor,** *n.*

re'flex, *adj.* **1.** denoting
involuntary action. **2.** bent.
—*n.* **3.** involuntary movement.

re•flex'ive, *adj.* **1.** (of verb)
having same subject and
object. **2.** (of pronoun)
showing identity with subject.
—**re•flex'ive•ly,** *adv.*

re•for'est, *v.* replant with
forest trees.
—**re'for•est•a'tion,** *n.*

re•form', *n.* **1.** correction of
what is wrong. —*v.* **2.** change
for better. —**re•form'er,** *n.*
—**ref'or•ma'tion,** *n.*

re•form'a•to•ry, *n., pl.* **-ries.**
prison for young offenders.

re•frac'tion, *n.* change of
direction of light or heat rays
in passing to another medium.
—**re•fract',** *v.* —**re•frac'tive,**
adj. —**re•frac'tor,** *n.*

re•frac'to•ry, *adj.* stubborn.

re•frain', *v.* **1.** keep oneself
(from). —*n.* **2.** recurring
passage in song, etc.

re•fresh', *v.* **1.** reinvigorate. **2.**
stimulate. —**re•fresh'ment,** *n.*
—**re•fresh'er,** *adj., n.*
—**re•fresh'ing,** *adj.*

re•frig′er•ate′, *v.*, -ated, -ating. make or keep cold. —**re•frig′er•ant**, *adj., n.* —**re•frig′er•a′tion**, *n.*

re•frig′er•a′tor, *n.* cabinet for keeping food cold.

ref′uge, *n.* shelter.

ref′u•gee′, *n.* person who flees for safety.

re•ful′gent (ri ful′jənt), *adj.* radiant. —**re•ful′gence**, *n.*

re•fund′, *v.* 1. give back (money). —*n.* (rē′fund). 2. repayment. —**re•fund′a•ble**, *adj.*

re•fur′bish, *v.* renovate. —**re•fur′bish•ment**, *n.*

re•fuse′, *v.*, -fused, -fusing, *n.* —*v.* 1. decline to accept. 2. deny (request). —*n.* 3. (ref′yo͞os). rubbish. —**re•fus′al**, *n.*

re•fute′, *v.*, -futed, -futing. prove false or wrong. —**ref′u•ta•ble**, *adj.* —**ref′u•ta′tion**, *n.*

re•gain′, *v.* get again.

re′gal, *adj.* royal. —**re′gal•ly**, *adv.*

re•gale′, *v.*, -galed, -galing. 1. entertain grandly. 2. feast.

re•ga′li•a, *n.pl.* emblems of royalty, office, etc.

re•gard′, *v.* 1. look upon with particular feeling. 2. respect. 3. look at. 4. concern. —*n.* 5. reference. 6. attention. 7. respect and liking.

re•gard′ing, *prep.* concerning.

re•gard′less, *adv.* 1. without regard; in spite of. —*adj.* 2. heedless.

re•gat′ta, *n.* 1. boat race. 2. organized series of boat races.

re•gen′er•ate′, *v.*, -ated, -ating, *adj.* —*v.* 1. make over for the better. 2. form anew. —*adj.* (-ət). 3. regenerated. —**re•gen′er•a′tion**, *n.* —**re•gen′er•a′tive**, *adj.*

re′gent, *n.* 1. person ruling in place of sovereign. 2. university governor. —**re′gen•cy**, *n.*

reg′gae (reg′ā), *n.* Jamaican music blending blues, calypso, and rock.

reg′i•cide′ (rej′-), *n.* killing of king.

re•gime′ (rā zhēm′), *n.* system of rule.

reg′i•men′, *n.* 1. course of diet, etc., for health. 2. rule.

reg′i•ment (-mənt), *n.* **1.** infantry unit. —*v.* (rej′ə ment′). **2.** subject to strict, uniform discipline. —**reg′i•men′tal,** *adj.* —**reg′i•men•ta′tion,** *n.*

re′gion, *n.* area; district. —**re′gion•al,** *adj.* —**re′gion•al•ly,** *adv.*

re′gion•al•ism, *n.* feature peculiar to region.

reg′is•ter, *n.* **1.** record. **2.** range of voice or instrument. **3.** device for controlling passage of warm air. —*v.* **4.** enter in register. **5.** show. **6.** enter oneself on list of voters. —**reg′is•tra′tion,** *n.*

reg′is•trar′, *n.* official recorder.

reg′is•try, *n., pl.* **-tries. 1.** registration. **2.** place where register is kept. **3.** register.

reg′nant, *adj.* **1.** ruling. **2.** widespread.

re•gress′, *v.* return to previous, inferior state. —**re•gres′sion,** *n.* —**re•gres′sive,** *adj.*

re•gret′, *v.,* **-gretted, -gretting,** *n.* —*v.* **1.** feel sorry about. —*n.* **2.** feeling of loss or sorrow. —**re•gret′ta•ble,** *adj.* —**re•gret′ful,** *adj.*

re•group′, *v.* form into new group.

reg′u•lar, *adj.* **1.** usual. **2.** symmetrical. **3.** recurring at fixed times. **4.** orderly. **5.** denoting permanent army. —*n.* **6.** regular soldier. —**reg′u•lar′i•ty,** *n.* —**reg′u•lar•ize′,** *v.* —**reg′u•lar•ly,** *adv.*

reg′u•late′, *v.,* **-lated, -lating. 1.** control by rule, method, etc. **2.** adjust. —**reg′u•la′tion,** *n.* —**reg′u•la•to′ry,** *adj.* —**reg′u•la′tor,** *n.*

re•gur′gi•tate′, *v.,* **-tated, -tating.** cast or surge back. —**re•gur′gi•ta′tion,** *n.*

re′ha•bil′i•tate′, *v.,* **-tated, -tating.** restore. —**re′ha•bil′i•ta′tion,** *n.*

re•hash′, *v.* **1.** rework or reuse in new form. —*n.* **2.** act of rehashing. **3.** something rehashed.

re•hearse′, *v.,* **-hearsed, -hearsing. 1.** practice for performance. **2.** recount in detail. —**re•hears′al,** *n.*

reign, *n.* **1.** royal rule. —*v.* **2.** have sovereign power or title.

re′im·burse′, *v.,* -bursed, -bursing. repay. —**re′im·burse′ment,** *n.*

rein, *n.* strap fastened to bridle for controlling animal.

re′in·car·na′tion, *n.* continuation of soul after death in new body.

rein′deer′, *n.* large arctic deer.

re′in·force′, *v.,* -forced, -forcing. strengthen. —**re′in·force′ment,** *n.*

re′in·state′, *v.,* -stated, -stating. put back into former position or state. —**re′in·state′ment,** *n.*

re·it′er·ate′, *v.,* -ated, -ating. repeat. —**re·it′er·a′tion,** *n.* —**re·it′er·a′tive,** *adj.*

re·ject′, *v.* 1. refuse. —*n.* (rē′jekt). 2. something rejected. —**re·jec′tion,** *n.*

re·joice′, *v.,* -joiced, -joicing. be or make glad.

re·join′, *v.* answer.

re·join′der, *n.* response.

re·ju′ve·nate′, *v.,* -nated, -nating. make vigorous again. —**re·ju′ve·na′tion,** *n.*

re·lapse′, *v.,* -lapsed, -lapsing. 1. fall back into former state or practice. —*n.* 2. act or instance of relapsing.

re·late′, *v.,* -lated, -lating. 1. tell. 2. establish relation.

re·lat′ed, *adj.* 1. associated. 2. connected by blood.

re·la′tion, *n.* 1. connection. 2. relative. 3. narrative. —**re·la′tion·ship′,** *n.*

rel′a·tive, *n.* 1. person connected with another by blood. —*adj.* 2. comparative. 3. designating word that introduces subordinate clause. —**rel′a·tive·ly,** *adv.*

relative humidity, ratio of water vapor in the air at a given temperature to the amount the air could hold.

rel′a·tiv′i·ty, *n.* principle that time, mass, etc. are relative, not absolute concepts.

re·lax′, *v.* 1. make or become less tense, firm, etc. 2. slacken. —**re′lax·a′tion,** *n.*

re′lay, *n.* 1. fresh supply of persons, etc., to relieve others. —*v.* 2. carry forward by relays.

re·lease′, *v.,* -leased, -leasing, *n.* —*v.* 1. let go; discharge. —*n.* 2. act of releasing.

rel′e·gate′, v., -gated, -gating. 1. consign. 2. turn over. —**rel′e·ga′tion**, n.

re·lent′, v. become more mild. —**re·lent′less**, adj.

rel′e·vant, adj. having to do with matter in question. —**rel′e·vance**, n.

re·li′a·ble, adj. trustworthy. —**re·li′a·bil′i·ty**, n. —**re·li′a·bly**, adv.

re·li′ance, n. 1. trust. 2. confidence. —**re·li′ant**, adj.

rel′ic, n. 1. object surviving from past. 2. personal memorial of sacred person.

re·lief′, n. 1. alleviation. 2. help. 3. pleasant change. 4. projection.

re·lieve′, v., -lieved, -lieving. 1. ease; alleviate. 2. break sameness of. 3. release or discharge from duty.

re·li′gion, n. 1. spiritual recognition and worship. 2. particular system of religious belief. —**re·li′gious**, adj. —**re·li′gious·ly**, adv. —**re·li′gious·ness**, n.

re·lin′quish, v. give up. —**re·lin′quish·ment**, n.

rel′i·quar′y (rel′i kwer′ē), n., pl. -quaries. receptacle for religious relics.

rel′ish, n. 1. enjoyment. 2. chopped pickles, etc. —v. 3. take enjoyment in.

re·live′, v., n. -lived, -living. experience again.

re·lo′cate, v., -cated, -cating. move. —**re′lo·ca′tion**, n.

re·luc′tant, adj. unwilling. —**re·luc′tance**, n. —**re·luc′tant·ly**, adv.

re·ly′, v., -lied, -lying. put trust in.

REM, n. quick movement of eyes during sleep.

re·main′, v. 1. continue to be. 2. stay; be left. —n.pl. 3. that which remains. 4. corpse.

re·main′der, n. that which remains.

re·mand′, v. send back, as to jail. —**re·mand′ment**, n.

re·mark′, v. 1. say casually. 2. perceive; observe. —n. 3. casual comment. 4. notice.

re·mark′a·ble, adj. extraordinary. —**re·mark′a·bly**, adv.

rem′e·dy, *v.,* **-died, -dying,** *n.,* *pl.* **-dies.** —*v.* **1.** cure or alleviate. **2.** correct. —*n.* **3.** something that remedies. —**re·me′di·al,** *adj.*

re·mem′ber, *v.* **1.** recall to or retain in memory. **2.** mention as sending greetings. —**re·mem′brance,** *n.*

re·mind′, *v.* cause to remember. —**re·mind′er,** *n.*

rem′i·nisce′, *v.,* **-nisced, -niscing.** recall past experiences. —**rem′i·nis′cence,** *n.* —**rem′i·nis′cent,** *adj.*

re·miss′, *adj.* negligent.

re·mit′, *v.,* **-mitted, -mitting. 1.** send money. **2.** pardon. **3.** abate. —**re·mis′sion,** *n.*

re·mit′tance, *n.* money sent.

re·mit′tent, *adj.* (of illness) less severe at times.

rem′nant, *n.* **1.** small remaining part. **2.** trace.

re·mod′el, *v.,* **-eled, -eling.** renovate.

re·mon′strate, *v.,* **-strated, -strating.** protest; plead in protest. —**re′mon·stra′tion, re·mon′strance,** *n.*

re·morse′, *n.* regret for wrongdoing. —**re·morse′ful,** *adj.* —**re·morse′less,** *adj.*

re·mote′, *adj.* **1.** far distant. **2.** faint. —*n.* **3.** remote control (def. 2). —**re·mote′ly,** *adv.* —**re·mote′ness,** *n.*

remote control, 1. control of an apparatus from a distance. **2.** Also, **remote.** device used for such control.

re·move′, *v.,* **-moved, -moving,** *n.* —*v.* **1.** take away or off. **2.** move to another place. —*n.* **3.** distance of separation. —**re·mov′al,** *n.* —**re·mov′a·ble,** *adj.*

re·mu′ner·ate′, *v.,* **-ated, -ating.** pay for work, etc. —**re·mu′ner·a′tion,** *n.* —**re·mu′ner·a′tive,** *adj.*

ren′ais·sance′ (ren′ə säns′), *n.* **1.** revival. **2.** (*cap.*) cultural period of the 14th–17th century.

re′nal (rēn′l), *adj.* of or near the kidneys.

re·nas′cent (ri nā′sənt), *adj.* being reborn.

rend, *v.* **1.** tear apart. **2.** disturb with noise. **3.** distress.

ren′der, *v.* **1.** cause to be. **2.** show. **3.** deliver officially. **4.** perform. **5.** give back. **6.** melt (fat). —**ren•di′tion,** *n.*

ren′dez•vous′ (rän′də vōō′, -dā-), *n., pl.* **-vous.** appointment or place to meet.

ren′e•gade′, *n.* deserter.

re•nege′ (ri nig′, -neg′), *v.,* **-neged, -neging.** *Informal.* break promise.

re•new′, *v.* **1.** begin or do again. **2.** make like new; replenish. —**re•new′a•ble,** *adj.* —**re•new′al,** *n.*

ren′net, *n.* **1.** membrane lining stomach of calf or other animal. **2.** preparation of this used in making cheese.

re•nounce′, *v.,* **-nounced, -nouncing.** give up voluntarily. —**re•nounce′ment,** *n.*

ren′o•vate′, *v.,* **-vated, -vating.** repair; refurbish. —**ren′o•va′tion,** *n.*

re•nown′, *n.* fame. —**re•nowned′,** *adj.*

rent, *n.* **1.** Also, **rent′al.** payment for use of property. **2.** tear; break. —*v.* **3.** grant in return for rent. —**rent′er,** *n.*

rent′al, *n.* **1.** amount given or received as rent. **2.** act of renting. **3.** property rented.

re•nun′ci•a′tion, *n.* act of renouncing.

Rep., 1. Representative. **2.** Republic. **3.** Republican.

re•pair′, *v.* **1.** restore to good condition. **2.** go. —*n.* **3.** work of repairing. **4.** condition. —**rep′a•ra•ble,** *adj.*

rep′a•ra′tion, *n.* amends for injury.

rep′ar•tee′, *n.* banter.

re•past′, *n.* meal.

re•pa′tri•ate′, *v.,* **-ated, -ating.** send back to one's native country. —**re•pa′tri•a′tion,** *n.*

re•pay, *v.,* **-paid, -paying.** pay back. —**re•pay′ment,** *n.*

re•peal′, *v.* **1.** revoke officially. —*n.* **2.** revocation.

re•peat′, *v.* **1.** say, tell, or do again. —*n.* **2.** act of repeating. **3.** passage to be repeated.

re•peat′ed, *adj.* said or done again and again. —**re•peat′ed•ly,** *adv.*

re•peat′er, *n.* **1.** one that repeats. **2.** gun firing several shots in rapid succession.

re•pel′, *v.*, **-pelled, -pelling. 1.** drive back; thrust away. **2.** excite disgust or suspicion. —**re•pel′lent**, *adj., n.*

re•pent′, *v.* feel contrition. —**re•pent′ance**, *n.* —**re•pent′ant**, *adj.* —**re•pent′ant•ly**, *adv.*

re′per•cus′sion, *n.* **1.** indirect result. **2.** echo.

rep′er•toire′ (rep′ər twär′), *n.* group of works that company can perform. Also, **rep′er•to′ry.**

rep′e•ti′tion, *n.* repeated action, utterance, etc. —**rep′e•ti′tious**, *adj.* —**re•pet′i•tive**, *adj.*

re•pine′, *v.*, **-pined, -pining. 1.** complain. **2.** yearn.

re•place′, *v.*, **-placed, -placing. 1.** take place of. **2.** provide substitute for. —**re•place′ment**, *n.* —**re•place′a•ble**, *adj.*

re•play′, *v.*, **-played, -playing. 1.** play again. —*n.* (rē′ plā). **2.** act of replaying. **3.** something replayed.

re•plen′ish, *v.* make full again. —**re•plen′ish•ment**, *n.*

re•plete′, *adj.* abundantly filled. —**re•ple′tion**, *n.*

rep′li•ca, *n.* copy.

rep′li•cate, *v.*, **-cated, -cating.** duplicate or reproduce.

rep′li•ca′tion, *n.* **1.** reply. **2.** replica. **3.** act of replicating.

re•ply′, *v.*, **-plied, -plying,** *n.*, *pl.* **-plies.** answer.

re•port′, *n.* **1.** statement of events or findings. **2.** rumor. **3.** loud noise. —*v.* **4.** tell of. **5.** present oneself. **6.** inform against. **7.** write about for newspaper. —**re•port′er**, *n.*

re•port′age, *n.* **1.** act of reporting. **2.** reported news.

re•pose′, *n., v.*, **-posed, -posing.** —*n.* **1.** rest or sleep. **2.** tranquillity. —*v.* **3.** rest or sleep. **4.** put, as trust. —**re•pose′ful**, *adj.*

re•pos′i•tor′y, *n., pl.* **-tories.** place where things are stored.

re′pos•sess′, *v.* take back.

rep′re•hen′si•ble, *adj.* blameworthy. —**rep′re•hen′si•bly**, *adv.*

rep′re•sent′, *v.* **1.** signify. **2.** act or speak for. **3.** portray. —**rep′re•sen•ta′tion**, *n.* —**rep′re•sen•ta′tion•al**, *adj.*

rep′re•sent′a•tive, *n.* **1.** one that represents another or others. **2.** member of legislative body. —*adj.* **3.** representing. **4.** typical.

re·press', *v.* **1.** inhibit. **2.** suppress. —**re·pres'sive**, *adj.* —**re·pres'sion**, *n.*

re·prieve', *v.*, **-prieved, -prieving**, *n.* respite.

rep'ri·mand', *n.* **1.** severe reproof. —*v.* **2.** scold.

re·pris'al, *n.* infliction of injuries in retaliation.

re·proach', *v.* **1.** blame; upbraid. —*n.* **2.** discredit. —**re·proach'ful**, *adj.*

rep'ro·bate', *n., adj., v.,* **-bated, -bating.** —*n.* **1.** hopelessly bad person. —*adj.* **2.** depraved. —*v.* **3.** condemn. —**rep'ro·ba'tion**, *n.*

re'pro·duce', *v.*, **-duced, -ducing. 1.** copy or duplicate. **2.** produce by propagation. —**re'pro·duc'tion**, *n.* —**re'pro·duc'tive**, *adj.*

re·proof', *n.* censure.

re·prove', *v.*, **-proved, -proving.** blame.

rep'tile, *n.* creeping animal, as lizard or snake.

re·pub'lic, *n.* state governed by representatives elected by citizens.

re·pub'li·can, *adj.* **1.** favoring republic. **2.** (*cap.*) of **Republican Party,** major political party of U.S. —*n.* **3.** (*cap.*) member of Republican Party.

re·pu'di·ate', *v.*, **-ated, -ating.** reject as false. —**re·pu'di·a'tion**, *n.*

re·pug'nant, *adj.* distasteful. —**re·pug'nance**, *n.*

re·pulse', *v.*, **-pulsed, -pulsing,** *n.* —*v.* **1.** drive back with force. —*n.* **2.** act of repulsing. **3.** rejection. —**re·pul'sion**, *n.*

re·pul'sive, *adj.* disgusting.

rep'u·ta·ble, *adj.* of good repute. —**rep'u·ta·bly**, *adv.*

rep'u·ta'tion, *n.* **1.** public estimation of character. **2.** good name.

re·pute', *n., v.,* **-puted, -puting.** —*n.* **1.** reputation. —*v.* **2.** give reputation to. —**re·put'ed·ly**, *adv.*

re·quest', *v.* **1.** ask for. —*n.* **2.** act of requesting. **3.** what is requested.

Req'ui·em (rek'wē əm), *n. Rom. Cath. Ch.* mass for dead.

re·quire', *v.*, **-quired, -quiring. 1.** need. **2.** demand. —**re·quire'ment**, *n.*

req′ui·site, *adj.* **1.** necessary. —*n.* **2.** necessary thing.

req′ui·si′tion, *n.* **1.** formal order or demand. —*v.* **2.** take for official use.

re·quite′, *v.,* **-quited, -quiting.** make return to or for. —**re·quit′al** (-kwī′təl), *n.*

re′run′, *n.* **1.** showing of program after its initial run. **2.** the program shown.

re·scind′ (-sind′), *v.* annul; revoke. —**re·scis′sion,** *n.*

res′cue, *v.,* **-cued, -cuing,** *n.* —*v.* **1.** free from danger, capture, etc. —*n.* **2.** act of rescuing. —**res′cu·er,** *n.*

re·search′, *n.* investigate. —**re·search′er,** *n.*

re·sec′tion, *n.* surgical removal of part of organ.

re·sem′ble, *v.,* **-bled, -bling.** be similar to. —**re·sem′blance,** *n.*

re·sent′, *v.* feel indignant or injured at. —**re·sent′ful,** *adj.* —**re·sent′ment,** *n.*

res′er·va′tion, *n.* **1.** act of withholding or setting apart. **2.** doubt or misgiving. **3.** advance assurance of accommodations. **4.** land for use of an Indian tribe.

re·serve′, *v.,* **-served, -serving,** *n., adj.* —*v.* **1.** keep back. —*n.* **2.** something reserved. **3.** part of military force held in readiness to support active forces. **4.** reticence. —*adj.* **5.** kept in reserve.

re·served′, *adj.* **1.** held for future use. **2.** self-restrained. —**re·serv′ed·ly,** *adv.*

re·serv′ist, *n.* member of military reserves.

res′er·voir′ (rez′ər vôr′), *n.* **1.** place where water is stored for use. **2.** supply.

re·side′, *v.,* **-sided, -siding. 1.** dwell. **2.** be vested, as powers.

res′i·dence, *n.* **1.** dwelling place. **2.** act or fact of residing. —**res′i·dent,** *n.* —**res′i·den′tial,** *adj.*

res′i·den·cy, *n., pl.* **-cies. 1.** residence (def. 2). **2.** period of advanced medical training.

res′i·due′, *n.* remainder. —**re·sid′u·al,** *adj.*

re·sign′, *v.* **1.** give up (job, office, etc.) **2.** submit, as to fate. —**res′ig·na′tion,** *n.*

re·signed′, *adj.* acquiescent.

re·sil′i·ent (ri zil′yənt), *adj.* **1.** springing back. **2.**

recovering readily from adversity. —**re•sil′i•ence,** *n.*

res′in, *n.* exudation from some plants. —**res′in•ous,** *adj.*

re•sist′, *v.* withstand; offer opposition to. —**re•sist′ant,** *adj.* —**re•sist′ance,** *n.* —**re•sist′er,** *n.*

re•sis′tor, *n.* device that introduces resistance into electrical circuit.

res′o•lute′, *adj.* determined on action or result. —**res′o•lute′ly,** *adv.* —**res′o•lute′ness,** *n.*

res′o•lu′tion, *n.* 1. expression of group opinion. 2. determination. 3. solution of problem.

re•solve′, *v.,* -solved, -solving, *n.* —*v.* 1. decide firmly. 2. state formally. 3. clear away. 4. solve. —*n.* 5. resolution.

res′o•nant, *adj.* 1. resounding. 2. rich in sound. —**res′o•nance,** *n.* —**res′o•nant•ly,** *adv.*

res′o•nate, *v.,* -nated, -nating. 1. resound. 2. produce resonance.

re•sort′, *v.* 1. turn (to) for use, help, etc. 2. go often. —*n.* 3.

place frequented for recreation. 4. recourse.

re•sound′ (-zound′), *v.* echo.

re•sound′ing, *adj.* impressively complete. —**re•sound′ing•ly,** *adv.*

re′source (rē′sôrs, ri sôrs′), *n.* 1. source of aid or supply. 2. (*pl.*) wealth.

re•source′ful, *adj.* clever. —**re•source′ful•ly,** *adv.* —**re•source′ful•ness,** *n.*

re•spect′, *n.* 1. detail. 2. reference. 3. esteem. —*v.* 4. revere. —**re•spect′er,** *n.*

re•spect′a•ble, *adj.* 1. worthy of respect. 2. decent. —**re•spect′a•bil′i•ty,** *n.* —**re•spect′a•bly,** *adv.*

re•spect′ful, *adj.* showing respect. —**re•spect′ful•ly,** *adv.* —**re•spect′ful•ness,** *n.*

re•spect′ing, *prep.* concerning.

re•spec′tive, *adj.* in order previously named. —**re•spec′tive•ly,** *adv.*

res′pi•ra′tor, *n.* apparatus to produce artificial breathing.

re•spire′, *v.,* -spired, -spiring. breathe. —**res′pi•ra′tion,** *n.* —**res′pi•ra•to′ry,** *adj.*

res'pite, *n., v.,* **-pited, -piting.**
—*n.* 1. temporary relief. —*v.*
2. relieve temporarily.

re•splend'ent, *adj.* gleaming.
—**re•splend'ence,** *n.*

re•spond', *v.* answer.

re•spond'ent, *adj.* 1.
answering. —*n.* 2. *Law.*
defendant.

re•sponse', *n.* reply.
—**re•spon'sive,** *adj.*
—**re•spon'sive•ly,** *adv.*
—**re•spon'sive•ness,** *n.*

re•spon'si•bil'i•ty, *n., pl.*
-ties. 1. state of being
responsible. 2. obligation. 3.
initiative.

re•spon'si•ble, *adj.* 1.
causing things to happen. 2.
capable of rational thought. 3.
reliable. —**re•spon'si•bly,**
adv.

rest, *n.* 1. refreshing quiet. 2.
cessation from motion, work,
etc. 3. support. 4. *Music.*
interval of silence. 5. others.
—*v.* 6. be at ease. 7. cease
from motion. 8. lie or lay. 9.
be based. 10. rely. 11.
continue to be. —**rest'ful,** *adj.*
—**rest'ful•ly,** *adv.*
—**rest'ful•ness,** *n.*

—**rest'less,** *adj.*
—**rest'less•ly,** *adv.*
—**rest'less•ness,** *n.*

res'tau•rant, *n.* public eating
place.

res'tau•ra•teur', *n.*
restaurant owner.

res'ti•tu'tion, *n.* 1.
reparation. 2. return of rights.

res'tive, *adj.* restless.
—**res'tive•ly,** *adv.*

re•store', *v.,* **-stored, -storing.**
1. bring back, as to use or
good condition. 2. give back.
—**res'to•ra'tion,** *n.*
—**re•stor'a•tive,** *adj., n.*

re•strain', *v.* 1. hold back. 2.
confine.

re•straint', *n.* 1. restraining
influence. 2. confinement. 3.
constraint.

re•strict', *v.* confine; limit.
—**re•stric'tion,** *n.*
—**re•stric'tive,** *adj.*

rest room, room in building
with washbowls and toilets.

re•sult', *n.* 1. outcome. —*v.* 2.
occur as result. 3. end.
—**re•sult'ant,** *adj., n.*

re•sume', *v.,* **-sumed, -suming.**
1. go on with again. 2. take
again. —**re•sump'tion,** *n.*

re·sur′face, *v.,* **-faced,
-facing. 1.** give new surface to.
2. come to the surface again.

ré·su·mé (rez′ ŏŏ mā′), *n.*
summary, esp. of work.

re·sur′gent, *adj.* rising again.
—re·sur′gence, *n.*

res′ur·rect′, *v.* bring to life
again. **—res′ur·rec′tion,** *n.*

re·sus′ci·tate′ (-sus′ə-), *v.*
revive. **—re·sus′ci·ta′tion,** *n.*

re′tail, *n.* **1.** sale of goods to
consumer. **—v. 2.** sell at retail.
—re′tail·er, *n.*

re·tain′, *v.* **1.** keep or hold. **2.**
engage. **—re·tain′a·ble,** *adj.*

re·tain′er, *n.* **1.** fee paid to
secure services. **2.** old servant.

re·take′, *v.,* **-took, -taken,
-taking. 1.** take again. **2.**
photograph again. **—n.** (rē′
tāk). **3.** picture photographed
again.

re·tal′i·ate′, *v.,* **-ated, -ating.**
return like for like, esp. evil.
—re·tal′i·a′tion, *n.*
—re·tal′i·a·to′ry, *adj.*

re·tard′, *v.* delay; hinder.
—re′tar·da′tion, *n.*

re·tard′ant, *n.* substance
slowing chemical reaction.

re·tard′ed, *adj.* **1.** slow or
weak in mental development.
—n.pl. 2. retarded persons.

retch, *v.* try to vomit.

re·ten′tion, *n.* **1.** retaining. **2.**
power of retaining. **3.**
memory. **—re·ten′tive,** *adj.*

ret′i·cent, *adj.* saying little.
—ret′i·cence, *n.*
—ret′i·cent·ly, *adv.*

ret′i·na, *n.* coating on back
part of eyeball that receives
images. **—ret′i·nal,** *adj.*

ret′i·nue′ (-nyŏŏ′), *n.* train of
attendants.

re·tire′, *v.,* **-tired, -tiring. 1.**
withdraw. **2.** go to bed. **3.** end
working life. **4.** put out (a
batter, etc.) **—re·tire′ment,** *n.*

re·tired′, *adj.* **1.** withdrawn
from occupation. **2.** secluded.

re·tir′ee′, *n.* retired person.

re·tir′ing, *adj.* shy.

re·tool′, *v.* replace tools of.

re·tort′, *v.* **1.** reply smartly.
—n. 2. sharp or witty reply. **3.**
vessel used in distilling.

re·touch′, *v.* touch up.

re·trace′, *v.,* **-traced, -tracing.**
go back over.

re·tract', *v.* withdraw.
—**re·trac'tion**, *n.*
—**re·tract'a·ble**, *adj.*

re'tread, *n.* **1.** tire that has had new tread added. **2.** *Informal.* person returned to former occupation. **3.** reworking of old idea.

re·treat', *n.* **1.** forced withdrawal. **2.** private place. —*v.* **3.** make a retreat. **4.** withdraw.

re·trench', *v.* economize. —**re·trench'ment**, *n.*

ret'ri·bu'tion, *n.* requital according to merits, esp. for evil. —**re·trib'u·tive**, *adj.*

re·trieve', *v.,* **-trieved, -trieving**, *n.* —*v.* **1.** regain or restore. **2.** make amends for. **3.** recover (killed game). —*n.* **4.** recovery. —**re·triev'er**, *n.*

ret'ro·ac'tive, *adj.* applying also to past.
—**ret'ro·ac'tive·ly**, *adv.*

ret'ro·fit', *v.,* **-fitted, -fitting.** refit with new equipment.

ret'ro·grade', *adj., v.,* **-graded, -grading.** —*adj.* **1.** moving backward. —*v.* **2.** move backward. **3.** decay.

ret'ro·gress', *v.* return to earlier or more primitive condition. —**ret'ro·gres'sion**, *n.* —**ret'ro·gres'sive**, *adj.*

ret'ro·spect', *n.* occasion of looking back.
—**ret'ro·spec'tive**, *adj.*
—**ret'ro·spec'tion**, *n.*

re·turn', *v.* **1.** go or come back to former place or condition. **2.** put or bring back. **3.** reply. —*n.* **4.** act or fact of returning. **5.** recurrence. **6.** requital. **7.** reply. **8.** (*often pl.*) profit. **9.** report. —**re·turn'a·ble**, *adj.*

re·turn'ee, *n., pl.* **-ees.** person who has returned.

re'u·nite', *v.,* **-nited, -niting.** unite after separation.
—**re·un'ion**, *n.*

rev, *n., v.,* **revved, revving.** *Informal.* —*n.* **1.** revolution (in machinery). —*v.* **2.** increase speed of (motor).

Rev., Reverend.

re·vamp', *v.* renovate.

re·veal', *v.* disclose.

rev'eil·le (rev'ə lē), *n. Mil.* signal for awakening.

rev'el, *v.,* **-eled, -eling. 1.** enjoy greatly. **2.** make merry. —*n.* **3.** merry-making. —**rev'e·ler**, *n.*
—**rev'el·ry**, *n.*

rev′e·la′tion, *n.* disclosure.

re·venge′, *n., v.,* **-venged, -venging.** —*n.* 1. retaliation. 2. vindictiveness. —*v.* 3. take revenge. —**re·venge′ful,** *adj.* —**re·veng′er,** *n.*

rev′e·nue′, *n.* income.

re·ver′ber·ate′, *v.,* **-ated, -ating.** 1. echo back. 2. reflect. —**re·ver′ber·a′tion,** *n.*

re·vere′, *v.,* **-vered, -vering.** hold in deep respect.

rev′er·ence, *n., v.,* **-enced, -encing.** —*n.* 1. deep respect and awe. —*v.* 2. regard with reverence. —**rev′er·ent, rev′er·en′tial,** *adj.* —**rev′er·ent·ly,** *adv.*

Rev′er·end, *adj.* title used with member of the clergy.

rev′er·ie, *n.* fanciful musing. Also, **rev′er·y.**

re·verse′, *adj., n., v.,* **-versed, -versing.** —*adj.* 1. opposite in position, action, etc. 2. of or for backward motion. —*n.* 3. reverse part, position, etc. 4. misfortune. —*v.* 5. turn in the opposite position, direction, or condition. —**re·ver′sal,** *n.* —**re·vers′i·ble,** *adj.*

re·vert′, *v.* go back to earlier state. —**re·ver′sion,** *n.*

re·view′, *n.* 1. critical article. 2. repeated viewing. 3. inspection. —*v.* 4. view again. 5. inspect. 6. survey. 7. write a review of. —**re·view′er,** *n.*

re·vile′, *v.,* **-viled, -viling.** speak abusively to or about. —**re·vile′ment,** *n.*

re·vise′, *v.,* **-vised, -vising.** change or amend content of. —**re·vi′sion,** *n.* —**re·vis′er,** *n.*

re·vi′sion·ism, *n.* departure from accepted doctrine. —**re·vi′sion·ist,** *n., adj.*

re·vi′tal·ize′, *v.,* **-ized, -izing.** bring new vitality to. —**re·vi′tal·i·za′tion,** *n.*

re·viv′al, *n.* 1. restoration to life, use, etc. 2. religious awakening. —**re·viv′al·ist,** *n.*

re·vive′, *v.,* **-vived, -viving.** bring back to life.

re·viv′i·fy, *v.,* **-fied, -fying.** bring back to life. —**re·viv′i·fi·ca′tion,** *n.*

re·voke′, *v.,* **-voked, -voking.** annul or repeal. —**rev′o·ca·ble,** *adj.* —**rev′o·ca′tion,** *n.*

re·volt′, *v.* 1. rebel. 2. feel disgust. 3. fill with disgust. —*n.* 4. rebellion. 5. loathing. —**re·volt′ing,** *adj.*

rev′o‧lu′tion, *n.* 1. overthrow of established government. 2. fundamental change. 3. rotation. —**rev′o‧lu′tion‧ar′y,** *adj., n.* —**rev′o‧lu′tion‧ist,** *n.*

rev′o‧lu′tion‧ize′, *v.,* **-ized, -izing.** effect radical change.

re‧volve′, *v.,* **-volved, -volving.** 1. turn round, as on axis. 2. consider.

re‧volv′er, *n.* pistol with revolving cylinder.

re‧vue′, *n.* theatrical show.

re‧vul′sion, *n.* violent change of feeling, esp. to disgust.

re‧ward′, *n.* 1. recompense for merit. —*v.* 2. give reward.

re‧ward′ing, *adj.* gratifying.

re‧word′, *v.* use other words.

re‧write′, *v.,* **-wrote, -written, -writing.** 1. revise. 2. write again.

RFD, rural free delivery.

rhap′so‧dize′, *v.* **-dized, -dizing.** talk ecstatically.

rhap′so‧dy, *n., pl.* **-dies.** 1. exaggerated expression of enthusiasm. 2. irregular musical composition.

rhe′o‧stat′, *n.* device for regulating electric current.

rhe′sus, *n.* kind of monkey.

rhet′o‧ric, *n.* 1. skillful use of language. 2. exaggerated speech. —**rhe‧tor′i‧cal,** *adj.*

rhetorical question, question asked for effect, not answer.

rheum, *n.* thin discharge of mucous membranes.

rheu′ma‧tism′, *n.* disease affecting joints or muscles. —**rheu‧mat′ic,** *adj., n.*

Rh factor (är′āch′), antigen in blood that may cause severe reaction in individual lacking the substance.

rhine′stone′, *n.* artificial diamondlike gem.

rhi‧ni′tis, *n.* inflammation of the nose.

rhi‧noc′er‧os, *n.* large mammal with horned snout.

rhi′zome (rī′zōm), *n.* rootlike stem.

rho′do‧den′dron, *n.* flowering evergreen shrub.

rhom′boid, *n.* oblique-angled parallelogram with only the opposite sides equal.

rhom′bus, *n., pl.* **-buses, -bi.** oblique-angled parallelogram with all sides equal.

rhu′barb, *n.* garden plant with edible leaf stalks.

rhyme, *n., v.,* **rhymed, rhyming.** —*n.* **1.** agreement in end sounds of lines or words. **2.** verse with such agreement. —*v.* **3.** make or form rhyme.

rhythm, *n.* movement with uniformly recurring beat. —**rhyth′mic, rhyth′mi•cal,** *adj.* —**rhyth′mi•cal•ly,** *adv.*

RI, Rhode Island. Also, **R.I.**

rib, *n., v.,* **ribbed, ribbing.** —*n.* **1.** one of the slender curved bones enclosing chest. **2.** riblike part. —*v.* **3.** furnish with ribs. **4.** *Informal.* tease.

rib′ald, *adj.* bawdy in speech. —**rib′ald•ry,** *n.*

rib′bon, *n.* strip of silk, rayon, etc.

ri′bo•fla′vin (rī′bō flā′vin), *n.* important vitamin.

rice, *n.* edible starchy grain.

rich, *adj.* **1.** having great possessions. **2.** abounding. **3.** costly. **4.** containing butter, cream, etc. **5.** strong. **6.** mellow. —*n.* **7.** rich people. —**rich′ly,** *adv.* —**rich′ness,** *n.*

rich′es, *n.pl.* wealth.

Rich′ter scale, scale for indicating intensity of earthquake.

rick, *n.* stack of hay, etc.

rick′ets, *n.* disease often marked by bone deformities.

rick′et•y, *adj.,* **-etier, -etiest.** shaky.

rick′shaw, *n.* two-wheeled passenger vehicle pulled by person.

ric′o•chet′ (rik′ə shā′), *v.,* **-cheted, -cheting,** *n.* —*v.* **1.** rebound from a flat surface. —*n.* **2.** such a movement.

ri•cot′ta, *n.* soft cheese.

rid, *v.,* **rid** or **ridded, ridding.** clear of. —**rid′dance,** *n.*

rid′dle, *n., v.,* **-dled, -dling.** —*n.* **1.** puzzling question or matter. **2.** coarse sieve. —*v.* **3.** speak perplexingly. **4.** pierce with many holes. **5.** put through sieve.

ride, *v.,* **rode, ridden, riding,** *n.* —*v.* **1.** be carried in traveling. **2.** sit on and manage (horse, etc.). **3.** rest on something. —*n.* **4.** journey on a horse, etc. **5.** device in which people ride for amusement.

rid′er, *n.* **1.** person that rides. **2.** clause attached to legislative bill before passage.

ridge, *n., v.,* **ridged, ridging.** —*n.* **1.** long narrow elevation. —*v.* **2.** form with ridge.

ridge′pole′, *n.* horizontal beam on roof to which rafters are attached.

rid′i·cule′, *n., v.,* **-culed, -culing.** —*n.* **1.** derision. —*v.* **2.** deride.

ri·dic′u·lous, *adj.* absurd. —**ri·dic′u·lous·ly**, *adv.*

rife, *adj.* **1.** widespread. **2.** abounding.

riff, *n.* **1.** repeated phrase in jazz or rock music. **2.** variation or improvisation. —*v.* **3.** perform a riff.

riff′raff′, *n.* rabble.

ri′fle, *n., v.,* **-fled, -fling.** —*n.* **1.** shoulder firearm with spirally grooved barrel. —*v.* **2.** cut spiral grooves in (gun barrel). **3.** search through to rob. **4.** steal. —**ri′fle·man**, *n.*

rift, *n.* split.

rig, *v.,* **rigged, rigging,** *n.* —*v.* **1.** fit with tackle and other parts. **2.** put together as makeshift. **3.** manipulate fraudulently. —*n.* **4.** arrangement of masts, booms, tackle, etc. **5.** equipment. —**rig′ger**, *n.*

rig′ging, *n.* ropes and chains that work masts, sails, etc.

right, *adj.* **1.** just or good. **2.** correct. **3.** in good condition. **4.** on side that is toward the east when one faces north. **5.** straight. —*n.* **6.** that which is right. **7.** right side. **8.** that justly due one. **9.** conservative side in politics. —*adv.* **10.** directly. **11.** set correctly. **12.** in right position. **13.** correct. —**right′ly**, *adv.* —**right′ness**, *n.* —**right′ist**, *adj., n.*

right angle, 90-degree angle.

right′eous, *adj.* virtuous. —**right′eous·ly**, *adv.* —**right′eous·ness**, *n.*

right′ful, *adj.* having just claim. —**right′ful·ly**, *adv.*

right′-hand′ed, *adj.* **1.** using the right hand more easily. **2.** for the right hand. —**right′-hand′edness**, *n.*

right of way, **1.** right of one vehicle to proceed ahead of another. **2.** path or route that may lawfully be used. **3.** strip of land acquired for use.

right′-to-life′, *adj.* advocating laws making abortion illegal. —**right′-to-lif′er**, *n.*

right wing, conservative element in organization. —**right′-wing′**, *adj.* —**right′-wing′er**, *n.*

rig′id, *adj.* 1. stiff; inflexible. 2. rigorous. —**ri•gid′i•ty,** *n.* —**rig′id•ly,** *adv.*

rig′ma•role′, *n.* confused talk.

rig′or, *n.* 1. strictness. 2. hardship. —**rig′or•ous,** *adj.* —**rig′or•ous•ly,** *adv.*

ri′gor mor′tis, stiffening of body after death.

rile, *v.,* **riled, riling.** *Informal.* vex.

rill, *n.* small brook.

rim, *n., v.,* **rimmed, rimming.** —*n.* 1. outer edge. —*v.* 2. furnish with rim.

rime, *n., v.,* **rimed, riming.** —*n.* 1. rhyme. 2. rough white frost. —*v.* 3. cover with rime.

rind, *n.* firm covering, as of fruit or cheese.

ring, *n., v.,* **rang, rung** (for 11, **ringed**), **ringing.** —*n.* 1. round band for a finger. 2. any circular band. 3. enclosed area. 4. group cooperating for selfish purpose. 5. ringing sound. 6. telephone call. —*v.* 7. sound resonantly. 8. appear. 9. be filled with sound. 10. signal by bell. 11. form ring around.

ring′er, *n.* 1. person or thing that closely resembles another. 2. athlete entered in competition in violation of eligibility rules.

ring′lead′er, *n.* leader in mischief.

ring′let, *n.* curl of hair.

ring′mas′ter, *n.* person in charge of performances in circus ring.

ring′worm′, *n.* contagious skin disease.

rink, *n.* floor or sheet of ice for skating on.

rinse, *v.,* **rinsed, rinsing,** *n.* —*v.* 1. wash lightly. —*n.* 2. rinsing act. 3. preparation for rinsing.

ri′ot, *n.* 1. disturbance by mob. 2. wild disorder. —*v.* 3. take part in riot. —**ri′ot•ous,** *adj.*

rip, *v.,* **ripped, ripping,** *n.* tear. —**rip′per,** *n.*

R.I.P., may he, she, or they rest in peace.

rip cord, cord that opens parachute.

ripe, *adj.,* **riper, ripest.** 1. fully developed; mature. 2. ready. —**rip′en,** *v.* —**ripe′ness,** *n.*

rip′off′, *n. Slang.* theft or exploitation.

ri•poste′ (ri pōst′), *n.* quick, sharp reply or reaction.

rip′ple, v., **-pled, -pling,** n. —v.
1. form small waves. —n. 2.
pattern of small waves.

ripple effect, spreading effect.

rip′-roar′ing, adj. boisterously
exciting.

rip′saw′, n. saw for cutting
wood with the grain.

rip′tide′, n. tide that opposes
other tides.

rise, v., **rose, risen, rising,** n.
—v. 1. get up. 2. revolt. 3.
appear. 4. originate. 5. move
upward. 6. increase. 7. (of
dough) expand. —n. 8.
upward movement. 9. origin.
10. upward slope. —**ris′er,** n.

ris′i•ble (riz′ə bəl), adj.
causing laughter.

risk, n. 1. dangerous chance.
—v. 2. expose to risk. 3. take
risk of. —**risk′y,** adj.

ris•qué′ (-kā′), adj. bawdy.

rite, n. ceremonial act.

rite of passage, event
marking passage from one
stage of life to another.

rit′u•al, n. system of religious
or other rites. —**rit′u•al•ism′,**
n. —**rit′u•al•is′tic,** adj.

ri′val, n., adj., v., **-valed,**
-valing. —n. 1. competitor. 2.

equal. —adj. 3. being a rival.
—v. 4. compete with. 5.
match. —**ri′val•ry,** n.

rive, v., **rived, rived** or **riven,**
riving. split.

riv′er, n. large natural stream.

riv′et, n., v., **-eted, -eting.** —n.
1. metal bolt hammered after
insertion. —v. 2. fasten with
rivets.

riv′u•let, n. small stream.

RN, registered nurse.

roach, n. cockroach.

road, n. 1. open way for travel.
2. Also, **road′stead′.**
anchorage near shore.

road′block′, n. 1. obstruction
placed across road to halt
traffic. 2. obstacle to progress.

road′run′ner, n. terrestrial
cuckoo of western U.S.

road show, show, as a play,
performed by touring actors.

roam, v. wander; rove.

roan, adj. 1. horse with gray or
white spots. —n. 2. roan
horse.

roar, v. 1. make loud, deep
sound. —n. 2. loud, deep
sound. 3. loud laughter.

roast, *v.* 1. cook by dry heat. —*n.* 2. roasted meat. —**roast′er,** *n.*

rob, *v.,* **robbed, robbing.** deprive of unlawfully. —**rob′ber,** *n.* —**rob′ber•y,** *n.*

robe, *n., v.,* **robed, robing.** —*n.* 1. long loose garment. 2. wrap or covering. —*v.* 3. clothe.

rob′in, *n.* red-breasted bird.

ro′bot, *n.* 1. humanlike machine that performs tasks. 2. person who acts in mechanical manner.

ro•bot′ics, *n.* technology of computer-controlled robots.

ro•bust′, *adj.* healthy.

rock, *n.* 1. mass of stone. 2. Also, **rock-'n'-roll.** popular music with steady, insistent rhythm. —*v.* 3. move back and forth. —**rock′y,** *adj.*

rock bottom, lowest level.

rock′er, *n.* curved support of cradle or **rock′ing chair.**

rock′et, *n.* tube propelled by discharge of gases from it.

rock′et•ry, *n.* science of rocket design.

rock′-ribbed′, *adj.* 1. having ridges of rock. 2. unyielding.

rock salt, salt occurring in rocklike masses.

ro•co′co, *n.* elaborate decorative style of many curves. —**ro•co′co,** *adj.*

rod, *n.* 1. slender shaft. 2. linear measure of 5½ yards.

ro′dent, *n.* small gnawing or nibbling mammal.

ro′de•o′, *n., pl.* **-deos.** exhibition of cowboy skills.

roe, *n., pl.* **roes, roe.** 1. small deer. 2. fish eggs or spawn.

roent•gen (rent′gən, -jən), *n.* unit for measuring radiation dosage.

rog′er, *interj.* (message) received.

rogue, *n.* rascal. —**ro′guish,** *adj.* —**ro′guer•y,** *n.*

roil, *v.* 1. make muddy. 2. vex. —**roil′y,** *adj.*

roist′er, *v.* 1. swagger. 2. carouse. —**roist′er•er,** *n.*

role, *n.* part of function, as of character in play. Also, **rôle.**

role model, person imitated by others.

roll, *v.* 1. move by turning. 2. rock. 3. have deep, loud sound. 4. flatten with roller. 5.

form into roll or ball. —*n.* **6.** list; register. **7.** anything cylindrical. **8.** small cake. **9.** deep long sound. —**roll′er,** *n.*

roll′back′, *n.* return to lower level.

roll call, calling of names for checking attendance.

roller coaster, 1. small railroad that moves along winding route with steep inclines. **2.** experience with sharp ups and downs.

roller skate, skate with four wheels. —**roller-skate,** *v.*

rol′lick•ing, *adj.* jolly.

rolling pin, cylinder for rolling out dough.

roll′o′ver, *n.* reinvestment of funds.

roll′-top desk, desk with flexible sliding cover.

ro′ly-po′ly, *adj.* short and round.

ROM, read-only memory: non-modifiable part of computer memory containing instructions to system.

ro•maine′, *n.* kind of lettuce.

Ro′man, 1. native or citizen of Rome or Roman Empire. **2.**

(*l.c.*) upright style of printing type. —**Ro′man,** *adj.*

Roman candle, kind of firework.

Roman Catholic Church, Christian Church of which pope (Bishop of Rome) is head. —**Roman Catholic.**

ro•mance′, *n., v.,* **-manced, -mancing.** —*n.* **1.** colorful, imaginative tale. **2.** colorful, fanciful quality. **3.** love affair. —*v.* **4.** act romantically. **5.** tell fanciful, false story.

Roman numerals, system of numbers using letters as symbols: I = 1, V = 5, X = 10, L = 50, C = 100, D = 500, M = 1,000.

ro•man′tic, *adj.* **1.** of romance. **2.** impractical or unrealistic. **3.** imbued with idealism. **4.** preoccupied with love. **5.** passionate; fervent. **6.** of a style of art stressing imagination and emotion. —*n.* **7.** romantic person. —**ro•man′ti•cal•ly,** *adv.*

ro•man′ti•cism, *n.* (*often cap.*) romantic spirit or artistic style or movement. —**ro•man′ti•cist,** *n.*

ro•man′ti•cize′, *v.,* **-cized, -cizing.** invest with romantic character.

romp, *v., n.* frolic.

romp′ers, *n.pl.* child's loose outer garment.

rood (rood), *n.* **1.** crucifix. **2.** one-quarter of an acre.

roof, *n., pl.* **roofs. 1.** upper covering of building. —*v.* **2.** provide with roof. —**roof′er,** *n.* —**roof′ing,** *n.*

rook (rook), *n.* **1.** European crow. **2.** chess piece; castle. —*v.* **3.** cheat.

rook′ie, *n. Slang.* recruit or beginner.

room, *n.* **1.** separate space within building. **2.** space. —*v.* **3.** lodge. —**room′er,** *n.* —**room′mate′,** *n.* —**room′y,** *adj.*

roost, *n.* **1.** perch where fowls rest. —*v.* **2.** sit on roost.

roost′er, *n.* male chicken.

root, *n.* **1.** part of plant growing underground. **2.** embedded part. **3.** origin. **4.** quantity that, when multiplied by itself so many times, produces given quantity. —*v.* **5.** establish roots. **6.** implant. **7.**

root out, exterminate. **8.** dig with snout. **9.** *Informal.* cheer encouragingly. —**root′er,** *n.*

root beer, soft drink flavored with extracts of roots, barks, and herbs.

root canal, root portion of the pulp cavity of a tooth.

rope, *n., v.,* **roped, roping.** —*n.* **1.** strong twisted cord. —*v.* **2.** fasten or catch with rope.

Roque′fort, *n. Trademark.* strong cheese veined with mold, made from sheep's milk.

Ror′schach test (rôr′shäk), diagnostic test of personality based on interpretations of inkblot designs.

ro′sa•ry, *n., pl.* **-ries.** *Rom. Cath. Ch.* **1.** series of prayers. **2.** string of beads counted in saying rosary.

rose, *n.* thorny plant having showy, fragrant flowers.

ro•sé′ (rō zā′), *n.* pink wine.

ro′se•ate, *adj.* **1.** rosy. **2.** promising; bright.

rose′mar′y, *n.* aromatic shrub used for seasoning.

ro•sette′, *n.* rose-shaped ornament.

Rosh' Ha·sha'na (rōsh' hä shä'nə), Jewish New Year.

ros'in, *n.* solid left after distilling pine resin.

ros'ter, *n.* list of persons, groups, events, etc.

ros'trum, *n., pl.* **-trums, -tra.** speakers' platform.

ros'y, *adj.,* **rosier, rosiest. 1.** pinkish-red. **2.** cheerful; optimistic. **3.** bright. —**ros'i·ly,** *adv.* —**ros'i·ness,** *n.*

rot, *v.,* **rotted, rotting,** *n.* —*v.* **1.** decay. —*n.* **2.** decay. **3.** decay of tissue.

ro'tate, *v.,* **-tated, -tating.** turn on or as on axis. —**ro'ta·ry,** *adj.* —**ro·ta'tion,** *n.* —**ro·ta'tor,** *n.*

ROTC, Reserve Officers Training Corps.

rote, *n.* **1.** routine way. **2. by rote,** from memory in mechanical way.

ro·tis'ser·ie, *n.* rotating machine for roasting.

ro'tor, *n.* rotating part.

ro'to·till'er, *n.* motorized device with spinning blades for tilling soil.

rot'ten, *adj.* **1.** decaying. **2.** corrupt. —**rot'ten·ly,** *adv.* —**rot'ten·ness,** *n.*

ro·tund', *adj.* round. —**ro·tun'di·ty,** *n.*

ro·tun'da, *n.* round room.

rou·é' (rōō ā'), *n.* dissolute man; rake.

rouge, *n., v.,* **rouged, rouging.** —*n.* **1.** red cosmetic for cheeks and lips. **2.** red polishing agent for metal. —*v.* **3.** color with rouge.

rough, *adj.* **1.** not smooth. **2.** violent in action or motion. **3.** harsh. **4.** crude. —*n.* **5.** rough thing or part. —*v.* **6.** make rough. —**rough'ly,** *adv.* —**rough'ness,** *n.*

rough'age, *n.* coarse or fibrous material in food.

rough'en, *v.* make or become rough.

rou·lette' (rōō-), *n.* gambling game based on spinning disk.

round, *adj.* **1.** circular, curved, or spherical. **2.** complete. **3.** expressed as approximate number. **4.** sonorous. —*n.* **5.** something round. **6.** complete course, series, etc. **7.** part of beef thigh between rump and leg. 8. song in which voices enter at intervals. 9. stage of competition, as in tournament. —*adv.* 10. in or as in a circle. 11. in circumference. —*prep.* 12. around. —*v.* 13. make round. 14. complete. 15. bring together. —**round'ness,** *n.*

round'a•bout', *adj.* indirect.

roun'de•lay, *n.* song in which phrase is staggered and repeated.

round'house', *n.* building for servicing locomotives.

round'ly, *adv.* unsparingly.

round table, group gathered for conference.

round trip, trip to and back.

round'worm', *n.* nematode that infests intestines of mammals.

round'up', *n.* 1. bringing together. 2. summary.

rouse, *v.,* **roused, rousing.** stir up; arouse.

roust'a•bout', *n.* laborer.

rout, *n.* 1. defeat ending in disorderly flight. —*v.* 2. force to flee in disorder.

route (roōt), *n., v.,* **routed, routing.** —*n.* 1. course of travel. —*v.* 2. send by route.

rou•tine', *n.* 1. regular order of action. —*adj.* 2. like or by routine. 3. ordinary. —**rou•tine'ly,** *adv.*

rove, *v.,* **roved, roving.** wander aimlessly. —**rov'er,** *n.*

row (rō), *v.* 1. propel by oars. 2. (rou). dispute noisily. —*n.* 3. trip in rowboat. 4. persons or things in line. 5. (rou). noisy dispute. —**row'boat',** *n.*

row'dy, *adj.,* **-dier, -diest,** *n.,* *pl.* **-dies.** —*adj.* 1. rough and disorderly. —*n.* 2. rowdy person. —**row'di•ness,** *n.*

roy'al, *adj.* of kings or queens. —**roy'al•ly,** *adv.*

roy'al•ist, *n.* person favoring royal government. —**royalist,** *adj.* —**roy'al•ism,** *n.*

roy'al•ty, *n., pl.* **-ties.** 1. royal persons. 2. royal power. 3. share of proceeds, paid to an author, inventor, etc.

rpm, revolutions per minute.

RR, 1. railroad. 2. rural route.

RSVP, please reply.

rub, *v.,* **rubbed, rubbing,** *n.* —*v.* 1. apply pressure to in cleaning, smoothing, etc. **2.** press against with friction. —*n.* **3.** act of rubbing. **4.** difficulty.

rub′ber, *n.* **1.** elastic material from a tropical tree. **2.** *pl.* overshoes. —**rub′ber•ize′,** *v.* —**rub′ber•y,** *adj.*

rubber band, band of rubber used for holding things together.

rubber cement, adhesive.

rub′ber•neck′, *Informal.* —*v.* **1.** stare curiously. —*n.* **2.** curious onlooker. **3.** sightseer.

rubber stamp, 1. stamp with rubber printing surface.

rub′bish, *n.* **1.** waste. **2.** nonsense.

rub′ble, *n.* broken stone.

rub′down′, *n.* massage.

ru•bel′la (roo bel′ə), *n.* usu. mild viral infection. Also, **German measles.**

ru′bi•cund′ (roo′bə kund′), *adj.* red.

ru′ble (roo′bəl), *n.* monetary unit of Russia and of some former Soviet states.

ru′bric (roo′brik), *n.* **1.** title or heading. **2.** class or category.

ru′by, *n., pl.* **-bies.** red gem.

ruck′sack′, *n.* knapsack.

ruck′us, *n.* noisy commotion.

rud′der, *n.* turning flat piece for steering vessel or aircraft.

rud′dy, *adj.,* **-dier, -diest.** having healthy red color.

rude, *adj.,* **ruder, rudest. 1.** discourteous. **2.** unrefined; crude. —**rude′ly,** *adv.* —**rude′ness,** *n.*

ru′di•ment (roo′-), *n.* basic thing to learn. —**ru′di•men′ta•ry,** *adj.*

rue, *v.,* **rued, ruing,** *n.* regret. —**rue′ful,** *adj.*

ruff, *n.* deep full collar.

ruf′fi•an, *n.* rough or lawless person.

ruf′fle, *v.,* **-fled, -fling,** *n.* —*v.* **1.** make uneven. **2.** disturb. **3.** gather in folds. **4.** beat (drum) softly and steadily. —*n.* **5.** break in evenness. **6.** band of cloth, etc., gathered on one edge. **7.** soft steady beat.

rug, *n.* floor covering.

Rug′by, *n.* English form of football.

rug′ged, *adj.* **1.** roughly irregular. **2.** severe. —**rug′ged•ly,** *adv.* —**rug′ged•ness,** *n.*

ru′in, *n.* 1. destruction. 2. (*pl.*) remains of fallen building, etc. —*v.* 3. bring or come to ruin or ruins. —**ru′in•a′tion,** *n.* —**ru′in•ous,** *adj.*

rule, *n., v.,* **ruled, ruling.** —*n.* 1. principle; regulation. 2. control. 3. ruler (def. 2). —*v.* 4. control. 5. decide in the manner of a judge. 6. mark with ruler. —**rul′ing,** *n., adj.*

rul′er, *n.* 1. person who rules. 2. straight-edged strip for measuring, drawing lines, etc.

rum, *n.* alcoholic liquor.

rum′ba, *n.* Cuban dance.

rum′ble, *v.,* **-bled, -bling,** *n.* —*v.* 1. make long, deep, heavy sound. —*n.* 2. such sound.

ru′mi•nant, *n.* 1. cud-chewing mammal, as cows. —*adj.* 2. cud-chewing.

ru′mi•nate′, *v.,* **-nated, -nating.** 1. chew cud. 2. meditate. —**ru′mi•na′tion,** *n.* —**ru′mi•na′tive,** *adj.*

rum′mage, *v.,* **-maged, -maging.** search.

rum′my, *n., pl.* **-mies.** 1. card game. 2. *Slang.* drunkard.

ru′mor, *n.* 1. unconfirmed but widely repeated story. —*v.* 2. tell as rumor.

rump, *n.* hind part of body.

rum′pus, *n. Informal.* noise.

run, *v.,* **ran, run, running,** *n.* —*v.* 1. advance quickly. 2. be candidate. 3. flow; melt. 4. extend. 5. operate. 6. be exposed to. 7. manage. —*n.* 8. act or period of running. 9. raveled line in knitting. 10. freedom of action. 11. scoring unit in baseball.

run′a•round′, *n. Informal.* evasive treatment.

run′a•way′, *n.* 1. fugitive; deserter. 2. something that has broken away from control. —*adj.* 3. escaped; fugitive. 4. uncontrolled.

run′-down′, *adj.* 1. fatigued; weary. 2. fallen into disrepair. 3. not running because of not being wound.

run′down′, *n.* short summary.

rune, *n.* ancient Germanic alphabet character. —**ru′nic,** *adj.*

rung, *n.* 1. ladder step. 2. bar between chair legs.

run′-in′, *n.* confrontation.

run′ner, *n.* 1. one that runs. 2. messenger. 3. blade of skate. 4. strip of fabric, carpet, etc.

run′ner-up′, *n.* competitor finishing in second place.

run′off′, *n.* final contest held to break tie.

run′-of-the-mill′, *adj.* mediocre.

run′-on′, *adj.* 1. of something that is added. —*n.* 2. run-on matter.

runt, *n.* undersized thing.

run′way′, *n.* strip where airplanes take off and land.

rup′ture, *n., v.,* **-tured, -turing.** —*n.* 1. break. 2. hernia. —*v.* 3. break. 4. cause breach of.

ru′ral, *adj.* of or in the country.

ruse, *n.* trick.

rush, *v.* 1. move with speed or violence. —*n.* 2. act of rushing. 3. hostile attack. 4. grasslike herb growing in marshes. —*adj.* 5. requiring or marked by haste.

rusk, *n.* sweet raised bread dried and baked again.

rus′set, *n.* reddish brown.

Rus′sian, *n.* native or language of Russia. —**Russian,** *adj.*

rust, *n.* 1. red-orange coating that forms on iron and steel exposed to air and moisture. 2. plant disease. —*v.* 3. make or become rusty. —**rust′y,** *adj.*

rus′tic, *adj.* 1. rural. 2. simple. —*n.* 3. country person.

rus′ti•cate′, *v.,* **-cated, -cating.** go to or live in the country.

rus′tle, *v.,* **-tled, -tling,** *n.* —*v.* 1. make small soft sounds. 2. steal (cattle, etc.). —*n.* 3. rustling sound. —**rus′tler,** *n.*

rut, *n., v.,* **rutted, rutting.** —*n.* 1. furrow or groove worn in the ground. 2. period of sexual excitement in male deer, goats, etc. —*v.* 3. make ruts in. 4. be in rut. —**rut′ty,** *adj.*

ru′ta•ba′ga (roo′tə bā′gə), *n.* yellow turnip.

ruth′less, *adj.* pitiless. —**ruth′less•ness,** *n.*

RV, recreational vehicle.

Rx, prescription.

rye, *n.* cereal grass used for flour, feed, and whiskey.

S, s, *n.* nineteenth letter of English alphabet.

S south, southern.

Sab'bath, *n.* day of religious observance and rest, observed on Saturday by Jews and on Sunday by most Christians.

sab·bat'i·cal, *n.* 1. paid leave of absence for study. —*adj.* 2. (*cap.*) of the Sabbath.

sa'ber, *n.* one-edged sword. Also, **sa'bre.**

saber saw, portable electric jigsaw.

sa'ble, *n.* small mammal with dark-brown fur.

sab'o·tage', *n., v.,* **-taged, -taging.** —*n.* 1. willful injury to equipment, etc. —*v.* 2. attack by sabotage. —**sab'o·teur',** *n.*

sac, *n.* baglike part.

sac'cha·rin (sak'ə rin), *n.* sweet substance used as sugar substitute.

sac'cha·rine, *adj.* overly sweet.

sac'er·do'tal (sas'ər-), *adj.* priestly.

sa·chet' (-shā'), *n.* small bag of perfumed powder.

S

sack, *n.* 1. large stout bag. 2. bag. 3. *Slang.* dismissal. 4. plundering. —*v.* 5. put into a sack. 6. *Slang.* dismiss. 7. plunder; loot. —**sack'ing,** *n.*

sack'cloth', *n.* coarse cloth worn for penance or mourning.

sac'ra·ment, *n.* 1. rite in Christian church. 2. (*cap.*) Eucharist. —**sac'ra·men'tal,** *adj.*

sa'cred, *adj.* 1. holy. 2. secured against violation. —**sa'cred·ness,** *n.*

sac'ri·fice', *n., v.,* **-ficed, -ficing.** —*n.* 1. offer of life, treasure, etc., to deity. 2. surrender of something for purpose. —*v.* 3. give as sacrifice. —**sac'ri·fi'cial,** *adj.*

sac'ri·lege (-lij), *n.* profanation of anything sacred. —**sac'ri·le'gious,** *adj.*

sac'ris·tan (sak'ri stan), *n.* sexton.

sac'ris·ty, *n., pl.* **-ties.** room in church, etc., where sacred objects are kept.

sac′ro·il′i·ac′, *n.* joint in lower back.

sac′ro·sanct′, *adj.* sacred.

sac′rum, *n.*, *pl.* **sacra.** bone forming rear wall of pelvis.

sad, *adj.*, **sadder, saddest.** sorrowful. —**sad′den**, *v.* —**sad′ly**, *adv.* —**sad′ness**, *n.*

sad′dle, *n.*, *v.*, **-dled, -dling.** —*n.* **1.** seat for rider on horse, etc. **2.** anything resembling saddle. —*v.* **3.** put saddle on. **4.** burden.

sad′dle·bag′, *n.* pouch laid over back of horse or mounted over rear wheel of bicycle or motorcycle.

sad′ism, *n.* sexual or other enjoyment in causing pain. —**sad′ist**, *n.* —**sa·dis′tic**, *adj.*

sa′do·mas′o·chism′ (sā′dō mas′ə kiz′əm), *n.* sexual or other enjoyment in causing or experiencing pain. —**sa′do·mas′o·chist′**, *n.* —**sa′do·mas′o·chis′tic**, *adj.*

sa·fa′ri (sə fär′ē), *n.* (in E. Africa) journey; hunting expedition.

safe, *adj.*, **safer, safest**, *n.* —*adj.* **1.** secure or free from danger. **2.** dependable. —*n.* **3.** stout box for valuables. —**safe′ty**, *n.* —**safe′ly**, *adv.* —**safe′keep′ing**, *n.*

safe′-con′duct, *n.* document authorizing safe passage.

safe′-de·pos′it, *adj.* providing safekeeping for valuables.

safe′guard′, *n.* **1.** something that ensures safety. —*v.* **2.** protect.

safe sex, sexual activity in which precautions are taken to avoid sexually transmitted diseases.

safety glass, shatter-resistant glass.

safety match, match that ignites only when struck on special surface.

safety pin, pin bent back on itself with guard for point.

safety razor, razor with blade guard.

saf′flow·er, *n.* thistle-like plant whose seeds yield cooking oil.

saf′fron, *n.* bright yellow seasoning.

sag, *v.*, **sagged, sagging**, *n.* —*v.* **1.** bend, esp. in middle, from weight or pressure. **2.** hang loosely. —*n.* **3.** sagging place.

sa′ga, *n.* heroic tale.

sa•ga′cious, *adj.* shrewd and practical. —**sa•gac′i•ty,** *n.*

sage, *n., adj.,* **sager, sagest.** —*n.* 1. wise person. 2. herb used in seasoning. —*adj.* 3. wise; prudent. —**sage′ly,** *adv.* —**sage′ness,** *n.*

sage′brush′, *n.* sagelike, bushy plant of dry plains of western U.S.

sa′go, *n.* starchy substance from some palms.

sa′hib (sä′ib), *n.* (in colonial India) term of respect for European.

said, *adj.* named before.

sail, *n.* 1. sheet spread to catch wind to propel vessel or windmill. 2. trip on sailing vessel. —*v.* 3. move by action of wind. 4. travel over water. —**sail′or,** *n.*

sail′cloth′, *n.* fabric used for boat sails or tents.

sail′fish′, *n.* large fish with upright fin.

saint, *n.* holy person. —**saint′hood,** *n.* —**saint′ly,** *adj.* —**saint′li•ness,** *n.*

sake, *n.* 1. benefit. 2. purpose. 3. (sä′kē). rice wine.

sa•laam (sə läm′), *n.* 1. Islamic salutation. 2. low bow with hand on forehead.

sal′a•ble, *adj.* subject to or fit for sale. Also, **sale′a•ble.**

sa•la′cious (-lā′shəs), *adj.* lewd.

sal′ad, *n.* dish esp. of raw vegetables or fruit.

sal′a•man′der, *n.* small amphibian.

sa•la′mi, *n.* kind of sausage.

sal′a•ry, *n., pl.* **-ries.** fixed payment for regular work. —**sal′a•ried,** *adj.*

sale, *n.* 1. act of selling. 2. opportunity to sell. 3. occasion of selling at reduced prices. —**sales′man,** *n.* —**sales′la′dy, sales′wom′an,** *n.fem.* —**sales′per′son,** *n.* —**sales′people,** *n.pl.* —**sales′room′,** *n.*

sales′man•ship′, *n.* skill of selling a product or idea.

sal′i•cyl′ic acid (sal′ə sil′ik), substance used in aspirin.

sa′li•ent (sā′-), *adj.* 1. conspicuous. 2. projecting. —*n.* 3. projecting part. —**sa′li•ence,** *n.* —**sa′li•ent•ly,** *adv.*

sa′line (sā′līn), *adj.* salty.
—**sa•lin′i•ty,** *n.*

sa•li′va, *n.* fluid secreted into mouth by glands.
—**sal′i•var′y,** *adj.*
—**sal′i•vate′,** *v.*
—**sal′i•va′tion,** *n.*

Salk vaccine, vaccine against poliomyelitis.

sal′low, *adj.* having sickly complexion.

sal′ly, *n., pl.* **-lies,** *v.,* **-lied, -lying.** —*n.* **1.** sudden attack by besieged troops. **2.** outward burst or rush. **3.** witty remark. —*v.* **4.** make sally.

salm′on, *n.* pink-fleshed food fish of northern waters.

sal′mo•nel′la (sal′mə nel′ə), *n., pl.* **-lae** (-ē), **-las.** bacillus that causes various diseases, including food poisoning.

sa•lon′, *n.* **1.** drawing room. **2.** art gallery.

sa•loon′, *n.* **1.** place where intoxicating liquors are sold and drunk. **2.** public room.

sal′sa (säl′sə, -sä), *n.* **1.** Latin-American music with elements of jazz, rock, and soul. **2.** sauce, esp. hot sauce containing chilies.

salt, *n.* **1.** sodium chloride, occurring as mineral, in sea water, etc. **2.** chemical compound derived from acid and base. **3.** wit. **4.** *Informal.* sailor. —*v.* **5.** season or preserve with salt. —**salt′y,** *adj.* —**salt′i•ness,** *n.*

SALT, *n.* Strategic Arms Limitation Talks.

salt′cel′lar, *n.* shaker or dish for salt.

sal•tine′, *n.* crisp, salted cracker.

salt lick, place where animals lick salt deposits.

salt of the earth, someone thought to embody best human qualities.

salt′pe′ter, *n.* potassium nitrate.

sa•lu′bri•ous, *adj.* healthful.
—**sa•lu′bri•ous•ly,** *adv.*
—**sa•lub′ri•ty,** *n.*

sal′u•tar′y, *adj.* healthful; beneficial.

sal′u•ta′tion, *n.* **1.** greeting. **2.** formal opening of letter.

sa•lute′, *v.,* **-luted, -luting,** *n.* —*v.* **1.** express respect or goodwill, esp. in greeting. —*n.* **2.** act of saluting.

sal′vage, *n., v.,* **-vaged, -vaging.** —*n.* **1.** act of saving ship or cargo at sea. **2.** property saved. —*v.* **3.** save from destruction.

sal•va′tion, *n.* **1.** deliverance. **2.** deliverance from sin.

salve (sav), *n., v.,* **salved, salving.** —*n.* **1.** ointment for sores. —*v.* **2.** apply salve to.

sal′ver, *n.* tray.

sal′vi•a, *n.* plant of mint family.

sal′vo, *n., pl.* **-vos, -voes.** discharge of guns, bombs, etc., in rapid series.

sam′ba (sam′bə, säm′-), *n., v.,* **-baed, -baing.** —*n.* **1.** Brazilian dance of African origin. —*v.* **2.** dance the samba.

same, *adj.* **1.** identical or corresponding. **2.** unchanged. **3.** just mentioned. —*n.* **4.** same person or thing. —**same′ness,** *n.*

sam′o•var′, *n.* metal urn.

sam′pan, *v.* small Far Eastern boat.

sam′ple, *n., adj., v.,* **-pled, -pling.** —*n.* **1.** small amount to show nature or quality. —*adj.* **2.** as sample. —*v.* **3.** test by sample.

sam′pler, *n.* needlework done to show skill.

sam′u•rai′, *n., pl.* **-rai.** member of hereditary warrior class in feudal Japan.

san′a•to′ri•um, *n., pl.* **-riums, -ria.** sanitarium.

sanc′ti•fy′, *v.,* **-fied, -fying. 1.** make holy. **2.** give sanction to. —**sanc′ti•fi•ca′tion,** *n.*

sanc′ti•mo′ny, *n.* hypocritical devoutness. —**sanc′ti•mo′ni•ous,** *adj.*

sanc′tion, *n.* **1.** permission or support. **2.** legal action by one state against another. —*v.* **3.** authorize; approve.

sanc′ti•ty, *n., pl.* **-ties. 1.** holiness. **2.** sacred character.

sanc′tu•ar′y, *n., pl.* **-aries. 1.** holy place. **2.** area around altar. **3.** place of immunity from arrest or harm.

sanc′tum, *n., pl.* **-tums, -ta.** private place.

sand, *n.* **1.** fine grains of rock. **2.** (*pl.*) sandy region. —*v.* **3.** smooth with sandpaper. —**sand′er,** *n.* —**sand′y,** *adj.*

san′dal, *n.* shoe consisting of sole and straps.

san′dal•wood′, *n.* fragrant wood.

sand′bag′, *n.* sand-filled bag used as fortification, ballast, or weapon.

sand′bank′, *n.* large mass of sand.

sand bar, bar of sand formed by tidal action.

sand′blast′, *v.* clean with blast of air or steam laden with sand.

sand′box′, *n.* receptacle holding sand for children to play in.

sand dollar, disklike sea animal.

sand′lot′, *n.* **1.** vacant lot used by youngsters for games. —*adj.* **2.** played in a sandlot.

sand′man′, *n.* figure in folklore who puts sand in children's eyes to make them sleepy.

sand′pa′per, *n.* **1.** paper coated with sand. —*v.* **2.** smooth with sandpaper.

sand′pip′er, *n.* small shore bird.

sand′stone′, *n.* rock formed chiefly of sand.

sand′storm′, *n.* windstorm with clouds of sand.

sand′wich, *n.* **1.** two slices of bread with meat, etc., between. —*v.* **2.** insert.

sane, *adj.,* **saner, sanest.** free from mental disorder; rational. —**sane′ly,** *adv.*

sang-froid′ (*Fr.* sän frwa′), *n.* composure.

san•gri′a, *n.* iced drink of red wine, sugar, fruit, and soda water.

san′gui•nar′y, *adj.* **1.** bloody. **2.** bloodthirsty.

san′guine (-gwin), *adj.* **1.** hopeful. **2.** red.

san′i•tar′i•um, *n., pl.* **-iums, -ia.** place for treatment of invalids and convalescents.

san′i•tar′y, *adj.* of health. —**san′i•tar′i•ly,** *adv.*

sanitary napkin, pad worn to absorb menstrual flow.

san′i•ta′tion, *n.* application of sanitary measures.

san′i•tize′, *v.,* **-tized, -tizing. 1.** free from dirt. **2.** make less offensive by removing objectionable elements.

san′i•ty, *n.* **1.** soundness of mind. **2.** good judgment.

San′skrit, *n.* extinct language of India.

sap, *n., v.,* **sapped, sapping.**
—*n.* **1.** trench dug to
approach enemy's position. **2.**
juice of woody plant. **3.** *Slang.*
fool. —*v.* **4.** weaken;
undermine. —**sap'per,** *n.*

sa'pi•ent, *adj.* wise.
—**sa'pi•ence,** *n.*

sap'ling, *n.* young tree.

sap'phire, *n.* deep-blue gem.

sap'suck'er, *n.* kind of
woodpecker.

sar'casm, *n.* **1.** harsh derision.
2. ironical gibe. —**sar•cas'tic,**
adj. —**sar•cas'ti•cal•ly,** *adv.*

sar•co'ma, *n., pl.* **-mas, -mata.**
type of malignant tumor.

sar•coph'a•gus, *n., pl.* **-gi.**
stone coffin.

sar•dine', *n.* small fish.

sar•don'ic, *adj.* sarcastic.
—**sar•don'i•cal•ly,** *adv.*

sa'ri (sär'ē), *n.* length of cloth
used as dress in India.

sa•rong', *n.* skirtlike garment.

sar'sa•pa•ril'la (sas'pə ril'ə),
n. **1.** tropical American plant.
2. soft drink flavored with
roots of this plant.

sar•to'ri•al, *adj.* of tailors or
tailoring.

SASE, self-addressed stamped
envelope.

sash, *n.* **1.** band of cloth
usually worn as belt. **2.**
framework for panes of
window, etc.

Sas'quatch (sas'kwoch,
-kwach), *n.* large, hairy
humanoid creature said to
inhabit wilderness areas of
U.S. and Canada. Also,
Bigfoot.

sass, *Informal.* —*n.* **1.**
impudent back talk. —*v.* **2.**
answer back impudently.
—**sas'sy,** *adj.*

sas'sa•fras', *n.* American tree
with aromatic root bark.

Sa'tan, *n.* chief evil spirit;
devil. —**sa•tan'ic,** *adj.*

satch'el, *n.* handbag.

sate, *v.,* **sated, sating.** satisfy
or surfeit.

sa•teen', *n.* glossy fabric.

sat'el•lite', *n.* **1.** body that
revolves around planet. **2.**
subservient follower.

satellite dish, dish-shaped
reflector, used esp. for
receiving satellite and
microwave signals.

sa′ti•ate′ (-shē-), *v.,* **-ated, -ating.** surfeit. **—sa′ti•a′tion, sa•ti′e•ty,** *n.*

sat′in, *n.* glossy silk or rayon fabric. **—sat′in•y,** *adj.*

sat′ire, *n.* use of irony or ridicule in exposing vice, folly, etc. **—sa•tir′i•cal, sa•tir′ic,** *adj.* **—sa•tir′i•cal•ly,** *adv.* **—sat′i•rist,** *n.*

sat′i•rize′, *v.,* **-rized, -rizing.** subject to satire.

sat′is•fy′, *v.,* **-fied, -fying. 1.** fulfill desire, need, etc. **2.** convince. **3.** pay. **—sat′is•fac′tion,** *n.* **—sat′is•fac′to•ry,** *adj.* **—sat′is•fac′to•ri•ly,** *adv.*

sa′trap, *n.* subordinate ruler, often despotic.

sat′u•rate′, *v.,* **-rated, -rating.** soak completely. **—sat′u•ra′tion,** *n.*

Sat′ur•day, *n.* seventh day of week.

Sat′urn, *n.* major planet.

sat′ur•nine′ (-nīn′), *adj.* gloomy.

sa′tyr (sā′tər), *n.* **1.** woodland deity, part man and part goat. **2.** lecherous person.

sauce, *n.* **1.** liquid or soft relish. **2.** stewed fruit.

sauce′pan′, *n.* cooking pan with handle.

sau′cer, *n.* small shallow dish.

sau′cy, *adj.,* **-cier, -ciest.** impertinent. **—sau′ci•ly,** *adv.* **—sau′ci•ness,** *n.*

sauer′kraut′, *n.* chopped fermented cabbage.

sau′na (sô′-), *n.* bath heated by steam.

saun′ter, *v., n.* stroll.

sau′ri•an, *adj.* of or resembling a lizard.

sau′ro•pod′, *n.* huge dinosaur with small head and long neck and tail.

sau′sage, *n.* minced seasoned meat, often in casing.

sau•té′ (sō tā′), *v.,* **-téed, -téeing.** cook in a little fat.

sau•terne′ (sō tûrn′), *n.* sweet white wine.

sav′age, *adj.* **1.** wild; uncivilized. **2.** ferocious. **—n. 3.** uncivilized person. **—sav′age•ly,** *adv.* **—sav′age•ry,** *n.*

sa•van′na, *n.* grassy plain with scattered trees. Also, **sa•van′nah.**

sa•vant′ (sə vänt′), *n.* learned person.

save, *v.,* **saved, saving,** *prep., conj.* —*v.* 1. rescue or keep safe. 2. reserve. —*prep., conj.* 3. except.

sav′ing, *adj.* 1. rescuing; redeeming. 2. economical. —*n.* 3. economy. 4. (*pl.*) money put by. —*prep.* 5. except. 6. respecting.

sav′ior, *n.* 1. one who rescues. 2. (*cap.*) Christ. Also, **sav′iour.**

sa′voir-faire′ (sav′wär fâr′), *n.* competence in social matters.

sa′vor, *n., v.* taste or smell.

sa′vor•y, *adj., n., pl.,* **-ories.** —*adj.* 1. pleasing in taste or smell. —*n.* 2. aromatic plant.

sav′vy, *n., adj.,* **-vier, -viest.** —*n.* 1. practical understanding. —*adj.* 2. shrewd and well-informed.

saw, *n.* 1. toothed metal blade. —*v.* 2. cut with saw. —**saw′mill,** *n.* —**saw′yer,** *n.*

saw′buck′, *n.* 1. sawhorse. 2. *Slang.* ten-dollar bill.

saw′dust′, *n.* fine particles of wood produced in sawing.

saw′horse′, *n.* movable frame for supporting wood while it's being sawed.

sax, *n.* saxophone.

Sax′on, *n.* member of Germanic people who invaded Britain in the 5th–6th centuries.

sax′o•phone′, *n.* musical wind instrument.

say, *v.,* **said, saying,** *n.* —*v.* 1. speak; declare; utter. 2. declare as truth. —*n.* 3. *Informal.* right to speak or choose.

say′ing, *n.* proverb.

say′-so′, *n., pl.* **-sos.** *Informal.* personal assurance; word.

SC, South Carolina. Also, **S.C.**

scab, *n., v.,* **scabbed, scabbing.** —*n.* 1. crust forming over sore. 2. worker who takes striker's place. —*v.* 3. form scab. —**scab′by,** *adj.*

scab′bard, *n.* sheath for sword blade, etc.

sca′bies, *n.* infectious skin disease.

scab′rous (skab′rəs), *adj.* 1. having a rough surface. 2. indecent; obscene.

scad, *n. (usually pl.)* great quantity.

scaf′fold, *n.* **1.** Also, **scaf′fold•ing.** temporary framework used in construction. **2.** platform on which criminal is executed.

scal′a•wag′, *n.* rascal.

scald, *v.* **1.** burn with hot liquid or steam. **2.** heat just below boiling. —*n.* **3.** burn caused by scalding.

scale, *n., v.,* **scaled, scaling.** —*n.* **1.** one of flat hard plates covering fish, etc. **2.** flake. **3.** device for weighing. **4.** series of measuring units. **5.** relative measure. **6.** succession of musical tones. —*v.* **7.** remove or shed scales. **8.** weigh. **9.** climb with effort. **10.** reduce proportionately. —**scal′y,** *adj.* —**scal′i•ness,** *n.*

scal′lion, *n.* small green onion.

scal′lop (skol′əp, skal′-), *n.* **1.** bivalve mollusk. **2.** one of series of curves on a border. —*v.* **3.** finish with scallops.

scalp, *n.* **1.** skin and hair of top of head. —*v.* **2.** cut scalp from. **3.** buy and resell at unofficial price. —**scalp′er,** *n.*

scal′pel, *n.* small surgical knife.

scam, *n., v.,* **scammed, scamming.** —*n.* **1.** fraudulent scheme; swindle. —*v.* **2.** cheat; defraud.

scamp, *n.* rascal.

scam′per, *v.* **1.** go quickly. —*n.* **2.** quick run.

scam′pi (skam′pē, skäm-), *n., pl.* **-pi. 1.** large shrimp. **2.** dish of scampi.

scan, *v.,* **scanned, scanning. 1.** examine closely. **2.** glance at. **3.** analyze verse meter.

scan′dal, *n.* **1.** disgraceful act; disgrace. **2.** malicious gossip. —**scan′dal•ous,** *adj.* —**scan′dal•mon′ger,** *n.*

scan′dal•ize′, *v.,* **-ized, -izing.** offend; shock.

scan′ner, *n.* **1.** person or thing that scans. **2.** device that monitors selected radio frequencies and reproduces any signal detected. **3.** device that optically scans bar codes, etc., and identifies data.

scan′sion, *n.* metrical analysis of verse.

scant, *adj.* barely adequate. Also, **scant′y.** —**scant′i•ly,** *adv.* —**scant′i•ness,** *n.*

scape′goat′, *n.* one made to bear blame for others.

scape′grace′, *n.* rascal.

scar, *n., v.,* **scarred, scarring.** —*n.* 1. mark left by wound, etc. —*v.* 2. mark with scar.

scar′ab, *n.* beetle.

scarce, *adj.,* **scarcer, scarcest.** 1. insufficient. 2. rare. —**scar′ci•ty, scarce′ness,** *n.*

scarce′ly, *adv.* 1. barely. 2. definitely not.

scare, *v.,* **scared, scaring, *n.*** —*v.* 1. frighten. —*n.* 2. sudden fright.

scare′crow′, *n.* object set up to frighten birds away from planted seed.

scarf, *n., pl.* **scarfs, scarves.** band of cloth esp. for neck.

scar′i•fy′, *v.,* **-fied, -fying.** 1. scratch (skin, etc.). 2. loosen (soil).

scar′let, *n.* bright red.

scarlet fever, disease marked by fever and rash.

scar′y, *adj.* **-ier, -iest.** causing fear.

scat, *v.,* **scatted, scatting.** run off.

scathe, *v.,* **scathed, scathing.** criticize harshly.

scat′o•log′i•cal, *adj.* concerned with excrement or obscenity. —**sca•tol′o•gy,** *n.*

scat′ter, *v.* throw loosely about.

scat′ter•brain′, *n.* person incapable of coherent thought. —**scat′ter-brained′,** *adj.*

scatter rug, small rug.

scav′enge, *v.,* **-enged, -enging.** 1. search for food. 2. cleanse. —**scav′en•ger,** *n.*

sce•nar′i•o′, *n., pl.* **-ios.** plot outline.

scene, *n.* 1. location of action. 2. view. 3. subdivision of play. 4. display of emotion. —**sce′nic,** *adj.*

scen′er•y, *n.* 1. features of landscape. 2. stage set.

scent, *n.* 1. distinctive odor. 2. trail marked by this. 3. sense of smell. —*v.* 4. smell. 5. perfume.

scep′ter (sep′-), *n.* rod carried as emblem of royal power. Also, **scep′tre.**

scep′tic, *n.* skeptic.

sched′ule (skej′-), *n., v.,* **-uled, -uling.** —*n.* 1. timetable or list. —*v.* 2. enter on schedule.

scheme, *n., v.,* **schemed, scheming.** —*n.* **1.** plan; design. **2.** intrigue. —*v.* **3.** plan or plot. —**schem′er,** *n.* —**sche•mat′ic,** *adj.*

scher′zo (skert′sō), *n., pl.* **-zos, -zi** (-sē). playful musical movement.

Schick test, diphtheria test.

schil′ling, *n.* monetary unit of Austria.

schism (siz′əm), *n.* division within church, etc.; disunion. —**schis•mat′ic,** *adj., n.*

schist (shist), *n.* layered crystalline rock.

schiz′oid (skit′soid), *adj.* having personality disorder marked by depression, withdrawal, etc.

schiz′o•phre′ni•a (skit′sə frē′nē ə), *n.* kind of mental disorder. —**schiz′o•phren′ic,** *adj., n.*

schle•miel′, *n. Slang.* awkward and unlucky person.

schlep (shlep), *v.,* **schlepped, schlepping,** *n. Slang.* —*v.* **1.** carry with great effort. —*n.* **2.** slow or awkward person. **3.** tedious journey.

schlock (shlok), *n. Informal.* inferior merchandise. —**schlock′y,** *adj.*

schmaltz (shmälts), *n. Informal.* sentimental art, esp. music. —**schmaltz′y,** *adj.*

schnapps, *n.* strong alcoholic liquor.

schol′ar, *n.* **1.** learned person. **2.** pupil. —**schol′ar•ly,** *adj.*

schol′ar•ship′, *n.* **1.** learning. **2.** aid granted to promising student.

scho•las′tic, *adj.* of schools or scholars. —**scho•las′ti•cal•ly,** *adv.*

school, *n.* **1.** place for instruction. **2.** regular meetings of teacher and pupils. **3.** believers in doctrine or theory. **4.** group of fish, whales, etc. —*v.* **5.** educate; train. —**school′house′,** *n.* —**school′room′,** *n.* —**school′teach′er,** *n.*

schoon′er, *n.* kind of sailing vessel.

schuss, *n.* **1.** straight downhill ski run at high speed.

schwa (shwä), *n.* vowel sound in certain unstressed syllables, as *a* in *sofa;* usually represented by ə.

sci•at′i•ca (sī-), *n.* neuralgia in hip and thigh. —**sci•at′ic,** *adj.*

sci′ence, *n.* systematic knowledge, esp. of physical world. —**sci′en•tif′ic,** *adj.* —**sci′en•tif′i•cal•ly,** *adv.* —**sci′en•tist,** *n.*

science fiction, fiction dealing with space travel, robots, etc.

sci-fi (sī′fī′), *n., adj. Informal.* science fiction.

scim′i•tar (sim′-), *n.* curved sword.

scin•til′la (sin-), *n.* particle, esp. of evidence.

scin′til•late′, *v.,* -lated, -lating. sparkle. —**scin′til•la′tion,** *n.*

sci′on (sī′ən), *n.* **1.** descendant. **2.** shoot cut for grafting.

scis′sors, *n.* cutting instrument with two pivoted blades.

scle•ro′sis (skli-), *n.* hardening, as of tissue. —**scle•rot′ic,** *adj.*

scoff, *v.* **1.** jeer. —*n.* **2.** derision. —**scoff′er,** *n.*

scoff′law′, *n.* person who flouts the law, as by ignoring traffic tickets.

scold, *v.* **1.** find fault; reprove. —*n.* **2.** scolding person.

sco′li•o′sis, *n.* lateral curvature of the spine.

sconce, *n.* wall bracket for candles, etc.

scone, *n.* small flat cake.

scoop, *n.* **1.** small deep shovel. **2.** bucket of steam shovel, etc. **3.** act of scooping. **4.** quantity taken up. **5.** *Informal.* earliest news report. —*v.* **6.** take up with scoop. **7.** *Informal.* best (competing news media) with scoop (def. 5).

scoot, *v.* go swiftly.

scoot′er, *n.* low two-wheeled vehicle.

scope, *n.* extent.

scorch, *v.* **1.** burn slightly. —*n.* **2.** superficial burn.

score, *n., pl.* **scores,** (for 3) **score,** *v.,* **scored, scoring.** —*n.* **1.** points made in game, etc. **2.** notch. **3.** group of twenty. **4.** account; reason. **5.** written piece of music. —*v.* **6.** earn points in game. **7.** notch or cut. **8.** criticize. —**scor′er,** *n.*

scorn, *n.* 1. contempt. 2. mockery. —*v.* 3. regard or refuse with scorn. —**scorn'ful,** *adj.* —**scorn'ful•ly,** *adv.*

scor'pi•on, *n.* small venomous spiderlike animal.

Scot, *n.* native or inhabitant of Scotland. —**Scot'tish,** *adj., n.pl.*

Scotch, *adj.* 1. (loosely) Scottish. —*n.* 2. (*pl.*) (loosely) Scottish people. 3. whiskey made in Scotland.

scotch, *v.* 1. make harmless. 2. put an end to.

scot'-free', *adj.* avoiding punishment or obligation.

Scots, *n.* English spoken in Scotland.

scoun'drel, *n.* rascal.

scour, *v.* 1. clean by rubbing. 2. range in searching.

scourge (skûrj), *n., v.,* **scourged, scourging.** —*n.* 1. whip. 2. cause of affliction. —*v.* 3. whip.

scout, *n.* 1. person sent ahead to examine conditions. —*v.* 2. examine as scout. 3. reject with scorn.

scow, *n.* flat-bottomed, flat-ended boat.

scowl, *n.* 1. fierce frown. —*v.* 2. frown fiercely.

scrab'ble, *v.,* **-bled, -bling.** 1. scratch with hands, etc. 2. scrawl.

scrag, *n.* scrawny creature. —**scrag'gy,** *adj.*

scrag'gly, *adj.,* **-glier, -gliest.** shaggy.

scram, *v.,* **scrammed, scramming.** *Informal.* go away quickly.

scram'ble, *v.,* **-bled, -bling,** *n.* —*v.* 1. move with difficulty, using feet and hands. 2. mix together. —*n.* 3. scrambling progression. 4. struggle for possession.

scrap, *n., adj., v.,* **scrapped, scrapping.** —*n.* 1. small piece. 2. discarded material. 3. *Informal.* fight. —*adj.* 4. discarded. 5. in scraps or as scraps. —*v.* 6. break up; discard. —**scrap'py,** *adj.*

scrap'book', *n.* blank book for clippings, etc.

scrape, *v.,* **scraped, scraping,** *n.* —*v.* 1. rub harshly. 2. remove by scraping. 3. collect laboriously. —*n.* 4. act or sound of scraping. 5. scraped

place. 6. predicament.
—**scrap'er,** *n.*

scrap'ple, *n.* sausagelike food of pork, corn meal, and seasonings.

scratch, *v.* 1. mark, tear, or rub with something sharp. 2. strike out. —*n.* 3. mark from scratching. 4. standard. —**scratch'y,** *adj.*

scrawl, *v.* 1. write carelessly or awkwardly. —*n.* 2. such handwriting.

scraw'ny, *adj.,* -nier, -niest. thin. —**scraw'ni•ness,** *n.*

scream, *n.* 1. loud sharp cry. —*v.* 2. utter screams.

screech, *n.* 1. harsh shrill cry. —*v.* 2. utter screeches.

screen, *n.* 1. covered frame. 2. anything that shelters or conceals. 3. wire mesh. 4. surface for displaying motion pictures. —*v.* 5. shelter with screen. 6. sift through screen.

screen'play', *n.* outline or full script of motion picture.

screw, *n.* 1. machine part or fastener driving or driven by twisting. 2. propeller. 3. coercion. —*v.* 4. hold with screw. 5. turn as screw.

screw'ball', *Slang.* —*n.* 1. eccentric or wildly whimsical person. —*adj.* 2. eccentric.

screw'driv'er, *n.* tool for turning screws.

screw'y, *adj.,* **screwier, screwiest.** *Slang.* 1. crazy. 2. absurd. —**screw'i•ness,** *n.*

scrib'ble, *v.,* -bled, -bling, *n.* —*v.* 1. write hastily or meaninglessly. —*n.* 2. piece of such writing.

scribe, *n.* professional copyist.

scrim, *n.* fabric of open weave.

scrim'mage, *n., v.,* -maged, -maging. —*n.* 1. rough struggle. 2. play in football. —*v.* 3. engage in scrimmage.

scrimp, *v.* economize.

scrim'shaw', *n.* carved articles, esp. of whalebone.

scrip, *n.* certificate, paper money, etc.

script, *n.* 1. handwriting. 2. manuscript.

Scrip'ture, *n.* 1. Bible. 2. (*l.c.*) sacred or religious writing or book. —**scrip'tur•al,** *adj.*

scrive'ner (skriv'-), *n.* scribe.

scrod, *n.* young codfish or haddock.

scrof'u•la, *n.* tuberculous disease, esp. of lymphatic glands. —**scrof'u•lous,** *adj.*

scroll, *n.* roll of inscribed paper.

scro'tum, *n., pl.* **-ta, -tums.** pouch of skin containing testicles. —**scro'tal,** *adj.*

scrounge, *v.,* **scrounged, scrounging.** *Informal.* 1. beg or mooch. 2. search. —**scroung'er,** *n.*

scrub, *v.,* **scrubbed, scrubbing,** *n., adj.* —*v.* 1. clean by rubbing. —*n.* 2. low trees or shrubs. 3. anything small or poor. —*adj.* 4. small or poor. —**scrub'by,** *adj.*

scruff, *n.* nape.

scruff'y, *adj.,* **scruffier, scruffiest.** untidy.

scrump'tious, *adj.* extremely pleasing.

scru'ple, *n.* restraint from conscience.

scru'pu•lous, *adj.* 1. having scruples. 2. careful. —**scru'pu•lous•ly,** *adv.*

scru'ti•nize', *v.,* **-nized, -nizing.** examine closely. —**scru'ti•ny,** *n.*

scu'ba, *n.* self-contained breathing device for swimmers.

scud, *v.,* **scudded, scudding.** move quickly.

scuff, *v.* 1. shuffle. 2. mar by hard use.

scuf'fle, *n., v.,* **-fled, -fling.** —*n.* 1. rough, confused fight. —*v.* 2. engage in scuffle.

scull, *n.* 1. oar used over stern. 2. light racing boat. —*v.* 3. propel with scull.

scul'ler•y, *n., pl.* **-leries.** workroom off kitchen.

scul'lion, *n.* kitchen servant.

sculp'ture, *n.* 1. three-dimensional art of wood, marble, etc. 2. piece of such work. —**sculp'tor,** *n.* —**sculp'tress,** *n.fem.*

scum, *n.* 1. film on top of liquid. 2. worthless persons. —**scum'my,** *adj.*

scup'per, *n.* opening in ship's side to drain off water.

scurf, *n.* 1. loose scales of skin. 2. scaly matter on a surface. —**scurf'y,** *adj.*

scur'ril•ous, *adj.* coarsely abusive or derisive. —**scur'ril•ous•ly,** *adv.*

—**scur•ril′i•ty,
scur′ril•ous•ness,** *n.*

scur′ry, *v.,* **-ried, -rying,** *n., pl.*
-ries. hurry.

scur′vy, *n., adj.,* **-vier, -viest.**
—*n.* **1.** disease from
inadequate diet. —*adj.* **2.**
contemptible.

scut′tle, *n., v.,* **-tled, -tling.**
—*n.* **1.** covered opening, esp.
on flat roof. **2.** coal bucket.
—*v.* **3.** sink intentionally. **4.**
scurry.

scut′tle•butt′, *n. Informal.*
rumor; gossip.

scythe (sīth), *n.* curved,
handled blade for mowing by
hand.

SD, South Dakota. Also, **S.D.**

S. Dak., South Dakota.

SE, southeast.

sea, *n.* **1.** ocean. **2.** body of salt
water smaller than ocean. **3.**
turbulence of water.
—**sea′board′, sea′shore′,** *n.*
—**sea′coast′,** *n.* —**sea′port′,**
n. —**sea′go′ing,** *adj.*

sea anemone, solitary marine
polyp.

sea bass (bas), marine food
fish.

sea′bed′, *n.* ocean floor.

sea cow, manatee.

sea′far′ing, *adj.* traveling by
or working at sea.
—**sea′far′er,** *n.*

sea′food′, *n.* edible marine
fish or shellfish.

sea gull, gull.

sea horse, small fish with
beaked head.

seal, *n., pl.* **seals,** (also for 3)
seal, *v.* —*n.* **1.** imprinted
device affixed to document. **2.**
means of closing. **3.** marine
animal with large flippers. —*v.*
4. affix seal to. **5.** close by
seal. —**seal′ant,** *n.*

sea legs, ability to adjust
balance to motion of ship.

sea level, position of the sea's
surface at mean level between
low and high tides.

sea lion, large seal.

seam, *n.* **1.** line formed in
sewing two pieces together.
—*v.* **2.** join with seam.

sea′man, *n., pl.* **-men.** sailor.
—**sea′man•ship′,** *n.*

seam′stress, *n.* woman who
sews.

seam′y, *adj.,* **seamier,
seamiest. 1.** sordid. **2.** having
seams. —**seam′i•ness,** *n.*

sé'ance (sā'äns), *n.* meeting to attempt communication with spirits.

sea'plane', *n.* airplane equipped with floats.

sea'port', *n.* port for seagoing vessels.

sear, *v.* 1. burn. 2. dry up.

search, *v.* 1. examine, as in looking for something. 2. investigate. —*n.* 3. examination or investigation. —**search'er,** *n.*

search'light', *n.* device for throwing strong beam of light.

sea'shell', *n.* shell of marine mollusk.

sea'sick'ness, *n.* nausea from motion of ship. —**sea'sick'**, *adj.*

sea'son, *n.* 1. any of four distinct periods of year. 2. best or usual time. —*v.* 3. flavor with salt, spices, etc. —**sea'son•al,** *adj.*

sea'son•a•ble, *adj.* appropriate to time of year.

sea'son•ing, *n.* flavoring, as salt, spices, or herbs.

seat, *n.* 1. place for sitting. 2. right to sit, as in Congress. 3. site; location. 4. established center. —*v.* 5. place on seat. 6. find seats for. 7. install.

seat belt, strap to keep passenger secure in vehicle.

seat'ing, *n.* 1. arrangement of seats. 2. material for seats.

sea urchin, small, round sea animal with spiny shell.

sea'way', *n.* waterway giving oceangoing ships access to inland port.

sea'weed', *n.* plant growing in sea.

sea'wor'thy, *adj.,* **-thier, -thiest.** fit for sea travel.

se•ba'ceous (-shəs), *adj.* of, resembling, or secreting a fatty substance.

seb'or•rhe'a (seb'ə rē'ə), *n.* abnormally heavy discharge from sebaceous glands.

se•cede', *v.,* **-ceded, -ceding.** withdraw from nation, alliance, etc. —**se•ces'sion,** *n.* —**se•ces'sion•ist,** *n.*

se•clude', *v.,* **-cluded, -cluding.** locate in solitude. —**se•clu'sion,** *n.*

sec'ond, *adj.* 1. next after first. 2. another. —*n.* 3. one that is second. 4. person who aids another. 5. (*pl.*) imperfect

goods. **6.** sixtieth part of minute of time or degree. —*v.* **7.** support; further. —*adv.* **8.** in second place.
—**sec′ond•ly,** *adv.*

sec′ond•ar′y, *adj.* **1.** next after first. **2.** of second rank or stage. **3.** less important.
—**sec′ond•ar′i•ly,** *adv.*

sec′ond-guess′, *v.* use hindsight in criticizing or correcting.

sec′ond•hand′, *adj.* **1.** not new. **2.** not original.

second nature, deeply ingrained habit or tendency.

sec′ond-rate′, *adj.* of lesser or minor quality or importance.

second string, squad of players available to replace those who start a game.

second wind, energy for renewed effort.

se′cret, *adj.* **1.** kept from knowledge of others. —*n.* **2.** something secret or hidden.
—**se′cre•cy,** *n.* —**se′cret•ly,** *adv.*

sec′re•tar′i•at, *n.* group of administrative officials.

sec′re•tar′y, *n., pl.* **-taries. 1.** office assistant. **2.** head of

department of government. **3.** tall writing desk.
—**sec′re•tar′i•al,** *adj.*

se•crete′, *v.,* **-creted, -creting. 1.** hide. **2.** discharge or release by secretion.

se•cre′tion, *n.* **1.** glandular function of secreting, as bile or milk. **2.** product secreted.
—**se•cre′to•ry,** *adj.*

se•cre′tive, *adj.* **1.** disposed to keep things secret. **2.** secretory. —**se•cre′tive•ly,** *adv.* —**se•cre′tive•ness,** *n.*

sect, *n.* group with common religious faith.
—**sec•tar′i•an,** *adj., n.*

sec′tion, *n.* **1.** separate or distinct part. —*v.* **2.** divide.
—**sec′tion•al,** *adj.*

sec′tor, *n.* **1.** plane figure bounded by two radii and an arc. **2.** part of combat area.

sec′u•lar, *adj.* worldly; not religious. —**sec′u•lar•ism,** *n.* —**sec′u•lar•ize′,** *v.*

se•cure′, *adj., v.,* **-cured, -curing.** —*adj.* **1.** safe. **2.** firmly in place. **3.** certain. —*v.* **4.** get. **5.** make secure.
—**se•cure′ly,** *adv.*

se•cu′ri•ty, *n., pl.* **-ties. 1.** safety. **2.** protection. **3.** pledge given on loan. **4.** certificate of stock, etc.

security blanket, something that gives feeling of security.

se•dan′, *n.* closed automobile for four or more.

se•date′, *adj.* **1.** quiet; sober. —*v.* **2.** give sedative to. —**se•date′ly,** *adv.* —**se•date′ness,** *n.*

sed′a•tive, *adj.* **1.** soothing. **2.** relieving pain or excitement. —*n.* **3.** sedative medicine.

sed′en•tar′y, *adj.* characterized by sitting.

Se′der (sā′dər), *n.* ceremonial dinner at Passover.

sedge, *n.* grasslike marsh plant.

sed′i•ment, *n.* matter settling to bottom of liquid. —**sed′i•men′ta•ry,** *adj.*

se•di′tion, *n.* incitement to rebellion. —**se•di′tious,** *adj.*

se•duce′, *v.,* **-duced, -ducing. 1.** corrupt; tempt. **2.** induce to have sexual intercourse. —**se•duc′er,** *n.* —**se•duc′tion,** *n.* —**se•duc′tive,** *adj.*

sed′u•lous, *adj.* diligent.

see, *v.,* **saw, seen, seeing,** *n.* —*v.* **1.** perceive with the eyes. **2.** find out. **3.** make sure. **4.** escort. —*n.* **5.** office or jurisdiction of bishop.

seed, *n.* **1.** propagating part of plant. **2.** offspring. —*v.* **3.** sow seed. **4.** remove seed from. —**seed′less,** *adj.*

seed′ling, *n.* plant grown from seed.

seed money, capital for beginning an enterprise.

seed′y, *adj.,* **seedier, seediest. 1.** having many seeds. **2.** shabby. —**seed′i•ness,** *n.*

see′ing, *conj.* inasmuch as.

seek, *v.,* **sought, seeking. 1.** search for. **2.** try; attempt. —**seek′er,** *n.*

seem, *v.* appear (to be or do).

seem′ing, *adj.* apparent. —**seem′ing•ly,** *adv.*

seem′ly, *adj.,* **-lier, -liest.** decorous. —**seem′li•ness,** *n.*

seep, *v.* ooze; pass gradually. —**seep′age,** *n.*

seer, *n.* **1.** person who sees. **2.** prophet. —**seer′ess,** *n.fem.*

seer′suck′er, *n.* crinkled cotton fabric.

see′-through′, *adj.* transparent.

see′saw′, *n.* **1.** children's sport played on balancing plank. —*v.* **2.** alternate, waver, etc.

seethe, *v.,* **seethed, seething.** boil; foam.

seg′ment, *n.* **1.** part; section. —*v.* **2.** divide into segments. —**seg′men·ta′tion,** *n.* —**seg·men′ta·ry,** *adj.*

seg′re·gate′, *v.,* **-gated, -gating.** separate from others. —**seg′re·ga′tion,** *n.* —**seg′re·ga′tion·ist,** *n.*

se′gue (sā′gwā, seg′wā), *v.,* **segued, segueing,** *n.* —*v.* **1.** continue at once with the next section, as in piece of music. **2.** make smooth transition. —*n.* **3.** smooth transition.

sei′gnior (sēn′ yər), *n.* lord. —**sei·gnio′ri·al, sei·gno′ri·al,** *adj.*

seine (sān), *n., v.,* **seined, seining.** —*n.* **1.** kind of fishing net. —*v.* **2.** fish with seine.

seis′mic (sīz′-), *adj.* of or caused by earthquakes.

seis′mo·graph′, *n.* instrument for recording earthquakes. —**seis·mog′ra·phy,** *n.*

seis·mol′o·gy, *n.* science of earthquakes. —**seis′mo·log′ic, seis′mo·log′i·cal,** *adj.* —**seis·mol′o·gist,** *n.*

seize, *v.,* **seized, seizing. 1.** take by force or authority. **2.** understand.

seiz′ure (sē′zhər), *n.* **1.** act of seizing. **2.** attack of illness.

sel′dom, *adv.* not often.

se·lect′, *v.* **1.** choose. —*adj.* **2.** selected. **3.** choice. —**se·lec′tion,** *n.* —**se·lec′tive,** *adj.* —**se·lec·tiv′i·ty,** *n.*

se·lect′man, *n., pl.* **-men.** town officer in New England.

self, *n., pl.* **selves,** *adj.* —*n.* **1.** person's own nature. **2.** personal advantage or interests. —*adj.* **3.** identical.

self′-ad·dressed′, *adj.* addressed for return to sender.

self′-as·ser′tion, *n.* expression of one's own importance, etc. —**self′-as·ser′tive,** *adj.*

self′-as·sur′ance, *n.* confidence in one's ability or rightness. —**self′as·sured′,** *adj.*

self′-cen′tered, *adj.* interested only in oneself.

self′-con′fi•dence, *n.* faith in one's own judgment, ability, etc. —**self′con′fi•dent,** *adj.*

self′-con′scious, *adj.* excessively aware of being observed by others; embarrassed or uneasy. —**self′-con′scious•ly,** *adv.* —**self′-con′scious•ness,** *n.*

self′-con•tained′, *adj.* **1.** containing within itself all that is necessary. **2.** reserved in behavior.

self′-con•trol′, *n.* restraint of one's actions. —**self′-con•trolled′,** *adj.*

self′-de•fense′, *n.* **1.** act of defending oneself or one's property. **2.** plea that use of force was necessary in defending one's person.

self′-de•ni′al, *n.* sacrifice of one's desires.

self′-de•ter′mi•na′tion, *n.* right or ability to choose government or actions.

self′-ef•fac′ing, *adj.* keeping oneself in the background.

self′-ev′i•dent, *adj.* obvious.

self′-im′age, *n.* conception or evaluation of oneself.

self′-im•por′tant, *adj.* having or showing exaggerated sense of one's own importance.

self′-in′ter•est, *n.* one's personal benefit.

self′ish, *adj.* caring only for oneself. —**self′ish•ly,** *adv.* —**self′ish•ness,** *n.*

self′less, *adj.* having little concern for oneself; unselfish.

self′-made′, *adj.* owing success entirely to one's own efforts.

self′-pos•sessed′, *adj.* calm; poised. —**self′-pos•ses′sion,** *n.*

self′-pres•er•va′tion, *n.* instinctive desire to guard one's safety.

self′-re•spect′, *n.* proper esteem for oneself. —**self′-re•spect′ing,** *adj.*

self′-re•straint′, *n.* self-control.

self′-right′eous (-rī′chəs), *adj.* convinced one is morally right. —**self′-right′eous•ly,** *adv.* —**self′right′eous•ness,** *n.*

self′same′, *adj.* identical.

self′-sat′is•fied′, *adj.* complacent. —**self′-sat•is•fac′tion,** *n.*

self'-seek'ing, *n.* **1.** selfish seeking of one's own interests or ends. —*adj.* **2.** given to or characterized by self-seeking.

self'-serv'ice, *adj.* **1.** of a commercial establishment in which customers serve themselves. **2.** designed to be used without the aid of an attendant.

self'-serv'ing, *adj.* serving to further one's own interests.

self'-styled', *adj.* so called only by oneself.

self'-suf•fi'cient, *adj.* able to supply one's own needs without external assistance. —**self'-suf•fi'ciency,** *n.*

self'-willed', *adj.* obstinate.

sell, *v.,* **sold, selling. 1.** part with for payment. **2.** betray. **3.** be for sale. —**sell'er,** *n.*

selt'zer, *n.* effervescent mineral water.

sel'vage, *n.* finished edge on fabric.

se•man'tics, *n.* study of meanings of words.

sem'a•phore', *n.* apparatus for signaling.

sem'blance, *n.* **1.** appearance. **2.** copy.

se'men, *n.* male reproductive fluid.

se•mes'ter, *n.* half school year.

semi-, prefix meaning half or partly.

sem'i•an'nu•al, *adj.* occurring every half-year. —**sem'i•an'nu•al•ly,** *adv.*

sem'i•cir'cle, *n.* half circle. —**sem'i•cir'cu•lar,** *adj.*

sem'i•co'lon, *n.* mark of punctuation (;) between parts of sentence.

sem'i•con•duc'tor, *n.* substance, as silicon, with electrical conductivity between that of an insulator and a conductor.

sem'i•fi'nal, *adj.* **1.** of the next to last round in a tournament. —*n.* **2.** semifinal round or bout.

sem'i•nal, *adj.* **1.** of or consisting of semen. **2.** influencing future development.

sem'i•nar', *n.* class of advanced students.

sem'i•nar'y, *n., pl.* **-naries.** school, esp. for young women or for divinity students.

Sem′i·nole, *n., pl.* **-nole, -noles.** member of American Indian people of Florida and Oklahoma.

sem′i·pre′cious, *adj.* of moderate value.

Se·mit′ic, *n.* **1.** language family of Africa and Asia, including Hebrew and Arabic. —*adj.* **2.** of Semitic languages or their speakers.

sem′i·tone′, *n.* musical pitch halfway between two whole tones.

sem′o·li·na, *n.* ground durum.

sen′ate, *n.* legislative body, esp. (*cap.*) upper house of legislatures of United States, Canada, etc. —**sen′a·tor,** *n.* —**sen′a·to′ri·al,** *adj.*

send, *v.,* **sent, sending. 1.** cause to go. **2.** have conveyed. **3.** emit. —**send′er,** *n.*

send′-off′, *n.* farewell demonstration of good wishes.

se·nes′cent, *adj.* aging. —**se·nes′cence,** *n.*

se′nile (sē′nīl), *adj.* feeble, esp. because of old age. —**se·nil′i·ty,** *n.*

sen′ior, *adj.* **1.** older. **2.** of higher rank. **3.** denoting last year in school. —*n.* **4.** senior person.

senior citizen, person 65 years of age or more.

sen·ior′i·ty, *n., pl.* **-ties.** status conferred by length of service.

se·ñor′ (se nyôr′), *n., pl.* **-ñores.** *Spanish.* **1.** gentleman. **2.** Mr. or sir. —**se·ño′ra,** *n.fem.*

se′ño·ri′ta (se′nyô rē′tä), *n. Spanish.* **1.** Miss. **2.** young lady.

sen·sa′tion, *n.* **1.** operation of senses. **2.** mental condition from such operation. **3.** cause of excited interest.

sen·sa′tion·al, *adj.* **1.** startling; exciting. **2.** of senses or sensation. —**sen·sa′tion·al·ly,** *adv.*

sen·sa′tion·al·ism, *n.* use of sensational subject matter.

sense, *n., v.,* **sensed, sensing.** —*n.* **1.** faculty for perceiving physical things (sight, hearing, smell, etc.). **2.** feeling so produced. **3.** (*pl.*) consciousness. **4.** (*often pl.*)

rationality; prudence. **5.** meaning. —*v.* **6.** perceive by senses. —**sense'less,** *adj.*

sen·si·bil'i·ty, *n., pl.* **-ties. 1.** capacity for sensation. **2.** (*often pl.*) sensitive feeling.

sen'si·ble, *adj.* **1.** wise or practical. **2.** aware. —**sen'si·bly,** *adv.*

sen'si·tive, *adj.* **1.** having sensation. **2.** easily affected. —**sen'si·tiv'i·ty,** *n.*

sen'si·tize', *v.,* **-tized, -tizing.** make sensitive.

sen'sor, *n.* device sensitive to light, temperature, or radiation level that transmits signal to another instrument.

sen'so·ry, *adj.* of sensation or senses.

sen'su·al, *adj.* **1.** inclined to pleasures of the senses. **2.** lewd. —**sen'su·al·ist,** *n.* —**sen'su·al'i·ty,** *n.* —**sen'su·al·ly,** *adv.*

sen'su·ous, *adj.* **1.** of or affected by senses. **2.** giving or seeking enjoyment through senses. —**sen'su·ous·ly,** *adv.* —**sen'su·ous·ness,** *n.*

sen'tence, *n., v.,* **-tenced, -tencing.** —*n.* **1.** group of words expressing complete thought. **2.** judgment; opinion. **3.** assignment of punishment. —*v.* **4.** pronounce sentence upon.

sen·ten'tious, *adj.* **1.** using maxims. **2.** affectedly judicious. **3.** pithy.

sen'tient (-shənt), *adj.* having feeling. —**sen'tience,** *n.*

sen'ti·ment, *n.* **1.** opinion. **2.** emotion. **3.** expression of belief or emotion.

sen'ti·men'tal, *adj.* expressing or showing tender emotion. —**sen'ti·men'tal·ist,** *n.* —**sen'ti·men'tal·ism,** *n.* —**sen'ti·men·tal'i·ty,** *n.* —**sen'ti·men'tal·ly,** *adv.*

sen'ti·nel, *n.* guard.

sen'try, *n., pl.* **-tries.** soldier on watch.

se'pal (sē'pəl), *n.* leaflike part of flower.

sep'a·rate', *v.,* **-rated, -rating,** *adj.* —*v.* (-rāt'). **1.** keep, put, or come apart. —*adj.* (-rit). **2.** not connected; being apart. —**sep'a·ra'tion,** *n.* —**sep'a·ra·ble,** *adj.* —**sep'a·rate·ly,** *adv.*

sep′a•ra•tist, *n.* advocate of separation.
—**sep′a•ra•tism,** *n.*

sep′a•ra′tor, *n.* apparatus for separating ingredients.

se′pi•a, *n.* 1. brown pigment. 2. dark brown.

sep′sis, *n.* infection in blood.
—**sep′tic,** *adj.*

Sept., September.

Sep•tem′ber, *n.* ninth month of year.

sep•tet′, *n.* group of seven. Also, **sep•tette′.**

sep′ti•ce′mi•a, *n.* blood poisoning.

septic tank, tank for decomposition of sewage.

sep′tu•a•ge•nar′i•an (sep′chōo ə-), *n.* person 70 to 79 years old.

Sep′tu•a•gint (-jint), *n.* oldest Greek version of Old Testament.

sep′tum, *n., pl.* **-ta.** dividing wall in plant or animal structure.

sep′ul•cher (-kər), *n.* burial place. Also, **sep′ul•chre.**
—**se•pul′chral,** *adj.*

seq., 1. sequel. 2. the following.

se′quel, *n.* 1. subsequent event. 2. literary work, film, etc., continuing earlier one.

se′quence, *n.* 1. succession; series. 2. result.
—**se•quen′tial,** *adj.*

se•ques′ter, *v.* 1. seclude. 2. seize and hold.
—**se′ques•tra′tion,** *n.*

se′quin, *n.* small spangle.

se•quoi′a, *n.* very large tree of northwest U.S.

se•ra′glio (-ral′yō), *n., pl.* **-glios.** harem.

se•ra′pe (sə rä′pē), *n.* wrap used in Mexico.

ser′aph, *n., pl.* **-aphs, -aphim.** angel of highest order.
—**se•raph′ic,** *adj.*

sere, *adj.* withered.

ser′e•nade′, *n., v.,* **-naded, -nading.** —*n.* 1. music performed as compliment outside at night. —*v.* 2. compliment with serenade.

ser′en•dip′i•ty, *n.* luck in making discoveries.

se•rene′, *adj.* 1. calm. 2. fair.
—**se•ren′i•ty,** *n.*
—**se•rene′ly,** *adv.*

serf, *n.* 1. person in feudal servitude. 2. slave. —**serf'dom,** *n.*

serge, *n.* stout twilled fabric.

ser'geant, *n.* noncommissioned officer above corporal.

sergeant at arms, officer whose chief duty is to preserve order.

se'ri•al, *n.* 1. story, etc., appearing in installments. —*adj.* 2. of serial. 3. of or in series. —**se'ri•al•ly,** *adv.*

se'ries, *n.* things in succession.

ser'if, *n.* smaller line used to finish off main stroke of letter.

ser'i•graph', *n.* silkscreen print.

se'ri•ous, *adj.* 1. solemn. 2. important.

ser'mon, *n.* religious discourse.

ser'pent, *n.* snake. —**ser'pen•tine'** (-tēn'), *adj.*

ser'rat•ed (ser'ā tid), *adj.* toothed; notched. Also, **ser'rate** (ser'it).

se'rum, *n.*, *pl.* **-rums, -ra.** 1. pale-yellow liquid in blood. 2.

such liquid from animal immune to certain disease.

serv'ant, *n.* 1. person employed at domestic work.

serve, *v.*, **served, serving.** 1. act as servant. 2. help. 3. do official duty. 4. suffice. 5. undergo (imprisonment, etc.). 6. deliver.

serv'ice, *n.*, *v.*, **-iced, -icing.** —*n.* 1. helpful activity. 2. domestic employment. 3. armed forces. 4. act of public worship. 5. set of dishes, etc. —*v.* 6. keep in repair.

serv'ice•a•ble, *adj.* usable.

serv'ice•man, *n.*, *pl.* **-men.** 1. person in armed forces. 2. gasoline station attendant.

ser'vile (-vil, -vīl), *adj.* slavishly obsequious. —**ser•vil'i•ty,** *n.*

ser'vi•tor, *n.* servant.

ser'vi•tude', *n.* bondage.

ses'a•me, *n.* small edible seed of tropical plant.

ses'qui•cen•ten'ni•al, *n.* 150th anniversary. —**ses'qui•cen•ten'ni•al,** *adj.*

ses'sion, *n.* sitting, as of a court or class.

set, *v.,* **set, setting,** *n., adj.* —*v.* 1. put or place. 2. put (broken bone) in position. 3. arrange (printing type). 4. pass below horizon. 5. become firm. —*n.* 6. group; complete collection. 7. radio or television receiver. 8. represented setting of action in drama. —*adj.* 9. prearranged. 10. fixed. 11. resolved.

set′back′, *n.* return to worse condition.

set•tee′, *n.* small sofa.

set′ter, *n.* kind of hunting dog.

set′ting, *n.* 1. surroundings. 2. music for certain words.

set′tle, *v.,* **-tled, -tling.** 1. agree. 2. pay. 3. take up residence. 4. colonize. 5. quiet. 6. come to rest. 7. deposit dregs. —**set′tle•ment,** *n.* —**set′tler,** *n.*

set′-to′, *n., pl.* **-tos.** brief, sharp fight.

set′up′, *n. Informal.* situation in detail.

sev′en, *n., adj.* six plus one. —**sev′enth,** *adj., n.*

sev′en•teen′, *n., adj.* sixteen plus one. —**sev′en•teenth′,** *adj., n.*

seventh heaven, bliss.

sev′en•ty, *n., adj.* ten times seven. —**sev′en•ti′eth,** *adj., n.*

sev′er, *v.* separate; break off. —**sev′er•ance,** *n.*

sev′er•al, *adj.* 1. some, but not many. 2. respective. 3. various. —*n.* 4. some. —**sev′er•al•ly,** *adv.*

se•vere′, *adj.,* **-verer, -verest.** 1. harsh. 2. serious. 3. plain. 4. violent or hard. —**se•ver′i•ty,** *n.* —**se•vere′ly,** *adv.*

sew (sō), *v.,* **sewed, sewed** or **sewn, sewing.** join or make with thread and needle. —**sew′er,** *n.*

sew′age (soo′-), *n.* wastes carried by sewers.

sew′er, *n.* conduit for waste water, refuse, etc.

sex, *n.* 1. character of being male or female. 2. sexual intercourse. —**sex′less,** *adj.* —**sex′u•al,** *adj.* —**sex′u•al•ly,** *adv.* —**sex′u•al′i•ty,** *n.*

sex′a•ge•nar′i•an, *n.* person 60 to 69 years old.

sex chromosome, chromosome that determines individual's sex.

sex'ism, *n.* bias because of sex, esp. against women. —**sex'ist,** *n., adj.*

sex'tant, *n.* astronomical instrument for finding position.

sex•tet', *n.* group of six. Also, **sex•tette'.**

sex'ton, *n.* church caretaker.

sex'tu•ple, *adj.* sixfold.

sexual harassment, unwelcome sexual advances, esp. by a superior.

sexually transmitted disease, disease transmitted by sexual contact.

sex'y, *adj.,* **sexier, sexiest.** sexually interesting or exciting; erotic.

Sgt., Sergeant.

shab'by, *adj.,* **-bier, -biest. 1.** worn; wearing worn clothes. **2.** mean. —**shab'bi•ly,** *adv.* —**shab'bi•ness,** *n.*

shack, *n.* rough cabin.

shack'le, *n., v.,* **-led, -ling.** —*n.* **1.** iron bond for wrist, ankle, etc. **2.** ∪-shaped bolt of padlock. —*v.* **3.** restrain.

shad, *n.* kind of herring.

shade, *n., v.,* **shaded, shading.** —*n.* **1.** slightly dark, cool place. **2.** ghost. **3.** degree of color. **4.** slight amount. —*v.* **5.** protect from light.

shad'ow, *n.* **1.** dark image made by body intercepting light. **2.** shade. **3.** trace. —*v.* **4.** shade. **5.** follow secretly. —**shad'ow•y,** *adj.*

shad'ow•box', *v.* go through motions of boxing without an opponent, as in training.

shad'y, *adj.,* **shadier, shadiest. 1.** in shade. **2.** arousing suspicion. —**shad'i•ness,** *n.*

shaft, *n.* **1.** long slender rod. **2.** beam. **3.** revolving bar in engine. **4.** vertical space.

shag, *n.* **1.** matted wool, hair, etc. **2.** napped cloth. —**shag'gy,** *adj.*

shah, *n.* (formerly) ruler of Persia (now Iran).

shake, *v.,* **shook, shaken, shaking,** *n.* —*v.* **1.** move with quick irregular motions. **2.** tremble. **3.** agitate. —*n.* **4.** act of shaking. **5.** tremor. —**shak'er,** *n.*

shake'down', *n.* **1.** extortion, as by blackmail. **2.** thorough search.

shake'up', *n. Informal.* organizational reform.

shak'y, *adj.,* **shakier, shakiest.**
1. not firm; insecure. 2.
quavering. 3. affected by
fright. —**shak'i•ly,** *adv.*
—**shak'i•ness,** *n.*

shale, *n.* kind of layered rock.

shall, *v.* 1. am (is, are) going
to. 2. am (is, are) obliged or
commanded to.

shal•lot', *n.* small onionlike
plant.

shal•low, *adj.* not deep.

sham, *n. adj., v.,* **shammed,**
shamming. —*n.* 1. pretense or
imitation. —*adj.* 2. pretended.
—*v.* 3. pretend.

sham'ble, *v.,* **-bled, -bling,** *n.*
—*v.* 1. walk awkwardly. —*n.*
2. shambling gait. 3. (*pl.*)
scene of confusion.

shame, *n., v.,* **shamed,**
shaming. —*n.* 1. painful
feeling from wrong or foolish
act or circumstance. 2.
disgrace. —*v.* 3. cause to feel
shame. —**shame'ful,** *adj.*
—**shame'less,** *adj.*

shame'faced', *adj.* 1. bashful.
2. showing shame.

sham•poo', *v.* 1. wash (hair,
rugs, or upholstery). —*n.* 2.
act of shampooing. 3. soap,
etc., for shampooing.

sham'rock, *n.* plant with
three-part leaf.

shang'hai, *v.,* **-haied, -haiing.**
(formerly) abduct for service
as sailor.

shank, *n.* part of leg between
knee and ankle.

shan'tung', *n.* silk.

shan'ty, *n., pl.* **-ties.** rough
hut.

shape, *n., v.,* **shaped, shaping.**
—*n.* 1. form. 2. nature. —*v.* 3.
give form to; take form. 4.
adapt. —**shape'less,** *adj.*

shape'ly, *adj.,* **-lier, -liest.**
handsome in shape.
—**shape'li•ness,** *n.*

shard, *n.* fragment, esp. of
broken earthenware.

share, *n., v.,* **shared, sharing.**
—*n.* 1. due individual portion.
2. portion of corporate stock.
—*v.* 3. distribute. 4. use,
enjoy, etc., jointly. —**shar'er,**
n. —**share'hold'er,** *n.*

share'crop'per, *n.* tenant
farmer who pays as rent part
of the crop.

shark, *n.* 1. marine fish, often
ferocious. 2. person who
victimizes.

shark'skin', *n.* smooth, silky
fabric with dull surface.

sharp, *adj.* **1.** having thin cutting edge or fine point. **2.** abrupt. **3.** keen. **4.** shrewd. **5.** raised in musical pitch. —*adv.* **6.** punctually. —*n.* **7.** musical tone one half step above given tone. —**sharp′en,** *v.* —**sharp′en•er,** *n.* —**sharp′ly,** *adv.* —**sharp′ness,** *n.*

sharp′er, *n.* swindler.

sharp′-eyed′, *adj.* having keen sight.

sharp′shoot′er, *n.* skilled shooter.

sharp′-tongued′, *adj.* harsh in speech.

shat′ter, *v.* break in pieces.

shat′ter•proof′, *adj.* made to resist shattering.

shave, *v.,* **shaved, shaved** or **shaven, shaving,** *n.* —*v.* **1.** remove hair with razor. **2.** cut thin slices. —*n.* **3.** act of shaving.

shav′ings, *n.pl.* thin slices of wood.

shawl, *n.* long covering for head and shoulders.

she, *pron.* female last mentioned.

sheaf, *n., pl.* **sheaves.** bundle.

shear, *v.,* **sheared, sheared** or **shorn, shearing.** clip, as wool.

shears, *n.pl.* large scissors.

sheath, *n.* **1.** case for sword blade. **2.** any similar covering.

sheathe, *v.,* **sheathed, sheathing.** put into or enclose in sheath.

she•bang′, *n. Informal.* organization or contrivance.

shed, *v.,* **shed, shedding,** *n.* —*v.* **1.** pour forth. **2.** cast (light). **3.** throw off. —*n.* **4.** simple enclosed shelter.

sheen, *n.* brightness.

sheep, *n., pl.* **sheep.** mammal valued for fleece and flesh.

sheep dog, dog trained to herd sheep.

sheep′fold′, *n.* enclosure for sheep.

sheep′ish, *adj.* embarrassed or timid.

sheer, *adj.* **1.** very thin. **2.** complete. **3.** steep. —*v., n.* **4.** swerve.

sheet, *n.* **1.** large piece of cloth used as bedding. **2.** broad thin mass or piece. **3.** rope or chain to control sail.

sheik, *n.* (Arab) chief. —**sheik′dom,** *n.*

shek′el (shek′əl), *n.* ancient Hebrew and modern Israeli monetary unit.

shelf, *n., pl.* **shelves. 1.** horizontal slab on wall, etc., for holding objects. **2.** ledge.

shelf life, period during which commodity remains fit for use.

shell, *n.* **1.** hard outer covering. **2.** shotgun cartridge. **3.** explosive missile from cannon. **4.** light racing boat. —*v.* **5.** remove shell from. **6.** take from shell. **7.** bombard with shells.

shel·lac′, *n., v.,* **-lacked, -lacking.** —*n.* **1.** substance used in varnish. **2.** varnish. —*v.* **3.** coat with shellac.

shell′fish′, *n.* aquatic animal having shell.

shell shock, combat fatigue.

shel′ter, *n.* **1.** place of protection. —*v.* **2.** protect.

shelve, *v.,* **shelved, shelving. 1.** put on shelf. **2.** lay aside. **3.** furnish with shelves. **4.** slope.

she·nan′i·gans, *n.pl. Informal.* mischief.

shep′herd, *n.* **1.** person who tends sheep. —*v.* **2.** guide while guarding. —**shep′herd·ess,** *n.fem.*

sher′bet, *n.* frozen fruit-flavored dessert.

sher′iff, *n.* county law-enforcement officer.

sher′ry, *n., pl.* **-ries.** strong wine served as cocktail.

shib′bo·leth (shib′ə lith, -leth′), *n.* **1.** peculiarity of pronunciation or usage that distinguishes a group. **2.** slogan; catchword.

shield, *n.* **1.** plate of armor carried on arm. —*v.* **2.** protect.

shift, *v.* **1.** move about. **2.** change positions. —*n.* **3.** act of shifting. **4.** period of work.

shift′less, *adj.* resourceless or lazy.

shift′y, *adj.,* **shiftier, shiftiest.** tricky; devious. —**shift′i·ly,** *adv.* —**shift′i·ness,** *n.*

shill, *n.* person who poses as a customer to lure others.

shil·le′lagh (shə lā′lē), *n.* rough Irish walking stick or cudgel.

shil′ling, *n.* former British coin, 20th part of pound.

shil'ly-shal'ly, *v.,* **-lied, -lying.** be irresolute.

shim'mer, *v.* **1.** glow faintly; flicker. —*n.* **2.** faint glow. —**shim'mer•y,** *adj.*

shim'my, *n., pl.* **-mies,** *v.,* **-mied, -mying.** *Informal.* —*n.* **1.** vibration. —*v.* **2.** vibrate.

shin, *n.* front of leg from knee to ankle.

shin'bone', *n.* tibia.

shin'dig', *n. Informal.* elaborate and usu. large party.

shine, *v.,* **shone** or (for 4) **shined, shining,** *n.* —*v.* **1.** give forth light. **2.** sparkle. **3.** excel. **4.** polish. —*n.* **5.** radiance. **6.** polish. —**shin'y,** *adj.*

shin'er, *n. Informal.* black eye.

shin'gle, *n., v.,* **-gled, -gling.** —*n.* **1.** thin slab used in overlapping rows as covering. **2.** close haircut. **3.** (*pl.*) viral skin disease marked by blisters. —*v.* **4.** cover with shingles. **5.** cut (hair) short.

shin'ny, *n.* form of hockey.

shin splints, painful condition of shins associated with strenuous activity.

Shin'to, *n.* native religion of Japan.

ship, *n., v.,* **shipped, shipping.** —*n.* **1.** vessel for use on water. —*v.* **2.** send as freight. **3.** engage to serve on ship. **4.** send away. —**ship'board',** *n.* —**ship'mate',** *n.* —**ship'ment,** *n.* —**ship'per,** *n.*

-ship, suffix meaning: **1.** state or quality, as *friendship.* **2.** position or rank, as *lordship.* **3.** skill or art, as *horsemanship.*

ship'shape', *adj., adv.* in good order.

ship'wreck', *n.* destruction of ship.

ship'wright', *n.* carpenter in ship repair or construction.

ship'yard', *n.* place where ships are built or repaired.

shire, *n. Brit.* county.

shirk, *v.* **1.** evade (obligation). —*n.* **2.** Also, **shirk'er.** person who shirks.

shirr, *v.* **1.** gather (cloth) on parallel threads. **2.** bake (eggs).

shirt, *n.* garment for upper body.

shirt'ing, *n.* fabric used to make shirts.

shirt'tail', *n.* part of shirt below waistline.

shirt'waist', *n.* tailored blouse.

shish' ke•bab', cubes of meat broiled on a skewer.

shiv'er, *v.* 1. tremble as with cold. 2. splinter. —*n.* 3. quiver. 4. splinter. —**shiv'er•y**, *adj.*

shoal, *n.* 1. shallow part of stream. 2. large number, esp. of fish.

shoat, *n.* young pig.

shock, *n.* 1. violent blow, impact, etc. 2. anything emotionally upsetting. 3. state of nervous collapse. 4. group of sheaves of grain. 5. bushy mass of hair, etc. —*v.* 6. strike with force, horror, etc.

shock absorber, device for damping sudden rapid motion.

shock'er, *n.* 1. something that shocks. 2. sensational novel, play, etc.

shock therapy, treatment for mental disorders in which drug or electricity is used to induce convulsions.

shod'dy, *adj.*, **-dier, -diest.** of poor quality. —**shod'di•ly,** *adv.* —**shod'di•ness,** *n.*

shoe, *n., v.*, **shod, shoeing.** —*n.* 1. external covering for foot. 2. shoelike machine part. —*v.* 3. provide with shoes.

shoe'horn', *n.* shaped object to assist in slipping into shoe.

shoe'mak'er, *n.* person who makes or mends shoes.

shoe'string', *n.* 1. lace or string for tying shoes. 2. very small amount of money.

shoe'tree', *n.* device placed in shoe to hold its shape.

sho'gun (shō'gən), *n.* chief military commander of Japan from 8th to 12th centuries.

shoo, *v.*, **shooed, shooing.** drive away by shouting "shoo."

shoo'-in', *n.* one regarded as certain to win.

shoot, *v.* 1. hit or kill with bullet, etc. 2. discharge (firearm, bow, etc.). 3. pass or send rapidly along. 4. emit. 5. grow; come forth. —*n.* 6. shooting contest. 7. young twig, etc. —**shoot'er**, *n.*

shooting star, meteor.

shop, *n., v.*, **shopped, shopping.** —*n.* 1. store. 2. workshop. —*v.* 3. inspect or purchase goods. —**shop'per**, *n.*

shop′lift′er, *n.* person who steals from shops while posing as customer.

shop′talk′, *n.* conversation about one's work or occupation.

shop′worn′, *adj.* worn-out.

shore, *v.,* **shored, shoring,** *n.* —*v.* 1. prop. —*n.* 2. prop. 3. land beside water. 4. land or country.

shorn, *v.* pp. of **shear.**

short, *adj.* 1. not long or tall. 2. rudely brief. 3. scanty. 4. inferior. 5. crumbly, as pastry. —*adv.* 6. abruptly. —*n.* 7. anything short. 8. (*pl.*) short, loose trousers. 9. short circuit. —**short′en,** *v.* —**short′ness,** *n.*

short′age, *n.* scarcity.

short′bread′, *n.* rich butter cookie.

short′cake′, *n.* rich biscuit topped with fruit and cream.

short′change′, *v.,* **-changed, -changing.** 1. give less than the correct change to. 2. cheat; defraud.

short circuit, *Elect.* abnormal connection between two points in circuit.

short′com′ing, *n.* defect.

short′cut′, *n.* shorter way to goal.

short′en·ing, *n.* 1. butter or other fat used to make pastry short. 2. act of making or becoming short.

short′hand′, *n.* system of swift handwriting.

short′-hand′ed, *adj.* not having enough workers.

short′-lived′ (-līvd′, -livd′), *adj.* lasting but short time.

short′ly, *adv.* in short time.

short shrift, little attention or consideration.

short′·sight′ed, *adj.* lacking foresight.

short′stop′, *n. Baseball.* player or position between second and third base.

short′-tem′pered, *adj.* irascible.

short′wave′, *n.* radio frequencies used for long-distance transmission.

Sho·sho′ne, *n., pl.* **-ne, -nes.** member of an American Indian people.

shot, *n., pl.* **shots** or (for 3), **shot.** 1. discharge of firearm, bow, etc. 2. range of fire. 3.

(*often pl.*) lead pellets. **4.** act or instance of shooting. **5.** person who shoots. **6.** heavy metal ball.

shot'gun', *n.* kind of smoothbore gun.

shot put, competition in which heavy metal ball is thrown for distance. —**shot'-put'ter,** *n.*

should, *v.* pt. of **shall.**

shoul'der, *n.* **1.** part of body from neck to upper joint of arm or foreleg. **2.** unpaved edge of road. —*v.* **3.** push as with shoulder. **4.** take up, as burden.

shout, *v.* **1.** call or speak loudly. —*n.* **2.** loud cry.

shove, *v.,* **shoved, shoving,** *n.* —*v.* **1.** push hard. —*n.* **2.** hard push.

shov'el, *n., v.,* **-eled, -eling.** —*n.* **1.** implement with broad scoop and handle. —*v.* **2.** dig or clear with shovel. —**shov'el•er,** *n.*

show, *v.,* **showed, shown** or **showed, showing,** *n.* —*v.* **1.** display. **2.** guide. **3.** explain. **4.** prove. **5.** be visible. —*n.* **6.** exhibition. **7.** acted entertainment. **8.** appearance.

show'boat', *n.* boat used as traveling theater.

show'case', *n., v.,* **-cased, -casing.** —*n.* **1.** setting for displaying something. —*v.* **2.** exhibit to best advantage.

show'down', *n.* decisive confrontation.

show'er, *n.* **1.** short fall of rain. **2.** any similar fall. **3.** bath in which water falls from above. —*v.* **4.** rain briefly. **5.** give liberally. —**show'er•y,** *adj.*

show'-off', *n.* person who seeks attention.

show'piece', *n.* something worthy of being exhibited.

show'place', *n.* place notable for its beauty or historical interest.

show'y, *adj.,* **showier, showiest.** conspicuous; ostentatious.

shrap'nel, *n.* shell filled with missiles.

shred, *n., v.,* **shredded** or **shred, shredding.** —*n.* **1.** torn piece or strip. **2.** bit. —*v.* **3.** reduce to shreds.

shrew, *n.* **1.** quarrelsome woman. **2.** small mouselike mammal. —**shrew'ish,** *adj.*

shrewd, *adj.* astute.
—**shrewd•ly,** *adv.*
—**shrewd'ness,** *n.*

shriek, *n.* **1.** loud shrill cry.
—*v.* **2.** utter shrieks.

shrike, *n.* predatory bird.

shrill, *adj.* **1.** high-pitched;
piercing. —*v.* **2.** cry shrilly.
—**shril'ly,** *adv.* —**shrill'ness,**
n.

shrimp, *n.* small long-tailed
edible shellfish.

shrine, *n.* place for sacred
relics.

shrink, *v.,* **shrank** or **shrunk,**
shrunk or **shrunken, shrinking.**
1. draw back. **2.** become
smaller.

shrink'age, *n.* **1.** act of
shrinking. **2.** amount of
shrinking.

shrinking violet, shy person.

shrink'-wrap', *v.,* **-wrapped,**
-wrapping, *n.* —*v.* **1.** seal in
plastic film that when exposed
to heat shrinks tightly around
object. —*n.* **2.** plastic used to
shrink-wrap.

shrive, *v.,* **shrove** or **shrived,**
shriven or **shrived, shriving. 1.**
impose penance on. **2.** grant
absolution to.

shriv'el, *v.,* **-eled, -eling.**
wrinkle in drying.

shroud, *n.* **1.** burial gown or
cloth. **2.** (*pl.*) set of ropes
supporting masts of vessel.
—*v.* **3.** wrap; cover.

shrub, *n.* woody perennial
plant. —**shrub'ber•y,** *n.*

shrug, *v.,* **shrugged, shrugging,**
n. —*v.* **1.** move shoulders to
show ignorance, indifference,
etc. —*n.* **2.** this movement.

shtick, *n. Slang.* **1.**
show-business routine. **2.**
special interest, talent, etc.
Also, **shtik.**

shuck, *n.* **1.** husk. **2.** shell. —*v.*
3. remove shucks from.

shud'der, *v.* **1.** tremble, as
from horror. —*n.* **2.** this
movement.

shuf'fle, *v.,* **-fled, -fling,** *n.* —*v.*
1. drag feet in walking. **2.** mix
(playing cards). **3.** shift. —*n.*
4. shuffling gait. **5.** act of
shuffling of cards.

shuf'fle•board', *n.* game
played on marked floor
surface.

shun, *v.,* **shunned, shunning.**
avoid.

shunt, *v.* divert; sidetrack.

shut, *v.,* **shut, shutting,** *adj.*
—*v.* **1.** close. **2.** confine. **3.** exclude. —*adj.* **4.** closed.

shut′-in′, *n.* person confined, as by illness, to the house, a hospital, etc.

shut′out′, *n.* game in which one side does not score.

shut′ter, *n.* **1.** cover for window. **2.** device for opening and closing camera lens.

shut′ter•bug′, *n.* amateur photographer.

shut′tle, *n., v.,* **-tled, -tling.**
—*n.* **1.** device for moving thread back and forth in weaving. **2.** bus, plane, etc., moving between two destinations. —*v.* **3.** move quickly back and forth.

shut′tle•cock′, *n.* feathered object hit back and forth in badminton.

shy, *adj.,* **shyer** or **shier, shyest** or **shiest,** *v.,* **shied, shying,** *n.,* *pl.* **shies.** —*adj.* **1.** bashful. **2.** wary. **3.** short. —*v.* **4.** start aside, as in fear. **5.** throw suddenly. —*n.* **6.** shying movement. **7.** sudden throw.
—**shy′ly,** *adv.* —**shy′ness,** *n.*

shy′ster, *n.* *Informal.* unscrupulous lawyer.

Si′a•mese′ twins, twins joined together by body part.

sib′i•lant, *adj.* **1.** hissing. —*n.* **2.** hissing sound.
—**sib′i•lance,** *n.*

sib′ling, *n.* brother or sister.

sib′yl (sib′əl), *n.* female prophet. —**sib′yl•line,** *adj.*

sic, *v.,* **sicked, sicking,** *adv.*
—*v.* **1.** urge to attack. —*adv.* **2.** *Latin.* so (it reads).

sick, *adj.* **1.** ill; not well. **2.** of sickness. **3.** nauseated. —*n.pl.* **4.** sick people. —**sick′ness,** *n.*
—**sick′en,** *v.*

sick′le, *n.* reaping implement with curved blade.

sick′ly, *adj.,* **-lier, -liest,** *adv.* **1.** ailing. **2.** faint; weak. —*adv.* **3.** in sick manner.

side, *n., adj., v.,* **sided, siding.**
—*n.* **1.** edge. **2.** surface. **3.** part other than front, back, top, or bottom. **4.** aspect. **5.** region. **6.** faction. —*adj.* **7.** at, from, or toward side. **8.** subordinate.
—*v.* **9.** align oneself.

side′bar′, *n.* short news feature highlighting longer story.

side′board′, *n.* dining-room cupboard.

side′burns′, *n.pl.* short whiskers in front of ears.

side effect, *n.* often adverse secondary effect.

side′kick′, *n.* **1.** close friend. **2.** confederate or assistant.

side′light′, *n.* item of incidental information.

side′line′, *n., v.,* **-lined, -lining.** —*n.* **1.** business or activity in addition to one's primary business. **2.** additional line of goods. **3.** line defining the side of an athletic field. —*v.* **4.** remove from action.

side′long′, *adj., adv.* to or toward the side.

si•de′re•al, *adj.* of or determined by stars.

side′sad′dle, *adv.* with both legs on one side of a saddle.

side′show′, *n.* **1.** minor show connected with principal one, as at circus. **2.** subordinate event or spectacle.

side′split′ting, *adj.* extremely funny.

side′-step′, *v.,* **-stepped, -stepping.** avoid, as by stepping aside.

side′swipe′, *v.,* **-swiped, -swiping.** strike along side.

side′track′, *v.* divert.

side′walk′, *n.* paved walk along street.

side′ward, *adj.* toward one side. —**side′ward, side′wards,** *adv.*

side′ways′, *adj., adv.* **1.** with side foremost. **2.** toward or from a side. Also, **side′wise′.**

sid′ing, *n.* short railroad track for halted cars.

si′dle, *v.,* **-dled, -dling.** move sideways or furtively.

SIDS, sudden infant death syndrome.

siege, *n.* surrounding of place to force surrender.

si•en′na, *n.* yellowish- or reddish-brown pigment.

si•er′ra, *n.* chain of hills or mountains whose peaks suggest the teeth of a saw.

si•es′ta, *n.* midday nap or rest.

sieve (siv), *n., v.,* **sieved, sieving.** —*n.* **1.** meshed implement for separating coarse and fine loose matter. —*v.* **2.** sift.

sift, *v.* separate with sieve. —**sift′er,** *n.*

sigh, *v.* **1.** exhale audibly in grief, weariness, etc. **2.** yearn. —*n.* **3.** act or sound of sighing.

sight, *n.* **1.** power of seeing. **2.** glimpse; view. **3.** range of vision. **4.** device for guiding aim. **5.** interesting place. —*v.* **6.** get sight of. **7.** aim by sights. —**sight′less,** *adj.*

sight′ed, *adj.* not blind.

sight′ly, *adj.,* **-lier, -liest.** pleasing to sight. —**sight′li•ness,** *n.*

sight′read′, *v.,* **-read, -reading.** perform without previous study.

sight′see′ing, *n.* visiting new places and things of interest. —**sight′se′er,** *n.* —**sight′see′,** *v.*

sign, *n.* **1.** indication. **2.** conventional mark, figure, etc. **3.** advertising board. **4.** trace. **5.** omen. —*v.* **6.** put signature to. —**sign′er,** *n.*

sig′nal, *n., adj., v.,* **-naled, -naling.** —*n.* **1.** symbolic communication. —*adj.* **2.** serving as signal. **3.** notable. —*v.* **4.** communicate by symbols. —**sig′nal•er,** *n.*

sig′nal•ize′, *v.,* **-ized, -izing.** make notable.

sig′nal•ly, *adv.* notably.

sig′na•to′ry, *n., pl.* **-ries.** signer.

sig′na•ture, *n.* **1.** person's name in own handwriting. **2.** *Music.* sign indicating key or time of piece.

sig′net, *n.* small seal.

sig•nif′i•cance, *n.* **1.** importance. **2.** meaning. —**sig•nif′i•cant,** *adj.*

significant other, spouse or cohabiting lover.

sig′ni•fy′, *v.,* **-fied, -fying. 1.** make known. **2.** mean. —**sig′ni•fi•ca′tion,** *n.*

Sikh (sēk), *n.* member of religion of India that rejects Hindu caste system. —**Sikh′ism,** *n.*

si′lage (sī′lij), *n.* fodder preserved in silo.

si′lence, *n., v.,* **-lenced, -lencing.** —*n.* **1.** absence of sound. **2.** muteness. —*v.* **3.** bring to silence. —**si′lent,** *adj.* —**si′lent•ly,** *adv.*

si′lenc•er, *n.* device for deadening report of a firearm.

sil'hou•ette' (sil'oo et'), *n.,
v.,* **-etted, -etting.** —*n.* **1.**
filled-in outline. —*v.* **2.** show
in silhouette.

sil'i•ca, *n.* silicon dioxide,
appearing as quartz, sand,
flint, etc.

sil'i•cate, *n.* mineral
consisting of silicon and
oxygen with a metal.

sil'i•con, *n.* abundant
nonmetallic element.

sil'i•cone', *n.* polymer with
silicon and oxygen atoms,
used in adhesives, lubricants,
etc.

sil'i•co'sis, *n.* lung disease
caused by inhaling silica.

silk, *n.* **1.** fine soft fiber
produced by silkworms. **2.**
thread or cloth made of it.
—*adj.* **3.** Also, **silk'en, silk'y.**
of silk.

silk'worm', *n.* caterpillar that
spins silk to make its cocoon.

sill, *n.* horizontal piece
beneath window, door, or
wall.

sil'ly, *adj.,* **-lier, -liest. 1.**
stupid. **2.** absurd.
—**sil'li•ness,** *n.*

si'lo, *n., pl.* **-los.** airtight
structure to hold green
fodder.

silt, *n.* **1.** earth, etc., carried
and deposited by a stream.
—*v.* **2.** fill with silt.

Si•lu'ri•an, *adj.* pertaining to
the third period of the
Paleozoic Era.

sil'ver, *n.* **1.** valuable white
metallic element. **2.** coins,
utensils, etc., of silver. **3.**
whitish gray. —*adj.* **4.** of or
plated with silver. **5.** eloquent.
6. indicating 25th anniversary.
—**sil'ver•y,** *adj.*

sil'ver•fish', *n.* wingless,
silvery-gray insect that
damages books, etc.

silver lining, prospect of hope
or comfort.

silver nitrate, poisonous
powder used in photography
and as astringent.

sil'ver-tongued', *adj.*
eloquent.

sil'ver•ware', *n.* eating and
serving utensils of silver or
other metal.

sim'i•an, *n.* **1.** ape or monkey.
—*adj.* **2.** of apes or monkeys.

sim′i•lar, *adj.* with general likeness. —**sim′i•lar′i•ty,** *n.* —**sim′i•lar•ly,** *adv.*

sim′i•le′, *n.* phrase expressing resemblance.

si•mil′i•tude′, *n.* 1. likeness. 2. comparison.

sim′mer, *v.* remain or keep near boiling.

si′mo•ny, *n.* buying or selling of ecclesiastical preferments.

sim•pa′ti•co′, *adj.* like-minded.

sim′per, *v.* 1. smile affectedly. —*n.* 2. affected smile.

sim′ple, *adj.,* **-pler, -plest.** 1. easy to grasp, use, etc. 2. plain. 3. mentally weak. —**sim•plic′i•ty,** *n.* —**sim′ply,** *adv.*

simple interest, interest payable only on the principle.

sim′ple-mind′ed, *adj.* 1.unsophisticated. 2. mentally deficient.

sim′ple•ton, *n.* fool.

sim′pli•fy′, *v.,* **-fied, -fying.** make simpler. —**sim′pli•fi•ca′tion,** *n.*

sim•plis′tic, *adj.* foolishly or naïvely simple. —**sim•plis′ti•cal•ly,** *adv.*

sim′u•late′, *v.,* **-lated, -lating.** feign; imitate. —**sim′u•la′tion,** *n.* —**sim′u•la′tive,** *adj.*

si′mul•cast′, *n., v.,* **-cast, -casted, -casting.** —*n.* 1. program broadcast simultaneously on radio and television. —*v.* 2. broadcast a simulcast.

si′mul•ta′ne•ous, *adj.* occurring at the same time. —**si′mul•ta′ne•ous•ly,** *adv.* —**si′mul•ta•ne′i•ty,** *n.*

sin, *n., v.,* **sinned, sinning.** —*n.* 1. offense, esp. against divine law. —*v.* 2. commit sin. —**sin′ner,** *n.* —**sin′ful,** *adj.* —**sin′ful•ly,** *adv.* —**sin′ful•ness,** *n.*

since, *adv.* 1. from then till now. 2. subsequently. —*conj.* 3. from time when. 4. because.

sin•cere′, *adj.,* **-cerer, -cerest.** honest; genuine. —**sin•cer′i•ty,** *n.* —**sin•cere′ly,** *adv.*

si′ne•cure′ (sī′ni kyŏŏr′), *n.* job without real responsibilities.

si′ne di′e (sī′nē dī′ē), without fixing a day for future action.

si′ne qua non′ (sin′ā kwä nōn′, non′, kwā), indispensable condition or element.

sin′ew, *n.* 1. tendon. 2. strength. —**sin′ew•y,** *adj.*

sing, *v.,* **sang** or **sung, sung, singing. 1.** utter words to music. **2.** make musical sounds. **3.** acclaim. —**sing′er,** *n.*

singe, *v.,* **singed, singeing,** *n.* scorch.

sin′gle, *adj., v.,* **-gled, -gling,** *n.* —*adj.* **1.** one only. **2.** unmarried. —*v.* **3.** select. —*n.* **4.** something single. **5.** unmarried person.

single file, line of persons or things one behind the other.

sin′gle-hand′ed, *adj.* **1.** accomplished by one person. **2.** by one's own effort; unaided. —*adv.* **3.** by one person alone. —**sin′gle-hand′ed•ly,** *adv.*

sin′gle-mind′ed, *adj.* having or showing a single aim or purpose.

sin′gly, *adv.* **1.** separately. **2.** one at a time. **3.** single-handed.

sing′song′, *adj.* monotonous in rhythm.

sin′gu•lar, *adj.* **1.** extraordinary. **2.** separate. **3.** denoting one person or thing. —*n.* **4.** singular number or form. —**sin′gu•lar′i•ty,** *n.* —**sin′gu•lar•ly,** *adv.*

sin′is•ter, *adj.* threatening evil.

sink, *v.,* **sank** or **sunk, sunk** or **sunken, sinking,** *n.* —*v.* **1.** descend or drop. **2.** deteriorate gradually. **3.** submerge. **4.** dig (a hole, etc.). **5.** bury (pipe, etc.). —*n.* **6.** basin connected with drain. —**sink′er,** *n.*

sink′hole′, *n.* **1.** hole in rock through which surface water drains into underground passage. **2.** depressed area in which drainage collects.

sinking fund, fund for extinguishing indebtedness.

sin′u•ous, *adj.* winding.

si′nus, *n.* cavity or passage, esp. one in the skull connecting with the nasal cavities.

sip, *v.,* **sipped, sipping,** *n.* —*v.* **1.** drink little at a time. —*n.* **2.**

act of sipping. **3.** amount taken in sip.

si'phon, *n.* **1.** tube for drawing liquids by gravity and suction to another container. —*v.* **2.** move by siphon.

sir, *n.* **1.** formal term of address to man. **2.** title of knight or baronet.

sire, *n., v.,* **sired, siring.** —*n.* **1.** male parent. —*v.* **2.** beget.

si'ren, *n.* **1.** mythical, alluring sea nymph. **2.** noise-making device used on emergency vehicles.

sir'loin, *n.* cut of beef from the loin.

si'sal, *n.* fiber used in ropes.

sis'sy, *n., pl.* **-sies. 1.** effeminate boy or man. **2.** timid or cowardly person.

sis'ter, *n.* **1.** daughter of one's parents. **2.** nun. —**sis'ter•hood',** *n.* —**sis'ter•ly,** *adj.*

sis'ter-in-law', *n., pl.* **sisters-in-law. 1.** sister of one's spouse. **2.** wife of one's brother.

sit, *v.,* **sat, sitting. 1.** rest on lower part of trunk of body. **2.** be situated. **3.** pose. **4.** be in session. **5.** seat. —**sit'ter,** *n.*

si•tar', *n.* Indian lute.

sit'-down', *n.* strike in which workers occupy their place of employment and refuse to work.

site, *n.* position; location.

sit'-in', *n.* protest by demonstrators who occupy premises refused to them.

sitting duck, easy target.

sit'u•ate', *v.,* **-ated, -ating.** settle; locate.

sit'u•a'tion, *n.* **1.** location. **2.** condition. **3.** job.

sitz bath, bath in which only the thighs and hips are immersed.

six, *n., adj.* five plus one. —**sixth,** *adj., n.*

six'teen', *n., adj.* ten plus six. —**six•teenth',** *adj., n.*

sixth sense, power of intuition.

six'ty, *n., adj.* ten times six. —**six'ti•eth,** *adj., n.*

siz'a•ble, *adj.* fairly large. Also, **size'a•ble.**

size, *n., v.,* **sized, sizing.** —*n.* **1.** dimensions or extent. **2.** great magnitude. **3.** Also, **sizing.** coating for paper, cloth, etc.

—*v.* 4. sort according to size. 5. treat with sizing.

siz′zle, *v.,* **-zled, -zling,** *n.* —*v.* 1. make hissing sound, as in frying. —*n.* 2. sizzling sound.

skate, *n., pl.* **skates** or (for 3) **skate,** *v.,* **skated, skating.** —*n.* 1. steel runner fitted to shoe for gliding on ice. 2. roller skate. 3. flat-bodied marine fish; ray. —*v.* 4. glide on skates. —**skat′er,** *n.*

skate′board′, *n.* oblong board on roller-skate wheels.

ske•dad′dle, *v.,* **-dled, -dling.** *Informal.* run away hurriedly.

skeet, *n.* sport of shooting at clay targets hurled to simulate flight of game birds.

skein (skān), *n.* coil of yarn or thread.

skel′e•ton, *n.* bony framework of human or animal. —**skel′e•tal,** *adj.*

skeleton key, key that opens various simple locks.

skep′tic, *n.* person who doubts or questions. —**skep′ti•cal•ly,** *adv.* —**skep′ti•cal,** *adj.* —**skep′ti•cism′,** *n.*

sketch, *n.* 1. simple hasty drawing. 2. rough plan. —*v.* 3. make sketch (of).

sketch′y, *adj.,* **sketchier, sketchiest.** vague; approximate. —**sketch′i•ly,** *adv.*

skew (skyo͞o), *v.* turn aside; swerve or slant.

skew′er, *n.* 1. pin for holding meat, etc., while cooking. —*v.* 2. fasten with skewer.

ski, *n.* 1. slender board fastened to shoe for traveling over snow. —*v.* 2. travel by skis. —**ski′er,** *n.*

skid, *n., v.,* **skidded, skidding.** —*n.* 1. surface on which to support or slide heavy object. 2. act of skidding. —*v.* 3. slide on skids. 4. slip.

skid row, run-down urban area frequented by vagrants.

skiff, *n.* small boat.

skill, *n.* expertness; dexterity. —**skilled,** *adj.* —**skill′ful,** *adj.* —**skill′ful•ly,** *adv.*

skil′let, *n.* frying pan.

skim, *v.,* **skimmed, skimming.** 1. remove from surface of liquid. 2. move lightly on surface.

skim milk, milk from which cream has been removed. Also, **skimmed milk.**

skimp, *v.* scrimp.

skimp'y, *adj.,* **skimpier, skimpiest.** scant. —**skimp'i•ness,** *n.*

skin, *n., v.,* **skinned, skinning.** —*n.* **1.** outer covering, as of body. —*v.* **2.** strip of skin. —**skin'ner,** *n.*

skin diving, underwater swimming with flippers and face mask, sometimes with scuba gear. —**skin diver,** *n.*

skin'flint', *n.* stingy person.

skin'ny, *adj.,* **-nier, -niest.** very thin.

skin'ny-dip', *v.,* **-dipped, -dipping,** *n. Informal.* swim in the nude.

skip, *v.,* **skipped, skipping,** *n.* —*v.* **1.** spring; leap. **2.** omit; disregard. —*n.* **3.** light jump.

skip'per, *n.* **1.** master of ship. —*v.* **2.** act as skipper of.

skir'mish, *n.* **1.** brief fight between small forces. —*v.* **2.** engage in skirmish. —**skir'mish•er,** *n.*

skirt, *n.* **1.** part of gown, etc., below waist. **2.** woman's garment extending down from waist. **3.** (*pl.*) outskirts. —*v.* **4.** pass around edge of. **5.** border.

skit, *n.* short comedy.

skit'ter, *v.* go or glide rapidly.

skit'tish, *adj.* apt to shy; restless.

skiv'vy, *n., pl.* **-vies. 1.** man's cotton T-shirt. **2.** (*pl.*) men's underwear consisting of T-shirt and shorts.

skul•dug'ger•y, *n., pl.* **-geries.** trickery.

skulk, *v.* sneak about; lie hidden. —**skulk'er,** *n.*

skull, *n.* bony framework around brain.

skull'cap', *n.* brimless, close-fitting cap.

skunk, *n.* **1.** small, striped, fur-bearing mammal that sprays acrid fluid to defend itself. **2.** contemptible person.

sky, *n., pl.* **skies.** region well above earth. —**sky'ward',** *adv., adj.*

sky'cap', *n.* airport porter.

sky'dive', *v.,* **-dived, -diving.** make parachute jump with longest free fall possible. —**sky'div'er,** *n.*

sky′jack′, v. Informal. seize (aircraft) while in flight. —**sky′jack′er**, n.

sky′light′, n. window in roof, ceiling, etc.

sky′line′, n. 1. outline against sky. 2. apparent horizon.

sky′rock′et, n. firework that rises into air before exploding.

sky′scrap′er, n. building with many stories.

sky′writ′ing, n. writing in sky formed by smoke released from airplane.

slab, n. broad flat piece of material.

slack, adj. 1. loose. 2. inactive. —adv. 3. slackly. —n. 4. slack part. 5. inactive period. —v. 6. slacken. —**slack′ly**, adv. —**slack′ness**, n.

slack′en, v. 1. make or become slack. 2. weaken.

slack′er, n. person who evades work.

slacks, n.pl. loose trousers.

slag, n. refuse matter from smelting metal from ore.

slake, v., slaked, slaking. 1. allay (thirst, etc.). 2. treat (lime) with water.

sla′lom (slä′ləm, -lōm), n. downhill ski race over winding course, around numerous barriers.

slam, v., slammed, slamming, n. —v. 1. shut noisily. —n. 2. this sound.

slam′mer, n. Slang. prison.

slan′der, n. 1. false, defamatory spoken statement. —v. 2. utter slander against. —**slan′der•ous**, adj.

slang, n. markedly informal language. —**slang′y**, adj.

slant, v. 1. slope. —n. 2. slope. 3. opinion.

slap, v., slapped, slapping, n. —v. 1. strike, esp. with open hand. —n. 2. such blow.

slap′dash′, adj. hasty and careless.

slap′hap′py, adj., -pier, -piest. 1. befuddled. 2. agreeably foolish.

slap′stick′, n. boisterous comedy with broad farce and horseplay.

slash, v. 1. cut, esp. violently and at random. —n. 2. such cut. —**slash′er**, n.

slat, n., v., slatted, slatting. —n. 1. thin narrow strip. —v. 2. furnish with slats.

slate, *n., v.,* **slated, slating.**
—*n.* **1.** kind of layered rock. **2.** dark bluish gray. **3.** list of nominees. —*v.* **4.** put in line for appointment.

slath′er, *v.* spread thickly.

slat′tern, *n.* untidy woman. —**slat′tern•ly,** *adj.*

slaugh′ter, *n.* **1.** killing of animals, esp. for food. **2.** brutal killing of people, esp. in great numbers. —*v.* **3.** kill for food. **4.** massacre. —**slaugh′ter•house′,** *n.*

slave, *n., v.,* **slaved, slaving.**
—*n.* **1.** person owned by another. —*v.* **2.** drudge. —**slav′er•y,** *n.*

slav′er, *v.* **1.** let saliva run from mouth. —*n.* **2.** saliva coming from mouth.

Slav′ic, *n.* **1.** language family that includes Russian, Polish, Czech, etc. —*adj.* **2.** of these languages or their speakers.

slav′ish (slāv′-), *adj.* **1.** without originality. **2.** servile. —**slav′ish•ly,** *adv.*

slaw, *n.* chopped seasoned raw cabbage.

slay, *v.,* **slew, slain, slaying.** kill. —**slay′er,** *n.*

slea′zy (slē′zē), *adj.,* **-zier, -ziest.** shoddy.

sled, *n., v.,* **sledded, sledding.**
—*n.* **1.** vehicle traveling on snow. —*v.* **2.** ride on sled.

sledge, *n., v.,* **sledged, sledging.** —*n.* **1.** heavy sledlike vehicle. **2.** Also, **sledge′ham′mer.** large heavy hammer. —*v.* **3.** travel by sledge.

sleek, *adj.* **1.** smooth; glossy. —*v.* **2.** smooth. —**sleek′ly,** *adv.* —**sleek′ness,** *n.*

sleep, *v.,* **slept, sleeping,** *n.*
—*v.* **1.** rest during natural suspension of consciousness. —*n.* **2.** state or period of sleeping. —**sleep′less,** *adj.* —**sleep′y,** *adj.* —**sleep′i•ly,** *adv.*

sleep′er, *n.* **1.** person who sleeps. **2.** railroad car equipped for sleeping. **3.** raillike foundation member. **4.** unexpected success.

sleeping bag, warmly lined bag in which a person can sleep.

sleeping car, railroad car with sleeping accommodations.

sleeping sickness, infectious disease of Africa, characterized by lethargy.

sleet, *n.* hard frozen rain.

sleeve, *n.* part of garment covering arm. —**sleeve′less,** *adj.*

sleigh, *n.* light sled.

sleight of hand (slīt), skill in conjuring or juggling.

slen′der, *adj.* 1. small in circumference. 2. scanty or weak. —**slen′der•ize′,** *v.* —**slen′der•ness,** *n.*

sleuth, *n.* detective.

slew, pt. of **slay.**

slice, *n., v.,* **sliced, slicing.** —*n.* 1. broad flat piece. —*v.* 2. cut into slices. —**slic′er,** *n.*

slick, *adj.* 1. sleek. 2. sly. 3. slippery. —*n.* 4. oil-covered area. —*v.* 5. smooth. —**slick′ness,** *n.*

slick′er, *n.* raincoat.

slide, *v.,* **slid, sliding,** *n.* —*v.* 1. move easily; glide. —*n.* 2. act of sliding. 3. area for sliding. 4. landslide. 5. glass plate used in microscope. 6. transparent picture.

sliding scale, scale, as of prices, that varies with such conditions as the ability of individuals to pay.

slight, *adj.* 1. trifling; small. 2. slim. —*v.* 3. treat as unimportant. —*n.* 4. such treatment; snub. —**slight′ness,** *n.*

slight′ly, *adv.* barely; partly.

sli′ly, *adv.* slyly.

slim, *adj.,* **slimmer, slimmest.** 1. slender. 2. poor. —*v.* 3. make or become slim. —**slim′ly,** *adv.* —**slim′ness,** *n.*

slime, *n.* 1. thin sticky mud. 2. sticky secretion of plants or animals. —**slim′y,** *adj.*

sling, *n., v.,* **slung, slinging.** —*n.* 1. straplike device for hurling stones. 2. looped rope, bandage, etc., as support. —*v.* 3. hurl. 4. hang loosely.

sling′shot′, *n.* Y-shaped stick with elastic strip between prongs, for shooting small missiles.

slink, *v.,* **slunk, slinking.** go furtively. —**slink′y,** *adj.*

slip, *v.,* **slipped, slipping,** *n.* —*v.* 1. move or go easily. 2. slide accidentally. 3. escape.

4. make mistake. —*n.* **5.** act of slipping. **6.** mistake. **7.** undergarment. **8.** space between piers for vessel. **9.** twig for propagating. —**slip′page,** *n.*

slip case, box open at one end for a book.

slip cover, easily removable cover for piece of furniture.

slip′knot′, *n.* knot that slips easily along cord.

slipped disk, abnormal protrusion of spinal disk between vertebrae.

slip′per, *n.* light shoe.

slip′per•y, *adj.* **1.** causing slipping. **2.** tending to slip.

slip′shod′, *adj.* careless.

slip′-up′, *n.* mistake.

slit, *v.,* **slit, slitting,** *n.* —*v.* **1.** cut apart or in strips. —*n.* **2.** narrow opening.

slith′er, *v.* slide. —**slith′er•y,** *adj.*

sliv′er, *n., v.* splinter.

slob, *n.* slovenly or boorish person.

slob′ber, *v., n.* slaver.

sloe, *n.* small sour fruit of blackthorn.

sloe′-eyed′, *adj.* **1.** having very dark eyes. **2.** having slanted eyes.

slog, *v.,* **slogged, slogging.** plod heavily. —**slog′ger,** *n.*

slo′gan, *n.* motto.

sloop, *n.* kind of sailing vessel.

slop, *v.,* **slopped, slopping,** *n.* —*v.* **1.** spill liquid. —*n.* **2.** spilled liquid. **3.** swill.

slope, *v.,* **sloped, sloping,** *n.* —*v.* **1.** incline; slant. —*n.* **2.** amount of inclination. **3.** sloping surface.

slop′py, *adj.* **-pier, -piest. 1.** untidy. **2.** careless. —**slop′pi•ly,** *adv.* —**slop′pi•ness,** *n.*

slosh, *v.* splash.

slot, *n.* narrow opening.

sloth (slôth), *n.* **1.** laziness. **2.** tree-living South American mammal. —**sloth′ful,** *adj.* —**sloth′ful•ness,** *n.*

slot machine, gambling machine.

slouch, *v.* **1.** move or rest droopingly. —*n.* **2.** drooping posture. —**slouch′y,** *adj.*

slough, *n.* **1.** (slou). muddy area. **2.** (slōō). marshy pond or inlet. 3. (sluf). cast-off skin or dead tissue. —*v.* (sluf). 4. be shed. 5. cast off.

slov′en (sluv′ən), *n.* untidy or careless person.
—**slov′en•li•ness,** *n.*
—**slov′en•ly,** *adj., adv.*

slow, *adj.* 1. not fast. 2. not intelligent or perceptive. 3. running behind time. —*adv.* 4. slowly. —*v.* 5. make or become slow. —**slow′ly,** *adv.*

slow burn, *Informal.* gradual build-up of anger.

slow′down′, *n.* slackening of pace or speed.

slow motion, process of projecting or replaying film or television sequence so that action appears to be slowed down.

slow′poke′, *n. Informal.* person who moves, works, or acts very slowly.

slow′-wit′ted, *adj.* slow in comprehension.

sludge, *n.* mud.

slue, *v.,* **slued, sluing.** turn round.

slug, *v.,* **slugged, slugging,** *n.* —*v.* 1. hit with fists. —*n.* 2. slimy, crawling mollusk

having no shell. 3. billet. 4. counterfeit coin. 5. hard blow, esp. with fist. —**slug′ger,** *n.*

slug′gard, *n.* lazy person.

slug′gish, *adj.* inactive; slow.
—**slug′gish•ly,** *adv.*
—**slug′gish•ness,** *n.*

sluice (slo͞os), *n.* channel with gate to control flow.

slum, *n.* squalid, overcrowded residence or neighborhood.

slum′ber, *v., n.* sleep.

slum′lord′, *n.* landlord who charges exorbitant rents in slums.

slump, *v.* 1. drop heavily or suddenly. —*n.* 2. act of slumping.

slur, *v.* **slurred, slurring,** *n.* —*v.* 1. say indistinctly. 2. disparage. —*n.* 3. slurred sound. 4. disparaging remark.

slurp, *v.* eat or drink with loud sucking noises.

slush, *n.* partly melted snow.
—**slush′y,** *adj.*

slush fund, money used for illicit political purposes.

slut, *n.* slatternly woman.

sly, *adj.,* **slyer, slyest** or **slier, sliest.** 1. cunning. 2. stealthy.
—**sly′ly,** *adv.* —**sly′ness,** *n.*

smack, *v.* 1. separate (lips) noisily. 2. slap. 3. have taste or trace. —*n.* 4. smacking of lips. 5. loud kiss. 6. slap. 7. taste. 8. trace. 9. small fishing boat. 10. *Slang.* heroin.

small, *adj.* 1. not big; little. 2. not great in importance, value, etc. 3. ungenerous. —*adv.* 4. in small pieces. —*n.* 5. small part, as of back. —**small'ness,** *n.*

small fry, 1. young children. 2. unimportant people.

small'-mind'ed, *adj.* petty or selfish.

small'pox', *n.* contagious disease marked by fever and pustules.

small'-scale', *adj.* 1. of limited scope. 2. being a small version of an original.

small talk, light conversation.

small'-time', *adj.* of little importance.

smart, *v.* 1. cause or feel sharp superficial pain. —*adj.* 2. sharp; severe. 3. clever. 4. stylish. —*n.* 5. sharp local pain. —**smart'ly,** *adv.*

smart al'eck, *Informal.* obnoxiously conceited and impertinent person. Also, **smart al'ec.**

smart bomb, air-to-surface missile guided by laser beam.

smart'en, *v.* improve in appearance.

smash, *v.* 1. break to pieces. —*n.* 2. act of smashing; destruction.

smat'ter•ing, *n.* slight knowledge.

smear, *v.* 1. rub with dirt, grease, etc. 2. sully. —*n.* 3. smeared spot. 4. slanderous attack.

smell, *v.* 1. perceive with nose. 2. have odor. —*n.* 3. faculty of smelling. 4. odor. —**smell'y,** *adj.*

smelling salts, preparation used as restorative.

smelt, *n., pl.* **smelts, smelt,** *v.* —*n.* 1. small edible fish. —*v.* 2. melt (ore or metal). —**smelt'er,** *n.*

smid'gen (smij'ən), *n.* very small amount. Also, **smid'gin, smid'geon.**

smi'lax, *n.* delicate twining plant.

smile, *v.,* **smiled, smiling,** *n.* —*v.* 1. assume look of pleasure, etc. 2. look favorably. —*n.* 3. smiling look.

smirch, *v.* 1. soil or sully. —*n.* 2. stain.

smirk, *v.* 1. smile smugly or affectedly. —*n.* 2. such a smile.

smite, *v.,* **smote, smitten** or **smit, smiting.** 1. strike. 2. charm.

smith, *n.* worker in metal.

smith′er•eens′, *n.pl.* fragments.

smith′y, *n., pl.* **smithies.** blacksmith's shop.

smock, *n.* long, loose overgarment.

smog, *n.* smoke and fog.

smoke, *n., v.,* **smoked, smoking.** —*n.* 1. visible vapor from burning. —*v.* 2. emit smoke. 3. draw into mouth and puff out tobacco smoke. 4. treat with smoke. —**smok′er,** *n.* —**smoke′less,** *adj.* —**smok′y,** *adj.*

smoke detector, alarm activated by presence of smoke.

smoke′house′, *n.* building in which meat or fish is cured with smoke.

smoke screen, 1. mass of dense smoke for concealment from enemy. 2. something intended to deceive.

smoke′stack′, *n.* 1. pipe for escape of smoke, combustion gases, etc. —*adj.* 2. engaged in heavy industry, as steelmaking.

smol′der, *v.* 1. burn without flame. 2. exist suppressed. Also, **smoul′der.**

smooch, *n., v. Informal.* kiss.

smooth, *adj.* 1. even in surface. 2. easy; tranquil. —*v.* 3. make smooth. —*n.* 4. smooth place. —**smooth′ly,** *adv.* —**smooth′ness,** *n.*

smooth′bore′, *adj.* (of gun) not rifled.

smor′gas•bord′, *n.* table of assorted foods.

smoth′er, *v.* suffocate.

smudge, *n., v.,* **smudged, smudging.** —*n.* 1. dirty smear. 2. smoky fire. —*v.* 3. soil.

smug, *adj.* 1. self-satisfied. 2. trim. —**smug′ly,** *adv.* —**smug′ness,** *n.*

smug′gle, *v.,* **-gled, -gling.** 1. import or export secretly and illegally. 2. bring or take secretly. —**smug′gler,** *n.*

smut, *n.* 1. soot. 2. smudge. 3. obscenity. 4. plant disease. —**smut′ty,** *adj.*

snack, *n.* light meal.

snaf′fle, *n.* kind of bit used on bridle.

snag, *n., v.,* **snagged, snagging.** —*n.* 1. sharp projection. 2. obstacle. —*v.* 3. catch on snag.

snail, *n.* crawling, spiral-shelled mollusk.

snake, *n., v.,* **snaked, snaking.** —*n.* 1. scaly limbless reptile. —*v.* 2. move like snake. 3. drag. —**snak′y,** *adj.*

snap, *v.,* **snapped, snapping,** *n., adj.* —*v.* 1. make sudden sharp sound. 2. break abruptly. 3. bite (at). 4. photograph. —*n.* 5. snapping sound. 6. kind of fastener. 7. *Informal.* easy thing. —*adj.* 8. unconsidered.

snap′drag′on, *n.* plant with spikes of flowers.

snap′pish, *adj.* cross.

snap′py, *adj.* **-pier, -piest.** 1. quick. 2. smart; stylish.

snap′shot′, *n.* unposed photograph.

snare, *n., v.,* **snared, snaring.** —*n.* 1. kind of trap. 2. strand across skin of small drum. —*v.* 3. entrap.

snarl, *v., n.* 1. growl. 2. tangle.

snatch, *v.* 1. grab. —*n.* 2. grabbing motion. 3. scrap of melody, etc. —**snatch′er,** *n.*

sneak, *v.* 1. go or act furtively. —*n.* 2. person who sneaks. —**sneak′y,** *adj.*

sneak′er, *n.* rubber-soled shoe.

sneak preview, preview of a motion picture, often shown in addition to an announced film.

sneer, *v.* 1. show contempt. —*n.* 2. contemptuous look or remark.

sneeze, *v.,* **sneezed, sneezing,** *n.* —*v.* 1. emit breath suddenly and forcibly from nose. —*n.* 2. act of sneezing.

snick′er, *n.* derisive, stifled laugh. —**snick′er,** *v.* Also, **snig′ger.**

snide, *adj.,* **snider, snidest.** derogatory in nasty, insinuating way.

sniff, *v.* 1. inhale quickly and audibly. —*n.* 2. such an inhalation. Also, **snif′fle.**

snif′ter, *n.* pear-shaped glass for brandy.

snip, *v.,* **snipped, snipping,** *n.*
—*v.* **1.** cut with small, quick strokes. —*n.* **2.** small piece cut off. **3.** cut. **4.** (*pl.*) large scissors.

snipe, *n., v.,* **sniped, sniping.**
—*n.* **1.** shore bird. —*v.* **2.** shoot from concealment.
—**snip′er,** *n.*

snip′pet, *n.* small bit, scrap, or fragment.

snip′py, *adj.,* **-pier, -piest.** sharp or curt, esp. in haughty or contemptuous way.

snit, *n.* agitated state.

snitch, *Informal.* —*v.* **1.** steal; pilfer. **2.** turn informer; tattle. —*n.* **3.** informer.

sniv′el, *v.* **1.** weep weakly. **2.** run at nose.

snob, *n.* person overconcerned with position, wealth, etc.
—**snob′bish,** *adj.*
—**snob′ber•y,** *n.*

snood, *n.* band or net for hair.

snoop, *Informal.* —*v.* **1.** prowl or pry. —*n.* **2.** Also, **snoop′er.** person who snoops.

snoot′y, *adj.,* **snootier, snootiest.** *Informal.* snobbish; condescending.
—**snoot′i•ness,** *n.*

snooze, *v.,* **snoozed, snoozing,** *n. Informal.* nap.

snore, *v.,* **snored, snoring,** *n.*
—*v.* **1.** breathe audibly in sleep. —*n.* **2.** sound of snoring. —**snor′er,** *n.*

snor′kel, *n.* **1.** tube through which swimmer can breathe while underwater. **2.** ventilating device for submarines.

snort, *v.* **1.** exhale loudly and harshly. —*n.* **2.** sound of snorting.

snot, *n. Informal.* **1.** nasal mucus. **2.** impudently disagreeable young person.
—**snot′ty,** *adj.*

snout, *n.* projecting nose and jaw.

snow, *n.* **1.** white crystalline flakes that fall to earth. —*v.* **2.** fall as snow. —**snow′drift′,** *n.*
—**snow′fall′,** *n.*
—**snow′flake′,** *n.*
—**snow′storm′,** *n.* —**snow′y,** *adj.*

snow′ball′, *n.* **1.** ball of snow. **2.** flowering shrub. —*v.* **3.** grow rapidly.

snow′bound′, *adj.* immobilized by snow.

snow'drop', *n.* early-blooming plant with white flowers.

snow'man', *n.* figure of person made of packed snow.

snow'mo•bile', *n.* motor vehicle for travel on snow.

snow'shoe', *n.* racketlike shoe for walking on snow.

snow'suit', *n.* child's warmly insulated outer garment.

snow tire, tire with deep tread.

snub, *v.,* **snubbed, snubbing,** *n., adj.* —*v.* **1.** treat with scorn. **2.** check or stop. —*n.* **3.** rebuke or slight. —*adj.* **4.** (of nose) short and turned up.

snuff, *v.* **1.** inhale. **2.** smell. **3.** extinguish. —*n.* **4.** powdered tobacco.

snuf'fle, *v.,* **-fled, -fling,** *n.* sniff.

snug, *adj.,* **snugger, snuggest. 1.** cozy. **2.** trim; neat. —**snug'ly,** *adv.*

snug'gle, *v.,* **-gled, -gling.** nestle.

so, *adv.* **1.** in this or that way. **2.** to such degree. **3.** as stated. —*conj.* **4.** consequently. **5.** in order that.

soak, *v.* **1.** wet thoroughly. **2.** absorb. —**soak'er,** *n.*

so'-and-so', *n., pl.* **so-and-sos.** person or thing not definitely named.

soap, *n.* **1.** substance used for washing. —*v.* **2.** rub with soap. —**soap'y,** *adj.*

soap'box', *n.* improvised platform on which speaker stands.

soap'stone', *n.* variety of talc.

soar, *v.* fly upward.

sob, *v.,* **sobbed, sobbing,** *n.* —*v.* **1.** weep convulsively. —*n.* **2.** convulsive breath.

so'ber, *adj.* **1.** not drunk. **2.** quiet; grave. —*v.* **3.** make or become sober. —**so•bri'e•ty, so'ber•ness,** *n.* —**so'ber•ly,** *adv.*

so'bri•quet' (sō'bri kā', -ket'), *n.* nickname.

so'-called', *adj.* called thus.

soc'cer, *n.* game resembling football.

so'cia•ble, *adj.* friendly. —**so'cia•bly,** *adv.* —**so'cia•bil'i•ty,** *n.*

so'cial, *adj.* **1.** devoted to companionship. **2.** of human society. —**so'cial•ly,** *adv.*

so'cial·ism, *n.* theory advocating community ownership of means of production, etc. —**so'cial·ist,** *n.* —**so'cial·is'tic,** *adj.*

socialized medicine, system to provide nation with complete medical care through government subsidization.

so'cial·ite', *n.* socially prominent person.

so'cial·ize', *v.,* -ized, -izing. 1. associate with others. 2. put on socialistic basis.

social security, (*often caps.*) federal program of old age, unemployment, health, disability, and survivors' insurance.

social work, services or activities designed to improve social conditions among poor, sick, or troubled persons.

so·ci'e·ty, *n., pl.* -ties. 1. group of persons with common interests. 2. human beings generally. 3. fashionable people. —**so·ci'e·tal,** *adj.*

Society of Friends, sect founded 1650; Quakers.

so'ci·o·ec·o·nom'ic, *adj.* pertaining to a combination of social and economic factors.

so'ci·ol'o·gy, *n.* science of social relations and institutions. —**so'ci·o·log'i·cal,** *adj.* —**so'ci·ol'o·gist,** *n.*

sock, *n. Informal.* short stocking.

sock'et, *n.* holelike part for holding another part.

sod, *n.* grass with its roots.

so'da, *n.* 1. drink made with soda water. 2. preparation containing sodium.

soda cracker, crisp cracker.

soda fountain, counter at which ice cream, sodas, etc., are served.

so·dal'i·ty, *n., pl.* -ties. association.

soda water, water charged with carbon dioxide.

sod'den, *adj.* 1. soaked. 2. stupid. —**sod'den·ness,** *n.*

so'di·um, *n.* soft whitish metallic element.

sodium bicarbonate, baking soda.

sodium chloride, salt.

sod'o•my (sod'-), *n.* anal or oral copulation.

so'fa (sō'fə), *n.* couch with back and arms.

soft, *adj.* **1.** yielding readily. **2.** gentle; pleasant. **3.** not strong. **4.** (of water) free from mineral salts. **5.** without alcohol. —**sof'ten**, *v.* —**soft'ly**, *adv.*

soft'ball', *n.* **1.** form of baseball played with larger, softer ball. **2.** the ball used.

soft'-boiled', *adj.* boiled only until the egg's yolk is partially set.

soft'-core', *adj.* sexually provocative without being explicit.

soft drink, nonalcoholic drink, often carbonated.

soft'-heart'ed, *adj.* very sympathetic.

soft'-ped'al, *v.*, **-aled, -aling.** make less obvious.

soft sell, quietly persuasive method of selling.

soft soap, persuasive talk.

soft'ware', *n.* programs for use with a computer.

sog'gy, *adj.*, **-gier, -giest. 1.** soaked. **2.** damp and heavy. —**sog'gi•ness**, *n.*

soi•gné' (swän yā'), *adj.* elegant. Also, **soi•gnée'.**

soil, *v.* **1.** dirty; smudge. —*n.* **2.** spot or stain. **3.** sewage. **4.** earth; ground.

soi•rée' (swä rā'), *n.* evening party.

so'journ, *v.* **1.** dwell briefly. —*n.* **2.** short stay.

sol'ace (sol'is), *n., v.* comfort in grief.

so'lar, *adj.* of the sun.

solar cell, cell that converts sunlight into electricity.

so•lar'i•um (-lâr'-), *n., pl.* **-iums, -ia.** glass-enclosed room for enjoying sunlight.

solar plexus, point on stomach wall just below sternum.

solar system, sun and all the celestial bodies revolving around it.

sol'der (sod'ər), *n.* **1.** fusible alloy for joining metal. —*v.* **2.** join with solder.

sol'dier, *n.* **1.** member of army. —*v.* **2.** serve as soldier. —**sol'dier•ly**, *adj.* —**sol'dier•y**, *n.*

sole, *n., v.,* **soled, soling,** *adj.*
—*n.* **1.** bottom of foot or shoe. **2.** edible flatfish. —*v.* **3.** put sole on. —*adj.* **4.** only.
—**sole'ly,** *adv.*

sol'e·cism, *n.* **1.** nonstandard usage. **2.** breach of etiquette.

sol'emn, *adj.* **1.** grave; serious. **2.** sacred. —**so·lem'ni·ty,** *n.* —**sol'emn·ly,** *adv.*

sol'em·nize', *v.,* **-nized, -nizing.** observe with ceremonies. —**sol'em·ni·za'tion,** *n.*

so·lic'it (-lis'-), *v.* **1.** entreat; request. **2.** lure; entice, as to a prostitute. **3.** solicit trade or sex. —**so·lic'i·ta'tion,** *n.*

so·lic'i·tor, *n.* **1.** person who solicits. **2.** *Brit.* lawyer.

so·lic'it·ous, *adj.* anxious; concerned. —**so·lic'it·ous·ly,** *adv.* —**so·lic'i·tude',** *n.*

sol'id, *adj.* **1.** having length, breadth, and thickness. **2.** not hollow. **3.** dense. **4.** substantial. **5.** entire. —*n.* **6.** solid body. —**so·lid'i·fy',** *v.* —**so·lid'i·ty,** *n.*

sol'i·dar'i·ty, *n., pl.* **-ties.** unanimity of attitude or purpose.

sol'id·ly, *adv.* **1.** so as to be solid. **2.** whole-heartedly; fully.

so·lil'o·quy (-kwē), *n., pl.* **-quies.** speech when alone. —**so·lil'o·quize',** *v.*

sol'i·taire', *n.* **1.** card game for one person. **2.** gem set alone.

sol'i·tar'y, *adj.* **1.** alone. **2.** single. **3.** secluded. —**sol'i·tude',** *n.*

so'lo, *n., pl.* **-los.** performance by one person. —**so'lo·ist,** *n.*

sol'stice, *n.* time in summer (June 21) or winter (Dec. 21) when sun is at its farthest from equator.

sol'u·ble, *adj.* able to be dissolved. —**sol'u·bil'i·ty,** *n.*

sol'ute (sol'yoot), *n.* dissolved substance.

so·lu'tion, *n.* **1.** explanation or answer. **2.** dispersion of one substance in another. **3.** resulting substance.

solve, *v.,* **solved, solving.** find explanation of. —**solv'a·ble,** *adj.* —**solv'er,** *n.*

sol'vent, *adj.* **1.** able to pay one's debts. **2.** causing dissolving. —*n.* **3.** agent that dissolves. —**sol'ven·cy,** *n.*

so·mat′ic, *adj.* of or affecting the body.

som′ber, *adj.* gloomy; dark. —**som′ber·ly,** *adv.*

som·bre′ro (-brâr′ō), *n., pl.* **-ros.** tall, broad-brimmed hat.

some, *adj.* 1. being an unspecified one or number. 2. certain. —*pron.* 3. unspecified number or amount.

some′bod′y, *pron.* some person. Also, **some′one′.**

some′day′, *adv.* at some distant time.

some′how′, *adv.* in some way.

som′er·sault′, *n.* heels-over-head turn of body.

some′thing′, *n.* unspecified thing.

some′time′, *adv.* 1. at indefinite time. —*adj.* 2. former.

some′times′, *adv.* at times.

some′what′, *adv.* to some extent.

some′where′, *adv.* in, at, or to unspecified place.

som·nam′bu·lism, *n.* sleep-walking. —**som·nam′bu·list,** *n.*

som′no·lent, *adj.* sleepy. —**som′no·lence,** *n.*

son, *n.* male offspring.

so′nar, *n.* method or apparatus for detecting objects in water by means of sound waves.

so·na′ta, *n.* instrumental composition.

song, *n.* music or verse for singing. —**song′ster,** *n.* —**song′stress,** *n.fem.*

son′ic, *adj.* of sound.

sonic boom, loud noise caused by aircraft moving at supersonic speed.

son′-in-law′, *n., pl.* **sons-in-law.** husband of one's daughter.

son′net, *n.* fourteen-line poem in fixed form.

so·no′rous, *adj.* 1. resonant. 2. grandiose in expression. —**so·nor′i·ty,** *n.* —**so·no′rous·ly,** *adv.*

soon, *adv.* in short time.

soot, *n.* black substance in smoke. —**soot′y,** *adj.*

soothe, *v.,* **soothed, soothing.** calm; allay.

sooth′say′er, *n.* person who predicts.

sop, *n., v.,* **sopped, sopping.** —*n.* 1. food dipped in liquid.

2. something given to pacify. —*v.* 3. soak (food). 4. absorb.

soph′ism, *n.* specious but plausible argument. —**soph′ist,** *n.*

so·phis′ti·cat′ed, *adj.* worldly; not simple. —**so·phis′ti·cate** (-kit), *n.* —**so·phis′ti·ca′tion,** *n.*

soph′ist·ry, *n., pl.* **-ries.** clever but unsound reasoning.

soph′o·more′, *n.* second-year high school or college student.

soph′o·mor′ic, *adj.* intellectually immature.

so′po·rif′ic, *adj.* 1. causing sleep. —*n.* 2. soporific agent.

sop′py, *adj.,* **-pier, -piest.** 1. drenched. 2. sentimental.

so·pran′o, *n., pl.* **-pranos.** 1. highest singing voice. 2. singer with such voice.

sor·bet′ (sôr bā′), *n.* fruit or vegetable ice.

sor′cer·er, *n.* magician; wizard. —**sor′cer·y,** *n.*

sor′did, *adj.* 1. dirty. 2. ignoble.

sore, *adj.,* **sorer, sorest,** *n.* —*adj.* 1. painful or tender. 2. grieved. 3. causing misery. 4.

Informal. annoyed. —*n.* 5. sore spot. —**sore′ly,** *adv.* —**sore′ness,** *n.*

sore′head′, *n. Informal.* disgruntled person.

sor′ghum (-gəm), *n.* cereal used in making syrup, etc.

so·ror′i·ty, *n., pl.* **-ties.** club of women or girls.

sor′rel, *n.* 1. reddish brown. 2. sorrel horse. 3. salad plant.

sor′row, *n.* 1. grief; regret; misfortune. —*v.* 2. feel sorrow. —**sor′row·ful,** *adj.* —**sor′row·ful·ly,** *adv.* —**sor′row·ful·ness,** *n.*

sor′ry, *adj.* 1. feeling regret or pity. 2. wretched.

sort, *n.* 1. kind or class. 2. character. 3. manner. —*v.* 4. separate; classify. —**sort′er,** *n.*

sor′tie (sôr′tē), *n.* 1. attack by defending troops. 2. combat mission.

SOS, call for help.

so′-so′, *adj.* 1. neither good nor bad. —*adv.* 2. tolerably.

sot, *n.* drunkard.

sot′to vo′ce (sot′ō vō′chē), in a low voice; softly.

sou•brette′ (soo-), *n.* coquettish maidservant in play or opera.

souf•fle′ (soo flā′), *n.* fluffy baked dish.

sough (sou), *v.* **1.** rustle or murmur, as wind. —*n.* **2.** act of soughing.

sought, pt. and pp. of **seek.**

soul, *n.* **1.** human spiritual quality. **2.** essential quality. **3.** person. **4.** Also, **soul music.** black popular music drawing on church influences. —*adj.* **5.** of black customs and culture. —**soul′ful,** *adj.* —**soul′less,** *adj.*

sound, *n.* **1.** sensation affecting organs of hearing, produced by vibrations (**sound waves**). **2.** special tone. **3.** noise. **4.** inlet or passage of sea. —*v.* **5.** make sound. **6.** say. **7.** give certain impression. **8.** measure depth of. **9.** examine; question. —*adj.* **10.** healthy; strong. **11.** reliable. **12.** valid. —**sound′proof′,** *adj.* —**sound′ly,** *adv.* —**sound′ness,** *n.*

sound barrier, abrupt increase in drag experienced by aircraft approaching speed of sound.

sound bite, brief, memorable statement excerpted for broadcast news.

sounding board, 1. thin board placed in musical instrument to enhance resonance. **2.** person whose reactions reveal acceptability of an idea.

sound′proof′, *adj.* **1.** impervious to sound. —*v.* **2.** make soundproof.

sound′track′, *n.* band on motion-picture film on which sound is recorded.

soup, *n.* liquid food of meat, vegetables, etc.

soup•çon′ (soop sôn′), *n.* slight trace.

soup′y, *adj.,* **soupier, soupiest. 1.** resembling soup in consistency. **2.** dense. **3.** overly sentimental.

sour, *adj.* **1.** acid in taste; tart. **2.** spoiled. **3.** disagreeable. —*v.* **4.** turn sour. —**sour′ly,** *adv.* —**sour′ness,** *n.*

source, *n.* origin.

sour′dough′, *n.* fermented dough used as leavening agent.

sour grapes, pretended disdain for something unattainable.

souse, *v.,* **soused, sousing,** *n.* —*v.* **1.** immerse; drench. **2.** pickle. —*n.* **3.** act of sousing. **4.** pickled food. **5.** *Slang.* drunkard.

south, *n.* **1.** point of compass opposite north. **2.** this direction. **3.** territory in this direction. —*adj., adv.* **4.** toward, in, or from south. —**south′er•ly,** *adj., adv.* —**south′ern,** *adj.* —**south′ern•er,** *n.* —**south′ward,** *adj., adv.*

south′east′, *n.,* point or direction midway between south and east. —**south′east′,** *adj., adv.*

south′paw′, *n. Informal.* left-handed person.

south′west′, *n.* point or direction midway between south and west. —**south′west′,** *adj., adv.*

sou′ve•nir′ (sōō′və nēr′), *n.* memento.

sov′er•eign (sov′rin), *n.* **1.** monarch. **2.** (formerly) British gold coin worth one pound. —*adj.* **3.** of a sovereign; supreme. —**sov′er•eign•ty,** *n.*

so′vi•et′, *n.* **1.** (in USSR) governing body. —*adj.* **2.** (*cap.*) of USSR.

sow, *v.* **1.** (sō). plant seed. —*n.* **2.** (sou). female hog. —**sow′er,** *n.*

soy′bean′, *n.* nutritious seed of leguminous plant.

soy sauce, salty sauce made from soybeans.

spa, *n.* resort at mineral spring.

space, *n., v.,* **spaced, spacing.** —*n.* **1.** unlimited expanse. **2.** particular part of this. **3.** linear distance. **4.** interval of time. —*v.* **5.** divide into space. **6.** set at intervals.

space′craft′, *n., pl.* **-craft.** vehicle for traveling in outer space.

spaced′-out′, *adj. Slang.* dazed by or as if by drugs.

space heater, device for heating small area.

space′ship′, *n.* rocket vehicle for travel between planets.

space shuttle, reusable spacecraft.

space station, manned spacecraft orbiting the earth and serving as base for research.

spa′cious, *adj.* large; vast. —**spa′cious•ly,** *adv.* —**spa′cious•ness,** *n.*

Spack′le, *n. Trademark.* brand of plasterlike material for patching cracks.

spade, *n., v.,* **spaded, spading.** —*n.* 1. tool with blade for digging. 2. (*pl.*) suit of playing cards. —*v.* 3. dig with spade.

spa•ghet′ti, *n.* pasta in form of long strings.

span, *n., v.,* **spanned, spanning.** —*n.* 1. distance between extended thumb and little finger. 2. space between two supports. 3. full extent. 4. team of animals. —*v.* 5. extend over.

span′dex, *n.* elastic synthetic fiber.

span′gle, *n., v.,* **-gled, -gling.** —*n.* 1. small bright ornament. —*v.* 2. decorate with spangles.

span′iel, *n.* kind of dog.

Span′ish, *n.* language or people of Spain. —**Spanish,** *adj.*

Spanish fly, preparation of powdered green European beetles once used as aphrodisiac.

Spanish moss, plant that grows in long strands over trees.

spank, *v.* 1. strike on buttocks. —*n.* 2. such a blow.

spank′ing, *adj.* brisk; vigorous.

spar, *v.,* **sparred, sparring,** *n.* —*v.* 1. box. 2. bandy words. —*n.* 3. *Naut.* mast, yard, etc. 4. bright crystalline mineral.

spare, *v.,* **spared, sparing,** *adj.,* **sparer, sparest.** —*v.* 1. deal gently with. 2. part with easily. —*adj.* 3. kept in reserve. 4. extra. 5. lean.

spare′rib′, *n.* cut of pork ribs.

spark, *n.* 1. burning particle. 2. flash of electricity. 3. trace.

spar′kle, *v.,* **-kled, -kling,** *n.* —*v.* 1. emit sparks. 2. glitter. 3. produce little bubbles. —*n.* 4. little spark. 5. brightness.

spark plug, device in internal-combustion engine that ignites fuel.

spar′row, *n.* small, common, hardy bird.

sparse, *adj.*, **sparser, sparsest.** thinly distributed. —**spar′si•ty, sparse′ness**, *n.* —**sparse′ly**, *adv.*

Spar′tan, *adj.* austere.

spasm, *n.* sudden involuntary muscular contraction.

spas•mod′ic, *adj.* **1.** of spasms. **2.** intermittent. —**spas•mod′i•cal•ly**, *adv.*

spas′tic, *adj.* of or marked by spasms.

spat, *n.* petty quarrel.

spate (spāt), *n.* sudden outpouring.

spa′tial, *adj.* of or in space.

spat′ter, *v., n.* sprinkle in many fine drops.

spat′u•la (spach′-), *n.* broad-bladed implement.

spav′in (spav′ən), *n.* disease of hock joint in horses.

spawn, *n.* **1.** eggs of fish, mollusks, etc. —*v.* **2.** produce spawn.

spay, *v.* neuter (female dog, cat, etc.).

speak, *v.*, **spoke, spoken, speaking. 1.** talk; say. **2.** deliver speech.

speak′eas′y, *n., pl.* **-easies.** place selling alcoholic beverages illegally.

speak′er, *n.* **1.** person who speaks. **2.** presiding officer.

spear, *n.* **1.** long staff bearing sharp head. —*v.* **2.** pierce with spear.

spear′head′, *n.* **1.** head of spear. **2.** leader. —*v.* **3.** lead.

spear′mint′, *n.* aromatic herb.

spe′cial, *adj.* **1.** particular in nature or purpose. **2.** unusual. —*n.* **3.** special thing or person. —**spe′cial•ly**, *adv.*

spe′cial•ize′, *v.*, **-ized, -izing.** study of work in special field. —**spe′cial•ist**, *n.* —**spe′cial•i•za′tion**, *n.*

spe′cial•ty, *n., pl.* **-ties.** field of special interest or competence.

spe′cie (spē′shē), *n.* coined money.

spe′cies, *n.* class of related individuals.

spe•cif′ic, *adj.* definite. —**spe•cif′i•cal•ly**, *adv.*

spec′i•fi•ca′tion, *n.* **1.** act of specifying. **2.** detailed requirement.

specific gravity, ratio of density of substance to density of standard substance, water being the standard.

spec'i•fy', *v.,* **-fied, -fying.** mention or require specifically.

spec'i•men, *n.* anything typical of its kind.

spe'cious (spē'shəs), *adj.* plausible but deceptive. —**spe'cious•ly,** *adv.* —**spe'cious•ness,** *n.*

speck, *n.* **1.** spot or particle. —*v.* **2.** spot.

speck'le, *n., v.,* **-led, -ling.** —*n.* **1.** small spot. —*v.* **2.** mark with speckles.

specs, *n.pl. Informal.* **1.** spectacles; eyeglasses. **2.** specifications (def. 2).

spec'ta•cle, *n.* **1.** anything presented to sight. **2.** public display. **3.** (*pl.*) eyeglasses.

spec•tac'u•lar, *adj.* dramatic; thrilling. —**spec•tac'u•lar•ly,** *adv.*

spec'ta•tor, *n.* observer.

spec'ter, *n.* ghost. Also, **spec'tre. —spec'tral,** *adj.*

spec'tro•scope', *n.* instrument for producing and examining spectra.

spec'trum, *n., pl.* **-tra** (-trə), **-trums.** band of colors formed when light ray is dispersed.

spec'u•late', *v.,* **-lated, -lating. 1.** think; conjecture. **2.** invest at some risk. —**spec'u•la'tion,** *n.* —**spec'u•la'tive,** *adj.* —**spec'u•la'tor,** *n.*

speech, *n.* **1.** power of speaking. **2.** utterance. **3.** talk before audience. **4.** language. —**speech'less,** *adj.*

speed, *n., v.,* **sped** or **speeded, speeding.** —*n.* **1.** swiftness. **2.** rate of motion —*v.* **3.** increase speed of. **4.** move swiftly. —**speed'er,** *n.* —**speed'y,** *adj.* —**speed'i•ly,** *adv.*

speed•om'e•ter, *n.* device for indicating speed.

speed'well', *n.* plant having spikes of small flowers.

spe'le•ol'o•gy (spē'lē-), *n.* exploration and study of caves. —**spe'le•ol'o•gist,** *n.*

spell, *v.,* **spelled** or **spelt, spelling,** *n.* —*v.* **1.** give letters of in order. **2.** (of letters) form. **3.** signify. **4.** relieve at work. —*n.* **5.** enchantment. **6.** brief period. —**spell'er,** *n.*

spell'bound', *adj.* fascinated.

spe·lunk′er (spi lung′kər), *n.* person who explores caves. —**spe·lunk′ing,** *n.*

spend, *v.,* **spent, spending. 1.** pay out. **2.** pass (time). **3.** use up. —**spend′er,** *n.*

spend′thrift′, *n.* extravagant spender.

sperm, *n.* male reproductive cell. —**sper·mat′ic,** *adj.*

sper′ma·cet′i (-set′ē), *n.* waxy substance from large square-headed whale (**sperm whale**).

sper·mat′o·zo′on, *n., pl.* **-zoa.** mature male reproductive cell.

sper′mi·cide′, *n.* sperm-killing agent.

spew, *v.* **1.** vomit. **2.** gush or pour out. —*n.* **3.** something spewed.

sphere, *n.* **1.** round ball. **2.** particular field of influence or competence. —**spher′i·cal,** *adj.*

sphe′roid, *n.* body approximately spherical.

sphinc′ter, *n.* muscle closing anus or other body opening. —**sphinc′ter·al,** *adj.*

sphinx, *n.* figure of creature with human head and lion's body.

spice, *n., v.,* **spiced, spicing.** —*n.* **1.** aromatic plant substance used as seasoning. —*v.* **2.** season with spice. —**spic′y,** *adj.*

spick′-and-span′, *adj.* **1.** spotlessly clean. **2.** perfectly new.

spic′ule, *n.* small, needlelike part or process.

spi′der, *n.* wingless, web-spinning insectlike animal. —**spi′der·y,** *adj.*

spiel, *n. Slang.* high-pressure sales talk.

spiff′y, *adj.,* **spiffier, spiffiest.** *Informal.* smart; fine.

spig′ot, *n.* faucet.

spike, *n., v.,* **spiked, spiking.** —*n.* **1.** large strong nail. **2.** stiff, pointed part. **3.** ear of grain. **4.** stalk of flowers. —*v.* **5.** fasten with spikes. **6.** frustrate or stop. —**spik′y,** *adj.*

spill, *v.,* **spilled** or **spilt, spilling. 1.** run or let run over. **2.** shed (blood). —**spil′lage,** *n.*

spill′way′, *n.* overflow passage.

spin, *v.,* **spun, spinning,** *n.* —*v.*
1. make yarn or thread from
fiber. 2. secrete filament. 3.
whirl. —*n.* 4. spinning
motion. 5. short ride. 6. *Slang.*
particular viewpoint or bias.
—**spin'ner,** *n.*

spin'ach (-ich), *n.* plant with
edible leaves.

spinal column, series of
vertebrae forming axis of
skeleton.

spinal cord, cord of nerve
tissue extending through
spinal column.

spin control, *Slang.* attempt to
give a bias to news coverage.

spin'dle, *n.* 1. tapered rod. 2.
any shaft or axis.

spin'dling, *adj.* tall and thin.
Also, **spin'dly.**

spin doctor, *Slang.* press agent
or spokesperson skilled at
spin control.

spine, *n.* 1. Also, **spinal
column.** connected series of
bones down back. 2. any
spinelike part. 3. stiff bristle
or thorn. —**spi'nal,** *adj.*
—**spin'y,** *adj.*

spine'less, *adj.* weak in
character.

spin'et, *n.* small piano.

spin'na•ker, *n.* large sail.

spinning wheel, device for
spinning yarn or thread.

spin'-off', *n.* by-product or
secondary development from
primary effort or product.

spin'ster, *n.* unmarried
woman, esp. elderly.

spi'ra•cle, *n.* blowhole.

spi'ral, *n., adj., v.,* **-raled,
-raling.** —*n.* 1. curve made by
circling a point while
approaching or receding from
it. —*adj.* 2. like or of spiral.
—*v.* 3. move spirally.
—**spi'ral•ly,** *adv.*

spire, *n.* tall tapering structure,
esp. on tower or roof.

spi•re'a (spī rē'ə), *n.* common
garden shrub. Also, **spiraea.**

spir'it, *n.* 1. vital principle in
humanity; soul. 2.
supernatural being. 3. feelings.
4. vigor. 5. intent. 6. (*pl.*)
alcoholic liquor. 7. (*cap.*)
Holy Ghost. —*v.* 8. carry off
secretly. —**spir'it•ed,** *adj.*
—**spir'it•less,** *adj.*

spir'it•u•al, *adj.* 1. of or in
spirit; ethereal. 2. religious.
—*n.* 3. religious song.
—**spir'it•u•al•ly,** *adv.*
—**spir'it•u•al'i•ty,** *n.*

spir′it·u·al·ism, *n.* belief that spirits of dead communicate with living. —**spir′it·u·al·ist,** *n., adj.*

spir′it·u·ous, *adj.* 1. alcoholic. 2. distilled.

spi′ro·chete′, *n.* mobile, spiral bacteria.

spit, *v.,* **spat** or **spit** (for 2 **spitted**), **spitting,** *n.* —*v.* 1. eject from mouth. 2. pierce. —*n.* 3. saliva. 4. *Informal.* image. 5. rod for roasting meat. 6. point of land.

spite, *n., v.,* **spited, spiting.** —*n.* 1. malice; grudge. —*v.* 2. annoy out of spite. —**spite′ful,** *adj.* —**spite′ful·ly,** *adv.* —**spite′ful·ness,** *n.*

spit′fire′, *n.* person with fiery temper.

spit′tle, *n.* saliva.

spit·toon′, *n.* cuspidor.

splash, *v.* 1. dash water, etc. —*n.* 2. act or sound of splashing. 3. spot. —**splash′y,** *adj.*

splash′down′, *n.* landing of space vehicle in ocean.

splat, *n.* 1. broad piece forming part of chair back. 2. sound made by splattering.

splat′ter, *v.* splash widely.

splay, *v., adj.* spread out.

spleen, *n.* 1. ductless organ near stomach. 2. ill humor.

splen′did, *adj.* gorgeous; superb; fine. —**splen′did·ly,** *adv.* —**splen′dor,** *n.*

sple·net′ic, *adj.* 1. of the spleen. 2. irritable or spiteful.

splice, *v.,* **spliced, splicing,** *n.* —*v.* 1. join, as ropes or boards. —*n.* 2. union made by splicing.

splint, *n.* 1. brace for broken part of body. 2. strip of wood for weaving. —*v.* 3. brace with splints.

splin′ter, *n.* 1. thin sharp fragment. —*v.* 2. break into splinters.

split, *v.,* **split, splitting,** *n., adj.* —*v.* 1. separate; divide. 2. burst. —*n.* 3. crack or breach. —*adj.* 4. cleft; divided.

split′-lev′el, *adj.* 1. having rooms on levels a half story apart. —*n.* 2. split-level house.

split pea, dried green pea.

split personality, mental disorder in which person acquires several personalities that function independently.

splotch, *n., v.,* blot; stain. —**splotch'y,** *adj.*

splurge, *n., v.,* **splurged, splurging.** —*n.* **1.** big display or expenditure. —*v.* **2.** make splurge; be extravagant.

splut'ter, *v.* **1.** talk vehemently and incoherently. —*n.* **2.** spluttering talk.

spoil, *v.,* **spoiled** or **spoilt, spoiling,** *n.* —*v.* **1.** damage; ruin. **2.** become tainted. —*n.* **3.** (*pl.*) booty. **4.** waste material. —**spoil'age,** *n.* —**spoil'er,** *n.*

spoil'sport', *n.* person who spoils the pleasure of others.

spoils system, practice of filling nonelective public offices with supporters of victorious party.

spoke, *n.* bar between hub and rim of wheel.

spokes'man, *n., pl.* **-men.** person speaking for others.

spo'li•a'tion, *n.* act of plundering.

sponge, *n., v.,* **sponged, sponging.** —*n.* **1.** marine animal. **2.** its light skeleton or an imitation, used to absorb liquids. —*v.* **3.** clean with sponge. **4.** impose or live on another. —**spong'er,** *n.* —**spon'gy,** *adj.*

sponge cake, light cake without shortening.

spon'sor, *n.* **1.** one that recommends or supports. **2.** godparent. **3.** advertiser on radio or television. —*v.* **4.** act as sponsor for. —**spon'sor•ship',** *n.*

spon•ta'ne•ous, *adj.* **1.** arising without outside cause. **2.** impulsive. —**spon•ta'ne•ous•ly,** *adv.* —**spon'ta•ne'i•ty,** *n.*

spontaneous combustion, ignition of a substance without heat from external source.

spoof, *n.* **1.** parody. **2.** prank. —*v.* **3.** make fun of lightly.

spook, *Informal.* —*n.* **1.** ghost. —*v.* **2.** frighten. —**spook'y,** *adj.*

spool, *n.* cylinder on which something is wound.

spoon, *n.* **1.** utensil for stirring or taking up food. —*v.* **2.** lift in spoon. —**spoon'ful,** *n.*

spoon'bill', *n.* large wading bird.

spoon'er•ism, *n.* inadvertent transposition of initial sounds of words.

spoon'-feed', *v.,* **-fed, -feeding. 1.** feed with a spoon. **2.** provide information in a simplified way.

spoor (spo͞or), *n.* trail of wild animal.

spo•rad'ic, *adj.* occasional; scattered. —**spo•rad'i•cal•ly,** *adv.*

spore, *n.* seed, as of ferns.

sport, *n.* **1.** athletic pastime. **2.** diversion. **3.** abnormally formed plant or animal. —*adj.* **4.** of or for sport. —*v.* **5.** play. —**sports'man,** *n.* —**sports'man•ly,** *adj.* —**sports'man•ship',** *n.* —**sports'wear',** *n.*

spor'tive, *adj.* playful. —**spor'tive•ly,** *adv.*

sports car, small, high-powered car.

sport'y, *adj.,* **sportier, sportiest.** flashy or showy.

spot, *n., v.,* **spotted, spotting,** *adj.* —*n.* **1.** blot; speck. **2.** locality. —*v.* **3.** stain with spots. **4.** notice. —*adj.* **5.** made, done, etc., at once.

—**spot'less,** *adj.* —**spot'ter,** *n.* —**spot'ty,** *adj.*

spot check, random sampling or investigation. —**spot'-check',** *v.*

spot'light', *n.* **1.** intense light focused on person or thing, as on stage. **2.** intense public attention.

spouse, *n.* husband or wife.

spout, *v.* **1.** discharge (liquid, etc.) with force. **2.** utter insincerely. —*n.* **3.** pipe or lip on container.

sprain, *v.* **1.** injure by wrenching. —*n.* **2.** such injury.

sprat, *n.* herringlike fish.

sprawl, *v.* **1.** stretch out ungracefully. —*n.* **2.** sprawling position.

spray, *n.* **1.** liquid in fine particles. **2.** appliance for producing spray. **3.** branch of flowers, etc. —*v.* **4.** scatter as spray. **5.** apply spray to. —**spray'er,** *n.*

spread, *v.,* **spread, spreading,** *n.* —*v.* **1.** stretch out. **2.** extend. **3.** scatter. —*n.* **4.** extent. **5.** diffusion. **6.** cloth cover. **7.** preparation for

eating on bread.
—**spread′a•ble,** *adj.*
—**spread′er,** *n.*

spread′-ea′gle, *adj., v.,* **-gled,
-gling.** —*adj.* **1.** suggesting
form of eagle with
outstretched wings. —*v.* **2.**
stretch out in this position.

spread′sheet′, *n.* **1.** outsize
ledger sheet used by
accountants. **2.** such a sheet
simulated electronically by
computer software.

spree, *n.* frolic.

sprig, *n.* twig or shoot.

spright′ly, *adj.,* **-lier, -liest.**
lively. —**spright′li•ness,** *n.*

spring, *v.,* **sprang** or **sprung,
sprung, springing,** *n., adj.* —*v.*
1. leap. **2.** grow or proceed. **3.**
disclose. —*n.* **4.** leap; jump. **5.**
natural fountain. **6.** season
after winter. **7.** elastic device.
—*adj.* **8.** of or for spring (def.
6). —**spring′time′,** *n.*
—**spring′y,** *adj.*

spring′board′, *n.* **1.** flexible
board used in diving and
gymnastics. **2.** starting point.

spring fever, restless feeling
associated with spring.

sprin′kle, *v.,* **-kled, -kling,** *n.*
—*v.* **1.** scatter in drops. **2.** rain

slightly. —*n.* **3.** instance of
sprinkling. **4.** something
sprinkled. —**sprin′kler,** *n.*

sprint, *v.* **1.** run fast. —*n.* **2.**
short fast run. —**sprint′er,** *n.*

sprite, *n.* elf; fairy.

spritz, *v.* **1.** spray briefly. —*n.*
2. squirt.

sprock′et, *n.* tooth on wheel
for engaging with chain.

sprout, *v.* **1.** begin to grow;
bud. —*n.* **2.** plant shoot.

spruce, *adj.,* **sprucer, sprucest,**
v., n. —*adj.* **1.** trim; neat. —*v.*
2. make spruce. —*n.* **3.**
cone-bearing evergreen tree.

spry, *adj.,* **spryer** or **sprier,
spryest** or **spriest.** nimble.
—**spry′ly,** *adv.* —**spry′ness,** *n.*

spud, *n.* **1.** spadelike tool. **2.**
Informal. potato.

spume, *n.* foam.

spu•mo′ni, *n.* variously
flavored ice cream containing
fruit and nuts.

spunk, *n. Informal.* courage;
spirit. —**spunk′y,** *adj.*

spur, *n., v.,* **spurred, spurring.**
—*n.* **1.** sharp device worn on
heel to goad horse. **2.** spurlike
part. —*v.* **3.** prick with spur. **4.**
urge.

spu'ri•ous (spyo͝or'-), *adj.* not genuine. —**spu'ri•ous•ly,** *adv.* —**spu'ri•ous•ness,** *n.*

spurn, *v.* scorn; reject.

spurt, *v.* **1.** gush or eject in jet. **2.** speed up briefly. —*n.* **3.** forceful gush. **4.** brief increase of effort.

sput'nik, *n.* first earth-orbiting satellite, launched by USSR in 1957.

sput'ter, *v.* **1.** emit violently in drops. **2.** splutter. —*n.* **3.** act or sound of sputtering.

spu'tum (spyo͞o'-), *n.* spittle, esp. mixed with mucus.

spy, *n., pl.* **spies,** *v.,* **spied, spying.** —*n.* **1.** secret observer, esp. one employed by government. —*v.* **2.** watch secretly. **3.** sight.

spy glass, small telescope.

squab, *n.* young pigeon.

squab'ble, *n., v.,* **-bled, -bling.** —*n.* **1.** petty quarrel. —*v.* **2.** have squabble.

squad, *n.* small group.

squad car, police car.

squad'ron, *n.* unit in Navy, Air Force, etc.

squal'id (skwol'id), *adj.* dirty or wretched. —**squal'id•ly,** *adv.* —**squal'id•ness,** *n.*

squall (skwôl), *n.* **1.** strong gust of wind, etc. **2.** loud cry. —*v.* **3.** cry loudly. —**squall'y,** *adj.*

squal'or (skwol'ər), *n.* squalid state.

squan'der, *v.* use or spend wastefully.

square, *n., v.,* **squared, squaring,** *adj.,* **squarer, squarest,** *adv.* —*n.* **1.** plane figure with four equal sides and four right angles. **2.** anything square. **3.** tool for checking right angles. **4.** product of number multiplied by itself. **5.** *Slang.* conventional, conservative, unimaginative person. —*v.* **6.** make square. **7.** adjust; agree. **8.** multiply by itself. —*adj.* **9.** being a square. **10.** level. **11.** honest. —*adv.* **12.** directly. —**square'ly,** *adv.*

square dance, dance by sets of four couples arranged in squares.

square'-rigged', having square sails.

square root, quantity of which a given quantity is the square.

squash, *v.* **1.** crush; suppress. —*n.* **2.** game resembling tennis. **3.** fruit of vinelike plant.

squat, *v.,* **squatted** or **squat, squatting,** *adj., n.* —*v.* **1.** sit with legs close under body. **2.** settle on land illegally or to acquire title. —*adj.* **3.** Also, **squat'ty.** stocky. —*n.* **4.** squatting position. —**squat'ter,** *n.*

squaw, *n. Often Offensive.* American Indian woman.

squawk, *n.* **1.** loud harsh cry. —*v.* **2.** utter squawks. —**squawk'er,** *n.*

squeak, *n.* **1.** small shrill sound. —*v.* **2.** emit squeaks. —**squeak'y,** *adj.* —**squeak'er,** *n.* —**squeak'i•ness,** *n.*

squeal, *n.* **1.** long shrill cry. —*v.* **2.** utter squeals. —**squeal'er,** *n.*

squeam'ish, *adj.* **1.** prudish. **2.** overfastidious. —**squeam'ish•ly,** *adv.* —**squeam'ish•ness,** *n.*

squee'gee, *n.* implement for cleaning glass surfaces.

squeeze, *v.,* **squeezed, squeezing,** *n.* —*v.* **1.** press together. **2.** cram. —*n.* **3.** act of squeezing. **4.** hug.

squelch, *v.* **1.** crush. **2.** silence. —*n.* **3.** crushing retort.

squib, *n.* **1.** short witty item. **2.** hissing firecracker.

squid, *n.* marine mollusk.

squig'gle, *n.* short, irregular curve or twist. —**squig'gly,** *adj.*

squint, *v.* **1.** look with eyes partly closed. **2.** be cross-eyed. —*n.* **3.** squinting look. **4.** cross-eyed condition.

squire, *n., v.,* **squired, squiring.** —*n.* **1.** country gentleman. **2.** escort. —*v.* **3.** escort.

squirm, *v., n.* wriggle.

squir'rel, *n.* bushy-tailed, tree-living rodent.

squirt, *v.* **1.** gush; cause to gush. —*n.* **2.** jet of liquid.

squish, *v.* **1.** make gushing sound when squeezed. **2.** squash (def. 1). —*n.* **3.** squishing sound.

Sr., 1. Senior. **2.** Sister.

SRO, 1. single-room occupancy. **2.** standing room only.

SS, social security.

SST, supersonic transport.

St., 1. Saint 2. Street.

stab, *v.,* **stabbed, stabbing,** *n.*
—*v.* 1. pierce with pointed
weapon. —*n.* 2. thrust with or
wound from pointed weapon.

sta′bi•lize′, *v.,* **-lized, -lizing.**
make or keep stable.
—**sta′bi•li•za′tion,** *n.*
—**sta′bi•liz′er,** *n.*

sta′ble, *n., v.,* **-bled, -bling,**
adj. —*n.* 1. building for
horses, etc. —*v.* 2. keep in
stable. —*adj.* 3. steady;
steadfast. —**stab′ly,** *adv.*
—**sta•bil′i•ty,** *n.*

stac•ca′to (stə kä′tō), *adj.*
Music. disconnected;
detached.

stack, *n.* 1. orderly heap. 2.
(*often pl.*) book storage area.
3. funnel for smoke. —*v.* 4.
pile in stack. 5. arrange
unfairly.

sta′di•um, *n., pl.* **-diums, -dia**
(-ə). large open structure for
games.

staff, *n., pl.* **staves** (stāvz) or
staffs (for 1, 3); **staffs** (for 2);
v. —*n.* 1. stick carried as
support, weapon, etc. 2. body
of administrators or assitants.

3. set of five lines on which
music is written. —*v.* 4.
provide with staff.

staff′er, *n.* member of a staff.

stag, *n.* 1. adult male deer.
—*adj.* 2. for men only. —*adv.*
3. without a date.

stage, *n., v.,* **staged, staging.**
—*n.* 1. single step or degree.
2. raised platform. 3. theater.
—*v.* 4. exhibit on stage.

stage′coach′, *n.* horse-drawn
public coach that traveled
over fixed route.

stage′hand′, *n.* worker in
theater who deals with
properties and scenery.

stage′struck′, *adj.* obsessed
with desire to act.

stag′ger, *v.* 1. move
unsteadily. 2. cause to reel. 3.
arrange at intervals. —*n.* 4.
staggering movement. 5. (*pl.*)
disease of horses, etc.
—**stag′ger•ing,** *adj.*

stag′ing, *n.* scaffolding.

stag′nant, *adj.* 1. not flowing;
foul. 2. inactive. —**stag′nate,**
v. —**stag•na′tion,** *n.*

staid, *adj.* sedate. —**staid′ly,**
adv. —**staid′ness,** *n.*

stain, *n.* 1. discolored patch. 2. kind of dye. —*v.* 3. mark with stains. 4. color with stain.

stain′less, *adj.* 1. unstained. 2. not liable to rusting.

stainless steel, steel allied with chromium to resist rust.

stair, *n.* series of steps between levels. —**stair′case′, stair′way′,** *n.*

stair′well′, *n.* vertical shaft containing stairs.

stake, *n., v.,* **staked, staking.** —*n.* 1. pointed post. 2. something wagered. 3. (*pl.*) prize. 4. hazard. —*v.* 5. mark off with stakes. 6. wager.

stake′out′, *n.* surveillance by police.

sta•lac′tite, *n.* icicle-shaped formation hanging from cave roof.

sta•lag′mite, *n.* cone-shaped deposit on cave floor.

stale, *adj.,* **staler, stalest,** *v.,* **staled, staling.** —*adj.* 1. not fresh. —*v.* 2. make or become stale. —**stale′ness,** *n.*

stale′mate′, *n., v.,* **-mated, -mating.** —*n.* 1. deadlocked position, orig. in chess. —*v.* 2. bring to stalemate.

stalk, *v.* 1. pursue stealthily. 2. walk in haughty or menacing way. —*n.* 3. plant stem. —**stalk′er,** *n.*

stall, *n.* 1. compartment for one animal. 2. sales booth. 3. (of airplane) loss of air speed. 4. *Slang.* pretext for delay. —*v.* 5. keep in stall. 6. stop; become stopped. 7. lose necessary air speed. 8. *Slang.* delay.

stal′lion (stal′yən), *n.* male horse.

stal′wart (stôl′wərt), *adj.* 1. robust. 2. brave. 3. steadfast. —*v.* 4. stalwart person.

sta′men, *n.* pollen-bearing organ of flower.

stam′i•na, *n.* endurance.

stam′mer, *v.* 1. speak with involuntary breaks or repetitions. —*n.* 2. such speech. —**stam′mer•er,** *n.*

stamp, *v.* 1. trample. 2. mark. 3. put paper stamp on. —*n.* 4. act of stamping. 5. marking device. 6. adhesive paper affixed to show payment of fees.

stam•pede′, *n., v.,* **-peded, -peding.** —*n.* 1. panicky flight. —*v.* 2. flee in stampede.

stamping ground, favorite haunt.

stance, *n.* position of feet.

stanch (stônch), *adj.* **1.** staunch. —*v.* **2.** stop flow, esp. of blood. —**stanch′ly,** *adv.* —**stanch′ness,** *n.*

stan′chion, *n.* upright post.

stand, *v.,* **stood, standing,** *n.* —*v.* **1.** rise or be upright. **2.** remain firm. **3.** be located. **4.** be candidate. **5.** endure. —*n.* **6.** firm attitude. **7.** place of standing. **8.** platform. **9.** support for small articles. **10.** outdoor salesplace. **11.** area of trees. **12.** stop.

stand′ard, *n.* **1.** approved model or rule. **2.** flag. **3.** upright support. —*adj.* **4.** being model or basis for comparison.

stan′dard-bear′er, *n.* leader of a cause.

stand′ard·ize′, *v.,* **-ized, -izing.** make standard. —**stand′ard·i·za′tion,** *n.*

standard time, civil time officially adopted for a region.

stand′·by′, *n., pl.* **-bys,** *adj.* —*n.* **1.** chief support. —*adj.* **2.** substitute.

stand′-in′, *n.* substitute.

stand′ing, *n.* **1.** status or reputation. **2.** duration. —*adj.* **3.** upright. **4.** stagnant. **5.** lasting; fixed.

stand′off′, *n.* tie or draw; situation in which neither side has advantage.

stand′off′ish, *adj.* tending to be aloof.

stand′out′, *n.* one that is conspicuously superior.

stand′pipe′, *n.* vertical pipe into which water is pumped to obtain required pressure.

stand′point′, *n.* point of view.

stand′still′, *n.* complete halt.

stand′-up′, *adj.* **1.** erect. **2.** performing a comic monologue while standing alone before audience.

stan′za, *n.* division of poem.

staph′y·lo·coc′cus (staf′ə lə kok′əs), *n., pl.* **-ci** (-sī, -sē). any of several spherical bacteria occurring in clusters.

sta′ple, *n., v.,* **-pled, -pling,** *adj.* —*n.* **1.** bent wire fastener. **2.** chief commodity. **3.** textile fiber. —*v.* **4.** fasten with staple. —*adj.* **5.** basic. —**sta′pler,** *n.*

star, *n., adj., v.,* **starred, starring.** —*n.* **1.** heavenly body luminous at night. **2.** figure with five or six points. **3.** asterisk. **4.** principal performer. **5.** famous performer. —*adj.* **6.** principal. —*v.* **7.** mark with star. **8.** have leading part. —**star′ry,** *adj.* —**star′dom,** *n.*

star′board′, *n.* right-hand side of vessel, facing forward. —**star′board′,** *adj., adv.*

starch, *n.* **1.** white tasteless substance used as food and as a stiffening agent. **2.** preparation from starch. —*v.* **3.** stiffen with starch. —**starch′y,** *adj.*

stare, *v.,* **stared, staring,** *n.* —*v.* **1.** gaze fixedly. —*n.* **2.** fixed look.

star′fish′, *n.* star-shaped marine animal.

star′gaze′, *v.,* **-gazed, -gazing. 1.** gaze at stars. **2.** daydream. —**star′gaz′er,** *n.*

stark, *adj.* **1.** utter; sheer. **2.** stiff. —*adv.* **3.** bleak. **4.** blunt; harsh. **5.** utterly. —**stark′ly,** *adv.* —**stark′ness,** *n.*

star′let, *n.* young movie actress.

star′light′, *n.* light emanating from the stars. —**star′lit′,** *adj.*

star′ling, *n.* small bird.

star′ry-eyed′, *adj.* overly romantic or idealistic.

start, *v.* **1.** begin. **2.** move suddenly. **3.** establish. —*n.* **4.** beginning. **5.** startled movement. **6.** lead. —**start′er,** *n.*

star′tle, *v.,* **-tled, -tling.** disturb suddenly.

starve, *v.,* **starved, starving. 1.** die or suffer severely from hunger. **2.** kill or weaken by hunger. —**star•va′tion,** *n.*

stash, *v.* **1.** hide away. —*n.* **2.** something hidden away. **3.** hiding place.

stat, *n.* statistic.

state, *n., adj., v.,* **stated, stating.** —*n.* **1.** condition. **2.** pomp. **3.** nation. **4.** commonwealth of a federal union. **5.** civil government. —*adj.* **6.** ceremonious. —*v.* **7.** declare. —**state′hood,** *n.* —**state′house,** *n.*

state′craft′, *n.* art of government.

state′less, *adj.* lacking nationality.

state′ly, *adj.,* **-lier, -liest.** dignified. —**state′li•ness,** *n.*

state′ment, *n.* **1.** declaration. **2.** report on business account.

state of the art, most advanced stage.

state′room′, *n.* quarters on ship, etc.

states′man, *n.* leader in government. —**states′man•ship′,** *n.*

stat′ic, *adj.* **1.** fixed; at rest. —*n.* **2.** atmospheric electricity. **3.** interference caused by it.

sta′tion, *n.* **1.** place of duty. **2.** depot for trains, buses, etc. **3.** status. **4.** place for sending or receiving radio or television broadcasts. —*v.* **5.** assign place to.

sta′tion•ar′y, *adj.* not moving; not movable; fixed.

sta′tion•er, *n.* dealer in stationery.

sta′tion•er′y, *n.* writing materials.

sta•tis′tics, *n.* science of collecting, classifying, and using numerical facts. —**sta•tis′ti•cal,** *adj.* —**sta•tis′ti•cal•ly,** *adv.* —**stat′is•ti′cian,** *n.*

stat′u•ar′y, *n.* statues.

stat′ue, *n.* carved, molded, or cast figure.

stat′u•esque′, *adj.* like statue; of imposing figure.

stat′u•ette′, *n.* little statue.

stat′ure, *n.* **1.** height. **2.** achievement.

sta′tus (stā′-, sta′-), *n.* **1.** social standing. **2.** present condition.

status quo, existing state.

status symbol, possession believed to indicate high social status.

stat′ute, *n.* law enacted by legislature. —**stat′u•to′ry,** *adj.*

statute of limitations, statute defining period within which legal action may be taken.

staunch (stônch), *adj.* **1.** firm; steadfast; strong. —*v.* **2.** stanch. —**staunch′ly,** *adv.* —**staunch′ness,** *n.*

stave, *n., v.,* **staved** or (for 3) **stove, staving.** —*n.* **1.** one of curved vertical strips of barrel, etc. **2.** *Music.* staff. —*v.* **3.** break hole in. **4.** ward (off).

stay, *v.* **1.** remain; continue. **2.** stop or restrain. **3.** support. —*n.* **4.** period at one place. **5.** stop; pause. **6.** support; prop. **7.** rope supporting mast.

staying power, endurance.

STD, sexually transmitted disease.

std., standard.

stead, *n.* **1.** place taken by another. **2.** advantage.

stead'fast', *adj.* **1.** fixed. **2.** firm or loyal. —**stead'fast'ly,** *adv.* —**stead'fast'ness,** *n.*

stead'y, *adj.,* **steadier, steadiest,** *v.,* **steadied, steadying.** —*adj.* **1.** firmly fixed. **2.** uniform; regular. **3.** steadfast. —*v.* **4.** make or become steady. —**stead'i•ly,** *adv.* —**stead'i•ness,** *n.*

steak, *n.* slice of meat or fish.

steal, *v.,* **stole, stolen, stealing. 1.** take wrongfully. **2.** move very quietly.

stealth, *n.* secret procedure. —**stealth'y,** *adj.* —**stealth'i•ly,** *adv.*

steam, *n.* **1.** water in form of gas or vapor. —*v.* **2.** pass off as or give off steam. **3.** treat with steam, as in cooking.

—*adj.* **4.** operated by steam. **5.** conducting steam. —**steam'boat', steam'ship',** *n.*

steam'er, *n.* **1.** vessel moved by steam. **2.** device for cooking, treating, etc., with steam.

steam'roll'er, *n.* **1.** heavy vehicle with roller used for paving roads. —*v.* **2.** crush, flatten, or overwhelm as if with steamroller.

steam shovel, machine for excavating.

steed, *n.* horse, esp. for riding.

steel, *n.* **1.** iron modified with carbon. —*adj.* **2.** of or like steel. —*v.* **3.** make resolute. —**steel'y,** *adj.*

steel wool, mass of stringlike woven steel, used esp. for scouring and smoothing.

steel'yard', *n.* kind of scale.

steep, *adj.* **1.** sloping sharply. **2.** exorbitant. —*v.* **3.** soak. **4.** absorb. —**steep'ly,** *adv.*

stee'ple, *n.* **1.** lofty tower on church, etc. **2.** spire.

stee'ple•chase', *n.* horse race over obstacle course.

stee'ple•jack', *n.* person who builds steeples.

steer, *v.* **1.** guide; direct. —*n.* **2.** ox.

steer'age, *n.* part of ship for passengers paying cheapest rate.

steg'o•saur', *n.* plant-eating dinosaur with bony plates along back.

stein, *n.* mug, esp. for beer.

stel'lar, *adj.* of or like stars.

stem, *n., v.,* **stemmed, stemming.** —*n.* **1.** supporting stalk of plant or of leaf, flower, or fruit. **2.** ancestry. **3.** part of word not changed by inflection. **4.** *Naut.* bow. —*v.* **5.** remove stem of. **6.** originate. **7.** stop or check. **8.** make headway against.

stem'ware', *n.* glassware with footed stems.

stench, *n.* bad odor.

sten'cil, *n., v.,* **-ciled, -ciling.** —*n.* **1.** sheet cut to pass design through when colored over. —*v.* **2.** print with stencil.

ste•nog'ra•pher, *n.* person skilled at shorthand and typing.

ste•nog'ra•phy, *n.* writing in shorthand. —**sten'o•graph'ic,** *adj.*

sten•to'ri•an, *adj.* very loud.

step, *n., v.,* **stepped, stepping.** —*n.* **1.** movement of foot in walking. **2.** distance of such movement. **3.** pace. **4.** footprint. **5.** stage in process. **6.** level on stair or ladder. —*v.* **7.** move by steps. **8.** press with foot.

step-, prefix showing relation by remarriage of parent. —**step'child,** *n.* —**step'son',** *n.* —**step'daugh'ter,** *n.* —**step'par'ent,** *n.* —**step'fath'er,** *n.* —**step'moth'er,** *n.* —**step'broth'er,** *n.* —**step'sis'ter,** *n.*

step'lad'der, *n.* ladder with flat treads.

steppe, *n.* vast plain.

-ster, suffix meaning one who is, one who is associated with, or one who makes or does.

ster'e•o, *n., pl.* **-eos.** stereophonic sound or equipment.

ster'e•o•phon'ic, *adj.* (of recorded sound) played through two or more speakers.

ster'e•op'ti•con, *n.* projector for slides, etc.

ster′e•o•scope′, *n.* device for viewing two pictures at once to give impression of depth. —**ster′e•o•scop′ic**, *adj.*

ster′e•o•type′, *n.*, *v.*, **-typed, -typing.** —*n.* **1.** process of making printing plates from mold taken from composed type. **2.** idea, etc., without originality. **3.** simplified image of person, group, etc. —*v.* **4.** make stereotype of. **5.** give fixed, trite form to.

ster′ile, *adj.* **1.** free from living germs. **2.** unable to produce offspring; barren. —**ste•ril′i•ty**, *n.*

ster′i•lize′, *v.*, **-lized, -lizing.** make sterile. —**ster′i•li•za′tion**, *n.* —**ster′i•liz′er**, *n.*

ster′ling, *adj.* **1.** containing 92.5% silver. **2.** of British money. **3.** excellent.

stern, *adj.* **1.** strict; harsh; grim. —*n.* **2.** hind part of vessel. —**stern′ly**, *adv.* —**stern′ness**, *n.*

ster′num, *n.*, *pl.* **-na, -nums.** flat bone in chest connecting with clavicle and ribs.

ste′roid, *n.* any of a group of fat-soluble organic compounds.

stet, *v.*, **stetted, stetting. 1.** let it stand (direction to retain material previously deleted). **2.** mark with word "stet."

steth′o•scope′, *n.* medical instrument for listening to sounds in body.

ste′ve•dore′, *n.* person who loads and unloads ships.

stew, *v.* **1.** cook by simmering. —*n.* **2.** food so cooked.

stew′ard, *n.* **1.** person who manages another's affairs, property, etc. **2.** person in charge of food, supplies, etc., for ship, club, etc. **3.** domestic employee on ship or airplane. —**stew′ard•ship′**, *n.*

stick, *v.*, **stuck, sticking**, *n.* —*v.* **1.** pierce; stab. **2.** thrust. **3.** cause to adhere. **4.** adhere. **5.** persist. **6.** extend. —*n.* **7.** small length of wood, etc.

stick′er, *n.* **1.** one that sticks. **2.** adhesive label. **3.** thorn.

stick′-in-the-mud′, *n.* person who avoids change.

stick′le, *v.*, **-led, -ling. 1.** argue over trifles. **2.** insist on correctness. —**stick′ler**, *n.*

stick′pin′, *n.* ornamental pin.

stick shift, manual transmission.

stick′y, *adj.,* **stickier, stickiest. 1.** adhering. **2.** humid. —**stick′i•ness**, *n.*

stiff, *adj.* **1.** rigid. **2.** not moving easily. **3.** formal. —**stiff′en**, *v.* —**stiff′ly**, *adv.* —**stiff′ness**, *n.*

stiff′-necked′, *adj.* obstinate.

sti′fle, *v.,* **-fled, -fling. 1.** smother. **2.** repress.

stig′ma, *n., pl.* **-mata, -mas. 1.** mark of disgrace. **2.** pollen-receiving part of pistil. —**stig′ma•tize′**, *v.*

stile, *n.* set of steps over fence, wall, etc.

sti•let′to, *n., pl.* **-tos, -toes.** dagger.

still, *adj.* **1.** motionless. **2.** silent. **3.** tranquil. —*adv.* **4.** as previously. **5.** until now. **6.** yet. —*conj.* **7.** nevertheless. —*v.* **8.** make or become still. —*n.* **9.** distilling apparatus. —**still′ness**, *n.*

still′born′, *adj.* born dead.

still life, picture of inanimate objects.

stilt, *n.* one of two poles enabling user to walk above the ground.

stilt′ed, *adj.* stiffly dignified.

stim′u•lant, *n.* food, medicine, etc., that stimulates briefly.

stim′u•late′, *v.,* **-lated, -lating. 1.** rouse to action. **2.** invigorate. —**stim′u•la′tion**, *n.* —**stim′u•la′tive**, *adj.*

stim′u•lus, *n., pl.* **-li.** something that stimulates.

sting, *v.,* **stung, stinging,** *n.* —*v.* **1.** wound with pointed organ, as bees do. **2.** pain sharply. **3.** goad. —*n.* **4.** wound caused by stinging. **5.** sharp-pointed organ. —**sting′er**, *n.*

sting′ray′, *n.* ray with flexible tail armed with bony spine.

stin′gy (stin′jē), *adj.,* **-gier, -giest. 1.** miserly. **2.** scanty. —**stin′gi•ness**, *n.*

stink, *v.,* **stank** or **stunk, stunk, stinking,** *n.* —*v.* **1.** emit bad odor. —*n.* **2.** bad odor.

stint, *v.* **1.** limit. **2.** limit oneself. —*n.* **3.** limitation. **4.** allotted task. —**stint′ing**, *adj.*

sti′pend (stī′pend), *n.* regular pay.

stip′ple, *v.,* **-pled, -pling,** *n.* —*v.* 1. paint or cover with tiny dots. —*n.* 2. such painting.

stip′u•late′, *v.,* **-lated, -lating.** require as condition of agreement. —**stip′u•la′tion,** *n.* —**stip′u•la•to′ry,** *adj.*

stir, *v.,* **stirred, stirring,** *n.* —*v.* 1. mix or agitate (liquid, etc.), esp. with circular motion. 2. move. 3. rouse; excite. —*n.* 4. movement; commotion. 5. *Slang.* prison.

stir′-cra′zy, *adj. Slang.* restless from long confinement.

stir′-fry′, *v.,* **-fried, -frying.** fry quickly while stirring constantly over high heat.

stir′rup, *n.* looplike support for foot, suspended from saddle.

stitch, *n.* 1. complete movement of needle in sewing, knitting, etc. 2. sudden pain. —*v.* 3. sew.

stock, *n.* 1. goods on hand. 2. livestock. 3. stem or trunk. 4. line of descent. 5. meat broth. 6. part of gun supporting barrel. 7. (*pl.*) framework in which prisoners were publicly confined. 8. capital or shares of company. —*adj.* 9. standard; common. 10. of stock. —*v.* 11. supply. 12. store. —**stock′brok′er,** *n.* —**stock′hold′er,** *n.*

stock•ade′, *n., v.,* **-aded, -ading.** —*n.* 1. barrier of upright posts. —*v.* 2. protect with stockade.

stock company, theatrical company acting repertoire of plays.

stock exchange, place where securities are bought and sold. Also, **stock market.**

stock′i•nette′, *n.* stretchy fabric.

stock′ing, *n.* close-fitting covering for foot and leg.

stocking cap, conical knitted cap with tassel or pompom.

stock′pile′, *n., v.,* **-piled, -piling.** —*n.* 1. stock of goods. —*v.* 2. accumulate for eventual use.

stock′-still′, *adj.* motionless.

stock′y, *adj.,* **stockier, stockiest.** sturdily built. —**stock′i•ly,** *adv.* —**stock′i•ness,** *n.*

stock′yard′, *n.* enclosure for livestock about to be slaughtered.

stodg′y, *adj.*, **stodgier, stodgiest.** pompous and uninteresting. —**stodg′i•ly,** *adv.* —**stodg′i•ness,** *n.*

sto′gy (stō′gē), *n., pl.* -**gies.** long, slender, cheap cigar.

sto′ic, *adj.* **1.** Also, **sto′i•cal.** not reacting to pain. —*n.* **2.** person who represses emotion. —**sto′i•cal•ly,** *adv.* —**sto′i•cism′,** *n.*

stoke, *v.*, **stoked, stoking.** tend (fire). —**stok′er,** *n.*

stole, *n.* scarf or narrow strip worn over shoulders.

stol′id, *adj.* unemotional; not easily moved. —**sto•lid′i•ty,** *n.* —**stol′id•ly,** *adv.*

stom′ach, *n.* **1.** organ of food storage and digestion. **2.** appetite; desire. —*v.* **3.** take into stomach. **4.** tolerate.

stomp, *v.* tread or tread on heavily.

stone, *n., pl.* **stones** or (for 4) **stone,** *adj., v.*, **stoned, stoning,** *adv.* —*n.* **1.** hard, nonmetallic mineral substance. **2.** small rock. **3.** gem. **4.** *Brit.* unit of weight = 14 pounds. **5.**
stonelike seed. **6.** concretion formed in body. —*adj.* **7.** of stone. —*v.* **8.** throw stones at. **9.** remove stones from. —*adv.* **10.** entirely. —**ston′y,** *adj.* —**ston′i•ly,** *adv.*

Stone Age, prehistoric period before use of metals.

stone′wall′, *v.* be evasive or uncooperative.

stooge, *n.* **1.** assistant to comedian. **2.** person acting in obsequious obedience.

stool, *n.* seat without arms or back.

stool pigeon, *Slang.* decoy or informer.

stoop, *v.* **1.** bend forward. **2.** condescend. —*n.* **3.** stooping posture. **4.** small doorway or porch.

stop, *v.*, **stopped, stopping,** *n.* —*v.* **1.** cease; halt. **2.** prevent. **3.** close up. **4.** stay. —*n.* **5.** act, instance, or place of stopping. **6.** hindrance. **7.** device on musical instrument to control tone. —**stop′page,** *n.*

stop′gap′, *n., adj.* makeshift.

stop′o′ver, *n.* temporary stop on journey.

stop'per, *n.* 1. plug. —*v.* 2. close with stopper. Also, **stop'ple.**

stop'watch', *n.* watch with hand that can be stopped or started instantly.

stor'age, *n.* 1. place for storing. 2. act of storing. 3. state of being stored. 4. fee for storing.

store, *n., v.,* **stored, storing.** —*n.* 1. place where merchandise is kept for sale. 2. supply. —*v.* 3. lay up; accumulate. 4. put in secure place. —**store'keep'er,** *n.*

store'front', *n.* small, street-level store.

store'house', *n.* building for storage. —**store'room',** *n.*

sto'ried, *adj.* famed in history or story.

stork, *n.* wading bird with long legs and bill.

storm, *n.* 1. heavy rain, snow, etc., with strong winds. 2. violent assault. —*v.* 3. blow, rain, etc., strongly. 4. rage. 5. attack. —**storm'y,** *adj.* —**storm'i•ly,** *adv.*

sto'ry, *n., pl.* **-ries.** 1. fictitious tale. 2. plot. 3. newspaper report. 4. *Informal.* lie. 5. horizontal section of building.

stoup (stoop), *n.* basin for holy water.

stout, *adj.* 1. solidly built. 2. strong. 3. firm. —*n.* 4. dark, sweet ale. —**stout'ly,** *adv.* —**stout'ness,** *n.*

stout'-heart'ed, *adj.* brave and resolute.

stove, *n.* apparatus for giving heat.

stow, *v.* 1. put away, as cargo. 2. stow away, hide on ship, etc., to get free trip. —**stow'age,** *n.* —**stow'a•way',** *n.*

stra•bis'mus, *n.* visual defect; cross-eye.

strad'dle, *v.,* **-dled, -dling,** *n.* —*v.* 1. have one leg on either side of. —*n.* 2. straddling stance.

strafe, *v.,* **strafed, strafing.** shoot from airplanes.

strag'gle, *v.,* **-gled, -gling.** stray from course; ramble. —**strag'gler,** *n.*

straight, *adj.* 1. direct. 2. even. 3. honest. 4. right. 5. *Informal.* heterosexual. —*adv.* 6. directly. 7. in straight line. 8.

honestly. —*n.* **9.** five-card consecutive sequence in poker. —**straight′en,** *v.*

straight′-arm′, *v.* deflect an opponent by pushing away with the arm held straight.

straight arrow, often righteously conventional person.

straight′a•way′, *adv.* at once. Also, **straight′way′.**

straight′edge′, *n.* bar with straight edge for use in drawing or testing lines.

straight face, expression that conceals feelings, as when keeping a secret.

straight′for′ward, *adj.* direct; frank.

straight man, entertainer who acts as foil for comedian.

strain, *v.* **1.** exert to utmost. **2.** injure by stretching. **3.** sieve; filter. **4.** constrain. —*n.* **5.** great effort. **6.** injury from straining. **7.** severe pressure. **8.** melody. **9.** descendants. **10.** ancestry. **11.** hereditary trait. —**strain′er,** *n.*

strained, *adj.* not natural.

strait, *n.* **1.** narrow waterway. **2.** (*pl.*) distress.

strait′en, *v.* **1.** put into financial troubles. **2.** restrict.

strait′jack′et, *n.* **1.** garment of strong material designed to bind arms and restrain violent person. **2.** anything that severely confines or hinders.

strait′-laced′, *adj.* excessively strict in conduct or morality.

strand, *v.* **1.** run aground. —*n.* **2.** shore. **3.** twisted component of rope. **4.** tress. **5.** string, as of beads.

strange, *adj.,* **stranger, strangest. 1.** unusual; odd. **2.** unfamiliar. —**strange′ly,** *adv.*

stran′ger, *n.* person not known or acquainted.

stran′gle, *v.,* **-gled, -gling. 1.** kill by choking. **2.** choke. —**stran′gler,** *n.* —**stran′gu•la′tion,** *n.*

stran′gle•hold′, *n.* **1.** illegal wrestling hold in which opponent is choked. **2.** restrictive force.

stran′gu•late′, *v.,* **-lated, -lating.** constrict. —**stran′gu•la′tion,** *n.*

strap, *n., v.,* **strapped, strapping.** —*n.* **1.** narrow strip or band. —*v.* **2.** fasten with strap.

strapped, *adj.* needing money.

strat′a•gem (-jəm), *n.* plan; trick.

strat′e•gy, *n., pl.* **-gies. 1.** planning and direction of military operations. **2.** plan for achieving goal. —**stra•te′gic,** *adj.* —**stra•te′gi•cal•ly,** *adv.* —**strat′e•gist,** *n.*

strat′i•fy′, *v.,* **-fied, -fying.** form in layers. —**strat′i•fi•ca′tion,** *n.*

strat′o•sphere′, *n.* upper region of atmosphere. —**strat′o•spher′ic,** *adj.*

stra′tum (strā′təm, strat′əm), *n., pl.* **-ta, -tums.** layer of material.

straw, *n.* **1.** stalk of cereal grass. **2.** mass of dried stalks.

straw′ber′ry, *n., pl.* **-ries.** fleshy fruit of stemless herb.

straw boss, assistant foreman.

straw vote, unofficial vote taken to determine general trend of opinion.

stray, *v.* **1.** ramble; go from one's course or rightful place. —*adj.* **2.** straying. —*n.* **3.** stray creature.

streak, *n.* **1.** long mark or smear. **2.** vein; stratum. —*v.* **3.** mark with streaks. **4.** flash rapidly. —**streak′y,** *adj.*

stream, *n.* **1.** flowing body of water. **2.** steady flow. —*v.* **3.** move in stream. **4.** wave.

stream′er, *n.* long narrow flag.

stream′line′, *adj., n., v.,* **-lined, -lining.** —*adj.* **1.** having shape past which fluids move easily. —*n.* **2.** streamline shape. —*v.* **3.** shape with streamline. **4.** reorganize efficiently.

street, *n.* public city road.

street′car′, *n.* public conveyance running on rails.

street smarts, shrewd awareness of how to survive in urban environment. —**street′-smart′,** *adj.*

street′walk′er, *n.* prostitute who solicits on the streets.

street′wise′, *adj.* possessing street smarts.

strength, *n.* **1.** power of body, mind, position, etc. **2.** intensity.

strength′en, *v.* make or grow stronger.

stren′u•ous, *adj.* vigorous; active. —**stren′u•ous•ly,** *adv.*

strep throat, acute sore throat caused by streptococci.

strep'to•coc'cus, *n., pl.* **-ci.** one of group of disease-producing bacteria. —**strep'to•coc'cal,** *adj.*

strep'to•my'cin, *n.* antibiotic drug.

stress, *v.* **1.** emphasize. —*n.* **2.** emphasis. **3.** physical, mental, or emotional strain.

stretch, *v.* **1.** extend; spread. **2.** distend. **3.** draw tight. —*n.* **4.** act of stretching. **5.** extension; expansion. **6.** continuous length.

stretch'er, *n.* **1.** canvas-covered frame for carrying sick, etc. **2.** device for stretching.

strew, *v.,* **strewed, strewed** or **strewn, strewing.** scatter; sprinkle.

stri'at•ed, *adj.* furrowed; streaked. —**stri•a'tion,** *n.*

strick'en, *adj.* **1.** wounded. **2.** afflicted, as by disease or sorrow.

strict, *adj.* **1.** exacting; severe. **2.** precise. **3.** careful. **4.** absolute. —**strict'ly,** *adv.* —**strict'ness,** *n.*

stric'ture, *n.* **1.** adverse criticism. **2.** morbid contraction of body passage.

stride, *v.,* **strode, stridden, striding,** *n.* —*v.* **1.** walk with long steps. **2.** straddle. —*n.* **3.** long step. **4.** steady pace.

stri'dent, *adj.* harsh in sound. —**stri'dent•ly,** *adv.* —**stri'den•cy,** *n.*

strife, *n.* conflict or quarrel.

strike, *v.,* **struck, struck** or **stricken, striking,** *n.* —*v.* **1.** deal a blow. **2.** hit forcibly. **3.** cause to ignite. **4.** impress. **5.** efface; mark out. **6.** afflict or affect. **7.** sound by percussion. **8.** discover in ground. **9.** encounter. **10.** (of workers) stop work to compel agreement to demands. **11. strike out,** *Baseball.* put or be put out on three strikes. —*n.* **12.** act of striking. **13.** *Baseball.* failure of batter to hit pitched ball; anything ruled equivalent. **14.** *Bowling.* knocking-down of all pins with first bowl. —**strik'er,** *n.*

strik'ing, *adj.* **1.** conspicuously attractive or impressive. **2.** noticeable; conspicuous.

string, *n., v.,* **strung, stringing.** —*n.* **1.** cord, thread, etc. **2.** series or set. **3.** cord on musical instrument. **4.** plant fiber. —*v.* 5. furnish with strings. 6. arrange in row. 7. mount on string. —**stringed,** *adj.* —**string'y,** *adj.*

string bean, bean with edible pod.

strin'gent (strin'jənt), *adj.* 1. very strict. 2. urgent. —**strin'gen•cy,** *n.* —**strin'gent•ly,** *adv.*

string'er, *n.* 1. horizontal timber connecting upright posts. 2. part-time news reporter.

strip, *v.,* **stripped, stripping,** *n.* —*v.* 1. remove covering or clothing. 2. rob. 3. cut into strips. —*n.* 4. long narrow piece.

stripe, *n., v.,* **striped, striping.** —*n.* 1. band of different color, etc. 2. welt from whipping. —*v.* 3. mark with stripes.

strip'ling, *n.* youth.

strip mine, mine in open pit. —**strip'-mine',** *v.*

strip'tease', *n.* act, as in burlesque, in which performer gradually removes clothing. —**strip'per,** *n.*

strive, *v.,* **strove, striven, striving.** try hard; struggle.

strobe, *n.* electronic flash producing rapid bursts of light. Also, **strobe light.**

stroke, *v.,* **stroked, stroking,** *n.* —*v.* 1. rub gently. —*n.* 2. act of stroking. 3. blow. 4. blockage or hemorrhage of blood vessel leading to brain. 5. one complete movement. 6. piece of luck, work, etc. 7. method of swimming.

stroll, *v.* 1. walk idly. 2. roam.

stroll'er, *n.* chairlike carriage in which young children are pushed.

strong, *adj.* 1. vigorous; powerful; able. 2. intense; distinct. —**strong'ly,** *adv.*

strong'-arm', *adj.* 1. involving physical force. —*v.* 2. use physical force.

strong'box', *n.* strongly made box for money.

strong'hold', *n.* fortress.

strong'-mind'ed, *adj.* 1. having vigorous mental powers. 2. determined.

stron'ti•um (-shē əm), *n.* metallic chemical element.

strop, *n., v.,* **stropped, stropping.** —*n.* 1. flexible strap. —*v.* 2. sharpen on strop.

struc′ture, *n.* **1.** form of building or arrangement. **2.** something built.
—**struc′tur•al,** *adj.*
—**struc′tur•al•ly,** *adv.*

stru′del, *n.* fruit-filled pastry.

strug′gle, *v.,* **-gled, -gling,** *n.*
—*v.* **1.** contend; strive. —*n.* **2.** strong effort. **3.** combat.

strum, *v.,* **strummed, strumming.** play carelessly on (stringed instrument).

strum′pet, *n.* prostitute.

strut, *v.,* **strutted, strutting,** *n.*
—*v.* **1.** walk in vain, pompous manner. —*n.* **2.** strutting walk. **3.** prop; truss.

strych′nine (strik′nin, -nīn), *n.* colorless poison.

stub, *n., v.,* **stubbed, stubbing.**
—*n.* **1.** short remaining piece. **2.** stump. —*v.* **3.** strike (one's toe) against something.
—**stub′by,** *adj.*

stub′ble, *n.* **1.** short stumps, as of grain stalks. **2.** short growth of beard. —**stub′bly,** *adj.*

stub′born, *adj.* **1.** unreasonably obstinate. **2.** persistent. —**stub′born•ly,** *adv.* —**stub′born•ness,** *n.*

stuc′co, *n., pl.* **-coes, -cos,** *v.,* **-coed, -coing.** —*n.* **1.** plaster for exteriors. —*v.* **2.** cover with stucco.

stuck′-up′, *adj. Informal.* snobbishly conceited.

stud, *n., v.,* **studded, studding.**
—*n.* **1.** projecting knob, pin, etc. **2.** upright prop. **3.** detachable button. **4.** collection of horses or other animals for breeding. **5.** stallion. —*v.* **6.** set or scatter with studs.

stu′dent, *n.* person who studies.

stud′ied, *adj.* deliberate.

stu′di•o′, *n., pl.* **-dios. 1.** artist's workroom. **2.** place equipped for radio or television broadcasting.

stud′y, *n., pl.* **studies,** *v.,* **studied, studying.** —*n.* **1.** effort to learn. **2.** object of study. **3.** deep thought. **4.** room for studying, writing, etc. —*v.* **5.** make study of
—**stu′di•ous,** *adj.*
—**stu′di•ous•ly,** *adv.*
—**stu′di•ous•ness,** *n.*

stuff, *n.* **1.** material. **2.** worthless matter. —*v.* **3.** cram full; pack.

stuffed shirt, pompous, self-satisfied person.

stuff'ing, *n.* material stuffed in something.

stuff'y, *adj.,* **stuffier, stuffiest.** 1. lacking fresh air. 2. pompous; pedantic. —**stuff'i•ness,** *n.*

stul'ti•fy', *v.,* **-fied, -fying.** 1. cause to look foolish 2. make futile.

stum'ble, *v.,* **-bled, -bling.** 1. lose balance. 2. come unexpectedly upon.

stumbling block, obstacle.

stump, *n.* 1. lower end of tree after top is gone. 2. any short remaining part. —*v.* 3. baffle. 4. campaign politically. 5. walk heavily.

stun, *v.,* **stunned, stunning.** 1. render unconscious. 2. amaze.

stun'ning, *adj.* strikingly attractive.

stunt, *v.* 1. check growth. 2. do stunts. —*n.* 3. performance to show skill, etc.

stu'pe•fy', *v.,* **-fied, -fying.** 1. put into stupor. 2. stun. —**stu'pe•fac'tion,** *n.*

stu•pen'dous, *adj.* 1. amazing; marvelous. 2. immense.

stu'pid, *adj.* having or showing little intelligence. —**stu•pid'i•ty,** *n.* —**stu'pid•ly,** *adv.*

stu'por, *n.* dazed or insensible state.

stur'dy, *adj.,* **-dier, -diest.** 1. strongly built. 2. firm. —**stur'di•ly,** *adv.* —**stur'di•ness,** *n.*

stur'geon, *n.* large fish of fresh and salt water.

stut'ter, *v., n.* stammer. —**stut'ter•er,** *n.*

sty, *n., pl.* **sties.** 1. pig pen. 2. inflamed swelling on eyelid.

style, *n., v.,* **styled, styling.** —*n.* 1. particular kind. 2. mode of fashion. 3. elegance. 4. distinct way of writing or speaking. 5. pointed instrument. —*v.* 6. name; give title to. —**sty•lis'tic,** *adj.*

styl'ish, *adj.* fashionable. —**styl'ish•ly,** *adv.*

styl'ist, *n.* person who cultivates distinctive style.

styl'ize, *v.,* **-ized, -izing.** cause to conform to conventionalized style.

sty'lus, *n.* pointed tool for writing, etc.

sty′mie, *v.,* -mied, -mying. hinder or obstruct, as in golf.

styp′tic, *adj.* **1.** checking bleeding. —*n.* **2.** styptic substance. —**styp′sis,** *n.*

Sty′ro•foam′, *n. Trademark.* lightweight plastic.

sua′sion, *n.* persuasion.

suave (swäv), *adj.* smoothly agreeable. —**suave′ly,** *adv.* —**suav′i•ty, suave′ness,** *n.*

sub-, prefix meaning under; below; beneath; less than.

sub•al′tern (-ôl′-), *n. Brit.* low-ranking officer.

sub′a•tom′ic, *adj.* of particles within an atom.

sub′com•mit′tee, *n.* committee appointed out of main committee.

sub•con′scious, *adj.* **1.** existing beneath consciousness. —*n.* **2.** ideas, feelings, etc., of which one is unaware. —**sub•con′scious•ly,** *adv.*

sub•con′ti•nent, *n.* large subdivision of continent.

sub′cul′ture, *n.* group with social, economic, or other traits distinguishing it from others within larger society.

sub′cu•ta′ne•ous, *adj.* beneath the skin.

sub′di•vide′, *v.,* -vided, -viding. divide into parts. —**sub′di•vi′sion,** *n.*

sub•due′, *v.,* -dued, -duing. **1.** overcome. **2.** soften.

sub•fam′i•ly, *n., pl.* -lies. **1.** category of related organisms within a family. **2.** group of related languages within a family.

sub′head′, *n.* **1.** heading of a subdivision. **2.** subordinate division of a title.

sub′ject, *n.* **1.** matter of thought, concern, etc. **2.** person under rule of government. **3.** *Gram.* noun or pronoun that performs action of predicate. **4.** one undergoing action, etc. —*adj.* **5.** being a subject. **6.** liable; exposed. —*v.* (səb jekt′). **7.** cause to experience. **8.** make liable. —**sub•jec′tion,** *n.*

sub•jec′tive, *adj.* **1.** personal. **2.** existing in mind. —**sub′jec•tiv′i•ty,** *n.* —**sub•jec′tive•ly,** *adv.*

sub•join′, *v.* append.

sub′ju•gate′, *v.*, **-gated, -gating.** subdue; conquer.
—**sub′ju•ga′tion,** *n.*
—**sub′ju•ga′tor,** *n.*

sub•junc′tive, *adj.* **1.** designating verb mode of condition, impression, etc. —*n.* **2.** subjunctive mode.

sub′lease′, *n., v.,* **-leased, -leasing.** —*n.* **1.** lease granted by tenant. —*v.* (sub lēs′). **2.** rent by sublease.

sub•let′, *v.,* **-let, -letting.** (of lessee) let to another person.

sub′li•mate′, *v.,* **-mated, -mating,** *n.* —*v.* **1.** deflect (biological energies) to other channels. **2.** sublime. —*n.* (-mit). **3.** substance obtained in subliming.
—**sub′li•ma′tion,** *n.*

sub•lime′, *adj., n., v.,* **-limed, -liming.** —*adj.* **1.** lofty; noble. —*n.* **2.** that which is sublime. —*v.* **3.** heat (substance) to vapor that condenses to solid on cooling. —**sub•lim′i•ty,** *n.*
—**sub•lime′ly,** *adv.*

sub•lim′i•nal, *adj.* below threshold of consciousness.
—**sub•lim′i•nal•ly,** *adv.*

sub′ma•chine′ gun, automatic weapon.

sub′ma•rine′, *n.* **1.** vessel that can navigate under water. —*adj.* (sub′mə rēn′). **2.** of submarines. **3.** being under sea.

sub•merge′, *v.,* **-merged, -merging.** plunge under water.
—**sub•mer′gence,** *n.*

sub•merse′, *v.,* **-mersed, -mersing.** submerge.
—**sub•mer′sion,** *n.*
—**sub•mers′i•ble,** *adj.*

sub•mis′sive, *adj.* yielding or obeying readily.
—**sub•mis′sive•ly,** *adv.*
—**sub•mis′sive•ness,** *n.*

sub•mit′, *v.,* **-mitted, -mitting. 1.** yield; surrender. **2.** offer for consideration.
—**sub•mis′sion,** *n.*

sub•nor′mal, *adj.* of less than normal intelligence.

sub•or′bit•al, *adj.* making less than a complete orbit.

sub•or′di•nate, *adj., n., v.,* **-nated, -nating.** —*adj.* (-nit). **1.** of lower rank or importance. —*n.* (-nit). **2.** subordinate person or thing. —*v.* (-nāt′). **3.** treat as subordinate.
—**sub•or′di•na′tion,** *n.*

sub•orn', *v.* bribe or incite to crime, esp. to perjury.

sub'plot', *n.* secondary plot.

sub•poe'na (sə pē'nə), *n., v.,* **-naed, -naing.** —*n.* 1. summons to appear in court. —*v.* 2. serve with subpoena.

sub ro'sa, secretly.

sub•scribe', *v.,* **-scribed, -scribing.** 1. promise contribution. 2. agree; sign in agreement. 3. contract to receive periodical regularly. —**sub•scrib'er**, *n.* —**sub•scrip'tion**, *n.*

sub'script, *n.* letter, number, etc. written low on line.

sub'se•quent, *adj.* later; following. —**sub'se•quent•ly**, *adv.*

sub•serve', *v.,* **-served, -serving.** promote; assist.

sub•ser'vi•ent, *adj.* 1. servile; submissive. 2. useful. —**sub•ser'vi•ence**, *n.* —**sub•ser'vi•ent•ly**, *adv.*

sub•side', *v.,* **-sided, -siding.** 1. sink; settle. 2. abate. —**sub•sid'ence**, *n.*

sub•sid'i•ar'y, *adj., n., pl.* **-aries.** —*adj.* 1. auxiliary. 2. subordinate. —*n.* 3. anything subsidiary.

sub'si•dy, *n., pl.* **-dies.** direct pecuniary aid, esp. by government. —**sub'si•dize'**, *v.*

sub•sist', *v.* 1. exist. 2. live (as on food). —**sub•sist'ence**, *n.*

sub'soil, *n.* layer of earth immediately underneath surface soil.

sub•son'ic, *adj.* of a speed below the speed of sound.

sub'stance, *n.* 1. matter or material. 2. density. 3. meaning. 4. likelihood.

sub•stand'ard, *adj.* below standard; not good enough.

sub•stan'tial, *adj.* 1. actual. 2. fairly large. 3. strong. 4. of substance. 5. prosperous. —**sub•stan'tial•ly**, *adv.*

sub•stan'ti•ate', *v.,* **-ated, -ating.** support with evidence. —**sub•stan'ti•a'tion**, *n.*

sub'stan•tive, *n.* 1. noun, pronoun, or word used as noun. —*adj.* 2. of or denoting substantive. 3. independent. 4. essential.

sub'sti•tute', *v.,* **-tuted, -tuting**, *n.* —*v.* 1. put or serve in place of another. —*n.* 2. substitute person or thing. —**sub'sti•tu'tion**, *n.*

sub′struc•ture, *n.* structure forming a foundation.

sub•sume′, *v.,* **-sumed, -suming.** consider or include as part of something larger.

sub′ter•fuge′, *n.* means used to evade or conceal.

sub′ter•ra′ne•an, *adj.* underground.

sub′text, *n.* underlying or implicit meaning.

sub′tile, *adj.* subtle.

sub′ti′tle, *n., v.,* **-tled, -tling.** —*n.* **1.** secondary or subordinate title, as of book. **2.** text of dialogue, etc., appearing at bottom of motion picture screen, etc. —*v.* **3.** give subtitles to.

sub′to•tal, *n., v.,* **-totaled, -totaling.** —*n.* **1.** total of part of a group of figures. —*v.* **2.** determine subtotal for.

sub′tle (sut′əl), *adj.,* **-tler, -tlest. 1.** delicate; faint. **2.** discerning. **3.** crafty. —**sub′tle•ty,** *n.* —**sub′tly,** *adv.*

sub•tract′, *v.* take from another; deduct. —**sub•trac′tion,** *n.*

sub•tra•hend′, *n.* number subtracted from another number.

sub•trop′i•cal, *adj.* bordering on tropics.

sub′urb, *n.* district just outside city. —**sub•ur′ban,** *adj.* —**sub•ur′ban•ite,** *n.*

sub•ur′bi•a, *n.* **1.** suburbs or suburbanites collectively. **2.** life in the suburbs.

sub•ven′tion, *n.* grant of money.

sub•vert′, *v.* overthrow; destroy. —**sub•ver′sion,** *n.* —**sub•ver′sive,** *adj., n.*

sub′way′, *n.* underground electric railway.

sub•ze′ro, *adj.* indicating lower than zero on some scale.

suc•ceed′, *v.* **1.** end or accomplish successfully. **2.** follow and replace.

suc•cess′, *n.* **1.** favorable achievement. **2.** good fortune. **3.** successful thing or person. —**suc•cess′ful,** *adj.* —**suc•cess′ful•ly,** *adv.*

suc•ces′sion, *n.* **1.** act of following in sequence. **2.** sequence of persons or things.

3. right or process of succeeding another. —**suc·ces'sive,** *adj.* —**suc·ces'sive·ly,** *adv.*

suc·ces'sor, *n.* one that succeeds another.

suc·cinct' (sək singkt'), *adj.* without useless words; concise. —**suc·cinct'ly,** *adv.* —**suc·cinct'ness,** *n.*

suc'cor, *n., v.* help; aid.

suc'co·tash', *n.* corn and beans cooked together.

suc'cu·lent, *adj.* juicy. —**suc'cu·lence,** *n.*

suc·cumb', *v.* 1. yield. 2. die.

such, *adj.* 1. of that kind, extent, etc. —*n.* 2. such person or thing.

suck, *v.* 1. draw in by using lips and tongue. 2. absorb. —*n.* 3. act of sucking.

suck'er, *n.* 1. one that sucks. 2. fresh-water fish. 3. *Informal.* lollipop. 4. shoot from underground stem or root. 5. *Informal.* gullible person.

suck'le, *v.,* -led, -ling. nurse at breast.

suck'ling, *n.* 1. infant. 2. unweaned animal.

su'crose (soo'krōs), *n.* sugar obtained esp. from sugar cane or sugar beet.

suc'tion, *n.* tendency to draw substance into vacuum.

sud'den, *adj.* abrupt; quick; unexpected. —**sud'den·ly,** *adv.* —**sud'den·ness,** *n.*

sudden death, overtime period in which tied contest is won after one contestant scores.

suds, *n.pl.* 1. lather. 2. soapy water. —**suds'y,** *adj.*

sue, *v.,* **sued, suing.** 1. take legal action. 2. appeal.

suede (swād), *n.* soft, napped leather.

su'et, *n.* hard fat about kidneys, etc., esp. of cattle.

suf'fer, *v.* 1. undergo (pain or unpleasantness). 2. tolerate. —**suf'fer·er,** *n.*

suf'fer·ance, *n.* 1. tolerance. 2. endurance.

suf·fice', *v.,* -ficed, -ficing. be enough.

suf·fi'cient, *adj.* enough. —**suf·fi'cien·cy,** *n.* —**suf·fi'cient·ly,** *adv.*

suf′fix, *n.* element added to end of word to form another word.

suf′fo·cate′, *v.,* **-cated, -cating.** kill or choke by cutting off air to lungs. —**suf′fo·ca′tion,** *n.*

suf′fra·gan (-gən), *n.* assistant bishop.

suf′frage, *n.* right to vote. —**suf′fra·gist,** *n.*

suf·fuse′, *v.* overspread.

sug′ar, *n.* **1.** sweet substance, esp. from sugar cane or sugar beet. —*v.* **2.** sweeten with sugar. —**sug′ar·less,** *adj.* —**sug′ar·y,** *adj.*

sugar beet, beet with white root having high sugar content.

sugar cane, tall grass that is the chief source of sugar.

sug′ar·coat′, *v.* make more pleasant or acceptable.

sugar maple, maple with sweet sap.

sugar plum, candy.

sug·gest′, *v.* **1.** offer for consideration or action. **2.** imply. —**sug·ges′tion,** *n.*

sug·gest′i·ble, *adj.* easily led or influenced. —**sug·gest′i·bil′i·ty,** *n.*

sug·ges′tive, *adj.* suggesting, esp. something improper. —**sug·ges′tive·ly,** *adv.* —**sug·ges′tive·ness,** *n.*

su′i·cide′, *n.* **1.** intentional killing of oneself. **2.** person who commits suicide. —**su′i·cid′al,** *adj.*

su′i ge′ne·ris (soo′ē jen′ər is), being one of a kind.

suit, *n.* **1.** set of clothes. **2.** legal action. **3.** division of playing cards. **4.** petition. **5.** wooing. —*v.* **6.** clothe. **7.** adapt. **8.** please.

suit′a·ble, *adj.* appropriate; fitting. —**suit′a·bly,** *adv.*

suit′case′, *n.* oblong valise.

suite (swēt), *n.* **1.** series or set, as of rooms. **2.** retinue.

suit′ing, *n.* fabric for making suits.

suit′or, *n.* wooer.

su′ki·ya′ki, *n.* Japanese dish of meat and vegetables cooked in soy sauce.

sul′fa drugs, group of antibacterial substances used to treat diseases, wounds, etc.

sul′fate, *n.* salt of sulfuric acid.

sul′fide, *n.* sulfur compound.

sul′fur, *n.* yellow nonmetallic element.

sul·fur′ic, *adj.* of or containing sulfur. Also, **sul′fur·ous.**

sulfuric acid, corrosive liquid used in fertilizers, chemicals, and explosives.

sulk, *v.* **1.** hold sullenly aloof. —*n.* **2.** fit of sulking.

sulk′y, *adj.,* **sulkier, sulkiest,** *n.* —*adj.* **1.** sullen; ill-humored. —*n.* **2.** two-wheeled racing carriage for one person. —**sulk′i·ly,** *adv.* —**sulk′i·ness,** *n.*

sul′len, *adj.* **1.** silently ill-humored. **2.** gloomy. —**sul′len·ly,** *adv.* —**sul′len·ness,** *n.*

sul′ly, *v.,* **-lied, -lying.** soil; defile.

sul′phur, *n.* sulfur.

sul′tan, *n.* ruler of Muslim country. —**sul′tan·ate′,** *n.*

sul·tan′a, *n.* raisin.

sul′try, *adj.,* **-trier, -triest.** hot and close. —**sul′tri·ness,** *n.*

sum, *n., v.,* **summed, summing.** —*n.* **1.** aggregate of two or more numbers, etc. **2.** total amount. **3.** gist. —*v.* **4.** total. **5.** summarize.

su′mac (shoo′-), *n.* small tree with long pinnate leaves.

sum′ma·rize′, *v.,* **-rized, -rizing.** make or be summary of.

sum′ma·ry, *n., pl.* **-ries,** *adj.* —*n.* **1.** concise presentation of main points. —*adj.* **2.** concise. **3.** prompt. —**sum·mar′i·ly,** *adv.*

sum·ma′tion, *n.* **1.** act of summing up. **2.** total.

sum′mer, *n.* **1.** season between spring and fall. —*adj.* **2.** of, like, or for summer. —*v.* **3.** spend summer. —**sum′mer·y,** *adj.*

sum′mer·house, *n.* structure in garden to provide shade.

sum′mit, *n.* highest point.

sum′mon, *v.* order to appear.

sum′mons, *n.* message that summons.

su′mo, *n.* Japanese form of wrestling featuring extremely heavy contestants.

sump, *n.* pit for collecting water, etc.

sump'tu•ous, *adj.* revealing great expense; luxurious. —**sump'tu•ous•ly,** *adv.* —**sump'tu•ous•ness,** *n.*

sun, *n., v.,* **sunned, sunning.** —*n.* **1.** heat- and light-giving body of solar system. **2.** sunshine. —*v.* **3.** expose to sunshine. —**sun'beam',** *n.*

Sun., Sunday.

sun'bathe', *v.,* **-bathed, -bathing.** expose body to sunlight.

Sun'belt', *n. Informal.* southern and southwestern U.S. Also, **Sun Belt.**

sun'block', *n.* substance, as a cream, to protect skin from sunburn. Also, **sun'screen'.**

sun'burn', *n., v.,* **-burned** or **-burnt, -burning.** —*n.* **1.** superficial burn from sun's rays. —*v.* **2.** affect with sunburn.

sun'dae, *n.* ice cream topped with fruit, etc.

Sun'day, *n.* first day of week.

sun'der, *v.* separate.

sun'di'al, *n.* outdoor instrument for telling time by shadow.

sun'dry (-drē), *adj., n., pl.* **-dries.** —*adj.* **1.** various. —*n.* **2.** (*pl.*) small items of merchandise.

sun'fish', *n.* fresh-water fish.

sun'flow'er, *n.* tall plant with yellow flowers.

sun'glass'es, *n.pl.* eyeglasses with tinted lenses to permit vision in bright sun.

sun'light', *n.* light from sun.

sun'lit', *adj.* lighted by the sun.

sun'ny, *adj.,* **-nier, -niest. 1.** with much sunlight. **2.** cheerful; jolly. —**sun'ni•ly,** *adv.* —**sun'ni•ness,** *n.*

sun'rise', *n.* ascent of sun above horizon. Also, **sun'up'.**

sun'roof', *n.* section of automobile roof that can be opened.

sun'screen', *n.* substance that protects skin from ultraviolet rays of sun.

sun'set', *n.* descent of sun below horizon. Also, **sun'down'.**

sun'shine', *n.* light of sun.

sun'spot', *n.* dark spot on face of sun.

sun′stroke′, *n.* illness from overexposure to sun's rays.

sun′tan′, *n.* darkening of skin caused by exposure to sun.

sup, *v.*, **supped, supping.** eat supper.

su′per, *n.* **1.** superintendent. —*adj.* **2.** very good; first-rate.

su′per-, prefix meaning above or over; exceeding; larger or more.

su′per·a·bun′dant, *adj.* exceedingly abundant. —**su′per·a·bun′dance**, *n.*

su′per·an′nu·at′ed, *adj.* **1.** retired. **2.** too old for work or use. **3.** antiquated; obsolete.

su·perb′, *adj.* very fine. —**su·perb′ly**, *adv.*

su′per·charge′, *v.*, **-charged, -charging. 1.** charge with abundant or excess energy, etc. **2.** supply air to (engine) at high pressure. —**su′per·charg′er**, *n.*

su′per·cil′i·ous (-sil′-), *adj.* haughtily disdainful. —**su′per·cil′i·ous·ly**, *adv.* —**su′per·cil′i·ous·ness**, *n.*

su′per·con′duc·tiv′i·ty, *n.* disappearance of electrical resistance in certain metals at extremely low temperatures. —**su′per·con·duct′or**, *n.*

su′per·e′go, *n.* part of personality representing conscience.

su′per·fi′cial, *adj.* **1.** of, on, or near surface. **2.** shallow, obvious, or insignificant. —**su′per·fi′ci·al′i·ty**, *n.* —**su′per·fi′cial·ly**, *adv.*

su·per′flu·ous, *adj.* **1.** being more than is necessary. **2.** unnecessary. —**su′per·flu′i·ty**, *n.* —**su·per′flu·ous·ly**, *adv.*

su′per·high′way, *n.* highway for travel at high speeds.

su′per·hu′man, *adj.* **1.** beyond what is human. **2.** exceeding human strength.

su′per·im·pose′, *v.*, **-posed, -posing.** place over something else.

su′per·in·tend′, *v.* oversee and direct. —**su′per·in·tend′ence, su′per·in·tend′en·cy**, *n.* —**su′per·in·tend′ent**, *n., adj.*

su·pe′ri·or, *adj.* **1.** above average; better. **2.** upper. **3.** arrogant. —*n.* **4.** superior person. **5.** head of convent, etc. —**su·pe′ri·or′i·ty**, *n.*

su·per'la·tive, *adj.* **1.** of highest kind; best. **2.** highest in comparison. —*n.* **3.** anything superlative. —**su·per'la·tive·ly,** *adv.*

su'per·man', *n., pl.* **-men.** person of extraordinary or superhuman powers.

su'per·mar'ket, *n.* self-service food store with large variety.

su'per·nat'u·ral, *adj.* **1.** outside the laws of nature; ghostly. —*n.* **2.** realm of supernatural beings or things.

su'per·no'va, *n., pl.* **-vas, -vae.** nova millions of times brighter than the sun.

su'per·nu'mer·ar'y, *adj., n., pl.* **-aries.** —*adj.* **1.** extra. —*n.* **2.** extra person or thing. **3.** actor with no lines.

su'per·pow'er, *n.* large, powerful nation greatly influencing world affairs.

su'per·script', *n.* letter, number, or symbol written high on line of text.

su'per·sede', *v.,* **-seded, -seding.** replace in power, use, etc.

su'per·son'ic, *adj.* faster than speed of sound.

su'per·star', *n.* entertainer or sports figure of world renown.

su'per·sti'tion, *n.* irrational belief in ominous significance of particular thing, event, etc. —**su'per·sti'tious,** *adj.* —**su'per·sti'tious·ly,** *adv.*

su'per·store', *n.* very large store that stocks wide variety of merchandise.

su'per·struc'ture, *n.* upper part of building or vessel.

su'per·vene', *v.,* **-vened, -vening. 1.** come as something extra. **2.** ensue. —**su'per·ven'tion,** *n.*

su'per·vise', *v.,* **-vised, -vising.** direct and inspect. —**su'per·vi'sion,** *n.* —**su'per·vi'sor,** *n.* —**su'per·vi'so·ry,** *adj.*

su'per·wom'an, *n., pl.* **-women. 1.** woman of extraordinary or superhuman powers. **2.** woman who copes successfully with demands of career, marriage, and motherhood.

su·pine' (soo-), *adj.* **1.** lying on back. **2.** passive. —**su·pine'ly,** *adv.*

sup'per, *n.* evening meal.

sup·plant', *v.* supersede.

sup'ple, *adj.,* **-pler, -plest.** flexible; limber. —**sup'ple•ly,** *adv.* —**sup'ple•ness,** *n.*

sup'ple•ment (-mənt), *n.* **1.** something added to complete or improve. —*v.* (-ment'). **2.** add to or complete. —**sup'ple•men'tal, sup'ple•men'ta•ry,** *adj.*

sup'pli•cate', *v.,* **-cated, -cating.** beg humbly. —**sup'pli•ant, sup'pli•cant,** *n., adj.* —**sup'pli•ca'tion,** *n.*

sup•ply', *v.,* **-plied, -plying,** *n., pl.* **-plies.** —*v.* **1.** furnish; provide. **2.** fill (a lack). —*n.* **3.** act of supplying. **4.** that supplied. **5.** stock. —**sup•pli'er,** *n.*

supply'-side', *adj.* of economic theory that reduced taxes will stimulate economic growth.

sup•port', *v.* **1.** hold up; bear. **2.** provide living for. **3.** uphold; advocate. **4.** corroborate. —*n.* **5.** act of supporting. **6.** maintenance; livelihood. **7.** thing or person that supports. —**sup•port'a•ble,** *adj.* —**sup•port'ive,** *adj.*

support group, group of people who meet regularly to support each other by discussing shared problems.

sup•pose', *v.,* **-posed, -posing. 1.** assume; consider. **2.** take for granted. —**sup•pos'ed•ly,** *adv.* —**sup'po•si'tion,** *n.* —**sup'po•si'tion•al,** *adj.*

sup•pos'i•to'ry, *n., pl.* **-ries.** solid mass of medication that melts on insertion into rectum or vagina.

sup•press', *v.* **1.** end forcibly; subdue. **2.** repress. **3.** withhold from circulation. —**sup•pres'sant,** *n.* —**sup•pres'sion,** *n.* —**sup•pres'si•ble,** *adj.*

sup'pu•rate' (sup'yə-), *v.,* **-rated, -rating.** form or discharge pus. —**sup'pu•ra'tion,** *n.* —**sup'pu•ra'tive,** *adj.*

su'pra, *adv.* above, esp. in text.

su•prem'a•cist, *n.* person who advocates supremacy of particular group.

su•preme', *adj.* chief; greatest. —**su•prem'a•cy,** *n.* —**su•preme'ly,** *adv.*

sur•cease', *n.* end.

sur′charge′, *n., v.,* **-charged, -charging.** —*n.* **1.** extra or excessive charge, load, etc. —*v.* (sûr chärj′). **2.** put surcharge on. **3.** overburden.

sur′cin′gle, *n.* girth that passes around horse's belly.

sure, *adj.,* **surer, surest. 1.** certain; positive. **2.** reliable. **3.** firm. —**sure′ly,** *adv.* —**sure′ness,** *n.*

sure′fire′, *adj. Informal.* certain to succeed.

sure′foot′ed, *adj.* not likely to stumble.

sure′ty (shŏŏr′i tē), *n., pl.* **-ties. 1.** security against loss, etc. **2.** person who accepts responsibility for another.

surf, *n.* **1.** waves breaking on shore. —*v.* **2.** ride on crest of wave while standing or lying on surfboard. —**surf′er,** *n.*

sur′face, *n., adj., v.,* **-faced, -facing.** —*n.* **1.** outer face; outside. —*adj.* **2.** superficial. —*v.* **3.** finish surface of. **4.** come to surface.

surf′board′, *n.* board on which person rides in surfing.

sur′feit (-fit), *n.* **1.** excess, esp. of food or drink. **2.** disgust at excess. —*v.* **3.** overeat; satiate.

surf′ing, *n.* sport of riding the surf, usu. on a **surf′board′.**

surge, *n., v.,* **surged, surging.** —*n.* **1.** swelling or rolling movement or body. —*v.* **2.** rise and fall.

surge protector, device to protect computer, etc., from damage by high-voltage electrical surges.

sur′geon, *n.* person skilled in surgery.

sur′ger•y, *n., pl.* **-geries. 1.** treatment of disease, etc., by cutting and other manipulations. **2.** room for surgical operations. —**sur′gi•cal,** *adj.* —**sur′gi•cal•ly,** *adv.*

sur′ly, *adj.,* **-lier, -liest.** rude; churlish. —**sur′li•ness,** *n.*

sur•mise′, *v.,* **-mised, -mising,** *n.* guess.

sur•mount′, *v.* **1.** get over or on top of. **2.** overcome. —**sur•mount′a•ble,** *adj.*

sur′name′, *n.* family name.

sur•pass′, *v.* **1.** exceed. **2.** transcend. —**sur•pass′ing,** *adj.*

sur′plice (-plis), *n.* white, loose-fitting robe worn over cassock.

sur′plus, *n.* **1.** amount beyond that needed; excess. —*adj.* **2.** being a surplus.

sur•prise′, *v.,* **-prised, -prising,** *n.* —*v.* **1.** come upon unexpectedly; astonish. —*n.* **2.** act of surprising. **3.** something that surprises. **4.** feeling of being surprised.

sur•re′al•ism, *n.* art attempting to express the subconscious. —**sur•re′al•ist,** *n., adj.* —**sur′re•al•is′tic,** *adj.*

sur•ren′der, *v.* **1.** yield. —*n.* **2.** act of yielding.

sur′rep•ti′tious, *adj.* stealthy; secret. —**sur′rep•ti′tious•ly,** *adv.*

sur′rey, *n.* light carriage.

sur′ro•gate′, *n.* **1.** substitute. **2.** judge concerned with wills, estates, etc.

surrogate mother, woman who bears child for another couple.

sur•round′, *v.* encircle; enclose.

sur•round′ings, *n.pl.* environment.

sur′tax′, *n.* additional tax, esp. on high incomes.

sur•veil′lance (-vā′ləns), *n.* close watch.

sur•vey′, *v.* (sər vā′). **1.** view. **2.** measure or determine dimensions or nature of. —*n.* (sûr′vā). **3.** methodical investigation. **4.** description from surveying.

sur•vey′ing, *n.* science of making land surveys. —**sur•vey′or,** *n.*

sur•vive′, *v.,* **-vived, -viving. 1.** remain alive. **2.** outlive. —**sur•viv′al,** *n.* —**sur•vi′vor,** *n.*

sus•cep′ti•ble (sə sep′-), *adj.* apt to be affected; liable. —**sus•cep′ti•bil′i•ty,** *n.* —**sus•cep′ti•bly,** *adv.*

su′shi (soo′shē), *n.* Japanese dish of rice cakes with raw fish, vegetables, etc.

sus•pect′, *v.* **1.** imagine to be guilty, false, etc. **2.** surmise. —*n.* (sus′pekt). **3.** one suspected. —*adj.* (sus′pekt). **4.** liable to doubt.

sus•pend′, *v.* **1.** hang. **2.** keep temporarily inactive. **3.** refuse work to temporarily.

sus•pend′ers, *n.pl.* straps for holding up trousers.

sus•pense′, *n.* uncertainty; anxiety. —**sus•pense′ful**, *adj.*

sus•pen′sion, *n.* **1.** act of suspending. **2.** temporary inactivity. **3.** state in which undissolved particles are dispersed in fluid.

suspension bridge, bridge with deck suspended from cables.

sus•pi′cion, *n.* **1.** act or instance of suspecting. **2.** trace.

sus•pi′cious, *adj.* **1.** having suspicions. **2.** causing suspicion. —**sus•pi′cious•ly**, *adv.*

sus•tain′, *v.* support; maintain. —**sus•tain′er**, *n.*

sus′te•nance, *n.* **1.** food. **2.** maintenance.

su′ture (soo′chər), *n., v.,* **-tured, -turing.** —*n.* **1.** closing of wound. **2.** stitch used to close wound. **3.** line joining two bones, esp. of the skull. —*v.* **4.** join by suture.

su′ze•rain•ty (soo′zə rin tē), *n., pl.* **-ties.** sovereignty of one state over another.

svelte, *adj.* slender.

SW, southwest.

swab, *n., v.,* **swabbed, swabbing.** —*n.* **1.** bit of cloth, etc., esp. on stick. —*v.* **2.** clean with swab.

swad′dle, *v.,* **-dled, -dling.** bind with strips of cloth.

swag, *n.* something fastened at each end and hanging down in the middle.

swag′ger, *v.* **1.** walk with insolent air. —*n.* **2.** swaggering gait.

Swa•hi′li (-hē′lē), *n.* Bantu language of Africa.

swain, *n.* **1.** country lad. **2.** male admirer or lover.

swal′low, *v.* **1.** take into stomach through throat. **2.** assimilate. **3.** suppress. —*n.* **4.** act of swallowing. **5.** small graceful migratory bird.

swal′low•tail′, *n.* **1.** deeply forked tail like that of swallow. **2.** kind of butterfly.

swa′mi, *n.* Hindu religious teacher.

swamp, *n.* **1.** marshy ground. —*v.* **2.** drench with water. **3.** overwhelm. —**swamp′y**, *adj.*

swan, *n.* large long-necked swimming bird.

swank, *adj.,* **swanker, swankest. 1.** stylish or elegant. **2.** pretentiously stylish. Also, **swank′y.**

swan song, final act or farewell appearance.

swap, *v.,* **swapped, swapping,** *n.* trade.

sward (swôrd), *n.* turf.

swarm, *n.* **1.** group of bees. —*v.* **2.** fly off to start new colony. **3.** cluster; throng.

swarth′y, *adj.,* **swarthier, swarthiest.** (esp. of skin) dark. —**swarth′i•ness,** *n.*

swash′buck′ler, *n.* swaggering fellow. —**swash′buck′ling,** *adj., n.*

swas′ti•ka, *n.* **1.** kind of cross used as symbol and ornament. **2.** emblem of Nazi Party.

swat, *v.,* **swatted, swatting,** *n. Informal.* —*v.* **1.** strike. —*n.* **2.** sharp blow. —**swat′ter,** *n.*

swatch, *n.* sample of material or finish.

swath (swoth), *n.* long cut made by scythe or mowing machine.

swathe (swoᵺ), *v.,* **swathed, swathing,** *n.* —*v.* **1.** wrap closely. —*n.* **2.** bandage.

sway, *v.* **1.** swing to and fro. **2.** influence or incline. —*n.* **3.** act of swaying. **4.** rule.

sway′back′, *n.* excessive downward curvature of the back, esp. of horses. —**sway′backed′,** *adj.*

swear, *v.,* **swore, sworn, swearing. 1.** affirm on oath; vow. **2.** use profane language. **3.** bind by oath.

sweat, *v.,* **sweat** or **sweated, sweating,** *n.* —*v.* **1.** excrete moisture through pores. **2.** gather moisture. —*n.* **3.** secretion of sweat glands. **4.** process of sweating. —**sweat′y,** *adj.*

sweat′er, *n.* knitted jacket.

sweat gland, tubular gland in skin that secretes sweat.

sweat′pants′, *n.* pants of absorbent fabric.

sweat′shirt′, *n.* loose pullover of absorbent fabric.

sweat′shop′, *n.* manufacturing establishment employing workers at low wages, for long hours, under poor conditions.

Swed′ish, *n.* language or people of Sweden. —**Swed′ish,** *adj.*

sweep, *v.,* **swept, sweeping,** *n.*
—*v.* **1.** move or clear with broom, etc. **2.** clear or pass over with forceful, rapid movement. —*n.* **3.** act of sweeping. **4.** extent; range.

sweep'ing, *adj.* of wide range or scope.

sweep'stakes', *n.* **1.** race for stakes put up by competitors. **2.** lottery.

sweet, *adj.* **1.** having taste of sugar. **2.** fragrant. **3.** fresh. **4.** pleasant in sound. **5.** amiable. —*n.* **6.** anything sweet. —**sweet'en,** *v.* —**sweet'ly,** *adv.* —**sweet'ness,** *n.*

sweet'bread', *n.* thymus or pancreas, esp. of calf or lamb, used for food.

sweet'bri'er, *n.* fragrant wild rose.

sweet'en•er, *n.* substance, esp. a substitute for sugar, to sweeten food or drink.

sweet'heart', *n.* beloved.

sweet'meat', *n.* confection.

sweet pea, annual vine with fragrant blooms.

sweet pepper, mild-flavored bell-shaped pepper.

sweet potato, plant with sweet edible root.

sweet'-talk', *v.* cajole; flatter.

sweet tooth, liking or craving for sweets.

sweet' wil'liam, low plant with dense flower clusters.

swell, *v.,* **swelled, swelled** or **swollen, swelling,** *n., adj.* —*v.* **1.** grow in degree, force, etc. —*n.* **2.** act of swelling. **3.** wave. —*adj.* **4.** *Informal.* excellent.

swel'ter, *v.* perspire or suffer from heat.

swel'ter•ing, *adj.* **1.** suffering from heat. **2.** oppressively hot.

swerve, *v.,* **swerved, swerving,** *n.* —*v.* **1.** turn aside. —*n.* **2.** act of swerving.

swift, *adj.* **1.** moving with speed. **2.** prompt or quick. —*n.* **3.** small bird. —**swift'ly,** *adv.* —**swift'ness,** *n.*

swig, *n., v.,* **swigged, swigging.** *Informal.* —*n.* **1.** deep drink. —*v.* **2.** drink heartily.

swill, *n.* **1.** moist garbage fed to hogs. —*v.* **2.** guzzle.

swim, *v.,* **swam, swum, swimming,** *n.* —*v.* **1.** move in water by action of limbs, etc. **2.** be immersed. **3.** be dizzy. —*n.* **4.** period of swimming. —**swim'mer,** *n.*

swimming hole, place with water deep enough for swimming.

swim′suit′, *n.* bathing suit.

swin′dle, *v.,* **-dled, -dling,** *n.* —*v.* **1.** cheat; defraud. —*n.* **2.** act of swindling; fraud. —**swin′dler,** *n.*

swine, *n., pl.* **swine.** hog.

swing, *v.,* **swung, swinging,** *n.* —*v.* **1.** move to and fro around point. **2.** brandish. —*n.* **3.** act, way, or extent of swinging. **4.** operation. **5.** scope. **6.** suspended seat for swinging. **7.** style or quality in jazz marked by smooth beat and flowing phrasing.

swing′er, *n. Slang.* **1.** person with modern attitudes. **2.** sexually uninhibited person.

swing shift, work shift from midafternoon until midnight.

swipe, *n., v.,* **swiped, swiping.** —*n.* **1.** sweeping blow. —*v.* **2.** deal such blow. **3.** *Informal.* steal.

swirl, *v., n.* whirl; eddy.

swish, *v.* **1.** rustle. —*n.* **2.** swishing sound.

Swiss cheese, firm, pale yellow cheese with holes.

switch, *n.* **1.** flexible rod. **2.** device for turning electric current on or off. **3.** device for moving trains from one track to another. **4.** change. —*v.* **5.** whip with switch. **6.** shift; divert. **7.** turn (electric current) on or off.

switch′back′, *n.* zigzag highway or railroad track arrangement for climbing steep grade.

switch′blade′, *n.* pocketknife with blade released by spring.

switch′board′, *n.* panel for controlling electric circuits.

swiv′el, *n., v.,* **-eled, -eling.** —*n.* **1.** device permitting rotation of thing mounted on it. —*v.* **2.** rotate.

swiz′zle stick, small wand for stirring mixed drinks.

swol′len, pp. of **swell.**

swoon, *v., n.* faint.

swoop, *v.* **1.** sweep down upon. —*n.* **2.** sweeping descent.

sword (sōrd), *n.* weapon with blade fixed in hilt or handle. —**sword′play′,** *n.* —**swords′man,** *n.*

sword′fish′, *n.* marine fish with swordlike upper jaw.

syb′a•rite′, *n.* person devoted to pleasure. —**syb′a•rit′ic**, *adj.*

syc′a•more′, *n.* plane tree.

syc′o•phant (sik′ə fənt), *n.* flatterer; parasite. —**syc′o•phan•cy**, *n.*

syl•lab′i•cate′, *v.*, **-cated**, **-cating.** divide into syllables. Also, **syl•lab′i•fy′.** —**syl•lab′i•ca′tion**, *n.*

syl′la•ble, *n.* single unit of speech. —**syl•lab′ic**, *adj.*

syl′la•bus, *n.*, *pl.* **-buses, -bi** (-bī′). outline of course of study.

syl′lo•gism, *n.* three-part chain of logical reasoning.

sylph, *n.* **1.** graceful woman. **2.** imaginary being supposed to inhabit the air.

syl′van, *adj.* **1.** of forests. **2.** wooded.

sym′bi•o′sis (sim′bē ō′sis, -bī-), *n.*, *pl.* **-ses** (-sēz). living together of two dissimilar organisms. —**sym′bi•ot′ic**, *adj.*

sym′bol, *n.* **1.** emblem; token; sign. **2.** thing that represents something else. —**sym•bol′ic**, **sym•bol′i•cal**, *adj.* —**sym′bol•ize′**, *v.*

sym′bol•ism, *n.* **1.** representing things by symbols. **2.** symbolic meaning of a character.

sym′me•try, *n.*, *pl.* **-tries.** pleasing balance or proportion. —**sym•met′ri•cal**, *adj.* —**sym•met′ri•cal•ly**, *adv.*

sympathetic nervous system, that part of autonomic nervous system that regulates involuntary reactions to stress.

sym′pa•thize′, *v.*, **-thized**, **-thizing. 1.** be in sympathy. **2.** feel or express sympathy. —**sym′pa•thiz′er**, *n.*

sym′pa•thy, *n.*, *pl.* **-thies. 1.** agreement in feeling; accord. **2.** compassion. —**sym′pa•thet′ic**, *adj.* —**sym′pa•thet′i•cal•ly**, *adv.*

sym′pho•ny, *n.*, *pl.* **-nies. 1.** composition for orchestra. **2.** harmonious combination. —**sym•phon′ic**, *adj.*

sym•po′si•um, *n.*, *pl.* **-siums, -sia.** meeting to present essays on one subject.

symp′tom, *n.* sign or indication, esp. of disease. —**symp′to•mat′ic**, *adj.*

syn·a·gogue′ (-gog′), *n.* 1. assembly of Jews for worship. 2. place of such assembly.

syn′apse, *n.* region where nerve impulses are transmitted from axon terminal to adjacent structure. —**syn·ap′tic**, *adj.*

sync, *n., v.,* **synced, syncing.** —*n.* 1. synchronization. 2. harmonious relationship. —*v.* 3. synchronize.

syn′chro·nize′, *v.,* **-nized, -nizing.** 1. occur at same time. 2. show or set to show same time. —**syn′chro·ni·za′tion**, *n.* —**syn′chro·nous**, *adj.*

syn′co·pate′, *v.,* **-pated, -pating.** 1. *Music.* play by accenting notes normally unaccented. 2. *Gram.* omit middle sound in (word). —**syn′co·pa′tion**, *n.*

syn′di·cate, *n., v.,* **-cated, -cating.** —*n.* (sin′də kit). 1. combination of persons or companies for large joint enterprise. 2. agency dealing in news stories, etc. —*v.* (sin′di kāt′). 3. publish as syndicate. —**syn′di·ca′tion**, *n.*

syn′drome, *n.* characteristic group of symptoms.

syn′er·gism, *n.* joint action of agents so that their combined effect is greater than sum of individual effects.

syn′fu′el, *n.* synthetic fuel.

syn′od (sin′əd), *n.* meeting of church delegates.

syn′o·nym, *n.* word meaning same as another. —**syn·on′y·mous**, *adj.* —**syn·on′y·mous·ly**, *adv.*

syn·op′sis, *n., pl.* **-ses.** brief summary.

syn′tax, *n.* arrangement of words into sentences, etc.

syn′the·sis, *n., pl.* **-ses.** 1. combination of parts into whole. 2. such whole.

syn′the·size′, *v.,* **-sized, -sizing.** make by combining parts.

syn′the·siz′er, *n.* electronic, usu. computerized device for creating or modifying musical sounds.

syn·thet′ic, *adj.* 1. produced artificially rather than by nature. 2. of synthesis. —**syn·thet′i·cal·ly**, *adv.*

synthetic fuel, fuel made esp. from coal or shale.

syph′i•lis, *n.* infectious venereal disease. —**syph•i•lit′ic,** *adj., n.*

sy•rin′ga (sə ring′gə), *n.* shrub with fragrant flowers, as lilac.

syr•inge′, *n.* device for drawing in and ejecting fluids.

syr′up, *n.* sweet thick liquid. —**syr′up•y,** *adj.*

sys′tem, *n.* 1. orderly assemblage of facts, parts, etc. 2. plan. 3. organization of body. —**sys′tem•at′ic,** *adj.* —**sys′tem•at′i•cal•ly,** *adv.*

sys′tem•a•tize′, *v.,* -tized, -tizing. arrange in or by system.

sys•tem′ic, *adj.* affecting entire body.

systems analysis, study of data-processing needs of project.

sys′to•le′ (sis′tə lē′), *n.* regular contraction of the heart. —**sys•tol′ic,** *adj.*

T, t, *n.* twentieth letter of English alphabet.

tab, *n., v.,* **tabbed, tabbing. —***n.* 1. small flap. 2. tag. —*v.* 3. furnish with tab.

Ta·bas'co, *n. Trademark.* pungent condiment sauce.

tab'by, *n., pl.* **-bies,** *adj.* —*n.* 1. striped or brindled cat. 2. silk fabric. —*adj.* 3. striped.

tab'er·nac'le, *n.* 1. temporary temple, esp. Jewish. 2. church for large congregation. 3. receptacle for Eucharist.

ta'ble, *n., v.,* **-bled, -bling. —***n.* 1. piece of furniture consisting of level part on legs. 2. food. 3. company at table. 4. compact arrangement of information in parallel columns. —*v.* 5. place on or enter in table. 6. postpone deliberation on. —**ta'ble·cloth',** *n.*

tab·leau' (tab lō'), *n., pl.* **-leaux.** picture.

ta'ble d'hôte' (täb'əl dōt'), meal fixed in courses and price.

ta'ble·land', *n.* elevated, level region of considerable extent.

T

ta'ble·spoon', *n.* 1. large spoon in table service. 2. tablespoonful.

ta'ble·spoon·ful', *n., pl.* **-fuls.** quantity tablespoon holds, about ½ fluid ounce or 3 teaspoonfuls.

tab'let, *n.* 1. pad of writing paper. 2. small slab. 3. pill.

table tennis, game resembling tennis, played on table with paddles and small hollow ball.

ta'ble·ware', *n.* dishes, etc., used at table.

tab'loid, *n.* newspaper about half ordinary size.

ta·boo', *adj., n., pl.* **-boos,** *v.* —*adj.* 1. forbidden. —*n.* 2. prohibition. —*v.* 3. prohibit.

ta'bor (tā'bər), *n.* small drum.

tab'u·late', *v.,* **-lated, -lating.** arrange in table. —**tab'u·lar,** *adj.* —**tab'u·la'tion,** *n.* —**tab'u·la'tor,** *n.*

ta·chom'e·ter (tə kom'ə tər), *n.* instrument for measuring velocity.

tach'y·car'di·a, *n.* excessively rapid heartbeat.

tac′it (tas′it), *adj.* **1.** silent. **2.** implied. **3.** unspoken.
—**tac′it•ly,** *adv.*

tac′i•turn, *adj.* inclined to silence. —**tac′i•tur′ni•ty,** *n.*
—**tac′i•turn•ly,** *adv.*

tack, *n.* **1.** short nail with flat head. **2.** straight windward run of sailing ship. —*v.* **3.** fasten by tack. **4.** navigate by tacks.

tack′le, *n., v.,* **-led, -ling.** —*n.* **1.** fishing equipment. **2.** hoisting apparatus. —*v.* **3.** undertake to deal with.
—**tack′ler,** *n.*

tack′y, *adj.,* **tackier, tackiest. 1.** *Informal.* shabby; dowdy. **2.** slightly sticky. **3.** in poor taste.
—**tack′i•ness,** *n.*

ta′co (tä′kō), *n.* fried tortilla folded and filled with chopped meat, cheese, lettuce, etc.

tact, *n.* skill in handling delicate situations. —**tact′ful,** *adj.* —**tact′ful•ly,** *adv.*
—**tact′less,** *adj.*
—**tact′less•ly,** *adv.*

tac•ti′cian (tak tish′ən), *n.* person versed in tactics.

tac′tics, *n.* **1.** maneuvering of armed forces. **2.** methods for attaining success.

—**tac′ti•cal,** *adj.*
—**tac′ti•cal•ly,** *adv.*

tac′tile, *adj.* of sense of touch.
—**tac•til′i•ty,** *n.*

tad, *n. Informal.* **1.** small child. **2.** small amount or degree.

tad′pole′, *n.* immature form of frogs, toads, etc.

taf′fe•ta, *n.* lustrous silk or rayon fabric.

taf′fy, *n., pl.* **-fies.** molasses candy.

tag, *n., v.,* **tagged, tagging.** —*n.* **1.** small paper, etc., attached as mark or label. **2.** game in which players chase and touch each other. —*v.* **3.** furnish with tag. **4.** touch in playing tag.

t′ai chi ch′uan (tī′ jē′ chwän′), *n.* Chinese system of meditative exercises. Also, **tai′ chi′.**

tail, *n.* **1.** appendage at rear of animal's body. **2.** something resembling this. **3.** bottom or end part. —*v.* **4.** follow.

tail′bone′, *n.* coccyx.

tail′gate′, *n., v.,* **-gated, -gating.** —*n.* **1.** hinged board at back of vehicle. —*v.* **2.** drive too closely behind.

tail′light′, *n.* light at the rear of automobile, train, etc.

tai′lor, *n.* maker or mender of outer garments.

tail′piece′, *n.* piece, design, etc., added at end; appendage.

tail′pipe′, *n.* exhaust pipe at rear of motor vehicle.

tail′spin′, *n.* descent of airplane in steep spiral course.

tail′wind′, *n.* wind from directly behind.

taint, *n.* 1. unfavorable trace. —*v.* 2. contaminate.

take, *v.,* **took, taken, taking.** 1. seize, catch, or embrace. 2. receive; obtain. 3. select. 4. remove. 5. deduct. 6. conduct. 7. travel by. 8. occupy. 9. assume. 10. require.

take′off′, *n.* 1. leaving of ground in leaping or flying. 2. place at which one takes off. 3. *Informal.* piece of mimicry.

take′out′, *adj.* intended to be taken from restaurant and eaten elsewhere.

take′o′ver, *n.* 1. act of seizing authority or control. 2. acquisition of corporation through purchase of stock.

talc, *n.* soft mineral, used for lubricants, etc. Also, **tal′cum.**

talcum powder, powder for the skin made of purified talc.

tale, *n.* story or lie.

tale′bear′er, *n.* gossip.

tal′ent, *n.* natural ability. —**tal′ent•ed,** *adj.*

tal′is•man, *n.* amulet.

talk, *v.* 1. speak; converse. 2. gossip. —*n.* 3. speech; conversation. 4. conference. 5. gossip. —**talk′a•tive,** *adj.* —**talk′er,** *n.*

talk′ing-to′, *n., pl.* **-tos.** scolding.

talk′y, *adj.,* **talkier, talkiest.** 1. containing too much talk, dialogue, etc. 2. talkative. —**talk′i•ness,** *n.*

tall, *adj.* high.

tal′low, *n.* 1. suet. 2. hardened fat for soap, etc.

tal′ly, *n., pl.* **-lies,** *v.,* **-lied, -lying.** —*n.* 1. notched stock indicating amount. 2. mark on tally. 3. record of amounts. —*v.* 4. record.

tal′ly•ho′, *n., pl.* **-hos,** *interj.* —*n.* 1. *Chiefly Brit.* mail or pleasure coach. —*interj.* (tal′ē hō′). 2. cry in hunting on catching sight of fox.

Tal′mud (täl′mŏŏd), *n.* collection of Jewish laws. —**Tal•mud′ic**, *adj.*

tal′on, *n.* claw.

tal′us, *n., pl.* **-li.** anklebone.

tam, *n.* tam-o′-shanter.

ta•ma′le (tə mä′lē), *n.* Mexican dish of cornmeal, meat, red peppers, etc.

tam′a•rack, *n.* N American larch.

tam′a•rind, *n.* tropical fruit.

tam′bou•rine′ (tam′bə rēn′), *n.* small drum with metal disks in frame.

tame, *adj.,* **tamer, tamest,** *v.,* **tamed, taming.** —*adj.* **1.** not wild; domesticated. **2.** uninterestingly conventional. —*v.* **3.** domesticate. —**tam′a•ble, tame′a•ble**, *adj.* —**tame′ly**, *adv.* —**tame′ness,** *n.* —**tam′er**, *n.*

tam′-o′-shan′ter, *n.* cap with flat crown.

tamp, *v.* force down or in. —**tamp′er**, *n.*

tam′per, *v.* meddle.

tam′pon, *n.* plug of cotton or the like for insertion into wound or body cavity to absorb blood.

tan, *v.,* **tanned, tanning,** *n., adj.* —*v.* **1.** convert into leather. **2.** make or become brown by exposure to sun. —*n.* **3.** light brown. **4.** Also, **tan′bark′.** bark used in tanning hides. —*adj.* **5.** light brown. —**tan′ner**, *n.* —**tan′ner•y**, *n.*

tan′a•ger, *n.* small, brightly colored bird.

tan′dem, *adv.* **1.** one behind another. —*adj.* **2.** having one following behind another. —*n.* **3.** team of horses so harnessed.

tang, *n.* strong flavor.

tan′ge•lo, *n., pl.* **-los.** fruit that is a cross between grapefruit and tangerine.

tan′gent, *adj.* **1.** touching. —*n.* **2.** tangent line, etc. **3.** sudden change of course, thought, etc. —**tan′gen•cy**, *n.*

tan•gen′tial, *adj.* **1.** being tangent; touching. **2.** not relevant. —**tan•gen′tial•ly,** *adv.*

tan′ge•rine′, *n.* loose-skinned fruit similar to orange.

tan′gi•ble, *adj.* **1.** discernible by touch. **2.** real. **3.** definite. —**tan′gi•bil′i•ty**, *n.* —**tan′gi•bly**, *adv.*

tan′gle, *v.,* **-gled, -gling,** *n.* —*v.* **1.** come or bring together in confused mass. **2.** involve. **3.** snare. **4.** *Informal.* come into conflict. —*n.* **5.** tangled state or mass.

tan′go, *n., pl.* **-gos,** *v.,* **-goed, -going.** —*n.* **1.** Spanish-American dance. —*v.* **2.** dance the tango.

tank, *n.* **1.** large receptacle. **2.** armored combat vehicle on caterpillar treads.

tank′ard, *n.* large cup.

tank′er, *n.* ship, truck, or airplane for transporting liquid bulk cargo.

tank top, sleeveless shirt.

tan′nin, *n.* astringent compound used in tanning. Also, **tan′nic ac′id.**

tan′ta•lize′, *v.,* **-lized, -lizing.** torment by prospect of something desired. —**tan′ta•liz′ing•ly,** *adv.*

tan′ta•mount′, *adj.* equivalent.

tan′trum, *n.* noisy outburst of ill-humor.

tap, *n., v.,* **tapped, tapping.** —*n.* **1.** plug or faucet through which liquid is drawn. **2.** light blow. —*v.* **3.** draw liquid from. **4.** reach or pierce to draw something off. **5.** strike lightly.

tap dance, dance in which rhythm is audibly tapped out by toe or heel. —**tap′-dance′,** *v.* —**tap′-danc′er,** *n.*

tape, *n., v.,* **taped, taping.** —*n.* **1.** narrow strip of flexible material. —*v.* **2.** furnish or tie with tape. **3.** record on tape.

tape deck, audio system component for playing tapes.

tape measure, tape marked for measuring. Also, **tape′line′.**

ta′per, *v.* **1.** make or become narrower toward end. —*n.* **2.** gradual decrease. **3.** small candle.

tape recorder, electrical device for recording or playing back sound recorded on magnetic tape.

tap′es•try, *n., pl.* **-tries.** woven, figured fabric for wall hanging, etc.

tape′worm′, *n.* parasitic worm in alimentary canal.

tap′i•o′ca, *n.* granular food from starch of tuberous plants.

ta′pir (tā′pər), *n.* tropical swinelike animal.

tap′room′, *n.* barroom.

tap′root′, *n.* main, central root pointing downward and giving off small lateral roots.

taps, *n.* bugle signal sounded at night as order to extinguish lights, and sometimes at military funerals.

tar, *n., v.,* **tarred, tarring.** —*n.* **1.** dark viscid product made from coal, wood, etc. **2.** sailor. —*v.* **3.** cover with tar. —**tar′ry** (tär′ē), *adj.*

tar′an·tel′la (tar′ən tel′ə), *n.* rapid, whirling southern Italian dance.

ta·ran′tu·la (-chə lə), *n.* large hairy spider.

tar′dy, *adj.,* **-dier, -diest.** late. —**tar′di·ly,** *adv.* —**tar′di·ness,** *n.*

tare (târ), *n.* **1.** weed. **2.** weight of a wrapping or receptacle.

tar′get, *n.* something aimed at.

tar′iff, *n.* **1.** list of export or import duties. **2.** one such duty.

tar′nish, *v.* **1.** lose luster. **2.** sully. —*n.* **3.** tarnished coating or state.

ta′ro, *n.* tropical plant cultivated for edible tuber.

ta′rot (tar′ō, ta rō′), *n.* any of set of 22 playing cards used for fortune-telling.

tar·pau′lin (tär pô′lin), *n.* waterproof covering of canvas, etc.

tar′pon, *n.* large game fish.

tar′ra·gon′, *n.* plant with aromatic leaves used as seasoning.

tar′ry (tar′ē), *v.,* **-ried, -rying.** **1.** stay. **2.** linger.

tar′sus, *n., pl.* **-si.** bones forming ankle joint.

tart, *adj.* **1.** sour; acid. **2.** caustic. —*n.* **3.** pastry shell filled with fruit, etc. —**tart′ly,** *adv.* —**tart′ness,** *n.*

tar′tan, *n.* cloth worn by natives of N Scotland, having crisscross pattern.

tar′tar, *n.* **1.** hard deposit on teeth. **2.** savage, intractable person. —**tar·tar′ic, tar′tar·ous,** *adj.*

tartar sauce, mayonnaise sauce containing chopped pickles, onions, etc.

task, *n.* **1.** assigned piece of work. —*v.* **2.** put strain on.

task force, 1. temporary group of armed units for carrying out specific mission. 2. temporary committee for solving specific problem.

task′mas′ter, *n.* assigner of tasks.

tas′sel, *n.* fringed ornament hanging from roundish knot.

taste, *v.,* **tasted, tasting,** *n.* —*v.* 1. try flavor by taking in mouth. 2. eat or drink a little of. 3. perceive flavor. 4. have particular flavor. —*n.* 5. act of tasting. 6. sense by which flavor is perceived. 7. flavor. 8. sense of fitness or beauty. —**taste′ful,** *adj.* —**taste′less,** *adj.* —**tast′er,** *n.*

taste bud, one of numerous small bodies, chiefly in tongue, that are organs for sense of taste.

tast′y, *adj.,* **tastier, tastiest.** 1. savory. 2. tasting good. —**tast′i•ness,** *n.*

tat, *v.,* **tatted, tatting.** to do, or make by, tatting.

tat′ter, *n.* 1. torn piece. 2. (*pl.*) ragged clothing.

tat′ting, *n.* 1. the making of a kind of knotted lace with a shuttle. 2. such lace.

tat′tle, *v.,* **-tled, -tling,** *n.* —*v.* 1. tell another's secrets. —*n.* 2. chatter; gossip. —**tat′tler, tat′tle•tale′,** *n.*

tat•too′, *n.* 1. indelible marking on skin by puncturing and dyeing. 2. design so made. 3. military signal on drum, bugle, etc., to go to quarters. —*v.* 4. mark by tattoo.

taunt, *v.* 1. reproach insultingly or sarcastically. —*n.* 2. insulting or sarcastic gibe.

taupe (tōp), *n.* dark gray usually tinged with brown, purple, yellow, or green.

taut, *adj.* tight; tense. —**taut′ly,** *adv.* —**taut′ness,** *n.*

tau•tol′o•gy, *n.,* *pl.* **-gies.** needless repetition. —**tau′to•log′i•cal,** *adj.*

tav′ern, *n.* 1. saloon. 2. inn.

taw (tô), *n.* 1. choice playing marble with which to shoot. 2. game of marbles.

taw′dry, *adj.,* **-drier, -driest.** gaudy; cheap. —**taw′dri•ly,** *adv.* —**taw′dri•ness,** *n.*

taw′ny, *adj.,* **-nier, -niest,** *n.* —*adj.* 1. of a dark-yellow or yellow-brown color. —*n.* 2. tawny color.

tax, *n.* 1. money regularly paid to government. 2. burdensome duty, etc. —*v.* 3. impose tax. 4. burden. 5. accuse. —**tax'a•ble,** *adj.* —**tax•a'tion,** *n.*

tax'i, *n., v.,* **taxied, taxiing.** —*n.* 1. taxicab. —*v.* 2. go in taxicab. 3. (of airplane) move on ground or water under its own power.

tax'i•cab', *n.* automobile carrying paying passengers.

tax'i•der'my, *n.* art of preserving and mounting skins of animals. —**tax'i•der'•mist,** *n.*

tax•on'o•my, *n., pl.* **-mies.** classification, esp. in relation to principles or laws.

tax'pay'er, *n.* person who pays tax.

tax shelter, financial arrangement that reduces or eliminates taxes due.

TB, tuberculosis. Also, **T.B.**

tbs., tablespoon. Also, **tbsp.**

T cell, cell involved in regulating immune system's response to infected or malignant cells.

tea, *n.* 1. dried aromatic leaves of Oriental shrub. 2. beverage made by infusion of these leaves in hot water. 3. similar beverage made by steeping leaves or flowers of other plants. 4. afternoon meal or reception. —**tea'cup',** *n.* —**tea'ket'tle,** *n.* —**tea'pot',** *n.*

teach, *v.,* **taught, teaching.** impart knowledge to. —**teach'er,** *n.* —**teach'a•ble,** *adj.*

teak, *n.* East Indian tree with hard wood.

teal, *n.* 1. any of certain small fresh-water ducks. 2. greenish blue.

team, *n.* 1. persons, etc., associated in joint action. —*v.* 2. join in team. —**team'mate',** *n.* —**team'work',** *n.*

team'ster, *n.* driver of team.

tear, *v.,* **tore, torn, tearing,** *n.* —*v.* 1. pull apart by force. 2. distress. 3. divide. 4. lacerate. 5. rend. —*n.* 6. act of tearing. 7. torn place. 8. (tēr). Also, **tear'drop'.** drop of fluid secreted by eye duct. —**tear'ful,** *adj.*

tear gas (tēr), gas that makes eyes smart and water.

tear'jerk•er, *n. Informal.* sentimental story, etc.

tease, *v.,* **teased, teasing,** *n.*
—*v.* **1.** annoy by raillery. —*n.*
2. person who teases.
—**teas'er,** *n.*

tea'sel, *n.* plant with prickly
leaves and flower heads.

tea'spoon', *n.* small spoon.
—**tea'spoon•ful'**, *n.*

teat, *n.* nipple.

tech'ni•cal, *adj.* **1.** pertaining
to skilled activity. **2.**
considered in strict sense.
—**tech'ni•cal•ly,** *adv.*

tech'ni•cal'i•ty, *n., pl.* **-ties.**
1. technical point or detail. **2.**
technical character.

Tech'ni•col'or (tek'-), *n.*
Trademark. system of making
color motion pictures.

tech•nique' (-nēk'), *n.* skilled
method. Also, **tech•nic'**.

tech•noc'ra•cy, *n., pl.* **-cies.**
government by technological
experts. —**tech'no•crat'**, *n.*

tech•nol'o•gy, *n., pl.* **-gies. 1.**
practical application of
science. **2.** technological
invention or method.
—**tech•no•log'i•cal,** *adj.*
—**tech•nol'o•gist,** *n.*

tech'no•thrill'er, *n.* suspense
novel in which sophisticated
technology is prominent.

tec•ton'ic, *adj.* **1.** of building
or construction. **2.** of the
structure and movements of
the earth's crust.

teddy bear, stuffed toy bear.

Te De'um (tā dā'əm), hymn of
praise and thanksgiving.

te'di•ous, *adj.* long and
tiresome. —**te'di•um,** *n.*
—**te'di•ous•ly,** *adv.*
—**te'di•ous•ness,** *n.*

tee, *n., v.,* **teed, teeing.** *Golf.*
—*n.* **1.** hard mound of earth at
beginning of play for each
hole. **2.** object from which ball
is driven. —*v.* **3.** place on tee.
4. strike from tee.

teem, *v.* abound; swarm.

teens, *n.pl.* years (13–19) of
ages ending in *-teen.*
—**teen'-ag'er, teen,** *n.*
—**teen'age', teen'aged',** *adj.*

tee'ter, *Informal.* —*v.* **1.**
seesaw. **2.** walk unsteadily.
—*n.* **3.** seesaw.

teethe, *v.,* **teethed, teething.**
grow or cut teeth.

tee•to'tal•er, *n.* person who
does not drink alcoholic
beverages.

Tef'lon, *n. Trademark.* **1.**
polymer with nonsticking

properties, used to coat cookware. —*adj.* **2.** impervious to blame or criticisms.

tel., **1.** telegram. **2.** telegraph. **3.** telephone.

tel′e•cast′, *v.,* **-cast** or **-casted, -casting,** *n.* —*v.* **1.** broadcast by television. —*n.* **2.** television broadcast.

tel′e•com•mu′ni•ca′tions, *n.* science and technology of transmitting information in the form of electromagnetic signals.

tel′e•con′fer•ence, *n.* conference of participants in different locations via telecommunications equipment.

tel′e•gen′ic, *adj.* having physical qualities that televise well.

tel′e•graph′, *n.* **1.** electrical apparatus or process for sending message (**tel′e•gram′**). —*v.* **2.** send by telegraph. —**te•leg′ra•pher,** *n.* —**tel′e•graph′ic,** *adj.* —**te•leg′ra•phy,** *n.*

tel′e•mar′ket•ing, *n.* selling or advertising by telephone.

te•lep′a•thy, *n.* communication between minds without physical means. —**te•lep′a•thist,** *n.* —**tel′e•path′ic,** *adj.* —**tel′e•path′i•cal•ly,** *adv.*

tel′e•phone′, *n., v.,* **-phoned, -phoning.** —*n.* **1.** electrical apparatus or process for transmitting sound or speech. —*v.* **2.** speak to or transmit by telephone. —**tel′e•phon′ic** (-fon′-), *adj.* —**tel′e•phon′i•cal•ly,** *adv.* —**te•leph′o•ny,** *n.*

tel′e•pho′to, *adj.* of a lens producing large image of small or distant object.

tel′e•scope′, *n., v.,* **-scoped, -scoping.** —*n.* **1.** optical instrument for enlarging image of distant objects. —*v.* **2.** force or slide one object into another. —**tel′e•scop′ic,** *adj.*

tel′e•thon′, *n.* lengthy television broadcast, usu. to raise money for charity.

Tel′e•type′, *n. Trademark.* teletypewriter.

tel′e•type′writ′er, *n.* telegraphic apparatus with typewriter terminals.

tel′e•van′ge•list, *n.* evangelist who conducts religious services on television.
—**tel′e•van′ge•lism,** *n.*

tel′e•view′, *v.* view with a television receiver.
—**tel′e•view′er,** *n.*

tel′e•vise′, *v.,* **-vised, -vising.** send or receive by television.

tel′e•vi′sion, *n.* radio or electrical transmission of images.

Tel′ex, *n. Trademark.* two-way teletypewriter system.

tell, *v.,* **told, telling. 1.** relate. **2.** communicate. **3.** say positively. **4.** distinguish. **5.** inform. **6.** divulge. **7.** order. **8.** produce marked effect.
—**tell′ing,** *adj.*

tell′-all′, *adj.* thoroughly revealing.

tell′er, *n.* bank cashier.

tell′tale′, *n.* **1.** divulger of secrets. —*adj.* **2.** revealing.

te•mer′i•ty, *n.* rash boldness.

temp, *n.* temporary worker.

tem′per, *n.* **1.** state or habit of mind. **2.** heat or passion. **3.** control of one's anger. **4.** state of metal after tempering. —*v.*

5. moderate. **6.** heat and cool metal to obtain proper hardness, etc.

tem′per•a, *n.* technique of painting using media containing egg.

tem′per•a•ment, *n.* mental disposition.

tem′per•a•men′tal, *adj.* **1.** moody or sensitive. **2.** of one's personality.
—**tem′per•a•men′tal•ly,** *adv.*

tem′per•ance, *n.* **1.** moderation. **2.** total abstinence from alcohol.

tem′per•ate, *adj.* moderate.
—**tem′per•ate•ly,** *adv.*
—**tem′per•ate•ness,** *n.*

Temperate Zone, part of earth's surface lying between either tropic and nearest polar circle.

tem′per•a•ture, *n.* degree of warmth or coldness.

tem′pest, *n.* violent storm, commotion, or disturbance.
—**tem•pes′tu•ous,** *adj.*
—**tem•pes′tu•ous•ly,** *adv.*

tem′plate (tem′plit), *n.* pattern, mold, etc., serving as gauge or guide in mechanical work.

tem′ple, *n.* **1.** place dedicated to worship. **2.** flat region at side of forehead.

tem′po, *n., pl.* **-pos, -pi. 1.** rate of speed of musical work. **2.** any characteristic rate or rhythm.

tem′po•ral, *adj.* **1.** of time. **2.** worldly. —**tem′po•ral•ly,** *adv.*

tem′po•rar′y, *adj.* not permanent. —**tem′po•rar′i•ly,** *adv.*

tem′po•rize′, *v.,* **-rized, -rizing. 1.** delay by evasion or indecision. **2.** compromise. —**tem′po•ri•za′tion,** *n.* —**tem′po•ri′zer,** *n.*

tempt, *v.* **1.** entice. **2.** appeal strongly. —**temp•ta′tion,** *n.* —**tempt′er,** *n.* —**tempt′ress,** *n.fem.*

tem•pur′a (tem po͝or′ə), *n.* Japanese deep-fried dish of vegetables or seafood.

ten, *n., adj.* nine plus one.

ten′a•ble, *adj.* defensible in argument. —**ten′a•bil′i•ty,** *n.* —**ten′a•bly,** *adv.*

te•na′cious, *adj.* **1.** holding fast. **2.** retentive. **3.** obstinate. **4.** sticky. —**te•na′cious•ly,** *adv.* —**te•nac′i•ty, te•na′cious•ness,** *n.*

ten′an•cy, *n., pl.* **-cies.** holding; tenure.

ten′ant, *n.* **1.** one renting from landlord. **2.** occupant.

Ten Commandments, precepts spoken by God to Israel (Exodus 20, Deut. 10) or delivered to Moses (Exodus 24:12, 34) on Mount Sinai.

tend, *v.* **1.** incline in action or effect. **2.** lead. **3.** take care of.

tend′en•cy, *n., pl.* **-cies. 1.** disposition to behave or act in certain way. **2.** predisposition; preference.

ten•den′tious, *adj.* having or showing bias. —**ten•den′tious•ly,** *adv.*

ten′der, *adj.* **1.** soft; delicate; weak. **2.** immature. **3.** soft-hearted. **4.** kind. **5.** loving. **6.** sensitive. —*v.* **7.** present formally. **8.** offer. —*n.* **9.** something offered. **10.** person who tends. **11.** auxiliary vehicle or vessel. —**ten′der•er,** *n.* —**ten′der•ly,** *adv.* —**ten′der•ness,** *n.* —**ten′der•ize′,** *v.*

ten′der•foot′, *n., pl.* **-foots, -feet.** *Informal.* **1.**

inexperienced person; novice. **2.** *Western U.S.* newcomer to ranching and mining regions.

ten′der-heart′ed, *adj.* soft-hearted; sympathetic. —**ten′der-heart′ed•ness,** *n.*

ten′der•loin′, *n.* **1.** tender meat on loin of beef, pork, etc. **2.** brothel district of city.

ten′di•ni′tis, *n.* inflammation of tendon.

ten′don, *n.* band of fibrous tissue connecting muscle to bone or part.

ten′dril, *n.* clinging threadlike organ of climbing plants.

ten′e•ment, *n.* **1.** dwelling place. **2.** Also, **tenement house.** cheap apartment house.

ten′et, *n.* principle, doctrine, dogma, etc.

Tenn., Tennessee.

ten′nis, *n.* game of ball played with rackets (**tennis rackets**) on rectangular court (**tennis court**).

ten′on, *n.* projection inserted into cavity (**mortise**) to form joint.

ten′or, *n.* **1.** continuous course or progress. **2.** perceived meaning or intention. **3.** male voice between bass and alto. **4.** singer with this voice.

ten′pins′, *n.* bowling game played with ten pins.

tense, *adj.,* **tenser, tensest,** *v.,* **tensed, tensing,** *n.* —*adj.* **1.** taut; rigid. **2.** emotionally strained. —*v.* **3.** make or become tense. —*n.* **4.** verb inflection indicating time of action or state. —**tense′ly,** *adv.* —**tense′ness,** *n.*

ten′sile (-səl), *adj.* **1.** of tension. **2.** ductile.

ten′sion, *n.* **1.** stretching or being stretched. **2.** strain. **3.** strained relations.

tent, *n.* portable shelter, usually canvas.

ten′ta•cle, *n.* slender, flexible organ for feeling, etc. —**ten′ta•cled,** *adj.*

ten′ta•tive, *adj.* in trial; experimental. —**ten′ta•tive•ly,** *adv.*

ten′ter•hook′, *n.* **1.** hook to hold cloth stretched on frame. **2. on tenterhooks,** in suspense.

tenth, *adj., n.* next after ninth.

ten′u•ous, *adj.* **1.** lacking a sound basis. **2.** thin, slender.

3. rarefied. —**ten′u•ous•ly,** *adv.* —**ten•u′i•ty, ten′u•ous•ness,** *n.*

ten′ure (-yər), *n.* **1.** holding of something. **2.** assurance of permanent work.

te′pee, *n.* American Indian tent.

tep′id, *adj.* lukewarm. —**te•pid′i•ty, tep′id•ness,** *n.* —**tep′id•ly,** *adv.*

te•qui′la (-kē′-), *n.* Mexican liquor.

ter′cen•ten′ni•al, *n.* 300th anniversary or its celebration. Also, **ter′cen•ten′a•ry.**

term, *n.* **1.** name for something. **2.** period, as of school instruction. **3.** (*pl.*) conditions of agreement or bargain. —*v.* **4.** name; designate.

ter′ma•gant, *n.* shrew (def. 1).

ter′mi•nal, *adj.* **1.** at end; concluding. **2.** leading to death. —*n.* **3.** end or extremity. **4.** terminating point for trains, buses, etc. **5.** point of electrical connection. **6.** device for entering information into or receiving information from computer. —**ter′mi•nal•ly,** *adv.*

ter′mi•nate′, *v.,* -nated, -nating. **1.** end or cease. **2.** occur at end. —**ter′mi•na•ble,** *adj.* —**ter′mi•na•bly,** *adv.* —**ter′mi•na′tion,** *n.*

ter′mi•nol′o•gy, *n., pl.* -gies. terms of technical subject.

ter′mi•nus, *n.* **1.** terminal. **2.** goal. **3.** limit.

ter′mite, *n.* destructive woodeating insect.

tern, *n.* gull-like aquatic bird.

ter′na•ry, *adj.* consisting of or involving three.

terp′si•cho•re′an (tûrp′si kə rē′ən, -kôr′ē ən), *adj.* of dancing.

ter′race, *n., v.,* -raced, -racing. —*n.* **1.** raised level with abrupt drop at front. **2.** flat roof. **3.** open area connected with house. —*v.* **4.** make or furnish as or with terrace.

ter′ra cot′ta, 1. hard, usually unglazed earthenware. **2.** brownish red.

ter′ra fir′ma (ter′ə fûr′mə), solid land.

ter•rain′, *n.* area of land of specified nature.

ter′ra•pin, *n.* edible North American turtle.

ter·rar′i·um, *n., pl.* **-iums, -ia.** glass tank for raising plants or land animals.

ter·raz′zo (tə rä′tsō, -raz′ō), *n.* mosaic flooring composed of stone chips and cement.

ter·res′tri·al, *adj.* of or living on earth.

ter′ri·ble, *adj.* 1. dreadful. 2. severe. —**ter′ri·ble·ness,** *n.* —**ter′ri·bly,** *adv.*

ter′ri·er, *n.* hunting dog.

ter·rif′ic, *adj.* 1. excellent. 2. terrifying. —**ter·rif′i·cal·ly,** *adv.*

ter′ri·fy′, *v.,* **-fied, -fying.** fill with terror. —**ter′ri·fy′ing·ly,** *adv.*

ter′ri·to′ry, *n., pl.* **-ries.** 1. region. 2. land and waters of state. 3. region not a state but having elected legislature and appointed officials. —**ter′ri·to′ri·al,** *adj.* —**ter′ri·to′ri·al·ly,** *adv.*

ter′ror, *n.* intense fear.

ter′ror·ism, *n.* use of violence and threats to obtain political demands. —**ter′ror·ist,** *n., adj.*

ter′ror·ize′, *v.,* **-ized, -izing.** fill with terror. —**ter′ror·i·za′tion,** *n.*

ter′ry, *n., pl.* **-ries.** pile fabric with loops on both sides. Also, **terry cloth.**

terse, *adj.* 1. concise. 2. curt; brusque. —**terse′ly,** *adv.* —**terse′ness,** *n.*

ter′ti·ar′y (tûr′shē-), *adj.* of third rank or stage.

tes′sel·late′, *v.,* **-lated, -lating.** form mosaic pattern from small squares.

test, *n.* 1. trial of or substance used to try quality, content, etc. 2. examination to evaluate student or class. —*v.* 3. subject to test.

tes′ta·ment, *n.* legal will. —**tes′ta·men′ta·ry,** *adj.*

tes′tate, *adj.* having left a valid will. —**tes′ta·tor,** *n.*

tes′ti·cle, *n.* either of two male sex glands located in scrotum. Also, **testis.**

tes′ti·fy′, *v.,* **-fied, -fying.** 1. give evidence. 2. give testimony.

tes′ti·mo′ni·al, *n.* writing certifying character, etc.

tes′ti·mo′ny, *n., pl.* **-nies.** 1. statement of witness under oath. 2. proof.

tes·tos′ter·one, *n.* male sex hormone.

test tube, *Chem.* small cylindrical glass container.

tes′ty, *adj.,* **-tier, -tiest.** irritable. —**tes′ti•ly,** *adv.* —**tes′ti•ness,** *n.*

tet′a•nus, *n.* infectious disease marked by muscular rigidity.

tête′-à-tête′ (tāt′ə tāt′), *n.* private conversation.

teth′er, *n.* **1.** rope, chain, etc., for fastening animal to stake. —*v.* **2.** fasten with tether.

tet′ra, *n., pl.* **-ras.** small, brightly colored fish of tropical American waters.

tet′ra•cy′cline, *n.* antibiotic.

tet′ra•he′dron (-hē′-), *n., pl.* **-drons, -dra.** solid contained by four plane faces.

te•tram′e•ter, *n.* verse of four feet.

Tex., Texas.

text, *n.* **1.** main body of matter in book or manuscript. **2.** quotation from Scripture, esp. as subject of sermon, etc. —**tex′tu•al,** *adj.* —**tex′tu•al•ly,** *adv.*

text′book′, *n.* student's book of study.

tex′tile (-tīl, -til), *n.* **1.** woven material. —*adj.* **2.** woven. **3.** of weaving.

tex′ture, *n.* characteristic surface or composition. —**tex′tur•al,** *adj.*

thal′a•mus, *n.* part of brain that transmits and integrates sensory impulses.

tha•lid′o•mide′, *n.,* drug formerly used as sedative, found to cause fetal abnormalities.

thal′li•um, *n.* rare metallic element.

than, *conj.* particle introducing second member of comparison.

than′a•top′sis, *n.* view or contemplation of death.

thane, *n. Early Eng. Hist.* person ranking between earl and ordinary freeman, holding lands of king or lord by military service.

thank, *v.* **1.** express gratitude for. —*n.* **2.** (*usually pl.*) expression of gratitude. —**thank′ful,** *adj.* —**thank′less,** *adj.* —**thanks′giv′ing,** *n.*

Thanksgiving Day, festival in acknowledgment of divine

favor, celebrated in U.S. on fourth Thursday of November and in Canada on second Monday of October.

that, *pron., pl.* **those,** *adj., adv., conj.* —*pron., adj.* **1.** demonstrative word indicating **a.** the person, thing, etc., more remote. **b.** one of two persons, etc., pointed out or mentioned before (opposed to **this**). **2.** relative pronoun used as: **a.** subject or object of relative clause. **b.** object of preposition. —*adv.* **3.** to that extent. —*conj.* **4.** word used to introduce dependent clause or one expressing reason, result, etc.

thatch, *n.* **1.** rushes, leaves, etc., for covering roofs. —*v.* **2.** cover with thatch.

thaw, *v.* **1.** melt. **2.** remove ice or frost from. —*n.* **3.** act or instance of thawing.

the, *def. article.* **1.** word used, esp. before nouns, with specifying effect. —*adv.* **2.** word used to modify comparative or superlative form of adjective or adverb.

the′a•ter, *n.* **1.** building for dramatic presentations, etc. **2.** dramatic art. **3.** place of action. Also, **the′a•tre.** —**the•at′ri•cal,** *adj.* —**the•at′ri•cal•ly,** *adv.*

thee, *pron. Archaic.* you.

theft, *n.* act or instance of stealing.

their, *pron.* **1.** possessive form of **they** used before noun. **2.** (*pl.*) that which belongs to them.

the′ism, *n.* belief in one God. —**the′ist,** *n.* —**the•is′tic,** *adj.*

them, *pron.* objective case of **they.**

theme, *n.* **1.** subject of discourse, etc. **2.** short essay. **3.** melody. —**the•mat′ic,** *adj.*

them•selves′, *pron.* emphatic or reflexive form of **them.**

then, *adv.* **1.** at that time. **2.** soon afterward. **3.** at another time. **4.** besides. **5.** in that case. —*adj.* **6.** being such at that time.

thence, *adv.* **1.** from that place or time. **2.** therefore.

thence′forth′, *adv.* from that place or time on. Also, **thence′for′ward.**

the•oc′ra•cy, *n., pl.* **-cies. 1.** government in which authorities claim to carry out divine law. **2.** government by priests. —**the′o•crat′ic,** *adj.*

the•ol′o•gy, *n.* study dealing with God and God's relations to universe. —**the′o•lo′gian,** *n.* —**the′o•log′i•cal,** *adj.* —**the′o•log′i•cal•ly,** *adv.*

the′o•rem (thē′ə rəm), *n.* **1.** *Math.* statement embodying something to be proved. **2.** rule or law, esp. one expressed by equation or formula.

the′o•ret′i•cal, *adj.* **1.** in theory. **2.** not practical. **3.** speculative. —**the′o•ret′i•cal•ly,** *adv.*

the′o•ry, *n., pl.* **-ries. 1.** proposition used to explain class of phenomena. **2.** proposed explanation. **3.** principles. —**the′o•rist,** *n.* —**the′o•rize′,** *v.*

the•os′o•phy, *n.* any of various forms of thought based on mystical insight into the divine nature.

ther′a•py, *n., pl.* **-pies. 1.** treatment of disease. **2.** psychotherapy. —**ther′a•pist,** *n.* —**ther′a•peu′tic**

(-pyo͞o′tik), *adj.* —**ther′a•peu′ti•cal•ly,** *adv.* —**ther′a•peu′tics,** *n.*

there, *adv.* **1.** in or at that place, point, matter, respect, etc. **2.** to that place. —**there′a•bout′, there′a•bouts′,** *adv.* —**there•af′ter,** *adv.* —**there•by′,** *adv.* —**there•for′,** *adv.* —**there•from′,** *adv.* —**there•in′,** *adv.* —**there•in′to,** *adv.* —**there•to′,** *adv.* —**there•un′der,** *adv.*

there′fore′, *adv.* consequently.

there•of′, *adv.* of or from that.

there•on′, *adv.* **1.** on that. **2.** immediately after that.

there′up•on′, *adv.* **1.** immediately after that. **2.** because of that. **3.** with reference to that.

there•with′, *adv.* with or in addition to that.

ther′mal, *adj.* of heat.

ther′mo•dy•nam′ics, *n.* science concerned with relations between heat and mechanical energy or work.

ther·mom'e·ter, *n.* instrument for measuring temperature.
—**ther'mo·met'·ric,** *adj.*

ther'mo·nu'cle·ar, *adj.* of nuclear-fusion reactions at extremely high temperatures.

ther'mo·plas'tic, *adj.* **1.** soft and pliable whenever heated, as some plastics, without change of inherent properties. —*n.* **2.** such plastic.

Ther'mos, *n. Trademark.* container with vacuum between double walls for heat insulation.

ther'mo·sphere', *n.* region of upper atmosphere in which temperature increases continually with altitude.

ther'mo·stat', *n.* device regulating temperature of heating system, etc.
—**ther'mo·stat'ic,** *adj.*

the·sau'rus, *n., pl.* **-ruses, -ri.** book of synonyms and antonyms.

these, *pron.* pl. of **this.**

the'sis, *n., pl.* **-ses. 1.** proposition to be proved. **2.** essay based on research.

thes'pi·an, *adj.* **1.** of dramatic art. —*n.* **2.** actor or actress.

they, *pron.* nominative plural of **he, she,** and **it.**

thi'a·mine (thī'ə min), *n.* vitamin B. Also, **thi'a·min.**

thick, *adj.* **1.** not thin. **2.** in depth. **3.** compact. **4.** numerous. **5.** dense. **6.** husky. **7.** slow-witted. —*adv.* **8.** so as to be thick. —*n.* **9.** something thick. —**thick'en,** *v.*
—**thick'en·er,** *n.*
—**thick'en·ing,** *n.* —**thick'ly,** *adv.* —**thick'ness,** *n.*

thick'et, *n.* thick growth of shrubs, bushes, etc.

thick'set', *adj.* **1.** set thickly; dense. **2.** with heavy or solid body.

thick'-skinned', *adj.* **1.** having thick skin. **2.** not sensitive to criticism or contempt.

thief, *n., pl.* **thieves.** person who steals. —**thieve,** *v.*
—**thiev'er·y,** *n.*

thigh, *n.* part of leg between hip and knee.

thigh'bone', *n.* femur.

thim'ble, *n.* cap to protect finger while sewing.

thin, *adj.,* **thinner, thinnest,** *v.,* **thinned, thinning.** —*adj.* **1.** having little extent between opposite sides; slender. **2.** lean. **3.** scanty. **4.** rarefied; diluted. **5.** flimsy. **6.** weak. —*v.* **7.** make or become thinner. —**thin•ner,** *n.* —**thin'ly,** *adv.* —**thin•ness,** *n.*

thing, *n.* **1.** inanimate object. **2.** entity. **3.** matter. **4.** item.

think, *v.,* **thought, thinking. 1.** conceive in mind. **2.** meditate. **3.** believe. —**think'er,** *n.* —**think'a•ble,** *adj.*

think tank, research organization employed to analyze problems and plan future developments.

thin'-skinned', *adj.* **1.** having thin skin. **2.** sensitive to criticism or contempt.

third, *adj.* **1.** next after second. —*n.* **2.** next after the second. **3.** any of three equal parts.

third'-class', *adj.* of the lowest class or quality.

third degree, *Chiefly U.S.* use of brutal measures by police (or others) in extorting information or confession.

third dimension, 1. thickness or depth. **2.** aspect that heightens reality.

third party, 1. party to case or quarrel who is incidentally involved. **2.** in two-party political system, usu. temporary party composed of independents.

third'-rate', *adj.* distinctly inferior.

Third World, developing countries of Asia, Africa, and Latin America.

thirst, *n.* **1.** sensation caused by need of drink. —*v.* **2.** be thirsty. —**thirst'y,** *adj.* —**thirst'i•ly,** *adv.* —**thirst'i•ness,** *n.*

thir'teen', *n., adj.* ten plus three. —**thir•teenth',** *adj., n.*

thir'ty, *n., adj.* ten times three. —**thir'ti•eth,** *adj., n.*

this, *pron., pl.* **these,** *adj., adv.* —*pron., adj.* **1.** demonstrative word indicating something as just mentioned, present, near, etc. —*adv.* **2.** to the indicated extent.

this'tle, *n.* prickly plant.

thith'er, *adv.* to that place, point, etc.

tho (*th ō*), *conj., adv. Informal.* though.

thong, *n.* strip of hide or leather.

tho'rax, *n., pl.* **-raxes, -races.** part of trunk between neck and abdomen. —**tho•rac'ic,** *adj.*

thor'i•um, *n.* grayish-white radioactive metallic element.

thorn, *n.* sharp spine on plant. —**thorn'y,** *adj.*

thor'ough (thûr'-), *adj.* complete. —**thor'ough•ly,** *adv.* —**thor'ough•ness,** *n.*

thor'ough•bred', *adj.* **1.** of pure breed. **2.** well-bred. —*n.* **3.** thoroughbred animal or person.

thor'ough•fare', *n.* road, street, etc., open at both ends.

thor'ough•go•ing, *adj.* doing things thoroughly.

those, *pron., adj.* pl. of **that.**

thou, *pron.* you (now little used except provincially, archaically, in poetry or elevated prose, in addressing God, and by Friends).

though, *conj.* **1.** notwithstanding that. **2.** even if. **3.** nevertheless. —*adv.* **4.** however.

thought, *n.* **1.** mental activity. **2.** idea. **3.** purpose. **4.** regard.

thought'ful, *adj.* **1.** meditative. **2.** heedful. **3.** considerate. —**thought'ful•ly,** *adv.* —**thought'ful•ness,** *n.*

thought'less, *adj.* **1.** showing lack of thought. **2.** careless; inconsiderate. —**thought'less•ly,** *adv.*

thou'sand, *n., adj.* ten times one hundred. —**thou'sandth,** *adj., n.*

thrall, *n.* **1.** person in bondage; slave. **2.** slavery; bondage. —**thrall'dom, thral'dom,** *n.*

thrash, *v.* **1.** beat thoroughly. **2.** toss wildly. —**thrash'er,** *n.*

thread, *n.* **1.** fine spun cord of flax, cotton, etc. **2.** filament. **3.** helical ridge of screw. **4.** connected sequence. —*v.* **5.** pass end of thread through needle's eye. **6.** fix beads, etc., on thread.

thread'bare', *adj.* shabby.

threat, *n.* menace. —**threat'en,** *v.* —**threat'en•er,** *n.*

three, *n., adj.* two plus one.

three'-di•men'sion•al, *adj.* having or seeming to have depth as well as width and height.

three'fold', *adj.* **1.** having three parts. **2.** three times as great.

three R's, reading, writing, and arithmetic.

three' score', *adj.* sixty.

thren'o•dy, *n., pl.* **-dies.** song of lamentation.

thresh, *v.* separate grain or seeds from a plant. —**thresh'er**, *n.*

thresh'old, *n.* **1.** doorway sill. **2.** entrance. **3.** beginning; border.

thrice, *adv.* three times.

thrift, *n.* frugality. —**thrift'less**, *adj.*

thrift shop, store that sells secondhand goods.

thrift'y, *adj.*, **thriftier**, **thriftiest.** saving; frugal. —**thrift'i•ly**, *adv.* —**thrift'i•ness**, *n.*

thrill, *v.* **1.** affect with sudden keen emotion. **2.** vibrate. —*n.* **3.** sudden wave of keen emotion or excitement.

thrill'er, *n.* suspenseful play or story.

thrive, *v.*, **thrived, thriving.** flourish.

throat, *n.* passage from mouth to stomach or lungs.

throat'y, *adj.*, **throatier**, **throatiest.** (of sound) husky; hoarse.

throb, *v.*, **throbbed, throbbing**, *n.* —*v.* **1.** beat violently or rapidly. **2.** vibrate. —*n.* **3.** act of throbbing.

throe, *n.* **1.** spasm. **2.** (*pl.*) pangs.

throm•bo'sis, *n.* clotting of blood in circulatory system.

throm'bus, *n., pl.* **-bi.** clot formed in thrombosis.

throne, *n.* official chair of sovereign, bishop, etc.

throng, *n., v.* crowd.

throt'tle, *n., v.*, **-tled, -tling.** —*n.* **1.** device controlling flow of fuel. —*v.* **2.** choke. **3.** check.

through, *prep.* **1.** in at one end and out at other. **2.** during all of. **3.** having finished. **4.** by means or reason of. —*adv.* **5.** in at one end and out at other. **6.** all the way. **7.** to the end. **8.** finished. —*adj.* **9.** passing through.

through•out', *prep.* **1.** in all parts of. —*adv.* **2.** in every part, etc.

throw, *v.,* **threw, thrown, throwing,** *n.* —*v.* **1.** propel or cast. **2.** fell in wrestling. **3.** host. **4.** confuse. —*n.* **5.** act of throwing. —**throw′er,** *n.*

throw′a•way′, *adj.* **1.** to be discarded after use. —*n.* **2.** notice distributed free.

throw′back′, *n.* **1.** setback or check. **2.** reversion to ancestral type.

thru, *prep., adv., adj. Informal.* through.

thrum, *v.,* **thrummed, thrumming,** *n.* —*v.* **1.** to play on stringed instrument, as guitar, by plucking strings. **2.** to tap with fingers. —*n.* **3.** act or sound of thrumming. —**thrum′mer,** *n.*

thrush, *n.* **1.** migratory singing bird. **2.** fungal disease of mouth.

thrust, *v.,* **thrust, thrusting,** *n.* —*v.* **1.** push; shove. **2.** stab. —*n.* **3.** push; lunge. **4.** stab.

thru′way′, *n.* expressway providing direct route between distant areas.

thud, *n., v.,* **thudded, thudding.** —*n.* **1.** dull striking sound. —*v.* **2.** make thudding sound.

thug, *n.* violent criminal.

thumb, *n.* **1.** short, thick finger next to the forefinger. —*v.* **2.** manipulate with thumb.

thumb′nail′, *n.* **1.** nail of thumb. —*adj.* **2.** brief and concise.

thumb′screw′, *n.* **1.** instrument of torture that compresses thumbs. **2.** screw turned by thumb and finger.

thumb′tack′, *n.* **1.** tack with large, flat head. —*v.* **2.** secure with thumbtack.

thump, *n.* **1.** blow from something thick and heavy. —*v.* **2.** pound.

thump′ing, *adj.* **1.** exceptional. **2.** of or like a thump.

thun′der, *n.* **1.** loud noise accompanying lightning. —*v.* **2.** give forth thunder. **3.** speak loudly. —**thun′der•ous,** *adj.* —**thun′der•storm′,** *n.* —**thun′der•show′er,** *n.*

thun′der•bolt′, *n.* flash of lightning with thunder.

thun′der•clap′, *n.* crash of thunder.

thun′der•cloud′, *n.* electrically charged cloud producing lightning and thunder.

thun′der•head′, *n.* mass of cumulus clouds warning of thunderstorms.

thun′der•struck′, *adj.* astonished.

Thurs., Thursday.

Thurs′day, *n.* fifth day of week.

thus, *adv.* **1.** in this way. **2.** consequently. **3.** to this extent.

thwack, *v.* **1.** strike hard with something flat. —*n.* **2.** thwacking blow.

thwart, *v.* **1.** frustrate; prevent. —*n.* **2.** seat across a boat.

thy, *adj. Archaic.* your.

thyme (tīm), *n.* plant of mint family.

thy′mus, *n.* gland at base of neck that aids in production of T cells.

thy′roid, *adj.* of thyroid gland.

thyroid gland, ductless gland near windpipe, involved in controlling metabolism and growth.

thy•self′, *pron.* **1.** emphatic appositive to **thou** or **thee. 2.** substitute for reflexive **thee.**

ti•ar′a (tē âr′ə), *n.* woman's ornamental coronet.

Ti•bet′an, *n.* native or language of Tibet. —**Tibetan,** *adj.*

tib′i•a, *n., pl.* **-iae, -ias.** bone from knee to ankle. —**tib′i•al,** *adj.*

tic, *n.* sudden twitch.

tick, *n.* **1.** soft, recurring click. **2.** bloodsucking mitelike animal. **3.** cloth case of mattress, pillow, etc. —*v.* **4.** produce tick (def. 1).

tick′er, *n.* **1.** one that ticks. **2.** telegraphic instrument that prints stock prices and market reports, etc., on tape (**ticker tape**). **3.** *Slang.* heart.

tick′et, *n.* **1.** slip indicating right to admission, transportation, etc. **2.** tag. **3.** summons for traffic or parking violation. —*v.* **4.** attach ticket to.

tick′ing, *n.* cotton fabric for ticks (def. 3).

tick′le, *v.,* **-led, -ling,** *n.* —*v.* **1.** touch lightly so as to make tingle or itch. **2.** gratify. **3.** amuse. —*n.* **4.** act of tickling. —**tick′lish,** *adj.* —**tick′lish•ly,** *adv.*

tickler file, file for reminding user at appropriate times of matters needing attention.

tick′-tack-toe′, *n.* game for two players, each trying to complete row of three X's or three O's on nine-square grid.

tidal wave, large, destructive ocean wave produced by earthquake or the like.

tid′bit′, *n.* choice bit.

tid′dly•winks′, *n.* game in which small disks are snapped with larger disks into cup.

tide, *n., v.,* **tided, tiding.** —*n.* 1. periodic rise and fall of ocean waters. 2. stream. —*v.* 3. help over difficulty. —**tid′al,** *adj.*

tide′land′, *n.* land alternately exposed and covered by tide.

tide′wa′ter, *n.* 1. water affected by tide. —*adj.* 2. of lowland near sea.

ti′dings, *n.pl.* news.

ti′dy, *adj.,* **-dier, -diest,** *v.,* **-died, -dying.** —*adj.* 1. neat; orderly. 2. fairly large. —*v.* 3. make tidy. —**ti′di•ly,** *adv.* —**ti′di•ness,** *n.*

tie, *v.,* **tied, tying,** *n.* —*v.* 1. bind with cord, etc. 2. confine. 3. equal or be equal. —*n.* 4. something used to tie or join. 5. necktie. 6. equality in scores, votes, etc. 7. contest in which this occurs. 8. bond of kinship, affection, etc.

tie′-dye′ing, *n.* method of dyeing with sections of garment bound so as not to receive dye. —**tie′-dyed′,** *adj.*

tie′-in′, *n.* link, association, or relationship.

tier (tēr), *n.* row or rank.

tie′-up′, *n.* 1. undesired stoppage of business, traffic, etc. 2. connection.

tiff, *n.* petty quarrel.

ti′ger, *n.* large striped Asian feline. —**ti′gress,** *n.fem.*

tiger lily, lily with flowers of dull-orange color spotted with black.

tight, *adj.* 1. firmly in place. 2. taut. 3. fitting closely. 4. impervious to fluids. 5. stingy. —**tight′en,** *v.* —**tight′ly,** *adv.* —**tight′ness,** *n.*

tight′-fist′ed, *adj.* stingy.

tight′-lipped′, *adj.* reluctant to speak.

tight′rope′, *n.* taut wire or cable on which acrobats perform.

tights, *n.pl.* close-fitting pants, worn esp. by acrobats, etc.

tight′wad′, *n. Slang.* stingy person.

til′de (til′də), *n.* diacritical mark (˜) placed over letter.

tile, *n., v.,* **tiled, tiling.** —*n.* **1.** thin piece of baked clay, etc., used as covering. —*v.* **2.** cover with tiles.

til′ing, *n.* **1.** operation of covering with tiles. **2.** tiles collectively.

till, *prep., conj.* **1.** until. —*v.* **2.** labor on to raise crops. **3.** plow. —*n.* **4.** drawer in back of counter for money. —**till′a•ble,** *adj.* —**till′age,** *n.*

till′er, *n.* **1.** one that tills. **2.** handle on head of rudder.

tilt, *v.* **1.** lean; slant. **2.** charge or engage in joust. —*n.* **3.** act of tilting. **4.** slant.

tim′bale (tim′bəl), *n.* **1.** a preparation of minced meat, etc., cooked in mold. **2.** this mold, usually of paste, and sometimes fried.

tim′ber, *n.* **1.** wood of growing trees. **2.** trees. **3.** wood for building. **4.** wooden beam, etc. —*v.* **5.** furnish or support with timber. —**tim′bered,** *adj.*

tim′ber•line′, *n.* altitude or latitude at which timber ceases to grow.

timber wolf, large brindled wolf of forested Canada and northern United States.

tim′bre, *n.* characteristic quality of a sound.

time, *n., v.,* **timed, timing.** —*n.* **1.** duration. **2.** period of time. **3.** occasion. **4.** point in time. **5.** appointed or proper time. **6.** meter of music. **7.** rate. —*v.* **8.** determine or record time. —**tim′er,** *n.*

time clock, clock with attachment that records times of arrival and departure of employees.

time′-hon′ored, *adj.* long valued or used; traditional.

time′keep′er, *n.* **1.** person who keeps time. **2.** timepiece, esp. as regards accuracy.

time′less, *adj.* **1.** eternal. **2.** referring to no particular time.

time line, **1.** linear representation of events in the order in which they occurred. **2.** schedule.

time′ly, *adj.,* **-lier, -liest,** *adv.* —*adj.* **1.** opportune. —*adv.* **2.** opportunely.

time′-out′, *n*. brief suspension of activity, as in sports contest.

time′piece′, *n*. clock; watch.

times, *prep*. multiplied by.

time′-shar′ing, *n*. 1. plan in which several people share cost of vacation home. 2. system in which users at different terminals simultaneously use a single computer.

time′ta′ble, *n*. schedule of times of departures, work completion, etc.

time′worn′, *adj*. 1. impaired by time. 2. trite.

time zone, one of 24 divisions of globe coinciding with meridians at successive hours from observatory at Greenwich, England.

tim′id, *adj*. 1. easily alarmed. 2. shy. —**tim′id•ly**, *adv*. —**ti•mid′i•ty**, **tim′id•ness**, *n*.

tim′ing, *n*. control of speed or occasion of an action, event, etc., so that it occurs at the proper moment.

tim′or•ous, *adj*. 1. fearful. 2. timid. —**tim′or•ous•ly**, *adv*. —**tim′or•ous•ness**, *n*.

tim′o•thy, *n., pl*. **-thies**. coarse fodder grass.

tim′pa•ni′ (-nē′), *n.pl*. kettledrums. —**tim′pa•nist**, *n*.

tin, *n., v.*, **tinned, tinning**. —*n*. 1. malleable metallic element. —*v*. 2. cover with tin. —**tin′ny**, *adj*.

tinc′ture, *n*. medicinal solution in alcohol.

tin′der, *n*. inflammable substance. —**tin′der•box′**, *n*.

tine, *n*. prong of fork.

tin′foil′, *n*. tin or alloy in thin sheet, used as wrapping.

tinge, *v.*, **tinged, tingeing** or **tinging**, *n*. —*v*. 1. impart trace of color, taste, etc., to. —*n*. 2. slight trace.

tin′gle, *v.*, **-gled, -gling**, *n*. —*v*. 1. feel or cause slight stings. —*n*. 2. tingling sensation.

tink′er, *n*. 1. mender of pots, kettles, pans, etc. —*v*. 2. do the work of a tinker. 3. work or repair unskillfully or clumsily.

tin′kle, *v.*, **-kled, -kling**, *n*. —*v*. 1. make light ringing sounds. —*n*. 2. tinkling sound.

tin plate, thin iron or steel sheet coated with tin.

tin′sel, *n.* **1.** glittering metal in strips, etc. **2.** anything showy and worthless.

tint, *n.* **1.** color or hue. —*v.* **2.** apply tint to.

tin′tin·nab′u·la′tion, *n.* ringing or sound of bells.

tin′type′, *n.* old type of positive photograph made on sensitized sheet of iron or tin.

ti′ny, *adj.,* **-nier, -niest.** very small.

-tion, suffix meaning action or process, result of action, or state or condition.

tip, *n., v.,* **tipped, tipping.** —*n.* **1.** small gift of money. **2.** piece of private information. **3.** useful hint. **4.** tap. **5.** slender or pointed end. **6.** top. —*v.* **7.** give tip to. **8.** furnish with tip. **9.** tilt. **10.** overturn. **11.** tap. —**tip′per,** *n.*

tip′-off′, *n. Slang.* hint or warning.

tip′pet, *n.* scarf.

tip′ple, *v.,* **-pled, -pling.** drink alcoholic liquor. —**tip′pler,** *n.*

tip′ster, *n.* person who sells tips.

tip′sy, *adj.,* **-sier, -siest.** slightly intoxicated.

—**tip′si·ly,** *adv.*
—**tip′si·ness,** *n.*

tip′toe′, *n., v.,* **-toed, -toeing.** —*n.* **1.** tip of toe. —*v.* **2.** move on tiptoes.

tip′top′, *n.* **1.** extreme top. —*adj.* **2.** situated at very top. **3.** *Informal.* of highest excellence.

ti′rade, *n.* long denunciation or speech.

ti′ra·mi′su (tir′ə mē′soo), *n.* Italian dessert.

tire, *v.,* **tired, tiring,** *n.* —*v.* **1.** exhaust strength, interest, patience, etc. —*n.* **2.** hoop of metal, rubber, etc., around wheel. —**tire′less,** *adj.* —**tire′some,** *adj.*

tired, *adj.* **1.** exhausted; fatigued. **2.** weary. —**tired′ly,** *adv.* —**tired′ness,** *n.*

tis′sue, *n.* **1.** substance composing organism. **2.** light, gauzy fabric.

tissue paper, very thin paper.

ti′tan (tīt′n), *n.* person or thing of great size or power. —**ti·tan′ic,** *adj.*

ti·tan′i·um (tī tā′nē əm), *n.* corrosion-resistant metallic element, used to toughen steel.

tit for tat, equivalent given in retaliation, repartee, etc.

tithe, *n.* tenth part.

ti′tian (tish′ən), *n., adj.* yellowish or golden brown.

tit′il•late′, *v.,* -lated, -lating. 1. tickle. 2. excite agreeably. —**tit′il•la′tion,** *n.*

tit′i•vate′, *v.,* -vated, -vating. make smart or spruce. —**tit′i•va′tion,** *n.*

ti′tle, *n., v.,* -tled, -tling. —*n.* 1. name of book, picture, etc. 2. caption. 3. appellation, esp. of rank. 4. championship. 5. right to something. 6. document showing this. —*v.* 7. furnish with title.

tit′mouse′, *n., pl.* -mice. small bird having crest and conical bill.

tit′ter, *n.* 1. restrained laugh. —*v.* 2. laugh in this way.

tit′tle, *n.* very small thing.

tit′u•lar, *adj.* 1. of or having a title. 2. being so in title only. —**tit′u•lar•ly,** *adv.*

tiz′zy, *n., pl.* -zies. *Slang.* dither.

TN, Tennessee.

TNT, trinitrotoluene.

to, *prep.* 1. particle specifying point reached. 2. sign of the infinitive. —*adv.* 3. toward. 4. to and fro, to and from place or thing.

toad, *n.* tailless, froglike amphibian.

toad′stool′, *n.* fungus with umbrellalike cap.

toad′y, *n., pl.* **toadies,** *v.,* **toadied, toadying.** —*n.* 1. fawning flatterer. —*v.* 2. be toady.

toast, *n.* 1. person whose health is proposed and drunk. 2. the proposal. 3. sliced bread browned by heat. —*v.* 4. propose as toast. 5. make toast.

toast′er, *n.* appliance for toasting bread.

toast′mas′ter, *n.* person who introduces the after-dinner speakers or proposes toasts. —**toast′mis′tress,** *n.fem.*

toast′y, *adj.,* **toastier, toastiest.** cozily warm.

to•bac′co, *n., pl.* -cos, -coes. 1. plant with leaves prepared for smoking or chewing. 2. the prepared leaves.

to•bac′co•nist, *n.* dealer in or manufacturer of tobacco.

to•bog′gan, *n.* **1.** long, narrow, flat-bottomed sled. —*v.* **2.** coast on toboggan.

toc•ca′ta (tə kä′tə), *n. Music.* keyboard composition in style of improvisation.

toc′sin, *n.* signal, esp. of alarm.

to•day′, *n.* **1.** this day, time, or period. —*adv.* **2.** on this day. **3.** at this period. Also, **to-day′.**

tod′dle, *v.,* **-dled, -dling.** go with short, unsteady steps. —**tod′dler,** *n.*

tod′dy, *n., pl.* **-dies.** drink made of alcoholic liquor and hot water, sweetened and sometimes spiced.

to-do′ (tə dōō′), *n., pl.* **-dos.** *Informal.* fuss.

toe, *n.* **1.** terminal digit of foot. **2.** part covering toes. —**toe′nail′,** *n.*

toe′hold′, *n.* **1.** small niche that supports the toes. **2.** any slight advantage.

tof′fee, *n.* taffy.

to′fu (tō′fōō), *n.* soft cheeselike food made from curdled soybean milk.

to′ga, *n.* ancient Roman outer garment.

to•geth′er, *adv.* **1.** into or in proximity, association, or single mass. **2.** at same time. **3.** in cooperation.

to•geth′er•ness, *n.* warm fellowship.

togs, *n.pl. Informal.* clothes.

toil, *n.* **1.** hard, exhausting work. —*v.* **2.** work hard. —**toil′er,** *n.*

toi′let, *n.* **1.** receptacle for excretion. **2.** bathroom. **3.** Also, **toi•lette′.** act or process of dressing.

toi′let•ry, *n., pl.* **-ries.** article or preparation used in grooming oneself.

toilet water, scented liquid used as light perfume.

toil′some, *adj.* laborious or fatiguing. —**toil′some•ly,** *adv.* —**toil′some•ness,** *n.*

to•kay′ (tō kā′), *n.* **1.** rich, sweet, aromatic wine. **2.** the variety of grape from which it is made.

toke, *n., v.,* **toked, toking.** *Slang.* —*n.* **1.** puff on marijuana cigarette. —*v.* **2.** puff or smoke (marijuana).

to′ken, *n.* **1.** thing expressing or representing something else. **2.** metal disk used as ticket, etc. —*adj.* **3.** being merely a token; minimal.

to'ken·ism, *n.* minimal conformity to law or social pressure.

tole, *n.* enameled or lacquered metal.

tol'er·a·ble, *adj.* **1.** endurable. **2.** fairly good. —**tol'er·a·bly,** *adv.*

tol'er·ance, *n.* fairness toward different opinions, etc. —**tol'er·ant,** *adj.* —**tol'er·ant·ly,** *adv.*

tol'er·ate', *v.,* -ated, -ating. **1.** allow. **2.** put up with. —**tol'er·a'tion,** *n.*

toll, *v.* **1.** sound bell slowly and repeatedly. —*n.* **2.** payment, as for right to travel. **3.** payment for long-distance telephone call.

toll'booth', *n.* booth where toll is collected.

tol'u·ene', *n.* flammable liquid.

tom, *n.* male of various animals.

tom'a·hawk', *n.* light ax used by North American Indians.

Tom and Jerry, hot drink of rum, milk, and beaten eggs.

to·ma'to, *n., pl.* -toes. cultivated plant with pulpy, edible fruit.

tomb, *n.* burial place for dead body; grave. —**tomb'stone',** *n.*

tom'boy', *n.* boisterous, romping girl. —**tom'boy'ish,** *adj.*

tom'cat', *n.* male cat.

Tom Col'lins, tall iced drink containing gin, lemon or lime juice, and carbonated water.

tome, *n.* large book.

tom'fool'er·y, *n., pl.* -eries. foolish or silly behavior.

Tommy gun, *Slang.* type of submachine gun.

tom'my·rot', *n. Slang.* nonsense.

to·mog'ra·phy, *n.* method of making x-rays of selected plane of the body.

to·mor'row, *n.* **1.** day after this day. —*adv.* **2.** on day after this day. Also, **to-mor'row.**

tom'-tom', *n.* primitive drum.

ton, *n.* **1.** unit of weight, equal to 2000 pounds (**short ton**) in U.S. and 2240 pounds (**long ton**) in Great Britain. **2.** *Naut.* unit of volume, equal to 100 cubic feet.

to·nal'i·ty, *n., pl.* **-ties. 1.** relation between tones of musical scales. **2.** the tones.

tone, *n., v.,* **toned, toning.** —*n.* **1.** sound. **2.** quality of sound. **3.** quality, etc., of voice. **4.** firmness. **5.** expressive quality. **6.** elegance; amenity. —*v.* **7.** give proper tone to. —**ton'al,** *adj.* —**ton'al·ly,** *adv.*

tone'-deaf', *adj.* unable to distinguish differences in musical pitch.

tongs, *n.pl.* two-armed implement for grasping.

tongue (tung), *n.* **1.** organ on floor of mouth, used for tasting, etc. **2.** language. **3.** tonguelike thing.

tongue'-lash'ing, *n.* severe scolding.

tongue'-tied', *adj.* unable to speak, as from shyness.

tongue twister, sequence of words difficult to pronounce rapidly.

ton'ic, *n.* **1.** invigorating medicine. —*adj.* **2.** invigorating.

to·night', *n.* **1.** this night. —*adv.* **2.** on this night.

ton'nage, *n.* **1.** carrying capacity or total volume of vessel. **2.** duty on cargo or tonnage. **3.** ships.

ton·neau' (tu nō'), *n., pl.* **-neaus, -neaux** (-nōz'). rear compartment of automobile with seats for passengers.

ton'sil, *n.* oval mass of tissue in throat.

ton'sil·lec'to·my, *n., pl.* **-mies.** removal of tonsils.

ton'sil·li'tis, *n.* inflammation of tonsils.

ton·so'ri·al, *adj.* of barbers.

ton'sure, *n.* **1.** shaving of head. **2.** shaved part of cleric's head.

to'ny, *adj.,* **-ier, -iest.** swank.

too, *adv.* **1.** also. **2.** excessively.

tool, *n.* **1.** mechanical instrument, as hammer or saw. **2.** exploited person; dupe. —*v.* **3.** decorate with tool.

toot, *v.* sound horn.

tooth, *n., pl.* **teeth. 1.** hard body attached to jaw, used in chewing, etc. **2.** projection. **3.** taste, relish, etc. —**tooth'ache',** *n.* —**tooth'brush',** *n.* —**tooth'paste',** *n.* —**tooth'pick',** *n.*

tooth and nail, with all one's resources and energy.

tooth′some, *adj.* tasty.

tooth′y, *adj.,* **toothier, toothiest.** having or displaying conspicuous teeth.

top, *n., v.,* **topped, topping.** —*n.* 1. highest point, part, rank, etc. 2. lid. 3. child's spinning toy. 4. separable upper part of clothing. —*v.* 5. put top on. 6. be top of. 7. surpass.

to′paz, *n.* colored crystalline gem.

top brass, high-ranking officials.

top′coat′, *n.* light overcoat.

top′er (tō′pər), *n.* drunkard.

top′flight′, *adj.* excellent.

top hat, man's tall silk hat.

top′-heav′y, *adj.* disproportionately heavy at top.

top′ic, *n.* subject of discussion or writing.

top′i•cal, *adj.* 1. of or dealing with matters of current interest. 2. of topics. 3. applied to local area. —**top′i•cal•ly,** *adv.*

top kick, *Mil. Slang.* first sergeant.

top′mast′, *n.* mast next above lower mast on sailing ship.

top′most, *adj.* highest.

top′notch′, *adj. Informal.* first-rate.

to•pog′ra•phy, *n., pl.* **-phies.** description of features of geographical area. —**to•pog′ra•pher,** *n.* —**top′o•graph′ic, top′o•graph′i•cal,** *adj.*

top′per, *n.* 1. one that tops. 2. *Slang.* top hat. 3. short coat worn by women.

top′ping, *n.* sauce or garnish placed on food.

top′ple, *v.,* **-pled, -pling.** fall; tumble.

top′sail′ (top′sāl′; *Naut.* -səl), *n.* square sail next above lowest or chief sail.

top′-se′cret, *adj.* extremely secret.

top′soil′, *n.* fertile upper soil.

top′sy-tur′vy, *adv., adj.* 1. upside down. 2. in confusion.

toque (tōk), *n.* hat with little or no brim.

tor, *n.* hill.

To′rah (tōr′ə), *n.* 1. five books of Moses; Pentateuch. 2. (*also l.c.*) whole Jewish Scripture.

torch, *n.* light carried in hand.

torch'bear'er, *n.* **1.** person who carries torch. **2.** leader in movement.

tor'e·a·dor', *n.* bullfighter.

tor·ment', *v.* **1.** afflict with great suffering. —*n.* (tôr'ment). **2.** agony. —**tor·men'tor, tor·ment'er,** *n.*

tor·na'do, *n., pl.* **-does, -dos.** destructive storm.

tor·pe'do, *n., pl.* **-does,** *v.,* **-doed, -doing.** —*n.* **1.** self-propelled missile launched in water and exploding on impact. —*v.* **2.** strike with torpedo.

torpedo boat, small fast warship used to launch torpedoes.

tor'pid, *adj.* **1.** inactive; sluggish. **2.** dull; apathetic; lethargic. —**tor·pid'i·ty,** *n.* —**tor'pid·ly,** *adv.*

tor'por, *n.* **1.** suspension of physical activity. **2.** apathy.

torque (tôrk), *n.* rotating force.

tor'rent, *n.* rapid, violent stream. —**tor·ren'tial,** *adj.* —**tor·ren'tial·ly,** *adv.*

tor'rid, *adj.* **1.** very hot. **2.** passionate.

Torrid Zone, part of earth's surface between tropics.

tor'sion, *n.* **1.** act of twisting. **2.** twisting by two opposite torques. —**tor'sion·al,** *adj.*

tor'so, *n., pl.* **-sos, -si.** trunk of body.

tort, *n. Law.* civil wrong (other than breach of contract or trust) for which law requires damages.

torte (tôrt), *n., pl.* **tortes.** rich cake, made with eggs, nuts, and usu. no flour.

tor'tel·li'ni, *n. (used with sing. or pl. v.)* small ring-shaped pieces of pasta filled with meat or cheese.

tor·til'la (tôr tē'yä), *n.* flat, round bread of Mexico, made from cornmeal or wheat flour.

tor'toise, *n.* turtle.

tor'toise·shell', *n.* **1.** horny brown and yellow shell of certain turtles, used for making combs, etc. **2.** synthetic tortoiseshell. —*adj.* **3.** colored like tortoiseshell.

tor'tu·ous, *adj.* **1.** twisting; winding. **2.** indirect. —**tor'tu·ous·ly,** *adv.* —**tor'tu·ous·ness,** *n.*

tor′ture, *n., v.,* **-tured, -turing.** —*n.* **1.** infliction of great pain. —*v.* **2.** subject to torture. —**tor′tur•er,** *n.* —**tor′tur•ous,** *adj.*

To′ry, *n., pl.* **-ries. 1.** (*also l.c.*) conservative. **2.** American supporter of Great Britain during Revolutionary period. —**To′ry•ism,** *n.*

toss, *v.* **1.** throw or pitch. **2.** pitch about. **3.** throw upward. —*n.* **4.** throw or pitch.

toss′up′, *n.* **1.** tossing of coin to decide something by its fall. **2.** *Informal.* even chance.

tot, *n.* small child.

to′tal, *adj., n., v.,* **-taled, -taling.** —*adj.* **1.** entire. **2.** utter; outright. —*n.* **3.** total amount. —*v.* **4.** add up. —**to•tal′i•ty,** *n.* —**to′tal•ly,** *adv.*

to•tal′i•tar′i•an, *adj.* of centralized government under sole control of one party. —**to•tal′i•tar′i•an•ism,** *n.*

tote, *v.,* **toted, toting,** *n. Informal.* —*v.* **1.** carry or bear, as burden. —*n.* **2.** act or course of toting. **3.** that which is toted. **4.** tote bag.

tote bag, open handbag.

to′tem, *n.* object in nature assumed as emblem of clan, family, or related group. —**to•tem′ic,** *adj.*

totem pole, pole with totemic figures, erected by Indians of northwest coast of North America.

tot′ter, *v.* **1.** falter. **2.** sway as if about to fall.

tou′can (to͞o′kan), *n.* large-beaked tropical American bird.

touch, *v.* **1.** put hand, finger, etc., in contact with something. **2.** come or be in contact. **3.** reach. **4.** affect with sympathy. **5.** refer to. —*n.* **6.** act or instance of touching. **7.** perception of things through contact. **8.** contact. —**touch′a•ble,** *adj.* —**touch′ing,** *adj.*

touch′ and go′, precarious condition.

touch′down′, *n. Football.* act of player in touching ball down to ground behind opponent's goal line.

tou•ché′ (to͞o shā′), *interj.* (used to acknowledge telling remark or rejoinder).

touched, *adj.* **1.** moved; stirred. **2.** slightly crazy; unbalanced.

touch'-me-not', *n.* yellow-flowered plant whose ripe seed vessels burst open when touched.

touch'stone', *n.* **1.** stone used to test purity of gold and silver by color produced when it is rubbed with them. **2.** any criterion.

touch'y, *adj.,* **touchier, touchiest. 1.** irritable. **2.** requiring tact. —**touch'i•ness,** *n.*

tough, *adj.* **1.** not easily broken. **2.** difficult to chew. **3.** sturdy. **4.** pugnacious. **5.** trying. —*n.* **6.** ruffian. —**tough'en,** *v.* —**tough'ly,** *adv.* —**tough'ness,** *n.*

tou•pee' (too pā', -pē'), *n.* wig or patch of false hair worn to cover bald spot.

tour, *v.* **1.** travel or travel through, esp. for pleasure. —*n.* **2.** trip. **3.** period of duty. —**tour'ist,** *n.* —**tour'ism,** *n.*

tour' de force', *n., pl.* **tours de force.** exceptional achievement.

tour'ma•line' (-lin), *n.* mineral occurring in various gems.

tour'na•ment, *n.* **1.** meeting for contests. **2.** contest between mounted knights. **3.** competition involving number of rounds. Also, **tour'ney.**

tour'ni•quet (tûr'nə kit), *n.* bandlike device for arresting bleeding by compressing blood vessels.

tou'sle, *v.,* **-sled, -sling.** dishevel.

tout, *Informal. v.* **1.** solicit (business, votes, etc.) importunately. **2.** proclaim; advertise. **3.** give tip on (race horse, etc.). —*n.* **4.** person who touts. —**tout'er,** *n.*

tow, *v.* **1.** drag by rope or chain. —*n.* **2.** act of towing. **3.** thing towed.

to•ward', *prep.* Also, **to•wards'. 1.** in direction of. **2.** with respect to. **3.** nearly.

tow'boat', *n.* boat for pushing barges.

tow'el, *n.* cloth or paper for wiping.

tow'el•ing, *n.* fabric of cotton or linen used for towels.

tow'er, *n.* **1.** tall structure. —*v.* **2.** rise high.

tow'er•ing, *adj.* **1.** very high or great. **2.** violent; furious.

tow'head' (tō'hed'), *n.* **1.** head of light-colored hair. **2.** person with such hair. —**tow'-head'ed,** *adj.*

tow'line' (tō'līn'), *n.* cable for towing.

town, *n.* **1.** small city. **2.** center of city. —**towns'man,** *n.* —**towns'wom'an,** *n.fem.* —**towns'peo'ple, towns'folk',** *n.pl.*

town house, one of group of similar houses joined by common side walls.

town meeting, meeting of voters of town.

town'ship, *n.* **1.** division of county. **2.** (in U.S. surveys) district 6 miles square.

tow'path', *n.* path along bank of canal or river.

tox•e'mi•a, *n.* blood poisoning resulting from presence of toxins in blood. —**tox•e'mic,** *adj.*

tox'ic, *adj.* **1.** of toxin. **2.** poisonous. —**tox•ic'i•ty,** *n.*

tox'i•col'o•gy, *n.* science of poisons. —**tox'i•col'o•gist,** *n.*

toxic shock syndrome, rapidly developing toxemia.

tox'in, *n.* poisonous product of microorganism, plant, or animal.

toy, *n.* **1.** plaything. —*v.* **2.** play.

trace, *n., v.,* **traced, tracing.** —*n.* **1.** mark or track left by something. **2.** small amount. **3.** pulling part of harness. —*v.* **4.** follow trace of. **5.** find out. **6.** draw. —**trace'a•ble,** *adj.* —**trac'er,** *n.*

trac'er•y, *n., pl.* **-eries.** ornamental pattern of interlacing lines, etc.

tra'che•a (trā'kē ə), *n., pl.* **-cheae** (-kē ē'). air-conveying tube from larynx to bronchi.

tra'che•ot'o•my, *n., pl.* **-mies.** operation of cutting into trachea, usu. to relieve difficulty in breathing.

track, *n.* **1.** parallel rails for railroad. **2.** wheel rut. **3.** footprint or other mark left. **4.** path. **5.** course. —*v.* **6.** follow; pursue.

track'ball', *n.* computer input device for controlling pointer on screen by rotating ball set inside case.

track record, record of achievements or performance.

tract, *n.* 1. region. 2. brief treatise.

trac′ta•ble, *adj.* easily managed. —**trac′ta•bil′i•ty,** *n.* —**trac′ta•bly,** *adv.*

trac′tion, *n.* 1. act or instance of pulling. 2. adhesive friction.

trac′tor, *n.* self-propelled vehicle for pulling farm machinery, etc.

trade, *n., v.,* **traded, trading.** —*n.* 1. buying, selling, or exchange of commodities; commerce. 2. exchange. 3. occupation. —*v.* 4. buy and sell. 5. exchange. —**trad′er,** *n.* —**trades′man,** *n.*

trade′-in′, *n.* goods given in whole or part payment for purchase.

trade′mark′, *n.* name, symbol, etc., identifying brand or source of things for sale.

trade name, word or phrase whereby particular class of goods is designated.

trade′-off′, *n.* exchange of one thing for another.

trade union, labor union.

trade wind, sea wind blowing toward equator from latitudes up to 30° away.

tra•di′tion, *n.* 1. handing down of beliefs, customs, etc., through generations. 2. something so handed down. —**tra•di′tion•al,** *adj.* —**tra•di′tion•al•ly,** *adv.* —**tra•di′tion•al•ist,** *n., adj.* —**tra•di′tion•al•ism,** *n.*

tra•duce′, *v.,* -duced, -ducing. slander.

traf′fic, *n., v.,* -ficked, -ficking. —*n.* 1. traveling persons and things. 2. trade. —*v.* 3. trade. —**traf′fick•er,** *n.*

traffic circle, circular roadway at multiple intersection.

traffic light, set of signal lights at intersection.

tra•ge′di•an, *n.* actor or writer of tragedy. —**tra•ge′di•enne′,** *n.fem.*

trag′e•dy, *n., pl.* -dies. 1. serious drama with unhappy ending. 2. sad event. —**trag′ic, trag′i•cal,** *adj.* —**trag′i•cal•ly,** *adv.*

trail, *v.* 1. draw or drag. 2. be drawn or dragged. 3. track.

—*n.* 4. path. 5. track, scent, etc., left.

trail′blaz′er, *n.* pioneer.

trail′er, *n.* 1. van attached to truck for hauling freight, etc. 2. vehicle attached to car or truck with accommodations for living, working, etc.

train, *n.* 1. railroad locomotive with cars. 2. moving line of persons, vehicles, etc. 3. series of events, ideas, etc. 4. trailing part. 5. retinue. —*v.* 6. instruct or undergo instruction. 7. make fit. 8. aim; direct. —**train′a•ble,** *adj.* —**train•ee′,** *n.* —**train′er,** *n.*

train′man, *n., pl.* **-men.** member of crew of railroad train.

traipse, *v.,* **traipsed, traipsing.** *Informal.* walk aimlessly.

trait, *n.* characteristic.

trai′tor, *n.* 1. betrayer of trust. 2. person guilty of treason. —**trai′tor•ous,** *adj.*

tra•jec′to•ry, *n, pl.* **-ries.** curve described by projectile in flight.

tram, *n. Brit.* streetcar or trolley car.

tram′mel, *n., v.* **-meled, -meling.** —*n.* 1. impediment to action. —*v.* 2. hamper.

tramp, *v.* 1. tread or walk firmly. 2. march. —*n.* 3. firm, heavy tread. 4. hike. 5. vagabond.

tram′ple, *v.,* **-pled, -pling.** step roughly on.

tram′po•line′ (-lēn′), *n.* cloth springboard for tumblers.

trance, *n.* half-conscious or hypnotic state.

tran′quil, *adj.* peaceful; quiet. —**tran′quil•ly,** *adv.* —**tran•quil′li•ty,** *n.* —**tran′quil•ize′,** *v.*

tran′quil•iz′er, *n.* drug to reduce tension.

trans-, prefix meaning across; through; on the other side; changing thoroughly; beyond or surpassing.

trans•act′, *v.* carry on business. —**trans•ac′tion,** *n.* —**trans•ac′tor,** *n.*

trans′at•lan′tic, *adj.* 1. passing across Atlantic. 2. on other side of Atlantic.

trans•ceiv′er, *n.* radio transmitter and receiver combined in one.

tran·scend′ (-send′), *v.* **1.** go or be beyond. **2.** excel.

tran·scend′ent, *adj.* **1.** extraordinary. **2.** superior; supreme.

tran′scen·den′tal, *adj.* beyond ordinary human experience. —**tran′scen·den′tal·ly,** *adv.*

trans′con·ti·nen′tal, *adj.* across a continent.

tran·scribe′, *v.,* **-scribed, -scribing. 1.** copy. **2.** make recording of. —**tran·scrip′tion, tran′script,** *n.* —**tran·scrib′er,** *n.*

trans·duc′er, *n.* device that converts signal from one form of energy to another.

tran′sept, *n.* transverse portion of cross-shaped church.

trans·fer′, *v.,* **-ferred, -ferring,** *n.* —*v.* (trans fûr′). **1.** convey, hand over, or transport. **2.** be transferred. —*n.* (trans′fər). **3.** means or act of transferring. —**trans·fer′a·ble,** *adj.* —**trans·fer′al,** *n.* —**trans·fer′ence,** *n.*

trans·fig′ure, *v.,* **-ured, -uring. 1.** transform. **2.** glorify. —**trans′fig·u·ra′tion,** *n.*

trans·fix′, *v.* **1.** pierce. **2.** paralyze with terror, etc.

trans·form′, *v.* change in form, nature, etc. —**trans′for·ma′tion,** *n.*

trans·form′er, *n.* device for converting electrical currents.

trans·fuse′, *v.,* **-fused, -fusing. 1.** transmit, as by pouring. **2.** transfer blood from one person to another. —**trans·fu′sion,** *n.*

trans·gress′, *v.* **1.** go beyond limit. **2.** violate law, etc. —**trans·gres′sion,** *n.* —**trans·gres′sor,** *n.*

tran′sient, *adj.* **1.** transitory. —*n.* **2.** transient person. —**tran′sient·ly,** *adv.*

tran·sis′tor, *n.* small electronic device replacing vacuum tube.

trans′it, *n.* passage or conveyance.

tran·si′tion, *n.* passage from one condition, etc., to another. —**tran·si′tion·al,** *adj.* —**tran·si′tion·al·ly,** *adv.*

tran′si·tive, *adj.* (of verb) regularly accompanied by direct object. —**tran′si·tive·ly,** *adv.*

tran′si•to′ry, *adj.* 1. not enduring. 2. brief. —**tran′si•to′ri•ness,** *n.*

trans•late′, *v.,* -lated, -lating. change from one language into another. —**trans•la′tion,** *n.* —**trans•lat′a•ble,** *adj.* —**trans•lat′or,** *n.*

trans•lit′er•ate′, *v.,* -ated, -ating. change into corresponding characters of another alphabet or language. —**trans′lit•er•a′tion,** *n.*

trans•lu′cent (-lōō′sənt), *adj.* transmitting light diffusely. —**trans•lu′cence, trans•lu′cen•cy,** *n.*

trans′mi•gra′tion, *n.* passage of soul into another body.

trans•mis′sion, *n.* 1. act or process of transmitting. 2. something transmitted. 3. set of gears to transfer force between mechanisms, as in automobile. 4. broadcast.

trans•mit′, *v.,* -mitted, -mitting. 1. send over or along. 2. communicate. 3. hand down. 4. cause or permit light, heat, etc., to pass through. 5. emit radio waves. —**trans•mis′si•ble,**

trans•mit′ta•ble, *adj.* —**trans•mit′tal,** *n.* —**trans•mit′ter,** *n.*

trans•mog′ri•fy, *v.,* -fied, -fying. change in appearance or form; transform. —**trans•mog′ri•fi•ca′tion,** *n.*

trans•mute′, *v.,* -muted, -muting. change from one nature or form to another. —**trans•mut′a•ble,** *adj.* —**trans•mu•ta′tion,** *n.*

trans•na′tion•al, *adj.* going beyond national boundaries or interests.

trans′o•ce•an′ic, *adj.* across or beyond ocean.

tran′som, *n.* 1. window above door. 2. crosspiece separating door from window, etc.

tran•son′ic, *adj.* close to speed of sound; moving 700–780 miles per hour.

trans′pa•cif′ic, *adj.* 1. passing across Pacific. 2. on other side of Pacific.

trans•par′ent, *adj.* 1. allowing objects to be seen clearly through it. 2. frank. 3. obvious. —**trans•par′en•cy,** *n.* —**trans•par′ent•ly,** *adv.*

tran·spire′, *v.,* **-spired, -spiring. 1.** occur. **2.** give off waste matter, etc., from surface.

trans·plant′, *v.* **1.** remove and put or plant in another place. —*n.* **2.** (trans′plant′). act of transplanting. **3.** something transplanted. —**trans′plan·ta′tion**, *n.*

trans·port′, *v.* **1.** convey from one place to another. **2.** enrapture. —*n.* (trans′pōrt). **3.** something that transports. —**trans′por·ta′tion**, *n.* —**trans·port′er**, *n.*

trans·pose′, *v.,* **-posed, -posing.** alter relative position, order, musical key, etc. —**trans′po·si′tion**, *n.*

trans·sex′u·al, *n.* **1.** person with sex surgically altered. **2.** person feeling identity with opposite sex.

trans·ship′, *v.,* **-shipped, -shipping.** transfer from one conveyance to another. —**trans·ship′ment**, *n.*

trans′sub·stan′ti·a′tion, *n.* (in the Eucharist) conversion of whole substance of bread and wine into body and blood of Christ.

trans·verse′, *adj.* **1.** lying across. —*n.* **2.** something transverse. —**trans·verse′ly**, *adv.*

trans·ves′tite, *n.* person who dresses like opposite sex.

trap, *n., v.,* **trapped, trapping. —*n.* 1.** device for catching animals. **2.** scheme for catching a person unawares. **3.** ∪-shaped section in pipe to prevent escape of air or gases. —*v.* **4.** catch in or set traps. —**trap′per**, *n.*

tra·peze′, *n.* suspended bar used in gymnastics.

trap′e·zoid′, *n.* four-sided figure with two parallel sides.

trap′pings, *n.pl.* equipment or dress.

trap′shoot·ing, *n.* sport of shooting at clay pigeons hurled from trap.

trash, *n.* rubbish. —**trash′y**, *adj.*

trau′ma (trou′-), *n., pl.* **-mata, -mas. 1.** externally produced injury. **2.** experience causing permanent psychological harm. —**trau·mat′ic**, *adj.*

tra·vail′ (trə vāl′), *n.* **1.** toil. **2.** labor pains.

trav′el, *v.,* **-eled, -eling,** *n.* —*v.* **1.** journey. **2.** move. —*n.* **3.** journeying. —**trav′el•er,** *n.*

trav′e•logue′ (trav′ə lôg′, -log′), *n.* lecture describing travel, usually illustrated. Also, **trav′e•log′.**

trav′erse, *v.,* **-ersed, -ersing,** *n.* —*v.* **1.** pass over or through. —*n.* **2.** act of traversing.

trav′es•ty, *n., pl.* **-ties,** *v.,* **-tied, -tying.** —*n.* **1.** literary burlesque. **2.** debased likeness. —*v.* **3.** make travesty on.

trawl, *n.* **1.** fishing net dragged on bottom of water. —*v.* **2.** fish with trawl. —**trawl′er,** *n.*

tray, *n.* flat, shallow receptacle or container.

treach′er•y, *n., pl.* **-eries.** betrayal; treason. —**treach′er•ous,** *adj.* —**treach′er•ous•ly,** *adv.* —**treach′er•ous•ness,** *n.*

tread, *v.,* **trod, trodden** or **trod, treading,** *n.* —*v.* **1.** step, walk, or trample. **2.** crush. —*n.* **3.** manner of walking. **4.** surface meeting road or rail. **5.** horizontal surface of step. —**tread′er,** *n.*

trea′dle, *n.* lever, etc., worked by foot to drive machine.

tread′mill′, *n.* apparatus worked by treading on moving steps, as for exercise.

trea′son, *n.* violation of allegiance to sovereign or state. —**trea′son•a•ble, trea′son•ous,** *adj.*

treas′ure, *n., v.,* **-ured, -uring.** —*n.* **1.** accumulated wealth. **2.** thing greatly valued. —*v.* **3.** prize. **4.** put away for future use.

treas′ure-trove′, *n.* **1.** anything valuable that one finds. **2.** treasure of unknown ownership, found hidden.

treas′ur•y, *n., pl.* **-uries. 1.** place for keeping public or private funds. **2.** the funds. **3.** (*cap.*) government department that handles funds. —**treas′ur•er,** *n.*

treat, *v.* **1.** behave toward. **2.** deal with. **3.** relieve or cure. **4.** discuss. **5.** entertain. —*n.* **6.** entertainment. —**treat′ment,** *n.* —**treat′a•ble,** *adj.*

trea′tise, *n.* writing on particular subject.

trea′ty, *n., pl.* **-ties.** formal agreement between states.

tre′ble, *adj., n., v.,* **-bled, -bling.** —*adj.* 1. triple. 2. of highest pitch or range. 3. shrill. —*n.* 4. treble part, singer, instrument, etc. —*v.* 5. triple. —**tre′bly,** *adv.*

tree, *n., v.,* **treed, treeing.** —*n.* 1. plant with permanent, woody, usually branched trunk. —*v.* 2. drive up tree.

tre′foil, *n.* 1. herb with leaf divided in three parts. 2. ornament based on this leaf.

trek, *v.,* **trekked, trekking,** *n.* journey.

trel′lis, *n.* lattice.

trem′a•tode′, *n.* parasitic flatworm.

trem′ble, *v.,* **-bled, -bling,** *n.* —*v.* 1. quiver. —*n.* 2. act or state of trembling.

tre•men′dous, *adj.* extraordinarily great. —**tre•men′dous•ly,** *adv.*

trem′o•lo, *n., pl.* **-los.** vibrating effect on instrument or in voice.

trem′or, *n.* 1. involuntary shaking. 2. vibration.

trem′u•lous, *adj.* 1. trembling. 2. fearful. —**trem′u•lous•ly,** *adv.*

trench, *n.* ditch or cut.

trench′ant, *adj.* 1. incisive. 2. vigorous. —**trench′ant•ly,** *adv.*

trench coat, belted raincoat with epaulets.

trench′er, *n.* flat piece of wood on which meat is served or carved.

trench′er•man, *n., pl.* **-men.** person with hearty appetite.

trench foot, disease of feet due to prolonged exposure to cold and moisture.

trench mouth, acute ulcerating infection of gums and teeth.

trend, *n.* 1. tendency. 2. increasingly popular fashion.

trend′y, *adj.,* **trendier, trendiest.** *Informal.* following current fads. —**trend′i•ly,** *adv.* —**trend′i•ness,** *n.*

trep′i•da′tion, *n.* tremulous alarm.

tres′pass, *v.* 1. enter property illicitly. 2. sin. —*n.* 3. act of trespassing. —**tres′pass•er,** *n.*

tress, *n.* braid of hair.

tres′tle, *n.* supporting frame or framework.

trey, *n.* *Cards* or *Dice.* three.

tri-, prefix meaning three.

tri′ad, *n.* group of three.

tri•age′ (trē âzh′), *n.* sorting victims to determine priority of medical treatment.

tri′al, *n.* **1.** examination before judicial tribunal. **2.** test. **3.** attempt. **4.** state of being tested. **5.** source of suffering.

tri′an′gle, *n.* figure of three straight sides and three angles. —**tri•an′gu•lar**, *adj.*

tri•an′gu•late, *v.,* **-lated, -lating. 1.** survey by using trigonometric principles. **2.** divide into triangles. —**tri•an′gu•la′tion**, *n.*

Tri•as′sic, *adj.* pertaining to period of Mesozoic Era.

tribe, *n.* people united by common descent, etc. —**trib′al**, *adj.*

tribes′man, *n., pl.* **-men.** man belonging to tribe. —**tribes′wom′an**, *n.fem.*

trib′u•la′tion, *n.* **1.** trouble. **2.** affliction.

tri•bu′nal, *n.* **1.** court of justice. **2.** place of judgment.

trib′une, *n.* **1.** person who defends rights of the people. **2.** rostrum.

trib′u•tar′y, *n., pl.* **-taries,** *adj.* —*n.* **1.** stream flowing into larger body of water. **2.** payer of tribute. —*adj.* **3.** flowing as tributary.

trib′ute, *n.* **1.** personal offering, etc. **2.** sum paid for peace, etc.

trice, *n.* instant.

tri′cen•ten′ni•al, *n.* tercentennial.

tri′ceps (trī′seps), *n.* muscle at back of upper arm.

trich′i•no′sis (trik′ə-), *n.* disease due to parasitic worm.

trick, *n.* **1.** artifice or stratagem. **2.** prank. **3.** knack. **4.** cards won in one round. —*v.* **5.** deceive or cheat by tricks. —**trick′er•y**, *n.* —**trick′ster**, *n.* —**trick′y**, *adj.*

trick′le, *v.,* **-led, -ling,** *n.* —*v.* **1.** flow in small amounts. —*n.* **2.** trickling flow.

tri′col′or, *adj.* **1.** of three colors. —*n.* **2.** three-colored flag, esp. of France.

tri•cus′pid, *adj.* having three cusps or points, as tooth.

tri′cy•cle, *n.* child's vehicle with large front wheel and two smaller rear wheels.

tri′dent, *n.* three-pronged spear.

tried, *adj.* tested; proved.

tri•en′ni•al (trī-), *adj.* **1.** lasting three years. **2.** occurring every three years. —*n.* **3.** period of three years. **4.** third anniversary.

tri′fle, *n., v.,* **-fled, -fling.** —*n.* **1.** article of small value. **2.** trivial matter or amount. —*v.* **3.** deal without due respect. **4.** act idly or frivolously. —**tri′fler,** *n.* —**tri′fling,** *adj.*

tri•fo′li•ate (trī-), *adj.* having three leaves or leaflike parts.

trig′ger, *n.* **1.** projecting tongue pressed to fire gun. **2.** device to release spring. —*v.* **3.** precipitate.

tri•glyc′er•ide′, *n.* ester forming much of fats and oils stored in tissues.

tri•go•nom′e•try, *n.* mathematical study of relations between sides and angles of triangles. —**trig′o•no•met′ric,** *adj.*

trill, *v.* **1.** sing or play with vibratory effect. —*n.* **2.** act or sound of trilling.

tril′lion, *n., adj.* 1 followed by 12 zeroes.

tril′li•um, *n.* plant of lily family.

tril′o•gy, *n., pl.* **-gies.** group of three plays, operas, etc., on related theme.

trim, *v.,* **trimmed, trimming,** *n., adj.,* **trimmer, trimmest.** —*v.* **1.** make neat by clipping, paring, etc. **2.** adjust (sails or yards). **3.** dress or ornament. —*n.* **4.** proper condition. **5.** adjustment of sails, etc. **6.** dress or equipment. **7.** trimming. —*adj.* **8.** neat. **9.** in good condition. —**trim′ly,** *adv.* —**trim′mer,** *n.* —**trim′ness,** *n.*

tri′ma•ran′, *n.* boat with three hulls.

tri•mes′ter, *n.* **1.** period of three months. **2.** one of three divisions of academic year.

trim′ming, *n.* something used to trim.

tri•ni′tro•tol′u•ene′, *n.* high explosive, known as TNT.

Trin′i•ty, *n.* unity of Father, Son, and Holy Ghost.

trin′ket, *n.* **1.** bit of jewelry, etc. **2.** trifle.

tri′o, *n., pl.* **trios.** group of three.

trip, *n., v.,* **tripped, tripping.** —*n.* **1.** journey. **2.** stumble. **3.** *Slang.* drug-induced event. *v.* **4.** stumble or cause to stumble. **5.** slip. **6.** tread quickly. —**trip′per,** *n.*

tri•par′tite (trī-), *adj.* **1.** divided into or consisting of three parts. **2.** participated in by three parties.

tripe, *n.* **1.** ruminant's stomach, used as food. **2.** *Slang.* worthless statements or writing.

tri′ple, *adj., n., v.,* **-pled, -pling.** —*adj.* **1.** of three parts. **2.** three times as great. —*n.* **3.** *Baseball.* hit allowing batter to reach third base. —*v.* **4.** make or become triple. —**tri′ply,** *adv.*

tri′plet, *n.* one of three children (**triplets**) born at a single birth.

trip′li•cate (-kit), *adj.* **1.** triple. —*n.* **2.** set of three copies.

tri′pod, *n.* three-legged stool, support, etc.

trip′tych (trip′tik), *n.* set of three panels side by side, with pictures or carvings.

trite, *adj.,* **triter, tritest.** commonplace; hackneyed. —**trite′ly,** *adv.* —**trite′ness,** *n.*

trit′u•rate′, *v.,* **-rated, -rating,** *n.* —*v.* **1.** to reduce to fine particles or powder; pulverize. —*n.* **2.** triturated substance. —**trit′u•ra′tion,** *n.*

tri′umph, *n.* **1.** victory. **2.** joy over victory. —*v.* **3.** be victorious or successful. **4.** rejoice over this. —**tri•um′phal,** *adj.* —**tri•um′phant,** *adj.*

tri•um′vir (trī um′vər), *n., pl.* **-virs, -viri** (-və rī′). *Rom. Hist.* any of three magistrates exercising same public function. —**tri•um′vi•ral,** *adj.*

tri•um′vi•rate (trī um′və rit), *n.* **1.** *Rom. Hist.* the office of triumvir. **2.** government of three joint magistrates. **3.** association of three, as in office.

triv′et, *n.* device protecting table top from hot objects.

triv′i•a, *n.* things that are very unimportant.

triv′i•al, *adj.* trifling. —**triv′i•al′i•ty,** *n.* —**triv′i•al•ly,** *adv.*

tro′che (-kē), *n.* small tablet of medicinal substance.

tro′chee (-kē), *n.* verse foot of two syllables, long followed by short. —**tro•cha′ic,** *adj.*

trog′lo•dyte′ (trog′lə dīt′), *n.* 1. cave dweller. 2. person living in seclusion. 3. person unacquainted with affairs of the world.

troi′ka, *n.* 1. Russian vehicle drawn by three horses. 2. ruling group of three.

troll, *v.* 1. sing in rolling voice. 2. sing as round. 3. fish with moving line. —*n.* 4. *Music.* round. 5. underground monster.

trol′ley, *n.* 1. trolley car. 2. pulley on overhead track or wire.

trolley bus, bus drawing power from overhead wires.

trolley car, electric streetcar receiving current from a trolley.

trol′lop (trol′əp), *n.* 1. untidy or slovenly woman; slattern. 2. prostitute.

trom•bone′, *n.* brass wind instrument with long bent tube. —**trom•bon′ist,** *n.*

troop, *n.* 1. assemblage. 2. cavalry unit. 3. body of police, etc. —*v.* 4. gather or move in numbers. 5. walk, as if in a march. —**troop′er,** *n.*

troop′ship′, *n.* ship for conveyance of military troops; transport.

trope, *n.* figure of speech.

tro′phy, *n., pl.* **-phies.** 1. memento taken in hunting, war, etc. 2. silver cup, etc., given as prize.

trop′ic, *n.* 1. either of two latitudes (**tropic of Cancer** and **tropic of Capricorn**) bounding torrid zone. 2. (*pl.*) region between these latitudes. —**trop′i•cal,** *adj.* —**trop′i•cal•ly,** *adv.*

tro′pism, *n.* response of plant or animal, as in growth, to influence of external stimuli. —**tro•pis′tic,** *adj.*

trop′o•sphere′, *n.* lowest layer of atmosphere.

trot, *v.,* **trotted, trotting,** *n.* —*v.* 1. go at gait between walk and run. 2. go briskly. 3. ride at trot. —*n.* 4. trotting gait. —**trot′ter,** *n.*

troth (trôth), *n.* 1. fidelity. 2. promise.

trou′ba•dour′ (trōō′bə dōr′), *n.* medieval lyric poet of W Mediterranean area who wrote on love and gallantry.

trou′ble, *v.,* -bled, -bling, *n.* —*v.* 1. distress. 2. put to or cause inconvenience. 3. bother. —*n.* 4. annoyance or difficulty. 5. disturbance. 6. inconvenience. —**trou′bler,** *n.* —**trou′ble•some,** *adj.*

trou′bled, *adj.* 1. emotionally or mentally distressed. 2. economically or socially distressed.

trou′ble•mak′er, *n.* person who causes trouble.

troub′le•shoot′er, *n.* expert in eliminating causes of trouble.

trough (trôf), *n.* 1. open boxlike container. 2. long hollow or channel.

trounce, *v.,* **trounced, trouncing.** beat severely.

troupe (trōōp), *n.* company of performers. —**troup′er,** *n.*

trou′sers, *n.pl.* outer garment divided into two separate leg coverings.

trous′seau (trōō′sō), *n., pl.* -seaux, -seaus (-sōz), bride's outfit.

trout, *n.* fresh-water game fish.

trow′el, *n.* 1. tool for spreading or smoothing. 2. small digging tool.

troy, *adj.* expressed in troy weight.

troy weight, system of weights for precious metals and gems.

tru′ant, *n.* 1. student absent from school without leave. —*adj.* 2. absent from school without leave. —**tru′an•cy,** *n.*

truce, *n.* suspension of military hostilities.

truck, *n.* 1. hand or motor vehicle for carrying heavy loads. 2. vegetables raised for market. 3. miscellaneous articles. —*v.* 4. transport by or drive a truck. 5. trade. —**truck′er,** *n.*

truck farm, farm on which vegetables are grown for market.

truck′le, *v.,* -led, -ling. submit humbly.

truckle bed, trundle bed.

truc′u•lent, *adj.* fierce. —**truc′u•lence,** *n.* —**truc′u•lent•ly,** *adv.*

trudge, *v.,* **trudged, trudging,** *n.* —*v.* 1. walk, esp. wearily. —*n.* 2. tiring walk.—**trudg′er,** *n.*

true, *adj.,* **truer, truest. 1.** conforming to fact. **2.** real. **3.** sincere. **4.** loyal. **5.** correct. —**tru′ly,** *adv.* —**true′ness,** *n.*

true′-blue′, *adj.* staunch; true.

truf′fle, *n.* **1.** edible fungus. **2.** chocolate confection resembling truffle.

tru′ism, *n.* obvious truth.

trump, *n.* **1.** playing card of suit outranking other suits. **2.** the suit. —*v.* **3.** take with or play trump. **4.** fabricate.

trump′er•y, *n., pl.* **-eries. 1.** something without use or value. **2.** nonsense; twaddle.

trum′pet, *n.* **1.** brass wind instrument with powerful, penetrating tone. —*v.* **2.** blow trumpet. **3.** proclaim. —**trum′pet•er,** *n.*

trun′cate, *v.,* **-cated, -cating.** shorten by cutting. —**trun•ca′tion,** *n.*

trun′cheon, *n.* club.

trun′dle, *v.,* **-dled, -dling,** *n.* —*v.* **1.** roll, as on wheels. —*n.* **2.** small roller, wheel, etc.

trun′dle bed′, low bed on casters, usually pushed under another bed when not in use. Also, **truckle bed.**

trunk, *n.* **1.** main stem of tree. **2.** box for clothes, etc. **3.** body of person or animal, excepting head and limbs. **4.** main body of anything. **5.** elephant's long flexible nasal appendage.

trunk line, 1. major long-distance transportation line. **2.** telephone line between two switching devices.

truss, *v.* **1.** bind or fasten. **2.** furnish or support with a truss. —*n.* **3.** rigid supporting framework. **4.** apparatus for confining hernia. **5.** bundle.

trust, *n.* **1.** reliance on person's integrity, justice, etc. **2.** confident hope. **3.** credit. **4.** responsibility. **5.** care. **6.** something entrusted. **7.** holding of legal title for another's benefit. **8.** combination of companies, often monopolistic, controlled by central board. —*v.* **9.** place confidence in. **10.** rely on. **11.** hope. **12.** believe. **13.** give credit. —**trust′ful,** *adj.* —**trust′wor′thy,** *adj.*

trus•tee′, *n.* **1.** administrator of company, etc. **2.** holder of trust (def. 7).

trus•tee′ship, *n.* 1. office of trustee. 2. control of territory granted by United Nations. 3. the territory.

trust fund, money, etc., held in trust.

trust territory, territory which United Nations has placed under administrative control of a country.

trust′y, *adj.,* **trustier, trustiest,** *n., pl.* **trusties.** —*adj.* 1. reliable. —*n.* 2. trusted one. 3. trustworthy convict given special privileges. —**trust′i•ly,** *adv.* —**trust′i•ness,** *n.*

truth, *n.* 1. true facts. 2. conformity with fact. 3. established fact, principle, etc. —**truth′ful,** *adj.* —**truth′ful•ly,** *adv.* —**truth′ful•ness,** *n.*

try, *v.,* **tried, trying.** 1. attempt. 2. test. 3. examine judicially. 4. strain endurance, patience, etc., of.

try′ing, *adj.* annoying; irksome.

try′out′, *n. Informal.* trial or test to ascertain fitness for some purpose.

tryst (trist), *n.* 1. appointment, as of lovers, to meet. 2. the meeting. 3. place of meeting. —*v.* 4. meet.

tsar (zär), *n.* czar.

tset′se fly (tset′sē), African fly transmitting disease.

T′-shirt′, *n.* short-sleeved knitted undershirt. Also, **tee′-shirt′.**

tsp., teaspoon.

T square, T-shaped ruler used in mechanical drawing.

tsu•na′•mi (tsoo nä′mē), *n.* huge wave caused by undersea earthquake or volcano.

tub, *n.* 1. bathtub. 2. deep, open-topped container.

tu′ba, *n.* low-pitched brass wind instrument.

tub′by, *adj.,* **-bier, -biest.** short and fat.

tube, *n.* 1. hollow pipe for fluids, etc. 2. compressible container for toothpaste, etc. 3. railroad or vehicular tunnel. —**tu′bu•lar,** *adj.* —**tub′ing,** *n.*

tu′ber, *n.* fleshy thickening of underground stem or shoot. —**tu′ber•ous,** *adj.*

tu′ber•cle, *n.* small roundish projection, nodule, or swelling.

tu•ber′cu•lin, *n.* liquid prepared from tuberculosis bacillus, used in test for tuberculosis.

tu•ber′cu•lo′sis, *n.* infectious disease marked by formation of tubercles. —**tu•ber′cu•lar, tu•ber′cu•lous,** *adj.*

tube′rose′, *n.* cultivated flowering plant.

tu′bule, *n.* small tube.

tuck, *v.* **1.** thrust into narrow space or retainer. **2.** cover snugly. **3.** draw up in folds. —*n.* **4.** tucked piece or part.

tuck′er, *n.* **1.** piece of cloth formerly worn by women about neck and shoulders. —*v.* **2.** *Informal.* tire; exhaust.

Tues., Tuesday. Also, **Tue.**

Tues′day, *n.* third day of week.

tuft, *n.* **1.** bunch of feathers, hairs, etc., fixed at base. **2.** clump of bushes, etc., —*v.* **3.** arrange in or form tufts. —**tuft′ed,** *adj.*

tug, *v.,* **tugged, tugging,** *n.* —*v.* **1.** drag; haul. —*n.* **2.** act of tugging. **3.** tugboat.

tug′boat′, *n.* powerful vessel used for towing.

tug of war, 1. contest between teams pulling opposite ends of rope. **2.** struggle for supremacy.

tu•i′tion, *n.* charge for instruction.

tu′lip, *n.* plant bearing showy, cup-shaped flowers.

tulle (tool), *n.* thin silk or rayon net.

tum′ble, *v.,* **-bled, -bling,** *n.* —*v.* **1.** fall over or down. **2.** perform gymnastic feats. **3.** roll about; toss. —*n.* **4.** act of tumbling.

tum′ble-down′, *adj.* dilapidated; rundown.

tum′bler, *n.* **1.** drinking glass. **2.** performer of tumbling feats. **3.** lock part engaging bolt.

tum′ble•weed′, *n.* plant whose upper part becomes detached and is driven about by wind.

tum′brel, *n.* farmer's cart that can be tilted to discharge its load. Also, **tum′bril.**

tu′mid, *adj.* **1.** swollen. **2.** turgid; bombastic. —**tu•mid′i•ty,** *n.* —**tu•mes′cent,** *adj.*

tum′my, *n., pl.* **-mies.** *Informal.* stomach or abdomen.

tu′mor, *n.* abnormal swelling of cells in part of body. —**tu′mor•ous,** *adj.*

tu′mult, *n.* disturbance, commotion, or uproar. —**tu•mul′tu•ous,** *adj.*

tun, *n.* large cask.

tu′na, *n.* 1. large oceanic fish. 2. tunny. Also, **tuna fish.**

tun′dra, *n.* vast, treeless, arctic plain.

tune, *n., v.,* **tuned, tuning.** —*n.* 1. melody. 2. state of proper pitch, frequency, or condition. 3. harmony. —*v.* 4. adjust to correct pitch. 5. adjust to receive radio or television signals. —**tune′ful,** *adj.* —**tun′a•ble, tune′a•ble,** *adj.* —**tune′less,** *adj.* —**tun′er,** *n.*

tune′-up′, *n.* adjustment, as of motor, to improve working condition.

tung′sten, *n.* metallic element used for electric-lamp filaments, etc.

tu′nic, *n.* 1. coat of uniform. 2. ancient Greek and Roman garment. 3. woman's upper garment.

tun′ing fork, steel instrument struck to produce pure tone of constant pitch.

tun′nel, *n., v.,* **-neled, -neling.** —*n.* 1. underground passage. —*v.* 2. make tunnel.

tun′ny, *n., pl.* **-ny, -nies.** large mackerellike fish.

tur′ban, *n.* head covering made of scarf wound round head.

tur′bid, *adj.* 1. muddy. 2. dense. 3. confused. —**tur•bid′i•ty,** *n.*

tur′bine, *n.* motor producing torque by pressure of fluid.

tur′bo•jet′, *n.* 1. jet engine that compresses air by turbine. 2. airplane with such engines.

tur′bo•prop′, *n.* 1. turbojet with turbine-driven propeller. 2. airplane with such engines.

tur′bot (-bət), *n.* flatfish.

tur′bu•lent, *adj.* 1. disorderly. 2. tumultuous. —**tur′bu•lence,** *n.* —**tur′bu•lent•ly,** *adv.*

tu•reen′ (tŏŏ rēn′), *n.* large covered dish for soup, etc.

turf, *n.* **1.** covering of grass and roots. **2.** familiar area, as of residence or expertise. —**turf'y,** *adj.*

tur'gid (tûr'jid), *adj.* **1.** swollen. **2.** pompous or bombastic. —**tur•gid'i•ty, tur'gid•ness,** *n.* —**tur'gid•ly,** *adv.*

tur'key, *n.* large, edible American bird.

turkey vulture, blackish brown New World vulture.

tur'mer•ic, *n.* aromatic powder prepared from Asian plant, used as condiment.

tur'moil, *n.* tumult.

turn, *v.* **1.** rotate. **2.** reverse. **3.** divert; deflect. **4.** depend. **5.** sour; ferment. **6.** nauseate. **7.** alter. **8.** become. **9.** use. **10.** pass. **11.** direct. **12.** curve. —*n.* **13.** rotation. **14.** change or point of change. **15.** one's due time or opportunity. **16.** trend. **17.** short walk, ride, etc. **18.** inclination or aptitude. **19.** service or disservice.

turn'a•bout', *n.* change of opinion, loyalty, etc.

turn'buck'le, *n.* link used to couple or tighten two parts.

turn'coat', *n.* renegade.

turning point, point at which decisive change takes place.

tur'nip, *n.* **1.** fleshy, edible root of cabbagelike plant. **2.** the plant.

turn'key, *n.* keeper of prison keys.

turn'off', *n.* small road that branches off from larger one.

turn'out', *n.* **1.** attendance at meeting, show, etc. **2.** output.

turn'o'ver, *n.* **1.** rate of replacement, investment, trade, etc. **2.** small pastry with filling.

turn'pike', *n.* **1.** barrier across road (**turnpike road**) where toll is paid. **2.** turnpike road.

turn'stile', *n.* horizontal crossed bars in gateway.

turn'ta'ble, *n.* rotating platform.

tur'pen•tine', *n.* **1.** type of resin from coniferous trees. **2.** oil yielded by this.

tur'pi•tude', *n.* depravity.

tur′quoise (-koiz), *n.* **1.** greenish-blue mineral used in jewelry. **2.** bluish green.

tur′ret, *n.* **1.** small tower. **2.** towerlike gun shelter.

tur′tle, *n.* marine reptile with shell-encased body.

tur′tle·dove′, *n.* small Old World dove.

tur′tle·neck′, *n.* **1.** high, close-fitting collar. **2.** garment with turtleneck.

tusk, *n.* very long tooth, as of elephant or walrus.

tus′sle, *v.,* **-sled, -sling.** fight; scuffle.

tus′sock, *n.* tuft of growing grass.

tu′te·lage, *n.* **1.** guardianship. **2.** instruction. —**tu′te·lar′y, tu′te·lar,** *adj.*

tu′tor, *n.* **1.** private instructor. **2.** college teacher (below instructor). —*v.* **3.** teach. —**tu·to′ri·al,** *adj.*

tut′ti-frut′ti (tōō′tē frōō′tē), *n.* confection, esp. ice cream, flavored with variety of fruits.

tu′tu′ (tōō′tōō′), *n.* short, full skirt worn by ballerina.

tux, *n. Informal.* tuxedo.

tux·e′do, *n., pl.* **-dos.** semiformal jacket or suit for men.

TV, television.

twad′dle, *n.* nonsense.

twain, *adj., n. Archaic.* two.

twang, *v.* **1.** sound sharply and ringingly. **2.** have nasal tone. —*n.* **3.** twanging sound.

tweak, *v.* **1.** seize and pull or twist. —*n.* **2.** sharp pull and twist.

tweed, *n.* coarse, colored wool cloth.

tweet, *n.* **1.** chirping sound. —*v.* **2.** chirp.

tweet′er, *n.* small loudspeaker reproducing high-frequency sounds.

tweez′ers, *n.pl.* small pincers.

twelve, *n., adj.* ten plus two. —**twelfth,** *adj., n.*

Twelve Step, of or based on program for recovery from addiction that provides 12 progressive levels toward attainment.

twen′ty, *n., adj.* ten times two. —**twen′ti·eth,** *adj., n.*

twerp, *n. Slang.* insignificant or despicable person.

twice, *adv.* **1.** two times. **2.** doubly.

twid'dle, *v.,* **-dled, -dling. 1.** turn round and round, esp. with the fingers. **2.** twirl (one's fingers) about each other.

twig, *n.* slender shoot on tree.

twi'light', *n.* light from sky when sun is down.

twill, *n.* **1.** fabric woven in parallel diagonal lines. **2.** the weave. —*v.* **3.** weave in twill.

twin, *n.* either of two children born at single birth.

twine, *n., v.,* **twined, twining.** —*n.* **1.** strong thread of twisted strands. **2.** twist. —*v.* **3.** twist or become twisted together. **4.** encircle.

twinge, *n., v.,* **twinged, twinging.** —*n.* **1.** sudden, sharp pain. —*v.* **2.** give or have twinge.

twin'kle, *v.,* **-kled, -kling,** *n.* —*v.* **1.** shine with light, quick gleams. —*n.* **2.** sly, humorous look. **3.** act of twinkling.

twin'kling, *n.* instant.

twirl, *v.* **1.** spin; whirl. —*n.* **2.** a twirling.

twist, *v.* **1.** combine by winding together. **2.** distort. **3.** combine in coil, etc. **4.** wind about. **5.** writhe. **6.** turn. —*n.* **7.** curve or turn. **8.** spin. **9.** wrench. **10.** spiral.

twist'er, *n.* **1.** person or thing that twists. **2.** *Informal.* whirlwind or tornado.

twit, *v.,* **twitted, twitting,** *n.* —*v.* **1.** taunt; tease. —*n.* **2.** *Informal.* insignificant or bothersome person.

twitch, *v.* **1.** jerk; move with jerk. —*n.* **2.** quick jerky movement, as of muscle.

twit'ter, *v.* **1.** utter small, tremulous sounds, as bird. **2.** tremble with excitement. —*n.* **3.** twittering sound. **4.** state of tremulous excitement.

two, *n., adj.* one plus one.

two'-bit', *adj. Informal.* inferior or unimportant.

two bits, *Informal.* 25 cents.

two'-faced', *adj.* deceitful or hypocritical.

two'-fist'ed, *adj.* strong and vigorous.

two'fold', *adj.* **1.** having two parts. **2.** twice as great. —*adv.* **3.** in two-fold measure.

two'-ply', *adj.* consisting of two layers, strands, etc.

two'some (-səm), *n.* pair.

two'-time', *v.*, **-timed, -timing.** *Informal.* be unfaithful to. —**two'-tim'er**, *n.*

two'-way', *adj.* **1.** allowing movement in two directions. **2.** involving two participants.

twp., township.

TX, Texas.

-ty, suffix meaning state or condition.

ty•coon', *n.* businessperson having great wealth and power.

tyke, *n.* small child.

tympanic membrane, membrane separating middle from external ear.

tym'pa•num (tim'pə nəm), *n.* **1.** middle ear. **2.** tympanic membrane. —**tym•pan'ic**, *adj.*

type, *n., v.,* **typed, typing.** —*n.* **1.** kind or class. **2.** representative specimen. **3.** piece bearing a letter in relief, used in printing. **4.** such pieces collectively. —*v.* **5.** typewrite. —**typ'ist**, *n.*

type'cast', *n.,* **-cast, -casting.** cast (actor) exclusively in same kind of role.

type'script', *n.* typewritten matter.

type'set'ter, *n.* **1.** person who sets type. **2.** machine for setting type. —**type'set'**, *v.*

type'writ'er, *n.* machine for writing mechanically. —**type'write'**, *v.*

ty'phoid, *n.* infectious disease marked by intestinal disorder. Also, **typhoid fever.**

ty•phoon', *n.* cyclone or hurricane of western Pacific.

ty'phus, *n.* infectious disease transmitted by lice and fleas.

typ'i•cal, *adj.* **1.** serving as a representative specimen. **2.** conforming to the characteristics of a particular group. —**typ'i•cal•ly**, *adv.*

typ'i•fy', *v.,* **-fied, -fying.** serve as typical example of.

ty'po (tī'pō), *n., pl.* **-pos.** error in typography or typing.

ty•pog'ra•phy, *n.* **1.** art or process of printing. **2.** general character of printed matter.

—**ty•pog′ra•pher,** *n.*
—**ty′po•graph′ic,**
ty′po•graph′i•cal, *adj.*

ty•ran′no•saur′, *n.* large
dinosaur that walked upright.

tyr′an•ny, *n., pl.* **-nies.** 1.
despotic abuse of authority. 2.
government or rule by tyrant.
—**ty•ran′ni•cal,** *adj.*
—**tyr′an•nize′,** *v.*

ty′rant, *n.* oppressive, unjust,
or absolute ruler.

ty′ro, *n., pl.* **-ros.** novice.

tzar, *n.* czar.

U, u, *n.* twenty-first letter of English alphabet.

u·biq′ui·tous, *adj.* simultaneously present everywhere. —**u·biq′ui·ty,** *n.*

U′-boat′, *n.* German submarine.

ud′der, *n.* mammary gland, esp. of cow.

UFO, unidentified flying object.

ug′ly, *adj.,* **-lier, -liest. 1.** repulsive. **2.** dangerous. —**ug′li·ness,** *n.*

u·kase (yōō kās′, -kāz′), *n.* order by absolute authority.

u′ku·le′le (yōō′kə lā′lē), *n.* small guitar.

ul′cer, *n.* open sore, as on stomach lining. —**ul′cer·ous,** *adj.* —**ul′cer·ate′,** *v.*

ul′na, *n.* larger bone of forearm. —**ul′nar,** *adj.*

ul·te′ri·or, *adj.* **1.** not acknowledged; concealed. **2.** later.

ul′ti·ma, *n.* last syllable of word.

ul′ti·mate, *adj.* **1.** final; highest. **2.** basic. —**ul′ti·mate·ly,** *adv.*

ul′ti·ma′tum (-mā′təm), *n., pl.* **-tums, -ta.** final demand.

U

ultra-, prefix meaning beyond; on the far side of; extremely.

ul′tra·con·serv′a·tive, *adj.* extremely conservative, esp. in politics.

ul′tra·fiche′, *n.* form of microfiche with images greatly reduced in size.

ultrahigh frequency, radio frequency between 300 and 3000 megahertz.

ul′tra·ma·rine′, *n.* deep blue.

ul′tra·sound′, *n.* **1.** sound above limit of human hearing. **2.** application of ultrasound to medical diagnosis and therapy. —**ul′tra·son′ic,** *adj.*

ul′tra·vi′o·let, *adj.* of invisible rays beyond violet in spectrum.

um′ber, *n.* **1.** reddish brown. —*adj.* **2.** of or like umber.

umbilical cord, cordlike structure connecting fetus with placenta, conveying nourishment and removing wastes.

um·bil′i·cus, *n., pl.* **-ci.** navel. —**um·bil′i·cal,** *adj.*

um′brage, *n.* resentment.

um•brel'la, *n.* cloth-covered framework carried for protection from rain, etc.

u'mi•ak ($\overline{oo}'$-), *n.* open Eskimo boat covered with skins.

um'laut, *n.* **1.** (in Germanic languages) assimilation in which vowel is influenced by following vowel. **2.** diacritical mark (··) used over vowel to indicate umlaut.

ump, *n., v.* umpire.

ump'teen, *adj. Informal.* innumerable. —**ump•teenth'**, *adj.*

um'pire, *n., v.,* **-pired, -piring.** —*n.* **1.** judge or arbitrator. —*v.* **2.** be umpire in.

UN, United Nations.

un-, prefix indicating negative or opposite sense, as in *unfair, unwanted,* and *unfasten.* See list below.

un•a'ble, *adj.* lacking necessary power, skill, or resources.

un'ac•count'a•ble, *adj.* **1.** inexplicable. **2.** not responsible. —**un'ac•count'a•bly,** *adv.*

un'af•fect'ed, *adj.* **1.** without affectation. **2.** not concerned or involved.

u•nan'i•mous, *adj.* completely agreed. —**u•nan'i•mous•ly,** *adv.* —**u'na•nim'i•ty,** *n.*

un'as•sum'ing, *adj.* modest; without vanity.

un•a'ble
un'ack•now'ledged
un'a•void'a•ble
un'a•ware'
un'be•liev'a•ble
un•born'
un•bound'ed
un•bur'den
un•but'ton
un•cer'tain
un•civ'il

un•clean'
un•cloak'
un•clothe'
un•com'fort•a•ble
un•com'mon
un•con'scious
un'con•trol'la•ble
un•cork'
un•cov'er
un'de•cid'ed
un'de•clared'

un′at•tached′, *adj.* 1. not attached. 2. not engaged or married.

un′a•vail′ing, *adj.* not effective; futile.

un′a•wares′, *adv.* not knowingly.

un•bal′anced, *adj.* 1. out of balance. 2. irrational; deranged.

un•bear′a•ble, *adj.* unendurable. —**un•bear′a•bly**, *adv.*

un′be•com′ing, *adj.* unattractive or unseemly.

un•bend, *v.,* -bent, -bending. 1. straighten. 2. act in genial, relaxed manner.

un•bend′ing, *adj.* rigidly formal or unyielding.

un•bid′den, *adj.* 1. not commanded. 2. not asked.

un•blush′ing, *adj.* showing no remorse; shameless.

un•bos′om, *v.* disclose (secrets, etc.).

un•bowed′ (-boud′), *adj.* 1. not bent. 2. not subjugated.

un•brid′led, *adj.* unrestrained.

un•bro′ken, *adj.* 1. not broken. 2. undisturbed. 3. not tamed.

un•bur′den, *v.* 1. free from burden. 2. relieve one's mind, conscience, etc., by confessing.

un•called′-for′, *adj.* not warranted.

un•can′ny, *adj.* unnaturally strange or good.

un′de•feat′ed
un′de•ni′a•ble
un•doubt′ed
un•dress′
un•due′
un•du′ly
un•e′qual
un•err′ing
un•e′ven
un′ex•pect′ed
un•fail′ing

un•fair′
un•faith′ful
un′fa•mil′iar
un•fas′ten
un•fit′
un•fold′
un′for•get′ta•ble
un′for•giv′a•ble
un•for′tu•nate
un•friend′ly
un•god′ly

un•cer′e•mo′ni•ous, *adj.* **1.** informal. **2.** rudely abrupt.

un•chart′ed, *adj.* not shown on map; unexplored.

un′ci•al (-shē-), *adj.* of a form of writing with a rounded shape, esp. in early Greek and Latin manuscripts.

un•clad′, *adj.* naked.

un′cle, *n.* brother of one's father or mother.

Uncle Sam, United States government.

un•com′pro•mis′ing, *adj.* refusing to compromise; rigid.

un′con•cern′, *n.* lack of concern; indifference.

un′con•di′tion•al, *adj.* absolute; without conditions or reservations.
—**un′con•di′tion•al•ly,** *adv.*

un•con′scion•a•ble (-shən-), *adj.* not reasonable or honest.

un•con′scious, *adj.* **1.** lacking awareness, sensation, or cognition. **2.** not perceived at level of awareness. **3.** done without intent. —*n.* **4. the unconscious,** part of psyche rarely accessible to awareness but influencing behavior.

un•couth′, *adj.* rude; boorish.

unc′tion, *n.* **1.** anointment with oil. **2.** soothing manner of speech.

unc′tu•ous (-choo əs), *adj.* **1.** oily. **2.** overly suave.

un•gra′cious	un•law′ful
un•guard′ed	un•like′
un•hap′py	un•like′ly
un•heard′-of′	un•load′
un•ho′ly	un•lock′
un′in•tel′lig•i•ble	un•mask′
un•in′ter•est•ed	un′mis•tak′a•ble
un′in•ter•rupt′ed	un•mor′al
un•kind′	un•nat′u•ral
un′known′	un•nec′es•sar′y
un•lace′	un•pack′

un•cut′, *adj.* **1.** not shortened; unabridged. **2.** not yet given shape, as a gemstone.

un•daunt′ed, *adj.* not discouraged or dismayed.

un′de•mon′stra•tive, *adj.* reserved.

un′der, *prep., adj., adv.* **1.** beneath; below. **2.** less than. **3.** lower.

under-, prefix meaning: **1.** below or beneath, as *underbrush.* **2.** lower in grade, as *understudy.* **3.** of lesser degree or amount, as *underestimate.*

un′der•a•chieve′, *v.,* **-achieved, -achieving.** perform below one's intellectual potential. **—un′der•a•chiev′er**, *n.*

un′der•age′, *adj.* being below legal or required age.

un′der•bel′ly, *n., pl.* **-ies. 1.** lower abdomen. **2.** vulnerable area.

un′der•brush′, *n.* low shrubs, etc., in forest.

un′der•car′riage, *n.* supporting framework underneath vehicle.

un′der•clothes′, *n.pl.* underwear. Also, **un′der•cloth′ing.**

un′der•cov′er, *adj.* secret.

un′der•cur′rent, *n.* **1.** hidden tendency or feeling. **2.** current below surface or beneath another current.

un′der•cut′, *v.,* **-cut, -cutting.** sell at lower price than.

un•pop′u•lar	un•twist′
un•rea′son•a•ble	un•typ′i•cal
un•roll′	un•used′
un•screw′	un•u′su•al
un•set′tle	un•veil′
un•shack′le	un•wind′
un•sight′ly	un•wise′
un•skilled′	un•worn′
un•tan′gle	un•wor′thy
un•true′	un•wrap′
un•truth′	un•yoke′

un′der•de•vel′oped, *adj.* **1.** insufficiently developed. **2.** having relatively low living standards and industrial development.

un′der•dog′, *n.* **1.** weaker contestant, etc. **2.** victim of injustice.

un′der•done′, *adj.* not cooked enough.

un′der•es′ti•mate′, *v.,* -mated, -mating. estimate too low.

un′der•ex•pose′, *v.,* -posed, -posing. expose (film) to insufficient light or for too short a period.

un′der•gar′ment, *n.* item of underwear.

un′der•go′, *v.,* -went, -gone, -going. experience; endure.

un′der•grad′u•ate, *n.* college student before receiving first degree.

un′der•ground′, *adj., adv.* **1.** under the ground. **2.** secret. —*n.* (un′dər ground′). **3.** secret resistance army.

un′der•growth′, *n.* underbrush.

un′der•hand′, *adj.* sly; secret. Also, **un′der•hand′ed.**

un′der•lie′, *v.,* -lay, -lain, -lying. **1.** lie beneath. **2.** be the cause or basis of.

un′der•line′, *v.,* -lined, -lining. **1.** draw line under. **2.** stress; emphasize.

un′der•ling′, *n.* subordinate.

un′der•mine′, *v.,* -mined, -mining. weaken or destroy, esp. secretly.

un′der•neath′, *prep., adv.* beneath.

un′der•pass′, *n.* passage running underneath.

un′der•pin′ning, *n.* **1.** system of supports. **2.** foundation; basis.

un′der•priv′i•leged, *adj.* denied normal privileges of society, esp. because poor.

un′der•score′, *v.,* -scored, -scoring. underline; stress.

un′der•sec′re•tar′y, *n., pl.* -taries. government official subordinate to principal secretary.

un′der•signed′, *n.* **the undersigned,** person signing document.

un′der•staffed′, *adj.* having insufficient number of workers.

un′der•stand′, *v.*, **-stood,
-standing. 1.** know meaning
of. **2.** accept as part of
agreement. **3.** sympathize.
—**un′der•stand′ing,** *n.*

un′der•state′, *v.*, **-stated,
-stating. 1.** state less strongly
than facts warrant. **2.** set forth
in restrained terms.
—**un′der•state′ment,** *n.*

un′der•stood′, *adj.* agreed or
assumed.

un′der•stud′y, *n., pl.* **-studies.**
substitute for performer.

un′der•take′, *v.*, **-took, -taken,
-taking. 1.** attempt. **2.**
promise. **3.** arrange funerals.

un′der•tak′er, *n.* funeral
director; mortician.

un′der•tak′ing, *n.* enterprise;
task.

un′der-the-coun′ter, *adj.*
illegal; unauthorized.

un′der•tone′, *n.* **1.** low tone.
2. underlying quality. **3.**
subdued color.

un′der•tow′, *n.* strong
subsurface current moving
opposite surface current.

un′der•wear′, *n.* garments
worn next to skin, under other
clothing.

un′der•world′, *n.* **1.** criminal
element. **2.** land of the dead.

un′der•write′, *v.*, **-wrote,
-written, -writing.** guarantee,
esp. expense.

un•do′, *v.*, **-did, -done, -doing.
1.** return to original state. **2.**
untie. **3.** destroy.

un•do′ing, *n.* **1.** reversing. **2.**
ruin. **3.** cause of ruin.

un′du•late′, *v.*, **-lated, -lating.**
have wavy motion or form.
—**un′du•lant,** *adj.*
—**un′du•la′tion,** *n.*

un•dy′ing, *adj.* eternal;
unending.

un•earned′, *adj.* **1.** not earned
by service. **2.** not deserved. **3.**
(of income) derived from
investments.

un•earth′, *v.* discover.

un•earth′ly, *adj.* **1.** not of this
world. **2.** supernatural; weird.
3. unreasonable; absurd.

un•eas′y, *adj.*, **-easier,
-easiest.** anxious.
—**un•eas′i•ly,** *adv.*
—**un•eas′i•ness,** *n.*

un′e•quiv′o•cal, *adj.*
unambiguous.

un′e•vent′ful, *adj.* routine.

un'ex·cep'tion·al, *adj.* ordinary.

un·feel'ing, *adj.* lacking sympathy. —**un·feel'ing·ly,** *adv.*

un·flap'pa·ble, *adj.* not easily upset.

un·fledged', *adj.* **1.** lacking sufficient feathers for flight. **2.** immature.

un·found'ed, *adj.* not supported by evidence.

un·frock', *v.* deprive of ecclesiastical rank, authority, and function.

un·gain'ly, *adj.* clumsy.

un'guent (ung'gwənt), *n.* salve.

un'gu·late (ung'gyə lit), *adj.* **1.** having hoofs. —*n.* **2.** hoofed mammal.

un·hand', *v.* release from grasp.

un·hinge', *v.,* **-hinged, -hinging. 1.** take off hinges. **2.** upset reason of; unbalance.

uni-, prefix meaning one.

u'ni·corn', *n.* mythical horselike animal with one horn.

u'ni·form', *adj.* **1.** exactly alike. **2.** even. —*n.* **3.** distinctive clothing of specific group. —*v.* **4.** put in uniform. —**u'ni·form'i·ty,** *n.*

u'ni·fy', *v.,* **-fied, -fying.** make into one. —**u'ni·fi·ca'tion,** *n.*

u'ni·lat'er·al, *adj.* one-sided.

un'im·peach'a·ble, *adj.* above reproach.

un'in·hib'it·ed, *adj.* unrestrained by convention.

un'ion, *n.* **1.** uniting; combination. **2.** labor group for mutual aid on wages, etc. —**un'ion·ism',** *n.* —**un'ion·ist,** *n., adj.* —**un'ion·ize',** *v.*

Union Jack, British flag.

u·nique', *adj.* **1.** only. **2.** most unusual or rare. —**u·nique'ly,** *adv.*

u'ni·sex', *adj.* of type or style used by both sexes.

u'ni·son, *n.* agreement.

u'nit, *n.* one of number of identical or similar things.

U'ni·tar'i·an, *n.* **1.** member of Christian denomination asserting unity of God. —*adj.* **2.** concerning Unitarians or their beliefs.

u·nite', *v.,* **united, uniting.** join, make, etc., into one.

United Nations, organization of nations to preserve peace and promote human welfare.

u'ni•ty, *n., pl.* **-ties. 1.** state of being one. **2.** agreement. **3.** uniformity.

u'ni•va'lent, *adj.* having chemical valence of one.

u'ni•valve', *n.* mollusk with single valve.

u'ni•ver'sal, *adj.* **1.** of all; general. **2.** of universe. **3.** having many skills, much learning, etc.
—**un'i•ver'sal•ly,** *adv.*
—**u'ni•ver•sal'i•ty,** *n.*

Universal Product Code, standardized bar code.

u'ni•verse', *n.* all things that exist, including heavenly bodies.

u'ni•ver'si•ty, *n., pl.* **-ties.** institution composed of various specialized colleges.

un•kempt', *adj.* untidy.

un•lead'ed (-led'id), *adj.* (of gasoline) free of pollution-causing lead.

un•less', *conj., prep.* except that.

un•let'tered, *adj.* illiterate.

un•mit'i•gat'ed, *adj.* **1.** not lessened. **2.** absolute.

un•nerve', *v.,* **-nerved, -nerving.** deprive of courage, strength, or determination.

un•par'al•leled', *adj.* without equal.

un•plumbed', *adj.* not explored in depth.

un•prin'ci•pled, *adj.* without principles or ethics.

un•print'a•ble, *adj.* unfit for print, esp. because obscene.

un•rav'el, *v.,* **-eled, -eling. 1.** disentangle. **2.** solve.

un•read', *adj.* **1.** not read. **2.** lacking in knowledge gained by reading.

un're•con•struct'ed, *adj.* stubbornly maintaining beliefs considered out of date.

un're•mit'ting, *adj.* not abating; incessant.

un•rest', *n.* **1.** restless state. **2.** strong, almost rebellious, dissatisfaction.

un•ruf'fled, *adj.* calm.

un•ru'ly, *adj.,* **-lier, -liest.** lawless.

un•sa'vo•ry, *adj.* **1.** tasteless; insipid. **2.** unpleasant in taste or smell. 3. morally objectionable.

un·sea′son·a·ble, *adj.* 1. being out of season. 2. inopportune.

un·seat′, *v.* 1. dislodge from seat. 2. remove from political office.

un·seem′ly, *adj.,* -lier, -liest. improper.

un·set′tle, *v.,* -tled, -tling. 1. cause to be unstable; disturb. 2. agitate mind or emotions of.

un·sound′, *adj.* 1. unhealthy. 2. not solid. 3. not valid. 4. not secure.

un·spar′ing, *adj.* 1. profuse. 2. unmerciful.

un·speak′a·ble, *adj.* 1. exceeding the power of speech. 2. inexpressibly bad.

un·sta′ble, *adj.* 1. unsteady. 2. changeable. 3. emotionally unsettled.

un·strung′, *adj.* nervously upset; unnerved.

un·sung′, *adj.* not celebrated, as in song; unappreciated.

un·taught′, *adj.* 1. natural. 2. not educated.

un·ten′a·ble, *adj.* not defensible as true.

un·think′a·ble, *adj.* not to be imagined; impossible.

un·ti′dy, *adj.,* -dier, -diest. not tidy or neat. —**un·tid′i·ly,** *adv.*

un·tie′, *v.,* -tied, -tying. loosen or open (something tied).

un·til′, *conj., prep.* 1. up to time when. 2. before.

un′to, *prep. Archaic.* to.

un·told′, *adj.* countless.

un·touch′a·ble, *adj.* 1. beyond control or criticism. 2. too vile to touch. —**un·touch′a·ble,** *n.*

un·to·ward′, *adj.* unfavorable or unfortunate.

un·well′, *adj.* ill or ailing.

un·wield′y, *adj.,* -wieldier, -wieldiest. awkward to handle.

un·wit′ting, *adj.* not aware. —**un·wit′ting·ly,** *adv.*

un·wont′ed, *adj.* not habitual or usual.

up, *adv., prep., n., v.,* **upped, upping.** —*adv.* 1. to higher place, etc. 2. erectly. 3. out of bed. 4. at bat. —*prep.* 5. to

higher place, etc., on or in.
—*n.* 6. rise. —*v.* 7. increase.

up'-and-com'ing, *adj.* likely
to succeed; promising.

up'beat', *adj.* optimistic;
happy.

up•braid', *v.* chide.

up'bring'ing, *n.* care and
training of children.

UPC, Universal Product Code.

up'com'ing, *adj.* about to take
place or appear.

up'coun'try, *adj., adv.* of,
toward, or situated in the
interior of a region.

up'date', *v.,* -dated, -dating.
modernize, esp. in details.

up'draft', *n.* upward
movement of air.

up•end', *v.* set on end.

up'-front', *adj.* 1. invested or
paid in advance. 2. honest;
candid.

up'grade', *n., v.,* -graded,
-grading. —*n.* 1. upward
incline. 2. increase, rise, or
improvement. —*v.* 3. raise in
rank, position, quality, or
value.

up•heav'al, *n.* sudden and
great movement or change.

up'hill', *adv.* up a slope or
incline. —**up'hill',** *adj.*

up•hold', *v.,* -held, -holding.
support. —**up•hold'er,** *n.*

up•hol'ster, *v.* provide
(furniture) with coverings, etc.
—**up•hol'ster•er,** *n.*
—**up•hol'ster•y,** *n.*

up'keep', *n.* maintenance.

up'land (up'lənd), *n.* elevated
region.

up•lift', *v.* 1. improve; exalt.
—*n.* 2. (up'lift').
improvement. 3. inspiration.

up•on', *prep.* on.

up'per, *adj.* higher.
—**up'per•most',** *adj.*

up'per•case', *adj.* 1. (of a
letter) capital. —*n.* 2. capital
letter.

upper hand, controlling
position; advantage.

up'pi•ty, *adj. Informal.*
haughty, snobbish, or
arrogant.

up'right', *adj.* 1. erect. 2.
righteous. —**up'right'ness,** *n.*

up'ris'ing, *n.* revolt.

up'roar', *n.* tumult; noise; din.
—**up•roar'i•ous,** *adj.*

up•root', *v.* tear up by roots.

up′scale′, *adj.* of or for people at upper end of economic scale.

up•set′, *v.*, **-set, -setting**, *n.*, *adj.* —*v.* **1.** turn over. **2.** distress emotionally. **3.** defeat. —*n.* (up′set′). **4.** overturn. **5.** defeat. —*adj.* **6.** disorderly. **7.** distressed.

up′shot′, *n.* final result.

up′side down, **1.** with upper part undermost. **2.** in or into complete disorder. —**up′side-down′**, *adj.*

up′stage′, *adv.*, *v.*, **-staged, -staging**. —*adv.* **1.** at or toward back of stage. —*v.* **2.** draw attention away from by moving upstage. **3.** outdo professionally or socially.

up′stairs′, *adv.*, *adj.* on or to upper floor.

up′start′, *n.* person newly risen to wealth or importance.

up′-to-date′, *adj.* **1.** until now. **2.** modern; latest.

up′ward, *adv.* to higher place. Also, **up′wards. —up′ward**, *adj.*

u•ra′ni•um, *n.* white, radioactive metallic element, important in development of atomic energy.

U′ra•nus (yŏŏr′ə nəs, yŏŏ rā′-), *n.* planet seventh in order from the sun.

ur′ban, *adj.* of or like a city.

ur•bane′, *adj.* polite or suave. —**ur•ban′i•ty**, *n.*

ur′chin, *n.* ragged child.

u•re′a (yŏŏ rē′ə, yŏŏr′ē ə), *n.* compound occurring in body fluids, esp. urine.

u•re′mi•a, *n.* presence in blood of products normally excreted in urine.

u•re′ter, *n.* duct that conveys urine from kidney to bladder.

u•re′thra (yŏŏ rē′thrə), *n.*, *pl.* **-thrae** (-thrē), **-thras**. duct that conveys urine and, in most male animals, semen.

urge, *v.*, **urged, urging**, *n.* —*v.* **1.** force, incite, or advocate. **2.** entreat. —*n.* **3.** desire; impulse.

ur′gent, *adj.* vital; pressing. —**ur′gent•ly**, *adv.* —**ur′gen•cy**, *n.*

u′ri•nal, *n.* wall fixture used by men for urinating.

u′ri•nal′y•sis, *n.*, *pl.* **-ses**. diagnostic analysis of urine.

u′ri·nar′y, *adj.* 1. of urine. 2. of organs that secrete and discharge urine.

u′ri·nate′, *v.,* -nated, -nating. pass urine. —**u′ri·na′tion,** *n.*

u′rine, *n.* secretion of kidneys. —**u′ric,** *adj.*

urn, *n.* vase or pot.

u·rol′o·gy, *n.* medical study of urinary or genitourinary tract. —**u·rol′o·gist,** *n.*

us, *pron.* objective case of **we.**

us′age, *n.* 1. custom. 2. treatment.

use, *v.,* used, using, *n.* —*v.* (yōoz). 1. do something with aid of. 2. expend. 3. make practice of. 4. treat. 5. accustom. —*n.* (yōos). 6. act or way of using. 7. service or value. —**us′a·ble,** *adj.* —**use′ful,** *adj.* —**use′ful·ness,** *n.* —**use′less,** *adj.* —**use′less·ness,** *n.* —**us′er,** *n.*

us′er-friend′ly, *adj.* easy to operate or understand.

ush′er, *n.* person who escorts people to seats, as in theater.

u′su·al, *adj.* 1. customary. 2. common. —**u′su·al·ly,** *adv.*

u·surp′ (yōo zûrp′), *v.* seize without right. —**u·surp′er,** *n.*

u′su·ry (yōo′zhə rē), *n.* lending money at exorbitant rates of interest. —**u′sur·er,** *n.* —**u·su′ri·ous** (-zhŏor′ē-), *adj.*

UT, Utah. Also, **Ut.**

u·ten′sil, *n.* device, container, etc., esp. for kitchen.

u′ter·us, *n.,* pl. -teri. part of woman's body in which fertilized ovum develops. —**u′ter·ine,** *adj.*

u·til′i·tar′i·an, *adj.* of practical use.

u·til′i·ty, *n.,* pl. -ties. 1. usefulness. 2. public service.

u′ti·lize′, *v.,* -lized, -lizing. use. —**u′ti·li·za′tion,** *n.*

ut′most′, *adj.* 1. greatest. 2. furthest.

U·to′pi·an, *adj.* impossibly perfect.

ut′ter, *v.* 1. speak; say. —*adj.* 2. complete; total. —**ut′ter·ance,** *n.*

ut′ter·ly, *adv.* completely; absolutely.

u′vu•la (yōō′vyə lə), *n., pl.*
-las, -lae. small, fleshy part on
soft palate.

ux•o′ri•ous (uk sōr′ē əs), *adj.*
foolishly or excessively fond
of one's wife.

V, v, *n.* twenty-second letter of English alphabet.

VA, Virginia. Also, **Va.**

va'can·cy, *n., pl.* **-cies. 1.** state of being vacant. **2.** vacant space.

va'cant, *adj.* **1.** empty. **2.** devoid. **3.** unintelligent. —**va'cant·ly,** *adv.*

va'cate, *v.,* **-cated, -cating. 1.** empty. **2.** quit. **3.** annul.

va·ca'tion, *n.* **1.** freedom from duty, business, etc. **2.** holiday. —*v.* **3.** take a vacation. —**va·ca'tion·ist,** *n.*

vac'ci·nate', *v.,* **-nated, -nating.** inoculate against smallpox, etc. —**vac'ci·na'tion,** *n.*

vac·cine' (vak sēn'), *n.* substance injected into bloodstream to give immunity. —**vac'ci·nal,** *adj.*

vac'il·late' (vas'ə-), *v.,* **-lated, -lating. 1.** waver; fluctuate. **2.** be irresolute. —**vac'il·la'tion,** *n.* —**vac'il·la'tor,** *n.*

va·cu'i·ty, *n., pl.* **-ties. 1.** emptiness. **2.** lack of intelligence. —**vac'u·ous,** *adj.* —**vac'u·ous·ly,** *adv.*

V

vac'u·um, *n.* space from which all matter has been removed.

vacuum bottle, bottle with double wall enclosing vacuum to retard heat transfer.

vacuum cleaner, apparatus for cleaning by suction.

vac'uum-packed', *adj.* packed with as much air as possible evacuated before sealing.

vacuum tube, sealed bulb, formerly used in radio and electronics.

vag'a·bond', *adj.* **1.** wandering; homeless. —*n.* **2.** vagrant.

va·gar'y (və gâr'ē), *n., pl.* **-garies.** capricious act or idea.

va·gi'na (və jī'nə), *n., pl.* **-nas, -nae.** passage from uterus to vulva. —**vag'i·nal,** *adj.*

va'grant, *n.* **1.** idle wanderer. —*adj.* **2.** wandering. —**va'gran·cy,** *n.*

vague, *adj.,* **vaguer, vaguest. 1.** not definite. **2.** indistinct. —**vague'ly,** *adv.* —**vague'ness,** *n.*

vain, *adj.* 1. futile. 2. conceited. —**vain′ly,** *adv.* —**vain′ness,** *n.*

vain′glo′ry, *n.* boastful pride. —**vain·glo′ri·ous,** *adj.*

val′ance (val′əns, vā′ləns), *n.* drapery across top of window.

vale, *n.* valley.

val′e·dic·to′ri·an, *n.* graduating student who delivers valedictory.

val′e·dic′to·ry, *n., pl.* **-ries.** farewell address, esp. one delivered at commencement.

va′lence (vā′ləns), *n.* combining capacity of atom or radical.

val′en·tine′, *n.* 1. affectionate card or gift sent on February 14 (**Saint Valentine's Day**). 2. sweetheart chosen on that day.

val′et (val′it, val′ā), *n.* personal manservant.

val′iant, *adj.* brave. —**val′iance,** *n.* —**val′iant·ly,** *adv.*

val′id, *adj.* 1. sound; logical. 2. legally binding. —**val′i·date′,** *v.* —**val′i·da′tion,** *n.* —**va·lid′i·ty,** *n.* —**val′id·ly,** *adv.*

va·lise′ (-lēs′), *n.* traveling bag.

val′ley, *n.* long depression between uplands or mountains.

val′or, *n.* bravery, esp. in battle. —**val′o·rous,** *adj.* —**val′o·rous·ly,** *adv.*

val′u·a·ble, *adj.* 1. of much worth, importance, etc. —*n.* 2. (*usually pl.*) valuable articles. —**val′u·a·bly,** *adv.*

val′u·a′tion, *n.* estimation or estimated value.

val′ue, *n., v.,* **-ued, -uing.** —*n.* 1. worth or importance. 2. equivalent or estimated worth. 3. conception of what is good. —*v.* 4. estimate worth of. 5. esteem. —**val′ue·less,** *adj.*

valve, *n.* device controlling flow of liquids, etc. —**val′vu·lar,** *adj.*

va·moose′, *v.,* **-moosed, -moosing.** *Slang.* leave hurriedly.

vamp, *n.* 1. upper front part of shoe or boot. 2. *Slang.* seductive woman. —*v.* 3. improvise (as music).

vam′pire, *n.* 1. corpse supposed to be reanimated and to suck blood of living persons. 2. extortionist. 3.

Also, **vampire bat.** South and Central American bat.

van, *n.* **1.** vanguard. **2.** covered truck for moving furniture, etc. **3.** small closed trucklike vehicle.

va•na′di•um (və nā′-), *n.* rare silvery metallic element, used esp. to toughen steel.

van′dal, *n.* person who damages or destroys wantonly. —**van′dal•ism,** *n.* —**van′dal•ize′,** *v.*

Van•dyke′, *n.* short, pointed beard.

vane, *n.* **1.** weathervane. **2.** one of set of blades set diagonally on a rotor to move or be moved by fluid.

van′guard′, *n.* **1.** foremost part. **2.** leaders of a movement.

va•nil′la, *n.* **1.** tropical orchid, whose fruit (**vanilla bean**) yields flavoring extract. **2.** the extract.

van′ish, *v.* disappear. —**van′ish•er,** *n.*

van′i•ty, *n., pl.* **-ties. 1.** vainness. **2.** makeup table. **3.** compact (def. 4).

van′quish, *v.* conquer; defeat. —**van′quish•er,** *n.*

van′tage, *n.* superior position or situation.

vap′id, *adj.* **1.** insipid. **2.** dull. —**va•pid′i•ty,** *n.* —**vap′id•ly,** *adv.*

va′por, *n.* **1.** exhalation, as fog or mist. **2.** gas. —**va′por•ous,** *adj.*

va′por•ize′, *v.,* **-ized, -izing.** change into vapor. —**va′por•i•za′tion,** *n.* —**va′por•iz′er,** *n.*

var′i•a•ble, *adj.* **1.** changeable. **2.** inconstant. —*n.* **3.** something variable. —**var′i•a•bil′i•ty,** *n.* —**var′i•a•bly,** *adv.*

var′i•ance, *n.* **1.** divergence or discrepancy. **2.** disagreement.

var′i•ant, *adj.* **1.** varying. **2.** altered in form. —*n.* **3.** variant form, etc.

var′i•a′tion, *n.* **1.** change. **2.** amount of change. **3.** variant. **4.** transformation of melody with changes in harmony, etc. —**var′i•a′tion•al,** *adj.*

var′i•col′ored, *adj.* having various colors.

var′i•cose′, *adj.* abnormally swollen, as veins.

var′i•e•gate′, *v.*, **-gated, -gating. 1.** mark with different colors, etc. **2.** vary. —**var′i•e•gat′ed,** *adj.*

va•ri′e•ty, *n., pl.* **-ties. 1.** diversity. **2.** number of different things. **3.** kind; category. **4.** variant. —**va•ri′e•tal,** *adj.*

va•ri′o•la, *n.* smallpox.

var′i•ous, *adj.* **1.** of different sorts. **2.** several. —**var′i•ous•ly,** *adv.*

var′mint, *n.* **1.** undesirable, usu. verminous animal. **2.** obnoxious person.

var′nish, *n.* **1.** resinous solution drying in hard, glossy coat. **2.** gloss. —*v.* **3.** lay varnish on.

var′y, *v.,* **varied, varying. 1.** change; differ. **2.** cause to be different. **3.** deviate; diverge.

vas′cu•lar, *adj.* of vessels that convey fluids, as blood or sap.

vase, *n.* tall container, esp. for flowers.

vas•ec′to•my, *n., pl.* **-mies.** surgery for male sterilization.

vas′sal, *n.* **1.** feudal holder of land who renders service to superior. **2.** subject, follower, or slave. —**vas′sal•age,** *n.*

vast, *adj.* immense; huge. —**vast′ly,** *adv.* —**vast′ness,** *n.*

vat, *n.* large container for liquids.

vaude′ville (vôd′vil), *n.* theatrical entertainment made up of separate acts.

vault, *n.* **1.** arched ceiling or roof. **2.** arched space, chamber, etc. **3.** room for safekeeping of valuables. —*v.* **4.** build or cover with vault. **5.** leap. —**vault′ed,** *adj.* —**vault′er,** *n.*

vault′ing, *adj.* **1.** leaping. **2.** excessive.

vaunt, *v.* **1.** boast of. —*n.* **2.** boast.

VCR, videocassette recorder.

VD, venereal disease.

V′-Day′, *n.* day of military victory.

VDT, video display terminal.

veal, *n.* flesh of calf as used for food.

vec′tor, *n.* **1.** quantity possessing both magnitude and direction. **2.** person or animal that transmits disease-causing organism.

veep, *n. Informal.* Vice President, esp. of U.S.

veer, *v.* change direction.

veg'e·ta·ble, *n.* 1. plant used for food. 2. any plant. —**veg'e·ta·ble, veg'e·tal,** *adj.*

veg'e·tar'i·an, *n.* 1. person who eats only vegetable food on principle (**vegetarianism**). —*adj.* 2. of or advocating vegetarianism. 3. suitable for vegetarians.

veg'e·tate', *v.,* **-tated, -tating.** 1. grow as plants do. 2. live dull, inactive life. —**veg'e·ta'tive,** *adj.*

veg'e·ta'tion, *n.* 1. plants collectively. 2. act or process of vegetating.

ve'he·ment (vē'ə mənt), *adj.* 1. impetuous or impassioned. 2. violent. —**ve'he·mence, ve'he·men'cy,** *n.* —**ve'he·ment·ly,** *adv.*

ve'hi·cle, *n.* means of transport, etc. —**ve·hic'u·lar,** *adj.*

veil, *n.* 1. material concealing face. 2. part of headdress, as of nun or bride. 3. cover; screen. 4. pretense. —*v.* 5. cover with veil.

vein, *n.* 1. vessel conveying blood from body to heart. 2. tubular riblike thickening, as in leaf or insect wing. 3. stratum of ore, coal, etc. 4. mood. —*v.* 5. furnish or mark with veins.

Vel·cro, *n. Trademark.* fastening tape with opposing pieces of nylon that interlock.

veld (velt, felt), *n.* open grassy country in South Africa. Also, **veldt.**

vel'lum, *n.* parchment.

ve·loc'i·ty, *n., pl.* **-ties.** speed.

ve·lour' (və lo͝or'), *n.* velvetlike fabric used for clothing and upholstery. Also, **ve·lours'.**

vel'vet, *n.* fabric with thick, soft pile. —**vel'vet·y,** *adj.*

vel'vet·een', *n.* cotton fabric resembling velvet.

ve'nal, *adj.* corrupt; mercenary. —**ve'nal·ly,** *adv.* —**ve·nal'i·ty,** *n.*

vend, *v.* sell. —**ven'dor,** *n.*

ven·det'ta, *n.* long, bitter feud.

vending machine, coin-operated machine for selling small articles.

ve•neer′, *v.* 1. overlay with thin sheets of fine wood, etc. —*n.* 2. veneered layer of wood. 3. superficial appearance.

ven′er•a•ble, *adj.* worthy of reverence. —**ven′er•a•bil′i•ty**, *n.*

ven′er•ate′, *v.*, -ated, -ating. revere. —**ven′er•a′tion**, *n.*

ve•ne′re•al (və nēr′ē əl), *adj.* relating to or caused by sexual intercourse.

ve•ne′tian blind, window blind with horizontal slats.

venge′ance, *n.* revenge.

venge′ful, *adj.* seeking vengeance. —**venge′ful•ly**, *adv.*

ve′ni•al, *n.* pardonable.

ven′i•son, *n.* flesh of deer as used for food.

ven′om, *n.* 1. poisonous fluid secreted by some snakes, spiders, etc. 2. spite; malice. —**ven′om•ous**, *adj.* —**ven′om•ous•ly**, *adv.*

ve′nous (vē′-), *adj.* 1. of or having veins. 2. of or being blood carried back to heart by veins.

vent, *n.* 1. outlet, as for fluid. 2. expression. —*v.* 3. express freely.

ven′ti•late′, *v.*, -lated, -lating. 1. provide with fresh air. 2. submit to discussion. —**ven′ti•la′tion**, *n.* —**ven′ti•la′tor**, *n.*

ven′tral, *adj.* 1. of or near belly; abdominal. 2. on lower, abdominal plane of animal's body.

ven′tri•cle, *n.* either of two lower cavities of heart. —**ven•tric′u•lar**, *adj.*

ven•tril′o•quism′, *n.* art of speaking so that voice seems to come from another source. —**ven•tril′o•quist**, *n.*

ven′ture, *n.*, *v.*, -tured, -turing. —*n.* 1. hazardous undertaking. —*v.* 2. risk; dare. 3. enter daringly. —**ven′ture•some**, **ven′tur•ous**, *adj.*

ven′ue, *n.* 1. place of crime or cause of action. 2. place where jury is gathered and case tried. 3. scene or locale of action or event.

Ve′nus, *n.* second planet from sun.

Ven′us's-fly′trap, *n.* plant with hinged leaves that trap insects.

ve·ra′cious, *adj.* truthful. —**ve·rac′i·ty** (və ras′ə tē), *n.*

ve·ran′da, *n.* open porch. Also, **ve·ran′dah.**

verb, *n.* part of speech expressing action, occurrence, existence, etc., as "saw" in the sentence "I saw Tom."

ver′bal, *adj.* 1. of or in form of words. 2. oral. 3. word for word. 4. of verbs. —*n.* 5. word, as noun, derived from verb. —**ver′bal·ly,** *adv.*

ver′bal·ize′, *v.,* -ized, -izing. express in words. —**ver′bal·i·za′tion,** *n.*

ver·ba′tim, *adv.* word for word.

ver·be′na, *n.* plant with long spikes of flowers.

ver′bi·age, *n.* 1. wordiness. 2. manner of verbal expression.

ver·bose′, *adj.* wordy. —**ver·bose′ness, ver·bos′i·ty,** *n.*

ver·bo′ten, *adj.* forbidden.

ver′dant, *adj.* 1. green with vegetation. 2. inexperienced. —**ver′dan·cy,** *n.*

ver′dict, *n.* decision.

ver′di·gris′ (vûr′də grēs′), *n.* green or bluish patina.

ver′dure (vûr′jər), *n.* 1. greenness. 2. green vegetation.

verge, *n., v.,* **verged, verging.** —*n.* 1. edge or margin. —*v.* 2. border. 3. incline; tend.

ver′i·fy′, *v.,* -fied, -fying. 1. prove to be true. 2. ascertain correctness of. —**ver′i·fi′a·ble,** *adj.* —**ver′i·fi·ca′tion,** *n.* —**ver′i·fi′er,** *n.*

ver′i·ly, *adv. Archaic.* truly.

ver′i·si·mil′i·tude′, *n.* appearance of truth.

ver′i·ta·ble, *adj.* genuine. —**ver′i·ta·bly,** *adv.*

ver′i·ty, *n., pl.* -ties. truth.

ver′mi·cel′li (-chel′ē, -sel′ē), *n.* pasta in long threads.

ver·mil′ion, *n.* 1. bright red. —*adj.* 2. of or like vermilion.

ver′min, *n.pl. or sing.* troublesome animals collectively. —**ver′min·ous,** *adj.*

ver·mouth′ (vər mooth′), *n.* white wine flavored with herbs.

ver•nac′u•lar, *adj.* 1. (of language) used locally or in everyday speech. —*n.* 2. native speech. 3. language of particular group.

ver′nal, *adj.* of spring. —**ver′nal•ly,** *adv.*

ve•ron′i•ca, *n.* plant with opposite leaves and clusters of small flowers.

ver′sa•tile, *adj.* doing variety of things well. —**ver′sa•til′i•ty,** *n.*

verse, *n.* 1. line of poem. 2. type of metrical line, etc. 3. poem. 4. poetry. 5. division of Biblical chapter.

versed, *adj.* expert; skilled.

ver′si•fy′, *v.,* **-fied, -fying.** 1. treat in or turn into verse. 2. compose verses. —**ver′si•fi′er,** *n.* —**ver′si•fi•ca′tion,** *n.*

ver′sion, *n.* 1. translation. 2. account.

ver′so, *n., pl.* **-sos,** left-hand page of book.

ver′sus, *prep.* in opposition or contrast to.

ver′te•bra, *n., pl.* **-brae, -bras.** bone or segment of spinal column. —**ver′te•bral,** *adj.*

ver′te•brate′, *adj.* 1. having vertebrae. —*n.* 2. vertebrate animal.

ver′tex, *n., pl.* **-texes, -tices** (-tə sēz′). highest point.

ver′ti•cal, *adj.* 1. perpendicular to plane of horizon. —*n.* 2. something vertical. —**ver′ti•cal•ly,** *adv.*

ver•tig′i•nous (-tij′-), *adj.* 1. whirling. 2. affected with or liable to cause vertigo.

ver′ti•go′, *n., pl.* **-goes.** dizziness.

verve, *n.* vivaciousness, energy, or enthusiasm.

ver′y, *adv., adj.,* **verier, veriest.** —*adv.* 1. extremely. —*adj.* 2. identical. 3. mere. 4. actual. 5. true.

ves′i•cle, *n.* small sac in body.

ves′per, *n.* 1. *Archaic.* evening. 2. (*pl.*) evening prayer, service, etc.

ves′sel, *n.* 1. ship or boat. 2. hollow or concave container, as dish or glass. 3. tube or duct, as for blood.

vest, *n.* 1. sleeveless garment worn under jacket. —*v.* 2. clothe or robe. 3. put in someone's possession or control. 4. endow with powers, etc.

ves′tal, *adj*. chaste.

vest′ed, *adj*. held completely and permanently.

vested interest, special interest in system, arrangement, or institution for personal reasons.

ves′ti‧bule′, *n*. small room between entrance and main room. —**ves‧tib′u‧lar,** *adj*.

ves′tige, *n*. **1**. trace of something extinct. **2**. slight trace of something. —**ves‧tig′i‧al,** *adj*.

vest′ing, *n*. granting to employee of right to pension benefits despite early retirement.

vest′ment, *n*. ceremonial garment.

vest′-pock′et, *adj*. conveniently small.

ves′try, *n., pl*. **-tries. 1**. room in church for vestments or for meetings, etc. **2**. church committee managing temporal affairs. —**ves′try‧man,** *n*.

vet, *n. Informal*. **1**. veterinarian. **2**. veteran.

vetch, *n*. plant used for forage and soil improvement.

vet′er‧an, *n*. **1**. person who has seen service, esp. in armed forces. —*adj*. **2**. experienced.

vet′er‧i‧nar′i‧an, *n*. veterinary practitioner.

vet′er‧i‧nar′y, *n., pl*. **-naries,** *adj*. —*n*. **1**. veterinarian. —*adj*. **2**. of medical and surgical treatment of animals.

ve′to, *n., pl*. **-toes,** *v.,* **-toed, -toing.** —*n*. **1**. power or right to reject or prohibit. **2**. prohibition. —*v*. **3**. reject by veto.

vex, *v*. **1**. irritate. **2**. worry. **3**. discuss vigorously. —**vex‧a′tion,** *n*. —**vex‧a′tious,** *adj*. —**vexed,** *adj*. —**vex′ed‧ly,** *adv*.

vi′a (vī′ə), *prep*. by way of.

vi′a‧ble, *adj*. **1**. capable of living. **2**. practicable; workable.

vi′a‧duct′, *n*. long highway or railroad bridge.

vi′al (vī′əl), *n*. small glass container.

vi′and, *n*. **1**. article of food. **2**. (*pl*.) dishes of food.

vibes, *n.pl.* **1.** *Slang.* something, esp. an emotional aura, emitted as if by vibration. **2.** vibraphone.

vi′brant, *adj.* **1.** resonant. **2.** energetic; vital. —**vi′bran·cy,** *n.* —**vi′brant·ly,** *adv.*

vi′bra·phone (vī′brə fōn′), *n.* instrument like metal xylophone, with electrically enhanced resonance.

vi′brate, *v.,* **-brated, -brating.** **1.** move very rapidly to and fro; oscillate. **2.** tremble. **3.** resound. **4.** thrill. —**vi·bra′tion,** *n.* —**vi′bra·tor,** *n.* —**vi′bra·to′ry,** *adj.* —**vi·bra′tion·al,** *adj.*

vi·bra′to, *n., pl.* **-tos.** pulsating effect produced by rapid but slight alterations in pitch.

vi·bur′num (vī-), *n.* shrub bearing white flower clusters.

vic′ar, *n.* **1.** parish priest. **2.** representative of bishop. **3.** deputy. —**vic′ar·ship′,** *n.* —**vi·car′i·al,** *adj.*

vic′ar·age, *n.* residence or position of vicar.

vi·car′i·ous, *adj.* **1.** done or suffered in place of another. **2.** substitute. —**vi·car′i·ous·ly,** *adv.*

vice, *n.* **1.** evil habit or fault. **2.** immoral conduct. **3.** vise. —*prep.* **4.** instead of.

vice-, prefix meaning deputy.

vice′-ad′mi·ral, *n.* commissioned officer ranking above rear admiral.

vice·ge′rent (vīs jēr′-), *n.* deputy to sovereign or magistrate.

vice′ pres′i·dent, *n.* officer next in rank to president. —**vice′ pres′i·den·cy,** *n.*

vice′roy, *n.* ruler of country or province as deputy of sovereign. —**vice-re′gal,** *adj.*

vi′ce ver′sa, in opposite way.

vi′chys·soise′ (vish′ē swäz′), *n.* cold cream soup of potatoes and leeks.

vi·cin′i·ty, *n., pl.* **-ties.** neighborhood; nearby area.

vi′cious, *adj.* **1.** immoral; depraved. **2.** evil. **3.** malicious. —**vi′cious·ly,** *adv.* —**vi′cious·ness,** *n.*

vi·cis′si·tude′ (vi sis′ə tyood′), *n.* change, esp. in condition.

vic′tim, *n.* **1.** sufferer from action or event. **2.** dupe. **3.** sacrifice. —**vic′tim·ize′,** *v.*

vic′tor, *n.* conqueror or winner. —**vic•to′ri•ous,** *adj.* —**vic•to′ri•ous•ly,** *adv.*

vic′to•ry, *n., pl.* **-ries.** success in contest.

vict′ual (vit′əl), *n.* **1.** (*pl.*) food. —*v.* **2.** supply with victuals. —**vict′ual•er,** *n.*

vid′e•o′, *adj.* **1.** of television. —*n.* **2.** television. **3.** the visual elements of a telecast. **4.** videotape or videocassette.

vid′e•o′cas•sette′, *n.* cassette containing videotape.

videocassette recorder, electronic device for recording and playing videocassettes.

vid′e•o•disc′, *n.* disc on which pictures and sound are recorded for playback on TV set.

video game, electronic game played on video screen or television set.

vid′e•o•tape′, *n., v.,* **-taped, -taping.** —*n.* **1.** magnetic tape on which TV program, motion picture, etc., can be recorded. —*v.* **2.** record on this.

vie, *v.,* **vied, vying.** contend for superiority.

view, *n.* **1.** seeing or beholding. **2.** range of vision. **3.** landscape, etc., within one's sight. **4.** aspect. **5.** mental survey. **6.** purpose. **7.** notion, opinion, etc. —*v.* **8.** see; look at. **9.** regard. —**view′er,** *n.* —**view′less,** *adj.*

view′find′er, *n.* camera part for viewing what will appear in picture.

view′point′, *n.* **1.** place from which view is seen. **2.** attitude toward something.

vig′il, *n.* period of staying awake, esp. as watch.

vig′i•lant, *adj.* **1.** wary. **2.** alert. —**vig′i•lance,** *n.* —**vig′i•lant•ly,** *adv.*

vig′i•lan′te (-lan′tē), *n.* person who takes law into own hands.

vi•gnette′ (vin yet′), *n., v.,* **-gnetted, -gnetting.** —*n.* **1.** small decorative design. **2.** photograph, etc., shading off at edges. **3.** literary sketch. —*v.* **4.** make vignette of.

vig′or, *n.* **1.** active strength. **2.** energy. —**vig′or•ous,** *adj.* —**vig′or•ous•ly,** *adv.*

Vik′ing, *n.* medieval Scandinavian raider.

vile, *adj.,* **viler, vilest. 1.** very bad. **2.** offensive. **3.** evil. —**vile'ly,** *adv.* —**vile'ness,** *n.*

vil'i·fy', *v.,* **-fied, -fying.** defame. —**vil'i·fi·ca'tion,** *n.* —**vil'i·fi·er,** *n.*

vil'la, *n.* luxurious country residence.

vil'lage, *n.* small town. —**vil'lag·er,** *n.*

vil'lain, *n.* wicked person. —**vil'lain·ous,** *adj.* —**vil'lain·y,** *n.*

vil'lein (-ən), *n.* feudal serf.

vim, *n.* vigor.

vin'ai·grette' (vin'ə gret'), *n.* dressing, esp. for salad, of oil and vinegar, usu. with herbs.

vin'ci·ble, *adj.* capable of being conquered.

vin'di·cate', *v.,* **-cated, -cating. 1.** clear, as from suspicion. **2.** uphold or justify. —**vin'di·ca'tion,** *n.* —**vin'di·ca'tor,** *n.*

vin·dic'tive, *adj.* holding grudge; vengeful. —**vin·dic'tive·ly,** *adv.* —**vin·dic'tive·ness,** *n.*

vine, *n.* creeping or climbing plant with slender stem.

vin'e·gar, *n.* sour liquid obtained by fermentation. —**vin'e·gar·y,** *adj.*

vine'yard (vin'-), *n.* plantation of grapevines.

vin'tage, *n.* **1.** wine from one harvest. **2.** grape harvest.

vint'ner, *n.* person who makes wine.

vi'nyl (vī'nəl), *n.* type of plastic.

Vi·nyl·ite (vī'nə līt', vin'ə-), *n. Trademark.* vinyl.

vi'ol (vī'əl), *n.* stringed instrument of 16th and 17th centuries.

vi·o'la, *n. Music.* instrument resembling violin but slightly larger.

vi'o·la·ble, *adj.* capable of being violated.

vi'o·late', *v.,* **-lated, -lating. 1.** break or transgress. **2.** break through or into. **3.** desecrate. **4.** rape. —**vi'o·la'tion,** *n.* —**vi'o·la'tor,** *n.*

vi'o·lent, *adj.* **1.** uncontrolled, strong, or rough. **2.** of destructive force. **3.** intense; severe. —**vi'o·lence,** *n.* —**vi'o·lent·ly,** *adv.*

vi′o‧let, *n.* 1. low herb bearing flowers, usually purple or blue. 2. bluish purple.

vi′o‧lin′, *n. Music.* stringed instrument played with bow. —**vi′o‧lin′ist,** *n.*

vi′o‧lon‧cel′lo (vē′ə lən chel′ō), *n., pl.* **-los.** cello. —**vi′o‧lon‧cel′list,** *n.*

VIP, *Informal.* very important person.

vi′per, *n.* 1. Old World venomous snake. 2. malicious or treacherous person. —**vi′per‧ous,** *adj.*

vi‧ra′go (vi rä′gō, -rā′-), *n., pl.* **-goes, -gos.** shrewish woman.

vi′ral, *adj.* of or caused by virus.

vir′gin, *n.* 1. person, esp. woman, who has not had sexual intercourse. —*adj.* 2. being or like virgin. 3. untried; unused. —**vir′gin‧al,** *adj.* —**vir‧gin′i‧ty,** *n.*

vir′gule (vûr′gyool), *n.* oblique stroke (/) used as dividing line.

vir′ile (vir′əl), *adj.* 1. manly. 2. vigorous. 3. capable of procreation. —**vi‧ril′i‧ty,** *n.*

vi‧rol′o‧gy, *n.* study of viruses. —**vi‧rol′o‧gist,** *n.*

vir′tu‧al, *adj.* 1. such in effect, though not actually. 2. simulated by computer. —**vir′tu‧al‧ly,** *adv.*

virtual reality, realistic simulation by computer system.

vir′tue, *n.* 1. moral excellence. 2. chastity. 3. merit. —**vir′tu‧ous,** *adj.* —**vir′tu‧ous‧ly,** *adv.* —**vir′tu‧ous‧ness,** *n.*

vir′tu‧o′so, *n., pl.* **-sos, -si.** person of special skill, esp. in music. —**vir′tu‧os′i‧ty,** *n.*

vir′u‧lent (vir′yə-), *adj.* 1. poisonous; malignant. 2. hostile. —**vir′u‧lence, vir′u‧len‧cy,** *n.* —**vir′u‧lent‧ly,** *adv.*

vi′rus, *n.* 1. infective agent. 2. corrupting influence. 3. segment of self-replicating code planted illegally in computer program.

vi′sa (vē′zə), *n.* passport endorsement permitting foreign entry or immigration.

vis′age, *n.* 1. face. 2. aspect.

vis′-à-vis′ (vē′zə vē′), *prep.* 1. in relation to; compared with. 2. opposite.

vis′cer•a (vis′ər ə), *n.pl.* 1. soft interior organs of body. 2. intestines. —**vis′cer•al,** *adj.*

vis′cid (vis′id), *adj.* sticky; gluelike. Also, **vis′cous** (vis′kəs). —**vis•cos′i•ty,** *n.*

vis′count (vī′-), *n.* nobleman ranking below earl or count. —**vis′count•ess,** *n.fem.*

vise, *n.* device, usually with two jaws, for holding object firmly.

vis′i•ble, *adj.* 1. capable of being seen. 2. perceptible. 3. manifest. —**vis′i•bil′i•ty,** *n.* —**vis′i•bly,** *adv.*

vi′sion, *n.* 1. power or sense of sight. 2. imagination or unusually keen perception. 3. mental image of something supernatural or imaginary. —**vi′sion•al,** *adj.*

vi′sion•ar′y, *adj., n., pl.* **-aries.** —*adj.* 1. fanciful. 2. seen in vision. 3. unreal. —*n.* 4. seer of visions. 5. bold or impractical schemer.

vis′it, *v.* 1. go to for purposes of talking, staying, etc. 2. afflict. —*n.* 3. act of visiting. 4. stay as guest. —**vis′i•tor, vis′i•tant,** *n.*

vis′it•a′tion, *n.* 1. visit. 2. bringing of good or evil, as by supernatural force.

vi′sor, *n.* front piece, as of helmet or cap.

vis′ta, *n.* extended view in one direction.

vis′u•al, *adj.* 1. of or by means of sight. 2. visible. —**vis′u•al•ly,** *adv.*

vis′u•al•ize′, *v.,* **-ized, -izing.** 1. make visual. 2. form mental image of. —**vis′u•al•i•za′tion,** *n.*

vi′tal, *adj.* 1. of life. 2. living; energetic; vivid. 3. giving or necessary to life. 4. essential. —**vi′tal•ly,** *adv.*

vi•tal′i•ty, *n., pl.* **-ties.** 1. vital force. 2. physical or mental vigor. 3. power of continued existence.

vital signs, essential body functions, comprising pulse rate, body temperature, and respiration.

vital statistics, statistics concerning deaths, births, and marriages.

vi′ta•min, *n.* food element essential in small quantities to maintain life. —**vi′ta•min′ic,** *adj.*

vi′ti•ate′ (vish′ē āt′), *v.*, **-ated, -ating. 1.** impair. **2.** corrupt. **3.** invalidate. **—vi′ti•a′tion,** *n.*

vit′i•cul′ture, *n.* cultivation of grapes. **—vit′i•cul′tur•ist,** *n.*

vit′re•ous, *adj.* of or like glass.

vitreous humor, transparent gelatinous substance that fills eyeball.

vit′ri•fy′, *v.,* **-fied, -fying.** change to glass.

vi•trine′ (-trēn′), *n.* glass cabinet.

vit′ri•ol, *n.* **1.** glassy metallic compound. **2.** sulfuric acid. **3.** caustic criticism, etc. **—vit′ri•ol′ic,** *adj.*

vi•tu′per•ate′ (vī tyoo′-), *v.,* **-ated, -ating. 1.** criticize abusively. **2.** revile. **—vi•tu′per•a′tion,** *n.* **—vi•tu′per•a′tive** (-pə rā′tiv), *adj.*

vi•va′cious, *adj.* lively; animated. **—vi•va′cious•ly,** *adv.* **—vi•va′cious•ness, vi•vac′i•ty,** *n.*

viv′id, *adj.* **1.** bright, as color or light. **2.** full of life. **3.** intense; striking. **—viv′id•ly,** *adv.* **—viv′id•ness,** *n.*

viv′i•fy′, *v.,* **-fied, -fying.** give life to.

vi•vip′ar•ous (vī vip′ər əs, vi-) *adj.* bringing forth living young rather than eggs.

viv′i•sec′tion, *n.* dissection of live animal. **—viv′i•sec′tion•ist,** *n.*

vix′en, *n.* **1.** female fox. **2.** ill-tempered woman.

vi•zier′ (vi zēr′), *n.* high official in certain Muslim countries.

vo•cab′u•lar′y, *n., pl.* **-laries. 1.** words used by people, class, or person. **2.** collection of defined words, usually in alphabetical order.

vo′cal, *adj.* **1.** of the voice. **2.** of or for singing. **3.** articulate or talkative. **—***n.* **4.** vocal composition or performance. **—vo′cal•ize′,** *v.* **—vo′cal•i•za′tion,** *n.* **—vo′cal•ly,** *adv.*

vocal cords, membranes in larynx producing sound by vibration.

vo′cal•ist, *n.* singer.

vo•ca′tion, *n.* occupation, business, or profession. **—vo•ca′tion•al,** *adj.*

voc′a•tive (vok′-), *adj.* of or being grammatical case used to indicate one being addressed.

vo•cif′er•ate′ (-sif′ə-), *v.*, **-ated, -ating.** cry noisily; shout. —**vo•cif′er•a′tion,** *n.* —**vo•cif′er•ous,** *adj.* —**vo•cif′er•ous•ly,** *adv.*

vod′ka, *n.* colorless distilled liquor.

vogue, *n.* **1.** fashion. **2.** popular favor.

voice, *n., v.,* **voiced, voicing.** —*n.* **1.** sound uttered through mouth. **2.** speaking or singing voice. **3.** expression. **4.** choice. **5.** right to express opinion. **6.** verb inflection indicating whether subject is acting or acted upon. —*v.* **7.** express or declare. —**voice′less,** *adj.*

voice box, larynx.

voice mail, electronic system that routes voice messages to appropriate recipients.

voice′-o′ver, *n.* voice of off-screen narrator or announcer, as on television.

void, *adj.* **1.** without legal force. **2.** useless. **3.** empty. —*n.* **4.** empty space. —*v.* **5.** invalidate. **6.** empty out. —**void′a•ble,** *adj.* —**void′ance,** *n.*

voile (voil), *n.* lightweight, semisheer fabric.

vol., volume.

vol′a•tile, *adj.* **1.** evaporating rapidly. **2.** explosive. **3.** rapidly changeable in emotion. —**vol′a•til′i•ty,** *n.*

vol•ca′no, *n., pl.* **-noes, -nos. 1.** vent in earth from which lava, steam, etc., are expelled. **2.** mountain with such vent. —**vol•can′ic,** *adj.*

vole, *n.* short-tailed stocky rodent.

vo•li′tion, *n.* act or power of willing. —**vo•li′tion•al,** *adv.*

vol′ley, *n.* **1.** discharge of many missiles together. **2.** returning of ball before it hits ground. —*v.* **3.** hit or fire volley.

vol′ley•ball′, *n.* **1.** game in which large ball is volleyed back and forth over net. **2.** ball used in this game.

volt, *n.* unit of electromotive force. —**volt′age,** *n.* —**volt′me′ter,** *n.*

vol·ta′ic, *adj.* of or noting electricity produced by chemical action.

vol′u·ble, *adj.* glibly fluent. —**vol′u·bil′i·ty,** *n.* —**vol′u·bly,** *adv.*

vol′ume, *n.* 1. book. 2. size in three dimensions. 3. mass or quantity. 4. loudness or fullness of sound.

vo·lu′mi·nous, *adj.* 1. filling many volumes. 2. ample. —**vo·lu′mi·nous·ly,** *adv.*

vol′un·tar′y, *adj.* 1. done, made, etc., by free choice. 2. controlled by will. —**vol′un·tar′i·ly,** *adv.*

vol′un·teer′, *n.* 1. person who offers self, as for military duty. 2. worker forgoing pay. —*v.* 3. offer for some duty or purpose.

vo·lup′tu·ous, *adj.* luxurious; sensuous. —**vo·lup′tu·ous·ly,** *adv.* —**vo·lup′tu·ous·ness,** *n.*

vo·lute′ (və loōt′), *n.* spiral object.

vom′it, *v.* 1. eject from stomach through mouth. 2. eject with force. —*n.* 3. vomited matter.

voo′doo, *n.* polytheistic religion deriving chiefly from African cults.

vo·ra′cious, *adj.* greedy; ravenous. —**vo·ra′cious·ly,** *adv.* —**vo·rac′i·ty,** *n.*

vor′tex, *n., pl.* **-texes, -tices.** whirling movement or mass.

vo′ta·ry, *n., pl.* **-ries.** 1. worshiper. 2. devotee. 3. person bound by religious vows.

vote, *n., v.,* **voted, voting.** —*n.* 1. formal expression of wish or choice, as by ballot. 2. right to this. 3. votes collectively. —*v.* 4. cast one's vote. 5. cause to go or occur by vote. —**vot′er,** *n.*

vouch, *v.* 1. answer for. 2. give assurance, as surety or sponsor.

vouch′er, *n.* 1. one that vouches. 2. document, receipt, etc., proving expenditure.

vouch·safe′, *v.,* **-safed, -safing.** grant or permit.

vow, *n.* 1. solemn promise, pledge, or personal engagement. —*v.* 2. make vow.

vow'el, *n.* 1. speech sound made with clear channel through middle of mouth. 2. letter representing vowel.

voy'age, *n, v.,* **-aged, -aging.** —*n.* 1. journey, esp. by water. —*v.* 2. make voyage. —**voy'ag•er,** *n.*

vo•yeur' (vwä yûr', voi ûr'), *n.* person who obtains sexual gratification by looking at sexual objects or acts. —**vo•yeur'ism,** *n.* —**voy'eur•is'tic,** *adj.*

V.P., Vice President. Also, **VP.**

vs., versus.

VT, Vermont. Also, **Vt.**

vul'can•ize', *v.,* **-ized, -izing.** treat rubber with sulfur and heat. —**vul'can•i•za'tion,** *n.* —**vul'can•iz'er,** *n.*

vul'gar, *adj.* 1. lacking good breeding or taste; unrefined. 2. indecent; obscene. 3. plebeian. 4. vernacular. —**vul'gar•ly,** *adv.* —**vul•gar'i•ty,** *n.*

vul'gar•ism, *n.* 1. vulgarity. 2. vulgar word.

vul'ner•a•ble, *adj.* 1. liable to physical or emotional hurt. 2. open to attack. —**vul'ner•a•bly,** *adv.* —**vul'ner•a•bil'i•ty,** *n.*

vul'ture, *n.* large, carrion-eating bird.

vul'va, *n., pl.* **-vae, -vas.** external female genitals.

vy'ing, *adj.* competing.

W, w, *n.* twenty-third letter of English alphabet.

W, west, western.

WA, Washington.

wack'y, *adj.,* **wackier, wackiest.** *Slang.* odd or irrational. —**wack'i•ness,** *n.*

wad, *n., v.,* **wadded, wadding.** —*n.* **1.** small soft mass. —*v.* **2.** form into wad. **3.** stuff.

wad'dle, *v.,* **-dled, -dling,** *n.* —*v.* **1.** sway in walking, as duck. —*n.* **2.** waddling gait.

wade, *v.,* **waded, wading,** *n.* —*v.* **1.** walk through water, sand, etc. —*n.* **2.** act of wading. —**wad'er,** *n.*

wa'fer, *n.* **1.** thin crisp biscuit. **2.** small disk of bread used in Eucharist.

waf'fle, *n., v.,* **-fled, -fling.** —*n.* **1.** batter cake baked in a double griddle (**waffle iron**). —*v.* **2.** speak or write equivocally.

waft, *v.* **1.** float through air or over water. —*n.* **2.** sound, odor, etc., wafted.

wag, *v.,* **wagged, wagging,** *n.* —*v.* **1.** move rapidly back and forth. —*n.* **2.** act of wagging. **3.** joker. —**wag'gish,** *adj.*

W

wage, *n., v.,* **waged, waging.** —*n.* **1.** pay; salary. **2.** recompense. —*v.* **3.** carry on (war, etc.).

wa'ger, *v., n.* bet.

wag'ger•y, *n., pl.* **-geries. 1.** roguish wit of a wag. **2.** joke.

wag'gle, *v.,* **-gled, -gling,** *n.* wag.

wag'on, *n.* four-wheeled vehicle for drawing heavy loads. Also, *Brit.,* **wag'gon.**

wagon train, train of wagons and horses.

waif, *n.* homeless child.

wail, *n.* **1.** long mournful cry. —*v.* **2.** sound like this. **3.** utter wails. —**wail'er,** *n.*

wain'scot, *n., v.,* **-scoted, -scoting.** —*n.* **1.** woodwork lining wall. —*v.* **2.** line with wainscot.

waist, *n.* **1.** part of body between ribs and hips. **2.** garment or part of garment for upper part of body. —**waist'band',** *n.* —**waist'line',** *n.*

waist'coat' (wes'kət), *n. Brit.* vest.

wait, *v.* **1.** stay in expectation. **2.** be ready. **3.** await. **4.** wait on; serve. —*n.* **5.** act of waiting. **6.** delay. **7.** ambush.

wait′er, *n.* man who waits on table. —**wait′ress,** *n.fem.*

waiting list, list of persons waiting, as for reservations or admission.

waive, *v.,* **waived, waiving.** give up; forgo.

waiv′er, *n.* statement of relinquishment.

wake, *v.,* **waked** or **woke, waked, waking,** *n.* —*v.* **1.** stop sleeping; rouse from sleep. —*n.* **2.** vigil, esp. beside corpse. **3.** track or path, esp. of vessel.

wake′ful, *adj.* awake; alert. —**wake′ful•ly,** *adv.* —**wake′ful•ness,** *n.*

wak′en, *v.* wake.

wale, *n., v.,* **waled, waling.** —*n.* **1.** mark left on skin by rod or whip. **2.** vertical rib or cord in fabric. —*v.* **3.** mark with wales.

walk, *v.* **1.** go or traverse on foot. **2.** cause to walk. —*n.* **3.** act, course, or manner of walking. **4.** branch of activity. **5.** sidewalk or path. —**walk′er,** *n.*

walk′a•way′, *n.* easy victory.

walk′ie-talk′ie, *n.* portable radio transmitter and receiver.

walking stick, 1. stick used for support in walking. **2.** insect with long twiglike body.

walk′out′, *n.* strike in which workers leave place of work.

wall, *n.* **1.** upright structure that divides, encloses, etc. —*v.* **2.** enclose, divide, etc., with wall.

wall′board′, *n.* artificial material used to make or cover walls, etc.

wal′let, *n.* small flat case for paper money, etc.

wall′eye′, *n.* **1.** condition in which eye or eyes are turned outward. **2.** N American freshwater food fish. Also, **walleyed pike.**

wall′flow′er, *n.* **1.** person who, because of shyness, remains at side of party. **2.** perennial plant with fragrant flowers.

Wal•loon′, *n.* member of French-speaking population of S and E Belgium.

wal′lop, *Informal.* —*v.* **1.** thrash or defeat. —*n.* **2.** blow.

wal′lop•ing, *adj. Informal.* **1.** very large. **2.** impressive.

wal′low, *v.* **1.** lie or roll in mud, etc. —*n.* **2.** place where animals wallow.

wall′pa′per, *n.* decorative paper for covering walls and ceilings.

wal′nut′, *n.* northern tree valued for wood and edible nut.

wal′rus, *n.* large tusked mammal of Arctic seas.

waltz, *n.* **1.** dance in triple rhythm. —*v.* **2.** dance a waltz. —**waltz′er,** *n.*

wam′pum, *n.* shell beads, formerly used by North American Indians as money and ornament.

wan, *adj.,* **wanner, wannest.** pale; worn-looking. —**wan′ly,** *adv.*

wand, *n.* slender rod or shoot.

wan′der, *v.* move aimlessly; stray. —**wan′der•er,** *n.*

Wandering Jew, trailing plant with green or variegated leaves.

wan′der•lust′, *n.* desire to travel.

wane, *v.,* **waned, waning,** *n.* —*v.* **1.** (of moon) decrease periodically. **2.** decline or decrease. —*n.* **3.** decline or decrease.

wan′gle, *v.,* **-gled, -gling.** bring out or obtain by scheming or underhand methods.

Wan′kel engine, (wäng′kəl, wang′-), internal-combustion rotary engine with triangular motor that revolves in chamber.

wan′na•be′ (won′ə bē′, wô′nə-), *n. Informal.* one who aspires, often vainly, to emulate another's success or status.

want, *v.* **1.** feel need or desire for. **2.** lack; be deficient in. —*n.* **3.** desire or need. **4.** lack. **5.** poverty.

want′ing, *adj., prep.* lacking.

wan′ton, *adj.* **1.** malicious; unjustifiable. **2.** lewd. —*n.* **3.** lascivious person. —*v.* **4.** act in wanton manner. —**wan′ton•ly,** *adv.* —**wan′ton•ness,** *n.*

war, *n., v.,* **warred, warring,** *adj.* —*n.* **1.** armed conflict. —*v.* **2.** carry on war. —*adj.* **3.** of, for, or due to war.

war'ble, *v.,* **-bled, -bling,** *n.* —*v.* **1.** sing with trills, etc., as birds. —*n.* **2.** warbled song.

war'bler, *n.* small songbird.

ward, *n.* **1.** division of city. **2.** division of hospital. **3.** person under legal care of guardian or court. **4.** custody. —*v.* **5. ward off,** repel or avert.

ward'en, *n.* **1.** keeper. **2.** administrative head of prison.

ward'er, *n.* guard.

ward heeler, minor politician who does chores for political machine.

ward'robe', *n.* **1.** stock of clothes. **2.** clothes closet.

ward'room', *n.* living quarters for ship's officers other than captain.

ware, *n.* **1.** (*pl.*) goods. **2.** pottery. **3.** vessels for domestic use.

ware'house', *n., v.,* **-housed, -housing.** —*n.* **1.** (wâr'hous'). storehouse for goods. —*v.* (-houz'). **2.** store in warehouse.

war'fare', *n.* waging of war.

war'head', *n.* section of missile containing explosive or payload.

war'-horse', *n. Informal.* veteran of many conflicts.

war'like', *adj.* waging or prepared for war.

war'lock', *n.* male witch.

warm, *adj.* **1.** having, giving, or feeling moderate heat. **2.** cordial. **3.** lively. **4.** kind; affectionate. —*v.* **5.** make or become warm. —**warm'er,** *n.* —**warm'ly,** *adv.* —**warm'ness, warmth,** *n.*

warm'-blood'ed, *adj.* having relatively constant body temperature that is independent of environment.

warmed'-o'ver, *adj.* **1.** reheated. **2.** stale.

warm'heart'ed, *adj.* having emotional warmth.

war'mong'er, *n.* person who advocates or incites war.

warn, *v.* **1.** give notice of danger, evil, etc. **2.** caution. —**warn'ing,** *n., adj.* —**warn'ing•ly,** *adv.*

warp, *v.* **1.** bend out of shape; distort. **2.** guide by ropes. —*n.* **3.** bend or twist. **4.** lengthwise threads in loom.

war′rant, *n.* **1.** justification. **2.** guarantee. **3.** document certifying or authorizing something. —*v.* **4.** authorize or justify. **5.** guarantee. —**war′rant•a•ble,** *adj.*

warrant officer, military officer between enlisted and commissioned grades.

war′ran•ty, *n., pl.* **-ties.** guarantee.

war′ren, *n.* place where rabbits live.

war′ri•or, *n.* soldier.

war′ship′, *n.* ship for combat.

wart, *n.* small hard elevation on skin. —**wart′y,** *adj.*

war′y (wâr′ē), *adj.,* **warier, wariest. 1.** watchful. **2.** careful. —**war′i•ly,** *adv.* —**war′i•ness,** *n.*

was, *v.* first and third pers. sing., past indicative of **be.**

wash, *v.* **1.** cleanse in or with water. **2.** flow over. **3.** carry in flowing. **4.** cover thinly. —*n.* **5.** act of washing. **6.** Also, **wash′ing.** clothes, etc., to be washed. **7.** liquid covering. **8.** rough water or air behind moving ship or plane. —**wash′a•ble,** *adj.* —**wash′board′,** *n.*

—**wash′bowl′,** *n.*

—**wash′cloth′,** *n.*

—**wash′stand′,** *n.*

—**wash′room′,** *n.*

Wash., Washington.

washed′-out′, *adj.* **1.** faded. **2.** *Informal.* weary or tired-looking.

washed′-up′, *adj. Informal.* done for; having failed.

wash′er, *n.* **1.** machine for washing. **2.** flat ring of rubber, metal, etc., to give tightness.

wash′out′, *n.* **1.** destruction from action of water. **2.** *Slang.* failure.

wasn′t, contraction of **was not.**

wasp, *n.* **1.** stinging insect. **2.** *Slang.* (*cap. or caps.*) white Anglo-Saxon Protestant.

wasp′ish, *adj.* irritable; snappish.

was′sail (wos′əl), *n.* **1.** drinking party. **2.** toast (def. 2). —*v.* **3.** drink a toast.

waste, *v.,* **wasted, wasting,** *n., adj.* —*v.* **1.** squander. **2.** fail to use. **3.** destroy gradually. **4.** become wasted. —*n.* **5.** useless expenditure. **6.** neglect. **7.** gradual decay. **8.** devastation. **9.** anything left

over. —*adj.* **10.** not used. **11.** left over or worthless.
—**waste′ful,** *adj.*
—**waste′bas′ket,** *n.*
—**waste′pa′per,** *n.*

waste′land′, *n.* barren land.

wast′rel (wās′trəl), *n.* **1.** spendthrift. **2.** idler.

watch, *v.* **1.** look attentively. **2.** be careful. **3.** guard. —*n.* **4.** close, constant observation. **5.** guard. **6.** period of watching. **7.** *Naut.* period of duty. **8.** small timepiece.
—**watch′band′,** *n.* —**watch′er,** *n.* —**watch′ful,** *adj.*
—**watch′man,** *n.*
—**watch′tow′er,** *n.*

watch′dog′, *n.* **1.** dog that guards property. **2.** guardian, as against illegal conduct.

watch′word′, *n.* **1.** password. **2.** slogan.

wa′ter, *n.* **1.** transparent liquid forming rivers, seas, lakes, rain, etc. **2.** surface of water. **3.** liquid solution. **4.** liquid organic secretion. —*v.* **5.** moisten or supply with water. **6.** dilute. **7.** discharge water. —*adj.* **8.** of, for, or powered by water.

wa′ter·bed′, *n.* water-filled plastic bag used as bed.

water buffalo, domesticated Asian buffalo with curved horns.

water chestnut, aquatic plant with edible, nutlike fruit.

water closet, room containing flush toilet.

wa′ter·col′or, *n.* **1.** pigment mixed with water. **2.** painting using such pigments.

wa′ter·course′, *n.* **1.** stream of water. **2.** bed of stream.

wa′ter·craft′, *n.* **1.** skill in boating and water sports. **2.** boat.

wa′ter·cress′, *n.* plant that grows in streams and bears pungent leaves used in salad.

wa′ter·fall′, *n.* steep fall of water.

wa′ter·fowl′, *n., pl.* **-fowl, -fowls.** aquatic bird.

wa′ter·front′, *n.* part of city or town on edge of body of water.

water gap, transverse gap in mountain ridge.

water glass, 1. vessel for drinking. **2.** sodium silicate.

wa'ter·ing place, resort by water or having mineral springs.

water lily, aquatic plant with showy flowers.

water line, one of series of lines on ship's hull indicating level to which it is immersed.

wa'ter·logged', *adj.* filled or soaked with water.

wa'ter·mark', *n.* **1.** mark showing height reached by river, etc. **2.** manufacturer's design impressed in paper. —*v.* **3.** put watermark in (paper).

wa'ter·mel'on, *n.* large sweet juicy fruit of a vine.

water moccasin, cottonmouth.

wa'ter·proof', *adj.* **1.** impervious to water. —*v.* **2.** make waterproof.

water rat, aquatic rodent.

wa'ter-repel'lent, *adj.* repelling water but not entirely waterproof.

wa'ter·shed', *n.* **1.** area drained by river, etc. **2.** high land dividing such areas. **3.** important point of division or transition.

water ski, short, broad ski for gliding over water while being towed by boat. —**wa'ter-ski',** *v.,* **-skied, -skiing.** —**wa'ter·ski'er,** *n.*

wa'ter·spout', *n.* tornadolike storm over lake or ocean.

water table, underground level beneath which soil and rock are saturated with water.

wa'ter·tight', *adj.* **1.** constructed or fitted to be impervious to water. **2.** incapable of being nullified or discredited.

wa'ter·way', *n.* body of water as route of travel.

water wheel, wheel turned by water to provide power.

wa'ter·works', *n.pl.* apparatus for collecting and distributing water, as for city.

wa'ter·y, *adj.* of, like, or full of water. —**wa'ter·i·ness,** *n.*

watt, *n.* unit of electric power. —**watt'age,** *n.*

wat'tle, *n.* **1.** flesh hanging from throat or chin. **2.** interwoven rods and twigs.

wave, *n., v.,* **waved, waving.** —*n.* **1.** ridge on surface of liquid. **2.** surge; rush. **3.** curve.

4. vibration, as in transmission of sound, etc. **5.** sign with moving hand, flag, etc. —*v.* **6.** move with waves. **7.** curve. **8.** signal by wave. —**wav'y,** *adj.*

wave'length', *n.* distance between two successive points in wave.

wa'ver, *v.* **1.** sway. **2.** hesitate. **3.** fluctuate.

wax, *n.* **1.** yellowish substance secreted by bees. **2.** any similar substance. —*v.* **3.** rub with wax. **4.** (esp. of moon) increase. **5.** become. —**wax'en,** *adj.* —**wax'er,** *n.* —**wax'y,** *adj.*

wax bean, variety of string bean bearing yellowish, waxy pods.

wax museum, museum displaying wax effigies of famous persons.

wax myrtle, bayberry of southeastern U.S.

wax paper, paper made moisture-resistant by paraffin coating.

wax'wing', *n.* small crested bird.

way, *n.* **1.** manner; fashion. **2.** plan; means. **3.** direction. **4.** road or route. **5.** custom. **6.** (*pl.*) timbers on which ship is built.

way'bill, *n.* list of goods with shipping directions.

way'far'er, *n.* rover.

way•lay', *v.* ambush.

way'-out', *adj. Informal.* very unconventional.

ways and means, methods of raising revenue.

way'side', *n.* **1.** side of road. —*adj.* **2.** beside road.

way'ward, *adj.* capricious. —**way'ward•ness,** *n.*

we, *pron.* nominative plural of **I.**

weak, *adj.* **1.** not strong; fragile; frail. **2.** deficient. —**weak'en,** *v.* —**weak'ness,** *n.*

weak'-kneed', *adj.* yielding readily to opposition, pressure, or intimidation.

weak'ling, *n.* weak creature.

weak'ly, *adj.,* **-lier, -liest,** *adv.* —*adj.* **1.** sickly. —*adv.* **2.** in weak manner.

weal, *n. Archaic.* well-being.

wealth, *n.* **1.** great possessions or riches. **2.** profusion. —**wealth'y,** *adj.*

wean, *v.* **1.** accustom to food other than mother's milk. **2.** detach from obsession or vice.

weap'on, *n.* instrument for use in fighting.

weap'on•ry, *n.* weapons collectively.

wear, *v.,* **wore, worn, wearing,** *n.* —*v.* **1.** have on body for covering or ornament. **2.** impair or diminish gradually. **3.** weary. **4.** undergo wear. **5.** last under use. —*n.* **6.** use of garment. **7.** clothing. **8.** gradual impairment or diminution. —**wear'a•ble,** *adj.* —**wear'er,** *n.*

wea'ri•some, *adj.* **1.** tiring. **2.** tedious.

wea'ry, *adj.,* **-rier, -riest,** *v.,* **-ried, -rying.** —*adj.* **1.** tired. **2.** tedious. —*v.* **3.** tire. —**wea'ri•ly,** *adv.* —**wea'ri•ness,** *n.*

wea'sel, *n.* small carnivorous animal.

weath'er, *n.* **1.** state of atmosphere as to moisture, temperature, etc. —*v.* **2.** expose to weather. **3.** withstand. —*adj.* **4.** of or on windward side.

weath'er•beat'en, *adj.* worn or marked by weather.

weath'er•ing, *n.* action of natural agents, as wind and water, on exposed rock.

weath'er•ize', *v.,* **-ized, -izing.** make secure against cold weather.

weath'er•proof', *adj.* **1.** able to withstand all kinds of weather. —*v.* **2.** make weatherproof.

weather strip, narrow strip placed between door or window sash and frame.

weath'er•vane', *n.* device to show direction of wind.

weave, *v.,* **wove, woven** or **wove, weaving,** *n.* —*v.* **1.** interlace, as to form cloth. **2.** take winding course. —*n.* **3.** manner of weaving. —**weav'er,** *n.*

web, *n., v.,* **webbed, webbing.** —*n.* **1.** something woven. **2.** fabric spun by spiders. **3.** membrane between toes in ducks, etc. —*v.* **4.** cover with web. —**webbed',** *adj.* —**web'bing,** *n.*

web'foot', *n.* foot with webbed toes. —**web'foot'ed,** *adj.*

wed, *v.,* **wedded, wedded** or **wed, wedding. 1.** bind or join in marriage. **2.** attach firmly.

Wed., Wednesday.

wed'ding, *n.* marriage ceremony.

wedge, *n., v.,* **wedged, wedging.** —*n.* **1.** angled object for splitting. —*v.* **2.** split with wedge. **3.** thrust or force like wedge.

wed'lock, *n.* matrimony.

Wednes'day, *n.* fourth day of week.

wee, *adj.* tiny.

weed, *n.* **1.** useless plant growing in cultivated ground. **2.** (*pl.*) mourning garments. —*v.* **3.** free from weeds. **4.** remove as undesirable. —**weed'er,** *n.* —**weed'y,** *adj.*

weeds, *n.pl.* black clothes for mourning.

week, *n.* **1.** seven successive days. **2.** working part of week.

week'day', *n.* any day except Sunday, or, often, Saturday and Sunday. —**week'day',** *adj.*

week'end', *n.* **1.** Saturday and Sunday. —*adj.* **2.** of or for weekend.

week'ly, *adj., adv., n., pl.* **-lies.** —*adj.* **1.** happening, appearing, etc., once a week. **2.** lasting a week. —*adv.* **3.** once a week. **4.** by the week. —*n.* **5.** weekly periodical.

weep, *v.,* **wept, weeping. 1.** shed tears. **2.** mourn. —**weep'er,** *n.*

wee'vil, *n.* beetle destructive to grain, fruit, etc. —**wee'vi•ly,** *adj.*

weft, *n.* threads interlacing with warp.

weigh, *v.* **1.** measure heaviness of. **2.** burden. **3.** consider. **4.** lift. **5.** have heaviness. —**weigh'er,** *n.*

weight, *n.* **1.** amount of heaviness. **2.** system of units for expressing weight. **3.** heavy mass. **4.** pressure. **5.** burden. **6.** importance. —*v.* **7.** add weight to. —**weight'y,** *adj.* —**weight'i•ly,** *adv.* —**weight'less,** *adj.*

weir (wēr), *n.* **1.** dam in a stream. **2.** fence set in stream to catch fish.

weird, *adj.* **1.** supernatural. **2.** uncannily strange. —**weird'ly,** *adv.* —**weird'ness,** *n.*

weird'o, *n. Slang.* odd, eccentric, or abnormal person.

wel'come, *n., v.,* **-comed, -coming,** *adj.* —*n.* **1.** friendly reception. —*v.* **2.** receive or greet with pleasure. —*adj.* **3.** gladly received. **4.** given permission or consent.

weld, *v.* **1.** unite, esp. by heating and pressing. —*n.* **2.** welded joint. —**weld'er,** *n.*

wel'fare', *n.* **1.** well-being. **2.** provision of benefits to poor.

well, *adv., compar.* **better,** *superl.* **best,** *adj., n., v.* —*adv.* **1.** excellently; properly. **2.** thoroughly. —*adj.* **3.** in good health. **4.** good; proper. —*n.* **5.** hole made in earth to reach water, oil, etc. **6.** source. **7.** vertical shaft. —*v.* **8.** rise or gush.

well'-advised', *adj.* **1.** acting with care. **2.** based on wise consideration.

well'-appoint'ed, *adj.* attractively furnished.

well'-be'ing, *n.* good or prosperous condition.

well'born', *adj.* of good family.

well'-bred', *adj.* showing good manners.

well'-dis•posed', *adj.* feeling favorable, sympathetic, or kind.

well'-done', *adj.* **1.** performed accurately and skillfully. **2.** thoroughly cooked.

well'-found'ed, *adj.* having or based on good reasons, sound information, etc.

well'-ground'ed, *adj.* having good basic knowledge of a subject.

well'-heeled', *adj.* prosperous; well-off.

well'-informed', *adj.* having extensive knowledge.

well'-mean'ing, *adj.* intending good. —**well'-meant',** *adj.*

well'-nigh', *adv.* nearly.

well'-off', *adj.* **1.** in good or favorable condition. **2.** prosperous.

well'-round'ed, *adj.* desirably varied.

well'-spo'ken, *adj.* **1.** speaking well or fittingly. **2.** spoken in a pleasing manner.

well'spring', *n.* source.

well′-to-do′, *adj.* prosperous.

well′-worn′, *adj.* **1.** showing effects of extensive use. **2.** trite.

Welsh (welsh, welch), *n.* people or language of Wales.

welt, *n.* **1.** wale from lash. **2.** strip around edge of shoe. **3.** narrow border along seam. —*v.* **4.** put welt on.

wel′ter, *v.* **1.** roll, as waves. **2.** wallow.

wen, *n.* small cyst.

wench, *n.* girl or young woman.

wend, *v.,* **wended, wending.** *Archaic.* go.

went, *v.* pt. of **go.**

were, *v.* past plural and pres. subjunctive of **be.**

weren't, contraction of **were not.**

were′wolf′ (wēr′-), *n., pl.* **-wolves.** (in folklore) human turned into wolf.

west, *n.* **1.** point of compass opposite east. **2.** direction of this point. **3.** area in this direction. —*adj.* **4.** toward, from, or in west. —*adv.* **5.** toward or from west.

—**west′er•ly,** *adj., adv.*
—**west′ern,** *adj.*
—**west′ern•er,** *n.*

west′ern•ize′, *v.,* **-ized, -izing.** influence with or convert to western ideas and customs.

west′ward, *adj.* **1.** moving or facing west. —*adv.* **2.** Also, **west′wards.** toward west. —*n.* **3.** westward part. —**west′ward•ly,** *adj., adv.*

wet, *adj.,* **wetter, wettest,** *n., v.,* **wet** or **wetted, wetting.** —*adj.* **1.** covered or soaked with water. **2.** rainy. —*n.* **3.** moisture. —*v.* **4.** make or become wet. —**wet′ness,** *n.*

wet blanket, one that dampens enthusiasm.

wet′land′, *n.* low land with usu. wet soil.

wet nurse, woman hired to suckle another's infant.

wet suit, close-fitting rubber suit worn for body warmth, as by scuba divers.

whack, *Informal. v.* **1.** strike sharply. —*n.* **2.** smart blow.

whale, *n., pl.* **whales** or **whale,** *v.,* **whaled, whaling.** —*n.* **1.** large fishlike marine mammal. —*v.* **2.** kill and render whales. —**whal′er,** *n.*

whale′bone′, *n.* elastic horny substance in upper jaw of some whales.

wharf, *n., pl.* **wharves.** structure for mooring vessels.

wharf′age, *n.* **1.** use of wharf. **2.** charge for such use.

what, *pron., pl.* **what**, *adv.* —*pron.* **1.** which one? **2.** that which. **3.** such. —*adv.* **4.** how much. **5.** partly.

what•ev′er, *pron.* **1.** anything that. **2.** no matter what. —*adj.* **3.** no matter what.

what′not′, *n.* small open cupboard, esp. for knickknacks.

what′so•ev′er, *pron., adj.* whatever.

wheal, *n.* swelling, as from mosquito bite.

wheat, *n.* grain of common cereal grass, used esp. for flour.

whee′dle, *v.,* **-dled, -dling.** influence by artful persuasion.

wheel, *n.* **1.** round object turning on axis. —*v.* **2.** turn on axis. **3.** move on wheels. **4.** turn.

wheel′bar′row, *n.* one-wheeled vehicle lifted at one end.

wheel′base′, *n. Auto.* distance between centers of front and rear wheel hubs.

wheel′chair′, *n.* chair mounted on wheels for use by persons who cannot walk.

wheeze, *v.,* **wheezed, wheezing,** *n.* —*v.* **1.** whistle in breathing. —*n.* **2.** wheezing breath. **3.** trite saying.

whelm, *v.* **1.** engulf. **2.** overwhelm.

whelp, *n.* **1.** young of dog, wolf, bear, etc. —*v.* **2.** bring forth whelps.

when, *adv.* **1.** at what time. —*conj.* **2.** at time that. **3.** and then.

whence, *adv., conj.* from what place.

when•ev′er, *adv.* at whatever time.

where, *adv.* **1.** in, at, or to what place? **2.** in what respect? —*conj.* **3.** in, at, or to what place. **4.** and there.

where′a•bouts′, *adv.* **1.** where. —*n.* **2.** location.

where•as′, *conj.* **1.** while on the contrary. **2.** considering that.

where•at′, *conj.* **1.** at which. **2.** to which; whereupon.

where•by′, *conj.* by what or which; under the terms of which.

where′fore′, *adv., conj.* **1.** why; for what. —*n.* **2.** reason.

where•in′, *conj.* **1.** in what or in which. —*adv.* **2.** in what way or respect?

where•of′, *adv., conj.* of what.

where′up•on′, *conj.* **1.** upon which. **2.** at or after which.

wher•ev′er, *conj.* at or to whatever place.

where′with•al′, *n.* means.

wher′ry, *n., pl.* **-ries.** light rowboat for one person.

whet, *v.,* **whetted, whetting.** sharpen. —**whet′stone′**, *n.*

wheth′er, *conj.* (word introducing alternative.)

whey (hwā), *n.* watery part that separates out when milk curdles.

which, *pron.* **1.** what one? **2.** the one that. —*adj.* **3.** what one of (those mentioned).

which•ev′er, *pron.* any that.

whiff, *n.* **1.** slight puff or blast. —*v.* **2.** blow in whiffs.

while, *n., conj., v.,* **whiled, whiling.** —*n.* **1.** time. —*conj.*

2. in time that. —*v.* **3.** pass (time) pleasantly.

whim, *n.* irrational or fanciful decision or idea.

whim′per, *v.* **1.** cry softly and plaintively. —*n.* **2.** whimpering cry. —**whim′per•er**, *n.*

whim′sy, *n., pl.* **-sies.** fanciful idea; whim. —**whim′si•cal,** *adj.* —**whim′si•cal′i•ty**, *n.* —**whim′si•cal•ly**, *adv.*

whine, *n., v.,* **whined, whining.** —*n.* **1.** low complaining sound. —*v.* **2.** utter whines. —**whin′er**, *n.* —**whin′ing•ly**, *adv.*

whin′ny, *v.,* **-nied, -nying**, *n., pl.* **-nies.** neigh.

whip, *v.,* **whipped, whipping**, *n.* —*v.* **1.** strike repeatedly; flog. **2.** jerk; seize. **3.** cover with thread; overcast. **4.** beat (cream, etc.). **5.** move quickly; lash about. —*n.* **6.** instrument with lash and handle for striking. **7.** party manager in legislature. —**whip′per**, *n.*

whip′cord′, *n.* fabric with diagonal ribs.

whip′lash′, *n.* **1.** lash of whip. **2.** neck injury caused by sudden jerking of the head.

whip′per•snap′per, *n.* insignificant, presumptuous person, esp. young one.

whip′pet, *n.* small swift dog.

whip′poor•will′, *n.* nocturnal American bird.

whip′saw′, *n.* saw for two persons.

whir, *v.,* **whirred, whirring,** *n.* —*v.* **1.** move with buzzing sound. —*n.* **2.** such sound. Also, **whirr.**

whirl, *v.* **1.** spin or turn rapidly. **2.** move quickly. —*n.* **3.** whirling movement. **4.** round of events, etc. —**whirl′er,** *n.*

whirl′i•gig′, *n.* toy revolving in wind.

whirl′pool′, *n.* whirling current in water.

whirl′wind′, *n.* whirling mass of air.

whisk, *v.* **1.** sweep up. **2.** move or carry lightly. —*n.* **3.** act of whisking.

whisk′er, *n.* **1.** (*pl.*) hair on man's face. **2.** bristle on face of cat, etc.

whis′key, *n.* distilled alcoholic liquor made from grain or corn. Also, **whis′ky.**

whis′per, *v.* **1.** speak very softly. —*n.* **2.** sound of whispering. **3.** something whispered. —**whis′per•er,** *n.*

whist, *n.* card game.

whis′tle, *v.,* **-tled, -tling,** *n.* —*v.* **1.** make clear shrill sound with breath, air, or steam. —*n.* **2.** device for making such sounds. **3.** sound of whistling. —**whis′tler,** *n.*

whis′tle-blow′er, *n.* person who publicly discloses corruption or wrongdoing.

whistle stop, 1. small town. **2.** short talk from rear platform of train during political campaign.

whit, *n.* particle; bit.

white, *adj.* **1.** of color of snow. **2.** having light skin. **3.** pale. —*n.* **4.** color without hue, opposite to black. **5.** Caucasian. **6.** white or light part. —**whit′en,** *v.* —**white′ness,** *n.* —**whit′ish,** *adj.*

white blood cell, nearly colorless blood cell of immune system.

white′-bread′, *adj.* bland; conventional.

white′cap′, *n.* wave with foaming white crest.

white′-col′lar, *adj.* of professional or office workers whose jobs usu. do not involve manual labor.

white elephant, useless, expensive possession.

white′fish′, *n.* small food fish.

white flag, all-white flag used to signal surrender or truce.

white gold, gold alloy colored white esp. by presence of nickel.

white goods, household linens.

white lie, harmless lie; fib.

white′wash′, *n.* **1.** substance for whitening walls, etc. —*v.* **2.** cover with whitewash. **3.** cover up faults or errors of.

white water, frothy water, as in rapids.

whith′er, *adv., conj. Archaic.* where; to what (which) place.

whit′ing, *n.* **1.** small Atlantic food fish. **2.** ground chalk used to whiten.

whit′low, *n.* inflammation on finger or toe.

Whit′sun•day, *n.* seventh Sunday after Easter.

whit′tle, *v.,* **-tled, -tling. 1.** cut bit by bit with knife. **2.** reduce. —**whit′tler**, *n.*

whiz, *v.,* **whizzed, whizzing,** *n.* —*v.* **1.** move with hum or hiss. —*n.* **2.** whizzing sound. **3.** person who is very good at something. Also, **whizz.**

who, *pron.* **1.** what person? **2.** the person that.

whoa, *interj.* (stop!)

who•dun′it, *n.* detective story.

who•ev′er, *pron.* anyone that.

whole, *adj.* **1.** entire; undivided. **2.** undamaged. **3.** *Math.* not fractional. —*n.* **4.** entire amount or extent. **5.** complete thing. —**whol′ly**, *adv.* —**whole′ness**, *n.*

whole′-heart′ed, *adj.* sincere.

whole note, *Music.* note equivalent in value to four quarter notes.

whole′sale′, *n., adj., v.,* **-saled, -saling.** —*n.* **1.** sale of goods in quantity, as to retailers. —*adj.* **2.** of or engaged in wholesale. —*v.* **3.** sell by wholesale. —**whole′sal′er**, *n.*

whole′some, *adj.* beneficial; healthful. —**whole′some•ly**, *adv.* —**whole′some•ness**, *n.*

whole′-wheat′, *adj.* prepared with complete wheat kernel.

whom, *pron.* objective case of who.

whom·ev′er, *pron.* objective case of **whoever.**

whoop, *n.* **1.** loud shout or cry. **2.** gasping sound characteristic of whooping cough. —*v.* **3.** utter whoops.

whoop′ing cough, infectious disease characterized by short, convulsive coughs followed by whoops.

whop′per (hwop′ər, wop′-), *n. Informal.* **1.** something uncommonly large. **2.** big lie.

whop′ping, *adj. Informal.* uncommonly large.

whore (hōr), *n., v.,* **whored, whoring.** —*n.* **1.** prostitute. —*v.* **2.** consort with whores.

whorl, *n.* **1.** circular arrangement, as of leaves. **2.** any spiral part.

whose, *pron.* possessive case of who.

who′so·ev′er, *pron.* whoever.

why, *adv., n., pl.* **whys.** —*adv.* **1.** for what reason. —*n.* **2.** cause or reason.

WI, Wisconsin.

wick, *n.* soft threads that absorb fuel to be burned in candle, etc.

wick′ed, *adj.* **1.** evil; sinful. **2.** naughty. —**wick′ed·ly,** *adv.* —**wick′ed·ness,** *n.*

wick′er, *n.* **1.** slender pliant twig. —*adj.* **2.** made of wicker. —**wick′er·work′,** *n.*

wick′et, *n.* **1.** small gate or opening. **2.** framework in cricket and croquet.

wide, *adj.,* **wider, widest,** *adv.* —*adj.* **1.** broad. **2.** extensive. **3.** expanded. **4.** far. —*adv.* **5.** far. **6.** to farthest extent. —**wide′ly,** *adv.* —**wid′en,** *v.* —**wide′ness,** *n.*

wide′-awake′, *adj.* **1.** fully awake. **2.** alert or observant.

wide′-eyed′, *adj.* having eyes open wide, as in amazement or innocence.

wide′spread′, *adj.* occurring widely.

widg′eon, *n.* wigeon.

wid′ow, *n.* **1.** woman whose husband has died. —*v.* **2.** make widow of. —**wid′ow·er,** *n.masc.* —**wid′ow·hood,** *n.*

width, *n.* **1.** breadth. **2.** piece of full wideness.

wield, *v.* **1.** exercise (power, etc.). **2.** brandish. —**wield'er,** *n.* —**wield'y,** *adj.*

wie'ner, *n.* small sausage; frankfurter.

wife, *n., pl.* **wives.** married woman. —**wife'ly,** *adj.*

wig, *n.* artificial covering of hair for head.

wig'eon (wij'ən), *n., pl.* **-eons, -eon.** freshwater duck.

wig'gle, *v.,* **-gled, -gling,** *n.* —*v.* **1.** twist to and fro; wriggle. —*n.* **2.** wiggling movement. —**wig'gly,** *adj.* —**wig'gler,** *n.*

wig'wag', *v.,* **-wagged, -wagging,** *n.* —*v.* **1.** signal in code with flags, etc. —*n.* **2.** such signaling. **3.** message so sent.

wig'wam (-wom), *n.* American Indian dwelling.

wild, *adj.* **1.** not cultivated. **2.** uncivilized. **3.** violent. **4.** uninhabited. **5.** disorderly. —*adv.* **6.** wildly. —*n.* **7.** uncultivated or desolate tract. —**wild'ly,** *adv.* —**wild'ness,** *n.*

wild'cat', *n., v.,* **-catted, -catting.** —*n.* **1.** large North American feline. —*v.* **2.** prospect independently. —*adj.* not called or sanctioned by labor union.

wil'de•beest, *n.* gnu.

wil'der•ness, *n.* wild or desolate region.

wild'-eyed', *adj.* **1.** having a wild expression in the eyes. **2.** extreme or radical.

wild'fire', *n.* outdoor fire that spreads rapidly and is hard to extinguish.

wild'flow'er, *n.* flower of plant that grows wild.

wild'-goose' chase', senseless search for something unobtainable.

wild'life', *n.* animals living in nature.

wild rice, tall aquatic grass of N North America.

wile, *n.* cunning; artifice.

will, *n.* **1.** power of conscious action or choice. **2.** wish; pleasure. **3.** attitude, either hostile or friendly. **4.** declaration of wishes for disposition of property after death. —*v.* **5.** decide to influence by act of will. **6.** consent to. **7.** give by will. —*auxiliary verb.* **8.** am (is, are) about to. **9.** am (is, are) willing to.

will'ful, *adj.* **1.** intentional. **2.** headstrong. Also, **wil'ful.** —**will'ful•ly,** *adv.* —**will'ful•ness,** *n.*

wil'lies, *n.pl.* nervousness.

will'ing, *adj.* **1.** consenting. **2.** cheerfully done, given, etc. —**will'ing•ly,** *adv.* —**will'ing•ness,** *n.*

will'-o'-the-wisp', *n.* **1.** flitting, elusive light. **2.** something that fascinates and deludes.

wil'low, *n.* slender tree or shrub with tough, pliant branches.

wil'low•y, *adj.,* **-lowier, -lowiest.** tall and slender. —**wil'low•i•ness,** *n.*

wil'ly-nil'ly, *adv.* willingly or unwillingly.

wilt, *v.* **1.** wither or droop. —*n.* **2.** wilted state.

wil'y (wī'lē), *adj.,* **wilier, wiliest.** crafty; cunning. —**wil'i•ness,** *n.*

wimp, *n. Informal.* weak, ineffectual person. —**wimp'y,** *adj.*

win, *v.,* **won, winning,** *n.* —*v.* **1.** succeed or get by effort. **2.** gain (victory). **3.** persuade. —*n.* **4.** victory.

wince, *v.,* **winced, wincing,** *n.* —*v.* **1.** shrink, as from pain or blow. —*n.* **2.** wincing movement.

winch, *n.* **1.** windlass. **2.** crank.

wind (wind for 1–7; wīnd for 8–11), *n., v.,* **winded** (for 5–7) or **wound** (wound) (for 8–11), **winding.** —*n.* **1.** air in motion. **2.** gas in stomach or bowels. **3.** animal odor. **4.** breath. —*v.* **5.** make short of breath. **6.** let recover breath. **7.** expose to wind. **8.** change direction. **9.** encircle. **10.** roll into cylinder or ball. **11.** turn (handle, etc.). —**wind'y,** *adj.* —**wind'er,** *n.*

wind'bag', *n.* pompous talker.

wind'break', *n.* shelter from wind.

wind'chill factor, apparent temperature felt on exposed skin owing to combination of temperature and wind speed.

wind'ed, *adj.* **1.** having wind. **2.** out of breath.

wind'fall', *n.* **1.** something blown down. **2.** unexpected luck.

winding sheet (wīn′ding), shroud.

wind instrument, musical instrument sounded by breath or air.

wind′jam•mer, *n.* large sailing ship.

wind′lass (-ləs), *n.* drum mechanism for hoisting.

wind′mill′, *n.* mill operated by wind.

win′dow, *n.* opening for air and light, usually fitted with glass in frame.

window dressing, 1. art, act, or technique of decorating store display windows. **2.** something done solely to create favorable impression.

win′dow•pane′, *n.* pane of glass for window.

win′dow-shop′, *v.,* **-shopped, -shopping.** look at articles in store windows without making purchases. —**win′dow shop′per,** *n.*

wind′pipe′, *n.* trachea.

wind′shield′, *n.* glass shield above automobile, etc., dashboard.

wind′sock′, *n.* mounted cloth cone that catches wind to indicate wind direction.

wind′storm′, *n.* storm with heavy wind but little or no precipitation.

wind′surf′ing, *n.* sport of riding on surfboard mounted with a sail. —**wind′surf′,** *v.* —**wind′surf′er,** *n.*

wind′-swept′, *adj.* exposed to or blown by wind.

wind′up′ (wīnd′-), *n.* close; end.

wind′ward, *n.* **1.** quarter from which wind blows. —*adj.* **2.** of, in, or to windward. —*adv.* **3.** against wind.

wine, *n., v.,* **wined, wining.** —*n.* **1.** fermented juice, esp. of grape. **2.** dark purplish red. —*v.* **3.** entertain with wine. —**win′y,** *adj.*

win′er•y, *n., pl.* **-eries.** place for making wine.

wing, *n.* **1.** organ of flight in birds, insects, and bats. **2.** winglike or projecting structure. **3.** flight. **4.** supporting surface of airplane. —*v.* **5.** travel on wings. **6.** wound in wing or arm. —**wing′ed,** *adj.*

wing′ding′, *n. Slang.* noisy, exciting party.

wink, *v.* **1.** close and open (eye) quickly. **2.** signal by winking. **3.** twinkle. —*n.* **4.** winking movement.

win'ner, *n.* one that wins.

win'ning, *n.* **1.** (*pl.*) that which is won. —*adj.* **2.** charming. —**win'ning•ly,** *adv.*

win'now, *v.* **1.** free from chaff by wind. **2.** separate.

wi'no, *n., pl.* **-os.** person addicted to wine.

win'some, *adj.* sweetly or innocently charming. —**win'some•ly,** *adv.* —**win'some•ness,** *n.*

win'ter, *n.* **1.** last season of year. —*adj.* **2.** of, like, or for winter. —*v.* **3.** pass winter. **4.** keep during winter. —**win'try, win'ter•y,** *adj.*

win'ter•green', *n.* creeping aromatic shrub.

win'ter•ize', *v.,* **-ized, -izing.** prepare to withstand cold weather.

wipe, *v.,* **wiped, wiping,** *n.* —*v.* **1.** rub lightly. **2.** remove or blot. —*n.* **3.** act of wiping. —**wip'er,** *n.*

wire, *n., adj., v.,* **wired, wiring.** —*n.* **1.** slender, flexible piece of metal. **2.** telegram or telegraph. —*adj.* **3.** made of wires. —*v.* **4.** bind with wire. **5.** *Elect.* install system of wires in. **6.** telegraph.

wire'less, *adj.* **1.** activated by electromagnetic waves rather than wires. —*n.* **2.** *Brit.* radio.

wire service, agency that sends syndicated news by wire to its subscribers.

wire'tap', *v.,* **-tapped, -tapping,** *n.* —*v.* **1.** connect secretly into telephone. —*n.* **2.** act of wiretapping.

wir'ing, *n.* system of electric wires.

wir'y, *adj.,* **wirier, wiriest.** like wire; lean and strong. —**wir'i•ness,** *n.*

Wis., Wisconsin. Also, **Wisc.**

wis'dom, *n.* **1.** knowledge and judgment. **2.** wise sayings.

wisdom tooth, last tooth to erupt.

wise, *adj.* **1.** having knowledge and judgment. **2.** prudent. **3.** informed. —*n.* **4.** way; respect. —**wise'ly,** *adv.*

wise'a'cre (-ā'kər), *n.* conceited, often insolent person.

wise′crack′, *n.* **1.** smart or facetious remark —*v.* **2.** make or say as a wisecrack.

wish, *v.* **1.** want; desire. **2.** bid. —*n.* **3.** desire. **4.** that desired. —**wish′er,** *n.* —**wish′ful,** *adj.* —**wish′ful•ly,** *adv.* —**wish′ful•ness,** *n.*

wish′bone′, *n.* forked bone in front of breastbone in most birds.

wish′y-wash′y, *adj.* thin or weak.

wisp, *n.* small tuft. —**wisp′y,** *adj.*

wis•te′ri•a, *n.* climbing shrub with purple flowers. Also, **wis•tar′i•a.**

wist′ful, *adj.* **1.** pensive. **2.** longing. —**wist′ful•ly,** *adv.* —**wist′ful•ness,** *n.*

wit, *n.* **1.** power of combining perception with clever expression. **2.** person having this. **3.** (*pl.*) intelligence. —*v.* **4.** *Archaic.* know. **5. to wit,** namely.

witch, *n.* **1.** woman thought to practice magic. **2.** ugly or mean old woman. —**witch′craft′,** *n.*

witch doctor, person in some cultures who uses magic esp. to cure illness.

witch′er•y, *n., pl.* **-eries. 1.** magic. **2.** charm.

witch hazel, preparation for bruises, etc.

witch′ing, *adj.* suitable for sorcery.

with, *prep.* **1.** accompanied by. **2.** using. **3.** against.

with•draw′, *v.,* **-drew, -drawn, -drawing. 1.** draw back. **2.** retract. —**with•draw′al,** *n.*

with′er, *v.* shrivel; fade. —**with′er•ing•ly,** *adv.*

with′ers, *n.pl.* part of animal's back just behind neck.

with•hold′, *v.,* **-held, -holding.** hold or keep back.

withholding tax, that part of employee's tax liability withheld by employer from wages.

with•in′, *adv.* **1.** inside; inwardly. —*prep.* **2.** in; inside of. **3.** at point not beyond.

with•out′, *prep.* **1.** lacking. **2.** beyond. —*adv.* **3.** outside. **4.** outwardly. **5.** lacking.

with•stand′, *v.,* **-stood, -standing.** resist.

wit'less, *adj.* stupid.
—**wit'less•ly,** *adv.*
—**wit'less•ness,** *n.*

wit'ness, *v.* 1. see. 2. testify. 3. attest by signature. —*n.* 4. person who witnesses. 5. testimony.

wit'ti•cism', *n.* witty remark.

wit'ting, *adj.* knowing; aware.
—**wit'ting•ly,** *adv.*

wit'ty, *adj.,* -tier, -tiest. showing wit. —**wit'ti•ly,** *adv.*
—**wit'ti•ness,** *n.*

wive, *v.,* **wived, wiving.** marry.

wiz'ard, *n.* magician.
—**wiz'ard•ry,** *n.*

wiz'ened (wiz'-), *adj.* shriveled.

wk., week.

w/o, without.

wob'ble, *v.,* -bled, -bling. move unsteadily from side to side.
—**wob'bly,** *adj.*

woe, *n.* grief or affliction.
—**woe'ful,** *adj.* —**woe'ful•ly,** *adv.* —**woe'ful•ness,** *n.*

woe'be•gone', *adj.* showing woe.

wok, *n.* Chinese cooking pan.

wolf, *n., pl.* **wolves,** *v.* —*n.* 1. wild carnivorous animal of dog family. —*v.* 2. *Informal.* eat ravenously. —**wolf'ish,** *adj.* —**wolf'ish•ly,** *adv.*

wolf'hound', *n.* kind of hound.

wolfs'bane', *n.* poisonous plant.

wol'ver•ine', *n.* North American mammal of weasel family.

wom'an, *n., pl.* **women.** adult female human being.
—**wom'an•hood',** *n.*
—**wom'an•ish,** *adj.*
—**wom'an•ly,** *adj.*
—**wom'an•li•ness,** *n.*

womb (woom), *n.* uterus.

wom'bat, *n.* burrowing, herbivorous Australian marsupial.

won'der, *v.* 1. be curious about. 2. marvel. —*n.* 3. something strange. 4. Also, **won'der•ment.** amazement.
—**won'der•ing•ly,** *adv.*

won'der•ful, *adj.* 1. exciting wonder. 2. excellent.
—**won'der•ful•ly,** *adv.*

won'drous, *adj.* 1. wonderful.
—*adv.* 2. remarkably.
—**won'drous•ly,** *adv.*

wont (wunt, wōnt), *adj.* 1. accustomed. —*n.* 2. habit.
—**wont'ed,** *adj.*

won't, contraction of **will not.**

woo, *v.* seek to win, esp. in marriage. —**woo'er,** *n.*

wood, *n.* **1.** hard substance under bark of trees and shrubs. **2.** timber or firewood. **3.** (*often pl.*) forest. —*adj.* **4.** made of wood. **5.** living in woods. —*v.* **6.** plant with trees. —**wood'craft',** *n.* —**woods'man,** *n.* —**wood'y,** *adj.* —**wood'ed,** *adj.*

wood'bine', *n.* any of various vines, as the honeysuckle.

wood'chuck', *n.* bushy-tailed burrowing rodent. Also called **ground'hog'.**

wood'cut', *n.* print made from a carved block of wood.

wood'en, *adj.* **1.** made of wood. **2.** without feeling or expression. —**wood'en•ly,** *adv.* —**wood'en•ness,** *n.*

wood'land', *n.* forest.

wood'peck'er, *n.* bird with hard bill for boring.

wood'pile', *n.* stack of firewood.

wood'ruff, *n.* fragrant plant with small white flowers.

wood'shed', *n.* shed for storing firewood.

woods'y, *adj.,* **woodsier, woodsiest.** of or resembling woods.

wood'wind', *n.* musical instrument of group including flute, clarinet, oboe, and bassoon.

wood'work', *n.* wooden fittings inside building. —**wood'work'er,** *n.* —**wood'work'ing,** *n., adj.*

woof, *n.* **1.** yarns from side to side in loom. **2.** texture or fabric. —*v.* **3.** bark like a dog.

woof'er, *n.* loudspeaker to reproduce low-frequency sounds.

wool, *n.* **1.** soft curly hair, esp. of sheep. **2.** garments, yarn, etc., of wool. **3.** curly, fine-stranded substance. —**wool'en** or (esp. *Brit.*) **wool'len,** *adj., n.* —**wool'ly,** *adj.* —**wool'li•ness,** *n.*

wool'gath'er•ing, *n.* daydreaming.

woolly bear, caterpillar with woolly hairs.

word, *n.* **1.** group of letters or sounds that represents concept. **2.** talk or conversation. **3.** promise. **4.**

tidings. **5.** (*pl.*) angry speech.
—*v.* **6.** express in words.
—**word′less,** *adj.*

word′age, *n.* **1.** words collectively. **2.** number of words. **3.** choice of words.

word′ing, *n.* way of expressing.

word of mouth, oral communication.

word′play′, *n.* witty repartee.

word processing, production of letters, reports, etc., using computers.

word processor, computer program or system for word processing.

word′y, *adj.,* **wordier, wordiest.** using too many words. —**word′i•ness,** *n.*

work, *n.* **1.** exertion; labor. **2.** task. **3.** employment. **4.** place of employment. **5.** materials on which one works. **6.** result of work. **7.** (*pl.*) industrial plant. —*adj.* **8.** of or for work. —*v.* **9.** do work. **10.** operate successfully. **11.** move or give. **12.** solve. **13.** excite. **14.** ferment. —**work′a•ble,** *adj.* —**work′er,** *n.*

work′a•day′, *adj.* commonplace; uneventful.

work′a•hol′ic, *n.* person who works compulsively.

work′book′, *n.* book for students containing questions and exercises.

work′horse′, *n.* **1.** horse used for heavy labor. **2.** person who works tirelessly.

work′house′, *n.* penal institution for minor offenders.

working class, 1. persons working for wages, esp. in manual labor. **2.** social or economic class composed of these workers.

work′load′, *n.* amount of work that machine or employee is expected to perform.

work′man, *n., pl.* **-men.** worker; laborer. Also, **work′ing•man′,** *fem.* **work′ing•wom′an.** —**work′man•like′,** *adj.* —**work′man•ship′,** *n.*

work′out′, *n.* **1.** practice or test to maintain or determine physical ability or endurance. **2.** structured regime of physical exercise.

work′shop′, *n.* place where work is done.

work′sta′tion, *n.* **1.** work area for one person, as in office, usu. with electronic equipment. **2.** powerful small computer used for graphics-intensive processing.

work′up′, *n.* thorough medical diagnostic examination.

world, *n.* **1.** earth; globe. **2.** particular part of earth. **3.** things common to profession, etc.; milieu. **4.** humanity. **5.** universe. **6.** great quantity.

world′-class′, *adj.* of the highest caliber.

world′ling, *n.* worldly person.

world′ly, *adj.,* **-lier, -liest. 1.** secular or earthly. **2.** devoted to affairs of this world; sophisticated; shrewd. **3.** of this world. **—world′li•ness,** *n.*

world′ly-wise′, *adj.* wise as to the affairs of this world.

world′-wea′ry, *adj.* blasé.

worm, *n.* **1.** small slender creeping animal. **2.** something suggesting worm, as screw thread. **3.** (*pl.*) intestinal disorder. **—v. 4.** move like worm. **5.** extract (secret) craftily. **6.** free from worms. **—worm′y,** *adj.*

worm′wood′, *n.* bitter aromatic herb.

worn, *adj.* exhausted; spent.

worn′-out′, *adj.* **1.** exhausted. **2.** destroyed by wear.

wor′ry, *v.,* **-ried, -rying,** *n., pl.* **-ries. —v. 1.** make or feel anxious. **2.** seize with teeth and shake. **—n. 3.** anxiety. **4.** cause of anxiety. **—wor′ri•er,** *n.* **—wor′ri•some,** *adj.*

worse, *adj.* **1.** less good; less favorable. **—n. 2.** that which is worse. **—adv. 3.** in worse way. **—wors′en,** *v.*

wor′ship, *n., v.,* **-shiped, -shiping** or **-shipped, -shipping. —n. 1.** homage paid to God. **2.** rendering of such homage. **—v. 3.** render religious reverence to. **—wor′ship•er,** *n.* **—wor′ship•ful,** *adj.*

worst, *adj.* **1.** least satisfactory; least well. **—n. 2.** that which is worst. **—adv. 3.** in the worst way. **—v. 4.** defeat.

wor′sted (wŏos′tid), *n.* **1.** firmly twisted wool yarn or thread. **2.** fabric made of it.

wort (wûrt), *n.* malt infusion before fermentation.

worth, *adj.* **1.** good enough to justify. **2.** having value of. —*n.* **3.** excellence; importance. **4.** quantity of specified value. —**worth'less,** *adj.* —**worth'less•ness,** *n.*

worth'while', *adj.* repaying time and effort spent.

wor'thy, *adj.,* **-thier, -thiest,** *n.,* *pl.* **-thies.** —*adj.* **1.** of adequate worth. **2.** deserving. —*n.* **3.** person of merit. —**wor'thi•ly,** *adv.* —**wor'thi•ness,** *n.*

would, *v.* past of **will** (defs. 8, 9).

would'-be', *adj.* wishing, pretending, or intended to be.

wound (wo̅o̅nd), *n.* **1.** puncture from external violence. —*v.* **2.** inflict wound. **3.** grieve with insult or reproach.

wrack, *n.* ruin.

wraith, *n.* ghost.

wran'gle, *v.,* **-gled, -gling,** *n.* dispute. —**wran'gler,** *n.*

wrap, *v.,* **wrapped** or **wrapt, wrapping,** *n.* —*v.* **1.** enclose; envelop. **2.** wind or fold about. —*n.* **3.** (*often pl.*) outdoor clothes.

wrap'per, *n.* **1.** one that wraps. **2.** Also, **wrapping.** outer cover. **3.** long loose garment.

wrath, *n.* **1.** stern or fierce anger. **2.** vengeance. —**wrath'ful,** *adj.* —**wrath'ful•ly,** *adv.* —**wrath'y,** *adj.*

wreak, *v.* inflict.

wreath, *n.* circular band of leaves, etc.

wreathe, *v.,* **wreathed, wreathing.** encircle with wreath.

wreck, *n.* **1.** anything reduced to ruins. **2.** destruction. —*v.* **3.** cause or suffer wreck. —**wreck'age,** *n.* —**wreck'er,** *n.*

wren, *n.* small active bird.

wrench, *v.* **1.** twist forcibly. **2.** injure by wrenching. —*n.* **3.** wrenching movement. **4.** tool for turning bolts, etc.

wrest, *v.* **1.** twist violently. **2.** get by effort. —*n.* **3.** twist; wrench.

wres'tle, *v.,* **-tled, -tling,** *n.* —*v.* **1.** contend with by trying to force other person down. —*n.* **2.** this sport. **3.** struggle. —**wres'tler,** *n.*

wretch, *n.* **1.** pitiable person. **2.** scoundrel.

wretch'ed, *adj.* **1.** pitiable. **2.** despicable. **3.** pitiful. —**wretch'ed•ly,** *adv.* —**wretch'ed•ness,** *n.*

wrig'gle, *v.,* **-gled, -gling,** *n.* wiggle; squirm. —**wrig'gler,** *n.* —**wrig'gly,** *adj.*

wright, *n.* worker who builds.

wring, *v.,* **wrung, wringing,** *n.* —*v.* **1.** twist or compress. **2.** expel by wringing. **3.** clasp tightly. —*n.* **4.** twist or squeeze. —**wring'er,** *n.*

wrin'kle, *n., v.,* **-kled, -kling.** —*n.* **1.** ridge or furrow. —*v.* **2.** form wrinkles in. —**wrin'kly,** *adj.*

wrist, *n.* joint between hand and arm.

writ, *n.* **1.** formal legal order. **2.** writing.

write, *v.,* **wrote, written, writing. 1.** form (letters, etc.) by hand. **2.** express in writing. **3.** produce, as author or composer. —**writ'er,** *n.*

write'-in', *n.* candidate or vote for candidate not listed on ballot but written in by voter.

write'-off', *n.* something cancelled, as a debt.

writhe, *v.,* **writhed, writhing,** *n.* —*v.* **1.** twist, as in pain. —*n.* **2.** writhing movement. —**writh'er,** *n.*

wrong, *adj.* **1.** not right or good. **2.** deviating from truth or fact. **3.** not suitable. **4.** under or inner (side). —*n.* **5.** evil; injury; error. —*v.* **6.** do wrong to. **7.** misjudge. —**wrong'do'er,** *n.* —**wrong'do'ing,** *n.* —**wrong'ful,** *adj.* —**wrong'ly,** *adv.*

wroth (rôth), *adj.* angry.

wrought, *adj.* **1.** worked. **2.** shaped by beating.

wrought'-up', *adj.* perturbed.

wry, *adj.,* **wrier, wriest. 1.** twisted; distorted. **2.** ironic. —**wry'ly,** *adv.* —**wry'ness,** *n.*

WYSIWYG (wiz'ē wig'), *adj.* of or being computer display screen that shows text exactly as it will appear when printed.

WV, West Virginia. Also, **W. Va.**

WY, Wyoming. Also, **Wyo.**

X, Y, Z

X, x, *n.* **1.** twenty-fourth letter of English alphabet. **2.** motion-picture classification: those less than 17 years old not admitted.

xan′thic (zan′thik), *adj.* yellow.

X chromosome, sex chromosome that determines femaleness when paired with another X chromosome and that occurs singly in males.

xen′o•pho′bi•a (zen′ə fō′bē ə, zē′nə-), *n.* fear or hatred of foreigners or strangers or of anything foreign or strange. —**xen′o•pho′bic,** *adj.*

xe•rog′ra•phy (zi rog′rə fē), *n.* copying process in which resins are fused to paper electrically. —**xe′ro•graph′ic,** *adj.*

Xe′rox (zēr′oks), *n.* **1.** *Trademark.* brand name for copying machine using xerography. **2.** (*l.c.*) copy made on Xerox. —*v.* **3.** (*l.c.*) print or reproduce by Xerox.

Xmas, *n.* Christmas.

x′-ray′, *n.* **1.** highly penetrating type of electromagnetic ray, used esp. in medicine. —*v.* **2.** photograph or treat with x-rays.

xy′lem (zī′lem), *n.* woody tissue of plants.

xy′lo•phone′, *n.* musical instrument of wooden bars, played with small hammers. —**xy′lo•phon′ist,** *n.*

Y, y, *n.* twenty-fifth letter of English alphabet.

-y, suffix meaning: **1.** full of or like, as *cloudy*. **2.** inclined to, as *squeaky*. **3.** dear or little, as *kitty*. **4.** action of, as *inquiry*. **5.** quality or state, as *victory*.

yacht, *n.* **1.** pleasure ship. —*v.* **2.** sail in yacht. —**yacht′ing,** *n.* —**yachts′man,** *n.*

ya′hoo, *n.* coarse stupid person.

yak, *n., v.,* **yakked, yakking.** —*n.* **1.** long-haired Tibetan ox. **2.** *Slang.* incessant idle or gossipy talk. —*v.* **3.** *Slang.* gab; chatter.

yam, *n.* edible potatolike root.

yam′mer, *v. Informal.* whine or chatter.

yank, *v.* **1.** pull suddenly; jerk. —*n.* **2.** sudden pull; jerk.

Yan'kee, *n.* native or inhabitant of the United States, northern U.S., or New England.

yap, *v.,* **yapped, yapping,** *n.* yelp.

yard, *n.* **1.** linear unit (3 feet). **2.** long spar. **3.** enclosed outdoor area, used as a lawn, etc.

yard'age, *n.* amount in yards.

yard'arm', *n.* either of the yards of square sail.

yard'stick', *n.* **1.** measuring stick one yard long. **2.** criterion.

yar'mul•ke (yär'məl kə, -mə-, yä'-), *n.* cap worn by Jewish males, esp. during prayer.

yarn, *n.* **1.** many-stranded thread. **2.** story.

yar'row, *n.* plant with flat-topped clusters of white-to-yellow flowers.

yaw, *v.* **1.** deviate. —*n.* **2.** deviation.

yawl, *n.* small sailboat.

yawn, *v.* **1.** open mouth wide involuntarily, as from sleepiness or boredom. —*n.* **2.** act of yawning.

yawp, *v., n. Informal.* bawl.

yaws (yôz), *n.* infectious tropical disease characterized by raspberrylike eruptions of skin.

Y chromosome, sex chromosome present only in males and paired with X chromosome.

ye, *pron. Archaic.* **1.** you. **2.** the.

yea, *adv., n.* yes.

year, *n.* period of 365 or 366 days. —**year'ly,** *adv., adj.*

year'book', *n.* **1.** book published annually with information on past year. **2.** commemorative book published as by graduating class.

year'ling, *n.* animal in its second year.

yearn, *v.* desire strongly. —**yearn'ing,** *adj., n.*

year'-round', *adj.* **1.** continuing, available, or used throughout the year. —*adv.* **2.** throughout the year.

yeast, *n.* yellowish substance, used to leaven bread, ferment liquor, etc.

yell, *v.* shout loudly.

yel'low, *n.* **1.** color of butter, lemons, etc. —*adj.* **2.** of or like yellow. **3.** *Slang.* cowardly. —**yel'low•ish,** *adj.*

yellow fever, infectious tropical disease transmitted by certain mosquitoes. Also, **yellow jack.**

yellow jacket, yellow and black wasp.

yelp, *v.* **1.** give sharp, shrill cry. —*n.* **2.** such cry.

yen, *n. Informal.* desire.

yeo'man, *n.* **1.** petty officer in navy. **2.** independent farmer. —**yeo'man•ry,** *n.*

yes, *adv., n.* expression of affirmation or assent.

ye•shi'va, *n.* Orthodox Jewish school.

yes'-man', *n., pl.* **-men.** person who always agrees with superiors.

yes'ter•day, *adv., n.* day before today.

yet, *adv.* **1.** so far; up to this (or that) time. **2.** moreover. **3.** still. **4.** nevertheless. —*conj.* **5.** but.

yew, *n.* evergreen coniferous tree.

Yid'dish, *n.* German-based Jewish language.

yield, *v.* **1.** produce; give. **2.** surrender. **3.** give way. —*n.* **4.** that which is yielded; product. —**yield'er,** *n.*

yip, *v.,* **yipped, yipping.** *Informal.* bark sharply.

yo'del, *v.,* **-eled, -eling. 1.** sing with quick changes to and from falsetto. —*n.* **2.** song yodeled.

yo'ga, *n.* series of postures and breathing exercises practiced to attain physical and mental control and tranquillity.

yo'gi (-gē), *n.* Hindu practicing asceticism (**yo'ga**).

yo'gurt (-gərt), *n.* curdled milk product. Also, **yo'ghurt.**

yoke, *n., v.,* **yoked, yoking.** —*n.* **1.** piece put across necks of oxen pulling cart, etc. **2.** pair. —*v.* **3.** couple with, or place in, yoke.

yo'kel, *n.* rustic.

yolk (yōk), *n.* yellow part of egg.

yon'der, *adj., adv. Archaic.* over there. Also, **yon.**

yore, *n.* time past.

you, *pron.* person or persons addressed.

young, *adj.* **1.** in early stages of life, operation, etc. **2.** of youth. —*n.* **3.** young persons. **4.** young offspring. —**young'ish,** *adj.*

young'ster, *n.* child.

your, *pron., adj.* possessive of **you;** (without noun following) **yours.**

you're, contraction of **you are.**

your•self', *pron.* emphatic or reflexive form of **you.**

youth, *n.* **1.** young state. **2.** early life. **3.** young person or persons. —**youth'ful,** *adj.* —**youth'ful•ly,** *adv.* —**youth'ful•ness,** *n.*

yowl, *v., n.* howl.

yo'-yo, *n., pl.* **-yos,** *v.,* **-yoed, -yoing.** —*n.* **1.** spoollike toy spun out and reeled in by string looped on finger. —*v.* **2.** move up and down or back and forth; fluctuate.

yr., year.

yu•an' (yo͞o än'), *n.* Taiwanese dollar.

yuc'ca, *n.* tropical American plant.

yuck, *interj. Slang.* (exclamation of disgust or repugnance). —**yuck'y,** *adj.*

yule, *n.* Christmas.

yule'tide', *n.* Christmas season.

yum'my, *adj.,* **-mier, -miest.** very pleasing, esp. to taste.

yup'pie, *n.* young, ambitious, and affluent professional who lives in or near a city. Also, **yup'py.**

yurt (yo͞ort), *n.* tentlike dwelling of nomadic peoples of central Asia.

Z, z, *n.* twenty-sixth letter of English alphabet.

za'ny, *n., pl.* **-nies,** *adj.* **-nier, -niest.** —*n.* **1.** clown. —*adj.* **2.** silly. —**za'ni•ness,** *n.*

zap, *v.,* **zapped, zapping.** *Slang.* kill or defeat.

zeal, *n.* intense ardor or eagerness. —**zeal'ous** (zel'-), *adj.* —**zeal'ous•ly,** *adv.* —**zeal'ous•ness,** *n.*

zeal'ot (zel'-), *n.* excessively zealous person; fanatic. —**zeal'ot•ry,** *n.*

ze'bra, *n.* wild, striped horselike animal.

ze'bu (zē'byoo̅), *n., pl.* **-bus.** domesticated ox of India.

Zen, *n.* Buddhist movement emphasizing enlightenment by meditation and direct, intuitive insight. Also, **Zen Buddhism.**

ze'nith, *n.* **1.** celestial point directly overhead. **2.** highest point or state.

zeph'yr, *n.* mild breeze.

zep'pe•lin, *n.* large dirigible of early 20th century.

ze'ro, *n., pl.* **-ros, -roes. 1.** symbol (0) indicating nonquantity. **2.** nothing. **3.** starting point of a scale.

zero hour, starting time.

zero population growth, condition in which population remains constant because of equal number of births and deaths.

zest, *n.* something adding flavor, interest, etc. **—zest'ful,** *adj.* **—zest'ful•ly,** *adv.* **—zest'ful•ness,** *n.* **—zest'less,** *adj.*

zig'zag', *n., adj., adv., v.,* **-zagged, -zagging. —n. 1.** line going sharply from side to side. **—adj., adv. 2.** with sharp turns back and forth. **—v. 3.** go in zigzag.

zilch, *n. Slang.* zero; nothing.

zil'lion, *n. Informal.* extremely large, indeterminate number.

zinc, *n.* bluish metallic element. **—zinc'ous,** *adj.*

zinc oxide, salve made of zinc and oxygen.

zing, *n.* **1.** sharp singing sound. **—v. 2.** make such sound. **—interj. 3.** (descriptive of such sound.)

zin'ni•a, *n.* bright, full-flowered plant.

Zi'on, *n.* **1.** Jewish people. **2.** Palestine as Jewish homeland. **3.** heaven as final gathering place of true believers.

Zi'on•ism', *n.* advocacy of Jewish establishment of state of Israel. **—Zi'on•ist,** *n., adj.*

zip, *v.,* **zipped, zipping,** *n. Informal.* **—v. 1.** go very speedily. **—n. 2.** energy.

ZIP code, code numbers used with address to expedite mail.

zip'per, *n.* fastener with interlocking edges.

zip'py, *adj.,* **-pier, -piest.** *Informal.* lively; smart.

zir′con, *n.* mineral used as gem when transparent.

zir·co′ni·um (zûr kō′nē əm), *n.* metallic element used in metallurgy and ceramics.

zit, *n. Slang.* pimple.

zith′er, *n.* stringed musical instrument. Also, **zith′ern.**

zi′ti (zē′tē), *n.* short, tubular pasta.

zo′di·ac′, *n.* imaginary belt of heavens containing paths of all major planets, divided into twelve constellations. —**zo·di′a·cal** (-dī′ə kəl), *adj.*

zom′bie, *n.* reanimated corpse.

zone, *n., v.,* **zoned, zoning.** —*n.* 1. special area, strip, etc. —*v.* 2. mark or divide into zones. —**zon′al,** *adj.*

zonked, *adj. Slang.* stupefied from or as if from alcohol or drugs.

zoo, *n.* place where live animals are exhibited. Also, **zoological garden.**

zo·ol′o·gy, *n.* scientific study of animals. —**zo′o·log′i·cal,** *adj.* —**zo·ol′o·gist,** *n.*

zoom, *v.* speed sharply.

zoom lens, camera lens allowing continual change of magnification without loss of focus.

zo′o·pho′bi·a (zō′ə-), *n.* fear of animals.

zo′o·phyte′ (-fīt′), *n.* plantlike animal, as coral.

zuc·chi′ni (zoo kē′nē), *n.* cucumber-shaped squash.

zwie′back′ (swē′bak′), *n.* kind of dried, twice-baked bread.

zy′gote (zī′gōt), *n.* cell produced by union of two gametes. —**zy·got′ic,** *adj.*

zy′mur·gy, *n.* branch of applied chemistry dealing with fermentation.

Pronunciation Key

STRESS

Pronunciations are marked for stress to reveal the relative differences in emphasis between syllables. In words of two or more syllables, a primary stress mark (ˈ), as in **mother** (muth′ər), follows the syllable having greatest stress. A secondary stress mark (ˌ), as in **grandmother** (grand′muth′ər), follows a syllable having slightly less stress than primary but more stress than an unmarked syllable.

ENGLISH SOUNDS

a	act, bat marry	**j**	just, tragic, fudge
ā	age, paid, say	**k**	keep, token, make
â(r)	air, dare, Mary	**l**	low, mellow, bottle
ä	ah, part, balm		(bot′l)
b	back, cabin, cab	**m**	my, summer, him
ch	child, beach	**n**	now, sinner, button
d	do, madder, bed		(but′n)
e	edge, set, merry	**ng**	sing, Washington
ē	equal, bee, pretty	**o**	ox, bomb, wasp
ēr	ear, mere	**ō**	over, boat, no
f	fit, differ, puff	**ô**	order, ball, raw
g	give, trigger, beg	**oi**	oil, joint, joy
h	hit, behave	**o͝o**	book, tour
hw	which, nowhere	**o͞o**	ooze, fool, too
i	if, big, mirror	**ou**	out, loud, cow
ī	ice, bite, deny	**p**	pot, supper, stop

r read, hu**rr**y, nea**r**	**y** **y**es, on**i**on
s **s**ee, pa**ss**ing, mi**ss**	**z** **z**oo, la**z**y, tho**s**e
sh **sh**oe, fa**sh**ion, pu**sh**	**zh** trea**s**ure, mira**g**e
t **t**en, ma**tt**er, bi**t**	**ə** used in unaccented
th **th**in, e**th**er, pa**th**	syllables to indicate
ŧħ **th**at, ei**th**er, smoo**th**	the sound of the
u **u**p, s**u**n	reduced vowel in
û(r) **ur**ge, b**ur**n, c**ur**	**a**lone, syst**e**m,
v **v**oice, ri**v**er, li**v**e	eas**i**ly, gall**o**p, circ**u**s
w **w**itch, a**w**ay	

NON-ENGLISH SOUNDS

A as in French **ami**	**R** [a symbol for any non-English r, including a trill or flap in Italian and Spanish and a sound in French and German similar to **KH** but pronounced with voice]
KH as in Scottish **loch**	
N as in French **bon** [used to indicate that the preceding vowel is nasalized.]	
œ as in French **feu**	**Y** as in French **tu** (tY)

Chief American Holidays

New Year's Day   January 1

Martin Luther King Day   January 15[1]

Inauguration Day   January 20

Lincoln's Birthday   February 12

Valentine's Day   February 14

Washington's Birthday   February 22[2]

Good Friday   Friday before Easter

Mother's Day   Second Sunday in May

Memorial Day   May 30[3]

Father's Day   Third Sunday in June

Independence Day   July 4

Labor Day   First Monday in September

Columbus Day   October 12[4]

Veterans Day   November 11

Election Day   Tuesday after first Monday in
                                November

Thanksgiving Day   Fourth Thursday in November

Christmas Day   December 25

---

[1] officially observed on 3rd Monday in January

[2] officially observed as Presidents' Day on 3rd Monday in February

[3] officially observed on last Monday in May

[4] officially observed on 2nd Monday in October

World Time Differences†

Amsterdam	6:00 P.M.	Manila	1:00 A.M.*
Athens	7:00 P.M.	Mexico City	11:00 A.M.
Bangkok	12:00 Mid.	Montreal	12:00 Noon
Berlin	6:00 P.M.	Moscow	8:00 P.M.
Bombay	10:30 P.M.	Paris	6:00 P.M.
Brussels	6:00 P.M.	Prague	6:00 P.M.
Buenos Aires	2:00 P.M.	Rio de Janeiro	2:00 P.M.
Cape Town	7:00 P.M.	Rome	6:00 P.M.
Dublin	5:00 P.M.	Shanghai	1:00 A.M.*
Havana	12:00 Noon	Stockholm	6:00 P.M.
Honolulu	7:00 A.M.	Sydney (N.S.W.)	3:00 A.M.*
Istanbul	7:00 P.M.	Tokyo	2:00 A.M.*
Lima	12:00 Noon	Vienna	6:00 P.M.
London	5:00 P.M.	Warsaw	6:00 P.M.
Madrid	6:00 P.M.	Zurich	6:00 P.M.

† at 12:00 noon Eastern Standard Time
* morning of the following day